# FREE eGUIDE!

Enter this code at primagames.com/code to unlock your FREE eGuide:

NVVS-GDYC-FR8C-Z582

### Mobile Friendly

Access your eGuide on any web-enabled device.

----

### Searchable & Sortable

Quickly find the strategies you need.

----

### Added Value

Strategy where, when, and how you want it.

## Check Out Our Complete eGuide Library at primagames.com!

www.primagames.com

The Prima Games logo and Primagames.com are registered trademarks of Penguin Random House LLC, registered in the United States.
Prima Games is an imprint of DK, a division of Penguin Random House LLC, New York.

# VAULT DWELLER'S SURVIVAL GUIDE

### VDSG VTB-004-111 COMPLETE REFERENCE EDITION

PASSIVE CONTRACT VT111.29-Q

The act of reading this document (either partially or in its entirety) is a non-verbal agreement between all Vault-Dwelling Parties and Vault-Tec Industries stating that Vault-Tec is not liable for any damages, injuries, or mental anguish inflicted during or after the perusal of the Vault Dweller's Survival Guide, Complete Reference Edition. Vault Dwellers also agree to refrain from the reproduction, dissemination, or public interpretation of this guide. Furthermore, the availability of this material shall not be construed as approval for leaving the security of the vault. As stated within the Vault Dweller's Protection Agreement (in section 45.6b), "...no member of a vault community may leave the vault without the direct consent of a Vault Overseer or other Vault-Tec Official."

All visual representations and projections have been developed through the use of Science.

# GUIDE UTILIZATION AND INTRODUCTION: CONTENTS

This guide is sub-divided into chapters segmented in the same manner as your RobCo Industries Pip-Boy 9000. Expect information pertinent to this menu system in the chapters that share the same name.

## STAT

After a widespread nuclear event, you may feel anxiety and wander ineptly. There is little time for gnawing fear; instead you must focus on quickly understanding the basics of Pip-Boy manipulation, interactions (both violent and passive), and learn how to hone your S.P.E.C.I.A.L. abilities and Perks. Advice is also given about interacting with like-minded Companions, the hostiles known to be present in the Commonwealth, as well as a brief primer on Crafting.

## INV

Understanding the complex and unrecognizable world you once knew depends on your usage of tools, comestibles, and scavenging know-how. This chapter details the opportunities you can make for yourself while sifting through the Inventory of your life.

## DATA

While risking your life by emerging from your Vault may be an idea you've already ignored the dangers of, why not completing disregard Vault-Tec advice and jeopardize the lives of others, too? Should you agree to complete quests for them, it seems only prudent to offer advice on remaining alive during the multitude of tasks you may wish to complete. The most pressing of which are contained here. For a complete list of Quests in alphabetical order, please consult "Quests: A Big Table" at the start of this chapter. Please note some minor quests, usually self-contained within a Commonwealth location, are noted in the MAP chapter.

# MAP

A comprehensive field study of the estimated dangers present for those foolish enough to venture out of a Vault. The vast irradiated Commonwealth is segmented into Zones, for use in conjunction with your Pip-Boy's World Map feature. Trackable items are noted, as well as dangers and other pertinent danger. The latest in ground-penetrating radar was used to extrapolate topographical data for surface and interior locations. Be sure to use The Commonwealth Collection Appendix if you wish to search Primary Locations alphabetically.

# RADIO

A brief collection of snippets, tracking all important life goals you can undertake, collectibles and worthy items you can gather, Companions to befriend, and the most important scavenging opportunities across the Commonwealth. Be sure to use The Commonwealth Collection Appendix if you wish to search Primary Locations alphabetically.

# INTRODUCTION: TRAINING FOR THE COMMONWEALTH

**S**tart your exploration

**T**aking the time to learn

**A**ugment your attributes

**T**errifying abominations lurk on the surface

## VAULT-TEC RECOMMENDS

**READ THIS FIRST!**

Vault-Tec recommends you familiarize yourself with the Main menu and seek out the "Help" option. This provides a complete basic training in the arts of survival and allows this guide to focus on more involved tactical knowledge. If you need to know about Action Points, different types of Damage, changing your Difficulty level, Experience Points (XP), Fast-Travel, Power Armor, your Pip-Boy, and other areas of interest, read this before continuing!

# THE PIP-BOY: A ROBCO INDUSTRIES TECHNOLOGICAL WONDER!

Knowing your way around your Pip-Boy is one of the first lessons you learn after entering a vault, assuming nuclear obliteration hasn't hastened acclimatization activities. Study the following indicators and near-field enhancements, as your life may well depend on the wealth of important information contained within this wondrous device!

## OPTIMIZED VIEWING PORTAL

OPTIMIZED VIEWING PORTAL (NORMAL VIEW).

OPTIMIZED VIEWING PORTAL (POWER ARMOR).

This is your optimized viewing portal, where Pip-Boy functionality helps you navigate the hostile environment outside the safety of Vault 111.

Both views detail the following:

**[1] Target/Dot:** This changes from a dot to a target of varying dimensions, depending on the weapon you are carrying or have unholstered. Use this to point yourself in the correct direction or aim when firing from the hip.

**[2] Compass:** Spin around to view all directions. Use your World Map menu to add markers that show up on your compass. Quest objectives appear as the same square-shaped markers. Enemies appear as red dots. Primary locations appear as icons that are the same as the world map in both your Pip-Boy and this guide.

**[3] Health and Radiation:** This shows the percentage of your Health left, regardless of the number of Health Points you have (in Power Armor, this also shows the state of your armor sections). Any time you take radiation damage, the bar always shows how many of the 1000 rads you can take are left. Employ chems or medical treatment to alleviate any radiation poisoning or trauma you may be experiencing.

**Damage Type (not shown):** This appears if you're struck by radiation damage, although sometimes poison damage has an accompanying visual effect.

**[4] Ammunition:** This shows the number of total bullets, shells, or ammunition you have for the weapon you're using, along with the current number left in your chamber. Reload manually during brief periods of down-time in combat.

**[5] Action Points:** Every time you sprint or utilize a weapon in combat, you use Action Points, and this bar shows the percentage of your total that you have available. They refill when you refrain from attempting either activity. Keep an eye on this bar to determine how long you can sprint before tiring out or fire (or swing) a weapon.

**[6] Information:** Occasionally, your Pip-Boy may relay pertinent information in this corner of your viewing portal. It is usually a warning, hint, or quest activity to perform.

**[7] Core (Power Armor only):** This measures the remaining energy in the Fusion Core that provides the "juice" your Power Armor requires to function normally. Continuously locate Fusion Cores to keep your Power Armor recharged, or face an impeding lack of maneuverability (and no Action Points to sprint with). Fusion Cores are automatically swapped, so always carry a spare. Or six.

## STATUS SCREENS

Your personal status is measured on your Pip-Boy. It reveals the following:

**[1]** The condition of your various appendages (head, both arms and legs, and entire Health). If the Vault Boy is looking less than healthy (ghoulish or with a bandaged appendage), seek chems or medical attention. Check the Help menu for more information on penalties you receive while crippled.

**[2]** Your offensive capabilities, which is the damage your current weapon inflicts. Some weapons inflict additional radiation, energy, or poison damage and are listed as appropriate. Change your weapon, and this value changes.

**[3]** Your defensive capabilities, which is the Damage Resistance of the armor you are currently wearing. Power Armor obviously provides an impressive level of protection. If your apparel also offers resistance against radiation, energy, and poison, it is also listed here.

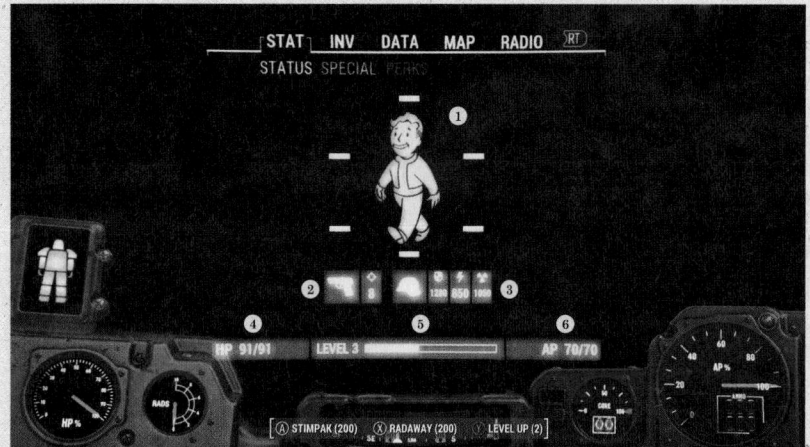

A RELATIVELY HEALTHY SPECIMEN, SHOWN WITHIN POWER ARMOR.

**[4] Health Points:** This shows the current and maximum Health Points you have. This is useful if you are, for example, administering a stimpak. You know the stimpak increases your Health by 30% of your health, so you may wish to use it when you're a little closer to death (when it is more effective). So you don't waste the additional Health Points, you may wish to then wait to heal yourself.

Remember your Health increases every time you level up.

**[5] Level:** This reveals your current level and a progression bar that fills up as you edge closer to your next level.

**[6] Action Points:** This shows your current and total number of Action Points. Simply rest to increase this back to the maximum total.

## OTHER SCREENS

Your SPECIAL screen details your attributes. This is detailed in the next section.

Your PERKS screen details any perks you have uncovered or unlocked. This is also detailed in the next section.

The INV chapter has more details regarding the associated Pip-Boy screens, but if you wish to know your Carry Weight and Caps total, look to the bottom left and bottom middle of this menu screen.

The DATA chapter has information on the Quests, Workshops, and Stats menus.

The MAP chapter has information on the world map and local map functionality, as well as marker and settlement information.

If you wish to know the date and current time, look to the bottom left and bottom middle of either of these menu screens.

The RADIO menu plays any current music or transmitting station within a specific radius. Aside from a variety of pleasant music, you can use the radio to locate distress calls from numerous sources and even track adversaries during specific quests. The available radio stations appear on your main screen as you near their range. As radio stations reveal locations already detailed in this guide's Map chapter, they aren't listed.

## FAVORITES

A FULLY STOCKED FAVORITES MENU, FILLED WITH THE ITEMS AND WEAPONS YOU USE THE MOST.

To ease and quicken the act of swapping between often-used items, be sure to access your Favorites menu every time you wish to switch between items. A total of 12 items can be given "Favorite" status within your INV menu. These include weapons, apparel, and aid. The objects you highlight as favorites are given a heart icon. Simply highlight them again and change to a new favorite as you wish.

## HELPFUL HINT *from Vault Boy!* — Now You Know!

HOW ABOUT CHOOSING YOUR TOP THREE MELEE WEAPONS, TOP THREE LONG-RANGE GUNS, THREE MOST-USED CHEMS, YOUR BEST GRENADES, OR EVEN A TRIO OF IMPORTANT APPAREL ITEMS FOR DIFFERENT OCCASIONS? UTILIZE THE BUILT-IN VERSATILITY OF THIS AT-A-GLANCE MENU.

### VAULT-TEC RECOMMENDS

#### SORTING ITEMS BY STATISTIC

As you gather more and more items, drop them off at a workbench or owned home, or make your own weapons or objects, you may wish to compare the potency of similar items. This is where the sorting part of your INV comes into play. Change the order of your items by their different statistics (also displayed on the screen) so you can, for example, compare fire rates, range, or weight of your weapons, and choose the one best-suited to your needs.

## HOLOTAPES

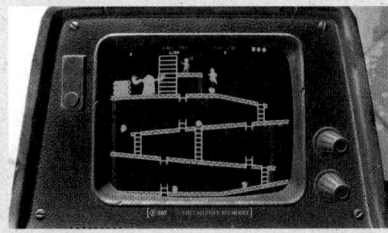

A CLASSIC HOLOTAPE GAME; ONE IS FOUND IN VAULT 111, AND THE OTHERS ARE FREE IN EVERY COPY OF ROBCO FUN! MAGAZINE.

Remember your Pip-Boy (and terminals) can play most Holotapes, which usually have audio recordings on them. Certain rare Holotapes have some classic video games to play. Have you found all five? You will if you check the Radio chapter of this guide.

## FLASHLIGHTS

EMPLOY THE FLASHLIGHT WHILE IN THE DARK, AND WITHOUT ANY SUBTLETY TO YOUR EXPLORATION.

Remember your Pip-Boy, certain mining helmets, and Power Armor all have flashlight capabilities for adventuring in dark and gloomy locations. Though you're more easily spotted (making this a less-than-ideal plan for the stealth expert), you're far less likely to get turned around, miss loot or foes, or remain in the dark for long.

## PRACTICE MAKES PERFECT

ACTIVATE IS A UBIQUITOUS COMMAND THAT HELPS YOU COMPLETE TASKS, FROM INSPECTING A LOOT TRUNK TO THE TROUSERS OF THE RECENTLY DECEASED. MOSTLY IT IS USED TO OPEN DOORS AND ACCESS TERMINALS.

THOUGH STRANGE TO HAVE AN OUT-OF-BODY EXPERIENCE, CHANGING YOUR POINT OF VIEW ALLOWS FOR GREATER PERIPHERAL VISION.

You may have woken from a period of enforced isolation. It is normal to feel a little light-headed and groggy. As your coordination returns, it is worth remembering the basic maneuvers you took for granted. Why not stay in the relative safety of Vault 111 and rid the corridors of the minor Radroach infestation while you familiarize yourself with the most basic of passive controls?

### Activate

Whether you're inspecting the contents of a desk, unlocking a door, activating a terminal, or disarming a trap, use this function.

### Reload or Transfer

If you want to transfer a large amount of loot, this is the function to complete. Otherwise, this reloads or holsters your weapon (if held).

### Toggle POV

Need to see behind you? That's a good idea, as you're able to enhance your peripheral vision quite considerably, while at the expense of completing more complex and pinpoint-accurate maneuvers (especially jumping).

### Jump

Leaping over low walls and across gaps and climbing rocky slopes is made not only more easy, but also actually possible if you jump.

## Pausing

Need to take a breather? Don't worry, we all need a little time to pause, check the Main menu, and perhaps look at the large number of incredibly astute hints in the Help menu.

**HELPFUL HINT**
*from Vault Boy!*

Did You Know?

IN NEED OF A REAL CHALLENGE? TRY SURVIVAL DIFFICULTY! HEALTH RESTORATION IS SEVERELY REDUCED, THOUGH THERE'S A GREATER CHANCE OF FINDING LEGENDARY ITEMS.

## VAULT-TEC RECOMMENDS

### SCAVENGING AND TAGGING ITEMS FOR SETTLEMENTS

Are you scavenging for component parts to help build items in a Workshop? Then employ Activate when scavenging for items used to build workshop components. Certain areas of scenery not usually of interest to past explorers, such as trees, tires, and junk items, now become incredibly important. Learn where the best junk is, head there and gather what you need, then return more than three days later and gather more.

If you are searching for scavengable items to break down into components for your settlement workshops, a small magnifying glass appears when you look at an object with the component you're after. This makes searching for components much less taxing. For more information, check the WORKSHOP chapter (page 218).

# SOCIAL STATUS:
# HOW TO REACT IF THE WORST HAPPENS

After surviving a nuclear blast, it is important to remain calm and wait for Vault-Tec (or other proper authorities) to contact your overseer. Should circumstances degenerate from optimal, you may be called upon to ascertain the situation from beyond the confines of your vault. At this point, the manner in which you conduct yourself in the chaotic topside environment becomes of paramount importance.

Begin a conversation, and you have four different choices to make, which can lead to a multitude of outcomes. Think about what you're about to say, as sometimes you can't take back a rude utterance or threat. Some friendly citizens have secrets or enjoy bantering with you. If this is the case, your conversations are color-coded with Speech Challenges. Such challenges are yellow (easy), orange (medium), or red (hard). Are you having problems convincing people and failing these challenges? Then increase your Charisma attribute or wear some Charisma-enhancing clothing.

**HELPFUL HINT**
*from Vault Boy!*

Did You Know?

REMEMBER, YOU ONLY NEED TO BRANDISH A WEAPON IF YOU SPOT AN IMMEDIATE THREAT. OTHERWISE, HOLSTER YOUR WEAPON, AS YOUR MOVEMENT SPEED IS SLOWER WITH A WEAPON OUT; THE HEAVIER THE WEAPON, THE SLOWER YOU MOVE; AND YOU'RE SLOWEST OF ALL WHILE LOOKING DOWN THE SIGHTS OF A WEAPON.

**HELPFUL HINT**
*from Vault Boy!*

Did You Know?

CRIMINAL ACTIVITY JUST ISN'T STOOD FOR IN THE COMMONWEALTH. COMMIT A CRIME (PICKING A LOCK, CONTAINER, OR DOOR; HACKING AN OWNED TERMINAL; ATTACKING AN INNOCENT; TRESPASSING; OR PICKPOCKETING), AND PREVIOUSLY FRIENDLY FOLK IMMEDIATELY TURN HOSTILE. LEARN MORE ABOUT THIS IN THE HELP MENU.

### OPTION 1: FRIEND OR FOE?

THIS GROTESQUE GHOULISH FACE OF FLAPPING SKIN MAY BE TERRIFYING TO WITNESS, BUT IT BELONGS TO A FRIENDLY SORT. APPEARANCES CAN SOMETIMES BE DECEPTIVE.

Many surface dwellers are simply attempting to eke out an existence and are little threat to you. They appear with a green health bar in V.A.T.S. if accidentally targeted and are sometimes gathered with other friendly sorts in (usually barricaded) settlements. Some like to converse with you, and some have tasks—quests—for you to complete. Others are traders.

### Traders

THE EASIEST WAY TO ACCRUE CAPS IS SELLING SCAVENGED LOOT WHILE WEARING A CHARISMA-IMPROVING BATHROBE.

To get some of the best gear going and start acquiring more than a meager collection of Caps, it is worth finding one of the many traders plying their wares across the Commonwealth. Simply find a trader, barter with them (the higher your Charisma, the better your deals), and come back another day for a different selection of items. There are different types of traders to find:

## MAJOR SETTLEMENT TRADERS

Seek out Deb in Bunker Hill, the vendors of Diamond City market, and the good folks of Goodneighbor for the very best (and rarest) items.

## MINOR SETTLEMENT TRADERS

Dealing in scrap, armor, and other bits and bobs, there are Commonwealth settlers attempting to trade from their own static locations—such as the scrap merchant perched by the freeway off-ramp near Forest Grove Marsh.

## RANDOMLY ENCOUNTERED TRADERS

Did you happen to spot a small girl and a large Sentry Bot while wandering? Then flag her down; she's a trader appearing as one of the multitude of random encounters. Find out more on page 214.

## TRADING CARAVANS

There are four traders who wander the Commonwealth with an armed guard, pack Brahmin, and a sense of purpose. They take the main thoroughfares between inhabitable locations, wait a few hours, and move on. Here's where they might be:

## TRADERS

| TRADER NAME | FIRST LOCATION | SECOND LOCATION | THIRD LOCATION | FOURTH LOCATION |
|---|---|---|---|---|
| Doc Weathers | County Crossing | Finch Farm | Salem | The Slog |
| Trashcan Carla | Sanctuary Hills | Drumlin Diner | — | — |
| Cricket | Diamond City | Vault 81 | Warwick Homestead | — |
| Lucas Miller | Covenant | Tenpines Bluff | Greentop Nursery | — |

## HELPFUL HINT *from Vault Boy!*

**Did You Know?**

DON'T JUST SAUNTER UP TO A TRADER WEARING POWER ARMOR AND EXPECT TO CLOSE A GREAT DEAL: COLLECT AN OUTFIT SPECIFICALLY FOR BARTERING. EVEN IF YOUR CHARISMA IS MEDIOCRE, PUTTING ON A BATHROBE (CHR +2), TRILBY HAT (CHR +1), AND SOME FASHIONABLE GLASSES (CHR +1) CAN REALLY TAKE YOUR VENDOR-FLEECING TO THE NEXT LEVEL!

TRADING CARAVANS GET A BOLSTER TO THEIR AVAILABLE CAPS IF YOU'VE MADE STRIDES IN YOUR SETTLEMENTS.

FINALLY, DO YOU DESPERATELY NEED TO TRADE WITH ONE OF THESE HARD-TO-FIND MERCHANTS? THEN HEAD TO BUNKER HILL, WHERE THERE'S A (RANDOM) CHANCE ONE OF THE CARAVANS WILL BE HERE, AS THIS IS WHERE THEY RESUPPLY.

## OPTION 2: JUST FOE

THERE IS LITTLE DOUBT THAT THIS LUMBERING SPECIMEN ISN'T HERE TO SELL YOU STIMPAKS. A MORE OFFENSIVE POSTURE IS THEREFORE CALLED FOR.

The vast majority of the time, you should be able to spot the telltale signs of a hostile encounter. Foes have red health bars. They usually have warnings to strangers, impaled skulls adorning their place of business, or a wild glint to their eye.

There could be blood or sacks of unpleasant entrails. Shots may be fired. At this point, it is wise to take action from the following options:

### General Hostile Actions

The situation has escalated. You should have prepared an offensive tool with which to calm the situation down. Early into your explorations, experiment with different weapon types—punching, melee, and the variety of ranged guns. Then choose perks that help you make the most of the weaponry you've chosen.

## MELEE COMBAT

CLOSE-RANGE COMBAT ISN'T FOR THE SQUEAMISH AND INVOLVES CHOOSING WHEN TO BASH, BLOCK, CHARGE IN, OR EXECUTE A MORE LUMBERING POWER ATTACK.

If you're using a punching or melee weapon, you must close the gap to the enemy and perform a "dance of death," countering your foe if they employ similar weapons or quickly cutting or bludgeoning the enemy if they're still carrying a gun. Remember you can:

– **BASH:** ATTACK NORMALLY TO INFLICT THE NORMAL DAMAGE FOR THE CLOSE-RANGE WEAPON YOU'RE USING AND TO QUICKLY HIT THEM IF THEY'RE TRYING A SLOWER POWER ATTACK WITH A MELEE WEAPON. THIS CAN LEAD TO THEM BEING STAGGERED.

– **POWER ATTACK:** BREAK A FOE'S BLOCK WITH A POWER ATTACK (AND HOPEFULLY STAGGER THEM), WHICH TAKES A LONGER TIME BUT PROVIDES MORE DEVASTATING DAMAGE. OR JUST BATTER THEM SENSELESS AS YOU CLOSE IN BY STARTING A POWER ATTACK EARLY.

– **BLOCK:** IF A FOE TAKES A SWING AT YOU (USING A MELEE STRIKE, AS YOU CAN'T BLOCK PROJECTILES), QUICKLY BLOCK JUST BEFORE THE SWING CONNECTS.

– **CHARGE!:** SPRINT INTO THE FRAY IF YOUR OPPONENT IS RELOADING, CONFUSED, HASN'T SEEN YOU, IS PREOCCUPIED IN SOME WAY, OR HAS BEEN STAGGERED. THEN BRING THEM DOWN WITH A BUMP IF YOU HAVE THE PAIN TRAIN PERK, OR STRIKE WITH MELEE OR PUNCHING ATTACKS BEFORE THEY CAN REACT.

## HELPFUL HINT *from Vault Boy!*

**Did You Know?**

UNLESS YOU'RE WIELDING A SILENCED WEAPON, MELEE IMPLEMENTS ARE MUCH QUIETER TO USE AND ARE EXCELLENT FOR SNEAKING. CONVERSELY, THEIR POTENCY IS INCREASED WITH THE STRENGTH ATTRIBUTE OR WHILE WEARING POWER ARMOR.

## RANGED COMBAT

CHOOSE JUST HOW FAR AWAY YOU WANT TO BE BY THE TYPE OF RANGED WEAPON YOU PICK.

Hip fire is any shooting done without pressing the aiming button. The crosshairs are wide when hip firing and tight when aiming. Aiming is more accurate, but you move slowly while aiming.

Firing from the hip is another option when neutralizing a situation that has gotten completely out of hand. This involves using your own mettle, manual dexterity (usually with a firearm or something that launches projectiles), and copious bullets. Are you focusing mainly on hip firing with no V.A.T.S. combat? Then Agility, Perception, and Luck are worth considerably less. The beauty of hip firing is you can now avoid those three stats and wind up with a devastating focused character.

However, if you're planning a focus on V.A.T.S., those stats are all vital. If you're pouring points into Luck, you also need high Agility and Perception to help the probability you'll score some crazy criticals!

The plan for hip firing is simple: Look for the most pertinent threats and nullify them. You can hip fire, but your accuracy is improved if you zoom in or look down the sights of a weapon. However, this comes at the cost of speed. Crouching and firing is even more accurate, though you're obviously a sitting duck. Also remember that the heavier the weapon, the more carry weight you'll need and the slower you'll be to react.

Both you and your enemies can inflict different types of damage:

- BALLISTIC: BULLET, SHELL, OR NORMAL PROJECTILE DAMAGE.
- ENERGY: POWERFUL BLASTS OF ELECTRICITY OR LASER FIRE.
- RADIATION: DAMAGE WITH A RADIOACTIVE ELEMENT, USUALLY ENVIRONMENTAL OR WHEN BEING STRUCK BY RADIOACTIVE CREATURES.
- POISON: USUALLY ATTACKS FROM CERTAIN TYPES OF UNCLEAN ENEMY CLAWS.

It's worth consulting the Combat chapter to see if the foes you're facing have resistance to any of these damage types and to plan to exploit their weaknesses instead.

Now simply fire on your foes until only one of you is standing. Let's hope it's you. Is the foe running? Aim for the legs. Better to earn some XP for your expended bullets by killing your target.

## VAULT-TEC RECOMMENDS

### GUN BASHING AND BACKPEDALING
Remember, foes that are too close for comfort can be physically battered using the weapon you're wielding; this usually allows you to step back afterward and fire.

### PROJECTILE COMBAT

GRENADES AND MINES ARE A GREAT WAY TO DAMAGE FOES WITHIN A LARGER AREA OR CREATE A DIVERSION.

Remember to utilize grenades at every possible opportunity to soften up the enemy as you close in (or if you have the Pickpocket perk, to place on a person you've snuck up to for an amusing and explosive demise). Remember to hold down to throw, and aim just in front of an enemy who is moving toward you, so the projectile explodes on them, not behind them.

Mines are another option, albeit a more stealthy plan. Place them on enemy patrol paths, in choke points, or at the perimeter of your settlements. And remember both grenades and mines can harm you (though mines only blow up on you when triggered by a foe), so don't drop one at your feet and stand there.

### VAULT-TEC ASSISTED TARGETING SYSTEM (V.A.T.S.) COMBAT

FROM THE SNIPER IN A FARAWAY NEST TO RAPID-FIRE MINIGUN MAYHEM, THE METHODS OF FOE DISPOSAL ARE SIMPLY STAGGERING.

V.A.T.S. allows you to slow down the lunacy of combat into more manageable time chunks. Use the targeting system to mark multiple enemies (or multiple areas of an enemy or enemies). This continues until you wish to stop choosing pieces of a foe to shoot at or you run out of bullets or Action Points. Remember! The larger the weapon, the more Action Points it is likely to use up for each hit. Successfully strike a foe, and your Critical meter is partly filled. Once completely full (and the speed of this depends on your Luck attribute), you can launch a critical hit—a high-powered and usually impressively messy attack.

## HELPFUL HINT
### from Vault Boy!

Did You Know?

NEED TO KNOW THE BEST WAYS TO IMPROVE YOUR V.A.T.S.? THE HIGHER YOUR AGILITY, THE MORE ACTION POINTS YOU HAVE. THE HIGHER YOUR PERCEPTION, THE MORE ACCURATE YOU ARE IN VATS. THE HIGHER YOUR LUCK, THE MORE QUICKLY YOUR CRITICAL METER FILLS. V.A.T.S. IS PREFERRED OVER FIRING FROM THE HIP IF YOU HAVE A TARGET AREA THAT'S PARTICULARLY TROUBLESOME TO HIT MANUALLY (SUCH AS A FAST-MOVING DEATHCLAW, OR DISTANT FOE WHO'S DIFFICULT TO AIM AT). YOU CAN ALSO SHOOT GRENADES OUT OF THE AIR, ONCE THROWN BY A FOE (BUT NOT OUT OF THEIR HANDS ON OR THEIR PERSON).
NEED TO MAXIMIZE YOUR V.A.T.S. POTENTIAL? THEN UTILIZE A WEAPON WITH LOW ACTION POINT USE (SUCH AS THE DELIVERER, THE SILENCED PISTOL FAVORED BY THE RAILROAD FACTION). BUILD YOUR CRITICAL METER WITH THIS, THEN QUICKLY SWAP IT FOR A WEAPON WITH A LARGE BASE DAMAGE VALUE (LIKE A FULLY CHARGED LASER MUSKET), AND EXECUTE THE CRITICAL WITH THAT WEAPON.
IS YOUR FOE FAR AWAY OR VERY DIFFICULT TO SCORE A HIT ON? THEN BUILD UP YOUR CRITICAL ON EASY-TO-TARGET FOES, AND UNLEASH THE CRITICAL ON THE FAR TARGET, AS CRITICALS ALWAYS HIT!
WORRIED ABOUT MINES? THEN ENTER V.A.T.S. AND YOU'LL AUTOMATICALLY SPOT ANY THAT ARE NEARBY.
DON'T SPRINT JUST BEFORE ENTERING V.A.T.S. COMBAT; YOU NEED ALL THE ACTION POINTS YOU CAN GET!

HIDING IN SHADOWS, WAITING TO STRIKE AFTER PLACING YOUR TRUST AND JUDGMENT IN ACCRUING ALL THE ABILITY-RELATED PERKS YOU CAN MUSTER.

Those with the necessary Agility and attire suitable for such antics may wish to try a spot of sneaking. This involves crouching, after which the level of detection appears.

**Hidden:** This means no nearby entities have detected you. Feel free to maneuver and attack with special damage bonuses, though you are at risk of being discovered. You may wish to try long-range takedowns with silenced weaponry instead. The farther apart the brackets are between the word "Hidden," the more successful your sneaking is.

**Detected:** A non-hostile entity has spotted you. The only immediate danger you face is possible embarrassment.

# HELPFUL HINT
## from Vault Boy!

WHAT MAKES A GOOD SNEAKING SPECIALIST? SOMEONE WHO STAYS IN THE SHADOWS, SWITCHES OFF ANY ILLUMINATION, SNEAKS ON ENEMIES OF A LOWER LEVEL, AND HAS MADE NUMEROUS PERK PURCHASES IN THE AGILITY SECTION OF THE PERK CHART. REMOVE POWER ARMOR AND DON APPAREL THAT GRANTS YOU BONUSES TO YOUR AGILITY (USUALLY LIGHTWEIGHT IN NATURE). STAY OUT OF A FOE'S LINE OF SIGHT. MOVE SLOWLY. USE SILENCED WEAPONRY. EMPLOY MISDIRECTION BY EXPLODING TRAPS OR SCENERY IN AREAS WHERE YOU AREN'T LOCATED. AND WATCH THE BRACKETS; IF THEY MOVE, YOU CAN BE ALERTED BEFORE YOU EVEN SEE AN ENEMY.

**Caution:** Enemies have detected but not pinpointed you. Evade them by watching the brackets around the word "Caution" expand, and return to Hidden status. Sneak attacks are still counted.

**Danger:** You have been spotted, and another type of combat is usually called for. Or run away.

# WHAT MAKES YOU S.P.E.C.I.A.L.?

Your Strength, Perception, Endurance, Charisma, Intelligence, Agility, and Luck, of course! These primary statistics, also known as attributes, are the bedrock from which you're chiseled. They range in value from 1 (woefully inadequate) to 10 (outlandishly prodigious). Each affects a different aspect of you and allows a specific list of 10 perks to be unlocked.

## THE VAULT-TEC REGISTRATION FORM: PRIMARY STATISTICS

Tell us about yourself! Vault-Tec needs to know what kind of citizen you are to ensure your future happiness. A Vault-Tec representative should have visited you recently, and you should have chosen the values of your primary statistics. You have 21 points to spend how you wish and another single point to spend if you locate the "You're S.P.E.C.I.A.L.!" book in your house in Sanctuary Hills (once you leave Vault 111).

# HELPFUL HINT
## from Vault Boy!

RONNIE HAS A CHARISMA OF 9. EVEN THOUGH HE'S LEVEL 1, HE CAN CHOOSE ANY OF THE CHARISMA PERKS, FROM 01 (CAP COLLECTOR) TO 09 (WASTELAND WANDERER). THE ONLY CHARISMA PERK HE CAN'T GET YET IS 10 (INTIMIDATION), BUT HE'S WORKING ON IT!

# HELPFUL HINT
## from Vault Boy!

STANLEY THINKS HE MADE A MISTAKE ON HIS REGISTRATION FORM AND WANTS TO CHANGE THE VALUE OF HIS S.P.E.C.I.A.L. ATTRIBUTES. FORTUNATELY, HE CAN DO THIS BEFORE LEAVING VAULT 111 FOR THE FIRST TIME. HE'S ALSO ENCOURAGED TO INVESTIGATE THE PERK CHART (ON HIS PIP-BOY), WHICH SHOWS THE PERKS THAT ARE UNLOCKED BASED ON THE VALUE OF EACH ATTRIBUTE.

# HELPFUL HINT
## from Vault Boy!

GAIL ANN HAS AN ENDURANCE OF 3 AND HAS BEEN HAVING TROUBLE RUNNING UP HILLS. LOOKING IN THE PERK CHART ON HER PIP-BOY, SHE WANTS TO GET FIT AND INCREASE HER ENDURANCE (TO ADD TO HER HEALTH AND LESSEN HER ACTION POINT DRAIN RATE FROM SPRINTING). SHE CAN SPEND POINTS AS SHE WISHES, INCREASING HER ENDURANCE (OR ANY OTHER ATTRIBUTE) EVERY TIME SHE LEVELS UP.

| NAME | | DESCRIPTION |
|------|--|-------------|
| Strength | | Strength is a measure of your raw physical power. It affects how much you can carry and the damage of all melee attacks. |
| | | Since every item you scavenge has a weight associated with it, the stronger you are, the more you can carry without becoming overburdened (which doesn't allow you to run). |
| | | Melee damage is inflicted by weapons you brandish with your hands, like a baseball bat. The higher your Strength, the more damage you inflict with such attacks. |
| Perception | | Perception is your environmental awareness and "sixth sense," and it affects weapon accuracy in V.A.T.S. If you employ this combat technique, the higher your Perception, the greater your chance of hitting a foe. A higher Perception also reveals detected threats (red dots on your compass) at a greater distance. |
| Endurance | | Endurance is a measure of your overall physical fitness. It affects your total Health and the Action Point drain from sprinting. Health is the amount of damage you can take before dying, and a higher Health is more helpful if you like to charge into battle rather than lurk and shoot from a distance. As Action Points (APs) and sprinting are both incredibly important, having larger reserves of APs (and therefore the ability to sprint greater distances) is most helpful. |
| Charisma | | Charisma is your ability to charm and convince others. It affects your success to persuade in dialogue and prices when you barter. Raise your Charisma if you wish to complete speech challenges—conversations in yellow (Easy), orange (Medium), or red (Hard)—during discussions with others. Better bartering prices also mean Caps you receive from your scavenging and trading goes farther. |
| Intelligence | | Intelligence is a measure of your overall mental acuity and affects the number of Experience Points earned. Intelligence also gives you access to the Hacker perk, allowing you to unlock more difficult terminals. As you receive a Perk Point each time you rise a level (which is spent to either increase an attribute, purchase a perk, or increase a perk by a rank), decreasing the time it takes to level up can only help you. Or can it? |
| Agility | | Agility is a measure of your overall finesse and reflexes. It affects the number of Action Points in V.A.T.S. and your ability to sneak. It is considered a particularly important attribute to those who value stealth as a viable way to maneuver around enemy territories without being seen (while crouching). As you need the largest number of Action Points as possible if you favor V.A.T.S. combat, this is another reason to never overlook this attribute. |
| Luck | | Luck is a measure of your general good fortune and affects the recharge rate of critical hits. While searching for loot, your Luck determines the (random) likelihood of receiving a rare item, mod, or high-value item. In combat, critical hits help remove targets in quicker, more violently impressive ways, and decreasing the time it takes to inflict such pain is obviously helpful. |

**The Benefits of Idiocy**

Intelligence is the one attribute you may wish to leave low, if you're interested in the benefits of the Idiot Savant perk, which requires a basic level of stupidity. Remember enemies become tougher as you level up, too, so expect to encounter more frightening foes if you lessen the time it takes to reach higher levels.

# VAULT LIFE HAS ITS PERKS!

Regularly study your Vault-Tec literature, as the Perk Chart that accompanies your Pip-Boy is the key to augmenting yourself for the better. When you increase a level, you receive a Perk Point. This can be saved, or you can spend them immediately, in one of three ways:

- PERK POINTS CAN BE SPENT ON RAISING ANY ATTRIBUTE (SO YOU CAN UNLOCK ANOTHER LEVEL OF PERKS).
- PERK POINTS CAN BE SPENT ON PURCHASING A NEW PERK, PROVIDING THE VALUE OF THE ASSOCIATED ATTRIBUTE HAS BEEN REACHED. A FEW PERKS REQUIRE YOU TO BE MALE OR FEMALE.
- PERK POINTS CAN BE SPENT TO INCREASE THE RANK OF AN ALREADY-PURCHASED PERK. PERKS CAN HAVE BETWEEN ONE AND FIVE RANKS, DENOTED BY STARS ON YOUR CHART. RANK 1 IS ALWAYS ACCESSIBLE (PROVIDING YOUR ATTRIBUTE REQUIREMENT HAS BEEN MET). RANK 2 AND HIGHER REQUIRES YOU TO BE A PARTICULAR LEVEL.

**HELPFUL HINT** from *Vault Boy!*  Did You Know?

JOEY IS FEELING PRETTY PLEASED WITH HIMSELF; HE'S JUST REACHED LEVEL 10! HE WANTS TO UNLOCK SOME COOL AGILITY PERKS, AND HE'S GOT THREE PERK POINTS TO SPEND (ONE FOR REACHING LEVEL 10 AND TWO PREVIOUSLY SAVED). CURRENTLY, HE HAS AN AGILITY OF 6. NOT BAD. HE ALREADY HAS THE SNEAK PERK (RANK 1 OF 5), SO HE USES A POINT TO INCREASE SNEAK TO RANK 2. BUT TO GET TO RANK 3, HE'LL NEED TO COMPLETE MORE ADVENTURING AND REACH LEVEL 12.

NEXT, HE REALLY WANTS THE NINJA PERK, BUT THAT REQUIRES AN AGILITY OF 7. SO HE CHECKS HIS AGILITY ATTRIBUTE, AND BECAUSE HE'S LEVEL 10, HE CAN ADD A POINT TO AGILITY. QUICK AS A FLASH, HE DOES JUST THAT! THIS OPENS UP THE NINJA PERK. HE UNLOCKS NINJA RANK 1 (RANK 2 REQUIRES HIM TO BE LEVEL 16, SO THAT'S GOING TO TAKE A WHILE).

**HELPFUL HINT** from *Vault Boy!*  Did You Know?

DAVE IS DEDICATED TO INCREASING HIS RAW, PHYSICAL POWER AND IS ALREADY AT STRENGTH 9. WAY TO GO, DAVE! BUT TO REACH THE PINNACLE OF BUFFNESS, HE'S PONDERING ON SPENDING YET ANOTHER PERK POINT ON STRENGTH TRAINING. HOWEVER, JUST BEFORE DECIDING, HE CHANCED UPON A SPECIAL VAULT-TEC LIMITED-EDITION STRENGTH BOBBLEHEAD, WHICH GRANTED HIM AN IMMEDIATE +1 TO HIS STRENGTH. NOW HE CAN SPEND HIS PERK POINT ON SOMETHING DIFFERENT! COULD DAVE TECHNICALLY HAVE RAISED HIS STRENGTH TO 11? YES, BUT THE BENEFITS ARE NEGLIGIBLE.

**HELPFUL HINT** from *Vault Boy!*  Did You Know?

MOLLY LIKES TO KEEP A STEALTHY DISTANCE FROM HER FOES AND HAS AN AGILITY OF 8. THAT'S AMAZING, MOLLY! RECENTLY, WHILE RUMMAGING AROUND, SHE DISCOVERED A SET OF MILITARY FATIGUES THAT BESTOWED A +2 AGILITY BONUS WHEN SHE WORE THEM. WOW! BUT THAT ONLY AFFECTED HER AGILITY BONUSES IN REGARDS TO HER ABILITY TO SNEAK AND THE ACTION POINTS IN V.A.T.S.; IT DIDN'T ALLOW HER TO UNLOCK ANY LEVEL 9 OR 10 AGILITY PERKS. RATS!

# STRENGTH-RELATED PERKS

## STRENGTH TRAINING

Strength is a measure of your raw physical power. It affects how much you can carry and the damage of all melee attacks.

Since every item you scavenge has a weight associated with it, the stronger you are, the more you can carry without becoming overburdened (which doesn't allow you to run).

Melee damage is inflicted by weapons you brandish with your hands, like a baseball bat. The higher your Strength, the more damage you inflict with such attacks.

Build those muscles! Spend a Perk Point and instantly gain 1 point of Strength to a maximum of 10.

There are no requirements for the training in this attribute.

## LEVEL 01: IRON FIST

Channel your chi to unleash devastating fury! If you're the pugilistic sort and favor unarmed weaponry to inflict pain and suffering to an ever-more impressive degree, this is the perk for you! Let's not dwell on the slight shortfall of the difficulty in fighting multiple opponents at once; this focuses all your muscle on one hapless fool. Consult the Weapons chapter for the variety of punching weapons available.

| RANK | REQUIREMENTS | DESCRIPTION |
|---|---|---|
| 1 | STR 1 | Punching attacks do 20 percent more damage to your opponent. |
| 2 | Level 9, STR 1 | Punching attacks now do 40 percent more damage and can disarm your opponent. |
| 3 | Level 18, STR 1 | Punching attacks now do 60 percent more damage. Unarmed Power Attacks have a chance to cripple one of your opponent's limbs. |
| 4 | Level 31, STR 1 | Punching attacks now do 80 percent more damage. Unarmed Power Attacks have an increased chance to cripple one of your opponent's limbs. |
| 5 | Level 46, STR 1 | Punching attacks now do double damage. Criticals in V.A.T.S. will paralyze your opponent. |

## LEVEL 02: BIG LEAGUES

Swing for the fences! If you design a bludgeoning or bladed method of bringing an end to your foes, this is the perk to take. Though difficult to battle against multiple enemies in the same space, close combat is much more impressive when your damage is increased. Check the Weapons chapter for more information on available melee weapons.

| RANK | REQUIREMENTS | DESCRIPTION |
|---|---|---|
| 1 | STR 2 | Does 20 percent more melee weapon damage. |
| 2 | Level 7, STR 2 | You now do 40 percent more melee weapon damage and gain a chance to disarm your opponent. |
| 3 | Level 15, STR 2 | You now do 60 percent more melee weapon damage and gain an increased chance to disarm your opponent. |
| 4 | Level 27, STR 2 | You now do 80 percent more melee weapon damage and hit all targets in front of you. |
| 5 | Level 42, STR 2 | You now do double damage with a melee weapon and gain a chance to cripple your opponent, or grand slam their head clean off! |

## LEVEL 03: ARMORER

Protect yourself from the dangers of the Wasteland. If you're the sort to tinkerer at an armor workbench and want to craft some impressively protective gear for yourself or your companions, choose this perk.

| RANK | REQUIREMENTS | DESCRIPTION |
|---|---|---|
| 1 | STR 3 | You gain access to base level and Rank 1 armor mods. |
| 2 | Level 13, STR 3 | You gain access to Rank 2 armor mods. |
| 3 | Level 25, STR 3 | You gain access to Rank 3 armor mods. |
| 4 | Level 39, STR 3 | You gain access to Rank 4 armor mods. |

This perk enhances your workshop settlements. This allows you to create the Power Armor station (Rank 1, with Local Leader Rank 2).

## LEVEL 04: BLACKSMITH

Fire up the forge! If you enjoy swinging a melee weapon into the skulls of your adversaries, it pays to craft modified variants at a weapons workbench, using these perks to make such implements with the very best bonuses.

| RANK | REQUIREMENTS | DESCRIPTION |
|---|---|---|
| 1 | STR 4 | You gain access to base level and Rank 1 melee weapon mods. |
| 2 | Level 16, STR 4 | You gain access to Rank 2 melee weapon mods. |
| 3 | Level 29, STR 4 | You gain access to Rank 3 melee weapon mods. |

## LEVEL 05: HEAVY GUNNER

Thanks to practice and conditioning, you're able to utilize the weightiest of weapons with an extra degree of precision. Check the Weapons chapter for the different types of heavy guns so you know which ones this perk affects. Combine with other weapon perks so you receive a bonus no matter which weapon you wield.

| RANK | REQUIREMENTS | DESCRIPTION |
|---|---|---|
| 1 | STR 5 | Heavy guns do 20 percent more damage. |
| 2 | Level 11, STR 5 | Heavy guns now do 40 percent more damage and have improved hip-fire accuracy. |
| 3 | Level 21, STR 5 | Heavy guns now do 60 percent more damage. Hip-fire accuracy is increased even more. |
| 4 | Level 35, STR 5 | Heavy guns now do 80 percent more damage and have a chance to stagger your opponent. |
| 5 | Level 47, STR 5 | Heavy guns now do double damage. |

## LEVEL 06: STRONG BACK

What are you, part pack mule? Though those favoring heavier weapons and armor are likely to take this perk on general principle, it's also hugely beneficial to scavengers; spend more time in the wilderness gathering loot to sell or trade! Carry a greater complement of killing equipment! And at higher levels, have some way of easily maneuvering back to safety without dropping your ill-gotten gains.

| RANK | REQUIREMENTS | DESCRIPTION |
|---|---|---|
| 1 | STR 6 | Gain +25 to carry weight. |
| 2 | Level 10, STR 6 | You now have +50 to carry weight. |
| 3 | Level 20, STR 6 | When overburdened, you can use Action Points to run. |
| 4 | Level 30, STR 6 | When overburdened, you can Fast-Travel. |

## LEVEL 07: STEADY AIM

Stay on target! If you enjoy the benefits of gunplay without entering V.A.T.S. to accomplish your violent goals, then increase the accuracy of any projectile weapon with this perk. This allows you just a little more leeway when manually firing at foes, and also without aiming down ironsights or scopes.

| RANK | REQUIREMENTS | DESCRIPTION |
|---|---|---|
| 1 | STR 7 | Hip-fire accuracy is improved when firing any gun. |
| 2 | Level 28, STR 7 | Hip-fire accuracy is improved even more when firing any gun. |

## LEVEL 08: BASHER

Get up close and personal! The amount of time you use the butt of your gun to inflict a bloody nose (or worse) at close quarters reflects how important you deem this perk to be. But it does increase the flexibility of more complex combat situations where you may not wish to switch between a favored firearm and a different weapon type (like a punching weapon).

| RANK | REQUIREMENTS | DESCRIPTION |
|---|---|---|
| 1 | STR 8 | Gun bashing does 25 percent more damage. |
| 2 | Level 5, STR 8 | Gun bashing now does 50 percent more damage and possibly cripples your opponent. |
| 3 | Level 14, STR 8 | Gun bashing now does 75 percent more damage and has an increased chance to cripple your opponent. |
| 4 | Level 26, STR 8 | Gun bashing does double damage and has an increased chance to cripple your opponent. It may also inflict a critical hit. |

## LEVEL 09: ROOTED

You're part tree! Though ostensibly used when you're standing there trading melee blows with a hapless idiot who's regretting challenging you to a close-quarter fight, this can also be employed if you're sneaking behind a foe, stopping, and delivering a killing blow.

| RANK | REQUIREMENTS | DESCRIPTION |
|---|---|---|
| 1 | STR 9 | While standing still, you gain +25 Damage Resistance and your melee and unarmed attacks deal 25 percent more damage. |
| 2 | Level 22, STR 9 | While standing still, you now gain +50 Damage Resistance and your melee and unarmed attacks deal 50 percent more damage. |
| 3 | Level 43, STR 9 | While standing still, you may automatically disarm enemies that use melee weapons against you. |

## LEVEL 10: PAIN TRAIN

Choo-choo! All aboard! Turning Power Armor into an offensive weapon? What an exceptional idea: As long as you have the Action Points to complete a sprint before switching to your favored weapon and you're focusing on Power Armor as a main source of protection, this can prove an excellent deterrent, at any time during combat.

| RANK | REQUIREMENTS | DESCRIPTION |
|---|---|---|
| 1 | STR 10 | While wearing Power Armor, sprinting into enemies hurts and staggers them. (Robots and oversized enemies are immune to the stagger.) |
| 2 | Level 24, STR 10 | Sprinting into enemies while wearing Power Armor now causes severe damage and a more powerful stagger. (Robots and oversized enemies are immune to the stagger.) |
| 3 | Level 50, STR 10 | Sprinting into enemies while wearing Power Armor now causes massive damage and knocks them down. Impact landing near enemies inflicts even more damage. |

# PERCEPTION-RELATED PERKS

## PERCEPTION TRAINING

Perception is your environmental awareness and "sixth sense," and it affects weapon accuracy in V.A.T.S. If you employ this combat technique, the higher your Perception, the greater your chance of hitting a foe. A higher Perception also reveals detected threats (red dots on your compass) at a greater distance.

Become more aware! Spend a Perk Point and instantly gain 1 point of Perception to a maximum of 10.

There are no requirements for the training in this attribute.

## LEVEL 01: PICKPOCKET

You have quick hands and sticky fingers, and for those favoring a stealthy method of foe disposal (or gathering items such as keys from folks without resorting to gunplay or fast-talking), this is a fine perk to take. Remember Rank 2 is the only way you're able to drop in a live grenade as a special present, and only if your adversaries haven't seen you.

| RANK | REQUIREMENTS | DESCRIPTION |
|---|---|---|
| 1 | PER 1 | Picking pockets is 25 percent easier. |
| 2 | Level 6, PER 1 | Picking pockets is now 50 percent easier. You can place a live grenade in a person's inventory. |
| 3 | Level 17, PER 1 | Picking pockets is now 75 percent easier, and you can steal equipped weapons. |
| 4 | Level 30, PER 1 | Picking pockets is now twice as easy, and you can steal equipped items. |

## LEVEL 02: RIFLEMAN

Keep your distance long and your kill count high. Though this only requires a Perception of 2, increasing this to a much greater degree allows you to spot and remove foes at a greater range, which is what these weapons are designed to do. Be certain you know which weapons nonautomatic rifles are; the Weapons chapter lists them all.

| RANK | REQUIREMENTS | DESCRIPTION |
|---|---|---|
| 1 | PER 2 | Attacks with nonautomatic rifles do 20 percent more damage. |
| 2 | Level 9, PER 2 | Attacks with nonautomatic rifles now do 40 percent more damage and ignore 15 percent of a target's armor. |
| 3 | Level 18, PER 2 | Attacks with nonautomatic rifles now do 60 percent more damage and ignore 20 percent of a target's armor. |
| 4 | Level 31, PER 2 | Attacks with nonautomatic rifles now do 80 percent more damage and ignore 25 percent of a target's armor. They also have a slight chance of crippling a limb. |
| 5 | Level 46, PER 2 | Attacks with nonautomatic rifles now do double damage and ignore 30 percent of a target's armor. They also have a slightly higher chance of crippling a limb. |

## LEVEL 03: AWARENESS

If additional information is what you crave, then this is a most helpful augmentation to your V.A.T.S. combat interface, as it allows you to see what a foe's resistances are and use weapons they are susceptible to.

| RANK | REQUIREMENTS | DESCRIPTION |
|---|---|---|
| 1 | PER 3 | To defeat your enemies, know their weaknesses! You can view a target's specific Damage Resistances in V.A.T.S. |

The following information is now imparted:

- Level: Your enemy's level.
- Shield: Your enemy's resistance to ballistic, explosive, or impact-related damage.
- Lightning: Your enemy's resistance to energy weapons.
- Radiation: Your enemy's resistance to weapons that inflict radiation damage.
- Poison Drop: Your enemy's resistance to weapons that inflict poison damage.

## LEVEL 04: LOCKSMITH

You have impressively nimble fingers. As there is a large number of doors that are locked, it is worth considering this perk if you must know what's behind every closet door, storage door, or secret door. Remember that sometimes a locked door can be opened via other means (a terminal, requiring the Hacker perk) or a key. The Map chapter shows every door's difficulty rating and the important items behind there, so figure out how important this is. It's usually better to focus on either Locksmith or Hacker.

| RANK | REQUIREMENTS | DESCRIPTION |
|---|---|---|
| 1 | PER 4 | You can pick Advanced locks. |
| 2 | Level 7, PER 4 | You can pick Expert locks. |
| 3 | Level 18, PER 4 | You can pick Master locks. |
| 4 | Level 41, PER 4 | Your bobby pins never break during lockpicking. |

## LEVEL 05: DEMOLITION EXPERT

The bigger the boom, the better! At the highest ranks, a proficient expert can craft a potent bomb or ten and lob them all at even the most dangerous of marauding foes, dropping the enemy before engaging in closer combat. Are you a fan of mines? Do you enjoy using V.A.T.S. to shoot grenades or mines close to or carried on an enemy? Then think about this perk.

| RANK | REQUIREMENTS | DESCRIPTION |
|---|---|---|
| 1 | PER 5 | Your explosives do 25 percent more damage, and you can craft explosives at any chemistry station. |
| 2 | Level 10, PER 5 | Your explosives now do 50 percent more damage, and grenades gain a throwing arc. |
| 3 | Level 22, PER 5 | Your explosives now do 75 percent more damage and affect a larger area. |
| 4 | Level 34, PER 5 | Your explosives now do double damage. Mines and grenades shot in V.A.T.S. explode for double damage, too. |

## LEVEL 06: NIGHT PERSON

You are a creature of the night! Though this doesn't allow you to spend Perk Points on perks you don't have the Intelligence or Perception to unlock, you do receive the impressive enhancements that a higher INT and PER allow you. For example, you have a greater distance to spot enemies and V.A.T.S. enhancements for Perception and the increase in XP that an Intelligence boost gives you.

| RANK | REQUIREMENTS | DESCRIPTION |
|---|---|---|
| 1 | PER 6 | Gain +2 to Intelligence and Perception between the hours of 6:00 p.m. and 6:00 a.m. |
| 2 | Level 25, PER 6 | You now have +3 to Intelligence and Perception between the hours of 6:00 p.m. and 6:00 a.m. and night vision when sneaking. |

## LEVEL 07: REFRACTOR

You must be part mirror! For enemies that favor weapons inflicting this type of damage (such as Institute synths, foes armed with cryo or energy weaponry, and tesla arc traps), this proves to be an impressive defense. To a Raider attempting to hit you with a baseball bat, this offers no protection. Further complement this resistance by taking the Moving Target, Robot Sympathy, and Shield Harmonics perks. The Toughness perk offers all-around protection and might be a better fit.

| RANK | REQUIREMENTS | DESCRIPTION |
|---|---|---|
| 1 | PER 7 | Instantly gain +10 Energy Resistance. |
| 2 | Level 11, PER 7 | You now have +20 Energy Resistance. |
| 3 | Level 21, PER 7 | You now have +30 Energy Resistance. |
| 4 | Level 35, PER 7 | You now have +40 Energy Resistance. |
| 5 | Level 42, PER 7 | You now have +50 Energy Resistance. |

## LEVEL 08: SNIPER

It's all about focus. Like Gunslinger and Commando (for your other weapon types), this allows further flexibility when utilizing any nonauto scoped rifle. A list of this weapon type is provided in the Weapons chapter. If you favor these type of guns, this is your first perk choice.

| RANK | REQUIREMENTS | DESCRIPTION |
|---|---|---|
| 1 | PER 8 | You have improved control and can hold your breath longer when aiming with scopes. This reduces wobble. |
| 2 | Level 13, PER 8 | Nonautomatic, scoped rifles have a chance of knocking down your target. |
| 3 | Level 26, PER 8 | Nonautomatic, scoped rifles gain +25 percent accuracy to head shots in V.A.T.S. |

## LEVEL 09: PENETRATOR

There's no place to hide! This doesn't allow shooting through impenetrable walls but does allow you to target partially obscured foes (like those behind trees, through windows, or behind barricades) if parts of them are visible. This is another good option to further enhance V.A.T.S. combat.

| RANK | REQUIREMENTS | DESCRIPTION |
|---|---|---|
| 1 | PER 9 | In V.A.T.S. you can target an enemy's body parts that are blocked by cover, with a decrease in accuracy. |
| 2 | Level 28, PER 9 | In V.A.T.S. when you target an enemy's body parts that are blocked by cover, there is no decrease in accuracy. |

## LEVEL 10: CONCENTRATED FIRE

Stay focused! This focus only stops when you run out of Action Points, so bolster APs to further enhance this perk. As you'll know how many APs it takes to fire off the bullets from your weapon, you should surmise that a heavier weapon, or one that fires slower and more damaging projectiles, is more likely to use up your Action Points more quickly and lessen the effectiveness of this perk. So play around with your favorite weapons to see which ones are most effective.

| RANK | REQUIREMENTS | DESCRIPTION |
|---|---|---|
| 1 | PER 10 | In V.A.T.S. every attack on the same body part gains +10 percent accuracy. |
| 2 | Level 26, PER 10 | In V.A.T.S. every attack on the same body part gains +15 percent accuracy. |
| 3 | Level 50, PER 10 | In V.A.T.S. every attack on the same body part gains +20 percent accuracy and does 20 percent more damage. |

# ENDURANCE-RELATED PERKS

## ENDURANCE TRAINING

Endurance is a measure of your overall physical fitness. It affects your total Health and the Action Point drain from sprinting. Health is the amount of damage you can take before dying, and a higher Health is more helpful if you like to charge into battle rather than lurk and shoot from a distance. As Action Points (APs) and sprinting are both incredibly important, having larger reserves of APs (and therefore the ability to sprint greater distances) is most helpful.

Get fit! Spend a Perk Point and instantly gain 1 point of Endurance to a maximum of 10.

There are no requirements for the training in this attribute.

## LEVEL 01: TOUGHNESS

If nothing else, you can take a beating! Assuming you'll be dealing with more than simple foul language hurled in your direction, gaining a permanent bolster to your Damage Resistance is just like having a thick skin of armor. A fantastic way to spend a Perk Point or five.

| RANK | REQUIREMENTS | DESCRIPTION |
|---|---|---|
| 1 | END 1 | Instantly gain +10 Damage Resistance. |
| 2 | Level 9, END 1 | You now have +20 Damage Resistance. |
| 3 | Level 18, END 1 | You now have +30 Damage Resistance. |
| 4 | Level 31, END 1 | You now have +40 Damage Resistance. |
| 5 | Level 46, END 1 | You now have +50 Damage Resistance. |

## LEVEL 02: LEAD BELLY

Your digestive tract has adjusted to the weirdness of the Wasteland! Are you sick of stimpaks? Detest chemistry stations and making your own chems, or constantly scavenging for them? Then look for comestibles and water sources throughout the Commonwealth without the usual "distaste"! Take this perk or ones that help you when you use chems (like Chem Resistant or Chemist).

| RANK | REQUIREMENTS | DESCRIPTION |
|---|---|---|
| 1 | END 2 | Take less radiation from eating or drinking. |
| 2 | Level 6, END 2 | You take even less radiation from eating or drinking. |
| 3 | Level 17, END 2 | You take no radiation from eating or drinking. |

## LEVEL 03: LIFE GIVER

You embody wellness! You also receive an instant Health increase, which has no downsides (except it takes slightly longer to inflict Nerd Rage! on a set of foes). If you need extra Health, this is a must-take perk.

| RANK | REQUIREMENTS | DESCRIPTION |
|---|---|---|
| 1 | END 3 | Instantly gain +20 maximum Health. |
| 2 | Level 8, END 3 | You instantly gain another +20 maximum Health. |
| 3 | Level 20, END 3 | You instantly gain another +20 maximum Health and slowly regenerate lost Health. |

## LEVEL 04: CHEM RESISTANT

All the rush without the hassle! Can't get enough of Jet, Psycho, or Buffout (or any other chem, including the ones you've made yourself at a chemistry station)? Then lessen (and finally remove) the downside of chem addiction completely. This is essential if you plan on enhancing your routines with chems.

| RANK | REQUIREMENTS | DESCRIPTION |
|---|---|---|
| 1 | END 4 | You're 50 percent less likely to get addicted when consuming chems. |
| 2 | Level 22, END 4 | You gain complete immunity to chem addiction. |

## LEVEL 05: AQUABOY / AQUAGIRL

Water is your ally. The Commonwealth has an impressive amount of it. Whether you're swimming the lakes or exploring the depths of the ocean, having the ability to use stealth and not suffer any ill effects from water is a most impressive feat indeed. It allows escape in any direction and sneak attacks on shoreline strongholds.

| RANK | REQUIREMENTS | DESCRIPTION |
|---|---|---|
| 1 | END 5 | You no longer take radiation damage from swimming and can breathe underwater. |
| 2 | Level 21, END 5 | You become totally undetectable while submerged. |

## LEVEL 06: RAD RESISTANT

Exposure to the Wasteland has made you more resilient. It also makes you less keen on consuming Rad-X, as this chem isn't anywhere near as necessary; so trade any you find before marching off into irradiated ponds or the infamous Glowing Sea.

| RANK | REQUIREMENTS | DESCRIPTION |
|---|---|---|
| 1 | END 6 | You are instantly granted +10 Radiation Resistance. |
| 2 | Level 13, END 6 | You now have +20 Radiation Resistance. |
| 3 | Level 26, END 6 | You now have +30 Radiation Resistance. |

## LEVEL 07: ADAMANTIUM SKELETON

Your skeleton has been infused with indestructible metal, which lessens the hobbling problems associated with crippling injuries. Sometimes your limbs are struck by foes, but most of the time such damage is caused by falling. Seek medical attention (or a bed) far less often than normal by choosing this perk.

| RANK | REQUIREMENTS | DESCRIPTION |
|---|---|---|
| 1 | END 7 | Your limb damage is reduced by 30 percent. |
| 2 | Level 13, END 7 | Your limb damage is now reduced by 60 percent. |
| 3 | Level 26, END 7 | Your limb damage is completely eliminated. |

## LEVEL 08: CANNIBAL

Feast on mortal flesh to heal your wounds! But don't do it around any polite folk (including companions, who aren't fans of chowing down on humans, Ghouls, or greenskin flesh), as you aren't seen in the best of lights. This is a good alternative to other forms of sustenance, though it requires you to be less caring in the way others perceive you. There's a chance you'll be openly attacked if you're gnawing on a citizen who lived in the establishment you're feasting at, too. So have some decorum, please!

| RANK | REQUIREMENTS | DESCRIPTION |
|---|---|---|
| 1 | END 8 | Eating human corpses restores Health. |
| 2 | Level 19, END 8 | Eating Ghoul or Super Mutant corpses restores Health. |
| 3 | Level 38, END 8 | Eating human, Ghoul, or Super Mutant corpses now restores a significant amount of Health. |

## LEVEL 09: GHOULISH

Sure, you're still human—on the outside! Inside, though, you're seemingly part Ghoul, which doesn't have a downside, except that the perk doesn't function away from radiation. This negates any Rad-X you may need to take (allowing you to sell it instead), and you can venture into the Glowing Sea in just your skivvies if you wish. Simply reference locations in this guide's Map chapter that mention radiation (especially severe) and you have an additional "recharge" point!

| RANK | REQUIREMENTS | DESCRIPTION |
|---|---|---|
| 1 | END 9 | Radiation now regenerates your lost Health. |
| 2 | Level 24, END 9 | Radiation now regenerates even more of your lost Health. |
| 3 | Level 48, END 9 | Radiation now regenerates even more of your lost Health, and some Feral Ghouls will randomly become friendly. |

## LEVEL 10: SOLAR POWERED

Catch some rays! A good perk for the extra melee damage, carry weight, Health, and Action Points you receive. When you're finally able to regenerate Health, combine this with Adamantium Skeleton (which heals limb damage) and snoozing on a bed during the night. Focus all your exploration during daytime hours.

| RANK | REQUIREMENTS | DESCRIPTION |
|---|---|---|
| 1 | END 10 | Gain +2 to Strength and Endurance between the hours of 6:00 a.m. and 6:00 p.m. |
| 2 | Level 27, END 10 | Sunlight slowly heals your radiation damage. |
| 3 | Level 50, END 10 | Sunlight regenerates your lost Health. |

# CHARISMA-RELATED PERKS

## CHARISMA TRAINING

Charisma is your ability to charm and convince others. It affects your success to persuade in dialogue and prices when you barter. Raise your Charisma if you wish to complete speech challenges—conversations in yellow (Easy), orange (Medium), or red (Hard)—during discussions with others. Better bartering prices also mean Caps you receive from your scavenging and trading goes farther.

Enhance your natural charm! Spend a Perk Point and instantly gain 1 point of Charisma to a maximum of 10.

There are no requirements for the training in this attribute.

### LEVEL 01: CAP COLLECTOR

You've mastered the art of the deal! This perk enhances your workshop settlements with better bartering power. It allows you to create the following:

- Trading Emporium (Rank 2, with Local Leader perk Rank 2)
- Armor Emporium (Rank 2, with Local Leader perk Rank 2)
- Weapons Emporium (Rank 2, with Local Leader perk Rank 2)
- Restaurant (Rank 2, with Local Leader perk Rank 2)a
- Clothing Emporium (Rank 2, with Local Leader perk, Rank 2)

Choose this if trading is your favored way to accrue wealth, and you have a bustling community of traders (including those you've attracted to any settlements you own).

| RANK | REQUIREMENTS | DESCRIPTION |
|------|--------------|-------------|
| 1 | CHR 1 | Buying and selling prices at vendors are better. |
| 2 | Level 20, CHR 1 | Buying and selling prices at vendors are now much better. |
| 3 | Level 41, CHR 1 | You can now invest a total of 500 Caps to raise a store's buying capacity. |

### LEVEL 02: BLACK WIDOW / LADY KILLER

"Come into my parlor," said the Black Widow. You're charming . . . and dangerous to those of the opposite sex. Though the gender of the Commonwealth's population is about evenly split, this perk won't affect those sporting a similar undercarriage to you. Don't forget the Intimidation perk; both of these perks in unison allows almost any situation to be handled your way, without (or with) violence.

| RANK | REQUIREMENTS | DESCRIPTION |
|------|--------------|-------------|
| 1 | CHR 2, Female | The opposite gender suffers +5 percent damage in combat and |
| 1 | CHR 2, Male | is easier to persuade in dialogue. |
| 2 | Level 7, CHR 2, Female | The opposite gender now suffers +10 percent damage in combat and is even easier to persuade in dialogue. They are |
| 2 | Level 7, CHR 2, Male | also easier to pacify with the Intimidation perk. |
| 3 | Level 22, CHR 2, Female | The opposite gender now suffers +15 percent damage in combat and is much easier to persuade in dialogue. They are |
| 3 | Level 22, CHR 2, Male | now even easier to pacify with the Intimidation perk. |

### LEVEL 03: LONE WANDERER

Who needs friends anyway? If you prefer a solo exploration, you can add value that would normally require Endurance and Strength bonuses at lower ranks. The relatively low CHR requirement means the first rank of this is an extremely attractive proposition.

| RANK | REQUIREMENTS | DESCRIPTION |
|------|--------------|-------------|
| 1 | CHR 3 | When adventuring without a companion, you take 15 percent less damage and carry weight increases by 50 |
| 2 | Level 17, CHR 3 | When adventuring without a companion, you take 30 percent less damage and carry weight increases by 100 |
| 3 | Level 40, CHR 3 | When adventuring without a companion, you do 25 percent more damage. |

### LEVEL 04: ATTACK DOG

If you're wandering the Commonwealth with Dogmeat, these improvements in his training allow him to help savage any foes you both come across. For the dog lover.

| RANK | REQUIREMENTS | DESCRIPTION |
|------|--------------|-------------|
| 1 | CHR 4 | Your faithful canine companion can hold an enemy, giving you a greater chance to hit them in V.A.T.S. |
| 2 | Level 9, CHR 4 | When your dog holds an enemy, there's a chance he'll cripple the limb he's biting. |
| 3 | Level 25, CHR 4 | When your dog holds an enemy, there's a chance he'll cause them to bleed. |

## LEVEL 05: ANIMAL FRIEND

Commune with beasts! But only if you're successful and aim your gun at the animal in question; you may wish to check the level of your target first in V.A.T.S. with the Awareness perk. The higher ranks allow you to use more interesting commands, allowing you to chance upon, say, a Yao Guai lair and bringing the beast with you into a nearby Raider camp. At Rank 3, the beast acts a little like a dumber pet, with more control over where you can send it, usually into areas to cause a distraction. Animals are beasts that were naturally occurring before the bombs dropped.

| RANK | REQUIREMENTS | DESCRIPTION |
| --- | --- | --- |
| 1 | CHR 5 | With your gun, aim at any animal below your level and gain a chance to pacify it. |
| 2 | Level 12, CHR 5 | When you successfully pacify an animal, you can incite it to attack. |
| 3 | Level 28, CHR 5 | When you successfully pacify an animal, you can give it specific commands. |

## LEVEL 06: LOCAL LEADER

This perk enhances your workshop settlements. It allows you to create the following:

- Trading Stand, Shop, Emporium*, (Rank 2)
- Armor Stand, Stop, Emporium* (Rank 2)
- Weapons Stand, Shop, Emporium* (Rank 2)
- Drink Stand, Bar, Restaurant* (Rank 2)
- First Aid Station**, Clinic**, Surgery Center** (Rank 2)
- Armor Workbench, Chemistry Station Type 1 & 2, Cooking Station Type 1 & 2, Cooking Stove, Power Armor Station***, Weapons Workbench 1 & 2 (Rank 2)
- (* Requires Cap Collector Perk, Rank 2)
- (** Requires Medic, Rank 1)
- (*** Requires Armorer, Rank 1)

As the ruler everyone turns to, this is a critically important perk to unlock as you work on improving the settlements you are running. Both ranks of this perk enhance your settlements, but Rank 2 is most dramatic. Consult the Workshop chapter for the specific benefits.

| RANK | REQUIREMENTS | DESCRIPTION |
| --- | --- | --- |
| 1 | CHR 6 | You are able to establish supply lines between your workshop settlements. |
| 2 | Level 14, CHR 6 | You can build stores and workstations at workshop settlements. |

## LEVEL 07: PARTY BOY / PARTY GIRL

Nobody has a good time like you! Simply look up the effects of your favorite wine, beer, vodka, or other alcoholic beverages, and employ them when you need to without the unpleasant side effects afterward. As Luck influences how quickly your critical hits recharge, fighting while drunk at Rank 3 now becomes even more beneficial, rather than an embarrassing kerfuffle.

| RANK | REQUIREMENTS | DESCRIPTION |
| --- | --- | --- |
| 1 | CHR 7 | There's no chance you'll get addicted to alcohol. |
| 2 | Level 15, CHR 7 | The effects of alcohol are doubled. |
| 3 | Level 37, CHR 7 | Your Luck is increased by 3 while you're under the influence of alcohol. |

## LEVEL 08: INSPIRATIONAL

Because you lead by example, your companions gain benefits from your methods of exploration. If you're concentrating on keeping a follower with you for the foreseeable future, it's well worth augmenting them as much as possible, though this always comes at the expense of spending points purely on yourself. But that's selfish.

| RANK | REQUIREMENTS | DESCRIPTION |
| --- | --- | --- |
| 1 | CHR 8 | Your companion does more damage in combat and cannot hurt you. |
| 2 | Level 19, CHR 8 | Your companion resists more damage in combat and can't be harmed by your attacks. |
| 3 | Level 43, CHR 8 | Your companion can carry more items. |

## LEVEL 09: WASTELAND WHISPERER

Master the post-apocalypse! This targets any critter you aim your gun at; you may wish to check the level of your target first in V.A.T.S. with the Awareness perk. The higher ranks allow you to seek more interesting commands, giving you the opportunity to, say, encounter a Feral Ghoul Glowing One and bring it with you into a nearby Gunner camp. At Rank 3, the creature acts a little like a dumber pet, with more control over where you can send it, usually into areas to cause a distraction.

| RANK | REQUIREMENTS | DESCRIPTION |
| --- | --- | --- |
| 1 | CHR 9 | With your gun, aim at any Wasteland creature below your level and gain a chance to pacify it. |
| 2 | Level 21, CHR 9 | When you successfully pacify a Wasteland creature, you can incite it to attack. |
| 3 | Level 49, CHR 9 | When you successfully pacify a Wasteland creature, you can give it specific commands. |

## LEVEL 10: INTIMIDATION

When you successfully pacify someone, you can give them specific commands. In the same way that Wasteland Whisperer and Animal Friend gave you the ability to control certain wild animals and critters, this ability is now available to any human you meet! Now you can turn Raiders on one another, make them enter areas they'd rather avoid falling into, and order them around like a subjugated follower, usually as a form of distraction to gain the upper hand on other enemies.

| RANK | REQUIREMENTS | DESCRIPTION |
| --- | --- | --- |
| 1 | CHR 10 | Time to show everyone who's boss! With your gun, aim at any human opponent below your level and gain a chance to pacify them. |
| 2 | Level 23, CHR 10 | When you successfully pacify someone, you can incite them to attack. |
| 3 | Level 50, CHR 10 | |

# INTELLIGENCE-RELATED PERKS

## INTELLIGENCE TRAINING

Intelligence is a measure of your overall mental acuity and affects the number of Experience Points earned. Intelligence also gives you access to the Hacker perk, allowing you to unlock more difficult terminals. As you receive a Perk Point each time you rise a level (which is spent to either increase an attribute, purchase a perk, or increase a perk by a rank), decreasing the time it takes to level up can only help you. Or can it?

Keep learning! Spend a Perk Point and instantly gain 1 point of Intelligence to a maximum of 10.

There are no requirements for the training in this attribute.

## LEVEL 01: V.A.N.S.

Let Vault-Tec guide you! The path to your closest quest target is displayed in V.A.T.S. In actuality, let Vault-Tec's Documentation Department guide you; learn your quest targets by checking this book instead, though without the compass flag to help. You could simply refer to this book and use a map marker on your world map, though.

| RANK | REQUIREMENTS | DESCRIPTION |
|---|---|---|
| 1 | INT 1 | |

## LEVEL 02: MEDIC

This perk enhances your workshop settlements. This allows you to create the following:

- First Aid Station, Clinic, Surgery Center (Rank 2, with Local Leader, Rank 2)

Is there a doctor in the house? Also employ the Chemist perk, this allows additional potency. Everyone needs a bit of extra Health (and radiation abatement), but to maximize this perk, make sure you're administering those chems, rather than using other perks to gain Health and negate radiation.

| RANK | REQUIREMENTS | DESCRIPTION |
|---|---|---|
| 1 | INT 2 | Stimpaks restore 40 percent of lost Health, and RadAway removes 40 percent of radiation. |
| 2 | Level 18, INT 2 | Stimpaks now restore 60 percent of lost Health, and RadAway removes 60 percent of radiation. |
| 3 | Level 30, INT 2 | Stimpaks restore 80 percent of lost Health, and RadAway removes 80 percent of radiation. |
| 4 | Level 49, INT 2 | Stimpaks and RadAway restore all lost Health and radiation and work much more quickly. |

## LEVEL 03: GUN NUT

This perk enhances your workshop settlements. This allows you to create the following:

- Heavy Machine-Gun Turret (Rank 1)
- Shotgun Turret (Rank 2)
- Missile Turret (Rank 3)

Shoot first, kill first, with access to an increasingly impressive range of gun mods. Consult the Mods chapter for a complete list. For those who like to tinker with armaments, this is a must-have. It is especially useful if you like variation in your settlement turret systems.

| RANK | REQUIREMENTS | DESCRIPTION |
|---|---|---|
| 1 | INT 3 | You gain access to base level and Rank 1 gun mods. |
| 2 | Level 13, INT 3 | You gain access to Rank 2 gun mods. |
| 3 | Level 25, INT 3 | You gain access to Rank 3 gun mods. |
| 4 | Level 39, INT 3 | You gain access to Rank 4 gun mods. |

## LEVEL 04: HACKER

Knowledge of cutting-edge computer encryption lets you hack an increasingly tricky number of terminals throughout the Commonwealth, and also allows you to build terminals in your workshop settlements. Beware of occasional redundancy with the Locksmith perk (this allows you to unlock doors, some of which are controlled by locked terminals) or the ability to circumvent some terminals by using passwords. You don't get the XP bonus using Holotapes, though, do you?

| RANK | REQUIREMENTS | DESCRIPTION |
|---|---|---|
| 1 | INT 4 | You can hack Advanced terminals. |
| 2 | Level 9, INT 4 | You can hack Expert terminals. |
| 3 | Level 21, INT 4 | You can hack Master terminals. |
| 4 | Level 33, INT 4 | When hacking, you never get locked out of a terminal when things go wrong. |

## LEVEL 05: SCRAPPER

Waste not, want not! This perk enhances your workshop settlements, as it makes locating rarer components much easier, and it allows you to build a wider variety of elements more quickly. If you're concentrating on building a settlement empire, consider this a must-have perk.

| RANK | REQUIREMENTS | DESCRIPTION |
|---|---|---|
| 1 | INT 5 | You can salvage uncommon components like screws, aluminum, and copper when scrapping weapons and armor. |
| 2 | Level 23, INT 5 | You can salvage rare components like circuitry, nuclear material, and fiber-optics when scrapping weapons and armor. Items with favorite components are highlighted. |

## LEVEL 06: SCIENCE!

This perk enhances your workshop settlements; it allows you to construct the following:

- Large Generator (Rank 1)
- Laser Tripwire (Rank 1)
- Strobe Light (Rank 1)
- Laser Turret (Rank 1)
- Heavy Laser Turret (Rank 3)
- Missile Turret (Rank 3)
- Water Purifier — Industrial (Rank 1)

Take full advantage of advanced technology with the ability to modify an increasing number of high-tech items. The exact items are discussed in the Mods chapter.

| RANK | REQUIREMENTS | DESCRIPTION |
|---|---|---|
| 1 | INT 6 | You gain access to base level and Rank 1 high-tech mods. |
| 2 | Level 17, INT 6 | You gain access to Rank 2 high-tech mods. |
| 3 | Level 28, INT 6 | You gain access to Rank 3 high-tech mods. |
| 4 | Level 41, INT 6 | You gain access to Rank 4 high-tech mods. |

## LEVEL 07: CHEMIST

Far out. Whether you're dabbling in Buffout, chewing down tins of grape Mentats, or even creating your own chem concoctions, the user and abuser of chems should never be without this perk.

| RANK | REQUIREMENTS | DESCRIPTION |
|---|---|---|
| 1 | INT 7 | Any chems you take last 50 percent longer. |
| 2 | Level 16, INT 7 | Any chems you take now last twice as long. |
| 3 | Level 32, INT 7 | Any chems you take now last an additional 150 percent longer. |
| 4 | Level 45, INT 7 | Any chems you take now last an additional 200 percent longer. |

## LEVEL 08: ROBOTICS EXPERT

Machines will always serve humans, if you have anything to say about it. If you're trying to power it down, destroy it afterward to claim the XP, rather than leaving it to rust. At higher ranks, you can send your metal pal off to cause a disturbance while you try a flank attack or sneak past a group of foes.

| RANK | REQUIREMENTS | DESCRIPTION |
|---|---|---|
| 1 | INT 8 | Hack a robot, and gain a chance to power it on or off or initiate a self-destruct. |
| 2 | Level 19, INT 8 | When you successfully hack a robot, you can incite it to attack. |
| 3 | Level 44, INT 8 | When you successfully hack a robot, you can give it specific commands. |

## LEVEL 09: NUCLEAR PHYSICIST

You've learned to split the atom...and command it. If you're a keen user of Power Armor, you know what a pain it is to constantly look for Fusion Cores. While there aren't a huge number of radiation weapons (the Weapons chapter flags the ones that use this damage type), this purchase is worth it for the extra energy it provides your Power Armor.

| RANK | REQUIREMENTS | DESCRIPTION |
|---|---|---|
| 1 | INT 9 | Radiation weapons do 50 percent more damage and Fusion Cores last an extra 25 percent longer. |
| 2 | Level 14, INT 9 | Radiation weapons now do double damage and Fusion Cores last an extra 50 percent longer. |
| 3 | Level 26, INT 9 | Fusion Cores can be ejected from Power Armor like devastating grenades, and Fusion Cores last twice as long. |

## LEVEL 10: NERD RAGE!

Genius. Is. ANGRY! This and any perks that increase your Damage Resistance allow you to spend more time below 20 percent of your Health. Watch perks like Ghoulish, Solar Powered, and Life Giver Rank 3; these raise your Health more quickly, and this makes it more difficult to drop to 20 percent of your Health and engage the rage!

| RANK | REQUIREMENTS | DESCRIPTION |
|---|---|---|
| 1 | INT 10 | When your Health drops below 20 percent, time slows and you gain +20 Damage Resistance and do 20 percent more damage while the effect lasts. |
| 2 | Level 31, INT 10 | You now gain 30 more Damage Resistance and do 30 percent more damage while Nerd Rage is in effect. |
| 3 | Level 50, INT 10 | You now gain 40 more Damage Resistance and do 40 percent more damage while Nerd Rage is in effect. Kills you make while enraged restore some lost Health. |

# AGILITY-RELATED PERKS

## AGILITY TRAINING

Agility is a measure of your overall finesse and reflexes. It affects the number of Action Points in V.A.T.S. and your ability to sneak. It is considered a particularly important attribute to those who value stealth as a viable way to maneuver around enemy territories without being seen (while crouching). As you need the largest number of Action Points as possible if you favor V.A.T.S. combat, this is another reason to never overlook this attribute.

Increase those reflexes! Spend a Perk Point and instantly gain 1 point of Agility to a maximum of 10.

There are no requirements for the training in this attribute.

## LEVEL 01: GUNSLINGER

Channel the spirit of the Old West! As long as you're familiar with exactly what constitutes a "nonautomatic pistol" (the Weapons chapter has a complete list), which is a one-handed gun that you fire once per shot, this becomes an impressively helpful perk. Shots now hit at farther ranges, meaning you save ammunition and reduce anxiety that a foe is getting too close for comfort.

| RANK | REQUIREMENTS | DESCRIPTION |
|---|---|---|
| 1 | AGI 1 | Nonautomatic pistols do 20 percent more damage. |
| 2 | Level 7, AGI 1 | Nonautomatic pistols now do 40 percent more damage and have increased range. |
| 3 | Level 15, AGI 1 | Nonautomatic pistols now do 60 percent more damage, and range is increased even farther. |
| 4 | Level 27, AGI 1 | Nonautomatic pistols now do 80 percent more damage, and their attacks can disarm opponents. |
| 5 | Level 42, AGI 1 | Nonautomatic pistols now do double damage. Their attacks have a much better chance to disarm opponents and may even cripple a limb. |

## LEVEL 02: COMMANDO

Rigorous combat training means that those favoring V.A.T.S. and who have a keen collection of automatic guns (the Weapons chapter lists the specific armaments) are bound to enjoy this perk. When firing from your hip (without V.A.T.S. or aiming down your sights), your accuracy is also improved, so fast-moving Bloatflies are much less of a pest, and more dangerous foes go down under a hail of more damaging bullets.

| RANK | REQUIREMENTS | DESCRIPTION |
|---|---|---|
| 1 | AGI 2 | Your automatic weapons do 20 percent more damage. |
| 2 | Level 11, AGI 2 | Your automatic weapons now do 40 percent more damage, with improved hip-fire accuracy. |
| 3 | Level 21, AGI 2 | Your automatic weapons now do 60 percent more damage. Hip-fire accuracy is improved even more. |
| 4 | Level 35, AGI 2 | Your automatic weapons now do 80 percent more damage and gain a chance to stagger opponents. |
| 5 | Level 49, AGI 2 | Your automatic weapons now do double damage and have a greater chance to stagger opponents. |

## LEVEL 03: SNEAK

Become whisper, become shadow. This self-explanatory perk diminishes your ability to be seen under sneaking circumstances. Do you like wading into combat yelling obscenities at the world and brandishing a Fat Man? Then this perk might not be for you. But if you enjoy keeping to the edges of areas, creeping around and behind enemies, and using perks like Ninja, Night Person, Mister Sandman, and Cloak & Dagger, you can slay multiple enemies without making a sound.

| RANK | REQUIREMENTS | DESCRIPTION |
|---|---|---|
| 1 | AGI 3 | You are 20 percent harder to detect while sneaking. |
| 2 | Level 5, AGI 3 | You are now 30 percent harder to detect while sneaking and no longer trigger floor-based traps. |
| 3 | Level 12, AGI 3 | You are now 40 percent harder to detect while sneaking and no longer trigger enemy mines. |
| 4 | Level 23, AGI 3 | You are now 50 percent harder to detect while sneaking, and running no longer adversely affects stealth. |
| 5 | Level 38, AGI 3 | Engaging stealth causes distant enemies to lose you. |

## LEVEL 04: MISTER SANDMAN

As an agent of death, combine this with the Night Person perk that allows enhancements during the cover of darkness (when most folk are asleep) and with perks that help you use surreptitiousness and surprise to your advantage (like Ninja and Sneak). If you favor the role of a quiet killer, this is an optimal perk to take, especially as the damage combines with other perks.

| RANK | REQUIREMENTS | DESCRIPTION |
|---|---|---|
| 1 | AGI 4 | You can instantly kill a sleeping person. Your silenced weapons do an additional 15 percent sneak attack damage. |
| 2 | Level 17, AGI 4 | Your silenced weapons do an additional 30 percent sneak attack damage. |
| 3 | Level 30, AGI 4 | Your silenced weapons now do 50 percent more sneak attack damage. |

## LEVEL 05: ACTION BOY / ACTION GIRL

There's no time to waste! Though this doesn't give you any more Action Points, it significantly lessens the time you spend waiting for them to regenerate, either during combat or after some sprinting. This is a great perk to take early into your adventuring, so you have more bursts of energy and less lengthy periods of tiring out.

| RANK | REQUIREMENTS | DESCRIPTION |
|---|---|---|
| 1 | AGI 5 | Your Action Points regenerate 25 percent faster. |
| 2 | Level 18, AGI 5 | Your Action Points now regenerate 50 percent faster. |

## LEVEL 06: MOVING TARGET

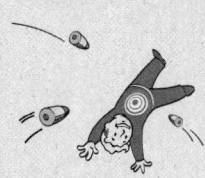

They can't hurt what they can't hit! Though you might wonder why expending Action Points (which occurs when sprinting) is helpful, consider attacks that require you to reach a foe in double-quick time, like melee or punching strikes, or the Power Armor charge of the Pain Train. Plus, if you're fleeing an area, it's good to have as much protection as possible.

| RANK | REQUIREMENTS | DESCRIPTION |
|---|---|---|
| 1 | AGI 6 | Get +25 Damage Resistance and +25 Energy Resistance when you're sprinting. |
| 2 | Level 24, AGI 6 | You now get +50 Damage Resistance and +50 Energy Resistance when you're sprinting. |
| 3 | Level 44, AGI 6 | Sprinting costs 50 percent fewer Action Points. |

## LEVEL 07: NINJA

If you're attacking foes without them seeing you, this is the pinnacle of your capabilities. Partner this perk with other clandestine perks (Sneak, Night Person, Mister Sandman, Cloak & Dagger) to create an unstoppable assassin.

| RANK | REQUIREMENTS | DESCRIPTION |
|---|---|---|
| 1 | AGI 7 | Your ranged sneak attacks do 2.5x normal damage and your melee sneak attacks do 4x normal damage. |
| 2 | Level 16, AGI 7 | Your ranged sneak attacks do 3x normal damage and your melee sneak attacks do 5x normal damage. |
| 3 | Level 33, AGI 7 | Your ranged sneak attacks now do 3.5x normal damage, and melee sneak attacks do 10x normal damage. |

## LEVEL 08: QUICK HANDS

In combat, there's no time to hesitate. Consider the weapons you're using; if you can comfortably take down a foe (or two) before needing to reload, this may not be a vital perk. But for the sniper, single-shot enthusiast, or gun-toter with few bullets or shells in their chambers, this helps you bring (usually more powerful) weapons to bear with increased potency.

| RANK | REQUIREMENTS | DESCRIPTION |
|---|---|---|
| 1 | AGI 8 | You can reload all guns faster. |
| 2 | Level 28, AGI 8 | Reloading guns costs no Action Points in V.A.T.S. |

## LEVEL 09: BLITZ

Find the gap and make the tackle! For those who enjoy the crunch of bone and sinew and want to start swinging from a little farther away, this is a critically important perk to take for the melee monster in you. Remember you can Blitz multiple targets in the same V.A.T.S. action.

| RANK | REQUIREMENTS | DESCRIPTION |
|---|---|---|
| 1 | AGI 9 | V.A.T.S. melee distance is increased significantly. |
| 2 | Level 29, AGI 9 | V.A.T.S. melee distance is increased even more, and the farther the Blitz distance, the greater the damage. |

## LEVEL 10: GUN-FU

You've learned to apply ancient martial arts to gunplay! Although many might balk at the Agility (and level) requirements, in cases where you're facing more than one foe (which, let's face it, is almost every occasion), a sizable damage augmentation is welcome. Remember this is for fans of V.A.T.S. only.

| RANK | REQUIREMENTS | DESCRIPTION |
|---|---|---|
| 1 | AGI 10 | Do 25 percent more damage to your second V.A.T.S. target and beyond. |
| 2 | Level 26, AGI 10 | In V.A.T.S. you do 50 percent more damage to your third target and beyond. |
| 3 | Level 50, AGI 10 | In V.A.T.S. you instantly do a critical hit against your fourth target and beyond. |

# LUCK-RELATED PERKS

## LUCK TRAINING

Luck is a measure of your general good fortune and affects the recharge rate of critical hits. While searching for loot, your Luck determines the (random) likelihood of receiving a rare item, mod, or high-value item. In combat, critical hits help remove targets in quicker, more violently impressive ways, and decreasing the time it takes to inflict such pain is obviously helpful.

To your good fortune! Spend a Perk Point and instantly gain 1 point of Luck to a maximum of 10.

There are no requirements for the training in this attribute.

## LEVEL 01: FORTUNE FINDER

You've discovered the Wasteland's hidden wealth, and this can certainly help you amass greater fortune. But there are other methods to make money (such as scavenging ammo and other equipment and selling it), too. "Containers" refers to any searchable piece of scenery.

| RANK | REQUIREMENTS | DESCRIPTION |
|---|---|---|
| 1 | LCK 1 | You find more Bottlecaps in containers. |
| 2 | Level 5, LCK 1 | You find even more Bottlecaps in containers. |
| 3 | Level 25, LCK 1 | You find even more Bottlecaps in containers. |
| 4 | Level 40, LCK 1 | You find even more Bottlecaps in containers, and there is a chance of enemies exploding in a shower of Caps when you kill them. |

## LEVEL 02: SCROUNGER

You know just how to scavenge to keep the fight going, and unlike the Fortune Finder perk, all that extra ammunition you find in the various containers of the Commonwealth can be employed in combat as well as traded for Caps: This means extra flexibility, depending on your ammo and money reserves.

| RANK | REQUIREMENTS | DESCRIPTION |
|---|---|---|
| 1 | LCK 2 | You find more ammunition in containers. |
| 2 | Level 7, LCK 2 | You find even more ammunition in containers. |
| 3 | Level 24, LCK 2 | You find even more ammunition in containers. |
| 4 | Level 37, LCK 2 | You find even more ammunition in containers. |

## LEVEL 03: BLOODY MESS

Watch out for flying eyeballs! Though more of an aesthetic at the initial rank, this becomes increasingly more potent, especially as the damage bonus is available to any weapon you're wielding. Spectacular gore-balls are also a real treat to watch explode.

| RANK | REQUIREMENTS | DESCRIPTION |
|---|---|---|
| 1 | LCK 3 | The +5 percent bonus damage means enemies will sometimes explode into a gory red paste. |
| 2 | Level 9, LCK 3 | You now inflict +10 percent damage in combat. |
| 3 | Level 31, LCK 3 | You now inflict +15 percent damage in combat. |
| 4 | Level 47, LCK 3 | When an enemy explodes, nearby enemies may suffer the same fate. |

## LEVEL 04: MYSTERIOUS STRANGER

Who is he? Why does he help? Who cares! This odd fellow is most helpful if you're trying to conserve every Action Point and bullet you can, especially at higher difficulty levels. Remember he's only appearing during V.A.T.S. combat, so spend a Perk Point if you favor this method of foe removal.

| RANK | REQUIREMENTS | DESCRIPTION |
|---|---|---|
| 1 | LCK 4 | The Mysterious Stranger will appear occasionally in V.A.T.S. to lend a hand, with deadly efficiency... |
| 2 | Level 22, LCK 4 | The Mysterious Stranger appears more often in V.A.T.S. |
| *** | Level 41, LCK 4 | The Mysterious Stranger appears more often in V.A.T.S. When he kills an opponent, there is a chance your Critical meter gets filled. |

## LEVEL 05: IDIOT SAVANT

You're not stupid! Just...different. The main advantage is the accrual of XP at a faster-than-normal pace, which allows you to level up, receive a Perk Point, and gain more levels and perks with haste. If you're going the Idiot Savant route for huge XP bumps, make sure you scour merchants. Since you'll never get Gun Nut or Science, you can still find mods for sale at pretty reasonable rates. Intelligence-reducing apparel also helps, too.

| RANK | REQUIREMENTS | DESCRIPTION |
|---|---|---|
| 1 | LCK 5 | Randomly receive 3x XP from any action, and the lower your Intelligence, the greater the chance. |
| 2 | Level 11, LCK 5 | You now randomly receive 5x XP from any action. The lower your Intelligence, the greater the chance. |
| 3 | Level 34, LCK 5 | Randomly receiving bonus XP from any action may trigger 3x XP for all kills for a short period of time. The lower your Intelligence, the greater the chance. |

## LEVEL 06: BETTER CRITICALS

Advanced training for enhanced combat effectiveness! Although you won't score criticals more frequently, they inflict a truly splendid amount of extra damage. If you favor this way of killing foes, this is a truly helpful perk.

| RANK | REQUIREMENTS | DESCRIPTION |
|---|---|---|
| 1 | LCK 6 | Criticals do 50 percent more extra damage. |
| 2 | Level 15, LCK 6 | Your criticals now do twice as much extra damage. |
| 3 | Level 40, LCK 6 | Your criticals now do 2.5x as much extra damage. |

## LEVEL 07: CRITICAL BANKER

You're a patient battlefield tactician and can wait to unleash a torrent of additional damage. But why save your criticals? During a protracted or difficult fight, you usually meet more dangerous enemies as you encroach farther into their territory, so keeping a couple of criticals just for a Raider boss, Glowing One, or Legendary enemy is just good combat sense.

| RANK | REQUIREMENTS | DESCRIPTION |
|---|---|---|
| 1 | LCK 7 | You can save a critical hit, to be used in V.A.T.S. when you need it the most. |
| 2 | Level 17, LCK 7 | You can now save 2 critical hits, to be used in V.A.T.S. when you need them the most. |
| 3 | Level 43, LCK 7 | You can now save 3 critical hits, to be used in V.A.T.S. when you need them the most. Banking a critical has a chance to save an additional critical. |

## LEVEL 08: GRIM REAPER'S SPRINT

Death becomes you! If you use V.A.T.S. and like your odds of clearing out a chamber full of foes without giving them a chance to respond, this is the perk to take.

| RANK | REQUIREMENTS | DESCRIPTION |
|---|---|---|
| 1 | LCK 8 | Any kill in V.A.T.S. has a 15 percent chance to restore all Action Points. |
| 2 | Level 19, LCK 8 | Any kill in V.A.T.S. now has a 25 percent chance to restore all Action Points. |
| 3 | Level 46, LCK 8 | Any kill in V.A.T.S. now has a 35 percent chance to restore all Action Points and refill your Critical meter. |

## LEVEL 09: FOUR LEAF CLOVER

Feeling lucky? You should! If you enjoy the different (and usually gore-filled) methods of taking down foes using critical hits in V.A.T.S. and want to ensure this happens every time, employ this perk. Naturally, combining this with Better Criticals and Critical Banker results in massive damage potential with increasing regularity.

| RANK | REQUIREMENTS | DESCRIPTION |
|---|---|---|
| 1 | LCK 9 | Each hit in V.A.T.S. has a chance of filling your Critical meter. |
| 2 | Level 13, LCK 9 | Each hit in V.A.T.S. now has an even better chance of filling your Critical meter. |
| 3 | Level 32, LCK 9 | Each hit in V.A.T.S. now has a very good chance of filling your Critical meter. |
| 4 | Level 48, LCK 9 | Each hit in V.A.T.S. now has an excellent chance of filling your Critical meter. |

## LEVEL 10: RICOCHET

What goes around comes around! Though it won't come around if your foe isn't using a ranged weapon, so be mindful of this fact. Don't worry about the "closer you are to death" part; there's still a chance of a ricochet when you're relatively unscathed, and leaving some enemies to kill themselves with their own projectiles frees you up to concentrate on other foes.

| RANK | REQUIREMENTS | DESCRIPTION |
|---|---|---|
| 1 | LCK 10 | An enemy's ranged attack will sometimes ricochet back and instantly kill them. The closer you are to death, the higher the chance. |
| 2 | Level 29, LCK 10 | There's an increased chance that an enemy's shot will ricochet back and kill them. |
| 3 | Level 50, LCK 10 | When an enemy's shot ricochets back and kills them, there is a chance your Critical meter gets filled. |

# OTHER PERKS: RESTING

If you've been exploring to the point of exhaustion, you need to take time to smell the roses. Or at least, try to remember what roses used to smell like before the bombs dropped.

| LOVER'S EMBRACE | QUIET REFLECTION | WELL RESTED |
|---|---|---|
| Requirements: Romancing one of your companions | Requirements: Sitting on a pew inside the All Faiths Chapel in Diamond City and waiting for a moment. | Requirements: Sleeping in a bed, usually after purchasing a bed for the night at a hotel such as the Dugout Inn (Diamond City) or Hotel Rexford (Goodneighbor) |
| After spending some quality time with your special someone, you feel completely relaxed and ready for anything! Earn +15 percent XP for a limited time. Romance is possible with Cait, Curie, Danse, Hancock, MacCready, Piper, and Preston. | After spending some quiet time reflecting on life's experiences, you feel more ready to continue your personal journey. Earn +5 percent XP for a limited time. | You had a great sleep and feel alert and invigorated! Earn +10 percent XP for a limited time. |

# COMPANION PERKS

Locate a friend in the Commonwealth, explore with them while making quest decisions and significant dialogue choices, complete small events to increase their affinity with you, engage in conversations with them, and (optionally, depending on the companion) complete their associated quest, and you receive a unique perk from each of them (except Dogmeat).

| BERSERK | CLOAK & DAGGER | CLOSE TO METAL | COMBAT MEDIC |
|---|---|---|---|
| Requirements: Gain maximum affinity with Strong | Requirements: Gain maximum affinity with Deacon | Requirements: Gain maximum affinity with Nick Valentine and complete Side Quest (Companion): Long Time Coming | Requirements: Gain maximum affinity with Curie and complete Side Quest (Companion): Emergent Behavior |
| Thanks to your relationship with Strong, when you fall below 25 percent Health, you deal +20 percent more melee weapon damage. | Thanks to your relationship with Deacon, you receive +40 percent Stealth Boy duration and deal +20 percent more sneak attack damage. | Thanks to your relationship with Nick Valentine, you get one extra guess and 50 percent faster terminal cooldown when hacking. | Thanks to your relationship with Curie, once per day you heal 100 Hit Points if your Health falls below 10 percent. |

| GIFT OF GAB | ISODOPED | KILLSHOT | KNOW YOUR ENEMY |
|---|---|---|---|
| Requirements: Gain maximum affinity with Piper | Requirements: Gain maximum affinity with Hancock | Requirements: Gain maximum affinity with MacCready, and complete Side Quest (Companion): Long Road Ahead | Requirements: Gain maximum affinity with Paladin Danse |
| Thanks to your relationship with Piper, you receive double XP for speech challenges and discovering new locations. | Thanks to your relationship with Hancock, at 250 rads or higher you get criticals 20 percent faster. | Thanks to your relationship with MacCready, headshot accuracy in V.A.T.S. is increased by 20 percent. | Thanks to your relationship with Danse, you deal +20 percent more damage against Feral Ghouls, Super Mutants, and synths. |

| ROBOT SYMPATHY | SHIELD HARMONICS | TRIGGER RUSH | UNITED WE STAND |
|---|---|---|---|
| Requirements: Gain maximum affinity with Codsworth | Requirements: Gain maximum affinity with X6-88 | Requirements: Gain maximum affinity with Cait, and complete Side Quest (Companion): Benign Intervention | Requirements: Gain maximum affinity with Preston Garvey |
| Thanks to your relationship with Codsworth, you receive +10 Damage Resistance against robot energy weapons. | Thanks to your relationship with X6-88, you receive +20 Energy Resistance. | Thanks to your relationship with Cait, Action Points regenerate faster if your Health is below 25 percent. | Thanks to your relationship with Preston, you deal +20 percent more damage and gain +20 Damage Resistance when facing three or more opponents. |

# REQUIRED READING (MAGAZINE) PERKS

The final set of perks cannot be overlooked, as some can augment your existing attributes and perks for even more potency! Note that some of the perk names differ slightly from the name of the magazine.

## ASTOUNDINGLY AWESOME TALES (1–14)

1. REGENERATE 1 POINT OF HEALTH PER MINUTE.
2. DO +5 PERCENT DAMAGE WITH SCOPED WEAPONS.
3. TAKE 5 PERCENT LESS DAMAGE FROM ROBOTS.
4. DO +5 PERCENT DAMAGE WITH THE ALIEN BLASTER.
5. GAIN +5 POISON RESISTANCE.
6. DO +5 PERCENT DAMAGE AGAINST MIRELURKS.
7. DO +5 PERCENT DAMAGE AT NIGHT.
8. GAIN +5 ACTION POINTS.
9. DO +5 DAMAGE WITH THE CRYOLATOR.
10. GAIN +5 RADIATION RESISTANCE.
11. RADAWAY HEALS +5 PERCENT RADIATION DAMAGE.
12. YOUR CANINE COMPANION PERMANENTLY TAKES 10 PERCENT LESS DAMAGE.
13. DO +5 PERCENT DAMAGE AGAINST GHOULS.
14. DO +5 PERCENT DAMAGE AGAINST SUPER MUTANTS.

Each copy of this magazine has a different perk.

| GROGNAK THE BARBARIAN | COVERT OPERATIONS | GUNS AND BULLETS | JUNKTOWN VENDOR |
|---|---|---|---|
| Rank: ********* | Rank: ********* | Rank: ********* | Rank: ******** |
| Each copy of this magazine has the same perk: Critical hits with unarmed and melee attacks permanently do +5 percent damage (per magazine found, up to 10 magazines, or +50 percent). | Each copy of this magazine has the same perk: Permanently more difficult to detect while sneaking (per magazine found, up to 10 times). | Each copy of this magazine has the same perk: Ballistic weapons do +5 percent critical damage (per magazine found, up to 10 magazines, or +50 percent). | Each copy of this magazine has the same perk: Get better prices when buying from vendors (up to eight times). |

## LIVE & LOVE (1-9)

1. COMPANIONS GAIN +10 HEALTH.
2. COMPANIONS DO +5 PERCENT DAMAGE.
3. COMPANIONS HAVE +10 CARRY WEIGHT.
4. GAIN +25 PERCENT XP FROM PERSUADING WOMEN.
5. GAIN +1 LUCK FROM ALCOHOL WHEN ADVENTURING WITH A COMPANION.
6. COMPANIONS GAIN +5 DAMAGE RESISTANCE AND ENERGY RESISTANCE.
7. GAIN +25 PERCENT XP FROM PERSUADING MEN.
8. GAIN +5 PERCENT XP WHILE ADVENTURING WITH A COMPANION.
9. ROBOT COMPANIONS PERMANENTLY INFLICT +5 PERCENT DAMAGE.

| MASSACHUSETTS SURGERY | TESLA SCIENCE | TUMBLERS TODAY | UNSTOPPABLE |
|---|---|---|---|
| Rank: ********* | Rank: ********* | Rank: ***** | Rank: ***** |
| Each copy of this magazine has the same perk: Permanently inflict +2 percent limb damage (per magazine found, up to 9 magazines, or +18 percent). | Each copy of this magazine has the same perk: Energy weapons permanently inflict +5 percent critical damage (per magazine found, up to 9 magazines, or +45 percent). | Each copy of this magazine has the same perk: Gain a bonus to lockpicking (up to five times). | Each copy of this magazine has the same perk: Permanently gain +1 percent chance of avoiding all damage from an attack (per magazine found, up to 5 magazines, or +5 percent). |

## WASTELAND SURVIVAL GUIDE (1–9)

1. HEAL 50 PERCENT MORE FROM FRUITS AND VEGETABLES.
2. TAKE 5 PERCENT LESS DAMAGE FROM INSECTS.
3. HEAL +50 PERCENT FROM IRRADIATED PACKAGED FOOD AND DRINK.
6. DISCOUNT OF +10 PERCENT FROM FOOD AND DRINK VENDORS.
7. SWIM +25 PERCENT FASTER.
8. TAKE 5 PERCENT LESS DAMAGE FROM MELEE ATTACKS.
9. COLLECT EXTRA MEAT FROM ANIMAL KILLS.

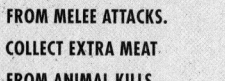

(Issues 4 and 5 of this magazine do not grant you a perk).

## BENEFITS OF OTHER MAGAZINES

The following magazines do not offer a perk:

- *HOT RODDER* (UNLOCKS UP TO THREE CUSTOM PAINT JOBS FOR YOUR POWER ARMOR).
- *LA COIFFE* (UNLOCKS UP TO TWO HAIRSTYLES).
- *PICKET FENCES* (BUILD NEW STATUES, PICKET FENCING, HIGH-TECH LIGHT, POTTED PLANTS, OR PATIO FURNITURE AT SETTLEMENT WORKSHOPS)
- *ROBCO FUN!* (UP TO FOUR HOLOTAPE GAMES).
- *TABOO TATTOOS* (UNLOCK UP TO FIVE DIFFERENT TATTOOS).
- *TOTAL HACK* (ALLOWING YOU TO HACK PROTECTRONS, SPOTLIGHTS, AND TURRETS).
- *WASTELAND SURVIVAL GUIDE*, ISSUE 4 (NEW DECORATION ITEMS FOR YOUR SETTLEMENT).
- *WASTELAND SURVIVAL GUIDE*, ISSUE 5 (DIAMOND CITY IS PERMANENTLY MARKED ON YOUR MAP).

# PERK AVAILABILITY BY LEVEL

Wouldn't it be helpful to know which perks are available when you reach a particular level? Fortunately, the following table reveals all:

| LEVEL | PERK NAME | RANK |
|---|---|---|
| 0 | All Rank * Perks (providing S.P.E.C.I.A.L. value has been achieved) | * |
| 1 | Friend of the Cats | None |
| 5 | Basher | ** |
| 5 | Fortune Finder | ** |
| 5 | Sneak | ** |
| 6 | Lead Belly | ** |
| 6 | Pickpocket | ** |
| 7 | Big Leagues | ** |
| 7 | Black Widow | ** |
| 7 | Gunslinger | ** |
| 7 | Lady Killer | ** |
| 7 | Locksmith | ** |
| 7 | Scrounger | ** |
| 8 | Life Giver | ** |
| 9 | Attack Dog | ** |
| 9 | Bloody Mess | ** |
| 9 | Hacker | ** |
| 9 | Iron Fist | ** |
| 9 | Rifleman | ** |
| 9 | Toughness | ** |
| 10 | Demolition Expert | ** |
| 10 | Strong Back | ** |
| 11 | Commando | ** |
| 11 | Heavy Gunner | ** |
| 11 | Idiot Savant | ** |
| 11 | Refractor | ** |
| 12 | Animal Friend | ** |
| 12 | Sneak | *** |
| 13 | Adamantium Skeleton | ** |
| 13 | Armorer | ** |
| 13 | Four Leaf Clover | ** |
| 13 | Gun Nut | ** |
| 13 | Rad Resistant | ** |
| 13 | Sniper | ** |
| 14 | Basher | *** |
| 14 | Local Leader | ** |
| 14 | Nuclear Physicist | ** |
| 15 | Better Criticals | ** |
| 15 | Big Leagues | *** |
| 15 | Gunslinger | *** |

| LEVEL | PERK NAME | RANK |
|---|---|---|
| 15 | Party Boy | ** |
| 15 | Party Girl | ** |
| 16 | Blacksmith | ** |
| 16 | Chemist | ** |
| 16 | Lady Killer | *** |
| 16 | Ninja | ** |
| 17 | Critical Banker | ** |
| 17 | Lead Belly | *** |
| 17 | Lone Wanderer | ** |
| 17 | Mister Sandman | ** |
| 17 | Pickpocket | *** |
| 17 | Science! | ** |
| 18 | Action Boy | ** |
| 18 | Action Girl | ** |
| 18 | Iron Fist | *** |
| 18 | Locksmith | *** |
| 18 | Medic | ** |
| 18 | Rifleman | *** |
| 18 | Toughness | *** |
| 19 | Cannibal | ** |
| 19 | Grim Reaper's Sprint | ** |
| 19 | Inspirational | ** |
| 19 | Robotics Expert | ** |
| 20 | Cap Collector | ** |
| 20 | Life Giver | *** |
| 20 | Strong Back | *** |
| 21 | Aquaboy | ** |
| 21 | Aquagirl | ** |
| 21 | Commando | *** |
| 21 | Hacker | *** |
| 21 | Heavy Gunner | *** |
| 21 | Refractor | *** |
| 21 | Wasteland Whisperer | ** |
| 22 | Black Widow | *** |
| 22 | Chem Resistant | ** |
| 22 | Demolition Expert | *** |
| 22 | Mysterious Stranger | ** |
| 22 | Rooted | ** |
| 23 | Intimidation | ** |
| 23 | Scrapper | ** |
| 23 | Sneak | **** |
| 24 | Ghoulish | ** |
| 24 | Moving Target | ** |

| LEVEL | PERK NAME | RANK |
|---|---|---|
| 24 | Pain Train | ** |
| 24 | Scrounger | *** |
| 25 | Armorer | *** |
| 25 | Attack Dog | *** |
| 25 | Fortune Finder | *** |
| 25 | Gun Nut | *** |
| 25 | Night Person | ** |
| 26 | Adamantium Skeleton | *** |
| 26 | Basher | **** |
| 26 | Concentrated Fire | ** |
| 26 | Gun-Fu | ** |
| 26 | Nuclear Physicist | *** |
| 26 | Rad Resistant | *** |
| 26 | Sniper | *** |
| 27 | Big Leagues | **** |
| 27 | Gunslinger | **** |
| 27 | Solar Powered | ** |
| 28 | Animal Friend | *** |
| 28 | Penetrator | ** |
| 28 | Quick Hands | ** |
| 28 | Science! | *** |
| 28 | Steady Aim | ** |
| 29 | Blacksmith | *** |
| 29 | Blitz | ** |
| 29 | Ricochet | ** |
| 30 | Medic | *** |
| 30 | Mister Sandman | *** |
| 30 | Pickpocket | **** |
| 30 | Strong Back | **** |
| 31 | Bloody Mess | *** |
| 31 | Iron Fist | **** |
| 31 | Nerd Rage! | ** |
| 31 | Rifleman | **** |
| 31 | Toughness | **** |
| 32 | Chemist | *** |
| 32 | Four Leaf Clover | *** |
| 33 | Hacker | **** |
| 33 | Ninja | *** |
| 34 | Demolition Expert | **** |
| 34 | Idiot Savant | *** |
| 35 | Commando | **** |
| 35 | Heavy Gunner | **** |
| 35 | Refractor | **** |

| LEVEL | PERK NAME | RANK |
|---|---|---|
| 37 | Party Boy | *** |
| 37 | Party Girl | *** |
| 37 | Scrounger | **** |
| 38 | Cannibal | *** |
| 38 | Sneak | ***** |
| 39 | Armorer | **** |
| 39 | Gun Nut | **** |
| 40 | Better Criticals | *** |
| 40 | Fortune Finder | **** |
| 40 | Lone Wanderer | *** |
| 41 | Cap Collector | *** |
| 41 | Locksmith | **** |
| 41 | Mysterious Stranger | *** |
| 41 | Science! | **** |
| 42 | Big Leagues | ***** |
| 42 | Gunslinger | ***** |
| 42 | Refractor | ***** |
| 43 | Critical Banker | **** |
| 43 | Inspirational | *** |
| 43 | Rooted | *** |
| 44 | Moving Target | *** |
| 44 | Robotics Expert | *** |
| 45 | Chemist | **** |
| 46 | Grim Reaper's Sprint | *** |
| 46 | Iron Fist | ***** |
| 46 | Rifleman | ***** |
| 46 | Toughness | ***** |
| 47 | Bloody Mess | **** |
| 47 | Heavy Gunner | ***** |
| 48 | Four Leaf Clover | *** |
| 48 | Ghoulish | *** |
| 49 | Commando | ***** |
| 49 | Medic | **** |
| 49 | Wasteland Whisperer | *** |
| 50 | Concentrated Fire | *** |
| 50 | Gun-Fu | *** |
| 50 | Intimidation | *** |
| 50 | Nerd Rage! | *** |
| 50 | Pain Train | *** |
| 50 | Ricochet | *** |
| 50 | Solar Powered | *** |

# YOU'RE NOT ALONE: COMPANIONS

Are you craving emotional support, a buddy to talk to, or a pal to get to know better? Or simply want to toy with someone for a bit before casting them away due to some deep-seated psychosis Vault-Tec's mental health professionals missed during your registration? Then you may wish to obtain a companion.

The following companions are available throughout the Commonwealth.

## HELPFUL HINT
*from Vault Boy!*

ARE YOU AWARE THAT THE GUN A COMPANION BEGINS WITH NEVER REQUIRES AMMUNITION? HOWEVER, IF YOU GIVE THEM A NEW WEAPON, THAT WILL REQUIRE AMMUNITION AS NORMAL. SHORT ON BULLETS? KEEP YOUR COMPANION'S ORIGINAL WEAPONRY!

## CAIT

- Description: Human female
- Location: Combat Zone
- Associated Quest: Side Quest (Companion): Benign Intervention
- Romance: Yes
- Perk: Trigger Rush

This fiery-tempered redheaded Irish pit-fighter has a nasty disposition and a dependence on chems. She's adept at picking locks, making her an invaluable resource in this respect. Her view of certain activities also changes once her quest is completed.

## CODSWORTH

- Description: Robot Mr. Handy
- Location: Sanctuary
- Associated Quest: None
- Romance: No
- Perk: Robot Sympathy

A faithful robot butler from a time long past, Codsworth may not have the most devastating salvos of weaponry or the ability to hack or pick locks, but he is unwaveringly loyal.

## CURIE

- Description: Robot "Mrs. Handy" Medic
- Location: Vault 81
- Associated Quest: Side Quest (Companion): Emergent Behavior
- Romance: Yes
- Perk: Combat Medic

This robotic laboratory assistant has become an independent wasteland researcher. The French accent is part of her programming, and she is highly adept at medical and scientific tasks. Her weapon of choice is a flamethrower.

## PALADIN DANSE

- Description: Human male
- Location: Cambridge Police Station
- Associated Quest: None
- Romance: Yes
- Perk: Know Your Enemy

A Brotherhood of Steel Paladin, it is Danse who sponsors your petition to become part of this faction. He is an expert battlefield tactician and is exceptional when it comes to providing backup during combat situations.

## DOGMEAT

- Description: A dog
- Location: Red Rocket Truck Stop
- Associated Quest: None
- Romance: No
- Perk: None

A faithful best friend, Dogmeat is unwaveringly loyal, always ready to help tackle any enemies you might need savaging, and he comes with his own particular perk (Attack Dog). Note that Dogmeat's natural affinity starts at maximum, so he doesn't need or react to your actions. Who's a good boy?

## DEACON

- Description: Human male
- Location: Old North Church
- Associated Quest: None
- Romance: No
- Perk: Cloak & Dagger

A companion initially sent to keep an eye on you as part of the clandestine operatives known as the Railroad, he enjoys disguises and is beneficial to those who enjoy a more stealthy outlook on life. He is the best field agent the Railroad has.

## HANCOCK

- Description: Ghoul male
- Location: Goodneighbor
- Associated Quest: Miscellaneous: Recruiting Hancock
- Romance: Yes
- Perk: Isodoped

Ever since Diamond City banished Ghouls, most of them have taken up residence in Goodneighbor. Cross him, and he'll torture you to death slowly. But don't, and he can be a great friend.

**MACCREADY**
- Description: Human male
- Location: The Third Rail (Goodneighbor)
- Associated Quest: Side Quest (Companion): Long Road Ahead
- Romance: Yes
- Perk: Killshot

A Commonwealth mercenary scouring the wasteland for a cure to an unknown disease. It's been a while since he left Little Lamplight. He's an expert with weapons, particularly the sniper rifle. He prefers to hang back in times of combat, but don't mistake that for cowardice; he's an exceptional help if you provide him with markers from where he can cover you.

**PIPER**
- Description: Human female
- Location: Diamond City
- Associated Quest: Location Quest: Story of the Century
- Romance: Yes
- Perk: Gift of Gab

As Piper's perk grants you double the XP for completing speech challenges and discovering new locations, she should be your first serious companion. She usually provides modest help with a custom pistol and is a pretty impressive shot. But her most impressive skill is her intrepid nature as a journalist and reporter.

**PRESTON GARVEY**
- Description: Human male
- Location: Museum of Freedom
- Associated Quest: None
- Romance: Yes
- Perk: United We Stand

Aside from providing the basis for your settlement expansions across the Commonwealth, Preston Garvey leads the Minutemen organization and is a crack shot with a laser musket. Help him establish trade routes and new settlements, and you'll have a friend to the end.

**STRONG**
- Description: Super Mutant male
- Location: Trinity Tower
- Associated Quest: None
- Romance: No
- Perk: Berserk

Having recently been introduced to the plays of William Shakespeare, Strong is intriguing, as he also has the brute strength and ability to level a battlefield with a missile launcher while also searching for "the milk of human kindness." He tags along during Side Quest: Curtain Call.

**NICK VALENTINE**
- Description: Synth male
- Location: Vault 114 (Park Street Station)
- Associated Quest: Side Quest: Long Time Coming
- Romance: No
- Perk: Close to Metal

Like any hard-boiled detective, Nick Valentine relies equally on his two weapons: his fists and his revolver. He's also extremely adept at hacking computers and runs a detective agency out of a modest building within Diamond City.

**X6-88**
- Description: Synth male
- Location: The Institute
- Associated Quest: None
- Romance: No
- Perk: Shield Harmonics

An Institute Courser and the pinnacle of technological advancements in the field of offensive capabilities, X6-88 is built for combat, can sense incoming enemies from an impressive distance, and is invaluable with his advanced energy weaponry.

## COMPANION AFFINITY

When you meet a companion for the first time, you may be unsure of one another. How do you break the ice? By completing significant decisions or events and seeing how your companion reacts to you. Companions have an active like or dislike for particular ways to solve problems, and they have reactions to your foibles. If you wish to unlock their perk, and further a meaningful conversation with them (and if flagged, attempt some flirting romance or perhaps a little more), you need to perform actions they like. Keep performing actions they aren't fond of, and your companion still provides help and support during explorations, but under protest.

### General Affinity Choices

The following chart details whether a companion likes or dislikes a quest decision or dialogue choice (either with them or a third party) that exhibits one of the following qualities:

| DECISION OR CHOICE QUALITY | CAIT | CODSWORTH | CURIE | DANSE | DEACON | HANCOCK | MACCREADY | PIPER | PRESTON | STRONG | VALENTINE | X6-88 |
|---|---|---|---|---|---|---|---|---|---|---|---|---|
| GENEROUS | 👎 | 👍 | — | — | — | 👍 | — | 👍 | 👍 | 👍 | — | 👎 |
| SELFISH | 👍 | 👎 | 👎 | — | — | 👍 | — | 👎 | 👎 | — | — | 👍 |
| NICE | — | 👍 | 👍 | 👍 | — | 👎 | — | — | 👍 | — | 👍 | 👎 |
| MEAN | 👎 | — | 👎 | 👎 | 👎 | 👎 | 👎 | 👎 | 👎 | 👍 | 👎 | — |
| PEACEFUL | 👎 | — | 👍 | 👍 | — | 👍 | 👍 | 👍 | 👍 | 👎 | 👍 | 👍 |
| VIOLENT | 👍 | — | 👎 | 👎 | 👍 | 👎 | 👍 | 👎 | 👎 | 👍 | 👎 | — |

### Specific Affinity Choices

The following chart details more specific choices you might make and how your companion reacts.

| EVENT | STRONG | MACCREADY | CURIE | NICK VALENTINE | PALADIN DANSE | PIPER | CAIT | PRESTON | X6-88 | DEACON | CODSWORTH | HANCOCK |
|---|---|---|---|---|---|---|---|---|---|---|---|---|
| CHEM ADDICTION | — | 👎 | 👎 | — | — | — | 👍👎 | 👎 | 👎 | 👎 | 👎 | — |
| CHEM USE | — | — | — | 👍 | — | — | 👍👎 | — | 👎 | 👍 | 👎 | 👍 |
| DONATE ITEM | — | 👎 | 👍 | 👍 | — | 👍 | 👍👎 | 👍 | 👍 | 👍 | 👍 | 👍 |
| DRINK ALCOHOL | — | — | — | — | — | — | 👍 | — | — | — | — | — |

| EVENT | STRONG | MACCREADY | CURIE | NICK VALENTINE | PALADIN DANSE | PIPER | CAIT | PRESTON | X6-88 | DEACON | CODSWORTH | HANCOCK |
|---|---|---|---|---|---|---|---|---|---|---|---|---|
| EAT CORPSE | ● | – | – | ● | ● | ● | ● | ● | – | ● | – | – |
| ENTER POWER ARMOR | ● | – | – | – | ● | – | – | – | ● | – | – | – |
| ENTER VERTIBIRD | ● | – | – | – | ● | – | – | – | ● | – | – | – |
| HACK COMPUTER | – | – | – | ● | – | – | – | – | ● | ● | – | – |
| HEAL DOGMEAT | ● | – | ● | ● | ● | ● | – | – | ● | – | ● | ● |
| MODIFY ARMOR | – | – | – | – | ● | – | – | – | – | – | ● | – |
| MODIFY WEAPON | – | – | – | – | ● | – | – | – | ● | – | ● | – |
| MURDER NON-HOSTILE | ● | ● | ● | ● | ● | ● | ● | ● | – | ● | ● | ● |
| PICK LOCK | ● | – | – | – | – | ● | ● | – | – | – | – | – |
| PICK LOCK OWNED | ● | ● | – | ● | – | ● | ● | ● | – | ● | ● | ● |
| SPEECH SUCCESS (MORE CAPS) | ● | ● | – | – | – | – | – | – | ● | ● | ● | – |
| STEALING | – | ● | ● | ● | ● | ● | – | ● | – | – | ● | ● |
| STEALING (PICKPOCKET) | – | – | ● | ● | ● | ● | ● | ● | – | – | ● | – |
| WALK AROUND UNCLOTHED | – | – | – | – | – | – | ● | – | ● | – | – | ● |

👍 / 👎 * This indicates Cait's state of mind before and after completing her quest.

So, when presented with your choice of response in conversation, look for answers that fit the qualities presented above. For quest decisions, look for peaceful or violent outcomes. When choosing more minor actions, be mindful that the previous actions may cause a like or dislike. Blank areas of the chart mean the companion isn't bothered by your answers one way or the other.

## Lending a Hand

Aside from helping you in combat and easing your anxiety about the torment of the Commonwealth wasteland, companions perform a number of other important functions:

– USE YOUR COMPANION TO CARRY YOUR EXTRA EQUIPMENT ONCE YOU REACH YOUR CARRYING CAPACITY; JUST TALK TO THEM AND TRADE.
– EQUIP MOST COMPANIONS WITH ARMOR TO ADD PROTECTION DURING COMBAT. ALTHOUGH YOUR COMPANIONS CAN'T BE KILLED, THEY CAN USE UP STIMPAKS JUST LIKE YOU DO. USE ONE IF THEY FALL IN COMBAT AND BRING THEM BACK INTO THE FIGHT.
– DISMISS COMPANIONS AND SEND THEM TO ANY OF YOUR LISTED WORKSHOP SETTLEMENTS. OR, YOU CAN SEND THEM BACK TO WHERE YOU ORIGINALLY FOUND THEM.

# CRAFTING

Are you making due with ramshackle gear and irradiated food? Is your settlement failing to meet the needs of a growing population? Are too many of your hard-earned Caps going toward stimpaks and RadAway? If you can't find the items you need, try making them yourself! Workshops and workstations make crafting a breeze.

Turn a bit of raw meat into a satisfying meal. Use junk items to expand your settlements and build powerful mods for your favorite gear. Craft chems and explosives, salvage valuable components, and keep your Power Armor in ready condition for combat. Advanced recipes often require specific perks—and some only become available after you complete certain tasks—but with the proper ingredients, you can craft useful items at any workstation.

– WORKSHOPS: USE WORKSHOPS TO BUILD STRUCTURES, FURNITURE, TURRETS, RESOURCES, AND MORE. WITH THE RIGHT COMPONENTS, YOU CAN BUILD ANYTHING AND EVERYTHING YOUR SETTLEMENT NEEDS. WITH THE RIGHT SELECTION OF PERKS, YOU CAN DO MUCH, MUCH MORE.
– ARMOR WORKBENCHES: USE THESE WORKBENCHES TO MODIFY, RENAME, OR SCRAP CUSTOMIZABLE APPAREL. INVEST IN ALL AVAILABLE RANKS OF THE ARMORER AND SCIENCE! PERKS TO TAKE FULL ADVANTAGE OF ARMOR WORKBENCHES.
– CHEMISTRY STATIONS: USE THESE WORKSTATIONS TO CRAFT CHEMS, EXPLOSIVES, SYRINGER AMMO, AND CUTTING FLUID. RANK 1 OF THE CHEMIST PERK IS REQUIRED TO CRAFT ADVANCED CHEMS. IF EXPLOSIVES PIQUE YOUR INTEREST, INVEST HEAVILY IN THE DEMOLITION EXPERT AND SCIENCE! PERKS—IT TAKES CONSIDERABLE SKILL TO CRAFT THE MOST ADVANCED MINES AND GRENADES.
– COOKING STATIONS: USE THESE WORKSTATIONS TO CRAFT FOOD, DRINK, AND VEGETABLE STARCH. COOKING DOESN'T REQUIRE ANY SPECIAL PERKS, BUT YOU'LL NEED A STEADY SUPPLY OF FRESH INGREDIENTS TO STAY WELL FED. MANY OF THE FRUITS, VEGETABLES, AND MEAT YOU COLLECT CAN BE USED TO PREPARE DISHES THAT ARE SAFER AND MORE SATISFYING THAN ANYTHING YOU'LL FIND IN THE WILD.
– POWER ARMOR STATIONS: USE THESE WORKSTATIONS TO MODIFY OR REPAIR POWER ARMOR. INVEST IN ALL AVAILABLE RANKS OF ARMORER, SCIENCE!, AND BLACKSMITH TO TAKE FULL ADVANTAGE OF POWER ARMOR STATIONS.
– WEAPONS WORKBENCHES: USE THESE WORKBENCHES TO MODIFY, RENAME, OR SCRAP CUSTOMIZABLE WEAPONS. TO MAKE THE MOST OF A WEAPONS WORKBENCH, INVEST IN ALL AVAILABLE RANKS OF THE GUN NUT, SCIENCE!, AND BLACKSMITH PERKS.

# ★ COMBAT

## OVERVIEW

### HUMANOID STATS

Most humanoid targets can utilize a wide variety of armor and weapons. This means that two seemingly identical targets can have significantly different resistances or offensive capabilities. For this reason, the following categories are used for most humanoid stats:

- NAME: THE NAME BY WHICH YOUR PIP-BOY IDENTIFIES A GIVEN TARGET.
- LEVEL: A TARGET'S LEVEL IS A GOOD INDICATOR OF ITS RELATIVE STRENGTH.
- INVENTORY: ITEMS THAT ARE SURE TO BE CARRIED BY A TARGET (ALTHOUGH MOST DEFEATED ENEMIES WILL ALSO DROP SEVERAL RANDOMLY SELECTED ITEMS).
- PERCEPTION: HOW EASILY A TARGET CAN DETECT HIDDEN THREATS. THE HIGHER A TARGET'S PERCEPTION, THE MORE DIFFICULT IT IS TO SNEAK PAST THEM.
- BASE HEALTH: A TARGET'S UNMODIFIED HEALTH.
- STANDARD ARMOR: THE TYPES OF ARMOR MOST COMMONLY WORN BY A TARGET.
- STANDARD WEAPONS: TYPES OF WEAPONS MOST COMMONLY CARRIED BY A TARGET.
- XP: THE UNMODIFIED XP GRANTED FOR DEFEATING A TARGET (SPECIFIC XP REWARDS ARE DETERMINED BY YOUR INTELLIGENCE, PERKS, AND ACTIVE BONUSES).

### NON-HUMANOID STATS

Because gear isn't a factor, non-humanoid targets tend to have much more predictable offensive and defensive capabilities. Stats for these targets are presented in the following categories:

- NAME: THE NAME BY WHICH YOUR PIP-BOY IDENTIFIES A GIVEN TARGET.
- LEVEL: A TARGET'S LEVEL IS A GOOD INDICATOR OF ITS RELATIVE STRENGTH.
- INVENTORY: ITEMS THAT ARE SURE TO BE CARRIED BY A TARGET (ALTHOUGH MOST DEFEATED ENEMIES WILL ALSO DROP SEVERAL RANDOMLY SELECTED ITEMS).
- PERCEPTION: HOW EASILY A TARGET CAN DETECT HIDDEN THREATS. THE HIGHER A TARGET'S PERCEPTION, THE MORE DIFFICULT IT IS TO SNEAK PAST THEM.
- BASE HEALTH: A TARGET'S UNMODIFIED HEALTH.
- DAMAGE RESISTANCE: RESISTANCE TO BALLISTIC/IMPACT DAMAGE.
- ENERGY RESISTANCE: RESISTANCE TO ENERGY DAMAGE.
- RADIATION RESISTANCE: RESISTANCE TO RADIATION DAMAGE.
- POISON RESISTANCE: RESISTANCE TO POISON.
- DAMAGE: DAMAGE CAUSED BY A TARGET'S PRIMARY ATTACK.
- SPECIAL ATTACK: A TARGET'S SECONDARY OR SITUATIONAL ATTACK.
- SA DAMAGE: DAMAGE DONE BY A TARGET'S SPECIAL ATTACK.
- XP: THE UNMODIFIED XP GRANTED FOR DEFEATING A TARGET (SPECIFIC XP REWARDS ARE DETERMINED BY YOUR INTELLIGENCE, PERKS, AND ACTIVE BONUSES).

### LEGENDARY ENEMIES

Most enemy types have Legendary variants that can appear at random. These enemies share the same base stats as their standard counterparts, but they also boast dormant Legendary abilities.

Legendary enemies that favor ranged damage tend to be much more accurate, while those that rely on melee damage usually hit twice as hard.

All Legendary enemies also have the ability to mutate after taking significant damage. Mutation replenishes an enemy's lost health and triggers its Legendary abilities.

Legendary enemies are formidable, but they always carry a piece of Legendary gear—weapons and armor that offer special bonuses.

One and Only Boston Baseball

# GROUPS, GANGS, AND FACTIONS

## BROTHERHOOD OF STEEL

Due to its considerable strength and unyielding conviction, the Brotherhood of Steel is one of the Commonwealth's most feared factions. Through the acquisition and preservation of prewar technology, the Brotherhood aims to ensure the future of the human race. However, this means that individual humans are often ignored or sacrificed if doing so can further the Brotherhood's goals.

Although the Brotherhood seeks to eradicate Ghouls and synths, its members don't generally attack humans without cause. However, any hostile action or open defiance is sure to result in bloodshed.

### Scribes

Scribes are tasked with cataloging and preserving any information considered valuable to the Brotherhood of Steel. When it comes to combat, Scribes lack the impressive skills and equipment of their front-line comrades. While they do have access to a small variety of armor and accessories, even the most effective combinations offer very little protection.

| NAME | LEVEL | INVENTORY | PERCEPTION | BASE HEALTH | STANDARD ARMOR | STANDARD WEAPONS | XP |
|---|---|---|---|---|---|---|---|
| Brotherhood Scribe Initiate | 1 | — | 4 | 40 | Scribe | Laser pistols | 4 |
| Brotherhood Scribe | 6 | — | 4 | 80 | Scribe | Laser pistols | 11 |
| Brotherhood Senior Scribe | 15 | — | 5 | 120 | Scribe | Laser pistols | 23 |

### Lancers

| NAME | LEVEL | INVENTORY | PERCEPTION | BASE HEALTH | STANDARD ARMOR | STANDARD WEAPONS | XP |
|---|---|---|---|---|---|---|---|
| Brotherhood Lancer-Initiate | 1 | — | 4 | 40 | Bomber jacket | Laser rifles | 4 |
| Brotherhood Lancer | 7 | — | 5 | 70 | Bomber jacket | Laser rifles | 12 |
| Brotherhood Lancer-Knight | 14 | — | 6 | 185 | Bomber jacket | Laser rifles | 21 |
| Brotherhood Lancer-Sergeant | 21 | — | 6 | 150 | Bomber jacket | Laser rifles | 31 |
| Brotherhood Lancer-Captain | 28 | — | 6 | 170 | Bomber jacket | Laser rifles | 40 |

Lancers are responsible for providing transportation and air support for the Brotherhood of Steel. With gear like bomber jackets and flight helmets, Lancers aren't particularly formidable, but every Lancer carries some sort of laser rifle in case a firefight breaks out.

### Soldiers

Soldiers are responsible for gathering technology and enforcing the will of the Brotherhood. Individuals who demonstrate exceptional loyalty and valor are promoted up the ranks, gaining more formidable gear along the way. Most Brotherhood of Steel soldiers rely on various laser rifles, but heavy guns such as miniguns, Gatling lasers, and missile launchers are sometimes used to overwhelm the opposition.

| NAME | LEVEL | INVENTORY | PERCEPTION | BASE HEALTH | STANDARD ARMOR | STANDARD WEAPONS | XP |
|---|---|---|---|---|---|---|---|
| Brotherhood Initiate | 2 | — | 4 | 50 | Brotherhood fatigues | Laser rifles | 6 |
| Brotherhood Aspirant | 9 | — | 4 | 115 | Brotherhood fatigues | Laser rifles | 15 |
| Brotherhood Knight | 17 | — | 5 | 200 | Combat armor | Laser rifles | 25 |
| Brotherhood Knight-Sergeant | 25 | — | 5 | 300 | Combat armor | Laser rifles | 36 |
| Brotherhood Knight-Captain | 33 | — | 6 | 375 | Combat armor | Laser rifles | 47 |
| Brotherhood Knight-Commander | 41 | — | 6 | 480 | Combat armor | Laser rifles | 58 |
| Brotherhood Paladin | 49 | — | 6 | 560 | Combat armor | Laser rifles | 70 |
| Brotherhood Paladin-Commander | 57 | — | 7 | 670 | Combat armor | Laser rifles | 81 |
| Brotherhood Star Paladin | 67+ | — | 8 | 800+ | Combat armor | Laser rifles | 96 |

Higher ranking soldiers sometimes employ T60 Power Armor, allowing them to absorb huge amounts of damage. Use powerful explosives, rifles, or heavy guns to engage from a safe distance, or equip a suit of Power Armor to even the odds in close combat.

### Vertibirds

Vertibirds are essentially mobile weapon platforms, providing air support to Brotherhood ground forces. Passengers can use the side-mounted miniguns to tear through enemy forces, and each Vertibird is also equipped with two front-mounted 5-mm cannons. Each projectile does relatively little damage, but even the toughest targets can be overwhelmed by a Vertibird's hail of bullets.

| NAME | LEVEL | PERCEPTION | BASE HEALTH | DAMAGE RESISTANCE | ENERGY RESISTANCE | RADIATION RESISTANCE | POISON RESISTANCE | DAMAGE | SPECIAL ATTACK | SA DAMAGE | XP |
|------|-------|------------|-------------|-------------------|-------------------|---------------------|-------------------|--------|----------------|-----------|-----|
| Vertibird | 20 | 10 | 910 | 60 | 60 | Immune | Immune | 108/sec | Minigun | 8 | 30 |
| Vertibird | 30 | 10 | 910 | 90 | 90 | Immune | Immune | 108/sec | Minigun | 8 | 43 |
| Vertibird | 40 | 10 | 1310 | 112 | 112 | Immune | Immune | 198/sec | Minigun | 8 | 75 |
| Vertibird | 50 | 10 | 1510 | 135 | 135 | Immune | Immune | 288/sec | Minigun | 8 | 71 |

If you find yourself in a Vertibird's crosshairs, check the area for any nearby structures that might offer cover. Target the pilot or use a missile launcher to quickly down one of these vehicles. Otherwise, chip away at its health with the most powerful weapon you have. During battle, a Vertibird tends to move in and out of any weapon's effective range. Monitor your ammunition and choose your shots wisely. A disabled Vertibird will stay in the air for several seconds before crashing down to the ground—use this time to get clear of the impending explosion.

## CHILDREN OF ATOM

Considered a cult by most outsiders, the Children of Atom worship nuclear material and the radiation it emits. While most members are compelled to spread the word of Atom, Children of Atom are wary of strangers and generally attack trespassers on sight. Unless important business takes you into their territory, approaching a Child of Atom will trigger a firefight.

Children of Atom congregate in the Crater of Atom, but smaller groups can be found throughout the Commonwealth.

| NAME | LEVEL | INVENTORY | PERCEPTION | BASE HEALTH | STANDARD ARMOR | STANDARD WEAPONS | XP |
|------|-------|-----------|------------|-------------|----------------|------------------|-----|
| Child of Atom | 10 | — | 9 | 280 | Child of Atom rags | Gamma guns, pipe guns | 16 |
| Child of Atom Cultist | 20 | — | 9 | 400 | Child of Atom rags | Gamma guns, pipe guns | 29 |
| Child of Atom Preacher | 30 | — | 9 | 500 | Child of Atom rags | Gamma guns, pipe guns | 43 |
| Child of Atom Zealot | 40 | — | 9 | 600 | Child of Atom rags | Gamma guns, pipe guns | 57 |
| Child of Atom Reborn | 50 | — | 9 | 700 | Child of Atom rags | Gamma guns, pipe guns | 71 |

Children of Atom wear rags that offer very little protection, but prolonged exposure has left them immune to radiation and able to withstand a considerable amount of punishment. Although some Children of Atom rely on a variety of handmade pipe guns, others favor the radiation damage offered by gamma guns. Whenever possible, equip armor that offers radiation resistance or stock up on RadAway before engaging these fanatics.

### Diamond City Security

Diamond City Security is responsible for keeping hostiles out of the city and maintaining order within its walls. Law-abiding visitors and residents have nothing to fear from Diamond City Security, but infractions like theft and violence are generally met with overwhelming force.

**HELPFUL HINT** *from Vault Boy!* Did You Know?

THE SPECIFIC LEVEL OF A DIAMOND CITY SECURITY GUARD IS DETERMINED BY THE PLAYER'S LEVEL AT THE TIME OF THE ENCOUNTER.

| NAME | LEVEL | INVENTORY | PERCEPTION | BASE HEALTH | STANDARD ARMOR | STANDARD WEAPONS | XP |
|------|-------|-----------|------------|-------------|----------------|------------------|-----|
| Diamond City Security | 20-50 | Stimpak | 7 | 285-435 | DC Guard | Pipe rifles, baseball bats | 30 |

For the most part, Diamond City Security uses repurposed baseball equipment to keep the peace. Their standard-issue armor favors damage resistance over energy resistance, and all guards carry some sort of baseball bat. Each guard also carries a pipe rifle and at least one stimpak, relying on superior numbers and emergency healing to overwhelm better-equipped enemies. Luckily, it's fairly easy to prevent confrontations with Diamond City Security—avoid committing criminal acts (or make sure such acts go unwitnessed) to ensure that these guards leave you in peace.

## DRIFTERS

Most of the people living in Goodneighbor are Drifters who have grown weary of wandering the wilderness. They aren't particularly aggressive, but they're quick to swarm on visitors who threaten the relative safety of their community.

| NAME | LEVEL | INVENTORY | PERCEPTION | BASE HEALTH | STANDARD ARMOR | STANDARD WEAPONS | XP |
|------|-------|-----------|------------|-------------|----------------|------------------|----|
| Drifter | 6 | — | 4 | 190 | Clothing | Pipe guns | 0 |

Wrapped in simple clothing and armed with only handmade pipe guns, Drifters aren't particularly effective in combat. However, attacking a Drifter will draw all of Goodneighbor into the skirmish. Considering that Drifters never carry anything of real value, there's not much to be gained from provoking them.

## FORGED

The Forged are similar to Raiders, set apart only by their small numbers and fanatic obsession with the destructive power of fire. These enemies can only be found in and around the Saugus Ironworks, and they'll attack any and all trespassers on sight.

| NAME | LEVEL | INVENTORY | PERCEPTION | BASE HEALTH | STANDARD ARMOR | STANDARD WEAPONS | XP |
|------|-------|-----------|------------|-------------|----------------|------------------|----|
| Forged | 1 | — | 4 | 30 | Wastelander | Ballistic guns, melee weapons, flamers | 5 |
| Forged | 4 | — | 4 | 45 | Wastelander | Ballistic guns, melee weapons, flamers | 8 |
| Forged | 9 | — | 4 | 70 | Wastelander | Ballistic guns, melee weapons, flamers | 15 |
| Forged | 14 | — | 4 | 125 | Wastelander | Ballistic guns, melee weapons, flamers | 21 |
| Forged | 30 | — | 4 | 390 | Wastelander | Ballistic guns, melee weapons, flamers | 43 |
| Forged | 39 | — | 4 | 540 | Wastelander | Ballistic guns, melee weapons, flamers | 55 |

Most Forged wear some form of cage armor, spiked armor, or Drifter outfit. Even when combined with a piece of headgear, a typical Forged has fairly low resistances. However, the Forged do carry a wide variety of weapons. Those who favor melee weapons tend to use baseball bats, sledgehammers, and even the occasional super sledge. They also have access to a large selection of pistols, rifles, and flamers, and most Forged carry a supply of Molotov cocktails.

Because Forged are limited to a single location, there's no need to engage them until you're adequately prepared. Forged are most effective at short to medium range, so it's usually best to pick them off from a distance. When that's not an option, be sure to watch for incoming Molotov cocktails as you deal with incoming Forged.

## GUNNERS

Gunners claim to be soldiers for hire, but throughout the Commonwealth, they have a well-earned reputation as being a highly militarized gang of thugs. Aggressive and fiercely territorial, Gunners are guaranteed to attack anyone who wanders into an area they've claimed as their own. They're well equipped and well organized, and a group of Gunners almost always includes at least one combat-ready robot.

Gunners can be found in Mass Bay Medical Center, Hub City Auto Wreckers, and many other locations throughout the Commonwealth.

### Gunner Humans

Low-ranking Gunners are usually limited to the protection offered by simple clothing, accessories, and the occasional piece of leather armor. Gunners who have reached the rank of Private sport a few pieces of combat armor. Further promotions grant Gunners better-quality pieces of combat armor. Gunners also enjoy a vast arsenal

of weapons. Combat rifles and laser rifles are popular choices—and no Gunner would ever be caught relying on a handmade pipe gun—but virtually any projectile weapon weapon has a chance of appearing in a Gunner's hands. Even valuable plasma weapons can be found on high-level Gunners. Batons and rippers are sometimes used, as are fragmentation grenades, Molotov cocktails, and a variety of heavy guns.

| NAME | LEVEL | INVENTORY | PERCEPTION | BASE HEALTH | STANDARD ARMOR | STANDARD WEAPONS | XP |
|---|---|---|---|---|---|---|---|
| Gunner | 8 | — | 4 | 120 | Clothing | Pistols, rifles | 13 |
| Gunner Conscript | 14 | — | 4 | 150 | Clothing | Pistols, rifles | 21 |
| Gunner Private | 22 | — | 4 | 240 | Combat armor | Pistols, rifles | 32 |
| Gunner Corporal | 30 | — | 5 | 400 | Combat armor | Pistols, rifles | 43 |
| Gunner Sergeant | 38 | — | 5 | 540 | Combat armor | Pistols, rifles | 54 |
| Gunner Lieutenant | 46 | — | 5 | 660 | Combat armor | Rifles | 65 |
| Gunner Captain | 58 | — | 6 | 780 | Combat armor | Rifles | 83 |
| Gunner Major | 70 | — | 6 | 890 | Combat armor | Rifles | 100 |
| Gunner Colonel | 82 | Stealth Boy | 6 | 1070 | Combat armor | Rifles | 118 |
| Gunner General | 94 | Stealth Boy | 7 | 1300 | Combat armor | Rifles | 137 |

### Gunner Robots

With the exception of custom paint jobs, Gunner robots are identical to their standard counterparts. When fighting a Mr. Gutsy, check its arms to estimate its offensive capabilities, then attack its eyes and torso. It's often best to slow an Assaultron by crippling its leg. Simply using your most powerful weapons against a Sentry Bot is usually your best option.

GUNNER MR. GUTSY — GUNNER ASSAULTRON — GUNNER SENTRY BOT

| NAME | LEVEL | PERCEPTION | BASE HEALTH | DAMAGE RESISTANCE | ENERGY RESISTANCE | RADIATION RESISTANCE | POISON RESISTANCE | DAMAGE | SPECIAL ATTACK | SA DAMAGE | XP |
|---|---|---|---|---|---|---|---|---|---|---|---|
| Gunner Mr. Gutsy | 22 | 6 | 250 | 60 | 40 | Immune | Immune | Varies | – | – | 32 |
| Gunner Lieutenant Gutsy | 32 | 7 | 350 | 75 | 50 | Immune | Immune | Varies | – | – | 51 |
| Gunner Major Gutsy | 50 | 8 | 550 | 90 | 60 | Immune | Immune | Varies | – | – | 83 |
| Gunner Colonel Gutsy | 52+ | 8 | 655+ | 110 | 70 | Immune | Immune | Varies | – | – | 130 |
| Gunner Assaultron | 24 | 5 | 300 | 75 | 40 | Immune | Immune | 60 | Head laser | 100 | 35 |
| Gunner Assaultron Invader | 36 | 5 | 400 | 105 | 60 | Immune | Immune | 90 | Head laser | 150 | 51 |
| Gunner Assaultron Dominator | 46 | 6 | 500 | 130 | 75 | Immune | Immune | 120 | Head laser | 200 | 65 |
| Gunner Sentry Bot | 30 | 10 | 750 | 125 | 85 | Immune | Immune | 109/sec | – | – | 43 |
| Gunner Siege Breaker Sentry Bot | 40 | 10 | 850 | 150 | 100 | Immune | Immune | 136/sec | Missile Launcher | 169 | 57 |
| Gunner Annihilator Sentry Bot | 50 | 10 | 1000 | 175 | 125 | Immune | Immune | 202 | – | – | 71 |
| Gunner Annihilator Sentry Bot Mk. II | 60+ | 10 | 1045+ | 135 | 125+ | Immune | Immune | 135 | Rocket Cluster | 5x30 | 86 |

# MERCENARIES

Mercenaries lack the Gunners' numbers and resources, but the two groups are similar in most respects. These enemies have been charged with guarding Parsons State Insane Asylum, which is the only place Mercenaries can be found in the Commonwealth. They take their work very seriously and are guaranteed to attack anyone who encroaches on their territory.

| NAME | LEVEL | INVENTORY | PERCEPTION | BASE HEALTH | STANDARD ARMOR | STANDARD WEAPONS | XP |
|------|-------|-----------|------------|-------------|----------------|------------------|-----|
| Mercenary | 8 | — | 4 | 120 | Combat armor | Combat rifles | 13 |
| Mercenary | 14 | — | 4 | 150 | Combat armor | Combat rifles | 21 |
| Mercenary | 22 | — | 4 | 240 | Combat armor | Combat rifles | 32 |
| Mercenary | 30 | — | 5 | 400 | Combat armor | Combat rifles | 43 |

Each Mercenary is equipped with at least a few pieces of combat armor and some type of combat rifle. This means all Mercenaries enjoy a good balance of damage resistance and energy resistance, and they all deal reliable damage from a decent range. Many Mercenaries also carry fragmentation grenades or Molotov cocktails to flush their targets out of cover. When battling a group of Mercenaries, try to keep track of enemy locations and keep an eye out for reinforcements that enter the skirmish.

# MINUTEMEN

The Minutemen were once a formidable and rather popular faction in the Commonwealth. Due to significant losses and internal squabbles, however, this people's militia has struggled to survive in recent years. By defending their friends and neighbors at every opportunity, the few remaining Commonwealth Minutemen hope

to bolster their numbers and bring some measure of peace and comfort to the average men and women scattered throughout the region.

Each Minuteman relies on whatever gear he or she can salvage, so the group's strength is determined by the allegiances it manages to forge. You first encounter Preston Garvey—who has spent years believing he's the last of the Commonwealth Minutemen—in the Museum of Freedom. With enough allies, however, Preston believes he can reestablish the Castle as the Minutemen's base of operations.

| NAME | LEVEL | INVENTORY | PERCEPTION | BASE HEALTH | STANDARD ARMOR | STANDARD WEAPONS | XP |
|------|-------|-----------|------------|-------------|----------------|------------------|-----|
| Minuteman | 1 | — | 4 | 30 | Clothing | Pistols, rifles | 5 |
| Minuteman | 9 | — | 4 | 70 | Clothing | Pistols, rifles | 15 |
| Minuteman | 14 | — | 4 | 125 | Clothing | Pistols, rifles | 21 |
| Minuteman | 22 | — | 4 | 240 | Clothing | Pistols, rifles | 32 |
| Minuteman | 30 | — | 5 | 400 | Clothing | Pistols, rifles | 43 |
| Minuteman | 39 | — | 4 | 540 | Clothing | Pistols, rifles | 55 |
| Minuteman | 46 | — | 5 | 660 | Clothing | Pistols, rifles | 65 |
| Minuteman | 58 | — | 6 | 100 | Clothing | Pistols, rifles | 83 |

Most Minutemen are limited to whatever protection is offered by simple clothing and headgear, but some members have managed to salvage a few pieces of leather armor or metal armor. The laser musket is the signature weapon of the Minutemen, but the average Minuteman is forced to rely on whatever weapons he or she has managed to salvage before joining. This means that patrolling Minutemen can be found carrying anything from humble pipe guns to heavily modified combat rifles.

While some of its members can seem a bit self-righteous, Minutemen never attack without provocation. In fact, because the group's strength is determined by the support of its allies, Minutemen are generally eager to lend a hand to anyone who doesn't pose a direct threat.

## NEIGHBORHOOD WATCH

The Neighborhood Watch is responsible for keeping order in Goodneighbor. Acts of theft or violence are answered with a hail of bullets, but visitors who stay out of trouble have nothing to fear from these local guards.

Wearing only patched three-piece suits and worn fedoras, members of the Neighborhood Watch aren't particularly well protected. The group does include both humans and Ghouls, however, so some members are immune to radiation damage. Most of these guards are surprisingly friendly, but they're always quick to deal with misbehaving visitors.

| NAME | LEVEL | INVENTORY | PERCEPTION | BASE HEALTH | STANDARD ARMOR | STANDARD WEAPONS | XP |
|------|-------|-----------|------------|-------------|----------------|------------------|-----|
| Neighborhood Watch | 1 | — | 7 | 40 | Patched three-piece suit | Submachine guns, assault rifles | 5 |
| Neighborhood Watch | 7 | — | 8 | 100 | Patched three-piece suit | Submachine guns, assault rifles | 12 |

## PILLARS OF THE COMMUNITY

The Pillars of the Community is a new movement based in the Charles View Amphitheater. Its leader claims to have discovered a path back to the prosperity of a prewar Commonwealth, and he's managed to gather a small flock of followers since founding the organization.

The Pillars of the Community aren't initially hostile, but they're easily provoked.

| NAME | LEVEL | PERCEPTION | BASE HEALTH | STANDARD ARMOR | STANDARD WEAPONS | XP |
|------|-------|------------|-------------|----------------|------------------|-----|
| Initiate | 3 | 4 | 50 | Clothing | Melee weapons | 7 |
| Mercenary | 6-25 | 4 | 130-320 | Clothing | Pipe guns | 12 |

### HELPFUL HINT from Vault Boy!

**Did You Know?**

INITIATES ARE ALWAYS LEVEL 3, BUT THE SPECIFIC LEVEL OF SENIOR MEMBERS IS DETERMINED BY THE PLAYER'S LEVEL AT THE TIME OF THE ENCOUNTER.

Pillars of the Community members have fairly unimpressive gear, but as a group, they can still be a handful. Missionaries carry pipe guns, but Initiates are limited to a variety of simple melee weapons. If you choose to engage this group in combat, keep moving to avoid being surrounded as you thin their numbers.

## RAIDERS

Raiders are plentiful, ruthless, and extremely aggressive—luckily, they're not particularly bright. Large groups can be a handful, and some gangs contain particularly strong members, but most Raiders are poorly equipped and all too accustomed to preying on the Commonwealth's most vulnerable residents. Raiders are predominantly human, but there are some Ghouls among their numbers. Many Raider gangs also include one or more attack dogs.

They've managed to maintain a strong presence throughout the Commonwealth, but check locations like Hardware Town, Combat Zone, and Dunwich Borers when you're itching to find a gang of Raiders.

### Common Raiders

Most Raiders possess at least one piece of Raider armor, but leather armor and metal armor are also quite common. More powerful Raiders even sport pieces of combat armor, so any two Raiders can have wildly different resistances. Because the weapons they carry are equally varied, it's just as difficult to gauge a specific Raider's offensive capabilities.

| NAME | LEVEL | INVENTORY | PERCEPTION | BASE HEALTH | STANDARD ARMOR | STANDARD WEAPONS | XP |
|------|-------|-----------|------------|-------------|----------------|------------------|-----|
| Raider | 1 | — | 4 | 30 | Raider armor | Ballistic guns, melee weapons | 5 |
| Raider Scum | 4 | — | 4 | 45 | Raider armor | Ballistic guns, melee weapons | 8 |
| Raider Psycho | 9 | — | 4 | 70 | Raider armor | Ballistic guns, melee weapons | 15 |
| Raider Scavver | 14 | — | 4 | 125 | Raider armor | Ballistic guns, melee weapons | 21 |
| Raider Waster | 21 | — | 4 | 175 | Raider armor | Ballistic guns, melee weapons | 31 |
| Raider Survivalist | 30 | — | 4 | 390 | Raider armor | Ballistic guns, melee weapons | 43 |

Most Raiders are limited to low-quality ballistic guns and melee weapons, but they will use any weapon they can salvage. Fragmentation grenades are also very popular with Raider gangs, so expect to dodge at least a few explosives when battling larger groups.

## Unnamed Raider Bosses

Like other groups and factions, Raiders have their share of Legendary members and infamous bosses. However, some groups contain at least one particularly powerful Raider who may not stand out from the pack. Raider Psychos equipped with Power Armor are easy enough to spot, but Raider Veterans often appear wearing gear you might find on any of their comrades. When in doubt, do a bit of reconnaissance before engaging a group of Raiders.

| NAME | LEVEL | INVENTORY | PERCEPTION | BASE HEALTH | STANDARD ARMOR | STANDARD WEAPONS | XP |
|------|-------|-----------|------------|-------------|----------------|------------------|-----|
| Raider Psycho | 9 | Stimpak | 4 | 80 | Raider Power Armor | Rifles | 15 |
| Raider Veteran | 10 | Stimpak | 4 | 85 | Raider armor | Rifles | 16 |
| Raider Veteran | 39 | — | 4 | 540 | Raider armor | Rifles | 55 |

## Raider Dogs

Raiders tend to equip their Attack Dogs with accessories and armor. These items may make their animals look more intimidating, but they offer no protection. Two Attack Dogs of the same level can have different strengths and weaknesses, but a quick look is usually all it takes to tell them apart. Dogs with full coats of fur have higher Perception and less Health than mangier Attack Dogs.

| NAME | LEVEL | INVENTORY | PERCEPTION | BASE HEALTH | DAMAGE RESISTANCE | ENERGY RESISTANCE | RADIATION RESISTANCE | POISON RESISTANCE | DAMAGE | SPECIAL ATTACK | SA DAMAGE | XP |
|------|-------|-----------|------------|-------------|-------------------|-------------------|----------------------|-------------------|--------|----------------|-----------|-----|
| Attack Dog | 1 | — | 10 | 30 | 5 | 5 | 0 | 0 | 5 | — | — | 5 |
| Attack Dog | 1 | — | 7 | 40 | 5 | 5 | 0 | 0 | 10 | — | — | 5 |
| Attack Dog | 7 | — | 10 | 80 | 10 | 10 | 0 | 0 | 15 | — | — | 12 |
| Attack Dog | 7 | — | 10 | 100 | 15 | 10 | 0 | 0 | 20 | — | — | 12 |
| Attack Dog | 14 | — | 10 | 120 | 15 | 15 | 0 | 0 | 20 | — | — | 21 |
| Attack Dog | 14 | — | 10 | 140 | 25 | 15 | 0 | 0 | 25 | — | — | 21 |
| Attack Dog | 21 | — | 10 | 170 | 20 | 20 | 0 | 0 | 25 | — | — | 31 |
| Attack Dog | 21 | — | 10 | 210 | 30 | 15 | 0 | 0 | 32 | — | — | 31 |

## RAILROAD AGENTS

The Railroad isn't the most powerful faction in the Commonwealth, but through the work of dedicated Railroad Agents, it has managed to gain a foothold in the Commonwealth.

Members of the Railroad offer aid to fugitive synths and hope that one day all synths will be free to live whatever life they please. These goals have put the Railroad at odds with both the Brotherhood of Steel and the Institute. The Railroad relies on secrecy and subterfuge to survive, but Railroad Agents won't hesitate to attack anyone who stands with their enemies.

| NAME | LEVEL | INVENTORY | PERCEPTION | BASE HEALTH | STANDARD ARMOR | STANDARD WEAPONS | XP |
|------|-------|-----------|------------|-------------|----------------|------------------|-----|
| Railroad Agent | 1 | — | 4 | 40 | Railroad armored coat | 10-mm pistols | 5 |
| Railroad Agent | 9 | — | 4 | 70 | Railroad armored coat | Hunting rifles | 15 |
| Railroad Agent | 21 | — | 4 | 175 | Railroad armored coat | Combat rifles | 31 |
| Railroad Agent | 30 | — | 4 | 390 | Railroad armored coat | Assault rifles | 43 |
| Railroad Agent | 38 | — | 5 | 540 | Railroad armored coat | Gauss rifles | 54 |
| Railroad Agent | 46 | — | 5 | 660 | Railroad armored coat | Gauss rifles | 65 |

Considering its simple appearance, Railroad armored coats offer fairly impressive resistances. All versions of this armor favor energy resistance over damage resistance, but the wearer even gains a small amount of radiation resistance. Each Railroad Agent carries some type of ballistic gun, but the most experienced operatives are issued Gauss rifles.

# ROBOTS

Robots are essentially tools, relying on their programming to determine friend from foe. Those designed for combat are equipped with particularly formidable weapons, but even those meant for more utilitarian tasks have some offensive capability. Any robot will take steps to protect itself from hostile actions. If a robot's weapons are destroyed during the skirmish, it will initiate a self-defense sequence and charge its target for a final attack.

Robots charged with defending specific locations tend to attack all trespassers, but others have been programmed with allegiances to groups or individuals. Additionally, many of the robots scattered throughout the Commonwealth have suffered malfunctions brought on by centuries of neglect—even seemingly friendly robots can turn hostile without warning. Whenever you encounter an unknown robot, regardless of the type, it's best to approach with caution.

Robots can be found in the General Atomics Galleria, Hester's Consumer Robotics, and various other locations throughout the Commonwealth.

## Eyebots

Eyebots are designed for reconnaissance and surveillance, but they're often used to broadcast information and propaganda to remote areas. The Minutemen and the Brotherhood of Steel sometimes utilize Eyebots for such reasons. Before you engage an Eyebot, consider any affiliated factions that might take offense. It's rare for an Eyebot to attack without provocation, but it does happen. Each Eyebot is equipped with a small laser weapon, but they're not particularly formidable enemies.

| NAME | LEVEL | INVENTORY | PERCEPTION | BASE HEALTH | DAMAGE RESISTANCE | ENERGY RESISTANCE | RADIATION RESISTANCE | POISON RESISTANCE | DAMAGE | SPECIAL ATTACK | SA DAMAGE | XP |
|------|-------|-----------|------------|-------------|-------------------|-------------------|----------------------|-------------------|--------|----------------|-----------|-----|
| Eyebot | 1 | — | 10 | 100 | 0 | 0 | Immune | Immune | 10 | — | — | 5 |

## Protectrons

Protectrons were designed to fill a variety of roles. Some are programmed for customer service, while others are responsible for maintenance, emergency response, or building security. Many Protectrons are linked to terminals through which you can issue basic commands or assign new protocols. While most Protectrons are equipped with some sort of energy weapons, many are limited to rudimentary melee strikes.

| NAME | LEVEL | PERCEPTION | BASE HEALTH | DAMAGE RESISTANCE | ENERGY RESISTANCE | RADIATION RESISTANCE | POISON RESISTANCE | DAMAGE | XP |
|------|-------|------------|-------------|-------------------|-------------------|----------------------|-------------------|--------|-----|
| Protectron Steward | 5 | 10 | 20 | 40 | 25 | Immune | Immune | Varies | 9 |
| Protectron | 5 | 10 | 100 | 40 | 25 | Immune | Immune | 22 | 9 |
| Utility Protectron | 14 | 10 | 190 | 75 | 50 | Immune | Immune | 15 | 10 |
| Protectron Watcher | 14 | 10 | 150 | 75 | 50 | Immune | Immune | 31 | 21 |
| Police Protectron | 14 | 10 | 190 | 75 | 50 | Immune | Immune | 22 | 21 |
| Protectron Guardian | 26 | 10 | 240 | 75 | 50 | Immune | Immune | 35 | 37 |

Protectrons move very slowly, and they're not particularly durable, but they can often be used to clear an area of vermin or distract more formidable enemies.

## Mr. Handy

A Mr. Handy's offensive capabilities are determined by the tools attached to its arms. Options include pinchers, saws, and miniature flamers. Each Mr. Handy can have up to three arms, so weapon combinations vary.

| NAME | LEVEL | INVENTORY | PERCEPTION | BASE HEALTH | DAMAGE RESISTANCE | ENERGY RESISTANCE | RADIATION RESISTANCE | POISON RESISTANCE | DAMAGE | XP |
|------|-------|-----------|------------|-------------|-------------------|-------------------|----------------------|-------------------|--------|-----|
| Mr. Handy | 7 | — | 0 | 150 | 30 | 0 | Immune | Immune | Varies | 12 |

Mr. Handy was designed as a consumer-model robot, so it's comparatively rare to encounter one that's outwardly hostile. If a fight does break out, though, it's usually best to simply overwhelm these robots. Most moderately powerful weapons can make short work of a Mr. Handy.

## Mr. Gutsy

Mr. Gutsy robots may look similar to the consumer-model Mr. Handy, but they boast a more durable design and more powerful weapons. Possible attachments include .44 pistols, combat rifles, laser guns, and saws. Each Mr. Gutsy can carry up to three attachments. All projectile-weapon attachments share a standard appearance, however, so it's impossible to determine a Mr. Gutsy's offensive capabilities until it opens fire.

| NAME | LEVEL | INVENTORY | PERCEPTION | BASE HEALTH | DAMAGE RESISTANCE | ENERGY RESISTANCE | RADIATION RESISTANCE | POISON RESISTANCE | DAMAGE | XP |
|------|-------|-----------|------------|-------------|-------------------|-------------------|----------------------|-------------------|--------|-----|
| Mr. Gutsy | 22 | — | 6 | 250 | 60 | 40 | Immune | Immune | Varies | 32 |
| Lieutenant Gutsy | 32 | — | 7 | 350 | 75 | 50 | Immune | Immune | Varies | 51 |
| Major Gutsy | 50 | — | 8 | 550 | 90 | 60 | Immune | Immune | Varies | 83 |
| Colonel Gutsy | 52+ | — | 8 | 655+ | 110 | 70 | Immune | Immune | Varies | 130 |

These robots are most effective at short to medium range, so long-range weapons are usually your best option. In close combat, try to target a Mr. Gutsy's eyes before focusing your attacks on its torso. Destroying all of its eyes will compromise its accuracy without triggering a self-destruct sequence.

## Assaultrons

Assaultrons are formidable combatants. These agile robots use powerful melee strikes to batter their enemies, but they can also fire charged laser blasts from the energy weapons hidden within their heads. Additionally, Assaultron Dominators can generate stealth fields, making them difficult to track in a firefight.

| NAME | LEVEL | PERCEPTION | BASE HEALTH | DAMAGE RESISTANCE | ENERGY RESISTANCE | RADIATION RESISTANCE | POISON RESISTANCE | DAMAGE | SPECIAL ATTACK | SA DAMAGE | XP |
|------|-------|------------|-------------|-------------------|-------------------|----------------------|-------------------|--------|----------------|-----------|-----|
| Assaultron | 24 | 5 | 300 | 75 | 40 | Immune | Immune | 60 | Head Laser | 100 | 31 |
| Assaultron Invader | 36 | 5 | 400 | 105 | 60 | Immune | Immune | 90 | Head Laser | 150 | 51 |
| Assaultron Dominator | 46 | 6 | 500 | 130 | 75 | Immune | Immune | 120 | Head Laser | 200 | 65 |

It's best to engage a hostile Assaultron from a distance. Target one of its legs with a long-range weapon and attempt to cripple it before it reaches you. Once you manage to down an Assaultron, keep moving to minimize the chances of being hit with a laser blast, and continue attacking until the robot is destroyed.

**Sentry Bots**

Sentry Bots are well armed and extremely durable. Armed with miniguns, missile launchers, and even custom shoulder launchers, these robots can be devastating in combat. Bait a Sentry Bot into moving while it attacks. Heavy activity eventually causes a Sentry Bot to overheat, leaving it temporarily incapacitated. When this happens, move behind the enemy and focus your attacks on its exposed Fusion Core to deliver greatly increased damage. It takes about six seconds for an incapacitated Sentry Bot to recover, so move quickly.

| NAME | LEVEL | PERCEPTION | BASE HEALTH | DAMAGE RESISTANCE | ENERGY RESISTANCE | RADIATION RESISTANCE | POISON RESISTANCE | DAMAGE | SPECIAL ATTACK | SA DAMAGE | XP |
|---|---|---|---|---|---|---|---|---|---|---|---|
| Sentry Bot | 30 | 10 | 750 | 85 | 80 | Immune | Immune | 109 | – | – | 43 |
| Siege Breaker Sentry Bot | 40 | 10 | 850 | 150 | 100 | Immune | Immune | 136 | Missile Launcher | 169 | 57 |
| Annihilator Sentry Bot | 50 | 10 | 1000 | 175 | 125 | Immune | Immune | 202 | – | – | 71 |
| Annihilator Sentry Bot Mk. II | 60+ | 10 | 1045+ | 175+ | 125+ | Immune | Immune | 135 | Rocket Cluster | 5x30 | 86 |

**Turrets**

Turrets are utilized by nearly every gang, faction, and organization in the Commonwealth. Connected terminals can sometimes be used to control nearby turrets, but that's not always an option.

Turrets that are mounted on walls or ceilings are protected by a shell of impenetrable armor. While they're inactive, these turrets can't be damaged. When one of these turrets opens fire, however, the exposed gun can be destroyed. Turrets mounted on tripods or resting in shopping carts are always vulnerable to attack.

Once alerted, it usually takes a moment for a turret to acquire its target. Use this time to destroy it or seek cover and wait for it to reset.

| NAME | LEVEL | INVENTORY | PERCEPTION | BASE HEALTH | DAMAGE RESISTANCE | ENERGY RESISTANCE | RADIATION RESISTANCE | POISON RESISTANCE | DAMAGE | XP |
|---|---|---|---|---|---|---|---|---|---|---|
| Machine-Gun Turret | 6 | – | 10 | 10 | 0 | 0 | Immune | Immune | 10/sec. | 10 |
| Machine Gun-Turret | 28 | – | 10 | 90 | 40 | 60 | Immune | Immune | 15/sec. | 40 |
| Laser Turret | 6 | – | 10 | 10 | 0 | 0 | Immune | Immune | 10/sec. | 10 |
| Laser Turret | 16 | – | 10 | 60 | 25 | 40 | Immune | Immune | 38/sec. | 24 |
| Laser Turret | 40 | – | 10 | 150 | 60 | 90 | Immune | Immune | 60/sec. | 57 |
| Machine-Gun Turret Mk. I | 6 | – | 10 | 80 | 20 | 10 | Immune | Immune | 10+/sec. | 10 |
| Machine-Gun Turret Mk. III | 16 | – | 10 | 125 | 35 | 25 | Immune | Immune | 10+/sec. | 10 |
| Machine-Gun Turret Mk. V | 28 | – | 10 | 160 | 50 | 35 | Immune | Immune | 10+/sec. | 10 |
| Machine-Gun Turret Mk. VI | 40 | – | 10 | 210 | 60 | 40 | Immune | Immune | 10+/sec. | 10 |

# SCAVENGERS

Scavengers roam the Commonwealth, generally looking to salvage anything of value. They aren't always hostile, but some Scavengers can be fiercely protective of areas they claim as their own. Give these anxious Scavengers their space, or use superior weaponry to clear them from your path.

Scavengers tend to move from spot to spot, so most Scavenger encounters happen at random locations in the Commonwealth's less populated areas.

| NAME | LEVEL | INVENTORY | PERCEPTION | BASE HEALTH | STANDARD ARMOR | STANDARD WEAPONS | XP |
|------|-------|-----------|------------|-------------|----------------|------------------|-----|
| Scavenger | 2 | — | 4 | 110 | Wastelander | Pipe guns | 6 |

Most Scavengers are limited to basic clothing, but they sometimes wear cage armor or a few leather armor pieces. With little protection and relatively shoddy weapons, hostile Scavengers aren't as formidable as they'd have you believe. They can make for easy prey out in the wilds, but Scavengers don't often carry much worth taking.

## SETTLERS

Settlers are ordinary men, women, and Ghouls looking for a place to call home. When these folks arrive at one of your workshop settlements, they're happy to take orders. Those you encounter in the wilds are usually on their way to your nearest workshop settlement. Either way, they'll only turn hostile if you attack them.

| NAME | LEVEL | INVENTORY | PERCEPTION | BASE HEALTH | STANDARD ARMOR | STANDARD WEAPONS | XP |
|------|-------|-----------|------------|-------------|----------------|------------------|-----|
| Settler | 2 | — | 4 | 110 | Wastelander | Pipe guns | 6 |

There isn't much to be gained by attacking your settlers. They're perfectly willing to give you anything they own, and they're crucial to the productivity of your workshop settlements. Additionally, attacking one settler draws the entire community into the fray. If you do choose to pick a fight, however, you will gain a small amount of XP for each settler you kill.

" EVERYBODY LOVES THAT NUKA! "

Super Mutants are massive, muscle-bound creatures with a natural immunity to radiation damage and an inherent hatred of humans. Most Super Mutants carry fairly crude gear, but they do have their share of powerful weapons, and many Super Mutant groups use trained Mutant Hounds to chase down trespassers. Super Mutants aren't particularly intelligent, but their physical strength and natural aggression have allowed them to establish a significant presence throughout the Commonwealth.

Super Mutants can be found in Fallon's Department Store, Fort Strong, and many other locations—most of which can be identified by the human remains and hanging meat bags scattered around the area.

### Standard Super Mutants

Super Mutant armor is fairly crude, but Super Mutants are inherently durable. Even the least powerful Super Mutants have natural damage, energy, and poison resistances, and these values increase significantly in high-ranking Super Mutants. Specifics vary based on equipped armor, but Super Mutants tend to prioritize damage resistance.

Melee weapons and fragmentation grenades are popular among Super Mutants. For ranged combat, they tend to favor pipe rifles, assault rifles, and laser rifles. When it comes to heavy guns, miniguns and missile launchers are fairly common.

| NAME | LEVEL | INVENTORY | PERCEPTION | BASE HEALTH | STANDARD ARMOR | STANDARD WEAPONS | XP |
|------|-------|-----------|------------|-------------|----------------|------------------|-----|
| Super Mutant | 10 | — | 7 | 120 | Super Mutant armor | Rifles, melee weapons | 7 |
| Super Mutant Skirmisher | 16 | — | 8 | 200 | Super Mutant armor | Rifles, melee weapons, heavy guns | 19 |
| Super Mutant Brute | 22 | — | 9 | 275 | Super Mutant armor | Rifles, melee weapons, heavy guns | 27 |
| Super Mutant Enforcer | 28 | — | 10 | 375 | Super Mutant armor | Rifles, melee weapons, heavy guns | 36 |
| Super Mutant Butcher | 35 | — | 10 | 500 | Super Mutant armor | Rifles, melee weapons, heavy guns | 46 |
| Super Mutant Master | 42 | — | 10 | 600 | Super Mutant armor | Rifles, melee weapons, heavy guns | 54 |
| Super Mutant Overlord | 48 | — | 11 | 750 | Super Mutant armor | Rifles, melee weapons, heavy guns | 63 |
| Super Mutant Primus | 59 | — | 11 | 950 | Super Mutant armor | Rifles, melee weapons, heavy guns | 77 |
| Super Mutant Warlord | 68+ | — | 12 | 1535+ | Super Mutant armor | Rifles, melee weapons, heavy guns | 91 |

Due to sensitive ears and a keen sense of smell, Super Mutants have relatively high Perception and a considerable amount of health. In most cases, it's best to target a Super Mutant's arms. This compromises their accuracy and improves your chances of surviving the encounter.

### Super Mutant Suiciders

A Super Mutant Suicider's strategy is simple but effective. Upon identifying a threat, a Suicider charges the target and detonates a Mini Nuke.

To identify these high-priority targets, look for the blinking red glow that appears near a Super Mutant Suicider's hip. If you have a sufficiently powerful weapon, try to eliminate these enemies before they detect your presence. An instant kill preserves the Mini Nuke, allowing you to collect it from the Suicider's corpse. Otherwise, focus your fire on a charging Suicider's right arm—this should allow you to detonate its Mini Nuke before it reaches you.

| NAME | LEVEL | INVENTORY | PERCEPTION | BASE HEALTH | STANDARD ARMOR | STANDARD WEAPONS | XP |
|------|-------|-----------|------------|-------------|----------------|------------------|-----|
| Super Mutant Suicider | 10 | Mini Nuke | 7 | 120 | Super Mutant armor | Mini Nuke | 7 |
| Super Mutant Suicider | 16 | Mini Nuke | 8 | 200 | Super Mutant armor | Mini Nuke | 19 |
| Super Mutant Suicider | 22 | Mini Nuke | 9 | 275 | Super Mutant armor | Mini Nuke | 27 |
| Super Mutant Suicider | 28 | Mini Nuke | 10 | 375 | Super Mutant armor | Mini Nuke | 36 |
| Super Mutant Suicider | 35 | Mini Nuke | 10 | 500 | Super Mutant armor | Mini Nuke | 46 |
| Super Mutant Suicider | 42 | Mini Nuke | 10 | 600 | Super Mutant armor | Mini Nuke | 54 |

## Mutant Hounds

Compared to a Super Mutant's lumbering gait, Mutant Hounds move very quickly. They also have powerful jaws and an impressive amount of health. Aim for the head to take them out as quickly as possible, or focus your fire on their legs to slow them down.

| NAME | LEVEL | INVENTORY | PERCEPTION | BASE HEALTH | DAMAGE RESISTANCE | ENERGY RESISTANCE | RADIATION RESISTANCE | POISON RESISTANCE | DAMAGE | SPECIAL ATTACK | SA DAMAGE | XP |
|---|---|---|---|---|---|---|---|---|---|---|---|---|
| Mutant Hound | 8 | Mutant Hound Meat | 7 | 120 | 15 | 10 | Immune | 0 | 35 | ? | ? | 13 |
| Glowing Mutant Hound | 28 | Mutant Hound Meat | 8 | 325 | 40 | 30 | Immune | 0 | 50 | ? | ? | 40 |

## Super Mutant Behemoths

Behemoths are by far the most powerful Super Mutants, but they're incredibly dumb—even by Super Mutant standards. They attack by tossing boulders at distant enemies, and they use massive fire hydrant bats to smash anything foolish enough to approach them. Your best option is to stay back and attack with a Fat Man and a few Mini Nukes.

If you're determined to find a Behemoth, check the area to the east of Sunshine Tidings Co-op.

| NAME | LEVEL | PERCEPTION | BASE HEALTH | DAMAGE RESISTANCE | ENERGY RESISTANCE | RADIATION RESISTANCE | POISON RESISTANCE | DAMAGE | SPECIAL ATTACK | SA DAMAGE | XP |
|---|---|---|---|---|---|---|---|---|---|---|---|
| Behemoth | 50 | 6 | 1000 | 135 | 100 | Immune | 100 | 125 | Throw Boulder | 75 | 100 |
| Glowing Behemoth | 65 | 6 | 1300 | 150 | 110 | Immune | 100 | 156 | Throw Boulder | 94 | 125 |
| Epic Behemoth | 80 | 6 | 1600 | 165 | 120 | Immune | 100 | 187 | Throw Boulder | 112 | 150 |
| Ancient Behemoth | 95 | 6 | 1900 | 180 | 130 | Immune | 100 | 187+ | Throw Boulder | 112+ | 175 |

# SYNTHS

Synths are synthetic humanoids manufactured by the Institute, and most of the synths you encounter are still controlled by this faction. However, there are plenty of renegade synths scattered throughout the Commonwealth. As such, even those who ally themselves with the Institute are sure to encounter hostile

synths. Combined with the shroud of mystery surrounding the Institute, stories of their unpredictable behavior have made synths hated and feared by most humans.

| NAME | LEVEL | INVENTORY | PERCEPTION | BASE HEALTH | STANDARD ARMOR | STANDARD WEAPONS | XP |
|---|---|---|---|---|---|---|---|
| Synth | 5 | — | 4 | 120 | Synth armor | Institute Laser guns, batons | 9 |
| Synth | 28 | — | 4 | 180 | Synth armor | Institute Laser guns, batons | 10 |
| Synth Strider | 13 | — | 4 | 140 | Synth armor | Institute Laser guns, batons | 20 |
| Synth Patroller | 21 | — | 4 | 265 | Synth armor | Institute Laser guns, batons | 32 |
| Synth Seeker | 29 | — | 4 | 300 | Synth armor | Institute Laser guns, batons | 42 |
| Synth Trooper | 39 | — | 4 | 425 | Synth armor | Institute Laser guns, batons | 55 |
| Synth Assaulter | 49 | — | 4 | 500 | Synth armor | Institute Laser guns, batons | 55 |
| Synth Stormer | 61 | — | 5 | 635 | Synth armor | Institute Laser guns, batons | 87 |
| Synth Eradicator | 71+ | — | 6 | 760+ | Synth armor | Institute Laser guns, batons | 102 |

Like Super Mutants, synths use armor to augment their natural resistances. While numbers vary, most synths maintain a balance between damage resistance and energy resistance, and all synths are immune to radiation and poison. However, synths do share many of the weaknesses found in human enemies. Headshots deal extra damage, and crippled limbs greatly reduce their effectiveness in combat.

Most synths carry some type of Institute pistol or Institute rifle, but shock batons are also fairly common.

### Institute Coursers

Institute Coursers are advanced synths used to carry out a variety of covert operations. Their primary duties include eliminating rogue synths, so they're considerably more formidable than the Institute's standard models. Coursers utilize relatively light armor, a variety of Institute laser pistols, and grenades that summon synth reinforcements. Each Courser also carries at least one Stealth Boy and one stimpak, making them particularly effective in prolonged battles. However, scoring a quick kill on an Institute Courser allows you to collect these items for yourself.

| NAME | LEVEL | INVENTORY | PERCEPTION | BASE HEALTH | STANDARD ARMOR | STANDARD WEAPONS | XP |
|---|---|---|---|---|---|---|---|
| Institute Courser | 15 | Stealth Boy, stimpak | 8 | 250 | Courser uniform | Institute pistols | 23 |
| Institute Courser | 21 | Stealth Boy, stimpak | 8 | 300 | Courser uniform | Institute pistols | 31 |
| Institute Courser | 28 | Stealth Boy, stimpak | 9 | 375 | Courser uniform | Institute pistols | 40 |
| Institute Courser | 36 | Stealth Boy, stimpak | 10 | 475 | Courser uniform | Institute pistols | 51 |
| Institute Courser | 44 | Stealth Boy, stimpak | 10 | 550 | Courser uniform | Institute pistols | 63 |
| Institute Courser | 52 | Stealth Boy, stimpak | 10 | 675 | Courser uniform | Institute pistols | 74 |
| Institute Courser | 60 | Stealth Boy, stimpak | 10 | 750 | Courser uniform | Institute pistols | 86 |
| Institute Courser | 70 | Stealth Boy, stimpak | 10 | 750+ | Courser uniform | Institute pistols | 100 |

## TRIGGERMEN

The Triggermen are a loosely organized group of thugs and criminals. Although some particularly enterprising individuals have hatched profitable schemes of their own, many Triggermen act as hired muscle for the various gangs and crime lords. Triggermen generally attack strangers on sight, but they aren't particularly formidable in small groups.

| NAME | LEVEL | INVENTORY | PERCEPTION | BASE HEALTH | STANDARD ARMOR | STANDARD WEAPONS | XP |
|---|---|---|---|---|---|---|---|
| Triggerman | 1 | — | 3 | 40 | Clothing | Pistols, automatic rifles | 5 |
| Triggerman | 7 | — | 4 | 100 | Clothing | Pistols, automatic rifles | 12 |
| Triggerman | 13 | — | 5 | 125 | Clothing | Pistols, automatic rifles | 20 |
| Triggerman | 19 | — | 6 | 170 | Clothing | Pistols, automatic rifles | 28 |
| Triggerman | 25 | — | 7 | 185 | Clothing | Pistols, automatic rifles | 36 |
| Triggerman | 31 | — | 7 | 200 | Clothing | Pistols, automatic rifles | 44 |
| Triggerman | 37 | — | 7 | 215 | Clothing | Pistols, automatic rifles | 53 |

Favoring style over substance, Triggermen don't have much in the way of armor. Aside from the natural radiation immunity enjoyed by Ghoul members, Triggermen are vulnerable to most attacks.

Submachine guns are particularly popular among Triggermen, but some members favor assault rifles or semiautomatic pistols. A single Triggerman is rarely dangerous, but large groups can deal significant damage fairly quickly. During heavy firefights, seek cover and pick off the Triggerman one at a time.

# CREATURES OF THE COMMONWEALTH

## ANIMALS

### Mongrels

Mongrels are fast and aggressive, but most varieties aren't particularly durable. They do tend to hunt in packs, however, and their quick attacks can deal significant damage. Be particularly wary of Alpha variants—they look just like standard Mongrels, but they're much more formidable.

| NAME | LEVEL | INVENTORY | PERCEPTION | BASE HEALTH | DAMAGE RESISTANCE | ENERGY RESISTANCE | RADIATION RESISTANCE | POISON RESISTANCE | DAMAGE | SPECIAL ATTACK | SA DAMAGE | XP |
|---|---|---|---|---|---|---|---|---|---|---|---|---|
| Wild Mongrel | 3 | Mongrel dog meat | 7 | 50 | 4 | 1 | Immune | 0 | 10 | — | — | 7 |
| Alpha Wild Mongrel | 12 | Mongrel dog meat | 8 | 140 | 25 | 15 | Immune | 0 | 25 | — | — | 19 |
| Vicious Mongrel | 12 | Mongrel dog meat | 8 | 140 | 25 | 15 | Immune | 0 | 25 | — | — | 19 |
| Alpha Vicious Mongrel | 20 | Mongrel dog meat | 8 | 210 | 30 | 15 | Immune | 0 | 35 | — | — | 29 |
| Feral Mongrel | 20 | Mongrel dog meat | 8 | 210 | 30 | 15 | Immune | 0 | 35 | — | — | 29 |
| Alpha Feral Mongrel | 30 | Mongrel dog meat | 8 | 275 | 40 | 20 | Immune | 0 | 50 | — | — | 43 |
| Albino Mongrel | 30 | Mongrel dog meat | 8 | 275 | 40 | 20 | Immune | 0 | 50 | — | — | 43 |
| Alpha Albino Mongrel | 40 | Mongrel dog meat | 8 | 380 | 50 | 25 | Immune | 0 | 65 | — | — | 57 |
| Rabid Mongrel | 40 | Mongrel dog meat | 8 | 380 | 50 | 25 | Immune | 0 | 65 | Poison | 10 | 57 |
| Alpha Rabid Mongrel | 40 | Mongrel dog meat | 8 | 500 | 60 | 35 | Immune | 0 | 75 | Poison | 10 | 71 |
| Glowing Mongrel | 50 | Mongrel dog meat | 8 | 425 | 60 | 35 | Immune | 0 | 80 | Rad Field | 3 rads/sec | 71 |
| Alpha Glowing Mongrel | 50 | Mongrel dog meat | 8 | 425 | 60 | 35 | Immune | 0 | 90 | Rad Field | 3 rads/sec | 80 |

## DEATHCLAWS

Deathclaws are among the most dangerous foes you're likely to encounter. They're incredibly fast, well armored, and capable of dealing tremendous damage. A Deathclaw's belly is the closest thing it has to a weak spot, but it's very difficult to target once the beast gets up to speed. Deathclaws can throw clods of dirt from a distance, but they're far more dangerous up close. In addition to their powerful melee strikes, Deathclaws will lift their prey into the air before slamming them into the ground.

STAT

COMBAT

| NAME | LEVEL | INVENTORY | PERCEPTION | BASE HEALTH | DAMAGE RESISTANCE | ENERGY RESISTANCE | RADIATION RESISTANCE | POISON RESISTANCE | DAMAGE | SPECIAL ATTACK | SA DAMAGE | XP |
|---|---|---|---|---|---|---|---|---|---|---|---|---|
| Deathclaw | 22 | Deathclaw hand, Deathclaw Meat | 10 | 510+ | 100 | 250 | Immune | 250 | 60 | Rubble throw | 40 | 35 |
| Alpha Deathclaw | 31 | Deathclaw hand, Deathclaw Meat | 10 | 800+ | 150 | 300 | Immune | 250 | 75 | Rubble throw | 40 | 48 |
| Glowing Deathclaw | 41 | Deathclaw hand, Deathclaw Meat | 10 | 1000+ | 200 | 350 | Immune | 250 | 90 | Rubble throw / Rad field | 40, 5 rad/sec | 64 |
| Deathclaw Matriarch | 51 | Deathclaw hand, Deathclaw Meat | 10 | 760+ | 225 | 375 | Immune | 250 | 105 | Rubble throw | 40 | 80 |
| Savage Deathclaw | 61 | Deathclaw hand, Deathclaw Meat | 10 | 910+ | 250 | 400 | Immune | 250 | 120 | Rubble throw | 40 | 96 |
| Albino Deathclaw | 71 | Deathclaw hand, Deathclaw Meat | 10 | 1060+ | 275 | 400 | Immune | 250 | 135 | Rubble throw | 40 | 112 |
| Chameleon Deathclaw | 81 | Deathclaw hand, Deathclaw Meat | 10 | 1210+ | 300 | 400 | Immune | 250 | 150 | Rubble throw | 40 | 129 |
| Mythic Deathclaw | 91+ | Deathclaw hand, Deathclaw Meat | 10 | 1360+ | 300 | 400 | Immune | 250 | 175 | Rubble throw | 40 | 145 |

Deathclaws have very high energy resistance, so it's usually best to stick with heavy guns and powerful ballistic rifles. Try to cripple one of the creature's legs, then concentrate your fire on its belly as it limps toward you.

## FERAL GHOULS

Feral Ghouls come in a variety of sizes and shapes, but they all share a singular purpose: to attack and consume any available prey. From a distance, these shambling creatures can seem almost docile—in fact, you'll often find them lying motionless or partially buried. Once Feral Ghouls spot a potential target, however, few enemies can match the pure ferocity shown by a swarm of these foes. Feral Ghouls use lunging strikes to deal direct damage, but each successful hit also inflicts a small amount of radiation damage. A suppressed long-range weapon is often the safest way to thin a group of Feral Ghouls. If you find yourself surrounded by multiple targets, it's generally best to use the most powerful rapid-fire weapon in your arsenal. But avoid using weapons that deal radiation damage, as each successful hit will heal a wounded Feral Ghoul.

| NAME | LEVEL | INVENTORY | PERCEPTION | BASE HEALTH | DAMAGE RESISTANCE | ENERGY RESISTANCE | RADIATION RESISTANCE | POISON RESISTANCE | DAMAGE | SPECIAL ATTACK | SA DAMAGE | XP |
|---|---|---|---|---|---|---|---|---|---|---|---|---|
| Feral Ghoul | 3 | — | 2 | 35 | 10 | 20 | 1000 | 200 | — | Radiation Damage | 10 | 5 |
| Feral Ghoul Roamer | 9 | — | 2 | 120 | 15 | 30 | 1000 | 200 | 15 | Radiation Damage | 10 | 13 |
| Feral Ghoul Stalker | 15 | — | 2 | 200 | 30 | 45 | 1000 | 50 | 30 | Radiation Damage | 20 | 22 |
| Feral Ghoul Reaver | 22 | — | 2 | 290 | 40 | 60 | 1000 | 200 | 40 | Radiation Damage | 30 | 32 |
| Withered Feral Ghoul | 32 | — | 3 | 350 | 50 | 75 | 1000 | 200 | 50 | Radiation Damage | 40 | 47 |
| Gangrenous Feral Ghoul | 42 | — | 3 | 500 | 60 | 90 | 1000 | 200 | 65 | Radiation Damage | 50 | 61 |
| Rotting Feral Ghoul | 52 | — | 4 | 700 | 70 | 100 | 1000 | 200 | 75 | Radiation Damage | 60 | 76 |
| Charred Feral Ghoul | 62+ | — | 5 | 855+ | 75 | 110 | 1000 | 200 | 85 | Radiation Damage | 70 | 90 |

### Glowing Ones

Glowing Ones are particularly dangerous Feral Ghoul variants. In addition to their lunging strikes, these creatures emit enough radiation to damage vulnerable targets from several feet away. This radiation also heals nearby Feral Ghouls, and Glowing Ones can even revive recently killed allies. Like Feral Ghouls, Glowing Ones are healed by radiation. Focusing your attacks on a Glowing One's legs can help you keep your distance, but it's best to finish them off as quickly as possible.

| NAME | LEVEL | INVENTORY | PERCEPTION | BASE HEALTH | DAMAGE RESISTANCE | ENERGY RESISTANCE | RADIATION RESISTANCE | POISON RESISTANCE | DAMAGE | SPECIAL ATTACK | SA DAMAGE | XP |
|---|---|---|---|---|---|---|---|---|---|---|---|---|
| Glowing One | 22 | — | 3 | 350 | 40 | 80 | 1000 | 200 | 40 | Radiation Damage | 35 | 32 |
| Putrid Glowing One | 40 | — | 4 | 650 | 75 | 150 | 1000 | 200 | 75 | Radiation Damage | 60 | 57 |
| Bloated Glowing One | 58 | — | 5 | 400 | 40+ | 80+ | 1000 | 200 | 35 | Radiation Damage | 75 | 83 |

# MIRELURKS

## Standard Mirelurks

Standard Mirelurks are large, crablike creatures with thick armor and powerful claws. They can sometimes be out in the open, but they're often lurking underwater or partially buried along the shoreline. A headshot is the best way to damage a Mirelurk, but due to their posture, it's often difficult to land a successful hit. In many cases, it's best to equip a powerful shotgun, wait for a Mirelurk to charge, then fire as many shots as you can manage as the creature raises it's head. Otherwise, focus your fire on a Mirelurk's legs. Above all, avoid targeting a Mirelurk's back—this protective shell can absorb massive amounts of damage.

| NAME | LEVEL | INVENTORY | PERCEPTION | BASE HEALTH | DAMAGE RESISTANCE | ENERGY RESISTANCE | RADIATION RESISTANCE | POISON RESISTANCE | DAMAGE | SPECIAL ATTACK | SA DAMAGE | XP |
|---|---|---|---|---|---|---|---|---|---|---|---|---|
| Mirelurk Hatchling | 1 | — | 4 | 3 | 0 | 0 | 0 | 0 | ? | — | — | 2 |
| Softshell Mirelurk | 5 | Mirelurk Meat | 3 | 100 | 45 | 40 | Immune | 0 | 25 | — | — | 9 |
| Mirelurk | 12 | Mirelurk Meat | 3 | 160 | 60 | 50 | Immune | 0 | 40 | — | — | 19 |
| Mirelurk Razorclaw | 18 | Mirelurk Meat | 3 | 215 | 100 | 85 | Immune | 0 | 65 | — | — | 27 |
| Mirelurk Killclaw | 26 | Mirelurk Meat | 3 | 380 | 125 | 100 | Immune | 0 | 75 | — | — | 37 |
| Glowing Mirelurk | 34 | Mirelurk Meat | 3 | 500 | 150 | 125 | Immune | 0 | 100 | Rad field/Rad damage | 1/sec, 15 | 48 |

Mirelurk Hatchlings only appear when you step on their eggs. They're extremely weak, but they can be a nuisance in the heat of battle. Whenever possible, shoot nearby eggs to prevent Mirelurk Hatchlings from joining the battle.

## Mirelurk Hunters

Mirelurk Hunters have fairly powerful melee strikes, but the acid they spit is a much greater threat. These projectile attacks can be difficult to anticipate, but you have a decent chance of avoiding them as long as you keep moving. Mirelurk

Hunters have less armor than the standard Mirelurks, but their claws are difficult to damage. Focus your attacks on a Hunter's head or legs to chip away at its health.

| NAME | LEVEL | INVENTORY | PERCEPTION | BASE HEALTH | DAMAGE RESISTANCE | ENERGY RESISTANCE | RADIATION RESISTANCE | POISON RESISTANCE | DAMAGE | SPECIAL ATTACK | SA DAMAGE | XP |
|---|---|---|---|---|---|---|---|---|---|---|---|---|
| Mirelurk Hunter | 24 | Mirelurk Meat | 9 | 410+ | 85+ | 85+ | Immune | 200 | 60 | Poison / Spit | 8 / 25 (Rad) | 35 |
| Glowing Mirelurk Hunter | 34 | Mirelurk Meat | 9 | 510 | 95 | 95 | Immune | 200 | 70 | Poison / Spit / Rad field | 8 / 50 (Rad) / 4 rad/sec | 48 |
| Albino Mirelurk Hunter | 46+ | Mirelurk Meat | 9 | 410+ | 90+ | 90+ | Immune | 200 | 90 | Poison / Spit | 8 / 75 (Rad) | 65 |

## Mirelurk Elites

Mirelurk Kings can deal significant damage, but it's their devastating Sonic Attack that makes them truly dangerous. Luckily, these shriekers are relatively easy to sidestep. Mirelurk Kings also have the ability to vanish. The effect only lasts a short time, but it can be difficult to keep track of your target. Aim for a Mirelurk King's head to deal maximum damage.

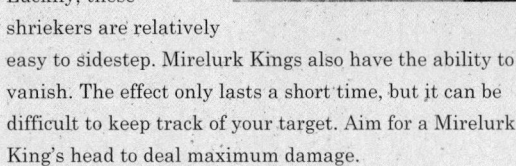

| NAME | LEVEL | INVENTORY | PERCEPTION | BASE HEALTH | DAMAGE RESISTANCE | ENERGY RESISTANCE | RADIATION RESISTANCE | POISON RESISTANCE | DAMAGE | SPECIAL ATTACK | SA DAMAGE | XP |
|---|---|---|---|---|---|---|---|---|---|---|---|---|
| Mirelurk King | 30 | – | 7 | 350 | 95 | 250 | Immune | 250 | 75 | Sonic / Poison | 75 (Energy) / 30 | 43 |
| Mirelurk Deep King | 40 | – | 8 | 400 | 110 | 275 | Immune | 250 | 35 | Sonic / Poison | 75 (Energy) / 35 | 57 |
| Glowing Mirelurk King | 50+ | – | 9 | 400+ | 110+ | 275+ | Immune | 250 | 45 | Sonic / Poison / Rad Field | 75 (Energy) / 40 / 6/sec | 71 |
| Mirelurk Queen | 50 | Mirelurk Queen Meat (5) | 10 | 1000 | 150 | 200 | Immune | Immune | 150 | Spit / Rad Field | 80 (Poison) / 10/sec | 200 |
| Mirelurk Spawn | 1 | – | 4 | 3 | 0 | 0 | 0 | 0 | 10 | – | – | 2 |

Mirelurk Queens are massive, and their acid spray makes them effective at a fairly long range. Sidestepping usually allows you to dodge the initial attack, but make sure to avoid stepping in the resulting acid puddles. Additionally, Queens release swarms of Mirelurk Spawn during combat. It's generally best to simply bombard a Mirelurk Queen with your best heavy weapon. Each time a new wave of Mirelurk Spawn appears, clear them out with an automatic weapon before resuming your attacks on the Queen.

## MUTATED ANIMALS

### Mole Rats

Mole Rats are among the weaker creatures you'll encounter in the wild, but they can be surprisingly dangerous in groups. These pests burrow underground, relocate, and spring up for a sudden attack. This behavior not only hinders your ability to target a Mole Rat, but it also makes it difficult to gauge the extent of a Mole Rat infestation.

| NAME | LEVEL | INVENTORY | PERCEPTION | BASE HEALTH | DAMAGE RESISTANCE | ENERGY RESISTANCE | RADIATION RESISTANCE | POISON RESISTANCE | DAMAGE | SPECIAL ATTACK | SA DAMAGE | XP |
|---|---|---|---|---|---|---|---|---|---|---|---|---|
| Mole Rat | 1 | Mole Rat Meat | 4 | 15 | 0 | 0 | Immune | 0 | 5 | – | – | 5 |
| Rabid Mole Rat | 7 | Mole Rat Meat | 4 | 50 | 10 | 10 | Immune | 0 | 1 | Poison | 10 | 11 |
| Glowing Mole Rat | 14 | Mole Rat Meat | 4 | 100 | 15 | 15 | Immune | 0 | 20 | Rad Field | 3 rads/sec | 21 |
| Mole Rat Brood Mother | 21 | Mole Rat Meat | 4 | 230 | 25 | 25 | Immune | 0 | 35 | – | – | 31 |

Bites from Rabid Mole Rats fester, causing damage over time. Glowing Mole Rats emit hazardous radiation fields, and Mole Rat Brood Mothers are the most powerful of the bunch, but all Mole Rat variants are vulnerable to headshots. When facing these enemies, keep moving to avoid being surrounded and improve your chances of dodging surprise attacks.

## Radstags

Lesser Radstags flee at the first sign of danger, but Albino Radstags, Rabid Radstags, and Glowing Radstags are considerably more aggressive. Radstags use their hooves and antlers to deal the bulk of their damage, but each hit that lands also inflicts a small amount of radiation damage.

Radstags are far from the fiercest creatures you'll encounter, and most of them are easily avoided. They are, however, a reliable source of Radstag

Meat and Radstag Hides. Use a long-range rifle to take them by surprise, and aim for a Radstag's right head to inflict maximum damage.

| NAME | LEVEL | INVENTORY | PERCEPTION | BASE HEALTH | DAMAGE RESISTANCE | ENERGY RESISTANCE | RADIATION RESISTANCE | POISON RESISTANCE | DAMAGE | SPECIAL ATTACK | SA DAMAGE | XP |
|---|---|---|---|---|---|---|---|---|---|---|---|---|
| Radstag Yearling | 1 | Radstag Mear, Radstag Hide | 10 | 40 | 10 | 20 | Immune | 0 | 5 | – | – | 4 |
| Radstag Doe | 4 | Radstag Mear, Radstag Hide | 10 | 60 | 10 | 20 | Immune | 0 | 10 | – | – | 8 |
| Radstag | 10 | Radstag Mear, Radstag Hide | 10 | 100 | 10 | 20 | Immune | 0 | 20 | – | – | 16 |
| Albino Radstag | 16 | Radstag Mear, Radstag Hide | 10 | 150 | 20 | 40 | Immune | 0 | 30 | – | – | 24 |
| Rabid Radstag | 24 | Radstag Mear, Radstag Hide | 10 | 250 | 30 | 60 | Immune | 100 | 45 | Poison | 10 | 35 |
| Glowing Radstag | 32 | Radstag Mear, Radstag Hide | 10 | 325 | 35 | 70 | Immune | 0 | 60 | Rad Field | 5 rads/sec | 46 |

## Yao Guai

Yao Guai are strong, durable, and fiercely territorial. They're capable of absorbing massive amounts of damage, and their powerful strikes can be difficult to survive. These bearlike creatures are also

surprisingly fast. Mines can be effective if you have a chance to prepare for a Yao Guai encounter. Otherwise, ready your most trusted weapon and prepare for a tough fight. Aiming for the head will grant a minor damage boost, but it's often best to focus your fire on a Yao Gaui's legs.

| NAME | LEVEL | INVENTORY | PERCEPTION | BASE HEALTH | DAMAGE RESISTANCE | ENERGY RESISTANCE | RADIATION RESISTANCE | POISON RESISTANCE | DAMAGE | SPECIAL ATTACK | SA DAMAGE | XP |
|---|---|---|---|---|---|---|---|---|---|---|---|---|
| Stunted Yao Guai | 16 | Yao Guai Meat, Yao Guai Hide | 14 | 350 | 40 | 25 | 0 | 55 | 50 | — | — | 24 |
| Yao Guai | 26 | Yao Guai Meat, Yao Guai Hide | 13 | 550 | 60 | 40 | Immune | 60 | 100 | — | — | 37 |
| Shaggy Yao Guai | 36 | Yao Guai Meat, Yao Guai Hide | 15 | 700 | 75 | 55 | Immune | 70 | 130 | — | — | 51 |
| Glowing Yao Guai | 46 | Yao Guai Meat, Yao Guai Hide | 13 | 900 | 90 | 60 | Immune | 80 | 165 | Rad Field | 4 rads/sec | 65 |
| Albino Yao Guai | 56 | Yao Guai Meat, Yao Guai Hide | 13 | 1000 | 100 | 70 | Immune | 90 | 175 | — | — | 80 |
| Rabid Yao Guai | 66 | Yao Guai Meat, Yao Guai Hide | 14 | 1100 | 100 | 85 | Immune | 100 | 185 | — | — | 94 |
| Dusky Yao Guai | 76+ | Yao Guai Meat, Yao Guai Hide | 15 | 1175+ | 100 | 100 | Immune | 125 | 200 | — | — | 109 |

### Bloatflies

Bloatflies are among the few wild creatures that use ranged attacks as their primary source of damage. They're not very durable, but their small size and erratic movements can make them troublesome. Whenever possible, use VATS to improve your chances of landing effective shots.

In addition to standard damage, each Bloatfly attack inflicts a small amount of radiation damage. Sidestepping should allow you to avoid the bulk of a Bloatfly's attacks, but doing so also makes it more difficult to keep your weapon aimed at such a small target.

| NAME | LEVEL | INVENTORY | PERCEPTION | BASE HEALTH | DAMAGE RESISTANCE | ENERGY RESISTANCE | RADIATION RESISTANCE | POISON RESISTANCE | DAMAGE | SPECIAL ATTACK | SA DAMAGE | XP |
|---|---|---|---|---|---|---|---|---|---|---|---|---|
| Bloatfly | 1 | Bloatfly Meat, Bloadfly Gland | 3 | 10 | 6 | 15 | Immune | 20 | 7 (Rad) | — | — | 5 |
| Black Bloatfly | 9 | Bloatfly Meat, Bloadfly Gland | 3 | 50 | 20 | 35 | Immune | 20 | 7 (Rad) | — | — | 15 |
| Festering Bloatfly | 17 | Bloatfly Meat, Bloadfly Gland | 3 | 25 | 25 | 45 | Immune | 20 | 7 (Rad) | Poison | 25 | 25 |
| Glowing Bloatfly | 27 | Bloatfly Meat, Bloadfly Gland | 3 | 195 | 30 | 55 | Immune | 20 | 7 (Rad) | Rad Field | 4 rads/sec | 39 |

### Bloodbugs

Despite their frail appearance, Bloodbugs can withstand a considerable amount of damage. They're also fast and extremely aggressive, making them particularly dangerous in large groups. Short-range strikes account for the bulk of a Bloodbug's damage, but these creatures will occasionally latch on to you and drain a fair amount of blood. Once this happens, there's a good chance the Bloodbug will spit the blood back in your face, temporarily obscuring your vision. Consider using VATS whenever you face these flying insects.

| NAME | LEVEL | INVENTORY | PERCEPTION | BASE HEALTH | DAMAGE RESISTANCE | ENERGY RESISTANCE | RADIATION RESISTANCE | POISON RESISTANCE | DAMAGE | SPECIAL ATTACK | SA DAMAGE | XP |
|---|---|---|---|---|---|---|---|---|---|---|---|---|
| Bloodbug Hatchling | 2 | Bloodbug Proboscis | 10 | 20 | 5 | 5 | Immune | 0 | 8 | Poison | 15 | 5 |
| Bloodbug | 10 | Bloodbug Proboscis | 10 | 120 | 15 | 15 | Immune | 0 | 25 | Poison | 15 | 16 |
| Red Widow Bloodbug | 18 | Bloodbug Proboscis | 10 | 240 | 30 | 30 | Immune | 0 | 35 | Poison | 15 | 27 |
| Infected Bloodbug | 26 | Bloodbug Proboscis | 10 | 350 | 40 | 40 | Immune | 0 | 45 | Poison | 15 | 37 |
| Glowing Bloodbug | 34 | Bloodbug Proboscis | 10 | 400 | 40 | 60 | Immune | 0 | 40 | Rad/Rad Field/ Poison | 20/3 rads/ sec/15 | 48 |
| Vampiric Bloodbug | 42+ | Bloodbug Proboscis | 10 | 450+ | 50 | 50 | Immune | 0 | 60 | Poison | 15 | 60 |

### Radroaches

Even in groups, Radroaches don't pose much of threat. Each hit a Radroach lands does inflict a bit of radiation damage, but they're relatively slow and extremely fragile.

| NAME | LEVEL | INVENTORY | PERCEPTION | BASE HEALTH | DAMAGE RESISTANCE | ENERGY RESISTANCE | RADIATION RESISTANCE | POISON RESISTANCE | DAMAGE | SPECIAL ATTACK | SA DAMAGE | XP |
|---|---|---|---|---|---|---|---|---|---|---|---|---|
| Radroach | 1 | Radroach Meat | 4 | 3 | 0 | 0 | Immune | 0 | 2 | — | — | 5 |
| Glowing Radroach | 5 | Radroach Meat | 4 | 15 | 0 | 0 | Immune | 0 | 3 | Rad Field | 3 rads/sec | 9 |

## Radscorpions

A single Radscorpion is formidable, but these creatures often hunt in packs. Radscorpions are able to burrow underground, usually hiding for several seconds at a time. Their powerful strikes inflict bonus radiation damage, and stingers at the end of their tails can inject foes with poison. They move very quickly for creatures of their size, and they boast a considerable amount of health.

| NAME | LEVEL | INVENTORY | PERCEPTION | BASE HEALTH | DAMAGE RESISTANCE | ENERGY RESISTANCE | RADIATION RESISTANCE | POISON RESISTANCE | DAMAGE | SPECIAL ATTACK | SA DAMAGE | XP |
|---|---|---|---|---|---|---|---|---|---|---|---|---|
| Radscorpion | 14 | Radscorpion Meat | 9 | 250 | 35 | 20 | Immune | 200 | 30 | Poison | 15 | 21 |
| Radscorpion Hunter | 22 | Radscorpion Meat | 9 | 350 | 45 | 25 | Immune | 200 | 35 | Poison | 20 | 32 |
| Glowing Radscorpion | 30 | Radscorpion Meat | 10 | 450 | 75 | 45 | Immune | 200 | 45 | Poison/ Rad Field | 25 / 3 rads/sec | 44 |
| Albino Radscorpion | 38 | Radscorpion Meat | 11 | 675 | 100 | 60 | Immune | 200 | 60 | Poison | 30 | 55 |
| Radscorpion Stalker | 46 | Radscorpion Meat | 11 | 850 | 120 | 85 | Immune | 200 | 90 | Poison | 35 | 67 |
| Radscorpion Predator | 54 | Radscorpion Meat | 11 | 950 | 135 | 100 | Immune | 250 | 100 | Poison | 40 | 78 |
| Deathskull Radscorpion | 64+ | Radscorpion Meat | 12 | 1115+ | 150 | 120 | Immune | 300 | 115 | Poison | 45 | 96 |

Radscorpions are vulnerable to headshots, but it takes a powerful weapon to finish even a low-level Radroach with a single shot. At short range, combat shotguns and powerful melee weapons are both good options.

## Stingwings

Stingwings tend to circle their targets, darting in to inject them with poison every few seconds. Using VATS is often the best way to deal with these flying insects.

| NAME | LEVEL | INVENTORY | PERCEPTION | BASE HEALTH | DAMAGE RESISTANCE | ENERGY RESISTANCE | RADIATION RESISTANCE | POISON RESISTANCE | DAMAGE | SPECIAL ATTACK | SA DAMAGE | XP |
|---|---|---|---|---|---|---|---|---|---|---|---|---|
| Stingwing | 10 | Stingwing Meat | 9 | 50 | 20 | 30 | Immune | 200 | 20 | Poison | 20 | 15 |
| Stingwing Darter | 18 | Stingwing Meat | 10 | 65 | 30 | 45 | Immune | 200 | 30 | Poison | 25 | 26 |
| Stingwing Skimmer | 30 | Stingwing Meat | 10 | 110 | 40 | 60 | Immune | 200 | 40 | Poison | 30 | 44 |
| Glowing Stingwing | 42 | Stingwing Meat | 10 | 140 | 50 | 75 | Immune | 200 | 50 | Poison/Rad Field | 35/ 5 rads/sec | 61 |
| Stingwing Chaser | 54+ | Stingwing Meat | 11 | 265+ | 60 | 90 | Immune | 200 | 70 | Poison | 40 | 78 |

## HELPFUL HINT
### from Vault Boy!

ALL STINGWING ATTACKS REDUCE PERCEPTION AND AGILITY BY 5 POINTS FOR 4 SECONDS.

# ★ WEAPONS

Range, accuracy, and overall damage are obviously important, but when it comes to choosing a weapon, there are a lot of other factors to consider. How much does a weapon weigh? How easy is it to acquire? What type of ammo does it use? How can it be modified? The list goes on. Maintaining a large arsenal is the best way to ensure you're prepared for any encounter.

Your own status is one of the most important things to consider when choosing a weapon. Your S.P.E.C.I.A.L. ranks significantly affect how a weapon performs. Strength determines the damage done by all melee weapons and punching weapons. Perception, Agility, and Luck all play a role in how well a weapon performs in V.A.T.S. However, your active perks will often determine which weapons prove most useful in a fight.

Perks like Bloody Mess, Four Leaf Clover, and Better Criticals improve the usefulness of all weapons. Some perks improve performance against specific targets or in specific situations. However, there are a few key perks that serve to divide weapons into seven distinct categories:

- **NON-AUTOMATIC PISTOLS: INCLUDES ALL WEAPONS THAT BENEFIT FROM THE GUNSLINGER PERK.**
- **NON-AUTOMATIC RIFLES: INCLUDES ALL WEAPONS THAT BENEFIT FROM THE RIFLEMAN PERK.**
- **AUTOMATIC WEAPONS: INCLUDES ALL WEAPONS THAT BENEFIT FROM THE COMMANDO PERK.**
- **HEAVY GUNS: INCLUDES ALL WEAPONS THAT BENEFIT FROM THE HEAVY GUNNER PERK.**
- **MELEE WEAPONS: INCLUDES ALL WEAPONS THAT BENEFIT FROM THE BIG LEAGUES PERK.**
- **PUNCHING WEAPONS: INCLUDES ALL WEAPONS THAT BENEFIT FROM THE IRON FIST PERK.**
- **EXPLOSIVES: INCLUDES ALL WEAPONS THAT BENEFIT FROM THE DEMOLITION EXPERT PERK.**

Each time you select or modify a weapon, consider whether it takes advantage of your active perks. Conversely, if you happen to find a particularly useful weapon, be mindful of any previously overlooked perks that could improve its performance in battle.

## HELPFUL HINT from Vault Boy!
**Did You Know?**

### WEAPON STATS
WEAPON STATS CAN VARY BASED ON YOUR S.P.E.C.I.A.L RANKS, ACTIVE PERKS, AND ANY MODS THAT ARE CURRENTLY ATTACHED TO THE ITEM IN QUESTION. THE DETAILS PROVIDED HERE APPLY TO STANDARD WEAPON CONFIGURATIONS AS WIELDED BY AN ADVENTURER WITH A RANK OF 4 IN ALL S.P.E.C.I.A.L. CATEGORIES AND NO DAMAGE-ENHANCING PERKS.

## GUNS

Nearly every available gun is essentially a selection of mods attached to a weapon frame. Other mods might better suit your needs, but even a seemingly underpowered gun can offer a weapon frame that belongs in your collection. It's also important to note that many guns can be modified to fit into different weapon categories. A non-automatic combat rifle is easily converted to an automatic weapon. Plasma guns can be modified to serve as anything from non-automatic pistols to heavy guns. When deciding whether a gun is worth using, consider all the possibilities its weapon frame offers.

### POSSIBLE GUN CONVERSIONS

| WEAPON FRAME | NON-AUTOMATIC PISTOL | NON-AUTOMATIC RIFLE | AUTOMATIC WEAPON | HEAVY GUN |
|---|---|---|---|---|
| .44 | | | | |
| 10 mm | | | | |
| Alien Blaster | | | | |
| Assault Rifle | | | | |
| Broadsider | | | | |
| Combat Rifle | | | | |
| Combat Shotgun | | | | |
| Cryolator | | | | |
| Deliverer | | | | |
| Double-Barrel Shotgun | | | | |
| Fat Man | | | | |
| Flamer | | | | |
| Gamma Gun | | | | |
| Gatling Laser | | | | |
| Gauss Rifle | | | | |
| Hunting Rifle | | | | |
| Institute Laser | | | | |
| Junk Jet | | | | |
| Laser Gun | | | | |
| Laser Musket | | | | |
| Minigun | | | | |
| Missile Launcher | | | | |
| Pipe Bolt-Action | | | | |
| Pipe Gun | | | | |
| Pipe Revolver | | | | |
| Plasma Gun | | | | |
| Railway Rifle | | | | |
| Submachine Gun | | | | |
| Syringer | | | | |

## NON-AUTOMATIC PISTOLS

In addition to dedicated non-automatic pistols like the .44, Alien Blaster, and Deliverer, you'll find numerous weapon frames that can benefit from any investments you make in the Gunslinger perk.

### ▶ .44  STANDARD MODEL: .44 PISTOL

| Damage: 48 (ballistic) | | Ammo: .44 | | |
|---|---|---|---|---|
| Fire Rate: 6 | Range: 119 | Accuracy: 66 | Weight: 5.2 | Value: 99 |

The .44 doesn't have as many customization options as most pistol frames, but these no-nonsense firearms boast considerable ballistic damage. For old-fashioned stopping power in a conveniently small package, it's hard to beat a heavily modified .44 pistol. These pistols are relatively common, and they can be found or purchased throughout the Commonwealth. They're also fairly popular with the Commonwealth's criminal element and can often be found on the bodies of slain Triggermen.

ATTACHED MODS

| Standard receiver | Standard barrel | Standard grip | Standard sights |
|---|---|---|---|

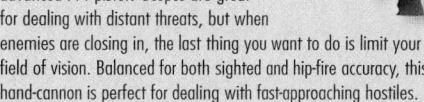

★ TIP ★

TACTICAL ADVANCED .44 PISTOL

| Damage: 48 (ballistic) | | Ammo: .44 | Fire Rate: 7 |
|---|---|---|---|
| Range: 119 | Accuracy: 73 | Weight: 6.4 | Value: 198 |

If you're looking for a pistol with stopping power, you're looking for the tactical advanced .44 pistol! Scopes are great for dealing with distant threats, but when enemies are closing in, the last thing you want to do is limit your field of vision. Balanced for both sighted and hip-fire accuracy, this hand-cannon is perfect for dealing with fast-approaching hostiles.

ATTACHED MODS

| Advanced receiver | Comfort grip |
|---|---|
| Bull barrel | Reflex sight |

### ▶ 10 mm
STANDARD MODEL: LONG 10-MM PISTOL

| Damage: 18 (ballistic) | | Ammo: 10 mm | Fire Rate: 46 |
|---|---|---|---|
| Range: 119 | Accuracy: 61 | Weight: 4.2 | Value: 53 |

The 10-mm weapon frame is fairly common, making it a popular choice among new adventurers. It isn't the most powerful base for a sidearm, but a heavily modified 10-mm pistol offers reliable damage with a comparatively high rate of fire.

There are multiple 10-mm pistols located in and around Vault 111, but you're sure to find many more scattered throughout the Commonwealth.

ATTACHED MODS

| Standard receiver | Standard grip | Standard sights |
|---|---|---|
| Long barrel | Standard magazine | No muzzle |

### ▶ Alien Blaster
STANDARD MODEL: ALIEN BLASTER PISTOL

| Damage: 50 (energy) | Ammo: Alien Blaster Round | Fire Rate: 100 |
|---|---|---|
| Range: 119 | Accuracy: 73 | Weight: 2.5 | Value: 1551 |

The Alien Blaster pistol is powerful, but it's also very rare, and anyone lucky enough to find one is likely to have trouble maintaining a supply of Alien Blaster rounds. Luckily, it can be modified to accept standard fusion cells.

This weapon is carried only by Aliens, so you'd do well to search any UFO crash sites you spot.

ATTACHED MODS

| Short barrel | Standard mag | Standard sights |
|---|---|---|
| Standard grip | | |

### ▶ Deliverer  STANDARD MODEL: DELIVERER

| Damage: 25 (ballistic) | | Ammo: 10 mm | |
|---|---|---|---|
| Fire Rate: 66 | Range: 119 | Accuracy: 61 | Weight: 4.4 | Value: 158 |

Using the same ammunition as the 10-mm pistol, the Deliverer outperforms comparably modified 10-mm pistols in almost every area. This unique weapon frame cannot accommodate a scope, however, so accuracy can be a bit of an issue at medium to long ranges.

The Deliverer is rewarded for completing The Railroad Quest: Tradecraft. By default, this weapon is equipped with a suppressor and a shorter barrel, but its remaining mod slots contain standard parts.

ATTACHED MODS

| Standard receiver | Standard grip | Standard sights |
|---|---|---|
| Extended barrel | Standard mag | No muzzle |

★ TIP ★

DELIVERER

| Damage: 43 (ballistic) | Ammo: 10 mm | Fire Rate: 99 |
|---|---|---|
| Range: 89 | Accuracy: 71 | Weight: 6.9 | Value: 479 |

This modified Deliverer may lack the bells and whistles found on other similar weapons, but no other suppressed pistol can squeeze so much damage from a 10-mm round. When you need to keep your enemies close and your gunfire quiet, it's hard to beat this handy pistol.

ATTACHED MODS

| Advanced receiver | Large quick-eject mag |
|---|---|
| Extended barrel | Glow sights |
| Sharpshooter's grip | Suppressor |

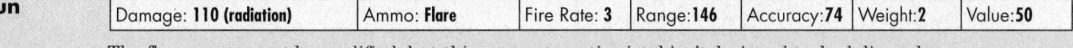

### ▶ Flare Gun

| Damage: 110 (radiation) | Ammo: Flare | Fire Rate: 3 | Range: 146 | Accuracy: 74 | Weight: 2 | Value: 50 |
|---|---|---|---|---|---|---|

The flare gun cannot be modified, but this non-automatic pistol isn't designed to deal direct damage. Instead, it summons nearby Minutemen to the area. Firing a flare directly at an enemy will cause a small amount of damage, but virtually every other weapon will yield better results in the heat of battle. You acquire the flare gun from Preston Garvey during The Minutemen Quest: When Freedom Calls.

## Gamma Gun   STANDARD MODEL: GAMMA GUN

| Damage: 110 (radiation) | | Ammo: **Gamma Round** | | |
|---|---|---|---|---|
| Fire Rate: **66** | Range: **119** | Accuracy: **69** | Weight: **3.0** | Value: **156** |

Even in their most basic form, gamma guns boast considerable radiation damage. Of course, this rare feature means most gamma guns have little effect on robots, Ghouls, Super Mutants, and the majority of wild creatures that plague the Commonwealth. However, most human enemies have limited Radiation Resistance. Even the most robust humans can often be defeated with several blasts from a properly modified gamma gun.

Gamma guns are popular with the Children of Atom. Whenever you defeat a group of these fanatics, you're likely to find at least one gamma gun among their possessions.

ATTACHED MODS

| Standard dish | Standard grip | No muzzle |
|---|---|---|

### ★ TIP ★

SHARPSHOOTER'S GAMMA GUN

| Damage: 40 (energy), 160 (radiation) | | Ammo: **Gamma Round** | Fire Rate: **66** |
|---|---|---|---|
| Range: **203** | Accuracy: **73** | Weight: **5.1** | Value: **292** |

This radiological wonder is the top choice of gamma gun enthusiasts — and for good reason! With this weapon, each blast of radiation also deals a good amount of energy damage. For maximum damage, hold the trigger to charge each shot before firing. Overwhelm vulnerable targets as you hedge your bets against radiation-immune critters. Put those gamma rounds to good use!

ATTACHED MODS

| Deep dish | Electric signal carrier |
|---|---|
| Sharpshooter's grip | antennae |

## Institute Laser (Pistol)

STANDARD MODEL: INSTITUTE PISTOL

| Damage: 15 (energy) | Ammo: **Fusion Cell** | Fire Rate: **66** | Range: **71** | Accuracy: **70** | Weight: **3.9** | Value: **50** |
|---|---|---|---|---|---|---|

Compared to similarly equipped laser guns, Institute lasers offer a superior rate of fire at the cost of per-shot damage. Even in pistol form, these energy weapons are highly customizable. More importantly, however, they're fairly common. Check the bodies of fallen synths to yield quite the collection of Institute laser weapons.

ATTACHED MODS

| Standard capacitor | Standard grip | No muzzle |
|---|---|---|
| Short barrel | Standard sights | |

## Laser Gun (Pistol)   STANDARD MODEL: LASER PISTOL

| Damage: **24** (energy) | | Ammo: **Fusion Cell** | Fire Rate: **50** |
|---|---|---|---|
| Range: **71** | Accuracy: **71** | Weight: **3.9** | Value: **66** |

Compared to similarly modified Institute laser weapons, laser guns offer superior damage with a lower rate of fire. They can be found throughout the Commonwealth, but they're particularly popular with the Brotherhood of Steel.

ATTACHED MODS

| Standard capacitor | Standard grip | No muzzle |
|---|---|---|
| Short barrel | Standard sights | |

### ★ TIP ★

RECON OVERCHARGED LASER PISTOL

| Damage: **72** (energy) | | Ammo: **Fusion Cell** | Fire Rate: **50** |
|---|---|---|---|
| Range: **263** | Accuracy: **105** | Weight: **7.3** | Value: **204** |

This highly modified energy pistol is like a long-range rifle you can hold in one hand! Use its high-tech scope to identify and track your targets, then deliver energy damage with laser beams that are both powerful and accurate! For maximum damage, allow the weapon to recharge between shots. Utilize rapid trigger-pulls to pepper your targets with a series of reduced-damage beams.

ATTACHED MODS

| Overcharged capacitor | Long recon scope |
|---|---|
| Improved sniper barrel | Fine-tuned beam focuser |
| Sharpshooter's grip | |

## Pipe Bolt-Action

STANDARD MODEL: PIPE BOLT-ACTION PISTOL

| Damage: **34** (ballistic) | | Ammo: **.308** | Fire Rate: **2** |
|---|---|---|---|
| Range: **131** | Accuracy: **64** | Weight: **3.9** | Value: **33** |

The pipe bolt-action weapon frame may not perform as well as other high-caliber options, but it's remarkably versatile and easily acquired. These makeshift guns are often carried by settlers and low-level enemies, but you'll find many pipe bolt-action weapons scattered throughout the Commonwealth.

ATTACHED MODS

| Standard receiver | Standard grip | No muzzle |
|---|---|---|
| Short barrel | Standard sights | |

## Pipe Revolver

STANDARD MODEL: PIPE REVOLVER PISTOL

| Damage: **24** (ballistic) | | Ammo: **.45** | Fire Rate: **6** |
|---|---|---|---|
| Range: **119** | Accuracy: **63** | Weight: **5.2** | Value: **27** |

The pipe revolver weapon frame is another low-tech option for self-defense. They lack the power of manufactured weapons, but they're fairly versatile and easy to acquire. Like other makeshift firearms, pipe revolvers are commonly carried by settlers and low-level enemies.

ATTACHED MODS

| Standard receiver | Standard grip | No muzzle |
|---|---|---|
| Short barrel | Standard sights | |

### Pipe Gun

STANDARD MODEL: PIPE PISTOL

| Damage: 13 (ballistic) | | Ammo: .38 | Fire Rate: 55 | Range: 119 | Accuracy: 58 | Weight: 2.8 | Value: 22 |
|---|---|---|---|---|---|---|---|

This admittedly humble weapon frame is best used to fill gaps in a new adventurer's arsenal. Like other makeshift firearms, pipe guns are inexpensive, versatile, and commonly carried by settlers and low-level enemies.

ATTACHED MODS

| | | |
|---|---|---|
| Standard receiver | Standard grip | Standard sights |
| Short barrel | Standard magazine | No muzzle |

### Plasma Gun (Pistol)

STANDARD MODEL: PLASMA PISTOL

| Damage: 24 (ballistic), 24 (energy) | Ammo: Plasma Cartridge | Fire Rate: 33 | Range: 119 | Accuracy: 142 | Weight: 3.9 | Value: 123 |
|---|---|---|---|---|---|---|

Plasma guns combine ballistic damage and energy damage, making these weapons very powerful and effective against most targets. Unfortunately, they're also quite rare, and it can be difficult to maintain a supply of the plasma cartridges they require.

For the most part, these weapons are only found on particularly formidable enemies. But once you acquire a plasma gun, you'll see it's one of the most powerful and versatile weapons in your arsenal.

ATTACHED MODS

| | |
|---|---|
| Standard capacitor | Standard grip |
| Short barrel | Standard sights |

## NON-AUTOMATIC RIFLES

Non-automatic rifles tend to offer better accuracy and per-shot damage than pistols and automatic weapons. Most non-automatic rifles can be equipped with scopes to benefit from all three ranks of the Sniper perk. Most importantly, non-automatic rifles are affected by any investments you make in the Rifleman perk.

### Assault Rifle

STANDARD MODEL: SHORT ASSAULT RIFLE

| Damage: 30 (ballistic) | Ammo: 5.56 | Fire Rate: 40 |
|---|---|---|
| Range: 119 | Accuracy: 72 | Weight: 13.1 | Value: 144 |

The standard assault rifle offers a nice balance of power and accuracy, making it a good choice in a variety of combat scenarios. Many of its available mods make this weapon particularly well suited to automatic fire, but a properly modified assault rifle can be turned into a serviceable sniper rifle with great ammo capacity and a comparatively high rate of fire.

Assault rifles are often carried by higher-level Super Mutants, but they can be found throughout the Commonwealth.

ATTACHED MODS

| | | |
|---|---|---|
| Standard receiver | Short stock | Standard sights |
| Short barrel | Standard magazine | No muzzle |

### Combat Rifle

STANDARD MODEL: SHORT COMBAT RIFLE

| Damage: 33 (ballistic) | Ammo: .45 | Fire Rate: 33 |
|---|---|---|
| Range: 119 | Accuracy: 70 | Weight: 11.1 | Value: 117 |

Standard combat rifles use .45 ammo to offer slightly higher damage than assault rifles but with a lower rate of fire and a minor drop in accuracy. Like assault rifles, however, combat rifles can be modified to meet a wide variety of offensive needs.

These weapons are particularly popular with Gunners, but they're commonly carried by higher-level enemies.

ATTACHED MODS

| | | |
|---|---|---|
| Standard receiver | Short stock | Standard sights |
| Short barrel | Standard magazine | No muzzle |

### Combat Shotgun  STANDARD MODEL: SHORT COMBAT SHOTGUN

| Damage: 50 (ballistic) | | Ammo: Shotgun Shell | |
|---|---|---|---|
| Fire Rate: 20 | Range: 47 | Accuracy: 23 | Weight: 11.1 | Value: 87 |

Combat shotguns deal significant damage, but they do so at the cost of accuracy and range. This isn't necessarily a bad thing. The wide spread from each shot can make it much easier to hit fast-moving targets—as long as they're relatively close. Even standard models can be effective, but a heavily modified combat shotgun offers enough firepower to overwhelm most targets in seconds.

ATTACHED MODS

| | | |
|---|---|---|
| Standard receiver | Short stock | Standard sights |
| Short barrel | Standard magazine | No muzzle |

### ★ TIP ★

RECOIL COMPENSATED ADVANCED COMBAT SHOTGUN

| Damage: 87 (ballistic) | | Ammo: Shotgun Shell | Fire Rate: 26 |
|---|---|---|---|
| Range: 53 | Accuracy: 54 | Weight: 22.3 | Value: 245 |

Whether you're surrounded by persistent pests or facing off against one formidable foe, this heavily modified combat shotgun can be a real lifesaver. When your back is to the wall and enemies are closing in, you don't need range—you need power! Increased ammo capacity means less-frequent reloads, but the attached bayonet ensures that even an empty weapon can deal serious damage. You might be outnumbered, but that doesn't have to mean you're outgunned.

ATTACHED MODS

| | |
|---|---|
| Advanced receiver | Quick-eject drum mag |
| Long ported and shielded barrel | Reflex sight (dot) |
| Recoil compensating stock | Large bayonet |

## Double-Barrel Shotgun

STANDARD MODEL: SHORT DOUBLE-BARREL SHOTGUN

| Damage: 45 (ballistic) | Ammo: Shotgun Shell | Fire Rate: 36 | Range: 47 | Accuracy: 16 | Weight: 9 | Value: 39 |
| --- | --- | --- | --- | --- | --- | --- |

Double-barrel shotguns are both powerful and plentiful, but they also require frequent reloads. This makes them less than ideal when you're outnumbered, but they're handy when a quick burst of damage is enough to end an encounter.

**ATTACHED MODS**

| | | |
| --- | --- | --- |
| Standard receiver | Short stock | No muzzle |
| Short barrel | Standard sights | |

## Gauss Rifle

STANDARD MODEL: GAUSS RIFLE

| Damage: 110 (ballistic) | Ammo: 2-mm Electromagnetic Cartridge | Fire Rate: 66 | Range: 191 | Accuracy: 39 | Weight: 15.8 | Value: 228 |
| --- | --- | --- | --- | --- | --- | --- |

Gauss rifles favor power over accuracy. Each shot must be charged for maximum damage, so this weapon is best used from the safety of cover. Most importantly, they're the only guns that utilize 2-mm electromagnetic cartridges. Depending on your ammo supply, a properly modified Gauss rifle can be a valuable addition to your arsenal.

**ATTACHED MODS**

| | | |
| --- | --- | --- |
| Standard barrel | Half capacitors | No muzzle |
| Standard stock | Standard sights | |

## Hunting Rifle    STANDARD MODEL: SHORT HUNTING RIFLE

| Damage: 37 (ballistic) | Ammo: .308 | Fire Rate: 3 |
| --- | --- | --- |
| Range: 131 | Accuracy: 71 | Weight: 9.6 | Value: 55 |

This weapon frame features high damage and accuracy with a low rate of fire. Hunting rifles are fairly common, but these seemingly simple weapons can be converted into extremely powerful sniper rifles.

**ATTACHED MODS**

| | | |
| --- | --- | --- |
| Standard receiver | Short stock | Standard sights |
| Short barrel | Standard magazine | No muzzle |

### ★ TIP ★

**RECON .50 SNIPER RIFLE**

| Damage: 64 (ballistic) | Ammo: .50 | Fire Rate: 4 |
| --- | --- | --- |
| Range: 185 | Accuracy: 112 | Weight: 19.2 | Value: 212 |

Let's face it—it's not always best to go in with guns blazing. This hunting rifle has been modified to use powerful .50-caliber rounds and has great accuracy over long distances, which means you can put every shot right where you want it. The increased ammo capacity minimizes pesky reloads, and the attached suppressor will help keep your enemies guessing. Stick to the shadows, and this modern take on the classic sniper rifle will let you end a firefight before it starts.

**ATTACHED MODS**

| | |
| --- | --- |
| .50 receiver | Large quick-eject mag |
| Long ported barrel | Long recon scope |
| Marksman's stock | Suppressor |

## Institute Laser

STANDARD MODEL: SHORT INSTITUTE RIFLE

| Damage: 15 (energy) | Ammo: Fusion Cell | Fire Rate: 66 |
| --- | --- | --- |
| Range: 71 | Accuracy: 75 | Weight: 4.8 | Value: 67 |

One simple mod is all it takes to convert an Institute pistol to an Institute rifle. This versatility means that standard Institute rifles lack the raw power offered by dedicated rifle weapon frames. When you're looking to deal long-distance energy damage, however, a properly modified Institute laser certainly fits the bill.

**ATTACHED MODS**

| | | |
| --- | --- | --- |
| Standard capacitor | Full stock | No muzzle |
| Short barrel | Standard sights | |

## Laser Gun (Rifle)

STANDARD MODEL: SHORT LASER RIFLE

| Damage: 24 (energy) | Ammo: Fusion Cell | Fire Rate: 50 |
| --- | --- | --- |
| Range: 71 | Accuracy: 75 | Weight: 4.5 | Value: 77 |

Like Institute lasers, laser guns are easily converted between pistol form and rifle form. However, a heavily modified laser rifle offers excellent per-shot damage, making it particularly effective as an energy-based sniper rifle.

**ATTACHED MODS**

| | | |
| --- | --- | --- |
| Standard capacitor | Short stock | No muzzle |
| Short barrel | Standard sights | |

## Laser Musket

STANDARD MODEL: SHORT LASER MUSKET

| Damage: 30 (energy) | Ammo: Fusion Cell | Fire Rate: 6 | Range: 71 | Accuracy: 70 | Weight: 12.6 | Value: 57 |
| --- | --- | --- | --- | --- | --- | --- |

The standard laser musket isn't quite as accurate as other energy rifles, but it does offer more power due to a unique reload process. A laser musket must be cranked before firing. The standard capacitor allows for a maximum of two cranks, but more advanced laser muskets can accommodate up to six cranks. The result is a massive boost in per-shot damage with greatly increased ammo usage.

**ATTACHED MODS**

| | |
| --- | --- |
| Standard capacitor | Short stock |
| Short barrel | Standard sights |

A slightly modified laser musket can be found just outside the Museum of Freedom.

## Pipe Bolt-Action

STANDARD MODEL: SHORT PIPE BOLT-ACTION RIFLE

| Damage: 34 (ballistic) | | Ammo: .308 | Fire Rate: 2 |
|---|---|---|---|
| Range: 131 | Accuracy: 71 | Weight: 4.8 | Value: 39 |

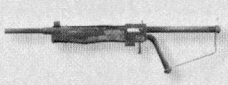

The pipe bolt-action weapon frame can be used to build a fairly powerful rifle, making it a good option for long-range damage until you can find a hunting rifle.

ATTACHED MODS

| | |
|---|---|
| Standard receiver | Standard sights |
| Short barrel | No muzzle |
| Standard stock | |

## Pipe Gun

STANDARD MODEL: SHORT PIPE RIFLE

| Damage: 13 (ballistic) | | Ammo: .38 | Fire Rate: 55 |
|---|---|---|---|
| Range: 119 | Accuracy: 69 | Weight: 3.4 | Value: 26 |

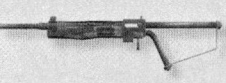

In rifle form, the pipe gun's true strength lies in its versatility. A few basic modifications should allow this weapon to fill gaps in your arsenal as you hunt down more powerful rifles.

ATTACHED MODS

| | |
|---|---|
| Standard receiver | Standard magazine |
| Short barrel | Standard sights |
| Standard stock | No muzzle |

## Pipe Revolver

STANDARD MODEL: SHORT PIPE REVOLVER RIFLE

| Damage: 24 (ballistic) | Ammo: .45 | Fire Rate: 6 | Range: 119 | Accuracy: 71 | Weight: 6.4 | Value: 32 |
|---|---|---|---|---|---|---|

Like other makeshift weapon frames, pipe revolvers are common and easily modified. It can't match the damage offered by more advanced rifles, but it's a good option for new adventurers.

ATTACHED MODS

| | | |
|---|---|---|
| Standard receiver | Standard stock | No muzzle |
| Short barrel | Standard sights | |

## Plasma Gun (Rifle)   STANDARD MODEL: SHORT PLASMA RIFLE

| Damage: 24 (ballistic), 24 (energy) | | Ammo: Plasma Cartridge | |
|---|---|---|---|
| Fire Rate: 33 | Range: 119 | Accuracy: 148 | Weight: 4.8 | Value: 154 |

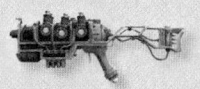

With its combination of ballistic damage and energy damage, the plasma gun is one of the most powerful and versatile options for small-arms fire. A properly modified plasma gun offers excellent range, accuracy, and per-shot damage, making it a particularly good sniper rifle. It can't support a suppressor, but a long-range plasma rifle is a great way to kick off a firefight.

ATTACHED MODS

| | |
|---|---|
| Standard capacitor | Standard stock |
| Short barrel | Standard sights |

## ★ TIP ★

RECON OVERCHARGED PLASMA SNIPER RIFLE

| Damage: 60 (ballistic), 60 (energy) | | Ammo: Plasma Cartridge | Fire Rate: 33 |
|---|---|---|---|
| Range: 233 | Accuracy: 184 | Weight: 8.1 | Value: 397 |

When you want to send a message to your enemies, let this overcharged rifle do the talking. What this high-tech weapon lacks in subtlety, it more than makes up for in range, accuracy, and per-shot damage.

ATTACHED MODS

| | |
|---|---|
| Overcharged capacitor | Recoil compensating stock |
| Improved sniper barrel | Long recon scope |

## Railway Rifle

STANDARD MODEL: RAILWAY RIFLE

| Damage: 100 (ballistic) | Ammo: Railway Spike | Fire Rate: 10 | Range: 119 | Accuracy: 69 | Weight: 14.4 | Value: 290 |
|---|---|---|---|---|---|---|

The railway rifle is less accurate than most non-automatic rifles, but it's extremely powerful. This steam-powered weapon launches railway spikes capable of crippling limbs and impaling enemies. It makes for an effective long-range weapon—especially after a few modifications—but it excels at short-to-medium range combat.

ATTACHED MODS

| | | |
|---|---|---|
| Standard receiver | Standard stock | No muzzle |
| Short barrel | Standard sights | |

The railway rifle is gained after completing The Railroad Quest: Underground Undercover.

## Syringer

STANDARD MODEL: SYRINGER RIFLE

| Damage: — | Ammo: Injectable | Fire Rate: 2 | Range: 119 | Accuracy: 72 | Weight: 6.2 | Value: 132 |
|---|---|---|---|---|---|---|

Rather than dealing direct damage, the Syringer is used to inflict your enemies with various effects. This weapon supports a wide variety of injectable ammo, all of which can be crafted at chemistry stations. Targets can be frenzied, paralyzed, weakened, poisoned, and more.

ATTACHED MODS

| | |
|---|---|
| Short barrel | Standard sights |
| Standard stock | |

There are several Syringers scattered across the Commonwealth. They can be found in the Greater Mass Blood Clinic, Medford Memorial Hospital, Mass Bay Medical Center, Sandy Coves Convalescent Home, Parsons State Insane Asylum, and various other locations. Vault 81 contains a Syringer that's easily collected during Side Quest: Hole in the Wall.

# AUTOMATIC WEAPONS

The Commando perk affects all automatic pistols and automatic rifles. It does not have any effect on automatic heavy guns.

## ▶ 10 mm

STANDARD MODEL: LONG 10-MM AUTO PISTOL

| Damage: 14 (ballistic) | Ammo: 10 mm | Fire Rate: 127 | Range: 107 | Accuracy: 49 | Weight: 4.7 | Value: 70 |
|---|---|---|---|---|---|---|

Even a heavily modified 10 mm offers limited ammo capacity, making it a poor choice for crowd control. But in short bursts, an automatic 10-mm pistol boasts impressive ballistic damage for a relatively compact weapon.

**ATTACHED MODS**

| | | |
|---|---|---|
| Automatic receiver | Standard grip | Standard sights |
| Long barrel | Standard magazine | No muzzle |

## ▶ Assault Rifle

STANDARD MODEL: SHORT AUTOMATIC ASSAULT RIFLE

| Damage: 20 (ballistic) | | Ammo: 5.56 | | |
|---|---|---|---|---|
| Fire Rate: 113 | Range: 107 | Accuracy: 71 | Weight: 14.6 | Value: 182 |

Automatic assault rifles offer a good balance of fire rate and per-shot damage. An automatic assault rifle is particularly effective at close range. Aim low and maintain a steady stream of fire, allowing the recoil to "walk" your shots toward your target's head.

**ATTACHED MODS**

| | | |
|---|---|---|
| Automatic receiver | Short stock | Standard sights |
| Short barrel | Standard magazine | No muzzle |

### ★ TIP ★

RECOIL COMPENSATED POWERFUL AUTOMATIC ASSAULT RIFLE

| Damage: 34 (ballistic) | | Ammo: 5.56 | Fire Rate: 113 |
|---|---|---|---|
| Range: 173 | Accuracy: 83 | Weight: 25.6 | Value: 445 |

Powerful, accurate, and tuned to minimize recoil, this customized assault rifle makes quick work of troublesome enemies. It offers a nice balance of fire rate and per-shot damage, and its impressive ammo capacity helps keep the bullets flying.

**ATTACHED MODS**

| | |
|---|---|
| Powerful automatic receiver | Quick-eject drum mag |
| Vented barrel | Reflex sight (circle) |
| Recoil compensating stock | Muzzle break |

## ▶ Combat Rifle

STANDARD MODEL: SHORT AUTOMATIC COMBAT RIFLE

| Damage: 22 (ballistic) | | Ammo: .45 | Fire Rate: 90 |
|---|---|---|---|
| Range: 107 | Accuracy: 67 | Weight: 12.4 | Value: 146 |

Compared to similarly modified assault rifles, automatic combat rifles offer better per-shot damage with slightly lower accuracy and a slower rate of fire. Combat rifles also lack the ammo capacity found in high-end assault rifles, but both guns make excellent automatic weapons.

**ATTACHED MODS**

| | | |
|---|---|---|
| Automatic receiver | Short stock | Standard sights |
| Short barrel | Standard magazine | No muzzle |

## ▶ Combat Shotgun

STANDARD MODEL: SHORT AUTOMATIC COMBAT SHOTGUN

| Damage: 50 (ballistic) | | Ammo: Shotgun Shell | Fire Rate: 23 |
|---|---|---|---|
| Range: 35 | Accuracy: 22 | Weight: 12.4 | Value: 112 |

Like most rapid-fire weapons, automatic combat shotguns offer a high rate of fire at the cost of per-shot damage. With a few modifications and a healthy supply of ammo, an automatic combat shotgun can be devastating in short-range firefights.

**ATTACHED MODS**

| | | |
|---|---|---|
| Automatic receiver | Short stock | Standard sights |
| Short barrel | Standard magazine | No muzzle |

## ▶ Gamma Gun

STANDARD MODEL: AUTOMATIC GAMMA GUN

| Damage: 110 (radiation) | Ammo: Gamma Round | Fire Rate: 90 |
|---|---|---|
| Range: 119 | Accuracy: 67 | Weight: 3.3 | Value: 216 |

The automatic gamma gun delivers short bursts of rapid-fire radiation damage. It's ineffective against radiation-immune enemies, and its limited ammo capacity means it requires frequent reloads, but this lightweight gun can devastate vulnerable targets.

**ATTACHED MODS**

| | | |
|---|---|---|
| Standard dish | Standard grip | Signal repeater |

## ▶ Institute Laser (Pistol)

STANDARD MODEL: AUTOMATIC INSTITUTE PISTOL

| Damage: 7 (energy) | Ammo: Fusion Cell | Fire Rate: 90 |
|---|---|---|
| Range: 203 | Accuracy: 63 | Weight: 5.0 | Value: 56 |

Automatic Institute lasers offer significantly lower per-shot damage than similarly modified laser guns. They make serviceable automatic energy weapons, but an automatic laser gun is sure to make better use of your fusion cells.

**ATTACHED MODS**

| | | |
|---|---|---|
| Standard capacitor | Standard grip | No muzzle |
| Automatic barrel | Standard sights | |

## ▶ Laser Gun (Pistol)
STANDARD MODEL: AUTOMATIC LASER PISTOL

| Damage: 18 (energy) | | Ammo: Fusion Cell | | |
|---|---|---|---|---|
| Fire Rate: 90 | Range: 203 | Accuracy: 63 | Weight: 5.0 | Value: 72 |

For rapid-fire energy damage, it's tough to beat an automatic laser gun. These weapons feature superior damage with the same range, accuracy, and fire rate as similarly modified Institute lasers.

ATTACHED MODS

| | | |
|---|---|---|
| Standard capacitor | Standard grip | No muzzle |
| Automatic barrel | Standard sights | |

### ★ TIP ★
RECOIL COMPENSATED OVERCHARGED IMPROVED AUTOMATIC LASER RIFLE

| Damage: 38 (energy) | | Ammo: Fusion Cell | Fire Rate: 113 |
|---|---|---|---|
| Range: 191 | Accuracy: 82 | Weight: 8.2 | Value: 174 |

When bullets just can't get the job done, give this high-tech wonder a whirl. Pelt your target with powerful, rapid-fire laser beams. Reduced recoil makes midrange combat a breeze, and the attached reflex sight improves accuracy without compromising your field of vision.

ATTACHED MODS

| | |
|---|---|
| Overcharged capacitor | Reflex sight |
| Improved automatic barrel | Quantum gyro compensating lens |
| Recoil compensating stock | |

## ▶ Pipe Gun
STANDARD MODEL: PIPE AUTO PISTOL

| Damage: 10 (ballistic) | | Ammo: .38 | | Fire Rate: 127 |
|---|---|---|---|---|
| Range: 107 | Accuracy: 47 | Weight: 3.2 | Value: 30 | |

Automatic pipe guns don't offer much power, but they do feature a high rate of fire and plenty of customization options. You're sure to find better weapons down the line, but an automatic pipe gun can be a useful tool for any new adventurer.

ATTACHED MODS

| | | |
|---|---|---|
| Automatic receiver | Standard grip | Standard sights |
| Short barrel | Standard magazine | No muzzle |

## ▶ Plasma Gun (Pistol)
STANDARD MODEL: AUTOMATIC PLASMA PISTOL

| Damage: 16 (ballistic), 15 (energy) | | Ammo: Plasma Cartridge | Fire Rate: 90 |
|---|---|---|---|
| Range: 203 | Accuracy: 128 | Weight: 5.0 | Value: 134 |

Automatic plasma guns combine ballistic damage and energy damage to deliver powerful rapid-fire shots. They're also accurate and highly customizable, making them a worthy addition to any arsenal.

ATTACHED MODS

| | |
|---|---|
| Standard capacitor | Standard grip |
| Automatic barrel | Standard sights |

## ▶ Railway Rifle
STANDARD MODEL: AUTOMATIC RAILWAY RIFLE

| Damage: 100 (ballistic) | | Ammo: Railway Spike | Fire Rate: 12 |
|---|---|---|---|
| Range: 107 | Accuracy: 68 | Weight: 15.9 | Value: 365 |

When it's equipped with an automatic piston receiver, the railway rifle offers a slightly higher rate of fire with small drops in range and accuracy. Overall damage output is roughly the same, so the choice between automatic and non-automatic fire is a matter of personal preference.

ATTACHED MODS

| | | |
|---|---|---|
| Automatic piston receiver | Short barrel | Standard sights |
| | Standard stock | No muzzle |

## ▶ Submachine Gun
STANDARD MODEL: SUBMACHINE GUN

| Damage: 10 (ballistic) | | Ammo: .45 | | Fire Rate: 127 |
|---|---|---|---|---|
| Range: 107 | Accuracy: 63 | Weight: 12.7 | Value: 109 | |

As the only dedicated automatic weapon frame, the submachine gun boasts an extremely high rate of fire and great ammo capacity. Its per-shot damage is relatively low, but a properly modified submachine gun is a great way to deal with swarming enemies.

ATTACHED MODS

| | | |
|---|---|---|
| Standard receiver | Short stock | Standard sights |
| Standard barrel | Medium magazine | No muzzle |

# HEAVY GUNS

It takes a strong back to carry more than one or two of these weapons, but any weapon that benefits from the Heavy Gunner perk qualifies as a heavy gun.

## ▶ Broadsider  STANDARD MODEL: BROADSIDER

As a handheld cannon, the Broadsider is about as simple as heavy guns get. Each shot launches a cannonball toward your target, causing impressive ballistic damage on impact. It takes quite a while to reload between shots, but the weapon can be modified to improve its rate of fire.

| Damage: 108 (ballistic) | | Ammo: Cannonball | Fire Rate: 2 |
|---|---|---|---|
| Range: 203 | Accuracy: 63 | Weight: 38.1 | Value: 245 |

ATTACHED MODS

| | | |
|---|---|---|
| Standard barrel | Standard grip | Standard shot canister |

The Broadsider is received as part of Side Quest: Last Voyage of the U.S.S. Constitution.

## Cryolator STANDARD MODEL: CRYOLATOR

| Damage: 20 (energy) | Ammo: **Cryo Cell** | Fire Rate: **90** |
|---|---|---|
| Range: **71** | Accuracy: **66** | Weight: **13.2** | Value: **302** |

| ATTACHED MODS | | |
|---|---|---|
| Standard barrel | Standard stock | Standard sights |

The Cryolator sprays a freezing mist that slows targets while dealing energy damage, and sustained blasts can temporarily freeze enemies, causing them to take additional damage from incoming attacks. Due to its limited ammo capacity, however, the Cryolator requires frequent reloads. This unique weapon does accommodate a Crystallizing Barrel mod, which allows it to fire cryogenic capsules for increased range and bonus ballistic damage.

The Cryolator is located in Vault 111.

## Fat Man

### STANDARD MODEL: FAT MAN

| Damage: **468 (ballistic)** | | Ammo: **Mini Nuke** | |
|---|---|---|---|
| Fire Rate: **1** | Range: **117** | Accuracy: **63** | Weight: **30.77** | Value: **512** |

| ATTACHED MODS |
|---|
| Standard Launcher |

Used to launch devastating Mini Nukes, the Fat Man boasts unrivaled per-shot damage. Once launched, a Mini Nuke quickly loses altitude. Aim slightly above your target or use V.A.T.S. to help ensure an accurate shot. Either way, make sure you're a safe distance away from your target—a Mini Nuke has a sizable blast radius.

### ★ TIP ★

**EXPERIMENTAL MIRV**

| Damage: **18 (ballistic)** | | Ammo: **Mini Nuke** | Fire Rate: **1** |
|---|---|---|---|
| Range: **117** | Accuracy: **63** | Weight: **36** | Value: **650** |

What do you do when a single Mini Nuke isn't enough to get the job done? You convert your Fat Man into an experimental MIRV! Each shot launches a cluster of Mini Nukes. Launch into the air to send Mini Nukes showering on your enemies, or aim for your target for a more contained explosion. This heavy gun packs more than enough power to make short work of the most formidable foes.

| ATTACHED MODS |
|---|
| MIRV Launcher |

## Flamer STANDARD MODEL: FLAMER

| Damage: **12 (energy damage)** | Ammo: **Flamer Fuel** | Fire Rate: **90** |
|---|---|---|
| Range: **47** | Accuracy: **53** | Weight: **16.1** | Value: **137** |

| ATTACHED MODS | | |
|---|---|---|
| Standard tank | Standard propellant | Standard nozzle |
| Standard barrel | tank | |

This classic heavy gun spews a stream of fire, dealing energy damage to any targets caught in the flame. It has a fairly short range, however, so it's best used against melee attackers and unarmed enemies.

## Gatling Laser STANDARD MODEL: GATLING LASER

| Damage: **14 (energy)** | Ammo: **Fusion Core** | Fire Rate: **272** |
|---|---|---|
| Range: **203** | Accuracy: **48** | Weight: **19.3** | Value: **804** |

| ATTACHED MODS | | |
|---|---|---|
| Gatling laser receiver | Standard barrel | No muzzle |
| | Standard sights | |

Gatling lasers are powerful, rapid-fire energy weapons, capable of dealing serious damage in a short amount of time. A standard Gatling laser fires comparatively weak beams at a very high rate, but these heavy guns can be modified for increased per-shot power at a slower rate of fire.

Gatling lasers are often carried by particularly powerful Brotherhood of Steel soldiers. Like Power Armor, these weapons are powered by Fusion Cores, so it can be difficult to maintain a good supply of ammunition.

## Junk Jet STANDARD MODEL: JUNK JET

| Damage: **40 (ballistic)** | Ammo: **Junk** | Fire Rate: **20** |
|---|---|---|
| Range: **119** | Accuracy: **75** | Weight: **29.9** | Value: **285** |

| ATTACHED MODS | |
|---|---|
| Short barrel | Standard sights |
| Standard stock | No muzzle |

The Junk Jet turns your unwanted items into powerful projectiles. Just fill this weapon with superfluous junk items and fire away. The standard Junk Jet deals ballistic damage, but it can be modified to add bonus energy damage to each shot.

The Junk Jet is located in ArcJet Systems, and it can be collected during or after Brotherhood of Steel Quest: Call to Arms.

## Minigun  STANDARD MODEL: MINIGUN

The Minigun combines low per-shot damage with an impressive rate of fire, resulting in a very effective ballistic weapon. Its high ammo capacity allows for sustained fire, and with the available barrel modifications you can improve its fire rate, accuracy, and overall damage.

| Damage: **8 (ballistic)** | Ammo: **5 mm** | Fire Rate: **272** |
| Range: **131** | Accuracy: **35** | Weight: **27.4** | Value: **382** |

ATTACHED MODS

| Standard barrel | Standard sights | No muzzle |

## Missile Launcher
### STANDARD MODEL: MISSILE LAUNCHER

| Damage: **150 (ballistic)** | Ammo: **Missile** | Fire Rate: **2** |
| Range: **203** | Accuracy: **65** | Weight: **21** | Value: **314** |

The missile launcher is less powerful than the Fat Man but has a better range and its ammunition is easier to come by. It can be customized to lock on to targets, improve damage, minimize reloads, and more. An appropriately modified missile launcher is generally your best defense against hostile Vertibirds.

ATTACHED MODS

| Standard barrel | Standard sights | No muzzle |

## Plasma Gun (Thrower)
### STANDARD MODEL: PLASMA THROWER

| Damage: **12 (ballistic), 12 (energy)** | Ammo: **Plasma cartridge** | Fire Rate: **90** |
| Range: **35** | Accuracy: **68** | Weight: **4.2** | Value: **146** |

The plasma gun can be used to make powerful pistols and rifles, but it also serves as a solid heavy gun. With an attached Flame Barrel mod, this weapon fires a stream of searing plasma. The combination of ballistic damage and energy damage ensures that it's effective against most enemies, and its comparatively low weight makes it an excellent choice as a secondary heavy gun.

ATTACHED MODS

| Standard capacitor | Standard grip |
| Flamer barrel | Standard sights |

# MELEE WEAPONS AND PUNCHING WEAPONS

Melee weapons and punching weapons share many similarities. They're only effective at short range, they deal damage without consuming ammo, and they leave you free to block enemy strikes. Their damage is affected by your Strength, and they all benefit from any investment in the Rooted perk. The primary difference between these two weapon categories is that only melee weapons benefit from the Big Leagues perk, while only punching weapons benefit from the Iron Fist perk.

## MELEE WEAPONS

All melee weapons benefit from the Big Leagues perk, but each one offers its own balance of power, speed, and weight. More importantly, two seemingly similar melee weapons can be modified to offer vastly different effects. Some melee weapons can be modified to increase the chances of stunning or disarming a target. Other melee weapons support attachments that can pierce armor or inflict bleeding damage. There are, of course, a few standout offerings, but the best melee weapon is the one you're most comfortable using.

## 2076 World Series Baseball Bat

| Damage: **30 (ballistic)** | Speed: **Medium** | Weight: **3** | Value: **25** |

Although it offers better speed and more raw damage than a standard baseball bat, the 2076 World Series baseball bat cannot be modified. This unique weapon is located with various other treasures hidden in Jamaica Plain.

## Baseball Bat  STANDARD MODEL: BASEBALL BAT

| Damage: **22 (ballistic)** | Speed: **Slow** | Weight: **3** | Value: **25** |

Baseball bats are relatively slow, but they offer fair damage and plenty of customization options. Like most blunt weapons, baseball bats can be modified to pierce armor or cause bleeding, but they also accommodate a wide variety of cosmetic mods.

ATTACHED MODS

| No upgrade | Natural |

### ★ TIP ★
**BLADED ALUMINUM BASEBALL BAT**

| Damage: **43 (ballistic)** | Speed: **Slow** | Weight: **3.9** | Value: **44** |

Why settle for an everyday baseball bat when you can wield this bladed beast? The attached saw blades add power to  every swing, and their razor-sharp teeth will leave your opponents bleeding. Aluminum construction increases power while decreasing weapon weight, giving it a clear edge over wooden baseball bats.

ATTACHED MODS

| Bladed | Aluminum |

## Baton    STANDARD MODEL: SECURITY BATON

| Damage: 15 (ballistic) | Speed: Medium | Weight: 2 | Value: 15 |

Security batons offer moderate damage and speed, but they can be modified to deliver bonus energy damage and a chance to stun your target.

ATTACHED MODS
No upgrade

## Board    STANDARD MODEL: BOARD

| Damage: 19 (ballistic) | Speed: Slow | Weight: 3 | Value: 20 |

Boards are slow and heavy with moderate damage. They're often found on low-level enemies, but they're very easy to come by. Basic upgrades can add armor piercing or bleed effects, but even the best board falls short of a similarly modified baseball bat.

ATTACHED MODS
No upgrade

## Chinese Officer Sword
STANDARD MODEL: CHINESE OFFICER SWORD

| Damage: 22 (ballistic) | Speed: Medium | Weight: 3 | Value: 50 |

The Chinese officer sword offers a good balance of speed and damage, and a fully upgraded model inflicts bonus bleeding and energy damage.

ATTACHED MODS
No upgrade

## Grognak's Axe

| Damage: 35 (ballistic) | Speed: Medium | Weight: 10 | Value: 100 |

This unique weapon is located within Hubris Comics. Grognak's Axe can't be modified, but it does boast high damage, an improved stagger effect, and the ability to inflict targets with additional bleed damage.

ATTACHED MODS
No upgrade

## Knife    STANDARD MODEL: COMBAT KNIFE

| Damage: 12 (ballistic) | Speed: Fast | Weight: 1 | Value: 25 |

These weapons are slightly more powerful than similarly modified switchblades, but the knife's most intriguing feature is its Stealth Blade mod. This customized blade increases damage from sneak attacks and causes targets to bleed.

ATTACHED MODS
No upgrade

★ TIP ★

STEALTH BLADE COMBAT KNIFE

| Damage: 21 (ballistic) | Speed: Fast | Weight: 1 | Value: 43 |

The perfect melee weapon for covert operatives, the stealth blade combat knife increases the damage you deal from sneak attacks. Fast, efficient, and very light, this weapon is a great addition to any arsenal.

ATTACHED MODS
Stealth blade

## Lead Pipe    STANDARD MODEL: LEAD PIPE

| Damage: 15 (ballistic) | Speed: Medium | Weight: 3 | Value: 15 |

Lead pipes offer moderate damage and speed, but a fully upgraded lead pipe deals extra limb damage with a chance to cripple targets.

ATTACHED MODS
No upgrade

## Machete    STANDARD MODEL: MACHETE

| Damage: 19 (ballistic) | Speed: Medium | Weight: 2 | Value: 25 |

The machete features moderate speed and damage, and it's a bit lighter than comparable melee weapons. Its only upgrade increases damage and causes targets to bleed.

ATTACHED MODS
No upgrade

## Pipe Wrench    STANDARD MODEL: PIPE WRENCH

| Damage: 18 (ballistic) | Speed: Medium | Weight: 2 | Value: 30 |

The pipe wrench offers moderate speed and damage, but it also accommodates some interesting modifications. Along with basic damage upgrades, this weapon can be customized to pierce armor, increase limb damage, or grant a chance to disarm targets.

ATTACHED MODS
Standard

## Pool Cue    STANDARD MODEL: POOL CUE

| Damage: 18 (ballistic) | Speed: Slow | Weight: 1 | Value: 10 |

Pool cues are slow, but they deal decent damage and they're extremely light. They're also quite common and easily modified.

ATTACHED MODS
No upgrade

### Revolutionary Sword
STANDARD MODEL: REVOLUTIONARY SWORD

| Damage: 22 (ballistic) | Speed: **Medium** | Weight: **3** | Value: **50** |
|---|---|---|---|

A fully upgraded revolutionary sword features a chance to stun with slightly less damage than a fully upgraded Chinese officer sword. Without modifications, however, the two weapons are very similar.

| ATTACHED MODS |
|---|
| No upgrade |

---

### Ripper   STANDARD MODEL: RIPPER

| Damage: 5 (ballistic) | Speed: **Very Fast** | Weight: **6** | Value: **50** |
|---|---|---|---|

The ripper is essentially a miniature chainsaw. While other melee weapons deal damage with each strike, the ripper deals low damage at a very high rate when you press it against your target. In addition to basic damage upgrades, a ripper can be modified for a chance to disarm targets or inflict bleeding.

| ATTACHED MODS |
|---|
| Standard |

---

### Rolling Pin   STANDARD MODEL: ROLLING PIN

| Damage: 15 (ballistic) | Speed: **Medium** | Weight: **1** | Value: **10** |
|---|---|---|---|

Rolling pins deal less damage than most blunt weapons, but they're very light and easily modified.

| ATTACHED MODS | |
|---|---|
| No upgrade | Wood |

---

### Shishkebab   STANDARD MODEL: SHISHKEBAB

| Damage: 18 (ballistic), 13 (energy) | Speed: **Medium** | Weight: **3** | Value: **200** |
|---|---|---|---|

The standard Shishkebab's combination of ballistic damage and energy damage make it a powerful bladed weapon, and it can be outfitted with additional flame jets for a significant boost in damage.

| ATTACHED MODS |
|---|
| No upgrade |

---

### Sledgehammer
STANDARD MODEL: SLEDGEHAMMER

| Damage: 32 (ballistic) | Speed: **Slow** | Weight: **12** | Value: **40** |
|---|---|---|---|

The sledgehammer is big, heavy, and slow—but it's also powerful and fairly common. They can be modified to penetrate armor or deal extra limb damage.

| ATTACHED MODS |
|---|
| Standard |

---

### Super Sledge   STANDARD MODEL: SUPER SLEDGE

| Damage: 56 (ballistic) | Speed: **Slow** | Weight: **20** | Value: **180** |
|---|---|---|---|

This rocket-assisted melee weapon is slow, heavy, and very powerful. A fully upgraded Super Sledge features added energy damage and a chance to stun your target. The Super Sledge is often carried by high-level Super Mutants and other formidable enemies.

| ATTACHED MODS |
|---|
| No upgrade |

### ★ TIP ★
STUNNING SUPER SLEDGE

| Damage: 56 (ballistic), 25 (energy) | Speed: **Slow** | Weight: **20** | Value: **540** |
|---|---|---|---|

Make each swing count with the Stunning Super Sledge. With this rocket-assisted hammer, ballistic damage is only the beginning. Each high-powered swing also delivers a jolt of energy damage with a chance to stun your target.

| ATTACHED MODS |
|---|
| Stun Pack |

---

### Switchblade
STANDARD MODEL: SWITCHBLADE

| Damage: 11 (ballistic) | Speed: **Fast** | Weight: **1** | Value: **20** |
|---|---|---|---|

The switchblade is light and fast, but it's less powerful than a standard combat knife.

| ATTACHED MODS |
|---|
| No upgrade |

### Tire Iron
STANDARD MODEL: TIRE IRON

| Damage: 16 (ballistic) | Speed: **Medium** | Weight: **2** | Value: **25** |
|---|---|---|---|

The tire iron offers a fair balance of speed and power, and it can be upgraded for a significant damage boost and the ability to inflict bleeding.

| ATTACHED MODS |
|---|
| No upgrade |

---

### Walking Cane
STANDARD MODEL: WALKING CANE

| Damage: 14 (ballistic) | Speed: **Medium** | Weight: **2** | Value: **10** |
|---|---|---|---|

The walking cane isn't particularly powerful, but this medium-speed weapon can be upgraded to pierce armor with a slight boost in damage.

| ATTACHED MODS |
|---|
| No upgrade |

Punching weapons aren't quite as common as melee weapons, and there aren't nearly as many to choose from. They do offer impressive damage for their speed and weight, and they all benefit from any investment you make in the Iron Fist perk.

### ▶ Boxing Glove

STANDARD MODEL: BOXING GLOVE

| Damage: 12 (ballistic) | Speed: Medium | Weight: 1 | Value: 10 |
|---|---|---|---|

A standard boxing glove deals less damage than other punching weapons. It can be upgraded to pierce armor, and the Lead Lining upgrade allows the boxing glove to deal extra limb damage with a chance to cripple enemies.

ATTACHED MODS

No upgrade

### ▶ Deathclaw Gauntlet    STANDARD MODEL: DEATHCLAW GAUNTLET

| Damage: 35 (ballistic) | Speed: Medium | Weight: 10 | Value: 75 |
|---|---|---|---|

The Deathclaw gauntlet is a high-damage punching weapon, but it's Extra Claw upgrade makes it much more powerful and grants a chance to disarm targets.

The Deathclaw gauntlet is possible reward for completing Side Quest: The Devil's Due.

ATTACHED MODS

No upgrade

#### ★ TIP ★

LARGE DEATHCLAW GAUNTLET

| Damage: 43 (ballistic) | Speed: Medium | Weight: 12 | Value: 97 |
|---|---|---|---|

Take a cue from one of the Commonwealth's most feared predators! The large Deathclaw gauntlet packs a serious punch, and each swing has a chance to disarm your target. This wrist-mounted weapon works wonders in close-quarter combat.

ATTACHED MODS

Extra claw

### ▶ Knuckles

STANDARD MODEL: KNUCKLES

| Damage: 14 (ballistic) | Speed: Medium | Weight: 0.5 | Value: 10 |
|---|---|---|---|

This compact punching weapon is very light, and its available upgrades focus on armor piercing and bleed effects.

ATTACHED MODS

No upgrade

### ▶ Power Fist    STANDARD MODEL: POWER FIST

| Damage: 28 (ballistic) | Speed: Medium | Weight: 4 | Value: 100 |
|---|---|---|---|

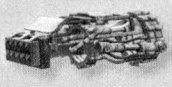

A standard Power Fist offers fairly high damage for a punching weapon, but it can also be modified to pierce armor or add a good amount of energy damage to each attack.

ATTACHED MODS

No upgrade

#### ★ TIP ★

HEATED POWER FIST

| Damage: 28 (ballistic), 20 (energy) | Speed: Medium | Weight: 4 | Value: 200 |
|---|---|---|---|

Put some pep in your punch with this modified Power Fist! As the powerful hydraulics batter your opponents, the attached heating coil delivers searing energy damage. With the best of both worlds strapped to your wrist, you'll give every enemy something to fear.

ATTACHED MODS

Heating coil

# EXPLOSIVES

Explosives are single-use devices, most of which are designed to deal heavy damage to any targets within a given area. However, some explosives deal almost no damage when they detonate; instead, they are meant to summon allies, mark targets, or inflict enemies with status effects. Regardless of its specific effect, any explosive that can be thrown is considered a grenade, and any explosive that can be set as a trap is considered a mine. All explosives are affected by the Demolition Expert perk.

## CRAFTED EXPLOSIVES

All explosives can be found somewhere in the Commonwealth, but many of them can be crafted at chemistry stations. Each explosive has its own list of components and perk prerequisites, but almost all of them demand at least some investment in the Demolition Expert perk.

### ▶ Baseball Grenade

| Damage: 101 (ballistic) | Fire Rate: 0 | Range: 93 | Accuracy: 0 | Weight: 1 | Value: 40 |
|---|---|---|---|---|---|

Low-tech and simple to make, the baseball grenade deals moderate ballistic damage to nearby enemies.

### ▶ Bottlecap Mine

| Damage: 301 (ballistic) | Fire Rate: 0 | Range: 93 | Accuracy: 0 | Weight: 0.5 | Value: 75 |
|---|---|---|---|---|---|

The Bottlecap Mine is extremely powerful, but its construction requires a Vault-Tec lunchbox along with other, more common components. Vault-Tech lunchboxes are comparatively rare, so Bottlecap Mines are best saved for tough encounters.

### Cryo Mine

| Damage: | Fire Rate: | Range: | Accuracy: | Weight: | Value: |
|---|---|---|---|---|---|
| 101 (ballistic) | 0 | 93 | 0 | 0.5 | 50 |

 When a cryo mine explodes, it has a chance to temporarily slow wounded targets that managed to survive the initial blast.

### Cryogenic Grenade

| Damage: | Fire Rate: | Range: | Accuracy: | Weight: | Value: |
|---|---|---|---|---|---|
| 101 (ballistic) | 0 | 93 | 0 | 0.5 | 125 |

 When a cryogenic grenade explodes, it has a chance to temporarily slow wounded targets that managed to survive the initial blast.

### Fragmentation Grenade

| Damage: | Fire Rate: | Range: | Accuracy: | Weight: | Value: |
|---|---|---|---|---|---|
| 151 (ballistic) | 0 | 93 | 0 | 0.5 | 50 |

 Fragmentation grenades are simple, effective, and widely used throughout the Commonwealth.

### Fragmentation Mine

| Damage: | Fire Rate: | Range: | Accuracy: | Weight: | Value: |
|---|---|---|---|---|---|
| 101 (ballistic) | 0 | 93 | 0 | 0.5 | 50 |

 Fragmentation mines aren't as powerful as most explosives, but they're often found scattered around enemy outposts.

### Molotov Cocktail

| Damage: | Fire Rate: | Range: | Accuracy: | Weight: | Value: |
|---|---|---|---|---|---|
| 51 (ballistic) | 0 | 93 | 0 | 0.5 | 20 |

 Molotov cocktails explode on impact, spreading flames across a small area. The initial explosion isn't very powerful, but affected targets take additional burning damage.

### Plasma Grenade

| Damage: | Fire Rate: | Range: | Accuracy: | Weight: | Value: |
|---|---|---|---|---|---|
| 150 (ballistic), 150 (energy) | 0 | 93 | 0 | 0.5 | 135 |

 Crafting plasma grenades requires considerable skill and some rare components, but the result is a compact explosive that deals a powerful combination of ballistic damage and energy damage.

### Plasma Mine

| Damage: 150 (ballistic), 150 (energy) | Fire Rate: | Range: | Accuracy: | Weight: | Value: |
|---|---|---|---|---|---|
| | 0 | 93 | 0 | 0.5 | 100 |

 Like plasma grenades, plasma mines offer a powerful combination of ballistic damage and energy damage. Crafting this explosive also requires considerable skill and some rare components.

### Pulse Grenade

| Damage: | Fire Rate: | Range: | Accuracy: | Weight: | Value: |
|---|---|---|---|---|---|
| 150 (energy) | 0 | 93 | 0 | 0.5 | 100 |

 The pulse grenade emits a burst of energy that only affects mechanical enemies.

### Pulse Mine

| Damage: | Fire Rate: | Range: | Accuracy: | Weight: | Value: |
|---|---|---|---|---|---|
| 150 (energy) | 0 | 93 | 0 | 0.5 | 100 |

 When triggered, the pulse mine emits a burst of energy that damages nearby mechanical targets.

## FACTION EXPLOSIVES

Some factions offer low-damage explosives that can be used to call for aid. The Demolition Expert perk doesn't affect the damage done by summoned allies or artillery fire, but the damage done by the initial explosion does receive a small boost.

### Artillery Smoke Grenade

| Damage: | Fire Rate: | Range: | Accuracy: | Weight: | Value: |
|---|---|---|---|---|---|
| 1 (ballistic) | 0 | 93 | 0 | 0.5 | 0 |

 You acquire the artillery smoke grenade during The Minutemen Quest: Old Guns. These explosives are used to mark high-priority targets for artillery support. They should only be used outside and within range of a workshop settlement that contains a manned artillery piece. If these conditions are met, the area marked by an artillery smoke grenade is bombarded with powerful explosives.

### Synth Relay Grenade

| Damage: | Fire Rate: | Range: | Accuracy: | Weight: | Value: |
|---|---|---|---|---|---|
| 1 (ballistic) | 0 | 93 | 0 | 0.5 | 50 |

 Toss a synth relay grenade to spawn synth reinforcements at a target location. This weapon can be obtained via a speech challenge during The Institute Quest: The Battle of Bunker Hill. Allies of the Institute can also purchase synth relay grenades from the Institute requisitions vendor after all Main Quests are completed.

### Vertibird Signal Grenade

| Damage: | Fire Rate: | Range: | Accuracy: | Weight: | Value: |
|---|---|---|---|---|---|
| 1 (ballistic) | 0 | 93 | 0 | 0.5 | 50 |

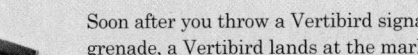 Soon after you throw a Vertibird signal grenade, a Vertibird lands at the marked location. You can then board the vehicle to take control of it's side-mounted minigun. When you're ready, exit the Vertibird or use your Pip-Boy's map to select a new destination. The Vertibird signal grenade can only be used outside, and only by Brotherhood of Steel members.

## MISCELLANEOUS EXPLOSIVES

Some explosives are only found in certain locations or must be used to accomplish specific tasks. Again, the Demolition Expert perk enhances the damage done when an explosive detonates, but any additional effects remain unchanged.

### ▶ HalluciGen Gas Grenade

| Damage: | Fire Rate: | Range: | Accuracy: | Weight: | Value: |
|---|---|---|---|---|---|
| 1 (ballistic) | 0 | 93 | 0 | 1 | 35 |

 Found only in HalluciGen, Inc., the HalluciGen gas grenade inflicts Frenzy on all targets within the blast radius.

### ▶ Institute EM Pulse Grenade

| Damage: | Fire Rate: | Range: | Accuracy: | Weight: | Value: |
|---|---|---|---|---|---|
| 150 (energy) | 0 | 93 | 0 | 0.5 | 100 |

 The Institute EM Pulse grenade sends out a blast of energy that only affects mechanical targets.

### ▶ Homing Beacon

| Damage: | Fire Rate: | Range: | Accuracy: | Weight: | Value: |
|---|---|---|---|---|---|
| 1 (ballistic) | 0 | 93 | 0 | 1 | 0 |

 Toss a homing beacon to call down a missile strike from Zao's sub. This item can only be used outside, and only after completing Side Quest: Here There Be Monsters.

### ▶ Nuka Grenade

| Damage: | Fire Rate: | Range: | Accuracy: | Weight: | Value: |
|---|---|---|---|---|---|
| 301 (ballistic), 100 (radiation) | 0 | 93 | 0 | 0.5 | 100 |

 Nuka grenades are rare and very powerful.

### ▶ Institute Beacon

| Damage: | Fire Rate: | Range: | Accuracy: | Weight: | Value: |
|---|---|---|---|---|---|
| 1 (ballistic) | 0 | 93 | 0 | 0.5 | 0 |

 Toss this grenade to spawn synth reinforcements at a target area. This weapon is given as a reward for completing The Institute Quest: Airship Down.

# LEGENDARY EFFECTS AND EXCEPTIONAL WEAPONS

## LEGENDARY EFFECTS

Each Legendary enemy you defeat has a chance of dropping a Legendary weapon with a randomly selected bonus effect.

### LEGENDARY WEAPON EFFECTS

| WEAPON NAME MODIFIER | DESCRIPTION |
|---|---|
| Assassin's | Does 50% more damage against humans. |
| Automatic | Automatic fire mode. |
| Berserker's | Does more damage the lower your damage resistance is. |
| Bloodied | Does more damage the lower your health is. |
| Cavalier's | Take 15% less damage while blocking or sprinting. |
| Crippling | 50% more limb damage. |
| Enraging | Critical hits cause target to frenzy. |
| Explosive | Bullets explode on impact doing 15 points area-of-effect damage. |
| Exterminator's | Does 50% more damage against Mirelurks and bugs. |
| Freezing | Does 10 points cryo damage and will freeze targets on critical hits. |
| Furious | Increased damage after each consecutive hit on the same target. |
| Ghoul Slayer's | Does 50% more damage against Ghouls. |
| Hunter's | Does 50% more damage against animals. |
| Incendiary | Sets target on fire for 15 points of damage. |
| Instigating | Does double damage if the target is at full health. |
| Irradiated | Does 50 points additional radiation damage. |
| Junkie's | Does increasing amounts of damage the more withdrawal effects you are suffering. |
| Kneecapper | Provides 20% chance to cripple the target's leg. |
| Lucky Weapon | Critical shots do double damage and the critical meter fills 15% faster. |
| Medic's | Heals targets instead of hurting them. |

| WEAPON NAME MODIFIER | DESCRIPTION |
|---|---|
| Mutant Slayer's | Does 50% more damage against Super Mutants. |
| Never Ending | Unlimited ammo capacity. |
| Nimble | Provides 75% faster movement while aiming. |
| Nocturnal | Does increasing amounts of damage as the night grows longer and less damage during the day. |
| Penetrating | Ignores 30% of the target's damage and energy resistance. |
| Plasma Infused | Adds 10 points of energy damage and can turn enemies into goo. |
| Poisoner's | Target is poisoned for 10 seconds. |
| Powerful | Provides 25% more damage. |
| Quickdraw | Costs 25% fewer Action Points. |
| Rapid | Provides 25% faster fire rate, 15% faster reload. |
| Relentless | Refills your Action Points on a critical hit. |
| Sentinel's | Take 15% less damage while standing and not moving. |
| Staggering | Chance to stagger on hit. |
| Stalker's | If you are not yet in combat, increases VATS accuracy but costs more AP. |
| Troubleshooter's | Does 50% more damage against robots. |
| Two Shot | Shoots an additional projectile. |
| VATS Enhanced | Improved VATS hit chance, 25% less Action Point cost. |
| VATS Enhanced | 40% less Action Point cost. |
| Violent | Deals +25% damage and limb damage, but has more recoil. |
| Wounding | Targets bleed for 25 points of additional damage. |

# EXCEPTIONAL WEAPONS

Exceptional weapons are uniquely powerful items with special bonus effects. Some Exceptional weapons can be purchased from vendors, but many of these prized possessions must be earned by completing quests or defeating specific enemies.

## UNIQUE WEAPONS

| NAME | WEAPON TYPE | BONUS | NOTES |
|---|---|---|---|
| 2076 World Series Baseball Bat | Baseball bat (cannot be modified) | Small chance to send targets flying. | Reward under Jamaica Plain City Hall. Sell it to Moe Cronin if you wish. |
| Ashmaker | MS16: The Big Dig | Chance to light targets on fire. | Reward for siding with Fahrenheit at the end of Side Quest: The Big Dig. |
| Automatic Laser Musket | Laser musket | Capable of automatic fire. | Given to you during the final assault, at the start of The Minutemen Quest: The Nuclear Option. |
| AX90 Fury | Plasma gun | 50% more damage vs Super Mutants | Sold by Teagan (The Prydwen). |
| Big Boy | Fat Man | Shoots an additional projectile. | Sold by Arturo (Diamond City). |
| Big Jim | Pipe wrench | 20% chance to cripple the target's leg. | Find this unique pipe wrench lying in Walden Pond. |
| Broadsider | Broadsider | — | Reward as part of Side Quest: Last Voyage of the U.S.S. Constitution. |
| Death From Above | Missile launcher | 75% faster movement while aiming. | Missile launcher sold by Proctor Teagan once you reach the rank of Paladin. |
| Deathclaw Gauntlet | Deathclaw Gauntlet | — | A possible reward for completing Side Quest: The Devil's Due |
| Deliverer | Deliverer | — | Reward after completing The Railroad Quest: Tradecraft. |
| Eddie's Peace | .44 | Deals extra limb damage. | Found during Side Quest: Detective Case Files: Long Time Coming |
| Experiment 18-A | Plasma gun | 25% faster fire rate, 15% faster reload. | Sold by Institute Requisitions (The Institute). |
| Final Judgment | Laser Gatling Gun | 25% faster fire rate, 15% faster reload. | Carried by Elder Maxson; remove it from him during Institute Quest: Airship Down, or The Railroad Quest: Precipice of War. |
| Furious Power Fist | Power Fist | Increased damage after each consecutive hit on the same target. | Remove the threat of Swan in Boston Common. |
| General Chao's Revenge | Chinese officer sword | Does 50% more damage against robots. | Sold by Trudy (Drumlin Diner). |
| Good Intentions | Laser gun | Critical hits cause target to frenzy | Carried by the Gunner leader Clint on the elevated freeway camp. |
| Grognak's Axe | Grognak's Axe | Hits cause more stagger and targets take bleed damage. | Found in a display case within Hubris Comics. |
| HalluciGen Gas Grenade | Grenade | Chance to Frenzy targets for 60 seconds. | Built with materials found in the basement laboratory of HalluciGen, Inc. |
| Homing Beacon | Grenade | Calls down a missile strike from Zao's sub. | A reward for completing Side Quest: Here There Be Monsters. |
| Institute Beacon | Grenade | Spawn Synths at beacon's location. | Reward for completing The Institute Quest: Airship Down. |
| Junk Jet | Junk Jet | — | Located in ArcJet Systems. Collect during or after Brotherhood of Steel Quest: Call to Arms. |
| Justice | Combat shotgun | Chance to stagger on hit. | Sold by Penny (Covenant). |
| Kellogg's Pistol | .44 | Refills your Action Points on a Critical Hit. | Found during Main Quest: Reunions |
| Les Fusil Teribles | Combat shotgun | +25% damage and limb damage, but has more recoil. | Found in the Captain's cabin in Libertalia. |
| Lorenzo's Artifact | Gamma gun | Uses telekinesis to push targets away. | Reward for completing Cabot House. |
| Old Faithful | Laser gun | Does double damage if the target is at full health. | Sold by Arturo (Diamond City). |
| Partystarter | Missile launcher | Does 50% more damage against humans. | Sold by KL-E-O (Goodneighbor). |
| Pickman's Blade | Knife | Increased damage from sneak attacks. Targets bleed. Exceptional damage. | A reward for siding with Pickman. |
| Prototype PA77 | Laser gun | Laser gun with infinite clip size | In the locked safe (Master) inside the University Credit Union. |
| Railway Rifle | Railway rifle | — | Reward after completing The Railroad Quest: Underground Undercover. |
| Reba II | Hunting rifle | Does 50% more damage against Mirelurks and bugs. | Reward for helping Barney during Miscellaneous Quest: Barney Rook. |
| Reckoning | Ripper | Take 15% Less Damage While Standing and not moving | Sold by Level 4 Workshop Merchant |
| Righteous Authority | Laser gun | Critical shots do double damage and the critical meter fills 15% faster. | A reward for completing Brotherhood of Steel Quest: Call to Arms. |
| Rockville Slugger | Baseball bat | 40% less Action Point cost. | Sold by Moe (Diamond City). |
| Sentinel's Plasmacaster | Plasma gun | Does double damage if the target is at full health. | Plasma Rifle sold by Proctor Teagan once you reach the rank of Sentinel. |
| Shem Drowne's Sword | Revolutionary Sword | Deals radiation damage. | Found during Side Quest: Detective Case Files: The Guilded Grasshopper |
| Shishkebab | Shishkebab | — | Found in the Blast Furnace, carried by Slag. |
| Spray'n'Pray | Submachine gun | Bullets explode on impact doing 15 points area effect damage. | Sold by Cricket (caravan trader). |
| Survivor's Special | Laser gun | Does more damage the lower your health is. | Kill Paladin Brandis, steal it from him, or receive it from him as a reward if you convince him to rejoin the Brotherhood as part of Brotherhood of Steel Quest: The Lost Patrol. |
| The Gainer | .44 | Sets target on fire for 15 points of damage. | Solve the Vitale Pumphouse number puzzle and this .44 Pistol is in the room with the steamer trunk. |
| The Last Minute | Gauss rifle | 50% more limb damage. | Sold by Level 4 Workshop Merchant |
| Tinker Tom Special | Hunting rifle | If you arenot yet in combat, increases VATS accuracy but costs more AP. | Sold by Tinker Tom (Railroad HQ). |
| Virgil's Rifle | Institute Laser rifle | Does 50% more damage against Super Mutants. | Kill Virgil or steal it from him. |
| Wastelander's Friend | 10mm | 50% more limb damage. | Sold by Deb (Bunker Hill). |
| Wazer Wifle | Laser gun | Unlimited ammo capacity. | Granted for completing Shaun's three quests once the Main and Faction quests are over. |

# APPAREL

From fashionable accessories to heavy-duty armor, apparel has a significant effect on your appearance, performance, and overall durability. The Commonwealth holds its share of dangers, and the right apparel can greatly increase your odds of survival. Of course, exactly how you choose to survive will ultimately determine the usefulness of any apparel item.

In general, heavier apparel items offer better protection. If you rely on speed or stealth, then protective metal armor will be too cumbersome to meet your needs. However, if you tend to charge into battle, you're sure to benefit from the most effective armor you can find, regardless of the extra weight. In either case, Legendary and Exceptional gear can make such decisions even more difficult—the bonus granted by a rare piece of armor might outweigh any concerns about weight or damage mitigation.

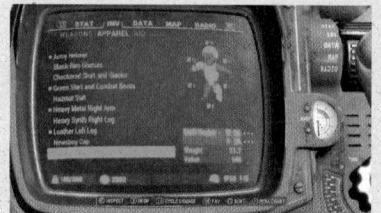

Use your Pip-Boy to review and equip the apparel items in your inventory. A quick glance is all it takes to gauge the protection offered by your current ensemble, but you can also see exactly how that protection is distributed. Tired of crippling injuries? Equip items that reinforce vulnerable limbs. Visiting the Crater of Atom? Make sure your Radiation Resistance is up to snuff. Just cycle the display to show how well you'd withstand different types of damage. You can even flag your favorite items for easy access.

Your choice of apparel also affects how people treat you. A head-turning ensemble often elicits comments from passersby, and especially pleasing apparel items make it easier to win friends and strike favorable deals. Combine items to create your own signature look, or keep a selection of clothes on hand to change your appearance as needed.

## HELPFUL HINT
### from Vault Boy!
**Did You Know?**

#### DRESS FOR SUCCESS

MANY OF THE ITEMS THAT GRANT S.P.E.C.I.A.L. BONUSES ARE LIGHT ENOUGH TO KEEP ON HAND. WHY NOT CREATE AN ENSEMBLE FOR EVERY OCCASION? BEFORE YOU BARTER WITH TRADERS OR ENGAGE IN A POTENTIALLY AWKWARD CONVERSATION, CHANGE INTO CLOTHES THAT INCREASE YOUR CHARISMA. BEFORE YOU TURN IN A QUEST OR SIT DOWN FOR A CRAFTING SESSION, BOOST YOUR INTELLIGENCE TO GAIN MORE XP. HEAVY ARMOR IS GREAT FOR COMBAT, BUT IT OFTEN PAYS TO SHOW YOUR MORE FASHIONABLE SIDE.

Many apparel pieces can be modified to better suit your needs. With the right skills and materials, you can craft mods for vault jumpsuits and most armor pieces at any armor workbench. However, many apparel items can only be modified with help from the Railroad. Complete the "Jackpot" radiant quest to unlock ballistic weave mods. Once you do, you can use armor workbenches to craft these protective linings and attach them to a variety of apparel items.

# CLOTHING

**VAULT 111 JUMPSUIT**    **ROAD LEATHERS**    **MINUTEMAN OUTFIT**

On its own, clothing doesn't offer much in the way of protection. However, these lightweight garments fit neatly under armor pieces. Many clothing options also grant bonus ranks to various S.P.E.C.I.A.L. stats, making them valuable additions to combat-oriented ensembles.

Many clothing items can be modified to offer extra protection. You can craft mods for vault jumpsuits at any armor workbench, but you'll need the Railroad's help to add protective linings to most clothing items.

## CLOTHING

| NAME | BONUS | DAMAGE RESISTANCE | ENERGY RESISTANCE | RADIATION RESISTANCE | WEIGHT | VALUE | MODS |
|---|---|---|---|---|---|---|---|
| Army Fatigues | Strength +1, Agility +1 | 0 | 0 | 0 | 3 | 12 | ✊ |
| Baseball Uniform | Strength +1, Agility +1 | 0 | 0 | 0 | 3 | 10 | ✊ |
| BOS Officer Uniform | — | 1 | 5 | 5 | 2 | 20 | ✊ |
| BOS Uniform | — | 1 | 5 | 5 | 2 | 20 | ✊ |
| Brotherhood of Steel Uniform | — | 1 | 5 | 5 | 2 | 20 | ✊ |
| Corset | Endurance +1 | 0 | 0 | 0 | 2 | 35 | ✊ |
| Dirty Army Fatigues | Strength +1, Agility +1 | 0 | 0 | 0 | 3 | 12 | ✊ |
| Flannel Shirt and Jeans | — | 1 | 0 | 0 | 2 | 20 | ✊ |
| Green Shirt and Combat Boots | Charisma +1, Endurance +1 | 0 | 0 | 0 | 3 | 11 | ✊ |
| Gunner Flannel Shirt and Jeans | — | 1 | 0 | 0 | 2 | 20 | ✊ |

| NAME | BONUS | DAMAGE RESISTANCE | ENERGY RESISTANCE | RADIATION RESISTANCE | WEIGHT | VALUE | MODS |
|---|---|---|---|---|---|---|---|
| Gunner Harness | — | 1 | 0 | 0 | 1 | 5 | |
| Gunner Leathers | — | 2 | 0 | 0 | 1 | 5 | |
| Harness | — | 1 | 0 | 0 | 1 | 5 | |
| Long Johns | — | 0 | 1 | 0 | 1 | 5 | |
| Military Fatigues | Agility +2 | 0 | 5 | 0 | 3 | 10 | |
| Minuteman Outfit | Agility +1, Perception +1 | 0 | 0 | 0 | 3 | 10 | |
| Raider Leathers | — | 2 | 0 | 0 | 1 | 5 | |
| Road Leathers | — | 2 | 0 | 0 | 1 | 5 | |
| Road Leathers | — | 0 | 0 | 0 | 1 | 5 | |
| Synth Uniform | Perception +1 | 0 | 0 | 0 | 3 | 10 | |
| Synth Uniform | Perception +1 | 20 | 0 | 0 | 3 | 65 | |
| Tattered Rags | Luck +1 | 0 | 0 | 0 | 2 | 1 | |
| Undershirt & Jeans | Luck +1 | 0 | 0 | 0 | 1 | 5 | |

| NAME | BONUS | DAMAGE RESISTANCE | ENERGY RESISTANCE | RADIATION RESISTANCE | WEIGHT | VALUE | MODS |
|---|---|---|---|---|---|---|---|
| Vault 101 Jumpsuit | — | 0 | 5 | 10 | 1 | 20 | |
| Vault 101 Jumpsuit—New | | 0 | 5 | 10 | 1 | 20 | |
| Vault 111 Jumpsuit | | 0 | 5 | 10 | 1 | 20 | |
| Vault 111 Jumpsuit—New | | 0 | 5 | 10 | 1 | 20 | |
| Vault 114 Jumpsuit | | 0 | 5 | 10 | 1 | 20 | |
| Vault 114 Jumpsuit—New | | 0 | 5 | 10 | 1 | 20 | |
| Vault 75 Jumpsuit | | 0 | 5 | 10 | 1 | 20 | |
| Vault 75 Jumpsuit—New | | 0 | 5 | 10 | 1 | 20 | |
| Vault 81 Jumpsuit | | 0 | 5 | 10 | 1 | 20 | |
| Vault 81 Jumpsuit—New | | 0 | 5 | 10 | 1 | 20 | |
| Vault 95 Jumpsuit | | 0 | 5 | 10 | 1 | 20 | |
| Vault 95 Jumpsuit—New | | 0 | 5 | 10 | 1 | 20 | |

# OUTFITS

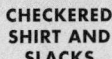

**CHECKERED SHIRT AND SLACKS**

**DRIFTER OUTFIT**

**HAZMAT SUIT**

Outfits are one-piece ensembles, most of which offer either basic protection or S.P.E.C.I.A.L. bonuses. Unlike clothing, however, outfits are too bulky to wear under a full set of armor. In fact, most outfits are too bulky to accommodate any armor pieces whatsoever. Full-body outfits even prevent the use of headgear and accessories.

The vast majority of outfits serve as fun cosmetic options, best used during friendly exchanges in relatively safe areas. However, some outfits do offer considerable utility. Railroad armored coats, for example, boast significant Damage Resistance. Equipping a hazmat suit makes you nearly immune to radiation damage. With the help of the Railroad, many outfits can be modified to offer better protection.

## OUTFITS

| NAME | BONUS | DAMAGE RESISTANCE | ENERGY RESISTANCE | RADIATION RESISTANCE | WEIGHT | VALUE | MODS |
|---|---|---|---|---|---|---|---|
| Agatha's Dress | Charisma +3 | 0 | 0 | 0 | 2 | 250 | |
| Athletic Outfit | — | 2 | 0 | 0 | 1 | 5 | |
| Atom Cats Jacket and Jeans | Luck +2 | 0 | 5 | 0 | 2 | 20 | |
| Bathrobe | Charisma +2 | 0 | 0 | 0 | 2 | 10 | |
| Beaded Blazer | Luck +1 | 0 | 0 | 0 | 2 | 5 | |
| Black Institute Lab Coat | Intelligence +2 | 0 | 0 | 0 | 3 | 65 | |
| Black Vest and Slacks | Endurance +2 | 0 | 0 | 0 | 0 | 10 | |
| Black Vest and Slacks | Endurance +2 | 0 | 0 | 0 | 3 | 10 | |
| Blue Institute Division Head Coat | Intelligence +1, Perception +1 | 0 | 0 | 0 | 3 | 65 | |
| Blue Institute Lab Coat | Intelligence +2 | 0 | 0 | 0 | 3 | 65 | |
| Bomber Jacket | — | 2 | 5 | 0 | 2 | 20 | |
| Brotherhood Fatigues | — | 5 | 10 | 10 | 4 | 20 | |

| NAME | BONUS | DAMAGE RESISTANCE | ENERGY RESISTANCE | RADIATION RESISTANCE | WEIGHT | VALUE | MODS |
|---|---|---|---|---|---|---|---|
| Brotherhood Fatigues | — | 10 | 10 | 10 | 4 | 20 | |
| Cabot's Lab Coat | Intelligence +1 | 0 | 0 | 0 | 2 | 17 | |
| Cage Armor | — | 24 | 27 | 0 | 27 | 90 | |
| Casual Outfit | — | 0 | 0 | 0 | 2 | 10 | |
| Casual Outfit | Perception +1, Charisma +1 | 0 | 0 | 0 | 3 | 16 | |
| Checkered Shirt and Slacks | Charisma +2 | 0 | 0 | 0 | 1 | 15 | |
| Child of Atom Long Rags | Endurance +2 | 0 | 0 | 25 | 2 | 10 | |
| Child of Atom Brown Rags | Endurance +2 | 0 | 0 | 25 | 2 | 10 | |
| Child of Atom Green Rags | Endurance +2 | 0 | 0 | 25 | 2 | 10 | |
| Child of Atom Long Brown Rags | Endurance +2 | 0 | 0 | 25 | 2 | 10 | |
| Child of Atom Long Green Rags | Endurance +2 | 0 | 0 | 25 | 2 | 10 | |
| Child of Atom Short Brown Rags | Endurance +2 | 0 | 0 | 25 | 2 | 10 | |

| NAME | BONUS | DAMAGE RESISTANCE | ENERGY RESISTANCE | RADIATION RESISTANCE | WEIGHT | VALUE | MODS |
|---|---|---|---|---|---|---|---|
| Child of Atom Short Green Rags | Endurance +2 | 0 | 0 | 25 | 2 | 10 | |
| Child of Atom Short Rags | Endurance +2 | 0 | 0 | 25 | 2 | 10 | |
| Child of Atom Simple Rags | Endurance +2 | 0 | 0 | 25 | 2 | 10 | |
| Clean Black Suit | Charisma +2 | 0 | 0 | 0 | 3 | 32 | |
| Clean Black Suit | Charisma +2 | 0 | 0 | 0 | 3 | 10 | |
| Clean Blue Suit | Charisma +2 | 0 | 0 | 0 | 3 | 32 | |
| Clean Gray Suit | Charisma +2 | 0 | 0 | 0 | 3 | 32 | |
| Cleanroom Suit | Endurance +2 | 0 | 0 | 0 | 3 | 65 | |
| Clean Striped Suit | Charisma +2 | 0 | 0 | 0 | 3 | 32 | |
| Clean Tan Suit | Charisma +2 | 0 | 0 | 0 | 3 | 32 | |
| Colonial Duster | — | 5 | 0 | 0 | 5 | 13 | |
| Courser Uniform | Endurance +1, Perception +1 | 30 | 15 | 15 | 15 | 200 | |
| Covert Sweater Vest | Charisma +1 | 10 | 10 | 0 | 2 | 10 | |
| Damaged Hazmat Suit | — | 0 | 0 | 500 | 5 | 55 | |
| DB Tech Varsity Uniform | Luck +2 | 1 | 0 | 0 | 2 | 20 | |
| Dirty Black Institute Lab Coat | Intelligence +2 | 0 | 0 | 0 | 3 | 65 | |
| Dirty Black Suit | Charisma +2 | 0 | 0 | 0 | 3 | 14 | |
| Dirty Blue Institute Division Head Coat | Intelligence +1, Perception +1 | 0 | 0 | 0 | 3 | 65 | |
| Dirty Blue Institute Lab Coat | Intelligence +2 | 0 | 0 | 0 | 3 | 65 | |
| Dirty Blue Suit | Charisma +2 | 0 | 0 | 0 | 3 | 14 | |
| Dirty Gray Suit | Charisma +2 | 0 | 0 | 0 | 3 | 14 | |
| Dirty Green Institute Division Head Coat | Intelligence +1, Perception +1 | 0 | 0 | 0 | 3 | 65 | |
| Dirty Green Institute Lab Coat | Intelligence +2 | 0 | 0 | 0 | 3 | 65 | |
| Dirty Institute Division Head Coat | Intelligence +1, Perception +1 | 0 | 0 | 0 | 3 | 65 | |
| Dirty Institute Jumper | Agility +2 | 0 | 0 | 0 | 3 | 65 | |
| Dirty Institute Lab Coat | Intelligence +2 | 0 | 0 | 0 | 3 | 65 | |
| Dirty Orange Institute Division Head Coat | Intelligence +1, Perception +1 | 0 | 0 | 0 | 3 | 65 | |
| Dirty Postman Uniform | Charisma +1, Endurance +1 | 0 | 0 | 0 | 3 | 10 | |
| Dirty Striped Suit | Charisma +2 | 0 | 0 | 0 | 3 | 14 | |
| Dirty Tan Suit | Charisma +2 | 0 | 0 | 0 | 3 | 14 | |
| Dirty Trench Coat | Charisma +1, Endurance +1 | 0 | 0 | 5 | 3 | 12 | |
| Dirty Yellow Institute Division Head Coat | Intelligence +1, Perception +1 | 0 | 0 | 0 | 3 | 65 | |
| Dirty Yellow Institute Lab Coat | Intelligence +2 | 0 | 0 | 0 | 3 | 65 | |
| Drifter Outfit | — | 5 | 7 | 0 | 10 | 35 | |
| Engineer's Armor | — | 2 | 5 | 0 | 2 | 15 | |
| Explorer Outfit | — | 1 | 0 | 0 | 4 | 13 | |
| Faded Trench Coat | Perception +1 | 0 | 0 | 0 | 2 | 14 | |
| Faded Trench Coat | Perception +2 | 0 | 0 | 0 | 3 | 15 | |
| Farmhand Clothes | Endurance +2 | 0 | 0 | 0 | 0 | 10 | |
| Farmhand Clothes | Endurance +2 | 0 | 0 | 0 | 3 | 10 | |
| Father's Lab Coat | Intelligence +2 | 0 | 0 | 0 | 2 | 35 | |
| Fatigues | Agility +1 | 0 | 0 | 0 | 2 | 30 | |
| Feathered Dress | Charisma +2 | 0 | 0 | 0 | 2 | 20 | |
| Field Scribe's Armor | — | 5 | 10 | 10 | 4 | 20 | |
| Flowery Dress | Charisma +1 | 0 | 0 | 0 | 2 | 10 | |
| Geneva's Ensemble | Perception +1, Charisma +1 | 0 | 0 | 0 | 3 | 16 | |
| Greaser Jacket and Jeans | Luck +2 | 0 | 5 | 0 | 2 | 20 | |
| Green Institute Division Head Coat | Intelligence +1, Perception +1 | 0 | 0 | 0 | 3 | 65 | |
| Green Institute Lab Coat | Intelligence +2 | 0 | 0 | 0 | 3 | 65 | |
| Grognak Costume | — | 10 | 15 | 15 | 2 | 24 | |
| Gunner Guard Outfit | — | 2 | 0 | 0 | 1 | 5 | |
| Hazmat Suit | — | 0 | 0 | 1000 | 5 | 85 | |
| Helmeted Cage Armor | — | 28 | 35 | 0 | 33 | 110 | |
| Helmeted Spike Armor | — | 13 | 15 | 0 | 17 | 65 | |
| Hooded Cleanroom Suit | Endurance +2 | 0 | 0 | 100 | 5 | 65 | |
| Hooded Rags | Endurance +2 | 0 | 0 | 0 | 2 | 7 | |
| Ingram's UnderArmor | — | 5 | 10 | 10 | 4 | 20 | |
| Institute Division Head Coat | Intelligence +1, Perception +1 | 0 | 0 | 0 | 3 | 65 | |
| Institute Jumper | Agility +2 | 0 | 0 | 0 | 3 | 65 | |
| Institute Lab Coat | Intelligence +2 | 0 | 0 | 0 | 3 | 65 | |
| Kellogg's Outfit | — | 30 | 30 | 0 | 2 | 100 | |
| Lab Coat | Intelligence +1 | 0 | 0 | 0 | 0 | 10 | |
| Lab Coat | Intelligence +2 | 0 | 0 | 0 | 2 | 10 | |
| Laundered Blue Dress | Charisma +2 | 0 | 0 | 0 | 2 | 19 | |
| Laundered Cream Dress | Charisma +2 | 0 | 0 | 0 | 2 | 19 | |
| Laundered Denim Dress | Charisma +2 | 0 | 0 | 0 | 2 | 21 | |
| Laundered Green Dress | Charisma +2 | 0 | 0 | 0 | 2 | 21 | |
| Laundered Loungewear | Charisma +2 | 0 | 0 | 0 | 0 | 30 | |
| Laundered Loungewear | Charisma +1, Endurance +1 | 0 | 0 | 0 | 1 | 15 | |
| Laundered Pink Dress | Charisma +2 | 0 | 0 | 0 | 2 | 19 | |
| Laundered Rose Dress | Charisma +2 | 0 | 0 | 0 | 2 | 21 | |
| Leather Coat | — | 1 | 0 | 0 | 2 | 13 | |
| Letterman's Jacket and Jeans | — | 1 | 0 | 0 | 2 | 20 | |
| Longshoreman Outfit | Energy Resist +10 | 0 | 0 | 0 | 2 | 10 | |
| Lorenzo's Suit | Charisma +2 | 0 | 0 | 0 | 3 | 10 | |
| MacCready's Duster | Agility +1 | 5 | 0 | 0 | 1 | 5 | |

| NAME | BONUS | DAMAGE RESISTANCE | ENERGY RESISTANCE | RADIATION RESISTANCE | WEIGHT | VALUE | MODS |
|---|---|---|---|---|---|---|---|
| Maxson's Battlecoat | Perception +1 | 50 | 0 | 0 | 20 | 400 | |
| Mechanic Jumpsuit | Intelligence +1, Perception +1 | 0 | 0 | 0 | 3 | 6 | |
| Mechanic Jumpsuit | Intelligence +1, Perception +1 | 0 | 0 | 0 | 3 | 11 | |
| Minutemen General's Uniform | Charisma +1 | 45 | 80 | 0 | 5 | 13 | |
| Nat's Dress | Charisma +1 | 0 | 0 | 0 | 1 | 5 | |
| Orange Institute Division Head Coat | Intelligence +1, Perception +1 | 0 | 0 | 0 | 3 | 65 | |
| Padded Blue Jacket | Charisma +2 | 0 | 0 | 0 | 0 | 10 | |
| Padded Blue Jacket | Charisma +1, Endurance +1 | 0 | 0 | 0 | 3 | 10 | |
| Pastor's Vestments | Charisma +1, Endurance +1 | 0 | 0 | 0 | 3 | 10 | |
| Patched Suit | Charisma +2 | 0 | 0 | 0 | 3 | 10 | |
| Patched Three-Piece Suit | Perception +1, Charisma +1 | 0 | 0 | 0 | 3 | 10 | |
| Postman Uniform | Charisma +1, Endurance +1 | 0 | 0 | 0 | 3 | 10 | |
| Quinlan's Armor | — | 1 | 15 | 0 | 2 | 15 | |
| Radstag Hide Outfit | — | 1 | 0 | 0 | 4 | 13 | |
| Railroad Armored Coat | — | 40 | 50 | 20 | 32 | 300 | |
| Railroad Armored Coat Mk I | — | 39 | 69 | 10 | 26 | 110 | |
| Railroad Armored Coat Mk II | — | 51 | 86 | 10 | 30 | 125 | |
| Railroad Armored Coat Mk III | — | 69 | 111 | 10 | 38 | 150 | |
| Railroad Armored Coat Mk IV | — | 81 | 128 | 10 | 44 | 170 | |
| Railroad Armored Coat Mk V | — | 93 | 150 | 10 | 50 | 185 | |
| Ratty Skirt | Charisma +2 | 0 | 0 | 0 | 2 | 11 | |
| Red Dress | Charisma +2 | 0 | 0 | 0 | 1.5 | 15 | |
| Red Frock Coat | Perception +1, Charisma +1 | 0 | 5 | 0 | 3 | 10 | |
| Red Leather Trench Coat | Charisma +1 | 0 | 5 | 0 | 3 | 10 | |
| Reginald's Suit | Charisma +3 | 0 | 0 | 0 | 3 | 250 | |
| Rex's Suit | — | 0 | 0 | 0 | 3 | 250 | |
| Scavenger Outfit | — | 1 | 0 | 0 | 4 | 13 | |
| Science Scribe's Armor | — | 1 | 15 | 0 | 2 | 15 | |
| Sequin Dress | Charisma +2 | 0 | 0 | 0 | 2 | 31 | |
| Silver Shroud Costume | Agility +1, Perception +1 | 0 | 15 | 15 | 2 | 40 | |
| Silver Shroud Costume | Agility +1, Perception +1 | 40 | 40 | 0 | 7 | 120 | |
| Silver Shroud Costume | Agility +1, Perception +1 | 55 | 55 | 0 | 7 | 150 | |
| Silver Shroud Costume | Agility +1, Perception +1 | 68 | 68 | 0 | 7 | 175 | |
| Silver Shroud Costume | Agility +1, Perception +1 | 85 | 85 | 0 | 7 | 200 | |
| Silver Shroud Costume | Agility +1 | 1 | 15 | 25 | 2 | 10 | |
| Spike Armor | — | 10 | 12 | 0 | 14 | 50 | |
| Submariner Uniform | Endurance +2 | 0 | 0 | 5 | 3 | 12 | |
| Summer Shorts | Charisma +2 | 0 | 0 | 0 | 2 | 16 | |

| NAME | BONUS | DAMAGE RESISTANCE | ENERGY RESISTANCE | RADIATION RESISTANCE | WEIGHT | VALUE | MODS |
|---|---|---|---|---|---|---|---|
| Surveyor Outfit | Endurance +1, Perception +1 | 0 | 0 | 0 | 3 | 10 | |
| Suspenders and Slacks | Endurance +2 | 0 | 0 | 0 | 3 | 10 | |
| Sweater Vest and Slacks | Charisma +2 | 0 | 0 | 0 | 3 | 17 | |
| Tattered Field Jacket | — | 1 | 0 | 0 | 2 | 13 | |
| Teagan's Armor | — | 2 | 5 | 0 | 2 | 15 | |
| Traveling Leather Coat | — | 1 | 0 | 0 | 2 | 13 | |
| T-Shirt and Slacks | Charisma +2 | 0 | 0 | 0 | 3 | 14 | |
| Tuxedo | Perception +1, Charisma +1 | 0 | 0 | 0 | 3 | 40 | |
| Utility Coveralls | Carry Weight +5 | 10 | 0 | 0 | 0 | 13 | |
| Utility Coveralls | Carry Weight +5 | 10 | 0 | 0 | 2 | 13 | |
| Vault-Tec Lab Coat | Intelligence +2 | 0 | 0 | 0 | 2 | 19 | |
| Weathered Outfit | Agility +2 | 0 | 0 | 0 | 0 | 10 | |
| Winter Jacket and Jeans | — | 2 | 0 | 0 | 2 | 20 | |
| Yellow Institute Division Head Coat | Intelligence +1, Perception +1 | 0 | 0 | 0 | 3 | 65 | |
| Yellow Institute Lab Coat | Intelligence +2 | 0 | 0 | 0 | 3 | 65 | |
| Yellow Trench Coat | Charisma +1, Endurance +1 | 0 | 0 | 5 | 3 | 24 | |
| Zeke's Jacket and Jeans | Charisma +1, Unarmed Damage +4 | 2 | 5 | 0 | 2 | 20 | |

# ARMOR PIECES

During your travels, you're sure to amass quite a collection of armor pieces. There are a few exceptions, but most armor pieces belong to one of five basic armor sets:

- COMBAT ARMOR
- LEATHER ARMOR
- METAL ARMOR
- RAIDER ARMOR
- SYNTH ARMOR

## HELPFUL HINT
### from Vault Boy!

### QUALITY CONTROL

ARMOR SET PIECES COME IN THREE DIFFERENT QUALITIES: STANDARD, STURDY, AND HEAVY. THE QUALITY OF AN ARMOR PIECE AFFECTS ITS STATS AND APPEARANCE, BUT IT DOESN'T HAVE ANY EFFECT ON WHICH MODS IT SUPPORTS. FOR EXAMPLE, A MOD THAT FITS INTO A LEATHER CHEST PIECE CAN BE ATTACHED TO A STURDY LEATHER CHEST PIECE, A HEAVY LEATHER CHEST PIECE, AND EVEN LEGENDARY AND EXCEPTIONAL LEATHER CHEST PIECES.

Each armor set offers a different balance of resistances and overall weight. And because each piece is equipped separately, you can mix and match pieces from different sets to meet your specific needs. You can even modify individual armor pieces for better protection or increased utility.

## COMBAT ARMOR

**COMBAT ARMOR**     **STURDY COMBAT ARMOR**     **HEAVY COMBAT ARMOR**

A full set of combat armor is fairly heavy, but it boasts an excellent balance of Damage Resistance and Energy Resistance. Combat armor can be found on a variety of powerful enemies, but these pieces are particularly popular among Gunners.

### COMBAT ARMOR PIECES

| NAME | DAMAGE RESISTANCE | ENERGY RESISTANCE | RADIATION RESISTANCE | WEIGHT | VALUE | MODS |
|---|---|---|---|---|---|---|
| **Chest** | | | | | | |
| Combat Armor Chest Piece | 15 | 15 | 0 | 8 | 60 | |
| Sturdy Combat Armor Chest Piece | 25 | 25 | 0 | 11.7 | 140 | |
| Heavy Combat Armor Chest Piece | 35 | 35 | 0 | 15.5 | 220 | |
| **Left Arm** | | | | | | |
| Combat Armor Left Arm | 9 | 9 | 0 | 2 | 25 | |
| Sturdy Combat Armor Left Arm | 13 | 13 | 0 | 4.5 | 85 | |
| Heavy Combat Armor Left Arm | 17 | 17 | 0 | 7 | 145 | |
| **Left Leg** | | | | | | |
| Combat Armor Left Leg | 8 | 8 | 0 | 2 | 25 | |
| Sturdy Combat Armor Left Leg | 12 | 12 | 0 | 4.5 | 105 | |
| Heavy Combat Armor Left Leg | 16 | 16 | 0 | 7 | 185 | |
| **Right Arm** | | | | | | |
| Combat Armor Right Arm | 9 | 9 | 0 | 2 | 25 | |
| Sturdy Combat Armor Right Arm | 13 | 13 | 0 | 4.5 | 85 | |
| Heavy Combat Armor Right Arm | 17 | 17 | 0 | 7 | 145 | |
| **Right Leg** | | | | | | |
| Combat Armor Right Leg | 8 | 8 | 0 | 4 | 25 | |
| Sturdy Combat Armor Right Leg | 12 | 12 | 0 | 6.5 | 105 | |
| Heavy Combat Armor Right Leg | 16 | 16 | 0 | 9 | 185 | |

## LEATHER ARMOR

**LEATHER ARMOR**

**STURDY LEATHER ARMOR**

**HEAVY LEATHER ARMOR**

Leather armor can't match the Damage Resistance offered by most armor sets, but it's an excellent option for those who prefer to travel light. It's also very common—low-level Raiders and Gunners often carry one or more pieces of leather armor, making it fairly easy to collect a complete set.

### LEATHER ARMOR PIECES

| NAME | DAMAGE RESISTANCE | ENERGY RESISTANCE | RADIATION RESISTANCE | WEIGHT | VALUE | MODS |
|---|---|---|---|---|---|---|
| **Chest** | | | | | | |
| Leather Chest Piece | 3 | 10 | 0 | 5 | 25 | 👍 |
| Sturdy Leather Chest Piece | 14 | 23 | 0 | 9.9 | 50 | 👍 |
| Heavy Leather Chest Piece | 24 | 36 | 0 | 14.8 | 75 | 👍 |
| **Left Arm** | | | | | | |
| Leather Left Arm | 1 | 3 | 0 | 2 | 8 | 👍 |
| Sturdy Leather Left Arm | 6 | 11 | 0 | 4.6 | 18 | 👍 |
| Heavy Leather Left Arm | 11 | 18 | 0 | 7.2 | 28 | 👍 |
| **Left Leg** | | | | | | |
| Leather Left Leg | 2 | 5 | 0 | 2 | 10 | 👍 |
| Sturdy Leather Left Leg | 7 | 13 | 0 | 4.6 | 20 | 👍 |
| Heavy Leather Left Leg | 13 | 20 | 0 | 7.2 | 30 | 👍 |
| **Right Arm** | | | | | | |
| Leather Right Arm | 1 | 3 | 0 | 2 | 8 | 👍 |
| Sturdy Leather Right Arm | 6 | 11 | 0 | 4.6 | 18 | 👍 |
| Heavy Leather Right Arm | 11 | 18 | 0 | 7.2 | 28 | 👍 |
| **Right Leg** | | | | | | |
| Leather Right Leg | 2 | 5 | 0 | 2 | 10 | 👍 |
| Sturdy Leather Right Leg | 7 | 13 | 0 | 4.6 | 20 | 👍 |
| Heavy Leather Right Leg | 13 | 20 | 0 | 7.2 | 30 | 👍 |

## METAL ARMOR

**METAL ARMOR**

**STURDY METAL ARMOR**

**HEAVY METAL ARMOR**

Metal armor pieces favor Damage Resistance over Energy Resistance. They also tend to be fairly heavy. Raiders are typically the best source of metal armor pieces, but you're sure to find these items scattered throughout the Commonwealth.

### METAL ARMOR PIECES

| NAME | DAMAGE RESISTANCE | ENERGY RESISTANCE | RADIATION RESISTANCE | WEIGHT | VALUE | MODS |
|---|---|---|---|---|---|---|
| **Chest** | | | | | | |
| Metal Chest Piece | 12 | 5 | 0 | 8 | 40 | 👍 |
| Sturdy Metal Chest Piece | 25 | 15 | 0 | 15.5 | 115 | 👍 |
| Heavy Metal Chest Piece | 37 | 25 | 0 | 23.1 | 190 | 👍 |
| **Left Arm** | | | | | | |
| Metal Left Arm | 7 | 3 | 0 | 3 | 15 | 👍 |
| Sturdy Metal Left Arm | 15 | 8 | 0 | 7.9 | 65 | 👍 |
| Heavy Metal Left Arm | 22 | 13 | 0 | 12.8 | 115 | 👍 |
| **Left Leg** | | | | | | |
| Metal Left Leg | 7 | 3 | 0 | 3 | 15 | 👍 |
| Sturdy Metal Left Leg | 15 | 8 | 0 | 7.9 | 65 | 👍 |
| Heavy Metal Left Leg | 22 | 13 | 0 | 12.8 | 115 | 👍 |
| **Right Arm** | | | | | | |
| Metal Right Arm | 7 | 3 | 0 | 3 | 15 | 👍 |
| Sturdy Metal Right Arm | 15 | 8 | 0 | 7.9 | 65 | 👍 |
| Heavy Metal Right Arm | 22 | 13 | 0 | 12.8 | 115 | 👍 |
| **Right Leg** | | | | | | |
| Metal Right Leg | 7 | 3 | 0 | 3 | 15 | 👍 |
| Sturdy Metal Right Leg | 15 | 8 | 0 | 7.9 | 65 | 👍 |
| Heavy Metal Right Leg | 22 | 13 | 0 | 12.8 | 115 | 👍 |

Mr. Handy

MAN'S BEST FRIEND. REINVENTED.

## RAIDER ARMOR

**RAIDER ARMOR**  **STURDY RAIDER ARMOR**  **HEAVY RAIDER ARMOR**

Considering its weight, a full set of Raider armor offers relatively little protection. However, most Raiders carry at least one of these ramshackle armor pieces, so it shouldn't take long to amass quite a collection.

### RAIDER ARMOR PIECES

| NAME | DAMAGE RESISTANCE | ENERGY RESISTANCE | RADIATION RESISTANCE | WEIGHT | VALUE | MODS |
|---|---|---|---|---|---|---|
| **Chest** | | | | | | |
| Raider Chest Piece | 4 | 2 | 0 | 7 | 18 | |
| Sturdy Raider Chest Piece | 14 | 11 | 0 | 12 | 33 | |
| Heavy Raider Chest Piece | 24 | 20 | 0 | 17 | 48 | |
| **Left Arm** | | | | | | |
| Raider Left Arm | 1 | 1 | 0 | 3 | 6 | |
| Sturdy Raider Left Arm | 6 | 6 | 0 | 7 | 81 | |
| Heavy Raider Left Arm | 11 | 11 | 0 | 10 | 156 | |
| **Left Leg** | | | | | | |
| Raider Left Leg | 2 | 2 | 0 | 3 | 8 | |
| Sturdy Raider Left Leg | 7 | 7 | 0 | 7 | 13 | |
| Heavy Raider Left Leg | 12 | 12 | 0 | 10 | 18 | |
| **Right Arm** | | | | | | |
| Raider Right Arm | 1 | 1 | 0 | 3 | 6 | |
| Sturdy Raider Right Arm | 6 | 6 | 0 | 7 | 81 | |
| Heavy Raider Right Arm | 11 | 11 | 0 | 10 | 156 | |
| **Right Leg** | | | | | | |
| Raider Right Leg | 2 | 2 | 0 | 3 | 8 | |
| Sturdy Raider Right Leg | 7 | 7 | 0 | 7 | 13 | |
| Heavy Raider Right Leg | 12 | 12 | 0 | 10 | 18 | |

## SYNTH ARMOR

**SYNTH ARMOR**  **STURDY SYNTH ARMOR**  **HEAVY SYNTH ARMOR**

Synth armor offers significant protection, but most pieces favor Energy Resistance over Damage Resistance. Appropriately enough, these armor pieces are most often found on defeated synths.

### SYNTH ARMOR PIECES

| NAME | DAMAGE RESISTANCE | ENERGY RESISTANCE | RADIATION RESISTANCE | WEIGHT | VALUE | MODS |
|---|---|---|---|---|---|---|
| **Chest** | | | | | | |
| Synth Chest Piece | 12 | 17 | 0 | 7 | 75 | |
| Sturdy Synth Chest Piece | 25 | 29 | 0 | 12 | 125 | |
| Heavy Synth Chest Piece | 37 | 42 | 0 | 17 | 175 | |
| **Left Arm** | | | | | | |
| Synth Left Arm | 7 | 10 | 0 | 3 | 30 | |
| Sturdy Synth Left Arm | 12 | 15 | 0 | 7 | 70 | |
| Heavy Synth Left Arm | 17 | 20 | 0 | 10 | 110 | |
| **Left Leg** | | | | | | |
| Synth Left Leg | 6 | 9 | 0 | 3 | 30 | |
| Sturdy Synth Left Leg | 11 | 14 | 0 | 7 | 80 | |
| Heavy Synth Left Leg | 16 | 19 | 0 | 10 | 130 | |
| **Right Arm** | | | | | | |
| Synth Right Arm | 7 | 10 | 0 | 3 | 30 | |
| Sturdy Synth Right Arm | 12 | 15 | 0 | 7 | 70 | |
| Heavy Synth Right Arm | 17 | 20 | 0 | 10 | 110 | |
| **Right Leg** | | | | | | |
| Synth Right Leg | 6 | 9 | 0 | 3 | 30 | |
| Sturdy Synth Right Leg | 11 | 14 | 0 | 7 | 80 | |
| Heavy Synth Right Leg | 16 | 19 | 0 | 10 | 130 | |

## MISCELLANEOUS ARMOR

**CAIT'S BANDOLIER**  **DC GUARD LEFT SHOULDER**  **VAULT-TEC SECURITY ARMOR**

You'll sometimes find bits of armor that don't belong to any of the major armor sets. These miscellaneous armor pieces aren't as common or customizable as set pieces, but some of them can be modified at armor workbenches.

### MISCELLANEOUS ARMOR PIECES

| NAME | BONUS | DAMAGE RESISTANCE | ENERGY RESISTANCE | RADIATION RESISTANCE | WEIGHT | VALUE | MODS |
|---|---|---|---|---|---|---|---|
| Cait's Bandolier | Strength +1 | 2 | 0 | 0 | 2 | 20 | |
| Covenant Security Armor | — | 6 | 0 | 0 | 5 | 13 | |
| DC Guard Left Arm Armor | — | 10 | 5 | 0 | 2 | 7 | |
| DC Guard Left Forearm | — | 4 | 2 | 0 | 1 | 5 | |
| DC Guard Left Shoulder | — | 5 | 2 | 0 | 1 | 5 | |
| DC Guard Right Arm Armor | — | 10 | 5 | 0 | 2 | 7 | |
| DC Guard Right Forearm | — | 4 | 2 | 0 | 1 | 5 | |
| DC Guard Right Shoulder | — | 5 | 2 | 0 | 1 | 5 | |
| DC Guard Umpire's Pads | — | 15 | 10 | 0 | 4 | 10 | |
| Vault 81 Security Armor | — | 6 | 0 | 0 | 5 | 13 | |
| Vault-Tec Security Armor | — | 6 | 0 | 0 | 5 | 13 | |

# HEADGEAR

**ASSAULT GAS MASK**

**COMBAT ARMOR HELMET**

**MILITIA HAT**

Whether you're looking to boost a S.P.E.C.I.A.L. rank or add a bit of extra protection to your ensemble, the right piece of headgear can improve both your performance and your appearance. These items come in a variety of styles, some of which cover part or all of your face.

You can use armor workbenches to modify mining helmets and any headgear associated with major armor sets. A few additional headgear items can be modified with help from the Railroad.

## HEADGEAR

| NAME | BONUS | DAMAGE RESISTANCE | ENERGY RESISTANCE | RADIATION RESISTANCE | WEIGHT | VALUE | MODS |
|---|---|---|---|---|---|---|---|
| Airship Captain's Hat | Charisma +1, Endurance +1 | 0 | 0 | 0 | 0.5 | 15 | |
| Army Helmet | — | 10 | 0 | 0 | 3 | 20 | |
| Assault Gas Mask | — | 1 | 0 | 15 | 3 | 25 | |
| Baseball Cap | Perception +1 | 0 | 0 | 0 | 0.25 | 15 | |
| Battered Fedora | Luck +1 | 0 | 0 | 0 | 0.5 | 6 | |
| Blue Batting Helmet | — | 2 | 5 | 0 | 1 | 5 | |
| BOS Hood | — | 0 | 2 | 0 | 0.5 | 12 | |
| Bowler Hat | Endurance +1 | 0 | 0 | 0 | 0.3 | 15 | |
| Brown Flight Helmet | — | 2 | 5 | 0 | 2 | 25 | |
| Captain Ironsides' Hat | Perception +1, Charisma +1 | 0 | 0 | 0 | 0.5 | 15 | |
| Chef Hat | Luck +1 | 0 | 0 | 0 | 0.5 | 15 | |
| Coast Guard Hat | Perception +1 | 0 | 0 | 0 | 0.4 | 20 | |
| Combat Armor Helmet | — | 10 | 10 | 0 | 4 | 25 | |
| Crumpled Fedora | Luck +1 | 0 | 0 | 0 | 0.5 | 15 | |
| DC Guard Heavy Helmet | — | 5 | 5 | 0 | 1 | 5 | |
| DC Guard Helm | — | 5 | 5 | 0 | 1 | 5 | |
| Dirty Army Helmet | — | 10 | 0 | 0 | 3 | 20 | |
| Dirty Fedora | Luck +1 | 0 | 0 | 0 | 0.5 | 8 | |
| Dirty Postman Hat | Endurance +1 | 0 | 0 | 0 | 0.4 | 15 | |
| Faded Visor | Perception +1 | 0 | 0 | 0 | 0.1 | 10 | |
| Field Scribe's Hat | — | 0 | 5 | 0 | 0.5 | 8 | |
| Flight Helmet | — | 3 | 5 | 0 | 2 | 25 | |
| Formal Hat | Charisma +1 | 0 | 0 | 0 | 0.4 | 15 | |
| Gas Mask | — | 1 | 0 | 15 | 3 | 10 | |
| Gas Mask with Goggles | — | 1 | 0 | 15 | 3 | 10 | |
| Grandpa Savoldi's Hat | Charisma +1 | 0 | 0 | 0 | 0.5 | 15 | |
| Gray Knit Cap | Luck +1 | 0 | 0 | 0 | 0.4 | 15 | |
| Green Hood | — | 1 | 0 | 0 | 3 | 5 | |
| Green Rag Hat | — | 0 | 0 | 0 | 0.5 | 2 | |
| Hard Hat | — | 4 | 0 | 0 | 0.5 | 15 | |
| Lieutenant's Hat | Charisma +1 | 0 | 0 | 0 | 0.5 | 15 | |
| Lorenzo's Crown | — | 4 | 0 | 0 | 3 | 20 | |
| MacCready's Hat | Perception +1 | 0 | 0 | 0 | 0.5 | 15 | |
| Mascot Head | — | 5 | 0 | 0 | 1 | 5 | |
| Medical Goggles | — | 0 | 10 | 0 | 0.5 | 12 | |
| Metal Helmet | — | 9 | 4 | 0 | 3 | 15 | |

| NAME | BONUS | DAMAGE RESISTANCE | ENERGY RESISTANCE | RADIATION RESISTANCE | WEIGHT | VALUE | MODS |
|---|---|---|---|---|---|---|---|
| Military Cap | Perception +1 | 0 | 0 | 0 | 0.2 | 15 | |
| Militia Hat | Charisma +1 | 0 | 0 | 0 | 0 | 15 | |
| Militia Hat | Charisma +1 | 0 | 0 | 0 | 0.5 | 15 | |
| Mining Helmet | — | 3 | 0 | 0 | 5 | 50 | |
| Minuteman Hat | — | 0 | 0 | 0 | 2 | 15 | |
| Minutemen General's Hat | Charisma +1 | 0 | 0 | 0 | 2 | 15 | |
| Newsboy Cap | Charisma +1 | 0 | 0 | 0 | 0 | 5 | |
| Newsboy Cap | Charisma +1 | 0 | 0 | 0 | 0.4 | 5 | |
| Pompadour Wig | Charisma +1 | 0 | 0 | 0 | 0 | 15 | |
| Pompadour Wig | Charisma +1 | 0 | 0 | 0 | 0.2 | 15 | |
| Postman Hat | Endurance +1 | 0 | 0 | 0 | 0.4 | 28 | |
| Press Cap | Intelligence +1 | 0 | 0 | 0 | 0.5 | 15 | |
| Red Flight Helmet | — | 2 | 5 | 0 | 2 | 25 | |
| Sack Hood | — | 0 | 0 | 2 | 0.75 | 5 | |
| Sack Hood with Hoses | — | 0 | 0 | 5 | 1 | 5 | |
| Sack Hood with Straps | — | 0 | 0 | 5 | 1.5 | 5 | |
| Sea Captain's Hat | Endurance +2 | 0 | 0 | 0 | 0.4 | 25 | |
| Security Helmet | — | 5 | 0 | 0 | 2 | 20 | |
| Silver Shroud Hat | Perception +1 | 0 | 0 | 0 | 0.5 | 15 | |
| Submariner Hat | — | 0 | 0 | 0 | 0.5 | 15 | |
| Synth Field Helmet | — | 9 | 11 | 0 | 3 | 33 | |
| Synth Helmet | — | 9 | 11 | 0 | 3 | 33 | |
| Tinker Headgear | Intelligence +1 | 5 | 5 | 0 | 1 | 5 | |
| Tricorn Hat | Charisma +1 | 0 | 0 | 0 | 0.5 | 15 | |
| Triggerman Bowler | Luck +1 | 0 | 0 | 0 | 0.3 | 15 | |
| Trilby Hat | Charisma +1 | 0 | 0 | 0 | 0.5 | 5 | |
| Ushanka Hat | Intelligence +1 | 0 | 0 | 0 | 0.3 | 15 | |
| Vault-Tec Security Helmet | — | 5 | 0 | 0 | 2 | 20 | |
| Welding Helmet | — | 3 | 5 | 0 | 4 | 20 | |
| Worn Fedora | Perception +1 | 0 | 0 | 0 | 0 | 15 | |
| Worn Fedora | Perception +1 | 0 | 0 | 0 | 0.5 | 15 | |
| Wrapped Cap | Perception +1 | 0 | 0 | 0 | 1 | 5 | |
| Yellow Fedora | Perception +1 | 0 | 0 | 0 | 0.5 | 16 | |
| Yellow Flight Helmet | Perception +1 | 2 | 5 | 0 | 2 | 25 | |
| Yellow Slicker hat | Luck +1 | 0 | 0 | 0 | 0.3 | 15 | |

APPAREL

# ACCESSORIES

**BLACK-RIM GLASSES**

**STARS AND STRIPES BANDANA**

**SURGICAL MASK**

Some accessories are purely cosmetic, but eyewear can boost various S.P.E.C.I.A.L. ranks. Most accessory items are very light and well worth collecting whenever they're found.

## ACCESSORIES

| NAME | BONUS | DAMAGE RESISTANCE | ENERGY RESISTANCE | RADIATION RESISTANCE | WEIGHT | VALUE | MODS |
|---|---|---|---|---|---|---|---|
| Black-Rim Glasses | Charisma +1 | 0 | 0 | 0 | 0.1 | 8 | 👊 |
| Blue Bandana | — | 0 | 0 | 0 | 0.1 | 1 | 👊 |
| Eyeglasses | Perception +1 | 0 | 0 | 0 | 0.1 | 7 | 👊 |
| Fashionable Glasses | Charisma +1 | 0 | 0 | 0 | 0.2 | 27 | 👊 |
| Gunner's Camo Bandana | — | 0 | 0 | 0 | 0.1 | 1 | 👊 |
| Gunner's Green Bandana | — | 0 | 0 | 0 | 0.1 | 1 | 👊 |
| Jangles Bandana | — | 0 | 0 | 0 | 0.1 | 1 | 👊 |
| Leopard Print Bandana | — | 0 | 0 | 0 | 0.1 | 1 | 👊 |
| Liam's Glasses | Intelligence +2, Charisma -1 | 0 | 0 | 0 | 0.5 | 80 | 👊 |
| Patrolman Sunglasses | Perception +1 | 0 | 0 | 0 | 0.1 | 8 | 👊 |
| Red Bandana | — | 0 | 0 | 0 | 0.1 | 1 | 👊 |
| Road Goggles | Intelligence +1 | 0 | 0 | 0 | 0.2 | 8 | 👊 |
| Robotic Bits | Perception +1 | 0 | 0 | 0 | 2 | 14 | 👊 |
| Skull Bandana | — | 0 | 0 | 0 | 0.1 | 1 | 👊 |
| Stars and Stripes Bandana | — | 0 | 0 | 0 | 0.1 | 1 | 👊 |
| Striped Bandana | — | 0 | 0 | 0 | 0.1 | 1 | 👊 |
| Sunglasses | Perception +1 | 0 | 0 | 0 | 0 | 20 | 👊 |
| Sunglasses | Perception +1 | 0 | 0 | 0 | 0.1 | 7 | 👊 |
| Surgical Mask | — | 0 | 0 | 0 | 0.2 | 5 | 👊 |
| Wedding Ring | — | 0 | 0 | 0 | 0 | 250 | 👊 |
| Welding Goggles | Perception +1 | 0 | 0 | 0 | 0.3 | 10 | 👊 |
| Wraparound Goggles | Perception +1 | 0 | 0 | 0 | 0.1 | 4 | 👊 |

# POWER ARMOR

When it comes to damage mitigation, no collection of conventional apparel items can match a functioning suit of Power Armor. More vehicle than clothing, Power Armor makes even the most fragile combatant a powerhouse on the battlefield. You'll find a variety of interchangeable, highly customizable parts scattered throughout the Commonwealth.

It takes considerable resources to modify such complex components, but with the right perks and materials, you can assemble a suit of Power Armor that provides unbeatable protection and impressive utility. Here are just a few of the benefits Power Armor enthusiasts enjoy:

- ENTERING A BASIC SUIT OF POWER ARMOR AUTOMATICALLY GRANTS YOU A STRENGTH RATING OF 11. EQUIPPING STRENGTH-BOOSTING MODS CAN INCREASE THE EFFECT. THIS BONUS LASTS AS LONG AS YOU REMAIN IN THE SUIT.

- EVEN THE SIMPLEST SUIT OF POWER ARMOR OFFERS EXCELLENT RADIATION RESISTANCE. LEAD PLATING MODS IMPROVE THE EFFECT.

- POWER ARMOR NEGATES ALL FALLING DAMAGE. IN FACT, FALLING FROM A SIGNIFICANT HEIGHT TRIGGERS AN IMPACT LANDING. THIS POWERFUL ATTACK DAMAGES ALL TARGETS LOCATED NEAR THE POINT OF IMPACT.

- MOST MODELS OF POWER ARMOR CAN ACCOMMODATE JETPACK MODS. SOME ITEMS AND LOCATIONS CAN ONLY BE REACHED WITH A ROCKET-ASSISTED JUMP.

- PERKS LIKE PAIN TRAIN AND NUCLEAR PHYSICIST MAKE POWER ARMOR EVEN MORE EFFECTIVE IN COMBAT, AND HOT RODDER MAGAZINES UNLOCK CUSTOM POWER ARMOR PAINT SCHEMES.

Of course, the benefits of Power Armor come at a cost. If you plan on using and maintaining even one suit of Power Armor, there are a few things you should keep in mind:

- POWER ARMOR IS FUELED BY FUSION CORES. THESE VALUABLE ITEMS ARE HARD TO COME BY, BUT YOU'LL NEED TO MAINTAIN A GOOD SUPPLY OF THEM TO KEEP YOUR POWER ARMOR BATTLE-READY. WHEN YOU'RE WEARING POWER ARMOR, ANYTHING THAT CONSUMES ACTION POINTS ALSO DEPLETES THE INSTALLED FUSION CORE.

- POWER ARMOR CAN BE DAMAGED. UNLIKE OTHER APPAREL ITEMS, POWER ARMOR PARTS NEED FREQUENT REPAIRS. THE REQUIRED MATERIALS VARY FROM PART TO PART, BUT YOU'D DO WELL TO KEEP YOUR POWER ARMOR STATION STOCKED WITH PLENTY OF STEEL, ALUMINUM, COPPER, AND PLASTIC.

- WHILE YOU'RE INSIDE A SUIT OF POWER ARMOR, YOU LOSE ANY BENEFITS GRANTED BY OTHER APPAREL ITEMS.

- POWER ARMOR CAN BE STOLEN. WHENEVER YOU LEAVE YOUR POWER ARMOR, REMOVE THE FUSION CORE TO PREVENT ANY UNAUTHORIZED USERS FROM COMMANDEERING YOUR VALUABLE EQUIPMENT.

- PUNCHING WEAPONS CAN'T BE USED WITH POWER ARMOR. POWER ARMOR IS CAPABLE OF DELIVERING IMPRESSIVE UNARMED DAMAGE, BUT IT'S TOO BULKY TO ACCOMMODATE KNUCKLES, GLOVES, OR WRIST-MOUNTED WEAPONS.

- CRAFTING POWER ARMOR MODS TAKES A GOOD SUPPLY OF RARE MATERIALS AND CONSIDERABLE KNOW-HOW. YOU CAN EARN CUSTOMIZED PARTS BY COMPLETING QUESTS OR DEFEATING APPROPRIATELY EQUIPPED ENEMIES, BUT YOU'LL NEED TO INVEST IN ALL AVAILABLE RANKS OF THE SCIENCE!, BLACKSMITH, AND ARMORER PERKS IF YOU WANT TO CRAFT YOUR OWN ADVANCED POWER ARMOR MODS.

## POWER ARMOR FRAMES

Power Armor frames can't be carried—and therefore never appear in your Pip-Boy's Apparel tab—but you can't build a suit of Power Armor without one. A bare Power Armor frame provides 60 Damage Resistance and 60 Energy Resistance. Attach and modify parts to create your ideal suit of Power Armor.

When not in use, a Power Armor frame acts much like a container—simply transfer parts from your inventory to mount them in place. While you're inside a frame, use the Pip-Boy to equip Power Armor parts the same way you'd equip clothing and armor. You can only equip Power Armor parts that are in working order; badly damaged parts must be repaired at a Power Armor station before they can be used.

### POWER ARMOR FRAMES: RECOMMENDED LOCATIONS

| LOCATION | NOTES |
|---|---|
| Crashed Vertibird (Covenant Lake) | Located in the water, near the Vertibird wreckage. |
| Crashed Vertibird (Elevated Freeway) | Near the Vertibird wreckage at the edge of the overpass. |
| Crashed Vertibird (Near Robotics Disposal Ground) | Located near the Vertibird wreckage. |
| Diamond City | Purchased from Arturo. |
| Fiddler's Green Trailer Estates | Located in a locked trailer (Master). |
| Mass Pike Interchange | Located in the Gunner camp on the overpass. |
| Military APCs (near Poseidon Energy Turbine #18-F) | Located near the crashed plane beside the APCs. |
| Military Armor Transport (Lexington) | Located behind a security door. Hack the terminal (Advanced) in the nearby train car. |
| Military Armor Transport (North Wilderness) | Located behind a security door. Hack the terminal (Advanced) in the nearby train car. |
| Military Checkpoint (Cambridge Outskirts) | In a locked cage. Use the nearby terminal (Advanced) to open the security door. |
| Military Convoy (Training Yard) | Located inside the convoy trailer. |
| Museum of Freedom | Located on the roof. Plays a key role in The Minutemen Quest: When Freedom Calls. |
| National Guard Training Yard | In the locked (Master) National Guard Armory. Use the terminal (Novice) to unlock the security door. |
| Revere Satellite Array | Located atop one of the dish towers. |
| The Prydwen | Purchased from Teagan. |

If you're interested in owning and maintaining multiple suits, you'll need to collect multiple frames. You'll find several Power Armor frames scattered across the Commonwealth, but additional frames can be purchased from vendors or earned by completing quests.

## POWER ARMOR PARTS

Every piece of Power Armor you find belongs to one of five sets. Raider Power Armor is the least advanced, X-01 Power Armor is the most advanced, and everything else falls somewhere in the middle. This hierarchy makes it fairly easy to determine whether a newly acquired part is an upgrade. A modified Raider Power Left Arm can offer more protection than a standard T-45 Left Arm, but barring bonuses granted by unique items, a more-advanced part can always be modified to outperform a less-advanced part.

Although most Power Armor parts offer identical customization options, it's important to note that each mod is set-specific. All Power Armor sets can accommodate rad scrubbers, but rad scrubbers pulled from a T-51 Helm can only be applied to another T-51 Helm. Luckily, there's no need to commit to a specific model of Power Armor. Simply equip the parts that seem most useful at any given time.

## Raider Power Armor

Raider Power Armor offers far fewer customization options than other Power Armor sets—most notably, the Raider Power Torso doesn't support jetpacks or Stealth Boy mods available on more advanced Power Armor. Still, even the most basic suit of Raider Power Armor provides far more protection than standard apparel.

Any Raider clad in Power Armor is likely to have several of these parts equipped.

### RAIDER POWER PARTS

| NAME | DAMAGE RESISTANCE | ENERGY RESISTANCE | RADIATION RESISTANCE | WEIGHT | VALUE | MODS |
|------|------|------|------|------|------|------|
| Raider Power Helm | 100 | 50 | 150 | 14 | 50 | 👍 |
| Raider Power Left Arm | 50 | 25 | 150 | 16 | 75 | 👍 |
| Raider Power Left Leg | 50 | 25 | 150 | 17 | 75 | 👍 |
| Raider Power Right Arm | 50 | 25 | 150 | 16 | 75 | 👍 |
| Raider Power Right Leg | 50 | 25 | 150 | 17 | 75 | 👍 |
| Raider Power Torso | 200 | 100 | 300 | 22 | 100 | 👍 |

## T-45 Power Armor

T-45 Power Armor can't match the protection offered by more advanced models, but it supports a full complement of mods. This Power Armor isn't widely used, but you'll find a complete set atop the Museum of Freedom.

### T-45 PARTS

| NAME | DAMAGE RESISTANCE | ENERGY RESISTANCE | RADIATION RESISTANCE | WEIGHT | VALUE | MODS |
|------|------|------|------|------|------|------|
| T-45 Helm | 100 | 60 | 150 | 12 | 60 | 👍 |
| T-45 Left Arm | 50 | 30 | 150 | 15 | 100 | 👍 |
| T-45 Left Leg | 50 | 30 | 150 | 15 | 100 | 👍 |
| T-45 Right Arm | 50 | 30 | 150 | 15 | 100 | 👍 |
| T-45 Right Leg | 50 | 30 | 150 | 15 | 100 | 👍 |
| T-45 Torso | 200 | 130 | 300 | 20 | 140 | 👍 |

## X-01 Power Armor

The X-01 is the most advanced Power Armor available. It's also the rarest. This makes it extremely difficult to assemble a complete set of X-01 Power Armor, but it's well worth using any parts you're lucky enough to find.

## T-51 Power Armor

T-51 Power Armor offers better protection than the T-45 model. These parts aren't favored by any particular group, but you can find bits and pieces scattered throughout the Commonwealth.

### T-51 PARTS

| NAME | DAMAGE RESISTANCE | ENERGY RESISTANCE | RADIATION RESISTANCE | WEIGHT | VALUE | MODS |
|------|------|------|------|------|------|------|
| T-51 Helm | 140 | 90 | 150 | 12 | 80 | 👍 |
| T-51 Left Arm | 90 | 60 | 150 | 15 | 130 | 👍 |
| T-51 Left Leg | 90 | 60 | 150 | 15 | 130 | 👍 |
| T-51 Right Arm | 90 | 60 | 150 | 15 | 130 | 👍 |
| T-51 Right Leg | 90 | 60 | 150 | 15 | 130 | 👍 |
| T-51 Torso | 240 | 160 | 300 | 20 | 180 | 👍 |

## T-60 Power Armor

T-60 Power Armor is favored by the Brotherhood of Steel and the Atom Cats, so these durable parts are relatively easy to find. You can take them by force if you're so inclined, but searching military bases and Vertibird crash sites tends to be just as effective.

This model's popularity also means you'll find T-60 parts that feature custom paint jobs. Atom Cat parts, in particular, offer a paint scheme you can't find anywhere else.

### T-60 PARTS

| NAME | DAMAGE RESISTANCE | ENERGY RESISTANCE | RADIATION RESISTANCE | WEIGHT | VALUE | MODS |
|------|------|------|------|------|------|------|
| T-60 Helm | 180 | 120 | 150 | 12 | 120 | 👍 |
| T-60 Left Arm | 130 | 85 | 150 | 15 | 160 | 👍 |
| T-60 Left Leg | 130 | 85 | 150 | 15 | 160 | 👍 |
| T-60 Right Arm | 130 | 85 | 150 | 15 | 160 | 👍 |
| T-60 Right Leg | 130 | 85 | 150 | 15 | 160 | 👍 |
| T-60 Torso | 280 | 185 | 300 | 20 | 200 | 👍 |

### X-01 PARTS

| NAME | DAMAGE RESISTANCE | ENERGY RESISTANCE | RADIATION RESISTANCE | WEIGHT | VALUE | MODS |
|------|------|------|------|------|------|------|
| X-01 Helm | 220 | 140 | 150 | 12 | 140 | 👍 |
| X-01 Left Arm | 170 | 110 | 150 | 15 | 200 | 👍 |
| X-01 Left Leg | 170 | 110 | 150 | 15 | 200 | 👍 |
| X-01 Right Arm | 170 | 110 | 150 | 15 | 200 | 👍 |
| X-01 Right Leg | 170 | 110 | 150 | 15 | 200 | 👍 |
| X-01 Torso | 320 | 210 | 300 | 20 | 280 | 👍 |

# SPECIALTY ITEMS

You'll sometimes find apparel you can't equip yourself. Save these specialty items for a more suitable user or sell them for a few extra caps.

## DOG APPAREL

Guard dogs are often equipped with collars and custom armor. These items don't offer any protection, but you can use them to give your canine companion a new look.

### DOG APPAREL

| NAME | DAMAGE RESISTANCE | ENERGY RESISTANCE | RADIATION RESISTANCE | WEIGHT | VALUE | MODS |
|---|---|---|---|---|---|---|
| Chain Dog Collar | 0 | 0 | 0 | 1 | 7 | 👊 |
| Dog Armor | 0 | 0 | 0 | 4 | 20 | 👊 |
| Dog Collar | 0 | 0 | 0 | 1 | 7 | 👊 |
| Double Dog Collar | 0 | 0 | 0 | 1 | 7 | 👊 |
| Heavy Dog Armor | 0 | 0 | 0 | 5 | 30 | 👊 |
| Light Dog Armor | 0 | 0 | 0 | 3 | 10 | 👊 |
| Reinforced Dog Collar | 0 | 0 | 0 | 1 | 7 | 👊 |
| Spiked Dog Collar | 0 | 0 | 0 | 1 | 7 | 👊 |

**HELPFUL HINT** *from Vault Boy!* **Did You Know?**

IN ADDITION TO DOG-SPECIFIC APPAREL, DOGMEAT CAN USE WELDING GOGGLES AND ANY BANDANAS YOU HAPPEN TO COLLECT.

## SUPER MUTANT APPAREL

Super Mutant Armor is too cumbersome for you to wear, but you can use it to give your Super Mutant companion a new look.

# LEGENDARY EFFECTS AND UNIQUE APPAREL

## LEGENDARY EFFECTS

Each Legendary enemy you defeat has a chance of dropping a Legendary armor piece with a randomly selected bonus effect. Legendary armor can accommodate all of the mods used by similar items.

| ARMOR NAME MODIFIER | DESCRIPTION |
|---|---|
| Cunning | Agility +1, Perception +1. |
| V.A.T.S. Enhanced | 10% reduction in Action Point costs in V.A.T.S. |
| Powered | Increases Action Point refresh speed. |
| Chameleon | Enemies have a harder time detecting you while you're sneaking and not moving. |
| Sharp | Charisma +1, Intelligence +1. |
| Duelist's | 10% chance to disarm melee attacker on hit. |
| Freefall | Prevents falling damage. |
| Cavalier's | Reduces damage while blocking or sprinting by 15%. |
| Titan's | Reduces damage while standing and not moving by 15%. |
| Hunter's | Reduces damage from animals by 15%. |
| Exterminator's | Reduces damage from Mirelurks and bugs by 15%. |
| Ghoul Slayer's | Reduces damage from Ghouls by 15%. |
| Assassin's | Reduces damage from humans by 15%. |
| Troubleshooter's | Reduces damage from robots by 15%. |
| Mutant Slayer's | Reduces damage from Super Mutants by 15%. |
| Acrobat's | Reduces falling damage by 50%. |
| Safecracker's | Increases size of sweet spot while picking locks. |
| Martyr's | Temporarily slows time during combat when you are at 20% or less Health. |
| Lucky | Luck +2. |
| Herbalist's | +25 poison resistance. |
| Punishing | Reflects 10% of melee damage back on attacker. |
| Bolstering | Grants increasing energy and damage resistance the lower your Health (up to +35). |
| Sprinter's | Increases wearer's movement speed by 15%. |
| Fortifying | Strength +1, Endurance +1. |
| Low Weight | Low carry weight. |
| Almost Unbreakable | Quadruples durability. |

### SUPER MUTANT APPAREL

| NAME | BONUS | DAMAGE RESISTANCE | ENERGY RESISTANCE | RADIATION RESISTANCE | WEIGHT | VALUE | MODS | LOCATIONS |
|---|---|---|---|---|---|---|---|---|
| Super Mutant Arm Guards | — | 7 | 5 | 0 | 5 | 10 | 👊 | Big John's Salvage, Gwinnett Brewery |
| Super Mutant Aviator Cap | — | 2 | 0 | 0 | 1 | 10 | 👊 | Wilson Atomatoys Factory, Rocky Cave (Virgil's Laboratory) |
| Super Mutant Bladed Helmet | — | 4 | 0 | 0 | 1 | 8 | 👊 | Weston Water Treatment Plant, West Roxbury Station |
| Super Mutant Bracers | — | 5 | 3 | 0 | 6 | 18 | 👊 | West Roxbury Station, Rocky Cave (Virgil's Laboratory) |
| Super Mutant Cage Helmet | — | 3 | 0 | 0 | 1 | 8 | 👊 | West Everett Estates, Gwinnett Brewery |
| Super Mutant Chains | — | 3 | 5 | 0 | 10 | 30 | 👊 | West Everett Estates, Revere Satellite Array |
| Super Mutant Chest Harness | — | 3 | 0 | 0 | 7 | 25 | 👊 | Breakheart Banks, Shaw High School |
| Super Mutant Cowl Armor | — | 10 | 5 | 0 | 10 | 30 | 👊 | Trinity Tower, Wilson Atomatoys Factory |
| Super Mutant Heavy Armor | — | 10 | 5 | 0 | 12 | 50 | 👊 | Trinity Tower, Medford Memorial Hospital |
| Super Mutant Heavy Gauntlets | — | 10 | 5 | 0 | 4 | 5 | 👊 | Weston Water Treatment Plant, Boston Public Library |
| Super Mutant Helmet | — | 3 | 0 | 0 | 1 | 8 | 👊 | Medford Memorial Hospital, Fraternal Post 115 |
| Super Mutant Leg Armor | — | 7 | 5 | 0 | 6 | 18 | 👊 | Trinity Tower, Revere Satellite Array |
| Super Mutant Leg Guards | — | 5 | 3 | 0 | 5 | 10 | 👊 | Scrap Palace, Trinity Tower |
| Super Mutant Light Body Armor | — | 12 | 10 | 0 | 8 | 15 | 👊 | Wilson Atomatoys Factory, Shaw High School |
| Super Mutant Shoulder Rags | — | 3 | 0 | 0 | 6 | 20 | 👊 | Scrap Palace, Wilson Atomatoys Factory |
| Super Mutant Waistcloth | — | 4 | 0 | 0 | 2 | 8 | 👊 | Breakheart Banks, Trinity Tower |
| Super Mutant Wrist Wraps | — | 3 | 0 | 0 | 2 | 8 | 👊 | Mass Fusion Disposal Site, Trinity Church (Trinity Plaza) |

# UNIQUE APPAREL

From Exceptional armor to stylish garments, you'll find a variety of unique apparel items during your time in the Commonwealth. Some of these items can be found or purchased from vendors, while others must be earned by completing quests or defeating specific enemies.

## UNIQUE APPAREL ITEMS

| NAME | ITEM TYPE | BONUS | NOTES |
|------|-----------|-------|-------|
| Agatha's Dress | Outfit | Charisma +3 | Complete "Curtain Call" as a female. |
| Apocalypse Chestplate | Metal Chest Piece | Temporarily slows time during combat when you are at 20% or less health. | Sold by Level 4 Workshop Armor Merchant |
| Apocalypse Left Greave | Metal Left Leg | Grants increasing energy and damage resistance the lower your health (up to +35). | Sold by Level 4 Workshop Armor Merchant |
| Black Ops Chestpiece | Combat Armor Chest Piece | Strength +1, Endurance +1 | Sold by Deb (Bunker Hill). |
| Black Ops Right Shinguard | Combat Armor Right Leg | Increases wearer's movement speed by 10% | Sold by Deb (Bunker Hill). |
| Captain Ironsides' Hat | Headgear | Perception +1, Charisma +1 | Complete "The Last Voyage of the USS Constitution." |
| Champion Chestpiece | Metal Chest Piece | Reduces damage from robots by 15%. | Sold by Myrna in Diamond City. |
| Champion Left Arm | Metal Left Arm | Strength +1, Endurance +1 | Sold by Lucas Miller (caravan trader). |
| Champion Right Arm | Metal Right Arm | Agility +1, Perception +1 | Sold by Becky Fallon (Fallon's Basement, Diamond City). |
| Commando Chest Piece | Combat Armor Chest Piece | Increases Action Point refresh speed. | Sold by Teagan (the Prydwen). |
| Commando Helmet | Combat Helmet | 10% reduction in Action Point costs in VATS. | Sold by Teagan (the Prydwen). |
| DB Tech Varsity Uniform | Outfit | — | Located in DB Tech High School. |
| Destroyer's Chest Piece | Combat Armor Chest Piece | Reduces damage from humans by 15% | Sold by Daisy (Goodneighbor). |
| Destroyer's Helmet | Combat Helmet | Charisma +1, Intelligence +1 | Sold by Penny Fitzgerald (Covenant). |
| Destroyer's Left Arm | Combat Armor Left Arm | Reduces damage while blocking or sprinting by 15%. | Sold by Deb (Bunker Hill). |
| Destroyer's Left Leg | Combat Armor Left Leg | Increases wearer's movement speed by 10%. | Sold by Daisy (Goodneighbor). |
| Destroyer's Right Leg | Combat Armor Right Leg | Increases wearer's movement speed by 10%. | Sold by Alexis Combes (Vault 81). |
| Devastator's Chestpiece | Metal Chest Piece | Reflects 10% of melee damage back on attacker. | Sold by KL-E-O (Goodneighbor). |
| Devastator's Right Greave | Metal Right Leg | Temporarily slows time during combat when you are at 20% or less health. | Sold by KL-E-O (Goodneighbor). |
| Exemplar's T-60c Torso | T-60c Torso | 10% reduction in Action Point costs in V.A.T.S. | Complete "Duty or Dishonor" by persuading Clarke to turn himself in. |
| Freefall Armor Left Leg | Combat Armor Left Leg | When both Freefall Legs are worn together, prevents fall damage. | Located in Mass Fusion, within the safe in Jack Rockford's office (28th floor). |
| Freefall Armor Right Leg | Combat Armor Right Leg | When both Freefall Legs are worn together, prevents fall damage. | Located in Mass Fusion, within the safe in Jack Rockford's office (28th floor). |
| Grognak Costume | Outfit | Increased Strength and melee damage. | Located within a locker on the fourth floor of Hubris Comics. |
| Honor | T-60 Left Leg | Increases Action Point refresh speed. | Sold by Teagan (the Prydwen). Requires Paladin rank within the Brotherhood of Steel. |
| Liam's Glasses | Accessory | Intelligence +2, Charisma -1 | Complete "Plugging a Leak." |
| Lieutenant's Hat | Headgear | Charisma +1 | Complete "The Last Voyage of the USS Constitution." |
| Mantis Left Armguard | Leather Left Arm | 10% chance to disarm melee attacker on hit. | Sold by Lucas Miller (caravan trader). |
| Mantis Left Greave | Leather Left Leg | Agility +1, Perception +1 | Sold by Lucas Miller (caravan trader). |
| Mark 2 Synth Chest Piece | Synth Chest Piece | Enemies have a harder time detecting you while you're sneaking and not moving. | Sold by Institute requisitions (the Institute). |
| Mark 2 Synth Helmet | Synth Helmet | Agility +1, Perception +1 | Sold by Institute requisitions (the Institute) |
| Mark 3 Synth Chest Piece | Synth Chest Piece | Grants increasing energy and damage resistance the lower your Health (up to +35) | Sold by Institute requisitions (the Institute). |
| Mark 3 Synth Right Arm | Synth Right Arm | Increases Action Point refresh speed. | Sold by Institute requisitions (the Institute). |
| Mark 4 Synth Chest Piece | Synth Chest Piece | Enemies have a harder time detecting you while you're sneaking and not moving. | Sold by Level 4 Workshop Armor Merchant. |
| Mark 4 Synth Left Leg | Synth Left Leg | Luck +2 | Sold by Level 4 Workshop Armor Merchant. |
| Mascot Head | Headgear | — | Located in DB Tech High School. |
| Minutemen General's Hat | Headgear | Charisma +1 | Found on a corpse in the Castle. |
| Minutemen General's Uniform | Outfit | Charisma +1 | Found on a corpse in the Castle. |

| NAME | ITEM TYPE | BONUS | NOTES |
| --- | --- | --- | --- |
| Nucleostrictive Torso Armor | T-60 Torso | Reduces the rate of Fusion Core depletion by 10%. | Complete the experiment Cambridge Polymer Labs. |
| Overseer's Left Armguard | Combat Armor Left Arm | 10% reduction in Action Point costs in VATS. | Sold by Alexis Combes (Vault 81). |
| Overseer's Right Armguard | Combat Armor Right Arm | Reduces damage while standing and not moving by 15%. | Sold by Alexis Combes (Vault 81). |
| Protector's Left Armguard | Leather Left Arm | Reduces damage from humans by 15%. | Sold by Arturo (Diamond City). |
| Protector's Right Armguard | Leather Right Arm | Reduces damage from Super Mutants by 15%. | Sold by Arturo (Diamond City). |
| Reginald's Suit | Outfit | Charisma +3 | Complete "Curtain Call" as a male. |
| Silver Shroud Armor | Outfit | Agility +1, Perception +1 | Complete "The Silver Shroud." Item stats are determined by your current level. |
| Silver Shroud Hat | Headgear | Perception +1 | Complete "The Silver Shroud." |
| Steadfast BOS Combat Armor Chest Piece | Combat Armor Chest Piece | Grants increasing energy and damage resistance the lower your Health (up to +35). | Complete "The Lost Patrol for Captain Kells." |
| Tessa's Fist | Raider Power Right Arm | Increases unarmed damage. | Defeat Tessa in the Quincy Ruins and collect the part from her body. |
| Vengeance | T-60 Right leg | Reflects 10% of melee damage back on attacker. | Sold by Teagan (the Prydwen). Requires Sentinel rank within the Brotherhood of Steel. |
| Visionary's T-60c Helm | T-60c Helm | Increases Action Point refresh speed. | Complete "A Loose End." |
| Wastelander's Chest Piece | Leather Chest Piece | Agility +1, Perception +1 | Sold by Becky Fallon (Fallon's Basement, Diamond City). |
| Wastelander's Right Leg | Leather Right Leg | Reduces damage from Super Mutants by 15%. | Sold by Lucas Miller (caravan trader). |
| Zeke's Jacket and Jeans | Outfit | Charisma +1, Unarmed Damage +4 | Located at the Atom Cats Garage. |

# AID

Even the most cautious adventurers need a little extra help from time to time. Luckily, you'll find a wide variety of consumables and single-use devices that can help you survive hostile gangs, radiation storms, and anything else the Commonwealth throws at you. Be warned: many aid items have addictive properties. Each time you consume alcohol, performance-enhancing chems, and even some food items, you increase your chances of developing an addiction.

## HELPFUL HINT from Vault Boy! Did You Know?

AN UNTREATED ADDICTION CAN HAVE A SERIOUS IMPACT ON YOUR PERFORMANCE. YOU CAN CURE ADDICTIONS WITH CHEMS LIKE ADDICTOL AND REFRESHING BEVERAGE, OR YOU CAN SEEK HELP FROM A MEDICAL PROFESSIONAL. AS A TEMPORARY SOLUTION, YOU CAN SIMPLY FEED YOUR ADDICTION — YOU WON'T SUFFER ANY WITHDRAWAL SYMPTOMS AS LONG AS THE SUBSTANCE IS IN YOUR SYSTEM.

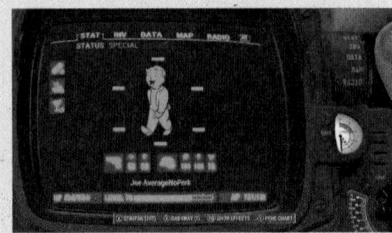

Many aid items grant bonuses or penalties that last several minutes. Some effects last considerably longer. Use your Pip-Boy's Status tab to review the effects of any aid items that are currently in your system.

### TIP

Aid items tend to be very light, but the food, chems, and alcohol you collect can quickly add up. Store or sell any unneeded items to keep them from weighing you down.

## FOOD

**SUGAR BOMBS** | **BLOATFLY MEAT** | **YAO GUAI RIBS** | **NUKA COLA QUANTUM**

Nearly all food items replenish some amount of Health, but many of these dishes offer special bonuses. Unfortunately, many foods also contain harmful radiation. Foods you cook are generally more effective (and much safer) than foods you find. If you're hankering for a satisfying meal, it's best to visit a well-stocked cooking station.

### FOOD

| NAME | EFFECT | WEIGHT | VALUE | ADDICTION % | DURATION (SEC) | CRAFTED |
|---|---|---|---|---|---|---|
| Ash blossom | HP +10, Rads +3 | 1 | 6 | — | 10 | ● |
| Baked Bloatfly | HP +40, Rad Resist +20 | 0.5 | 15 | — | 10 (heal), 600 (Rad Resist) | ● |
| Blamco Brand Mac and Cheese | HP +20, Rads +6 | 0.1 | 10 | — | 10 | ● |
| Blamco Brand Mac and Cheese | HP +40 | 0.1 | 15 | — | 10 | ● |
| Bloatfly Meat | HP +5, Rads +6 | 0.5 | 8 | — | 10 | ● |
| Bloodbug Meat | HP +45, Rads +9 | 0.5 | 18 | — | 10 | ● |
| Bloodbug Steak | +15 Max HP for 1 hour, HP +105 | 0.5 | 24 | — | 10 (heal), 3600 (HP boost) | ● |
| Bloodleaf | HP +10, Rads +2 | 0.1 | 5 | — | 10 | ● |
| Blood Pack | HP +50 | 0.1 | 10 | — | 10 | ● |
| Brahmin Meat | HP +10, Rads +8 | 1 | 28 | — | 10 | ● |
| Brain Fungus | HP +10, Rads +3 | 0.1 | 6 | — | 10 | ● |
| Bubblegum | HP +10, Rads +1 | 0.1 | 5 | — | 10 | ● |
| Canned Dog Food | HP +10, Rads +2 | 0.5 | 6 | — | 10 | ● |
| Carrot | HP +10, Rads 3 | 0.1 | 3 | — | 10 | ● |
| Carrot Flower | HP +10, Rads 3 | 0.1 | 6 | — | 10 | ● |
| Cat Meat | HP +15, Rads 8 | 0.5 | 8 | — | 10 | ● |
| Cave Fungus | HP +10, Rads -10 | 0.1 | 8 | — | 10 | ● |
| Cooked Softshell Meat | HP +85, Max AP +15 | 0.5 | 40 | — | 10 (heal), 3600 (AP boost) | ● |

| NAME | EFFECT | WEIGHT | VALUE | ADDICTION % | DURATION (SEC) | CRAFTED |
|---|---|---|---|---|---|---|
| Corn | HP +10, Rads +3 | 0.1 | 6 | — | 10 | ● |
| Cram | HP +25, Rads +5 | 0.5 | 25 | — | 10 | ● |
| Crispy Squirrel Bits | HP +35 | 0.1 | 6 | — | 10 | ● |
| Dandy Boy Apples | HP +10, Rads +3 | 0.5 | 7 | — | 10 | ● |
| Deathclaw Egg | HP +45, Rads +7 | 0.1 | 69 | — | 10 | ● |
| Deathclaw Egg Omelet | Increases heal rate for 2 hours, HP +115 | 0.1 | 80 | — | 10 (heal), 7200 (heal rate) | ● |
| Deathclaw Meat | HP +90, Rads +6 | 1 | 110 | — | 10 | ● |
| Deathclaw Steak | HP +185, Agility +1 | 1 | 130 | — | 10 (heal), 3600 (Agility) | ● |
| Deathclaw Wellingham | Increases heal rate, HP +115 | 0.1 | 120 | — | 10 (heal), 7200 (heal rate) | ● |
| Deezer's Lemonade | HP +50 | 0.5 | 1 | — | 10 | ● |
| Dirty Water | HP +20, Rads +7 | 0.5 | 5 | — | 10 | ● |
| Drugged Water | HP +20, Rads +7, Perception -1 | 0.5 | 8 | 50% | 10 (heal), 120 (Perception) | ● |
| Experimental Plant | HP +10, Rads +5 | 0.1 | 5 | — | 10 | ● |
| Fancy Lads Snack Cakes | HP +10, Rads +4 | 0.1 | 18 | — | 10 | ● |
| Fancy Lads Snack Cakes | HP +25 | 0.1 | 18 | — | 10 | ● |
| Food Paste | HP +50, Endurance +1 | 0.3 | 0 | — | 10 (heal), 3600 (Endurance) | ● |
| Fresh Carrot | HP +20 | 0.1 | 36 | — | 10 | ● |
| Fresh Corn | HP +20 | 0.1 | 36 | — | 10 | ● |

| NAME | EFFECT | WEIGHT | VALUE | ADDICTION % | DURATION (SEC) | CRAFTED |
|---|---|---|---|---|---|---|
| Fresh Melon | HP +20 | 1 | 36 | — | 10 | |
| Fresh Mutfruit | HP +20 | 0.1 | 8 | — | 10 | |
| Ghoul Meat | HP +10, Rads +10 | 0.3 | 4 | — | 10 | |
| Glowing Fungus | HP +10, Rads +3 | 0.1 | 6 | — | 10 | |
| Gourd | HP +10, Rads +3 | 1 | 6 | — | 10 | |
| Gourd | HP +20 | 1 | 36 | — | 10 | |
| Gourd Blossom | HP +10, Rads +3 | 1 | 6 | — | 10 | |
| Grilled Radroach | HP +30 | 0.5 | 7 | — | 10 | |
| Grilled Radstag | +25 Carry Weight | 1 | 60 | — | 10 (heal), 3600 (Carry Weight) | |
| Ground Mole Rat | HP +20, Rads +5 | 0.1 | 4 | — | 10 | |
| Gum Drops | HP +10, Rads +1 | 0.1 | 5 | — | 10 | |
| Happy Birthday Sweet Roll | HP +20, Rads +4 | 0 | 0 | — | 10 | |
| Hubflower | HP +10, Rads +2 | 0.1 | 5 | — | 10 | |
| Ice Cold Nuka Cherry | HP +75, Rads +5, AP +35 | 1 | 40 | — | 10 | |
| Ice Cold Nuka Cola | HP +45, Rads +5, AP +20 | 1 | 20 | — | 10 | |
| Ice Cold Nuka Cola Quantum | HP +650, Rads +5, AP +125 | 1 | 50 | 10% | 10 | |
| Iguana Bits | HP +15, Rads +5 | 0.1 | 8 | — | 10 | |
| Iguana Soup | HP +95 | 1 | 21 | — | 10 | |
| Iguana on a Stick | HP +40 | 0.1 | 33 | — | 10 | |
| InstaMash | HP +20 | 0.5 | 20 | — | 10 | |
| Institute Bottled Water | HP +40 | 0.5 | 15 | — | 10 | |
| Institute Food Packet | HP +25 | 0.5 | 10 | — | 10 | |
| Melon | HP +10, Rads +3 | 1 | 6 | — | 10 | |
| Melon | HP +20, Rads +3 | 1 | 18 | — | 10 | |
| Melon Blossom | HP +10, Rads +3 | 1 | 6 | — | 10 | |
| Mirelurk Cake | You can breathe underwater, HP +140 | 0.1 | 35 | — | 10 (heal), 1800 (breathing) | |
| Mirelurk Egg | HP +9, Rads +12 | 1 | 0 | — | 10 | |
| Mirelurk Egg Omelet | HP +45, AP +50 | 0.1 | 30 | — | 10 | |
| Mirelurk Meat | HP +35, Rads +10 | 0.5 | 18 | — | 10 | |
| Mirelurk Queen Steak | HP +200, Endurance +2 | 1 | 130 | — | 10 (heal), 3600 (Endurance) | |
| Moldy Food | HP +5, Rads +6 | 0.5 | 1 | — | 10 | |
| Mole Rat Chunks | HP +50, Max AP +5 | 0.5 | 8 | — | 10 (heal), 900 (AP boost) | |
| Mole Rat Meat | HP +25, Rads +7 | 0.5 | 5 | — | 10 | |
| Mongrel Dog Meat | HP +20, Rads +8 | 0.5 | 8 | — | 10 | |
| Mutant Hound Chops | HP +60, Rads -50 | 0.5 | 12 | — | 10 | |
| Mutant Hound Meat | HP +30, Rads +8 | 0.5 | 8 | — | 10 | |
| Mutated Fern Flower | HP +10, Rads +1 | 0.1 | 4 | — | 10 | |
| Mutfruit | HP +10, Rads +2 | 0.1 | 8 | — | 10 | |
| Mutt Chops | HP +40 | 0.5 | 12 | — | 10 | |
| Noodle Cup | HP +40 | 0.5 | 20 | — | 10 | |
| Nuka Cherry | HP +50, Rads +5, AP +25 | 1 | 40 | — | 10 | |
| Nuka Cola | HP +20, Rads +5, AP +10 | 1 | 20 | — | 10 | |
| Nuka Cola Quantum | HP +400, Rads +5, AP +100 | 1 | 50 | 10% | 10 | |
| Perfectly Preserved Pie | HP +30 | 0.5 | 20 | — | 10 | |
| Pork n' Beans | HP +20, Rads +6 | 0.5 | 10 | — | 10 | |
| Potato Crisps | HP +10, Rads +7 | 0.1 | 7 | — | 10 | |
| Potted Meat | HP +40, Rads +12 | 1 | 25 | — | 10 | |
| Preserved InstaMash | HP +45 | 0.5 | 23 | — | 10 | |
| Pristine Deathclaw Egg | HP +45, Rads +7 | 0.1 | 69 | — | 10 | |
| Purified Water | HP +40 | 0.5 | 20 | — | 10 | |
| Queen Mirelurk Meat | HP +10, Rads +25, Endurance +1 | 0.5 | 22 | — | 10 (heal), 3600 (Endurance) | |

| NAME | EFFECT | WEIGHT | VALUE | ADDICTION % | DURATION (SEC) | CRAFTED |
|---|---|---|---|---|---|---|
| Radroach Meat | HP +15, Rads +11 | 0.1 | 3 | — | 10 | |
| Radscorpion Egg | HP +35, Rads +11 | 0.1 | 48 | — | 10 | |
| Radscorpion Egg Omelet | Cure all addictions, HP +75 | 0.1 | 65 | — | 10 | |
| Radscorpion Meat | HP +75, Rads +13 | 1 | 55 | — | 10 | |
| Radscorpion Steak | HP +150, Energy Resist +25 | 1 | 65 | — | 10 (heal), 3600 (Energy Resist) | |
| Radstag Meat | HP +60, Rads +13 | 1 | 50 | — | 10 | |
| Radstag Stew | HP +150, Energy Resist +30 | 1 | 60 | — | 10 (heal), 3600 (Energy Resist) | |
| Razorgrain | HP +10, Rads +2 | 0.1 | 5 | — | 10 | |
| Ribeye Steak | HP +110 | 1 | 40 | — | 10 | |
| Roasted Mirelurk Meat | HP +70, Max AP +10 | 0.5 | 40 | — | 10 (heal), 1800 (AP boost) | |
| Salisbury Steak | HP +30, Rads +9 | 0.5 | 20 | — | 10 | |
| Salisbury Steak | HP +60 | 0.5 | 25 | — | 10 | |
| Silt Bean | HP +10, Rads +3 | 0.1 | 6 | — | 10 | |
| Slocum's BuzzBites | HP -10, Max AP +25, Perception +1 | 0.5 | 0 | — | 3600 (AP boost), 3600 (Perception) | |
| Softshell Mirelurk Meat | HP +40, Rads +15 | 0.5 | 22 | — | 10 | |
| Squirrel Bits | HP +15, Rads +5 | 0.1 | 4 | — | 10 | |
| Squirrel Stew | +2% XP gain for 2 hours, HP +105 | 1 | 24 | — | 10 (heal), 7200 (XP boost) | |
| Squirrel on a Stick | HP +45 | 0.1 | 15 | — | 10 | |
| Stingwing Filet | HP +130, Perception +1 | 0.5 | 35 | — | 10 | |
| Stingwing Meat | HP +65, Rads +9 | 0.5 | 30 | — | 10 (heal), 3600 (Perception) | |
| Sugar Bombs | HP +15, Rads +7 | 0.5 | 11 | — | 10 | |
| Sugar Bombs | HP +30 | 0.5 | 14 | — | 10 | |
| Sweet Roll | HP +20, Rads +4 | 0.1 | 9 | — | 10 | |
| Synthetic Gorilla Meat | HP +30 | 1 | 28 | — | 10 | |
| Tarberry | HP +10, Rads +2 | 0.1 | 5 | — | 10 | |
| Tasty Deathclaw Omelet | Increases heal rate, HP +115, Max HP +50 | 0.1 | 100 | — | 10 (heal), 7200 (heal rate), 7200 (HP boost) | |
| Tato | HP +10, Rads 5 | 0.5 | 7 | — | 10 | |
| Tato Flower | HP +10, Rads +5 | 0.5 | 7 | — | 10 | |
| Thistle | HP +10, Rads +5 | 0.1 | 5 | — | 10 | |
| Vegetable Soup | +25 Rad Resist for 1 hour, HP +55 | 1 | 13 | — | 10 (heal), 3600 (Rad Resist) | |
| Wild Corn | HP +10, Rads +3 | 0.1 | 6 | — | 10 | |
| Wild Mutfruit | HP +10, Rads +2 | 0.1 | 8 | — | 10 | |
| Wild Razorgrain | HP +10, Rads +2 | 0.1 | 5 | — | 10 | |
| Wild Tarberry | HP +10, Rads +2 | 0.1 | 5 | — | 10 | |
| Yao Guai Meat | HP +80, Rads +6 | 1 | 85 | — | 10 | |
| Yao Guai Ribs | HP +165, Damage Resist +15 | 1 | 90 | — | 10 (heal), 3600 (Damage Resist) | |
| Yao Guai Roast | +10 melee damage, HP +210 | 1 | 110 | — | 10 (heal), 3600 (Melee boost) | |
| Yum Yum Deviled Eggs | HP +15, Rads +5 | 0.5 | 20 | — | 10 | |

## HELPFUL HINT
*from Vault Boy!*

**Did You Know?**

MOST CRAFTED MEALS CAN BE PREPARED WHENEVER YOU HAVE THE RIGHT MATERIALS AND ACCESS TO A COOKING STATION. HOWEVER, SOME DISHES CAN ONLY BE COOKED ONCE YOU'VE LEARNED SPECIAL RECIPES. RECIPES FOR DEATHCLAW WELLINGTON AND TASTY DEATHCLAW OMELET CAN BE EARNED DURING "THE DEVIL'S DUE" QUEST. THE RECIPE FOR SLOCUM'S BUZZBITES IS LOCATED IN SLOCUM'S JOE CORPORATE HQ.

# ALCOHOL

**GWINNETT PALE**  **RUM**

**WINE**  **WHISKEY**

Specifics vary by drink, but most alcoholic beverages boost your Strength and Charisma at the cost of Intelligence. These effects are temporary, but each serving of alcohol also carries a chance of addiction. Most alcoholic drinks must be found or purchased, but with a supply of Mutfruit, Nuka Cola, and whiskey, you can brew your own Dirty Wastelanders at any cooking station.

## ALCOHOL

| NAME | EFFECT | WEIGHT | VALUE | ADDICTION % | DURATION (SEC) | CRAFTED |
|---|---|---|---|---|---|---|
| Beer | Strength +1, Charisma +1, Intelligence -1 | 1 | 5 | 5% | 180 | 🖐 |
| Bobrov's Best Moonshine | Charisma +1, Strength +1, Intelligence -1, Max HP +25 | 0.5 | 30 | 15% | 300 | 🖐 |
| Bourbon | Endurance +1, Strength +1, Intelligence -1 | 1 | 7 | 5% | 240 | 🖐 |
| Dirty Wastelander | Intelligence -2, Strength +3, Charisma +1 | 0.5 | 10 | 10% | 300 | 🔨 |
| Gwinnett Ale | Strength +1, Charisma +1, Intelligence -1 | 1 | 5 | 5% | 180 | 🖐 |
| Gwinnett Brew | Strength +1, Charisma +1, Intelligence -1 | 1 | 5 | 5% | 180 | 🖐 |
| Gwinnett Lager | Strength +1, Charisma +1, Intelligence -1 | 1 | 5 | 5% | 180 | 🖐 |
| Gwinnett Pale | Strength +1, Charisma +1, Intelligence -1 | 1 | 5 | 5% | 180 | 🖐 |
| Gwinnett Pilsner | Strength +1, Charisma +1, Intelligence -1 | 1 | 5 | 5% | 180 | 🖐 |
| Gwinnett Stout | Strength +1, Charisma +1, Intelligence -1 | 1 | 5 | 5% | 180 | 🖐 |
| Ice Cold Beer | Strength +1, Charisma +1, Intelligence -1, AP +35 | 1 | 5 | 5% | 180 | 🖐 |
| Ice Cold Gwinnett Ale | Strength +1, Charisma +1, Intelligence -1, AP +35 | 1 | 5 | 5% | 180 | 🖐 |
| Ice Cold Gwinnett Brew | Strength +1, Charisma +1, Intelligence -1, AP +35 | 1 | 5 | 5% | 180 | 🖐 |
| Ice Cold Gwinnett Lager | Strength +1, Charisma +1, Intelligence -1, AP +35 | 1 | 5 | 5% | 180 | 🖐 |
| Ice Cold Gwinnett Pale | Strength +1, Charisma +1, Intelligence -1, AP +35 | 1 | 5 | 5% | 180 | 🖐 |
| Ice Cold Gwinnett Pilsner | Strength +1, Charisma +1, Intelligence -1, AP +35 | 1 | 5 | 5% | 180 | 🖐 |
| Ice Cold Gwinnett Stout | Strength +1, Charisma +1, Intelligence -1, AP +35 | 1 | 5 | 5% | 180 | 🖐 |
| Poisoned Wine | Strength +1, Intelligence -1, Max AP +15 | 1 | 50 | 5% | 180 | 🖐 |
| Rum | Agility +1, Strength +1, Intelligence -1 | 1 | 8 | 5% | 240 | 🖐 |
| Vodka | Max HP +25, Strength +1, Intelligence -1 | 1 | 5 | 5% | 240 | 🖐 |
| Whiskey | Strength +2, Intelligence -1 | 1 | 5 | 5% | 240 | 🖐 |
| Wine | Strength +1, Intelligence -1, Max AP +15 | 1 | 5 | 5% | 180 | 🖐 |

## VAULT-TEC RECOMMENDS

If you want a steady supply of ice-cold alcohol, retrieve Buddy from the Shamrock Taphouse basement. This modified Protectron can brew all of the Gwinnett recipes you manage to collect.

# CHEMS

**STIMPAK**  **RADAWAY**  **BUFFOUT**  **DADDY-O**

Medicinal items like stimpaks, RadAway, and Addictol can keep you safe and healthy. Performance-enhancing chems (most of which are addictive) grant a variety of temporary bonuses. You'll find chems throughout the Commonwealth, but you can make many of these useful items at chemistry stations.

## CHEMS

| NAME | EFFECT | WEIGHT | VALUE | ADDICTION % | DURATION (SEC) | CRAFTED |
|---|---|---|---|---|---|---|
| Addictol | Cures all addictions. | 0.1 | 125 | — | — | 🖐 |
| Berry Mentats | Highlights living targets. | 0.1 | 60 | 10% | 480 | 🔨 |
| Buffjet | Slows time for 15 seconds. Strength +3, Endurance +3, Max HP +65, Max AP +35 | 0.1 | 75 | 15% | 15 | 🔨 |
| Buffout | Strength +2, Endurance +2, Max HP +50 | 0.1 | 45 | 10% | 300 | 🖐 |
| Bufftats | Strength +3, Endurance +3, Max HP +65, Perception +3 | 0.1 | 75 | 15% | 480 | 🔨 |
| Calmex | x2 sneak attack multiplier, Perception +3, Agility +3 | 0.1 | 100 | 15% | 480 | 🔨 |
| Curie's Healthpak | HP +35, Rads -300 | 0.5 | 90 | — | — | 🖐 |
| Daddy-O | Intelligence +3, Perception +3, Charisma -2 | 0.1 | 50 | 15% | 600 | 🖐 |
| Day Tripper | Luck +3, Charisma +3, Strength -2 | 0.1 | 40 | 15% | 300 | 🔨 |
| Fury | Increases melee damage by 50%. | 0.1 | 70 | 15% | 480 | 🔨 |

| NAME | EFFECT | WEIGHT | VALUE | ADDICTION % | DURATION (SEC) | CRAFTED |
|------|--------|--------|-------|-------------|----------------|---------|
| Glowing Blood Pack | HP +40%, Rad Resist +75 | 0.1 | 30 | — | 5 (heal), 600 (Rad Resist) | |
| Grape Mentats | Buy for 10% lower, sell for 10% higher; Charisma +5 | 0.1 | 60 | 10% | 480 | |
| Irradiated Blood | HP +50, Rads +20 | 0.3 | 50 | — | 5 | |
| Jet | Slows time for 10 seconds. | 0.1 | 50 | 10% | 10 | |
| Jet Fuel | Increased AP recovery rate. | 0.1 | 60 | 15% | 480 | |
| Med-X | Damage Resist +25 | 0.1 | 50 | 10% | 300 | |
| Mentats | Intelligence +2, Perception +2 | 0.1 | 50 | 10% | 300 | |
| Mysterious Serum | Damage Resist +50, Rads +36,000 | 0.1 | 25 | — | 3600 | |
| Orange Mentats | +10% V.A.T.S. accuracy. | 0.1 | 60 | 10% | 480 | |
| Overdrive | +25% Critical Chance, Damage +25% | 0.1 | 55 | 15% | 480 | |
| Psycho | Damage +25%, Damage Resist +25 | 0.1 | 50 | 10% | 300 | |
| Psychobuff | Damage +25%, Strength +3, Endurance +3, Max HP +65 | 0.1 | 70 | 15% | 480 | |
| Psycho Jet | Slows time for 15 seconds, Damage +25%, Damage Resist +35, Max AP +35 | 0.1 | 70 | 15% | 480 | |
| Psychotats | Damage +25%, Damage Resist +15, Perception +3 | 0.1 | 70 | 15% | 480 | |
| RadAway | Rads -300 | 0.1 | 80 | — | 5 | |
| Rad-X | Rad Resist +100 | 0.1 | 40 | — | 180 | |
| Refreshing Beverage | Cures all addictions, HP +500, Rads -1000 | 0.5 | 110 | — | — | |
| Skeeto Spit | Max HP +25 | 0.1 | 40 | — | 1200 | |
| Stimpak | HP +30% | 0 | 48 | — | 5 | |
| Ultra Jet | Slows time for 15 seconds, Max AP +100 | 0.1 | 67 | 15% | 15 | |
| Vault 81 Cure | HP +50% | 0.3 | 400 | — | 5 | |
| X-111 Compound | Rads -600 | 0.3 | 40 | — | — | |
| X-Cell | Strength +2, Perception +2, Endurance +2, Charisma +2, Intelligence +2, Agility +2, Luck +2 | 0.1 | 60 | 35% | 120 | |

# SYRINGER AMMO

The Syringer rifle can give you an edge in combat—but only when you have a good supply of ammunition. Use chemistry stations to craft these ballistic injectables.

## SYRINGER AMMO

| NAME | EFFECT | WEIGHT | VALUE | ADDICTION % | DURATION (SEC) | CRAFTED |
|------|--------|--------|-------|-------------|----------------|---------|
| Berserk Syringe | Chance to frenzy target for 2 minutes. | 0.1 | 50 | — | 120 | |
| Bleed Out Syringe | Does 30 points of damage over 10 seconds to target. | 0.1 | 17 | — | 10 | |
| Bloatfly Larva | Chance on death for target to spawn a Bloatfly. | 0.1 | 10 | — | — | |
| Endangerol Syringe | Reduces target's Damage Resistance by 25% for 2 minutes. | 0.1 | 60 | — | 120 | |
| Lock Joint Syringe | Chance to paralyze target for 10 seconds. | 0.1 | 40 | — | 10 | |
| Mind Cloud Syringe | Target believes you have vanished and has a reduced chance to detect you for 30 seconds. | 0.1 | 73 | — | 30 | |
| Pax Syringe | Chance to make the target nonviolent for 30 seconds. | 0.1 | 39 | — | 30 | |
| Radscorpion Venom Syringe | Does 40 points of damage over 10 seconds to target. | 0.1 | 65 | — | 10 | |
| Yellow Belly Syringe | Chance on hit to cause target to flee for 30 seconds. | 0.1 | 55 | — | 30 | |

# STEALTH BOYS

The Stealth Boy is a handy (and rare) high-tech device that makes you nearly invisible with the flip of a switch. Railroad Stealth Boys produce the same effect with a longer duration, but these special devices are only made available to trusted members of the Railroad.

## STEALTH BOYS

| NAME | EFFECTS | WEIGHT | VALUE | ADDICTION % | CRAFTED |
|------|---------|--------|-------|-------------|---------|
| Railroad Stealth Boy | Generates a stealth field for 40 seconds. | 1 | 150 | — | |
| Stealth Boy | Generates a stealth field for 30 seconds. | 1 | 100 | — | |

**HELPFUL HINT** from *Vault Boy!*  **Did You Know?**

COMPLETE THE "MEMORY INTERRUPTED" QUEST TO GAIN ACCESS TO THE RAILROAD STEALTH BOY.

# MISCELLANEOUS

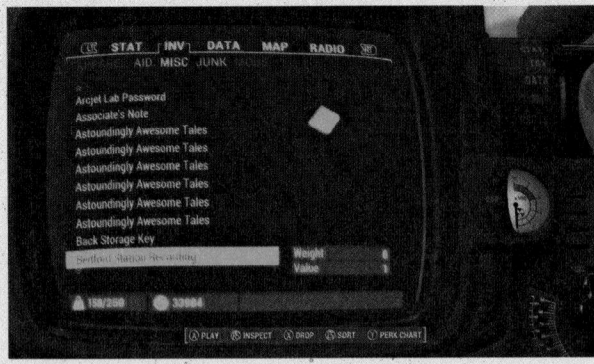

From bobby pins to posted notes, you're sure to amass quite a collection of miscellaneous items during your travels. Some of these items unlock doors and terminals, while others provide useful information. Items like Bobbleheads and magazines grant powerful bonuses, while other items don't serve any practical purpose. What should you keep? What's safe to sell? What's an adventurer to do?

Fret not! Most of the items that appear in your Pip-Boy's Misc tab are weightless. No matter how many Holotapes, notes, and access cards you carry, they're not likely to slow you down. Items that do add weight to your load are scarce enough that a quick scroll through the list makes it easy to identify curios that might be worth storing or selling. Of course, for those who like to keep a tidy inventory, it can be helpful to know exactly what some of these items are used for.

# UTILITY ITEMS

## BOBBY PINS

 Is a locked safe or door keeping you from unknown treasures? A few bobby pins might be just what you need. It takes a gentle touch to pick a lock without breaking a bobby pin, and complicated locks can only be attempted by those who've invested in various ranks of the Locksmith perk. Still, with a bit of patience and a good supply of bobby pins, even a novice can bypass simple locks.

### BOBBY PINS

| NAME | WEIGHT | VALUE |
|------|--------|-------|
| Bobby Pin | 0 | 1 |

## BOTTLECAPS

 Bottlecaps are the standard currency of the Commonwealth, so you can trade your collected Caps for a wide variety of goods and services. You'll find Caps stashed in containers or hidden in the pockets of defeated enemies. Of course, you can always earn extra Caps by completing quests and selling unwanted goods.

## VAULT-TEC LUNCHBOXES

 You can sell Vault-Tec Lunchboxes for extra Caps, but these rare items can also be used to craft powerful Bottlecap mines at chemistry stations. Making a Bottlecap mine takes a variety of components and some investment in the Demolition Expert perk, but these handmade explosives pack a serious wallop.

## HOLOTAPE GAMES

Life in the Commonwealth can be incredibly stressful—why not unwind with a Holotape game? These fun and challenging diversions can be played on any terminal, but you can also pop them into your Pip-Boy anytime you need a break. Most Holotape games are bundled with RobCo FUN! magazines, but the Red Menace can be found in a recreational terminal within Vault 111.

### HOLOTAPE GAMES

| NAME | WEIGHT | VALUE |
|------|--------|-------|
| Atomic Command | 0 | 300 |
| Grognak and the Ruby Ruins | 0 | 300 |
| Pipfall | 0 | 300 |
| Red Menace | 0 | 300 |
| Zeta Invaders | 0 | 300 |

# PERKS AND BONUSES

## BOBBLEHEADS

Each Bobblehead you collect grants a permanent perk. You're free to sell these valuable figurines, but proud collectors should consider displaying them on custom-made Bobblehead stands.

### BOBBLEHEADS

| BOBBLEHEAD | EFFECT | WEIGHT | VALUE |
|---|---|---|---|
| Agility | Your Agility has been permanently increased by 1. | 0 | 300 |
| Barter | Prices are permanently 5% better. | 0 | 300 |
| Big Guns | Permanently gain +25% critical damage with heavy weapons. | 0 | 300 |
| Charisma | Your Charisma has been permanently increased by 1. | 0 | 300 |
| Endurance | Your Endurance has been permanently increased by 1. | 0 | 300 |
| Energy Weapons | Permanently gain +25% critical damage with energy weapons. | 0 | 300 |
| Explosive | Permanently gain +15% damage with explosives. | 0 | 300 |
| Intelligence | Your Intelligence has been permanently increased by 1. | 0 | 300 |
| Lockpicking | Lockpicking is permanently easier. | 0 | 300 |
| Luck | Your Luck has been permanently increased by 1. | 0 | 300 |
| Medicine | Stimpaks permanently heal 10% more damage. | 0 | 300 |

| BOBBLEHEAD | EFFECT | WEIGHT | VALUE |
|---|---|---|---|
| Melee | Permanently gain +25% critical damage with melee weapons. | 0 | 300 |
| Perception | Your Perception has been permanently increased by 1. | 0 | 300 |
| Repair | Fusion Cores permanently last 10% longer. | 0 | 300 |
| Science | Get one extra guess when hacking terminals. | 0 | 300 |
| Small Guns | Permanently gain +25% critical damage with ballistic guns. | 0 | 300 |
| Sneak | You are permanently 10% harder to detect. | 0 | 300 |
| Speech | All vendors permanently have 100 more Caps for bartering. | 0 | 300 |
| Strength | Your Strength has been permanently increased by 1. | 0 | 300 |
| Unarmed | Permanently gain +25% critical damage with unarmed attacks. | 0 | 300 |

## MAGAZINES

You'll find informative magazines scattered across the Commonwealth. Each time you collect one of these items, you're rewarded with a permanent perk. When you're done with a magazine, you're free to display it on a magazine rack or sell it for some extra Caps.

INV

MISC.

### MAGAZINES

| NAME | EFFECT | WEIGHT | VALUE |
|---|---|---|---|
| Astoundingly Awesome Tales | Regenerate 1 point of health per minute. | 0 | 100 |
| Astoundingly Awesome Tales | Do +5% damage with scoped weapons. | 0 | 100 |
| Astoundingly Awesome Tales | Take 5% less damage from robots. | 0 | 100 |
| Astoundingly Awesome Tales | Do +5% damage with the Alien Blaster. | 0 | 100 |
| Astoundingly Awesome Tales | Gain +5 Poison Resistance. | 0 | 100 |
| Astoundingly Awesome Tales | Do +5% damage with against Mirelurks. | 0 | 100 |
| Astoundingly Awesome Tales | Do +5% damage at night. | 0 | 100 |
| Astoundingly Awesome Tales | Gain +5 Action Points. | 0 | 100 |
| Astoundingly Awesome Tales | Do +5 damage with the Cryolator. | 0 | 100 |
| Astoundingly Awesome Tales | Gain +5 Radiation Resistance. | 0 | 100 |
| Astoundingly Awesome Tales | RadAway heals +5% radiation damage. | 0 | 100 |
| Astoundingly Awesome Tales | Your canine companion permanently takes 10% less damage. | 0 | 100 |
| Astoundingly Awesome Tales | Do +5% damage against Ghouls. | 0 | 100 |
| Astoundingly Awesome Tales | Do +5% damage against Super Mutants. | 0 | 100 |
| Grognak the Barbarian (10 issues) | Critical Hits with unarmed and melee attacks permanently do +5% damage (per magazine found, up to 10 magazines, or +50%). | 0 | 100 |

| NAME | EFFECT | WEIGHT | VALUE |
|---|---|---|---|
| Guns and Bullets (10 issues) | Ballistic weapons do +5% critical damage (per magazine found, up to 10 magazines, or +50%). | 0 | 100 |
| Hot Rodder (3 issues) | Permanently unlock a new custom paint job for your Power Armor (1 paint job per magazine found, up to 3 magazines). | 0 | 100 |
| La Coiffe (2 issues) | Permanently unlock a new unique hairstyle (1 hairstyle per magazine found, up to two magazines). | 0 | 100 |
| Life & Love | Companions gain +10 health. | 0 | 100 |
| Life & Love | Companions do +5% damage. | 0 | 100 |
| Life & Love | Companions have +10 carry weight. | 0 | 100 |
| Life & Love | Gain +25% XP from persuading women. | 0 | 100 |
| Life & Love | Gain +1 Luck from alcohol when adventuring with a companion. | 0 | 100 |
| Life & Love | Companions gain +5 Damage Resistance and Energy Resistance. | 0 | 100 |
| Life & Love | Gain +25% XP from persuading men. | 0 | 100 |
| Life & Love | Gain +5% XP while adventuring with a companion. | 0 | 100 |
| Life & Love | Robot companions permanently inflict +5% damage. | 0 | 100 |
| Massachusetts Surgical Journal (9 issues) | Permanently inflict +2% limb damage. (per magazine found, up to 9 magazines, or +18%). | 0 | 100 |
| Picket Fences | You are now able to build picket fencing at settlement workshops. | 0 | 100 |
| Picket Fences | You are now able to build a high tech light at settlement workshops. | 0 | 100 |

| NAME | EFFECT | WEIGHT | VALUE |
|---|---|---|---|
| Picket Fences | You are now able to build new statues at settlement workshops. | 0 | 100 |
| Picket Fences | You are now able to build potted plants at settlement workshops. | 0 | 100 |
| Picket Fences | You are now able to build patio furniture at settlement workshops. | 0 | 100 |
| RobCo FUN! | Includes the Atomic Command holotape game. | 0 | 100 |
| RobCo FUN! | Includes the Grognak the Barbarian holotape game. | 0 | 100 |
| RobCo FUN! | Includes the Pipfall holotape game. | 0 | 100 |
| RobCo FUN! | Includes the Zeta Invaders holotape game. | 0 | 100 |
| Taboo Tattoos (5 issues) | Permanently unlock a new unique facial tattoo. | 0 | 100 |
| Tales of a Junktown Jerky Vendor (8 issues) | Permanently gain better prices when buying from a vendor (per magazine found, up to eight magazines). | 0 | 100 |
| Tesla Science (9 issues) | Energy Weapons permanently inflict +5% critical damage (per magazine found, up to 9 magazines, or +45%). | 0 | 100 |
| Total Hack | Includes the Protectron hacking source code. | 0 | 100 |
| Total Hack | Includes the spotlight hacking source code. | 0 | 100 |
| Total Hack | Includes the turret hacking source code. | 0 | 100 |

| NAME | EFFECT | WEIGHT | VALUE |
|---|---|---|---|
| Tumblers Today (5 issues) | Lockpicking is permanently easier (per magazine found, up to five magazines). | 0 | 100 |
| U.S. Covert Operations Manual (10 issues) | Permanently more difficult to detect while sneaking (per magazine found, up to 10 magazines). | 0 | 100 |
| Unstoppables (5 issues) | Permanently gain +1% chance of avoiding all damage from an attack (per magazine found, up to 5 magazines, or +5%). | 0 | 100 |
| Wasteland Survival Guide | Heal 50% more from fruits and vegetables. | 0 | 100 |
| Wasteland Survival Guide | Take 5% less damage from insects. | 0 | 100 |
| Wasteland Survival Guide | Heal +50% from irradiated packaged food and drink. | 0 | 100 |
| Wasteland Survival Guide | Permanently unlock new decoration items in workshop settlements. | 0 | 100 |
| Wasteland Survival Guide | Diamond City is now permanently marked on your map. | 0 | 100 |
| Wasteland Survival Guide | +10% discount from food and drink vendors. | 0 | 100 |
| Wasteland Survival Guide | Swim +25% faster. | 0 | 100 |
| Wasteland Survival Guide | Take 5% less damage from melee attacks. | 0 | 100 |
| Wasteland Survival Guide | Collect extra meat from animal kills. | 0 | 100 |

## TIP

YOU'RE S.P.E.C.I.A.L.!

This children's book is found in your old home in Sanctuary Hills. When you collect it, you gain one rank to a S.P.E.C.I.A.L. stat of your choosing. You're S.P.E.C.I.A.L.! is similar to collectible magazines, but it can't be displayed on a magazine rack and it isn't worth any Caps.

## RECIPES

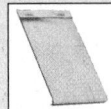

**SLOCUM'S BUZZBITES RECIPE**
**GWINNETT BREW RECIPE**

Whether they're written on paper or recorded on Holotapes, recipes grant access to previously unknown items. Slocum's BuzzBite recipe and Wellingham's recipe unlock new options at cooking stations as soon as you collect them. Gwinnett recipes can be given to Buddy to unlock a variety of alcoholic beverages.

**FEATURED RECIPES**

| NAME | WEIGHT | VALUE |
|---|---|---|
| Gwinnett Brew Recipe | 0 | 1 |
| Gwinnett Lager Recipe | 0 | 1 |
| Gwinnett Pils Recipe | 0 | 1 |
| Gwinnett Stout Recipe | 0 | 1 |
| Slocum's BuzzBites Recipe | 0 | 0 |
| Wellingham's Recipe | 0 | 0 |

# REDEEMABLES

## OVERDUE BOOKS

| NAME | WEIGHT | VALUE |
|---|---|---|
| Overdue Book | 0.5 | 2 |

There are overdue books scattered all across the Commonwealth. Deposit these items into book return terminals to receive book return tokens.

| LOCATION | NO. OF OVERDUE BOOKS |
|---|---|
| East Boston Preparatory School | 9 |
| Shaw High School | 8 |
| Boston Public Library | 6 |
| Suffolk County Charter School | 5 |
| Collegiate Administration Building | 4 |
| Sandy Coves Convalescence Home | 4 |

## BOOK RETURN TOKENS

You can exchange collected book return tokens for useful prizes at book return terminals. The terminal within the Boston Public Library even contains a Massachusetts Surgical Journal.

| NAME | WEIGHT | VALUE |
|---|---|---|
| Book Return Token | 0 | 1 |

# ACCESS AND INFORMATION

## HOLOTAPES

Some Holotapes contain passwords, protocols, or executable files, but many simply contain personal logs or long-forgotten messages. Load a Holotape into your Pip-Boy (or any terminal) to find out what secrets it holds. Most Holotapes are weightless and have little to no value to traders.

## KEYS AND PASSWORDS

Sometimes the only way to open a door is with a key. Sometimes the only way to access a terminal is with the right password. Collect keys and access cards whenever you find them, and check notes, terminals, and Holotapes for recorded passwords. Most of these items are weightless, and it's often impossible to sell them.

## LETTERS AND NOTES

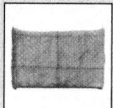

Some letters and notes provide valuable information, but many just offer insight into the lives of strangers. Of course, there's only one way to find out—pick it up and have a look!

# QUEST ITEMS

**EXPLOSIVE CHARGE**  **COURSER CHIP**  **HAPTIC DRIVE**

Why are you carrying a cybernetic brain augmenter? Why can't you sell a can of green paint? During your time in the Commonwealth, you're likely to collect dozens of items that are both bizarre and extremely important. Although many quests involve common items, most quest-specific items can only be removed from your inventory once you've completed the related objective.

# KNICKKNACKS

## MISCELLANEOUS TOYS

**BUTTERCUP TOY**  **SENTRY BOT MODEL**  **ROBOT PARTS MODEL**

Although many toys can be scrapped for useful components, there are a few toys that can't be salvaged.

Use these miscellaneous toys to decorate your settlements or sell them for some extra Caps. Robot models often appear in Vault-Tec Lunchboxes, but they can also be built from any robot model kits you're lucky enough to find. With model kits, you can also build some less valuable (but very interesting) custom robot parts models.

### FEATURED TOYS

| NAME | WEIGHT | VALUE |
|---|---|---|
| Buttercup Toy | 2 | 150 |
| Eyebot Model | 0 | 100 |
| Mr. Gutsy Model | 0 | 100 |
| Mr. Handy Model | 0 | 100 |
| Protectron Model | 0 | 100 |
| Robot Parts Model | 0 | 0 |
| Sentry Bot Model | 0 | 100 |

### ROBOT MODEL KIT LOCATIONS

| NAME | LOCATION | NOTES |
|---|---|---|
| Eyebot Model Kit | [6.12] Fallons Department Store | In the Level 2 Employees Only storage room (Novice) on the shelves near the Protectron and terminal. |
| Mr. Gutsy Model Kit | [3.14] Boston Mayoral Shelter | In the blue wallpapered bedroom, east of the stairs down from the bar and laundry room. |
| Mr. Handy Model Kit | [4.04] Hugo's Hole | On the metal shelf near the Hazmat Suit and Holotape. |
| Robot Model Kit Parts | [5.05] Lake Cochituate | Northeast shore, in the ramshackle settler shacks (next to the steamer trunk). |
| Robot Model Kit Parts | [4.02] Mahkra Fishpacking | Inside the small concrete exterior maintenance building (Advanced), in the metal storage hut. |
| Robot Model Kit Parts | [5.01] Poseidon Reservoir | Up the broken pipe between the plant and warehouse (south), to the Railroad dead drop. |
| Protectron Model Kit | [4.16] Revere Beach Station | In the locked garage (accessed via the fallen tree), by the power armor station. |
| SentryBot Model Kit | [5.30] O'Neill Family Manufacturing | Accessed via the concrete hole: In the buried room on the metal table by the wall terminal. |

## CLUTTER

**BURNT FASHION MAGAZINE**  **FOLDER**  **STINGWING BARB**

### MISCELLANEOUS CLUTTER

| NAME | WEIGHT | VALUE |
|---|---|---|
| Burnt Book | 1 | 0 |
| Burnt Fashion Magazine | 0 | 1 |
| Burnt Grognak Comic | 0 | 1 |
| Burnt Lifestyle Magazine | 0 | 1 |
| Burnt Manta-Man Comic | 0 | 1 |
| Burnt Textbook | 1 | 0 |
| Burnt Trade Magazine | 0 | 1 |
| Burnt Unstoppables Comic | 0 | 1 |
| Folder | 0 | 1 |
| Napkin | 0 | 1 |
| Ruined Book | 0 | 0 |
| Ruined History Book | 0 | 0 |
| Stingwing Barb | 0.5 | 6 |
| Subway Token | 0 | 1 |

Beauty is in the eye of the beholder. If you're looking to add a wasteland aesthetic to your living space, these items should certainly get the job done. But if your inventory could benefit from a little spring cleaning, keep an eye out for clutter like Stingwing barbs, folders, and burnt books. When sold in bulk, some of these items can yield a fair amount of Caps. Some only serve to weigh you down.

# JUNK

You'll find junk on defeated enemies, stashed in containers, and scattered around virtually every location you explore. You can, of course, sell these bits and bobs for extra Caps, but a junk item's true value lies in the components it yields. Battered clipboards are made from springs and wood; desk fans contain gears, screws, and steel; an old fuse can be salvaged for copper and glass. With the right junk items, you can build everything from simple floor mats to advanced Power Armor mods.

Whenever you build an item, the required components are automatically salvaged from the junk items that are currently in your inventory or stored within the related crafting station. If a settlement is under control, all of its workstations are linked to its workshop. This makes managing your collected junk items incredibly easy—when you attempt to craft an object, you'll instantly see which components can be salvaged from the available junk items.

When a lack of materials is holding up construction, use your Pip-Boy's Junk tab to mark your desperately needed components. Cycle the display to "Component View" to see all of the components offered by the junk items that are currently in your inventory. Highlight the desired component and select "Tag for Search." From that point on, your Pip-Boy automatically indicates if a targeted junk item contains the tagged component. Repeat the process at any time to add or remove tracked components from your list.

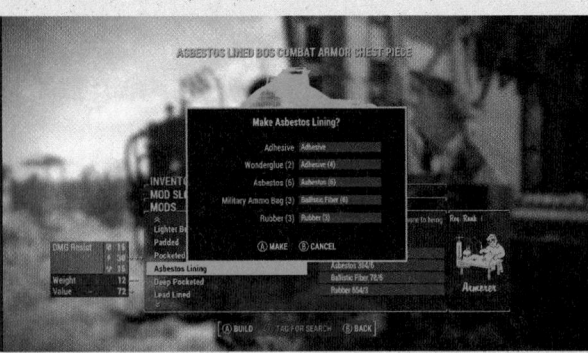

### HELPFUL HINT from *Vault Boy!* Did You Know?

WHEN A JUNK ITEM IS SALVAGED, ONLY THE REQUIRED COMPONENTS ARE CONSUMED. AFTER CONSTRUCTION, ANY UNUSED COMPONENTS ARE AUTOMATICALLY RETURNED TO STORAGE.

## VAULT-TEC RECOMMENDS

Tag components like aluminum, oil, adhesive fiberglass, and screws as early as possible. If you plan to modify your gear, you'll need to collect a good supply of these uncommon building materials.

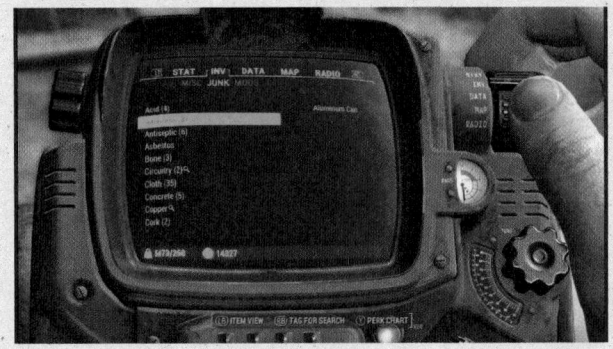

# BASE COMPONENTS

| COMPONENT | RARITY | DESCRIPTION |
|---|---|---|
| ACID | Rare | Acid is primarily used to craft chems, explosives, and cutting fluid at chemistry stations. |
| ADHESIVE | Special | This essential component is used in a wide variety of mods, explosives, and workshop items. Even with the Scrapper perk, this component can never be salvaged from weapons or armor. However, maintaining a good supply of adhesive makes it much easier to upgrade your gear and expand your settlements. |
| ALUMINUM | Uncommon | Aluminum is used in nearly every type of crafting, but it's an essential component of most complicated devices. If you plan on crafting ballistic weapon mods, Power Armor mods, explosives, turrets, and generators, you'll need to grab all the aluminum you can find. |
| ANTISEPTIC | Rare | Antiseptic is most often used to craft medicinal mods and chems. |
| ASBESTOS | Rare | Asbestos is most often used to boost an item's Energy Resistance, but it's needed for a variety of mods and chems. |

| COMPONENT | RARITY | DESCRIPTION |
|---|---|---|
| BALLISTIC FIBER | Rare | Ballistic fiber is an essential component of many armor mods—especially the ballistic weave mods used to reinforce many lightweight apparel items. |
| BONE | Common | Bone is needed to craft specialty items like Raider armor mods and cutting fluid. |
| CERAMIC | Common | Ceramic is used to craft some mods and workshop items, but it's an important part of most power-related items. You'll need ceramic to build radio recruitment beacons, smaller generators, and nearly all switches. |
| CIRCUITRY | Rare | Circuitry is used in most high-tech devices. Many advanced mods, turrets, and electronic devices require some amount of circuitry. You'll even find this component listed in recipes for some explosives and chems. |
| CLOTH | Common | Cloth is required for various mods and workshop items, but it's particularly important for armor modification and furniture production. |
| CONCRETE | Common | Concrete is primarily used to build shack foundations and water pumps. |
| COPPER | Uncommon | Copper is an important part of most electronic devices. Generators, switches, lights, and advanced mods all tend to use some amount of copper. But this component also has a variety of low-tech applications. |
| CORK | Uncommon | Cork is primarily used for weight-reducing armor mods. |
| CRYSTAL | Rare | Crystal is an important part of most laser-based devices. Laser tripwires, heavy laser turrets, and many laser gun mods require a good supply of crystal. It's also needed for advanced scopes and other high-tech items. |
| FERTILIZER | Uncommon | Fertilizer is primarily used to craft chems and explosives at chemistry stations. |
| FIBER-OPTICS | Rare | Fiber-optics are required to craft a variety of high-tech mods and devices. These components are particularly important to laser-based weapons and switches, but fiber-optics are used in the creation and modification of several items. |
| FIBERGLASS | Uncommon | Both lightweight and durable, fiberglass is used in a variety of weapon, armor, and Power Armor mods. Energy weapon mods, in particular, tend to require a good amount of fiberglass. This versatile component is also required to craft a small selection of explosives and workshop items. |
| GEAR | Uncommon | Gears are required for a variety of applications. From simple ceiling fans to massive generators, nearly any device that involves moving parts includes some amount of gears. These low-tech components are particularly important in turret production and gun modification, so restock your supply as often as possible. |
| GLASS | Uncommon | Glass is used in several recipes, but it's particularly important when crafting lights, scopes, syringes, and laser-based weapon mods. |
| GOLD | Rare | Gold is needed for a variety of high-tech mods and devices. It's particularly important for laser weapon enthusiasts, but any craftsman would do well to keep a supply of gold on hand. |
| LEAD | Uncommon | Most lead applications involve boosting the Radiation Resistance offered by a piece of apparel, but any item meant to reflect or contain radiation is likely to require some amount of lead. |
| LEATHER | Common | Leather has a few different uses, but it's most often used to craft mods at armor workbenches. |
| NUCLEAR MATERIAL | Rare | Nuclear material is required to craft a variety of mods, explosives, and workshop items. Most of the devices that use nuclear materials are fairly advanced, but this rare component is also needed to craft simple weapon sights. |
| OIL | Special | Oil is essential to most mechanical devices like gun mods, turrets, and water purifiers, but it's also used in a variety of armor mods and explosives. |

| COMPONENT | | RARITY | DESCRIPTION |
|---|---|---|---|
| | PLASTIC | Common | Plastic is involved in almost every type of crafting, but it's most commonly needed for building furniture or modifying armor and energy weapons. |
| | RUBBER | Common | The unique properties of rubber make it an essential part of many items. It serves as insulation for mechanical devices like generators and pylons, it adds flexibility to weapons and armor, and it's an important component of various furniture pieces and decorative items. |
| | SCREW | Uncommon | Whether you're constructing mechanical devices or reinforcing armor, you'll find a lot of uses for this component. Screws aren't as rare as some materials, but if you plan on modifying your gear, building turrets, or taking advantage of the workshop's most effective machines, you'll want to salvage as many screws as possible. |
| | SILVER | Rare | Silver is primarily used for modifying weapons. It's required for a wide variety of energy weapon mods, but it's also a featured component of most sights and scopes. |
| | SPRING | Uncommon | Springs are used in a variety of gear mods and mechanical devices. Whether you're building a simple pressure plate, extending the ammo capacity of your favorite gun, or customizing a suit of Power Armor, you'll find plenty of projects that require springs. |
| | STEEL | Common | Steel is one of the most essential building materials you'll find—luckily, it's also one of the most common. In addition to basic construction, steel is needed for a large variety of mods. |
| | WOOD | Common | Wood is most often used in basic construction. Structures, furniture, and decorative items all tend to require large amounts of wood. Most settlements contain enough trees to get you started, but wood-based junk items can help you better meet the needs of your settlers. |

# JUNK ITEMS

Over time, you'll develop an eye for junk you find particularly useful, but the Commonwealth is absolutely packed with discarded treasures. Every junk item has its uses, but some are far more valuable than you might expect.

## JUNK ITEMS

| NAME | WEIGHT | VALUE | SALVAGEABLE COMPONENTS |
|---|---|---|---|
| 40 lb Barbell | 40 | 7 | Lead (10) |
| 80 lb Barbell | 80 | 15 | Lead (20) |
| 20 lb Dumbbell | 20 | 5 | Lead (9) |
| 160 lb Dumbbell | 160 | 30 | Lead (40) |
| 80 lb Curlbar | 80 | 15 | Lead (20) |
| 10 lb Weight | 10 | 2 | Lead (3) |
| 25 lb Weight | 25 | 4 | Lead (50) |
| 5 lb Weight | 5 | 1 | Lead (2) |
| Abraxo Cleaner | 1 | 5 | Acid (1), Antiseptic (2), Fiberglass (1) |
| Abraxo Cleaner Industrial Grade | 1 | 15 | Acid (2), Antiseptic (4), Fiberglass (2) |
| Acid | 0.1 | 2 | Acid (1) |
| Adhesive | 0.1 | 8 | Adhesive (1) |
| Adjustable Wrench | 1 | 1 | Gear (1), Steel (2) |
| Alarm Clock | 1 | 10 | Aluminum (2), Glass (1), Spring (1), Nuclear Material (1) |
| Aluminum | 0.1 | 3 | Aluminum (1) |
| Aluminum Can | 0.1 | 1 | Aluminum (2) |
| Aluminum Canister | 3 | 12 | Aluminum (2), Fiberglass (2), Oil (1) |
| Aluminum Oil Can | 0.5 | 12 | Oil (2), Steel (1) |
| Aluminum Tray | 0.5 | 1 | Steel (1) |
| Amontillado Bottle | 1 | 2 | Glass (4) |
| Anchorage Veteran's Flag | 3 | 20 | Wood (2), Cloth (4) |
| Annika's Locket | 0.1 | 24 | Silver (2) |
| Antifreeze Bottle | 2 | 4 | Acid (2), Plastic (2) |
| Antique Globe | 3 | 3 | Cork (2), Plastic (2), Screw (1) |
| Antique Pocket Watch | 0.5 | 111 | Gear (2), Silver (2), Spring (1) |
| Antique Silver Locket | 0.1 | 60 | Silver (2) |
| Antique Table Knife | 0.1 | 3 | Steel (1) |
| Antiseptic | 0.1 | 3 | Antiseptic (1) |
| Applicator | 0.5 | 12 | Aluminum (1), Fiber-Optics (1) |
| Asbestos | 0.1 | 6 | Asbestos (1) |

| NAME | WEIGHT | VALUE | SALVAGEABLE COMPONENTS |
|---|---|---|---|
| Ashtray | 0.5 | 1 | Ceramic (1) |
| Assaultron Circuit Board | 2 | 100 | Circuitry (5), Silver (2) |
| Baby Bottle | 0.5 | 1 | Glass (2), Rubber (1) |
| Baby Rattle | 0.5 | 2 | Plastic (2) |
| Bag of Cement | 8 | 15 | Concrete (5) |
| Bag of Fertilizer | 4 | 25 | Acid (1), Fertilizer (4) |
| Ballistic Fiber | 0.1 | 5 | Ballistic Fiber (1) |
| Ball-Peen Hammer | 1.5 | 3 | Wood (1), Steel (2) |
| Bandage Scissors | 0.25 | 3 | Steel (1) |
| Baseball | 0.5 | 4 | Cork (2), Leather (1) |
| Baseball Base | 3 | 4 | Plastic (2), Cloth (2) |
| Baseball Glove | 1 | 4 | Leather (3) |
| Basketball | 1 | 2 | Rubber (3) |
| Battered Clipboard | 0.2 | 1 | Spring (1), Wood (1) |
| Beaker | 0.5 | 1 | Glass (1) |
| Beaker Stand | 0.5 | 4 | Copper (1) |
| Beer Bottle | 0.5 | 2 | Glass (2) |
| Biometric Scanner | 3 | 20 | Fiber-Optics (1), Asbestos (1), Nuclear Material (2) |
| Blacksmith Hammer | 3 | 3 | Wood (1), Steel (2) |
| Blast Radius Board Game | 1 | 21 | Wood (2), Nuclear Material (1) |
| Bloatfly Gland | 0.5 | 2 | Acid (2) |
| Bloodbug Proboscis | 0.2 | 10 | Acid (1) |
| Blood Can | 5 | 10 | Oil (2), Steel (2) |
| Blood Sac | 0.5 | 4 | Antiseptic (2), Fiberglass (1) |
| Blowtorch | 3 | 15 | Steel (2), Oil (1) |
| Blue Paint | 5 | 10 | Oil (2), Steel (2) |
| Blue Table Lamp | 3 | 5 | Copper (1), Glass (2) |
| Bone | 1 | 1 | Bone (1) |
| Bone Cutter | 3 | 8 | Plastic (1), Gear (2), Copper (1) |
| Bonesaw | 1.5 | 5 | Rubber (1), Steel (2) |
| Boston Bugle | 0 | 1 | Cloth (1) |

| NAME | WEIGHT | VALUE | SALVAGEABLE COMPONENTS |
| --- | --- | --- | --- |
| Boston Bugle | 0.1 | 2 | Cloth (1) |
| Bourbon | 1 | 4 | Glass (4) |
| Bourbon Bottle | 1 | 2 | Glass (4) |
| Bowl | 0.5 | 2 | Ceramic (2) |
| Bowling Ball | 8 | 5 | Plastic (7) |
| Bowling Pin | 3 | 3 | Plastic (2), Wood (2) |
| Box of San Francisco Sunlights | 0.5 | 40 | Wood (2), Cloth (3) |
| Brahmin Hide | 2 | 8 | Leather (4) |
| Brahmin Skull | 3 | 2 | Bone (5) |
| Bread Box | 1 | 2 | Plastic (3) |
| Broken Femur | 0.5 | 1 | Bone (2) |
| Broken Lamp | 3 | 5 | Copper (1), Glass (2) |
| Broken Lightbulb | 0.5 | 1 | Copper (1) |
| Broken Tibia | 0.5 | 1 | Bone (2) |
| Broom | 3 | 2 | Wood (2), Plastic (1) |
| Brotherhood of Steel Holotag | 0.1 | 1 | Steel (1) |
| Brown Bottle | 0.5 | 2 | Glass (2) |
| Bunsen Burner | 1 | 10 | Steel (2), Copper (1) |
| Burgundy Bottle | 0.5 | 2 | Glass (2) |
| Cafeteria Tray | 1 | 2 | Plastic (2) |
| Cake Pan | 0.5 | 5 | Aluminum (3) |
| Camera | 3 | 12 | Gear (2), Spring (2), Crystal (2) |
| Can | 0.1 | 1 | Steel (2) |
| Capless Skull | 0.1 | 1 | Bone (1) |
| Carlisle Typewriter | 5 | 20 | Gear (6), Screw (4), Spring (5), Aluminum (2) |
| Cat Bowl | 0.5 | 2 | Plastic (2) |
| Cauterizer | 0.5 | 19 | Aluminum (1), Nuclear Material (1), Spring (1) |
| Ceramic | 0.1 | 1 | Ceramic (1) |
| Ceramic Bowl | 1 | 2 | Ceramic (2) |
| Chalk | 0 | 2 | Asbestos (2) |
| Championship Bowling Ball | 8 | 21 | Plastic (7) |
| Championship Bowling Pin | 3 | 10 | Plastic (2), Wood (2) |
| Charge Card | 0 | 1 | Plastic (1) |
| Chemistry Jar | 0.5 | 1 | Glass (1) |
| Chessboard | 1 | 2 | Wood (2) |
| Cigar | 0 | 1 | Cloth (1) |
| Cigar Box | 0.5 | 40 | Wood (2), Fiberglass (1), Cloth (3) |
| Cigarette | 0 | 1 | Cloth (1) |
| Cigarette Carton | 1 | 50 | Plastic (2), Cloth (4), Asbestos (2) |
| Circuitry | 0.3 | 5 | Circuitry (1) |
| Classroom Globe | 3 | 28 | Cork (2), Plastic (2), Screw (1) |
| Claw Hammer | 3 | 3 | Wood (1), Steel (2) |
| Clean Bowl | 0.5 | 3 | Ceramic (2) |
| Clean Broom | 3 | 3 | Wood (2), Plastic (1) |
| Clean Cake Pan | 0.5 | 7 | Aluminum (2) |
| Clean Coffee Cup | 0.5 | 1 | Ceramic (1) |
| Clean Coffee Tin | 1 | 6 | Aluminum (2) |
| Clean Dog Bowl | 0.5 | 2 | Plastic (2) |
| Clean Drinking Glass | 0.5 | 1 | Glass (1) |
| Clean Globe | 3 | 5 | Cork (2), Plastic (2), Screw (1) |
| Clean Pepper Mill | 0.5 | 4 | Screw (1), Plastic (1) |
| Clean Red Plate | 1 | 1 | Ceramic (2) |
| Clean Salt Shaker | 0.5 | 1 | Plastic (1) |
| Clean Tea Kettle | 1.5 | 2 | Steel (2) |
| Clean Umbrella | 1.5 | 5 | Spring (2), Plastic (2) |
| Clean Umbrella Stand | 2 | 14 | Ceramic (2) |
| Clean White Plate | 1 | 1 | Ceramic (2) |
| Clipboard | 0.2 | 3 | Spring (2), Wood (1) |
| Cloth | 0.1 | 1 | Cloth (1) |
| Clothes Hanger | 0.5 | 1 | Steel (1) |
| Clothing Iron | 3 | 3 | Plastic (1), Steel (2) |
| Coffee Cup | 0.5 | 1 | Ceramic (1) |
| Coffee Pot | 1 | 1 | Plastic (1), Steel (2), Asbestos (1) |
| Coffee Tin | 1 | 3 | Aluminum (2) |

| NAME | WEIGHT | VALUE | SALVAGEABLE COMPONENTS |
| --- | --- | --- | --- |
| Colander | 0.5 | 1 | Steel (1) |
| Collectible Baseball | 0.5 | 8 | Cork (2), Leather (1) |
| Colonial Vase | 3 | 14 | Ceramic (2) |
| Combination Wrench | 1 | 1 | Steel (2) |
| Comfy Pillow | 1 | 3 | Cloth (3) |
| Concrete | 3 | 1 | Concrete (1) |
| Connecting Rod | 5 | 2 | Steel (2) |
| Cooking Oil | 0.5 | 4 | Oil (3), Plastic (1) |
| Cooking Pan | 0.5 | 2 | Steel (2) |
| Cooking Pot | 0.5 | 4 | Copper (1), Steel (2) |
| Coolant | 1 | 7 | Acid (2), Plastic (1) |
| Coolant Cap | 1 | 5 | Aluminum (2) |
| Copper | 0.1 | 4 | Copper (1) |
| Copper Bar | 0.5 | 200 | Copper (10) |
| Cork | 0.1 | 1 | Cork (1) |
| Cotton Yarn | 0.5 | 1 | Cloth (1) |
| Covered Sauce Pan | 1.5 | 2 | Steel (2) |
| Cracked Bowl | 1 | 1 | Ceramic (2) |
| Cracked Deathclaw Egg | 0.1 | 5 | Bone (2), Acid (1) |
| Cracked Glass Bowl | 1 | 1 | Glass (2) |
| Crystal | 0.2 | 4 | Crystal (1) |
| Crystal Liquor Decanter | 3 | 18 | Cork (1), Crystal (4) |
| Cue Ball | 0.5 | 3 | Plastic (2) |
| Cutting Board | 0.5 | 2 | Wood (2) |
| Cutting Fluid | 1 | 7 | Oil (3), Steel (1) |
| Danse's Holotags | 0.1 | 1 | Steel (1) |
| Dawnshire Vase | 3 | 14 | Ceramic (2) |
| Deathclaw Hand | 5 | 25 | Bone (2), Leather (2) |
| Deathclaw Hide | 8 | 15 | Leather (5) |
| Deflated Kickball | 0.5 | 1 | Rubber (3) |
| Derby-Winning Toy Car | 1 | 16 | Screw (1), Wood (2) |
| Desk Fan | 3 | 4 | Gear (2), Screw (2), Steel (2) |
| Desktop Picture Frame | 1 | 2 | Wood (2) |
| Dinner Fork | 0.1 | 1 | Steel (1) |
| Dinner Plate | 1 | 1 | Steel (1) |
| Dirty Ashtray | 0.5 | 1 | Ceramic (1) |
| Dishrag | 0.1 | 1 | Cloth (1) |
| Distress Pulser | 1 | 5 | Aluminum (2), Circuitry (1), Nuclear Material (1) |
| Dog Bowl | 0.5 | 1 | Plastic (2) |
| Dog Tags | 0.1 | 1 | Steel (1) |
| Drinking Glass | 0.5 | 1 | Glass (1) |
| Duct Tape | 0.1 | 12 | Adhesive (1), Cloth (1) |
| Ear Examiner | 0.75 | 15 | Aluminum (1), Fiber-Optics (1), Glass (1) |
| Economy Wonderglue | 0.75 | 40 | Adhesive (5) |
| Eight Ball | 0.5 | 2 | Plastic (2) |
| Eleven Ball | 0.5 | 2 | Plastic (2) |
| Empty Blood Pack | 0.5 | 1 | Plastic (1) |
| Empty Blood Sac | 0.1 | 1 | Antiseptic (1) |
| Empty Can | 0.5 | 1 | Steel (1) |
| Empty Coolant | 0.5 | 1 | Plastic (1) |
| Empty Floral Barrel Vase | 1 | 1 | Ceramic (2) |
| Empty Floral Bud Vase | 1 | 1 | Ceramic (2) |
| Empty Floral Flared Vase | 2 | 1 | Ceramic (2) |
| Empty Floral Rounded Vase | 3 | 1 | Ceramic (2) |
| Empty Floral Vaulted Vase | 3 | 1 | Ceramic (2) |
| Empty Milk Bottle | 1 | 1 | Glass (2) |
| Empty Paint Can | 0.5 | 5 | Steel (2) |
| Empty Teal Barrel Vase | 1 | 1 | Ceramic (2) |
| Empty Teal Bud Vase | 1 | 1 | Ceramic (2) |
| Empty Teal Flared Vase | 2 | 1 | Ceramic (2) |
| Empty Teal Rounded Vase | 3 | 1 | Ceramic (2) |
| Empty Teal Vaulted Vase | 3 | 1 | Ceramic (2) |
| Empty Willow Barrel Vase | 1 | 1 | Ceramic (2) |
| Empty Willow Bud Vase | 1 | 1 | Ceramic (2) |
| Empty Willow Flared Vase | 2 | 1 | Ceramic (2) |
| Empty Willow Rounded Vase | 3 | 1 | Ceramic (2) |

| NAME | WEIGHT | VALUE | SALVAGEABLE COMPONENTS |
|---|---|---|---|
| Empty Willow Vaulted Vase | 3 | 1 | Ceramic (2) |
| Enamel Bucket | 3 | 2 | Steel (2) |
| Enhanced Targeting Card | 0.25 | 9 | Plastic (1), Silver (1), Circuitry (2) |
| Extinguisher | 6 | 6 | Rubber (2), Steel (4), Asbestos (2) |
| Fancy Hairbrush | 0.5 | 9 | Plastic (1), Silver (2) |
| Feather Duster | 1 | 1 | Plastic (2), Cloth (1) |
| Femur | 1 | 1 | Bone (2) |
| Fertilizer | 0.1 | 1 | Fertilizer (1) |
| Fiberglass | 0.1 | 5 | Fiberglass (1) |
| Fiber-Optics | 0.1 | 6 | Fiber Optics (1) |
| Fifteen Ball | 0.5 | 2 | Plastic (2) |
| Fishing Rod | 3 | 4 | Gear (2), Spring (1), Wood (1) |
| Five Ball | 0.5 | 2 | Plastic (2) |
| Flask | 0.5 | 1 | Glass (1) |
| Flight Data Recorder | 3 | 17 | Circuitry (1), Fiber-Optics (2), Copper (1) |
| Flip Lighter | 0.5 | 12 | Oil (1), Spring (1), Steel (1) |
| FLL3 Turbopump Bearings | 0 | 300 | Aluminum (3), Circuitry (1) |
| Floral Barrel Vase | 1 | 1 | Ceramic (2) |
| Floral Bud Vase | 1 | 1 | Ceramic (2) |
| Floral Flared Vase | 2 | 1 | Ceramic (2) |
| Floral Rounded Vase | 3 | 1 | Ceramic (2) |
| Floral Vaulted Vase | 3 | 1 | Ceramic (2) |
| Flux Sensor | 0.1 | 1 | Steel (1) |
| Fork | 0.1 | 1 | Steel (1) |
| Four Ball | 0.5 | 2 | Plastic (2) |
| Fourteen Ball | 0.5 | 2 | Plastic (2) |
| Frying Pan | 1 | 2 | Steel (2) |
| Fumigus Blowtorch | 3 | 25 | Steel (3), Oil (3) |
| Fuse | 0.1 | 5 | Copper (1), Glass (1) |
| Fusion Pulse Charge | 3 | 31 | Circuitry (2), Copper (1), Nuclear Material (5) |
| Gas Canister | 3 | 10 | Steel (3), Oil (1) |
| Gear | 1 | 1 | Steel (1) |
| Gear | 0.2 | 3 | Gear (1) |
| Giddyup Buttercup | 8 | 177 | Gear (3), Steel (5), Spring (4), Screw (4) |
| Giddyup Buttercup Back Leg | 1 | 69 | Spring (2), Steel (1), Gear (2) |
| Giddyup Buttercup Body | 3 | 60 | Steel (2), Spring (2), Screw (2) |
| Giddyup Buttercup Front Leg | 1 | 69 | Gear (2), Steel (1), Spring (2) |
| Giddyup Buttercup Head | 3 | 36 | Steel (2), Spring (2) |
| Giddyup Buttercup Toy Parts | 1 | 45 | Plastic (1), Spring (1) |
| Gilded Grasshopper | 2 | 451 | Gold (5), Glass (2), Copper (10) |
| Glass | 0.1 | 2 | Glass (1) |
| Glass Barrel Red Vase | 3 | 26 | Glass (2) |
| Glass Barrel Teal Vase | 3 | 26 | Glass (2) |
| Glass Barrel Vase | 3 | 26 | Glass (2) |
| Glass Bowl | 1 | 2 | Glass (2) |
| Glass Bud Red Vase | 3 | 26 | Glass (2) |
| Glass Bud Teal Vase | 3 | 26 | Glass (2) |
| Glass Bud Vase | 3 | 26 | Glass (2) |
| Glass Flared Red Vase | 3 | 26 | Glass (2) |
| Glass Flared Teal Vase | 3 | 26 | Glass (2) |
| Glass Flared Vase | 3 | 26 | Glass (2) |
| Glass Pitcher | 1 | 1 | Glass (3) |
| Glass Rounded Red Vase | 3 | 26 | Glass (2) |
| Glass Rounded Teal Vase | 3 | 26 | Glass (2) |
| Glass Rounded Vase | 3 | 26 | Glass (2) |
| Glass Vaulted Red Vase | 3 | 26 | Glass (2) |
| Glass Vaulted Teal Vase | 3 | 26 | Glass (2) |
| Glass Vaulted Vase | 3 | 26 | Glass (2) |
| Globe | 3 | 2 | Screw (1), Cork (2), Plastic (2) |
| Gold | 0.1 | 9 | Gold (1) |
| Gold Bar | 0.5 | 450 | Gold (10) |
| Gold Plated Flip Lighter | 0.5 | 26 | Gold (1), Oil (1), Steel (1) |
| Gold Watch | 0.5 | 40 | Gear (2), Gold (2), Spring (1) |
| Graduated Cylinder | 0.5 | 1 | Glass (1) |
| Gwinnett Ale Bottle | 0.5 | 2 | Glass (2) |
| Gwinnett Brew Bottle | 0.5 | 2 | Glass (2) |

| NAME | WEIGHT | VALUE | SALVAGEABLE COMPONENTS |
|---|---|---|---|
| Gwinnett Lager Bottle | 0.5 | 3 | Glass (2) |
| Gwinnett Pale Ale Bottle | 0.5 | 2 | Glass (2) |
| Gwinnett Pilsner Bottle | 0.5 | 3 | Glass (2) |
| Gwinnett Stout Bottle | 0.5 | 2 | Glass (2) |
| Hack Saw | 2 | 3 | Steel (2), Wood (1) |
| Hairbrush | 0.5 | 2 | Plastic (2) |
| HalluciGen Gas Canister | 3 | 35 | Steel (1) |
| Hammer | 1.5 | 5 | Wood (1), Steel (2) |
| Handcuffs | 0.5 | 6 | Screw (1), Spring (1), Steel (2) |
| High-Powered Magnet | 5 | 13 | Copper (3), Ceramic (1), Nuclear Material (1) |
| High-Powered Microscope | 5 | 22 | Crystal (2), Fiber-Optics (1), Gear (2), Glass (2) |
| Hoe | 5 | 3 | Steel (3), Wood (3) |
| Home Plate | 3 | 4 | Plastic (2), Cloth (2) |
| Hot Plate | 3 | 7 | Circuitry (2), Copper (1), Screw (1) |
| Hubcap | 3 | 5 | Screw (2), Aluminum (2) |
| Human Jaw | 0.1 | 1 | Bone (2) |
| Ichor Sac | 0.5 | 15 | Acid (2), Nuclear Material (1) |
| Inactive Distress Pulser | 1 | 5 | Circuitry (1), Nuclear Material (1), Aluminum (2) |
| Industrial Oil Canister | 3 | 14 | Aluminum (2), Oil (2) |
| Industrial Size Shortening | 4 | 20 | Oil (5) |
| Industrial Solvent | 1 | 15 | Steel (3), Antiseptic (4) |
| Initiate Clarke's Holotag | 0.1 | 1 | Steel (1) |
| Injector | 0.5 | 8 | Aluminum (1) |
| IV Bag | 0.25 | 3 | Plastic (1) |
| Jangles the Moon Monkey | 2 | 12 | Cloth (3), Plastic (1), Fiberglass (1) |
| Jawless Brahmin Skull | 3 | 1 | Bone (4) |
| Kickball | 0.5 | 1 | Rubber (3) |
| Kitchen Scale | 2 | 6 | Steel (3), Spring (3) |
| Knight Rylan's Holotag | 0.1 | 1 | Steel (1) |
| Knight Varham's Holotag | 0.1 | 1 | Steel (1) |
| Lab Bottle | 0.5 | 1 | Glass (1) |
| Ladle | 0.5 | 2 | Steel (2) |
| Lantern | 3 | 15 | Glass (2), Oil (2), Steel (3) |
| Large Baby Bottle | 1 | 4 | Glass (2), Rubber (1) |
| Large Beaker | 0.5 | 1 | Glass (1) |
| Large Dinner Plate | 1 | 1 | Ceramic (3) |
| Large Plate | 1 | 1 | Ceramic (3) |
| Large Serving Plate | 1 | 1 | Ceramic (3) |
| Late Edition Newspaper | 0.1 | 2 | Cloth (2) |
| Lead | 0.3 | 1 | Lead (1) |
| League Bowling Pin | 3 | 3 | Plastic (2), Wood (2) |
| Leather | 0.1 | 2 | Leather (1) |
| Left Arm Bones | 1 | 1 | Bone (3) |
| Left Foot Bones | 1 | 1 | Bone (2) |
| Left Hand Bones | 1 | 1 | Bone (2) |
| Left Leg Bones | 1 | 1 | Bone (3) |
| Life Preserver | 3 | 6 | Plastic (3), Spring (1) |
| Lightbulb | 0.5 | 3 | Glass (1), Copper (1) |
| Liquor Bottle | 0.5 | 2 | Glass (2) |
| Lit Cigar | 0 | 1 | Cloth (1) |
| Lit Cigarette | 0 | 1 | Cloth (1) |
| Lit Stogie | 0 | 1 | Cloth (1) |
| Locket | 0 | 50 | Silver (2) |
| Luxobrew Coffee Pot | 1 | 5 | Plastic (2), Steel (3), Asbestos (2) |
| Magnifying Glass | 0.5 | 8 | Glass (2), Copper (1), Crystal (2) |
| Makeshift Battery | 6 | 17 | Lead (3), Wood (1), Acid (3) |
| Masonry Hammer | 3 | 3 | Wood (1), Steel (2) |
| Medical Liquid Nitrogen Dispenser | 5 | 12 | Steel (2) |
| Metal Bucket | 3 | 2 | Steel (2) |
| Microscope | 5 | 22 | Gear (2), Glass (2), Crystal (2), Fiber-Optics (1) |
| Military Ammo Bag | 3 | 4 | Ballistic Fiber (2) |
| Military-Grade Circuit Board | 2 | 25 | Circuitry (5) |
| Military-Grade Duct Tape | 0.1 | 30 | Ballistic Fiber (2), Adhesive (4) |

| NAME | WEIGHT | VALUE | SALVAGEABLE COMPONENTS |
|---|---|---|---|
| Mini Nuke Beryllium Cap | 0 | 0 | Steel (2), Nuclear Material (1) |
| Mini Nuke Detonator Shell | 0 | 0 | Nuclear Material (2), Steel (3) |
| Mini Nuke Hemisphere Core | 0 | 0 | Nuclear Material (1), Steel (2) |
| Mini Nuke Stabilizer Fins | 0 | 0 | Steel (3), Screw (2) |
| Mole Rat Hide | 0.5 | 8 | Leather (1) |
| Mole Rat Teeth | 0.5 | 1 | Bone (1) |
| Mop | 2 | 1 | Wood (2), Cloth (2) |
| Mr. Handy Fuel | 3 | 14 | Steel (3), Oil (2) |
| New Floral Barrel Vase | 1 | 1 | Ceramic (2) |
| New Floral Bud Vase | 1 | 1 | Ceramic (2) |
| New Floral Flared Vase | 2 | 1 | Ceramic (2) |
| New Floral Rounded Vase | 3 | 1 | Ceramic (2) |
| New Floral Vaulted Vase | 3 | 1 | Ceramic (2) |
| New Power Cables | 1 | 15 | Copper (2), Steel (3) |
| New Teal Barrel Vase | 1 | 1 | Ceramic (2) |
| New Teal Bud Vase | 1 | 1 | Ceramic (2) |
| New Teal Flared Vase | 2 | 1 | Ceramic (2) |
| New Teal Rounded Vase | 3 | 1 | Ceramic (2) |
| New Teal Vaulted Vase | 3 | 1 | Ceramic (2) |
| New Toy Car | 1 | 10 | Screw (1), Wood (2) |
| New Toy Truck | 1 | 15 | Steel (2), Screw (2) |
| New Willow Barrel Vase | 1 | 1 | Ceramic (2) |
| New Willow Bud Vase | 1 | 1 | Ceramic (2) |
| New Willow Flared Vase | 2 | 1 | Ceramic (2) |
| New Willow Rounded Vase | 3 | 1 | Ceramic (2) |
| New Willow Vaulted Vase | 3 | 1 | Ceramic (2) |
| Nine Ball | 0.5 | 2 | Plastic (2) |
| Nuclear Material | 0.1 | 10 | Nuclear Material (1) |
| Nuka Cola Bottle | 0.5 | 2 | Glass (2) |
| NX-42 Guidance Chip | 0 | 150 | Plastic (1), Silver (1) |
| Office Desk Fan | 3 | 4 | Gear (2), Screw (2), Steel (2) |
| Oil | 0.1 | 4 | Oil (1) |
| Oil Can | 0.5 | 15 | Oil (4), Aluminum (1) |
| Oil Canister | 3 | 12 | Steel (2), Oil (2) |
| One Ball | 0.5 | 2 | Plastic (2) |
| Oven Mitt | 1 | 1 | Asbestos (1), Cloth (2) |
| Pack of Cigarettes | 0.1 | 12 | Plastic (1), Cloth (2), Asbestos (1) |
| Pack of Duct Tape | 0.1 | 20 | Adhesive (4), Cloth (2) |
| Paintbrush | 0.5 | 2 | Wood (1), Cloth (1) |
| Paint Can | 5 | 10 | Oil (2), Steel (2) |
| Paladin Brandis' Holotag | 0.1 | 1 | Steel (1) |
| Peizonucleic Liner | 0 | 0 | Ballistic Fiber (2), Rubber (1), Steel (1) |
| Pelvis Bones | 1 | 1 | Bone (3) |
| Pen | 0 | 1 | Plastic (1) |
| Pencil | 0 | 1 | Lead (1), Wood (1) |
| Pepper Mill | 0.5 | 2 | Screw (1), Plastic (1) |
| Picture Frame | 1 | 4 | Wood (2) |
| Pint Glass | 0.5 | 3 | Glass (2) |
| Pip-Boy | 0 | 0 | Fiber-Optics (2), Nuclear Material (1) |
| Plastic | 0.1 | 1 | Plastic (1) |
| Plastic Bowl | 0.5 | 2 | Plastic (2) |
| Plastic Fork | 0.1 | 1 | Plastic (1) |
| Plastic Knife | 0.1 | 1 | Plastic (1) |
| Plastic Plate | 0.25 | 1 | Plastic (2) |
| Plastic Pumpkin | 1 | 2 | Plastic (2) |
| Plastic Spoon | 0.1 | 1 | Plastic (1) |
| Plate | 1 | 2 | Steel (1) |
| Plunger | 1 | 1 | Rubber (2), Wood (1) |
| Poseidon Radar Transmitter | 0 | 75 | Steel (3), Circuitry (1) |
| Power Relay Coil | 0.5 | 15 | Copper (2), Steel (2) |
| Preserved Cigarette Pack | 0.1 | 12 | Plastic (1), Cloth (2), Asbestos (1) |
| Pre-War Lamp | 3 | 15 | Copper (4), Glass (2) |
| Pre-War Money | 0 | 8 | Cloth (1) |
| Pristine Deathclaw Egg | 1 | 25 | Bone (2), Acid (1) |
| ProSnap Camera | 3 | 30 | Gear (4), Spring (4), Crystal (4) |
| Prototype Biometric Scanner | 3 | 164 | Fiber-Optics (1), Asbestos (1), Nuclear Material (2) |

| NAME | WEIGHT | VALUE | SALVAGEABLE COMPONENTS |
|---|---|---|---|
| Rack | 0.5 | 2 | Wood (2) |
| Radar Transmitter | 0 | 30 | Steel (3), Circuitry (1) |
| Radioactive Gland | 0.5 | 30 | Nuclear Material (2) |
| Radscorpion Stinger | 0.5 | 30 | Nuclear Material (2) |
| Radstag Hide | 2 | 8 | Leather (4) |
| Rat Poison | 0.5 | 6 | Steel (1), Asbestos (1), Fiberglass (2) |
| Recorder | 0.75 | 23 | Aluminum (1), Nuclear Material (1), Circuitry (1), Glass (1) |
| Red Plate | 1 | 1 | Ceramic (2) |
| Reflex Capacitor | 0.1 | 1 | Steel (1) |
| Reporter's Camera | 3 | 112 | Gear (2), Spring (2), Crystal (2) |
| Reporter's Pen | 0 | 3 | Plastic (1) |
| Reporter's Pencil | 0 | 10 | Lead (1), Wood (1) |
| Research Test Tube | 0.1 | 1 | Glass (1) |
| Restored Desk Fan | 3 | 8 | Steel (2), Screw (2), Gear (2) |
| RFID Device | 0 | 0 | Circuitry (1), Fiberglass (1) |
| Rib Cage | 1 | 1 | Bone (5) |
| Rib Cage and Pelvis | 1 | 1 | Bone (3) |
| Rib Cage and Spine | 1 | 1 | Bone (5) |
| Right Arm Bones | 1 | 1 | Bone (3) |
| Right Foot Bones | 1 | 1 | Bone (2) |
| Right Hand Bones | 1 | 1 | Bone (2) |
| Right Leg Bones | 1 | 1 | Bone (3) |
| Ring Stand | 3 | 2 | Steel (1), Aluminum (1) |
| Rolled Boston Bugle | 0.1 | 2 | Cloth (1) |
| Rubber | 0.1 | 2 | Rubber (1) |
| Rum Bottle | 1 | 2 | Glass (4) |
| Ruptured HalluciGen Gas Canister | 3 | 10 | Steel (1) |
| Sabotaged Turbopump Bearings | 0 | 15 | Aluminum (3), Circuitry (1) |
| Salt Shaker | 0.5 | 1 | Plastic (1) |
| Sauce Pan | 1 | 2 | Steel (2) |
| Sauce Pan Lid | 0.5 | 1 | Steel (1) |
| Saucer | 0.5 | 1 | Ceramic (1) |
| Saw | 3 | 3 | Steel (3), Rubber (1) |
| Scalpel | 0.25 | 5 | Steel (1) |
| Scissors | 0.25 | 3 | Plastic (1), Steel (2) |
| Screw | 0.1 | 2 | Screw (1) |
| Screwdriver | 0.5 | 3 | Steel (2), Wood (1) |
| Scribe Faris' Holotag | 0.1 | 1 | Steel (1) |
| Sealed Boston Bugle | 0 | 1 | Cloth (1) |
| Sealed Wonderglue | 0.1 | 25 | Adhesive (4) |
| Sensor | 0.5 | 20 | Aluminum (1), Nuclear Material (1) |
| Sensor Module | 2 | 30 | Steel (1), Circuitry (5), Copper (2) |
| Seven Ball | 0.5 | 2 | Plastic (2) |
| Shadeless Lamp | 3 | 5 | Copper (1), Glass (2) |
| Shadeless Table Lamp | 3 | 5 | Copper (1), Glass (2) |
| Shem Drowne's Skull | 0.1 | 10 | Bone (2) |
| Shopping Basket | 1 | 1 | Plastic (1), Steel (3) |
| Shot Glass | 0.1 | 1 | Glass (1) |
| Shovel | 5 | 3 | Steel (3), Wood (3) |
| Silver | 0.1 | 6 | Silver (1) |
| Silver Bar | 0.5 | 300 | Silver (10) |
| Silver Bowl | 1 | 15 | Silver (2) |
| Silver Fork | 0.1 | 4 | Silver (1) |
| Silver Hairbrush | 0.5 | 63 | Plastic (1), Silver (2) |
| Silver Locket | 0.1 | 10 | Silver (2) |
| Silver Plate | 1 | 7 | Silver (1) |
| Silver Pocket Watch | 0.5 | 25 | Gear (2), Silver (2), Spring (1) |
| Silver Shroud Costume | 0 | 0 | Cloth (3) |
| Silver Submachine Gun Prop | 1 | 1 | Wood (1), Steel (1), Spring (1) |
| Silver Table Knife | 0.1 | 4 | Silver (1) |
| Silver Table Spoon | 0.1 | 4 | Silver (1) |
| Six Ball | 0.5 | 2 | Plastic (2) |
| Skull | 1 | 1 | Bone (3) |
| Skull Cap Bone | 0.1 | 1 | Bone (2) |

| NAME | WEIGHT | VALUE | SALVAGEABLE COMPONENTS |
| --- | --- | --- | --- |
| Skull Eye Socket | 0.1 | 1 | Bone (2) |
| Skull Faceplate | 0.1 | 1 | Bone (2) |
| Skull Fragment | 0.1 | 1 | Bone (2) |
| Small Baby Bottle | 1 | 4 | Glass (2), Rubber (1) |
| Small Covered Sauce Pan | 1.25 | 1 | Steel (1) |
| Small Dinner Plate | 0.5 | 1 | Ceramic (2) |
| Small Picture Frame | 1 | 2 | Wood (2) |
| Small Plate | 0.5 | 1 | Ceramic (2) |
| Small Sauce Pan | 1 | 1 | Steel (1) |
| Small Sauce Pan Lid | 0.25 | 1 | Steel (1) |
| Small Serving Plate | 0.5 | 1 | Ceramic (2) |
| Soap | 0.5 | 4 | Oil (1) |
| Spanner | 0.5 | 8 | Aluminum (1) |
| Spatula | 0.5 | 1 | Rubber (1), Steel (1) |
| Spine | 1 | 5 | Bone (5) |
| Spring | 0.1 | 3 | Spring (1) |
| Steel | 0.2 | 1 | Steel (1) |
| Stew Pot | 3 | 8 | Steel (3), Copper (1) |
| Stogie | 0 | 1 | Cloth (1) |
| Straw Pillow | 1 | 1 | Cloth (2) |
| Suprathaw Antifreeze | 2 | 8 | Acid (4), Plastic (3) |
| Surgical Scalpel | 0.25 | 5 | Steel (1) |
| Surgical Tray | 0.5 | 2 | Aluminum (3) |
| Swan Boat Fragments | 0 | 12 | Fiberglass (5), Plastic (1), Steel (1) |
| Sweeper | 4 | 100 | Nuclear Material (2), Aluminum (3), Circuitry (2) |
| Synth Component | 0 | 20 | Plastic (1) |
| Table Knife | 0.1 | 1 | Steel (1) |
| Table Spoon | 0.1 | 1 | Steel (1) |
| Tabletop Picture Frame | 1 | 2 | Wood (2) |
| Tack Hammer | 1.5 | 2 | Wood (1), Steel (1) |
| Tall Flask | 0.5 | 1 | Glass (1) |
| Teacup | 0.5 | 1 | Ceramic (2) |
| Tea Kettle | 1.5 | 2 | Steel (2) |
| Teal Barrel Vase | 1 | 1 | Ceramic (2) |
| Teal Bud Vase | 1 | 1 | Ceramic (2) |
| Teal Flared Vase | 2 | 1 | Ceramic (2) |
| Teal Rounded Vase | 3 | 1 | Ceramic (2) |
| Teal Vaulted Vase | 3 | 1 | Ceramic (2) |
| Teapot | 1 | 2 | Ceramic (5), Asbestos (1) |
| Teddy Bear | 1 | 3 | Leather (1), Cloth (3) |
| Telephone | 3 | 5 | Circuitry (2), Copper (1), Fiberglass (2) |
| Ten Ball | 0.5 | 2 | Plastic (2) |
| Test Tube | 0.5 | 1 | Glass (1) |
| Test Tube Rack | 1 | 1 | Wood (2) |
| Thermal Coupler | 1 | 10 | Rubber (2) |
| Thin Beaker | 0.5 | 1 | Glass (1) |
| Thirteen Ball | 0.5 | 2 | Plastic (2) |
| Three Ball | 0.5 | 2 | Plastic (2) |
| Tibia | 1 | 1 | Bone (2) |
| Tin Can | 0.1 | 1 | Steel (2) |
| Toaster | 3 | 3 | Spring (2), Steel (2) |
| Tongs | 3 | 18 | Steel (2), Screw (1) |
| Toothbrush | 0.1 | 1 | Plastic (1) |
| Toothpaste | 0.25 | 3 | Plastic (1), Antiseptic (2) |
| Torque Rod End | 3 | 1 | Steel (1) |
| Toy Alien | 0.5 | 5 | Plastic (2), Rubber (1) |
| Toy Car | 1 | 5 | Screw (1), Wood (2) |
| Toy Rocketship | 0.5 | 7 | Aluminum (1), Plastic (2) |
| Toy Truck | 1 | 8 | Steel (2), Screw (1) |
| Tray | 1 | 12 | Aluminum (1) |
| Trifold American Flag | 3 | 3 | Wood (2), Cloth (4) |

| NAME | WEIGHT | VALUE | SALVAGEABLE COMPONENTS |
| --- | --- | --- | --- |
| Tri Tool | 0.5 | 15 | Aluminum (1), Nuclear Material (1) |
| Tube Flange | 5 | 2 | Steel (2) |
| Turpentine | 1 | 10 | Steel (2), Antiseptic (2) |
| TV Dinner Tray | 0.5 | 1 | Aluminum (3) |
| Tweezers | 0.2 | 8 | Aluminum (1) |
| Twelve Ball | 0.5 | 2 | Plastic (2) |
| Two Ball | 0.5 | 2 | Plastic (2) |
| Typewriter | 5 | 11 | Gear (3), Screw (2), Spring (3) |
| Umbrella | 1.5 | 3 | Spring (2), Plastic (2) |
| Umbrella Stand | 2 | 2 | Ceramic (2) |
| Undamaged Abraxo Cleaner | 1 | 10 | Acid (1), Antiseptic (2), Fiberglass (1) |
| Undamaged American Flag | 3 | 9 | Wood (2), Cloth (4) |
| Undamaged Baseball Glove | 1 | 6 | Leather (3) |
| Undamaged Camera | 3 | 18 | Gear (2), Spring (2), Crystal (2) |
| Undamaged Cigarettes | 1 | 50 | Plastic (2), Cloth (4), Asbestos (2) |
| Unfilled Kickball | 0.5 | 1 | Rubber (3) |
| Unrusted Tin Can | 0.1 | 1 | Steel (1), Aluminum (1) |
| Unscorched Oven Mitt | 1 | 1 | Asbestos (1), Cloth (2) |
| Untarnished Coffee Pot | 1 | 3 | Plastic (1), Steel (2), Asbestos (1) |
| Untarnished Metal Bucket | 3 | 3 | Steel (2) |
| Unused Ashtray | 0.5 | 3 | Ceramic (2) |
| Unused Enamel Bucket | 3 | 3 | Steel (2) |
| Unused Flip Lighter | 0.5 | 21 | Oil (1), Spring (1), Steel (1) |
| Upper Skull | 0.1 | 1 | Bone (1) |
| Used Oil Can | 0.5 | 2 | Steel (1), Oil (1) |
| Vacuum Tube | 0.25 | 3 | Copper (1), Glass (2) |
| Vase | 3 | 1 | Ceramic (3) |
| Vegetable Starch | 0.5 | 6 | Adhesive (5) |
| Vodka | 1 | 4 | Glass (4) |
| Vodka Bottle | 1 | 2 | Glass (4) |
| Wakemaster Alarm Clock | 1 | 15 | Aluminum (2), Glass (2), Spring (2), Nuclear Material (2) |
| Warwick Pump Part | 0.25 | 1 | Ceramic (2) |
| Warwick Pump Piece | 0.25 | 1 | Ceramic (2) |
| Whiskey | 1 | 2 | Glass (4) |
| Whiskey Bottle | 1 | 2 | Glass (4) |
| White Bottle | 0.5 | 2 | Glass (2) |
| White Plate | 1 | 1 | Ceramic (2) |
| Willow Barrel Vase | 1 | 1 | Ceramic (2) |
| Willow Bud Vase | 1 | 1 | Ceramic (2) |
| Willow Flared Vase | 2 | 1 | Ceramic (2) |
| Willow Rounded Vase | 3 | 1 | Ceramic (2) |
| Willow Vaulted Vase | 3 | 1 | Ceramic (2) |
| Wine Bottle | 1 | 2 | Glass (4) |
| Wonderglue | 0.1 | 20 | Adhesive (2) |
| Wood | 0.2 | 1 | Wood (1) |
| Wooden Block—B & Y | 0.1 | 1 | Wood (1) |
| Wooden Block—I & D | 0.1 | 1 | Wood (1) |
| Wooden Block—N & S | 0.1 | 1 | Wood (1) |
| Wooden Block—V & F | 0.1 | 1 | Wood (1) |
| Wooden Picture Frame | 1 | 4 | Wood (2) |
| Wooden Solider Toy | 1 | 1 | Ceramic (1) |
| Wooden Spoon | 0.1 | 1 | Wood (2) |
| Wrench | 1 | 1 | Steel (2) |
| Yao Guai Hide | 2.5 | 10 | Leather (4) |
| Yardstick | 0.75 | 1 | Wood (2) |
| Yellow Paint | 5 | 10 | Steel (2), Oil (2) |
| Yellow Plate | 1 | 1 | Ceramic (2) |
| Yellow Table Lamp | 3 | 5 | Copper (1), Glass (2) |
| Yellow-Trimmed Plate | 1 | 2 | Ceramic (2) |
| Youth League Baseball | 1 | 20 | Cork (2), Leather (1) |
| Youth League Glove | 1 | 30 | Leather (3) |

## JUNK SHIPMENTS

With a bit of time and effort, you can salvage materials for any and all of your crafting needs. However, many traders can ship components directly to a location of your choosing. After you purchase a shipment contract, place the contract in your desired workshop (or workstation) to receive your order.

### JUNK SHIPMENTS

| NAME | WEIGHT | VALUE | DELIVERED COMPONENTS |
|---|---|---|---|
| Shipment of Acid—25 | 0 | 250 | Acid (25) |
| Shipment of Adhesive—25 | 0 | 1000 | Adhesive (25) |
| Shipment of Adhesive—50 | 0 | 2000 | Adhesive (50) |
| Shipment of Aluminum—25 | 0 | 375 | Aluminum (25) |
| Shipment of Aluminum—50 | 0 | 750 | Aluminum (50) |
| Shipment of Antiseptic—25 | 0 | 375 | Antiseptic (25) |
| Shipment of Asbestos—25 | 0 | 750 | Asbestos (25) |
| Shipment of Ballistic Fiber—25 | 0 | 625 | Ballistic Fiber (25) |
| Shipment of Ceramic—25 | 0 | 175 | Ceramic (25) |
| Shipment of Circuitry—25 | 0 | 625 | Circuitry (25) |
| Shipment of Circuitry—50 | 0 | 1250 | Circuitry (50) |
| Shipment of Cloth—25 | 0 | 100 | Cloth (25) |
| Shipment of Concrete—50 | 0 | 150 | Concrete (50) |
| Shipment of Copper—25 | 0 | 500 | Copper (25) |
| Shipment of Cork—25 | 0 | 125 | Cork (25) |
| Shipment of Crystal—25 | 0 | 575 | Crystal (25) |
| Shipment of Fertilizer—25 | 0 | 300 | Fertilizer (25) |

| NAME | WEIGHT | VALUE | DELIVERED COMPONENTS |
|---|---|---|---|
| Shipment of Fiberglass—25 | 0 | 700 | Fiberglass (25) |
| Shipment of Fiber-Optics—25 | 0 | 850 | Fiber-Optics (25) |
| Shipment of Gears—25 | 0 | 450 | Gears (25) |
| Shipment of Glass—25 | 0 | 325 | Glass (25) |
| Shipment of Gold—25 | 0 | 1125 | Gold (25) |
| Shipment of Lead—25 | 0 | 200 | Lead (25) |
| Shipment of Leather—25 | 0 | 250 | Leather (25) |
| Shipment of Nuclear Material—25 | 0 | 1250 | Nuclear Material (25) |
| Shipment of Oil—25 | 0 | 500 | Oil (25) |
| Shipment of Plastic—25 | 0 | 75 | Plastic (25) |
| Shipment of Rubber—25 | 0 | 250 | Rubber (25) |
| Shipment of Screws—25 | 0 | 400 | Screw (25) |
| Shipment of Silver—25 | 0 | 750 | Silver (25) |
| Shipment of Springs—25 | 0 | 375 | Spring (25) |
| Shipment of Steel—50 | 0 | 150 | Steel (50) |
| Shipment of Steel—100 | 0 | 300 | Steel (100) |
| Shipment of Wood—50 | 0 | 100 | Wood (50) |
| Shipment of Wood—100 | 0 | 200 | Wood (100) |

## VAULT-TEC RECOMMENDS

### JUNK ITEMS

Some junk items are just too good to pass up! If you're serious about crafting, you'd do well to grab these items whenever you spot them:

| BIOMETRIC SCANNER | FIBER OPTICS (1), NUCLEAR MATERIAL (2) |
|---|---|
| Military Ammo Bag | Ballistic Fiber (2) |
| Military-Grade Circuit Board | Circuitry (5) |
| Military-Grade Duct Tape | Ballistic Fiber (2), Adhesive (4) |
| Institute Recorder | Circuitry (1), Nuclear Material (1) |
| Baseball Glove | Leather (3) |
| Camera | Crystal (2) |
| Bag of Fertilizer | Fertilizer (4) |
| Microscope | Crystal (2), Fiber Optics (1) |
| Liquid Decanter | Crystal (4) |
| Magnifying Glass | Crystal (2), Copper (1) |
| Telephone | Fiberglass (2), Copper (1) |
| Abraxo Cleaner | Antiseptic (2), Fiberglass (1) |
| Aluminum Canister | Fiberglass (2), Oil (1) |
| Mr Handy Fuel | Oil (2) |
| Gold Plated Flip Lighter | Oil (1), Gold (1) |
| Typewriter | Gears (3), Springs (3) |
| Giddyup Buttercup | Screws (4), Springs (4) |
| Fancy Hairbrush | Silver (2) |
| Silver Watch | Silver (2), Gears (2) |

# MODS

Mods are special attachments or alterations that can be added to weapons, armor, and Power Armor. You can purchase mods from some traders, and you'll find a few loose mods lying around the Commonwealth, but almost any mod can be hand-crafted or plucked from existing gear.

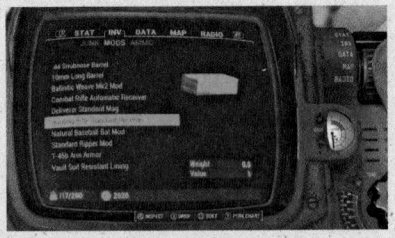

Your Pip-Boy's Mods tab displays all of the loose mods that are currently in your inventory. In most cases, a mod's name indicates the items with which it can be used. A pipe bolt-action suppressor can be attached to any pipe-bolt-action gun. A shadowed leather arm mod can be placed on any leather armor arm piece.

The Mod tab also displays the weight and value of each loose mod. Most of these items are relatively light, but a single crafting session can result in any number of loose mods; store or sell superfluous mods to keep them from weighing you down.

To attach an existing mod to a piece of gear, you simply need access to the appropriate workstation. With the required components and perks, you can build nearly any mod you'll find in the Commonwealth.

## TIP

Need a complete list of every mod? Then remember accessing this book grants you unfettered access to the central database, or "online", component of this guide, where Vault-Tec automated charts are available for just this purpose. Refer to the "MODS" section for the entire chart and statistics.

# WEAPON MODS

With the right mods and access to a weapons workbench, you can improve virtually every gun, blade, and club in your arsenal. You can craft variety simple mods as soon as you have the necessary components, but most advanced weapon mods require some combination of the Gun Nut, Blacksmith, and Science! perks.

## GUNS

Nearly every gun you find can be modified to better suit your needs. Most guns can even be altered to take advantage of specific perks. However, even simple gun mods tend to require a selection of uncommon components. Specifics vary, but you'd do well to stock up on adhesive, aluminum, gears, screws, and oil if you plan on crafting your own gun mods.

If you favor ballistic guns, invest in the Gun Nut perk as early as possible. If energy weapons are your passion, make the Science! perk a priority—just know that some advanced gun mods require all available ranks of both Gun Nut and Science!

### Barrel Mods

As applied to ballistic weapons, barrel mods tend to affect a gun's range, accuracy, and recoil. In general, longer barrels improve range and sighted accuracy while also increasing recoil. Shorter barrels usually reduce a gun's maximum range while improving hip-fire accuracy and weapon recoil.

On energy weapons, barrel mods can affect nearly every aspect of a gun's performance. Damage, range, accuracy, fire rate, and ammo capacity can all be altered with a single barrel mod. Barrel mods also have diverse effects on some heavy guns.

### Grip Mods

Grip mods generally affect a gun's accuracy and recoil. Enhanced pistol grips tend to improve hip-fire accuracy. Enhanced rifle stocks usually improve sighted accuracy. Most stock upgrades also improve a rifle's bash damage.

### Mag Mods

Mag mods usually determine a weapon's ammo capacity and reload speed. In rare cases, a mag mod can include a less conventional effect. A fusion mag, for example, allows an Alien Blaster to use fusion cells as ammunition; the gauss rifle's mag mods also affect overall weapon damage.

### Muzzle Mods

Different muzzle mods serve different purposes. For ballistic weapons, compensators and muzzle breaks improve recoil while reducing weapon range. Suppressors reduce range while improving recoil and—most importantly—minimizing the sound of gunfire. Bayonets increase bash damage while reducing weapon range.

Most energy weapon muzzle mods are lenses used to focus or split the projected beam. These mods usually affect an energy weapon's range, accuracy, and recoil. Some weapons, like the gamma gun and Junk Jet, offer muzzle mods that add bonus energy damage to each shot fired.

## HELPFUL HINT
### from Vault Boy!

**Did You Know?**

THE GAMMA GUN BARREL MOD "LORENZO'S ARTIFACT" CAN'T BE CRAFTED. COMPLETE THE "CABOT HOUSE" QUEST TO EARN A WEAPON THAT CONTAINS THIS UNIQUE MOD.

## Receiver Mods

Nearly all receivers play an important role in overall weapon damage, but these mods can dramatically change the way a weapon performs. Many ballistic gun receivers reduce per-shot damage to offer armor penetration or automatic fire. Some ballistic receivers increase accuracy or critical shot damage. Swapping a receiver mod can even change the ammo used by some guns.

Energy weapon receiver mods are just as diverse as those found on ballistic guns. There are plenty of options that alter accuracy or critical shot damage, but some energy weapon receivers affect ammo capacity, add burning damage, or allow for charged shots.

### Sight Mods

Sight mods primarily affect a weapon's sighted accuracy. Sight rings and reflex sights make it easier to focus on targets, and the magnification offered by scopes makes it much easier to hit distant targets. Many advanced scopes even offer features like night vision and target tracking.

## MELEE MODS

Melee and punching weapons don't feature the deep customization offered by most guns, but close-combat enthusiasts are sure to enjoy the benefits of a well-chosen mod. Again, different mods require different components, but maintaining a good supply of adhesive will make modifying your melee weapons considerably easier.

The most powerful melee mods can require up to Rank 3 of the Blacksmith perk; a small investment in Science! is also needed to craft a number of high-tech melee mods.

### Material Mods

Baseball bats and rolling pins are the only weapons that accommodate material mods. These mods change the entire look of a weapon. Often, the change is purely cosmetic. However, an aluminum material mod can significantly enhance the performance of a bat or rolling pin.

### Upgrade Mods

Most melee (and punching) weapons contain a single upgrade slot. The vast majority of upgrade mods increase weapon damage, but most upgrades also add special features. Even simple weapons can be modified to pierce armor, inflict bleeding, disarm targets, deal energy damage, and more. Of course, options vary by weapon, but some upgrade mods offer considerable utility.

# ARMOR MODS

Armor mods can dramatically improve your protective gear. Covert operators can benefit from mods that reduce armor weight and improve stealth; front-line combatants can reinforce armor for maximum protection. No matter how you engage your enemies, the right armor mods can greatly increase your chances of survival.

Pieces belonging to the major armor sets offer far more customization options than simpler garments. Each piece of armor that belongs to one of the major armor sets contains two mod slots—one for material mods and one for miscellaneous mods. However, for those with the proper skills, the Commonwealth contains a wide variety of customizable apparel.

If you plan to craft your own advanced armor mods, consider investing in all available ranks of the Armorer and Science! perks. Of course, the mods you build will also determine the components you need, but nearly all armor mods require some amount of adhesive.

## MATERIAL MODS

Most armor material mods affect Damage Resistance and Energy Resistance. However, there are a few material mods that include special features. Shadowed mods—which are available for combat, leather, and metal armor pieces—improve stealth in dark areas. The Brotherhood of Steel material mod even improves the Radiation Resistance offered by a piece of combat armor. The headgear associated with major armor sets can accommodate similar material mods.

## MISCELLANEOUS MODS

Miscellaneous mods are linings that further improve armor pieces. BioCommMesh mods increase the duration of chems; pocketed mods increase carrying capacity. Leg armor can be modified to improve sprinting or reduce falling damage. Arm mods can improve blocking or melee damage. Of course, every armor piece can be modified to improve resistances, but you'll find many more useful effects as you craft or collect new mods. Similar mods are available for miscellaneous armor pieces like DC umpire's pads and Vault-Tec security armor.

## HEADLAMPS

You can attach various headlamps to mining helmets. These handy little mods work similarly to your Pip-Boy's onboard flashlight.

## BALLISTIC WEAVE MODS

Ballistic weave mods reinforce lightweight garments that wouldn't otherwise offer much protection. You'll find clothing, outfits, and headgear that can accommodate these special linings. Unlike most mods, ballistic weaves aren't limited to a single item type. A ballistic weave mod that attaches to a battered fedora can also be placed in a set of farmhand clothes.

**HELPFUL HINT** *from Vault Boy!*  Did You Know?

BEFORE YOU CAN CRAFT BALLISTIC WEAVE MODS, YOU MUST PROVE YOUR LOYALTY TO THE RAILROAD. COMPLETE THE "JACKPOT" RADIANT QUEST; THEN SPEAK TO TINKER TOM TO LEARN ABOUT THESE VALUABLE UPGRADES. YOU CAN ALSO COMPLETE THE RAILROAD QUEST: RANDOLPH SAFEHOUSE 6 TO EARN THE INSTITUTE KILLER WEAVE MOD.

## THE MAGIC OF MODS
### SAMPLE ARMOR MODIFICATIONS

### MODIFIED LEATHER ARMOR

THE RIGHT MODS CAN MAKE IT MUCH EASIER TO STAY OUT OF SIGHT. EACH PIECE OF THIS LEATHER ARMOR SET IS EQUIPPED WITH A SHADOWED MATERIAL MOD, IMPROVING STEALTH IN DARK AREAS. THE CHEST PIECE'S ULTRALIGHT BUILD REDUCES WEIGHT AND GRANTS BONUS ACTION POINTS. SLEEK LEG MODS ALLOW YOU TO MOVE FASTER WHILE SNEAKING, AND THE ARMS' STABILIZER MODS MAKE SCOPED AIMING MORE STEADY.

### MODIFIED HEAVY COMBAT ARMOR

THIS COLLECTION OF HEAVY COMBAT ARMOR HAS BEEN MODIFIED TO GRANT EXTRA PROTECTION. EVERY PIECE IS EQUIPPED WITH A POLYMER MATERIAL MOD, RESULTING IN SIGNIFICANTLY INCREASED DAMAGE RESISTANCE AND ENERGY RESISTANCE. THE CHEST PIECE'S ASBESTOS LINING FURTHER IMPROVES ENERGY RESISTANCE AND MAKES IT IMPOSSIBLE FOR YOU TO BE SET ON FIRE. BOTH ARM PIECES HAVE BEEN STRENGTHENED TO REDUCE LIMB DAMAGE, AND THE LEAD-LINED LEGS GRANT A BIT OF RADIATION RESISTANCE.

### MODIFIED STURDY RAIDER ARMOR

THIS STURDY RAIDER ARMOR HAS BEEN CUSTOMIZED FOR CLOSE COMBAT. EVERY PIECE HAS BEEN BUTTRESSED TO PROVIDE EXTRA PROTECTION. THE CHEST PIECE'S PNEUMATIC MOD REDUCES THE MAGNITUDE OF INCOMING STAGGERS. WEIGHTED ARMS ALLOW PUNCHING ATTACKS AND MELEE ATTACKS TO IGNORE SOME OF YOUR TARGET'S ARMOR, AND CUSTOM-FITTED LEGS REDUCE THE ACTION POINT COST FOR SPRINTING.

# POWER ARMOR MODS

With the right mods, you can assemble a suit of Power Armor that provides unbeatable protection and unmatched utility. Damage mitigation is just the beginning—Power Armor mods can offer everything from custom paint jobs to integrated electronic devices.

You can earn modified parts by completing quests or defeating appropriately equipped enemies, but if you plan to craft your Power Armor mods, invest in all available ranks of the Science!, Blacksmith, and Armorer perks. You'll need a supply of rare components, but collecting adhesive, aluminum, and circuitry is a good place to start.

## BASE MODS

Base mods determine the Damage Resistance and Energy Resistance offered by a piece of Power Armor. Raider Power Armor only offers two base mods (standard and welded), but more advanced models of Power Armor offer six levels of protection.

## MATERIAL MODS

Most Power Armor parts offer slots for material mods. Options like lead plating, winterized coating, and explosive shielding grant bonuses as soon as they're applied. In many cases, you must apply matching material mods to all Power Armor parts before a bonus is activated. Unlock additional Power Armor material mods by collecting Hot Rodder magazines and earning the trust of various factions.

Aside from Raider Power Armor (for which there are no material mods), each model of Power Armor offers at least one unique paint scheme:

- COMPLETE THE MINUTEMEN QUEST: WHEN FREEDOM CALLS TO UNLOCK A MINUTEMEN PAINT SCHEME FOR T-45 POWER ARMOR.
- COMPLETE THE RAILROAD QUEST: TRADECRAFT TO UNLOCK A RAILROAD PAINT SCHEME FOR T-51 POWER ARMOR.
- COMPLETE MISCELLANEOUS QUEST: ATOM CATS TO UNLOCK AN ATOM CATS PAINT SCHEME FOR T-60 POWER ARMOR.
- COMPLETE BROTHERHOOD OF STEEL QUEST: SHADOW OF STEEL TO UNLOCK A BOS PAINT SCHEME FOR T-60 POWER ARMOR. EARN PROMOTIONS TO UNLOCK RANK-BASED VARIATIONS.
- COMPLETE THE INSTITUTE QUEST: NUCLEAR FAMILY TO UNLOCK AN INSTITUTE PAINT SCHEME FOR X-01 POWER ARMOR.

## MISCELLANEOUS MODS

Miscellaneous mods grant powerful bonuses to individual parts. Arm mods tend to improve different aspects of unarmed combat, while leg mods offer effects like improved sprinting, increased carrying capacity, and larger impact landings. In most Power Armor torsos, miscellaneous mods can add extra features like jetpacks, medic pumps, and tesla coils. Helmets can be modified to improve target acquisition or remove radiation from items you consume. Of course, this is only the beginning—you'll find a variety of useful mods for every piece of Power Armor.

## HEADLAMPS

Every Power Armor helmet can accommodate a variety of headlamps. Equip new headlamps to change the color of the projected beam.

## THE MAGIC OF MODS

SAMPLE POWER ARMOR MODIFICATIONS

### MODIFIED RAIDER POWER ARMOR

THIS SUIT OF RAIDER POWER ARMOR IS GEARED TOWARD UNARMED COMBAT. EVERY PIECE OF THIS SUIT HAS BEEN REINFORCED WITH WELDED PLATES. BOTH ARMS FEATURE RUSTY KNUCKLE MODS THAT ADD BLEEDING DAMAGE TO UNARMED ATTACKS, AND THE LEGS INCLUDE OVERDRIVE SERVOS TO INCREASE SPRINT SPEED. THE TORSO'S ONBOARD MEDIC PUMP AUTOMATICALLY USES A STIMPAK WHEN YOUR HEALTH GETS TOO LOW, AND THE HELMET'S RAD SCRUBBERS MAKE IT SAFE TO TOP OFF YOUR HEALTH WITH IRRADIATED WATER.

### MODIFIED T-60 POWER ARMOR

THIS SUIT OF T-60 POWER ARMOR HAS BEEN MODIFIED FOR EXTRA MOBILITY AND IMPROVED V.A.T.S. USAGE. EVERY PIECE OF THIS SUIT HAS BEEN UPGRADED WITH MODEL F MODS FOR BETTER PROTECTION. THE THE TORSO INCLUDES A JETPACK FOR INCREASED MOBILITY AND ON-DEMAND IMPACT LANDINGS. THE HELMET'S V.A.T.S. MATRIX INCREASES V.A.T.S.' HIT CHANCE, AND THE CUSTOM HOT-ROD FLAMES PAINT SCHEME BOOSTS AGILITY. BOTH ARMS ARE EQUIPPED WITH OPTIMIZED BRACERS THAT REDUCE THE ACTION POINT COST OF POWER ATTACKS, AND THE LEGS HAVE KINETIC SERVOS THAT INCREASE AP REFRESH SPEED WHILE YOU'RE IN MOTION.

### MODIFIED X-01 POWER ARMOR

THIS SUIT OF X-01 POWER ARMOR HAS BEEN CUSTOMIZED FOR MELEE COMBAT. EVERY PIECE HAS BEEN UPGRADED WITH MK. VI MODS AND TITANIUM PLATING FOR DAMAGE MITIGATION AND DURABILITY. THE TORSO'S TESLA COILS DEAL ENERGY DAMAGE TO NEARBY ENEMIES. THE HELMET'S TARGETING HUD HIGHLIGHTS LIVING CREATURES, MAKING IT MUCH EASIER TO SPOT POTENTIAL THREATS. THE LEGS' OPTIMIZED SERVOS REDUCE THE ACTION POINT COST FOR SPRINTING, AND THE ARMS' OPTIMIZED BRACERS REDUCE THE ACTION POINT COST FOR POWER ATTACKS.

# ★ AMMO

What good is a gun without ammo? All ammunition is weightless, so there's never a reason to avoid collecting it. Your level determines which ammo types can appear in containers or on defeated enemies. However, there are a few types of ammo that only appear at specific locations. You'll find plenty of ammo scattered throughout the Commonwealth, but when you're running low on a specific type, head to the nearest trader to see what's in stock.

## AMMO TYPES

| NAME | VALUE | MIN. LEVEL |
|---|---|---|
| .308 Round | 3 | 4 |
| .38 Round | 1 | 1 |
| .44 Round | 3 | 18 |
| .45 Round | 2 | 12 |
| .50 Caliber Round | 4 | 17 |
| 10 mm Round | 2 | 1 |
| 2 mm Electromagnetic Cartridge | 10 | 28 |

| NAME | VALUE | MIN. LEVEL |
|---|---|---|
| 5.56 Round | 2 | 24 |
| 5 mm Round | 1 | 24 |
| Alien Blaster Round | 1 | — |
| Cannonball | 8 | — |
| Cryo Cell | 10 | — |
| Flamer Fuel | 1 | 10 |
| Flare | 1 | — |
| Fusion Cell | 3 | 7 |

| NAME | VALUE | MIN. LEVEL |
|---|---|---|
| Fusion Core | 200 | 10 |
| Gamma Round | 10 | 10 |
| Mini Nuke | 100 | — |
| Missile | 25 | 9 |
| Plasma Cartridge | 5 | 17 |
| Railway Spike | 1 | 10 |
| Shotgun Shell | 3 | 14 |

## HELPFUL HINT
*from Vault Boy!*

Did You Know?

ALIEN BLASTER ROUNDS, CANNONBALLS, CRYO CELLS, FLARES, AND MINI NUKES DON'T APPEAR RANDOMLY. THESE RARE AMMO TYPES CAN ONLY BE FOUND AT SPECIFIC LOCATIONS OR ON SPECIFIC INDIVIDUALS. HOWEVER, MOST OF THEM CAN BE PURCHASED FROM VENDORS.

---
★
# QUESTS
---

## INTRODUCTION:
## HELPING OTHERS TO HELP YOURSELF

**Q**uality of life depends on the friends you make.

**U**nderstand the predicament you are facing.

**E**scape situations you find uncomfortable.

**S**tudy before making life-changing decisions.

**T**rust in yourself to adapt over time.

It has come to our attention that the vault dweller's continued well-being outside in the Commonwealth is dependent upon working on a variety of tasks. Some are simple activities designed to make friends, win favor, improve combat, seek an interesting item or two, or to stave off the feeling of hopelessness and dread you may be experiencing. Others are complex, multistage explorations that may lead to difficult decisions that you cannot take back and that change the Commonwealth forever.

At this time, you may be feeling overwhelmed. Don't worry; this is perfectly natural. Please consult your vault doctor for the correct dosage of chems to ease this anxiety.

The vast array of quests available show up in the Data > Quests menu of your Pip-Boy. RobCo Industries is proud to show a list of all activities you can undertake. On the left side of the Quests screen are the names of your quests. On the right side of the screen is a brief description of the objective you have reached in the highlighted quest, and underneath is the objective itself.

---

### HELPFUL HINT
*from Vault Boy!*   **Did You Know?**

MAKING THE MOST OF YOUR PIP-BOY SHOULD BE SECOND NATURE TO A SEASONED EXPLORER. BUT ARE YOU MORE OF A TIMID TIMMY? WELL, MAKE SURE YOU HIGHLIGHT THE QUEST YOU'RE INTERESTED IN, WHILE OPTIONALLY TURNING OFF ANY OTHER QUESTS THAT CAN WAIT UNTIL LATER. THAT WAY YOU CAN SEE HIGHLIGHTED MARKERS ON YOUR WORLD MAP AND COMPASS POINTING YOU IN THE CORRECT DIRECTION. THIS EVEN WORKS WITH MISCELLANEOUS QUESTS AS LONG AS YOU HIGHLIGHT THE OBJECTIVE FIRST. ARE THERE TOO MANY MARKERS CLOGGING UP YOUR VIEW? THEN HIGHLIGHT ONLY THE QUEST YOU NEED DIRECTIONS FOR. OR BETTER YET, REMAIN COMFORTABLY AND SENSIBLY UNDERGROUND.

---

If a quest doesn't have a name, it is noted as "miscellaneous." These are one or more objectives and aren't usually related to each other. Some of these may lead to quests. Others may lead to more straightforward, smaller victories. Or traps.

# QUESTING THE VAULT-TEC WAY

Comprehensive and thorough scientific testing projections using the SimTek 5000 indicate the necessity to further separate and define the types of quests available to you on your travels. These are divided into the following groupings:

## MAIN QUESTS

It appears you have woken from your cryogenetic slumber, Vault Dweller. These quests chart the progress you're likely to take to reunite yourself with your offspring, and as deemed to be the quests most important to you, they are referenced first.

## INSTITUTE QUESTS

This faction of important scientists has a distinct vision of the Commonwealth, and you're able to play an integral role in helping realize this. Meet a man named Father during your Main Quest, and seek further information then.

## BROTHERHOOD OF STEEL QUESTS

After an unequivocal arrival, this military fraternity of honor-bound technology salvagers requires your assistance in helping their cause. Should you wish to work with Paladin Danse and eventually Elder Maxson, find out more in this section.

## THE RAILROAD QUESTS

A clandestine group of synth sympathizers led by Desdemona, the Railroad needs your help in ferrying the downtrodden to safety. Latest data shows the Railroad recently left a compromised home base close to Lexington. Perhaps the Freedom Trail holds the answer?

## MINUTEMEN QUESTS

A ragtag band of surface dwellers, Preston Garvey and his crew want nothing more than a new society to blossom. Are you game to help establish settlements and trade routes and help fellow settlers build a new utopia? The aptly-named Museum of Freedom is where to find these folks.

## SIDE QUESTS

Perhaps you'd like to meet and greet (or eventually maim) potential companions, rescue hapless fools who have gotten themselves in a bind, or solve a conundrum not linked to the main factions? Then try this pot-luck selection of disparate and unrelated activities.

## LOCATION QUESTS

It's a large and frankly terrifying world out there. Fortunately, Vault-Tec is here to provide notes on which locations have one or more activities to undertake. Some are frivolous, but many offer monetary rewards, and some offer hope to those who need it. Seek them all in the Map chapter of this book.

## RANDOM ENCOUNTERS

You have every right to be suspicious, as danger may arrive in many guises, at any time, and in every place you might wander. But a list of probable encounters can ease your consternation.

### VAULT-TEC RECOMMENDS

**WHERE ARE YOUR MAPS?**

Each quest has a compilation of the most likely objectives available and the order you complete them. After that is a list of known locations to visit during the quest. Use the page numbers found in the location lists to find that area in the Map chapter. Usually it will be a schematic of the surface area, along with important items and an optimal path through the route. Combine both chapters while researching your quest and never be lost again!

DATA

QUESTS

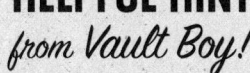  

**HELPFUL HINT** *from Vault Boy!* **Did You Know?**

LIKE A PEBBLE THROWN INTO A POND (A PREWAR POND OF COURSE, AS PRESENT-DAY PONDS ARE LIKELY TO DISSOLVE YOUR PEBBLE), YOUR ACTIONS CAUSE RIPPLE EFFECTS THAT MAY OR MAY NOT BE OBVIOUS TO YOU. CERTAIN FRIENDSHIPS WITH ONE SET OF PALS, AND THE TASKS THEY ASK YOU TO COMPLETE FOR THEM, MAY BE IN CONFLICT WITH ANOTHER GROUP'S WISHES. ARE YOU CONFLICTED ABOUT AN ACTION YOU'RE GOING TO UNDERTAKE? THEN PONDER THESE DECISIONS CAREFULLY AND CONSULT THIS CHAPTER. ALSO BE SURE TO MAKE EYE CONTACT WHEN TALKING TO OTHERS.

# QUESTS: A BIG TABLE

Here is a big table. It lists all the quests Vault-Tec has predicted may be available on your travels. As always, the Vault-Tec Documentation Department's simulations guarantee close (but not 100 percent) accuracy.

Have a great—and careful—day!

| QUEST NAME | QUEST TYPE | PAGE |
|---|---|---|
| Big Dig, The | Side Quest | 185 |
| Building a Better Crop | The Institute (Miscellaneous) | 129 |
| Butcher's Bill 2 | The Railroad Quest (Radiant) | 165 |
| Abernathy Farm: Retribution | Minutemen Quest (Radiant Recruitment) | 179 |
| Ad Victoriam | Brotherhood of Steel Quest (Main) | 145 |
| Airship Down | The Institute (Main) | 127 |
| Appropriation | The Institute (Radiant) | 133 |
| Banished from the Institute | The Institute (Miscellaneous) | 125 |
| Battle of Bunker Hill | The Institute (Main) | 122 |
| Benign Intervention | Side Quest | 184 |
| Blind Betrayal | Brotherhood of Steel Quest (Main) | 142 |
| Boston After Dark | The Railroad Quest (Miscellaneous) | 163 |
| Burning Cover | The Railroad Quest (Main) | 162 |
| Butcher's Bill 1 | The Railroad Quest (Radiant) | 165 |
| Call to Arms | Brotherhood of Steel Quest (Main) | 135 |
| Clean Equation, A | The Railroad Quest (Radiant) | 169 |
| Cleansing the Commonwealth | Brotherhood of Steel Quest (Radiant) | 153 |
| Clearing the Way | Minutemen Quest (Radiant Recruitment) | 180 |
| Combat Zone | Side Quest | 498 |
| Concierge | The Railroad Quest (Radiant) | 167 |
| Confidence Man | Side Quest | 187 |
| Curtain Call | Side Quest | 188 |
| Dangerous Minds | Main Quest (Act II) | 115 |
| Defend a Settlement | Minutemen Quest (Radiant Ownership) | 182 |
| Defend Artillery | Minutemen Quest (Radiant Ownership) | 182 |
| Defend the Castle | Minutemen Quest (Main) | 175 |
| Detective Case Files | Side Quest | 189-193 |
| Devil's Due, The | Side Quest | 197 |
| Diamond City Blues | Side Quest | 194 |
| Disappearing Act, The | Side Quest | 189 |
| Duty or Dishonor | Brotherhood of Steel Quest (Miscellaneous) | 150 |
| Emergent Behavior | Side Quest | 198 |
| End of the Line | The Institute (Main) | 126 |
| Feeding the Troops | Brotherhood of Steel Quest (Radiant) | 154 |
| Fire Support | Brotherhood of Steel Quest (Main) | 135 |
| First Step, The | Minutemen Quest (Radiant Recruitment) | 178 |
| Food | Minutemen Quest (Radiant Ownership) | 183 |
| Form Ranks | Minutemen Quest (Main) | 175 |
| From Within | Brotherhood of Steel Quest (Main) | 139 |
| Getting a Clue | Main Quest (Act I) | 113 |
| Ghoul Problem | Minutemen Quest (Radiant Recruitment) | 180 |
| Glowing Sea, The | Main Quest (Act II) | 116 |
| Greenskins | Minutemen Quest (Radiant Recruitment) | 179 |
| Guilded Grasshopper, The | Side Quest | 190 |
| Here There be Monsters | Side Quest | 199 |
| High Ground | The Railroad Quest (Radiant) | 169 |
| Hole in the Wall | Side Quest | 212 |
| House Divided, A | The Institute (Miscellaneous) | 131 |
| Human Error | Side Quest | 200 |
| Hunter/Hunted | Main Quest (Act II) | 117 |
| Hypothesis | The Institute (Radiant) | 132 |

| QUEST NAME | QUEST TYPE | PAGE |
|---|---|---|
| In Sheep's Clothing | Location Quest: Freeform (Diamond City) | 442 |
| Inside Job | Minutemen Quest (Main) | 175 |
| Institutionalized | Main Quest (Act II) | 120 |
| Jackpot | The Railroad Quest (Radiant) | 166 |
| Jewel of the Commonwealth | Main Quest (Act I) | 111 |
| Kicked out of the Railroad | The Railroad Quest (Miscellaneous) | 163 |
| Kid in a Fridge | Side Quest | 202 |
| Kidnapped Trader | Minutemen Quest (Radiant Ownership) | 183 |
| Kidnapping | Minutemen Quest (Radiant Recruitment) | 179 |
| Last Voyage of the U.S.S. Constitution | Side Quest | 203 |
| Leading by Example | Brotherhood of Steel Quest (Radiant) | 154 |
| Learning Curve | Brotherhood of Steel Quest (Radiant) | 154 |
| Liberty Reprimed | Brotherhood of Steel Quest (Main) | 140 |
| Long Road Ahead | Side Quest | 206 |
| Long Time Coming | Side Quest | 191 |
| Loose End, A | Brotherhood of Steel Quest (Miscellaneous) | 151 |
| Lost Patrol, The | Brotherhood of Steel Quest (Miscellaneous) | 148 |
| Lost Soul | The Railroad Quest (Radiant) | 169 |
| Mankind—Redefined | The Institute (Main) | 123 |
| Mass Fusion (the Institute) | The Institute (Main) | 123 |
| Memory Den, The | Location Quest: Freeform (Goodneighbor) | 488 |
| Memory Interrupted | The Railroad Quest (Miscellaneous) | 164 |
| Mercer Safehouse | The Railroad Quest (Radiant) | 166 |
| Miscellaneous (Atom Cats Garage): Atom Cats* | Location Quest (Atom Cats Garage) | 391 |
| Miscellaneous (Bunker Hill): Fallen Hero* | Location Quest: Freeform (Bunker Hill) | 425 |
| Miscellaneous (Bunker Hill): Meg's Tour | Location Quest: Freeform (Bunker Hill) | 425 |
| Miscellaneous (Bunker Hill): Prep School* | Location Quest: Freeform (Bunker Hill) | 425 |
| Miscellaneous (Bunker Hill): Traffic Jam* | Location Quest: Freeform (Bunker Hill) | 425 |
| Miscellaneous (Cambridge Polymer Labs): Cambridge Polymer Labs* | Location Quest (Cambridge Polymer Labs) | 408 |
| Miscellaneous (Charles View Amphitheater): A Pillar of the Community* | Location Quest (Charles View Amphitheater) | 447 |
| Miscellaneous (Chestnut Hillock Reservoir): Edwin's Terminal* | Location Quest (Chestnut Hillock Reservoir) | 320 |
| Miscellaneous (Combat Zone): Combat Zone* | Location Quest (Combat Zone) | 498 |
| Miscellaneous (Diamond City): Botany Class* | Location Quest: Freeform (Diamond City) | 440 |
| Miscellaneous (Diamond City): Brother Against Brother* | Location Quest: Freeform (Diamond City) | 440 |
| Miscellaneous (Diamond City): Diamond City's Most Wanted* | Location Quest: Freeform (Diamond City) | 439 |
| Miscellaneous (Diamond City): End Game* | Location Quest: Freeform (Diamond City) | 442 |
| Miscellaneous (Diamond City): Fly Fishing* | Location Quest: Freeform (Diamond City) | 441 |
| Miscellaneous (Diamond City): Holidays* | Location Quest: Freeform (Diamond City) | 442 |
| Miscellaneous (Diamond City): Home Run!* | Location Quest: Freeform (Diamond City) | 440 |
| Miscellaneous (Diamond City): New Hair, New Face* | Location Quest: Freeform (Diamond City) | 440 |
| Miscellaneous (Diamond City): Nuka Cola Needs* | Location Quest: Freeform (Diamond City) | 442 |
| Miscellaneous (Diamond City): Pool Cleaning* | Location Quest: Freeform (Diamond City) | 440 |
| Miscellaneous (Diamond City): Wedding Day* | Location Quest: Freeform (Diamond City) | 442 |
| Miscellaneous (Diamond City): World Series Win* | Location Quest: Freeform (Diamond City) | 441 |
| Miscellaneous (Drumlin Diner): Drumlin Diner Shakedown* | Location Quest (Drumlin Diner) | 264 |
| Miscellaneous (Dunwich Borers): Dunwich Borers* | Location Quest (Dunwich Borers) | 327 |
| Miscellaneous (Egret Tours Marina): Phyllis Daily* | Location Quest (Egret Tours Marina) | 373 |
| Miscellaneous (Fens Street Sewer): Dear Detective* | Location Quest (Fens Street Sewer) | 432 |
| Miscellaneous (General Atomics Factory): Quality Assurance* | Location Quest (General Atomics Factory) | 514 |
| Miscellaneous (General Atomics Galleria): Galleria* | Location Quest (General Atomics Galleria) | 280 |
| Miscellaneous (Goodneighbor): Art Appreciation* | Location Quest: Freeform (Goodneighbor) | 489 |
| Miscellaneous (Goodneighbor): The Cleaner* | Location Quest: Freeform (Goodneighbor) | 489 |
| Miscellaneous (Goodneighbor): Familiar Faces* | Location Quest: Freeform (Goodneighbor) | 489 |
| Miscellaneous (Goodneighbor): Hazardous Material* | Location Quest: Freeform (Goodneighbor) | 488 |
| Miscellaneous (Goodneighbor): MacCready for Action* | Location Quest: Freeform (Goodneighbor) | 489 |
| Miscellaneous (Goodneighbor): Recruiting Hancock* | Location Quest: Freeform (Goodneighbor) | 489 |
| Miscellaneous (Goodneighbor): Tough Times* | Location Quest: Freeform (Goodneighbor) | 488 |
| Miscellaneous (Graygarden): Supervisor Brown* | Location Quest (Graygarden) | 304 |

| QUEST NAME | QUEST TYPE | PAGE |
|---|---|---|
| Rogue Courser | Minutemen Quest (Radiant Recruitment) | 181 |
| Sanctuary | Minutemen Quest (Main) | 172 |
| Secret of Cabot House, The | Side Quest | 209 |
| Semper Invicta | Brotherhood of Steel Quest (Main) | 136 |
| Shadow of Steel | Brotherhood of Steel Quest (Main) | 137 |
| Shattered | Main Quest (Act II) | 115 |
| Show No Mercy | Brotherhood of Steel Quest (Main) | 138 |
| Sight, The | Minutemen Quest (Main) | 172 |
| Silver Shroud, The | Side Quest | 210 |
| Spoils of War | Brotherhood of Steel Quest (Main) | 144 |
| Stop the Raiding | Minutemen Quest (Radiant Ownership) | 182 |
| Story of the Century | Location Quest: Freeform (Diamond City) | 441 |
| Suspected Synth | Minutemen Quest (Radiant Ownership) | 183 |
| Synth Retention | The Institute (Main) | 121 |
| Tactical Thinking | Brotherhood of Steel Quest (Main) | 143 |
| Taking Independence | Minutemen Quest (Main) | 173 |
| Taking Point | Minutemen Quest (Radiant Recruitment) | 180 |
| To the Mattresses | The Railroad Quest (Radiant) | 168 |
| Tour of Duty | Brotherhood of Steel Quest (Main) | 137 |
| Tradecraft | The Railroad Quest (Main) | 156 |
| Trouble Brewin' | Location Quest: Freeform (Goodneighbor) | 490, 506 |
| Troubled Waters | Location Quest (Graygarden) | 304 |
| Underground Undercover | The Railroad Quest (Main) | 156 |
| Unlikely Valentine | Main Quest (Act I) | 112 |
| Variable Removal | The Railroad Quest (Radiant) | 168 |
| Vault 81 | Side Quest | 212 |
| War Never Changes | Main Quest (Act I) | 110 |
| Water | Minutemen Quest (Radiant Ownership) | 183 |
| Weathervane | The Railroad Quest (Radiant) | 167 |
| When Freedom Calls | Minutemen Quest (Main) | 170 |
| With Our Powers Combined | Minutemen Quest (Main) | 177 |

## VAULT-TEC RECOMMENDS

HOW DO I SEARCH FOR MISCELLANEOUS OBJECTIVES?

Glad you asked: Any quest with an asterisk (*) will not appear on your Pip-Boy. What should you do? First, remain calm. Second, any unnamed quest appears under "M" for "Miscellaneous" in this chart. Fortunately, the location of the occurring quest is also listed, enabling you to look up the quest by location. So if you've discovered a new place to explore, check this chart (or the Map chapter) for evidence of quest activities before continuing.

CLEANLINESS IS GODLINESS

STAY FIT, STAY FOCUSED

AMERICA LIVES ON ...IN YOU

# MAIN QUEST: ACT I

## Quest
## WAR NEVER CHANGES

## Quest
## OUT OF TIME

1. EXIT VAULT 111
2. GO HOME
3. TALK TO CODSWORTH
4. SEARCH THE NEIGHBORHOOD WITH CODSWORTH
5. KILL THE INSECTS
6. INVESTIGATE CONCORD

**Locations to Explore**

– VAULT 111 (PAGE 257)              – CONCORD (PAGE 262)
– SANCTUARY (PAGE 258)

---

### YOU'RE ONE S.P.E.C.I.A.L. FAMILY

Rise and shine! After making some changes to your appearance, explore your domicile until there's a knock at the door. Great news! The Vault-Tec representative is here to help secure your future.

### HELPFUL HINT
### from Vault Boy!

PLEASE FILL IN THE REGISTRATION FORM TO THE BEST OF YOUR ABILITIES. LITERALLY. MADE A MISTAKE? DON'T WORRY, YOU CAN REASSIGN YOUR SPECIALS JUST BEFORE LEAVING VAULT 111.

### VAULT-TEC RECOMMENDS

ESSENTIAL READING

 **GROGNAK THE BARBARIAN COMIC**

Peruse the Grognak the Barbarian comic in the kitchen and Shaun's You're S.P.E.C.I.A.L. book in your child's bedroom. Such reading materials offer excellent insights and statistical data to benefit your predicament, but only after exiting Vault 111.

When your day becomes a trifle more chaotic, follow the instructions of the government personnel and seek refuge inside Vault 111. Ignore the gnawing fear you might feel; this is quite natural. Please enter the decontamination pod.

---

### SEEKING SANCTUARY AND SHAUN

### HELPFUL HINT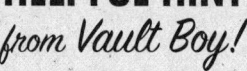
### from Vault Boy!

RISE AND SHINE! IT IS PERFECTLY NORMAL TO FEEL SOMEWHAT GROGGY AFTER SPENDING AN EXTENDED PERIOD OF TIME INSIDE A CRYOSTASIS CAPSULE. PLEASE LOCATE YOUR VAULT DOCTOR FOR FURTHER ASSISTANCE. YOU ARE ALSO ENCOURAGED TO LEARN AND PERFECT THE ART OF ASSIGNING ITEMS AND WEAPONS TO YOUR FAVORITES MENU. TRY IT!

There's little time to make sense of your predicament. Follow the corridors of the vault to the overseer's terminal and open the evacuation tunnel.

### VAULT-TEC RECOMMENDS

PEST CONTROL: INITIAL ARMAMENTS

 **10MM PISTOL**

Don't leave home without a 10-mm pistol, ammunition, and the Pip-Boy, which you find at the vault door. Test your gun (or punching) skills on the Radroaches that inhabit this vault. The lack of cleanliness here is far from the norm for a Vault-Tec structure. Please accept our apologies.

## VAULT-TEC RECOMMENDS

### LOOTING VAULT 111

#### HOLOTAPE GAME: RED MENACE
#### CRYOLATOR

Thoroughly inspect Vault 111. Find your first Holotape for the popular Red Menace video game in the cafeteria terminal. The overseer's chamber has an impressive weapon — the Cryolator — locked in a secure cabinet (Master). Return at your convenience with the necessary lockpicking skill to obtain this impressive armament.

Head east and discover the settlement of Sanctuary. Locate Codsworth outside your old home and explore Sanctuary with him (or clear the area beforehand). Watch out for the poisonous spit of any Bloatflies you encounter.

Codsworth recommends widening the search for Shaun. Head southeast; you're likely to run into a friendly dog at the Red Rocket Truck Stop. He's sure to be a faithful companion. Perhaps the first of many.

 **COMPANION: DOGMEAT**

The pond northwest of Concord is a breeding ground for Bloodbugs—a disgusting winged fly with filthy proboscis strikes. But the real threat are the Raiders holed up in the town. This foul-mouthed bunch of psychotic wastrels favors any sort of weapon that mangles. They cannot be reasoned with.

Search the Museum of Freedom here to encounter Preston Garvey of the Minutemen. Consider helping his faction before moving on.

Otherwise, your exploration toward Boston continues.

> ## HELPFUL HINT
> ### from Vault Boy! 〔Did You Know?〕
>
> FEELING LOST? OVERWHELMED? ALL ALONE? DON'T FRET! FURTHER ADVICE ON YOUR CURRENT EXPLORATION IS NOW AVAILABLE ON YOUR PIP-BOY. BRING UP THE QUEST MENU FOR MORE DETAILS. IF YOU WISH TO INTERACT WITH PRESTON GARVEY (AND SEARCH CONCORD MORE THOROUGHLY), CONSULT THE "MINUTEMEN QUESTS" SECTION OF THIS GUIDE.

DATA

QUESTS

## *Quest*
# JEWEL OF THE COMMONWEALTH

1. GO TO DIAMOND CITY
2. FIND INFORMATION ABOUT SHAUN
3. GO TO VALENTINE'S DETECTIVE AGENCY

**Locations to Explore**

– DIAMOND CITY (PAGE 433)

### DIAMOND IN THE ROUGH

It seems Diamond City is the best hope for gathering more information about Shaun. Getting there from Sanctuary is a long trek southeast. Once you cross the bridge into the remains of the city, look for signs pointing you in the direction of the Diamond.

> ## HELPFUL HINT
> ### from Vault Boy! 〔Did You Know?〕
>
> IT'S GOOD TO HAVE OPTIONS: IF THE HOSTILES OF DOWNTOWN BOSTON DON'T SCARE YOU, THERE'S ALWAYS THE TOWNSHIP OF GOODNEIGHBOR TO LOCATE FIRST. TRY SPEAKING TO IRMA AT THE MEMORY DEN THERE; SHE MIGHT BE ABLE TO POINT YOU IN THE RIGHT DIRECTION AFTER YOU SIT FOR A FEW MINUTES.

At the entrance, you run into a reporter named Piper. She tells you how to fool the guard on the intercom into letting you in.

At the entrance, speak with Mayor McDonough and get his thoughts on Piper. Then head into Diamond City Market.

 Like to influence the powerful? Chat to the mayor about his situation with Piper if you wish.

Who can help you in this bustling market? Most are friendly folks, and asking any of the following provides a clue to your next move:

– **DANNY SULLIVAN (THE GATE GUARD)**
– **PASTOR CLEMENTS (OF THE ALL FAITHS CHAPEL)**
– **NAT (PIPER'S KID SISTER, SELLING COPIES OF PUBLIC OCCURRENCES)**
– **PIPER (AFTER SHE INTERVIEWS YOU)**
– **MOE CRONIN (SWATTERS SALESMAN EXTRAORDINAIRE)**
– **JOHN THE BARBER**
– **ARTUO THE WEAPONS MERCHANT**
– **PROPRIETOR OF THE VALENTINE DETECTIVE AGENCY**

DIVERSIONS IN DIAMOND CITY

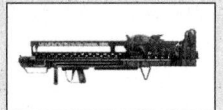  

**BIG BOY**
**OLD FAITHFUL**
**LIVE & LOVE 9**

Vault-Tec has determined that this township has a number of entertaining diversions. Some of the most helpful include:

Speaking to Moe Cronin at Swatters and completing a couple of tasks for him, then pocketing some Caps.

Purchasing a variety of impressive weaponry (such as Big Boy and Old Faithful) and equipment from Commonwealth Weaponry and Diamond City Surplus.

Purchasing Health and Chems from Chem-I-Care.

Chatting with the locals in the Dugout Inn.

Exploring the mayor's office and starting the cap-collecting you'll need to purchase your own shack for 2,000 Bottlecaps.

Experimenting with trespassing and stealing. Anything flagged with red text isn't yours, but occasionally, some items can be pilfered, like Live & Love from the schoolhouse. Be careful when stealing; you don't want the town to be furious with you!

Why not find out more about Freeform Activities while you're here? See page 433.

Visit the Valentine Detective Agency. It seems the hard-boiled detective Nick Valentine has gone missing. Ellie Perkins hopes you might lend a hand to help find him.

Charming Ellie Perkins allows you to shake her down for a few caps upon delivery of her boss.

## *Quest*
# UNLIKELY VALENTINE

1. FIND NICK VALENTINE
2. FREE NICK VALENTINE
3. TALK TO NICK VALENTINE
4. FOLLOW NICK VALENTINE

**Locations to Explore**
– PARK STREET STATION (PAGE 473)
– VAULT 114 (PAGE 454)

## FINDING AND FREEING NICK VALENTINE

Nick Valentine is your best lead in finding Shaun, but he's gone missing too. His last known location was Park Street Station, located at the northeast edge of Boston Common.

Gain access to the terminal either through hacking (Novice) or taking the password from Dino, the Triggerman guarding this area.

**HELPFUL HINT** from *Vault Boy!* **Did You Know?**

REACHING PARK STREET STATION WILL TAKE YOU INTO THE HEART OF DOWNTOWN BOSTON. CHOOSE YOUR ROUTE AND BATTLES CAREFULLY. SOME CONFLICTS ARE BEST AVOIDED.

Once inside Park Street Station, follow the subway tunnels and enter Vault 114. You'll face the Triggermen throughout, a group of armed thugs who favor submachine guns.

Shortly after entering Vault 114, you discover Nick Valentine is being held in the overseer's office. The door is locked and by a nearby terminal.

After a brief conversation, Nick will guide your escape from Vault 114.

LOOTING VAULT 114

**BOBBLEHEAD: SPEECH**
**ASTOUNDINGLY AWESOME TALES**

A thorough search of the subway and vault yields some surprises, such as a thirst-quenching Nuka Cola Quantum and some essential reading materials. But the overseer's office has perhaps the best prize: a limited-edition and official Vault-Tec Speech Bobblehead!

As you and Nick leave Vault 114, you're confronted by Skinny Malone, the gang's boss. He'll be joined by Darla and their bodyguards.

You can use your Charisma to influence how his confrontation plays out. It's possible to turn Darla and Malone against each other, or even talk your way out of the situation without any further violence.

You'll leave the way you came in, at which point Nick will return to his office in Diamond City. You can meet him there to continue your search for Shaun and receive your rewards for rescuing Nick.

 **FADED TRENCH COAT**

 **BOTTLECAPS (100)**

 **WORN FEDORA**

## Quest
# GETTING A CLUE

1. GO TO VALENTINE'S DETECTIVE AGENCY
2. TALK TO ELLIE
3. SIT DOWN
4. TELL NICK YOUR STORY
5. FOLLOW NICK
6. GET THE KEY TO KELLOGG'S HOUSE
7. INVESTIGATE KELLOGG'S HOUSE
8. FOLLOW NICK
9. SHOW DOGMEAT THE CIGAR

**Locations to Explore**
– DIAMOND CITY (PAGE 433)

## THE SECRETS OF KELLOGG'S HOUSE

Now that you and Nick are becoming acquainted, he invites you for a sit-down chat about Shaun. Apparently a man named Kellogg could be involved. Head over to Kellogg's house in Diamond City. The front door is locked.

Unlock the door by using a bobby pin (Master) or by visiting the mayor's office and asking for the key. They're understandably reluctant to hand out keys to strangers. Unless you bribe Geneva the receptionist with 250 Caps.

 Or, you can charm Geneva into handing you the keys, or use your Charisma on Mayor McDonough. It's the cheaper option.

**HELPFUL HINT** *from Vault Boy!* **Did You Know?**

FEELING CONFLICTED ABOUT FAST-TALKING THE SLOW-WITTED? DON'T BE! IT'S USUALLY BETTER TO USE YOUR CHARISMA (OR CAPS) TO SOLVE PROBLEMS, THOUGH STEALING THE KEY IS ALWAYS AVAILABLE FOR THOSE OF A SNEAKY DISPOSITION.

You enter Kellogg's house and poke around—literally, as there's a button under his desk to open a secret door. Press it.

Inspect the secret room for clues, including Kellogg's favorite brand of cigars. Exit and meet with Dogmeat. Show him a cigar to pick up the scent. Nick heads back to his office, though he can tag along with you if you wish.

 **COMPANION: NICK VALENTINE**

## Quest
# REUNIONS

1. FOLLOW DOGMEAT
2. SEARCH FOR CLUES TO KELLOGG (1-3)
3. CHECK ON DOGMEAT
4. FIND A WAY INTO FORT HAGEN
5. SEARCH FORT HAGEN
6. CONFRONT KELLOGG
7. KILL KELLOGG
8. SEARCH FOR MORE INFORMATION
9. DISCUSS YOUR FINDINGS WITH NICK
10. DISCUSS YOUR FINDINGS WITH PIPER

**Locations to Explore**
− FORT HAGEN (PAGE 308)

## DOGMEAT'S NOSE KNOWS

Dogmeat has the scent of Kellogg. Follow him out of the Fens, exit Diamond City, and head to the small pond to the southwest.

Something stinks on that ruined deck.

Dogmeat follows the trail along the railroad tracks. Search the freeway underpass for signs of Kellogg's blood. Prepare for more four-legged fiends; you encounter Wild Mongrels farther along the railroad tracks.

Search a metal railroad shack for evidence of a well-prepared trap expert, partial to a tipple of Gwinnett Stout.

The trail continues across a bridge. Fend off a shambling horde of Feral Ghouls. Locate the remains of an Assaultron and speak to it.

You'll head up into the woods to the perimeter of Fort Hagen, where more mutated wildlife (Wild Mongrels and Radstag Does) roam. Search for bloodied bandages. Then run to the exterior of Fort Hagen, where the trail goes cold at the blocked entrance.

### HELPFUL HINT
*from Vault Boy!*

 Did You Know?

WATCH FOR MACHINE-GUN TURRETS ON THE ROOF. HOWEVER, THEY AREN'T SO PROFICIENT AT PUNCTURING YOU IF YOU SCALE THE ROOF AND REMOVE THEM FROM BEHIND THEIR FIRING RADIUS.

## CONFRONTING KELLOGG

Enter Fort Hagen either by a roof hatch or by an underground parking lot exit door. Once inside, prepare to face numerous synths, humanoid machines that use laser weaponry. Also beware of laser turrets; check nearby terminals to shut them down.

Use the elevator to descend to the basement level. Expect fierce resistance from the synths. Access the command center and search for a wood-paneled office. It's here that Kellogg lets you in to face him.

## VAULT-TEC RECOMMENDS

LOOTING FORT HAGEN

**BOBBLEHEAD: ENERGY WEAPONS**
**GUNS AND BULLETS**
**U.S. COVERT OPERATIONS MANUAL**

A methodical approach to exploring Fort Hagen yields copious amounts of armaments and ammo, health and chems, and traps to disarm. Become well read by finding both Guns and Bullets (issue #2) and the U.S. Covert Operations Manual number 6. But the big prize is in the kitchens of the command center — another limited-edition and official Vault-Tec Bobblehead!

Deal with Kellogg and his synth bodyguards, and don't leave the area without Kellogg's terminal password or his Cybernetic Brain Augmenter.

Exit via a nearby elevator after accessing Kellogg's terminal and unlocking the security doors. There's a pistol here, too.

 **KELLOGG'S PISTOL**

Back at the Valentine Detective Agency in Diamond City, Piper has some ideas about your predicament. Nick mentions a place in Goodneighbor to visit and either of them are more than happy to accompany you.

 **COMPANION: PIPER**

# MAIN QUEST: ACT II

## Quest
# DANGEROUS MINDS

1. RETRIEVE A PIECE OF KELLOGG'S BRAIN
2. TALK TO DOCTOR AMARI
3. SIT IN THE MEMORY LOUNGER
.............................................
**Locations to Explore**
- GOODNEIGHBOR (PAGE 483)

## Quest
# SHATTERED

1. EXPLORE KELLOGG'S
   MEMORIES
2. TALK TO DOCTOR AMARI

---

## LOUNGING AROUND AT THE MEMORY DEN

Kellogg has kindly allowed you to use a bit of his brain—the Cybernetic Brain Augmenter—to delve deep into his memories. Gather it from Fort Hagen (as part of the previous quest, "Reunions").

### HELPFUL HINT
### from Vault Boy!

**Did You Know?**

HAVE YOU SAID HELLO TO THE VARIOUS FRIENDLY FACTIONS OF THE COMMONWEALTH YET? AFTER EMERGING FROM FORT HAGEN, YOU SEE A HUGE AIRSHIP HEADING FOR BOSTON AIRPORT. THAT MUST BELONG TO THE BROTHERHOOD OF STEEL, WHO ARE ALSO ACTIVE AT CAMBRIDGE POLICE STATION. YOU MIGHT HAVE HEARD OF THE FREEDOM TRAIL (IN BOSTON COMMON) FROM SCUTTLEBUTT IN DIAMOND CITY. WHY NOT LEARN SOME HISTORY AND CONTACT THE RAILROAD TOO? AND DON'T FORGET TO HELP OUT THE MINUTEMEN BACK IN CONCORD; NOW'S A GREAT TIME TO START MAKING FRIENDS!

Follow Nick Valentine's advice and locate Doctor Amari. This involves a trip into Boston, through the ruins of the Financial District, to the rough-and-tumble fortified settlement of Goodneighbor. Greet the locals, then head to the Memory Den. Irma owns this establishment.

Down in the basement, converse with Doctor Amari. After Nick Valentine volunteers to help out, you're invited to sit in the lounger to experience snippets of Kellogg's past.

## YOU'RE MORE THAN A MEMORY NOW

Wander through the ethereal strands of Kellogg's memory. You can watch the scene, interact with the figures in the memory, or find the continuation of the string path and skip the memory. The last memory (involving a child and an Institute Courser) seems most interesting.

Ready to leave? Then access the television in this memory. Back in the Memory Den, speak to Doctor Amari about an old Institute scientist to visit. Then depart the Memory Den, optionally talking to Nick on the way out for a different kind of conversation.

### VAULT-TEC RECOMMENDS

......................................................
#### GOODNEIGHBORLY ADVICE
Though Goodneighbor may seem to lack good social graces, spend some time here and you may discover the settlement's finer qualities. There's good trading opportunities at Daisy's Discount store. Mayor Hancock may be eccentric, but he seems like a decent fellow. The Memory Den houses Kent Connolly, the biggest Silver Shroud fan in the Commonwealth. For the variety of activities offered here, consult the Map Chapter entry for this location, on page 483.
......................................................

DATA

QUESTS

# Quest
# THE GLOWING SEA

## 1. FIND VIRGIL IN THE GLOWING SEA

................................

Locations to Explore

– CRATER OF ATOM (PAGE 361)

– ROCKY CAVE (VIRGIL'S LABORATORY) (PAGE 363)

---

### AN INHOSPITABLE OCEAN

Kellogg's memories and Doctor Amari's advice indicate you should locate an escaped Institute scientist. His last known position was deep in the most irradiated region of the Commonwealth—the Glowing Sea.

### HELPFUL HINT
### from Vault Boy!

Did You Know?

DID YOU KNOW THAT YOUR CHANCES OF SURVIVAL DECREASE DRAMATICALLY IF YOU'RE IMPROPERLY EQUIPPED FOR A TRIP INTO AN IRRADIATED ZONE? DON'T LET YOURSELF SUCCUMB TO RADIATION SICKNESS: REMEMBER THIS THREE-POINT PLAN:

1. PREVENTION! PURCHASE, SCAVENGE, OR CRAFT ALL THE RAD-X AND RADAWAY YOU'LL NEED FOR THIS JAUNT.

2. PROTECTION! HAZMAT SUITS MUST BE WORN AT ALL TIMES WHEN ENTERING IRRADIATED ZONES. HOWEVER, THEY OFFER LITTLE PROTECTION AGAINST ANY HOSTILES YOU MAY ENCOUNTER.

3. POWER! WANT THE VERY BEST IN BOTH PREVENTION AND PROTECTION? USE POWER ARMOR FOR THE DURATION OF YOUR TRIP.

Commence the long trek southwest, following the remains of the freeway until your Pip-Boy indicates a hike off-road is in order. Expect to face Radscorpions, Feral Ghouls, and other irradiated wildlife. When you reach the map marker, you are close to the Crater of the Atom.

---

Warning! You are trespassing when you enter the location of a strange cult, led by Mother Isolde. Though violence is always an option (search the area of a scrap of paper indicating a nearby cave), you can:

– LOWER YOUR WEAPON AND SPEAK TO MOTHER ISOLDE. ANSWER HER POLITELY. SHE DIRECTS YOU TO A NEARBY CAVE.

(Medium) Tell her you need information if you wish.

Locate the Rocky Cave roughly southwest of the Crater of the Atom. Watch for, or sneak past, the roaming Deathclaw.

You'll find Virgil inside this cave. He requests you help him locate a serum within the Institute in return for his knowledge.

(Medium) You have two opportunities to be inquisitive or secretive with your conversation.

### VAULT-TEC RECOMMENDS

SEEKING VIRGIL'S SERUM: MISCELLANEOUS QUESTING

Virgil mentions a serum he requires. Helping him won't achieve your overall goals, but if you're an amenable sort, you can help. Find out more about this Miscellaneous Quest on page 363.

.................................

    **VIRGIL'S RIFLE**

.................................

You also have the option to kill Virgil, or steal his unique laser rifle, which is a blast against super mutants!

# Quest
# HUNTER/HUNTED

1. TRAVEL TO C.I.T.
2. TUNE TO COURSER'S RADIO FREQUENCY
3. USE THE COURSER'S RADIO FREQUENCY TO TRACK COURSER
4. KILL THE COURSER
5. RECOVER COURSER CHIP

**Locations to Explore**
- GREENETECH GENETICS (PAGE 415)

## THE CAMBRIDGE COURSER

Virgil recommends infiltrating the Institute, an organization so secretive no surface dweller knows where their base of operations is. As they rely on teleportation, Virgil recommends you travel to the old C.I.T. ruins and use your Pip-Boy to pick up a signal from a Courser. Retrace your steps from the Glowing Sea, heading northeast into Cambridge. Locate the ruins of the old C.I.T. building.

Once here, select your Pip-Boy > Radio > Courser Signal. You hear a pinging noise. The pinging increases with frequency the closer you are to the Courser. Follow this audible trail to the Greenetech Genetics building. The structure is tall with a rusting green façade; you can't miss it.

## THE UNSYMPATHETIC SYNTH

Enter the Greenetech Genetics building. You stumble into a battle between Gunners, an armed militia who favor all types of weaponry as well as an abundance of turrets. There's also an unknown group farther up the tower.

Ascend the facility until you reach the Courser Z2-47. You can chat, but the conversation devolves into combat. Remove the chip from his corpse.

**COURSER CHIP**

## VAULT-TEC RECOMMENDS

### LOOTING GREENETECH GENETICS

  Did you make the most of your time at Greenetech Genetics? A thorough inspection of all rooms yields some excellent results, including three Fusion Cores for your Power Armor, a delicious Nuka Cola Quantum, and some required reading. There is also a synth named K1-98 to free, close to the Courser's location (Miscellaneous Quest, page 416).

# Quest
# THE MOLECULAR LEVEL

1. HAVE THE COURSER CHIP ANALYZED
2. SEARCH THE RAILROAD HQ
3. ANALYZE THE COURSER CHIP
4. RETURN TO VIRGIL
5. GET HELP TO BUILD THE SIGNAL INTERCEPTOR
6. (OPTIONAL) TALK TO THE BROTHERHOOD
7. (OPTIONAL) TALK TO THE MINUTEMEN
8. (OPTIONAL) TALK TO THE RAILROAD
9. TALK TO [FACTION SCIENTIST]
10. BUILD THE REFLECTOR PLATFORM
11. BUILD THE BEAM EMITTER

12. (OPTIONAL) SEARCH MILITARY SITES FOR
    A CIRCUIT BOARD
13. BUILD THE RELAY DISH
14. (OPTIONAL) SEARCH TELECOM SITES FOR
    A SENSOR MODULE
15. BUILD THE CONSOLE
16. (OPTIONAL) SEARCH HOSPITALS FOR
    A BIOMETRIC SCANNER
17. POWER UP THE SIGNAL INTERCEPTOR
18. TALK TO [FACTION SCIENTIST]
19. USE THE SIGNAL INTERCEPTOR

## Locations to Explore
- SANCTUARY (PAGE 258)
- CAMBRIDGE POLICE STATION (PAGE 403)
- PRYDWEN (PAGE 345)
- OLD NORTH CHURCH (PAGE 466)

## ON THE RIGHT TRACKS

Doctor Amari knows about synth technology, so visit her in Goodneighbor at the Memory Den. She suggests contacting the Railroad.

## VAULT-TEC RECOMMENDS

### FACTIONS AND THE ROAD TO FREEDOM

Have you made contact with the Railroad yet? If not, it is imperative you complete the Railroad Quest: Road to Freedom (page 155). You cannot advance your current quest until this occurs. This is also the last recommended opportunity to gain beneficial support from the Minutemen and the Brotherhood of Steel. Why not see what these three factions have to offer you? You'll be glad you did!

Enter the old church and access the Railroad HQ. A conversation with the Railroad leader, Desdemona, allows you to have the Courser Chip analyzed by Tinker Tom. Leave the Railroad HQ via the escape tunnel; this way you can remove the chain to the secret door and access this location more easily in the future.

Enter Virgil's laboratory back in the Glowing Sea. After updating him, he hands you some plans.

 **SIGNAL INTERCEPTOR PLANS**

## MAKING PLANS

You may have plans for a teleportation device, but building it is another matter. Fortunately, there are four different methods to accomplish this goal. The following assumes you are on friendly terms with each faction.

## Method #1: Brotherhood Steel

Head to the Cambridge Police Station, and fight off any Feral Ghouls as part of Brotherhood of Steel Quest: Fire Support. Speak to Paladin Danse about the signal interceptor. He'll allow Brotherhood resources to help you, providing you complete Brotherhood of Steel Quest: Call to Arms first.

Once you finish the quest, you can speak to the faction scientist Proctor Ingram about clues to constructing the signal interceptor.

## Method #2: Minutemen Mettle

Preston Garvey can help your cause, too, providing you finish the Minutemen Quest: When Freedom Calls. Head to Sanctuary (or whichever settlement you instructed him to move to) and ask Preston about the signal interceptor. He hopes you'll help out with some settlers first. Complete the Minutemen Quest: The First Step before you can receive help from this faction.

Once you finish the quest, you can speak to the faction scientist Sturges about clues to constructing the signal interceptor.

## Method #3: Railroad Resolution

Return to the Old North Church, and speak with Desdemona about the signal interceptor. She hopes you'll join the cause.

To prove yourself, you must complete the Railroad Quest: Tradecraft with Deacon before you can receive help from this faction.

Once you finish the quest, you can speak to the faction scientist Tinker Tom about clues to constructing the signal interceptor.

### Method #4: Misanthropic Moxie

Or, you can ignore all three factions and build a signal interceptor on your own, at any settlement workshop you have uncovered.

## BUILDING A BETTER TELEPORTER

Construction of the signal interceptor now begins in earnest. Clear an area of ground in one of your settlements (such as Sanctuary), and use the workshop to access the Special menu.

### Under Construction: Stabilized Reflector Platform

Time to construct the Stabilized Reflector Platform:

**Build with:**
- ALUMINUM (10)
- CIRCUITRY (3)
- STEEL (5)

**Requires:**
- POWER (3)

 **STABILIZED REFLECTOR PLATFORM**

Great work! Now chat with the faction scientist if you want to know about each special piece of junk required for the beam emitter, relay dish, and console. Remember you need to scavenge for the regular build parts, too.

## VAULT-TEC RECOMMENDS

### UNCOMMON SCAVENGING

Sourcing uncommon parts can be troublesome, so remember where to look to avoid unnecessary traipsing across the Commonwealth:

 The beam emitter requires a military-grade circuit board. These are located in military sites (usually shown on your Pip-Boy map as a star within a circle icon).

 The relay dish requires a sensor module. Acquire this in telecom sites or other tall structures, such as Trinity Tower.

 The Console requires a biometric scanner, usually found in hospitals (shown as a cross within a circle icon).

Don't worry! Your Pip-Boy is preprogrammed to point you toward the location where the item is guaranteed to be! Simply refer to the maps of the location for floor plans of the interior and other pertinent data. Thanks, Vault-Tec!

### Under Construction: Beam Emitter

**Build with:**
- RUBBER (2)
- STEEL (10)
- COPPER (1)
- MILITARY-GRADE CIRCUIT BOARD (1)
- CIRCUITRY (1)

**Requires:**
- POWER (20)

 **BEAM EMITTER**

Fantastic tinkering! Now for the next part of the teleport.

### Under Construction: Relay Dish

**Build with:**
- COPPER (3)
- STEEL (3)
- CLOTH (6)
- GOLD (3)
- SENSOR MODULE (1)

**Requires:**
- POWER (5)

 **RELAY DISH**

Amazing engineering abilities! Now fit the console together.

### Under Construction: Console

**Build with:**
- RUBBER (2)
- COPPER (3)
- STEEL (5)
- BIOMETRIC SCANNER (1)

**Requires:**
- POWER (2)

 **CONSOLE**

Truly first-class fabrication! Now be sure you connect everything: Access the Power > Generators part of your workshop, and build enough generators to power the entire device. Then attach wires from each generator to a component, so they power up. If you're correct, you can (optionally) talk to your faction scientist and use the signal interceptor.

## HELPFUL HINT from Vault Boy!

**Did You Know?**

DID YOU KNOW THAT EACH FACTION HAS ITS OWN REASONS FOR OBTAINING DATA FROM THE INSTITUTE? WHEN SPEAKING TO YOUR CHOSEN FACTION SCIENTIST, YOU MAY BE ASKED TO LOAD DATA FROM AN INSTITUTE TERMINAL ONTO A HOLOTAPE. BEFORE YOU AGREE, WHY NOT FIND OUT MORE BY CONSULTING THE RELATED QUESTS? REMEMBER: MENTAL CLARITY IS MOST IMPORTANT WHEN AGREEING TO TASKS YOU MIGHT NOT FULLY UNDERSTAND!

RELATED QUEST: BROTHERHOOD OF STEEL QUEST: FROM WITHIN (PAGE 139).

RELATED QUEST: THE MINUTEMEN QUEST: INSIDE JOB (PAGE 175).

RELATED QUEST: THE RAILROAD QUEST: UNDERGROUND UNDERCOVER (PAGE 156).

IF YOU'RE THINKING OF WORKING WITH THE INSTITUTE IN THE FUTURE, IT IS INADVISABLE TO REVEAL THEIR SECRETS TO OUTSIDE PARTIES, THOUGH IT IS POSSIBLE.

1. ENTER THE ELEVATOR
2. MEET THE DIVISION LEADERS

**Locations to Explore**
– THE INSTITUTE (PAGE 409)

---

## LIKE FATHER LIKE SON

The teleportation is a success. You reach the Institute. Listen to the voice directing you. Oblige the voice, and you soon find a man named Father, who runs the Institute.

After speaking with him and agreeing to join the Institute (an offer you can rescind at a later date), you are free to explore the facility.

Access Institute Bioscience and meet Doctor Clayton Holdren.

Find Chief Engineer Allie Filmore in the main concourse.

Access Institute SRB and meet acting director of the Synth Retention Bureau, Justin Ayo. He doesn't seem to trust you.

(Medium) Ask him about trusting you, if you wish.

Access Institute Advanced Systems and meet Doctor Madison Li, who installs a relay into your Pip-Boy, allowing Fast-Travel to and from this location.

### VAULT-TEC RECOMMENDS

FURTHER INSTITUTE INSIGHT

Once this quest is over, you have complete freedom to continue working for your chosen faction(s):

You can continue to help out the Brotherhood of Steel, the Railroad, or the Minutemen by installing the Holotape you were given in your previous quest. The terminal to download data from is close to your teleportation landing spot.

You can start to help out the Institute, too.

At some point (covered in the Faction quests), you need to choose a faction you deem most beneficial to your needs. When that happens, Main Quest: Act III begins. Remember: These decisions are not to be taken lightly!

### VAULT-TEC RECOMMENDS

THE FINAL ACT

Congratulations! You've made it to the end of Act II! But what about your continuing progress in your search for answers? Now your focus shifts to helping one (or more) of the major factions (literally) vying for power in the Commonwealth. You must now complete as many main faction quests as you wish, before picking a side to ally with: Only then will you feel a sense of true accomplishment.

# THE INSTITUTE QUESTS

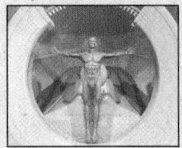

To begin the first of this faction's quests, you must complete Main Quest: Institutionalized, find Father, and agree to his request. You are free to continue Institute operations for as long as you wish. Please be aware that your relationships with the other main factions—the Brotherhood of Steel, the Railroad, and the Minutemen—may be negatively affected the more Institute quests you complete. It seems you can't be friends with everybody.

The following Institute quests become available:

| THE INSTITUTE QUESTS | | | |
|---|---|---|---|
| **Main Faction Quest** | **Location** | **Miscellaneous Faction Quest** | **Location** |
| Synth Retention | Page 121 | Building a Better Crop | Page 129 |
| Battle of Bunker Hill | Page 122 | Plugging a Leak | Page 130 |
| Mankind Redefined | Page 123 | A House Divided | Page 131 |
| Mass Fusion (Institute) | Page 123 | **Radiant Faction Quest** | **Location** |
| Pinned | Page 125 | Pest Control | Page 132 |
| Powering Up | Page 126 | Hypothesis | Page 132 |
| End of the Line | Page 126 | Appropriation | Page 133 |
| Airship Down | Page 127 | Reclamation | Page 133 |
| Nuclear Family | Page 128 | Political Leanings | Page 133 |

## Quest
# SYNTH RETENTION

1. TALK TO FATHER
2. MEET UP WITH THE COURSER
3. RECLAIM THE ROGUE SYNTH
4. RETURN TO FATHER
5. VISIT YOUR QUARTERS

**Locations to Explore**
- THE INSTITUTE (PAGE 409)
- NAHANT SHERIFF'S DEPARTMENT (PAGE 338)
- LIBERTALIA (PAGE 336)

### GIVE ME LIBERTALIA, OR GIVE ME DEATH

A rogue synth has been located, and you are tasked with reclaiming him. You have a Synth Courser named X6-88 to assist you with this task. Fast-Travel out from the Institute, and travel to Nahant township. This is almost due east but requires a long trek to the coast. The Nahant Sheriff's Department is deserted. Find your Courser buddy here.

Gabriel
So tell me, is the Institute so deviod of any resources that its stealing, plunder from hone-hard-working Commonwealth gangs?

## HELPFUL HINT
### from Vault Boy!

 Did You Know?

A DIRECT PATH ISN'T ALWAYS THE SAFEST PATH! TO REACH NAHANT, VAULT-TEC TOPOGRAPHICAL RADAR TECHNOLOGY SUGGESTS HEADING NORTHEAST THROUGH CHARLESTON, FOLLOWING THE MAIN ROAD TO COUNTY CROSSING, THEN CLEARING THE GIBSON POINT AREA OF HOSTILES. THEN IT'S A SHORT JAUNT TO LYNN PIER PARKING AND SOUTHEAST INTO THE COASTAL SETTLEMENT OF NAHANT. THE ALTERNATIVE? SWIMMING OUT FROM REVERE BEACH, WHICH IS BOTH DANGEROUS AND HIGHLY UNORTHODOX.

Begin your assault on this large Raider camp by sweeping the planks and rusting boats for enemies and neutralizing any turrets. You can swim to the rogue synth's location—the shanty tower built on the stern of a sunken tanker—or you can summon a small shack platform from the trash boat and ride it without getting your feet wet.

Climb up to and enter the captain's cabin, and X6-88 informs you of the rogue synth's reset code. Speak to Gabriel. You can:

- SLAY HIM AND HIS TWO LIEUTENANTS.
- RESET HIM, AND SLAY HIS TWO LIEUTENANTS.

LOOTING LIBERTALIA

 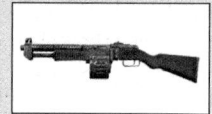

**U.S. COVERT OPERATIONS MANUAL**
**LE FUSIL TERRIBLES (SHOTGUN)**

Nahant township has been mostly picked clean of high-value collectibles, but the Libertalia Raider camp has loot to gather. There's some essential reading and a unique shotgun to claim from the captain's cabin area.

This mission is deemed successful either way. Return to the Institute and speak with Father. You're granted your own quarters with some useful supplies. Head there and speak to X6-88.

**REWARD: INSTITUTE QUARTERS AND GEAR**

## *Quest*
# THE BATTLE OF BUNKER HILL

1. SPEAK TO FATHER
2. (OPTIONAL) INFORM THE BROTHERHOOD
3. (OPTIONAL) INFORM THE RAILROAD
4. REACH BUNKER HILL
5. FIND THE ESCAPED SYNTHS
6. DEAL WITH THE ESCAPED SYNTHS
7. SPEAK WITH FATHER IN THE RUINS OF CIT

**Locations to Explore**
– BUNKER HILL (PAGE 423)
– C.I.T. RUINS (PAGE 408)

## RAISING HELL AT BUNKER HILL

Father has another task for you—recover the synths that have escaped from the Institute and fled to Bunker Hill. Optionally gather supplies and ammunition for this assault (trading at the Institute's synth equipment vendor). Then decide where your loyalties lie:

- THE INSTITUTE REQUIRES YOU TO RENDEZVOUS WITH A COURSER IN THE NARROW ALLEYS OF THE CHARLESTON NEIGHBORHOOD AND COMPLETE THE QUEST AS ORDERED.
- THE BROTHERHOOD OF STEEL REQUIRES YOU TO DESTROY THE SYNTHS: YOUR ENEMIES DURING THIS BATTLE ARE INSTITUTE AND RAILROAD FORCES.
- THE RAILROAD REQUIRES YOU TO FREE THE TRAPPED SYNTHS. YOUR ENEMIES DURING THIS BATTLE ARE INSTITUTE AND BROTHERHOOD OF STEEL FORCES.
- THE MINUTEMEN HAVE NO LOYALTY TO ANY OTHER FACTION, OR A DIRECT INVOLVEMENT IN THIS QUEST. BUNKER HILL BECOMES A SETTLEMENT YOU CAN DEVELOP ONCE THIS QUEST HAS BEEN COMPLETED.

Even if you're not loyal to the Institute, the Institute Quest: Mankind—Redefined will still be available after this quest.

(Hard) Request a clutch of Synth Beacon Grenades, allowing you to summon teleporting synths to aid you. They appear where you throw these projectiles.

 **SYNTH BEACON GRENADE (3)**

## HELPFUL HINT
*from Vault Boy!*

**Did You Know?**

SOMETIMES IT'S TRICKY TO KNOW WHO YOUR BUDDIES ARE IN THESE PARTS! WHO CAN YOU TRUST? THAT'S A JUDGMENT CALL ONLY YOU CAN MAKE, BUT IT'S ALWAYS BETTER TO MEET UP WITH THE LEADERS OF THE DIFFERENT FACTIONS, PAL AROUND WITH THEM FOR A FEW JAUNTS, AND WAIT UNTIL YOU'RE ASKED TO COMPLETE A TASK YOU FIND MORALLY REPREHENSIBLE. IF YOU'RE STILL FINE WITH FOLLOWING THOSE ORDERS, YOU KNOW YOU'VE MADE SOME FRIENDS FOR LIFE!

THE BONANZA AT BUNKER HILL

**LIVE & LOVE MAGAZINE**
**WASTELANDER'S FRIEND**

Keeping the residents of Bunker Hill on your side yields dividends if you're out to expand your magazine collection, your unique weapons armory, and even your settlements! Deb sells ammunition, Tony Savoldi offers you a place to stay, and Kay can patch you up. Bear that in mind before choosing sides; err on the side of the Minutemen if you're wanting to utilize these services.

The following assumes you are allied with the Institute. During your rendezvous with Courser X4-18, you receive some synth recall codes.

## SYNTH EXTRACTION DEPENDS ON YOUR FACTION

Working with the Courser, engage in a protracted firefight against your chosen enemies. Battle your way into this stronghold, and access the utility basement trapdoor.

The interior contains machine-gun turrets and additional enemies. Find the synths in a subterranean living quarters. Your definition of "freeing" each of them depends on your faction loyalties.

You can:

- **RESET THEM (AS PER INSTITUTE INSTRUCTIONS).**
- **KILL THEM (AS PER BROTHERHOOD OF STEEL INSTRUCTIONS).**
- **FREE THEM (AS PER RAILROAD INSTRUCTIONS).**

Optionally gather Caps from one when prompted—before your decision, if you wish. Then extract yourself from Bunker Hill.

Head west across Cambridge to the C.I.T. Ruins (north of the river), and find one of the many ground-floor entrances into the rotunda. Synths are advancing on a Super Mutant position throughout the three floors here. Ascend to the roof and explain yourself to Father.

### VAULT-TEC RECOMMENDS

QUICK ACCESS TO THE ROOF

With minimal scavenging opportunities, you may wish to ignore the fighting within the rotunda and simply head to the stairwell on the far eastern side. This offers direct access to the roof.

## Quest
# MANKIND REDEFINED

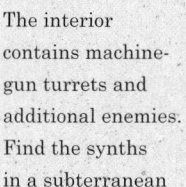

1. **ATTEND DIRECTORATE MEETING**
2. **SPEAK WITH FATHER**

Locations to Explore
- **THE INSTITUTE (PAGE 409)**

### YOUR PLASTIC PAL WHO'S FUN TO BE WITH

Following your rooftop chat, teleport into the Institute and head to the conference room. Engage in debate with the division heads, and agree to continue assisting this faction. The Courser X6-88 can now accompany you on any quest you wish.

 **COMPANION: X6-88**

## Quest
# MASS FUSION

1. **SPEAK WITH ALLIE FILMORE**
2A. **RELAY TO MASS FUSION**
2B. **INFORM THE BROTHERHOOD**
3. **LOCATE THE BERYLLIUM AGITATOR**
4. **RETRIEVE THE EXECUTIVE KEYCARD**
5. **PROCEED TO THE REACTOR LEVEL**
6. **(OPTIONAL) RESTORE POWER TO THE ELEVATOR**
7. **RETRIEVE THE BERYLLIUM AGITATOR**
8. **UNLOCK THE REACTOR**
9. **TAKE THE BERYLLIUM AGITATOR**
10. **ELIMINATE REACTOR LEVEL SECURITY**
11. **EXIT MASS FUSION**
12. **(OPTIONAL) ASSIST INSTITUTE FORCES IN THE LOBBY**
13. **SPEAK WITH ALLIE FILMORE**

Locations to Explore
- **MASS FUSION (PAGE 477)**

### TESTING YOUR LOYALTIES

After speaking to the scientist Allie Filmore, you agree to help her find something called a "Beryllium Agitator" from the ruins of Mass Fusion. Decide whether she'll accompany you or not; then you must make a potentially epoch-defining decision. You can:

- **RELAY TO MASS FUSION AND CONTINUE YOUR LOYALTY TO THE INSTITUTE. THIS QUEST CONTINUES (BELOW), SEVERAL BROTHERHOOD OF STEEL QUESTS FAIL, AND BROTHERHOOD OF STEEL QUEST: BROTHERHOOD OF STEEL SHUTDOWN BEGINS.**
- **LEAVE THE INSTITUTE, VISIT THE BROTHERHOOD OF STEEL, AND INFORM THEM, SWITCHING YOUR LOYALTIES TO THEM. THE BROTHERHOOD OF STEEL QUEST: SPOILS OF WAR BEGINS.**

## MASS CONFUSION

You relay to the Mass Fusion skyscraper roof, in the Financial District of Boston. After neutralizing all threats, descend one floor to the executive suites, and locate the balcony desk before the room with the Executive Research Lab Terminal. Gather the following from the desk:

**MASS FUSION EXECUTIVE LAB PASSWORD**

**MASS FUSION EXECUTIVE ID**

Now you can access the Executive Research Lab Terminal (Advanced) with a password. Read the personal intramails; the item you seek is in the facility's basement. And you're on the roof.

At the elevator, swipe the Mass Fusion Executive ID through the card reader. Ride the elevator all the way down, taking pot shots at enemy forces along the way. When the coast is clear, you can:

(Optional) Locate the circuit breaker in the chamber to the north and above your current position. Flip the breaker to power the elevator. Then return, swipe the ID card, and ride the elevator down to the lobby, maximizing enemy casualties as you go.

Locate the room to the north of your current position. Locate the Mass Fusion Labs Key on the desk. Use it to open the door to the adjacent chamber with the hole in the floor. Drop down, and continue a manual descent through the floors to the lobby, removing any potential enemy threats along the way.

**MASS FUSION LABS KEY**

Expect more enemy resistance in the lobby. Search for the service elevator, swiping your ID card to access it.

## VAULT-TEC RECOMMENDS

MASS HAUL AT MASS FUSION

**TESLA SCIENCE MAGAZINE
NUKA CHERRY**

As you fight through Mass Fusion, gather a few choice items—the Nuka Cherry in the laboratory on the roof; a copy of Tesla Science to the south on the uppermost accessible level once you're in the tower (grab it before you take the elevator down to the lobby); and a Steamer Trunk and Hazmat Suit in the reactor chamber, handy for the automated greeters you encounter once the Beryllium Agitator is yours.

## BERYLLIUM AGITATION

After stepping into the decontamination area (press that button!), move into the reactor chamber. Press the interlock release and activate the agitator receptacle. Grab what you came here for.

**BERYLLIUM AGITATOR**

The facility's robotic defenses are automatically activated. Reach the outer reactor room and engage a Sentry Bot and Protectron. After using your ID card to open the main door, bring your defenses to bear on an Assaultron. Then ascend the stairs to nullify another Protectron without being scorched by a laser turret.

Exit to the lobby. If you have the ammunition and abilities, help Institute forces rid the lobby of threats. Then rendezvous with Allie Filmore back inside the Institute.

## Quest
# PINNED

1. SPEAK TO FATHER
2. REACH THE HOUSE
3. SPEAK TO MINUTEMEN CONTACT
4. ELIMINATE THE OPPOSITION
5. SPEAK TO ENRICO THOMPSON
6. SPEAK TO WALLACE

**Locations to Explore**

– GRAYGARDEN (PAGE 304)

## DIPLOMACY AT WORK

Thanks to your success at Mass Fusion, plans to power up the Institute reactor are moving forward but the process has stalled somewhat as a scientist named Wallace hasn't arrived at the facility. Relay out from the Institute, and head west from Cambridge to Graygardens. Locate the homestead just west of the hydroponic garden. Depending on your previous actions, you meet one of the following factions here:

– IF YOU HAVE HAD NO DEALINGS WITH THE MINUTEMEN DURING YOUR ADVENTURE, YOU WILL HAVE GUNNERS TO REMOVE IN THIS LOCATION BEFORE YOU CAN RESCUE YOUR CONTACT.

– IF YOU HAVE HAD DEALINGS WITH THE MINUTEMEN, A NUMBER OF THEM ARE WAITING TO ATTACK THE STRUCTURE. SPEAK WITH THEM NOW. YOU CAN:

- AGREE TO THIS ATTACK, TURNING THE INSTITUTE HOSTILE. YOU CAN NO LONGER ALIGN WITH THEM. THE INSTITUTE QUEST: BANISHED FROM THE INSTITUTE BEGINS IF ANY INSTITUTE FORCES ARE KILLED.

- PERSUADE THE MINUTEMEN TO STAND DOWN. YOU CAN TELL THEM IT'S AN ORDER.

 (Easy, Medium) Or you can tell the Minutemen there's a misunderstanding, that they risk being wrong, there's no danger, threaten them, or tell them everyone is working together.

## HELPFUL HINT
### from Vault Boy!
**Did You Know?**

THOSE MINUTEMEN MAY HAVE GOOD INTENTIONS, BUT THEY FAIL TO SEE THE BIG PICTURE, DON'T THEY? DON'T WORRY ABOUT OFFENDING THESE FOLKS; IF YOU'RE HAPPY WORKING WITH THE INSTITUTE, THESE SETTLERS WON'T GET ANTSY AFTER SOME TOUGH-TALKING.

Inside the homestead, speak to your Institute contact Enrico Thompson. Wallace has barricaded himself behind a nearby door. Make verbal contact with this agitated fellow, and convince him to help out.

 (Medium, Hard) Calming or threatening are both options.

## VAULT-TEC RECOMMENDS

BECOMING SELF-SUFFICIENT IN GRAYGARDENS

 **MUTFRUIT**

Even though the settlement of Graygardens may not have highly prized collectibles, it grows an abundance of crops you can taste. Helping out the supervisor robots isn't only neighborly, but it can also add a special robot settlement to your Minutemen-related real estate empire!

DATA

QUESTS

125

## Quest
# POWERING UP

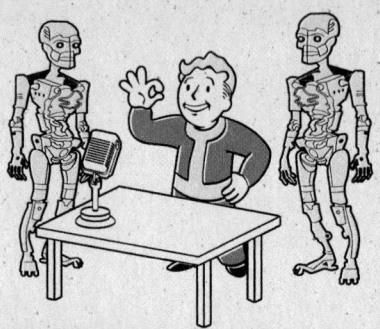

1. SPEAK TO FATHER
2. RECORD THE SPEECH
3. SPEAK WITH FATHER
4. RECONFIGURE THE TRANSMITTER
5. SPEAK WITH FATHER
6. ACTIVATE THE REACTOR
7. SPEAK WITH FATHER
8. ATTEND DIRECTORATE MEETING

**Locations to Explore**
− THE INSTITUTE (PAGE 409)

## THE POWER OF BENEVOLENCE

# HELPFUL HINT
## from Vault Boy!

**Did You Know?**

DESPITE VAULT-TEC'S BEST ATTEMPTS TO REMOVE INFORMATION DEEMED "SECRET," CERTAIN PIP-BOY OBJECTIVES MAY REVEAL ACTIVITIES BOTH SHOCKING AND GAME-CHANGING. YOU ARE ADVISED TO EXERCISE RETINAL CAUTION WHEN VIEWING THIS DATA.

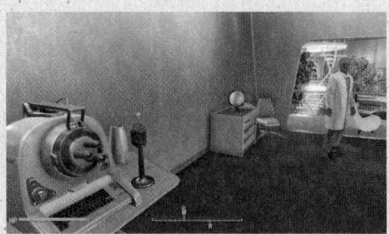

It seems the Institute is ready to reveal itself to those dwelling topside. To ensure a peaceful coexistence, you're to record a broadcast once the Institute's reactor is turned on. Speak with Father and record the speech in his quarters. The oratory style is up to you.

Teleport to Diamond City Market and travel to Diamond City Radio. You're here to modify the transmitter; fortunately there are radio parts in a crate. Slot them into the racks until the transmitter's power is increased.

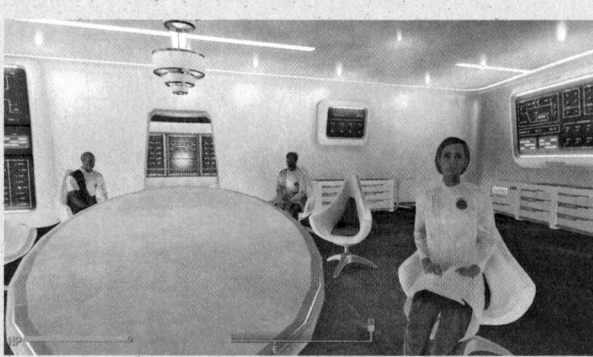

After a quick trip back to the Institute, head to Institute Advanced Systems and find the door to the reactor. If you're in agreement with Father, open the reactor door and activate the core. Then access the terminal and initiate the reactor start-up sequence.

## MASTERS OF THE COMMONWEALTH!

Now that the reactor is humming away, a directorate meeting is called, and you're here to answer any questions posed by the Division heads. You must decide where to focus the development manpower: on weapon development (better armaments for you) or on synth production (more friendly troops by your side). Whatever your choice, you've successfully allied with the Institute, to the detriment of your relationships with other factions.

## Quest
# END OF THE LINE

1. SPEAK WITH FATHER
2. KILL DESDEMONA
3. ELIMINATE THE RAILROAD LEADERS
4. SPEAK WITH FATHER (2)

**Locations to Explore**
− OLD NORTH CHURCH (PAGE 466)

## OFF THE RAILS

Well, you've made your bed and now you'll have to lie in it! Father demands you visit the members of the Railroad. Relay into the North End Neighborhood of Boston and locate the Old North Church.

Employ projectiles in place of platitudes as you maneuver into the crypts under the Old North Church. If the Freedom Trail Ring has not been activated, spin it to spell out the word RAILROAD. Head through the secret opening.

## Quest
# AIRSHIP DOWN

Now that all the Railroad leaders are hopefully gathered in one place, begin to introduce them to the Institute's way of thinking. This place was originally a crypt, so think of this as reverting the location back to its earliest use. When Desdemona, Drummer Boy, Glory, Tinker Tom, Deacon, and Doctor Carrington are all clued in, you're done.

1. SPEAK TO DOCTOR LI
2. SPEAK TO DOCTOR WATSON
3. USE THE RELAY TO REACH THE AIRPORT
4. INFILTRATE THE TERMINAL
5. DESTROY BROTHERHOOD GENERATORS (3)
6. REACH LIBERTY PRIME
7. (OPTIONAL) PLACE TELEPORT BEACONS
8. DEFEND THE SYNTH HACKING LIBERTY PRIME
9. EVACUATE THE AIRPORT

**Locations to Explore**
- BOSTON AIRPORT (PAGE 342)

## POWERING DOWN BOSTON AIRPORT

Contact the Brotherhood of Steel next and minimize their machinations. You need a plan to accomplish this: Visit Doctor Li (or, if she is not present, Evan Watson), in Institute Advanced Systems, and say "it's time." The enthusiastic Doctor Rosalind Orman explains the plan and hands some teleport beacons to bring synths to help you if necessary.

 **INSTITUTE BEACON (3)**

You're here to destroy three generators. The Boston Airport map (page 342) shows the exact location of each of them. Expect to receive returning fire from turrets and other entities. The generators can be bombed or shot at from any distance and in any order:

- THE FIRST IS AT THE FAR SIDE OF A VERTIBIRD LANDING PAD.
- THE SECOND IS GUARDED BY A PROTECTRON AND TURRETS ATOP THE CONTROL TOWER.
- THE THIRD IS AT ONE END OF A SKYWALK LEADING TO LIBERTY PRIME.

Relay over to Boston Airport, south of East Boston. Infiltrate the airport terminal via this hole in the wall. Employ stealth during this time or expect resistance to your maneuvers.

## HACK ATTACK

With the Brotherhood's defenses compromised, a synth reaches the top of Liberty Prime and sets about reprogramming. Your job is to keep this synth intact and uploading the virus. Defend the area around Liberty Prime during this time.

## VAULT-TEC RECOMMENDS

MAINTAINING THE UPLOAD

Use the height of the gantry to your advantage. Lob Institute teleport beacons into high-traffic areas, such as the corridor behind you and the ground-level entrances below. Stay behind Prime's head or in the covered corridor where you can easily watch the hacking synth. Descending to the ground below easily compromises your defenses and isn't recommended.

Once the synth hacking Liberty Prime has reached 100 percent, break off the confrontation and immediately evacuate the vicinity. Head to the ground, and back away to the north.

## VAULT-TEC RECOMMENDS

 **FINAL JUDGMENT**

If you managed to remove Elder Maxson as a threat, why not gather up his unique Laser Gatling? It sure fires fast!

# *Quest*
# NUCLEAR FAMILY

**1. SPEAK TO FATHER**

Locations to Explore

– THE INSTITUTE (PAGE 409)

## IN GOOD HANDS

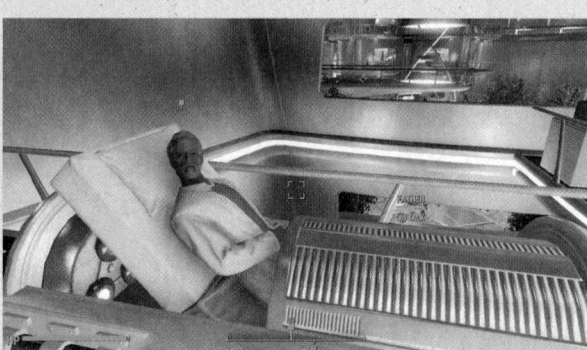

Father needs to know the Commonwealth is finally safe. Relay back to the Institute, and let him know of your successes. The Institute Main Quests are now concluded, though Miscellaneous and Radiant Quests are still available.

 **REWARD: FATHER'S QUARTERS**

## VAULT-TEC RECOMMENDS

 **WOW! A WAZER WIFLE!**

Once your questing is over, a small boy you've previous met at the Institute has three super-secret quests you can undertake for him. Think of it as some bonding you missed while you were in the deep freeze. Finish all three quest, and you're awarded with a special "wifle" that never runs out of ammo!

# THE INSTITUTE MISCELLANEOUS QUESTS

DATA

QUESTS

## HELPFUL HINT
### from Vault Boy!

**Did You Know?**

WHAT ARE MISCELLANEOUS INSTITUTE QUESTS? GREAT QUESTION! THE THREE QUESTS SHOWN HERE ARE PURELY OPTIONAL ANTICS TO UNDERTAKE FOR THIS FACTION WHILE YOU'RE OUT DOING YOUR MAIN QUESTING. EXPECT SOME TOUGH TASKS BUT ALSO SOME CHOICE REWARDS FOR HELPING THE GOOD FOLKS AT THE INSTITUTE! ARE YOU ON LESS-THAN-STELLAR TERMS WITH THIS FACTION? THEN THESE QUESTS AREN'T AVAILABLE. LET'S PLAY NICE OUT THERE!

## Quest
# BUILDING A BETTER CROP

1. TALK TO ISAAC KARLIN
2. DELIVER THE SEEDS TO ROGER WARWICK
3. FOLLOW ROGER WARWICK
4. TALK TO ROGER WARWICK

5. DISCOVER BILL'S PLANS
6. TALK TO CEDRIC HOPTON
7. TALK TO ROGER WARWICK

8. CONFRONT BILL SUTTON
9. TALK TO ROGER WARWICK
10. TALK TO ISAAC KARLIN

**Locations to Explore**
- THE INSTITUTE (PAGE 409)
- WARWICK HOMESTEAD (PAGE 393)
- GOODNEIGHBOR (PAGE 483)

## SEEDY ACTIVITIES AT THE WARWICK HOMESTEAD

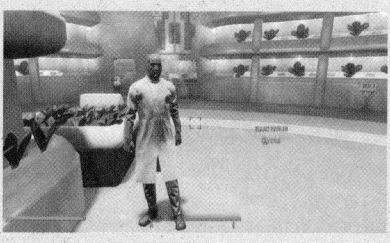

This quest is available once you ally yourself with the Institute and complete Main Quest: Institutionalized. Isaac Karlin (visit him in BioScience) has asked you to deliver some genetically modified seeds to Roger Warwick at the homestead that bears his name.

Warwick's place is on the southeast coast. Heading through South Boston, past Jamaica Plain and through Quincy is the easiest route

to take. Find Roger, whisper the passphrase to him, and agree to help.

## VAULT-TEC RECOMMENDS

SETTLING DOWN AT WARWICK HOMESTEAD

**TATO**
If you're also helping the Minutemen establish settlements throughout the Commonwealth, this location offers a couple of advantages: There's some concrete structures already in place, and there's a working farm of quality Mutfruit and Tatos.

Locate one of the Warwick clan—Wally, Janey, or June—and quiz them until they mention a man named Cedric Hopton.

(Medium) You can use your way with words to get the clue, too.

## HAVING YOUR FILL OF CEDRIC AND BILL

Cedric Hopton is currently mooching about the Third Rail, a popular watering hole in Goodneighbor. Cedric is a tougher nut to crack and requires one of the following to spill the beans:

- (500 CAPS) A BRIBE

(Medium) A sympathetic ear.

 (Medium) Call his bluff until he surrenders.

You learn that a settler back at Warwick Homestead named Bill Sutton doesn't have Roger Warwick's best interests at heart. When you stroll into the main sleeping quarters of the homestead, you stumble upon a confrontation to de-escalate. You can:

- CALM THE SITUATION WITH WORDS.
- ATTACK BILL AND KILL HIM WITH FISTS OR GUNS.

With the situation resolved, relay back to the Institute, inform Isaac Karlin what happened (answering as you wish), and receive the following reward:

 **STIMPACK (20)**

## Quest
# PLUGGING A LEAK

1. INVESTIGATE THE ROBOTICS TERMINALS
2. INVESTIGATE BINET'S QUARTERS
3. INVESTIGATE THE SRB TERMINALS
4. INVESTIGATE THE MAINTENANCE TERMINAL
5. CONFRONT LIAM BINET
6. REPORT YOUR FINDINGS TO JUSTIN AYO
7. DISABLE THE SAFEGUARDS ON JUSTIN AYO'S TERMINAL
8. RETURN TO LIAM BINET

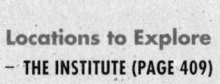

Locations to Explore
– THE INSTITUTE (PAGE 409)

## A PRECOCIOUS KID. A FEROCIOUS MOTHER.

This quest is available once you ally yourself with the Institute and complete Institute Quest: Mankind—Redefined. It is not available if you've already completed Railroad Quest: Tradecraft. Dr. Ayo (find him in the Synth Retention Bureau, or SRB) suspects that another colleague—Dr. Binet—is helping synths to escape the Institute.

Agree to help Ayo, wander over to the robotics laboratory, and access any terminal.

This leads you to Binet's quarters. You're greeted by his son Liam and Liam's mother. You can:

- CHECK THE BINET QUARTERS TERMINAL AND FIND THE ACCESS LOGS. OBJECTIVE 3 IS NOW AVAILABLE.

 (Hard) Or tell him you're only trying to help, and Liam reveals everything, allowing you to decide what to do now—Objective 5: Confront Liam Binet.

- ENTER THE INSTITUTE SRB AND ACCESS ANY TERMINAL IN THERE. A CLUE LEADS YOU TO THE MAINTENANCE ROOM. EVE BINET, LIAM'S MOTHER, ISN'T TOO HAPPY ABOUT YOU CHECKING THE TERMINAL IN HERE.

Resolve this peacefully or with combat. Optionally check Maintenance Terminal 6 afterward.

 (Hard) Keep the secret, and agree to help the Binets.

## REFUTING CLAIMS AND NAMING NAMES

When you confronted Liam Binet about his role in the synth escapes, he admitted his guilt and then asked you to help him frame Dr. Ayo. You have two options:

- PLAN A: IGNORE LIAM AND INFORM JUSTIN AYO. AFTER STATING YOUR FINDINGS, YOU RECEIVE AN IMPRESSIVE NUMBER OF BOTTLECAPS.
- PLAN B: AGREE TO FRAME JUSTIN AYO.

 (Medium) Agree in exchange for a gift. Liam agrees.

Enter Ayo's quarters and access his private terminal. Disable the safeguards, return to Liam, and tell him what you've done.

 (Easy) Ask him what happens now.

You're given a slightly less valuable reward from Liam—some glasses.

 BOTTLECAPS (1,000)  LIAM'S GLASSES

# Quest
# A HOUSE DIVIDED

1. TALK TO NEWTON OBERLY
2. FOLLOW NEWTON OBERLY
3. GO TO THE BIOSCIENCE OBSERVATION ROOM
4. TALK TO LAWRENCE HIGGS
5. RESOLVE THE STANDOFF IN HYDROPONICS
6. TALK TO NEWTON OBERLY

Locations to Explore
– THE INSTITUTE (PAGE 409)

## CONCLUDING THE STANDOFF (CHARISMATICALLY)

This quest is available once you ally yourself with the Institute and complete Institute Quest: Mankind—Redefined. Something is amiss in BioScience and Dr. Oberly has requested your help. After obtaining the BioScience Systems Access Holotape, enter the door Dr. Oberly opened.

Beware of hostile synths and turrets as you fight to the BioScience Observation room. Chat to Lawrence Higgs through the window. You can:

– COMPLETE YOUR CHAT WITHOUT REACHING A COMPROMISE.

 (Hard, Medium) Tell him to give you a chance, then convince him and Doctor Loken to stand down, completing the quest.

## CONCLUDING THE STANDOFF (DRAMATICALLY)

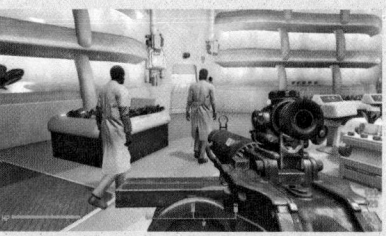

There are a variety of ways to conclude this standoff. You can:

– LOCATE THE TERMINAL IN THE OBSERVATION CHAMBER, AND INSERT THE BIOSCIENCE SYSTEMS ACCESS HOLOTAPE INTO IT. FROM THERE, YOU CAN TURN OFF THE TURRETS. BUT YOU CAN ALSO RELEASE THE SYNTH GORILLAS INSIDE THE LABORATORY SO THEY MAUL THE SYNTHS AND DOCTORS. OPEN THE DOOR TO THE LABORATORY, AND USE THE BIOSCIENCE TERMINAL TO UNLOCK THE OTHER DOOR, ENDING THE STANDOFF.
– OPEN THE DOOR INTO THE LABORATORY. BEWARE OF SYNTHS. AFTER THE ALTERCATION, SPEAK TO DOCTORS HIGGS AND LOKEN. THE LATTER SEES SENSE AND OPENS THE DOOR, ENDING THE STANDOFF.
– (NOVICE) WORK YOUR WAY THROUGH THE FEV LABORATORY (BEWARE OF SYNTHS, TURRETS, AND AN ASSAULTRON) TO A SECOND TERMINAL, WHERE YOU CAN ATTEMPT THE SAME ACTIONS.

Reach Dr. Oberly again. He's unhappy if the doctors are dead. If they survived, he asks you what punishment is befitting. You can:

– ANSWER HOW YOU WISH.

 – (MEDIUM) CHOOSE EXECUTION.

The quest concludes with Dr. Oberly offering you the following pick-me-ups:

 MENTATS (5), JET (5), RADAWAY (5)

# THE INSTITUTE RADIANT QUESTS

## HELPFUL HINT
*from Vault Boy!*

 **Did You Know?**

WHAT ARE RADIANT INSTITUTE QUESTS? A PERCEPTIVE QUESTION! THE FIVE QUESTS REFERENCED HERE ARE OPTIONAL ENGAGEMENTS YOU CAN TACKLE WHILE YOU WORK ON MORE IMPORTANT INSTITUTE MATTERS. THEY ARE "RADIANT," AS THE LOCATIONS YOU'RE SENT TO ARE RANDOM—YOU'LL RECEIVE CALLS FROM DIFFERENT SCIENTISTS WITHIN THE INSTITUTE BUILDING. THESE QUESTS ARE REPEATABLE, MAKING THEM A GREAT WAY TO ACCUMULATE REWARDS. YOUR HELP IS ALWAYS GRATEFULLY RECEIVED!

## VAULT-TEC RECOMMENDS

### RANDOM FACTS

Due to the random nature of the locations you are sent to, it is imperative you read up on the hostiles (as well as the valuables) you'll encounter at each one. Vault-Tec is proud to provide comprehensive cartography for just such a reconnoiter.

## Quest
# PEST CONTROL

1. ELIMINATE THE FERAL GHOULS
2. RETURN TO ALAN BINET

**Locations to Explore**
— THE INSTITUTE (PAGE 409)

### FINISHING OFF FERALS TOPSIDE

Speak with Dr. Binet over at Robotics, and agree to eliminate some Feral Ghouls causing problems for a synth scavenger team. Teleport to the location indicated on your Pip-Boy.

Enter the location and engage the enemies within. Not all foes need to be slain. Fight your way to the tagged enemy (in this example, a Glowing One) and kill it. Then return to Binet.

 (Easy) Request a reward, and you're given some funds that aren't quite as valuable as Dr. Binet believes they are.

 **PREWAR MONEY (10)**

## Quest
# HYPOTHESIS

1. COLLECT A FLESH SAMPLE
2. TAKE THE FLESH SAMPLE TO CLAYTON HOLDREN

**Locations to Explore**
— THE INSTITUTE (PAGE 409)

### SEEING RED AND KILLING GREEN

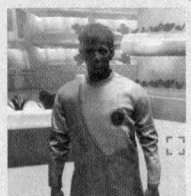

To aid in one of his experiments, Doctor Holdren of the BioScience division has asked you to obtain a tissue sample from a particularly tough Super Mutant. Teleport to the location indicated on your Pip-Boy.

Use stealth or blind, ugly violence to stay safe as you head to the enemy tagged on your Pip-Boy map. Remove the Super Mutant threat (not all enemies need to be slain), then pry out the tissue sample. Return it to Holdren.

 (Easy) Request a reward, and you're given the following:

**STIMPAK (4)**

## Quest
# APPROPRIATION

1. RETRIEVE THE BLUEPRINTS
2. TAKE THE BLUEPRINTS TO VAN WATSON

**Locations to Explore**
– THE INSTITUTE (PAGE 409)

## BROTHERHOOD OF STEAL

In an effort to learn more about their technology, Dr. Watson has asked you to obtain blueprints from the Brotherhood of Steel. Teleport to the random location indicated on your Pip-Boy. This quest presupposes a hostile relationship with the Brotherhood.

Beware of Brotherhood of Steel forces. Not all foes need to be slain. Remove all pertinent threats, and secure the blueprints from the marked crate. Return with them to Watson.

 (Easy) Request a reward, and you're given the following:

**FUSION CELL (4)**

## Quest
# RECLAMATION

1. TAKE THE TRANSMITTER TO THE CAPTURED SYNTH
2. RETURN TO DOCTOR SECORD

**Locations to Explore**
– THE INSTITUTE (PAGE 409)

## A BEACON OF HOPE

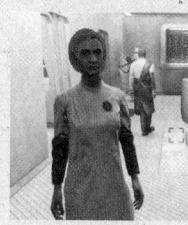

One of the Institute's synths was taken by Raiders. Doctor Secord of the SRB asks you to place a tracking beacon on the synth so she can plan a retrieval mission. Teleport to the location indicated on your Pip-Boy.

Beware of enemies, though it is not mission-critical to slay any of them. Maneuver your way to the captured synth and talk to it. With the beacon in place, return to Secord.

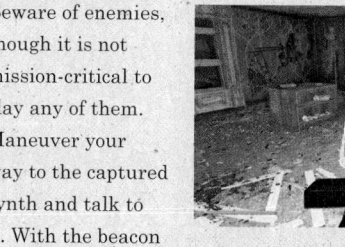

 (Easy) Request a reward, and you're given the following:

 **PLASMA GRENADE (5)**

DATA

QUESTS

## Quest
# POLITICAL LEANINGS

1. TALK TO MAYOR MCDONOUGH
2. TAKE THE MAYOR'S REPORT TO JUSTIN AYO

**Locations to Explore**
– DIAMOND CITY (PAGE 433)

## REPORTING IN

Once there, locate the mayor and obtain the report from him. Ask him specifically for it. Then return to Ayo with the report.

 (Easy) Request a reward, and you're given the following:

 **BOTTLECAPS (100)**

Dr. Ayo of the SRB has asked you to collect an intelligence report from Mayor McDonough in Diamond City.

# BROTHERHOOD OF STEEL QUESTS

Joining this well-armed (and some might say zealous) faction begins whenever you wish, after you (optionally) listen to Military Frequency AF95 and visit Cambridge Police Station, or you observe a giant airship flying overhead and mooring at Boston Airport. You can continue Brotherhood of Steel operations for as long as you wish. However, be aware that your relationships with the other main factions—the Institute, the Railroad, and the Minutemen—may be impacted negatively the more you pursue your career as a Brotherhood soldier. Be warned—you may need to learn some Latin.

The following Brotherhood of Steel Quests become available:

| BROTHERHOOD OF STEEL QUESTS | |
|---|---|
| **Main Faction Quest** | **Location** |
| Reveille | Page 134 |
| Fire Support | Page 135 |
| Call to Arms | Page 135 |
| Semper Invicta | Page 136 |
| Shadow of Steel | Page 137 |
| Tour of Duty | Page 137 |
| Show No Mercy | Page 138 |
| From Within | Page 139 |
| Outside the Wire | Page 140 |
| Liberty Reprimed | Page 140 |
| Blind Betrayal | Page 142 |
| Tactical Thinking | Page 143 |
| Spoils of War | Page 144 |
| Ad Victoriam | Page 145 |
| The Nuclear Option (Brotherhood of Steel) | Page 146 |
| A New Dawn | Page 147 |
| **Miscellaneous Faction Quest** | **Location** |
| The Lost Patrol | Page 148 |
| Duty or Dishonor | Page 149 |
| A Loose End | Page 150 |
| Getting Technical* | Page 152 |
| Blood Bank* | Page 152 |
| Reactor Coolant* | Page 152 |
| **Radiant Faction Quest** | **Location** |
| Cleansing the Commonwealth | Page 153 |
| Quartermastery | Page 153 |
| Leading by Example | Page 154 |
| Learning Curve | Page 154 |
| Feeding the Troops | Page 154 |

## Quest
# REVEILLE

1. INVESTIGATE THE BROTHERHOOD OF STEEL AIRSHIP
2. PROCEED TO CAMBRIDGE POLICE STATION

**Locations to Explore**
- BOSTON AIRPORT (PAGE 342)
- CAMBRIDGE NEIGHBORHOOD (PAGE 400)
- CAMBRIDGE POLICE STATION (PAGE 403)

## AN AWE-INSPIRING PRESENCE

As you emerge from Fort Hagen, you observe a huge Brotherhood of Steel airship pass overhead. It appears to be heading toward the city. You can:

- HEAD TO BOSTON AIRPORT AND SPEAK TO ANY BROTHERHOOD SOLDIER, WHO RECOMMENDS YOU TRY OUT AS A NEW RECRUIT OVER AT CAMBRIDGE POLICE STATION.
- OR HEAD DIRECTLY TO CAMBRIDGE POLICE STATION.

## HELPFUL HINT
### from Vault Boy!

THIS IS ONE WAY TO OBSERVE THE BROTHERHOOD OF STEEL'S PRESENCE AND BEGIN WORKING WITH THEM. THOUGH THE AIRSHIP ARRIVES JUST AFTER YOU EMERGE FROM FORT HAGEN AFTER COMPLETING MAIN QUEST: REUNIONS, THIS QUEST IS ONLY ACCESSIBLE IF YOU HAVEN'T TAKEN AN INTEREST IN RADIO SIGNAL MILITARY FREQUENCY AF95 OR VISITED CAMBRIDGE POLICE STATION YET. COME ON, SLOWPOKE!

Beware of Feral Ghouls at the station entrance. Expect a vicious battle with over a dozen foes. Then follow the objectives of

Brotherhood of Steel Quest: Fire Support from this point.

## Quest
# FIRE SUPPORT

1. LISTEN TO MILITARY FREQUENCY AF95
2. PROCEED TO CAMBRIDGE POLICE STATION
3. ASSIST THE SOLDIERS
4. SPEAK TO PALADIN DANSE

### Locations to Explore
- CAMBRIDGE NEIGHBORHOOD (PAGE 400)
- CAMBRIDGE POLICE STATION (PAGE 403)

## Quest
# CALL TO ARMS

1. SPEAK TO PALADIN DANSE
2. FOLLOW PALADIN DANSE
3. FIND A WAY TO OPEN THE DOOR
4. PROVIDE FIRE SUPPORT FOR PALADIN DANSE
5. FOLLOW PALADIN DANSE
6. RESTORE AUXILIARY POWER FOR PALADIN DANSE
7. PROCEED TO THE CONTROL ROOM
8. (OPTIONAL) ACTIVATE THE ENGINE CORE'S ROCKET
9. (OPTIONAL) ASSESS PALADIN DANSE'S CONDITION
10. CLEAR THE CONTROL ROOM
11. RETRIEVE THE DEEP RANGE TRANSMITTER
12. EXIT ARCJET SYSTEMS
13. SPEAK TO PALADIN DANSE

### Locations to Explore
- ARCJET SYSTEMS (PAGE 322)

## A FERAL GHOUL PESTILENCE

While traveling near Lexington and College Square (or just south of Corvega Assembly Plant if you're heading southeast from Concord), your Pip-Boy receives a military radio broadcast. Listen to it, then head to Cambridge Police Station.

Beware of Feral Ghouls at the station entrance. Expect a crazed battle with over a dozen foes. When the fight ends, speak to the commander here, Paladin Danse. Agree to assist him.

You may also persuade Paladin Danse to hire you. If successful, you receive a larger reward of caps at the end of Call to Arms.

## VAULT-TEC RECOMMENDS

### LOOTING CAMBRIDGE POLICE STATION
This forward recon base for the Brotherhood has a few scattered chems and ammunition, but nothing worth salivating over except for the large number of loose chems and a couple of containers in the Evidence Room at the back of the station. Don't overlook the garage, though; you can park your Power Armor here whenever you need to.

## GOING DEEP

Paladin Danse has asked you to follow him to ArcJet Systems where he hopes to get his hands on a Deep Range Transmitter to repair the Brotherhood of Steel communications array. After optionally talking with Scribe Haylen or Knight Rhys, head west to the abandoned ArcJet Systems building.

After a chat about the transmitter and automated security, provide fire support for the Paladin. He's dismayed to discover the presence of Institute synths. Head to the lab analysis room. You can:

- (ADVANCED) HACK INTO THE LAB CONTROL TERMINAL.
- USE THE LAB ANALYST'S TERMINAL TO RECEIVE THE LAB CONTROL TERMINAL PASSWORD.

Use the lab control terminal to open the door. When you reach the second-floor corridor just outside the CEO's office, you can fight through the turret-lined hallway with Paladin Danse, or head into the office nearby and use the terminal to disable them. Follow Paladin Danse to the elevator leading down to the ArcJet Engine Core.

## VAULT-TEC RECOMMENDS

### RANSACKING BEFORE THE CORE

**TESLA SCIENCE**

As you have a full run of the place, Paladin Danse won't mind if you take some extra time to flip through another issue of Tesla Science magazine. It's in the office just before those pesky turrets.

## HARD CORE

Paladin Danse and you need to reach the top of the engine core in ArcJet Systems. But first you'll have to search for a way to restore power to the access elevator. This is achieved by accessing the facilities terminal (Novice) and hacking it. Start the auxiliary generators before returning to help Paladin Danse with his synth problems.

Or if you want to see an impressive roasting, press the Engine Start button and remove the synth threats more easily. Then head to the elevator and ascend.

## VAULT-TEC RECOMMENDS

### LOOTING THE ARCJET ENGINE CORE

**JUNK JET**
**FAT MAN**

Aside from a Fusion Core to pry out, this rocket chamber has a couple of high-value pieces of killing equipment. Take the Junk Jet—an amazing device that turns trash into deadly projectiles—in the chamber with the button and viewing window! After you take the elevator to the upper level, you can jump down to the mid-level catwalks to reach two smaller side chambers. One of them contains your favorite portable nuclear launcher!

Battle to the control room, securing the Deep Range Transmitter from one of the synth corpses. Then leave the facility via the control room elevator.

 **DEEP RANGE TRANSMITTER**

Topside, speak to the Paladin:

 (Medium) Optionally ask about how smoothly the operation went.

To further your involvement with the Brotherhood of Steel, hand over the Deep Range Transmitter and receive the following:

 **RIGHTEOUS AUTHORITY**

## *Quest*
# SEMPER INVICTA

1. **RETURN TO CAMBRIDGE POLICE STATION**
2. **SPEAK WITH PALADIN DANSE**
3. **SUPPORT THE BROTHERHOOD RECON TEAM**

**Locations to Explore**
– **CAMBRIDGE (NEIGHBORHOOD) (PAGE 400)**
– **CAMBRIDGE POLICE STATION (PAGE 403)**

## THE NEW RECRUIT

After you agree to join the Brotherhood of Steel, Paladin Danse asks you to return to the Cambridge Police Station. You are formally inducted into the Brotherhood of Steel:

– **PRIOR TO MAIN QUEST: ACT II: YOU ARE INDUCTED AS AN INITIATE.**
– **IF MAIN QUEST: ACT II HAS BEGUN: YOU ARE INDUCTED AS A KNIGHT, AND BROTHERHOOD OF STEEL QUEST: SHADOW OF STEEL BEGINS.**

Afterward, report to both Scribe Haylen or Knight Rhys for further assignments:

– **BROTHERHOOD OF STEEL RADIANT QUEST: QUARTERMASTERY IS NOW ACCESSIBLE VIA SCRIBE HAYLEN.**
– **BROTHERHOOD OF STEEL RADIANT QUEST: CLEANSING THE COMMONWEALTH IS NOW ACCESSIBLE VIA KNIGHT RHYS.**

 (Medium) Optionally ask Haylen about her relationship with Rhys.

Brotherhood of Steel Misc Quest: The Lost Patrol is accessible after completing Quartermastery or Cleansing the Commonwealth via Paladin Danse.

## Quest
# SHADOW OF STEEL

1. LISTEN TO MILITARY FREQUENCY AF95
2. REPORT TO PALADIN DANSE
3. BOARD THE VERTIBIRD
4. ATTEND THE DEBRIEFING
5. SPEAK TO LANCER-CAPTAIN KELLS
6. ATTEND ELDER MAXSON'S ADDRESS
7. SPEAK TO ELDER MAXSON
8. MISCELLANEOUS: OPEN YOUR PERSONAL STORAGE CONTAINER
9. REPORT TO PALADIN DANSE

**Locations to Explore**
– PRYDWEN (PAGE 345)

## MEETING MAXSON

After observing a huge Brotherhood of Steel airship pass overhead, your Pip-Boy radio receives a transmission. You listen to it for further instructions before heading to Cambridge Police Station and following Paladin Danse to the roof.

Man the minigun turret, and feel free to rake the ground as you fly over Boston. Try to hit Raider encampments and create satisfying explosions. At the Brotherhood of Steel's flagship, the "Prydwen," disembark onto the flight deck and meet Lancer-Captain Kells.

You're ordered to attend an address being given by Elder Maxson, the supreme commander of the Brotherhood of Steel. Speak to Maxson afterward. Regardless of your earlier rank in the Brotherhood, Maxson now bestowed the title "Knight" to you and a shiny new suit of Power Armor. Find it in Power Armor Station 03 of the main deck.

 **POWER ARMOR (BOS II T-60B)**

 **COMPANION: PALADIN DANSE**

## Quest
# TOUR OF DUTY

1. MEET PROCTOR INGRAM
2. MEET PROCTOR TEAGAN
3. MEET PROCTOR QUINLAN
4. MEET KNIGHT-CAPTAIN CADE

**Locations to Explore**
– PRYDWEN (PAGE 345)

## MEET YOUR MENTORS

In order to become an effective part of the Brotherhood, Elder Maxson has ordered you to tour the Prydwen and familiarize yourself with her crew. Find Proctor Ingram near the Power Armor Stations. Don't forget your own Power Armor at Station 03.

 (Medium) Ask about her legs, and you have three opportunities to further the conversation.

Locate Proctor Teagan at the supply store. Aside from the impressive armaments he sells, you can ask him about extra work. Brotherhood of Steel Radiant Quest: Feeding the Troops becomes available.

Locate Proctor Quinlan at his office. Speak to him as you wish. If you're fine with foraging, agree to help locate some papers for him: Miscellaneous Objective: Getting Technical.

**HOLOTAPE: MAXSON WAS RIGHT**

Though it's bad manners to break into Proctor Teagan's supply store and steal his Mini Nuke collection, there are other items of interest; stocking up on caps to buy some of Teagan's more impressive wares is a good start. There are also Holotapes to listen to, and Scribe Neriah has a Miscellaneous quest to undertake on the lower level of the main deck.

Locate Knight-Captain Cade in the sickbay. Speak to him as you wish. Return here if you require medical attention in the future.

## Quest
# SHOW NO MERCY

1. MEET WITH ELDER MAXSON
2. BOARD THE VERTIBIRD GUNSHIP
3. KILL THE SUPER MUTANT BEHEMOTH
4. SECURE FORT STRONG

5. SECURE FORT STRONG ARMORY
6. SPEAK TO PALADIN DANSE
7. SPEAK TO ELDER MAXSON

**Locations to Explore**
– FORT STRONG (PAGE 347)

## THE BATTLE FOR FORT STRONG

Now that you've familiarized yourself with the Prydwen and her crew, meet Elder Maxson on the flight deck for your first mission.

You're to head out to nearby Fort Strong and cleanse it of all hostile Super Mutant forces. Step onto the Vertibird and man the minigun. Use this weapon to cut down the sizable Super Mutant roaming the exterior grounds of Fort Strong.

Alternatively, you can Fast-Travel elsewhere, or to Fort Strong, and engage the Super Mutant forces on foot.

The only good greenskin is a dead one! After the red mist has receded, chat to Paladin Danse before returning to the Prydwen for an impressive reward (aerial Fast-Travel via Vertibird).

(Medium) Ask about his hatred for Super Mutants.

Return to the Prydwen, and answer Elder Maxson as you wish. You are awarded with the following (aerial Fast-Travel via Vertibird):

**VERTIBIRD SIGNAL GRENADE (8)**

You may now purchase additional Vertibird Signal Grenades from Proctor Teagan.

## VAULT-TEC RECOMMENDS

**POWER ARMOR (LEVELED)**
**MINI NUKE**

Multiple Mini Nukes, a Fat Man, and a set of T-51 Power Armor are just some of the large quantities of armaments and ammo you can expect to find when you make a thorough sweep of Fort Strong.

Depending on your progress through the Main Quest, the following quests are available:

– BROTHERHOOD OF STEEL: FROM WITHIN BECOMES AVAILABLE IF YOU HAVEN'T COMPLETED MAIN QUEST: INSTITUTIONALIZED.
– BROTHERHOOD OF STEEL: OUTSIDE THE WIRE BECOMES AVAILABLE IF YOU HAVE ALREADY COMPLETED MAIN QUEST: INSTITUTIONALIZED.

# HELPFUL HINT
## from Vault Boy!

**Did You Know?**

THIS ISN'T LIKELY TO BE YOUR FIRST ENCOUNTER WITH THE GREEN ABOMINATIONS KNOWN AS SUPER MUTANTS. BUT IT COULD BE YOUR TOUGHEST! READ UP ON THE VAULT-TEC-APPROVED TAKEDOWN TACTICS (SEE PAGE 347) FOR THESE DEGENERATES SO YOU'RE FULLY PREPARED FOR CARNAGE.

Disembark and remove all indicated Super Mutant threats. Enter Fort Strong Armory and exterminate all hostiles on all floors of this location.

# Quest
# FROM WITHIN

1. LOCATE DOCTOR LI
2. SPEAK TO DOCTOR LI
3. RETRIEVE EVIDENCE TO CONVINCE DOCTOR LI
4. BRING THE HOLOTAPE TO DOCTOR LI
5. REPORT TO ELDER MAXSON

**Locations to Explore**
- **THE INSTITUTE (PAGE 409)**

---

## LAB WORK WITH DOCTOR LI

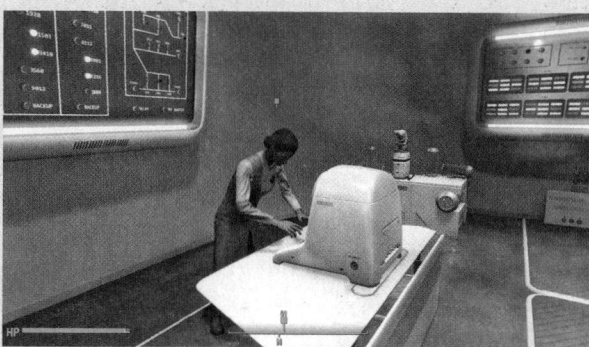

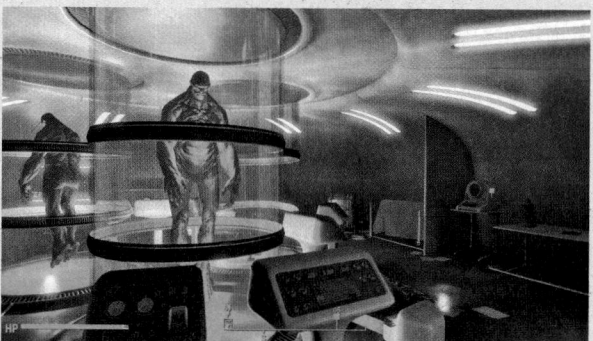

**HELPFUL HINT** *from Vault Boy!* **Did You Know?**

ARE YOU WANDERING THROUGH LIFE WITHOUT FULLY UNDERSTANDING YOUR ACTIONS? DON'T! THIS QUEST OCCURS CONCURRENTLY WITH MAIN QUEST: INSTITUTIONALIZED AND BROTHERHOOD OF STEEL QUEST: OUTSIDE THE WIRE. BE SURE YOU UNDERSTAND BOTH OF THOSE QUESTS BEFORE CONTINUING, OR YOU MIGHT HAVE TO MAKE DECISIONS YOU DON'T FULLY UNDERSTAND THE MAGNITUDE OF.

During your infiltration of the Institute, Elder Maxson orders you to make contact with a Doctor Madison Li and convince her to work on a "special project" for the Brotherhood of Steel. Find her within the Institute and let her know you've been sent to find her (or be direct and tell her the Brotherhood sent you). You can:

(Medium, Hard) Ask her if she's happy, and complete a series of difficult fast-talking challenges to convince her. If she agrees, you can skip to the final objective of this quest.

Or, agree to find evidence about Virgil's disappearance from his laboratory.

In order to ensure Doctor Li's trust, you've agreed to recover evidence regarding an accident that supposedly killed her colleague, Doctor Virgil. His former lab is in a sealed section of the BioSciences Division. To access it, you can:

- **(MASTER) UNLOCK THE FEV LAB ENTRY TERMINAL BY THE LASER GRID GATE.**
- **(NOVICE) UNLOCK THE FEV LAB DOOR.**

Venture through the FEV lab, which has automated turret security, synths, and an Assaultron. Locate the Holotape at the laboratory.

 **BRIAN VIRGIL PERSONAL LOG 0176**

Return to Doctor Li and hand over the Holotape. Then continue with Main Quest: Institutionalized. Once you leave the Institute, return to the Prydwen and inform Elder Maxson.

### VAULT-TEC RECOMMENDS

 While you're here, pick up the Experimental Serum for Miscellaneous Quest: Curing Virgil.*

## Quest
# OUTSIDE THE WIRE

1. INSERT NETWORK SCANNER HOLOTAPE INTO INSTITUTE TERMINAL
2. GIVE HOLOTAPE TO PROCTOR INGRAM

**Locations to Explore**
— THE INSTITUTE (PAGE 409)

## INSTITUTE ACCESS

During your infiltration of the Institute, Proctor Ingram has ordered you to steal data from one of their terminals using a special Holotape she's provided. This Holotape may also have been given to you by another faction.

Access the terminal at the Institute relay area and entrance, insert the Network Scanner Holotape, and remove the data. Then simply continue the rest of Main Quest: Institutionalized. Return to Proctor Ingram and give her the data.

**NETWORK SCANNER HOLOTAPE**

### HELPFUL HINT
### from Vault Boy! Did You Know?

WHY CAN'T EVERYBODY JUST GET ALONG? UNFORTUNATELY, IN THE POST-APOCALYPTIC WASTELAND, LIMITED RESOURCES AND SURVIVAL INSTINCTS USUALLY LEAD TO DISTRUST. SO PICK A FACTION YOU WANT TO WORK WITH, AND REMEMBER, YOU CAN GIVE THE HOLOTAPE TO A DIFFERENT FACTION IF YOU CHANGE YOUR ALLEGIANCE. BUT THIS IS THE TIME TO PICK A SIDE AND STICK WITH THEM!

## Quest
# LIBERTY REPRIMED

1. SPEAK TO PROCTOR INGRAM
2. FOLLOW PROCTOR INGRAM
3. SPEAK TO PROFESSOR SCARA
4. SEARCH FOR PROFESSOR SCARA
5. OR SPEAK TO DOCTOR LI
6. SPEAK TO PROCTOR INGRAM
7. LOCATE A HIGH-POWERED MAGNET
8. CONSTRUCT ELECTOMAGNETIC ACTUATORS (4)
9. SPEAK TO PROCTOR INGRAM
10. SPEAK TO SCRIBE HAYLEN
11. LOCATE THE BOMB STORAGE FACILITY
12. LOCATE THE MARK 28 NUKE STOCKPILE
13. ACTIVATE THE DISTRESS PULSER
14. SPEAK TO PALADIN DANSE
15. RETURN TO PROCTOR INGRAM
16. ACTIVATE LIBERTY PRIME
17. SPEAK TO PROCTOR INGRAM

**Locations to Explore**
— BOSTON AIRPORT (PAGE 342)
— GENERAL ATOMICS GALLERIA (PAGE 280)
— SENTINEL SITE PRESCOTT (PAGE 364)

## BUILDING A WAR MACHINE

Head to Boston Airport. Proctor Ingram's special project is the reconstruction of a massive war machine. It looks like it needs a lot of work to get up and running. In fact, a fellow scientist is required to help:

— IF YOU FAILED TO CONVINCE DOCTOR LI TO JOIN YOU (OR IF YOU KILLED HER) DURING BROTHERHOOD OF STEEL QUEST: FROM WITHIN, PLAN A OCCURS.
— IF YOU COMPLETED BROTHERHOOD OF STEEL QUEST: FROM WITHIN AND CONVINCED DOCTOR LI TO JOIN, PLAN B OCCURS.

### PLAN A: FINDING PROFESSOR SCARA

Proctor Ingram tells you to find Professor Scara. She hands you the following to help convince her to help.

**CEREBROFUSION ADAPTOR**

Proctor Ingram has tasked you with finding a robotics expert in Diamond City named Professor Scara and asking for her assistance. At the Science! Center (in Diamond City Market), converse with Doctor Duff. She hasn't seen her colleague Scara for over a week after she left for a field expedition. Perhaps you can help?

Journey to the General Atomics Galleria, north into the Commonwealth. Enter the Back Alley Bowling building and find Professor Scara inside.

 (Easy) Convince her using your charm.

 Or convince her using your Cerebrofusion Adaptor.

Plan A now concludes.

## VAULT-TEC RECOMMENDS

### LOOTING GENERAL ATOMICS GALLERIA

While you're here, you might as well play along with those General Atomics robots. Or mangle them into heaps of metal; the decision is yours to make. Don't exit the place without opening the steamer trunk, though.

## PLAN B: SPEAKING TO DOCTOR LI

In order to get the war machine's power systems stabilized, Proctor Ingram has asked you to speak to Doctor Li on the Prydwen. Head to

the main deck, and after a conversation with you, she seems tentatively convinced.

Plan B now concludes.

## MAGNETS. HOW DO THEY WORK?

Back at Boston Airport, Proctor Ingram requires the building of electromagnetic actuators. She hands you a build list. All of the components are stored in Boston Airport's workshop. Well, all of them except one: a high-powered magnet.

 **ELECTROMAGNETIC ACTUATORS LIST**

Or, as high-powered magnets can be scrapped, they may be found throughout the Commonwealth, or sold by vendors too.

You need to recover a high-powered magnet. One of the (random) hospital ruins should have the part that you need.

Head to the location indicated on your Pip-Boy, and beware of local dangers. Find the magnet, usually inside a marked trunk with other items.

 **HIGH-POWERED MAGNET**

Back at the airport's workshop, access the Special menu. Build four actuators, using the following components (required for each one, with the exception of the high-powered magnet):

– **BUILD WITH: CIRCUITRY (5), SCREW (1), STEEL (10), FIBER OPTICS (3), RUBBER (5), HIGH-POWERED MAGNET (1)**

## AN ALMOST UNATTAINABLE ARSENAL

Inform Proctor Ingram of your progress. Naturally, you're not done yet. You need fully loaded Mark 28 Nuclear Bomb packs for the war machine's weapons systems. Meet Scribe Haylen at the new Primary Location Waypoint Echo, on the edge of the Glowing Sea. You're given a distress pulser to pinpoint the position of the nukes when you find them. Haylen's team will extricate them.

---

**HELPFUL HINT**
*from Vault Boy!*  Did You Know?

AS YOU SHOULD ALREADY HAVE BRAVED THE INHOSPITABLE ELEMENTS OF THE GLOWING SEA, YOU SHOULD BE WELL VERSED IN PREVENTATIVE MEASURES TO REDUCE RADIATION SICKNESS. REMEMBER:

1. PREVENTION! PURCHASE, SCAVENGE, OR CRAFT ALL THE RAD-X AND RADAWAY YOU'LL NEED FOR THIS JAUNT.
2. PROTECTION! YOU MUST WEAR A HAZMAT SUIT AT ALL TIMES WHEN ENTERING IRRADIATED ZONES. HOWEVER, THEY OFFER LITTLE PROTECTION AGAINST ANY HOSTILES YOU MAY ENCOUNTER.
3. POWER! WANT THE VERY BEST IN BOTH PREVENTION AND PROTECTION? USE POWER ARMOR FOR THE DURATION OF YOUR TRIP.

---

 **DISTRESS PULSER**

Head roughly southwest into the Glowing Sea, and enter Sentinel Site Prescott (pictured). Beware of Radscorpions and other irradiated dangers along the way.

Descend the outer gantry. Locate the terminal at the base of the structure and abort the launch sequence, allowing all blast doors to be opened (via terminals). Open the adjacent blast door. Locate the cylindrical tunnel. Beware of Feral Ghouls.

Wind your way through cylindrical and concrete tunnels, through holes, and along waterlogged passages, watching for more ferals. At the warehouse control room, you encounter Brother Henri and Atom's Wrath (an Assaultron). You can kill them, either before or after the conversation. Locate the password on Henri's corpse and use it to unlock his terminal and open the doors.

**HENRI'S TERMINAL PASSWORD**

(Medium) Pretend you revere the Children of the Atom cult, and you're let past without incident. He opens the doors for you.

## VAULT-TEC RECOMMENDS

LOOTING THE SENTINEL SITE

**ASTOUNDINGLY AWESOME TALES**

Unfortunately, you can't take any of the Mark 28 nukes home with you, but the facility does have two copies of Astoundingly Awesome Tales, a few Holotapes, and a mini nuke to take.

The stockpile is now accessible. If Paladin Danse is your current companion, speak to him and he agrees to stay and defend the stockpile.

Return to Proctor Ingram to inform her of your progress. She's happy enough with your progress to let you press the power transfer switch and power up the war machine. Afterward, accept an impressive reward:

**T-60 MEDIC PUMP**

## Quest
# BLIND BETRAYAL

1. SPEAK TO ELDER MAXSON
2. SPEAK TO PROCTOR QUINLAN
3. FOLLOW SCRIBE HAYLEN
4. SPEAK TO SCRIBE HAYLEN
5. TRAVEL TO LISTENING POST BRAVO
6. LOCATE PALADIN DANSE
7. SPEAK TO PALADIN DANSE
8. AND/OR EXECUTE PALADIN DANSE
9. RETRIEVE PALADIN DANSE'S HOLOTAGS
10. WATCH DANSE'S EXECUTION
11. SPEAK TO ELDER MAXSON
12. RETURN TO THE PRYDWEN
13. SPEAK TO ELDER MAXSON

**Locations to Explore**
– LISTENING POST BRAVO (PAGE 282)

### AN ALARMING DEVELOPMENT

You've been informed that Elder Maxson has an urgent mission for you and you should report to him on the Prydwen immediately. Agree to his order.

(Medium) There are a few possible choices to make him believe you.

You need to find Paladin Danse and sort out the confusing news you've heard about him. Danse has disappeared, but Proctor Quinlan (on the main deck) has a way to track him down. Then speak to Scribe Haylen for a more private conversation.

Head into the northern Commonwealth wilderness, and locate Listening Post Bravo. Avoid or neutralize the turrets, power up the elevator, and ride it down.

Watch out for a small Protectron presence. Paladin Danse is nearby, and there are multiple options.

### PLAN A: THE LAST DANSE

Remove him as a threat immediately, without talking to him.

Or, speak to him, using a threatening tone. If your persuasion attempts fail, Paladin Danse gives you an order. Oblige him, then retrieve his dog tags.

**DANSE'S HOLOTAGS**

Return to the Prydwen, and inform Elder Maxson. You receive the rank of Paladin.

## PLAN B: ONE LAST CHANCE

Plan B: (Medium) Speak to him, with friendly answers. Refuse to remove him as a threat. When prompted, choose any persuasion attempt and succeed with it.

Paladin Danse sees your way of thinking and hands over his dog tags.

**DANSE'S HOLOTAGS**

Exit Listening Post Bravo, where your escape is interrupted. Answer the person responsible for your interruption. You can:

– AGREE TO HIS WAY OF THINKING, AND REMOVE PALADIN DANSE AS A THREAT.

– AGREE TO HIS WAY OF THINKING, AND WATCH AS PALADIN DANSE IS REMOVED AS A THREAT.

– DISAGREE WITH HIS WAY OF THINKING, AND CONVINCE HIM TO LET DANSE LIVE. AFTER A BEGRUDGING AGREEMENT, YOU'RE LEFT WITH PALADIN DANSE. YOU CAN:

  • TELL HIM TO STAY (HE REMAINS HERE) OR BECKON HIM TO ACCOMPANY YOU AS A COMPANION.

Whatever decision you make, return to the Prydwen, inform Elder Maxson, and receive the rank of Paladin.

### VAULT-TEC RECOMMENDS

**DEATH FROM ABOVE**
**HONOR**

Time to check in with Proctor Teagan, as he has a nasty-looking missile launcher and a piece of power armor to purchase!

## *Quest* TACTICAL THINKING

1. SPEAK TO LANCER-CAPTAIN KELLS
2. ENTER OLD NORTH CHURCH
3. KILL DOCTOR CARRINGTON
4. BREACH THE DOOR TO THE LOWER LEVELS
5. KILL GLORY
6. KILL TINKER TOM
7. KILL DEACON
8. KILL DESDEMONA
9A. REPROGRAM PAM
9B. DESTROY PAM
10. REPORT TO LANCER-CAPTAIN KELLS

**Locations to Explore**
– NORTH END (NEIGHBORHOOD) (PAGE 464)
– OLD NORTH CHURCH (PAGE 466)

### THE WRONG SIDE OF THE TRACKS

Stop! Ready to be kicked out of the Railroad? Accept Kell's forthcoming orders and this becomes permanent, so if you have any loose ends to tie up with the Railroad, do so before speaking to Kells. You've been informed that Lancer-Captain Kells wishes to speak with you on the command deck of the Prydwen. After agreeing to his orders, head north into the North End neighborhood of Boston, and enter the Old North Church. You have a Priority Kill Order list. It's time to check those priorities off.

Remove all threats in the initial church chamber. It's wise to eliminate all foes before continuing into the crypt. Fight down into the catacombs. Locate and activate the detonator and blow a hole in the wall. Your remaining primary targets are now acquired.

Enter through the hole in the wall and into the Railroad HQ. Dispatch all Railroad threats from the theater of combat

Locate the PAM mainframe terminal or the automaton herself. Either destroy the robot or use the terminal to reprogram her. Then return and report to Lancer-Captain Kells.

There is disappointment if PAM was deactivated rather than reprogrammed. If PAM was reprogrammed, she is later transported onto the Prydwen.

### VAULT-TEC RECOMMENDS

LOOTING OLD NORTH CHURCH
**ASTOUNDINGLY AWESOME TALES**

Great news! There's some required reading on one of the desks inside these headquarters. Even better! Usually you'd have to steal this magazine, but nobody's going to mind your light fingers now, are they?

## HELPFUL HINT *from Vault Boy!*

 **Did You Know?**

THE FOES YOU'RE GOING UP AGAINST ARE HEAVILY ARMED AND DESPERATE. THE INFILTRATION AREA IS NARROW WITH NUMEROUS CORNERS TO HIDE AROUND. LOB IN PROJECTILES TO SOFTEN UP YOUR TARGETS. FOCUS ON ONE FOE (IDEALLY ONE ARMED WITH THE NASTIEST WEAPON) AT A TIME. AND COME PACKING BOTH HEAT AND HEALTH. A METHODICAL APPROACH TO EXECUTIONS IS A GREAT WAY TO SPILL ALL THE BLOOD YOU WANT—JUST NONE OF YOUR OWN!

## Quest
# SPOILS OF WAR

Locations to Explore
– MASS FUSION (PAGE 477)

1. SPEAK TO PROCTOR INGRAM
2A. FLY TO MASS FUSION OR
2B. INFORM THE INSTITUTE
3. JUMP TO MASS FUSION'S ROOF
4. LOCATE THE BERYLLIUM AGITATOR
5. RETRIEVE THE EXECUTIVE KEY CARD
6. PROCEED TO THE REACTOR LEVEL
7. (OPTIONAL) RESTORE POWER TO THE ELEVATOR

8. ENTER THE REACTOR CHAMBER
9. UNLOCK THE REACTOR
10. TAKE THE BERYLLIUM AGITATOR
11. ELIMINATE REACTOR LEVEL SECURITY
12. EXIT MASS FUSION
13. (OPTIONAL) ASSIST BROTHERHOOD FORCES IN THE LOBBY
14. RETURN TO BOSTON AIRPORT
15. SPEAK TO PROCTOR INGRAM

## WHERE DO YOUR LOYALTIES LIE?

After speaking to Proctor Ingram, you agree to help her find something called a "Beryllium Agitator" from the ruins of Mass Fusion. After deciding whether she accompanies you or not, you must make a potentially epoch-defining decision. You can:

- FLY TO MASS FUSION BY BOARDING THE VERTIBIRD, MANNING THE MINIGUN UNTIL YOU'RE TOLD TO DROP, AND CONTINUING YOUR LOYALTY TO THE BROTHERHOOD OF STEEL. THIS QUEST CONTINUES (BELOW), A NUMBER OF INSTITUTE QUESTS FAIL, AND INSTITUTE QUEST: BANISHED FROM THE INSTITUTE BEGINS.
- LEAVE THIS AREA, VISIT THE INSTITUTE, AND INFORM THEM, CHANGING YOUR LOYALTY TO THE INSTITUTE. THE INSTITUTE QUEST: MASS FUSION BEGINS.

## HELPFUL HINT
### from Vault Boy!
**Did You Know?**

HAVE YOU PACKED ENOUGH PROVISIONS AND SUPPLIES? YOU KNOW YOUR LOVED ONES MIGHT WORRY IF YOU HAVEN'T HAD THE FORESIGHT TO GATHER ENOUGH HEALTHY SNACKS AND RADIATION-SUPPRESSING CHEMS. AS THE ENVIRONMENT INSIDE MASS FUSION IS EXTREMELY HOSTILE, WHY NOT BUNDLE UP IN PROPER PROTECTIVE ATTIRE? POWER ARMOR IS A GREAT CHOICE HERE.

## MASSACRE IN MASS FUSION

You drop to the roof of the building, in the Financial District of Boston. After you neutralize all threats, head to the second level, and locate the balcony desk before the room with the Executive Research Lab terminal. Gather the following from the desk:

MASS FUSION EXECUTIVE LAB PASSWORD

MASS FUSION EXECUTIVE ID

Now you can access the Executive Research Lab terminal (Advanced) with a password. Read the personal intramails; the item you seek is apparently in the facility's basement. And you're on the roof.

You have a third option to restore power to the elevator-- in the room with the Mass Fusion Labs Key, if you can hack the manager's terminal (Expert), you can restore the power without having to head up to the circuit breaker.

At the elevator, swipe the Mass Fusion Executive ID through the card reader. Ride the elevator down until you cannot descend farther, taking pot shots at enemy forces along the way. When the coast is clear, you can:

(Optional) Locate the circuit breaker in the chamber to the north and above your current position. Flip the breaker to power the elevator. Then return, swipe the ID card, and ride the elevator down to the lobby, maximizing enemy casualties as you go.

Or locate the room to the north of your current position. Locate the Mass Fusion labs key on the desk. Use it to open the door to the adjacent chamber with the hole in the floor. Drop down, and continue a manual descent through the floors to the lobby, removing any potential enemy threats along the way.

MASS FUSION LABS KEY

Expect more enemy resistance in the lobby. Search for the service elevator, swiping your ID card to access it.

MASS HAUL AT MASS FUSION

**TESLA SCIENCE MAGAZINE**    **NUKA CHERRY**

As you fight through Mass Fusion, you can gather a few choice items. Don't forget the Nuka Cherry in the laboratory on the roof. And be sure to read Tesla Science; there's a copy to the south on the uppermost level you can access without a jetpack, once you're in the tower. Is there time to fly to the floors even higher up this skyscraper interior for some cunningly hidden loot? You decide! Grab the magazine before you take the elevator down to the Lobby. Finally, there's a steamer trunk and hazmat suit in the reactor chamber — handy for the automated greeters you encounter once the Beryllium Agitator is yours.

## BERYLLIUM AGITATION

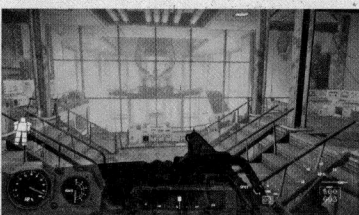

After stepping into the decontamination area (press that button!), move into the reactor chamber. Press the interlock release and activate the agitator receptacle. Grab what you came here for.

**BERYLLIUM AGITATOR**

---

### HELPFUL HINT
*from Vault Boy!*    **Did You Know?**

- IN THE REACTOR CONTROL ROOM (TO YOUR LEFT AS YOU ENTER), THERE'S A MASTER-LOCKED REACTOR SECURITY CONTROL TERMINAL. IF YOU CAN HACK THAT, YOU CAN UNLOCK THE DOORS TO THE FACILITIES OFFICE ON THE OPPOSITE SIDE OF THE ROOM. A TERMINAL THERE ALLOWS YOU TO DISABLE THE SECURITY SYSTEM ENTIRELY, PREVENTING THE ROBOTS AND TURRETS FROM ATTACKING WHEN YOU TAKE THE AGITATOR.
- CAN'T QUITE HACK IT? YOU CAN ALSO USE THE OTHER TERMINALS SCATTERED THROUGHOUT THE LEVEL TO RELEASE THE PROTECTRONS AND THE ASSAULTRON EARLY AND KILL THEM ONE AT A TIME.
- MAKE SURE YOU HAVE RADIATION PROTECTION BEFORE ENTERING THE REACTOR CHAMBER-- THE RADIATION LEVEL IS LETHAL. FOR BEST RESULTS, GRAB A HAZMAT SUIT-- THERE ARE SEVERAL SCATTERED AROUND THE REACTOR LEVEL, INCLUDING ONE IN THE LOCKER ROOM.

The facility's robotic defenses are automatically activated. Reach the outer reactor room and engage a Sentry Bot and Protectron. After using your ID card to open the main door, bring your defenses to bear on an Assaultron. Then ascend the stairs to nullify another Protectron without being scorched by a laser turret.

Exit to the lobby. If you have the ammunition and abilities, help Brotherhood of Steel forces rid the lobby of threats. Then rendezvous with Proctor Ingram back at Boston Airport.

DATA

QUESTS

## *Quest*
# AD VICTORIAM

1. FOLLOW PROCTOR INGRAM
2. SPEAK TO PROCTOR INGRAM
3. PLUG IN BERYLLIUM AGITATOR
4. ACTIVATE POWER TRANSFER SWITCH
5. FOLLOW LIBERTY PRIME
6. DEFEND LIBERTY PRIME
7. ENTER THE INSTITUTE

**Locations to Explore**
- EAST BOSTON POLICE STATION (PAGE 339)
- CHARLESTOWN (NEIGHBORHOOD) (PAGE 422)
- CAMBRIDGE (NEIGHBORHOOD) (PAGE 400)

## A STROLL THROUGH BOSTON. WITH SUPERIOR FIREPOWER.

In order to get the war machine running under its own power, you should speak to Proctor Ingram, then ascend the scaffold and insert the Agitator into the war machine's reactor port (behind the head). Return to the gantry computer and press the power transfer switch.

Escort Liberty Prime through the streets of Boston in a roughly northerly and then westerly direction. You can neutralize any synth threats, though you have impressive fire support. You may wish to use the bridge when the war machine crosses the river. Continue until you reach the C.I.T. ruins.

At the ruins of the C.I.T., expect multiple synth threats at once. Remove all of them. When the war machine successfully makes a hole in the Institute's defenses, it's time to drop into it.

## Quest
# THE NUCLEAR OPTION
# (BROTHERHOOD OF STEEL)

1. TALK TO ELDER MAXSON
2. REACH INSTITUTE REACTOR
3. USE TERMINAL TO OVERRIDE INSTITUTE LOCKDOWN
4. (OPTIONAL) ISSUE EVACUATION ORDER
5. REACH THE REACTOR
6. PLANT FUSION PULSE CHARGE INSIDE REACTOR

7. TALK TO ELDER MAXSON
8. TALK TO PROCTOR INGRAM
9. TALK TO SHAUN
10. STEP INTO THE RELAY
11. ACTIVATE DETONATOR
12. TALK TO ELDER MAXSON

Locations to Explore
− THE INSTITUTE (PAGE 409)

## EXERCISING YOUR OPTION

### VAULT-TEC RECOMMENDS

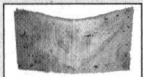

FOR THE BROTHERHOOD!

This conclusion to the Main Quest is available only if you sided with the Brotherhood of Steel. It commences once you complete Brotherhood of Steel Quest: Ad Victoriam.

You have previously agreed to Elder Maxson's way of thinking and must now enter the Institute. Speak with your leader, who hands you a device imperative to concluding these activities.

 **FUSION PULSE CHARGE**

You head through the Old Robotics area. Expect heavy synth resistance and laser turrets. Locate and drop through the hatch and enter the Institute BioScience laboratory. Work your way to the reactor entrance. Not surprisingly, the blast door has been activated.

At the central elevator, press the button. Enter Father's quarters and receive the override password from him. Use it, or hack the terminal (Novice). Activate the Master Security Lockdown Override.

 (Medium) There are three options if you answer Father regarding why he should help you.

## HELPFUL HINT
*from Vault Boy!*

DO YOU LIKE TO MINIMIZE CASUALTIES IN THE COMBAT ZONE? THEN TRIGGER THE EVACUATION OPTIONS AT FATHER'S TERMINAL SO YOU HAVE FEWER INSTITUTE SYNTHS TO ENCOUNTER. THIS IS A GREAT IDEA IF SAFETY (BUT NOT GATHERING EXPERIENCE POINTS) IS YOUR NUMBER ONE CONCERN.

## AN UNEQUIVOCAL REACTION

Approach the Institute Advanced Systems and maneuver to the reactor chamber. If no evacuation has been called, expect a heavy synth presence. Access the reactor door and activate the reactor housing.

Proctor Ingram teleports you to the Institute relay control room. Speak with Elder Maxson before Ingram interjects regarding an unexpected guest in the vicinity. Speak to the little fellow:

− AGREE TO TAKE HIM UNDER YOUR WING AND SAVE HIS LIFE. PROCTOR INGRAM ENSURES HIS SAFETY. FIND HIM AT BOSTON AIRPORT.
− INFORM PROCTOR INGRAM THAT THE CHILD MUST REMAIN HERE.

After speaking into the relay and teleporting to the roof of the Mass Fusion building, you're able to conclude this operation without room for interpretation. Your Main Questing ends after you speak to Elder Maxson about the future of the Commonwealth.

### VAULT-TEC RECOMMENDS

**WOW! A WAZER WIFLE!**

Once your questing is over, this diminutive fellow has three super-secret quests you can undertake for him. Think of it as some bonding you missed while you were in the deep freeze. Finish all three quest, and you're awarded with a special "wifle" that never runs out of ammo.

## Quest
# A NEW DAWN

1. RETURN TO THE PRYDWEN
2. SPEAK TO ELDER MAXSON

### UT IN POSTERUM

  **T-60 JETPACK**

Elder Maxson has ordered you back to the Prydwen for your final debriefing. You are awarded the title of Sentinel and granted a jetpack for your Power Armor. Lancer-Captain Kells informs you that Radiant Quests continue to be available at Cambridge Police Station. In addition, Miscellaneous Quest: Reactor Coolant (a request from Proctor Ingram) is now available.

DATA

QUESTS

*Lone Wanderer*

LEAVE WORK BEHIND.

# BROTHERHOOD OF STEEL: MISCELLANEOUS QUESTS

## HELPFUL HINT
### from Vault Boy!

**Did You Know?**

WHAT ARE MISCELLANEOUS BROTHERHOOD OF STEEL QUESTS? THAT'S ONE PERTINENT QUESTION, FRIEND! THE FIVE QUESTS DETAILED HERE ARE PURELY OPTIONAL REQUESTS FROM THIS FACTION. COMPLETE THEM DURING THE MAIN QUESTS. BEWARE OF SOME ELONGATED BATTLES, BUT PREPARE ALSO FOR SOME EXCELLENT REWARDS FOR MANAGING THESE EXTRA ORDERS. HOWEVER, IF YOU'RE ON SHAKY GROUND WITH THIS FACTION (IF YOU FIGHT OR ALLY AGAINST THEM), EXPECT YOUR PIP-BOY TO INDICATE A "BROTHERHOOD OF STEEL SHUTDOWN" HAS BEEN ACTIVATED, AND MOST OF THESE QUESTS WON'T BE ACCESSIBLE.

## Quest
# THE LOST PATROL

1. REPORT TO PALADIN DANSE
2. REPORT YOUR DISCOVERY TO THE BROTHERHOOD
3. SEARCH FOR THE RECON TEAM
4. FOLLOW THE RADIO DISTRESS SIGNAL
5. INVESTIGATE THE BATTLE SITE
6. LISTEN TO THE BATTLEFIELD HOLOTAPE
7. (OPTIONAL) REPORT BACK TO PALADIN DANSE
8. INVESTIGATE THE NATIONAL GUARD TRAINING YARD
9. FOLLOW THE RADIO DISTRESS SIGNAL
10. INVESTIGATE THE BATTLE SITE
11. LISTEN TO KNIGHT ASTLIN'S HOLOTAPE
12. INVESTIGATE THE SATELLITE ARRAY
13. FOLLOW THE RADIO DISTRESS SIGNAL
14. INVESTIGATE THE BATTLE SITE
15. LISTEN TO SCRIBE FARIS' HOLOTAPE
16. INVESTIGATE THE BUNKER
17. SPEAK TO PALADIN BRANDIS
18. KILL PALADIN BRANDIS OR
19. MEET PALADIN DANSE OUTSIDE
20. REPORT TO PALADIN DANSE
21. SPEAK TO PALADIN DANSE OR
22. REPORT TO CAPTAIN KELLS

**Locations to Explore**
- WEST EVERETT ESTATES (PAGE 292)
- NATIONAL GUARD TRAINING YARD (PAGE 293)
- REVERE SATELLITE ARRAY (PAGE 296)
- RECON BUNKER THETA (PAGE 276)

### KNIGHT VARHAM'S RESTING SPOT

Three years ago, the last Brotherhood recon team sent to the Commonwealth went missing. This quest begins in one of three ways:

- **YOU STUMBLE UPON ONE OF THE RECON TEAM WITHOUT KNOWLEDGE OF THIS QUEST. REPORT YOUR DISCOVERY TO PALADIN DANSE OR CAPTAIN KELLS AND BEGIN THIS QUEST.**
- **YOU COMPLETE EITHER BROTHERHOOD OF STEEL RADIANT QUEST: QUARTERMASTERY OR CLEANSING THE COMMONWEALTH, AND SPEAK TO PALADIN DANSE OR CAPTAIN KELLS.**
- **YOU COMPLETE BROTHERHOOD OF STEEL QUEST: SHOW NO MERCY AND SPEAK TO CAPTAIN KELLS.**

If you haven't met the Brotherhood yet (or sided against them), you can still complete this quest. If you later decide to join up, you can tell Danse or Kells about your discovery and receive your reward.

The following investigations can occur in any order.

Head to the West Everett Estates close to Malden Middle School, near Med-Tek Research, in North Central Commonwealth. Explore until you find a distress signal, and tune your radio to it. There are Super Mutants active in this area, so be careful.

Listen for the ping. Follow it to the Brotherhood of Steel Battle Site, a burned-out structure southeast of Med-Tek Research. Examine Knight Varham and listen to the Holotape you find on him. Report this or continue your searching.

**KNIGHT VARHAM'S HOLOTAPE**

**KNIGHT VARHAM'S HOLOTAG**

## VAULT-TEC RECOMMENDS

### LOOTING WEST EVERETT ESTATES

 **NUKA COLA QUANTUM**

The nearby vicinity of West Everett Estates may not hold a gargantuan pile of ammunition, but there's a hidden cellar area and various ruined homes to sift through. Top of the scavenging list are two bottles of Nuka Cola Quantum.

## THE RESTING PLACE OF KNIGHT ASTLIN

Head to the National Guard Training Yard in the North Central Commonwealth Zone. Beware of Feral Ghouls and turrets. Tune your radio to the distress signal and listen for the ping. Follow it to the National Guard Recruitment Office. Fend off any ferals before searching Knight Astlin and listening to her Holotape.

 **KNIGHT ASTLIN'S HOLOTAPE**

 **KNIGHT ASTLIN'S HOLOTAG**

## VAULT-TEC RECOMMENDS

### LOOTING THE NATIONAL GUARD TRAINING YARD

 **POWER ARMOR (LEVELED)**

Three suits of Power Armor and two Fusion Cores top the list of items you must gather before leaving this location. Of course, there's an automated Sentry Bot between you and the goods, so plan your hunt accordingly, and don't forget to check the cluster of cargo containers to the northwest.

## SITTING A SPELL WITH SCRIBE FARIS

Head to the nearby Revere Satellite Array. Beware of a heavy Super Mutant presence. Follow the distress signal to a shack perched on one

of the satellite arrays. Examine Scribe Faris and listen to his Holotape. You receive Recon Bunker Access Code 429A.

 **SCRIBE FARIS'S HOLOTAPE**

 **SCRIBE FARIS'S HOLOTAG**

## VAULT-TEC RECOMMENDS

### LOOTING REVERE SATELLITE ARRAY

 **U.S. COVERT OPERATIONS MANUAL**

What makes slogging through pools of congealed blood and hanging meat bags at this location worthwhile is some most informative reading material. Oh, and a suit of Power Armor, too.

## THE BUNKER OF BRANDIS

The Bunker Access Code refers to Recon Bunker Theta, also in the vast North Central Commonwealth. Input access code **429A** into the terminal to enter. Inside is Paladin Brandis. You can:

– **MENTION HIS NAME, AND SOLVE THE STANDOFF PEACEFULLY.**

 (Hard) Tell him you're here to talk or are with the Brotherhood. Fail and you may have to kill him. Succeed and the standoff ends peacefully.

(Hard) Tell him to back off. Fail and you must kill him. Succeed and the standoff ends peacefully.

If the standoff ends in violence, gather the Paladin's unique weapon after the fight:

 **PALADIN BRANDIS'S HOLOTAG**

 **SURVIVOR'S SPECIAL**

If you speak to him, you can:

– **FINISH THE CONVERSATION AS YOU WISH. GIVE HIM HIS TEAM'S HOLOTAGS IF YOU WISH.**

 (Medium) convince him to return to the Brotherhood.

## VAULT-TEC RECOMMENDS

### LOOTING RECON BUNKER THETA

 **FUSION CORE**

Paladin Brandis keeps a relatively tidy hovel, but aside from some foodstuffs and the usual scattering of chems and ammo, the only real item of value (especially as you're likely to be a Power Armor aficionado) is a Fusion Core.

If Paladin Danse is accompanying you on this quest, speak to him about Paladin Brandis afterward. If Main Quest: Act I is active, return to Cambridge Police Station for your reward from Paladin Danse:

 **BOTTLECAPS (200)**

If Main Quest: Act II is active, return to the Prydwen for your reward from Captain Kells:

 **STEADFAST BROTHERHOOD OF STEEL COMBAT ARMOR CHEST PIECE**

If you convinced Paladin Brandis to rejoin the Brotherhood, you can later meet him in the Prydwen's mess hall, where he will give you his unique gun—**Survivor's Special**. He will also fight with the Brotherhood during the Brotherhood of Steel Main Quests.

## Quest
# DUTY OR DISHONOR

**Locations to Explore**
- BOSTON AIRPORT (PAGE 342)
- PRYDWEN (PAGE 345)

## SUSPICIONS AT THE SUPPLY DEPOT

This quest becomes available once you complete both Brotherhood of Steel Quest: Show No Mercy and Brotherhood of Steel Miscellaneous Quest: The Lost Patrol. Captain Kells ordered you to investigate some missing supplies at the airport. Report to Knight-Sergeant Gavil in the Boston Airport supply depot for more information. Ask about Lucia and Clarke.

Your first suspect might be Knight Lucia, so talk to her about the recent activities.

(Medium) You can ask her about Clarke if you wish. If you succeed, she shares her suspicions, and much of the investigation can be skipped (Objective: Confront Initiate Clarke is now available).

Your second possible suspect is Initiate Clarke.

(Easy) You can ask him about Lucia if you wish.

Knight-Sergeant Gavil directs you to find evidence. Board the Prydwen, and find Clarke's and Lucia's sleeping quarters on the lower main deck.

Their footlockers are locked (Novice). You can:

- PICKPOCKET EITHER KEY FROM THEM IN THE SUPPLY DEPOT.
- (NOVICE, EXPERT) PICK THE LOCK OF CLARKE'S AND LUCIA'S FOOTLOCKERS.
- OR FIND CLARKE'S KEY ON HIS BED, OPEN HIS FOOTLOCKER, FIND LUCIA'S KEY INSIDE CLARKE'S FOOTLOCKER, THEN OPEN HER FOOTLOCKER. AMASS THE FOLLOWING, READ THE NOTE, AND READ HER LOG.

| 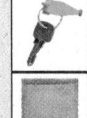 CLARKE'S PERSONAL KEY |  LUCIA'S PERSONAL KEY |
| --- | --- |
| NOTE: FROM LUCIA |  KNIGHT LUCIA'S LOG |

## SHADOWING THE SUSPECT

Now that one of your suspects has been acting suspiciously, return to the supply depot at Boston Airport. Lucia grants you more information.

Locate and follow your main suspect at a safe distance. Back away after speaking to them if you're seen. Your suspect disappears into Boston Airport Ruins.

There's a little-known underground area of ruins under the airport, including an old subway station and baggage claim area. The place is filled with Ghouls and some of the least pleasant water you've ever waded through. Along the way, dart into a dead-end corridor and discover Knight Rylan. Gather his Holotag. This enables more conversation choices when confronting your suspect.

 **KNIGHT RYLAN'S HOLOTAGS**

Continue to explore the ruins, culling Feral Ghouls. Destroy them all if you wish (or they are destroyed once the quest is complete).

When you finally catch up to your suspect, you can:

- **KILL THEM WITHOUT A CONVERSATION.**
- **PROVOKE THEM IN ANY WAY, TURNING THE SUSPECT HOSTILE.**

 (Varies) Persuade your suspect to allow you to kill the Ghouls, if you wish.

 (Medium) Convince your suspect to turn themselves in.

Or convince the suspect to go into exile. They leave the airport, though you may meet again during a random encounter later in your adventure.

Or promise to lie about your discovery.

If your suspect is killed or pickpocketed, you can gather the following:

 **AIRPORT EMPLOYEE ID CARD**

 **HOLOTAGS**

After dealing with the culprit, report to Lancer-Captain Kells on the Prydwen. Your options here will vary depending on how things went in the airport ruins, but basically, you can:

- **LIE ABOUT THE THEFTS. IF YOUR SUSPECT IS STILL ALIVE, THEY REMAIN WORKING AT THE AIRPORT.**
- **OR TELL THE TRUTH. IF YOUR SUSPECT IS STILL ALIVE, THEY ARE IMPRISONED AT CAMBRIDGE POLICE STATION. DURING RAILROAD QUEST: PRECIPICE OF WAR, YOU CAN OPTIONALLY FREE YOUR SUSPECT IF YOU SUBSEQUENTLY SIDE WITH THE RAILROAD.**

 (Hard) Or make up a lie about Ghouls stealing supplies.

You receive a reward from Kells. This is usually Bottlecaps. However, if you managed to persuade Clarke to turn himself in, you receive a special Power Armor part.

 **EXEMPLAR'S T60C TORSO**

 **BOTTLECAPS (0-200)**

# Quest
# A LOOSE END

| | **Locations to Explore** |
|---|---|
| 1. SPEAK TO CAPTAIN KELLS | – PRYDWEN (PAGE 345) |
| 2. KILL VIRGIL | – ROCKY CAVE (VIRGIL'S LABORATORY) (PAGE 363) |
| 3. REPORT TO CAPTAIN KELLS | – THE INSTITUTE (PAGE 409) |

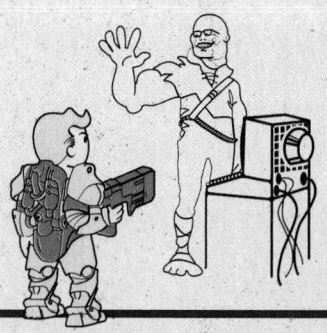

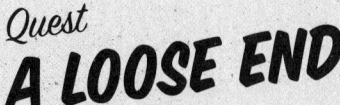

## THE FATE OF DOCTOR BRIAN VIRGIL

This quest becomes available during Brotherhood of Steel Quest: Liberty Reprimed. You must also have completed Brotherhood of Steel Miscellaneous Quest: Duty or Dishonor. Aboard the Prydwen, speak to Lancer-Captain Kells for your orders. He believes Virgil to be a threat to the Brotherhood, who must be eliminated.

 You have a number of different choices, some of which are related to Miscellaneous Quest: Curing Virgil.* If you want additional decisions, complete that optional quest (see page 363). Then visit the Rocky Cave within the Glowing Sea.

Meet Virgil. You can:

- **ALREADY HAVE KILLED HIM. REPORT IMMEDIATELY TO KELLS WITHOUT TRAVELING TO THE GLOWING SEA.**
- **ATTACK AND KILL HIM. BEWARE OF HIS PROTECTRON AND TURRETS.**
- **SPEAK TO HIM, AND AGREE TO KEEP HIM ALIVE AND TO LIE TO KELLS.**

**HELPFUL HINT** *from Vault Boy!* **Did You Know?**

WHAT EXACTLY DOES VIRGIL NEED TO BE CURED? YOU MUST JOURNEY TO THE INSTITUTE, ACCESS THE FEV LABORATORY, FIND THE EXPERIMENTAL SERUM THERE, AND RETURN IT TO VIRGIL. THIS IS A STRAIGHTFORWARD, IF LENGTHY, PROCESS.

 (Hard) If you haven't completed Miscellaneous Quest: Curing Virgil*, you can persuade Virgil that the serum has been destroyed, and that he would be better off dead. He agrees to let you kill him. This persuasion is easier is easier if you've read notes after searching Primary Location: Swan's Pond (in the Boston Common Neighborhood; see page 472).

Miscellaneous Quest: Curing Virgil*: Kill him after curing him with the serum. He is much easier to kill.

Miscellaneous Quest: Curing Virgil*: Cure him, and leave him alive (he cannot escape, as the radiation from the Glowing Sea would kill him). Now that Virgil has been dealt with, report back to Captain Kells. You can:

(Medium) Miscellaneous Quest: Curing Virgil*: Tell Kells that Virgil is cured and "no longer a threat."

- TELL KELLS THAT VIRGIL HAS BEEN KILLED.
- (LIE) TELL KELLS THAT VIRGIL HAS BEEN KILLED, IF YOU AGREED TO THIS WITH VIRGIL.

You receive a reward from Kells as this quest concludes.

**VISIONARY'S T-60C HELM**

## Quest
# GETTING TECHNICAL*

MISCELLANEOUS: COLLECT TECHNICAL DOCUMENTS FOR PROCTOR QUINLAN
(*THIS QUEST APPEARS IN THE MISCELLANEOUS PART OF YOUR QUEST MENU.)

### FILING SOME PAPERWORK

This quest is given by Proctor Quinlan aboard the Prydwen. It commences if you speak to him during Brotherhood of Steel Quest: Tour of Duty and agree to help.

During your adventure, gather any Technical Documents you may find, such as this one locked in a safe.

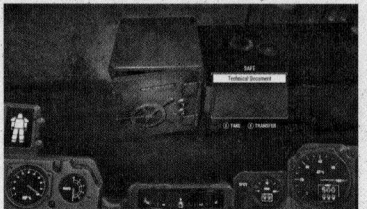

**TECHNICAL DOCUMENT**

Return to Proctor Quinlan and present any documents. The quest is repeatable.

**BOTTLECAPS
(25 PER SET OF DOCUMENTS)**

## Quest
# BLOOD BANK*

MISCELLANEOUS: SECURE VIABLE BLOOD SAMPLES FOR SCRIBE NERIAH
(*THIS QUEST APPEARS IN THE MISCELLANEOUS PART OF YOUR QUEST MENU.)

### YOU'VE GOT RED ON YOU

This quest is given by Scribe Neriah aboard the Prydwen. It commences once you finish Brotherhood of Steel Quest: Tour of Duty and agree to help her.

Your Pip-Boy is reprogrammed to recognize "Viable Blood Samples" from enemies you slay. Once you kill an entity, check its corpse for this new item and extract it.

**VIABLE BLOOD SAMPLE**

Return to Scribe Neriah and present the blood you've collected. The quest is repeatable.

**BOTTLECAPS
(25+ PER VIAL OF BLOOD)**

## Quest
# REACTOR COOLANT*

MISCELLANEOUS: MAKE REACTOR COOLANT FOR PROCTOR INGRAM
(*THIS QUEST APPEARS IN THE MISCELLANEOUS PART OF YOUR QUEST MENU.)

### KEEP THE BROTHERHOOD BLIMP AFLOAT

This quest is given by Proctor Ingram aboard the Prydwen. It starts once you conclude all the Main Brotherhood of Steel quests, speak with her, and agree to help her find components to mix into Reactor Coolant for the Prydwen's engines. You receive a note indicating what you need:

- GAS CANISTER
- NUCLEAR MATERIAL (2)
- ANTIFREEZE (3)
- DIRTY WATER (5)

Head to the nearest Chemistry Station and concoct the coolant, before returning to Proctor Ingram for your reward. The quest is repeatable.

**REACTOR COOLANT**

Head to the nearest Chemistry Station and concoct the coolant, before returning to Proctor Ingram for your reward. The quest is repeatable.

**BOTTLECAPS
(25+ PER REACTOR COOLANT)**

# BROTHERHOOD OF STEEL RADIANT QUESTS

## HELPFUL HINT
### *from Vault Boy!*

WHAT ARE RADIANT BROTHERHOOD OF STEEL QUESTS? AN INTERESTING ASIDE TO YOUR MAIN WORK FOR THIS ORGANIZATION, THE FIVE QUESTS REFERENCED HERE ARE OPTIONAL TASKS TO UNDERTAKE FROM DIFFERENT MEMBERS OF THE BROTHERHOOD. THEY ARE "RADIANT," AS THE LOCATIONS YOU'RE SENT TO ARE RANDOM. SOME QUESTS ARE ALSO REPEATABLE, MAKING THEM A GREAT WAY TO ACCUMULATE REWARDS.

## VAULT-TEC RECOMMENDS

### RANDOM FACTS

Due to the random nature of the locations you are sent to, it is imperative you read up on the hostiles (as well as the valuables) you'll uncover at each one. Vault-Tec is proud to provide comprehensive cartography for just such a reconnoiter.

---

## Quest
# CLEANSING THE COMMONWEALTH

1. CLEAR OUT [A RANDOM LOCATION]    2. REPORT TO KNIGHT RHYS

**Locations to Explore**
- CAMBRIDGE POLICE STATION (PAGE 403)
- PRYDWEN (PAGE 345)

### ANNIHILATE ALL ABOMINATIONS

Knight Rhys has given you an assignment to clear a location of "abominations." You need to find the location and eliminate any synths, ferals, Super Mutants, and Atom-worshipping cultists that you can find. The location given to you by Rhys is random. Only the tagged foes must be slain. Others are optional. Then return and claim your caps from Knight Rhys.

 **BOTTLECAPS (APPROX 100)**

## Quest
# QUARTERMASTERY

1. RECOVER THE [TECH ITEM] AT [A RANDOM LOCATION]
2. REPORT TO SCRIBE HAYLEN

**Locations to Explore**
- CAMBRIDGE POLICE STATION (PAGE 403)
- PRYDWEN (PAGE 345)

### ARTIFACT APPROPRIATION

Scribe Haylen has given you a mission to recover a piece of technology for her at a given location. You need to go there, find the artifact, and bring it back to her in one piece. Only the item—usually hidden inside a steamer trunk—needs to be found. A thorough exploration of the location is usually necessary. Consult the "Map" chapter for environmental hazards. Killing enemies is optional. Then return and claim your Caps reward from Scribe Haylen.

 **BOTTLECAPS (APPROX 100)**

## Quest
# LEADING BY EXAMPLE

1. SPEAK TO THE BROTHERHOOD SQUIRE (1)
2. CLEAR [A LOCATION] OF ALL HOSTILES WITH THE SQUIRE
3. SPEAK TO THE BROTHERHOOD SQUIRE (2)
4. RETURN TO LANCER-CAPTAIN KELLS

**Locations to Explore**
- CAMBRIDGE POLICE STATION (PAGE 403)
- PRYDWEN (PAGE 345)

### FRESH BLOOD

Speak to Lancer-Captain Kells (usually on the Prydwen) and agree to train one of the Brotherhood Squires by allowing him to accompany you on a mission. Meet the Squire in the airport, where he'll give you details on the mission's random location.

Head to the location the Squire indicated, and remove all the foes tagged on your Pip-Boy. Any other entities are optional kills. Speak to the enthusiastic Squire once combat is over.

Then return and explain how the Squire performed to Lancer-Captain Kells and claim your reward.

**BOTTLECAPS (APPROX 100)**

## Quest
# LEARNING CURVE

1. SPEAK TO THE BROTHERHOOD SCRIBE
2. ESCORT THE SCRIBE TO THE DATA AT [A LOCATION]
3. PROTECT THE BROTHERHOOD SCRIBE
4. RETURN TO PROCTOR QUINLAN

**Locations to Explore**
- CAMBRIDGE POLICE STATION (PAGE 403)
- PRYDWEN (PAGE 345)

### KNOWLEDGE IS POWER

Talk with Proctor Quinlan and agree to escort a Brotherhood Scribe on a research patrol. This conversation occurs once you complete Brotherhood of Steel Quest: Tour of Duty. Express interest in aiding a research patrol. Then locate the Scribe at Boston Airport.

Head to the Scribe's (random) location. Remove all threats while ensuring the Scribe isn't killed. Locate the terminal and guard the Scribe as he hacks it.

When the Scribe finishes collecting data, continue to protect him until you both depart the location. If he dies, the data will be lost and the mission fails. Exit the location. Fast-Travel to Proctor Quinlan to claim a Caps reward.

**BOTTLECAPS (APPROX 100)**

## Quest
# FEEDING THE TROOPS

1. SECURE SETTLEMENT CROPS AT [A SETTLEMENT LOCATION]
2. RETURN TO PROCTOR TEAGAN

**Locations to Explore**
- PRYDWEN (PAGE 345)
- SETTLEMENT (RANDOM)

### FARMING WITH OR WITHOUT THE MINUTEMEN

After you complete Brotherhood of Steel Quest: Tour of Duty, express interest in "extra work" for Proctor Teagan. He asks you to visit a Commonwealth farm and secure their crops for the Brotherhood. You've been told to "persuade" them by any means necessary.

Locate the (random) settlement Teagan indicates and speak to the tagged settler. You can:

**PURCHASE THE CROPS FROM THE SETTLER FOR 1,000 CAPS.**

(Medium) Or bargain the settler down to 500 Caps.

(Medium) Ask the settler to donate a portion of their crops to the Brotherhood.

(Medium) Threaten the settler into handing over a portion of their crops to the Brotherhood.

Or kill all the Settlers, take over and manage the settlement, and grow crops yourself. After you make a choice, return to Proctor Teagan and let him know of your in-roads. Caps are claimed once again.

**BOTTLECAPS (APPROX 50)**

# THE RAILROAD QUESTS

You can work with this clandestine faction after you find the clues leading to the Railroad's hidden hideout and complete Road to Freedom. You can continue Railroad missions for as long as you want. However, be aware that your relationships with the other main factions—the Brotherhood of Steel, the Institute, (though not the Minutemen)—may be negatively affected the more Railroad quests you complete. It seems war never changes.

The following Railroad Quests become available:

| THE INSTITUTE QUESTS | | | |
|---|---|---|---|
| **Main Faction Quest** | **Location** | **Radiant Faction Quest** | **Location** |
| Road to Freedom | Page 155 | Butcher's Bill 1 | Page 165 |
| Tradecraft | Page 156 | Butcher's Bill 2 | Page 165 |
| Underground Undercover | Page 158 | Mercer Safehouse | Page 166 |
| Operation Ticonderoga | Page 159 | Jackpot | Page 166 |
| Precipice of War | Page 160 | Concierge | Page 167 |
| Rockets' Red Glare | Page 161 | Weathervane | Page 167 |
| The Nuclear Option (Railroad) | Page 161 | Randolph Safehouse | Page 167 |
| Burning Cover | Page 162 | Variable Removal | Page 168 |
| **Miscellaneous Faction Quest** | **Location** | To the Mattresses | Page 168 |
| Boston After Dark | Page 163 | Lost Soul | Page 169 |
| Memory Interrupted | Page 164 | A Clean Equation | Page 169 |
| | | High Ground | Page 169 |

## Quest
# ROAD TO FREEDOM

1. FOLLOW THE FREEDOM TRAIL
2. CONTINUE FOLLOWING THE FREEDOM TRAIL
3. SEARCH FOR THE RAILROAD
4. TALK WITH DESDEMONA

**Locations to Explore**
- BOSTON COMMON (PAGE 472)
- NORTH END (PAGE 464)
- OLD NORTH CHURCH (PAGE 466)

### TRAIL OF TERROR

If you want to fight the Institute, you've been told you should find the Railroad. The only clue you have is "Follow the Freedom Trail." The tourist trail starts at Boston Common due east of Diamond City.

This quest can start in a variety of ways:

- YOU INVESTIGATE THE AREA AROUND PARK STREET STATION, EITHER DURING YOUR EXPLORATION OR DURING MAIN QUEST: UNLIKELY VALENTINE.
- IF YOU SPEAK WITH DOCTOR AMARI AT THE START OF MAIN QUEST: THE MOLECULAR LEVEL, SHE INDICATES THE RAILROAD FACTION WOULD BE HELPFUL TO YOUR CAUSE.
- YOU OVERHEAR FOLKS IN DIAMOND CITY MARKET (AT THE MARKET OR IN THE DUGOUT INN), OR GUARDS IN GOODNEIGHBOR

Head to Boston Common, adjacent to Park Street Station. Locate this fountain with the scrawled board that reads "At Journey's End Follow Freedom's Lantern." On the ground in front of that is a Freedom Trail marker reading "A7."

Follow the red brick line along the sidewalk around the perimeter of Boston Common. Locate Massachusetts State House and the marker "L4."

Follow the trail to the Old Granary Burying Ground and the marker "A2." Watch for the ferocious ferals.

Follow the trail to the Old State House and the marker "O6." The disgusting displays of entrails indicate Super Mutants are active here.

Follow the trail to the Old Corner Bookstore and the marker "3I." Expect confrontations with Wild Mongrels, Feral Ghouls, Super Mutants, and Raiders.

Follow the trail to Faneuil Hall and the marker "5R." There's not a friendly face to be found; deal with Feral Ghouls, Super Mutants, and Mutant Hounds. Be particularly careful of the Super Mutant Suicider here; shoot the bomb out of his hand, or backpedal to avoid a disgustingly messy and violent attack.

The trail continues to what's left of Paul Revere's House and the marker "8D." Beware of Mutant Hounds and Super Mutants.

## HELPFUL HINT
### from Vault Boy!

**Did You Know?**

THE FREEDOM TRAIL WAS ONCE A TOURIST TRAP. NOW IT'S JUST A TRAP. THE VARIOUS UNFRIENDLY FIENDS VYING FOR CONTROL OF BOSTON'S CENTRAL NEIGHBORHOODS MAY PUT YOU ON EDGE. HAVE YOU TRIED A MORE STEALTHY APPROACH? A TACTICAL WITHDRAWAL? BUILDING UP YOUR PERCEPTION SO YOU SEE PROBLEMS BEFORE YOU'RE OVERWHELMED BY THEM? DON'T FORGET TO STUDY THE NEIGHBORHOOD MAPS OF THIS GUIDE TOO—WE SHOW EVERY ALLEY!

The trail concludes at the Old North Church and the marker "1R." Note the lantern sign painted on the wall by the door. Enter the church.

## NEW FRIENDS IN NORTH END

The old ruined church has Feral Ghouls lurking throughout the hall and lower catacombs. Follow the lantern markers downstairs to the Freedom Trail Ring, and spin it either clockwise or counterclockwise to spell out "RAILROAD." Moments later, you make contact with the Railroad. Answer their leader Desdemona how you wish:

(Easy) If you want more information, ask her, "Who are you?"

(Hard) If you're being secretive, make something up when she asks about you.

After more talking and agreeing to help her cause, you're tentatively welcomed in.

## VAULT-TEC RECOMMENDS

### UP THE STEEPLE, DOWN IN THE CRYPT

**FUSION CORE**

**ASTOUNDINGLY AWESOME TALES**

A thorough inspection of the Old North Church yields some surprises. The steeple (accessed via the hall above the crypt) offers views of North End and a sniper rifle. The Railroad Headquarters has two traders (Tinker Tom and Doctor Carrington) who can help bolster your items and health. There's some light reading on one of the tables. And don't forget to pry the Fusion Core from its generator when you use the Escape Tunnels to exit the place.

## Quest
# TRADECRAFT

1. TALK WITH DEACON
2. MEET DEACON AT THE OLD HIGHWAY
3. FOLLOW DEACON AND FIND THE "TOURIST"
4. TALK TO DEACON
5. GET INSIDE THE ESCAPE TUNNEL
6. (OPTIONAL) ENTER BASE THROUGH FRONT ENTRANCE
7. GET CARRINGTON'S PROTOTYPE
8. LEAVE THE SWITCHBOARD
9. MEET DEACON AT THE OLD NORTH CHURCH
10. TALK TO DESDEMONA
11. FOLLOW DESDEMONA

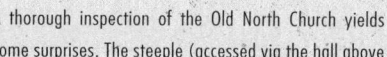

**Locations to Explore**

— NORTH END (PAGE 464)     — LEXINGTON (PAGE 267)     — SWITCHBOARD (PAGE 273)

## GOING INCOGNITO

If you want to have more dealings with the Railroad, talk with Deacon at the Railroad HQ. He's the mysterious man who vouched for you when you met with Desdemona, the Railroad's leader. He wants you to prove yourself first.

(Easy, Medium, Hard) Find out why he vouched for you.

Leave the Railroad HQ via the escape tunnel so you can unchain the door and return from this direction. Then set off on a long trek northwest toward Lexington. Use the elevated freeway and head west from the Corvega factory to rendezvous with Deacon.

Before you visit the Railroad's old base, Deacon wants to gleam some information from a "tourist" (a friend of this faction). Climb the ruined freeway and repel any corpses dashing in your direction. Meet up with Ricky Dalton. Give the Railroad password (you were told this earlier) or Deacon steps in.

(Easy, Medium, Hard) Talk with Ricky Dalton again for a variety of conversations; you can obtain more supplies, convince him to snipe the synths at the entrance, or convince him to make a suicide rush at the synths in front of the Slocum's Joe's.

## PRESSING THE RIGHT BUTTONS AT THE SWITCHBOARD

The news isn't good; the Railroad's old base (known as the Switchboard) is crawling with older model synths. You can:

- FOLLOW DEACON'S ADVICE AND ENTER VIA THE BACK "SEWER" ENTRANCE (PICTURE 1). THIS IS AN EMERGENCY ESCAPE ROUTE AND IS THE PREFERRED PATH.

- TRY TO ENTER VIA THE BASEMENT OF SLOCUM JOE'S ON THE OUTSKIRTS OF LEXINGTON. THIS IS HEAVILY TRAPPED AND DEFENDED WITH SYNTHS AND TURRETS. UNFORTUNATELY, WHEN YOU TRY TO ACCESS THE ELEVATOR VIA A HIDDEN BOOKCASE, IT IS INACCESSIBLE. LOOKS LIKE IT'S TIME TO WADE INTO THAT SEWER.

Work your way through the Switchboard, letting Deacon remove any security doors or terminals you can't access. Your target chamber is the Department X R&D room. Deacon accesses the terminal to open the safe security door.

**CARRINGTON'S PROTOTYPE**

## HELPFUL HINT
*from Vault Boy!*   **Did You Know?**

ARE YOU AWARE THAT THE RAILROAD HAS SPECIAL SECRET SIGNS TO INDICATE DANGEROUS LOCATIONS AND STASHES OF AMMUNITION? DEACON EXPLAINED THIS DURING YOUR FREEWAY WALK. THERE'S ONE STASH HIDDEN IN A PIPE IN THE SWITCHBOARD. FOR A LIST OF EVERY TYPE OF RAILROAD SIGN, LOOK AT THE CHALKBOARD AT RAILROAD HQ.

## VAULT-TEC RECOMMENDS

SCAVENGING THROUGH LEXINGTON TOWNSHIP

**NUKA CHERRY**
**U.S. COVERT OPERATIONS MANUAL**
**TALES OF A JUNKTOWN JERKY VENDOR**

Don't leave the Switchboard without a copy of the U.S. Covert Operations Manual. And while you're visiting Lexington, why not take in a few sights? There's the Super Duper Mart, which has a special offer on Nuka Cherries and Quantums (they're yours if you can survive the Feral Ghoul attacks). There's also some additional light reading to find at the Mystic Pines convalescent home, northeast of here. Otherwise, Lexington is a tough place to survive; Raiders are battling a large Feral threat, and neither party is particularly thrilled to see you!

After parting ways with Deacon, return to the Railroad HQ at your leisure. Desdemona is being debriefed by Deacon.

(Easy) Deacon tries to sell a lie to Desdesmona. Go with it.

Afterward, you are beckoned into the main headquarters and are formally given a codename. The choice is yours, unless you let Desdemona make the decision, in which case you're known as "The Wanderer." Welcome to the Railroad. Your first Railroad Miscellaneous Quest (Boston After Dark) is now available. You receive the following for your troubles:

 **DELIVERER**    **COMPANION: DEACON**

# Quest
# UNDERGROUND UNDERCOVER

1. TALK WITH TINKER TOM
2. UPLOAD ENCRYPTED MESSAGE ON ANY INSTITUTE TERMINAL
3. READ PATRIOT'S REPLY
4. MEET PATRIOT
5. FOLLOW LIAM
6. TALK WITH LIAM
7. TALK TO DESDEMONA
8. ENTER REPORT ON TERMINAL
9. TALK WITH PAM
10. GET PASSWORD FOR CODE DEFENDER
11. RETURN TO DESDEMONA
12. GIVE PASSWORD TO LIAM BINET
13. MEET WITH Z1-14
14. GIVE Z1-14 A DAY
15. MEET WITH Z1-14
16. KILL THE TUNNEL GUARDS
17. (OPTIONAL) DEPOSIT WEAPONS FOR REBELS
18. RETURN TO Z1-14
19. CONTINUE WORKING WITH FATHER
20. WAIT FOR Z1-14 TO CONTACT YOU
21. MEET WITH Z1-14
22. WARN DESDEMONA

**Locations to Explore**
- OLD NORTH CHURCH (PAGE 466)
- THE INSTITUTE (PAGE 409)
- CAMBRIDGE (PAGE 400)
- CAMBRIDGE POLYMER LABS (PAGE 407)

## A TRUE PATRIOT

Once you complete Main Quest: The Molecular Level—and you worked with the Railroad during that quest—you receive an encoded Holotape from Desdemona that you can use at any Institute terminal to contact the Railroad's guardian angel, Patriot. Tinker Tom also has some advice before handing you the Network Scanner Holotape.

 **NETWORK SCANNER**

Relay into the Institute, and locate any terminal (one example is pictured). Access it, insert the Network Scanner Holotape, then read the reply when it appears.

  **HELPFUL HINT** *from Vault Boy!* **Did You Know?**

WHY CAN'T EVERYBODY JUST GET ALONG? UNFORTUNATELY, IN THE POST-APOCALYPTIC WASTELAND, LIMITED RESOURCES AND SURVIVAL INSTINCTS USUALLY LEAD TO DISTRUST. SO PICK A FACTION YOU WANT TO WORK WITH, AND REMEMBER, YOU CAN GIVE THE HOLOTAPE TO A DIFFERENT FACTION IF YOU CHANGE YOUR ALLEGIANCES.

Patriot sends you an encrypted message requesting your presence at the Advanced Systems maintenance room. Say hello to Liam Binet, who subsequently introduces you to another friend on the inside, the synth Z1-14.

 (Medium) Tell Z1-14 you're fighting for them.

After another chat with Liam, relay back to Desdemona and inform her of your progress.

## LABORATORY LOCKDOWN

Patriot has a daring rescue plan, but this requires the login credentials for C.I.T.'s original security system, named "Code Defender." Return to the Railroad HQ, and speak with Desdemona. She points you in the direction of PAM, who offers some advice after you enter the report on her terminal.

It seems a man named Wilfred Bergman worked on the project and has the login credentials you need. Relay down to Cambridge Neighborhood, and enter Cambridge Polymer Labs. After a brief orientation with a robot named Molly, you're sealed inside this facility in the clean room. That isn't helpful, but it does begin the Miscellaneous quest at this location (see page 407 for advice). You're only here to access Bergman's terminal, though:

In the main mezzanine area (with the upper balcony), fight off the Feral Ghouls and look for the sign for laboratory C3. You enter this laboratory via lab C4. Access lab C5 through the hole in the wall. Get to lab C3 by climbing the "ramp" of ceiling debris, crawling across the ceiling crawlspace, and dropping down the third hole you spot in the floor. Drop in from the collapsed ceiling above.

- (EXPERT) OR HACK THE WALL TERMINAL TO OPEN THE LAB C3 DOOR.

Access Bergman's terminal and collect the password. Then return and speak with Desdemona.

## VAULT-TEC RECOMMENDS

### SCAVENGING CAMBRIDGE POLYMER LABS

**NUKA COLA QUANTUM**
**MASSACHUSETTS SURGICAL JOURNAL**
**PEIZONEUCLEIC POWER ARMOR CHEST**

While you're stuck inside the laboratory, you might as well make a thorough sweep of the area. Use the guidance on page 407 to identify six samples of matter that you can combine to make some impressive power armor. Along the way, grab some thirst-quenching sustenance and light reading.

## FREEDOM IS NEVER GIVEN—IT IS WON

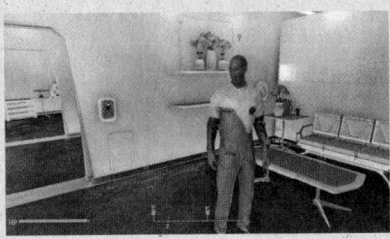

Back at Railroad HQ, Desdemona informs you of an even more daring rescue operation, but your plans remain unchanged: Relay back to the Institute, hand the login credentials to Patriot (Liam Benet), and then rendezvous with Z1-14.

Is he willing to fight for his freedom? He needs to process this information. Twenty-four hours later, he has an answer. Sit and wait if you wish.

 (Medium) Some persuasion is also available.

When you return, Z1-14 tells you many volunteers have joined the cause for freedom, but they require weapons. Optionally deposit any weapons and ammunition into the maintenance locker if you wish to arm the synths in the next fight. Then access a storage area and the elevator down to the tunnels. Repel all Institute-loyal synth guards at the tunnel entrance. Then return to Z1-14 and inform him of your victory. So you don't raise suspicion, continue to work with Father. Complete the Institute Quests: Mankind Redefined and Mass Fusion.

After continuing your other quests, you receive a cryptic message from Z1-14. Relay into the Institute, meet Z1-14's representative, and journey to your Institute quarters (given to you during Institute Quest: Synth Retention). He tells you of a worrying development regarding the Brotherhood of Steel. Immediately head back to the Railroad HQ. Desdemona is mobilizing the Railroad's defenses and hands you a weapon that might come in handy for the battle to come. This leads to Railroad Quest: Precipice of War.

 **RAILWAY RIFLE AND AMMO**

## Quest
# OPERATION TICONDEROGA

1. GO TO TICONDEROGA SAFEHOUSE
2. KILL ALL COURSERS
3. REPORT BACK TO DESDEMONA

**Locations to Explore**
- OLD NORTH CHURCH (PAGE 466)
- CAMBRIDGE (PAGE 400)
- TICONDEROGA SAFEHOUSE (PAGE 420)

## THE COURSE OF TICONDEROGA NEVER DID RUN SMOOTH

Once you complete Main Quest: Institutionalized but before Railroad Quest: Precipice of War has begun, Desdemona tells you that Institute Coursers have been spotted in the field. This means trouble. You're asked to check on Ticonderoga Safehouse, which has gone dark.

## HELPFUL HINT
### from Vault Boy!

 **Did You Know?**

YOUR PIP-BOY IS A MARVEL OF VAULT-TEC TECHNOLOGY, BUT EVEN IT HAS LIMITATIONS TO ITS CARTOGRAPHY. THE TICONDEROGA SAFEHOUSE IS AN UNMARKED "SECONDARY" LOCATION JUST SOUTH OF MONSIGNOR PLAZA IN THE CAMBRIDGE NEIGHBORHOOD. USE THE CAMBRIDGE NEIGHBORHOOD MAP (PAGE 400) AND YOUR PIP-BOY MARKER TO PINPOINT THIS, AND ANY OTHER UNMARKED LOCATION YOU WISH TO VISIT, SO YOU AREN'T WANDERING AROUND AIMLESSLY. BUT HAVE YOU TRIED SIMPLY WAITING IN COMPLETE SAFETY WITHIN A VAULT INSTEAD?

Though you can thoroughly search the entirety of the building for synths, you only need dispatch the two Institute Coursers. Beware of machine-gun turrets, synths, and Coursers. Be sure to locate the Courser leader X9-27 and slay him. Exit and mop up any additional foes. Then inform Desdemona.

**BOTTLECAPS (500)**

**TACTICAL HARDENED PIPE PISTOL AND AMMO**

## Quest
# PRECIPICE OF WAR

1. WARN DESDEMONA
2. DEFEND RAILROAD HQ
3. TALK WITH DESDEMONA
4. SECURE THE CATACOMBS
5. SECURE THE CHURCH
6. TALK WITH DESDEMONA
7. MEET TINKER TOM AT THE POLICE STATION
8. ELIMINATE BROTHERHOOD FORCES
9. TALK WITH TINKER TOM
10. DEFEND THE VERTIBIRD
11. TALK WITH DEACON

**Locations to Explore**
- OLD NORTH CHURCH (PAGE 466)
- CAMBRIDGE (PAGE 400)
- CAMBRIDGE POLICE STATION (PAGE 403)

## THROUGH THE PERILOUS FIGHT

You have hostiles at the Railroad HQ arriving from both directions! Initially, the escape tunnels are breached, so force your foes back and dispatch them quickly (laying mines in the narrow spaces or lobbing grenades can soften up your adversaries).

## HELPFUL HINT
*from Vault Boy!*   **Did You Know?**

DIPLOMACY IS A LOST ART. HAVE YOU TRIED REASONING WITH YOUR FOES? SURELY YOU HAVE MORE TO LOSE BY A FORCEFUL RESOLUTION OF PREVIOUS ANIMOSITIES? HOWEVER, IF YOU CAN'T BE FRIENDS ANYMORE, BE SURE TO BRING THE HEAVIEST, FINEST FIREPOWER IN MODDED WEAPONRY, THE BEST ARMOR YOU'VE FOUND OR CRAFTED, AND A PLENTIFUL SUPPLY OF CHEMS. THEN WIPE YOUR FOES OUT WITH EXTREME PREJUDICE.

Incoming! More enemies of the Railroad have infiltrated the Old North Church entrance. After speaking with Glory, enter the catacombs and fight your way to the main church hall. Every entity not recognized as a Railroad agent must be nullified!

The Railroad HQ has survived. But until the main base of your enemies is permanently removed from the Commonwealth, you'll never be safe. Head west across the Cambridge Neighborhood to rendezvous with Tinker Tom at the Cambridge Police Station.

The battle continues to rage through the police station interior, up the stairs, and onto the roof. After a lull in the combat, speak with Tinker Tom. A rather harebrained scheme is explained to you, and explosives are given out. Tinker Tom takes the pilot's seat of the Vertibird.

**EXPLOSIVE CHARGE**

Additional hostiles are incoming by air. Missile weaponry is favored. Shoot your foe's aircraft, and then find and destroy any remaining forces that may have jettisoned out. Once this final wave of foes has succumbed to your superior firepower, receive even more firepower courtesy of Deacon.

**PLASMA GUN (RANDOM NAME AND PROPERTIES) AND AMMO**

**PULSE AND PLASMA GRENADES**

## Quest
# ROCKETS' RED GLARE

**1. FLY TO PRYDWEN**
**2. PLANT EXPLOSIVES (3)**
**3. ESCAPE THE PRYDWEN**
**4. TALK TO DESDEMONA**

**Locations to Explore**
– PRYDWEN (PAGE 345)

### O'ER THE LAND OF THE FREE

Tinker Tom takes off in the Vertibird with Deacon, and you man the minigun. The plan—if you can call it that—is to bluff your way past the air traffic control and land the Vertibird on the flight deck. Sit back and stifle your worrying on the journey. Your cause is just!

Afterward, extricate yourself from this location (the same way you came in) as adeptly as possible. The severity of combat completely depends on your knowledge of the main deck layout and competence with weaponry. Expect this to be one of the most difficult battles of your adventure. Back at the still-smoldering Railroad HQ, Desdemona should be debriefed and a just reward is given.

 **RAILWAY RIFLE MOD**

### VAULT-TEC RECOMMENDS

 **TIDY UP BEFORE TAKING OFF**
**MINI NUKE**
This is obviously the last opportunity to pillage this place of weapons and equipment. If you're pressed for time, focus your attention on the locked (Expert) provisions area at the far end of the main deck. Loot everything you can, including mini nukes, before departing.

### HELPFUL HINT
*from Vault Boy!*

 **Did You Know?**

WHY NOT DRESS FOR SUCCESS? YOU MAY FIND THIS TASK SIGNIFICANTLY EASIER IF YOU'RE CLAD IN THE APPROPRIATE CLOTHING OR ARMOR OF THE FACTION YOU'RE ABOUT TO ANNIHILATE. AS LONG AS YOU HAVEN'T ALREADY JOINED THE BROTHERHOOD OF STEEL AND FLOWN TO THE PRYDWEN YOURSELF (IN WHICH CASE, YOU ARE ALREADY KNOWN TO THIS FACTION), YOU'RE SURE TO REMAIN INCOGNITO UNTIL AFTER YOU DOCK.

Step onto the gantry area. Use sneaking if you're skilled enough. If you're clad in enemy faction attire, feel free to talk to Brotherhood personnel if the opportunity arises.

### VAULT-TEC RECOMMENDS

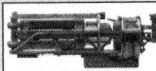 **FINAL JUDGMENT**
If you managed to remove Elder Maxson as a threat, why not gather up his unique Laser Gatling? It sure fires fast!

 (Hard) There are a number of difficult speech challenges to overcome in order to bluff your way through the decks to the explosive points. This is very difficult, but it is possible to set the explosives without resorting to violence at all.

Then move from the flight deck to the main deck, planting the three charges at the positions indicated on your Pip-Boy's map (head upstairs).

## Quest
# THE NUCLEAR OPTION (THE RAILROAD)

**1. TALK TO DESDEMONA**
**2. TALK TO Z1-14**
**3. KILL EVERYONE IN THE RELAY CONTROL ROOM**
**4. TALK TO DESDEMONA**
**5. REACH THE REACTOR**
**6. USE TERMINAL TO OVERRIDE INSTITUTE LOCKDOWN**
**7. (OPTIONAL) ISSUE EVACUATION ORDER**
**8. REACH THE REACTOR**
**9. PLANT FUSION PULSE CHARGE INSIDE REACTOR**
**10. TALK TO DESDEMONA**
**11. TALK TO TINKER TOM**
**12. TALK TO SHAUN**

**13. STEP INTO THE RELAY**
**14. ACTIVATE DETONATOR**
**15. TALK TO DESDEMONA**

**Locations to Explore**
– THE INSTITUTE (PAGE 409)

### THE TRAIL ENDS HERE

### VAULT-TEC RECOMMENDS

**FREE THE SYNTHS!**
 This conclusion to the Main Quest is only available if you sided with the Railroad. It commences once you complete Railroad Quest: Rockets' Red Glare.

DATA

QUESTS

It seems you've come around to Desdemona's way of thinking. At the Railroad HQ, you listen to her plan and agree with it.

After relaying into the Institute, you find Z1-14 removing threats in the relay control room to allow Desdemona and her crew to teleport in. Speak with your leader, who hands you a device critical to finishing these activities.

 **FUSION PULSE CHARGE**

Your infiltration takes you through the Old Robotics area, where you should expect heavy synth resistance and active laser turrets.

Locate and drop through the hatch to enter the Institute BioScience laboratory. Weave your way through to the reactor entrance. It isn't surprising that the blast door has sealed the reactor down.

Press the button at the central elevator. Access Father's quarters and receive the override password after speaking with him. Utilize it, or hack the terminal (Novice). Now activate the master security lockdown override.

 (Medium) There are three options if you answer Father regarding why he should help you.

## THE RAILROAD TERMINUS

Work your way to the Institute Advanced Systems and into the reactor chamber. A heavy synth presence is expected. Access the reactor door and activate the reactor housing.

Tinker Tom relays you back to the Institute relay control room. Speak with

Desdemona before Tom interrupts, announcing an unexpected arrival in the vicinity.

Speak to the tiny tyke:

– **AGREE TO TAKE HIM UNDER YOUR WING AND SAVE HIS LIFE. TINKER TOM ENSURES HIS SAFETY. FIND HIM AT THE RAILROAD HQ.**
– **TELL THE DIMINUTIVE FELLOW THAT HE MUST REMAIN HERE.**

Once you step into the relay and are teleported to the roof of the Mass Fusion building, you're able to definitively conclude the Institute's operations in Boston for the foreseeable future. Your Main Questing ends after you speak to Desdemona about the future of the Commonwealth.

## VAULT-TEC RECOMMENDS

 **WOW! A WAZER WIFLE!**
Once your questing is over, this diminutive fellow has three super-secret quests you can undertake for him. Think of it as some bonding you missed while you were in the deep freeze. Finish all three quest, and you're awarded with a special "wifle" that never runs out of ammo!

## Quest
# BURNING COVER

1. **TALK TO DESDEMONA**
2. **TALK TO PRESTON**

This quest becomes available only if your relationship with the Institute faction turns hostile at any point before Railroad Quest: Underground Undercover concludes. With no access to the Institute, there's nothing more the Railroad can do to thwart the Institute. Desdemona says your best chance to stop the Institute lies with the Minutemen. Find Preston Garvey, and begin working with his faction instead.

# THE RAILROAD MISCELLANEOUS QUESTS

**HELPFUL HINT** from *Vault Boy!* **Did You Know?**

WHAT ARE MISCELLANEOUS RAILROAD QUESTS? AN ASTUTE QUERY! BOTH THE QUESTS SHOWN HERE ARE PURELY OPTIONAL UNDERTAKINGS RELATED TO THIS FACTION. ATTEMPT THEM DURING THE MAIN QUESTS. EXPECT SOME TRICKY SITUATIONS, BUT ALSO SOME FINE REWARDS FOR HELPING THE FREEDOM-LOVING RAILROAD. HOWEVER, IF YOU'RE ON LESS-THAN-PLEASANT STANDING WITH THIS FACTION (IF YOU FIGHT OR ALLY AGAINST THEM), EXPECT YOUR PIP-BOY TO INDICATE YOU'VE BEEN "KICKED OUT OF THE RAILROAD" AND THESE QUESTS AREN'T AVAILABLE.

## Quest
# BOSTON AFTER DARK

1. GIVE CARRINGTON HIS PROTOTYPE
2. RETRIEVE THE DEAD DROP
3. MEET OLD MAN STOCKTON
4. SECURE THE RENDEZVOUS POINT
5. WAIT UNTIL NIGHTTIME FOR OLD MAN STOCKTON
6. WAIT FOR RAILROAD CONTACT
7. FOLLOW HIGH RISE
8. TALK WITH HIGH RISE
9. REPORT BACK TO DOCTOR CARRINGTON

### Locations to Explore
- CHARLESTOWN (PAGE 422)
- BUNKER HILL (PAGE 423)
- CAMBRIDGE (PAGE 400)
- MONSIGNOR PLAZA (PAGE 417)
- TICONDEROGA SAFEHOUSE (PAGE 420)

## DEAD DROP FOR BUNKER HILL

Speak to Doctor Carrington after you complete Railroad Quest: Tradecraft, as he has your first official assignment.

 (Medium) Get on Carrington's good side, if you can.

 **STOCKTON'S HOLOTAPE**

The dead drop mentions a contact at Bunker Hill. You're here to meet Old Man Stockton. Be sure to use the countersign so your talking continues to be covert in nature.

Stockton was supposed to deliver H2-22 to another Railroad agent, but Raiders prevented this. Head to the ruined church on the outskirts of Cambridge Neighborhood (marked on your Pip-Boy map), engaging or avoiding the Super Mutants along the way. As you arrive, dispatch the Raider threats.

For your first job you have to help out H2-22, a synth who is in trouble at Bunker Hill. Cross the river and head roughly north into Charleston Neighborhood. The dead drop is east of Monsignor Plaza. Watch for Mirelurks. Remove the item from the mailbox.

### VAULT-TEC RECOMMENDS

BONANZA AT BUNKER HILL

 **LIVE & LOVE**

Bunker Hill is a key settlement and ripe for Minutemen expansion. Traders arrive here from different parts of the Commonwealth. Kay (the vet) and Deb offer additional trading opportunities. And there's more than a great view at the top of the obelisk!

## HIGH RISE, HIGH RISK, AND HIGH REWARD

Wait on a pew until 11:00 p.m., when Stockton and the synth arrive. An agent named High Rise is summoned; he hopes you can help with some escorting duties. You're running roughly south, toward the Raider camp of Monsignor Plaza. Clear that location of foes entirely, and push toward the Ticonderoga Safehouse. Job well done! Check in with Carrington to gather up the following:

**BOTTLECAPS (180)**

**BOBBY PINS (5)**

**SNIPER RIFLE (RANDOM TYPE) AND AMMO**

### VAULT-TEC RECOMMENDS

MONSIGNOR PLAZA IS A BUST

**GRISWOLD'S POETRY COLLECTION**

Usually at this point, Vault-Tec offers excellent knowledge of high-value items known to be at a location you're set to clear. Unfortunately, Vault-Tec scanning has shown only low levels of ammunition and a Holotape of questionable poetry.

## Quest
# MEMORY INTERRUPTED

1. TALK TO DOCTOR AMARI
2. ELIMINATE THE GEN 1S
3. REPORT BACK TO DESDEMONA

**Locations to Explore**
- GOODNEIGHBOR (PAGE 483)
- MEMORY DEN (PAGE 488)
- MALDEN CENTER (PAGE 286)

---

## NO GUTS, NO GLORY

Converse with PAM at the Railroad HQ, and she mentions a synth stranded at the Memory Den. His escape route out of there has been compromised. Visit Goodneighbor and find Doctor Amari within the Memory Den to tell her you've been sent to clear a path. Optionally take the Holotape from H2-22 and listen to it.

**GOODBYE FROM H2-22**

Travel to Malden Center in the northern part of the Commonwealth. You're here to remove a group of Gen 1 synths that are preventing the Railroad's runners from getting H2-22 to safety. It seems Railroad agent Glory had a similar idea; she meets you at the Malden Center entrance. You can:

- REFUSE HER OFFER TO ASSIST YOU.
- AGREE FOR HER TO OFFER FIRE SUPPORT.

Enter Malden Center, and conduct a thorough sweep, slaying all synths indicated on your Pip-Boy. There are Raiders (including the one named Helter-Skelter) to optionally remove. Then return to Desdemona for your reward.

**BOTTLECAPS (200)**

**RAILROAD STEALTH BOY (2)**

Railroad Stealth Boys are now available for purchase from Tinker Tom.

### VAULT-TEC RECOMMENDS

MALDEN: A TOWNSHIP OF HIDDEN DEPTHS

**TUMBLERS TODAY**

The township of Malden holds many surprises. As you sweep Malden Center, locate a magazine and rare Nuka Cola bottle. But why stop there? The Medford Memorial Hospital has another magazine to gather, though the Super Mutants aren't the friendliest. But the area of most interest is Malden Middle School. Assuming this location hasn't been overrun by troublesome Gunners, another quality and completely safe Vault (number 75) was constructed here. Not only is your safety guaranteed, but there's also a Bobblehead, essential reading, and a ton of ammunition!

# THE RAILROAD RADIANT QUESTS

## HELPFUL HINT
### from Vault Boy!

Did You Know?

WHAT ARE RADIANT RAILROAD QUESTS? AN INTERESTING QUESTION! THE 12 QUESTS REFERENCED HERE ARE PURELY OPTIONAL ACTIVITIES YOU CAN ATTEMPT WHILE ASSISTING ON MORE IMPORTANT RAILROAD MATTERS. THEY ARE REQUESTS FROM DIFFERENT RAILROAD AGENTS AND ARE "RADIANT," AS SOME OF THE LOCATIONS YOU'RE SENT TO MAY BE RANDOM. SOME QUESTS ARE REPEATABLE, ALLOWING YOU TO ACCUMULATE REWARDS. ANY HELP IS ALWAYS GRATEFULLY RECEIVED!

## VAULT-TEC RECOMMENDS

### RANDOM FACTS

Due to the random nature of the locations you are sent to, it is imperative you read up on the hostiles (as well as the valuables) you'll find at each one. Vault-Tec is proud to provide comprehensive cartography for just such a reconnoiter.

## Quest
# BUTCHER'S BILL 1

1. GO TO THE DEAD DROP
2. DETERMINE STATUS OF AUGUSTA SAFEHOUSE
3. REPORT BACK TO DOCTOR CARRINGTON

**Locations to Explore**
- OLD NORTH CHURCH (RAILROAD HQ) (PAGE 466)
- BOSTON COMMON (PAGE 472)
- KENDALL HOSPITAL (PAGE 406)

### A SORRY STATE HOUSE

Since the fall of Switchboard and after you completed Railroad Miscellaneous Quest: Boston After Dark, the Railroad's been picking up the pieces. Carrington is sending you to check the status of Augusta Safehouse. Go to the indicated drop location, near Goodneighbor.

  **AUGUSTA REPORT**

### DETERMINE STATUS OF AUGUSTA SAFEHOUSE

The safehouse is in Cambridge, within the raider stronghold of the Kendall Hospital. The place is an absolute mess, so follow the maps in this guide if you become confused. Locate the Steamer Trunk inside.

  **AUGUSTA STATION LAST UPDATE**

Exit the Kendall Hospital, and report in at Railroad HQ. You receive some Caps for your troubles. This quest is not repeatable.

  **BOTTLECAPS (150)**

## Quest
# BUTCHER'S BILL 2

1. GO TO THE DEAD DROP FOR DOCTOR CARRINGTON
2. FIND AGENT BLACKBIRD
3. REPORT BACK TO DOCTOR CARRINGTON

**Locations to Explore**
- OLD NORTH CHURCH (RAILROAD HQ) (PAGE 466)

### FLOWN THE NEST

Start this after Radiant Quest: Butcher's Bill 1. A survivor potentially made it out of the Augusta Safehouse disaster. His name is Blackbird and he was spotted recently. Speak to Doctor Carrington, and head to the indicated drop location, which is in a random location.

**BLACKBIRD REPORT**

 **BOTTLECAPS (175)**

The report has some worrying information about Blackbird. Rush to the safehouse, which is randomly located, usually near an enemy stronghold. Defeat as many foes as you wish. Locate Agent Blackbird. Then find the note that Blackbird has, and report back to Doctor Carrington. You receive some armor and Caps for your troubles. This quest is not repeatable.

## Quest
# MERCER SAFEHOUSE

1. SECURE [A SETTLEMENT LOCATION] AND THEN USE WORKSHOP
2. BUILD DEFENSES
3. REPORT BACK TO PAM

**Locations to Explore**
- OLD NORTH CHURCH
  (RAILROAD HQ) (PAGE 466)

## SECURING A NEW SAFEHOUSE

This quest is available once you are aligned with the Railroad. Speak to PAM in the Railroad HQ. Go to the indicated location (a random settlement). Once there, remove any threats and access the workshop. Build defenses—in this case, two turrets.

Exit the area, and report in at Railroad HQ. You receive the following for your troubles. Mercer Safehouse now appears on your world map. This quest is not repeatable.

 **BOTTLECAPS (200)**

## Quest
# JACKPOT

1. SECURE THE DIA CACHE
2. REPORT BACK TO PAM

**Locations to Explore**
- OLD NORTH CHURCH (RAILROAD HQ) (PAGE 466)

## CACHING IN WITH PAM

Beware of enemies. Fight your way to the location. The RFID Device opens up a secret cubbyhole. Gather items from there if you wish. Report in at Railroad HQ. You receive the following for your troubles. This quest is repeatable.

 **BALLISTIC WEAVE MK 1**

 **VAULT-TEC RECOMMENDS**

TINKERING WITH TOM

The reward you receive is regular clothing with the properties of full armor. Now talk to Tinker Tom, and use crafting to modify clothing to achieve even higher armor ratings!

This quest is available once you are aligned with the Railroad. Speak to PAM at Railroad HQ. Go to the indicated location (a random location), and secure a DIA Cache inside.

 **RFID DEVICE**

# Quest
# CONCIERGE

1. GO TO MERCER SAFEHOUSE
2. ELIMINATE THE THREAT AT [A LOCATION]
3. REPORT BACK TO CARETAKER

Locations to Explore
– OLD NORTH CHURCH (RAILROAD HQ) (PAGE 466)
– MERCER STATION (RANDOM SETTLEMENT)

## TAKING CARE OF BUSINESS

This quest is available once you complete Railroad Radiant Quest: Mercer Safehouse. Mercer's new Railroad agent, Caretaker, needs to help a tourist so he in turn can help one of your synths escape the Commonwealth. Locate Caretaker. Answer with a Railroad countersign.

Head to the indicated location (an enemy stronghold). In this example, it is Back Street Apparel. Fight your way to the tagged enemy, and slay them. Then return to Caretaker. You receive the following for your troubles. This quest is not repeatable.

 STIMPAK (4)      BOTTLECAPS (150)

# Quest
# WEATHERVANE

1. SET UP MILA
2. REPORT BACK TO TINKER TOM

Locations to Explore
– OLD NORTH CHURCH (RAILROAD HQ) (PAGE 466)

## PRECARIOUS POSITIONING

Tinker Tom wants you to place MILA, a combination surveillance device and atmospheric sensor, at a high vantage point over the Commonwealth.

 MILA

Exit the area, and report in at Railroad HQ. You receive the following for your troubles. This quest is repeatable.

Go to the indicated (random) location, many of which are indicated throughout the maps. The location is always high up. Battle any foes and place MILA on the vantage point.

 CHANCE OF A RANDOM ITEM

 BOTTLECAPS (150-190)

# Quest
# RANDOLPH SAFEHOUSE

1. PICK UP THE DEAD DROP
2. CLEAR HOSTILES
3. REPORT BACK TO DESDEMONA

Locations to Explore
– OLD NORTH CHURCH (RAILROAD HQ) (PAGE 466)
– RANDOLPH SAFEHOUSE (RANDOM LOCATION)

## THE LIFE OF A HEAVY IS NEVER DULL

Randolph Safehouse has been dark since Switchboard fell. Speak to Drummer Boy, and he says the safehouse has left a message at a dead drop. Go to the indicated (random) dead drop location.

 RANDOLPH SAFEHOUSE UPDATE

Head to the indicated location, and remove all synths until the objective updates.

On the sixth (and last) time, you finally meet your contact—Mister Tims—in the flesh and disband the safehouse.

Exit the area, and report in at Railroad HQ. Desdemona requires you to check in with Drummer Boy from time to time as the situation at Randolph Safehouse is continually accessed. This quest then repeats five more times.

# Quest
# VARIABLE REMOVAL

1. ELIMINATE THE COURSER
2. REPORT BACK TO PAM

**Locations to Explore**
- OLD NORTH CHURCH (RAILROAD HQ) (PAGE 466)

## INTERCEPT AND ELIMINATE

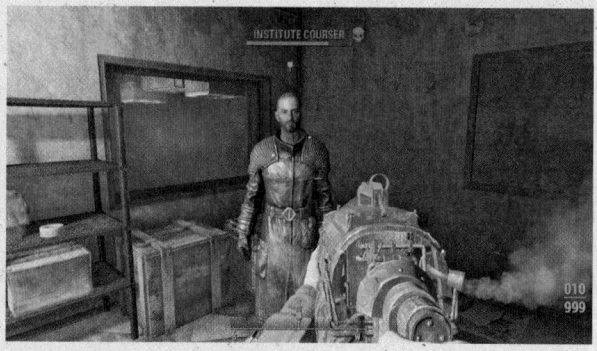

Speak with PAM; she has intel on a Courser in the field. An unchecked Courser can cause tremendous damage to the Railroad. Your job is to eliminate it at the indicated (random) location. Seek and destroy the tagged target. Other enemies are optional kills.

Report in at Railroad HQ. You receive the following for your troubles. This quest is repeatable.

**BOTTLECAPS (270)**

# Quest
# TO THE MATTRESSES

1. KILL [L&L GANG BOSS]
2. REPORT BACK TO DESDEMONA

**Locations to Explore**
- OLD NORTH CHURCH (RAILROAD HQ) (PAGE 466)
- L&L GANG HIDEOUT (RANDOM LOCATION)

## WIPING OUT THE L&L GANG

Once you complete Railroad Quest: The Nuclear Option, speak with Desdemona. With the Institute out of the picture, the synth-hating L&L Gang is the greatest single threat remaining to the Railroad. Go to the indicated (random) location. Seek and destroy the tagged target. In this case, it is a Raider boss named Lucky Tatum. Other enemies are optional kills.

Exit the area, and report in at Railroad HQ. You are rewarded. Check in again with Desdemona as the five other Raider bosses from the L&L Gang are located. This quest then repeats five more times. On the sixth (and last) time, you finish off the gang for good.

## Quest
# LOST SOUL

1. RESCUE THE SYNTH
2. REPORT BACK TO CARRINGTON

**Locations to Explore**
- OLD NORTH CHURCH (RAILROAD HQ) (PAGE 466)

### SHARING AND CARING

Once you complete Railroad Quest: The Nuclear Option, speak with Doctor Carrington. It seems not all synths that teleported out of the Institute made it to safety. Carrington has a lead on one synth that's in danger. After they're saved, you have a care package that'll help them get to safety. Then head to the indicated (random) location.

All enemies are optional but better off dead. Locate the synth, and speak with him or her.

 **SYNTH CARE PACKAGE**

Exit the area, and report in at Railroad HQ. You receive the following for your troubles. This quest is repeatable.

 **CHANCE OF A RANDOM ITEM**

 **BOTTLECAPS (100-300)**

## Quest
# A CLEAN EQUATION

1. ELIMINATE THE BROTHERHOOD PATROL
2. REPORT BACK TO PAM

**Locations to Explore**
- OLD NORTH CHURCH (RAILROAD HQ) (PAGE 466)

### MELTING STEEL

Once you complete Railroad Quest: Rockets' Red Glare, speak with PAM: Brotherhood stragglers are a threat to the Railroad, and a surviving patrol has been spotted. Go to the indicated (random) location and defeat the Brotherhood of Steel patrol there.

Exit the area, and report in at Railroad HQ. You receive the following for your troubles. This quest is repeatable.

 **BOTTLECAPS (100-300)**

 **CHANCE OF A RANDOM ITEM**

## Quest
# HIGH GROUND

1. ELIMINATE THE VERTIBIRD
2. REPORT BACK TO PAM

### CLIPPING SOME WINGS

PAM has spotted a surviving Vertibird that needs to be destroyed. Go to the indicated (random) location. Defeat the Vertibird there (and any other dangers if you wish). Projectile weaponry such as a missile launcher is recommended for this task.

Exit the area, and report in at Railroad HQ. You receive the following for your troubles. This quest is repeatable.

 **CHANCE OF A RANDOM ITEM**

 **BOTTLECAPS (100-300)**

Once you complete Railroad Quest: The Nuclear Option, speak with PAM: The Brotherhood still poses a threat to the Railroad.

# THE MINUTEMEN QUESTS

You can begin working with this faction almost immediately after you emerge from Vault 111: Simply wander down the road from Sanctuary, heading southeast until you reach the township of Concord. Visit the Museum of Freedom. You can continue Institute operations for as long as you wish. Please be aware that unlike your relationships with the other main factions—the Brotherhood of Steel, the Railroad, and the Institute—the other plans you're hatching tend not to affect the Minutemen negatively (unless specified). The Minutemen want to create a Commonwealth of hard-working patriots who trade and build strong bonds together.

The following Minutemen Quests become available:

| MINUTEMEN QUESTS | |
|---|---|
| **Main Faction Quest** | **Location** |
| When Freedom Calls | Page 170 |
| Sanctuary | Page 172 |
| The Sight | Page 172 |
| Taking Independence | Page 173 |
| Old Guns | Page 174 |
| Inside Job | Page 175 |
| Form Ranks | Page 175 |
| Defend the Castle | Page 175 |
| The Nuclear Option (Minutemen) | Page 176 |
| With Our Powers Combined | Page 177 |
| **Main Radiant Quest (Recruitment)** | **Location** |
| The First Step | Page 178 |
| Raider Troubles | Page 178 |
| Kidnapping | Page 179 |
| Abernathy Farm: Retribution | Page 179 |
| Greenskins | Page 179 |
| Clearing the Way | Page 180 |
| Taking Point | Page 180 |
| Ghoul Problem | Page 180 |
| Rogue Courser | Page 181 |
| Resettle Refugees | Page 181 |
| **Main Radiant Quest (Ownership)** | **Location** |
| Defend a Settlement | Page 182 |
| Defend Artillery at a Settlement | Page 182 |
| Stop the Raiding | Page 182 |
| Kidnapped Trader | Page 183 |
| Water, Food, or Power | Page 183 |
| Suspected Synth | Page 183 |

## Quest
# WHEN FREEDOM CALLS

1. ENTER THE MUSEUM
2. (OPTIONAL) TAKE THE LASER MUSKET
3. LOCATE THE TRAPPED SETTLERS
4. KILL THE RAIDERS (7)
5. TALK TO PRESTON GARVEY
6. UNLOCK THE SECURITY GATE
7. GET A FUSION CORE
8. PUT THE FUSION CORE IN THE POWER ARMOR
9. ENTER THE POWER ARMOR
10. GRAB THE MINIGUN
11. CLEAR CONCORD OF HOSTILES
12. REPORT BACK TO PRESTON
13. JOIN PRESTON GARVEY IN SANCTUARY

**Locations to Explore**
- CONCORD (PAGE 262)
- MUSEUM OF FREEDOM (PAGE 263)

## GOT A MINUTE?

On your travels through Concord, you spot a man protecting a group of people from Raider attacks on a balcony of a museum. Below the balcony is a short laser musket and some fusion cell ammunition in front of the doors. Pick it up if you're interested in disintegrating your enemies, and clear any foes from the streets. Then enter the Museum of Freedom.

**SHORT LASER MUSKET**

Armed Raiders are prowling the splintered interior of this museum. Weave your way through the remains of the displays. Your targets aren't red-coated; they have more of an "animal hide and leather studs" appearance. In between takedowns, feel free to read the freedom wall en route to a top-floor office where the defenders are.

Meet Preston Garvey and the remnants of his Minutemen forces. They seem like friendly sorts and are in a bind. Agree to help him and Sturges provide fire support to crush any remaining Raider opposition in town. Drop to the ground floor and into the basement. You can:

- (NOVICE) USE BOBBY PINS TO OPEN THE SECURITY GATE. THERE ARE SOME ON TOP OF THE COMPUTER TERMINAL MONITOR.
- (NOVICE) HACK THE COMPUTER TERMINAL AND UNLOCK THE SECURITY GATE.

 **FUSION CORE**

## VAULT-TEC RECOMMENDS

LOOTING THE MUSEUM OF FREEDOM

 **BOBBLEHEAD: PERCEPTION**
**ROBCO FUN**

In the museum, there are two exhibits that will catch your eye; a limited-edition Vault-Tec Bobblehead and one of the classic issues of RobCo FUN! magazine, with a free Holotape game to boot!

## LET FREEDOM REIGN

Access the roof to find an empty suit of T-45 Power Armor. It's not in the finest condition, but it's working well enough to clamber into once you insert the Fusion Core into the back of the unit. Detach the Vertibird minigun if you're craving rapid firepower. Then test the armor's cushioning by dropping into the street. Another option? Stay up here and snipe for a bit.

 **T-45 POWER ARMOR**

 **MINIGUN**

# HELPFUL HINT
## from Vault Boy!
**Did You Know?**

FUSION CORES SLOT INTO THE BACKS OF POWER ARMOR SUITS TO POWER THEM. RUN OUT OF THESE, AND YOU'RE STUCK! SO KEEP BOTH EYES OPEN FOR ADDITIONAL FUSION CORES THROUGHOUT YOUR TRAVELS. THE MAP CHAPTER OF THIS GUIDE FLAGS ALL TRACKABLE LOCATIONS, SO YOU'RE NEVER FAR AWAY FROM COPIOUS NUCLEAR POWER!

# HELPFUL HINT
## from Vault Boy!
**Did You Know?**

POWER ARMOR OFFERS TOP-NOTCH PROTECTION FROM BULLETS, CLAWS, SHORT FALLS, AND EVEN RADIATION. ALSO, THE HIGHER THE SERIAL NUMBER, THE HIGHER THE ARMOR'S QUALITY. DON'T FORGET YOUR SUITS REQUIRE UPKEEP AT POWER ARMOR STATIONS. VAULT-TEC HAS TAGGED EVERY COMMONWEALTH LOCATION WHERE BOTH POWER ARMOR AND STATIONS CAN BE FOUND. YOU'RE WELCOME!

Cut down any Raiders you see. Beware of a Deathclaw clambering out of a ground hatch. It is wise to back up while using the minigun or when coaxing the Raiders into a fight with the Deathclaw and mopping up the wounded survivors. Afterward, check in with Preston for a reward. To further your friendship, agree to join the Minutemen as they repopulate your old township of Sanctuary.

 **BOTTLECAPS (100)**

## VAULT-TEC RECOMMENDS

THE SECRETS OF CONCORD

 **TABOO TATTOOS**

Do you have time to take in the sights of Concord? Aside from the speakeasy and workshop in town, there's the Concord Civic Access tunnels. Try entering from the hatch by the Municipal Plutonium Well. Though hardly picturesque, this sewer tunnel links to two other parts of town, and there's some required reading to obtain.

# HELPFUL HINT
## from Vault Boy!
**Did You Know?**

THE POWER ARMOR YOU ARE WEARING INCLUDES A FRAME. THESE ARE THE SKELETONS WITH WHICH YOU CAN ATTACH VARIOUS PIECES OF POWER ARMOR YOU SCAVENGE, OR ARE REWARDED WITH. CONSULT THE POWER ARMOR FRAMES SECTION OF THE APPAREL CHAPTER FOR MORE INFORMATION, AND LOCATIONS OF OTHER FRAMES ACROSS THE COMMONWEALTH.

## Quest
# SANCTUARY

1. BUILD SHELTERED BEDS FOR SANCTUARY SETTLERS
2. TALK TO STURGES
3. PROVIDE CLEAN WATER FOR SANCTUARY SETTLERS
4. TALK TO STURGES
5. PROVIDE FOOD FOR SANCTUARY SETTLERS
6. TALK TO STURGES
7. BUILD DEFENSES FOR SANCTUARY SETTLERS
8. TALK TO STURGES

**Locations to Explore**

– SANCTUARY (PAGE 258)

---

### A NEW HOPE IN THE HILLS

When Preston Garvey and his friends reach Sanctuary, they're hoping for more than just a few ruined houses and a slightly eccentric Mr. Handy robot to befriend. It is time to rebuild Sanctuary as a shining beacon of hope! Or, at the bare minimum, a place where the Minutemen can call home.

Access the workshop (via the Furniture > Beds menu), and construct any of these beds (including mattresses or sleeping bags) in an acceptable location (indicated in green). This can be in a new or preexisting structure, or even outside, but must have a roof or shelter above. The number of beds you make should be equal to or greater than the number of people.

Continue to speak to Sturges about the needs of this motley crew. Build them any purifier you wish (from the Resources > Water menu). The number should bring a water value equal to the population of your settlement.

These folks are hungry too! Access the Resources > Food menu. Plant any of the food varieties you wish.

The number should bring a food value higher than the population (so a Food value of 4 is acceptable). Remember to assign a settler to tend these plants if no one is working this land.

Finally, Sturges is hoping for some kind of defense. Choose guard posts, turrets, or traps, as you wish. The Defense value should be 2 or greater, so a guard post or tower is acceptable. Remember to assign the task of patrolling a guard location to a settler. Build and link generators to certain turrets or traps if they require power.

### HELPFUL HINT
### from Vault Boy!
**Did You Know?**

DID YOU KNOW SETTLERS AREN'T TOO KEEN ON SLEEPING OUTSIDE? THAT'S JUST ONE OF THE MANY HELPFUL HINTS OFFERED IF YOU CONSULT THE "WORKSHOPS" CHAPTER OF THIS GUIDE. IF YOU'RE DETERMINED TO IGNORE THE ADVANTAGES OF VAULT DWELLING IN FAVOR OF LIFE ON THE SURFACE, LOOK HERE FOR MORE INFORMATION. YOU'LL BE GLAD YOU DID!

---

## Quest
# THE SIGHT

**Locations to Explore**
– SANCTUARY (PAGE 258)
– QUINCY RUINS (PAGE 387)

1. BRING JET TO MAMA MURPHY
2. BUILD MAMA MURPHY'S CHAIR IN SANCTUARY
3. BRING MENTATS TO MAMA MURPHY
4. BRING MED X TO MAMA MURPHY
5. BRING BUFFOUT TO MAMA MURPHY
6. BRING PSYCHO TO MAMA MURPHY

---

### OLD COOT OR SOOTHSAYER?

One of the Minutemen's members is Mama Murphy, a friendly old woman who insists she receives visions of the future. Of course, these come only after you find the necessary chems for her, and she needs at least eight hours of rest between each intake of chems.

If you speak to her, she hopes you'll find some Jet and bring it back to her. Oblige, and she reveals a revelation. Talk to her again, and she asks if you can build her a special chair.

This workshop item is in the Special menu, not the Furniture one. Now that she has a place to sit, those visions can keep coming.

At any point you can refuse her chem requests and tell her to go clean.

 (Medium) Some persuasion or light threatening might hammer the point home.

Or you can keep giving her chems and listening to her visions. This goes against the wishes of Preston Garvey and Sturges. You might not want to overdo it, though; that Psycho chem is a killer!

## HELPFUL HINT
### from Vault Boy!
**Did You Know?**

CHEMS ARE PART OF A WELL-ROUNDED MEDICAL REGIME IF ADMINISTERED IN CORRECT DOSES. SCAVENGE THEM THROUGHOUT THE COMMONWEALTH. OR YOU CAN BUY WHAT YOU NEED AT CHEM-I-CARE IN DIAMOND CITY MARKET. BUT MAMA MURPHY ALSO HAS A HIDDEN CHEM STASH IN QUINCY RUINS (SOUTHEAST OF BOSTON), WHERE PRESTON'S CREW USED TO RESIDE BEFORE THE PLACE WAS OVERRUN BY GUNNERS. LOOK FOR THIS CHEM COOLER IN THE "MAPS" CHAPTER, IN THE SECTION FOR THIS LOCATION.

## *Quest*
# TAKING INDEPENDENCE

1. MEET THE MINUTEMEN NEAR THE CASTLE
2. DECIDE ON A PLAN OF ATTACK
3. WAIT FOR THE MINUTEMEN TO GET INTO POSITION
4. CLEAR THE COURTYARD
5. DESTROY THE EGG CLUTCHES
6. KILL THE MURELURK QUEEN
7. MEET THE MINUTEMEN IN THE COURTYARD
8. POWER UP THE RADIO TRANSMITTER

**Locations to Explore**
- THE CASTLE (PAGE 517)

## KINGS OF THE CASTLE

Once the Minutemen are established at Sanctuary, and you've completed a few Radiant quests for Preston Garvey, he thinks it's time for the Minutemen to retake "the Castle," an old fort that used to be their main base of operations. Travel to the remains of the snack shop outside the perimeter of the Castle, located in South Boston (feel free to navigate around Boston city). Preston has gathered some Minutemen and wants to know your opinion on a plan of attack. Choose from the following:

- PINCER ATTACK: LIKE TO SNEAK? TRY THIS MORE SUBTLE APPROACH.
- DRAW THEM OUT: ENJOY SNIPING? ATTACK FROM AFAR.
- GUNS BLAZING: THINK TACTICS ARE FOR BRAINIACS? CHARGE!

Navigate toward the Castle, and clear the main courtyard of any irradiated aquatic life.

### VAULT-TEC RECOMMENDS

GUNS AND BULLETS?

 **GUNS AND BULLETS**
The Castle doesn't give up all of its secrets immediately, but there's a magazine to purloin by the central radio mast. You're also encouraged to read about guns and bullets and to bring a weighty supply of them too—the irradiated wildlife in these parts is tough! How tough? Consult the "Bestiary" chapter for best potshot practices. Need more ammo? Look to the Castle's interior corridors. That missile launcher might do the job!

Now to remove any hatchlings. Look to your Pip-Boy compass and destroy all the marked egg clutches. Oh dear. It seems that while you were clearing the eggs from the Castle, the beast that hatched them rose from the depths and is none too pleased. Remove this huge threat, finish destroying any remaining egg clutches, and claim this Castle!

Power up the old radio transmitter by building some generators. Attach wires from the transmitter to each generator so it is powered.

Medium Generator*

- BUILD WITH: SCREW (3), GEAR (3), STEEL (7), RUBBER (3), COPPER (3), CERAMIC (1)
- (*THE TRANSMITTER REQUIRES 10 POWER, SO YOU NEED TWO MEDIUM GENERATORS OR FOUR SMALL GENERATORS.)

The transmitter allows the Minutemen to broadcast Radio Freedom across the Commonwealth! Tune in for the latest reports and for Radiant Quests that require your attention.

## HELPFUL HINT
### from Vault Boy!
**Did You Know?**

IF YOU'RE HAVING A HARD TIME FRYING SOME EGGS, WHY NOT TRY THE FLAMER JUST INSIDE THE DOORWAY ON THE EASTERN WALL? THIS CLEARS AWAY THE CLUTCHES MORE QUICKLY.
HAVING TROUBLE KILLING THE QUEEN? GATHER THE MISSILE LAUNCHER IN THE GENERAL'S QUARTERS, AND STAND WELL BACK WHEN FIRING!

## Quest
# OLD GUNS

1. RETURN TO THE CASTLE
2. SPEAK TO RONNIE SHAW AT THE CASTLE
3. GAIN ACCESS TO THE CASTLE'S ARMORY
4. TALK TO RONNIE SHAW
5. BUILD AND ASSIGN ARTILLERY AT THE CASTLE
6. TALK TO RONNIE SHAW
7. FOLLOW RONNIE SHAW
8. HEAD TO THE TARGET AREA
9. (OPTIONAL) KEEP YOUR RADIO ON AND TUNED TO RADIO FREEDOM
10. THROW A SMOKE FLARE INTO THE TARGET AREA
11. SPEAK TO PRESTON GARVEY

Locations to Explore
– THE CASTLE (PAGE 517)

## RONNIE SHAW'S REVELATION

While speaking to Preston Garvey after another successful recruitment mission, he mentions someone named Ronnie Shaw has arrived at the Castle looking for you. Head over to the Castle (using the workshop here to build defenses is wise if you didn't think of this already).

Enter the armory and gather as many impressive pieces of killing equipment as you want to test out. Don't leave without the Artillery Schematic or smoke grenades.

 **ARTILLERY SCHEMATIC**

 **ARTILLERY SMOKE GRENADE (20)**

## BOMBS BURSTING IN AIR

An Artillery Piece would be a huge boost to the hitting power available to the Minutemen. Time to build one! Place it anywhere you wish within the Castle's perimeter.

– BUILD WITH: OIL (4), SCREW (8), GEAR (11), SPRING (5), STEEL (16), CONCRETE (4), WOOD (4)
– REQUIRES: PERSON (1)

Locate any settler within the Castle. Highlight them and press "Command." Move over to the Artillery Piece. Press "Assign."

Ronnie Shaw wishes to conduct a test fire of the artillery. Head down to the ruined snack shop, and lob a smoke grenade (access it just like any other projectile). Back up, and witness the artillery test fire. You can now return to Preston Garvey to finish this quest and secure additional Radiant activities.

### HELPFUL HINT from Vault Boy!

 **Did You Know?**

ARE YOU HELPING THE MINUTEMEN ACROSS THE COMMONWEALTH? YOU NEED TO BE, AS SETTING UP KEY SETTLEMENTS AND TRADING ROUTES BETWEEN THEM, AND KEEPING YOUR POPULATION HAPPY AND SAFE AFFECTS FUTURE MINUTEMEN QUESTS. YOU'RE HERE FOR THE LONG HAUL TOO; THIS QUEST DOESN'T BEGIN UNTIL THREE COMMONWEALTH DAYS AFTER THE CONCLUSION OF TAKING INDEPENDENCE.

Ronnie tells you about an old Minutemen armory located in the west bastion of the Castle. Unfortunately, the old entrance is covered in rubble. Fortunately, your Workshop skills allow you to scrap the rubble.

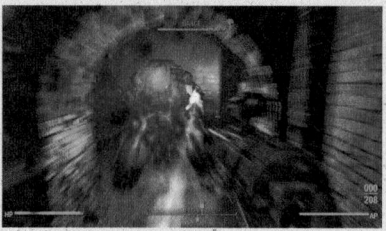

Venture into the Castle tunnels with Ronnie. Eliminate the defenses, including a vicious Sentry Bot named Sarge. After Ronnie opens the security door, you spot the previous leader of the Minutemen. Feel free to dress in his attire if you wish to look the part. Then find the button to open the piston door to the exterior courtyard.

 **GENERAL'S HAT**

 **MINUTEMEN GENERAL'S COAT**

## VAULT-TEC RECOMMENDS

ARTILLERY PIECES AND PATRIOTISM

 **FAT MAN**

Tune in to Radio Freedom for the patriotism and random radiant tasks. Check the armory for some heavy-weight armaments, like the Fat Man. Ronnie Shaw is now the Castle quartermaster for trading items. And don't forget that Artillery Piece; you can build it at any of your owned settlements before using smoke grenades to call in strikes if enemies are idiotic enough to challenge you; as the range of this artillery can hit anywhere in the Commonwealth, if you place them across settlements you own, This can be very useful for clearing out surface strongholds of foes. As for the rusting old artillery dotted around The Castle? Scrap them to build new ones!

## Quest
# INSIDE JOB

1. INSERT NETWORK SCANNER HOLOTAPE INTO INSTITUTE TERMINAL
2. GIVE HOLOTAPE TO STURGES

**Locations to Explore**
- THE INSTITUTE (PAGE 409)

## INSTITUTE ACCESS

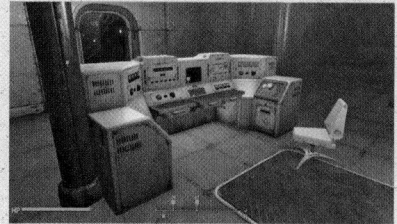

This quest is available if you had Sturges help you build the teleporter during Main Quest: The Molecular Level. Another faction may also have given you this Holotape.

**NETWORK SCANNER HOLOTAPE**

Begin Main Quest: Institutionalized. Access the terminal at the Institute relay area and entrance, or any other terminal you come across; insert the Network Scanner Holotape, and remove the data.

Then simply continue the rest of Main Quest: Institutionalized. Then return to Sturges and give him the data.

**HELPFUL HINT from Vault Boy!** **Did You Know?**

WHY CAN'T EVERYBODY JUST GET ALONG? UNFORTUNATELY, IN THE POST-APOCALYPTIC WASTELAND, LIMITED RESOURCES AND SURVIVAL INSTINCTS USUALLY LEAD TO DISTRUST. SO PICK A FACTION YOU WANT TO WORK WITH, AND REMEMBER YOU CAN GIVE THE HOLOTAPE TO A DIFFERENT FACTION IF YOU CHANGE YOUR ALLEGIANCE. THIS STILL ALLOWS YOU TO CONTINUE WORKING WITH THE MINUTEMEN.

## Quest
# FORM RANKS

1. TALK TO PRESTON GARVEY ABOUT THE INSTITUTE
2. RECRUIT MORE SETTLEMENTS FOR THE MINUTEMEN

**Locations to Explore**
- THE CASTLE (PAGE 517)

## Quest
# DEFEND THE CASTLE

1. TRAVEL TO THE CASTLE
2. BUILD DEFENSES
3. DEFEND THE CASTLE
4. SPEAK TO RONNIE SHAW
5. TALK TO PRESTON GARVEY

**Locations to Explore**
- THE CASTLE (PAGE 517)

## STRENGTH IN NUMBERS

This quest is available if you've been kicked out of the Institute for any reason (declining Father's initial offer, during a chat with Father when The Battle of Bunker Hill occurs, or by exercising violence against a scientist. Speak to Preston Garvey about this predicament. He has two answers:

- HE BELIEVES THE MINUTEMEN AREN'T STRONG ENOUGH TO TACKLE THE INSTITUTE YET. YOU MUST RECRUIT AND BUILD UP MORE SETTLEMENTS, SUCH AS THIS ONE AT KINGSPORT LIGHTHOUSE.
- OR, IF YOU HAVE EIGHT OR MORE SETTLEMENTS, HE IMMEDIATELY WARNS YOU ABOUT AN INSTITUTE ATTACK ON THE CASTLE, AND MINUTEMEN QUEST: DEFEND THE CASTLE BECOMES AVAILABLE.

## A PROTRACTED PUMMELING

You've received word that Institute synths are gathering to attack the Castle! Once you have eight Settlements, you can start this quest by:

- LISTENING TO RADIO FREEDOM.
- VISITING THE CASTLE.
- SPEAKING TO PRESTON GARVEY.

Tune in to Radio Freedom for information on the direction of the attackers. Use the height of the walls. Beware of failing defenses as the enemy targets your generators (repair them). Beware of synths teleporting through any walled defenses. Repel all attackers in this protracted battle. Assuming you survive, chat to Ronnie and Preston after you've driven back this mechanical menace.

## VAULT-TEC RECOMMENDS

FOREWARNED IS FOREARMED

Prior to the beginning of this quest, constructing a number of well-defended areas of the Castle to help repel foes is critical. Think about proper placement of important machinery, as the synths aren't Super Mutants; they are cunning enough to, for example, take out generators that are powering your turrets. So why not store generators behind defenses that aren't immediately accessible? Those synths like to teleport into the fray, too, so defensive choke points aren't as helpful.

## Quest
# THE NUCLEAR OPTION (THE MINUTEMEN)

1. TALK TO PRESTON GARVEY
2. TALK TO STURGES
3. GAIN ACCESS TO THE INSTITUTE
4. ACTIVATE INSTITUTE RELAY
5. TALK TO PRESTON GARVEY
6. REACH INSTITUTE REACTOR
7. USE TERMINAL TO OVERRIDE INSTITUTE LOCKDOWN
8. (OPTIONAL) ISSUE EVACUATION ORDER
9. REACH THE REACTOR
10. PLANT FUSION CHARGE INSIDE REACTOR
11. TALK TO PRESTON GARVEY
12. TALK TO STURGES
13. TALK TO SHAUN
14. STEP INTO THE RELAY
15. USE THE DETONATOR
16. TALK TO PRESTON GARVEY

## EVERY MINUTE COUNTS

You feel an affinity to Preston Garvey's way of thinking and must now enter the Institute. Speak with Preston, then Sturges, who has figured out a way into the Institute you were banished from. The data you stole during Minutemen Quest: Inside Job reveals the location of a teleporter. He hands you a Holotape to use in the same terminal, and an impressive piece of firepower to help get the job done.

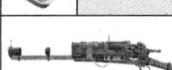
**INSTITUTE RELAY TARGETING SEQUENCE**

**AUTOMATIC LASER MUSKET**

## VAULT-TEC RECOMMENDS

FOR THE COMMONWEALTH!

This version of Main Quest: The Nuclear Option is only available if you declined to work with Father and declined to work with the Railroad or Brotherhood of Steel (though you don't need to be hostile to either faction). It commences once you complete Minutemen Quests: Inside Job and Defend the Castle and when Preston deems the Minutemen to be strong enough to take on the Institute.

Travel to the irradiated river's edge in the Cambridge Neighborhood, west of Greenetech Genetics. There's a Raider camp by the river you may wish to clear first. Dive into the water, swim into the Public Works Maintenance Area, and activate the keypad. A hazmat suit or Power Armor negates the radiation here.

Open the grate and drop through the effluent pipe into the old sewer. Locate a second pipe with a hatch at the end of it. Wind your way through the sewer, following the large white "inflow" pipe with arrows on it. Hack the security terminal (Expert) or pick the lock of the security door (Expert), and head through the hole in the wall to the southeast. Or, head through the open security door (northeast of the security door). Battle your way to the open inflow pipe and enter it. This accesses the Institute facility. Open the subsequent hatch and infiltrate the premises.

## A FEW GOOD MEN

Load the Institute Relay Targeting Sequence into the relay terminal, and Preston (plus a few Minutemen) teleport in. Chat to Preston again; he hands you a device vital to completing these activities.

**FUSION PULSE CHARGE**

Your route takes you through the Old Robotics area. Expect numerous synth adversaries and laser turrets. Locate and drop through the hatch and enter the Institute BioScience laboratory.

Head to the reactor entrance. As you might have expected, the blast door has been activated.

At the central elevator, press the button. Enter Father's quarters and obtain the override password from him. Use it, or hack the terminal (Novice). Activate the Master Security Lockdown Override.

(Medium) There are three options if you answer Father regarding why he should help you.

## HELPFUL HINT
### from Vault Boy!

 Did You Know?

YOU LIKE FOLLOWING ORDERS, DON'T YOU? WELL PRESTON GARVEY WANTS MINIMAL CASUALTIES AND HOPES YOU'LL TRIGGER THE EVACUATION OPTIONS AT FATHER'S TERMINAL SO YOU AREN'T FORCED TO KILL MORE SYNTHS AND SCIENTISTS. FOLLOW THIS IF YOU'RE SICKENED BY FURTHER VIOLENCE. IGNORE THIS IF YOU AREN'T.

## KING OF THE COMMONWEALTH

Weave your way to the Institute Advanced Systems and enter the reactor chamber. If no evacuation has been called, expect a cluster of synths and scientists. Access the reactor door and activate the reactor housing.

Sturges teleports you to the Institute Relay Control Room. Speak with Preston Garvey before Sturges mentions an unplanned visitor in close proximity. Speak to the little guy. You can:

- AGREE TO TAKE HIM UNDER YOUR WING AND SAVE HIS LIFE. STURGES ENSURES HIS SAFETY. FIND HIM AT SANCTUARY (OR WHEREVER YOU SENT STURGES TO LIVE).
- INFORM STURGES THAT THE CHILD MUST REMAIN HERE.

After speaking into the relay and teleporting to the roof of the Mass Fusion building, you can press a button and put on a spectacular light show. Your Main Questing ends after a conversation with Preston Garvey about the future of the Commonwealth.

## VAULT-TEC RECOMMENDS

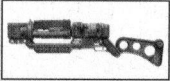

**WOW! A WAZER WIFLE!**

Once your questing is over, this diminutive fellow has three super-secret quests you can undertake for him. Think of it as some bonding you missed while you were in the deep freeze. Finish all three quest, and you're awarded with a special "wifle" that never runs out of ammo!

## Quest
# WITH OUR POWERS COMBINED

1. TALK TO PRESTON GARVEY
2. BUILD ARTILLERY IN FIVE SETTLEMENT LOCATIONS
3. LAUNCH ARTILLERY STRIKE ON PRYDWEN
4. DESTROY PRYDWEN
5. DEFEAT BROTHERHOOD ATTACK ON THE CASTLE
6. TALK TO PRESTON GARVEY

Locations to Explore
– THE CASTLE (PAGE 517)

## PUTTING THE "ART" IN ARTILLERY

It's time for the Minutemen to remove the Brotherhood of Steel as a threat to the Commonwealth. This quest is available only after you turn the Brotherhood of Steel hostile. Talk to Preston, and agree to build artillery defenses. You must build an Artillery Piece and then assign a settler to man it, in five different settlements you own.

## VAULT-TEC RECOMMENDS

BURNING THE BROTHERHOOD

It may have occurred to you that the Brotherhood of Steel isn't a particularly passive bunch of zealots. So a well-defended fortification, with numerous turrets and well-protected generators, is key to repelling any foes sent after you've watched the fireworks.

Afterward, return to the Castle, speak to the Minutemen radio operator. Request that he gives the order to fire. Watch the fireworks. Then brace for a final assault from the Brotherhood of Steel. Repel these forces, and speak to Preston again to conclude this quest.

 **REWARD: VERTIBIRD FAST-TRAVEL**

# THE MINUTEMEN RADIANT QUESTS: RECRUITMENT

## Quest
# THE FIRST STEP AND RAIDER TROUBLES

1. TALK TO THE SETTLERS AT [A RANDOM SETTLEMENT LOCATION]
2. KILL THE RAIDERS IN [A LOCATION]
3. REPORT YOUR SUCCESS TO SETTLERS AT [THE SETTLEMENT]
4. TALK TO PRESTON GARVEY

## RADIANT RAIDER TROUBLES

Recruitment Quest: The First Step is given immediately after you complete Minutemen Quest: When Freedom Calls. It is not repeatable.

Recruitment Quest: Raider Troubles is given randomly and is repeatable. This quest is also available from owned settlements.

Head to the indicated settlement and speak to one of the settlers. They are having problems with Raiders. Agree to help them.

Wipe out the tagged foes and (optionally) any other enemies. Return to the settlement with the good news before reporting back to Preston Garvey. You receive some caps, and the settlement is now ripe for expansion!

Workshop available at this settlement.

 **BOTTLECAPS (APPROX. 100)**

## Quest
# KIDNAPPING

1. TALK TO THE SETTLERS AT [A RANDOM SETTLEMENT LOCATION]
2. (OPTIONAL) PAY THE RANSOM
3. RESCUE THE KIDNAPPED SETTLER FROM [A LOCATION]
4. REPORT BACK TO THE SETTLERS AT [THE SETTLEMENT]
5. TALK TO PRESTON GARVEY

### A STOLEN SETTLER

This quest is also available from owned settlements. Head to the settlement requesting assistance and speak to one of the settlers. One of their ilk has been kidnapped. You can:

- (OPTIONAL) PAY OFF THE RANSOM AND COMPLETE THE QUEST.
- AGREE TO RESCUE THE KIDNAPPED SETTLER.

Visit the indicated enemy stronghold. Wipe out as many foes as you wish, ideally any close to the intended kidnapped settler. Locate them, and bring them out of the stronghold.

This quest fails if the kidnap victim dies. Return to the settlement with the good news before reporting back to Preston Garvey.

Workshop available at this settlement.

 **BOTTLECAPS (APPROX. 100)**

## Quest
# ABERNATHY FARM: RETRIBUTION

1. TRAVEL TO ABERNATHY FARM
2. RETRIEVE MARY'S LOCKET IN USAF SATELLITE STATION OLIVIA
3. REPORT YOUR SUCCESS TO BLAKE ABERNATHY
4. TALK TO PRESTON GARVEY

### IN MARY'S MEMORY

This quest is available when you visit Abernathy Farm for the first time. It is not repeatable. Speak to Blake Abernathy and agree to help him.

Visit the Raider stronghold of USAF Satellite Station Olivia. Remove all the threats you wish, and locate the locket in the toolbox. Return to  Blake Abernathy with the good news before reporting back to Preston Garvey.

 **MARY'S LOCKET**

Workshop available at Abernathy Farm.

 **BOTTLECAPS (APPROX. 100)**

## Quest
# GREENSKINS

1. TALK TO THE SETTLERS AT [A RANDOM SETTLEMENT LOCATION]
2. KILL THE SUPER MUTANTS IN [A LOCATION]
3. REPORT YOUR SUCCESS TO SETTLERS AT [THE SETTLEMENT]
4. TALK TO PRESTON GARVEY

### SUPER MUTANT SLAUGHTER

This quest is also available from owned settlements. Visit the indicated settlement and speak to one of the settlers. They are having troubles with Super Mutants. Agree to help them.

Visit the indicated Super Mutant stronghold. Wipe out the tagged foes and (optionally) any other of his brethren. Return to the settlement with the good news before reporting back to Preston Garvey.

Workshop available at this settlement.

 **BOTTLECAPS (APPROX. 100)**

## Quest
# CLEARING THE WAY

1. TALK TO THE SETTLERS AT [A RANDOM SETTLEMENT LOCATION]
2. SECURE THE WORKSHOP AT [A RANDOM SETTLEMENT LOCATION]

3. REPORT YOUR SUCCESS TO THE SETTLERS AT [THE FIRST SETTLEMENT LOCATION]
4. REPORT TO PRESTON GARVEY

## UNWANTED INTERLOPERS

This quest is also available from owned settlements. Speak to the settler and agree to their request. In this case, it is to clear a potential settlement of foes.

Enter the indicated settlement and remove all threats. Expect one or more troublesome foes—Feral Ghouls, Radroaches, Raiders, Super Mutants, or even Deathclaws. Once complete, you may use the settlement workshop immediately. Speak to the settler, as this enables them to inform their friends, who leave for the new settlement you cleared. Now return to Preston.

Workshop available at this settlement.

 **BOTTLECAPS (APPROX. 100)**

## Quest
# TAKING POINT

1. CLEAR [A RANDOM SETTLEMENT LOCATION]
2. BUILD AND ACTIVATE RECRUITMENT RADIO BEACON

3. TALK TO PRESTON GARVEY

## RANSACKING BEFORE RECRUITMENT

A settlement has been discovered that looks great for expansion. Of course, the current occupants need to be removed first. Visit the settlement and clear all threats. Once cleared, you must do the following:

Access the workshop and build the following:

**Recruitment Radio Beacon**
- BUILD WITH: CIRCUITRY (2), CRYSTAL (2), COPPER (6), STEEL (10), CERAMIC (3), RUBBER (1)
- REQUIRES: POWER (1)

**Generator—Small***
- BUILD WITH: GEAR (2), STEEL (4), RUBBER (2), COPPER (2), CERAMIC (1)
- (*ANY GENERATOR IS ACCEPTABLE.)

Now attach a wire from the beacon to the generator so it is powered. Then return to Preston Garvey.

Workshop available at this settlement.

 **BOTTLECAPS (APPROX. 100)**

## Quest
# GHOUL PROBLEM

1. TALK TO THE SETTLERS AT [A RANDOM SETTLEMENT LOCATION]
2. KILL THE GHOULS IN [A LOCATION]

3. REPORT YOUR SUCCESS TO SETTLERS AT [THE SETTLEMENT]
4. TALK TO PRESTON GARVEY

## FERAL DWELLERS MUST DIE!

This quest is also available from owned settlements. Visit the settlement and ask more about the problem. You're pointed in the direction of [a random location] where the Ghouls lurk.

Visit the indicated Feral Ghoul haven. Wipe out the tagged foes and (optionally) any other of their brethren. Return to the settlement with victory assured before reporting back to Preston Garvey.

Workshop available at this settlement.

 **BOTTLECAPS (APPROX. 100)**

## Quest
# ROGUE COURSER

1. KILL THE COURSER
2. TALK TO PRESTON GARVEY

### THE SYNTHETIC RAIDER

This only occurs when speaking to Preston and after you destroy the Institute during the Main Quest. You're pointed in the direction of [a random

 **BOTTLECAPS (APPROX. 100)**

location], where a Courser has joined a Raider gang. Wipe out the tagged foe and (optionally) any other of his Raider friends. Then report back to Preston Garvey for more caps to add to your collection.

## Quest
# RESETTLE REFUGEES

1. TALK TO THE SETTLERS AT [A RANDOM SETTLEMENT LOCATION]
2. SECURE THE WORKSHOP AT [A RANDOM SETTLEMENT LOCATION]
3. REPORT YOUR SUCCESS TO THE SETTLERS AT [THE FIRST SETTLEMENT LOCATION]
4. REPORT TO PRESTON GARVEY

### IRRADIATION, THEN REPOPULATION

This only occurs when speaking to Preston and after you destroy the Institute during the Main Quest. You must also have evacuated the Institute, or you cannot begin this quest. Speak to the settler and agree to their request.

Enter the settlement tagged on your map and remove all threats. Expect one or more of the following: Feral Ghouls, Radroaches, Raiders, Super Mutants or even Deathclaws. Once complete, you may use the settlement workshop immediately. Speak to the settler, as this enables them to send refugees for the new settlement you cleared. Now return to Preston.

Workshop available at this settlement:

 **BOTTLECAPS (APPROX. 100)**

# THE MINUTEMEN
# RADIANT QUESTS: OWNERSHIP

## HELPFUL HINT
### *from Vault Boy!*

WHAT ARE MINUTEMEN RADIANT OWNERSHIP QUESTS? A PERTINENT QUESTION! THE SIX QUESTS LISTED HERE ARE RANDOMLY AVAILABLE (UNLESS OTHERWISE STATED) AND ARE GIVEN EITHER BY PRESTON GARVEY OR RADIO FREEDOM (AT THE CASTLE). THEY ARE CALLS TO ASSIST SETTLEMENTS THAT HAVE ALREADY ALLIED WITH YOU. YOU MAY ALSO SOMETIMES TRIGGER THESE QUESTS BY STUMBLING INTO A SETTLEMENT NEEDING A PARTICULAR TYPE OF HELP. THESE QUESTS ARE "RADIANT," AS THE LOCATIONS YOU'RE SENT TO ARE RANDOM. THESE QUESTS ARE USUALLY REPEATABLE, MAKING THEM A GREAT WAY TO ACCUMULATE REWARDS. TIME TO REMAIN IN CONTROL OF YOUR SHANTY SETTLEMENT EMPIRE! ASIDE FROM SPEAKING TO PRESTON GARVEY, START THESE QUESTS BY LISTENING TO RADIO FREEDOM, OR JUST SHOWING UP AT A SETTLEMENT LOCATION. PRESTON NEED NOT BE SPOKEN TO, IF THIS IS THE CASE.

## VAULT-TEC RECOMMENDS

### RANDOM FACTS

Due to the random nature of the locations you are sent to, it is imperative you read up on the hostiles (as well as the valuables) you'll uncover at each one. Vault-Tec is proud to provide comprehensive cartography for just such adventuring.

## Quest
## DEFEND A SETTLEMENT OR DEFEND ARTILLERY AT A SETTLEMENT

1. TRAVEL TO [AN OWNED SETTLEMENT]
2. BUILD DEFENSES
3. HELP DEFEND [THE OWNED SETTLEMENT]
4. TALK TO PEOPLE OF [THE OWNED SETTLEMENT]
5. TALK TO PRESTON GARVEY

### TURRETS SYNDROME

Visit the indicated settlement and immediately access their workshop. Build defenses until the objective is satisfied.

Wait (sit or sleep if no enemies arrive immediately) awhile after a job well done. Then help defeat one of the following types of foes: Raiders, Feral Ghouls, Super Mutants, Gunners, the Brotherhood of Steel (if this faction is hostile to you), synths (if the Institute is hostile to you or has been destroyed). After you wipe out the incursion, speak to the settlers; then report back to Preston Garvey for some Caps.

BOTTLECAPS (APPROX. 100)

## Quest
## STOP THE RAIDING

1. TRAVEL TO [AN OWNED SETTLEMENT]
2. KILL THE RAIDERS IN [A LOCATION]
3. REPORT YOUR SUCCESS TO SETTLERS AT [THE SETTLEMENT]

### WE'LL DO THE RAIDING, THANK YOU

This is given randomly. Head to the indicated settlement and speak to one of the settlers. They are having problems with Raiders. Aren't they always? Agree to help them.

Visit the indicated Raider stronghold. Wipe out the tagged foes and (optionally) any other enemies. Return to the settlement with the good news.

BOTTLECAPS (APPROX. 100)

## Quest
# KIDNAPPED TRADER

1. TRAVEL TO [AN OWNED SETTLEMENT]
2. (OPTIONAL) PAY THE RANSOM
3. RESCUE THE KIDNAPPED TRADER FROM [A LOCATION]
4. REPORT BACK TO THE PEOPLE OF [THE SETTLEMENT]

## A CAPS PAYMENT, OR BLOODY REVENGE

Head to the settlement requesting assistance and speak to one of the settlers. One of their traders has been kidnapped. You can:

- (OPTIONAL) PAY OFF THE RANSOM AND COMPLETE THE QUEST.
- AGREE TO RESCUE THE KIDNAPPED TRADER.

Visit the indicated enemy stronghold. Wipe out as many foes as you wish—ideally any close to the kidnapped trader. Locate them and bring them out

of the stronghold. This quest fails if the trader dies. Assuming the trader survives, return to the settlement with the good news.

 **BOTTLECAPS (APPROX. 100)**

## Quest
# WATER, FOOD, OR POWER

1. TRAVEL TO [AN OWNED SETTLEMENT]    3. REPORT YOUR SUCCESS
2. BUILD [THE REQUIRED RESOURCE]

## AMENABLE WITH YOUR AMENITIES

Visit your rather impoverished settlement and immediately access their workshop. Add one of the following resources until the objective is satisfied: water, food, power.

Speak to the settlers after the resource is available. Then report back to the quest giver for the great Bottlecap giveaway.

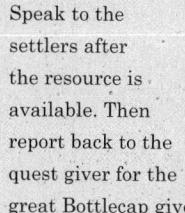 **BOTTLECAPS (APPROX. 100)**

## Quest
# SUSPECTED SYNTH

1. DECIDE WHAT TO DO ABOUT SUSPECTED SYNTH

## MERCY OR MURDER

This only occurs if the Institute has not been destroyed. An alert from one of your owned settlements indicates a synth has infiltrated the citizens there. Speak to the people and decide the synth's fate. You can either banish the synth or kill it.

 **BOTTLECAPS (APPROX. 100)**

# SIDE QUESTS

The following Side Quests are available:

## SIDE QUESTS

| Side Quest | Location | Side Quest | Location |
|---|---|---|---|
| Benign Intervention | Page 184 | Emergent Behavior | Page 198 |
| The Big Dig | Page 185 | Here There Be Monsters | Page 199 |
| Confidence Man | Page 187 | Human Error | Page 200 |
| Curtain Call | Page 188 | Kid in a Fridge | Page 202 |
| Detective Case Files: The Disappearing Act | Page 189 | Last Voyage of the U.S.S. Constitution | Page 203 |
| Detective Case Files: The Gilded Grasshopper | Page 190 | Long Road Ahead | Page 206 |
| Detective Case Files: Long Time Coming | Page 191 | The Secret of Cabot House | Page 207 |
| Diamond City Blues | Page 194 | The Silver Shroud | Page 210 |
| The Devil's Due | Page 197 | Vault 81 and Hole in the Wall | Page 212 |

## Quest
# BENIGN INTERVENTION

1. MISCELLANEOUS: ELIMINATE THE REMAINING RAIDERS
2. MISCELLANEOUS: TALK TO TOMMY
3. BRING CAIT TO VAULT 95
4. LOCATE THE CLEAN ROOM
5. SPEAK TO CAIT
6. WAIT FOR CAIT TO GET INTO THE CLEAN ROOM CHAIR
7. CURE CAIT'S ADDICTION
8. SPEAK TO CAIT

**Locations to Explore**
- COMBAT ZONE (PAGE 497)
- THEATER DISTRICT (NEIGHBORHOOD) (PAGE 496)
- VAULT 95 (PAGE 358)

## MISCELLANEOUS: COMPANION CAIT

During your exploration of Boston, take in a show at the Combat Zone. This is a Raider stronghold, so you'll need to fight your way in. Once inside, there are more Raiders to attend to before entering the arena.

Once in the arena, speak with Tommy Lonegan. He's hoping you'll partner up with Cait while he gets his arena back in order.

(Medium) Ask why you should partner with Cait.

**COMPANION: CAIT**

## A REFORMED PSYCHO KILLER

Speak to her periodically until she confides in you about her dependency on Psycho. It's taking its toll on her health. She mentions an old Vault where she might be able to cure this addiction. Head southeast to Vault 95, and set upon the Gunners and Assaultrons at the entrance. Watch for turrets, too.

Make your way through Vault 95, mopping up more Gunners until you locate a "Clean Room," an area dedicated to drug rehabilitation. Speak with Cait and convince her to go through with the detoxification.

 (Easy) You can use your friendship to help convince her.

When she is seated, use the Clean Room terminal and begin the detox. Afterwards, you can affinity with Cait (until her perk becomes available), but her outlook to certain actions she likes and dislikes changes. Look to the Companions section of STAT Chapter for more information.

## VAULT-TEC RECOMMENDS

WHAT'S THERE TO LOOT?

**NUKA CHERRY**
**BOBBLEHEAD: BIG GUNS**

There's little left that the Raiders haven't picked over at the Combat Zone (except a Nuka Cherry). However, the Gunners in Vault 95 are guarding a limited-edition official Vault-Tec Bobblehead! Bring home the Big Guns!

## Quest
# THE BIG DIG

1. TALK TO BOBBI
2. MEET BOBBI INSIDE
3. JOIN THE DIG
4. EXTERMINATE THE MIRELURKS
5. MEET BOBBI IN DIAMOND CITY
6. GET MEL OUT OF JAIL
7. RECRUIT MEL
8. MEET THE GANG IN THE DIG
9. DIG INTO THE STRONG ROOM
10. DIG THROUGH THE SUBWAY AREA
11. DIG THROUGH THE BASEMENT AREA
12. MEET WITH THE GANG IN THE STRONG ROOM BASEMENT
13. GET OUT OF THE BASEMENT
14. ENTER THE STRONG ROOM
15. KILL FAHRENHEIT AND HER MEN
16. OR KILL BOBBI
17. OPEN THE TRAIN CAR AND GET PAID
18. OR TALK TO FAHRENHEIT

**Locations to Explore**
- GOODNEIGHBOR (PAGE 483)
- BOBBI'S HOUSE (PAGE 486)
- THE BIG DIG (PAGE 486)
- NH&M FREIGHT DEPOT (PAGE 371)

## GOING UNDERGROUND

Over in Goodneighbor, behind the two locked warehouses to the southeast, is a dingy alley with a metal door at the end of it. Bobbi No-Nose lives here, and she's looking for someone to help her with some tunneling work. Agree to start this quest.

 (Easy, Medium, Hard) You can ask for more information and then press her (twice) for better payment options up front. This leads her to giving you some caps right away.

 **BOTTLECAPS (100-200)**

Enter the basement, into the Dig area, and join in. You won't be using a shovel, though; there's a small infestation of Mirelurks to remove. Bobbi comes in afterward and promotes you.

Head west across Boston to visit Diamond City, where Bobbi is hanging out at the market. She tells you the real nature of the job—or heist—and needs you to recruit someone named Mel who's locked up in Diamond City Security.

Enter the security office, and speak with Mel, who's behind bars. You can:

- **(EXPERT) HACK THE TERMINAL AND START THE PROTECTRON UNIT, KEEPING THE SECURITY GUARDS BUSY WHILE YOU FREE MEL.**
- **SPEAK TO A SECURITY GUARD: (300 CAPS) BRIBE THE GUARD.**
- **OR PICKPOCKET A KEY FROM A THE GUARD, OR STEAL A KEY FROM THE DESK INSIDE THE SECURITY OFFICE, AND UNLOCK THE CELL.**

 (Medium, Hard) Or ask nicely or threaten the guard to let Mel out.

After recruiting Mel in Diamond City, return to the dig site under Goodneighbor, where you're introduced to Mel's digging friend, Sonya. What follows is a lengthy and dangerous series of tunneling stops interspersed with some underground exploration. In each chamber, inspect the rock wall for a "fragile" section, send Sonya to dig the wall out, and proceed deeper into the sewers. Mirelurks are active here.

Keep digging until you break into a section of old subway tracks and a station populated by Feral Ghoul commuters. The plan is still to find fragile walls, dig them out, and proceed to new areas. Continue until you reach the wall to the strong room. This last dig tires Sonya out considerably.

---

**HELPFUL HINT** *from Vault Boy!* **Did You Know?**

LOST? DISORIENTATED? IN NEED OF A MAP? WELL, VAULT-TEC IS PROUD TO PROVIDE COMPLETE BLUEPRINTS OF THIS TUNNEL AND SUBWAY COMPLEX, ON PAGE 487. IN ADDITION, BE SURE YOU FOLLOW THE GLOWING RED LIGHTS THAT LEAD THE WAY OUT OF THIS MODERATELY UNPLEASANT HELLHOLE.

---

### LOOTING THE TUNNELS

  **FUSION CORE**
**NUKA COLA QUANTUM (2)**
Digging into the strong room isn't a time-sensitive issue, allowing you to explore a side passage to the east that contains a suit of Power Armor. There are also three Fusion Cores (one in the power armor) and a couple of Nuka Cola Quantums to pick up during your exploration.

## THE FULL STORY IN THE STRONG ROOM

Look for the metal "exit" door into the strong room and climb out into NH&M Freight Depot. Be ready for a confrontation with Fahrenheit, Mayor Hancock's main squeeze. It seems the situation regarding whose valuables you were stealing wasn't fully explained to you. You can:

- **SIDE WITH BOBBI AND REMOVE ANY THREATS IN THE CHAMBER (WATCH FOR FLAMERS AND EXPLODING BARRELS IN YOUR VICINITY), AND CLAIM YOUR SHARE OF THE LOOT.**

 **BOTTLECAPS (APPROX. 200)**

- **SIDE WITH FAHRENHEIT, REMOVE ANYONE HAVING A PROBLEM WITH YOUR CHANGE OF ALLEGIANCE, AND SPEAK WITH FAHRENHEIT, WHO'S HAPPY YOU MADE THE CHOICE AND GRANTS YOU THE FOLLOWING:**

 **UNIQUE WEAPON: ASHMAKER**

 (Medium) Feel free to convince Bobbi to leave and resolve the situation without bloodshed.

Once your decision is made, the quest is over. Of course, your choices directly affect your standing with Mayor Hancock of Goodneighbor, so expect repercussions. These post-quest activities are detailed in the Goodneighbor quest—Miscellaneous: Recruiting Hancock (on page 489).

# Quest
# CONFIDENCE MAN

1. SPEAK TO VADIM
2. MEET TRAVIS IN THE DUGOUT INN AFTER 6 P.M.
3. HELP TRAVIS
4. TALK TO VADIM
5. CONVINCE SCARLETT TO MEET TRAVIS
6. TALK TO YEFIM
7. TALK TO TRAVIS
8. MEET TRAVIS AT THE BEANTOWN BREWERY
9. HELP TRAVIS RESCUE VADIM
10. SPEAK TO TRAVIS

**Locations to Explore**
– DIAMOND CITY (PAGE 433)   – DUGOUT INN (PAGE 438)   – BEANTOWN BREWERY (PAGE 316)

## THIS CHARMING MAN

Vadim, the jocular owner of the Dugout Inn, is hoping you'll help him improve the confidence of Diamond City Radio's DJ, Travis Miles. Agree to help, and return to the inn after 6:00 p.m. You witness Travis being harassed by a greaser named Bull. Speak to Travis and encourage him as you wish. A fistfight starts. Pummel Bull (and his sidekick, Gouger) if necessary. Chat to both Travis and Vadim afterward. That went reasonably well, they reckon.

Vadim's next plan involves Scarlett, the Dugout Inn's waitress, who needs to be talked into spending some quality time with Travis Miles. Find her in the Dugout Inn or around Diamond City. Answer her without your usual witty charm, or:

(Easy) Threaten or persuade her.
(Medium) Bribe her.

Return to the Dugout Inn and speak with Yefim. He tells you that Bull had an altercation with Vadim and the barkeeper has disappeared!

## BEATDOWN AT BEANTOWN

Travis knows the score. Find him in Diamond City, and he reveals Vadim has been kidnapped. He agrees to meet you at old Beantown Brewery. Make sure he comes home in one piece. Well, both of them really.

Beware of Raiders. Battle your way to Vadim's location. A named Raider "Tower Tom," Bull, and Gouger need more than a swift talking to. After you spray their blood across the brewery walls, untie Vadim and he rewards you for your help. A chat with Travis indicates he's a lot more confident now. But hardened. As you'll hear if you tune into his future broadcasts on Diamond City Radio.

 **BOTTLECAPS (200)**

 **BUFFOUT (4), JET (2)**

## VAULT-TEC RECOMMENDS

LOOTING BEANTOWN BREWERY

  **PICKET FENCES MAGAZINE**
**GWINNETT BREW RECIPE**

Have you read the latest issue of Picket Fences magazine? Those interior designs are to die for! Did you find the Gwinnett Brew Recipe too? Your Drinkin' Buddy can mix this up for you (find him in the Shamrock Taphouse). Cheers!

DATA

QUESTS

187

## Quest
# CURTAIN CALL

1. INVESTIGATE RADIO BROADCAST
2. UNLOCK CAGE
3. GET REX TO SAFETY
4. TALK TO REX GOODMAN

**Locations to Explore**
- TRINITY TOWER (PAGE 454)
- BACK BAY (PAGE 450)
- WRVR BROADCAST STATION (PAGE 356)

## SOMETHING WICKED THIS WAY COMES

Did you hear the latest broadcast from Trinity Tower Radio? Tune your Pip-Boy when you can receive the signal. A good place to try for a signal is in Diamond City Market or close to Trinity Tower. Or, if you're traveling in the southwest Commonwealth, visit WRVR Broadcast Station, where the folks there have Rex's broadcast on a loop. He's begging to be rescued from super mutants who have taken him captive in Trinity Tower.

Enter the plaza area at the base of the skyscraper, and rid yourself of any Super Mutants and Mutant Hounds. Ride the elevator to the middle interior. Make slow but steady progress up through the Super Mutants until you arrive at a second elevator. Ride that up to the exposed top of the structure. Fight more Super Mutants, ascending to the open skyscraper roof.

### VAULT-TEC RECOMMENDS

**LOOTING TRINITY TOWER**

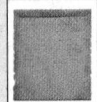 

**MACBETH SCRIPT**
**BOBBLEHEAD: MELEE**
Aside from the assortment of items inside the steamer trunk, don't leave the tower's roof without peeking inside Rex's cage. Grab Strong's MacBeth Script and a Melee Bobblehead before you go!

## HOVER THROUGH FOG AND FILTHY AIR

Locate the cage where Rex Goodman and his Super Mutant friend Strong are imprisoned. Unlock the cage by:

- **(MASTER) USING YOUR EXTREME SKILL.**
- **USING YOUR REGULAR CUNNING BY TAKING THE TRINITY TOWER CELL KEY FROM THE NEARBY STEAMER TRUNK AND USING IT.**

 **TRINITY TOWER CELL KEY**

The only way back down, aside from a death plummet, is to battle to the window-washer lift. Press the button once the three of you are on it. Ride this down while laying suppressing fire on the Super Mutants you can see. Repeat this plan until all threats are abated and you're on the ground level. Back on terra firma, with anything green except Strong dispatched, speak to Rex. While he returns to his career in the WRVR building, Strong is available to become a companion.

 **REGINALD'S SUIT (IF YOU'RE MALE)**

 **AGATHA'S DRESS (IF YOU'RE FEMALE)**

 **COMPANION: STRONG**

*Quest*

# MISCELLANEOUS: DETECTIVE CASE FILES

1. TALK TO ELLIE
2. CHECK THE DETECTIVE CASES
3. READ EARL STERLING'S CASE FILE
4. READ MARTY BULLFINCH'S CASE FILE
5. LISTEN TO MARTY'S HOLOTAPE
6. REPORT BACK TO VALENTINE'S DETECTIVE AGENCY

**Locations to Explore**

– DIAMOND CITY (PAGE 433)

## A COLD CASE CLOSE TO HOME BASE

While you're in Diamond City, you might as well enter the Valentine Detective Agency (usually as part of Main Quest: Jewel of the Commonwealth) and chat with Ellie the assistant. She's come across some unsolved case files:

**EARL STERLING CASE FILE**

**MARTY BULLFINCH'S HOLOTAPE**

Picking up Earl Sterling's case file starts Side Quest: The Disappearing Act. Listening to Marty Bullfinch's Holotape is one way to start Side Quest: The Gilded Grasshopper.

*Quest*

# DETECTIVE CASE FILES: THE DISAPPEARING ACT

1. SEARCH EARL STERLING'S HOUSE FOR CLUES
2. (OPTIONAL) OBTAIN THE KEY TO EARL STERLING'S HOUSE
3. SEARCH THE MEGA SURGERY CENTER FOR CLUES
4. INVESTIGATE THE SURGERY CELLAR
5. (OPTIONAL) OBTAIN THE KEY TO SURGERY CELLAR
6. TALK TO ELLIE

**Locations to Explore**

– DIAMOND CITY (PAGE 433)

## A STERLING START

You've offered to help Nick and Ellie find out what happened to Earl Sterling, a bartender at the Dugout Inn. You need to get into Earl's home, see if you can find any clues to his whereabouts. Try the following:

- (NOVICE) PICK THE LOCK TO EARL STERLING'S HOUSE (IN DIAMOND CITY).
- ENTER THE DUGOUT INN, SPEAK TO VADIM BOBROV, AND RECEIVE THE KEY FROM HIM.

(Easy) In addition, chat to Yefim about Earl Sterling.

**EARL STERLING'S HOUSE KEY**

Enter Earl Sterling's house. If you've brought Nick along, he might be able to lend a hand looking for clues. Rummage under the sofa to find something of interest:

**FOLDER AND RECEIPT**

## BODY DECONSTRUCTION SURGERY

Clues lead you to a facial reconstruction specialist who works at the Mega Surgery Center. Maybe he knows what happened to Earl. Speak to Doctor Sun about him.

(Medium) Ask about your suspect.

Inspect the interesting marks on the ground leading to the surgery cellar. Ask Doctor Sun about this.

(Hard) Ask for an explanation regarding the marks.

At this point, you can:

- (ADVANCED) PICK THE LOCK TO THE MEGA SURGERY CELLAR.

(Medium) Threaten Doctor Sun into opening the cellar, or mention your investigation and request he opens the cellar.

(100 Bottlecaps) Bribe him into opening the cellar.

**SURGERY CELLAR KEY**

You make a possibly case-solving discovery in the cellar. Speak to your suspect. You can:

(Medium) Arrest him, or end the standoff peacefully.

Or kill him.

After a more indignant chat with Doctor Sun, return to Ellie and explain how you solved the case for the following reward:

**BOTTLECAPS (APPROX. 200)**

## Quest
# DETECTIVE CASE FILES: THE GILDED GRASSHOPPER

1. FIND THE GILDED GRASSHOPPER
2. READ "FOOD FOR THE GRASSHOPPER"
3. FIND SHEM DROWNE'S GRAVE

**Locations to Explore**
- DIAMOND CITY (PAGE 433)
- FINANCIAL DISTRICT (NEIGHBORHOOD) (PAGE 476)
- FANEUIL HALL (PAGE 482)
- NORTH END (NEIGHBORHOOD) (PAGE 464)
- NORTH END GRAVEYARD (PAGE 468)

## CATCHING A GRASSHOPPER

Nick's former partner, Marty Bullfinch, believes there's a treasure map hidden in the Gilded Grasshopper on top of Faneuil Hall. Pay the hall a visit. Head into the hellhole that is Boston's Financial District, and assault this Super Mutant stronghold.

Ascend through the structure's interior, looking for the ladder to the roof. Locate the Gilded Grasshopper there and read the note inside.

**GILDED GRASSHOPPER**

**NOTE: FOOD FOR THE GRASSHOPPER**

**HELPFUL HINT** *from Vault Boy!* *Did You Know?*

COLLECTING TINY INSECTS IS FUN, ESPECIALLY AS MOST OF THEM NOWADAYS HAVE MUTATED INTO HIDEOUS, BLOOD-SUCKING PARASITES. THE GILDED GRASSHOPPER IS UP ON THIS ROOF AND CAN BE DISCOVERED AT ANY TIME, EVEN IF THE QUEST ISN'T ACTIVE. JUST POP UP HERE AND GRAB HIM!

### LOOTING FANEUIL HALL
### LIVE & LOVE

You shouldn't leave your tour of this historic mansion without at least pilfering a Fusion Core and obtaining the latest issue of Live & Love magazine. Also search the gift shop magazine rack for some notes about other interesting places to visit in the Commonwealth.

The note inside the Gilded Grasshopper seems to point toward Shem Drowne's grave, located in a small cemetery between Cabot House and Pickman Galley in North End Neighborhood. Watch for Feral Ghouls before inspecting the grave.

 **NOTE: FEAR NOT**

 **COPPER, SILVER, AND GOLD BARS**

 **UNIQUE WEAPON: SHEM DROWNE'S SWORD**

## Quest
# DETECTIVE CASE FILES: LONG TIME COMING

1–10. FIND EDDIE WINTER'S HOLOTAPES (10)

11. TALK TO NICK

12. TRAVEL TO EDDIE'S HIDEOUT

13. CONFRONT EDDIE WINTER

14. FOLLOW NICK

**Locations to Explore**

- DIAMOND CITY (PAGE 433)
- BADTFL REGIONAL OFFICE (PAGE 423)
- MALDEN CENTER (PAGE 286)
- QUINCY POLICE STATION (PAGE 390)
- NATICK POLICE DEPARTMENT (PAGE 355)

- NAHANT SHERIFF'S DEPARTMENT (PAGE 338)
- EAST BOSTON POLICE STATION (PAGE 339)
- SOUTH BOSTON POLICE STATION (PAGE 515)
- POLICE PRECINCT 8 (PAGE 430)
- COAST GUARD PIER (PAGE 369)

- ANDREW STATION (PAGE 514)
- JOE'S SPUCKIES COFFEE SHOP (SOUTHIE SPEAKEASY) (PAGE 520)

## COLD CASES: SOLVED!

Once both cases are closed, and you've palled around with Nick and gained affinity with him, he will speak to you about a cold case. Speak to both Ellie and Nick. Side Quest: Long Time Coming is now available.

## HOLOTAPE HUNT

Nick asked for your help in recovering 10 Holotapes belonging to Eddie Winter. He thinks the Commonwealth's police evidence terminals should be able to point you toward the tapes. You receive the first from Nick. Read the notes, and look at the world map for the locations of the remaining nine tapes.

 **WELCOME HOME!**

 **EDDIE WINTER CASE NOTES**

 **EDDIE WINTER HOLOTAPE 1**

## HELPFUL HINT
### *from Vault Boy!*

ISN'T NICK VALENTINE A STAND-UP FELLA? A SALT-OF-THE-EARTH TYPE, WITH A HEALTHY SKEPTICISM AND A STRONG, CHISELED CHIN (WELL, BEFORE HIS PLASTIC FACE MELTED). REMEMBER IF YOU WANT A DEEPER FRIENDSHIP WITH HIM AND START THIS QUEST, YOU NEED TO HAVE ACHIEVED THE FOLLOWING:

- RESCUED NICK FROM VAULT 114 AND RECEIVE THE REWARD FROM ELLIE.
- GAINED NICK AS A COMPANION.
- GAINED AFFINITY WITH NICK SO HE TALKS TO YOU ABOUT HAVING MEMORY FLASHES OF THE "OLD NICK".
- GAINED ADMIRATION LEVEL OF AFFINITY WITH HIM.
- SPOKE TO NICK AFTER FINISHING MAIN QUEST: DANGEROUS MINDS. THE COMPANIONS SECTION OF THIS GUIDE (PAGE 29) PUTS YOU ON THE RIGHT TRACK REGARDING AFFINITY.

Visit each of the following locations. At each one, find the police evidence terminal, and access the file on Eddie Winter. Then search the building for the Holotape.

## HOLOTAPE HUNT: BADTFL REGIONAL OFFICE

Find this location in Charleston Neighborhood. Beware of Raiders. The tape is on a filing cabinet.

 **EDDIE WINTER HOLOTAPE 0**

## HOLOTAPE HUNT: MALDEN CENTER POLICE STATION

Look for this unmarked location near Malden Center in North Central Commonwealth. The tape is on a desk.

 **EDDIE WINTER HOLOTAPE 2**

## HOLOTAPE HUNT: QUINCY POLICE STATION

Beware of Gunners (and their leader, Tessa). The tape is in a nearby locker.

 **EDDIE WINTER HOLOTAPE 3**

## HOLOTAPE HUNT: NATICK POLICE DEPARTMENT

Watch out for the Deathclaw. The tape is inside an evidence locker.

 **EDDIE WINTER HOLOTAPE 4**

## HOLOTAPE HUNT: NAHANT SHERIFF'S DEPARTMENT

The tape is on a filing cabinet.

 **EDDIE WINTER HOLOTAPE 5**

## HOLOTAPE HUNT: EAST BOSTON POLICE STATION

The tape is in a desk.

**EDDIE WINTER HOLOTAPE 6**

## HOLOTAPE HUNT: SOUTH BOSTON POLICE DEPARTMENT

Beware of Vicious Mongrels and a Police Protectron. The tape is on an office desk.

**EDDIE WINTER HOLOTAPE 7**

## HOLOTAPE HUNT: POLICE PRECINCT 8

This location is just west of Boston Public Library in Back Bay Neighborhood. The tape is in a nearby cell.

**EDDIE WINTER HOLOTAPE 8**

## HOLOTAPE HUNT: COAST GUARD PIER

Mow down the Super Mutants, Mutant Hounds, and Vicious Mongrels. The tape is on a safe.

**EDDIE WINTER HOLOTAPE 9**

## VAULT-TEC RECOMMENDS

LOOTING COAST GUARD PIER

**ASTOUNDINGLY AWESOME TALES 2**
You'll have an astoundingly awesome time if you pick up this magazine and pry some major chems from the evidence locker. There's a Mini Nuke and Nuka Cherry too.

## THE WINTER OF YOUR DISCONTENT

After finding all of Eddie Winter's Holotapes, turn them over to Nick. He'll use the Holotapes to decipher the code to Eddie Winter's bunker. Now it's time to head to Andrew Station and put an end to Eddie. Fight the Raiders and descend into the subway tunnels and sewer passages. Search for a metal door with a keypad. Input the code Nick mentioned.

 **HELPFUL HINT** *from Vault Boy!*  Did You Know?

WANT TO MAKE LESS OF A GRAND ENTRANCE? THEN FIND THE METAL HATCH IN THE FLOOR OF JOE'S SPUCKIES COFFEE SHOP. THE PLACE IS SEALED TIGHT (MASTER), BUT IF YOU'RE THE SNEAKING SORT, YOU CAN INFILTRATE THE SOUTHIE SPEAKEASY WITHOUT YOUR RAIDER PALS REALIZING UNTIL IT'S TOO LATE! WAY TO GO!

## VAULT-TEC RECOMMENDS

LOOTING ANDREW STATION

**NUKA CHERRY (2)**
The Raider gang, led by Chancer, is hanging around under here. They have some reasonably good ammo to take, but the real prize are a couple of thirst-quenching Nuka Cherries, in the Foodstuffs counter, just as you enter the Station.

It's time for Eddie Winter to face the music. Afterward, pry the small arms from his withered hands.

 **UNIQUE WEAPON: EDDIE'S PEACE**

Afterward, Nick has one more matter to attend to. Exit via the ladder to Joe's Spuckies Coffee Shop. Speak to Nick when he finds the location he's looking for. Now continue your companionship with Nick until you reach the highest affinity, after which you receive the following Perk:

**PERK: CLOSE TO METAL**

# Quest
## DIAMOND CITY BLUES

1. INTIMIDATE HENRY COOKE
2. HELP PAUL PEMBROKE INTIMIDATE HENRY COOKE
3. TALK TO HENRY COOKE
4. OR KILL HENRY COOKE
5. REPORT BACK TO PAUL PEMBROKE
6. SEARCH COOKE'S BODY AND READ HIS NOTE
7. AMBUSH NELSON LATIMER'S CHEM DEAL
8. INTERROGATE TRISH
9. OR KILL TRISH
10. SEARCH TRISH AND READ HER NOTE
11. DIVIDE THE SPOILS
12. GAIN ACCESS TO MAROWSKI'S CHEMS LAB

### Locations to Explore

## THREE TO TANGO

After entering the Colonial Taphouse in Diamond City (upstairs in the "fancy" part of town), you observe an argument between husband (Paul Pembroke) and wife (Darcy Pembroke) and a fight between Paul and Henry Cooke, the barkeep. Paul storms out, leaving you to chat to either Darcy or Henry. But outside, Paul asks whether you could help intimidate Cooke for him. You can:

- **AGREE TO HELP.**

(Easy, Medium) Request a reward and tell him you'll go alone.

- **(AFTER WHICH EITHER A CONFRONTATION WILL PLAY OUT BETWEEN THEM THE NEXT TIME YOU ENTER THE TAPHOUSE, OR -- IF YOU LEAVE DIAMOND CITY BEFORE VISITING THE TAPHOUSE AGAIN -- COOKE WILL KILL PAUL PRIOR TO YOUR RETURN).**

Plan A (Alone): Head up to the taphouse alone, and speak with Cooke about his infraction with the Pembrokes. Cooke feels it's none of your business. You can:

(Easy, Medium) Win a speech challenge (with three options) and resolve the situation peacefully (though if you fail, you are attacked).

- **OR YOU CAN SAY "YOUR MOVE", AFTER WHICH HE ATTACKS.**

Plan B (with Paul): Head up to the taphouse with a seething Paul in tow. With some "muscle" behind him, Paul is more enthusiastic with his hatred for Cooke. You can egg him on or calm him down.

If the conversation ends diplomatically, Cooke tells you of a chems deal he's involved in.

If the conversation ends in fisticuffs or worse, check his body for a note regarding a chem deal Cooke was involved in. The deal is with Nelson Latimer, a wannabe gangster. There's a reward if you ambush Latimer at the deal spot.

## THE DEAL GOES SOUTH

Head north to the river just west of Back Street Apparel, where Nelson's chem deal is going down. Cooke, Paul, a companion, or no one might be with you. Nelson isn't happy about your intrusion and the conversation ends with bullets flying.

Speak to the only survivor, a ghoul (and Nelson's supplier) named Trish, who works for a local (and very real) gangster named Marowski. You can:

- **AGREE TO LET HER LIVE, AFTER WHICH SHE REVEALS THE LOCATION OF A SECRET CHEMS LAB.**
- **REMOVE HER AS A THREAT, SEARCHING HER FOR A NOTE REVEALING THE LOCATION OF A SECRET CHEMS LAB.**
- **PROMISE TO LET HER GO, SO SHE GIVES YOU A PASSWORD FOR THE TERMINAL AT THE SECRET CHEMS LAB, ALLOWING YOU EASIER ACCESS.**

 **FOUR LEAF SECURITY PASSWORD**

Trish always tries to flee, and you can let her (though Cooke won't let that happen if he's with you), or gun her down (ideally after she mentions that password).

## PAUL TAKES A CUT

If Cooke is alive at this point, he says he's going to leave town. He's not about to stick around and incur the wrath of the real gangster Marowski.

If Paul Pembroke is still in the picture and attended the chem deal, he'll want you to split the spoils of the chem deal with him. He's usually at the Dugout Inn at Diamond City. You can:

– **SPLIT THE LOOT 50-50.**

(Easy, Medium) Split the loot 70-30 in your favor. Or all in your favor.

– **HE STILL WANTS MORE. REFUSE, OR GIVE HIM 500 CAPS AND HE'LL BE ON HIS WAY. YOU'LL NEED TO FIGHT HIM IF YOU WANT TO KEEP ALL THE LOOT.**

If Paul Pembroke is still in the picture but you talked to Cooke alone and Paul didn't attend the chem deal, you can inform him of the fate of Cooke, and part ways.

## A COOLER OF CHEMS AND A CAN OF WORMS

Travel southeast across town to South Boston, and find the Ghoul-infested Four Leaf Fishpacking Plant. There's some advanced trip-wire security for a place that's seemingly abandoned. The interior of the plant isn't your focus (unless you enjoy mowing down living corpses). Instead, climb the exterior walkway to the roof, secure the area from any outside ferals, and locate the wall terminal on the side of the roof. You can:

– **SOLVE THE PUZZLE OF THE TRIPWIRES BY SHUTTING THEM DOWN IN THE CORRECT ORDER. READ THE NOTE FROM TRISH TO FIGURE OUT THE ORDER TO TRIP THE TRIPWIRES IN, SO THAT THE SECRET DOOR OPENS.**
– **(MASTER) HACK THIS IMPRESSIVELY DIFFICULT TERMINAL.**
– **OR USE THE SECURITY PASSWORD TRISH GAVE YOU, IF YOU DIDN'T IMMEDIATELY RESORT TO KILLING HER.**

Once inside the lab, there are a few of Marowski's chem lab workers who aren't happy to see you. But the wealth of chems inside is reason enough to slay them. The quest ends. Or does it?

**MAROWSKI'S CHEMS**

## VAULT-TEC RECOMMENDS

CHEMS AND CORES AT THE FISHPACKING PLANT

**FUSION CORE**

You might as well fully explore this plant, as there are three Fusion Cores to pick up and more chems than you can safely ingest in a week. Are you sure no one's going to miss those chems, though?

## AFTER THE QUEST: THE LATIMER SITUATION

1. KILL MAROWSKI OR KILL PAUL PEMBROKE
2. COLLECT REWARD FROM MALCOLM LATIMER

About 24 hours after you dealt with Nelson Latimer at the chem ambush, his father Malcolm becomes aware of his son's fate.

He's close to the taphouse area of Diamond City. Try to ignore Latimer, and a few of his thugs might rough you up when you next enter Diamond City. Assuming you don't want the entire city to turn hostile, speak with Malcolm Latimer. He lays down some options for you. You can:

– **AGREE TO KILL MAROWSKI AFTER PINNING THE DEATH ON THE GANGSTER.**
– **AGREE TO KILL PAUL PEMBROKE BY BLAMING HIM (IF PAUL IS STILL ALIVE).**
– **END THE CONVERSATION AT AN IMPASSE, AND EXPECT LATIMER TO SEND THUGS TO THWART YOU.**
– **END THE CONVERSATION WITH MALCOLM FURIOUS AT YOU; PAYING HIM OFF OR KILLING HIM ARE YOUR ONLY TWO OPTIONS.**

Assuming you ended the talk diplomatically, find your target, slay them (which solves the "Marowski situation" if this gangster is targeted but causes subsequent problems if Paul is slain) and claim your reward.

**BOTTLECAPS (50+)**

## AFTER THE QUEST: THE MAROWSKI SITUATION

1. TALK TO MAROWSKI ABOUT HIS MISSING CHEMS
2. PAY MAROWSKI 2,000 (OR 1,000) CAPS

If you let anyone live (Nelson or Trish) during the chem ambush, around 24 hours later you receive word that Marowski wants to talk to you at Hotel Rexford in Goodneighbor. You can head there on your own volition, or receive a stern warning from some of Marowski's thugs that their boss wants to see you.

Ignore Marowski's wishes, and expect periodic encounters with his thugs in both Goodneighbor and across the Commonwealth.

Meet Marowski, and he isn't pleased with you snooping around in his chem lab and wants reparations—2,000 Caps' worth. You can:

(Medium) Convince him you only need pay 1,000 Caps.

– **PAY UP, ENDING THE CONFLICT WITH MAROWSKI.**
– **ASK FOR A WEEK TO PAY, WHICH MAROWSKI GRANTS YOU. AFTER THAT, THE THUG ATTACKS START UP AGAIN UNTIL YOU PAY.**
– **OR SHOW MAROWSKI A HEIST PHOTO YOU OBTAINED DURING "THE DARCY SITUATION" (BELOW). THIS STARTS A SUBSEQUENT TASK: "MAROWSKI'S MERCENARY."**

## AFTER THE QUEST: THE COLETTE SITUATION

Did Henry Cooke die during the quest (for any reason)? Then his daughter Colette appears in the Dugout Inn, around one week after the quest concludes, investigating what happened. Your responses are based on Cooke's fate. You can:

- CONFESS TO KILLING COOKE (IF YOU DID THE DEED), THEN DIPLOMATICALLY TALK WITH HER OR RESORT TO VIOLENCE (YOU NEED TO KILL HER).
- TELL HER COOKE IS DEAD OR VANISHED, WITH SUBSEQUENT DIPLOMATIC TALKING; SHE EITHER ACCEPTS YOUR STORY, IS SUSPICIOUS, OR STARTS A FIGHT WITH YOU.
- TELL HER YOU DON'T KNOW ANYTHING. SHE EITHER SUSPECTS YOU (BUT DOESN'T RESORT TO VIOLENCE) OR THINKS YOU'RE TELLING THE TRUTH. EITHER WAY, SHE STILL HANGS AROUND TO INVESTIGATE FURTHER.

Is Colette still sniffing around in town? Then if Paul Pembroke is alive, he tries to speak with you, worried he'll be found out. You can:

- CALM HIM DOWN.
- AGREE TO LET PAUL GO OFF AND KILL COLETTE.
- AGREE TO KILL COLETTE YOURSELF.

Another week passes in Diamond City. If Colette is still investigating, you can run into her again (usually at the Dugout Inn).

If you split the chem ambush deal with Paul Pembroke at 70/30 percent, or if you took it all, he'll squeal on you and tell Colette you killed Cooke. She is very confrontational.

Or if she was suspicious when you first met her, she still thinks you had a hand in her father's murder.

End this conversation in several ways:

- COMBAT (USING VIOLENCE OR NOT ANSWERING HER QUESTIONS).
- YOUR CONFESSION (IF YOU KILLED HIM), WHICH LEADS TO COMBAT OR HER LEAVING TOWN.
- YOU TELL THE TRUTH (IF YOU DIDN'T KILL HIM) AND SHE LEAVES TOWN.
- YOU TELL HER PAUL IS THE MURDERER (IF HE ACCUSED YOU) AND SHE LEAVES TOWN, NOT SURE WHO TO BELIEVE.

Finally, if Colette leaves town still suspicious of you, be wary of her turning up at one of your settlements in the future, which leads to combat.

Or, if Colette leaves town still suspicious of Paul, you later hear of his death and can speak to Darcy about it.

## AFTER THE QUEST: THE DARCY SITUATION

Darcy Pembroke isn't some wilting flower in all of this, either! Sometime in the 72 hours after the completion of this quest, and if you weren't rude to her both times you had a chance to talk to her (at the start of the quest), she tries to talk and wants to know what happened. You can:

- TELL THE TRUTH.
- ANSWER WITH EVASIVE OR UNPLEASANT RESPONSES. SHE ENDS HER TALKING WITH YOU.
- AGREE TO HELP HER FIND OUT WHAT HAPPENED TO COOKE AND PAUL.
- OR TELL HER YOU DON'T KNOW ANYTHING.

Do you actually know what happened to Paul (if he isn't in Diamond City)? You can:

- CONFRONT COOKE ABOUT PAUL'S DISAPPEARANCE AND OBTAIN A CONFESSION BEFORE INFORMING DARCY.
- STUMBLE UPON PAUL'S BODY IN TOWN AND TELL DARCY HE'S DEAD.

One week later, and if you've been helpful to Darcy, she finds a heist photo—some incriminating evidence of past malfeasance that Marowski, Cooke, and Malcolm Latimer were involved in.

 **HEIST PHOTO**
..............................................................................

The following Miscellaneous objectives are available:

1. TALK TO MAROWSKI, COOKE, OR LATIMER ABOUT THE PHOTO
2. KILL COOKE AND LATIMER
3. TALK TO MAROWSKI

You have a few options, which obviously depend on who's still alive in both Diamond City and Goodneighbor. You can:

- TALK TO MAROWSKI IN HOTEL REXFORD (GOODNEIGHBOR). YOU CAN SELL THE PHOTO TO MAROWSKI, OR USE IT TO PAY OFF YOUR REPARATIONS. MAROWSKI WANTS THE OTHER TWO FELLOWS DEAD. OBLIGE HIM FOR A CAPS REWARD.
- TALK TO COOKE OR LATIMER ABOUT THE PHOTO. THEY OFFER TO PAY YOU FOR THE PHOTO. AGREE IF YOU WANT THE CAPS.

Then return to Darcy and split the caps with her, if you're a kind soul.

 **BOTTLECAPS**
..............................................................................

# Quest
# THE DEVIL'S DUE

1. MISCELLANEOUS: INVESTIGATE THE BUTCHERED BODY
2. LISTEN TO PRIVATE HART'S HOLOTAPE
3. EXPLORE THE MUSEUM
4. TAKE THE EGG
5. COMPLETE DELIVERY OF THE EGG OR
6. RETURN THE EGG TO ITS NEST

**Locations to Explore**
- MUSEUM OF WITCHCRAFT (PAGE 329)
- DIAMOND CITY MARKET (PAGE 433)
- COLONIAL TAPHOUSE (PAGE 438)
- LYNN WOODS (PAGE 276)

## HORRORS AT THE WITCHCRAFT MUSEUM

Visit the Witchcraft Museum, which has two firmly sealed front doors. In the side yard, you find a Holotape on a mutilated body.

 **PRIVATE HART'S HOLOTAPE**

Aha! There is a way inside! Access the side hatch and climb into the Museum of Witchcraft basement. As you proceed, there are some strange and frightening sounds. Keep your composure and follow the debris trail upstairs. Face the horror you heard earlier. Assuming you aren't torn to shreds, locate and gather the Holotape from Sergeant Lee. Listen to it. Pick up the Deathclaw Egg from the same location.

 **SERGEANT LEE'S HOLOTAPE**

 **PRISTINE DEATHCLAW EGG**

These Gunners were delivering a case of Deathclaw Eggs from their nest in Lynn Woods to Diamond City. You've got a decision to make—complete the delivery (Plan A) or return the egg to its nest (Plan B).

### VAULT-TEC RECOMMENDS ◀▣▶

 LOOTING THE WITCHCRAFT MUSEUM
**GROGNAK THE BARBARIAN**
Those Gunners were voracious comic readers. How else do you explain the copy of Grognak the Barbarian you find here?

### Plan A: A Recipe for Success

Head to Diamond City Market, and locate the Colonial Taphouse.

Speak to Wellingham, who looks down his nose at you when he speaks (if he had a nose) and mention the egg.

(Easy) Ask about his plans for the egg or for money.

(Medium) Ask for even more money.

You are given some Caps and a special recipe from Wellingham (which you can make yourself). The quest concludes. Why not return here later to see if Wellingham has made this recipe too?

 **BOTTLECAPS (200 APPROX)**

 **WELLINGHAM'S RECIPE**

### Plan B: Eggs Placed in a Nest

Head to Lynn Woods in the northern Commonwealth, and locate the nearby Deathclaw Nest. Place the egg there, and be

extremely careful of the beasts that hatched it. Pick up the egg again afterward if you decide to complete Plan A. Amazingly, you usually aren't attacked if you return an intact egg. You can only pick up the Deathclaw Gauntlet if you visit this nest before completing the quest.

 **DEATHCLAW GAUNTLET**

### VAULT-TEC RECOMMENDS ◀▣▶

 LOOTING LYNN WOODS
**WASTELAND SURVIVAL GUIDE**
Your woodland frolics don't end there. Did you explore the strange tower and Raider camp nearby? Some required reading makes the carnage worth the trip!

## Quest
# EMERGENT BEHAVIOR

1. FIND SOMEONE TO HELP CURIE
2. BRING CURIE TO DOCTOR AMARI
3. WAIT FOR DOCTOR AMARI
4. TALK TO THE CARETAKER
5. WATCH THE DOWNLOAD PROCEDURE
6. TALK TO CURIE

**Locations to Explore**
– GOODNEIGHBOR (PAGE 483)
– MEMORY DEN (PAGE 488)

## VIVRE SANS AIMER N'EST PAS PROPREMENT VIVRE

This quest has the following prerequisites: You must have completed Side Quests: Vault 81 and Hole in the Wall and have Curie as a companion. After spending some time with her as a Companion, and her gaining affinity for you, she tells you she really wants to become human, or as close to it so she can better pursue her studies.

 **COMPANION: CURIE**

### HELPFUL HINT
### from Vault Boy!
*Did You Know?*

CURIE IS A FINE FRIEND TO HAVE, DESPITE HER QUIRKS AND SLIGHTLY RUSTY SKIN TONE. REMEMBER IF YOU WANT A DEEPER FRIENDSHIP WITH HER, YOU NEED TO MAKE DECISIONS SHE SEES AS POSITIVE. THE COMPANIONS SECTION OF THIS GUIDE (PAGE 29) HAS THE RIGHT CHOICES TO MAKE.

Becoming more human might involve an operation involving the transference of memories. Wasn't there a specialist inside the Memory Den in Goodneighbor? Find Doctor Amari by:

– **COMPLETING GOODNEIGHBOR FREEFORM ACTIVITY: MEMORY DEN.**
– **COMPLETING MAIN QUEST: DANGEROUS MINDS.**

Doctor Amari is willing to help and even has a synth—G5-19—whose body could potentially be donated for this task. Amari requires a day to set everything up. Return to the Memory Den after 24 hours.

## C'EST CELA L'AMOUR, TOUT DONNER, TOUT SACRIFIER SANS ESPOIR DE RETOUR

Head down to the Memory Loungers downstairs. You're met by G5-19's caretaker, which is Glory from the Railroad, or another Railroad member if you've completed Railroad Quest: Precipice of War. Answer her how you wish.

(Medium) You have two optionally and convincing reasons why the operation should occur. Afterward, speak with Curie, who seems to be more human than ever.

Tell the caretaker this helps science.

# Quest
# HERE THERE BE MONSTERS

1. FIND THE SEA MONSTER
2. INVESTIGATE THE SUBMARINE
3. TALK TO CAPTAIN ZAO
4. GET THE DAMPENING RODS
5. TALK TO CAPTAIN ZAO
6. GET THE WARHEAD
7. TALK TO CAPTAIN ZAO
8. INSTALL DAMPENING RODS
9. INSTALL WARHEAD
10. TALK TO ZAO

**Locations to Explore**
– BOSTON HARBOR (NEIGHBORHOOD) (PAGE 504)   – YANGTZE (PAGE 407)   – SAUGUS IRONWORKS (PAGE 283)

---

## SWALLOWED BY A METAL MONSTER

Visit the docks between the Harbormaster Hotel and the Shamrock Taphouse down on Boston Harbor. Speak to Donny Kowalski; the tyke claims he saw a sea monster in the bay. Swim out to the trash barge. Swim to the hatch and enter.

Open the bulkhead door. There's a submarine captain who's been here for a very long time; speak and agree to help Captain Zao.

 (Easy) Ask for payment.

You've agreed to get a nuclear dampening coil from the Saugus Ironworks to repair the submarine's reactor. Trek roughly north and prepare yourself for a battering, courtesy of the Forged, a group of toughened Raiders who favor fire-based weapons. Ascend the interior to the blast furnace. Inside is Slag and a young man named Jake Finch.

You're here to activate the dampening rod sleeve and grab a dampening coil. Leave (via the roof if you grab the key from Slag or Jake), and traipse back to the Yangtze.

 **DAMPENING COIL**

## VAULT-TEC RECOMMENDS

LOOTING SAUGUS IRONWORKS

    **BOBBLEHEAD: EXPLOSIVES**
**SHISH KEBAB**

Any conversations you have with Slag or Jake aren't related to this quest; it's part of Location Quest: Out of the Fire, on page 296. But what's of paramount interest is Slag's infamous weapon and the Bobblehead he covets. Why not take both?

## YOU'RE NO MATE OF MINE

Access the bulkhead terminal and open the door. Wind your way down into the lower bulkhead, watching for Zao's crew, who have turned more than a little "bitey." Work your way to the ICBM, watching for the first mate nearby. Scavenge the ICBM to obtain the warhead.

 **WARHEAD**

Move to and activate the reactor core. Install the dampening coil, then the warhead. That seems to have pleased the captain!

 **PRE-WAR MONEY (4)**

 **HOMING BEACON**

DATA

QUESTS

199

## HELPFUL HINT
### *from Vault Boy!*

WERE YOU AWARE THAT THE HOMING BEACON ALLOWS YOU TO REQUEST THAT A FRIENDLY MISSILE BE FIRED FROM THE SUBMARINE TO AID YOU IN COMBAT? USE THE TRANSPONDER AS YOU WOULD A GRENADE. OUTDOOR TARGETS ONLY, TO AVOID DISAPPOINTMENT.

## VAULT-TEC RECOMMENDS

LOOTING THE YANGTZE

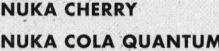

**NUKA CHERRY**
**NUKA COLA QUANTUM**

It seems our Chinese chum did more than a little investigating into western culture from his metal coffin; aside from the Fusion Core to find, there's some Commonwealth Cola to take back for Uncle Sam.

## *Quest*
# HUMAN ERROR

1. SEARCH COVENANT FOR CLUES
2. (OPTIONAL) SEARCH DESTROYED CARAVAN FOR CLUES
3. (OPTIONAL) TALK WITH HONEST DAN
4. (OPTIONAL) ASK DAN ABOUT SYNTHS
5. FIND THE LOCATION OF THE SECRET COMPOUND
6. (OPTIONAL) TALK WITH HONEST DAN
7. FIND THE COVENANT COMPOUND
8. SEARCH FOR ANY CARAVAN SURVIVORS
9. RESCUE AMELIA STOCKTON
10. (OPTIONAL) WAIT FOR CHAMBERS TO KILL AMELIA
11. TALK WITH HONEST DAN
12. FIND OLD MAN STOCKTON
13. TALK WITH DR. CHAMBERS

**Locations to Explore**
– COVENANT (PAGE 290)
– COVENANT COMPOUND (SEWER) (PAGE 267-268)
– BUNKER HILL (PAGE 423)

## WELCOME TO COVENANT. YOU'LL NEVER LEAVE!

On your travels, you might stumble across the walled community of Covenant in the northern part of the Commonwealth. Speak to the guard outside, a gruff but amenable chap named Swanson, who requests you take a SAFE test before entering. Agree.

(Medium) Ask about the "SAFE" and "Undesirables" for more pertinent information.

Answer Swanson as you wish while you take the test. You're deemed worthy and may enter.

Hey, everything's great in here! The folks are so friendly! Well, except Honest Dan, who's got a face like a slapped arse. He's been hired to find Stockon's missing caravan. That's Old Man Stockton, who's living in Bunker Hill. Want to help with the investigation? Start by chatting to the villagers after speaking with Dan first.

(Medium) Ask for Bottlecaps up front.

## MAKING LEMONS OUT OF LEMONADE

Either before or after interrogating the villagers, leave Covenant and locate the remains of the caravan. Check the cooler for the following:

**DEEZER'S LEMONADE**

Return to Covenant. You can question any and all villagers, in any order you like. Talia McGovern and Penny Fitzgerald provide some subtle clues. Ask everyone about their problem with synths and about some secret compound as these conversation choices become available. Talk to Deezer until he offers you some free lemonade—the same lemonade that you found at the caravan! Be sure to exhaust your conversation choices with Honest Dan and ask about synths.

(Medium) Persuade or flatter either Talia or Penny to mention some kind of "compound" that the Covenant has nearby.

Back at Covenant, find the locked building. You can:

**– (ADVANCED) UNLOCK IT WITHOUT BEING SEEN.**

Or steal the Covenant House Keys from the table near Penny, in Doctor Patricia's office.

Search this dormitory for another set of keys and the following:

**COVENANT HOUSE KEYS**

**NOTE: JACOB'S PASSWORD**

Now enter the office building (to the rear, behind the tree) and access the office terminal on the desk. You can:

**– (MASTER) HACK THE TERMINAL.    – OR ACCESS IT USING JACOB'S PASSWORD.**

The information on the terminal is most illuminating. Talk to Dan about it if you wish before setting off to find the compound. On the way out of the compound, you may be stopped by Jacob Orden. Answer how you wish, playing dumb, being rude, or taking a bribe.

(Medium) Or asking to reach a compromise.

Exit the compound, and head west across the lake (or around the shore) to a sewer pipe entrance.

## COMPOUND FRACTURE

You may have tried convincing Jacob Orden to give you the Stockton caravan survivors peacefully. Or attempted other means. He may have sent word ahead so you can make your case to them. Meet up with the compound guards, Manny and Blythe. Look for a Compound Key on either of them. Use it to unlock the subsequent door. Explore (with or without Honest Dan) until you reach the laboratory of Dr. Roslyn Chambers.

(Various) Instead of violence, feel free to ask Manny to escort you to Doctor Chambers. The difficulty of this speech challenge depends on whether you succeeded in asking for a compromise with Jacob Orden, earlier.

Have a frank discussion with the Doctor. You can:

**– REJECT HER OFFER, OPTIONALLY KILL HER, USE HER TERMINAL TO FREE AMELIA FROM CELL BLOCK 1, AND SPEAK TO HONEST DAN FOR A REWARD.**

(Easy, Medium) But ask for a bigger cut of the reward. Or an even bigger cut!

**BOTTLECAPS (300-520)**

**– REJECT HER OFFER, OPTIONALLY KILL HER, USE HER TERMINAL TO FREE AMELIA FROM CELL BLOCK 1, AND THEN TRAVEL ALL THE WAY INTO CHARLESTON NEIGHBORHOOD, TO BUNKER HILL, AND FIND OLD MAN STOCKTON FOR A BIGGER REWARD.**

**BOTTLECAPS (300)**

**– OR ACCEPT HER OFFER, WAIT FOR HER TO DEAL WITH AMELIA, THEN END YOUR WORKING RELATIONSHIP WITH HONEST DAN (IF HE'S WITH YOU). SPEAK TO DOCTOR CHAMBERS FOR YOUR REWARD.**

**BOTTLECAPS (300)**

## Quest
# KID IN A FRIDGE

1. INVESTIGATE THE VOICE
2. TALK TO BILLY
3. TAKE BILLY HOME
4. TALK TO BULLET
5. SELL BILLY TO BULLET
6. OR TAKE CARE OF BILLY
7. TALK TO MATT PEABODY

**Locations to Explore**
- JAMAICA PLAIN (PAGE 379)
- UNIVERSITY POINT (PAGE 518)
- QUINCY RUINS (PAGE 387)
- THE FRIDGE (PAGE 397)
- THE PEABODY RESIDENCE (PAGE 390)

## TAKING A BULLET FOR BILLY PEABODY

While exploring west of Jamaica Plain and south of University Point, you hear a voice coming from a rusty fridge among some junk. Speak to it:

(Easy) Ask, "Who are you?" if you wish.

Shoot the door off its hinges and free Billy. Speak to Billy the Ghoul child, answering how you wish.

(Easy) Tell him his parents are dead if you wish. They aren't, though.

Agree to take him home, after clearing the area of Mirelurks. Find the Peabody residence south of Quincy ruins in the marsh.

At this point, you'll be approached by a Gunner named Bullet, who offers to buy Billy.

(Medium) You can succeed in some speech challenges and up the caps count for handing Billy over to Bullet.

Or you can refuse. Killing Bullet now avoids a thougher confrontation later.

### VAULT-TEC RECOMMENDS

LOOTING QUINCY RUINS

**POWER ARMOR (T-60)**
**GUNS AND BULLETS MAGAZINE**
**FAT MAN AND MINI NUKE**

The ruins of Quincy Township are brimming with both sought-after items and heavily armed Gunners. There's a sizable contingency throughout the rooftops and atop the ruined freeway. Are the prizes (including a sizable ammo and chem haul) worth the mayhem? You bet they are!

Enter and speak with Carol and Matt Peabody. Investigate the subsequent commotion. Locate Bullet (and his contingent of three Gunners) and speak to him. You can:

(Hard) Tell him the ghouls are gone.

- AGREE TO SELL THEM, AND LEAVE THE FAMILY TO THEIR FATE. SPEAK TO BULLET FOR A REWARD.
- AGREE TO SELL THEM, RETURN, AND TALK TO THE PEABODY FAMILY, THEN AGREE TO RESCUE BILLY AND KILL BULLET (PLUS HIS GUNNERS).
- TELL BULLET THE GHOULS ARE UNDER YOUR PROTECTION, DEFEAT GUNNER AND HIS COHORTS, AND SPEAK TO MATT PEABODY FOR A REWARD.

 **BOTTLECAPS (250)**

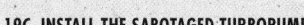

# Quest
# LAST VOYAGE OF THE USS CONSTITUTION

## Locations to Explore

1. MEET THE CAPTAIN
2. (OPTIONAL) FIRE THE CANNONS
3. REPULSE SCAVENGER ATTACK
4. TALK WITH THE BOSUN
5. (OPTIONAL) GRAB POWER CABLES
6. REPAIR OR REPLACE POWER CABLES (3)
7. REPAIR OR BUY A REPLACEMENT POWER RELAY COIL
8. TALK WITH THE NAVIGATOR
9. RECOVER THE GUIDANCE CHIP
10. INSTALL THE POWER RELAY COIL

11. TALK WITH THE BOSUN
12. INSTALL THE GUIDANCE CHIP
13. TALK WITH THE NAVIGATOR
14. REPAIR OR REPLACE POSEIDON RADAR TRANSMITTER
15. INSTALL THE POSEIDON RADAR TRANSMITTER
16. TALK WITH THE NAVIGATOR
17. TALK WITH IRONSIDES
18. FIND FLL3 TURBOPUMP BEARINGS
19A. INSTALL TURBOPUMP BEARINGS
19B. (OPTIONAL) SABOTAGE TURBOPUMP WITH MANDY

19C. INSTALL THE SABOTAGED TURBOPUMP
20. RETURN TO IRONSIDES
21A. DEFEND THE USS CONSTITUTION
21B. RETURN TO IRONSIDES
22A. FIRE UP AUXILIARY POWER
22B. TALK TO MANDY
23A. DEFEAT IRONSIDES
23B. DEFEAT THE SCAVENGERS

## REQUESTING PERMISSION TO COME ABOARD

While exploring the Charleston Neighborhood, you may be stopped by Lookout, a Mr. Handy robot at the foot of an ancient seafaring vessel called the USS Constitution, now embedded in buildings overlooking Boston Harbor. Locate the hull door in the ruined building the ship is sitting on, and work your way up through the interior to the exterior main deck.

Speak to Ironsides. Agree to help him assist in repairing his vessel.

 (Easy) Ask for a reward up-front for your troubles.

Scurvy dogs from below! The ship is under attack from Scavengers. You must defend it. You can:

– PREP THE STREETS BELOW WITH TRAPS BEFORE BOARDING THE VESSEL.
– FIRE THE CANNONS BY COMPLETING THE CIRCUIT BREAKER AND SOFTENING THE TARGETS BELOW.
– ATTACK WITH RANGED OR SNIPER WEAPONS FROM THE DECK.
– USE THE AFT ROWBOAT TO QUICKLY DESCEND AND ASCEND, AND CHARGE AT THE FOES. OR SIMPLY DROP DOWN IF YOU HAVE MORE ROBUST ARMOR ON.

After the battle, speak to either the Bosun, the Navigator, or both. The next few objectives can be completed in either order.

## CHOSEN BY THE BOSUN

Head below deck and talk to the Bosun. You have three power cable wiring boxes to fix. You can:

– FIND A METAL BOX (BELOW DECK) WITH THREE POWER CABLES IN IT, AND USE THEM TO REPAIR THE CABLES.

 **POWER CABLES**

(Jury Rig, Intelligence 3+) Salvage the replacement power cables without needing the power cables from the metal box. Then return to Bosun; he has another job for you (regarding the Power Relay Coil objective).

## THE CHIPS ARE DOWN

Head up on deck and speak to Mr. Navigator. He requires you to obtain a guidance chip from some Scavengers and requests you don't use force. But that's up to you. Now go shopping.

Visit Mandy Stiles and her scavenger sidekick Davies at her store/hideout, close to the ship. Answer her how you wish. You can:

- AGREE TO WORK WITH HER TO BRING DOWN IRONSIDES AND HIS CREW. THIS IS RECOMMENDED, AS YOU CAN ALWAYS CHANGE YOUR MIND LATER, AND MANDY WON'T BE HOSTILE. TAKE THE GUIDANCE CHIP.
- AGREE TO WORK WITH IRONSIDES. THIS IS ONLY RECOMMENDED IF YOU JUST WANT TO HELP THE SHIP'S CREW. KILL EVERYONE AND TAKE THE GUIDANCE CHIP.
- IGNORE HER, SNEAK INTO THE RUINED BUILDING BEHIND HER, AND STEAL THE GUIDANCE CHIP FROM THE CABINET. IF YOU'RE SPOTTED, MANDY AND THE SCAVENGERS TURN HOSTILE.

 **NX-42 GUIDANCE CHIP**

While you're on shore leave, you should also visit Bunker Hill and purchase a power relay coil from Deb, if you don't want to repair it on the ship.

 **POWER RELAY COIL**

Return to the ship and head below deck. Access the power relay. You can:

- INSTALL THE POWER RELAY COIL YOU ACQUIRED.
- (REPAIR, INTELLIGENCE 5+) REPAIR THE DAMAGED COIL WITHOUT NEEDING TO FIND A NEW ONE.

Then talk with the Bosun and conclude his tasks.

Head to the deck and activate the Core Guidance System. Speak to Mr. Navigator, who rewards you and gives you another job.

 **BOTTLECAPS (250): INSTALLING GUIDANCE CHIP**

## GETTING GUIDANCE

Mr. Navigator requires a radar transmitter. You can repair the one on the ship or find a new one from a random location, such as the Poseidon Energy Turbine #18-F. Locate the steamer trunk at the location and obtain the following:

 **POSEIDON RADAR TRANSMITTER**

Return to the ship and head on deck to the guidance radar and begin fiddling with it. If you have the best Repair skill, you can fix this. Otherwise, install the new Poseidon Radar Transmitter.

Report in to Mr. Navigator for a reward; then you're directed to talk to the captain.

 **BOTTLECAPS (250): INSTALLING POSEIDON RADAR TRANSMITTER**

## GETTING YOUR BEARINGS

Ironsides needs one last component to repair the USS Constitution: turbopump bearings. Find them at a nearby factory. After that, maybe he can tell you what the hell he's up to. He gives you a key to enter his cabin to install the device.

 **CAPTAIN'S QUARTERS KEY**

## VAULT-TEC RECOMMENDS

LOOTING THE USS CONSTITUTION

 **U.S. COVERT OPERATIONAL MANUAL**
Now that you can enter the captain's cabin inside the hull, purloin whatever scattered items you wish, including some quality covert reading material.

Travel to the indicated (random) location; it is always one with a steamer trunk–sized crate to open. Rummage around inside after abating any immediate threats and grab the following:

 **FLL3 TURBOPUMP BEARINGS**

## OPTIONAL: LOSING YOUR BEARINGS

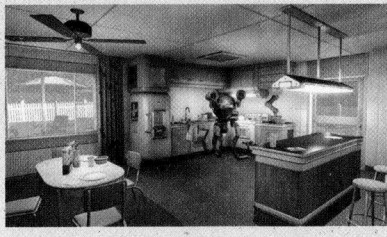

At this point, you have one of two plans to commit to:

- PLAN A: RETURN TO THE SHIP AND INSTALL THE TURBOPUMP BEARINGS AS IRONSIDES REQUESTED. THIS OCCURS WHETHER YOU AGREED TO SIDE WITH THE SCAVENGERS OR NOT.
- PLAN B: STOP OFF AT MANDY'S LOCATION, SABOTAGE THE TURBOPUMP FIRST, AND THEN INSTALL IT. THIS IS ONLY AVAILABLE IF YOU SIDED WITH THE SCAVENGERS EARLIER AND KEPT YOUR WORD TO MANDY.

Return to Ironsides and speak to him about his next harebrained scheme. At this point, there are two possible conclusions: Plan A and B. You receive the following reward for installing the Turbopump:

 BOTTLECAPS (500)

## PLAN A: SETTING SAIL!

Before the arguably insane Ironsides can start his plan, you have to fend off a last-ditch attack from the Scavengers.

Fend them off, optionally using the cannons, previously laid traps, and more devastating weapons in your arsenal—if Ironsides dies, the quest fails.

After the Scavengers are dead, speak to Ironsides, who grants you the following and has one last request: To fire up the auxiliary power.

  UNIQUE WEAPON: BROADSIDER

 BOTTLECAPS (1,500)

Leave the ship and ascend the ruins of the building the Scavengers attacked from, south of the street. Flip the circuit breaker and watch the voyage of the ship. Afterwards, if you've watched where the ship ended up, you can visit the new location and have another chat with Captain Ironsides, and receive a special Charisma-improving Lieutenant's Hat, and the use of the Captain's quarters.

 LIEUTENANT'S HAT (AND CAPTAIN'S QUARTERS)

## PLAN B: ENGINE FAIL!

Did you sabotage the USS Constitution's rockets? Now Ironsides needs more power before everything goes to hell. You should check in with Mandy Stiles before setting things in motion, and agree to her request to slay Ironsides.

Ascend the ruins of the building the Scavengers attacked from, south of the street. Flip the circuit breaker and watch the engines explode. Board the ship and defeat Ironsides and any other crew members you wish. Then return to Mandy, who promptly betrays you. Kill her and all other Scavengers, and loot the salvage for yourself, as your disastrous decisions finally catch up with you.

CAPTAIN IRONSIDE'S HAT

# Quest
# LONG ROAD AHEAD

1. BRING MACCREADY TO THE MASS PIKE INTERCHANGE
2. KILL WINLOCK
3. KILL BARNES
4. SPEAK TO MACCREADY
5. CONTINUE TRAVELING WITH MACCREADY
6. BRING MACCREADY TO MED-TEK RESEARCH
7. ENTER MED-TEK RESEARCH
8. LOCATE THE EXECUTIVE TERMINAL
9. OVERRIDE CONTAINMENT LOCKDOWN
10. ENTER MED-TEK SUB-LEVEL
11. RETRIEVE CURE FOR MACCREADY
12. SPEAK TO MACCREADY
13. BRING CURE TO DAISY IN GOODNEIGHBOR

**Locations to Explore**

- FINANCIAL DISTRICT (NEIGHBORHOOD) (PAGE 476)
- GOODNEIGHBOR (PAGE 483)
- THE THIRD RAIL (PAGE 485)
- MASS PIKE INTERCHANGE (PAGE 317)
- MED-TEK RESEARCH (PAGE 288)
- DAISY'S DISCOUNT (PAGE 484)

## MACCREADY AT THE READY

After visiting Goodneighbor, you hired MacCready despite a verbal altercation with Winlock and Barnes in the VIP room of the Third Rail.

(Easy) When hiring him, knock his price down from 250 to 200 caps.

After some exploration (and numerous talks that you initiate), MacCready asks you to bring him to the Mass Pike Interchange to hunt down and kill the two Gunners that were threatening him in Goodneighbor.

**COMPANION: MACCREADY**

# HELPFUL HINT
## from Vault Boy!

**Did You Know?**

MACCREADY SEEMS A BIT ROUGH AROUND THE EDGES, BUT HE'S SURE HELPFUL IN A FIGHT! HE'LL NEED TO BE WITH THE NUMBER OF GUNNERS HE HAS VEXED. REMEMBER IF YOU WANT A DEEPER FRIENDSHIP WITH HIM, YOU NEED TO MAKE DECISIONS HE SEES AS POSITIVE. THE COMPANIONS SECTION OF THIS GUIDE (PAGE 29) HAS ADVICE ON THIS.

MacCready finally feels ready to hunt down the Gunners. Travel to the Mass Pike Interchange (west and slightly north of Greater Boston), and locate the lift slightly north of the world map marker.

Then wade through the Gunners' camp, massacring anyone named Winlock or Barnes and anyone else in your way.

Afterward, you must continue to make decisions that MacCready deems positive. Continue this until he's ready to speak again. He tells you about his son.

## VAULT-TEC RECOMMENDS

LOOTING MASS PIKE INTERCHANGE

**GROGNAK THE BARBARIAN POWER ARMOR (LEVELED)**

While you're up here, quickly scout the Gunners' base, especially as they're tinkering with some Power Armor that you can take. Don't forget a Fusion Core and copy of Grognak the Barbarian. To the victor goes the spoils!

## PREVENTATIVE MEASURES

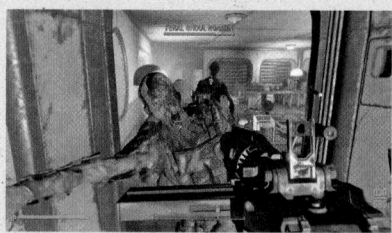

MacCready confided in you that his son is extremely ill and needs a cure that can only be found within a place called Med-Tek Research. The place is close to Malden Township, in the northern part of the Commonwealth.

Enter the facility and fill any Feral Ghouls with lead. The structure is in partial ruins and under a containment alert, but accessing the executive terminal on the upper floor and using a scrap of paper that MacCready gives you shuts down the alarm.

Access the airlock terminal and open it, allowing you to reach an elevator down deeper into the facility. There are still gormless feral corpses to destroy.

Locate the Med-Tek Lab Terminal to open the lab doors. Pick up the vial of "Prevent" from the central lab work surface.

**PREVENT**

## VAULT-TEC RECOMMENDS

### LOOTING MED-TEK RESEARCH

**MASSACHUSETTS SURGICAL JOURNAL**
**NUKA CHERRY**

Even though you're here for some antidote, MacCready won't mind if you make a thorough search for a good haul of ammo, a thirst-quenching Nuka Cherry, and some fascinating medical reading.

With the antidote for MacCready's son in hand, travel to Goodneighbor and visit Daisy's Discounts, where MacCready hands over the serum to Daisy so she can send it on to his son. Your help does not go unnoticed; now continue to explore with MacCready until you gain enough affinity to obtain his perk. See the Companions section of the STAT Chapter for more information (page 29).

*Quest*

## THE SECRET OF CABOT HOUSE: SPECIAL DELIVERY

1. TALK TO JACK CABOT
2. TALK TO EDWARD
3. TALK TO GUARD CAPTAIN
4. RECOVER PACKAGE
5. RETURN SERUM TO CABOT HOUSE

**Locations to Explore**
- BEACON HILL (NEIGHBORHOOD) (PAGE 460)
- CABOT HOUSE (PAGE 462)
- PARSONS STATE INSANE ASYLUM (PAGE 276)
- PARSONS CREAMERY (PAGE 276)

## SEARCHERS AFTER HORROR HAUNT STRANGE, FAR PLACES

While in Diamond City Market, visit the Dugout Inn and speak to a friendly Ghoul named Edward Deegan. He has some work for you to agree to, as well as the name of the man who's hiring—Jack Cabot.

(Medium) Ask about a reward, too. If you wish.

## HELPFUL HINT
*from Vault Boy!*

**Did You Know?**

THAT EDWARD DEEGAN GETS AROUND TOWN. HE'S BEEN SPOTTED IN COLONIAL TAPHOUSE, DUGOUT INN (DIAMOND CITY MARKET), THE THIRD RAIL (GOODNEIGHBOR), AND THE MARKET IN BUNKER HILL. BUT HE DOESN'T APPEAR UNTIL:
- YOU REACH LEVEL 10, AND
- YOU ATTACK THE GUARDS AFTER VISITING PARSONS STATE INSANE ASYLUM.

Mosey on over to the Beacon Hill Neighborhood in northeast Boston and locate the impressively intact Cabot House.

Activate the intercom. Mention Jack Cabot by name and you're let in and introductions are made. Feel free to ask any questions before agreeing to your first mission. You receive a key allowing free passage to and from this residence.

**CABOT HOUSE KEY**

You're supposed to recover a missing "package." Edward suggested that the guard captain at Parsons State Insane Asylum may know where to start looking for it. Travel roughly north into the Commonwealth, to the ominous-looking structure.

Meet Maria the guard captain at the main entrance door. Mention Edward sent you and you're given the location of some Raiders at the adjacent creamery. Head there and remove the Raider marked on your Pip-Boy. They are carrying an item most interesting:

**MYSTERIOUS SERUM**

Return to Cabot House and chat to Edward. You can:

(Easy) Tell him the serum is all gone or you didn't find any.

**– OR HAND THE SERUM OVER.**

You receive a reward and a bonus if you hand over the serum.

 **BOTTLECAPS (100)**

 **BOTTLECAPS (BONUS) (50)**

*Quest*
## THE SECRET OF CABOT HOUSE: EMOGENE TAKES A LOVER

1. TALK TO EDWARD
2. FIND EMOGENE CABOT
3. (OPTIONAL) ASK AROUND THE THIRD RAIL ABOUT EMOGENE
4. RETURN TO CABOT HOUSE
5. TALK TO JACK

**Locations to Explore**
- FINANCIAL DISTRICT (NEIGHBORHOOD) (PAGE 476)
- GOODNEIGHBOR: THE THIRD RAIL (PAGE 483)
- ESPLANADE (NEIGHBORHOOD) (PAGE 446)
- CHARLES VIEW AMPHITHEATER (PAGE 447)

### PRELUDE: A VAIN PRESENCE ON THE TERRAQUEOUS GLOBE

Back at the Cabot House, Jack's aged mother Wilhelmina makes an appearance, worried about her daughter, Emogene. Edward reckons she liked to hang out at the Third Rail in Goodneighbor.

Head inside the Third Rail. Speak to Whitechapel Charlie at the bar, asking about Emogene. He directs you to Magnolia. Ask her, and she brings in her friend Ham to confirm Emogene's whereabouts; she's taken up with a cult leader named Brother Thomas.

The cult operates out of the Charles View Amphitheater. Visit this place and speak with Brother Thomas.

He evades all of your questions. You can:

- JOIN THE PILLARS (HIS CULT), SHEDDING ALL OF YOUR CLOTHING AND EQUIPMENT AND GIVING IT TO HIM. PERHAPS NOT THE MOST TACTICALLY SAVVY OF PLANS.
- (ADVANCED) REFUSE TO JOIN HIS CULT. THEN SNEAK INTO HIS OFFICE AND OPEN THE LOCKED DOOR.
- REFUSE TO JOIN HIS CULT. THEN SNEAK BEHIND AND PICKPOCKET THE AMPHITHEATER KEY; UNLOCK THE DOOR IN THE SIDE OFFICE.
- OR GUN DOWN BROTHER THOMAS AND HIS CULTISTS. SEARCH HIS CORPSE FOR AN AMPHITHEATER KEY. USE IT ON THE DOOR IN HIS SIDE OFFICE.

 You have several chances to ask about Emogene, and some additional speech challenges; you can Bribe, Threaten, or Persuade Brother Thomas into revealing more about Emogene. Succeed, and he unlocks the door. Fail, and he refuses to let you see her (or attacks if you've threatened him).

Behind the locked door is Emogene Cabot. She knows why you're here. Speak with her, and she agrees to return.

 (Easy, Medium) Comment on her age and the serum's effects. Or tell her she's ungrateful.

Back at the Cabot House, tell Jack you've found Emogene. The joy is short-lived, however; there's trouble at the asylum.

 **BOTTLECAPS (BONUS) (200)**

# Quest
# THE SECRET OF CABOT HOUSE

1. MEET JACK OUTSIDE PARSONS STATE INSANE ASYLUM
2. HELP JACK REACH HIS OFFICE
3. HELP JACK REACH THE BASEMENT
4. STOP THE RAIDERS FROM FREEING LORENZO CABOT
5. KILL OR FREE LORENZO CABOT
6A. TALK TO JACK CABOT
6B. MISCELLANEOUS: TALK TO JACK CABOT ABOUT THE ARTIFACT
7A. TALK TO LORENZO CABOT
7B. RETURN TO CABOT HOUSE
8A. KILL THE CABOTS
8B. KILL LORENZO CABOT
9A. TALK TO JACK CABOT
9B. TALK TO LORENZO CABOT

**Locations to Explore**
– PARSONS STATE INSANE ASYLUM (PAGE 276)

## PAST, PRESENT, FUTURE—ALL ARE ONE

There's been some kind of attack on Jack's facility at the Parsons State Insane Asylum. You and Jack need to deal with it. After meeting him outside the main entrance, you realize Raiders have overrun the facility. Battle through the administration rooms, following Jack and removing Raider threats. After a loop upstairs and down, unchain the door and enter Jack's office.

Edward has shut down the elevator to the lower levels, but the Raiders have still managed to infiltrate the basement. Jack certainly isn't happy about that. Push out into the courtyard, up the scaffolding, and into the main asylum.

The place is in shambles. Locate the section of fallen floor and descend. Work your way to a hole behind the wallpaper wall in the southeast corner, and rampage through the cell block. Drop down the hole in the cell to a sublevel that leads to an elevator to the basement.

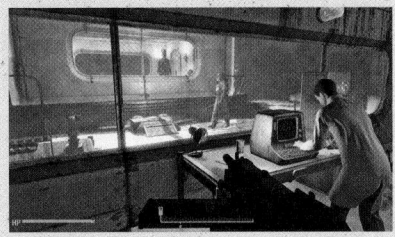

Follow Jack into a strange laboratory and listen to his instructions. There's a Cabot named Lorenzo here, and Raiders are trying to free him. Apparently, that's not a great idea. Enter the series of doors Jack opens, and cut down the Raiders, including a tough old boot named Lefty. Access the four Abremalin Generators on each of the walls, and set two of them to manual override. Lorenzo's voice seems more forceful and persuasive now: He's hoping you'll free him. What a conundrum!

## VAULT-TEC RECOMMENDS

## PLAN A: PUTTING LORENZO TO BED

Lorenzo isn't to be trusted, so flip the remaining Abremalin Generators to manual override, and then speak with Jack. He's very pleased you saw sense, thanks you with a Caps reward, and tells you to head back to Cabot House in a week; he might have something else for you. One week later, visit Jack, and he hands you a contraption called Lorenzo's Artifact Gun. This weapon is only awarded if you've been consistently polite to Jack throughout this quest.

**BOTTLECAPS (APPROX. 200)**

**UNIQUE WEAPON: LORENZO'S ARTIFACT GUN**

## PLAN B: WAKING LORENZO UP

That Lorenzo character sure is charismatic, isn't he? Why not release him from his quarters? Opening the door doesn't win you any favors from Jack Cabot. Lorenzo doesn't need any help escaping and lets you know he's off to Beacon Hill for a spot of house cleaning. You can:

– LET THE CABOT FAMILY KNOW THEY HAVE A GUEST COMING AND HELP THEM WITH THEIR PREDICAMENT. AFTER THE DUST HAS SETTLED, JACK SAYS HE HAS SOMETHING FOR YOU, BUT YOU'LL HAVE TO COME BACK FOR IT IN A WEEK. RETURN THEN, AND HE HANDS YOU HIS "GAMMA GUN."

**UNIQUE WEAPON: LORENZO'S ARTIFACT GUN**

– OR YOU CAN ENTER CABOT HOUSE WITH LORENZO AND HELP HIM WITH HIS HOUSE CLEANING. AFTERWARD, HE'S THANKFUL FOR YOUR HELP AND GRANTS YOU A VIAL OF THE SERUM MADE FROM HIS BLOOD.

**MYSTERIOUS SERUM**

DATA

QUESTS

## Quest
# THE SILVER SHROUD

1. TALK WITH KENT CONNOLLY
2. GET THE SILVER SHROUD COSTUME
3. GIVE KENT THE SILVER SHROUD COSTUME
4. TALK WITH KENT
5. LISTEN TO SILVER SHROUD STATION IN GOODNEIGHBOR
6. KILL WAYNE DELANCY
7. PUT CALLING CARD ON WAYNE'S BODY
8. DEAL WITH AJ
9. PUT CALLING CARD ON AJ'S BODY
10. TALK WITH WHITECHAPEL CHARLIE

11. KILL KENDRA
12. PUT CALLING CARD ON KENDRA'S BODY
13. LISTEN TO SILVER SHROUD STATION IN GOODNEIGHBOR
14. (OPTIONAL) ASSASSINATE SHELLY TILLER
15. (OPTIONAL) COLLECT ASSASSINATION PAYMENT
16. MEET WITH HANCOCK AS THE SHROUD
17. KILL SMILING KATE
18. KILL NORTHY
19. SEARCH BODY FOR CLUES
20. FIND KENT
21. LISTEN TO SILVER SHROUD STATION

22. KILL SHINJIN
23. (OPTIONAL) SAVE KENT CONNOLLY
24. TALK WITH KENT
25. MEET WITH HANCOCK AS THE SHROUD

### Locations to Explore

## KENT CONNOLLY: SILVER SHROUD SUPERFAN

There's all sorts of folks to meet in Goodneighbor. Over in the Memory Den, for example, is a friendly Ghoul called Kent Connolly. Obsessed isn't a strong enough word to describe how he feels about the Hubris Comics superhero, the Silver Shroud. In fact, he wants to play caped crusader, though he's missing the actual costume. The one in Hubris Comics that you're going to get for him.

 (Easy) Ask for payment.

Head on over to Hubris Comics (to the west, close to Boston Common), and work your way up the interior of the building. The place is overrun with ferals and features some open-air flooring to fall through if you aren't careful. Climb to the top-floor recording studio. Dash and grab the costume. Flee via the roof ladder or descend back down.

 **SILVER SHROUD COSTUME**

 **SILVER SHROUD HAT**

## VAULT-TEC RECOMMENDS

LOOTING HUBRIS COMICS

**ASTOUNDINGLY AWESOME TALES**
**UNSTOPPABLES**
**GROGNAK'S AXE**

You'd expect some graphic novels at a comic store, and you're not disappointed; there are two (and a load more burned beyond recognition). Wait, isn't that a replica Grognak's Axe in the display cabinet? No way! Hold on, is that a Grognak Costume near the roof ladder? Awesome! And a signed Silver Shroud Photo too? What a haul!.

## THE SILVER SHROUD RISES AGAIN!

Return to Kent and you're given a reward. He's so excited about the costume, he has a slight change of plan: Kent's going to use his radio station like a police scanner. You're supposed to wear the costume, patrol Goodneighbor's streets, tune in, and fight crime. What could go wrong?

 (Medium) Request more caps for this ignominy.

 **BOTTLECAPS (125)**

 **SUBMACHINE GUN AND AMMO**

 **SILVER SHROUD CALLING CARDS**

The costume is optional, but tuning your Pip-Boy to Radio > Silver Shroud Radio is mandatory. Listen for Kent informing you of a problem citizen who needs a comeuppance:

- THERE'S WAYNE DELANCY, A LOWLIFE WHO MURDERED A MOTHER AND HER KID. KENT WANTS YOU TO DEAL OUT SOME SILVER SHROUD JUSTICE, THEN LEAVE A CALLING CARD ON HIS CORPSE. WAYNE IS IN THE ALLEY BEHIND HOTEL REXFORD. OBLIGE KENT, THEN LISTEN FOR FURTHER RADIO BULLETINS.
- THERE'S AJ, A CHEM DEALER WHO HAS BEEN PEDDLING HIS GARBAGE TO KIDS. SO KENT WANTS THE SILVER SHROUD TO STRIKE AGAIN. AND LEAVE ANOTHER CALLING CARD. FIND HIM IN AN ALLEYWAY IN FRONT OF BOBBI'S HOUSE, BETWEEN THE TWO WAREHOUSES. YOU CAN:
- IGNORE HIM AND SKIP THESE TWO OBJECTIVES.

(Easy, Medium) Bribe AJ for caps. Then more caps. Slay him afterward if you wish.

- SLAY HIM AND HIS BODYGUARDS. LEAVE A CALLING CARD ON HIS BODY. CONTINUE TO LISTEN FOR FURTHER RADIO BULLETINS.

So it sounds like you're targeting another psychopath— an assassin named Kendra. Whitechapel Charlie at the Third Rail (in Goodneighbor) can help you track her down. Costume optional. Chinwag with Whitechapel Charlie about your quarry:

(Easy) Ask specifically about Kendra.

- OR BRIBE CHARLIE FOR INFORMATION (60 CAPS).
- OR SPEAK AS THE SHROUD.

Whitechapel Charlie backs up Kent's tale about Kendra. She's at Water Street Apartments, close by in the ruins of the city. Enter Water Street Apartments. Remain on the lower levels, offing any Raiders. Pin Kendra in her room and drop her. Oh, what's this? A contract on her corpse?

CONTRACT: SHELLY TILLER

## (OPTIONAL) THE SILVER SHROUD GOES ROGUE: KILLER OF SHELLY TILLER

Though Kent won't be happy, you can optionally track Kendra's last target to the National Guard Training Facility. Beware of Feral Ghouls. Enter the recruitment office. Find Shelly and kill her. Then claim the bounty yourself. A tool case is located just west of the entrance to Goodneighbor and northeast of the Old Granary Burying Ground. Open it and claim the reward:

BOTTLECAPS (500)

## VAULT-TEC RECOMMENDS

LOOTING THE NATIONAL GUARD TRAINING YARD

POWER ARMOR (LEVELED)
Three suits of Power Armor and two Fusion Cores top the list of items you should grab before you leave. Of course, there's an automated Sentry Bot standing between you and a complete ransacking, so plan your hunt accordingly, and don't forget to check the cluster of cargo containers to the northwest.

## THE SILVER SHROUD: KILL ME, KATE

Kendra and her goons have been dispatched. It's back to Goodneighbor and Kent's radio station to learn what's next. Back in Goodneighbor, meet up with Mayor Hancock. Feel free to dress and act as the Silver Shroud when speaking with him. Agree to help rid the area of more scum.

(Medium) Ask for caps. Shooting scum is expensive.

Your next target is radioed in: Though Smiling Kate can't lose her grin, she can certainly be taken down a peg or two. Head north into Charleston Neighborhood, close to Bunker Hill. Beware of Sinjin's Gang (Raiders). Defeat all foes.

## THE SILVER SHROUD: NORTHY'S NOT WORTHY

Find Northy just south of Wattz Consumer Electronics in the Cambridge Neighborhood. Beware of his bodyguards (Raiders). Chase after Northy and slay him. Check his corpse and read the note you find.

**NOTE: FIND THE SILVER SHROUD**

## THE SILVER SHROUD: SINJIN'S LAST STAND

The local crime boss whose underlings you've been offing—Sinjin—is heading to Goodneighbor to pay a "special" visit to Kent. Alas, you're too late! Use the radio to find out where Kent's been taken: Milton General Hospital, south of the city. Bring your best combat gear and prepare for a protracted battle with Raiders. Work your way through the floors and elevators to a final elevator down.

> **HELPFUL HINT** *from Vault Boy!*  **Did You Know?**
>
> THAT MILTON GENERAL HOSPITAL SURE IS A MAZE! THANK GOODNESS VAULT-TEC HAS SUPPLIED THE MOST RECENT FLOOR PLANS FOR YOU TO LOOK OVER. NO TIME FOR MAPS? THEN MAKE SURE YOU'RE LOOKING FOR HOLES IN FLOORS AND CEILINGS AND AN ELEVATOR TO CALL.

LOOTING MILTON GENERAL HOSPITAL

 **NUKA CHERRY**

If you're hankering for some fizzy beverages, you've come to the right ruined hospital. As well as the usual random ammo, health, and chems, there's a couple of Quantums and three Nuka Cherries to slowly dissolve your teeth with.

Use V.A.T.S. and high-damage weaponry to remove Sinjin and the Raider named Avery to avoid a more depressing end to Kent's story. When you've mown down anyone not excited to see you, end this caper.

 (Hard) Or, you can end this with a tricky speech challenge to save Kent, which is actually much safer. "Kill me first" save's Kent's life. "Scare Sinjin's Men causes his men to flee, leading to some amusing hostage negotiations, though Kent doesn't usually survive.

If Kent is still alive, he offers to upgrade your armor at Levels 25, 35, and 45. Now conclude the quest by speaking to Hancock in Goodneighbor; he hands over a reward too—an impressive haul of caps.

 **KENT CONNOLLY: ARMOR UPGRADES**

 **BOTTLECAPS (750)**

## Quest
# VAULT 81 AND HOLE IN THE WALL

1. TALK TO OVERSEER MCNAMARA
2. DELIVER FUSION CORES TO OVERSEER MCNAMARA
3. MISCELLANEOUS: FOLLOW AUSTIN
4. MISCELLANEOUS: TALK TO DR. FORSYTHE
5. MISCELLANEOUS: SIT TO DONATE BLOOD

**Locations to Explore**
- VAULT 81 (PAGE 318)

### PART 1: VAULT 81

While traveling in the western Commonwealth, locate the Caravan Stop and entrance to Vault 81 and enter. Try to activate the vault door controls, and you're stopped by Officer Edwards and Overseer McNamara. You can:

 (Hard) Ask them to help a Vault Dweller. They let you in.

 Give them three Fusion Cores in return for letting you in.

> **HELPFUL HINT** *from Vault Boy!*  **Did You Know?**
>
> THREE FUSION CORES PROVIDE AN AWFUL LOT OF JUICE FOR YOUR POWER ARMOR! REMEMBER YOU CAN FIND TRADERS WITH FUSION CORES, OR CONSULT THE LOCATION GUIDE TO FLAG PERTINENT AREAS WHERE THESE ITEMS CAN BE SCAVENGED.

You're welcomed into Vault 81, which impressively seems to still be fully functioning. Speak to the Overseer, receiving payment for your Fusion Cores. You are now free to move about the vault, and Side Quest: Vault 81 concludes.

 **BOTTLECAPS (100)**

## MISCELLANEOUS: THE FRIENDLY FOLKS OF VAULT 81

 Say hello to Miranda, Neil, and Officer Edwards if you wish. Access the elevator to the atrium. At this point you are accosted by Austin, a child who offers to show you around the vault (Vault 81 Freeform Quest: Vault 81 Tour). You can:

- **ACCEPT OR REFUSE.**

 (Easy) Accept without paying him.

Complete this objective by following him to the end of his tour. If you break off the tour, the objective fails. During or after the tour, you can optionally meet the following Vault Dwellers (Location Quests):

- **CALVIN THE MAINTENANCE MAN. HE NEEDS TOOLS YOU SCAVENGE AND WILL PAY YOU FOR ANY YOU BRING BACK.**
- **ALEXIS AND HOLT COMBES WHO RUN THE DEPOT. SHE IS A TRADER.**
- **HORATIO: YOU CAN CHANGE YOUR APPEARANCE AT HIS BARBER'S SHOP.**
- **MARIA, WHO RUNS THE CAFETERIA. SHE IS A TRADER.**
- **KATY, THE TEACHER IN THE CLASSROOM. COMPLETE MISCELLANEOUS QUEST: SHORT STORIES FOR A COPY OF GROGNAK THE BARBARIAN.**
- **DR. PENSKE RUNS THE HYDROPONICS LAB. SHE ASKS YOU TO TASTE A MUTFRUIT FOR HER. ANSWER HOW YOU WISH. SHE NEEDS FERTILIZER YOU SCAVENGE AND WILL PAY YOU FOR ANY YOU BRING BACK.**
- **BOBBY AND TINA DELUCA ARE IN THE REACTOR AREA. BOBBY WILL BUY CHEMS OFF YOU. TINA WANTS BOBBY OFF THE JET AND BUFFOUT.**

## VAULT-TEC RECOMMENDS
LOOTING VAULT 81

 **TABOO TATTOOS MAGAZINE**
**GROGNAK THE BARBARIAN**

Though it's unwise to steal anything that isn't bolted down, as this doesn't ingratiate you with the inhabitants, there are a couple of items you should think about grabbing right now, including Taboo Tattoos over at Horatio's. A simple short story for the classroom of kids nets you a comic, too.

As you explore Vault 81, the dwellers start to request you go see Dr. Forsythe in the clinic. Ready for a syringe without a load of chems? Then agree to give blood.

 (Easy) For some caps.

You can also eavesdrop on the Vault Dwellers, listening to conversations through one-way windows, and learning about the original purpose of the Vault.

## HOLE IN THE WALL

 Leave Vault 81, explore for for a little while, beyond the rock walls of the entrance, then return to Vault 81. The situation seems a little more frantic; dwellers are talking about Austin's condition. Visit the clinic to witness a discussion between Forsythe, Penske, and Bobby about a newly discovered secret part of the vault.

Agree to help. Follow Bobby DeLuca until he opens a secret wall to a hidden part of Vault 81. Put on your best Molerat exterminating gear and enter Secret Vault 81. Though there are machine-gun turrets and a Protectron to worry about, your main threats are some specially bred Vault 81 Lab Molerats.

 Head steadily through the secret vault until you find the Vault 81 Secure Access Terminal. You can:

- **(EXPERT) HACK THIS TO UNLOCK THE DOOR.**
- **LOCATE A HOLOTAPE FROM THE LAB CHAMBER ON THIS LEVEL, AND USE THAT TO ACCESS THE TERMINAL AND UNLOCK THE DOOR.**

Once inside the inner laboratory area, you're greeted by the one remaining scientist in this part of the vault. After you abate all Molerat threats, Curie unlocks the door. When you explain what you're here for, she gives it to you.

 **VAULT 81 CURE**

## VAULT-TEC RECOMMENDS
LOOTING SECRET VAULT 81

 **BOBBLEHEAD: MEDICINE**
While you may be attracted to Curie's quarters by her accent alone, there's another reason to befriend this scientist; she's keeping a limited-edition Vault-Tec warm for you!

Ride up the elevator with Curie, returning to Dr. Forsythe. You can:

- **KEEP THE CURE.**
- **OR CONCLUDE THIS QUEST AND HAND OVER THE CURE, BUT SUFFER A PERMANENT -10 TO YOUR HEALTH. AUSTIN IS HEALED, A GRATEFUL DR. FORSYTHE REWARDS YOU WITH A UNIQUE WEAPON, AND OVERSEER MCNAMARA GIVES YOU A ROOM IN VAULT 81.**

 **UNIQUE WEAPON: SYRINGER RIFLE**

 **YOUR OWN PERSONAL VAULT QUARTERS**

 **COMPANION: CURIE**

# RANDOM ENCOUNTERS

## THE COMMONWEALTH: NOT AS DESOLATE AS FIRST POSTULATED

**A CHANCE ENCOUNTER IN THE COMMONWEALTH. ONE OF MANY.**

Vault-Tec simulations have gathered a vast number of probable encounters based on your location, quest choices, and even companion choices. These can occur almost anywhere, and are always at random. The image to the left is one example; a Brahmin trader you may meet on your travels. You may wish to check off an encounter once it occurs. The following types of encounters can occur:

### STATIC ENCOUNTERS

These usually occur in a specific area, which could be anywhere in the Commonwealth.

| ENCOUNTER | NOTES |
|---|---|
| Deceased Fellow | You chance upon a dead guy. Check his pockets for a note mentioning treasure in a [random] location. |
| Raiders versus Farmers | A farmer runs to ask for help as you witness a fracas. |
| Wounded Dog | Why not patch this dog up and name her? Later on, she might appear to help you. |
| Mole Rat Ambush | Whack those pesky mutations when they pop out of their holes. |
| Dead Meat | A dead Brahmin, Yao Guai, or other carcass you can loot. |
| Wild Pack of Dogs | During an exploration, you chance upon a resting pack of dogs. |
| Gene the Reluctant Dog Vendor | If you own a settlement with a workshop, you may chance upon this trader. Use your Charisma and he'll sell you a dog. |
| Super Mutants and Prisoner | A victorious raiding party of greenskins returns with a victim. Free the victim if you wish. |
| Deathclaws Duel | Two of these powerful beasts are battling. |
| Vicious Dogs and Farmer | Three vicious dogs are attacking a farmer ill-equipped to defend himself. |
| Traveling Vault Merchant | You meet a guard and merchant on their way to a vault. Speak, and the vault's location is revealed. |
| Raiders and the Pink Paste | A dead Raider or two have some strange paste on them. Apparently this came from Suffolk County Charter School. Why not visit there? |
| You've Got Crabs | Mirelurks occasionally scuttle around and ambush you. Time to crack a few shells. |
| The Postman | Despicable foes have slain this postman, who has letters you can read. Some reveal locations to explore. |
| Stingwing versus Radscorpion | Two examples of mutated wildlife aren't getting along. |
| Pickman's Prey | A pile of dead Raiders, evocatively staged, each marked with a strange calling card, and the location of Pickman Gallery. |
| Vertibird versus Raiders | If the Prydwen has arrived, and the Brotherhood of Steel are active, expect death to Raiders from above before the craft heads back to Boston Airport. |
| Vertibird Patrol Drop | If the Prydwen has arrived, and the Brotherhood of Steel are active, expect two Brotherhood of Steel soldiers, or a soldier and scribe, to be dropped off. |

| ENCOUNTER | NOTES |
|---|---|
| Super Mutant Raiding Party | Up to four greenskins are returning to a Super Mutant stronghold. Check the leader's corpse for a note. After you kill them, of course. |
| Roving Eyebot | A still-functioning Eyebot plays a verbal advertisement for job openings as the Cambridge Polymer Labs. Why not head there? |
| Unfriendly Deathclaws | Occasionally you stumble into the frighteningly sharp fangs and claws of a roaming Deathclaw. |
| The Return of Manta Man! | An amateurish superhero is seen fighting Mole Rats, or a variety of enemies. Usually badly. He's no Silver Shroud, though he only appears after you finish Side Quest: The Silver Shroud. |
| Jack Is Back | If you sided with Jack Cabot during Side Quest: The Secret of Cabot House, you'll find him with Edward Deegan and can sell him items he requires. |
| Lorenzo Is Undying | If you sided with Lorenzo Cabot during Side Quest: The Secret of Cabot House, you'll find him investigating dead Ghouls. How pleasant. |
| Vault 81 Dead Dweller | One example of how living underground extends your life is when you encounter a dead vault dweller with a note for Vault 81 and a mention of Doctor Penske. |
| Mutant Hound versus Yao Guai | Two brawling and sinewy animal mutations take a distinct dislike for one another. |
| Bloated Animal Corpse | A dead Radstag Doe, Yao Guai, or Brahmin is feeding a few Bloatflies, Bloodbugs, or Radroaches. Yuck. |
| Super Mutant versus Stingwings | Can a greenskin and his hound survive a nasty sting or two? You're about to find out. |
| Feral Ghoul Ambush | A dead farmer and Brahmin are decoys for a Feral Ghoul, who lies in wait to pounce on anyone investigating. |
| Resting Radstags | Two Radstags are snoozing in a wilderness location. Unless you arrive and make noise. |
| Eyebot Advertisement | An Eyebot still outputs prewar advertising. |
| Two Faces. One Synth | You stumble into two men with the same face. Each claims the other is a synth. Who do you believe? |

# FLUID ENCOUNTERS

The entities you may encounter are moving, and the location cannot be pinpointed. Expect a higher chance of these occurring if you stay on roads.

| ENCOUNTER | NOTES |
|---|---|
| Smiling Larry | Have you bought anything from this trader? His two guards look tough. But if you've built a Level 3 Weapons Store at one of your settlements, you can offer to have him come live at any of your workshop locations. |
| Mister Gutsy | A Mister Gutsy is on patrol, looking for Chinese infiltrators. Have you seen any? |
| Workshop Armor Vendor | Are your workshops impressive enough? If they aren't, hire this chap. If they are, just barter with him. But if you've built a Level 3 Armor Store at one of your settlements, you can offer to have him come live at any of your workshop locations. |
| Brotherhood of Steel versus Raiders | If the Prydwen has arrived, these two factions encounter each other. Diplomatic relations are strained to nonexistent. |
| Brotherhood of Steel versus Deathclaw | If the Prydwen has arrived, three Brotherhood of Steel scouts find themselves facing an apex predator. |
| The Gossiping Trader | Chance upon a trader who has some pertinent rumors regarding the some primary locations across the Commonwealth. |
| Super Mutants versus Raiders | These two factions are constantly battling for territory. Usually, though, the territory is a stronghold and not out in the open. |
| Deathclaw Hunting | My, that's a big-clawed, scaly beast you've inadvertently stumbled into. |
| The Brahmin Vendor | Do you need a Brahmin for your workshop settlement? Then you're in luck. |
| The Brahmin Farmer | A livestock farmer is making his way in the world. |
| Ness Encounter | You encounter a woman named Ness. For more information, consult Primary Location: Skylanes Flight 1981 (page 279). |
| Radstag Herd | Up to four of these majestic, mutated beasts can be witnessed. |
| "Preston Garvey" | If you finished Minutemen Quest: When Freedom Calls, some chancer appears asking for a donation to the Minutemen. Pay up, refuse, or confront him. |
| Feral Ghoul Pack | You see a pack of frothing ferals. You'd better get back because it'll be dark soon, and they mostly come at night. Mostly. |
| Sated Radscorpion | A mutated wildlife encounter with these vicious stingers. |
| Dogs versus Mole Rats | A pack of dogs chasing a Mole Rat. |
| Revenge of the Forged | Complete Location Quest: Out of the Fire and you may be attacked by the Forged. |
| Bobbi's Recruiter | You're stopped and asked to help out in Goodneighbor; there's a Ghoul named Bobbi who needs your help starting Side Quest: The Big Dig. |
| One Man and His Robot | Once Side Quest: The Big Dig is over, you may meet Mel again. |

| ENCOUNTER | NOTES |
|---|---|
| Swanson's Revenge | Did you complete Side Quest: Human Error? Then you may have angered Swanson, who turns up all hot under the collar. |
| Vault 81 Prisoner | A group of Raiders are holding a vault dweller hostage. Can you help, and find out the vault's location in the process? |
| Darla Goes Home | If you finished Main Quest: Unlikely Valentine and Darla isn't dead, you may see her heading home. |
| Heading to Trinity Tower | Super Mutants are taking a prisoner to their highest stronghold. Side Quest: Curtain Call now begins. |
| The Exile | If Brotherhood of Steel Quest: Duty or Dishonor is complete, you may see Clarke fleeing from a group of Feral Ghouls. They aren't so friendly now, are they? |
| Gruel's Recipes | Did you kill a strange Raider with a chef's hat on? Then check his corpse for some rare ingredients and recipes. |
| Escaped Synth | If the Institute is still active and Railroad Quest: Boston After Dark hasn't been completed, you spot a synth in Institute janitorial attire who requests the location of Bunker Hill. Provide this information if you've discovered this location, or ask for Caps. |
| Radstags versus Dogs | An interesting conundrum: Which animal will be victorious? |
| Super Mutants versus Mister Gutsy | Can the greenskins overpower the pride of RobCo Industries? |
| Kat and Gus | A child merchant named Kat and her impressively dangerous protector Sentry Bot Gus are wandering the landscape. Time to trade? |
| Predator's Lunch | Did you see that Yao Guai or Deathclaw chasing down that dog? Glad it wasn't you! |
| Radscorpion's Lunch | A Radscorpion deems a Raider to be the tastiest morsel around. |
| Stash, Lexa, and Simon | Did you meet the merchant Stash and her bodyguards? You might want to talk to Stash about Simon's chem addiction. A previous encounter with these folks must have been completed without you attacking or stealing. |
| Simon's Side | Simon gave in to his addiction; later you find he's sided with some Raiders. |
| Paranoid Scavengers | A group of Scavengers aren't that welcoming, though the note on the leader's corpse reveals a rethink in tactics. Too late now, though. |
| Wattz Electronics Protectron Barker | Have you heard about the bargains at Wattz Electronics? You will if you meet this Protectron. |
| Gunner Patrol | Two gunners and an Assaultron (or two Gunners and a leader clad in Power Armor) are patrolling the Commonwealth. |
| Brotherhood of Steel Patrol | If the Prydwen has arrived and the Brotherhood of Steel are active, you may encounter two soldiers and a scribe on patrol. If attacked, they call for backup. A Vertibird arrives and drops off two soldiers in Power Armor. Gulp! |

BOSTON BUGLE — Trumpeting Truth for Over 50 Years

DATA

QUESTS

215

## GENERAL ENCOUNTERS

You can find these encounters almost anywhere in the Commonwealth.

| ENCOUNTER | NOTES |
|---|---|
| The Locked Fridge | Someone is trying to open a locked fridge. Will they be successful? |
| The Hatch | A scavenger blows open the doors of a bomb shelter. Deal with him, then head inside and see what you find. |
| Feral Ghoul Ambush | A rusting car is as good a place as any for ferals to test their ambushing skills out on you. |
| Glowing Anomaly | A type of "glowing" creature is found near some radioactive barrels. |
| Thirsty Guy | A parched chap hopes you have water. Offer some if you're a kindhearted sort. |
| Poisoned Gal | An irradiated dame hopes you have some RadAway. Offer some if you're a kindhearted type. |
| Vertibird Pick-up | If this faction is active and the Prydwen has arrived, you watch a Brotherhood of Steel patrol get airlifted at the end of their patrol. A battle with Gunners may be occurring. Sometimes the Vertibird subsequently crashes. |
| The Minefield | A cluster of mines strewn about. Instead of crippling a leg, why not gather them up? |
| Atomcats Scavenger | A greaser from the Atomcats Garage is scavenging for parts and invites you to this location if you haven't been already. |
| Tire Fire | Someone's set some tires alight. That noxious cloud is only slightly more unpleasant than the regular air you're breathing. Get too close and fire burns. |
| Safe Landing | Did you find a locked safe lying in a small crater? Then unlock it! |

| ENCOUNTER | NOTES |
|---|---|
| Radioactive Barrels | A group of leaky barrels add to the already-insurmountable radiation leakage in the Commonwealth. |
| Giddyup Buttercup | A popular toy is found, along with a note from Arlen Glass, who left The Slog after Miscellaneous: Arlen Glass quest was completed. |
| Radio and Refuse Pile | Along with a toolbox and safe, a radio is broadcasting from a pile of trash. |
| Vault-Tec Van | If anyone knows the whereabouts of Larry, last seen heading to a Commonwealth Vault, please inform the Documentation Department. He has a note regarding the Vault on his person. |
| Scavenger Guard | Sometimes, items needed to complete Main Quest: The Molecular Level are guarded by a stationary Scavenger. |
| Deathclaw Mother | One of these giant predators is guarding a cluster of (delicious) eggs. |
| Brahmin Corpse and Mines | A few items are hidden close to a Brahmin corpse, with mines to dissuade the curious. |
| Gunners and Tank | Some Gunners are removing scrap from a tank. They aren't happy to see you. |
| Commonwealth Funeral | A group of settlers are burying a friend. |
| Mac's Bar | Mac is setting up a bar. Is this a strange place for a bar? You decide. |

## CAMPSITE ENCOUNTERS

Expect these encounters at any campfires you might stumble upon. One example would be just east of Concord, in the small parking lot.

| ENCOUNTER | NOTES |
|---|---|
| Deserted Campsite | A small camp with a few beds and containers to loot. There's a chance the Raiders who made this camp may return. Only occurs at night (20:00 to 06:00). |
| Dead Scavengers | A pair of Scavengers have succumbed to Bloodbug prodding. Loot the camp if you're able to finish off the insects. Only occurs at night (20:00 to 06:00). |
| Merchant of Dreth | An arms dealer named Dreth and her two guards occupy this camp. Buy any armaments you wish from her. |
| The Walking Wounded | A wandering doctor has finished treating a patient. |
| Time to Party | A bartender and friends ask you to join their camp party. Only occurs at night (20:00 to 06:00). |
| Chems Vendor | Need a little pick-me-up? A chem vendor can be found with just the wares you need. |
| Dirty Laundry | A Raider is boiling some attire to clean them. He's rather ill-prepared for combat. Only occurs at night (20:00 to 06:00). |
| Drug Overdose | Too many chems have killed these Scavengers. Now their corpses feed the Radroaches. Only occurs at night (20:00 to 06:00). |
| Daddy and Daughter | A father and daughter share a campsite. |
| That's Not a Sandwich | Two (vaguely idiotic) settlers argue over some food. |
| Synth Attack Aftermath | A camp of Scavengers is looking distinctly worse for wear after a recent synth massacre. |
| Synth Ambush I | Have you chanced upon an empty camp with a container? It may be a trap! This occurs once Main Quest: Hunter/Hunted is complete and the Institute are still active. |
| Synth Ambush II | Three settlers are in camp. Moments later, synths teleport in and a massacre begins. This occurs once Main Quest: Hunter/Hunted is complete and the Institute are still active. |
| Super Mutant Camp | A group of greenskins is camping out. Only occurs at night (20:00 to 06:00). |

| ENCOUNTER | NOTES |
|---|---|
| Mirelurk Bake | A group of Raiders is eating some delicious Mirelurk bake. Why not help yourself? |
| Exiled Scientists | Scientists Lawrence Higgs and Max Loken may be spotted at a campfire if you exiled them during Institute Quest: A House Divided. Only occurs at night (20:00 to 06:00). |
| Skinny Malone, All Alone | Did you keep this guy alive during Main Quest: Unlikely Valentine? Then you might see him at a campsite. Only occurs at night (20:00 to 06:00). |
| Sick Scavenger, Mystery Meat | An ill Scavenger mentions some bad meat he consumed. He took it from Longneck Lukowski's Cannery. Why not see what's going on there? |
| Rylee the Trader | Once you visit Longneck Lukowski's Cannery and meet Rylee, you can barter with her again at a camp. Only occurs at night (20:00 to 06:00). |
| Deserted Feral Camp | This camp looks devoid of human contact. This is technically correct, as you're subsequently ambushed by ferals. |
| Occupied Feral Camp | Two dead Scavengers and four feasting ferals. You probably know what happened here. |
| Vicious Dog Camp | A dead Raider and masterless dog are encountered. Down, boy. |
| Deserted Camp with Mines | Watch your step and disarm the mines scattered around this camp, or face a crippling injury. |
| Yao Guai Camp | A ferocious clawing beast has wandered into a Scavenger camp. The scavengers came off second best. |
| Raider Camp and Dogs | Vicious dogs are gnawing at a couple of camping Raiders. |
| Stash and Lexa's Camp | You witness the final encounter with these two traders if you encountered them previously. |
| Runaway Synth Camp | A group of settlers has discovered one of their own isn't as "fleshy" as they once thought. Quest: The Nuclear Option must not be completed. |

## ANIMOSITY ENCOUNTERS

These encounters occur anywhere and typically involve two factions or enemy types that have particularly strained or nonexistent diplomatic relations with one another.

| ENCOUNTER | NOTES |
|---|---|
| Super Mutants versus Ghouls | Sit back and watch infected bony fingernails scrape against overly large green hides. |
| Super Mutants versus Scavengers | A one-sided battle, with Super Mutants already victorious and moving back to a nearby stronghold. |
| Raiders versus Scavengers | Come for the fighting. Stay for the loot one of the Scavengers had collected. |
| Dogs versus Farmers | Only the dogs are hostile. |
| Scavengers versus Robots | Both groups are hostile if you barge in uninvited. |
| Minutemen versus [Other Faction] | Once you ally with the Minutemen, you may encounter a group of them defending a settlement from Brotherhood of Steel soldiers, Institute synths (who may use relaying to ambush), or one or more Institute Coursers. Help out your chosen faction. You must have been kicked out of the faction that is attacking. |
| Brotherhood of Steel versus [Other Faction] | Once you ally with the Brotherhood of Steel, you may encounter a group of them defending a settlement from Minutemen, Institute synths (who may use relaying to ambush), or one or more Institute Coursers. Help out your chosen faction. You must have been kicked out of the Institute if they are attacking. |
| Minutemen versus [enemy] | Once you ally with the Minutemen, expect to see them defending random locations in the Commonwealth. These small outposts may be attacked by Raiders or Gunners; lend them a hand if you can. |
| Brotherhood of Steel versus [Enemy] | Once you ally with the Brotherhood of Steel, expect to see them at a random location, attacked by Feral Ghouls or Super Mutants. |
| Institute Relay Ambush | If you've been kicked out of the Institute and the faction is still active, you may be attacked by teleporting synths as you near a location. |
| Vicious Dogs versus Bloodbugs | A human corpse serves as a rag doll being torn between dogs and bugs, both parties wishing to devour it. |
| Feral Ghouls versus Raiders | A group of wandering corpses do battle against the idiotic wastrels of the Commonwealth. |
| Active Sniper | Some lunatic with a sniper rifle enjoys shooting up the location you're entering. |
| Ricky Dalton and the Raiders | Once Railroad Quest: Tradecraft is complete, you may see him fighting off Raiders. |
| Gunners versus Children of the Atom | Feel free to watch both these enemy factions make (lightly irradiated) mincemeat of each other. |
| Gunners versus Behemoth or Mirelurk Queen | A trio of Gunners are making impressive inroads against one of the Commonwealth's true giants. |

## TREASURE HUNT ENCOUNTERS

These follow a similar pattern; you encounter a dead person with a note on their corpse. If you read the note, you're pointed in the direction of a (random) location, and a map marker appears to reveal where a steamer trunk is located.

| ENCOUNTER | REWARD |
|---|---|
| A dead Raider's note | Caps |
| A dead junkie's note | Chems |
| A dead Gunner's note | Gun and impressive mod |
| Three dead Scavengers | Scrap and junk. |
| A dead farmer's note | A synth with an impressively modded gun, scrap, and junk in a trunk. |
| Hadrian's note | This starts Miscellaneous Quest: Treasure of Jamaica Plain. |

## CHOKEPOINT ENCOUNTERS

Expect the following to occur in areas where you have limited maneuverability, such as a bridge crossing.

| ENCOUNTER | NOTES |
|---|---|
| None Shall Pass! | Three Raiders (or Gunners) are manning a choke point, demanding Caps for you to pass. Use your speech to reduce the amount (Easy to Hard); this can allow free passage if you're a good fast-talker. You're attacked if you leave without paying or if you attack them. If you have a Luck of 8 or more and fewer Caps than the Raiders demand, choose the "fake it" option and the Raiders take whatever Caps you have. |
| Mister Gutsy's Curfew | This robot demands you return to your home. A speech challenge allows you to convince the robot you're on military business, and you're let through. Attempt to pass and you're attacked. If you have a Luck of 7 or more, select the same questions for the robot multiple times until it explodes. |
| Raiders Accosting Farmers | Three Raiders are trying to extract a toll from some farmers. Help the farmers out if you wish. |
| Synth Relay Choke Point | If you've been kicked out of the Institute and the faction is still active, you may be attacked by teleporting synths (and sometimes a Courser) as you near a choke point. |
| Minutemen Defenses | A small group of Minutemen are defending a choke point, once you ally with this faction. |
| Brotherhood of Steel Defenses | A small contingent of Brotherhood soldiers is defending a choke point once the Prydwen arrives. How they react to you depends on how your alliance is going. |
| Synth Defenses | A small contingent of synths is defending a choke point once Institute Quest: Airship Down is complete. How they react to you depends on how your alliance is going. |
| Nervous Farmers | A group of farmers asks you to holster any weapon you're carrying. Comply and you can pass. If not, expect hostility. |
| Super Mutant Blockage | A couple of lumbering green mutants are preventing your progress. |
| Stash, Lexa, and Simon | A merchant and two bodyguards are found here, and bartering can occur. |
| Choke Point Mines | Disarm a set of mines at this location, or face a crippling injury. |
| Unconstitutional | If you completed Side Quest: Last Voyage of the U.S.S. Constitution, some disgruntled Scavengers are furious that you jumped their claim on the ship. |
| Bullet's Ambush | If you finished Side Quest: Kid in a Fridge and Bullet is still alive, he may jump you with a couple of cohorts. |

## COMPANION ENCOUNTERS

Do you have a particular companion by your side? Then expect the following to occur during your time with them.

| COMPANION | ENCOUNTER | NOTES |
|---|---|---|
| Strong | Hunting for Strong | You encounter Super Mutants who are looking for Strong once you complete Side Quest: Curtain Call. |
| MacCready | Gunners' Revenge | A few Gunners are looking for revenge once you slay the Gunner leaders during Side Quest: Long Road Ahead. |
| Nick Valentine | Profuse Thanks | After you're ambushed by Raiders, one realizes who Nick is and the situation turns remarkably less violent. Accept a small collection of items afterward. |
| Piper | One Tough Critic | You're stopped by a group of rough-looking types who are here on behalf of someone Piper wrote an unpleasant article about. They attack, thus proving Piper's journalistic integrity. |
| Preston Garvey | Preston's Friend | If Preston is your current companion, and you own four settlements, you may encounter an old friend of Preston's fighting some Raiders. If the chap survives, they reminisce. |
| Cait | Drug Runner Revenge | Apparently Cait owes some Raiders Caps for the Jet she bought. They are here to collect. Show them the error of this plan. |
| Hancock | Bar Room Buddy | Visit a bar at a settlement, and there's a chance Hancock recognizes an old friend. They converse. |

# WORKSHOPS

Workshops are powerful construction tools that allow you to build, scrap, and rearrange items within a specified area. Whether you create an idyllic utopia or a fortified stronghold, it all starts with a workshop.

## WORKSHOP SETTLEMENTS

Once you control a workshop, you control the settlement that holds it. Build farming communities to feed settlers and produce cooking ingredients. Build industrial complexes packed with salvage stations. Build stores to turn a humble settlement into productive and profitable center of commerce. Or, if you prefer, don't build anything. The choice is yours.

Open the Workshop menu to reveal a settlement's buildable area. This border represents the workshop's maximum reach. You can build and move items anywhere within this area. Each settlement also has a size limit, meaning that it can only accommodate so much construction.

### UNLOCKING WORKSHOPS

If a settlement is occupied by an enemy gang or dangerous creatures, you generally have to eliminate all threats before  you can access a workshop. When a workshop is located in an established settlement, you usually have two options: earn the right to use the workshop, or eliminate the current population and claim the workshop as your own. There are, of course, exceptions. Some workshops can only be used once you've completed certain quests. In rare cases, unlocking a workshop is as simple as walking up and activating it.

**HELPFUL HINT** *from Vault Boy!*   **Did You Know?**

#### ACTIONS HAVE CONSEQUENCES
ALLIED SETTLEMENTS (THOSE THAT START WITH AN EXISTING POPULATION) WILL REVOKE YOUR WORKSHOP PRIVILEGES IF THEY FEEL IT'S NECESSARY TO DO SO.

Most workshops share a standard set of features and options, but some offer limited functionality. In all cases, you can use a workshop to build new items or store unneeded gear. Junk items stored in a workshop are automatically applied to any crafting and construction projects within the settlement.

## AVAILABLE WORKSHOPS

| LOCATION | PREREQUISITE | NOTES |
|---|---|---|
| Abernathy Farm | Complete the quest "Returning the Favor." | Offers a large buildable area and plenty of dirt. |
| Boston Airport | Complete the quest "Shadow of Steel." | An unestablished settlement that can't support crops or artillery. |
| Bunker Hill | Complete the quest "The Battle of Bunker Hill." | Features several established structures and a variety of vendors. |
| Castle, the | Clear the area of hostiles. | Features a large structure, a radio transmitter, and a variety of useful items Plays a key role in several quests. |
| Coastal Cottage | Clear the area of hostiles. | An unestablished settlement. |
| County Crossing | Complete the offered radiant quest. | A simple settlement. |
| Covenant | Complete the quest "Human Error" or defeat the current residents. | A small but well-established settlement. The existing population includes some vendors. |
| Croup Manor | Clear the area of hostiles. | An unestablished settlement featuring a large three-story structure. |
| Egret Tours Marina | Placate or defeat Phyllis Daily. | Features multiple buildings, a large body of water, and numerous booby traps. |
| Finch Farm | Complete the quest "Out of the Fire." | A simple settlement. |
| Graygarden | Complete the quest "Troubled Waters." | Features an established robot population, high food production, and a vendor. |
| Greentop Nursery | Complete the offered radiant quest. | Features two large buildings and well-established crops. |
| Hangman's Alley | Clear the area of hostiles. | An enclosed settlement featuring several simple structures to modify or scrap. |
| Home Plate (Diamond City House) | Purchase a housing permit from Geneva in the Mayor's office (2000 Caps). | A personal space that offers limited workshop functionality. |
| Jamaica Plain | Clear the area of hostiles. | Features a two-story building and a sizable parking lot. |
| Kingsport Lighthouse | Clear the area of hostiles. | Features multiple large structures, open water, and uneven terrain. |
| Murkwater Construction Site | Clear the area of hostiles. | An unestablished settlement with a large body of water. |
| Nordhagen Beach | Complete the offered radiant quest. | A simple settlement with plenty of dirt and access to open water. |
| Oberland Station | Complete the offered radiant quest. | A simple settlement featuring a small two-story structure and established crops. |
| Outpost Zimonja | Clear the area of hostiles. | A small settlement with some basic structures and an established power grid. |
| Red Rocket Truck Stop | — | Features a well-equipped service station. |
| Sanctuary Hills | — | Offers several established structures, a variety of workstations, access to open water, and a very large buildable area. |
| Slog, the | Complete the offered radiant quest. | Contains a sizable Ghoul population and a variety of established crops. |
| Somerville Place | Complete the offered radiant quest. | A simple settlement featuring established crops and a large buildable area. |
| Spectacle Island | Clear the area of hostiles. | Features multiple structures and an established power grid within a massive buildable area. Activate the circuit breakers to reveal hidden enemies. |
| Starlight Drive-in | Clear the area of hostiles. | Features multiple structures within a very large buildable area. |
| Sunshine Tidings Co-op | Clear the area of hostiles. | Offers several structures, a large buildable area, and a unique robot resident. |
| Taffington Boathouse | Clear the area of hostiles. | Features two established structures and access to open water. |
| Tenpines Bluff | Complete the offered radiant quest. | A simple settlement. |
| Warwick Homestead | Complete the offered radiant quest. | Offers multiple structures and a variety of crops within a large buildable area. |

Some settlements are located along caravan trade routes. You don't need to control a settlement to barter with a visiting trader, but it does allow you to create some safe, convenient stops along their designated routes.

### VISITED SETTLEMENTS

| SETTLEMENT | TRADER |
|---|---|
| County Crossing | Doc Weathers |
| Covenant | Lucas Miller |
| Finch Farm | Doc Weathers |
| Greentop Nursery | Lucas Miller |
| Oberland Station | Trashcan Carla |
| Sanctuary Hills | Trashcan Carla |
| Slog, the | Doc Weathers |
| Somerville Place | Trashcan Carla |
| Tenpines Bluff | Lucas Miller |
| Warwick Homestead | Cricket |

## NOTEWORTHY SETTLEMENTS

Every settlement offers something of value, but there are some particularly interesting locations. As you expand your influence in the Commonwealth, consider the benefits and challenges offered by these noteworthy settlements.

### Abernathy Farm

Abernathy Farm is one of your better options for large-scale food production. This family-run settlement features an impressive collection of tato plants, a small patch of melons, and plenty of room to expand. Most importantly, it's located in the comparatively safe area surrounding Sanctuary Hills. It gets its share of unwanted visitors, of course, but Abernathy Farm is far away from the more powerful enemies you'll encounter on the other side of the Commonwealth.

Some fresh crops and a few new settlers can dramatically increase food production, and the buildable area has more than enough room to accommodate additional shelters, water pumps, and whatever amenities you deem appropriate—just remember to upgrade the settlement's defenses as food production increases. Flourishing farms are among the most popular targets of roving gangs.

## Boston Airport

The Boston Airport workshop isn't a true settlement. It can't accommodate crops, salvage stations, stores, artillery pieces, or recruitment beacons. However, it does contain a fair amount of scrap.

Water pumps can be placed in various piles of gravel, but the lack of food means that you'll need to establish supply lines if you hope to keep the population happy.

The Boston Airport workshop becomes available during the "Shadow of Steel" quest.

## Bunker Hill

Bunker Hill serves as a base of operations for various caravan traders, and its many vendors offer a variety of goods. It's a small but well-established settlement with enough beds, food, and water to meet the needs of its current residents. The residents will do business with any peaceful visitors, but they'll only grant you access to their workshop after you complete the "The Battle of Bunker Hill" quest.

## The Castle

The Castle once served as a stronghold for the Commonwealth Minutemen, and many of the items from that era are still intact. The settlement features a first-aid station and a couple of guard posts. Interior lights and an industrial water purifier are already tied to pylons in the courtyard—simply attach a suitable generator to complete the power grid. The existing structures can accommodate plenty of beds, and the courtyard has more than enough space for crops.

The Castle plays a key role in several Minutemen quests. These are all optional, but completing them will unlock many of this location's best features. The "Taking Independence" quest provides allies in the battle to reclaim the Castle—completing this quest activates Radio Freedom, which then broadcasts news and alerts about allied settlements. Complete "Old Guns" to unlock the armory and gain access to workstations, weapons, and powerful artillery pieces. This hidden structure even contains laser turrets and Tesla arcs that you can use to bolster the settlement's defenses.

## Covenant

Covenant is another small but well-established settlement—whether it stays that way is largely up to you. The "Human Error" quest begins and ends at this location, and how (or if) you choose to resolve that quest will determine if the current residents are willing to ally with you. Gaining their trust results in a relatively self-sufficient settlement with a few vendors. Otherwise, you're free to clear out the current residents, take control of the workshop, and draw new settlers into the area.

## Graygarden

Graygarden is another excellent farming settlement, but what sets it apart is that its starting population is made up entirely of robots. Once you earn their trust, you'll have a small group of workers that don't need sleep, food, or water.

By default, Graygarden produces enough food to support several smaller settlements. If you place a few powerful turrets in the area, this high-tech farm can easily serve as one of your most self-sufficient settlements. New settlers will allow you to increase production, but this supplemental workforce will expect amenities the robots can do without.

## Hangman's Alley

Hangman's Alley has the distinction of being the only big-city workshop settlement in the Commonwealth. This Raider-controlled camp may not have the pleasant views offered by other locations, but the urban setting does have its advantages. Due to the surrounding buildings, attackers can only approach from two directions. Once you've dealt with the original occupants, Hangman's Alley is sure to rank among the most easily defended areas you control.

Hangman's Alley doesn't start with any water or food, but it does offer several ramshackle structures, most of which include pieces that can be moved, stored, or scrapped. The terrain isn't ideal for farming, but patches of cracked asphalt can support crops or water pumps. The buildable area extends far beyond the fence on the enclosure's eastern edge, so Hangman's Alley has a fair amount of room to expand.

## Home Plate

This Diamond City house isn't actually a settlement, and it won't appear in your Pip-Boy's list of workshops. It does, however, contain some handy items, an established power grid, and a workshop with limited functionality. The rights to Home Plate can be purchased once you've gained entry to Diamond City. Simply visit Geneva in the mayor's office to discuss the transaction.

Home Plate can't accommodate structures or resource-production, but its workshop can be used to build a selection of furniture, decorations, and power-related items. Home Plate offers ample space, and it includes a fuse box wired directly into the Diamond City power grid. With the right materials, you can turn this simple space into your dream home.

## Red Rocket Truck Stop

Located just outside Sanctuary Hills, the Red Rocket Truck Stop is an unestablished but very well-equipped settlement. It features numerous workstations, a good amount of scrap, and one of the Commonwealth's few friendly canines.

In its initial state, the Red Rocket Truck Stop serves as a great place to store surplus Power Armor. With a bit of time and effort, you can transform this abandoned service station into a thriving settlement.

## Sanctuary Hills

Located just outside of Vault 111, Sanctuary Hills is likely to be the first workshop settlement you discover. This sprawling suburban neighborhood offers multiple structures, a variety of workstations, access to open water, and a considerable amount of scrap. It also plays an important role in several quests. All of these factors combine to make Sanctuary Hills an excellent choice as a base of operations. At the very least, it's a great place to learn the basics of settlement management.

You can take control of Sanctuary Hills at any time after you leave Vault 111, and some of the early Minutemen quests will task you with improving Sanctuary Hills to accommodate new residents. Even if you opt to ignore Preston Garvey and the people he's protecting, Sanctuary Hills can easily serve as a productive and easily defended settlement.

## The Slog

The Slog is a humble but productive farming settlement populated entirely by Ghouls. This isn't a matter of policy, however. Once you gain access to its workshop, the Slog welcomes any and all new settlers you draw to the area.

The Slog features one large structure and a considerable number of crops. The settlement can accommodate several upgrades, but items like turrets and junk fences can quickly push the buildable area to capacity. Scrapping the existing workstations can free up a bit of space, but careful planning is the best way to ensure that your settlers' needs can always be met.

## Spectacle Island

Spectacle Island features a massive buildable area with plenty of open water. It also contains some formidable enemies, so it's likely to be one of the last settlements to fall under your control.

Spectacle Island contains several structures and a variety of useful objects. The ship near the island's southern edge holds an onboard generator that produces a small amount of power, and there are a few workstations scattered around the area. Even with all of these elements in place, Spectacle Island is largely undeveloped. If you're looking for a chance to flex your creative muscle, you'd be hard-pressed to find a better option.

## Sunshine Tidings Co-op

The Sunshine Tidings Co-op features a large buildable area with several structures—many of which already contain beds. With ample shelter and plenty of scrap items, Sunshine Tidings Co-op makes it fairly easy to properly support new settlers.

Convenience aside, this settlement's most interesting feature is Professor Goodfeels—a malfunctioning Mr. Handy unit linked to the Sunshine Tidings terminal. Unlock the terminal to learn more about Professor Goodfeels or alter its protocols. If you haven't yet discovered Hesters Consumer Robotics, you can even use Professor Goodfeels's maintenance protocols to mark the location on your Pip-Boy's map.

# THE WORKSHOP ITEMS

A well-stocked workshop makes even the most ambitious construction project a simple affair. Just select an item from the Workshop menu, choose a location, and construction is done in an instant. Many workshop items snap together for perfect placement, but all items can be moved and rotated to meet your exacting standards. All workshop items require construction materials, and many items can only be built after you've completed certain quests or invested in specific perks. Plan ahead to ensure that your settlement lives up to your expectations.

## SPECIAL ITEMS

This category contains buildable quest-related items. Many of these special items can only be built at certain times or in certain locations, and the category only appears in the workshop menu when you can build at least one of these items at the settlement in question.

| NAME | BUILD WITH | PREREQUISITE | NOTES |
|---|---|---|---|
| Mama Murphy's Chair | Wood (4), Cloth (3), Steel (1) | Mama Murphy requests a chair. | Build this chair for Mama Murphy. |
| Artillery Piece | Oil (4), Screw (4), Gear (6), Spring (5), Steel (16), Concrete (4), Wood (4) | Artillery Schematic (collected in the Castle armory during the "Old Guns" quest) | Use Artillery Smoke Grenades to call in artillery strikes on your enemies. Produces 6 Defense. Requires an assigned worker. |
| Control Console | Rubber (2), Copper (3), Steel (5), Biometric Scanner (1) | Progress through the "The Molecular Level" quest. | Wire this into the same power grid as the Beam Emitter. Requires 2 Power. |
| Molecular Beam Emitter | Rubber (2), Steel (10), Copper (5), Military-Grade Circuit Board (1), Circuitry (3) | Progress through the "The Molecular Level" quest. | Snap this in place over the Reflector Platform. Requires 20 Power. |
| Relay Dish | Copper (3), Steel (3), Cloth (6), Gold (3) | Progress through the "The Molecular Level" quest. | Wire this into the same power grid as the Beam Emitter. Requires 5 Power. |
| Stabilized Reflector Platform | Aluminum (10), Circuitry (3), Steel (5) | Progress through the "The Molecular Level" quest. | The first piece of a very large machine. |
| Electromagnetic Actuator | Circuitry (5), Screw (1), Steel (10), Fiber Optics (3), Rubber (5), High Powered Magnet (1) | Progress through the "Liberty Reprimed" quest. | A special request from the Brotherhood of Steel. |

## STRUCTURES

This category contains items geared toward basic construction. Here, you'll find basic items like floors, walls, and roofs, but this category also contains doors, fences, completed structures, and more. Whether you're looking to build a simple shelter or a stately manor, this is likely to be your first stop in the workshop menu.

### Subcategories

- STRUCTURES > WOOD
- STRUCTURES > METAL
- STRUCTURES > DOORS
- STRUCTURES > FENCES
- STRUCTURES > MISCELLANEOUS

### Structures > Wood

The Workshop menu contains a wide variety of woods structures. In addition to the basic floors, walls, and roofs, this subcategory contains items like stairs, bridges, and railings. On the whole, wood structures are efficient, versatile, and made from relatively common materials.

### Subcategories

- STRUCTURES > WOOD > PREFABS
- STRUCTURES > WOOD > FLOORS
- STRUCTURES > WOOD > WALLS
- STRUCTURES > WOOD > ROOFS
- STRUCTURES > WOOD > STAIRS
- STRUCTURES > WOOD > MISCELLANEOUS

### STRUCTURES > WOOD > PREFABS

This subcategory features convenient, readymade structures. These items vary in size, shape, and complexity. Some prefabs are easily combined to build larger structures, while others are a bit more difficult to modify. Every prefab features some sort of roof, however, so they can serve as a basic shelter without any additional construction.

## WOOD PREFABS

| NAME | BUILD WITH | PREREQUISITES | NOTES |
|---|---|---|---|
| Floor and Roof | Wood (10), Steel (10) | — | A simple structure. |
| Wall and Roof | Wood (12), Steel (10) | — | A simple structure. |
| Hallway | Wood (12), Steel (10) | — | A simple structure. |
| Hallway End | Wood (14), Steel (10) | — | A simple structure. |
| Corner | Wood (15), Steel (12) | — | A simple structure. |
| Wall and Roof | Wood (16), Steel (10) | — | A simple structure. |
| Corner | Wood (20), Steel (15) | — | A simple structure. |
| Small Shack | Wood (30), Steel (20) | — | A completed shack. |
| Large Shack | Wood (40), Steel (20) | — | A completed shack. |

### STRUCTURES > WOOD > FLOORS

When you're building a structure from scratch, it's usually best to start with the floor. In addition to simple floor tiles, this category contains some particularly handy items. The foundation pieces can sink into the ground, serving as a level base for structures on uneven terrain. The stairwell features a one-story flight of stairs anchored between two floor tiles. Once a stairwell is in place, constructing a second story is as simple as snapping a few floor tiles to the top of the steps.

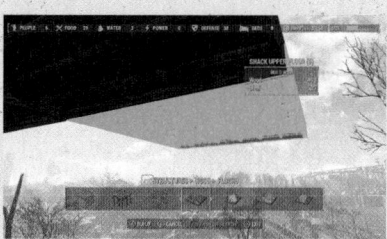

Another noteworthy item is the "Shack Upper Floor" piece. This floor tile is thick enough to meet any walls placed on the level beneath it. You're free to use thinner tiles on upper floors, but doing so will leave gaps along the exterior of multistory structures.

### WOOD FLOORS

| NAME | BUILD WITH | PREREQUISITES | NOTES |
|---|---|---|---|
| Shack Floor | Wood (7), Steel (2) | — | A standard floor. |
| Shack Foundation | Wood (12), Concrete (3) | — | Used to level uneven ground. |
| Shack Foundation | Wood (12), Steel (3) | — | Used to level uneven ground. |
| Shack Stairwell | Wood (12), Steel (3) | — | Two floors connected by stairs. |
| Shack Upper Floor | Wood (8), Steel (2) | — | A double-thick floor. |
| Floor—Small | Wood (3), Steel (1) | — | A small floor tile. |
| Floor—Small | Wood (3), Steel (1) | — | A small floor tile. |
| Floor—Small | Wood (3), Steel (1) | — | A small floor tile. |
| Floor—Small | Wood (3), Steel (1) | — | A small floor tile. |
| Floor—Small | Wood (3), Steel (1) | — | A small floor tile. |

### STRUCTURES > WOOD > WALLS

Wood walls come in a wide variety of shapes and sizes. Here you'll find everything from simple panels to elaborate wall/roof combinations. Most walls can snap neatly to floors and other wall panels, but there are a few exceptions. End pieces don't snap to any items, and they're a bit taller than standard walls. Covered corner pieces only snap to covered wall panels. Every wood wall has its uses, however, making this a very important section of the Workshop menu.

### WOOD WALLS

| NAME | BUILD WITH | PREREQUISITES | NOTES |
|---|---|---|---|
| Shack Wall—Doorway | Wood (5), Steel (3) | — | Includes a slight overhang. |
| Shack Wall—Outer Cap | Wood (4), Steel (9) | — | Includes a slight overhang. |
| Shack Wall—Corner | Wood (12), Steel (8) | — | A large, open corner piece. |
| Shack Wall—Corner | Wood (5), Steel (8) | — | A small, covered corner piece. |
| Shack Wall—Corner | Wood (6), Steel (3) | — | A small, covered corner piece. |
| Shack Wall and Roof | Wood (5), Steel (4) | — | A narrow, covered structure. |
| Shack Wall and Roof | Wood (4), Steel (4), Cloth (2) | — | A narrow, covered structure. |
| Wall | Wood (8), Steel (5) | — | A narrow, covered structure. |
| Wall | Wood (8) Steel (5) | — | A narrow, covered structure. |
| Wall | Wood (5), Steel (9) | — | A narrow, covered structure. |
| Wall | Wood (5), Steel (9) | — | A narrow, covered structure. |
| Wall | Wood (8), Steel (5) | — | A narrow, covered structure. |

| NAME | BUILD WITH | PREREQUISITES | NOTES |
|------|------------|---------------|-------|
| Wall | Wood (8), Steel (5) | — | A narrow, covered structure. |
| Wall | Wood (8), Steel (5) | — | A narrow, covered structure. |
| Wall | Wood (5), Steel (9) | — | A narrow, covered structure. |
| Wall—Corner | Wood (7), Steel (3) | — | A small, covered corner piece. |
| Wall—Corner | Wood (10), Steel (4) | — | A small, covered corner piece. |
| Wall—Corner | Wood (10), Steel (4) | — | A small, covered corner piece. |
| Wall—Corner | Wood (10), Steel (4) | — | A small, covered corner piece. |
| Wall—Corner | Wood (7), Steel (3) | — | A small, covered corner piece. |
| Wall—Corner | Wood (7), Steel (3) | — | A small, covered corner piece. |
| Wall—End | Wood (4), Steel (1) | — | A narrow, uneven wall. |
| Wall—End | Wood (4), Steel (1) | — | A narrow, uneven wall. |
| Wall—Small | Wood (8), Steel (2) | — | A basic wall. |
| Wall—Small | Wood (8), Steel (2) | — | A basic wall. |
| Wall—Small | Wood (8), Steel (2) | — | A basic wall. |
| Wall—Small | Wood (4), Steel (9) | — | Includes a slight overhang. |
| Wall—Small | Wood (4), Steel (9) | — | Includes a slight overhang. |

## STRUCTURES > WOOD > ROOFS

Every settler expects a roof over his or her head, and this area of the Workshop menu has plenty of options. Roofs snap to each other and to the tops of most wall panels. Wood roofs come in a variety of shapes, but they all serve the same purpose in shelter construction.

## WOOD ROOFS

| NAME | BUILD WITH | PREREQUISITES | NOTES |
|------|------------|---------------|-------|
| Shack Roof | Wood (3), Steel (6) | — | A flat roof. |
| Shack Roof | Wood (5), Cloth (5), Steel (2) | — | A sloped roof. |
| Shack Roof | Wood (4), Steel (6) | — | A sloped roof. |
| Shack Roof | Wood (3), Steel (6) | — | A flat roof. |
| Shack Roof | Wood (5), Steel (6) | — | A sloped roof. |
| Shack Roof | Wood (4), Cloth (6), Steel (2) | — | A sloped roof. |
| Shack Roof | Wood (4), Steel (6) | — | A sloped roof. |
| Shack Roof | Wood (5), Steel (6) | — | A sloped roof. |
| Shack Roof | Wood (5), Steel (6) | — | A sloped roof. |

## STRUCTURES > WOOD > STAIRS

Stairs are obviously an important part of any multistory building, but they also make it much easier to move in and out of structures built on raised foundations. Stairs can be placed anywhere, but they snap to floors and sometimes to each other. Most stairs can also sink into the ground.

## WOOD STAIRS

| NAME | BUILD WITH | PREREQUISITES | NOTES |
|------|------------|---------------|-------|
| Shack Stairs | Wood (9), Steel (2) | — | A long set of stairs between two anchor points. |
| Stairs | Wood (7), Steel (2) | — | A small set of stairs. |
| Stairs | Wood (7), Steel (2) | — | A medium set of stairs. |
| Stairs | Wood (7), Steel (2) | — | A long set of stairs. |

## STRUCTURES > WOOD > MISCELLANEOUS

This subcategory includes a bridge and an assortment of railing pieces. Bridges snap to each other, but they can also sink into the ground. They make excellent walkways, of course, but they're also handy when you want to build a few turret platforms or place some support beams under an existing structure. Railings are also quite versatile, but they're an excellent way to mark hazardous areas and prevent accidental falls.

## MISCELLANEOUS WOOD STRUCTURES

| NAME | BUILD WITH | PREREQUISITES | NOTES |
|------|-----------|---------------|-------|
| Bridge | Wood (6), Steel (2) | — | A narrow bridge. |
| Railing | Railing (2), Steel (1) | — | A short railing. |
| Railing | Wood (2), Steel (1) | — | A long railing. |
| Railing | Wood (2), Steel (1) | — | A short railing. |
| Railing | Wood (2), Steel (1) | — | A short railing. |
| Railing | Wood (2), Steel (1) | — | A short railing. |

## Structures > Metal

The Workshop menu contains far fewer options for metal structures than you'll find for wood structures—there are no metal-based floors, stairs, or miscellaneous items, and there are only two options for roofs. Of course, your stock of materials will likely determine which structures are the best fit for a settlement, but metal boasts an industrial aesthetic that wood simply can't match.

### Subcategories

- STRUCTURES > METAL > PREFABS
- STRUCTURES > METAL > WALLS
- STRUCTURES > METAL > ROOFS

### STRUCTURES > METAL > PREFABS

Like wood prefabs, metal prefabs are ready-made structures. Many of these items are easily incorporated into larger structures, but some metal prefabs feature rounded shapes that prohibit some walls and roofs from snapping into place.

## METAL PREFABS

| NAME | BUILD WITH | PREREQUISITES | NOTES |
|------|-----------|---------------|-------|
| Corner | Steel (10), Wood (4) | — | A simple structure. |
| Doorway | Steel (10), Wood (4) | — | Features an interior doorway. |
| Floor and Roof | Steel (10), Wood (4) | — | A simple structure. |
| Floor and Roof | Steel (10), Wood (4) | — | A simple structure. |
| Floor and Roof | Steel (10), Wood (4) | — | A simple structure. |
| Hallway | Steel (10), Wood (4) | — | A simple structure. |
| Hallway End | Steel (10), Wood (4) | — | A simple structure. |
| Wall and Roof | Steel (12), Wood (8) | — | A simple structure. |
| Wall and Roof | Steel (10), Wood (4) | — | A simple structure. |
| Small Metal Shack | Wood (20), Steel (30) | — | A completed shack. |
| Small Metal Shack | Wood (20), Steel (30) | — | A completed shack. |
| Large Metal Shack | Wood (20), Steel (40) | — | A completed shack. |

### STRUCTURES > METAL > WALLS

For the most part, a metal wall can be used anywhere a similarly shaped wood wall can be placed. The rounded walls found in this area of the Workshop menu don't have a wooden counterpart. Rather than snapping to floors, round metal walls snap to the framework found in most prefabs and wall/roof combos.

## METAL WALLS

| NAME | BUILD WITH | PREREQUISITES | NOTES |
|------|-----------|---------------|-------|
| Shack Wall | Wood (3), Steel (4) | — | A basic wall. |
| Shack Wall—Doorway | Wood (5), Steel (3) | — | Includes a slight overhang. |
| Shack Wall—Outer Cap | Wood (4), Steel (9) | — | Includes a slight overhang. |
| Shack Wall—Corner | Wood (12), Steel (8) | — | A large, open corner piece. |
| Shack Wall—Corner | Wood (5), Steel (8) | — | A small, covered corner piece. |
| Shack Wall—Corner | Wood (6), Steel (3) | — | A small, covered corner piece. |
| Shack Wall and Roof | Wood (5), Steel (4) | — | A narrow, covered structure. |
| Shack Wall and Roof | Wood (4), Steel (4), Cloth (2) | — | A narrow, covered structure. |
| Wall | Wood (8), Steel (5) | — | A narrow, covered structure. |
| Wall | Wood (8), Steel (5) | — | A narrow, covered structure. |

| NAME | BUILD WITH | PREREQUISITES | NOTES |
|------|-----------|---------------|-------|
| Wall | Wood (5), Steel (9) | — | A narrow, covered structure. |
| Wall | Wood (5), Steel (9) | — | A narrow, covered structure. |
| Wall | Wood (8), Steel (5) | — | A narrow, covered structure. |
| Wall | Wood (8), Steel (5) | — | A narrow, covered structure. |
| Wall | Wood (8), Steel (5) | — | A narrow, covered structure. |
| Wall | Wood (5), Steel (9) | — | A narrow, covered structure. |
| Wall—Corner | Wood (7), Steel (3) | — | A small, covered corner piece. |
| Wall—Corner | Wood (10), Steel (4) | — | A small, covered corner piece. |
| Wall—Corner | Wood (10), Steel (4) | — | A small, covered corner piece. |
| Wall—Corner | Wood (10), Steel (4) | — | A small, covered corner piece. |
| Wall—Corner | Wood (7), Steel (3) | — | A small, covered corner piece. |
| Wall—Corner | Wood (7), Steel (3) | — | A small, covered corner piece. |
| Wall—End | Wood (4), Steel (1) | — | A narrow, uneven wall. |
| Wall—End | Wood (4), Steel (1) | — | A narrow, uneven wall. |
| Wall—Small | Wood (8), Steel (2) | — | A basic wall. |
| Wall—Small | Wood (8), Steel (2) | — | A basic wall. |
| Wall—Small | Wood (8), Steel (2) | — | A basic wall. |
| Wall—Small | Wood (4), Steel (9) | — | Includes a slight overhang. |
| Wall—Small | Wood (4), Steel (9) | — | Includes a slight overhang. |

## STRUCTURES > METAL > ROOFS

All roofs snap to walls and to each other, so a metal roof can be used anywhere a wood roof would fit.

## METAL ROOFS

| NAME | BUILD WITH | PREREQUISITES | NOTES |
|------|-----------|---------------|-------|
| Shack Roof | Wood (3), Steel (10) | — | A rounded roof. |
| Shack Roof | Wood (3), Steel (10) | — | A flat roof. |

## STRUCTURES > DOORS

Doors snap to any wall or prefab that features a doorway. There are several doors to choose from, but the differences are purely cosmetic.

## DOORS

| NAME | BUILD WITH | PREREQUISITES | NOTES |
|------|-----------|---------------|-------|
| Door | Wood (3), Steel (3) | — | A basic door. |
| Door | Wood (3), Steel (3) | — | A basic door. |
| Door | Wood (3), Steel (3) | — | A basic door. |
| Door | Wood (3), Steel (3) | — | A basic door. |
| Door | Wood (3), Steel (3) | — | A basic door. |
| Door | Wood (3), Steel (3) | — | A basic door. |
| Door | Wood (3), Steel (3) | — | A basic door. |
| Door | Wood (3), Steel (3) | — | A basic door. |
| Door | Wood (3), Steel (3) | — | A basic door. |

## Structures > Fences

Fences are largely cosmetic, but they do have some practical uses. Well-placed fences can keep residents where you want them and limit enemy access to a settlement.

### Subcategories

- STRUCTURES > FENCES > JUNK FENCE
- STRUCTURES > FENCES > PICKET FENCE
- STRUCTURES > FENCES > WIRE FENCE

STRUCTURES > FENCES > JUNK FENCE

Junk fences are large and relatively costly, but they're great for fortifying vulnerable settlements. Fences don't contribute to a settlement's Defense rating, but well-positioned junk fences can funnel invaders into heavily defended areas. Forcing attackers toward a settlement's turrets and guard posts is one of the best ways to guarantee a raid ends quickly.

### JUNK FENCES

| NAME | BUILD WITH | PREREQUISITES | NOTES |
|------|-----------|--------------|-------|
| Gate | Wood (10), Steel (15) | — | A large gate. |
| Junk Fence | Wood (15), Steel (4) | — | A large, corner piece. |
| Junk Fence | Wood (6), Steel (9), Rubber (4) | — | A makeshift fence. |
| Junk Fence | Wood (10), Steel (4) | — | A makeshift fence. |
| Junk Fence | Wood (10), Steel (4), Rubber (2) | — | A makeshift fence. |
| Junk Fence | Wood (10), Steel (4), Rubber (2) | — | A makeshift fence. |
| Junk Fence | Wood (10), Steel (4) | — | A makeshift fence. |
| Junk Fence | Wood (6), Steel (9), Rubber (4) | — | A makeshift fence. |
| Junk Fence | Wood (15), Steel (4) | — | A large corner piece. |
| Junk Fence | Wood (2), Steel (6) | — | Features a doorway. |
| Junk Fence | Wood (2), Steel (6) | — | Features a doorway. |

STRUCTURES > FENCES > PICKET FENCE

Picket fences not only offer a classic aesthetic, but they also snap together for easy installation. Just place a post between each fence panel to maintain a perfect line. Picket fences must be unlocked before they can be built. This subcategory only appears in the Workshop menu after you've collected the *Picket Fences* magazine located in the Beantown Brewery.

### PICKET FENCES

| NAME | BUILD WITH | PREREQUISITES | NOTES |
|------|-----------|--------------|-------|
| Gate | Wood (3) | Picket Fences (Issue #1, located in Beantown Brewery) | A small gate. |
| Picket Fence Post | Wood (2) | Picket Fences (Issue #1, located in Beantown Brewery) | A single fence post. |
| Picket Fence | Wood (3) | Picket Fences (Issue #1, located in Beantown Brewery) | A short fence. |
| Picket Fence | Wood (3) | Picket Fences (Issue #1, located in Beantown Brewery) | A short fence. |
| Picket Fence | Wood (3) | Picket Fences (Issue #1, located in Beantown Brewery) | A short fence. |
| Picket Fence | Wood (3) | Picket Fences (Issue #1, located in Beantown Brewery) | A short fence. |
| Picket Fence—Long | Wood (6) | Picket Fences (Issue #1, located in Beantown Brewery) | A long fence. |
| Picket Fence—Long | Wood (6) | Picket Fences (Issue #1, located in Beantown Brewery) | A long fence. |
| Picket Fence | Wood (3) | Picket Fences (Issue #1, located in Beantown Brewery) | A long fence. |
| Picket Fence | Wood (3) | Picket Fences (Issue #1, located in Beantown Brewery) | A short fence. |
| Picket Fence | Wood (3) | Picket Fences (Issue #1, located in Beantown Brewery) | A short fence. |
| Picket Fence | Wood (3) | Picket Fences (Issue #1, located in Beantown Brewery) | A short fence. |

These rustic fences are often found in farming settlements. Wire fence pieces snap together whenever the edge of a mesh panel is moved toward a post.

## WIRE FENCES

| NAME | BUILD WITH | PREREQUISITES | NOTES |
|------|-----------|---------------|-------|
| Wire Fence | Wood (2) | — | A single fence post. |
| Wire Fence | Wood (2), Steel (2) | — | A basic fence. |
| Wire Fence | Wood (2), Steel (4) | — | A long fence. |
| Wire Fence | Wood (4), Steel (4) | — | A corner piece. |
| Wire Fence | Wood (4), Steel (2) | — | A wide gate. |
| Wire Fence | Wood (2), Steel (4) | — | A long fence. |
| Wire Fence | Wood (2), Steel (2) | — | A basic fence. |
| Wire Fence | Wood (2) | — | A single fence post. |
| Wire Fence | Steel (2) | — | A wire mesh panel. |

## Structures > Miscellaneous

This subcategory only contains two items, both of which are tall poles wrapped in razor wire. These items are purely cosmetic, but they certainly make a statement.

## MISCELLANEOUS STRUCTURES

| NAME | BUILD WITH | PREREQUISITES | NOTES |
|------|-----------|---------------|-------|
| Spiked Pole | Steel (6), Skull (3) | — | A pole covered in razor wire and skulls. |
| Spiked Pole | Steel (6) | — | A pole covered in razor wire. |

# FURNITURE

This category contains a variety of beds, chairs, shelves, and more. Although furniture plays an important role in a settlement's overall aesthetic, each type of furniture offers at least one useful feature.

### Subcategories

- FURNITURE > BEDS
- FURNITURE > CHAIRS
- FURNITURE > CONTAINERS
- FURNITURE > SHELVES
- FURNITURE > TABLES
- FURNITURE > MISCELLANEOUS

## Furniture > Beds

If you hope to keep the residents of your settlement happy and productive, you must provide one bed for each one. If you wish, you can even assign a settler to a specific bed. You're also free to use any bed you build—remember that each time you sleep, you receive the Well Rested perk. This temporary perk grants a 10 percent bonus to earned XP for a limited time, so it pays to take regular naps.

## BEDS

| NAME | BUILD WITH | PREREQUISITES | NOTES |
|------|-----------|---------------|-------|
| Bed | Steel (4), Cloth (5) | — | Accommodates one person. |
| Bed | Steel (4), Cloth (5) | — | Accommodates one person. |
| Bed | Steel (4), Cloth (5) | — | Accommodates one person. |
| Bed | Steel (4), Cloth (5) | — | Accommodates one person. |
| Mattress | Cloth (6) | — | Accommodates one person. |
| Sleeping Bag | Cloth (3) | — | Accommodates one person. |

## Furniture > Chairs

This subcategory contains a wide variety of benches, chairs, couches, and stools. These items are largely decorative, but idle settlers often seek out places to sit. You can also use these items to wait for hours at a time. Chairs don't offer the Well Rested perk granted by beds, but after you sit down, you're free to relax as time flies by.

### CHAIRS

| NAME | BUILD WITH | PREREQUISITES | NOTES |
|------|-----------|---------------|-------|
| Airplane Seat | Cloth (6), Aluminum (4) | — | A row of two airplane seats. |
| Airplane Seat | Cloth (8), Aluminum (5) | — | A row of three airplane seats. |
| Airplane Seat | Cloth (4), Aluminum (3) | — | A single airplane seat. |
| Bench | Steel (3), Wood (4) | — | A simple bench. |
| Bench | Wood (5), Steel (1) | — | A simple bench. |
| Chair | Leather (4), Steel (4) | — | A simple chair. |
| Chair | Cloth (4), Steel (4) | — | A small seat. |
| Chair | Cloth (4), Steel (4) | — | A basic chair. |
| Chair | Cloth (4), Steel (4) | — | A basic chair. |
| Chair | Cloth (4), Steel (4) | — | A small seat. |
| Chair | Cloth (4), Steel (4) | — | Three connected seats. |
| Chair | Cloth (3), Wood (5) | — | A basic chair. |
| Chair | Wood (4), Cloth (4) | — | A basic chair. |
| Chair | Wood (4), Cloth (2) | — | A basic chair. |
| Chair | Wood (4), Plastic (1) | — | A basic chair. |
| Chair | Steel (3), Cloth (1), Plastic (1) | — | A basic chair. |
| Chair | Steel (3), Cloth (2), Plastic (2) | — | A basic chair. |
| Chair | Wood (3), Cloth (5), Steel (1) | — | A basic chair. |
| Chair | Wood (4), Steel (1) | — | A basic chair. |
| Chair | Steel (3), Cloth (2), Plastic (2) | — | A basic chair. |
| Chair | Wood (4), Cloth (4) | — | A basic chair. |
| Chair | Cloth (4), Steel (4) | — | A basic chair. |
| Chair | Cloth (4), Steel (4) | — | Three connected seats. |
| Chair | Steel (4) | — | A basic chair. |
| Couch | Wood (5), Cloth (9) | — | A basic couch. |
| Couch | Wood (5), Cloth (10) | — | A basic couch. |
| Couch | Wood (4), Cloth (7), Steel (2) | — | A basic couch. |
| Couch | Wood (6), Cloth (10), Steel (2) | — | A basic couch. |
| Couch | Wood (6), Cloth (9) | — | A basic couch. |
| Patio Chair | Steel (4), Plastic (2) | Picket Fences (Issue #5, located in Weston Water Treatment Plant) | A basic chair. |
| Stool | Steel (3) | — | A simple stool. |
| Stool | Steel (3) | — | A simple stool. |
| Stool | Steel (2), Wood (1) | — | A simple stool. |
| Stool | Wood (3), Steel (1) | — | A simple stool. |
| Stool | Steel (4) | — | A simple stool. |
| Stool | Steel (3) | — | A simple stool. |
| Stool | Steel (5) | — | A stool with an attached back. |
| Stool | Steel (3), Plastic (1) | — | A simple stool. |

## Furniture > Containers

Containers come in all shapes and sizes, but from the massive bureau to the compact toolbox, all containers can store as many items as you choose. Simply approach a container and begin transferring items to or from your inventory.

### CONTAINERS

| NAME | BUILD WITH | PREREQUISITES | NOTES |
|------|-----------|---------------|-------|
| Bureau | Wood (4) | — | A tall bureau. |
| Cabinet | Steel (8) | — | A narrow cabinet. |
| Cabinet | Steel (8) | — | A wide cabinet. |

| NAME | BUILD WITH | PREREQUISITES | NOTES |
|---|---|---|---|
| Cabinet | Steel (8) | — | A tall cabinet. |
| Cabinet | Steel (8) | — | A wall-mounted cabinet. |
| Cabinet | Steel (8) | — | A long cabinet. |
| Cooler | Steel (2), Fiberglass (1) | — | A small cooler. |
| Desk | Steel (6) | — | A simple desk. |
| Desk | Steel (2), Wood (4) | — | A simple desk. |
| Dresser | Wood (4), Steel (2) | — | A narrow dresser. |
| Dresser | Wood (4), Steel (2) | — | A wide dresser. |
| File Cabinet | Steel (4) | — | A short file cabinet. |
| File Cabinet | Steel (4) | — | A tall file cabinet. |
| File Cabinet | Steel (4) | — | A tall file cabinet. |
| Filing Cabinet | Steel (2), Wood (6) | — | A large filing cabinet. |
| Footlocker | Steel (2), Wood (4) | — | A small box. |
| Metal Box | Steel (4) | — | A large box. |
| Safe | Spring (5), Steel (10), Gear (3) | — | A simple floor safe. |
| Steamer Trunk | Steel (4) | — | A large trunk. |
| Suitcase | Steel (1), Cloth (2) | — | A simple suitcase. |
| Tool Chest | Steel (4) | — | A large tool chest. |
| Toolbox | Steel (2) | — | A small toolbox. |
| Wooden Crate | Wood (3) | — | A large box. |

## Furniture > Shelves

Use shelves to hold and display items from your inventory. Just drop an item on the ground, activate the Workshop menu, then grab the item and place it wherever you like.

This subcategory also contains two magazine racks. Use these special shelves to store and display any magazines you collect as you explore the Commonwealth.

### SHELVES

| NAME | BUILD WITH | PREREQUISITES | NOTES |
|---|---|---|---|
| Bookcase | Wood (7), Steel (1) | — | A tall bookcase. |
| Bookcase | Wood (3), Steel (1) | — | A short bookcase. |
| Magazine Rack | Screw (1), Steel (4) | — | A small rack that only holds magazines. |
| Magazine Rack | Screw (1), Steel (4) | — | A large rack that only holds magazines. |
| Shelf | Steel (4) | — | A simple shelf unit. |
| Shelf | Wood (10), Steel (3) | — | A large shelf unit. |
| Shelf | Wood (13), Steel (4) | — | A large, double-sided shelf unit. |
| Wall Shelf | Steel (2) | — | A wall-mounted shelf. |
| Wall Shelf | Steel (2) | — | A wall-mounted shelf. |
| Wall Shelf | Wood (2) | — | A wall-mounted shelf. |
| Wall Shelf | Wood (2) | — | A wall-mounted shelf. |

## Furniture > Tables

Like shelves, tables can hold and display items from your inventory. This subcategory contains everything from coffee tables to pool tables, so you're sure to find something to match any décor.

### TABLES

| NAME | BUILD WITH | PREREQUISITES | NOTES |
|---|---|---|---|
| Coffee Table | Wood (3), Steel (1) | — | A low coffee table. |
| Coffee Table | Wood (4) | — | A high coffee table. |
| End Table | Wood (3), Steel (1) | — | A small end table. |
| End Table | Wood (4), Steel (1) | — | A large end table. |
| Kitchen Table | Wood (4), Steel (3) | — | A short table. |
| Kitchen Table | Wood (4), Steel (2) | — | A medium table. |

| NAME | BUILD WITH | PREREQUISITES | NOTES |
|------|-----------|---------------|-------|
| Kitchen Table | Wood (4), Steel (3) | — | A long table. |
| Patio Table | Steel (10) | Picket Fences (Issue #5, located in Weston Water Treatment Plant) | A round table with an attached umbrella. |
| Picnic Table | Wood (8), Steel (2) | Picket Fences (Issue #5, located in Weston Water Treatment Plant) | A large picnic table. |
| Pool Table | Cloth (3), Wood (8), Plastic (2), Rubber (1), Steel (2) | — | A large pool table. |
| Table | Wood (4), Steel (1) | — | A small table. |
| Table | Wood (4) | — | A small table. |
| Table | Wood (4), Steel (1) | — | A short table. |
| Table | Wood (7), Steel (1) | — | A large table. |
| Table | Steel (5) | — | A small table. |
| Table | Wood (7), Steel (1) | — | A large table. |
| Table | Wood (4), Steel (1) | — | A small table. |
| Table | Wood (3), Steel (1) | — | A small table. |
| Table | Wood (7), Steel (1) | — | A large table. |
| Table | Wood (4), Steel (1) | — | A small table. |
| Table | Wood (3), Steel (1) | — | A small table. |
| Table | Wood (6), Steel (1) | — | A large table. |
| Table | Wood (2), Steel (2) | — | A small table. |
| Table | Wood (3), Steel (2) | — | A large table. |
| Table | Wood (2), Steel (2) | — | A medium table. |
| Table | Steel (5) | — | A small table. |
| Table | Steel (2) | — | A small table. |
| Table | Wood (4) | — | A high table. |
| Wet Bar | Wood (4), Steel (1) | — | An open wet bar. |
| Wet Bar | Wood (4), Steel (1) | — | A closed wet bar. |

## Furniture > Miscellaneous

This area of the Workshop menu contains miscellaneous furniture items like televisions, bathroom fixtures, and more. Dedicated explorers would do well to build the Bobblehead stand—this stylish piece of furniture is a great way to proudly display your Bobblehead collection.

## MISCELLANEOUS FURNITURE

| NAME | BUILD WITH | PREREQUISITES | NOTES |
|------|-----------|---------------|-------|
| Bathtub | Ceramic (8), Steel (2) | — | A damaged bathtub. |
| Bobblehead Stand | Screw (3), Steel (4), Fiberglass (3) | — | A unit to hold and display collected Bobbleheads. |
| Counter | Wood (6), Steel (2) | — | A large counter. |
| Ottoman | Wood (2), Cloth (3), Steel (1) | — | A small ottoman. |
| Television | Steel (2), Circuitry (3), Wood (2), Glass (2), Aluminum (2) | — | Requires power. |
| Television | Steel (2), Circuitry (3), Wood (3), Glass (2), Aluminum (2) | — | Requires power. |
| Television | Steel (2), Circuitry (3), Wood (2), Glass (2), Aluminum (2) | — | Requires power. |
| Toilet | Ceramic (5), Plastic (1) | — | A damaged toilet. |

# DECORATIONS

This category features an impressive assortment of decorative items. When you just want to add a bit of flair to a settlement, make sure you visit this section of the Workshop menu.

**Subcategories**

- DECORATIONS > FLOOR COVERINGS
- DECORATIONS > WALL DECORATIONS
- DECORATIONS > STATUES
- DECORATIONS > MISCELLANEOUS

## Decorations > Floor Coverings

This section of the Workshop menu contains a variety of rugs and floor mats.

### FLOOR COVERINGS

| NAME | BUILD WITH | PREREQUISITES | NOTES |
|------|-----------|---------------|-------|
| Floor Mats | Cloth (2), Rubber (1) | — | A small mat. |
| Floor Mats | Cloth (2), Rubber (1) | — | A small mat. |
| Floor Mats | Cloth (2), Rubber (1) | — | A small mat. |
| Floor Mats | Cloth (2), Rubber (1) | — | A small mat. |
| Floor Mats | Cloth (2), Rubber (1) | — | A small mat. |
| Floor Mats | Cloth (2), Rubber (1) | — | A small mat. |
| Rug | Cloth (6) | — | A large rug. |
| Rug | Cloth (3) | — | A small rug. |
| Rug | Cloth (4) | — | A small rug. |
| Rug | Cloth (6) | — | A large rug. |
| Rug | Cloth (6) | — | A large rug. |

## Decorations > Wall Decorations

This section of the Workshop menu contains wall-mounted items like flags, trophies, and paintings.

**Subcategories**

- DECORATIONS > WALL DECORATIONS > FLAGS
- DECORATIONS > WALL DECORATIONS > MOUNTED CREATURES
- DECORATIONS > WALL DECORATIONS > PAINTINGS
- DECORATIONS > WALL DECORATIONS > SIGNS
- DECORATIONS > WALL DECORATIONS > MISCELLANEOUS

### DECORATIONS > WALL DECORATIONS > FLAGS

Initially, the Workshop menu only offers the U.S. flag, but more flags become available as you gain new allies. You're only able to build a faction's flag while you're a recognized member—if you're kicked out of a faction, the related flag is removed from the Workshop menu.

### FLAGS

| NAME | BUILD WITH | PREREQUISITES | NOTES |
|------|-----------|---------------|-------|
| Brotherhood of Steel Flag | Cloth (5) | Complete the "Fire Support" quest and be part of the Brotherhood of Steel faction. | A wall-mounted flag. |
| Institute Flag | Cloth (5) | Complete the "Institutionalized" quest and be part of the Institute faction. | A wall-mounted flag. |
| Railroad Flag | Cloth (5) | Complete the "Tradecraft" quest and be part of the Railroad faction. | A wall-mounted flag. |
| Minutemen Flag | Cloth (5) | Complete the quest "When Freedom Calls." | A wall-mounted flag. |
| U.S. Flag | Cloth (5) | — | A wall-mounted flag. |

## DECORATIONS > WALL DECORATIONS > MOUNTED CREATURES

This subcategory offers a small collection of wall-mounted hunting trophies.

### MOUNTED CREATURES

| NAME | BUILD WITH | PREREQUISITES | NOTES |
|---|---|---|---|
| Mounted Brahmin Heads | Wood (1), Cloth (2), Brahmin Skull (2) | — | A wall-mounted trophy. |
| Mounted Mirelurk Claw | Wood (1), Cloth (1), Mirelurk Meat (1) | — | A wall-mounted trophy. |
| Mounted Mole Rat Head | Wood (1), Cloth (1), Mole Rat Meat (1), Mole Rat Teeth (1) | — | A wall-mounted trophy. |
| Mounted Radstag Heads | Wood (1), Cloth (2), Radstag Meat (1) | — | A wall-mounted trophy. |

## DECORATIONS > WALL DECORATIONS > PAINTINGS

This section of the Workshop menu offers paintings of various styles and sizes.

### PAINTINGS

| NAME | BUILD WITH | PREREQUISITES | NOTES |
|---|---|---|---|
| Painting | Wood (5) | — | A wall-mounted painting. |
| Painting | Wood (5) | — | A wall-mounted painting. |
| Painting | Wood (5) | — | A wall-mounted painting. |
| Painting | Wood (5) | — | A wall-mounted painting. |
| Painting | Wood (5) | — | A wall-mounted painting. |
| Painting | Wood (5) | — | A wall-mounted painting. |
| Painting | Wood (5) | — | A wall-mounted painting. |
| Painting | Wood (5) | — | A wall-mounted painting. |
| Painting | Wood (5) | — | A wall-mounted painting. |
| Painting | Wood (5) | — | A wall-mounted painting. |
| Painting | Wood (5) | — | A wall-mounted painting. |
| Painting | Wood (5) | — | A wall-mounted painting. |
| Painting | Wood (5) | — | A wall-mounted painting. |
| Painting | Wood (5) | — | A wall-mounted painting. |
| Painting | Wood (5) | — | A wall-mounted painting. |
| Painting | Wood (5) | — | A wall-mounted painting. |
| Painting | Wood (5) | — | A wall-mounted painting. |
| Painting | Wood (5) | — | A wall-mounted painting. |
| Painting | Wood (5) | — | A wall-mounted painting. |

## DECORATIONS > WALL DECORATIONS > SIGNS

In this section of the Workshop menu, you'll find signs in a variety of shapes, styles, and sizes.

### SIGNS

| NAME | BUILD WITH | PREREQUISITES | NOTES |
|---|---|---|---|
| Signs | Steel (4) | — | A wall-mounted sign. |
| Signs | Steel (4) | — | A wall-mounted sign. |
| Signs | Steel (4) | — | A wall-mounted sign. |
| Signs | Steel (4) | — | A wall-mounted sign. |

| NAME | BUILD WITH | PREREQUISITES | NOTES |
|------|-----------|---------------|-------|
| Signs | Steel (4) | — | A wall-mounted sign. |
| Signs | Steel (4) | — | A wall-mounted sign. |
| Signs | Steel (4) | — | A wall-mounted sign. |
| Signs | Steel (4) | — | A wall-mounted sign. |
| Signs | Steel (4) | — | A wall-mounted sign. |
| Signs | Steel (4) | — | A wall-mounted sign. |
| Signs | Steel (4) | — | A wall-mounted sign. |

## DECORATIONS > WALL DECORATIONS > MISCELLANEOUS

This section of the Workshop menu features two miscellaneous wall decorations: a mountable basketball hoop and a stylish Eat-O-Tronic unit.

### MISCELLANEOUS WALL DECORATIONS

| NAME | BUILD WITH | PREREQUISITES | NOTES |
|------|-----------|---------------|-------|
| Basketball Hoop | Steel (4) | — | A wall-mounted basketball hoop. |
| Eat-O-Tronic | Steel (4), Glass (2) | — | A wall-mounted vending machine. |

## Decorations > Statues

This subcategory only appears in the Workshop menu after you collect the *Picket Fences* magazine located in the Saugus Ironworks. Once you unlock these items, you can use workshops to build some rather impressive statues.

### STATUES

| NAME | BUILD WITH | PREREQUISITES | NOTES |
|------|-----------|---------------|-------|
| Statue | Copper (10) | Picket Fences (Issue #3, located in Saugus Ironworks) | A small statue. |
| Statue | Copper (10) | Picket Fences (Issue #3, located in Saugus Ironworks) | A large statue. |
| Statue | Copper (20) | Picket Fences (Issue #3, located in Saugus Ironworks) | A very large statue. |
| Statue | Copper (20) | Picket Fences (Issue #3, located in Saugus Ironworks) | A very large statue. |
| Fountain | Copper (20) | Picket Fences (Issue #3, located in Saugus Ironworks) | A very large fountain. |

## Decorations > Miscellaneous

This section of the Workshop menu contains some particularly interesting decorations, many of which offer additional functionality. Some vending machines and trash receptacles can be used as containers. The doghouse gives your canine companion a place to relax between outings. Radios and jukeboxes add a bit of life to any settlement. Initially, the workshop offers a good selection of miscellaneous decorations, but many more can be unlocked as you explore the Commonwealth.

### MISCELLANEOUS DECORATIONS

| NAME | BUILD WITH | PREREQUISITES | NOTES |
|------|-----------|---------------|-------|
| Ashtray | Steel (4) | — | A standing ashtray. |
| Basketball Hoop | Steel (6) | — | A standing basketball hoop. |
| Cigarette Machine | Steel (4), Rubber (1) | — | A small vending machine. |
| Crib | Steel (1), Wood (5), Cloth (2) | — | A baby's crib. |
| Doghouse | Wood (3), Steel (1) | — | A simple doghouse. |
| Grill | Steel (4), Rubber (1) | Picket Fences (Issue #5, located in Weston Water Treatment Plant) | A small grill. |
| Ice Cooler | Steel (4), Rubber (1) | — | A large ice machine. |
| Lawn Flamingos | Steel (1), Plastic (4) | Wasteland Survival Guide (Issue #5, located in Lynn Woods) | A lawn Flamingo. |
| Lawn Flamingos | Steel (1), Plastic (4) | Wasteland Survival Guide (Issue #5, located in Lynn Woods) | A lawn Flamingo. |
| Milk Vending Machine | Steel (4), Rubber (1) | — | A large vending machine. |
| Nuka-Cola Machine | Steel (2), Rubber (1), Plastic (2) | — | A large vending machine. |
| Potted Plant | Steel (2), Wood (2) | Picket Fences (Issue #4, located in Combat Zone) | A small potted plant. |
| Potted Plant | Steel (2), Wood (2) | Picket Fences (Issue #4, located in Combat Zone) | A small potted plant. |

| NAME | BUILD WITH | PREREQUISITES | NOTES |
|------|-----------|---------------|-------|
| Potted Plant | Steel (2), Wood (2) | Picket Fences (Issue #4, located in Combat Zone) | A large potted plant. |
| Potted Plant | Steel (2), Wood (2) | Picket Fences (Issue #4, located in Combat Zone) | A small potted plant. |
| Potted Plant | Steel (2), Wood (2) | Picket Fences (Issue #4, located in Combat Zone) | A large potted plant. |
| Potted Plant | Steel (2), Wood (2) | Picket Fences (Issue #4, located in Combat Zone) | A small potted plant. |
| Potted Plant | Steel (2), Wood (2) | Picket Fences (Issue #4, located in Combat Zone) | A large potted plant. |
| Potted Plant | Steel (2), Wood (2) | Picket Fences (Issue #4, located in Combat Zone) | A large potted plant. |
| Radio | Circuitry (1), Plastic (2), Copper (1), Rubber (2) | — | Tuned to Diamond City Radio. |
| Radio | Circuitry (1), Plastic (2), Copper (1), Rubber (2) | — | Tuned To Classical Radio. |
| Radio | Circuitry (1), Plastic (2), Copper (1), Rubber (2) | Complete The Minutemen Quest: Taking Independence. | Tuned to Radio Freedom. |
| Sign | Steel (4), Rubber (1) | — | A large, freestanding sign. |
| Trash Bin | Steel (4), Rubber (1) | — | A large trash receptacle. |
| Trash Can | Steel (4) | — | A small trash receptacle. |
| Jukebox | Circuitry (2), Plastic (2), Copper (2), Glass (2), Steel (2) | — | Requires 2 Power. |
| Shaun's Crib | Cloth (2), Steel (1), Wood (5) | Scrap Shaun's crib. | Unique item. Can only be built in Sanctuary Hills. |

## POWER

This category contains all of the items you'll need to generate and deliver power, but it also offers some very useful high-tech devices. With this selection of generators, switches, lights, and special electronics, you can build a power grid that rivals anything found in the Commonwealth.

### Subcategories

- POWER > GENERATORS
- POWER > CONNECTORS AND SWITCHES
- POWER > LIGHTS
- POWER > MISCELLANEOUS

### Power > Generators

Generators produce the power needed to run lights, turrets, and all of a settlement's electronic devices. Each generator features its own size, output, and building materials, and the most powerful generator requires an investment in the Science! perk.

### GENERATORS

| NAME | BUILD WITH | PREREQUISITES | NOTES |
|------|-----------|---------------|-------|
| Generator—Small | Gear (2), Steel (4), Rubber (2), Copper (2), Ceramic (1) | — | Produces 3 Power |
| Generator—Medium | Screw (3), Gear (3), Steel (7), Rubber (3), Copper (3), Ceramic (1) | — | Produces 5 Power |
| Generator—Large | Gear (6), Screw (5), Rubber (4), Copper (10), Aluminum (12), Nuclear Material (3) | Rank 1: Science! | Produces 10 Power |
| Generator—Windmill | Steel (15), Copper (4), Aluminum (10), Gear (2) | — | Produces 3 Power |

### Power > Connectors and Switches

This section of the Workshop menu offers an assortment of pylons, conduits, and switches. By connecting these devices to a power source, you can expand and control the flow of electricity within a settlement. Pylons and conduits serve as anchor points for wires, and you can link them to deliver power to buildings and devices located anywhere within a settlement. As long as they're attached to a suitable power source, these connectors also radiate energy needed to power televisions, jukeboxes, and most lights.

Use switches to determine when and if power is transmitted to specific areas or devices. You'll find everything from basic on/off switches to programmable power counters. Connect switches to terminals to access additional options; combine switches to create new effects. Like basic connectors, switches radiate the energy needed to power simple devices. Of course, this energy field is only active while a switch is turned on.

## CONNECTORS AND SWITCHES

| NAME | BUILD WITH | PREREQUISITES | NOTES |
|---|---|---|---|
| Power Pylon | Copper (2), Wood (2), Ceramic (1), Steel (1) | — | A short pylon |
| Power Pylon—Large | Copper (4), Ceramic (3), Steel (8), Rubber (1) | — | A tall pylon. Requires power. |
| Power Conduit | Copper (2), Ceramic (2), Steel (2) | — | Mounts to floors |
| Power Conduit | Copper (2), Ceramic (2), Steel (2) | — | Mounts to walls |
| Power Conduit | Copper (2), Ceramic (2), Steel (2) | — | Mounts to ceilings |
| Switched Power Pylon | Copper (3), Wood (2), Steel (2), Ceramic (1), Rubber (1) | — | Features an on/off switch. Requires power. |
| Switched Power Pylon—Large | Copper (5), Steel (9), Ceramic (3), Rubber (1) | — | Features an on/off switch. Requires power. |
| Switch | Steel (2), Copper (1), Rubber (1) | — | A wall-mounted on/off switch. Requires power. |
| Pressure Plate | Copper (3), Steel (3), Spring (2) | — | Transmits power when activated. Requires power. |
| Laser Tripwire | Fiber Optics (2), Steel (4), Crystal (1), Fusion Cell (6) | Rank 1: Science! | Transmits power when disarmed. Use a connected terminal to access additional functionality. Requires power. |
| Laser Tripwire | Fiber Optics (2), Steel (4), Crystal (1), Fusion Cell (6) | Rank 1: Science! | Transmits power when disarmed. Use a connected terminal to access additional functionality. Requires power. |
| Delayed Off Switch | Copper (2), Wood (2), Ceramic (1) | — | Stops transmitting power after a short delay. Use a connected terminal to change the delay. Requires power. |
| Delayed On Switch | Copper (2), Wood (2), Ceramic (1) | — | Transmits power after a short delay. Use a connected terminal to change the delay. Requires power. |
| Interval Switch | Copper (2), Wood (2), Ceramic (1) | — | Switches on and off repeatedly. Use a connected terminal to change the on/off intervals. Requires power. |
| Power Counter | Copper (1), Wood (1), Ceramic (1), Steel (2) | — | Transmits power briefly after cycling power 10 times. Use a connected terminal to change the max count. Requires power. |

## Power > Lights

Initially, the Workshop menu contains a good variety of lighting options, but you can unlock many more by collecting the *Picket Fences* magazine located in Hardware Town. Nearly all lights are powered by radiant energy—the one exception is the construction light. This freestanding light must be wired directly to a power grid in order to function.

## LIGHTS

| NAME | BUILD WITH | PREREQUISITES | NOTES |
|---|---|---|---|
| Lightbulb | Glass (1), Copper (1), Steel (2) | — | A hanging light. Requires power. |
| Industrial Wall Light | Glass (1), Copper (1), Steel (2) | — | A wall-mounted light. Requires power. |
| Construction Light | Glass (2), Copper (1), Steel (4) | — | A freestanding light. Requires 1 Power. |
| Ceiling Fan | Glass (1), Copper (1), Gear (1), Wood (1), Steel (2) | — | A hanging fan. Requires power. |
| Lamp | Glass (1), Copper (1), Steel (2) | — | A freestanding light. Requires power. |
| High Tech Lights | Glass (1), Copper (1), Steel (2) | Picket Fences (Issue #2, located in Hardware Town) | A freestanding light. Requires power. |
| High Tech Lights | Glass (1), Copper (1), Steel (2) | Picket Fences (Issue #2, located in Hardware Town) | A freestanding light. Requires power. |
| High Tech Lights | Glass (1), Copper (1), Steel (2) | Picket Fences (Issue #2, located in Hardware Town) | A freestanding light. Requires power. |
| High Tech Lights | Glass (1), Copper (1), Steel (2) | Picket Fences (Issue #2, located in Hardware Town) | A hanging light. Requires power. |
| High Tech Lights | Glass (1), Copper (1), Steel (2) | Picket Fences (Issue #2, located in Hardware Town) | A hanging light. Requires power. |
| High Tech Lights | Glass (1), Copper (1), Steel (2) | Picket Fences (Issue #2, located in Hardware Town) | A hanging light. Requires power. |
| High Tech Lights | Glass (1), Copper (1), Steel (2) | Picket Fences (Issue #2, located in Hardware Town) | A hanging light. Requires power. |
| High Tech Lights | Glass (1), Copper (1), Steel (2) | Picket Fences (Issue #2, located in Hardware Town) | A freestanding light. Requires power. |
| High Tech Lights | Glass (1), Copper (1), Steel (2) | Picket Fences (Issue #2, located in Hardware Town) | A freestanding light. Requires power. |
| High Tech Lights | Glass (1), Copper (1), Steel (2) | Picket Fences (Issue #2, located in Hardware Town) | A freestanding light. Requires power. |
| High Tech Lights | Glass (1), Copper (1), Steel (2) | Picket Fences (Issue #2, located in Hardware Town) | A freestanding light. Requires power. |
| Mirror Ball | Glass (6), Copper (1), Steel (2) | — | A hanging light. Requires power. |
| Strobe Light | Glass (1), Copper (1), Steel (2), Circuitry (1) | Rank 1: Science! | A hanging light. Requires power. |

## Power > Miscellaneous

This section of the Workshop menu contains a small selection of interesting items. The recruitment radio beacon is particularly useful—this powered transmitter draws new residents to a specific settlement, allowing your population to grow fairly quickly.

Use terminals to access additional functionality on attached devices. Not every powered device offers extra features, but all terminals can be used with switches, lightboxes, powered speakers, and powered turrets.

### MISCELLANEOUS POWER ITEMS

| NAME | BUILD WITH | PREREQUISITES | NOTES |
|------|-----------|---------------|-------|
| Recruitment Radio Beacon | Circuitry (2), Crystal (2), Copper (6), Steel (10), Ceramic (3), Rubber (1) | — | Attracts new settlers to your settlement when turned on. Requires 1 Power. |
| Terminal | Rubber (2), Copper (2), Circuitry (2), Aluminum (4) | Rank 1: Hacker | Access additional functionality on connected objects. Requires 1 Power. |
| Lightbox | Glass (1), Copper (1), Steel (2) | — | Use a connected terminal to access additional functionality. Requires 1 Power. |
| Powered Speaker | Copper (1), Wood (1), Steel (2), Circuitry (1) | — | Plays a musical tone when powered. Use a connected terminal to change the pitch. Requires 1 Power. |

## DEFENSE

Use the items in this category to boost your settlement's Defense rating. A high Defense rating makes your settlement a much less appealing target for would-be attackers. This, in turn, results in a more self-sufficient settlement with a happier, more productive population.

### Subcategories

- DEFENSE > GUARD POSTS
- DEFENSE > TURRETS
- DEFENSE > TRAPS

### Defense > Guard Posts

Guard posts are made from common materials—in most cases, a newly acquired settlement contains more than enough scrap to build at least a few of these defensive items. You must assign a worker to a guard post before it contributes to a settlement's Defense rating, but because each guard can generate a maximum of 6 Defense, a single guard can man up to three posts.

### GUARD POSTS

| NAME | BUILD WITH | PREREQUISITES | NOTES |
|------|-----------|---------------|-------|
| Guard Post | Wood (10), Steel (4) | — | Provides 2 Defense. Requires an assigned worker. |
| Guard Tower | Wood (12), Steel (6) | — | Provides 2 Defense. Requires an assigned worker. |

### Defense > Turrets

The Workshop menu offers a variety of turrets. These automated weapons boost a settlement's Defense rating without compromising its workforce. It does, however, take a fair amount of uncommon and rare materials to build them, and most turrets require power to function. Still, if you have the required resources and skills, building a collection of powerful turrets will go a long way toward keeping your settlements safe.

### TURRETS

| NAME | BUILD WITH | PREREQUISITES | NOTES |
|------|-----------|---------------|-------|
| Machine-Gun Turret | Steel (8), Circuitry (1), Gear (2), Oil (2) | — | Provides 5 Defense. |
| Heavy Machine-Gun Turret | Steel (10), Circuitry (2), Gear (2), Oil (4) | Rank 1: Gun Nut | Provides 8 Defense. |

| NAME | BUILD WITH | PREREQUISITES | NOTES |
|------|-----------|---------------|-------|
| Laser Turret | Aluminum (5), Circuitry (3), Screw (3), Fiber Optics (4), Gear (2), Nuclear Material (2), Steel (5), Glass (3) | Rank 1: Science! | Requires 2 Power. Produces 8 Defense. |
| Shotgun Turret | Aluminum (4), Circuitry (5), Screw (4), Gear (4), Oil (5), Steel (6) | Rank 2: Gun Nut | Requires 2 Power. Produces 8 Defense. |
| Spotlight | Circuitry (1), Screw (1), Gear (2), Steel (6), Oil (1), Glass (2) | — | Requires 2 Power. Produces 2 Defense. |
| Heavy Laser Turret | Crystal (4), Aluminum (7), Circuitry (4), Screw (4), Fiber Optics (4), Gear (3), Nuclear Material (4), Steel (3) | Rank 3: Science! | Requires 2 Power. Produces 12 Defense. |
| Missile Turret | Aluminum (6), Circuitry (6), Screw (5), Gear (5), Oil (6), Steel (6) | Rank 3: Gun Nut | Requires 2 Power. Produces 15 Defense. |

## Defense > Traps

Like turrets, traps function without the help of assigned workers. Unlike turrets, traps must be repaired after each use. A trap triggers the moment it receives power, and it will continue to attack until it breaks. Use switches like pressure plates and laser tripwires to better control when and how trap can be activated. To count toward a settlement's Defense rating, a trap must be undamaged and wired to a power grid.

## TRAPS

| NAME | BUILD WITH | PREREQUISITES | NOTES |
|------|-----------|---------------|-------|
| Tesla Arc | Steel (2), Copper (3), Circuitry (1) | — | Requires power. Produces 2 Defense. |
| Radiation Emitter | Screw (2), Nuclear Material (3), Lead (2), Steel (2) | — | Requires power. Produces 2 Defense. |
| Flamethrower Trap | Screw (2), Rubber (4), Aluminum (4), Oil (6) | — | Requires power. Produces 3 Defense. |

# RESOURCES

Most of the items in this category are geared toward water collection and food production, but you'll also find an assortment of items that can make a settlement more productive and easier to manage.

### Subcategories

- RESOURCES > WATER
- RESOURCES > FOOD
- RESOURCES > MISCELLANEOUS

## Resources > Water

To keep your settlements happy, it's important to provide enough water for the current population. Water pumps are simple devices that generate a small amount of water. They can only be placed in dirt, but virtually every settlement has terrain that can accommodate at least a few water pumps. Water purifiers, on the other hand, can only be placed in water. These machines are more difficult to build, and they require power, but they're able to generate an impressive amount of drinkable water.

## WATER ITEMS

| NAME | BUILD WITH | PREREQUISITES | NOTES |
|------|-----------|---------------|-------|
| Water Pump | Concrete (1), Steel (4), Gear (1) | — | Can only be placed in dirt. Produces 3 Water. |
| Water Purifier | Oil (2), Ceramic (2), Rubber (5), Copper (2), Steel (10), Cloth (2) | — | Must be placed in the water. Requires 2 Power. Produces 10 Water. |
| Water Purifier—Industrial | Oil (4), Ceramic (2), Rubber (10), Copper (4), Steel (20), Cloth (4), Screw (6) | Rank 1: Science! | Must be placed in the water. Requires 5 Power. Produces 40 Water. |

### Resources > Food

Like water, food is an important factor in a settlement's overall happiness. The crops found in the Workshop menu can only be placed in dirt, and they only count toward your settlement's Food rating if workers are assigned to care for them. A single worker can generate up to 6 Food, and he or she can tend any combination of crops that doesn't exceed this limit.

Assigned crops also produce food that you can harvest yourself. You can consume this food, sell it, or use it to plant new crops and create items at workstations. Harvesting food has no effect on your settlement's Food rating.

#### FOOD ITEMS

| NAME | BUILD WITH | PREREQUISITES | NOTES |
|------|-----------|---------------|-------|
| Carrot | Carrot (1) | — | Can only be placed in dirt. Produces 0.5 Food. Requires an assigned worker. |
| Corn | Corn (1) | — | Can only be placed in dirt. Produces 0.5 Food. Requires an assigned worker. |
| Corn | Corn (1) | — | Can only be placed in dirt. Produces 0.5 Food. Requires an assigned worker. |
| Gourd | Gourd (1) | — | Can only be placed in dirt. Produces 0.5 Food. Requires an assigned worker. |
| Melon | Melon (1) | — | Can only be placed in dirt. Produces 0.5 Food. Requires an assigned worker. |
| Mutfruit Plant | Mutfruit (1) | — | Can only be placed in dirt. Produces 1 Food. Requires an assigned worker. |
| Razorgrain | Razorgrain (1) | — | Can only be placed in dirt. Produces 0.5 Food. Requires an assigned worker. |
| Razorgrain | Razorgrain (1) | — | Can only be placed in dirt. Produces 0.5 Food. Requires an assigned worker. |
| Tato Plant | Tato (1) | — | Can only be placed in dirt. Produces 0.5 Food. Requires an assigned worker. |
| Tato Plant | Tato (1) | — | Can only be placed in dirt. Produces 0.5 Food. Requires an assigned worker. |

### Resources > Miscellaneous

This section of the Workshop menu contains some very useful items. Scavenging stations increase the amount of scrap salvaged by the workers assigned to them. Feed troughs keep Brahmin from wandering around your settlements. Bells and sirens make it easier to manage your settlers, and the Fast-Travel target adjusts your arrival point at a given settlement.

#### MISCELLANEOUS RESOURCE ITEMS

| NAME | BUILD WITH | PREREQUISITES | NOTES |
|------|-----------|---------------|-------|
| Scavenging Station | Wood (5), Steel (3) | — | Extra scavenging production. Requires an assigned worker. |
| Brahmin Feed Trough | Steel (2), Ceramic (8) | — | Brahmin will tend to stay near their feed trough. |
| Bell | Wood (4), Steel (4) | — | Ring to gather nearby settlers. |
| Siren | Copper (5), Steel (9), Ceramic (3), Rubber (1) | — | Alerts nearby settlers to danger when triggered. Requires 1 Power. |
| Fast-Travel Target | Cloth (2), Rubber (1) | — | Only 1 per location. Moves the Fast-Travel arrival point. |

## STORES

In addition to buying and selling goods, stores you build within a settlement generate income based on the current population. Many stores even increase a settlement's total Happiness rating. You must assign a worker to a store before it can be used—once you do, a worker stays at his or her store during its hours of operation. You must have both ranks of the Local Leader perk before you can build a store, and many stores have additional perk requirements.

#### Subcategories

- STORES > TRADER
- STORES > ARMOR
- STORES > WEAPONS
- STORES > FOOD AND DRINK
- STORES > CLINIC
- STORES > CLOTHING

### Stores > Trader

Trading stores specialize in junk items. Larger stores offer a better selection of rarer goods and keep more money on hand. These stores also increase a settlement's Happiness rating.

**TRADING STORES**

| NAME | BUILD WITH | PREREQUISITES | NOTES |
|------|-----------|---------------|-------|
| Trading Stand | Wood (5), Bottlecap (300), Steel (3) | Rank 2: Local Leader | Produces income based on the total population. Makes settlements happier. Requires an assigned worker. |
| Trading Shop | Wood (5), Bottlecap (600), Steel (3) | Rank 2: Local Leader | Produces income based on the total population. Makes settlements happier. Requires an assigned worker. |
| Trading Emporium | Wood (5), Bottlecap (1500), Steel (3) | Rank 2: Cap Collector, Rank 2: Local Leader | Produces income based on the total population. Makes settlements happier. Requires an assigned worker. |

### Stores > Armor

Armor stores specialize in protective apparel. Larger stores offer a better selection of rarer goods and keep more money on hand.

**ARMOR STORES**

| NAME | BUILD WITH | PREREQUISITES | NOTES |
|------|-----------|---------------|-------|
| Armor Stand | Wood (5), Bottlecap (500), Steel (3) | Rank 2: Local Leader | Produces income based on the total population. Requires an assigned worker. |
| Armor Shop | Wood (5), Bottlecap (1000), Steel (3) | Rank 2: Local Leader | Produces income based on the total population. Requires an assigned worker. |
| Armor Emporium | Wood (5), Bottlecap (3000), Steel (3) | Rank 2: Cap Collector, Rank 2: Local Leader | Produces income based on the total population. Requires an assigned worker. |

### Stores > Weapons

Weapon stores specialize in weapons and ammunition. Larger stores offer a better selection of rarer goods and keep more money on hand.

**WEAPON STORES**

| NAME | BUILD WITH | PREREQUISITES | NOTES |
|------|-----------|---------------|-------|
| Weapons Stand | Wood (5), Bottlecap (500), Steel (3) | Rank 2: Local Leader | Produces income based on the total population. Requires an assigned worker. |
| Weapons Shop | Wood (5), Bottlecap (1000), Steel (3) | Rank 2: Local Leader | Produces income based on the total population. Requires an assigned worker. |
| Weapons Emporium | Wood (5), Bottlecap (3000), Steel (3) | Rank 2: Cap Collector, Rank 2: Local Leader | Produces income based on the total population. Requires an assigned worker. |

### Stores > Food and Drink

Food and drink stores specialize in comestible aid items. Larger stores offer a better selection of rarer goods and keep more money on hand. These stores also increase a settlement's Happiness rating.

## FOOD AND DRINK STORES

| NAME | BUILD WITH | PREREQUISITES | NOTES |
|------|-----------|---------------|-------|
| Drink Stand | Wood (5), Bottlecap (250), Steel (3) | Rank 2: Local Leader | Produces income based on the total population. Makes settlements happier. Requires an assigned worker. |
| Bar | Wood (5), Bottlecap (500), Steel (3) | Rank 2: Local Leader | Produces income based on the total population. Makes settlements happier. Requires an assigned worker. |
| Restaurant | Wood (5), Bottlecap (1500), Steel (3) | Rank 2: Cap Collector, Rank 2: Local Leader | Produces income based on the total population. Makes settlements happier. Requires an assigned worker. |

### Stores > Clinic

Clinics restore health and offer cures for chem addiction and radiation sickness. They also sell medicinal aid items. Larger stores offer a better selection of rarer goods and keep more money on hand. Clinics also increase a settlement's Happiness rating.

## CLINICS

| NAME | BUILD WITH | PREREQUISITES | NOTES |
|------|-----------|---------------|-------|
| First Aid Station | Wood (5), Bottlecap (600), Steel (3) | Rank 2: Local Leader, Rank 1: Medic | Produces income based on the total population. Makes settlements happier. Requires an assigned worker. |
| Clinic | Wood (5), Bottlecap (1200), Steel (3) | Rank 2: Local Leader, Rank 1: Medic | Produces income based on the total population. Makes settlements happier. Requires an assigned worker. |
| Surgery Center | Wood (5), Bottlecap (1800), Steel (3) | Rank 2: Local Leader, Rank 1: Medic | Produces income based on the total population. Makes settlements happier. Requires an assigned worker. |

### Stores > Clothing

Clothing stores specialize in cosmetic apparel. Larger stores offer a better selection of rarer goods and keep more money on hand. These stores also increase a settlement's Happiness rating.

## CLOTHING STORES

| NAME | BUILD WITH | PREREQUISITES | NOTES |
|------|-----------|---------------|-------|
| Clothing Stand | Wood (5), Bottlecap (200), Steel (3) | Rank 2: Local Leader | Produces income based on the total population. Makes settlements happier. Requires an assigned worker. |
| Clothing Shop | Wood (5), Bottlecap (400), Steel (3) | Rank 2: Local Leader | Produces income based on the total population. Makes settlements happier. Requires an assigned worker. |
| Clothing Emporium | Wood (5), Bottlecap (1000), Steel (3) | Rank 2: Cap Collector, Rank 2: Local Leader | Produces income based on the total population. Makes settlements happier. Requires an assigned worker. |

## VAULT-TEC RECOMMENDS

### LEVEL 4 WORKSHOP MERCHANTS

Even the best stores can benefit from expert traders. Recruit these special merchants to join a settlement, assign them to the appropriate stores, and you'll have access to some rare and unique items. Some of these individuals are harder to convince than others, and some demand a minimum population before they'll offer their services. Luckily, any settlements connected (by supply lines) to the target location count toward minimum population requirements.

| CATEGORY | REQUIRED STORE | MERCHANT | MIN. POPULATION | NOTES |
|----------|---------------|----------|-----------------|-------|
| Armor | Armor Emporium | The Scribe | 10 | Met during Random Encounter: Workshop Armor Vendor. |
| Clinic | Surgery Center | Doc Anderson | 20 | Met during Random Encounter: The Walking Wounded. |
| Clothing | Clothing Emporium | Ann Hargraves | — | Found in Vault 81. |
| Food & Drink | Restaurant | Ron Staples | 20 | Met during Random Encounter: Time to Party. |
| General | Trading Emporium | Vault-Tec Rep | — | Found in Goodneighbor. |
| General | Trading Emporium | Rylee | — | Met during Random Encounter: Rylee the Trader |
| General | Trading Emporium | Holt Combes | — | Found in Vault 81. |
| Weapons | Weapons Emporium | Smiling Larry | 30 | Met during Random Encounter: Smiling Larry. |

## CRAFTING

If you invest in both ranks of the Local Leader perk, you can build workstations in any of your settlements.

### WORKSTATIONS

| NAME | BUILD WITH | PREREQUISITES | NOTES |
|---|---|---|---|
| Armor Workbench | Wood (3), Gear (5), Spring (4), Screw (4), Aluminum (8) | Rank 2: Local Leader | Used to modify or scrap armor. |
| Chemistry Station | Wood (8), Steel (6), Glass (6), Rubber (3), Screw (4) | Rank 2: Local Leader | Used to craft chems and explosives. |
| Chemistry Station | Wood (3), Steel (6), Copper (4), Rubber (3), Screw (3), Glass (4) | Rank 2: Local Leader | Used to craft chems and explosives. |
| Cooking Station | Steel (5), Concrete (3), Wood (3), Screw (3) | Rank 2: Local Leader | Used to cook consumables. |
| Cooking Station | Steel (4), Gear (3), Wood (2), Screw (2) | Rank 2: Local Leader | Used to cook consumables. |
| Cooking Stove | Steel (4), Gear (3), Wood (2), Screw (2) | Rank 2: Local Leader | Used to cook consumables. |
| Power Armor Station | Gear (6), Oil (4), Screw (4), Plastic (4), Aluminum (12), Fiberglass (6), Circuitry (3) | Rank 2: Local Leader | Used to modify or repair Power Armor. |
| Weapons Workbench | Wood (4), Gear (4), Screw (3), Aluminum (7), Rubber (4) | Rank 2: Local Leader | Used to modify or scrap weapons. |
| Weapons Workbench | Wood (3), Gear (3), Screw (4), Aluminum (6), Rubber (6) | Rank 2: Local Leader | Used to modify or scrap weapons. |

# MANAGING SETTLEMENTS

You're free to run a settlement in whatever manner you see fit. You can address problems as they arise or ignore them completely—your settlers will survive with or without your help. For a settlement to thrive, however, you'll need to play a more active role. Developing a settlement takes effort; juggling the needs of multiple settlements takes careful planning and a watchful eye.

## RECOMMENDED PERKS

Effective management takes time, effort, and ample resources, but rebuilding the Commonwealth also takes considerable know-how. If you're looking to make the most of your settlements, you'd do well to invest in these perks:

- LOCAL LEADER: AT RANK 1, THIS CHARISMA-BASED PERK GRANTS THE ABILITY TO ESTABLISH SUPPLY LINES BETWEEN YOUR SETTLEMENTS. RANK 2 IS REQUIRED TO BUILD THE STORES AND WORKSTATIONS FOUND IN THE WORKSHOP MENU. IF YOU'RE SERIOUS ABOUT SETTLEMENTS, MAKE THIS PERK A PRIORITY.
- HACKER: RANK 1 OF THIS INTELLIGENCE-BASED PERK IS REQUIRED TO BUILD TERMINALS. TERMINALS CAN INTERACT WITH A VARIETY OF DEVICES, BUT THEY'RE MOST USEFUL WHEN COMBINED WITH SWITCHES. WHETHER YOU'RE LOOKING TO STREAMLINE YOUR AUTOMATED DEFENSES OR DESIGN CUSTOM AUDIO/VISUAL ELEMENTS, YOU'LL NEED AT LEAST ONE TERMINAL TO ACCESS ALL OF THE AVAILABLE OPTIONS.
- SCIENCE!: RANK 1 OF THIS INTELLIGENCE-BASED PERK IS REQUIRED TO BUILD LARGE GENERATORS, INDUSTRIAL WATER PURIFIERS, LASER TRIPWIRES, AND MANY OTHER PARTICULARLY HANDY ITEMS. RANK 3 IS REQUIRED TO BUILD HEAVY LASER TURRETS.
- GUN NUT: RANK 3 OF THIS INTELLIGENCE-BASED PERK IS REQUIRED TO BUILD MISSILE TURRETS. THESE POWERFUL WEAPON SYSTEMS GENERATE MORE DEFENSE THAN ANY OF THE OTHER ITEMS CONTAINED IN THE WORKSHOP MENU.

Of course, these perks are just the beginning. Medic is needed to build any clinic, and most of the largest stores require Rank 2 of the Cap Collector perk. Perks like Scrapper, Fortune Finder, and Strong Back make it easier to maintain a supply of building materials. Balance your needs against those of the settlers to determine which perks are right for you.

## BASIC CONSTRUCTION

Workshops make building fun and easy—just open the Workshop menu and select the desired item. As long as you have the required materials, construction is done in a flash. But where should you build an item? When should you build it? Is it the best use of your materials? How will it affect your settlers?

Of course, the answers to these questions are determined by your specific goals. Whether you favor form or function, there are a few steps you can take to minimize wasted time, effort, and resources.

## Scrap for Success

Once you take control of a settlement, open the Workshop menu and search the area for items to scrap. Most settlements contain several items that serve no practical purpose. Scrap trees and crates for wood. Scrap cars and mailboxes for steel. Scrap cinder blocks for concrete and tires for rubber. If you feel an item adds to a settlement's aesthetic, by all means, keep it. Otherwise, scrap it for materials. Old appliances, broken furniture, damaged fences—scrap anything and everything that you don't need.

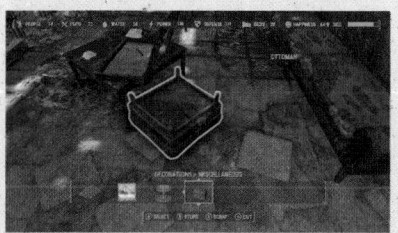

After you finish with scrap items, decide what to do with a settlement's usable items. Again, if you feel an item has some decorative value, leave it where it lies. Otherwise, scrap, sell, store, or rearrange usable items until you're satisfied.

## Plan for the Future

Before you start building, consider your goals for a specific settlement. If you aim to develop a self-sufficient settlement, set aside areas for farming and water collection. If you plan on establishing a supply line, decide which resources a settlement will contribute or require. Look for ways to exploit the terrain or utilize existing structures. Imagine the completed settlement before you place so much as a floor panel.

## Start Small

Efficiency is important when you're juggling multiple settlements—building a massive bunkhouse for a few settlers probably isn't the best use of materials. But even if you can spare the materials for massive projects, it's usually best to improve a settlement a bit at a time. Each settlement can only accommodate so many items. Reaching a settlement's size limit halfway through construction can turn your glorious vision into a costly miscalculation.

## When in Doubt, Start from Scratch

When it comes to convenience, it's hard to beat a prefabricated structure. If you have the space and materials to construct a ready-to-use shack, you can have a settlement up and running in no time. It is, however, much easier to modify a structure built from scratch. Rearrange walls, floors, and roofs to change a building's layout, or build new pieces to turn a humble shack into an ornate tower.

## Build from the Ground Up

Use shack foundations to level rocky terrain. If you want a structure with a clean, sleek look, you'll want to start your project with these versatile floor pieces.

## Waste Not, Want Not

Most settlements contain established structures that can't be moved or altered. They can, however, be incorporated into larger structures. Try building on or around existing structures when you need to save space or reduce construction costs.

## Think Vertically

In some smaller settlements, farmable dirt is hard to come by. When space is at a premium, consider building raised platforms or narrow, multistory structures to leave enough room for crops and water pumps.

How you run a settlement is entirely up to you, but your residents do expect a certain level of comfort and security. Happy settlers are productive settlers, and over time, effective management can yield significant rewards.

The state of a settlement is determined by a combination of factors:

- PEOPLE: THE NUMBER OF PEOPLE LIVING WITHIN THE SETTLEMENT.
- FOOD: THE AMOUNT OF FOOD PRODUCED BY A SETTLEMENT.
- WATER: THE AMOUNT OF WATER PRODUCED BY A SETTLEMENT.
- POWER: THE AMOUNT OF POWER PRODUCED BY A SETTLEMENT.
- DEFENSE: THE DEFENSIVE STRENGTH OF A SETTLEMENT.
- BEDS: THE NUMBER OF BEDS IN A SETTLEMENT.
- HAPPINESS: THE OVERALL HAPPINESS OF A SETTLEMENT'S RESIDENTS.

**HELPFUL HINT** *from Vault Boy!* **Did You Know?**

MANAGEMENT MADE EASY

A SETTLEMENT'S RATINGS ARE PROVIDED WHENEVER THE WORKSHOP MENU IS ACTIVE. ANY RATING THAT FALLS BELOW YOUR SETTLERS' EXPECTATIONS IS DISPLAYED IN RED. YOUR PIP-BOY'S WORKSHOP TAB LISTS ALL OF THE SETTLEMENTS YOU CONTROL. ALERTS APPEAR NEAR ANY SETTLEMENT WITH AT LEAST ONE SUBSTANDARD RATING. SELECT THAT SETTLEMENT FROM THE LIST TO SEE WHICH RATINGS COULD STAND TO BE IMPROVED.

**People**

A settlement's population determines the amount of food and water needed, as well as how many beds you're expected to provide. Meeting their needs can take time, effort, and a considerable amount of building materials, but your people also serve as a valuable resource. Many workshop items only function when a worker is assigned. People without assigned tasks automatically generate salvage, so a large, happy population can provide a steady stream of building materials.

Settlers are naturally drawn to well-established settlements, but populations tend to grow very slowly. Build recruitment radio beacons at key locations to accelerate population growth. Some of the people you encounter during your travels can also be convinced to join one of your settlements.

**HELPFUL HINT** *from Vault Boy!* **Did You Know?**

CHARISMA COUNTS

YOUR CHARISMA RANK DETERMINES A SETTLEMENT'S MAXIMUM POPULATION. A SINGLE WORKSHOP CAN ACCOMMODATE 10 RESIDENTS, PLUS ONE ADDITIONAL RESIDENT FOR EACH RANK OF YOUR CHARISMA. NEW SETTLERS STOP ARRIVING ONCE YOUR POPULATION REACHES THIS NUMBER.

Speak to settlers to receive available quests, hear about their concerns, or initiate trades. During a trade, you can have a settler equip any clothes, armor, or weapons you're willing to provide. Weapons and armor don't affect a settlement's Defense rating, but well-equipped settlers are much more effective in combat.

**HELPFUL HINT** *from Vault Boy!* **Did You Know?**

UNAUTHORIZED ACQUISITIONS

SETTLERS SOMETIMES COLLECT WEAPONS THAT ARE LEFT OUT IN THE OPEN. IN SOME CASES, A SETTLER WILL EVEN COMMANDEER AN UNUSED SUIT OF POWER ARMOR. IT'S EASY ENOUGH TO RECLAIM THESE ITEMS ONCE YOU IDENTIFY THE CULPRIT, BUT YOU CAN ALSO TAKE MEASURES TO KEEP YOUR PRIZED POSSESSIONS SAFE—SIMPLY STORE VALUABLE WEAPONS IN CONTAINERS AND REMOVE FUSION CORES FROM IDLE POWER ARMOR.

Use the Workshop menu to issue commands to a specific settler. You can assign settlers to items like beds, guard posts, artillery pieces, salvage stations, and stores. You can also command a settler to walk to a specific spot or relocate to a different workshop settlement.

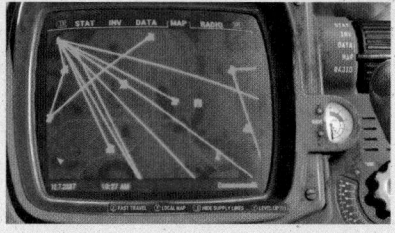

If you've invested in the Local Leader perk, you can also assign a settler to a supply line. Two settlements connected by a supply line can share food, water, and any of the building materials stored in their respective workshops. Settlers you assign to supply lines become provisioners, moving back and forth along their assigned routes. To cancel a supply line, simply assign its provisioner to a different task.

Not all of the people in your settlements can be relocated or assigned to specific tasks. The available commands depend on the individual in question, but key figures like settlement leaders and idle traveling companions tend to be less flexible than common settlers. It's important to note, however, that these people still count toward a settlement's total population.

## Food

A settlement's Food rating reflects how much food a settlement produces. In most cases, it's best to maintain a Food rating that's at least as high as a settlement's current population. Establishing supply lines splits the burden between multiple settlements. Settlers will be satisfied with a very low Food rating as long as the connected settlements produce enough food to make up the difference. In either case, food shortages lower a settlement's overall happiness and productivity.

To raise a settlement's Food rating, simply plant and assign crops. A single worker can generate up to 6 Food, and he or she can tend any combination of crops that doesn't exceed this limit. Assigned crops also produce food that you can harvest yourself. These aid items can be eaten, sold, stored, replanted, or used to craft new items at workstations.

## HELPFUL HINT
### from Vault Boy!
**Did You Know?**

#### FOOD FOR THOUGHT
ADHESIVE CAN BE HARD TO COME BY, SO WHY NOT CRAFT YOUR OWN? USE YOUR CROPS TO PROVIDE CORN, MUTFRUIT, AND TATOS. ALONG WITH A BIT OF PURIFIED WATER, YOU CAN USE THESE INGREDIENTS TO CRAFT VEGETABLE STARCH AT COOKING STATIONS.

Brahmin often appear in settlements with high Food ratings. These bovine beasts are docile enough, but they can get in the way from time to time. Build feed troughs to prevent Brahmin from aimlessly wandering around your settlements.

Crops are vulnerable to attack, and they're often damaged during enemy raids. Use the Workshop menu to repair damaged crops to resume food production.

## Water

A settlement's Water rating reflects how much water a settlement produces. Your settlers expect a Water rating that's at least as high as the current population. Again, establishing supply lines splits the burden between connected settlements, but any water shortages will make affected settlers less productive.

Water-producing items don't require assigned workers. The moment you build a water pump, it raises a settlement's Water rating. Water purifiers only function when they're connected to an adequate power supply. Still, with the right materials and appropriate terrain, it's fairly easy to meet a settlement's water needs.

Like crops, water pumps and water purifiers are susceptible to damage. Use the Workshop menu to make repairs as needed.

## Power

A settlement's Power rating indicates how much power a settlement produces. You obviously need to provide enough power for connected devices to function, but your settlers will be satisfied with any Power rating.

Use the Workshop menu to attach wires to generators, connectors, switches, or powered devices. It takes 1 Copper to create a wire. The Workshop menu can also be used to remove and store unwanted wires. Any device that can accommodate a wire can transmit power. This means that you can link powered devices to each other—as long as enough power is available, all of the devices in the chain will function.

Generators are susceptible to attacks, and they're often targeted during raids. This can be a serious issue for settlements that rely on traps and powered turrets to keep hostiles at bay. Place key generators safely out of sight and use the Workshop menu to make repairs as needed.

## Defense

A settlement's Defense rating represents the combined strength of its defensive items. A settlement's Defense rating should be at least as high as its current population. Anything less not only makes settlers less productive, but it also increases the odds of a settlement being attacked.

Requiring only wood and steel, guard posts are relatively easy to build. They're easily incorporated into fences and structures, and they provide decent cover from enemy fire. A single guard assigned to three posts produces 6 Defense. Even when you have the materials for more powerful defensive items, it's usually worth building a few guard posts.

With an assigned worker, an artillery piece generates 6 Defense. Of course, its real value is in the utility it provides while you're out in the field. If you can spare the space and materials, build an artillery piece to boost a settlement's Defense and improve the coverage of your artillery support.

Unlike guard posts and artillery pieces, turrets are fully automated. If you can spare the materials, building a turret is the simplest way to boost a settlement's Defense rating. Special perks and rare materials are required to build most turrets, but these powerful weapons are well worth the cost.

Traps break each time they're triggered, and they'll damage any friendly units within range. However, a trap only needs to be undamaged and wired to a power grid to count toward a settlement's Defense rating. Install a switch between a trap and its power source to control exactly when it's triggered.

---

**HELPFUL HINT** *from Vault Boy!*

### TRAPS, TRIGGERS, AND YOU

YOU CAN MANUALLY CONTROL A TRAP WITH A SIMPLE ON/OFF SWITCH. AN ATTACHED PRESSURE SWITCH TURNS A TRAP INTO AN AUTOMATED DEFENSE SYSTEM THAT'S JUST AS LIKELY TO BE TRIGGERED BY SETTLERS AS IT IS BY ENEMIES. IF YOU WANT TO MAKE THE MOST OF A TRAP, USE A LASER TRIPWIRE AS THE TRIGGER. CONNECT A TERMINAL TO ACCESS THE TRIPWIRE'S OPTIONS. THEN SIMPLY SET IT TO IGNORE FRIENDLY TARGETS.

---

Guard posts and artillery pieces don't take damage, but turrets are vulnerable to attack and traps break after each use. Watch for any drops in a settlement's Defense rating and use the Workshop menu to make any necessary repairs.

Maintaining an appropriate Defense rating will cut down on enemy raids, but every settlement is likely to be attacked from time to time. Use structures and junk fences to funnel invaders toward turrets and traps. Build Fast-Travel targets to ensure that you arrive in the safest possible location whenever you visit a settlement, and equip your settlers with high-quality weapons for a little extra firepower.

## Beds

A settlement's Beds rating simply indicates how many beds are located in the area. You're expected to have one bed for each resident. A shortage of beds lowers a settlement's productivity.

The Workshop menu contains a variety of beds, but they all serve the same function. It isn't necessary to assign settlers to specific beds, but doing so can prevent others from sleeping in a bed you've claimed as your own.

To keep your settlers happy, it's important to place each bed under some sort of roof. Placing beds outside doesn't affect your Beds rating, but it does reduce your settlement's happiness and productivity.

## Happiness

A settlement's Happiness rating indicates the residents' overall satisfaction. A high Happiness rating improves food production, and the salvage generated by idle settlers and workers assigned to salvage stations. Your rewards are automatically deposited in related workshops.

The best way to keep your settlers happy is to meet their basic needs. Provide enough food, water, and beds for all of your residents, and make sure a settlement's Defense rating meets or exceeds expectations.

Actively helping a settlement also improves its Happiness rating. Monitor Radio Freedom and check your Pip-Boy for updates and alerts about the settlements you control. Help fend off invading enemies and complete any quests your settlers offer.

Some of the items in the Workshop menu can increase a settlement's Happiness ratings. Clinics, clothing stores, trading stores, and stores that sell food and drink all improve your settlers' moods. If you manage to purchase a dog for one of your settlements, its arrival will have a similar effect.

# MAP

## LOCATION TYPES

To avoid confusion, Vault-Tec has divided the land of the Commonwealth into various areas, from large to small. Let us begin with zones:

### ZONES

These are large-scale areas where approximately 20 primary locations can be found. Boundaries are drawn based on the topography of the area. These aren't shown on your Pip-Boy and are only so we can focus on chunks of areas at a time in this guide. There are six exterior (Wasteland) zones.

### Zones: Neighborhoods

If you venture into the Greater Boston area, you'll enter one of the neighborhoods. These neighborhoods follow the old prewar boundaries and are built-up areas. When using an exterior door after visiting a primary location interior, you'll be informed which neighborhood you're in. Expect fewer primary locations here but a larger concentration of exploration opportunities.

### Townships

Outside Greater Boston are older settlements with prewar names such as Quincy and Salem. These are clusters of primary locations in close proximity to each other, and they often share the same boundary.

## MAP LEGENDS

Before continuing, familiarize yourself with what the different map icons mean.

### WORLD MAP LEGEND

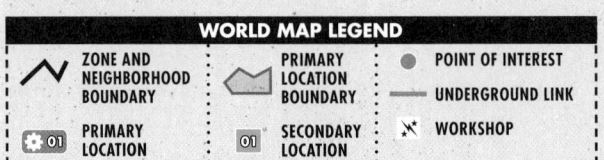

This legend is shown at the beginning of each zone (or neighborhood) and refers to the overview map.

### ZONE AND NEIGHBORHOOD BOUNDARY

This is the perimeter of the zone. Outside of Boston, this usually follows an easy-to-see landmark, such as a winding river, main thoroughfare, or elevated freeway.

### PRIMARY LOCATIONS

These are usually sizable locations that, once discovered, appear and remain on your Pip-Boy's world map. You are fortunate that Vault-Tec's ground-penetrating radar and the latest in topographical advancements have allowed purveyors of this guide to see every single primary location prior to discovery. Primary locations may require an interior investigation; if they do, an interior map is provided where necessary. Each location has a Vault-Tec–approved number code. For example, Vault 111 has the number [1.01], indicating it is in Zone 1 and is Primary Location 01 within the zone.

#### Primary Location Boundary

If primary locations or townships have a perimeter, a reasonably accurate boundary will be shown on the zone map so you can see how big the location is in a general sense before visiting it. If primary locations merge together, such as with townships, the entire area will be in a single boundary.

### SECONDARY LOCATIONS

These are smaller locations that rarely require an interior investigation. They are color-coded, do not feature a Pip-Boy icon, and do not ever appear on your Pip-Boy world map. Each location has a similar number code. For example, the Dry Creek Bed north of Vault 111 is [1.01], indicating it is in Zone 1 and is secondary location 01 within the zone.

#### Points of Interest

There are dozens of small, strange, and interesting areas you may wish to investigate that are too tiny to be a secondary location but may yield a random encounter, small stash of goods, or other item of use.

### TIP

**LOOKING FOR LOCATIONS IN ALL THE RIGHT PLACES #1**

Want to pinpoint a secondary location on your Pip-Boy? Sure you do! Simply use the Map Marker functionality, place the marker at the secondary location you want to find, and travel there without the hassle of finding it by chance!

#### Underground Link

While adventuring across the Commonwealth, it is often worth knowing if one location has a hidden underground link to another. If you see this line, you'll know two (or more) locations are linked.

## WORKSHOPS

Certain primary locations have the additional benefit of having a workshop on the premises, which are used to build defenses and power and to attract settlers as part of the Minutemen faction's plan for the future. Find and connect all the locations with this icon and create a Commonwealth community of farmers and traders, all looking out for one another.

## LOCAL MAP LEGEND

| MAP LEGEND | | | | | |
|---|---|---|---|---|---|
| 13     20 OPTIMAL ROUTE | BOTTLECAPS | HEALTH OR CHEMS | FUSION CORE | Collectibles: BOBBLEHEAD | NUKA COLA QUANTUM |
| | SAFE | TERMINAL | POWER ARMOR | NUKA CHERRY | HOLOTAPE |
| AREA OF INTEREST | ARMAMENTS AND AMMO DOOR | STEAMER TRUNK | REQUIRED READING | MINI NUKE | A KEY |

| | | | |
|---|---|---|---|
| N – Novice (Locked) | E – Expert (Locked) | T – Terminal required to unlock | IN – Inaccessible | CB – Circuit Breaker |
| A – Advanced (Locked) | M – Master (Locked) | KEY – Key or ID Card required to unlock | C – Chained | B – Button |

This legend is shown whenever a location is large enough to require an interior map. Most of the icons are self-explanatory, as they show doors, safes, terminals, ammo, and a variety of collectibles. The letter by some doors, terminals, or safes indicates how it is accessed.

### Optimal Route

This is a series of waypoints that charts one method of completing a thorough investigation of the premises. It doesn't usually involve stealth but does result in the location receiving a "Cleared" rating on your Pip-Boy afterward. If you get lost, use this to find your way out. Here's how it works:

– THE USUAL START LOCATION IS FLAGGED, THOUGH SOMETIMES A LOCATION MAY HAVE MORE THAN ONE STARTING POINT.

– THE WAYPOINTS ARE NUMBERED: WHEN THE NUMBER AND ROUTE STOP AND THE SAME NUMBER IS SEEN ON ANOTHER LEVEL OF THE INTERIOR MAP, IT MEANS THE ROUTE HAS CHANGED FLOORS (YOU'VE GONE UPSTAIRS OR DOWN OR USED AN ELEVATOR).

– WHEN THE NUMBER IS SHOWN AND A SUBSEQUENT NUMBER ON THE SAME LEVEL MAP IS SHOWN AFTERWARD, THIS WAYPOINT USUALLY INDICATES AN IMPORTANT EVENT MUST OCCUR, LIKE USING A TERMINAL TO UNLOCK A PATH TO CONTINUE OR LOCATING A KEY.

# AREA STATISTICS

Every location in the Commonwealth has a list of pertinent information to better inform you of what to expect when you visit it. The following list explains what all of this is. Remember that most items (such as mods, types of ammunition, and health) are randomly obtained and thus cannot be tracked. For information on the best way to scavenge these, consult the appropriate chapters (INV, MOD, WORKSHOP) in this guide.

## ARMAMENTS AND AMMO

 **Armaments and Ammo (+++)***

 The immediate area has weapons, ammunition, or both. The bullets, firepower, or bludgeoning weapon could be loose on the ground, sitting on a table, in a toilet, or inside an ammo box, duffel bag, locked suitcase, locked toolbox, or other interesting container. Low on ammo? Look for these icons!

**Armaments and Ammo: Mini Nuke or Fat Man**

 You'll find either a large, rotund missile at this location, specifically designed to be fired from the infamous Fat Man, or an elongated launcher in the indicated area or location. A portable nuclear weapon, this has the added bonus of coming with a Mini Nuke already prepped!

 **Armaments and Ammo: Trunk**

 This location has a type of steamer trunk that holds a large amount of (random) loot. It is basically a "reward" for clearing the area of undesirables. Trunks come in a few varieties—red, green, military, and even with a Vault 81 insignia—and they are all shown by this icon. Want to make your life easier? Hunt down these repositories of rare items, recipes, and other treasures!

MAP

INTRODUCTION

**HELPFUL HINT** *from Vault Boy!*

**Did You Know?**

*(+++) WHAT DOES THIS THIS STRANGE SET OF "+" SYMBOLS MEAN? WELL, IT DENOTES HOW PLENTIFUL A SUPPLY OF A PARTICULAR ITEM IS AND REFERS TO AMMO, BOTTLECAPS, HEALTH, OR CHEMS. IF YOU SEE A "+", "++", OR "+++" NEXT TO THESE ITEM CALLOUTS, YOU KNOW THERE'S A LOT, AN IMPRESSIVE AMOUNT, OR A MASSIVE NUMBER OF THESE ITEMS AT A LOCATION. SO LOOK FOR THESE SIGNS IF YOU'RE AFTER SOME EXTRA-SWELL GOODIES!

###  Armor Part: Fusion Core

 Fusion Cores are worth a good deal of bartering currency, but mostly they are useful for slotting into the back of your Power Armor suits; therefore, they are critical for the continuing operation of your protective exoskeleton. You usually find them powering generators, but they are also loose in a location or already plugged into existing Power Armor.

###  Armor Part: Power Armor (Type)

 To keep your Power Armor in working order, you'll want to cannibalize parts from other suits you find. Locations with this flag have such a suit. This armor could be a frame (from which you can build another suit), it may be in parts, underwater, or still attached to a Raider you're beating to death with a power fist.

###   BOTTLECAPS (+++) AND SAFES

 This location has a good number of Bottlecaps to add to your currency collection. Receive them after bartering from a trader or as a quest reward, or find them in Caps stashes or on recently slain settlers. If an area has Caps, it is duly noted. Also flagged are any safes and the difficulty of the lock.

## COLLECTIBLES

###  Collectible: Bobblehead

 A limited-edition, one-of-a-kind Vault-Tec official Bobblehead is at this location! Why not collect all of them? Each one has a specific statistical improvement, and any you collect can be displayed at a settlement you own. But finding them can be tricky, unless you know where to look.

###  Collectible: Holotape

 If you wish to learn more about a location you're visiting, find clues that lead to quests, or listen to stories about squirrels, seek out these Holotapes strewn about the location.

###  Collectible: Holotape Game

Your first incredible RobCo FUN! Holotape game is in Vault 111. But what about the other four? They are free with copies of the RobCo FUN! magazine. If there's a Holotape game to collect, it will be flagged.

###  Collectible: Nuka Cola Quantum

 When your thirst won't quit, quench it with a Quantum! Make time for a Nuka break by finding these glowing blue bottles, and drink up like your life depends on it. Delicious? Yes! Nutritious? Of course!

### HELPFUL HINT from *Vault Boy*! Did You Know?

GREAT NEWS, NUKA COLA FANS! ALTHOUGH THIS CHAPTER HAS SPECIFIC LOCATIONS FOR NUKA CHERRY AND NUKA COLA QUANTUMS, THESE DELICIOUS BEVERAGES MAY ALSO APPEAR RANDOMLY IN NUKA COLA MACHINES OR IN CRATES OR COOLERS. THEY ARE ALSO CARRIED BY FOLKS YOU'VE MOWN DOWN IN A FRENZY. SO EXPECT TO GATHER MORE OF THESE DRINKS THAN THIS CHAPTER TRACKS.

###  Collectible: Nuka Cherry

 Need to satisfy your craving for the intense and delicious flavor of cherries? Then look for the glowing red bottles found across the Commonwealth.

###  Required Reading: Skill Magazine

Scattered throughout the wasteland are over 100 books that offer a great deal of information and some excellent bonuses to your various statistics. Need to know the reward for finding each magazine? Check page 27-28.

## CRAFTING

 Armor workbenches, chemistry stations, cooking stations, Power Armor stations, and weapons workbenches are all flagged if a location has one to tinker on.

## COMPANIONS

Occasionally, a location has a special friend you can pal around with, order about, and have lengthy chats with. Mostly, though, they're helpful with providing fire support and lugging scavenged equipment around.

## DANGERS

 A vast majority of locations feature one or more of the following dangers. Just another reason why leaving the safety of your Vault is a decision not to be taken lightly.

**Can Chimes!**

These hanging cans can be disarmed for scrap or jingled to attract attention.

**Escaping Gas!**

The area has a thick wavy malaise about the air; explosive projectiles can cause this to explode in a highly damaging blast.

**Explosive Barrels!**

The area has one or more red barrels or thin canisters that are designed to explode when shot at. Try not to be standing close by during a detonation.

**Flamethrowers!**

At this location, you encounter a flamethrower turret designed to burn you alive.

**Grenades!**

Tension traps, or bathroom scale traps, usually release grenades when triggered. Instead, look for these grenade bouquets and pocket them for use against the enemies that prepped them.

**Long Drop!**

This location is high up. It features a lengthy drop to the ground, which is fine to take while wearing Power Armor but can lead to a horrific crushing death if you're less well armored.

**Madness!**

This place has a strange oddness about it. Did you hear the rumors? What was that sound? Who is that? It might be time to flee before events you cannot explain take a toll on your sanity.

**Makeshift Bombs!**

These are attached to doors or around corners and are sometimes triggered by tension traps; disarm them so they don't go off in your face.

## Mines!

That beeping sound indicates you're about to be crippled by a mine if you don't disarm or flee the immediate area. Beware of these at the location.

## Oil!

A rainbow hue of leaking fluid, usually from age-old machinery in various stages of disrepair, can go up in flames if you use flammable projectiles or explode barrels. Be sure foes—not you—are standing over oil.

## Radiation (Mild)!

This location is mildly radioactive, usually in areas of water or with a few scattered barrels improperly disposed of. Take reasonable care and a Rad-X afterward.

## Radiation (Severe)!

This location is very radioactive, especially the Glowing Sea, areas where radioactive barrels have been dumped, or at the remains of a massive crater created when the bombs dropped. Exercise extreme caution and wrap up properly before entering.

## Tension Trigger!

A spring has been set against a door or other object, and when released, a grenade or makeshift bomb (or other wounding device) is set to go off. Disarm these with haste.

## Tesla Arcs!

An electrical device that's as impressive to look at as it is foolish to take damage from. Quickly disarm these wall-mounted devices or face a nasty singe of energy damage.

## Tripwires!

A length of wire or laser has been activated in this location, and tripping it usually releases another type of trap; sometimes it's a weapon firing at you, a tesla arc, a makeshift bomb, or grenades. Disarm these instead.

## Turrets!

The location features unmanned turrets, usually controlled by a nearby terminal you can hack, if you don't wish to sneak by or manually destroy these machine guns.

## FACTION

The type of enemy that lives at this location is listed. There could be multiple types, and these range from enemy types (such as Bloatflies and Raiders) to more robust factions (such as the Brotherhood of Steel or Institute) as appropriate.

## CHARACTERS

This lists characters that appear, or have been known to appear, at a location, in case you wish to strike up a conversation or simply strike them.

## THREAT LEVEL

| | | | | | | | |
|---|---|---|---|---|---|---|---|
| 1-5 | 6-14 | 15-25 | 20+ | 25+ | 30+ | 35+ | 40+ | 45+ |

This indicates the typical level range of the enemies at this location. The higher the range, the more dangerous the foes will tend to be. Obviously, a Super Mutant stronghold is going to be tougher to tackle than a single, gibbering Ghoul, but this indicates the toughness of any creature in the vicinity. Avoid these areas until you feel competent to tackle the foes inhabiting them.

##  HEALTH OR CHEMS (+++)

Whether you're scavenging for white first-aid boxes, yellow chem boxes, scattered health or chems in a loose cluster, or the contents of a chem cooler, if there's a sizable amount of chems, these are shown. Single chems or stimpaks aren't tracked, just the larger collections.

## QUEST START

This indicates a quest begins at this location, so if you're looking for a new adventure, seek out these locations.

## QUEST VISIT

This indicates a quest already in progress may have an objective that requires you to visit this location. If you haven't started the mentioned quest, it may be wise to wait until visiting this location, as some areas of it may not be accessible.

## SERVICES: TRADERS

A trader is known to operate from this area. This person may sell a variety of goods and can be bartered with. You may have better luck finding quality merchandise in larger settlements rather than lone shacks. But any trader who isn't wandering or randomly encountered is flagged for your attention.

## SERVICES: WORKSHOPS

 This indicates a location is a settlement with a workshop, allowing you to build a defensive, and hopefully idyllic, stronghold; set up trade routes; and create a post-apocalyptic utopia with the help of the Minutemen.

## SERVICES: RADIO

A radio signal can be heard at this location. It may require you to search for the source of the signal nearby. Some radio stations simply play music or have chatter to listen to. Others may be distress signals.

## UNIQUE OR EXCEPTIONAL ITEMS

 This location has an item of extreme interest to obtain: Perhaps it is carried by the leader of the location, sold by a trader, or found by particularly cunning means. Whatever the method of obtaining it, you usually can't get this item anywhere else. Whether this is a unique weapon, piece of armor, disgusting pink paste, or toy buttercup horse, be sure to check out these items and add them to your collection of interesting, rare, and entertaining equipment.

---

**TIP**

**LOOKING FOR LOCATIONS IN ALL THE RIGHT PLACES #2**

This atlas is functional, providing you can understand where in the Commonwealth wasteland you are standing and can learn the arbitrary zone borders (main roads, water, and the elevated freeway). But what if you want to quickly look up a location and don't know where it is? Then cross-reference the Commonwealth Collection appendix (page 528), which lists every primary location in alphabetical order, along with the zone number so you can quickly look it up. Simple!

# THE COMMONWEALTH: WORLD MAP

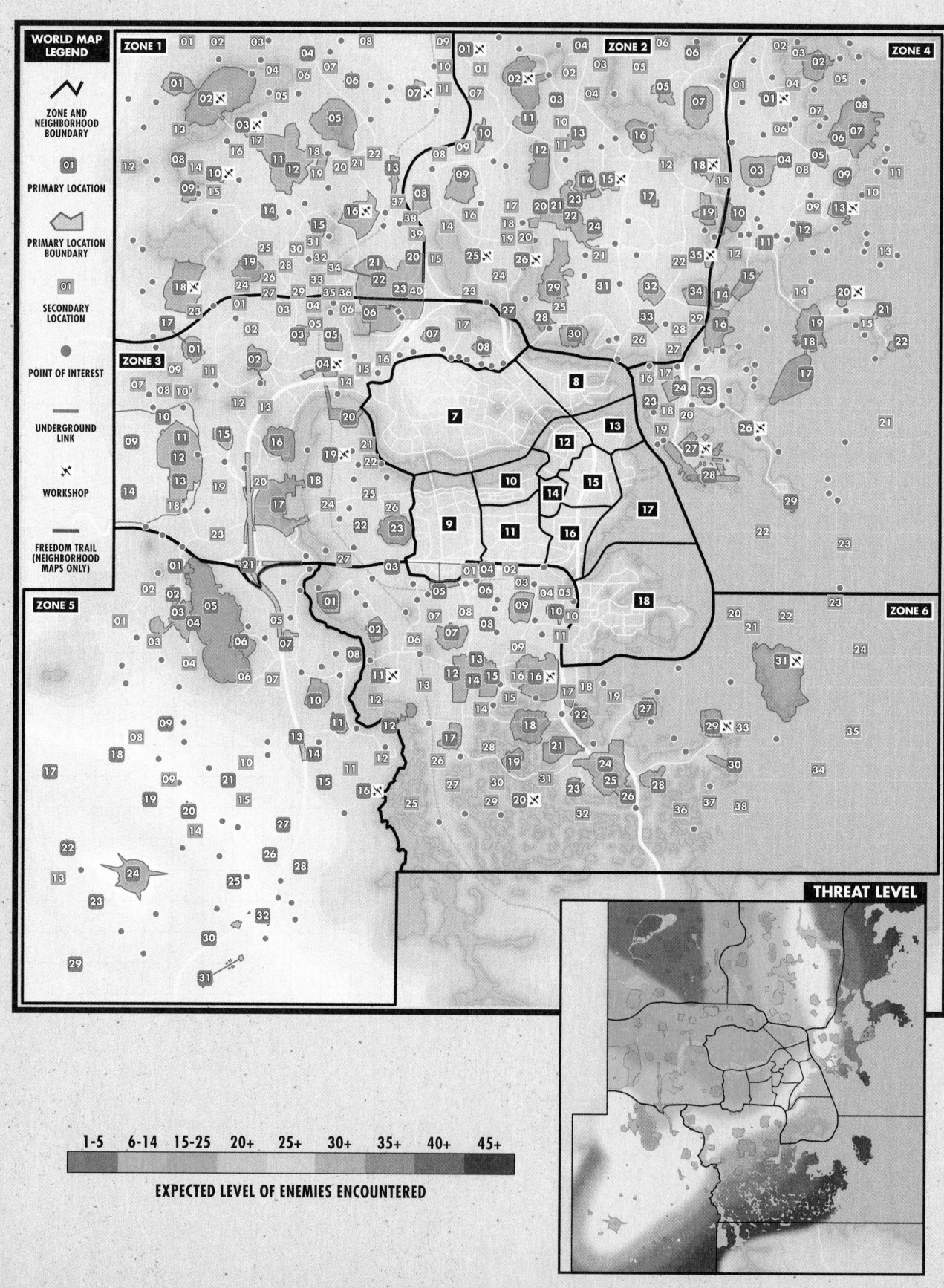

**WORLD MAP LEGEND**

Zone and Neighborhood Boundary

01 — Primary Location

Primary Location Boundary

01 — Secondary Location

Point of Interest

Underground Link

Workshop

Freedom Trail (Neighborhood Maps Only)

**THREAT LEVEL**

1-5  6-14  15-25  20+  25+  30+  35+  40+  45+

EXPECTED LEVEL OF ENEMIES ENCOUNTERED

## ZONE 1: LEXINGTON AND NORTHWEST COMMONWEALTH

### Primary Locations

[1.01] Vault 111
[1.02] Sanctuary
[1.03] Red Rocket Truck Stop
[1.04] Robotics Disposal Ground
[1.05] Thicket Excavations
[1.06] USAF Satellite Station Olivia
[1.07] Tenpines Bluff
[1.08] Ranger Cabin
[1.09] Wicked Shipping Fleet Lockup
[1.10] Abernathy Farm
[1.11] Concord
[1.12] Museum of Freedom
[1.13] Bedford Station
[1.14] Gorski Cabin
[1.15] Drumlin Diner
[1.16] Starlight Drive-In
[1.17] Lonely Chapel
[1.18] Sunshine Tidings Co-op
[1.19] Walden Pond
[1.20] Mystic Pines
[1.21] Super Duper Mart
[1.22] Lexington
[1.23] Lexington Apartments

### Secondary Locations

[1.01] Dry Creek Bed
[1.02] Raider Shack
[1.03] Old Firing Range
[1.04] Sunken Rowboat Stash
[1.05] Water Filtration Caps Stash
[1.06] Raider Hilltop Den
[1.07] Crashed Vertibird (Near Robotics Disposal Ground)
[1.08] Scavenger's Shack
[1.09] Pond and Freeway Shack
[1.10] Elevated Freeway Access (North Wilderness)
[1.11] Military Armor Transport (North Wilderness)
[1.12] Trader's Shack (West of Ranger Cabin)
[1.13] Military APC (Sanctuary Lake)
[1.14] Abandoned Caravan
[1.15] Dry Creek Shack
[1.16] Half-Buried Stash
[1.17] Concord Outskirts Ruined House
[1.18] Concord Campfire
[1.19] Shopping Cart of Goodies
[1.20] Radroach Outhouse
[1.21] A Cooking Spot
[1.22] Dilapidated Trailer Shack
[1.23] Construction Lift to Gunners' Den
[1.24] Settlers' Tent
[1.25] Raider Chem Lab Shack
[1.26] Small Trading Shack
[1.27] Elevated Gunners' Den
[1.28] On-Ramp Gunners' Den
[1.29] Bus Ramp
[1.30] Military Pillbox (Walden)
[1.31] Vending Machine Truck Transport
[1.32] Wicked Shipping Container Truck #2
[1.33] Military Armor Transport (Lexington)
[1.34] Switchboard Entrance (Sewer)
[1.35] Elevated Freeway: Derelict Bus
[1.36] Elevated Freeway Access (Lexington)
[1.37] Freeway Shack and Cage
[1.38] Military Checkpoint (Lexington)
[1.39] Elevated Freeway Access (Lexington)
[1.40] Elevated Jumping-Off Point

## ZONE 2: MEDFORD AND NORTH CENTRAL COMMONWEALTH

### Primary Locations

[2.01] Outpost Zimonja
[2.02] Lake Quannapowitt
[2.03] Radio Tower 3SM-U81
[2.04] Recon Bunker Theta
[2.05] Lynn Woods
[2.06] Parsons Creamery
[2.07] Parsons State Insane Asylum
[2.08] Rotten Landfill
[2.09] Wildwood Cemetery
[2.10] Skylanes Flight 1981
[2.11] General Atomics Galleria
[2.12] Dark Hollow Pond
[2.13] Mass Fusion Containment Shed
[2.14] Old Gullet Sinkhole
[2.15] Greentop Nursery
[2.16] Breakheart Banks
[2.17] Listening Post Bravo
[2.18] The Slog
[2.19] Saugus Ironworks
[2.20] Medford Memorial Hospital
[2.21] Malden Center
[2.22] Slocum's Joe Corporate HQ
[2.23] Malden Middle School (Vault 75)
[2.24] Med-Tek Research
[2.25] Covenant
[2.26] Taffington Boat House
[2.27] Tucker Memorial Bridge
[2.28] Poseidon Energy Turbine #18-F
[2.29] West Everett Estates
[2.30] Irish Pride Industries Shipyard
[2.31] Relay Tower OMC-810
[2.32] National Guard Training Yard
[2.33] County Crossing
[2.34] Revere Satellite Array
[2.35] Finch Farm

### Secondary Locations

[2.01] Container Truck Camp
[2.02] Hilltop Hut
[2.03] Car Tree Camp
[2.04] Deserted Picnic Area
[2.05] Deathclaw Nest (Lynn Woods)
[2.06] Rusty Trailer
[2.07] Bloatfly Camp
[2.08] Billboard Scavenger Shack
[2.09] Elevated Gunner Camp
[2.10] Wicked Shipping Container Truck #3
[2.11] Scavenger Camp
[2.12] Military Convoy (APCs and Trailer)
[2.13] Elevated Freeway: Elevated Trailer
[2.14] Crashed Vertibird (Covenant Lake)
[2.15] The Fishing Spot (Covenant Compound)
[2.16] Rusty Tractor
[2.17] Old Caravan Trailer
[2.18] The Locked Trailer
[2.19] Caravan Crossroads
[2.20] Malden Drainage
[2.21] Brotherhood of Steel Battle Site
[2.22] Military Convoy (Training Yard)
[2.23] Abandoned Raider Camp (Elevated Freeway)
[2.24] Derelict Mansion
[2.25] Military APCs
[2.26] Cooling Vats
[2.27] River's End Shack
[2.28] Protectron Trailer
[2.29] River's End Warehouse

## ZONE 3: WESTERN COMMONWEALTH

### Primary Locations

[3.01] Federal Ration Stockpile
[3.02] ArcJet Systems
[3.03] Rocky Narrows Park
[3.04] Graygarden
[3.05] Jalbert Brothers Disposal
[3.06] Corvega Assembly Plant
[3.07] Mass Gravel & Sand
[3.08] Wattz Consumer Electronics
[3.09] Fort Hagen Satellite Array
[3.10] Relay Tower 0BB-915
[3.11] Fort Hagen Filling Station
[3.12] Fort Hagen
[3.13] Greater Mass Blood Clinic
[3.14] Boston Mayoral Shelter
[3.15] Fiddler's Green Trailer Estates
[3.16] Weston Water Treatment Plant
[3.17] Forest Grove Marsh
[3.18] Relay Tower 1DL-109
[3.19] Oberland Station
[3.20] Beantown Brewery
[3.21] Mass Pike Interchange
[3.22] Vault 81
[3.23] Chestnut Hillock Reservoir

### Secondary Locations

[3.01] Car Wreckage
[3.02] Tractor Warehouse
[3.03] Gunner Camp On-ramp
[3.04] Raider Graves
[3.05] Carriage Den
[3.06] Ruined Brick Warehouse
[3.07] Scavenger's Trailer
[3.08] Rusting APC
[3.09] Mirelurk Pond
[3.10] Canister Launch Shack
[3.11] Schoelt Propane Store
[3.12] Bridge (South of ArcJet Systems)
[3.13] Elevated Freeway Access
[3.14] Pulowski Preservation Shelter Cluster
[3.15] Crashed Vertibird (Elevated Freeway)
[3.16] Construction Lift
[3.17] Military Checkpoint (Cambridge Outskirts)
[3.18] Power Armor Warehouse
[3.19] ArcJet Engine Transport
[3.20] Scrap Merchant
[3.21] Cave
[3.22] Crash Site
[3.23] Military Checkpoint (South Zone 3)
[3.24] Waystation
[3.25] Roadside Store
[3.26] Joe's Spuckies Coffee Shop (Fens Outskirts)
[3.27] Raider Lookout Camp (Elevated Freeway)

## ZONE 4: COASTAL COMMONWEALTH

### Primary Locations

[4.01] Coastal Cottage
[4.02] Mahkra Fishpacking
[4.03] Dunwich Borers
[4.04] Hugo's Hole
[4.05] Museum of Witchcraft
[4.06] Sandy Coves Convalescent Home
[4.07] Salem
[4.08] Rook Family House
[4.09] Crater House
[4.10] Hub City Auto Wreckers
[4.11] Lynn Pier Parking
[4.12] Longneck Lukowski's Cannery
[4.13] Kingsport Lighthouse
[4.14] Reeb Marina
[4.15] Gibson Point Pier
[4.16] Revere Beach Station
[4.17] Libertalia
[4.18] Nahant Wharf
[4.19] Nahant Sheriff's Department
[4.20] Croup Manor
[4.21] Nahant Chapel
[4.22] Nahant Oceanological Society
[4.23] East Boston Police Station
[4.24] East Boston Preparatory School
[4.25] Easy City Downs
[4.26] Nordhagen Beach
[4.27] Boston Airport
[4.28] Prydwen
[4.29] Fort Strong

### Secondary Locations

[4.01] Gunner Camp (Parsons Elevated Freeway)
[4.02] Milton General Billboard
[4.03] Coastal Vacationers
[4.04] Coastal Hideout
[4.05] The Sunken Bathtub
[4.06] Shanty Store
[4.07] Salem Coastal Diner and Dock
[4.08] Raider Shack (Salem Outskirts)
[4.09] Kingsport Restrooms
[4.10] Ocean Fishing Shack
[4.11] Sunken Fishing Boat
[4.12] Vitale Pumphouse
[4.13] Ocean Raft
[4.14] Unloading Barge
[4.15] Nahant Pier Restaurant
[4.16] Drumlin Diner (East Boston)
[4.17] Waterfront Warehouse
[4.18] East Boston Garage
[4.19] Container Crates Stash
[4.20] Freeway Rooftops
[4.21] Upside Down Rowboat
[4.22] Doomed Airlines Flight
[4.23] Floating Barge

## ZONE 5: NATICK AND THE GLOWING SEA

### Primary Locations

[5.01] Poseidon Reservoir
[5.02] Roadside Pines Motel
[5.03] Natick Banks
[5.04] Natick Police Department
[5.05] Lake Cochituate
[5.06] Mass Fusion Disposal Site
[5.07] Electrical Hobbyist's Club
[5.08] WRVR Broadcast Station
[5.09] Federal Supply Cache 84NE
[5.10] Robotics Pioneer Park
[5.11] Scrap Palace
[5.12] Cutler Bend
[5.13] Edge of the Glowing Sea
[5.14] Waypoint Echo
[5.15] Vault 95
[5.16] Somerville Place
[5.17] Forgotten Church
[5.18] Abandoned Shack
[5.19] Atlantic Offices
[5.20] Capsized Factory
[5.21] Cave (Red Rocket Filling Station)
[5.22] Decayed Reactor Site
[5.23] Decrepit Factory
[5.24] Crater of Atom
[5.25] Cave (Super Duper Mart)
[5.26] Vertibird Wreckage
[5.27] Hopesmarch Pentecostal Church
[5.28] Relay Tower 0DB-521
[5.29] Rocky Cave (Virgil's Laboratory)
[5.30] O'Neill Family Manufacturing
[5.31] Sentinel Site
[5.32] Skylanes Flight 1665

### Secondary Locations

[5.01] Natick Power Station
[5.02] Natick Hillside Home
[5.03] Settler Campsite (Natick Outskirts)
[5.04] Military Checkpoint (Lake Cochituate)
[5.05] The Mausoleum
[5.06] Fishing Cabin
[5.07] Two Cabins and an Outhouse
[5.08] Collapsed Billboard (Glowing Sea)
[5.09] Buried Mansion
[5.10] Radiation Lake
[5.11] Military Pillbox (Somerville)
[5.12] The Splintered Statue
[5.13] Derelict Bus
[5.14] Buried House
[5.15] Buckled Freeway

## ZONE 6: QUINCY AND SOUTHERN COMMONWEALTH

### Primary Locations

[6.01] Westing Estate
[6.02] Coast Guard Pier
[6.03] Mass Pike Tunnel West
[6.04] Mass Pike Tunnel East
[6.05] Boston Police Rationing Site
[6.06] NH&M Freight Depot
[6.07] Fairline Hill Estates
[6.08] Relay Tower 0SC-527
[6.09] Big John's Salvage
[6.10] South Boston Military Checkpoint
[6.11] Egret Tours Marina
[6.12] Fallon's Department Store
[6.13] Milton General Hospital
[6.14] West Roxbury Station
[6.15] Shaw High School
[6.16] Jamaica Plain
[6.17] Gunners Plaza
[6.18] Hyde Park
[6.19] Suffolk County Charter School
[6.20] Murkwater Construction Site
[6.21] Quincy Quarries
[6.22] Neponset Park
[6.23] Wilson Atomatoys Factory
[6.24] Quincy Ruins
[6.25] Quincy Police Station
[6.26] Peabody House
[6.27] Atom Cats Garage
[6.28] Poseidon Energy
[6.29] Warwick Homestead
[6.30] Wreck of the FMS Northern Star
[6.31] Spectacle Island

### Secondary Locations

[6.01] Red Rocket Filling Station (Mass Pike East)
[6.02] Layton Towers Underpass Entrance
[6.03] Crater and Shack
[6.04] Red Rocket Filling Station (Big John's Salvage)
[6.05] Wicked Shipping Container Truck #4
[6.06] Railroad Maintenance Shed
[6.07] The Trading Post
[6.08] Dog's Dinner
[6.09] Military Checkpoint (West Roxbury)
[6.10] Deserted Camp (Elevated Freeway)
[6.11] Raider Camp (University Point Outskirts)
[6.12] Island Cabin
[6.13] Waystation (West Roxbury)
[6.14] Moonshiner's Cabin
[6.15] The Hanging Tree
[6.16] Jamaica Plain Pond
[6.17] Military Convoy (Elevated Freeway)
[6.18] The Fridge
[6.19] Military Barge (University Point)
[6.20] Boating Platforms
[6.21] Sunken Fishing Boat (Spectacle Island)
[6.22] Barge Platform
[6.23] Deep Trench Wreckage
[6.24] Sunken Supertanker
[6.25] Sniper's Hideout
[6.26] Waystation (Gunners' Plaza)
[6.27] Ruined Grove Estates
[6.28] The Small Dig
[6.29] Crashed Vertibird (Marshland)
[6.30] Military Pillboxes
[6.31] Old Military Monument
[6.32] Overflow Outlet Camp (Atomatoys Factory)
[6.33] Scuppered Boat
[6.34] Floating Barge
[6.35] Skylines Flight Salvage
[6.36] Boat Graveyard
[6.37] Quincy Lighthouse
[6.38] Undersea Hatch Pipe

# GREATER BOSTON NEIGHBORHOODS

**7 NEIGHBORHOOD: CAMBRIDGE**

## Primary Locations

[7.01] College Square
[7.02] Cambridge Police Station
[7.03] Collegiate Administration Building
[7.04] Fraternal Post 115
[7.05] Cambridge Campus Diner
[7.06] Campus Law Offices
[7.07] Kendall Hospital
[7.08] Cambridge Polymer Labs
[7.09] C.I.T. Ruins
[7.10] The Institute
[7.11] Greenetech Genetics
[7.12] Cambridge Crater
[7.13] Monsignor Plaza

## Secondary Locations

[7.01] Bridge Den (Cambridge)
[7.02] Charles River Boathouse
[7.03] Red Rocket Filling Station (College Square)
[7.04] Union's Hope Cathedral
[7.05] Hardware Store (Cambridge)
[7.06] Plumber's Secret
[7.07] Raider Bonfire Camp
[7.08] Red Rocket Filling Station (North Central Cambridge)
[7.09] Raider Camp (Narrow Yard)
[7.10] Cambridge Park and Old Covered Alley
[7.11] Mass Chemical
[7.12] Super Mutant High Rise
[7.13] Raider Platforms (Cambridge)
[7.14] Raider Rooftop Apartments (Cambridge)
[7.15] Campus Office and Covered Bridge
[7.16] Kendall Parking
[7.17] Kendall Raider Apartments
[7.18] Ticonderoga Safehouse
[7.19] Public Works Maintenance Area
[7.20] Science Center Gift Shop

**8 NEIGHBORHOOD: CHARLESTOWN**

## Primary Locations

[8.01] BADTFL Regional Office
[8.02] Bunker Hill
[8.03] U.S.S. Constitution

## Secondary Locations

[8.01] Ruined Tavern (Charlestown)
[8.02] Back Alley Scaffold Steps
[8.03] Green Awning Mansion
[8.04] Drug Den
[8.05] South Alley and Garage
[8.06] Abandoned House
[8.07] Scavenger Camp (Charlestown)
[8.08] Shelled-Out Building
[8.09] Charlestown Laundry
[8.10] South Apartments (Charlestown)

**9 NEIGHBORHOOD: THE FENS**

## Primary Locations

[9.01] Wreck of the USS Riptide
[9.02] Hangman's Alley
[9.03] Back Street Apparel
[9.04] Police Precinct 8
[9.05] Parkview Apartments
[9.06] Fens Street Sewer
[9.07] Diamond City
[9.08] Diamond City Market
[9.09] Home Plate
[9.10] Hardware Town

## Secondary Locations

[9.01] Fens Subway Station (Outskirts)
[9.02] Fens Tunnel Entrance
[9.03] Super Mutant Alley Apartments
[9.04] Anna's Café
[9.05] Raider Back-Alley Camp (The Fens)
[9.06] Bridgeway Trust
[9.07] Bridgeway Garage
[9.08] Diner and Apartments (The Fens)
[9.09] Settler's Stop (The Fens)
[9.10] Raider Cul-de-Sac (The Fens)
[9.11] Scaffold Bridge (The Fens)
[9.12] Diamond City Scrap
[9.13] Scavenger's Rest (The Fens)

**10 NEIGHBORHOOD: ESPLANADE**

## Primary Locations

[10.01] Charles View Amphitheater
[10.02] HalluciGen, Inc.

## Secondary Locations

[10.01] Footbridge (Esplanade)
[10.02] Holy Mission Congregation Church
[10.03] Barricade and Rooftops
[10.04] Rooftop Den (Esplanade)
[10.05] Malborough House
[10.06] Raider Lookout (Esplanade)
[10.07] Gun Shop Garage
[10.08] Commonwealth Avenue

**11 NEIGHBORHOOD: BACK BAY**

## Primary Locations

[11.01] Boston Public Library
[11.02] Trinity Plaza
[11.03] Hubris Comics
[11.04] Vault 114 (Exit)
[11.05] Trinity Tower
[11.06] Dartmouth Professional Building
[11.07] Layton Towers
[11.08] Wilson Atomatoys Corporate HQ

## Secondary Locations

[11.01] The Corner of Mass and Newbury
[11.02] Half-Demolished Apartment (Back Bay)
[11.03] Trinity Plaza Parking
[11.04] Shenley's Oyster Bar
[11.05] The Patriot's Sleep Shack
[11.06] Trader Rooftop (Back Bay)
[11.07] Raider Rooftops (Back Bay)
[11.08] Warren Theater
[11.09] Raider Blockade (Southeast Back Bay)

**12 NEIGHBORHOOD: BEACON HILL**

## Primary Locations

[12.01] Vault-Tec Regional HQ
[12.02] Boston Bugle Building
[12.03] Cabot House

## Secondary Locations

[12.01] Beacon Hill Apartments
[12.02] Demolished Apartment Tower (Beacon Hill)
[12.03] Playground Garage
[12.04] Rooftop Generator (Beacon Hill)
[12.05] Destroyed Tenement (Beacon Hill)
[12.06] Rubble Overlook

**13 NEIGHBORHOOD: NORTH END**

## Primary Locations

[13.01] Pickman Gallery
[13.02] Old North Church

## Secondary Locations

[13.01] Rooftop Apartment (North End)
[13.02] North End Graveyard
[13.03] Railroad HQ Escape Tunnel Exit
[13.04] Raider Courtyard (North End)
[13.05] Hot Pizza Pie Shop
[13.06] Crashed Vertibird (Military Barge)
[13.07] Wharfside Cottage
[13.08] Rooftop Lounger
[13.09] Skytram (North End Elevated Freeway)
[13.10] Mean Pastries
[13.11] Pickman's Exit
[13.12] Boxing Gym
[13.13] Scaffold Stairs (North End)
[13.14] Billboard Alley
[13.15] Ruined Brick Apartment (North End)
[13.16] Subway Station (North End)
[13.17] Paul Revere's House

**14 NEIGHBORHOOD: BOSTON COMMON**

## Primary Locations

[14.01] Massachusetts State House
[14.02] Old Granary Burying Ground
[14.03] Swan's Pond
[14.04] Boston Common
[14.05] Park Street Station (Vault 114)
[14.06] Boylston Club

## Secondary Locations

[14.01] Super Mutant Hotel Shell
[14.02] Prost Bar

**15 NEIGHBORHOOD: FINANCIAL DISTRICT**

## Primary Locations

[15.01] Mass Fusion Building
[15.02] Old Corner Bookstore
[15.03] Haymarket Mall

## THREAT LEVEL

| 1-5 | 6-14 | 15-25 | 20+ | 25+ | 30+ | 35+ | 40+ | 45+ |

**EXPECTED LEVEL OF ENEMIES ENCOUNTERED**

## ZONE MAP

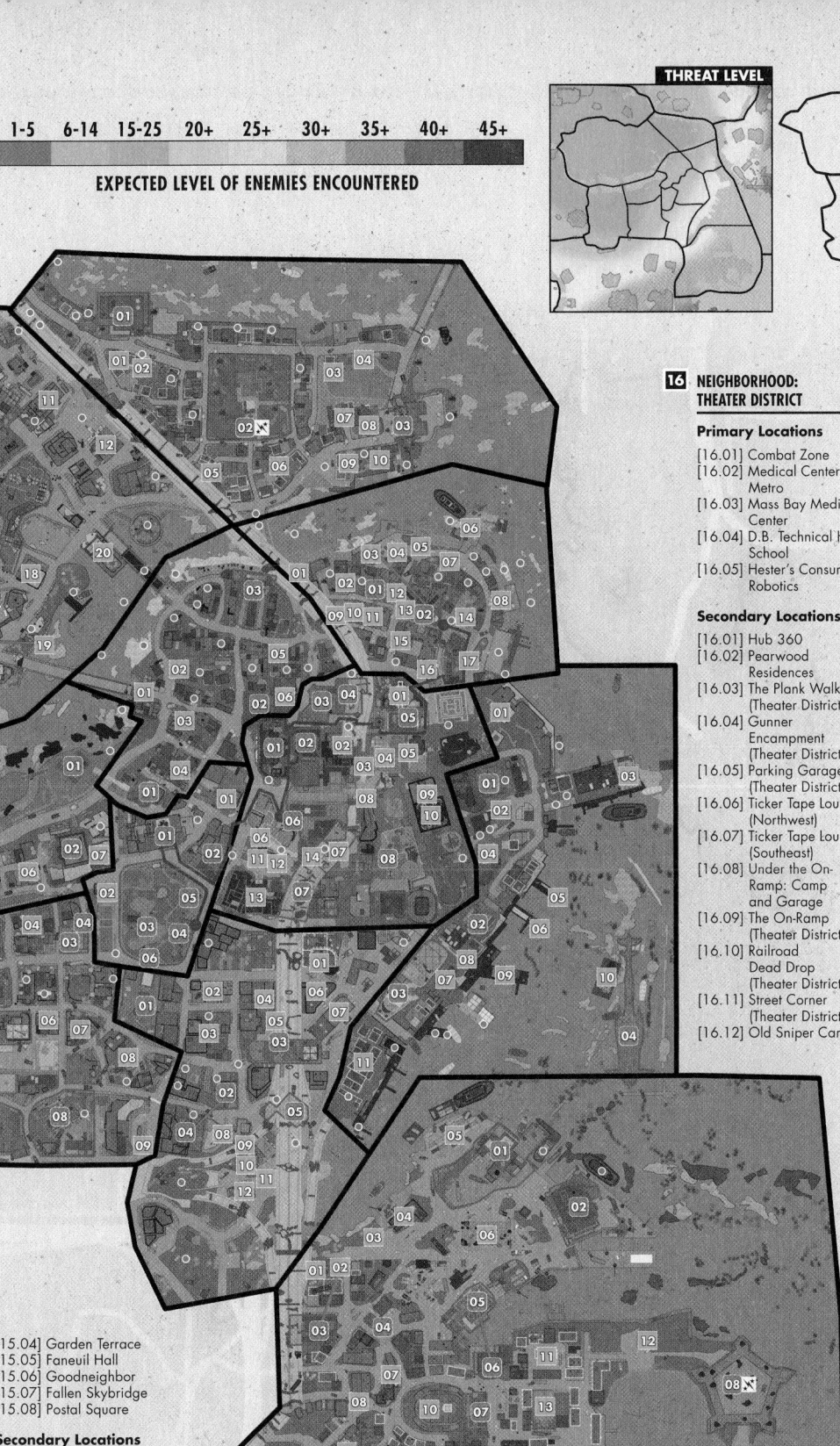

### 16 NEIGHBORHOOD: THEATER DISTRICT

**Primary Locations**

[16.01] Combat Zone
[16.02] Medical Center Metro
[16.03] Mass Bay Medical Center
[16.04] D.B. Technical High School
[16.05] Hester's Consumer Robotics

**Secondary Locations**

[16.01] Hub 360
[16.02] Pearwood Residences
[16.03] The Plank Walk (Theater District)
[16.04] Gunner Encampment (Theater District)
[16.05] Parking Garage (Theater District)
[16.06] Ticker Tape Lounge (Northwest)
[16.07] Ticker Tape Lounge (Southeast)
[16.08] Under the On-Ramp: Camp and Garage
[16.09] The On-Ramp (Theater District)
[16.10] Railroad Dead Drop (Theater District)
[16.11] Street Corner (Theater District)
[16.12] Old Sniper Camp

### 17 NEIGHBORHOOD: BOSTON HARBOR (WATERFRONT)

**Primary Locations**

[17.01] Custom House Tower
[17.02] The Shamrock Taphouse
[17.03] Harbormaster Hotel
[17.04] Yangtze

**Secondary Locations**

[17.01] Waterfront Park
[17.02] Custom House Tower Courtyard
[17.03] Warehouse and Wharf
[17.04] Scavengers' Rooftops (Waterfront)
[17.05] Tinkerer's Boathouse (Waterfront)
[17.06] Main Boathouse (Waterfront)
[17.07] Locked Diner
[17.08] Pedestrian Walkway (Waterfront)
[17.09] Waterfront Cabin
[17.10] Scrap Metal Barge
[17.11] Desolate Promenade

### 18 NEIGHBORHOOD: SOUTH BOSTON

**Primary Locations**

[18.01] Four Leaf Fishpacking Plant
[18.02] General Atomics Factory
[18.03] Andrew Station
[18.04] South Boston Police Department
[18.05] Gwinnett Brewery
[18.06] The Gwinnett Restaurant
[18.07] South Boston High School
[18.08] The Castle
[18.09] University Point

**Secondary Locations**

[18.01] Bus and Apartment Wreckage
[18.02] Joe's Spuckies (Southie Speakeasy)
[18.03] Dockside Warehouse (South Boston)
[18.04] Factory (South Boston)
[18.05] Four Leaf Fishpacking Container Yard
[18.06] Construction Yard
[18.07] Roof Generator (South Boston)
[18.08] Roundabout Raider Camp
[18.09] Hawthorne Estate
[18.10] Dorchester Height Monument
[18.11] Roof Camp (South Boston)
[18.12] The Candy Shop
[18.13] South Boston Church
[18.14] South Boston Wharf and Restrooms
[18.15] Rusting Ship and Stilt Cabin

[15.04] Garden Terrace
[15.05] Faneuil Hall
[15.06] Goodneighbor
[15.07] Fallen Skybridge
[15.08] Postal Square

**Secondary Locations**

[15.01] Weatherby Investment Trust
[15.02] Congress Street Garage
[15.03] Bus Wreckage
[15.04] Commonwealth Bank
[15.05] Skyscraper Stash
[15.06] Elevated Road (West Access)
[15.07] Elevated Raider Camp (Financial District)
[15.08] Elevated Road (Central Access)
[15.09] Railroad Hideout (Financial District)
[15.10] 35 Court
[15.11] Rooftop Hideaway (Financial District)
[15.12] Pedestrian Underpass
[15.13] Parking garage and Raider Rooftops
[15.14] Water Street Apartments

255

# ZONE 1: LEXINGTON AND NORTHWEST COMMONWEALTH

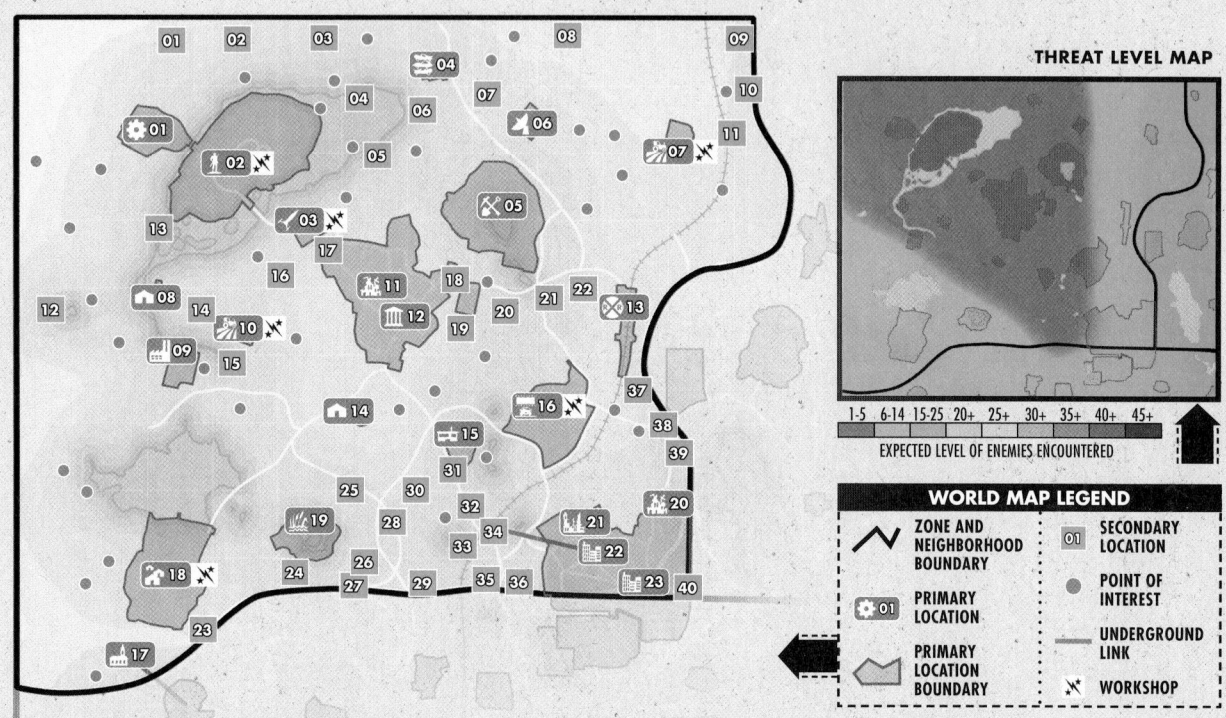

**THREAT LEVEL MAP**

1-5 | 6-14 | 15-25 | 20+ | 25+ | 30+ | 35+ | 40+ | 45+
EXPECTED LEVEL OF ENEMIES ENCOUNTERED

**WORLD MAP LEGEND**

| | | |
|---|---|---|
| ∿ | ZONE AND NEIGHBORHOOD BOUNDARY | 01 SECONDARY LOCATION |
| ⚙01 | PRIMARY LOCATION | ● POINT OF INTEREST |
| ⬟ | PRIMARY LOCATION BOUNDARY | ─ UNDERGROUND LINK |
| | | ⚔ WORKSHOP |

This section of the Commonwealth is comprised of your old stomping grounds of Sanctuary Hills and has reasonable road access southeast into the townships of Concord and Lexington. There are several settlements to visit and inhabitants to befriend, if you're planning on building a new cooperative of farms and strongholds. For those without combat readiness, it is advisable to stay within the confines of this zone while you practice, as enemy threats are the lowest. The border of this zone is easy to see; the east and south edges follow the path of the elevated freeway. Or at least, what's left of it. Both freeways converge at Lexington, your gateway to Boston.

## Primary Locations

- [1.01] VAULT 111
- [1.02] SANCTUARY
- [1.03] RED ROCKET TRUCK STOP
- [1.04] ROBOTICS DISPOSAL GROUND
- [1.05] THICKET EXCAVATIONS
- [1.06] USAF SATELLITE STATION OLIVIA
- [1.07] TENPINES BLUFF
- [1.08] RANGER CABIN
- [1.09] WICKED SHIPPING FLEET LOCKUP
- [1.10] ABERNATHY FARM
- [1.11] CONCORD
- [1.12] MUSEUM OF FREEDOM
- [1.13] BEDFORD STATION
- [1.14] GORSKI CABIN
- [1.15] DRUMLIN DINER
- [1.16] STARLIGHT DRIVE-IN
- [1.17] LONELY CHAPEL
- [1.18] SUNSHINE TIDINGS CO-OP
- [1.19] WALDEN POND
- [1.20] MYSTIC PINES
- [1.21] SUPER DUPER MART
- [1.22] LEXINGTON
- [1.23] LEXINGTON APARTMENTS

## Secondary Locations

- [1.01] DRY CREEK BED
- [1.02] RAIDER SHACK
- [1.03] OLD FIRING RANGE
- [1.04] SUNKEN ROWBOAT STASH
- [1.05] WATER FILTRATION CAPS STASH
- [1.06] RAIDER HILLTOP DEN
- [1.07] CRASHED VERTIBIRD (NEAR ROBOTICS DISPOSAL GROUND)
- [1.08] SCAVENGER'S SHACK
- [1.09] POND AND FREEWAY SHACK
- [1.10] ELEVATED FREEWAY ACCESS (NORTH WILDERNESS)
- [1.11] MILITARY ARMOR TRANSPORT (NORTH WILDERNESS)
- [1.12] TRADER'S SHACK (WEST OF RANGER CABIN)
- [1.13] MILITARY APC (SANCTUARY LAKE)
- [1.14] ABANDONED CARAVAN
- [1.15] DRY CREEK SHACK
- [1.16] HALF-BURIED STASH
- [1.17] CONCORD OUTSKIRTS RUINED HOUSE

**MAP LEGEND**

| 13 — 20 OPTIMAL ROUTE | | |
| --- | --- | --- |
| ○ AREA OF INTEREST | | |

- © BOTTLECAPS
- 🔒 SAFE
- ARMAMENTS AND AMMO
- DOOR

- HEALTH OR CHEMS
- TERMINAL
- STEAMER TRUNK

- FUSION CORE
- POWER ARMOR
- REQUIRED READING

Collectibles:
- BOBBLEHEAD
- NUKA CHERRY
- MINI NUKE
- NUKA COLA QUANTUM
- HOLOTAPE
- A KEY

| N – Novice (Locked) | E – Expert (Locked) | T – Terminal required to unlock | IN – Inaccessible | CB – Circuit Breaker |
| --- | --- | --- | --- | --- |
| A – Advanced (Locked) | M – Master (Locked) | KEY – Key or ID Card required to unlock | C – Chained | B – Button |

# PRIMARY LOCATIONS

## ⚙ [1.01] VAULT 111

THREAT LEVELS 1-5

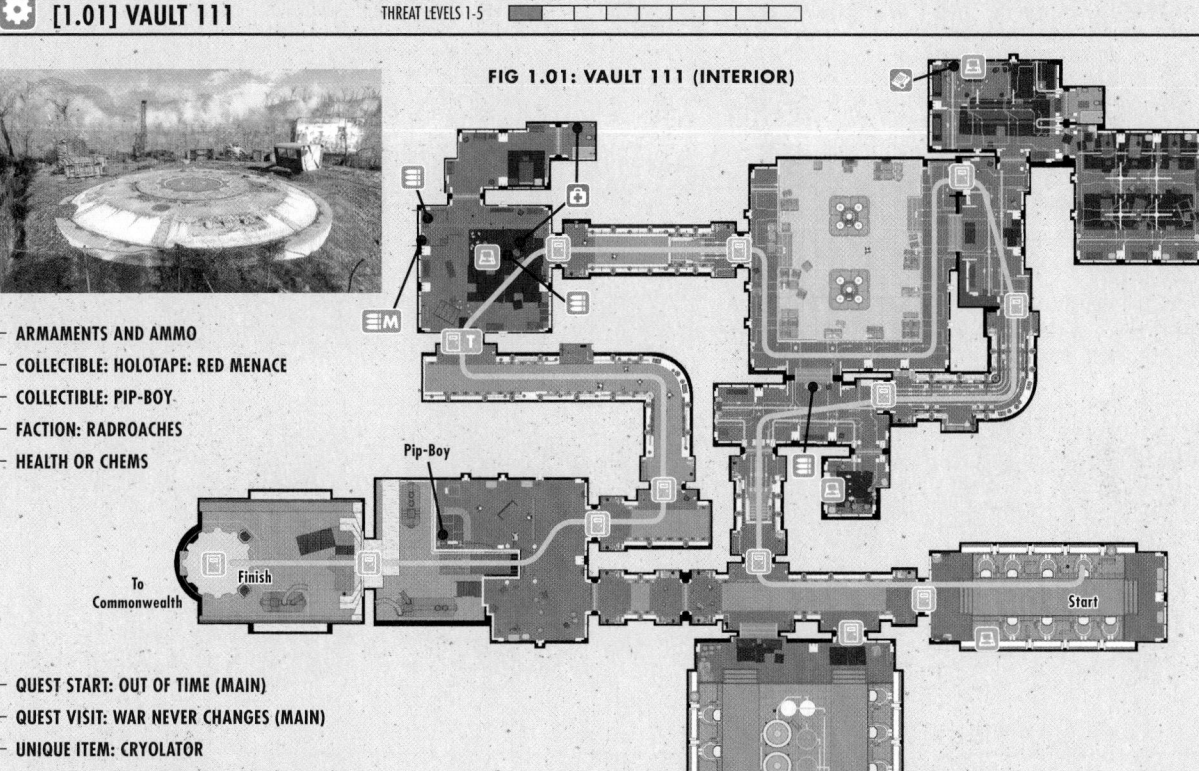

FIG 1.01: VAULT 111 (INTERIOR)

- ARMAMENTS AND AMMO
- COLLECTIBLE: HOLOTAPE: RED MENACE
- COLLECTIBLE: PIP-BOY
- FACTION: RADROACHES
- HEALTH OR CHEMS

Pip-Boy

To Commonwealth    Finish

Start

- QUEST START: OUT OF TIME (MAIN)
- QUEST VISIT: WAR NEVER CHANGES (MAIN)
- UNIQUE ITEM: CRYOLATOR

MAP

ZONE 1

LEXINGTON AND NORTHWEST COMMONWEALTH

### VAULT-TEC RECOMMENDED LOOT ⚙

HOLOTAPE: RED MENACE
UNIQUE ITEM: CRYOLATOR

Vault-Tec Calling! We are pleased to reveal your new home underground. Despite an initially chilly reception, you may find this location to be the safest around, especially as the population has thinned out quite considerably since you were frozen.

The Holotape in the cafeteria terminal is the popular game "Red Menace." Eject it so you can play it at your leisure!

The overseer's office has a firmly locked case (Master) with a prototype weapon, the Cryolator. Return here with bobby pins and an impressive lockpicking ability to obtain this rare item.

If you leave Vault 111, you may find some ammunition and a knife in a trailer to the north. Should you wish to return, simply press the Vault 111 Elevator Button in the outside pod to call the surface elevator. Have a great day!

**HELPFUL HINT** *from Vault Boy!*  Did You Know?

RED MENACE IS A HOLOTAPE GAME THAT USUALLY COMES FREE WITH ROBCO FUN! MAGAZINE. THERE ARE FOUR OTHER GAMES TO COLLECT, FREE IN EACH ISSUE! NEED TO FIND ALL OF THEM? CHECK THE REQUIRED READING APPENDIX AT THE BACK OF THIS BOOK.

## [1.02] SANCTUARY

THREAT LEVELS 1-5 ▮▮▯▯▯▯▯▯▯▯

(*The quest start location depends on where Preston Garvey is located. Unless you send him to another settlement, he is here.)

- ARMAMENTS AND AMMO
- BOTTLECAPS
- CRAFTING: ARMOR WORKBENCH
- CRAFTING: CHEMISTRY STATION
- CRAFTING: COOKING STATION
- CRAFTING: POWER ARMOR STATION
- CRAFTING: WEAPONS WORKBENCH
- COLLECTIBLE: NUKA CHERRY (2)
- COLLECTIBLE: REQUIRED READING: YOU'RE S.P.E.C.I.A.L.!
- COMPANION: CODSWORTH
- DANGER: MAKESHIFT BOMB!
- FACTION: BLOATFLIES
- FACTION: RADROACHES
- FACTION: SETTLER
- FACTION: CHARACTER: CODSWORTH
- HEALTH OR CHEMS+
- QUEST START: WAR NEVER CHANGES (MAIN)
- QUEST START: SANCTUARY (THE MINUTEMEN)
- QUEST START: TAKING INDEPENDENCE (THE MINUTEMEN)*
- QUEST START: RADIANT QUESTS (THE MINUTEMEN)*
- QUEST START: RECRUITMENT QUESTS (THE MINUTEMEN)*
- QUEST VISIT: OUT OF TIME (MAIN)
- QUEST VISIT: THE MOLECULAR LEVEL (MAIN)
- QUEST VISIT: WHEN FREEDOM CALLS (THE MINUTEMEN)
- SERVICES: WORKSHOP

### VAULT-TEC RECOMMENDED LOOT

REQUIRED READING:
YOU'RE S.P.E.C.I.A.L.!
REQUIRED READING:
GROGNAK THE BARBARIAN
COLLECTIBLE: NUKA CHERRY

### AVAILABLE COMPANION

COMPANION: CODSWORTH

Growing from the ruins of Sanctuary Hills, the prewar neighborhood your family used to call home, is a new settlement, a beacon of hope for the downtrodden and the new base of operations for the Minutemen.

You can level the more decrepit dwellings for building materials. There are excellent crafting opportunities, as all stations and workbenches are already here. The area is relatively safe and becomes safer after you fortify the area with defenses you build from your workshop. Attract settlers! Beckon the Minutemen to live here! Build another paradise!

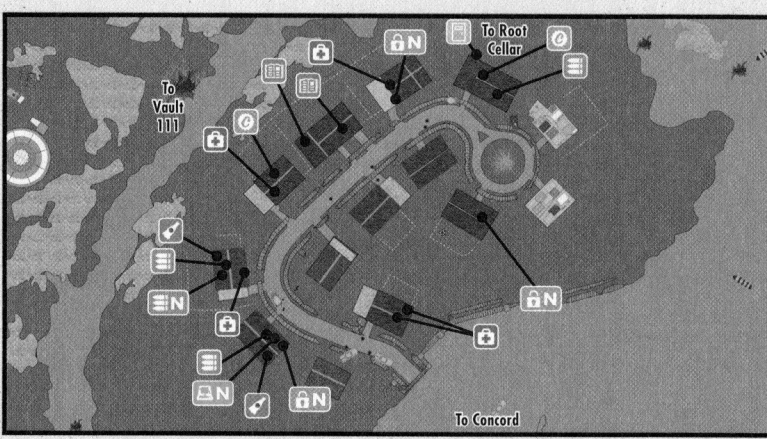

FIG 1.02: SANCTUARY (EXTERIOR)

Thoroughly search the area. The house to the north has a root cellar with a safe (Advanced) and first aid box to loot, as well as a place to sleep. A few homes have smaller items to scavenge, like bobby pins. Others have safes and health, and your own home has something S.P.E.C.I.A.L., too (as well as that Grognak the Barbarian you didn't have time to read). And finally, don't forget Codsworth!

## [1.03] RED ROCKET TRUCK STOP

THREAT LEVELS 1-5 ▮▮▯▯▯▯▯▯▯▯

- ARMAMENTS AND AMMO
- ARMOR PART: FUSION CORE
- BOTTLECAPS
- COMPANION: DOGMEAT

- CRAFTING: ARMOR WORKBENCH
- CRAFTING: CHEMISTRY STATION
- CRAFTING: COOKING STATION
- CRAFTING: POWER ARMOR STATION
- CRAFTING: WEAPONS WORKBENCH
- DANGER: EXPLOSIVE BARRELS!
- DANGER: RADIATION (MILD)!
- FACTION: MOLE RATS
- FACTION: CHARACTER: DOGMEAT
- HEALTH OR CHEMS
- SERVICES: WORKSHOP

### VAULT-TEC RECOMMENDED LOOT

ARMOR PART: FUSION CORE

### AVAILABLE COMPANION

COMPANION: DOGMEAT

This is a service station between Sanctuary Hills and Concord. It seems ex-employees of the company had a habit of dumping hazardous materials in the cave beneath the station instead of disposing of them properly. Check the hill to the south for an entrance to the cave (now a Mole Rat Den), but watch for explosive barrels in this confined burrow. There's a safe (Novice) in here, as well as an ironic Trashbusters Award (Note), a pipe pistol, and some ammo. Also of interest is a Fusion Core (by the note), which helps give continuous juice to your Power Armor.

##  [1.04] ROBOTICS DISPOSAL GROUND  THREAT LEVELS 1-5

- – ARMAMENTS AND AMMO+
- – ARMAMENTS AND AMMO: MINI NUKE
- – ARMAMENTS AND AMMO: MINI NUKE (FAT MAN)
- – ARMAMENTS AND AMMO: TRUNK
- – COLLECTIBLE: REQUIRED READING: HOT RODDER
- – CRAFTING: WEAPONS WORKBENCH
- – FACTION: MOLE RATS
- – FACTION: ROBOT
- – HEALTH OR CHEMS

### VAULT-TEC RECOMMENDED LOOT

**REQUIRED READING: HOT RODDER MAGAZINE**

**ARMAMENTS AND AMMO: MINI NUKE AND MINI NUKE (FAT MAN)**

A junkyard for failed assembly line robot prototypes, as well as rusting scrap. Use the holotape in the terminal to activate the Sentry Proto MKIV if you wish. How far away is the range of this activation? Why not test it out? Don't forget to rummage around by the tire pile (east entrance) for a Mini Nuke, and the Fat Man is among the rusting cars, northwest of the Sentry Bot.

##  [1.05] THICKET EXCAVATIONS  THREAT LEVELS 1-5

- – ARMAMENTS OR AMMO+
- – ARMAMENTS OR AMMO: TRUNK
- – BOTTLECAPS+
- – COLLECTIBLE: REQUIRED READING: TABOO TATTOOS
- – CRAFTING: COOKING STATION
- – CRAFTING: CHEMISTRY STATION
- – CRAFTING: WEAPONS STATION
- – DANGER: LONG DROP!
- – DANGER: RADIATION (MILD)!
- – FACTION: MIRELURKS
- – FACTION: RAIDERS
- – FACTION: CHARACTER: SULLY MATHIS
- – HEALTH OR CHEMS
- – QUEST START: PULL THE PLUG (LOCATION)

Pipe Valve

Pipe Valve

FIG 1.05: THICKET EXCAVATIONS (EXTERIOR)

MAP

ZONE 1

LEXINGTON AND NORTHWEST COMMONWEALTH

### VAULT-TEC RECOMMENDED LOOT

**REQUIRED READING: TABOO TATTOOS**

This marble quarry has gained a reputation as the source of the finest Mirelurk meat in the Commonwealth, thanks to the still water giving the meat a less brackish flavor.

**Pull the Plug**

1. REPAIR PIPES (3)     3. START THE PUMP
2. TALK TO SULLY MATHIS

Speak to Sully Mathis and agree to help repair some underwater pipes.

 (Easy, Medium) Ask for Caps, or what he's really doing here.

Dive into the quarry pond, locating the three valves. Return to Sully, then activate the circuit breaker to switch on the pump and drain the quarry. Deal with any Mirelurks before accepting some Caps for your troubles.

After reaching level 12, return here after 24 hours to find the water drained and a bunch of Raiders rearing Mirelurks. Descend and search the Raider shacks for more items, including a steamer trunk to pillage.

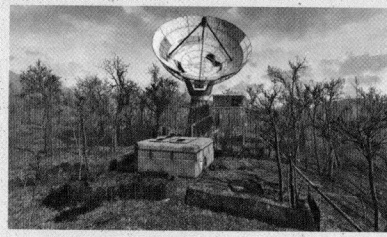

## [1.06] USAF SATELLITE STATION OLIVIA

THREAT LEVELS 1-5

### VAULT-TEC RECOMMENDED LOOT

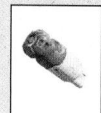

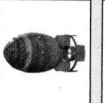

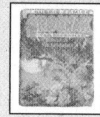

**ARMOR PART: FUSION CORE**

**ARMAMENTS AND AMMO: MINI NUKE**

**REQUIRED READING: U.S. COVERT OPERATIONS MANUAL**

- ARMAMENTS AND AMMO+
- ARMAMENTS AND AMMO: MINI NUKE
- ARMAMENTS AND AMMO: TRUNK
- ARMOR PART: FUSION CORE
- COLLECTIBLE: REQUIRED READING: U.S. COVERT OPERATIONS MANUAL
- CRAFTING: ARMOR WORKBENCH
- DANGER: OIL!
- DANGER: TRIPWIRE!
- FACTION: RADROACHES
- FACTION: RAIDERS
- FACTION: CHARACTER: ACK-ACK
- HEALTH OR CHEMS

Raiders are looting this inactive communications satellite station. Mount an attack on the exterior; the bunker has an Armor Workbench and an entrance inside. The dish gantry has some ammo to pilfer.

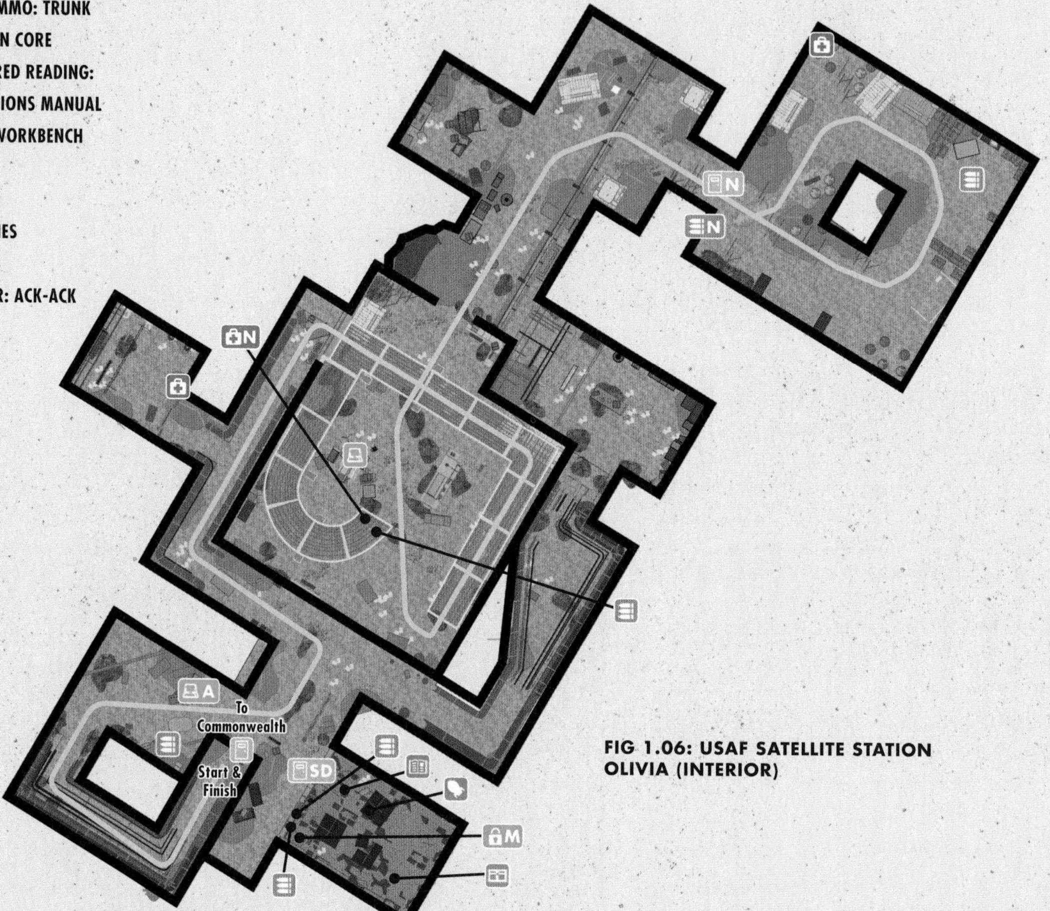


**FIG 1.06: USAF SATELLITE STATION OLIVIA (INTERIOR)**

Inside, the guard terminal opens the intel room (the security gate area), or find the key in the instrument case behind the locked double doors (Novice). The rest of the facility has Raiders led by Ack-Ack, who uses a nasty minigun.

## [1.07] TENPINES BLUFF

THREAT LEVELS 6-14

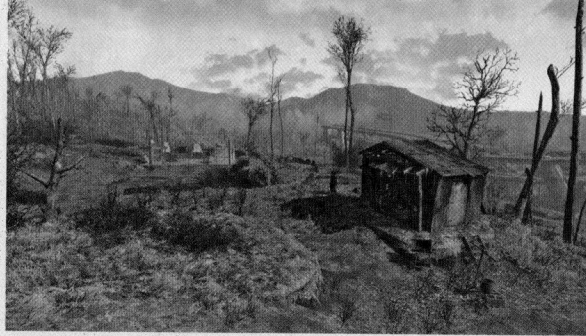

- CRAFTING: COOKING STATION
- FACTION: RADROACH
- FACTION: SETTLERS
- SERVICES: WORKSHOP

This small settlement of Tato farmers is ripe for an alliance, with a light Radroach infestation.

**[1.08] RANGER CABIN** THREAT LEVELS 1-5

- COLLECTIBLE: REQUIRED READING: WASTELAND SURVIVAL GUIDE
- CRAFTING: CHEMISTRY STATION
- CRAFTING: COOKING STATION
- FACTION: BLOATFLIES

**VAULT-TEC RECOMMENDED LOOT**

 COLLECTIBLE: REQUIRED READING: WASTELAND SURVIVAL GUIDE

This is the remains of a U.S. Forest Service cabin, the last known whereabouts of a young runaway.

 **[1.09] WICKED SHIPPING FLEET LOCKUP** THREAT LEVELS 1-5

**VAULT-TEC RECOMMENDED LOOT**

  COLLECTIBLE: REQUIRED READING: GROGNAK THE BARBARIAN

WICKED SHIPPING TRAILER KEY

Tim and Blake were two brothers who started their own shipping business. They had a small fleet of seven trucks and were out on deliveries when the bombs dropped.

One of the rusting big-rig containers has a safe to crack (Novice).

 **Miscellaneous: Wicked Shipments***

Listen to the Holotape in the garage by the Power Armor station. Check the Wicked Shipping terminal in the office for shipping manifests to three locations. Optionally head there (look in this guide for "Wicked Shipping Container Truck" Secondary Locations) to find any Wicked Shipping trucks to unlock. Grab the trailer key by the desk for easy access into the trailers. The first trailer is in the parking area at the front of the main warehouse (Expert). Inside is a steamer trunk to pillage.

- ARMAMENTS AND AMMO+
- ARMAMENTS AND AMMO: TRUNK
- COLLECTIBLE: REQUIRED READING: GROGNAK THE BARBARIAN
- COLLECTIBLE: HOLOTAPE: WICKED BUSINESS
- CRAFTING: ARMOR WORKBENCH
- CRAFTING: CHEMISTRY STATION
- CRAFTING: POWER ARMOR STATION
- FACTION: FERAL GHOULS
- HEALTH OR CHEMS
- QUEST START: WICKED SHIPMENTS (LOCATION MISCELLANEOUS)

 **[1.10] ABERNATHY FARM** THREAT LEVELS 1-5

- ARMAMENTS AND AMMO
- CRAFTING: CHEMISTRY STATION
- CRAFTING: COOKING STATION
- FACTION: SETTLER
- FACTION: CHARACTER: BLAKE ABERNATHY
- FACTION: CHARACTER: CONNIE ABERNATHY
- FACTION: CHARACTER: LUCY ABERNATHY
- QUEST START: RETURNING THE FAVOR (MINUTEMEN)
- SERVICES: TRADER (BLAKE ABERNATHY)
- SERVICES: TRADER (CONNIE ABERNATHY)
- SERVICES: WORKSHOP

Blake and his wife, Connie, tend to their tato and melon patches and mourn the loss of their eldest daughter Mary, killed in a recent Raider attack.

**MAP**

**ZONE 1**

LEXINGTON AND NORTHWEST COMMONWEALTH

## [1.11] CONCORD

THREAT LEVELS 1-5

### VAULT-TEC RECOMMENDED LOOT

**ARMOR PART: FUSION CORE**

**COLLECTIBLE: REQUIRED READING: TABOO TATTOOS**

- ARMAMENTS AND AMMO+
- ARMAMENTS AND AMMO: TRUNK (2)
- ARMOR PART: FUSION CORE
- COLLECTIBLE: REQUIRED READING: TABOO TATTOOS
- BOTTLECAPS++
- DANGER: RADIATION (MILD)!
- FACTION: DEATHCLAWS
- FACTION: MIRELURKS
- FACTION: MOLE RATS
- FACTION: RADROACHES
- FACTION: RAIDERS
- HEALTH OR CHEMS
- QUEST START: WHEN FREEDOM CALLS (MINUTEMEN)
- QUEST VISIT: OUT OF TIME (MAIN)

FIG 1.11: CONCORD (EXTERIOR)

To Concord Civic Access

To Concord Civic Access

To Concord Civic Access

This township is comprised of a once-quaint main thoroughfare, now overrun by a Raider gang. To the south is the Museum of Freedom, adjacent to a ruined church (use the steeple to snipe from and as a landmark). Aside from dilapidated structures with a few scavengable items, most of Concord's buildings are sealed up tight, with the exception of the following secondary locations:

### [01] Workhouse

This partly collapsed small factory has stairs to access, allowing you to reach the upper floors. Jump to the concrete floor ledges to access ammo and chems. Farther upstairs is a safe (Advanced) and roof access—an excellent sniping spot.

### [02] Concord Speakeasy

This small public house has a safe behind the bar (Advanced), a small cellar, and an upstairs area with some oddly placed mannequins and a roof exit. Open the locked door (Advanced) to reach a steamer trunk and small ammo stash.

## Concord Civic Access

Access this from three different locations on the surface. We recommend using the metal hatch the Deathclaw burst from by the municipal plutonium well, as you can open the chained door from this direction. This is a small but slightly confusing sewer tunnel with small branching corridors. Loot the trunk, find the Fusion Core at the base of the plutonium well, and grab the magazine before you leave (they're all close together).

If you enter via one of the two other entrances (not near the Deathclaw's exit), and do so prior to the Deathclaw fight in the township, you can actually hear the beast sleeping, but you're not able to access this area of the sewers. The fence is destroyed, and access is available only once the Deathclaw is disturbed.

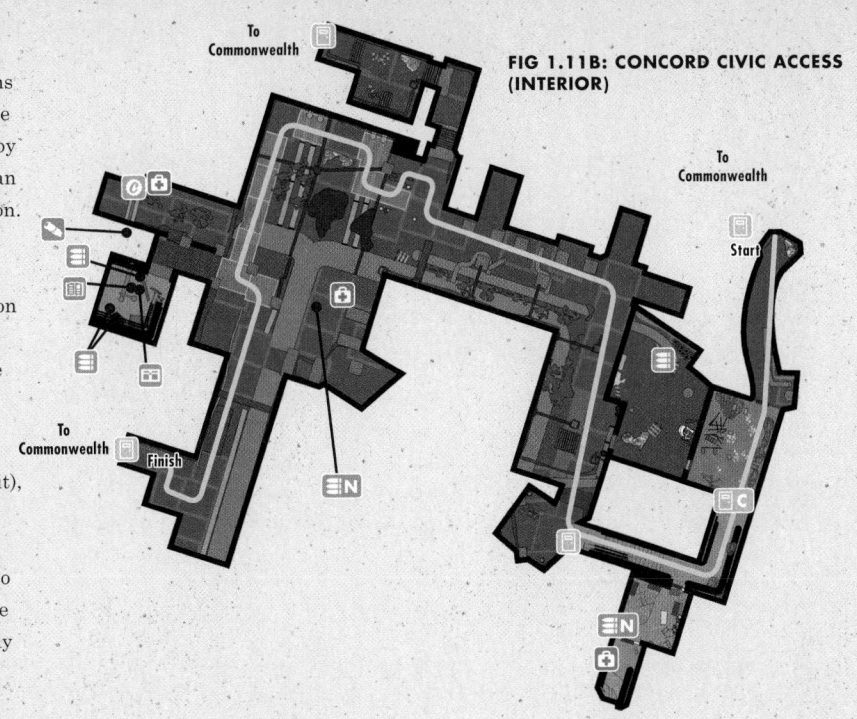

FIG 1.11B: CONCORD CIVIC ACCESS (INTERIOR)

## 🏛 [1.12] MUSEUM OF FREEDOM

THREAT LEVELS 1-5

**FIG 1.12: MUSEUM OF FREEDOM (INTERIOR)**

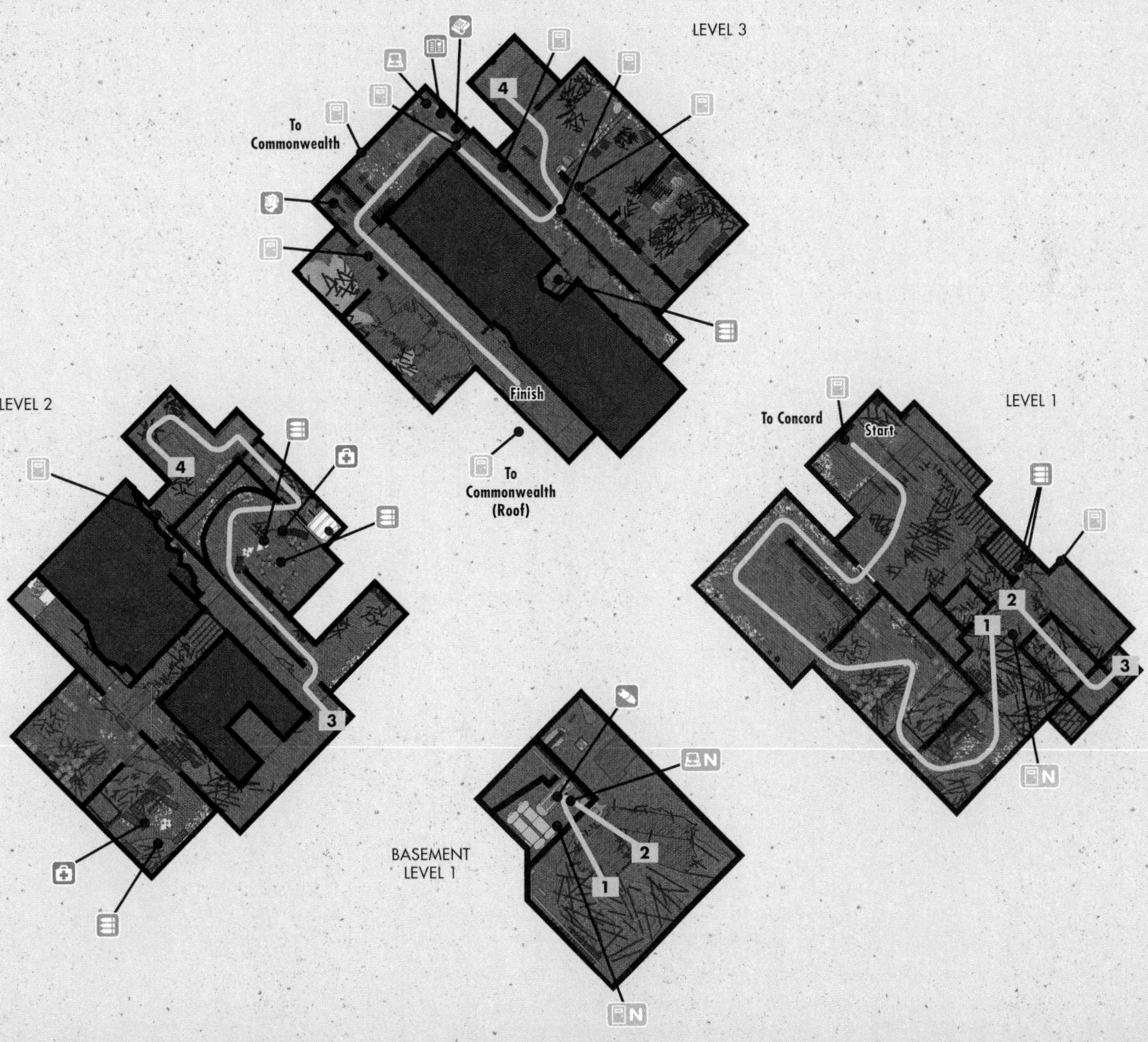

MAP

ZONE 1

LEXINGTON AND NORTHWEST COMMONWEALTH

- ARMAMENTS AND AMMO
- ARMOR PART: FUSION CORE
- ARMOR PART: POWER ARMOR (T-45)
- COLLECTIBLE: BOBBLEHEAD: PERCEPTION
- COLLECTIBLE: HOLOTAPE: ATOMIC COMMAND
- COLLECTIBLE: HOLOTAPE: LOG—SSG MICHAEL DALY
- COLLECTIBLE: REQUIRED READING: ROBCO FUN!
- COMPANION: PRESTON GARVEY
- BOTTLECAPS
- DANGER: LONG DROP!

- FACTION: MINUTEMEN
- FACTION: RAIDERS
- FACTION: SETTLERS
- FACTION: CHARACTER: JUN LONG
- FACTION: CHARACTER: MAMA MURPHY
- FACTION: CHARACTER: MARCY LONG
- FACTION: CHARACTER: PRESTON GARVEY
- FACTION: CHARACTER: STURGES
- HEALTH OR CHEMS
- QUEST START: WHEN FREEDOM CALLS (MINUTEMEN)

## VAULT-TEC RECOMMENDED LOOT

 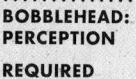

**BOBBLEHEAD: PERCEPTION**

**REQUIRED READING: ROBCO FUN! MAGAZINE**

**HOLOTAPE: ATOMIC COMMAND**

**POWER ARMOR (T-45)**

## AVAILABLE COMPANION

**COMPANION: PRESTON GARVEY**

It's rather apt that Preston Garvey has decided to take a stand here, in a place dedicated to reminding patrons that freedom is a privilege afforded to the many, yet hard won by a noble few. Rescue them (without forgetting the magazine and Bobblehead in the room they're in) and begin a long and fruitful relationship with the settlers of the Commonwealth. Access the door to the roof to reach the Vertibird. Use the previous Concord map to note the items to grab there.

## [1.13] BEDFORD STATION

THREAT LEVELS 6-14

- ARMAMENTS AND AMMO
- ARMAMENTS AND AMMO: TRUNK
- DANGER: OIL!
- FACTION: FERAL GHOUL

- FACTION: CHARACTER: DUTCHMAN
- FACTION: CHARACTER: HELENA
- HEALTH OR CHEMS

This was a train switching station serving Thicket Excavations. Recently, this location appears to have been used by the Railroad as a stopover. Look for the bodies of Helena and Dutchman, though the synth they were protecting is nowhere to be found. Locate a large trunk with items in the freight warehouse (north) and a Railroad dead drop in the blue carriage.

## [1.14] GORSKI CABIN

THREAT LEVELS 1-5

- ARMAMENTS AND AMMO
- COLLECTIBLE: REQUIRED READING: WASTELAND SURVIVAL GUIDE
- CRAFTING: CHEMISTRY STATION
- CRAFTING: WEAPONS WORKBENCH
- FACTION: FERAL GHOUL

### VAULT-TEC RECOMMENDED LOOT

**REQUIRED READING: WASTELAND SURVIVAL GUIDE**

The residence of one Wayne Gorski, a survivalist and keen patriot, though not a fan of electrical towers. Be sure to investigate his root cellar (the trapdoor within the cabin).

## [1.15] DRUMLIN DINER

THREAT LEVELS 1-5

In this small diner, Trudy attempts to eke out an existence, not helped by her chem-addled son.

- BOTTLECAPS
- FACTION: RAIDER
- FACTION: SCAVENGER
- FACTION: CHARACTER: PATRICK
- FACTION: CHARACTER: SIMONE
- FACTION: CHARACTER: TRUDY
- FACTION: CHARACTER: WOLFGANG
- HEALTH OR CHEMS
- QUEST START: DRUMLIN DINER SHAKEDOWN (LOCATION MISCELLANEOUS)
- SERVICES: TRADER (TRUDY)

 **Miscellaneous: Drumlin Diner Shakedown***

A couple of Raiders are active in this area and may be visiting the diner owner, Trudy, regarding her son's proclivity for chems. Sort that out if you'd like to trade with Trudy.

## [1.16] STARLIGHT DRIVE-IN

THREAT LEVELS 1-5

- ARMAMENTS AND AMMO
- ARMOR PART: FUSION CORE
- COLLECTIBLE: NUKA CHERRY
- COLLECTIBLE: NUKA-COLA QUANTUM
- CRAFTING: COOKING STATION
- DANGER: MAKESHIFT BOMB!
- DANGER: MINES!
- DANGER: RADIATION (MILD)!
- FACTION: MOLE RATS
- FACTION: RADROACHES
- SERVICES: WORKSHOP

A once-thriving drive-in movie theater and diner is now slightly less welcoming: Beware of the makeshift bomb on the diner door (then find the Nuka Cherry on the low shelf). Unlock the back storage shed (Novice) to access the workshop, or find the back storage key in the footlocker on top of the big screen gantry. Open the rear storage (Novice) behind the screen; this is where the Fusion Core and Quantum are stored.

## [1.17] LONELY CHAPEL

THREAT LEVELS 6-14

- FACTION: RAIDERS

Open the door and locate the trapdoor to enter the stockpile. This is an access point to the federal ration stockpile (in Zone 3). Consult that location for what to expect. Use this as an alternate route through the area.

## [1.18] SUNSHINE TIDINGS CO-OP

THREAT LEVELS 6-14

- ARMAMENTS AND AMMO: TRUNK
- BOTTLECAPS
- COLLECTIBLE: REQUIRED READING: WASTELAND SURVIVAL GUIDE
- CRAFTING: CHEMISTRY STATION
- CRAFTING: COOKING STATION
- FACTION: FERAL GHOUL
- FACTION: RADROACHES
- FACTION CHARACTER: PROFESSOR GOODFEELS
- HEALTH OR CHEMS
- SERVICES: WORKSHOP

A beatnik farming co-op of cabins and a trading warehouse. Local scuttlebutt suggests the place is haunted by its former residents. Meet Professor Goodfeels, who still rattles about the place. He'll be a good guard if you hack his protocols at the Sunshine Tidings terminal (Novice). There's a locked medical cabin here (Novice) too. Did you find the trunk in the western cabin yet?

## [1.19] WALDEN POND

THREAT LEVELS 1-5

THREAT LEVELS 6-14

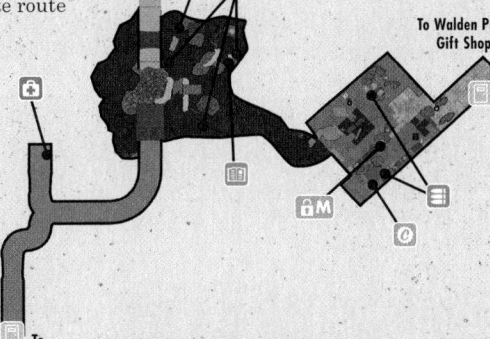

- ARMAMENTS AND AMMO
- BOTTLECAPS
- COLLECTIBLE: REQUIRED READING: TALES OF A JUNKTOWN JERKY VENDOR
- DANGER: CAN CHIMES!
- DANGER: MAKESHIFT BOMB!
- DANGER: MONKEY!
- DANGER: RADIOACTIVITY (MILD)!
- FACTION: RAIDER
- FACTION: CHARACTER: BEAR
- FACTION: CHARACTER: TWEEZ
- FACTION: CHARACTER: WALTER
- FACTION: CHARACTER: WHIPLASH
- HEALTH OR CHEMS
- UNIQUE ITEM: BIG JIM (WEAPON)

**FIG. 1.19 GIFT SHOP BASEMENT**

To Walden Pond Gift Shop

To Commonwealth

Once the home of a transcendentalist author, this is now home to a quartet of chem-addled Raiders. The gift shop has some traps, as well as a note near the locked basement door (Master). Walter the Raider has the key. Enter the basement via the drainage pipes. Don't forget to take the audio tour!

# [1.20–1.23] LEXINGTON TOWNSHIP

##  [1.20] MYSTIC PINES    THREAT LEVELS 6-14

- ARMOR PART: FUSION CORE
- COLLECTIBLE: REQUIRED READING:
- TALES OF A JUNKTOWN JERKY VENDOR 5
- COLLECTIBLE: NUKA CHERRY
- COLLECTIBLE: NUKA-COLA QUANTUM
- HEALTH OR CHEMS

### VAULT-TEC RECOMMENDED LOOT

**ARMOR PART: FUSION CORE**

**REQUIRED READING: TALES OF A JUNKTOWN JERKY VENDOR**

A small convalescence home on the outskirts of Lexington for the infirm or addled. Unlock the security gate (Advanced) in the greenhouse if you require medical items. Pry the Fusion Core from the basement generator, too.

## [1.21] SUPER DUPER MART    THREAT LEVELS 1-5

- ARMAMENTS AND AMMO+
- ARMAMENTS AND AMMO: TRUNK
- ARMOR PART: FUSION CORE
- BOTTLECAPS
- COLLECTIBLE: HOLOTAPE: EMMA'S HOLOTAPE
- COLLECTIBLE: NUKA CHERRY (3)
- COLLECTIBLE: NUKA COLA QUANTUM (2)
- COLLECTIBLE: REQUIRED READING: TALES OF A JUNKTOWN JERKY VENDOR
- CRAFTING: CHEMISTRY STATION
- DANGER: OIL!
- FACTION: FERAL GHOULS
- FACTION: CHARACTER: EMMA
- HEALTH OR CHEMS+

### VAULT-TEC RECOMMENDED LOOT

**ARMOR PART: FUSION CORE**
**COLLECTIBLE: NUKA CHERRY (3)**
**COLLECTIBLE: NUKA COLA QUANTUM (2)**
**REQUIRED READING: TALES OF A JUNKTOWN JERKY VENDOR**

The exterior of the mart has a terminal (Advanced) on the east unloading dock. Hack it to access the adjacent garage where Emma's Holotape and some ammo can be found.

Inside, this place is in remarkably good shape (except for the roof), albeit in complete disarray. The same could be said for the frothing ferals. There's a tiny basement access to the garage where Emma is. You can also grab some Nuka Cherries and Quantums here (don't leave without all five bottles).

**FIG 1.21: SUPER DUPER MART (INTERIOR)**

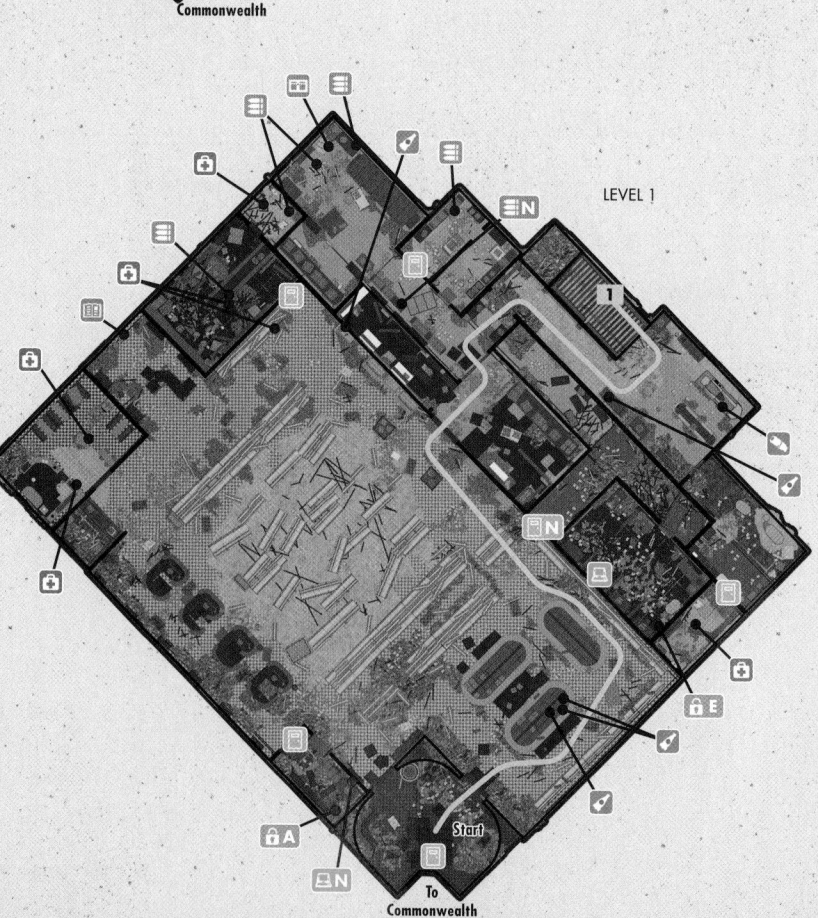

(*Asset list does not include Secondary Location 02: Slocum's Joe Coffee Shop [Switchboard])

- ARMAMENTS AND AMMO
- ARMAMENTS AND AMMO: TRUNK
- ARMAMENTS AND AMMO: MINI NUKE
- CRAFTING: ARMOR WORKBENCH
- CRAFTING: CHEMISTRY STATION
- CRAFTING: WEAPONS WORKBENCH (2)
- DANGER: EXPLOSIVE BARRELS!
- DANGER: LONG DROP!
- DANGER: OIL!

- FACTION: FERAL GHOULS
- FACTION: RAIDERS
- HEALTH OR CHEMS
- QUEST VISIT: TRADECRAFT (THE RAILROAD)

**VAULT-TEC RECOMMENDED LOOT**

ARMAMENTS AND AMMO: MINI NUKE

**FIG 1.22A: LEXINGTON (EXTERIOR)**

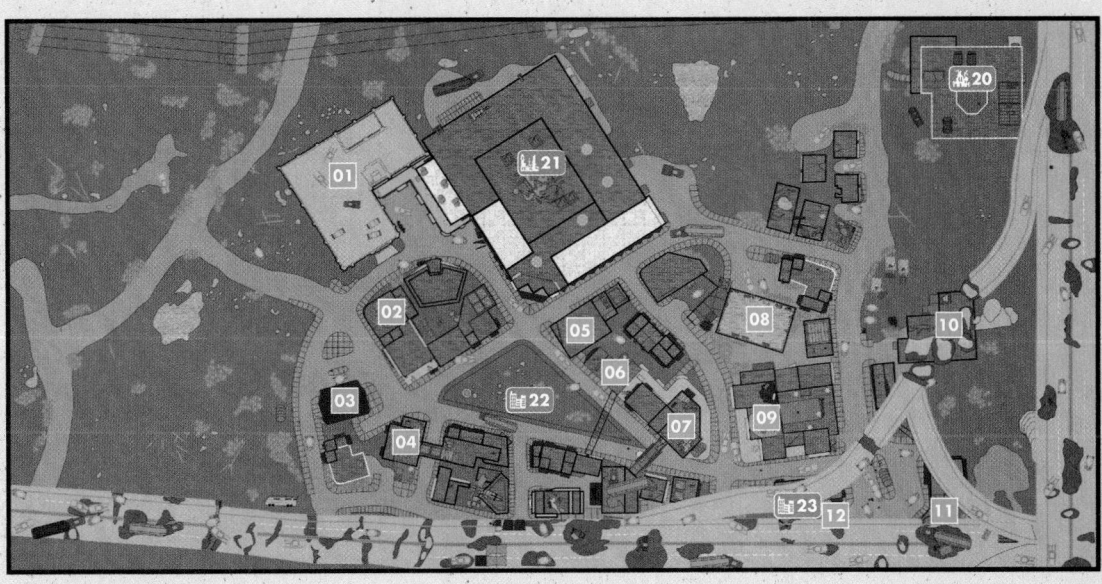

MAP

ZONE 1

LEXINGTON AND NORTHWEST COMMONWEALTH

Once known as Corvega Town, thanks to the large plant just south of here, Lexington was where the ancient Revolutionary War started. The statue of the Minuteman still stands in the town square (known as the Battle Green). This was once a Raider stronghold, but that faction fled due to an abundance of Feral Ghouls.

### [01] Super Duper Mart Parking Lot

The exterior has a pistol in the small maintenance room and a collection of rusting vehicles along with a forecourt. Access the parking garage interior from the makeshift door near the "out of order" sign or from the bottom of the concrete parking lot steps. Inside is the lower garage level, an oily mess with explosive barrels and a group of Feral Ghouls to dispatch. Hack the terminal (Novice) to control a Protectron. Open the security gate (Novice) to access explosives and first aid boxes.

### [02] Slocum's Joe Coffee Shop and Laundromat (Switchboard)

**VAULT-TEC RECOMMENDED LOOT**

ARMAMENTS AND AMMO: MINI NUKE
ARMOR PART: FUSION CORE (2)
REQUIRED READING: U.S. COVERT OPERATIONS MANUAL

- ARMAMENTS AND AMMO
- ARMAMENTS AND AMMO: TRUNK
- ARMAMENTS AND AMMO: MINI NUKE
- ARMOR PART: FUSION CORE (2)
- COLLECTIBLE: REQUIRED READING: U.S. COVERT OPERATIONS MANUAL
- BOTTLECAPS
- CRAFTING: ARMOR WORKBENCH
- CRAFTING: COOKING STATION
- CRAFTING: WEAPONS WORKBENCH
- DANGER: EXPLOSIVE BARRELS!
- DANGER: MINES!
- DANGER: TESLA ARC!
- DANGER: TRIPWIRES!
- DANGER: TURRETS!
- FACTION: RADROACHES
- FACTION: RADSCORPIONS (IF THE QUEST IS INACTIVE)
- FACTION: SYNTHS (INSTITUTE)
- HEALTH OR CHEMS
- QUEST VISIT: TRADECRAFT (THE RAILROAD)

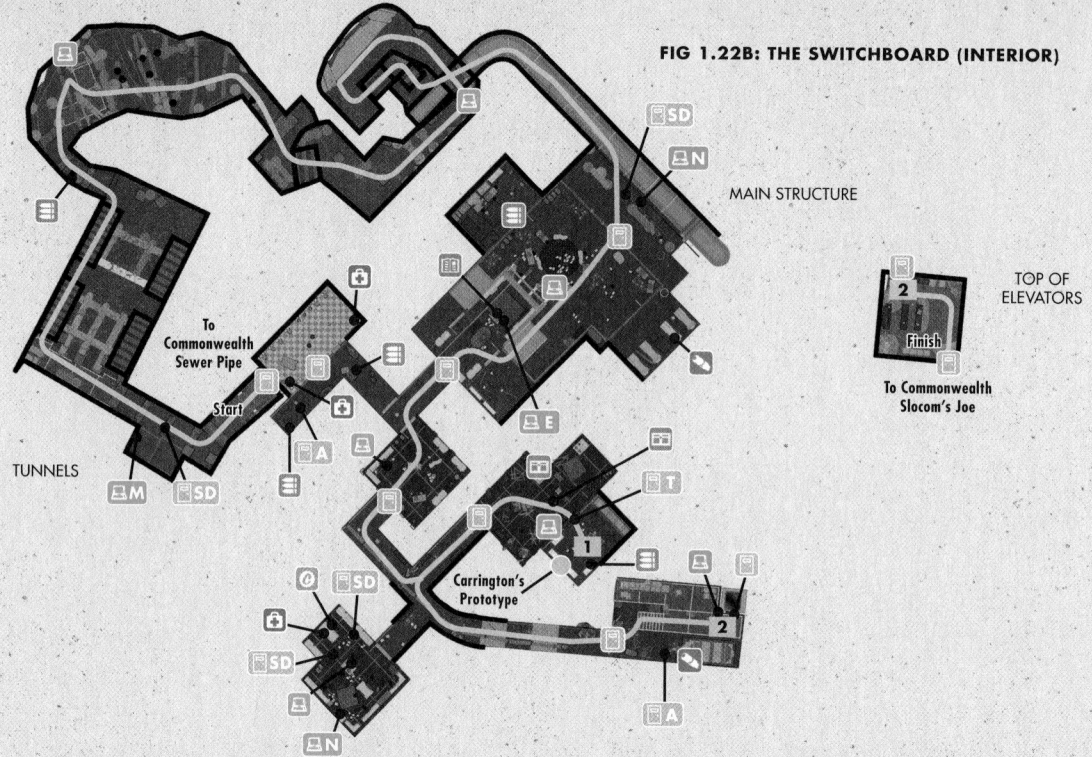

MAIN STRUCTURE

TOP OF
ELEVATORS

Finish

To Commonwealth
Slocom's Joe

To
Commonwealth
Sewer Pipe

Start

TUNNELS

Carrington's
Prototype

You cannot access areas of this location until the specified quest is active. This unassuming coffee shop is usually devoid of enemies. During the quest, expect turrets and synth threats. Find a Caps stash under the counter. Attached to the building is a Laundromat with some health. Of considerably more interest is the basement (known as the switchboard and shown on the adjacent map).

The switchboard was the secret base of the Railroad until it was overrun by Institute synths. Move the bookcase and try to call the elevator. It lacks power, forcing you to enter the switchboard from the old sewer pipe. This is Zone 1 Secondary Location: Switchboard Entrance (Sewer). You're able to access all rooms (providing your Hack skill is high enough; otherwise bring Deacon with you and start the indicated quest). Don't forget the Fusion Cores, magazine, and Mini Nuke before you emerge.

## [03] Red Rocket Gas Station

This dilapidated garage has been picked clean by countless previous scavengers.

## [04] Old Bridge and Ruins

An old shop and bridge are overrun by Ghouls. Follow the stairwell and cross some precarious planks to reach a rusting building and access to the rooftops overlooking the town square.

## [05] Lexington Bank

Hack the terminal (Novice) to open the safe room, which appears to have been compromised quite severely.

## [06] Ruined Apartment (Rusting)

This multifloor structure is teeming with ferals. There's a ground-floor terminal (Advanced) that opens a security door to a cubbyhole with a safe (Advanced). There's health and ammo to scrounge here, too. Upstairs is an Armor Workbench.

## [07] Bridge to Liquor Store

The apartment to the northwest has two stairwells, numerous Ghouls, and an outdoor roof with a chemistry station. The bridge across to the liquor store is Raider territory. Find ammo and chems on the bridge. There's been some creative parking by a big-rig driver above the liquor store and scaffold steps down to a nearby house porch with health in it. To the east is a ruined hardware store with chems and ammo.

## [08] Basketball Court

The municipal basketball court. A settler doesn't appear to understand the rules of the game.

## [09] Ruined Apartment (Pool)

There's fire escape access all the way up to the roof and a weapons workbench. Battle Raiders here. There's ammo, chems, and grotesque decorations in the bedroom, and a cunningly hidden steamer trunk on the upper roof area. With some nimble leaping onto the narrowest roof ledge, you can reach the eastern blown-out section and view the freeway.

Or if you want a quick dip in the slightly irradiated pool (where tarberry is growing), fight off the Raiders and Ghouls battling each other.

Don't forget to check the Pulowski Preservation Shelter for a Mini Nuke.

## [10] Crushed Building

A section of freeway has fallen and crushed a construction company building. The wandering Ghouls fail to see the irony.

## [11] Ruined Apartment (Under Freeway)

East of the Primary Location apartments is another ruined apartment structure with chems in a bathroom medicine cabinet and little else but the slight feeling of despair.

## [12] Freeway Apartment

If you accessed the elevated freeway (from Zone 1 Secondary Locations 36 or 39), you can step across a plank to reach this apartment from the freeway before (carefully) dropping down.

## [1.23] LEXINGTON APARTMENTS

THREAT LEVELS 6-14

- ARMAMENTS AND AMMO
- BOTTLECAPS
- DANGER: MINE!
- DANGER: TRIPWIRE!
- FACTION: RAIDERS

A Raider duo now makes this small apartment complex under the freeway their home. There's an explosives box in the kitchen and an open-air bathroom.

# SECONDARY LOCATIONS

## [1.01] DRY CREEK BED

**COLLECTIBLE: NUKA COLA QUANTUM**

Someone's lucky explorers find a thirst-quenching Nuka in the leaves at the base of this dry creek, below the rusting barrels.

## [1.02] RAIDER SHACK

- ARMAMENTS OR AMMO
- FACTION: RAIDER
- HEALTH OR CHEMS

A Raider and attack dog have overrun a small settler shack.

## [1.03] OLD FIRING RANGE

- ARMAMENTS OR AMMO
- FACTION: SCAVENGER

A Scavenger has set up a small shooting range with bottles.

## [1.04] SUNKEN ROWBOAT STASH

- ARMAMENTS AND AMMO: TRUNK
- DANGER: RADIATION (MILD)!

A lost rowboat has sunk along the north lake shore. Dive down for a locked trunk treat (Novice).

## [1.05] WATER FILTRATION CAPS STASH

- BOTTLECAPS+
- HEALTH OR CHEMS

Flip the circuit breaker at the water's edge to open a filtration unit with a hidden Caps stash inside.

## [1.06] RAIDER HILLTOP DEN

- FACTION: RAIDER
- HEALTH OR CHEMS

A collection of branches and bedding atop a rocky hill.

## [1.07] CRASHED VERTIBIRD (NEAR ROBOTICS DISPOSAL GROUND)

- ARMAMENTS AND AMMO: TRUNK
- ARMOR PART: POWER ARMOR
- FACTION: RADSTAG DOES

The remains of a Vertibird close to the road. Beware of Radstag Does. Don't forget to check the sloping ground behind the Vertibird tail for a half-buried trunk, near the wooden crates.

## [1.08] SCAVENGER'S SHACK

- ARMAMENTS OR AMMO
- FACTION: SCAVENGER
- HEALTH OR CHEMS

A Scavenger with a penchant for drink and views of the woods.

## [1.09] POND AND FREEWAY SHACK

- ARMAMENTS AND AMMO
- DANGER: RADIATION (MILD)
- HEALTH OR CHEMS

A dead settler has taken a permanent trip from his bathtub hut. South of here is a separate shack. Inside is a sink with a small collection of tatos in it, ready for tasting.

## [1.10] ELEVATED FREEWAY ACCESS (NORTH WILDERNESS)

- ARMAMENTS OR AMMO

Climb here. Check the bus at the north end of the freeway for an explosives stash (Novice). Follow the freeway south to Skylanes Flight 1981.

## [1.11] MILITARY ARMOR TRANSPORT (NORTH WILDERNESS)

- ARMOR PART: FUSION CORE
- ARMOR PART: POWER ARMOR

Hack the terminal in the carriage (Advanced) to access the armor and core in the security cage.

## [1.12] TRADER'S SHACK (WEST OF RANGER CABIN)

- SERVICES: TRADER

Trade here or steal a small garden of wild corn and tato fruit.

## [1.13] MILITARY APC (SANCTUARY LAKE)

- DANGER: RADIATION (MILD)
- FACTION: IRRADIATED WILDLIFE
- HEALTH OR CHEMS

Beware of Bloatflies. The corpse has an army helmet if you want it.

## [1.14] ABANDONED CARAVAN

- ARMAMENTS OR AMMO
- HEALTH OR CHEMS

West of Abernathy Farm is a rusting caravan with stuff to scavenge.

## [1.15] DRY CREEK SHACK

- HEALTH OR CHEMS

A small rickety shack overlooking the entrance to Wicked Shipping fleet lockup.

## [1.16] HALF-BURIED STASH

- ARMAMENTS AND AMMO: TRUNK

Southeast of the water tower is a copse of trees and a half-buried trunk to pillage.

## [1.17] CONCORD OUTSKIRTS RUINED HOUSE

- COLLECTIBLE: NUKA COLA QUANTUM

Thirsty on your way to Concord? Stop at the fridge inside this ruined house.

## [1.18] CONCORD CAMPFIRE

- CRAFTING: COOKING STATION
- FACTION: RAIDERS

An occasional caravan stop is usually overrun by a couple of Raiders and their emaciated hounds.

## [1.19] SHOPPING CART OF GOODIES

- COLLECTIBLE: NUKA CHERRY

Someone's left a collection of edibles and a delicious Nuka Cherry. They won't mind if you have them. They're probably dead, anyway.

## [1.20] RADROACH OUTHOUSE

- FACTION: IRRADIATED WILDLIFE
- HEALTH OR CHEMS

Watch your step; there are Radroaches in these rustic restrooms.

## [1.21] A COOKING SPOT

- CRAFTING: COOKING STATION
- ARMAMENTS OR AMMO

A deserted cooking station with a place to sleep and a trunk to pillage.

## [1.22] DILAPIDATED TRAILER SHACK

- ARMAMENTS OR AMMO
- FACTION: IRRADIATED WILDLIFE

Beware the Radroaches and Bloatfly in this shack built atop a rail trailer.

## [1.23] CONSTRUCTION LIFT TO GUNNERS' DEN

- ARMAMENTS OR AMMO
- ARMAMENTS OR AMMO: TRUNK
- CRAFTING: COOKING STATION
- CRAFTING WEAPONS WORKBENCH
- FACTION: GUNNERS

Watch for machine-gun turrets and Gunners. Ride the lift up to the elevated freeway, where you can mow down a few more Gunners. Explore the elevated section of freeway as you wish.

## [1.24] SETTLERS' TENT

- FACTION: SETTLER

CharlieTwo settlers lead a meager existence southwest of Walden Pond.

## [1.25] RAIDER CHEM LAB SHACK

- ARMAMENTS OR AMMO
- CRAFTING: CHEMISTRY STATION
- FACTION: RAIDER
- HEALTH OR CHEMS

A shack with a lookout and a couple of easily dispatched idiots.

## [1.26] SMALL TRADING SHACK

- SERVICE: TRADER

A shack with a friendly trader and a number of cats: some paintings, others purring.

## [1.27] ELEVATED GUNNERS' DEN

- ARMAMENTS OR AMMO
- FACTION: GUNNERS

Offering a good view of the vicinity. Beware of a machine-gun turret and a few Gunners. Access from the on-ramp to the northeast (Secondary Location 1.28).

## [1.28] ON-RAMP GUNNERS' DEN

- FACTION: GUNNERS

Scale the freeway on-ramp to explore the elevated road. Watch for the Gunner and machine-gun turret.

## [1.29] BUS RAMP

- FACTION: THE RAILROAD
- FACTION: FERAL GHOULS
- QUEST VISIT: TRADECRAFT (THE RAILROAD)

Meet Deacon here during the quest. Watch for Railroad signs. This leads up onto the elevated freeway, past a Ghoul-infested bus and Secondary Location 1.35.

## [1.30] MILITARY PILLBOX (WALDEN)

- ARMAMENTS OR AMMO

Watch for an Eyebot in here. Unlock the terminal (Novice) to open the security door.

## [1.31] VENDING MACHINE TRUCK TRANSPORT

- COLLECTIBLE: NUKA COLA QUANTUM

The transportation of some vending machines was stopped short by a big bomb. Fortunately, there's sometimes a Quantum still left in the Nuka Machine.

## [1.32] WICKED SHIPPING CONTAINER TRUCK #2

- ARMAMENTS AND AMMO: TRUNK
- QUEST VISIT: WICKED SHIPMENTS (LOCATION MISCELLANEOUS)

This is one of Wicked Shipping's trailers. Unlock it (Master) or use the key found at the fleet lockup to access the trunk inside.

## [1.33] MILITARY ARMOR TRANSPORT (LEXINGTON)

- ARMAMENTS AND AMMO
- ARMAMENTS AND AMMO: TRUNK
- ARMOR PART: FUSION CORE
- ARMOR PART: POWER ARMOR

Hack the terminal in the orange carriage (Advanced) to access the armor and core in the security cage. Don't forget the trunk in the blue carriage, too.

## [1.34] SWITCHBOARD ENTRANCE (SEWER)

- QUEST VISIT: TRADECRAFT (THE RAILROAD)

You can go into the sewer entrance to the Switchboard—the Railroad's old base of operations—from here, ideally during the quest. Your path soon ends at a terminal (Master). The main entrance—extremely well guarded during the quest—is underneath Slocum Joe's in Lexington (Primary Location 1.22) and connects to here. Consult that location for the interior map of the Switchboard.

## [1.35] ELEVATED FREEWAY: DERELICT BUS

- COLLECTIBLE: NUKA-COLA QUANTUM
- CRAFTING: COOKING STATION
- FACTION: THE RAILROAD
- FACTION: FERAL GHOULS
- QUEST VISIT: TRADECRAFT (THE RAILROAD)

Check the bus for a Quantum. Ricky Dalton is only here during the quest.

## [1.36] ELEVATED FREEWAY ACCESS (LEXINGTON)

- CRAFTING: COOKING STATION

Climb here and you can look down on Lexington, fire off sniper shots at the Raiders on the Corvega Assembly Plant, and explore the abandoned camp. This offers good (but precarious) access into Zones 2 and 3 and down onto the roofs of the Lexington buildings near the interchange overpass.

## [1.37] FREEWAY SHACK AND CAGE

- BOTTLECAPS
- FACTION: IRRADIATED WILDLIFE
- HEALTH OR CHEMS

Come for the big band sound on the radio. Leave when the Radscorpion ambushes you. Feel revulsion when you unlock the cage gate (Expert) and inspect the prisoner conditions inside.

## [1.38] MILITARY CHECKPOINT (LEXINGTON)

- ARMAMENTS OR AMMO
- ARMAMENTS AND AMMO: TRUNK

This area is under the remains of the elevated freeway and devoid of life. There's a trunk to scavenge, so turn that frown upside down!

## [1.39] ELEVATED FREEWAY ACCESS (LEXINGTON)

Climb here and you can look down on Mystic Pines, Lexington, fire off sniper shots at the Raiders on the Corvega Assembly Plant, and explore the rusting vehicles scattered across the interchange to the south. This offers good (but precarious) access into Zones 2 and 3 and down onto the roofs of the Lexington buildings near the interchange overpass.

## [1.40] ELEVATED JUMPING-OFF POINT

Jump from the upper roadway—accessed from Secondary Location 1.39—and explore the freeway above Lexington here.

# ZONE 2: NORTH CENTRAL COMMONWEALTH

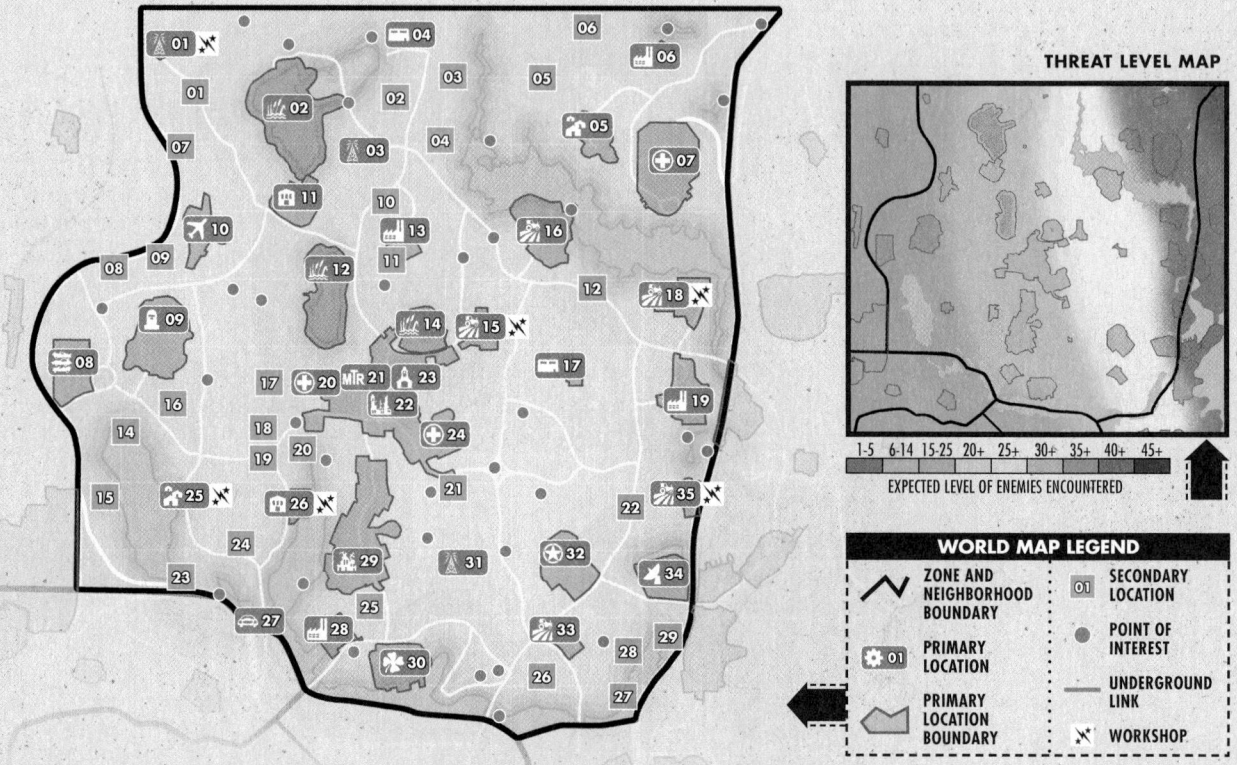

THREAT LEVEL MAP

1-5  6-14  15-25  20+  25+  30+  35+  40+  45+
EXPECTED LEVEL OF ENEMIES ENCOUNTERED

**WORLD MAP LEGEND**

| | | |
|---|---|---|
| ⋀ ZONE AND NEIGHBORHOOD BOUNDARY | ⬛ 01 | SECONDARY LOCATION |
| ⚙ 01 PRIMARY LOCATION | ● | POINT OF INTEREST |
| ▱ PRIMARY LOCATION BOUNDARY | — | UNDERGROUND LINK |
| | ✕ | WORKSHOP |

Bordered by the elevated freeway to the east and west and the Mystic River to the south, this part of the Commonwealth consists of the main township of Malden in its center, with various interesting and dangerous smaller locations surrounding it. The farther south you go, the more industrial the landscape becomes. The farther east you go, the more dangerous the inhabitants become. However, you are encouraged to chance a meeting at the more esoteric establishments in this zone, allowing you to befriend both robots and ghouls alike. And even Deathclaws! But not Super Mutants.

## Primary Locations

- [2.01] OUTPOST ZIMONJA
- [2.02] LAKE QUANNAPOWITT
- [2.03] RADIO TOWER 3SM-U81
- [2.04] RECON BUNKER THETA
- [2.05] LYNN WOODS
- [2.06] PARSONS CREAMERY
- [2.07] PARSONS STATE INSANE ASYLUM
- [2.08] ROTTEN LANDFILL
- [2.09] WILDWOOD CEMETERY
- [2.10] SKYLANES FLIGHT 1981
- [2.11] GENERAL ATOMICS GALLERIA
- [2.12] DARK HOLLOW POND

- [2.13] MASS FUSION CONTAINMENT SHED
- [2.14] OLD GULLET SINKHOLE
- [2.15] GREENTOP NURSERY
- [2.16] BREAKHEART BANKS
- [2.17] LISTENING POST BRAVO
- [2.18] THE SLOG
- [2.19] SAUGUS IRONWORKS
- [2.20] MEDFORD MEMORIAL HOSPITAL
- [2.21] MALDEN CENTER
- [2.22] SLOCUM'S JOE CORPORATE HQ
- [2.23] MALDEN MIDDLE SCHOOL (VAULT 75)
- [2.24] MED-TEK RESEARCH

- [2.25] COVENANT
- [2.26] TAFFINGTON BOAT HOUSE
- [2.27] TUCKER MEMORIAL BRIDGE
- [2.28] POSEIDON ENERGY TURBINE #18-F
- [2.29] WEST EVERETT ESTATES
- [2.30] IRISH PRIDE INDUSTRIES SHIPYARD
- [2.31] RELAY TOWER OMC-810
- [2.32] NATIONAL GUARD TRAINING YARD
- [2.33] COUNTY CROSSING
- [2.34] REVERE SATELLITE
- [2.35] FINCH FARM

## Secondary Locations

- [2.01] CONTAINER TRUCK CAMP
- [2.02] HILLTOP HUT
- [2.03] CAR TREE CAMP
- [2.04] DESERTED PICNIC AREA
- [2.05] DEATHCLAW NEST (LYNN WOODS)
- [2.06] RUSTY TRAILER
- [2.07] BLOATFLY CAMP
- [2.08] BILLBOARD SCAVENGER SHACK
- [2.09] ELEVATED GUNNER CAMP
- [2.10] WICKED SHIPPING CONTAINER TRUCK #3
- [2.11] SCAVENGER CAMP
- [2.12] MILITARY CONVOY (APCS AND TRAILER)
- [2.13] ELEVATED FREEWAY: ELEVATED TRAILER
- [2.14] CRASHED VERTIBIRD (COVENANT LAKE)
- [2.15] THE FISHING SPOT (COVENANT COMPOUND)
- [2.16] RUSTY TRACTOR
- [2.17] OLD CARAVAN TRAILER
- [2.18] THE LOCKED TRAILER
- [2.19] CARAVAN CROSSROADS
- [2.20] MALDEN DRAINAGE
- [2.21] BROTHERHOOD OF STEEL BATTLE SITE
- [2.22] MILITARY CONVOY (TRAINING YARD)
- [2.23] ABANDONED RAIDER CAMP
  (ELEVATED FREEWAY)
- [2.24] DERELICT MANSION
- [2.25] MILITARY APCS
- [2.26] COOLING VATS
- [2.27] RIVER'S END SHACK
- [2.28] PROTECTRON TRAILER
- [2.29] RIVER'S END WAREHOUSE

# PRIMARY LOCATIONS

 ### [2.01] OUTPOST ZIMONJA
THREAT LEVELS 15-25

- ARMAMENTS AND AMMO
- ARMAMENTS AND AMMO: MINI NUKE
- COLLECTIBLE: REQUIRED READING: ASTOUNDINGLY AWESOME TALES 7
- CRAFTING: COOKING STATION
- DANGER: TURRETS!
- FACTION: RAIDER
- FACTION: CHARACTER: BOOMER
- SERVICES: WORKSHOP

#### VAULT-TEC RECOMMENDED LOOT

ARMAMENTS AND AMMO: MINI NUKE
REQUIRED READING:
ASTOUNDINGLY AWESOME TALES

A settler camp built around an old relay station has recently been overridden by Raiders under the command of a heavily armed (and armored) ne'er-do-well named Boomer. Remember to pick that ripe Mini Nuke from the tato plant allotment afterward!

 ### [2.02] LAKE QUANNAPOWITT
THREAT LEVELS 20+

- ARMAMENTS AND AMMO
- ARMAMENTS AND AMMO: TRUNK
- DANGER: RADIATION (SEVERE)!
- FACTION: BLOATFLIES
- FACTION: BLOODBUGS
- FACTION: MIRELURKS

Suffering from a pollution problem even before the current inhospitable living conditions, this remote lake provides habitat for Mirelurks and a few airborne bugs. If you must swim, dive into the northern part of the lake where a sunken rowboat yields a steamer trunk of goods.

 ### [2.03] RADIO TOWER 3SM-U81
THREAT LEVELS 20+

- FACTION: BLOODBUGS
- RADIO: AUTOMATED RADIO ALARM
- RADIO: GREENBRIAR RADIO SIGNAL
- RADIO: NAUTICAL RADIO SIGNAL

This is part of the Commonwealth relay tower network. Authorized personnel only. Use the relay tower terminal to amplify three nearby radio signals.

MAP

**ZONE 2**

NORTH CENTRAL
COMMONWEALTH

**[2.04] RECON BUNKER THETA**

- ARMAMENTS AND AMMO
- ARMAMENTS AND AMMO: TRUNK
- ARMOR PART: FUSION CORE
- BOTTLECAPS

- DANGER: OIL!
- FACTION: CHARACTER: PALADIN BRANDIS
- QUEST VISIT: THE LOST PATROL
  (BROTHERHOOD OF STEEL)

### VAULT-TEC RECOMMENDED LOOT

**ARMOR PART: FUSION CORE**

This bunker has been sealed and cannot be accessed unless the specified quest is active. Inside is a small bunker stacked with scrap parts and other items of interest. With the quest active, the bedside trunk can be accessed.

 **[2.05] LYNN WOODS**

THREAT LEVELS 35+

- BOTTLECAPS
- DANGER: TRIPWIRE!
- FACTION: DEATHCLAWS
- FACTION: RAIDERS
- HEALTH OR CHEMS
- QUEST VISIT: THE DEVIL'S DUE (SIDE QUEST)

- ARMAMENTS AND AMMO
- ARMAMENTS AND AMMO: TRUNK
- COLLECTIBLE: REQUIRED READING: WASTELAND
  SURVIVAL GUIDE

### VAULT-TEC RECOMMENDED LOOT

 **REQUIRED READING: WASTELAND SURVIVAL GUIDE**

Dominated for centuries by an old stone lookout tower, this settler encampment was recently pillaged by Raiders. Why not return the favor? Expect reinforcements if you scale the tower; even the odds by flipping the circuit breaker atop the tower. The siren summons two Deathclaws from a nearby nest. Unlock the steamer trunk (Master) using good old-fashioned chuzpah, or use the key on the settler corpse at the top of the tower.

 **[2.06] PARSONS CREAMERY**

THREAT LEVELS 35+

- ARMAMENTS AND AMMO
- FACTION: RAIDERS

- QUEST VISIT: THE SECRET OF CABOT
  HOUSE (SIDE)

This company once provided milk for the Medford area and was part of the Little Cobb Creamery collective. Unless the specified quest is active, this place is deserted. Otherwise, expect a Raider presence. If you're adept at safecracking, expect a pleasant surprise here (Advanced). Explore the roof to locate a skeleton close to an assault rifle and locked wooden crate (Novice). If you're after a boatload of grenades, you've come to the right place.

 **[2.07] PARSONS STATE INSANE ASYLUM**

THREAT LEVELS 35+

- ARMAMENTS AND AMMO
- BOTTLECAPS
- COLLECTIBLE: BOBBLEHEAD: CHARISMA
- COLLECTIBLE: REQUIRED READING:
  MASSACHUSETTS SURGICAL JOURNAL
- CRAFTING: CHEMISTRY STATION
- DANGER: MADNESS!
- DANGER: MINES!
- DANGER: RADIATION (MILD)!
- DANGER: TURRETS!
- FACTION: RADROACHES (QUEST ONLY)
- FACTION: MERCENARIES (CABOT FAMILY)

- FACTION: RAIDERS (QUEST ONLY)
- FACTION: CHARACTER: LEFTY
- FACTION: CHARACTER: LORENZO
  CABOT
- HEALTH OR CHEMS
- QUEST VISIT: THE SECRET OF CABOT
  HOUSE (SIDE)
- UNIQUE ITEM: LORENZO'S SUIT
- UNIQUE ITEM: GAMMA GUN
- UNIQUE ITEM: MYSTERIOUS SERUM

**FIG 2.07A: PARSONS STATE INSANE ASYLUM (EXTERIOR)**

**FIG 2.07B: PARSONS STATE ADMINISTRATION (INTERIOR)**

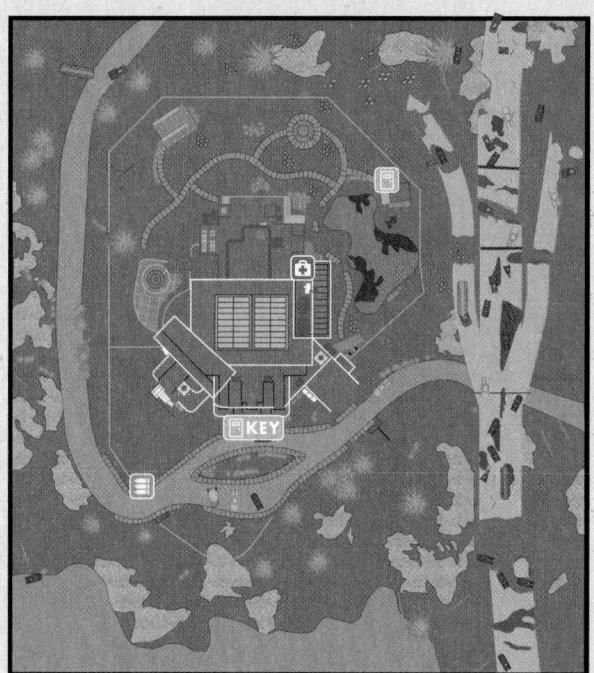

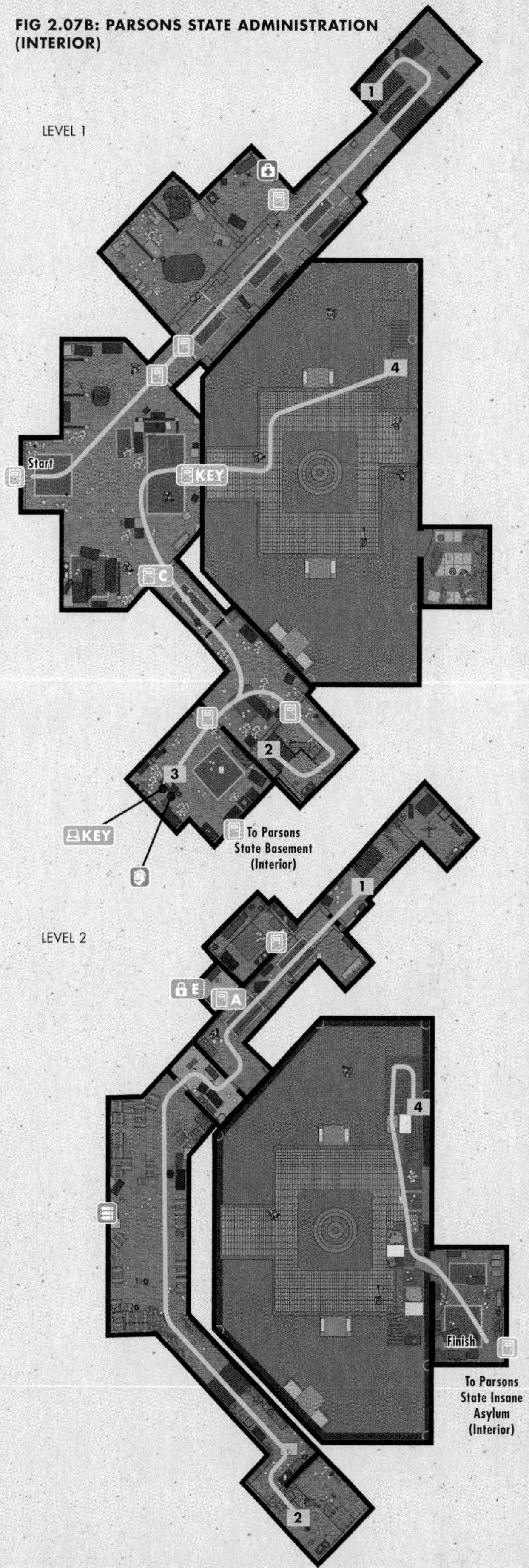

LEVEL 1

LEVEL 2

To Parsons
State Basement
(Interior)

To Parsons
State Insane
Asylum
(Interior)

MAP

**ZONE 2**

NORTH CENTRAL
COMMONWEALTH

## VAULT-TEC RECOMMENDED LOOT

**BOBBLEHEAD: CHARISMA**

**REQUIRED READING: MASSACHUSETTS SURGICAL JOURNAL**

You cannot enter this location unless the specified quest is active.

Before the Great War, this asylum was built to house the addled, weak of brain, and terminally confused folk of the Commonwealth. Old records state that additional subterranean rooms were created to house particularly difficult guests. The location appears to have been built by the Cabot family of the Beacon Hill neighborhood of Boston. Armed mercenary guards currently patrol the facility.

There's bloodleaf in the pond to the east. The only entrance is the ominous but grand doorway to the south, which is only accessed with a key, given to you during the specified quest.

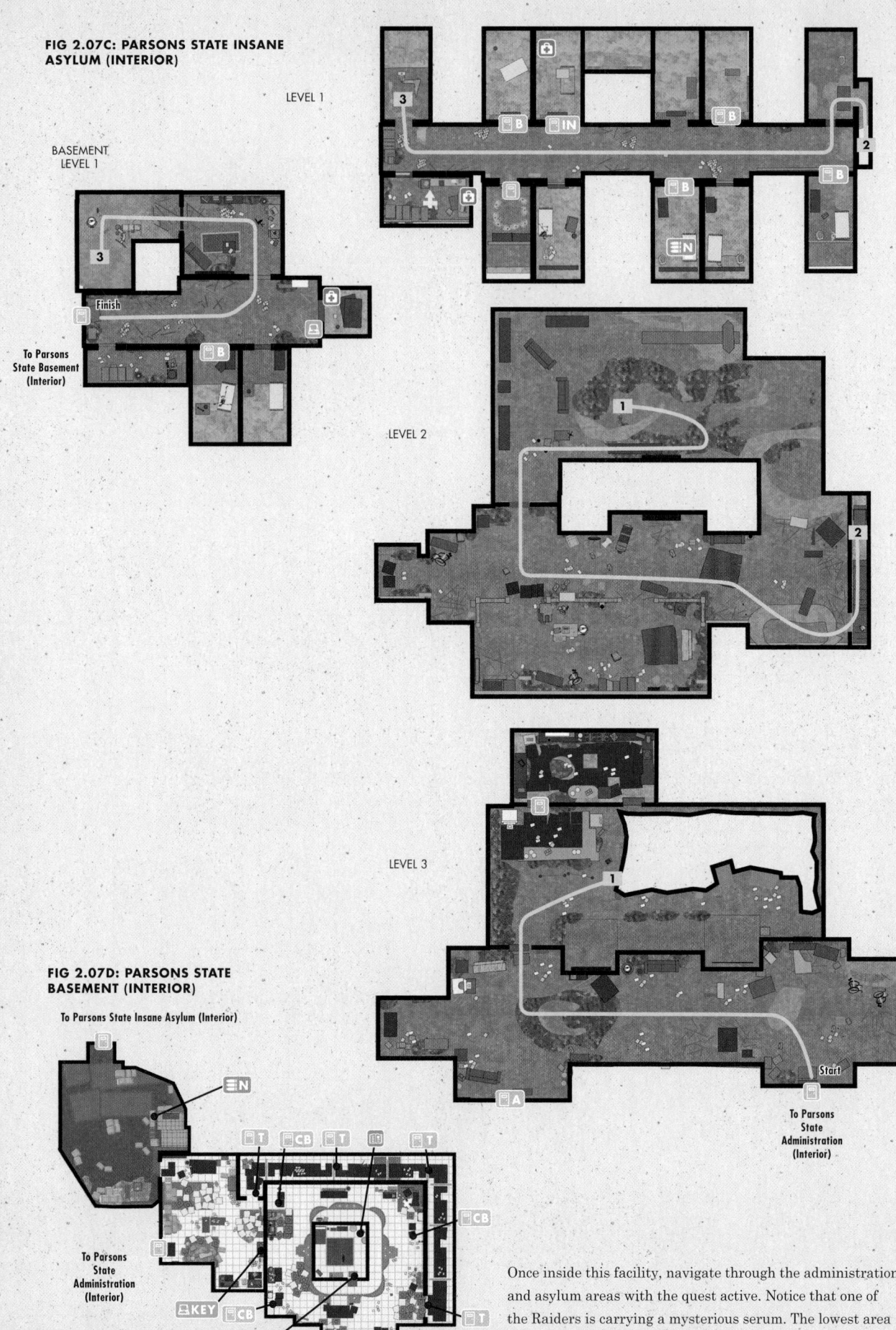

**FIG 2.07C: PARSONS STATE ASYLUM (INTERIOR)**

LEVEL 1

BASEMENT
LEVEL 1

3

Finish

To Parsons
State Basement
(Interior)

LEVEL 2

LEVEL 3

**FIG 2.07D: PARSONS STATE BASEMENT (INTERIOR)**

To Parsons State Insane Asylum (Interior)

To Parsons
State
Administration
(Interior)

Start

To Parsons
State
Administration
(Interior)

Once inside this facility, navigate through the administration and asylum areas with the quest active. Notice that one of the Raiders is carrying a mysterious serum. The lowest area basement contains a special living quarters.

##  [2.08] ROTTEN LANDFILL

THREAT LEVELS 6-14

- ARMAMENTS AND AMMO
- ARMAMENTS AND AMMO: TRUNK
- FACTION: MOLE RATS
- FACTION: SETTLER
- HEALTH OR CHEMS
- SERVICES: TRADER

Mole Rats are raising merry hell at this location and have overrun this refuse dump. Inspect the interior of the trash mound to fully eradicate these vermin; there's a trunk in this junk. If you return and settlers are still alive, they give you caps for your help.

##  [2.09] WILDWOOD CEMETERY

THREAT LEVELS 15-25

- ARMAMENTS AND AMMO
- COLLECTIBLE: REQUIRED READING: TOTAL HACK
- FACTION: MOLE RATS
- FACTION: RAIDERS
- HEALTH OR CHEMS

### VAULT-TEC RECOMMENDED LOOT

REQUIRED READING:
TOTAL HACK

The historic Wildwood Cemetery was founded in 1851, and numerous local dignitaries may be buried here. Confirmation is difficult due to the lack of prewar data.

##  [2.10] SKYLANES FLIGHT 1981

THREAT LEVELS 15-25

- ARMAMENTS AND AMMO
- ARMAMENTS AND AMMO: TRUNK
- BOTTLECAPS++
- COLLECTIBLE: REQUIRED READING: ASTOUNDINGLY AWESOME TALES
- DANGER: EXPLOSIVE BARRELS!
- FACTION: FERAL GHOULS
- FACTION: RAIDERS
- FACTION: CHARACTER: NESS
- FACTION: CHARACTER: MR. DONOGHUE
- HEALTH OR CHEMS
- HOLOTAPE: SKYLANES FLIGHT 1981 RECORDING
- QUEST VISIT: MISCELLANEOUS (RANDOM ENCOUNTER: NESS)

On October 23, 2077, Skylanes Flight 1981 (with service to Boston) had just begun its final descent when the bombs began to fall. The shock wave crippled the plane. Since the crash, the wreckage has been picked over by generations of Raiders and scavengers.

### VAULT-TEC RECOMMENDED LOOT

  REQUIRED READING: ASTOUNDINGLY AWESOME TALES

BOTTLECAPS

Scavenge the wings, engine, and fuselage for chems, ammo, and caps, as well as a Jangles the Moon Monkey. The front section of fuselage has a magazine to gather from the restroom, a steamer trunk you need to drop down from outside to reach, and a Holotape at the cockpit of the final moments of the flight. Underneath is a hidden compartment (Master) with a smuggling manifest.

 **Miscellaneous Quest (Random Encounter: Ness)**

1. INVESTIGATE THE CRASH SITE
2. MEET NESS NEAR THE CRASH SITE
3. SECURE THE CRASH SITE
4. COLLECT YOUR PAY

If you haven't picked the location clean, and if you've randomly stumbled upon Ness during your travels, she mentions some loot hidden at this location. Agree to find it.

 (Easy, Medium, Hard) Feel free to ask for more caps.

If you already found the compartment, the quest concludes.

Visit this location and remove any Raiders. Speak with Ness to receive your caps. If you kill Ness at any time, she has the compartment key on her. If you collect your pay from Ness and leave, she clears out the secret compartment herself.

Ness' key also unlocks a secret compartment at Primary Location [5.32] Skylines Flight 1665 in the Glowing Sea.

- ARMAMENTS AND AMMO
- BOTTLECAPS
- DANGER: ESCAPING GAS!
- DANGER: EXPLOSIVE BARRELS!
- DANGER: LONG DROP!
- DANGER: MINES!
- FACTION: ROBOTS
- FACTION: CHARACTER: BEAN
- FACTION: CHARACTER: COOK HANDY
- FACTION: CHARACTER: CRISP
- FACTION: CHARACTER: DANNY
- FACTION: CHARACTER: GREETER
- FACTION: CHARACTER: KINGPIN
- FACTION: CHARACTER: LANE
- FACTION: CHARACTER: MACK
- FACTION: CHARACTER: PROFESSOR SCARA (QUEST ONLY)
- FACTION: CHARACTER: REG
- FACTION: CHARACTER: SPARE

- FACTION: CHARACTER: SPROCKET
- FACTION: CHARACTER: SPLIT
- FACTION: CHARACTER: STRIKE
- FACTION: CHARACTER: TENPIN
- FACTION: CHARACTER: TORTE
- FACTION: CHARACTER: THE CHAMP
- FACTION: CHARACTER: THE DIRECTOR
- FACTION: CHARACTER: WAITRON
- HEALTH OR CHEMS
- QUEST START: MISCELLANEOUS (GALLERIA)
- QUEST VISIT: LIBERTY REPRIMED (BROTHERHOOD OF STEEL)
- SERVICES: TRADER (BEAN)
- SERVICES: TRADER (CRISP)
- SERVICES: TRADER (DANNY)
- SERVICES: TRADER (REG)
- SERVICES: TRADER (SPROCKET)
- SERVICES: TRADER (WAITRON)

**FIG 2.11: GENERAL ATOMICS GALLERIA (EXTERIOR)**

A fully automated model shopping center designed by General Atomics to showcase the versatility of their line of robots. The centerpiece is a towering Mr. Handy statue. The location is currently closed due to a series of lethal programming glitches.

## Miscellaneous Quest (Galleria)

### 1. REPORT TO THE DIRECTOR OF THE GENERAL ATOMICS GALLERIA

Speak to the greeter and agree to report to the director. He resides within the head of the Mr. Handy statue.

 (Medium, Hard) You can bluff your credentials.

Otherwise, the director deems you a threat and the situation dissolves into violence. You can override the director from his terminal. (Master)

### 01. Mister Handy Statue

This is where the director is stationed. Use the lift to enter and exit, and hack the terminal (Master) if you wish.

If you thoroughly explored [18.02] General Atomics Factory in South Boston, you may actually have a General Atomics ID. Present it, and all will be well.

If you kill the Director, you can use his terminal to choose from several options that will disable or destroy the robots, or trigger the Grand Reopening. Can't hack the (Master) terminal? There's a password on the supervisor's terminal in Back Alley Bowling.

## VAULT-TEC RECOMMENDS

The Grand Reopening resolves most of the glitches with the Galleria's robots. If they survived, many of the robots will now act as traders, although their supplies are rather limited. And as the Galleria's new owner, you're free to loot all of the stores.

### 02. Madden's Boxing Gym

Expect a fight at Madden's Gym. Step into the ring and face The Champ, but be wary of fouls—using any weapon other than boxing gloves or stepping out of the ring will cause all three robots to attack.

After the Grand Reopening, you can trade with Danny. There are chems to gather, and a back room (Advanced) where you can hack a terminal (Novice) to start a manager's sale, which improves Danny's prices.

After the Grand Reopening, you can also buy supplies from Sproket.

### 03. General Atomics Outlet

Visit Sprocket at the outlet store for a product demonstration. Scavenge the robots and area for parts and ammo. Access the workroom using chutzpah (Expert) or the key in the cash register. There's a locked toolbox (Novice) inside.

### 04. Handy Eats Diner

Visit the diner and speak to the waitron about taking your order. Cook is waiting to chef something up and is a miserable sod.

## 05. Back Alley Bowling

At Back Alley Bowling, Tenpin is happy to let you pass for a small fee (or if you have a General Atomics ID card). Otherwise, expect a fight with him, Lane, and Split. Check the restrooms for chems and caps. Find a safe (Advanced) and a Jangles the Moon Monkey in the storeroom behind Tenpin. Check behind the lanes to visit Kingpin, who's near a steamer trunk and other ammo to scavenge. Visit Strike at the upstairs bar, which needs a little freshening up. The stairwell provides access to the roof, a supervisor's room with chems, and a terminal (Advanced) that explains the history of the Galleria. You can find a password to this terminal near the Director in the Mister Handy Statue.

## 06. Fallon's Department Store

Visit Reg at Fallon's, but be careful not to touch the merchandise. After the Grand Reopening, he's a little more willing to part with his wares.

## 07. Pirelli's Bakery

You can visit Crisp at the bakery, but be warned-- it may be a long wait. Expect better service after the Grand Reopening.

## 08. Slocum's Joe

Visit Bean at Slocum's Joe for a quick cuppa. Wait, can you smell gas?

##  [2.12] DARK HOLLOW POND

THREAT LEVELS 20+

- DANGER: RADIATION (MILD)!
- FACTION: MIRELURKS
- FACTION: RAIDERS

A prime recreation spot for the inhabitants of Medford, now this is home to Mirelurks and a couple of Raider stragglers with their unpleasant dogs.

##  [2.13] MASS FUSION CONTAINMENT SHED

THREAT LEVELS 25+

- ARMAMENTS AND AMMO
- ARMOR PART: FUSION CORE
- DANGER: OIL!
- DANGER: RADIATION (SEVERE)!
- FACTION: RADROACHES
- FACTION: FERAL GHOULS

Mass Fusion is the leader in the safe handling and disposal of radioactive waste. Except here the place is overrun with Feral Ghouls and spilled barrels. Check the outside balcony for a cooler (Novice). Inspect the supervisor's terminal (Novice) to unlock the security door. Check the secure area for a toolbox (Novice) and a gate to a steamer trunk.

## [2.14] OLD GULLET SINKHOLE

THREAT LEVELS 25+

- ARMAMENTS AND AMMO
- ARMAMENTS AND AMMO: TRUNK
- BOTTLECAPS
- COLLECTIBLE: REQUIRED READING: WASTELAND SURVIVAL GUIDE
- CRAFTING: COOKING STATION
- DANGER: RADIATION (MILD)!
- FACTION: DEATHCLAW
- FACTION: FERAL GHOUL
- FACTION: RADROACHES
- HEALTH OR CHEMS
- QUEST VISIT: FOR JOE SAVOLDI
- (BUNKER HILL)
- UNIQUE ITEM: GRANDPA SAVOLDI'S HAT

The latest topographical radar indicates recent seismic activity in this area. Beware the Deathclaw on the surface, guarding a trunk near an overturned car. Drop into the sinkhole to uncover some answers regarding the quest, which must be active for the discovery to be made. Don't forget the reading materials on the cooking station! Exit via the cellar of the local residence with the red chained door, watching for feral folks on the way out. There's a safe to hack too (Novice).

## [2.15] GREENTOP NURSERY

THREAT LEVELS 25+

- CRAFTING: CHEMISTRY STATION
- CRAFTING: COOKING STATION
- FACTION: STINGWINGS
- FACTION: SETTLER
- SERVICES: WORKSHOP

This Mutfruit-growing operation on the outskirts of Malden may be beneficial to the enterprising Minuteman. The two gardeners here seem to be in need of protection and an alliance.

## [2.16] BREAKHEART BANKS

THREAT LEVELS 25+ | THREAT LEVELS 30+

FIG 2.16: BREAKHEART BANKS (EXTERIOR)

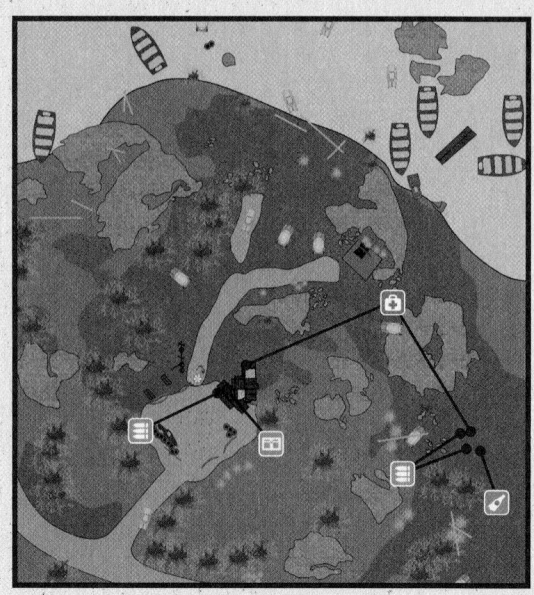

- ARMAMENTS AND AMMO
- ARMAMENTS AND AMMO: TRUNK
- BOTTLECAPS
- COLLECTIBLE: NUKA-COLA QUANTUM
- CRAFTING: COOKING STATION
- CRAFTING: WEAPONS WORKBENCH
- DANGER: CAN CHIMES!
- DANGER: MINES!
- FACTION: SUPER MUTANT
- HEALTH OR CHEMS

A small family farm on the banks of the Saugus River, with a corn field and melon patch, has fallen to the oversized hands of a Super Mutant gang. Remember to loot the trunk on the top floor of the central shack. Need a drink? Try a Quantum on the small lookout platform to the east.

### VAULT-TEC RECOMMENDED LOOT

COLLECTIBLE: NUKA COLA QUANTUM

## [2.17] LISTENING POST BRAVO

THREAT LEVELS 30+

- ARMAMENTS AND AMMO
- ARMAMENTS AND AMMO: TRUNK
- CRAFTING: ARMOR WORKBENCH
- CRAFTING: WEAPONS WORKBENCH
- DANGER: EXPLOSIVE BARRELS!
- DANGER: TURRETS!
- FACTION: BROTHERHOOD OF STEEL
- FACTION: IRRADIATED WILDLIFE (YAO GUAI)
- FACTION: ROBOTS
- HEALTH OR CHEMS
- QUEST VISIT: BLIND BETRAYAL
  (BROTHERHOOD OF STEEL)

This location has an additional accessible room if the quest is active.

An ex-military checkpoint to scavengers is like a porch lamp for bugs. It is currently devoid of human foes, with only robots active in this area. Below ground, the bunker abuts a Yao Guai cave.

Two machine-gun turrets dissuade the inquisitive. A Protectron waddles the interior, guarding a security gate (Advanced) with ammo inside. The elevator isn't working until the quest is active or you hack the terminal (Master). Below ground is a hidden bunker with chems and a terminal. Beware of the wildlife in the cave. The inaccessible section is only available during the quest; there's a military trunk there.

## [2.18] THE SLOG

THREAT LEVELS 35+

- BOTTLECAPS+++
- CRAFTING: ARMOR WORKBENCH
- CRAFTING: COOKING STATION
- FACTION: SETTLER (GHOULS)
- FACTION: CHARACTER: WISEMAN
- FACTION: CHARACTER: ARLEN GLASS
- FACTION: CHARACTER: HOLLY
- FACTION: CHARACTER: DEIDRE
- FACTION: CHARACTER: JONES
- QUEST START: MISCELLANEOUS (WISEMAN)
- QUEST START: MISCELLANEOUS (ARLEN GLASS)
- QUEST START: MISCELLANEOUS (MARLENE'S HOLOTAPE)
- QUEST START: MISCELLANEOUS (HOLLY)
- SERVICES: TRADER (DEIDRE)
- SERVICES: WORKSHOP
- UNIQUE ITEM: BUTTERCUP TOY

### VAULT-TEC RECOMMENDED LOOT

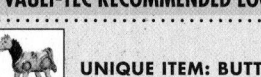

UNIQUE ITEM: BUTTERCUP TOY

The Middlesex County public swimming pool is now the only Tarberry Bog in the Commonwealth. Run by Ghoul settlers, they could provide much-needed trading goods to an enterprising (and open-minded) Minuteman. There's a small diner on the property to scavenge too (Advanced).

**Miscellaneous Quest (Wiseman)**

Rid the local area of Super Mutants, and Wiseman forms an alliance with you. Bring settlers here to improve the trading conditions for Deidre.

 **Miscellaneous Quest (Arlen Glass)**

Arlen Glass, the farm's handyman, has a special interest in repairing Giddyup Buttercup toys. If you're up for the challenge (and a very long trek), he sends you to retrieve a crate of parts from Location [6.23] Wilson Atomatoys Factory, south of Quincy. You can persuade him (Easy, Medium) for a better reward, or (Hard) for an Atomatoys ID Card, which will save you a bit of time at the factory. Expect 150-300 caps for your reward.

If you're just wanting Giddyup Buttercup toys for your collection (and who isn't?), find them here:

| GIDDYUP BUTTERCUP | |
|---|---|
| Location | Number of Toys |
| Wilson Atomatoys Factory | 5 |
| Wilson Atomatoys Corporate HQ | 14 |

 **Miscellaneous Quest (Marlene's Holotape)**

If you manage to find Marlene's Holotape at the Wilson Atomatoys Factory, return it to Arlen. After an emotional moment, you're awarded with around 350 caps and a unique item—a Buttercup Toy horse.

 **Miscellaneous Quest (Holly)**

Harvest tarberry from the swimming pool and she'll pay you.

 **[2.19] SAUGUS IRONWORKS**        THREAT LEVELS 30+

**VAULT-TEC RECOMMENDED LOOT**

**BOBBLEHEAD: EXPLOSIVES**          **COLLECTIBLE: NUKA CHERRY**
**REQUIRED READING: PICKET FENCES**      **UNIQUE ITEM: SHISHKEBAB**

- ARMAMENTS AND AMMO+
- ARMAMENTS AND AMMO: TRUNK
- COLLECTIBLE: BOBBLEHEAD: EXPLOSIVES
- COLLECTIBLE: HOLOTAPE: JAKE'S HOLOTAPE
- COLLECTIBLE: NUKA CHERRY
- COLLECTIBLE: REQUIRED READING: PICKET FENCES
- CRAFTING: ARMOR WORKBENCH
- CRAFTING: POWER ARMOR STATION
- CRAFTING: WEAPONS WORKBENCH
- DANGER: FLAMETHROWERS!
- DANGER: OIL!
- DANGER: MINES!
- DANGER: RADIATION (MILD)!
- DANGER: TENSION TRIGGER!
- DANGER: TURRETS!
- FACTION: FORGED (RAIDERS)
- FACTION: CHARACTER: SLAG
- FACTION: CHARACTER: JAKE FINCH
- HEALTH OR CHEMS
- QUEST VISIT: HERE THERE BE MONSTERS (SIDE)
- QUEST VISIT: OUT OF THE FIRE (LOCATION QUEST)
- UNIQUE ITEM: SHISHKEBAB

Once a historic pre–Revolutionary War ironworks, this location was reopened during the ramp-up to provide materials for the war with China. The location is now run by Slag, a particularly ferocious Raider and his clan, the Forged.

Pipe ramp to Roof

**FIG 2.19A: SAUGUS IRONWORKS (EXTERIOR)**

**FIG 2.19B: SAUGUS IRONWORKS (INTERIOR)**

LEVEL 1

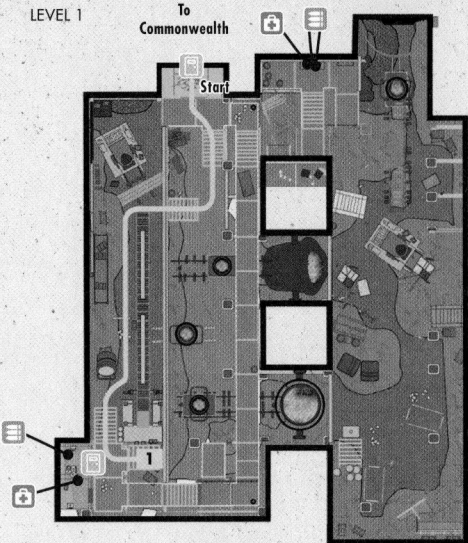

To
Commonwealth

Start

**FIG 2.19C: SAUGUS BLAST FURNACE (INTERIOR)**

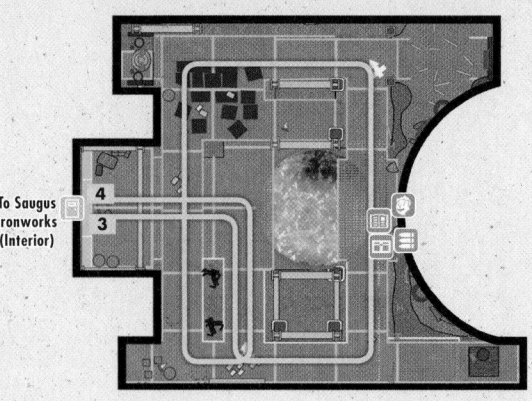

To Saugus
Ironworks
(Interior)

The interior is a confusing maze of catwalks and ramps, so take your time and try not to fall into the molten forges. Slag and Jake Finch both carry a Saugus roof key if you can't manage to unlock it (Expert), as well as his Holotape. Don't overlook the Bobblehead, trunk, and magazine in this fiery chamber. For details of the location quest, consult the Primary Location: Finch Farm.

LEVEL 2

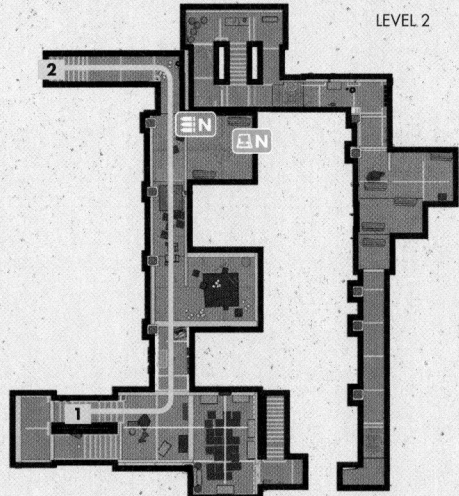

LEVEL 3

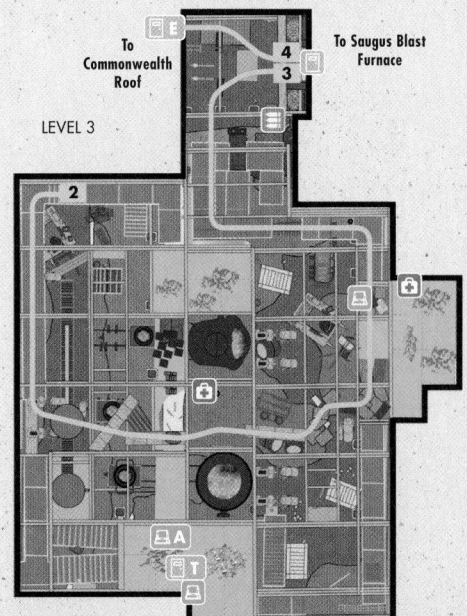

To
Commonwealth
Roof

To Saugus Blast
Furnace

**FIG 2.20–24: MALDEN TOWNSHIP (EXTERIOR) AND SURROUNDINGS**

The following cluster of Primary Locations makes up the township of Malden. Synths are active in this area. Also be aware of three Secondary Locations within the boundaries of this township, detailed below.

## [2.20] MEDFORD MEMORIAL HOSPITAL

**THREAT LEVELS 20+**

- ARMAMENTS AND AMMO
- ARMAMENTS AND AMMO: TRUNK (2)
- ARMOR PART: FUSION CORE
- BOTTLECAPS
- COLLECTIBLE: NUKA CHERRY
- COLLECTIBLE: NUKA COLA QUANTUM
- COLLECTIBLE: REQUIRED READING: MASSACHUSETTS SURGICAL JOURNAL
- CRAFTING: CHEMISTRY STATION
- DANGER: EXPLOSIVE BARRELS!
- DANGER: OIL!
- FACTION: SUPER MUTANT
- HEALTH OR CHEMS
- QUEST VISIT: RADIANT QUEST: JACKPOT (RAILROAD)

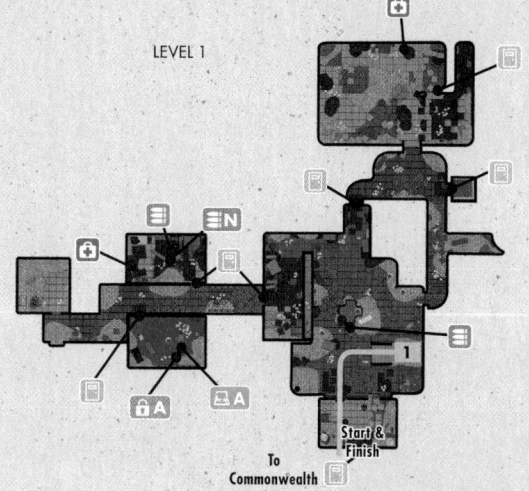

LEVEL 1

To Commonwealth

Start & Finish

LEVEL 2

**FIG 2.20: MEDFORD MEMORIAL HOSPITAL (INTERIOR)**

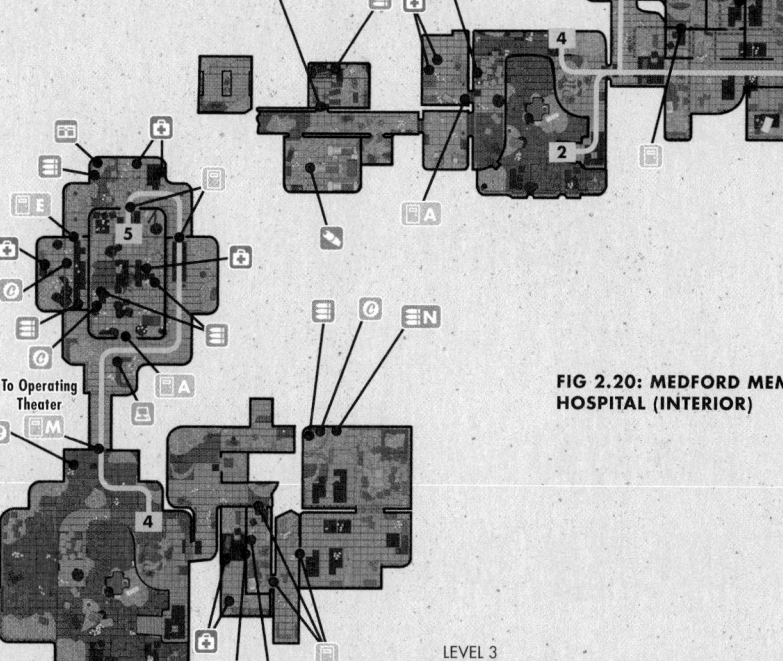

To Operating Theater

LEVEL 3

This plaza shows the telltale signs of Super Mutant fortification. Inside, if you make steady progress floor by floor, you can obtain the theater key from a toolbox in a northeast room, allowing access to the theater on the upper floor. Open the Level 2 balcony door to access the room with the magazine and one of the trunks. The other trunk is in a hidden room on the top floor in the southeast part of the interior, only accessed during the quest.

## [2.21] MALDEN CENTER

THREAT LEVELS 20+

- ARMAMENTS AND AMMO+
- ARMAMENTS AND AMMO: MINI NUKE
- ARMAMENTS AND AMMO: MINI NUKE (FAT MAN)
- ARMAMENTS AND AMMO: TRUNK
- ARMOR PART: FUSION CORE
- BOTTLECAPS+
- COLLECTIBLE: NUKA CHERRY
- COLLECTIBLE: REQUIRED READING: TUMBLERS TODAY
- CRAFTING: COOKING STATION
- CRAFTING: WEAPONS WORKBENCH

- DANGER: EXPLOSIVE BARRELS!
- DANGER: MINE!
- DANGER: TRIPWIRE!
- DANGER: TURRETS!
- FACTION: RAIDERS
- FACTION: SYNTHS (THE INSTITUTE)
- FACTION: CHARACTER: HELTER SKELTER
- HEALTH OR CHEMS
- QUEST VISIT: MEMORY INTERRUPTED (THE RAILROAD)

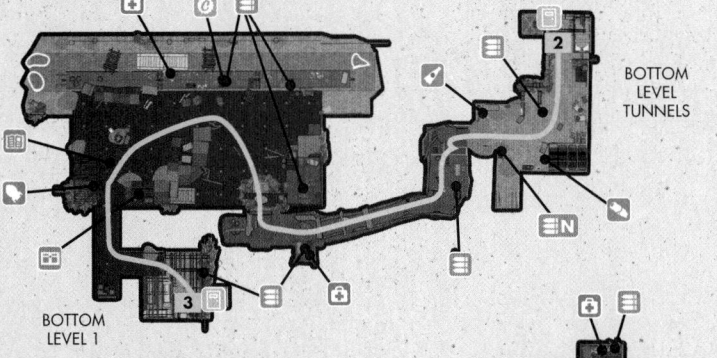

BOTTOM LEVEL TUNNELS

BOTTOM LEVEL 1

To Commonwealth

Start

Finish

PLATFORM LEVEL 1

STATION LEVEL 1

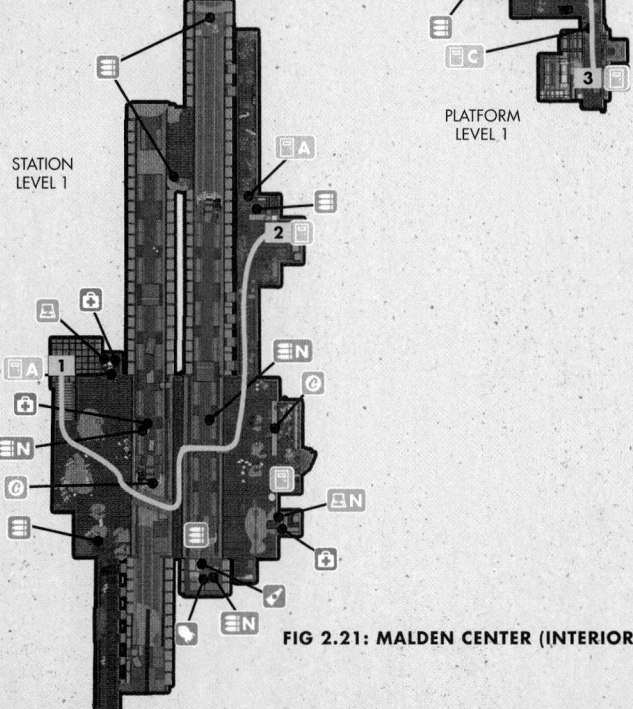

**FIG 2.21: MALDEN CENTER (INTERIOR)**

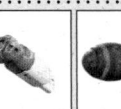

A public park surrounds the entrance to the subway, an attempt by the city to brighten up the area. The station park was clear and clean and a great place for families and children.

Previous to your arrival, a band of roving raiders moved into the subway, creating a small community of shacks and a broken subway car. They've lived here for a while, stealing from and murdering nearby caravans and living the good raiding life.

As you arrive, you may see synth units on the prowl, systematically removing all Raiders from the vicinity. Remember to carefully navigate the interior of this station; there are elevators to use if you wish to reach the main Raider base and the trunk.

## [2.22] SLOCUM'S JOE CORPORATE HQ

THREAT LEVELS 20+

- ARMAMENTS AND AMMO
- ARMAMENTS AND AMMO: TRUNK BOTTLECAPS
- CRAFTING: COOKING STATION
- CRAFTING: CHEMISTRY STATION
- CRAFTING: POWER ARMOR STATION
- FACTION: RAIDER
- UNIQUE ITEM: SLOCUM'S BUZZBITES RECIPE

### VAULT-TEC RECOMMENDED LOOT

UNIQUE ITEM: SLOCUM'S BUZZBITES RECIPE

Rumor has it a Slocum's Joe recipe—the company's boldest innovation in coffee and confectionary—is hidden inside a safe (Advanced) here. Outside is a three-floor ruined office building with an attached garage (with a Power Armor station) and views of the police station next door. Check the top exterior floor for a chemistry station and trunk.

## [2.23] MALDEN MIDDLE SCHOOL (VAULT 75)

THREAT LEVELS 20+

- ARMAMENTS AND AMMO+++
- ARMAMENTS AND AMMO: TRUNK
- BOTTLECAPS
- COLLECTIBLE: BOBBLEHEAD: SCIENCE
- COLLECTIBLE: REQUIRED READING: GROGNAK THE BARBARIAN
- CRAFTING: CHEMISTRY STATION

- DANGER: TESLA ARC!
- DANGER: TURRETS!
- FACTION: GUNNERS
- FACTION: BROTHERHOOD OF STEEL
- FACTION: THE INSTITUTE
- HEALTH OR CHEMS+
- QUEST START: VAULT 75

**FIG 2.23: VAULT 75 (INTERIOR)**

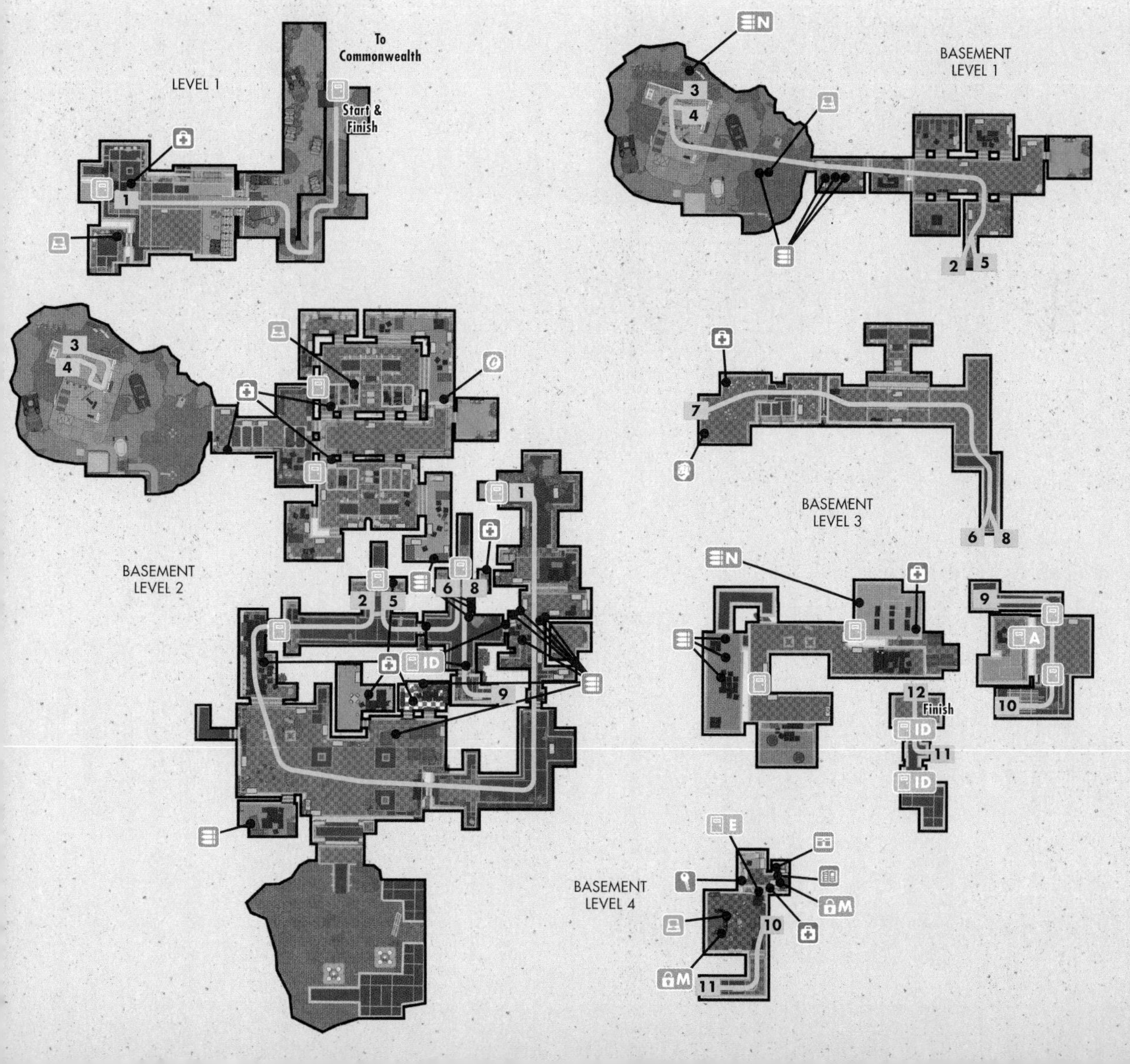

LEVEL 1

To Commonwealth

Start & Finish

1

BASEMENT LEVEL 1

N

3

4

2  5

BASEMENT LEVEL 2

3

4

1

2  5

6  8

9

BASEMENT LEVEL 3

7

6  8

N

9

A

12 Finish

ID

11

10

ID

ID

BASEMENT LEVEL 4

E

10

M

11

MAP

### ZONE 2

NORTH CENTRAL COMMONWEALTH

287

**BOBBLEHEAD: SCIENCE**

**REQUIRED READING: GROGNAK THE BARBARIAN**

According to some uncorroborated reports, Vault-Tec was commissioned by the U.S. military to experiment on and train children to become battle-ready super-soldiers who would obey orders without a second thought. The experiment did not end well. Gunners have moved into what remains of the vault.

If you are currently allied with the Brotherhood of Steel or the Institute, expect to encounter allied forces battling Gunners at this location. The entrance to the interior is located behind a cell door (watch for the trap) at the southern corner of the building.

 **Vault 75 (Miscellaneous Quest)**

1. EXPLORE VAULT 75
2. ACCESS LABORATORY AREA
3. EXPLORE LABORATORY
4. FIND ADMIN ACCESS CARD
5. EXPLORE ADMIN AREA

The interior of the vault is a rabbit warren of corridors. Take your time and locate two different access cards to further your exploration: The Gunner Commander, located in the simulation area, holds the Vault 75 Lab Access Card. One of the Gunners, located on the upper floor of the laboratory area (near the Bottlehead), holds the Vault 75 Admin Access Card. The key to the safe under the overseer's bed (Master) is on the blue crate by the toolbox.

## [2.24] MED-TEK RESEARCH

THREAT LEVELS 25+

- ARMAMENTS AND AMMO++
- ARMAMENTS AND AMMO: TRUNK
- ARMOR PART: FUSION CORE
- COLLECTIBLE: REQUIRED READING: MASSACHUSETTS SURGICAL JOURNAL 7
- COLLECTIBLE: NUKA CHERRY
- CRAFTING: CHEMISTRY STATION
- DANGER: RADIATION (MILD)!
- FACTION: FERAL GHOULS

- HEALTH OR CHEMS
- QUEST VISIT: LONG ROAD AHEAD (SIDE COMPANION)
- UNIQUE ITEM: PREVENT

**FIG 2.24A: MED-TEK RESEARCH (INTERIOR)**

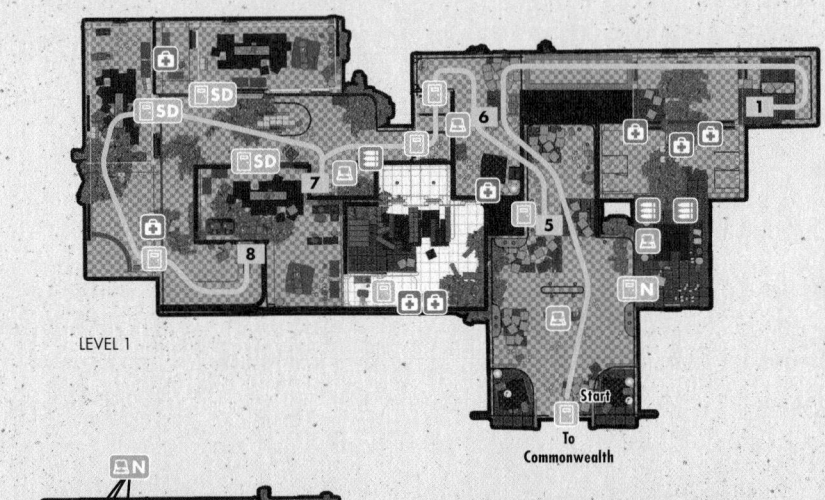

LEVEL 1

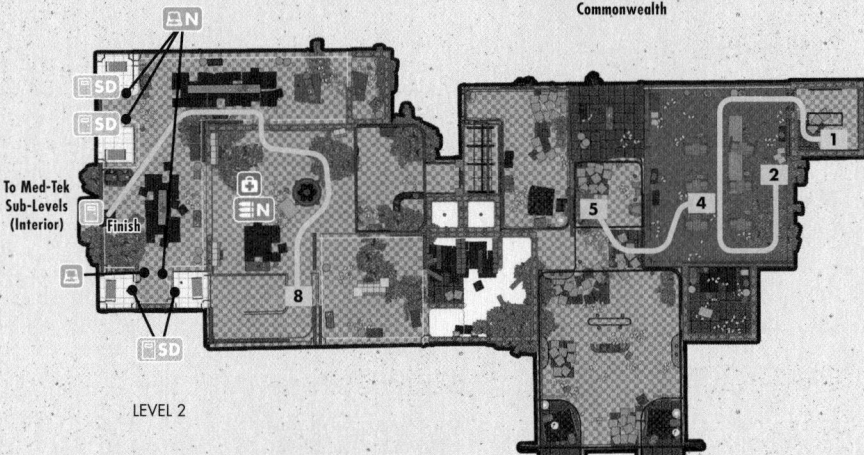

LEVEL 2

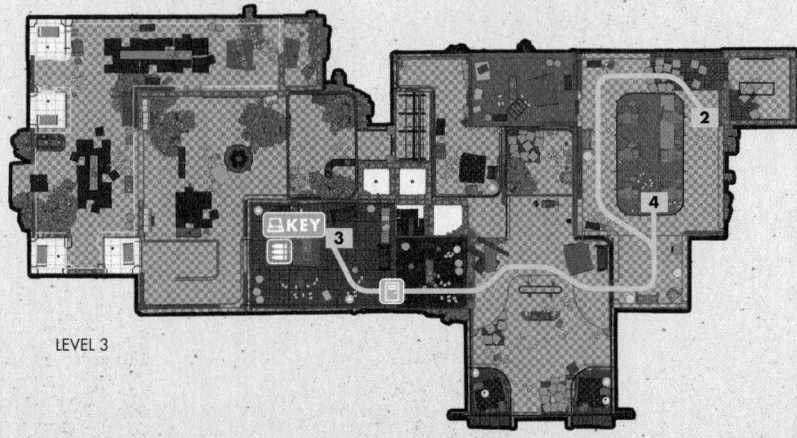

LEVEL 3

**FIG 2.24A: MED-TEK SUB-LEVELS (INTERIOR)**

LEVEL 1

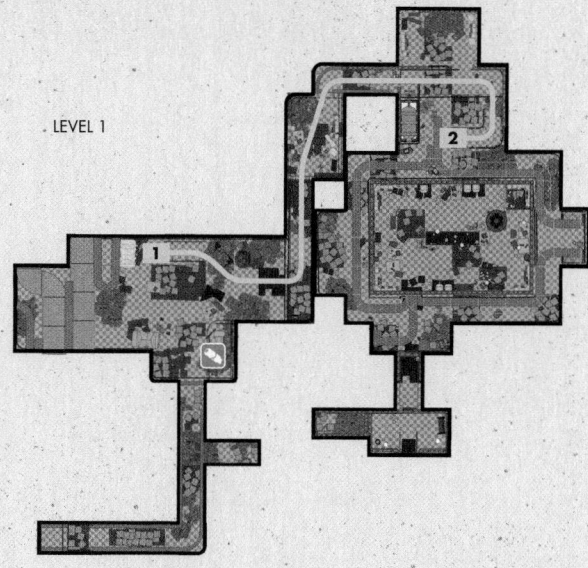

This location has areas that cannot be accessed if the specified quest is not active.

This private research laboratory owned by the Med-Tek Corporation began experimenting with infectious diseases. One was a virus that affected only teenagers and children. The entire facility went into lockdown when the bombs fell to prevent any contagion from spreading, trapping all the inhabitants. The lockdown was never lifted.

Outside, beware of Feral Ghouls in the forecourt. Inside, there is a lockdown in effect. There is a single, main entrance to enter. Inside, up on Level 3, you need a key to access the executive terminal, which you find during the specified quest. It is the only way to deactivate the alert and enter the sublevel.

LEVEL 2

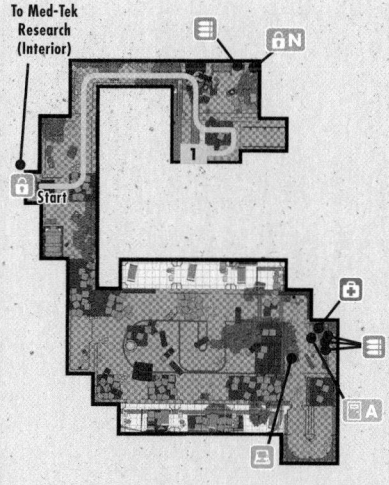

To Med-Tek
Research
(Interior)

Start

## MALDEN TOWNSHIP SECONDARY LOCATIONS

### [01] Garage Alcove

– **CRAFTING:
CHEMISTRY STATION**

Around the back and under the ice cream store is a small garage.

BASEMENT
LEVEL 1

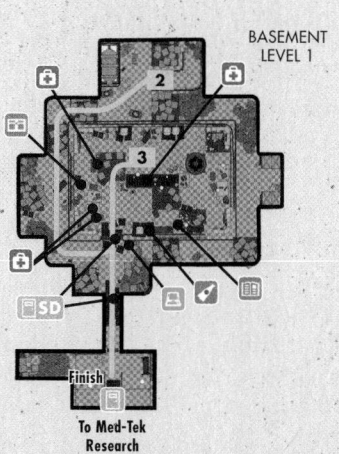

Finish

To Med-Tek
Research
(Interior)

### [02] Malden Police Station

– **ARMAMENTS AND AMMO**
– **HOLOTAPE: EDDIE WINTER HOLOTAPE**
– **HEALTH OR CHEMS**
– **QUEST: LONG TIME COMING (SIDE COMPANION)**

Find the quest-related Holotape by the evidence terminal, on the upper floor, southeast corner.

### [03] Med-Tek Parking Garage

– **CRAFTING: COOKING STATION**
– **CRAFTING: WEAPONS WORKBENCH**
– **FACTION: FERAL GHOULS**

Access this two-floor parking structure from inside the perimeter of the Med-Tek Research Facility yard.

- ARMAMENTS AND AMMO
- ARMAMENTS AND AMMO: TRUNK
- ARMOR PART: FUSION CORE
- BOTTLECAPS++
- COLLECTIBLE: HOLOTAPE: SUBJECT 12 TESTING
- CRAFTING: ARMOR WORKBENCH
- CRAFTING: CHEMISTRY STATION
- DANGER: TESLA ARC!
- DANGER: TURRETS!
- FACTION: SETTLERS (COVENANT)
- FACTION: COMPOUND GUARD (SEWER)

- FACTION: CHARACTER: AMELIA STOCKTON
- FACTION: CHARACTER: BLYTHE
- FACTION: CHARACTER: BRIAN FITZGERALD
- FACTION: CHARACTER: DEEZER
- FACTION: CHARACTER: DOCTOR PATRICIA
- FACTION: CHARACTER: DOCTOR ROSLYN CHAMBERS
- FACTION: CHARACTER: DORA
- FACTION: CHARACTER: HONEST DAN
- FACTION: CHARACTER: JACOB ORDEN
- FACTION: CHARACTER: MANNY
- FACTION: CHARACTER: PENNY FITZGERALD

- FACTION: CHARACTER: SWANSON
- FACTION: CHARACTER: TALIA MCGOVERN
- FACTION: CHARACTER: TED HUNTLEY
- HEALTH OR CHEMS
- QUEST START: HUMAN ERROR (SIDE)
- SERVICES: TRADER (DOCTOR PATRICIA)
- SERVICES: TRADER (DEEZER)
- SERVICES: TRADER (PENNY FITZGERALD)
- SERVICES: TRADER (TALIA MCGOVERN)
- SERVICES: WORKSHOP

## VAULT-TEC RECOMMENDED LOOT

**ARMOR PART: FUSION CORE**

### FIG 2.25A: COVENANT (EXTERIOR)

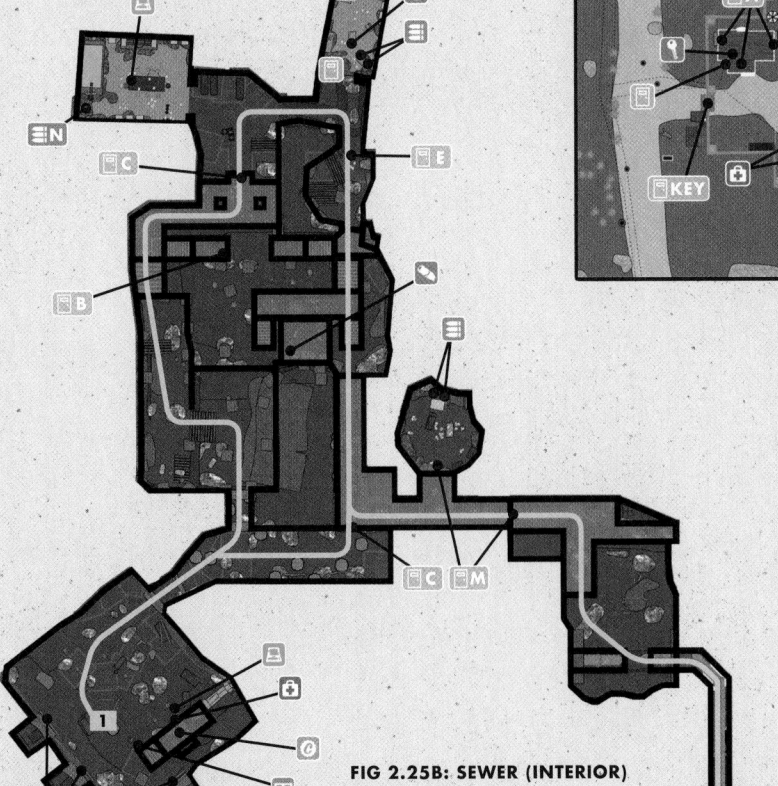

FIG 2.25B: SEWER (INTERIOR)

Start & Finish

To Commonwealth

Covenant is an impressively defended and seemingly prosperous community of settlers. The people are friendly, the amenities are quaint, and it appears to be safe. All you have to do is pass a simple test to enter. Many of the settlers at this location have keys to their own houses and the office establishments.

The Covenant also have commandeered a sewer tunnel area across the lake to the west, just below a lake lookout east of Mystic Pines. To progress farther into the Covenant's secret headquarters, open the door from the initial chamber (Master) or use the compound key that Manny or one of the compound guards is carrying.

## [2.26] TAFFINGTON BOAT HOUSE

THREAT LEVELS 15-25

- ARMAMENTS AND AMMO
- ARMAMENTS AND AMMO: TRUNK (2)
- ARMOR PART: FUSION CORE
- BOTTLECAPS+
- CRAFTING: CHEMISTRY STATION
- CRAFTING: COOKING STATION
- DANGER: MINES!
- DANGER: TRIPWIRES!
- FACTION: BLOODBUGS
- HEALTH OR CHEMS
- SERVICES: WORKSHOP

The residence of one Mary Sutton, this location may be cleared of hostiles and used as a settlement. There's a safe (Advanced) and steamer trunk (Novice) to unlock upstairs. Circumvent the door to the boathouse (Novice) by swimming under and up, watching for tripwires. The Bloodbugs sucking these settlers dry seem to be coming from the Malden Drainage area to the north.

**Malden Drainage**

### VAULT-TEC RECOMMENDED LOOT

 **ARMOR PART: FUSION CORE**

Clear this interior chem lab of its blood-sucking parasites before inspecting the area for Russell Sutton and a small security cell with a locked terminal (Advanced) and a trunk. There's a second trunk in the small upper laboratory area.

## [2.27] TUCKER MEMORIAL BRIDGE

THREAT LEVELS 15-25

## [2.28] POSEIDON ENERGY TURBINE #18-F

THREAT LEVELS 15-25

- ARMAMENTS AND AMMO: TRUNK
- COLLECTIBLE: REQUIRED READING: TUMBLERS TODAY
- DANGER: RADIATION (MILD)!
- FACTION: BLOATFLIES
- FACTION: MIRELURKS
- FACTION: RADROACHES
- HEALTH OR CHEMS
- QUEST VISIT: LAST VOYAGE OF THE U.S.S. CONSTITUTION (SIDE)

- DANGER: EXPLOSIVE BARRELS!
- DANGER: OIL!
- DANGER: MINES!

Offering an excellent thoroughfare from the Commonwealth across the river and into either Charleston (southeast) or Cambridge (southwest) Neighborhoods, this also offers less than stellar safety if you're hapless enough to set off the cascading explosive trap.

**FIG 2.28: POSEIDON ENERGY TURBINE #18-F (EXTERIOR)**

### VAULT-TEC RECOMMENDED LOOT

 **REQUIRED READING: TUMBLERS TODAY**

This is a small nuclear turbine used to the supply energy to much of the Commonwealth. The turbine is inactive. You find a quest item here if the quest is active. Clear the interior of disgusting mutant insects. Use the exterior roof as a defensive position if necessary.

FIG 2.29A: WEST EVERETT ESTATES (EXTERIOR)

- ARMAMENTS AND AMMO
- ARMAMENTS AND AMMO: TRUNK (2)
- BOTTLECAPS
- COLLECTIBLE: NUKA-COLA QUANTUM (2)
- CRAFTING: ARMOR WORKBENCH
- CRAFTING: COOKING STATION
- CRAFTING: WEAPONS WORKBENCH
- DANGER: CAN CHIMES!

- DANGER: GRENADE TRAP!
- DANGER: MINES!
- DANGER: OIL!
- DANGER: TURRETS!
- FACTION: SUPER MUTANT
- FACTION: CHARACTER: HAMMER
- HEALTH OR CHEMS

To Backyard Bunker (Interior)

**VAULT-TEC RECOMMENDED LOOT**

 **COLLECTIBLE: NUKA COLA QUANTUM (2)**

This once-picturesque suburban community is similar to Sanctuary Hills. Currently, it could best be described now as a "transitional" neighborhood. Recently, a Raider gang was overrun by Super Mutants under the leadership of "Hammer." They are clustered to the south. Be sure to thoroughly inspect the area for a safe (Master) and steamer trunk (Expert), Lance's terminal (Advanced), and a nearby safe (Advanced). Enter the backyard bunker to locate Wayne's terminal, another Quantum, and one more trunk.

 **[2.30] IRISH PRIDE INDUSTRIES SHIPYARD**     THREAT LEVELS 20+

- ARMAMENTS AND AMMO
- ARMAMENTS AND AMMO: TRUNK
- BOOK OR MAGAZINE: TABOO TATTOOS
- BOTTLECAPS
- CRAFTING: ARMOR WORKBENCH
- CRAFTING: POWER ARMOR STATION
- DANGER: RADIATION (MILD)!
- FACTION: BLOODBUGS
- FACTION: MIRELURKS
- HEALTH OR CHEMS

FIG 2.30A: IRISH PRIDE INDUSTRIES SHIPYARD (EXTERIOR)

**VAULT-TEC RECOMMENDED LOOT**

 **REQUIRED READING: TABOO TATTOOS**

This small shipyard produces midsized shipping vessels. Recently, the place was taken over by Rory Rigwell, lover of Mirelurks. He believed the mutated crustaceans weren't violent, just misunderstood.

The west warehouse has a Power Armor station, and you find some caps stashed on a boat moored to the south. There are two entrances—the main doors to the northwest and a side entrance (Master).

## FIG 2.30B: IRISH PRIDE INDUSTRIES SHIPYARD (INTERIOR)

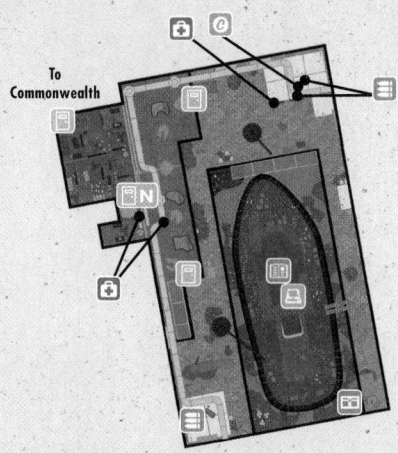

Through the office and locker room is a large yard where you find the remains of a rusty tugboat. The intermittent chatter of Rory can be heard (and turned off at the boat's terminal). Don't forget to check the metal roof of the workshops and the muddy base around the boat for a trunk.

## [2.31] RELAY TOWER OMC-810

THREAT LEVELS 20+

- RADIO: DEFAULT RADIO SIGNAL
- RADIO: SEPARATED FAMILY RADIO SIGNAL

This is part of the Commonwealth Relay Tower Network. Authorized personnel only. Use the relay tower terminal to amplify two nearby radio signals.

## [2.32] NATIONAL GUARD TRAINING YARD    THREAT LEVELS 25+

- ARMAMENTS AND AMMO+
- ARMAMENTS AND AMMO: TRUNK
- ARMOR PART: FUSION CORE (2)
- ARMOR PART: POWER ARMOR (LEVELED)
- ARMOR PART: POWER ARMOR (LEVELED)
- ARMOR PART: POWER ARMOR (LEVELED)
- COLLECTIBLE: HOLOTAPE:
  KNIGHT ASTLIN'S HOLOTAPE
- COLLECTIBLE: HOLOTAPE:
  NATIONAL GUARD OFFICER'S PASSWORD
- COLLECTIBLE: REQUIRED READING: U.S. COVERT
  OPERATIONS MANUAL
- CRAFTING: ARMOR WORKBENCH
- CRAFTING: COOKING STATION
- CRAFTING: POWER ARMOR STATION
- CRAFTING: WEAPONS WORKBENCH
- DANGER: OIL!
- DANGER: MINES!
- DANGER: TRIPWIRES!
- FACTION: BROTHERHOOD OF STEEL
- FACTION: FERAL GHOULS
- FACTION: ROBOTS
- FACTION: CHARACTER: KNIGHT ASTLIN
- FACTION: CHARACTER: SHELLY TILLER
- HEALTH OR CHEMS
- QUEST START: THE LOST PATROL
  (BROTHERHOOD OF STEEL)
- QUEST VISIT: THE LOST PATROL
  (BROTHERHOOD OF STEEL)
- QUEST VISIT: THE SILVER SHROUD (SIDE)

FIG 2.32A:
NATIONAL GUARD
TRAINING YARD
(EXTERIOR)

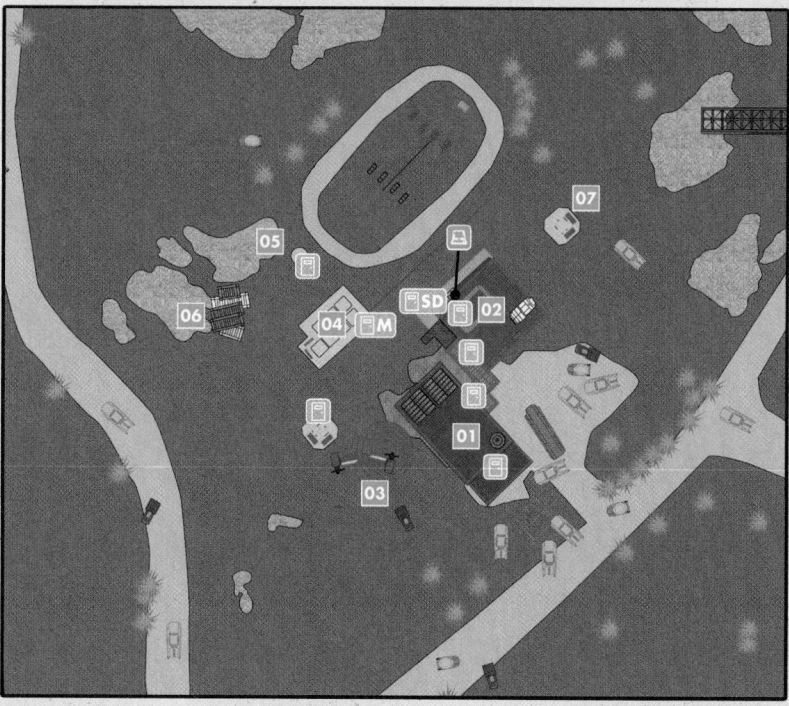

## VAULT-TEC RECOMMENDED LOOT

**ARMOR PART: FUSION CORE (2)**
**ARMOR PART: POWER ARMOR (LEVELED)**
**REQUIRED READING: U.S. COVERT OPERATIONS MANUAL**

Two hundred years ago, the National Guard was in higher demand than ever before. This facility was expanded just prior to the bombs falling. Currently, this location has recently been visited by the Brotherhood of Steel; they used this location to house and repair Power Armor.

### [01] National Guard Recruitment Office

The upper floor of this office has almost completely collapsed. The Brotherhood Knight in this location begins the specified quest if you inspect her. This is also the location of Shelly Tiller if the side quest is active. There's also some required reading in the ground floor cafeteria.

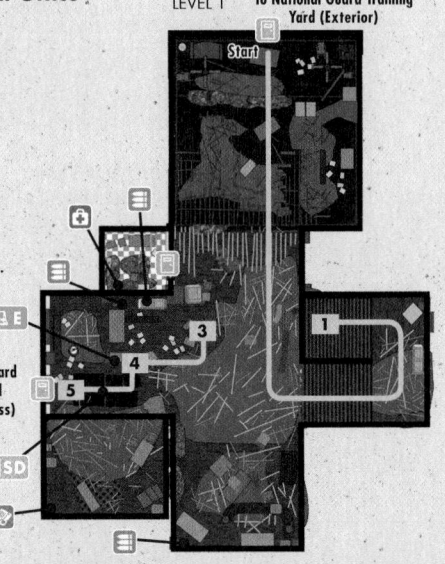
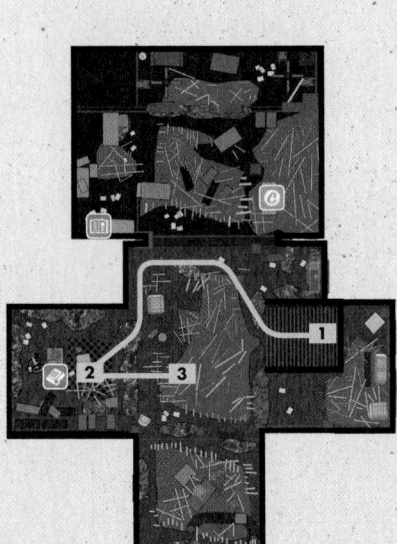

**FIG 2.32B: NATIONAL GUARD RECRUITMENT OFFICE (INTERIOR)**

## [02] National Guard Barracks

### FIG 2.32C: NATIONAL GUARD BARRACKS (INTERIOR)

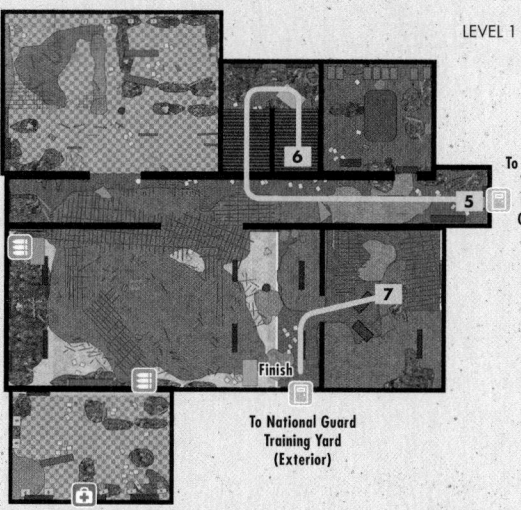

LEVEL 1

To National Guard Training Yard (Recruitment Office Access)

To National Guard Training Yard (Exterior)

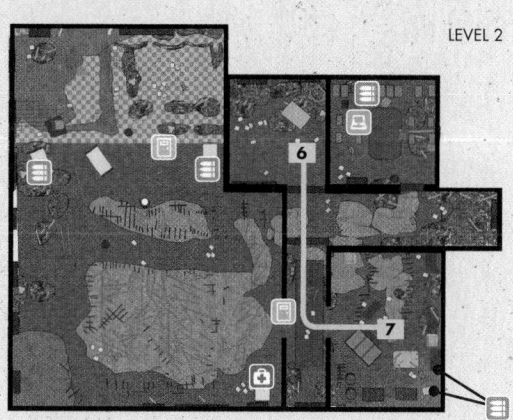

LEVEL 2

The exterior has scaffold steps to reach the roof, allowing for sniping opportunities against ferals and turrets. Once inside (accessed via the recruitment office), use the Holotape password found in the recruitment office to access the armory terminal (Master) if your hacking skills aren't up to par. Then unlock the door to the armory from here.

## [03] Crashed Vertibird and West Pillbox

The building has a wooden box to crack open, and the area offers protection against wandering ferals.

## [04] National Guard Armory

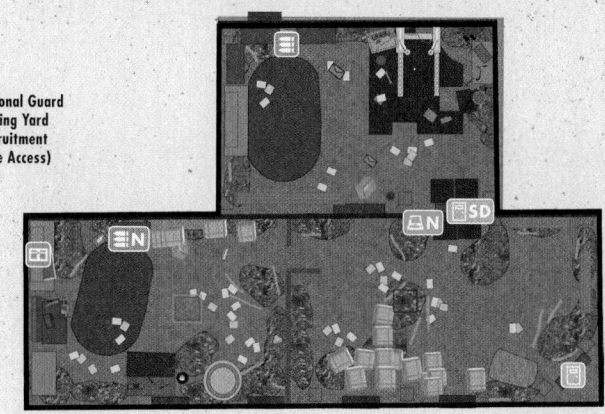

To National Guard Training Yard (Exterior)

### FIG 2.32D: NATIONAL GUARD ARMORY (INTERIOR)

Unless you used the armory terminal in the barracks (Master), this door is firmly locked (Master). If you access the Power Armor storage, a Sentry Bot will be released from the northwest pillbox when you exit.

## [05] Northwest Pillbox

The Sentry Bot within this location is not active until you visit the armory.

## [06] Rusting Cargo Containers

Don't overlook the open container with the security gate (Expert). Unlock it to access some Power Armor and a Fusion Core.

## [07] Northeast Pillbox

There's ammo inside here and more on the roof, courtesy of the Brotherhood of Steel, though you need the Power Armor Jetpack to land on the roof. The Jetpack is a reward given during the Brotherhood of Steel quests.

 ## [2.33] COUNTY CROSSING     THREAT LEVELS 25+

- CRAFTING: COOKING STATION          - SERVICES: WORKSHOP
- FACTION: SETTLER

Eking out an existence in some of the least defendable arable land, two settlers and their Mutfruit orchard are ready for your help.

## [2.34] REVERE SATELLITE ARRAY

- ARMAMENTS AND AMMO+
- ARMAMENTS AND AMMO: MINI NUKE
- ARMAMENTS AND AMMO: MINI NUKE (FAT MAN)
- ARMAMENTS AND AMMO: TRUNK
- ARMOR PART: POWER ARMOR (LEVELED)
- COLLECTIBLE: REQUIRED READING: U.S. COVERT OPERATIONS MANUAL
- CRAFTING: ARMOR WORKBENCH
- CRAFTING: COOKING STATION
- DANGER: LONG FALL!
- DANGER: OIL!
- FACTION: BROTHERHOOD OF STEEL
- FACTION: SUPER MUTANT
- FACTION: CHARACTER: SCRIBE FARIS
- HEALTH OR CHEMS
- QUEST START: THE LOST PATROL (BROTHERHOOD OF STEEL)
- QUEST VISIT: THE LOST PATROL (BROTHERHOOD OF STEEL)

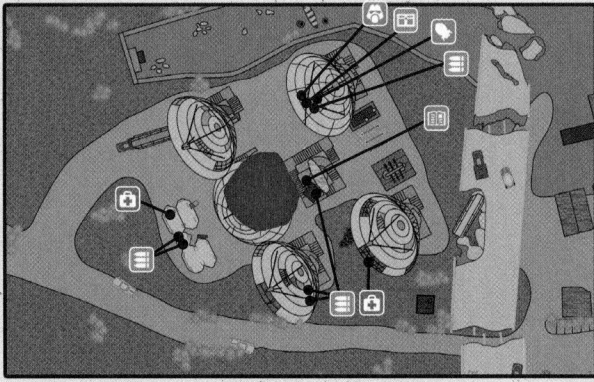

**FIG 2.34: REVERE SATELLITE ARRAY (EXTERIOR)**

### VAULT-TEC RECOMMENDED LOOT

ARMAMENTS AND AMMO: MINI NUKE (AND FAT MAN)

ARMOR PART: POWER ARMOR (LEVELED)

REQUIRED READING: U.S. COVERT OPERATIONS MANUAL

Super Mutants are advancing into Raider territory throughout this zone and are using this flooded array as a bone pit. Visit the wayward Brotherhood scribe Faris here to begin a quest. Find the Fat Man after a precarious ascent and a Mini Nuke after a disgustingly bloody wade.

## [2.35] FINCH FARM

- BOTTLECAPS+
- CRAFTING: COOKING STATION
- FACTION: SETTLER
- FACTION: CHARACTER: ABRAHAM FINCH
- FACTION: CHARACTER: ABIGAL FINCH
- FACTION: CHARACTER: DANIEL FINCH
- QUEST START: OUT OF THE FIRE (LOCATION QUEST)
- SERVICES: TRADER (FINCH)
- SERVICES: WORKSHOP

The Finch family farm this grim scrubland, and their youngest, Jake, has disappeared. Offer to help, complete the quest, and you may add this Mutfruit settlement to your burgeoning empire.

 **Out of the Fire**

1. RETRIEVE ABRAHAM FINCH'S SWORD FROM SAUGUS IRONWORKS
2. RETURN ABRAHAM FINCH'S SWORD TO HIM AT FINCH FARM

Speak to Abraham Finch and agree to help him.

 (Easy) Ask for more Caps.

Visit Saugus Ironworks and prepare for protracted combat with a Raider gang known as the Forged. Enter the blast furnace, slay the Raider leader Slag, then return to Finch (with or without Jake) for your reward; you get to keep the sword (Unique Weapon: Shishkebab, located at Saugus Ironworks).

MR. PEBBLES
THE FIRST CAT IN SPACE

# SECONDARY LOCATIONS

## [2.01] CONTAINER TRUCK CAMP

- ARMAMENTS AND AMMO
- CRAFTING: COOKING STATION
- DANGER: TURRETS!
- FACTION: RAIDER
- HEALTH OR CHEMS

On the road south of Outpost Zimonja is a parked trailer guarded by two Redcoat mannequins. The real threat is the Raider and his dog. Search the trailer for an explosives box (Novice) and other ammo.

## [2.02] HILLTOP HUT

- CRAFTING: WEAPONS WORKBENCH
- FACTION: ROBOT

A small stilt shack with a commanding view of the area has a locked terminal (Expert) to hack, if you want a spot of Protectron remote-controlling.

## [2.03] CAR TREE CAMP

- ARMAMENTS AND AMMO
- BOTTLECAPS+
- CRAFTING: COOKING STATION
- FACTION: RADSCORPIONS

Three settlers used this landmark as a camp. The Radscorpions use this as a feeding ground. Grab some caps from the settlers, and inspect their duffel bag.

## [2.04] DESERTED PICNIC AREA

- CRAFTING: COOKING STATION

This was once a picturesque rest stop for day-tripping picnickers. Now there's a rusty cooler (Novice) to scavenge from as you view the desolate scrub.

## [2.05] DEATHCLAW NEST (LYNN WOODS)

- QUEST VISIT: THE DEVIL'S DUE (SIDE)

A small collection of kills and a large nest indicates the presence of Deathclaws. Drop in an egg-shaped present so you're not mauled.

## [2.06] RUSTY TRAILER

- ARMAMENTS AND AMMO: TRUNK

Long ago, vacationers didn't get far. Look inside the rusting trailer for a steamer trunk.

## [2.07] BLOATFLY CAMP

- ARMAMENTS AND AMMO
- FACTION: BLOATFLIES

A shack under the elevated freeway houses a wooden crate, a settler, and a small swarm of Bloatflies.

## [2.08] BILLBOARD SCAVENGER SHACK

- CRAFTING: COOKING STATION

Beneath the large rusting billboard is a small shack with a cooking fire.

## [2.09] ELEVATED GUNNER CAMP

- ARMAMENTS AND AMMO
- CRAFTING: POWER ARMOR STATION
- DANGER: LONG DROP!
- HEALTH OR CHEMS

This Gunner camp has a construction lift to the south, but it is raised, meaning you need to approach from the fallen freeway section to the north. Gather chems, unlock the wooden crate, and ride the other construction lift to the upper part of the camp. There's usually a good weapon between the two large windmills.

## [2.10] WICKED SHIPPING CONTAINER TRUCK #3

- ARMAMENTS AND AMMO
- ARMAMENTS AND AMMO: TRUNK
- QUEST VISIT: WICKED SHIPMENTS (LOCATION MISCELLANEOUS)

This is one of Wicked Shipping's trailers; the hatch is unlocked. Access the trunk and explosives box inside.

## [2.11] SCAVENGER CAMP

– ARMAMENTS AND AMMO
– FACTION: YAO GUAI

A wild Yao Guai has interrupted a group of scavengers. Pick through the remains after anything violent attempts to gnaw on you.

## [2.12] MILITARY CONVOY (APCS AND TRAILER)

– ARMAMENTS AND AMMO
– ARMAMENTS AND AMMO: TRUNK

A rusting convoy of APCs and two big-rigs. The APC holds some ammunition and explosives, but the larger reward is in the green container trailer—a trunk.

## [2.13] ELEVATED FREEWAY: ELEVATED TRAILER

– ARMAMENTS AND AMMO: TRUNK

A green container trailer is attached to the big-rig, which is delicately balanced on a seemingly inaccessible "island" of elevated freeway. Jump here with a Brotherhood of Steel jetpack, and claim the trunk from inside the trailer.

## [2.14] CRASHED VERTIBIRD (COVENANT LAKE)

– ARMOR PART: POWER ARMOR (LEVELED)
– DANGER: RADIATION (MILD)

The remains of a Vertibird are sticking out of the north end of this lake. Swim by the vessel to scavenge the suit of Power Armor, fully submerged next to the craft.

## [2.15] THE FISHING SPOT (COVENANT COMPOUND)

– DANGER: RADIATION (MILD)!
– DANGER: TURRETS!
– FACTION: COVENANT
– FACTION: CHARACTER: BLYTHE
– FACTION: CHARACTER: MANNY
– QUEST VISIT: HUMAN ERROR (SIDE)

A grumpy fisherman sits on this sewer outlet. Investigate the sewer pipe and you stumble upon a strange compound allied to the Covenant (on the east side of the lake). Do not disturb Manny and Blythe unless you wish to get on their bad side. Instead, why not investigate Covenant first? The map to the sewers is listed in Primary Location 2.25:

## [2.16] RUSTY TRACTOR

– BOTTLECAPS
– FACTION: FERAL GHOUL

This is a pile of corpses and farm equipment. Though one of the corpses isn't quite dead. Find the caps on the tractor seat.

## [2.17] OLD CARAVAN TRAILER

– BOTTLECAPS
– DANGER: TURRET!
– FACTION: ROBOTS

A rather antisocial dame (who isn't home at the moment) has left her caravan with a turret and Sentry Bot on guard. Make it through to claim the caps inside.

## [2.18] THE LOCKED TRAILER

– ARMAMENTS AND AMMO

Open the trailer (Advanced) and discover a surprise inside.

## [2.19] CARAVAN CROSSROADS

– BOTTLECAPS
– CHARACTER: FRED O'CONNELL

The last known position of the O'Connell Caravan, which last stopped at Covenant.

## [2.20] MALDEN DRAINAGE

- FACTION: BLOODBUGS

This sewer drain entrance is populated by Bloodbugs. Related to Taffington Boathouse, south of here. Investigate there first, looking for information on Malden Drainage.

## [2.21] BROTHERHOOD OF STEEL BATTLE SITE

- ARMAMENTS AND AMMO
- FACTION: BROTHERHOOD OF STEEL
- FACTION: CHARACTER: KNIGHT VARHAM
- QUEST START: THE LOST PATROL (BROTHERHOOD OF STEEL)
- QUEST VISIT: THE LOST PATROL (BROTHERHOOD OF STEEL)

An explosion tore this building apart. Knight Varham's body may hold the clue to what happened here. There's a safe to unlock (Advanced) and a duffel bag to inspect.

## [2.22] MILITARY CONVOY (TRAINING YARD)

- ARMAMENTS AND AMMO
- ARMAMENTS AND AMMO: TRUNK
- ARMOR PART: FUSION CORE
- ARMOR PART: POWER ARMOR (LEVELED)
- FACTION: ROBOTS
- FACTION: STINGWINGS

A convoy of two APCs and a trailer didn't make it too far from the training yard; find it on the road to the north. There's a trunk inside the APC and Power Armor in the trailer.

## [2.23] ABANDONED RAIDER CAMP (ELEVATED FREEWAY)

- ARMAMENTS AND AMMO
- DANGER: LONG DROP!
- FACTION: RAIDERS

Access is available from the interchange above Lexington to the west or by using the construction lift from the ground. This two-level Raider camp has some ammo to scavenge, and not a soul about.

## [2.24] DERELICT MANSION

- ARMAMENTS AND AMMO
- HEALTH OR CHEMS

The attractively hued mansion on this desolate stretch of road is uninhabited, but there's a suitcase and wooden box to scavenge.

## [2.25] MILITARY APCS

- ARMOR PART: POWER ARMOR (LEVELED)
- FACTION: ROBOTS
- HEALTH OR CHEMS

Two parked APCs near a downed aircraft is where you'll find a patrolling utility Protectron. Check the back of the APC for health.

## [2.26] COOLING VATS

- ARMAMENTS AND AMMO - FACTION: BLOODBUGS

A wooden crate and a workman with a leisurely disregard for fire safety can be found between these two giant globelike cooling vats, now in complete disrepair.

## [2.27] RIVER'S END SHACK

- CRAFTING: WEAPONS WORKBENCH
- FACTION: FERAL GHOULS

A small locked shack (Novice) can be opened, if you want to interrupt a meal.

## [2.28] PROTECTRON TRAILER

- FACTION: ROBOTS

A police Protectron is still serving its masters, who are inside this rusty old trailer.

## [2.29] RIVER'S END WAREHOUSE

- CRAFTING: POWER ARMOR STATION

A small rusting warehouse close to the elevated freeway, this also was used as a boat dock. Now it sits in quiet decay.

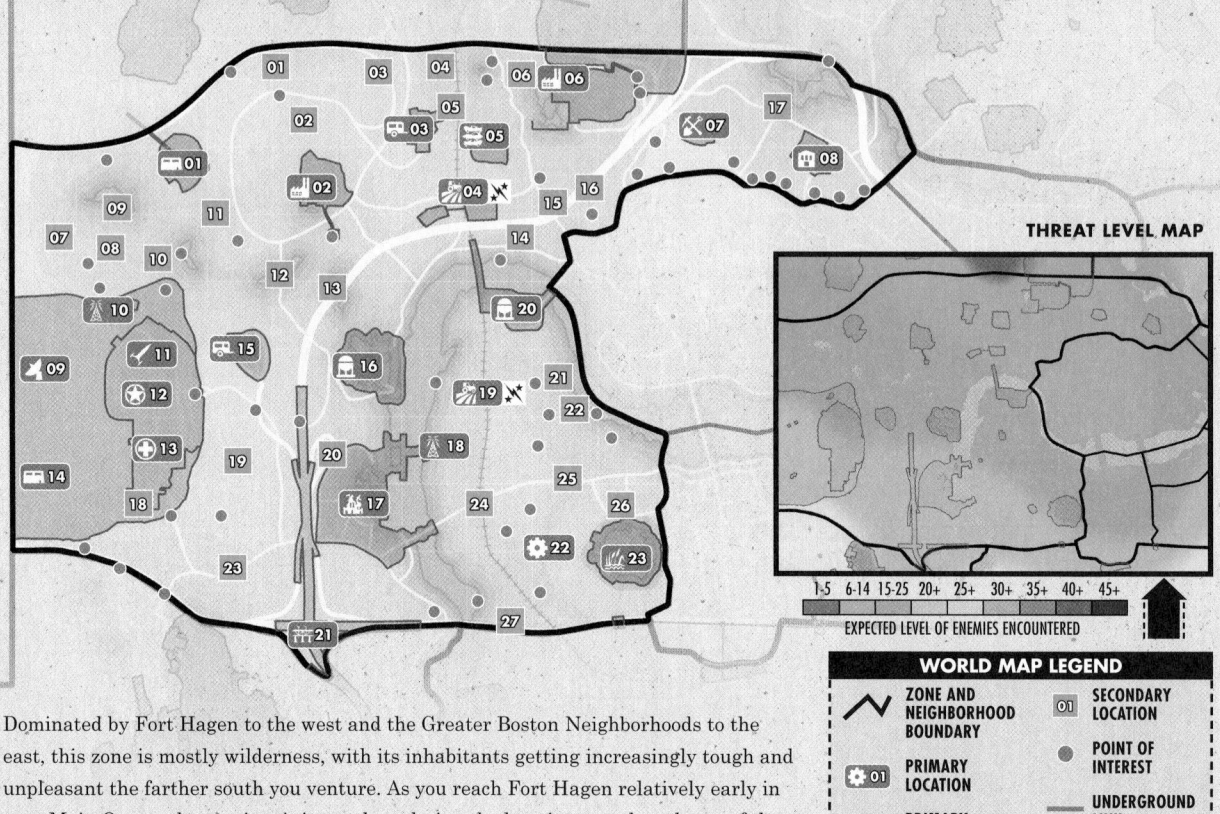

THREAT LEVEL MAP

1-5  6-14  15-25  20+  25+  30+  35+  40+  45+

EXPECTED LEVEL OF ENEMIES ENCOUNTERED

### WORLD MAP LEGEND

| | | | |
|---|---|---|---|
| ∧ | ZONE AND NEIGHBORHOOD BOUNDARY | 01 | SECONDARY LOCATION |
| ⚙ 01 | PRIMARY LOCATION | ● | POINT OF INTEREST |
| ▱ 01 | PRIMARY LOCATION BOUNDARY | — | UNDERGROUND LINK |
| | | ✕ | WORKSHOP |

Dominated by Fort Hagen to the west and the Greater Boston Neighborhoods to the east, this zone is mostly wilderness, with its inhabitants getting increasingly tough and unpleasant the farther south you venture. As you reach Fort Hagen relatively early in your Main Quest adventuring, it is worth exploring the locations north and east of the fort, venturing to the more soggy southern Charles River and back into Boston when you're ready for a breather at Diamond City. Follow the roads and the rail tracks to avoid getting lost. For the settlement wrangler, there's only two possible alliances to make, and one of those is with some gardening robots.

## Primary Locations

- [3.01] FEDERAL RATION STOCKPILE
- [3.02] ARCJET SYSTEMS
- [3.03] ROCKY NARROWS PARK
- [3.04] GRAYGARDEN
- [3.05] JALBERT BROTHERS DISPOSAL
- [3.06] CORVEGA ASSEMBLY PLANT
- [3.07] MASS GRAVEL & SAND
- [3.08] WATTZ CONSUMER ELECTRONICS

- [3.09] FORT HAGEN SATELLITE ARRAY
- [3.10] RELAY TOWER 0BB-915
- [3.11] FORT HAGEN FILLING STATION
- [3.12] FORT HAGEN
- [3.13] GREATER MASS BLOOD CLINIC
- [3.14] BOSTON MAYORAL SHELTER
- [3.15] FIDDLER'S GREEN TRAILER ESTATES
- [3.16] WESTON WATER TREATMENT PLANT

- [3.17] FOREST GROVE MARSH
- [3.18] RELAY TOWER 1DL-109
- [3.19] OBERLAND STATION
- [3.20] BEANTOWN BREWERY
- [3.21] MASS PIKE INTERCHANGE
- [3.22] VAULT 81
- [3.23] CHESTNUT HILLOCK RESERVOIR

## Secondary Locations

- [3.01] CAR WRECKAGE
- [3.02] TRACTOR WAREHOUSE
- [3.03] GUNNER CAMP ON-RAMP
- [3.04] RAIDER GRAVES
- [3.05] CARRIAGE DEN
- [3.06] RUINED BRICK WAREHOUSE
- [3.07] SCAVENGER'S TRAILER
- [3.08] RUSTING APC
- [3.09] MIRELURK POND

- [3.10] CANISTER LAUNCH SHACK
- [3.11] SCHOELT PROPANE STORE
- [3.12] BRIDGE (SOUTH OF ARCJET SYSTEMS)
- [3.13] ELEVATED FREEWAY ACCESS
- [3.14] PULOWSKI PRESERVATION SHELTER CLUSTER
- [3.15] CRASHED VERTIBIRD (ELEVATED FREEWAY)
- [3.16] CONSTRUCTION LIFT
- [3.17] MILITARY CHECKPOINT (CAMBRIDGE OUTSKIRTS)
- [3.18] POWER ARMOR WAREHOUSE

- [3.19] ARCJET ENGINE TRANSPORT
- [3.20] SCRAP MERCHANT
- [3.21] CAVE
- [3.22] CRASH SITE
- [3.23] MILITARY CHECKPOINT (SOUTH ZONE 3)
- [3.24] WAYSTATION
- [3.25] ROADSIDE STORE
- [3.26] JOE'S SPUCKIES COFFEE SHOP (FENS OUTSKIRTS)
- [3.27] RAIDER LOOKOUT CAMP (ELEVATED FREEWAY)

| | | | Collectibles: | |
|---|---|---|---|---|
| 13 ▬▬▬ 20 OPTIMAL ROUTE | C BOTTLECAPS | ✚ HEALTH OR CHEMS | ⚔ FUSION CORE | 💀 BOBBLEHEAD | 🥤 NUKA COLA QUANTUM |
| | 🔒 SAFE | ⬛ TERMINAL | 🛡 POWER ARMOR | 🚀 NUKA CHERRY | 📼 HOLOTAPE |
| | ARMAMENTS AND AMMO | STEAMER TRUNK | REQUIRED READING | MINI NUKE | A KEY |
| AREA OF INTEREST | DOOR | | | | |

| | | | | |
|---|---|---|---|---|
| N – Novice (Locked) | E – Expert (Locked) | T – Terminal required to unlock | IN – Inaccessible | CB – Circuit Breaker |
| A – Advanced (Locked) | M – Master (Locked) | KEY – Key or ID Card required to unlock | C – Chained | B – Button |

# PRIMARY LOCATIONS

## [3.01] FEDERAL RATION STOCKPILE

THREAT LEVELS 6-14 ▬▬▬▬▬▬▬▬▬▬

**FIG 3.01A: FEDERAL RATION STOCKPILE (EXTERIOR)**

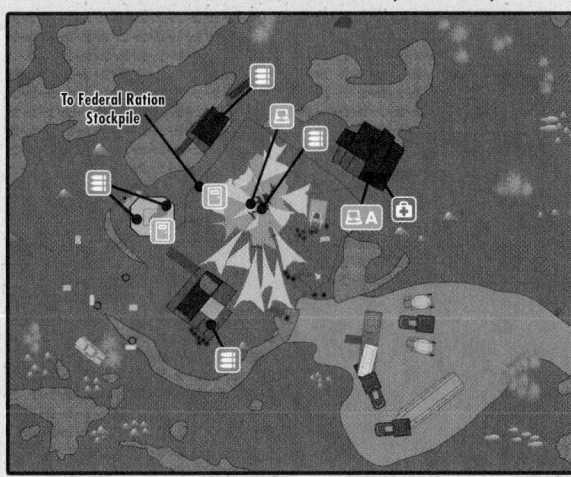

To Federal Ration Stockpile

- ARMAMENTS AND AMMO
- ARMAMENTS AND AMMO: MINI NUKE
- ARMAMENTS AND AMMO: MINI NUKE (FAT MAN)
- ARMAMENTS AND AMMO: TRUNK
- ARMOR PART: FUSION CORE
- ARMOR PART: POWER ARMOR
- BOTTLECAPS
- COLLECTIBLE: NUKA CHERRY
- COLLECTIBLE: NUKA COLA QUANTUM (2)
- COLLECTIBLE: REQUIRED READING: U.S.

- COVERT OPERATIONS MANUAL
- CRAFTING: ARMOR WORKBENCH
- CRAFTING: COOKING STATION
- CRAFTING: WEAPONS WORKBENCH
- DANGER: CAN CHIMES!
- DANGER: MINES!
- DANGER: TURRETS!
- FACTION: RAIDERS
- FACTION: CHARACTER: RED TOURETTE
- HEALTH OR CHEMS

**MAP**

**ZONE 3**

WESTERN COMMONWEALTH

### VAULT-TEC RECOMMENDED LOOT

**ARMOR PART: FUSION CORE**

**COLLECTIBLE: NUKA CHERRY**

**COLLECTIBLE: NUKA COLA QUANTUM**

 **REQUIRED READING: U.S. COVERT OPERATIONS MANUAL**

**ARMOR PART: POWER ARMOR (LEVELED)**

An old Federal bunker and tunnel system that links northwest to Zone 1 Primary Location: Lonely Chapel (it can also be approached from this direction if you wish to face Red Tourette first). It is the base for a gang of Raiders. The group underwent a recent change in leadership. Or was it mutiny? The exterior is a sprawling camp with a bunker and various shanty outbuildings. Check the container truck for power armor, and the generator at the back of the bunker for a Fusion Core.

Red Tourette's hideout in the southern part of the tunnels holds some choice items, as well as the federal ration stockpile password—the key to unlocking either of those two troublesome terminals (Master).

**FIG 3.01B: FEDERAL RATION STOCKPILE (INTERIOR)**

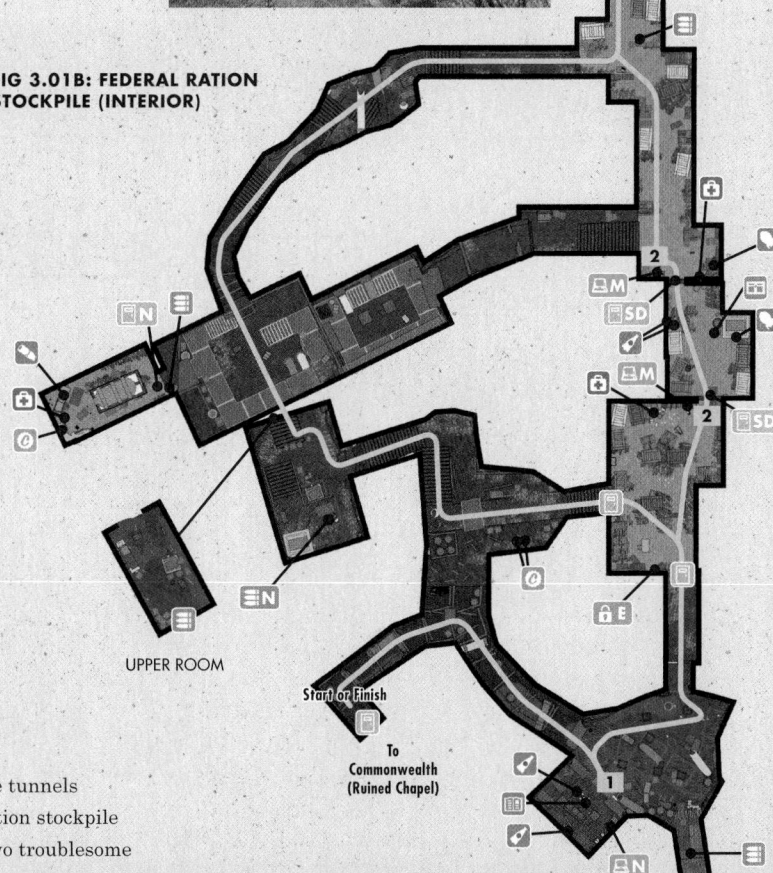

To Commonwealth

Start or Finish

UPPER ROOM

Start or Finish

To Commonwealth (Ruined Chapel)

**FIG 3.02A: ARCJET SYSTEMS (INTERIOR)**

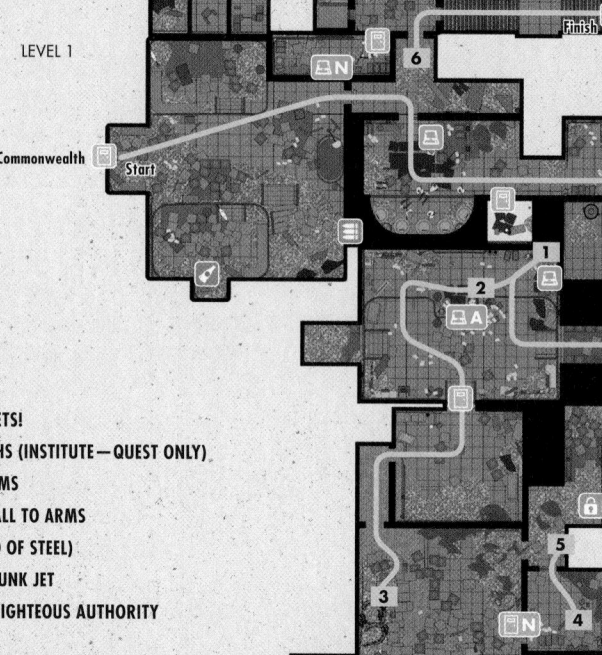

LEVEL 1

To Commonwealth

Start

To ArcJet Engine Core

Finish

- ARMAMENTS AND AMMO++
- ARMAMENTS AND AMMO: MINI NUKE (FAT MAN)
- ARMAMENTS AND AMMO: TRUNK (2)
- ARMOR PART: FUSION CORE
- COLLECTIBLE: REQUIRED READING: TESLA SCIENCE
- COLLECTIBLE: HOLOTAPE: TECHNICIAN'S PERSONAL LOG
- BOTTLECAPS
- CRAFTING: ARMOR WORKBENCH
- CRAFTING: WEAPONS WORKBENCH
- DANGER: EXPLOSIVE BARRELS!
- DANGER: OIL!
- DANGER: RADIATION (MILD)!
- DANGER: TESLA ARC!
- DANGER: TRIPWIRE!
- DANGER: TURRETS!
- FACTION: SYNTHS (INSTITUTE—QUEST ONLY)
- HEALTH OR CHEMS
- QUEST VISIT: CALL TO ARMS (BROTHERHOOD OF STEEL)
- UNIQUE ITEM: JUNK JET
- UNIQUE ITEM: RIGHTEOUS AUTHORITY

## VAULT-TEC RECOMMENDED LOOT

**ARMAMENTS AND AMMO: MINI NUKE (FAT MAN)**
**REQUIRED READING: TESLA SCIENCE**
**UNIQUE ITEM: JUNK JET**
**UNIQUE ITEM: RIGHTEOUS AUTHORITY**

**FIG 3.02: ARCJET SYSTEMS (EXTERIOR)**

LEVEL 2

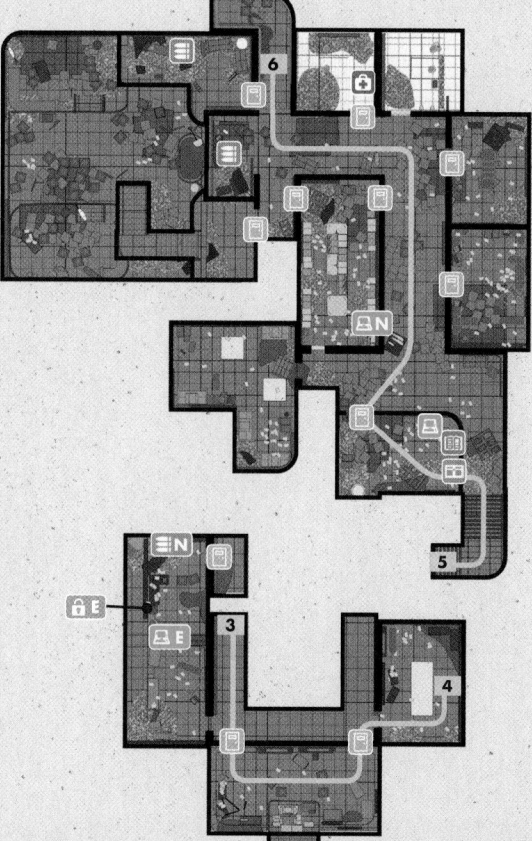

**FIG 3.02B: ARCJET ENGINE CORE (INTERIOR)**

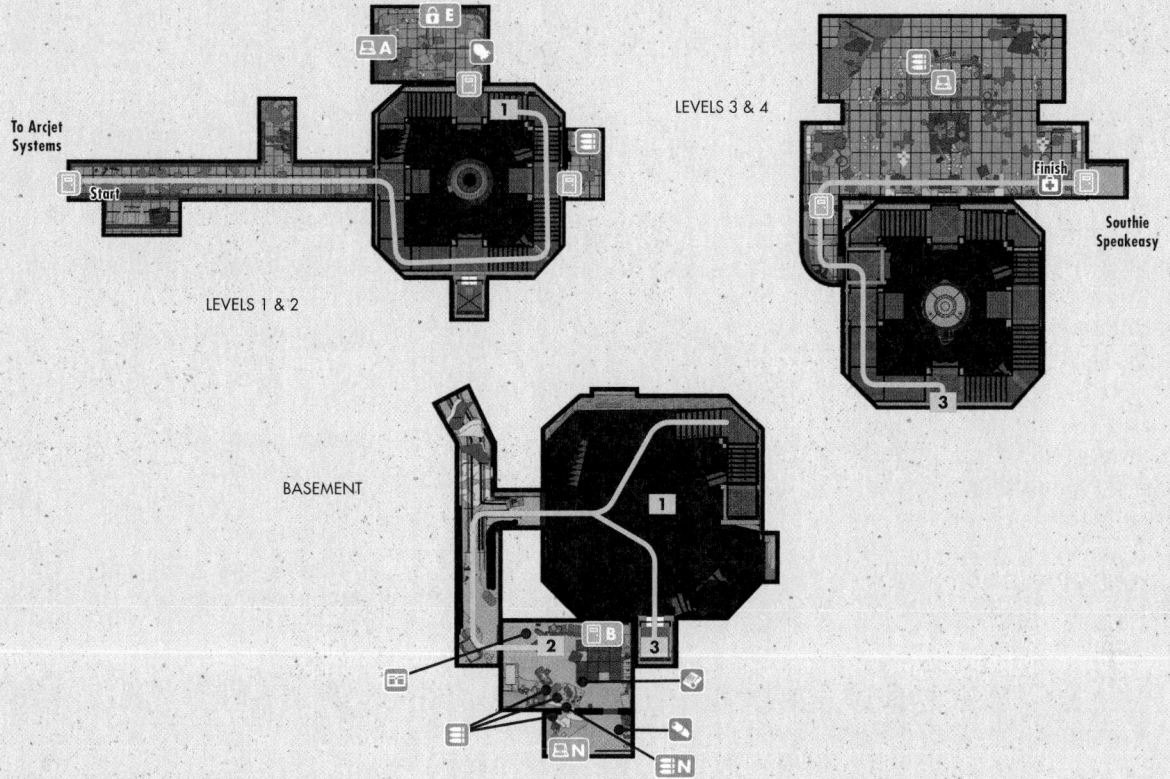

LEVELS 1 & 2

LEVELS 3 & 4

To Arcjet Systems

Start

Southie Speakeasy

Finish

BASEMENT

ArcJet was a contractor specializing in the design and development of custom-built high-tech aviation equipment. This particular facility included offices and labs for their staff, as well as a secure test chamber for new products in development. It has largely been abandoned since the war. Its security system, including turrets and Protectrons, was more than enough to fend off any Raiders.

Most of this facility is closed off prior to the specified quest. In particular, the Engine Core can only be accessed during the quest.

Before you enter, the workshop bunker behind the main structure has some first aid and an elevator, but the power is out. It can only be powered during the specified quest. The other unique weapon (the Junk Jet) is found in the engine core area.

Inside, the main offices and laboratories are set out on two sprawling floors you weave between, along with elevator access down to the engine core. Check every room so you don't miss some quality items, including a Fat Man and two steamer trunks (one in the main building, the other in the engine core area, though only one is available each time you visit)! If you're completing the Brotherhood of Steel quest, expect some righteous authority as you exit.

 **[3.03] ROCKY NARROWS PARK**       THREAT LEVELS 6-14

- ARMAMENTS AND AMMO
- ARMAMENTS AND AMMO: TRUNK
- CRAFTING: COOKING STATION
- FACTION: YAO GUAI
- FACTION: RADSTAG DOE

A small park and sad, bittersweet reminder of a world long gone. Please don't feed the bears. Check the eastern trailer for a trunk.

## [3.04] GRAYGARDEN

THREAT LEVELS 6-14

- BOTTLECAPS+
- CRAFTING: CHEMISTRY STATION
- FACTION: SETTLER (ROBOTS)
- FACTION: CHARACTER: SUPERVISOR GREENE
- FACTION: CHARACTER: SUPERVISOR BROWN
- FACTION: CHARACTER: SUPERVISOR WHITE
- HEALTH OR CHEMS
- QUEST START: MISCELLANEOUS (SUPERVISOR GREEN)
- QUEST START: MISCELLANEOUS (SUPERVISOR BROWN)
- QUEST START: TROUBLED WATERS (SUPERVISOR WHITE)
- QUEST VISIT: PINNED (THE INSTITUTE)
- SERVICES: TRADER (ROBOTS)
- SERVICES: WORKSHOP

### VAULT-TEC RECOMMENDED LOOT

 **BOTTLECAPS**

A fully automated hydroponic garden run by robots, this is the brainchild of Doctor Edward Gray. Even today, this is a remarkable example of self-sufficiency and features almost every crop: Mutfruit, tato, corn, melon, and gourd are growing here.

### Miscellaneous Quest (Supervisor Green)

Play along with Supervisor Greene for a fabulous cash prize.

### Miscellaneous Quest (Supervisor Brown)

Locate Mutfruit Seeds for Supervisor Brown for caps.

### Troubled Waters

1. INVESTIGATE THE WATER TREATMENT PLANT
2. DRAIN THE FLOODED WATER TREATMENT PLANT
3. RESTART THE MAIN PUMP
4. RETURN TO SUPERVISOR WHITE

Speak to Supervisor White and agree to help her. Visit the water treatment facility she indicates. Optionally remove all threats and enter the facility, flipping the breaker to bring all four pumps online. Once you restart the main pump, retreat and return to Supervisor White for caps, produce, an alliance, and a discount with Green when trading.

A ruined homestead sits to the west. Head inside and unlock the basement door (Expert) to explore a root cellar with a chemistry station and slightly more impressive salvage.

## [3.05] JALBERT BROTHERS DISPOSAL

THREAT LEVELS 6-14

### VAULT-TEC RECOMMENDED LOOT

**ARMAMENTS AND AMMO: MINI NUKE**

- ARMAMENTS AND AMMO
- ARMAMENTS AND AMMO: MINI NUKE
- ARMAMENTS AND AMMO: TRUNK
- CRAFTING: ARMOR WORKBENCH
- DANGER: TRIPWIRE!
- DANGER: RADIATION (SEVERE)!
- FACTION: MOLE RATS
- FACTION: CHILDREN OF THE ATOM
- HEALTH OR CHEMS

When wandering the Commonwealth, a follower of the Atom may find themselves in need of meditation and a chance to reflect. Or in the case of the cultists here, a pack of Mole Rats. The cultists have joined the Great Atom. You may, too, if you stay long enough in the irradiated garage. It is here you can read Brother Edmund's Journals (Advanced), unlock his floor safe (Expert), and locate the trunk and Mini Nuke.

## [3.06] CORVEGA ASSEMBLY PLANT

THREAT LEVELS 1-5          THREAT LEVELS 6-14

- ARMAMENTS AND AMMO+
- ARMAMENTS AND AMMO: TRUNK
- COLLECTIBLE: BOBBLEHEAD: REPAIR
- COLLECTIBLE: REQUIRED READING: GROGNAK THE BARBARIAN
- COLLECTIBLE: NUKA CHERRY
- CRAFTING: POWER ARMOR STATION
- DANGER: CAN CHIMES!
- DANGER: EXPLOSIVE BARRELS!
- DANGER: OIL!
- DANGER: MAKESHIFT BOMBS!
- DANGER: RADIATION (MILD)!
- DANGER: TRIPWIRES!
- DANGER: TURRETS!
- FACTION: FERAL GHOULS
- FACTION: RAIDERS
- FACTION: CHARACTER: JARED
- HEALTH OR CHEMS
- QUEST VISIT: WEATHERVANE (THE RAILROAD)

**FIG 3.06A: CORVEGA ASSEMBLY PLANT (EXTERIOR)**

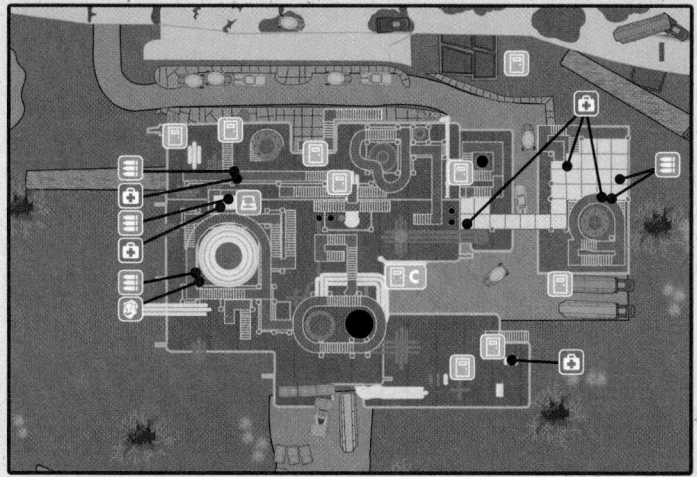

**FIG 3.06B: CORVEGA ASSEMBLY PLANT (INTERIOR)**

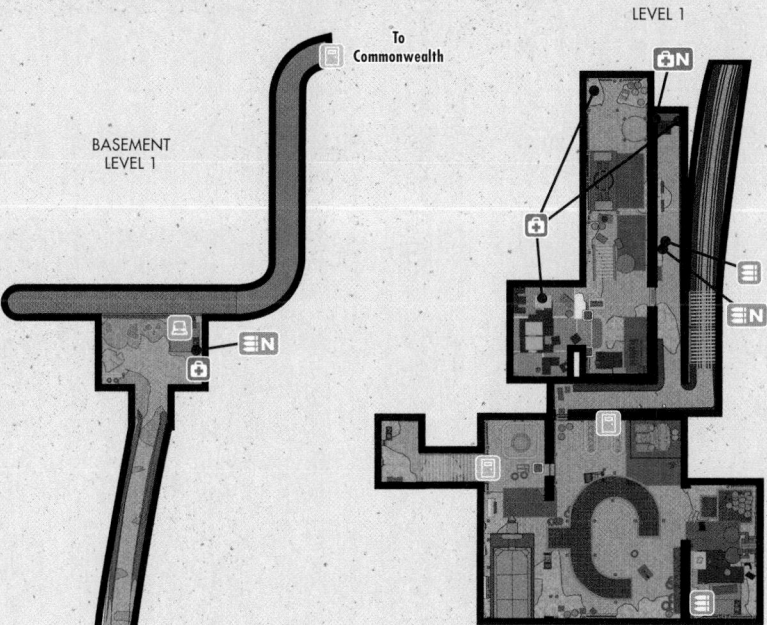

**BOBBLEHEAD: REPAIR**

**REQUIRED READING: GROGNAK THE BARBARIAN**

This was the pride of Lexington until the tourists departed. Now the south of the township is comprised of a sprawling assembly plant where the main bulk of the Raiders lurk, ready to push back the ferals that have swarmed the streets to the north.

There are four ground-level entrances into the factory. Of the three doors, the one on the eastern side is chained and an exit only. Choose either door on the north side (one is above the other). Or, look for the crack in the large sewer pipe to the northeast; head in here to access the basement level first.

To reach the roof, use the gantry to the east. There's an upper entrance into the plant just west of the covered bridge and road ramp (northeast). You can climb all the walkways to the top of the huge chimneys; the gantry around the massive cooling vat with the Corvega sign (to the southwest) has a place to put MILA (see quest), and there's a Bobblehead to snag. Finally, move to a hatch on the roof's northwestern corner—another way to enter this plant.

**MAP**

**ZONE 3**

WESTERN COMMONWEALTH

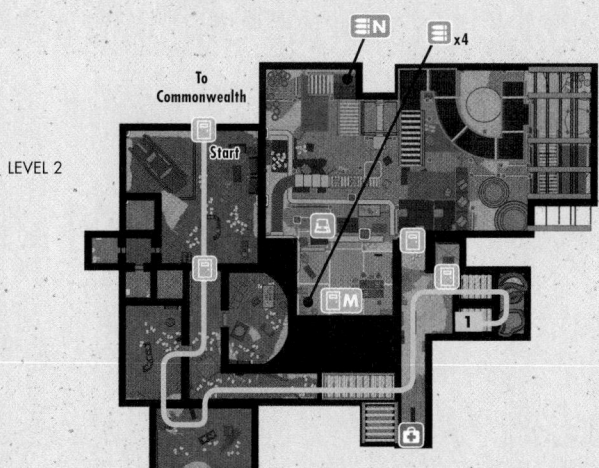

LEVEL 3
CATWALKS

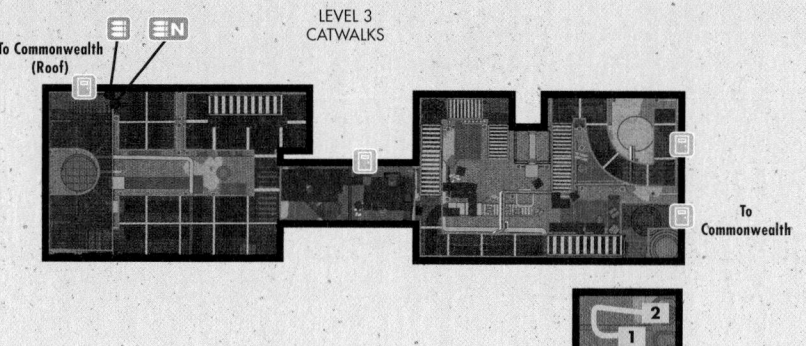

To Commonwealth (Roof)

To Commonwealth

Inside, the plant is very easy to get lost in, so carefully follow the map. The Raider Jared is on the upper assembly floor where Corvega vehicles used to be assembled. He holds the safe key, which opens his hidden safe (Advanced) located on the ground beneath the pod with his terminal, hidden behind a board.

## [3.07] MASS GRAVEL & SAND

THREAT LEVELS 6-14

- CRAFTING: WEAPONS WORKBENCH
- DANGER: LONG DROP!
- FACTION: MOLE RATS
- FACTION: RAIDER

Just north of Charleston is a small quarry serving as a lookout point for Raiders and a burrowing point for Mole Rats. Eradicating both will brighten your day.

LEVEL 4

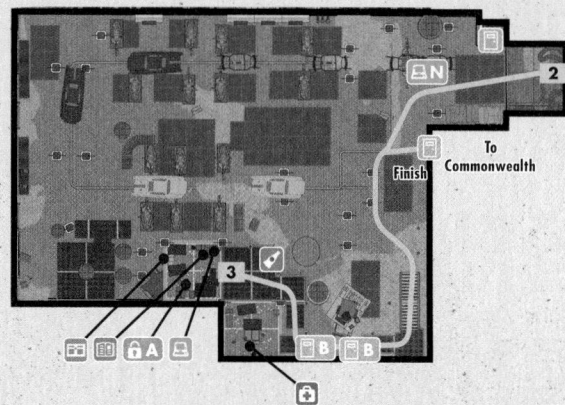

To Commonwealth

Finish

## [3.08] WATTZ CONSUMER ELECTRONICS

THREAT LEVELS 6-14

FIG 3.08: WATTZ
ELECTRONICS (INTERIOR)

BASEMENT

LEVEL 1

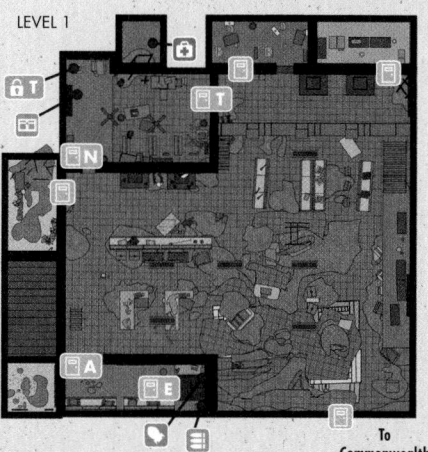

To Commonwealth

- ARMAMENTS AND AMMO
- ARMAMENTS AND AMMO: MINI NUKE
- ARMAMENTS AND AMMO: TRUNK
- COLLECTIBLE: REQUIRED READING: TOTAL HACK
- CRAFTING: ARMOR WORKBENCH
- FACTION: RADROACHES
- FACTION: ROBOTS
- HEALTH OR CHEMS

### VAULT-TEC RECOMMENDED LOOT

ARMAMENTS AND
AMMO: MINI NUKE
REQUIRED READING:
TOTAL HACK

With the large electromagnetic pulse sent out by the nuclear bombs, many of the robots at this store have reactivated in Demo Mode, leaving them wandering around, showing off their best features. Fair warning: tinkering with the terminals or safes at this location may cause these robots to turn hostile. Be sure you tinker with the basement terminal, though, if only to grab the magazine there.

# [3.09–3.13] FORT HAGEN TOWNSHIP

##  [3.09] FORT HAGEN SATELLITE ARRAY  THREAT LEVELS 15-25

— ARMAMENTS AND AMMO

Two large radar dishes and a small interior bunker (accessed via the metal trapdoor at the base of the south dish) stand ominously above Fort Hagen. There's little else here but desiccated woodland.

##  [3.10] RELAY TOWER 0BB-915  THREAT LEVELS 15-25

— RADIO: DISTRESS SIGNAL
— RADIO: RAIDER RADIO SIGNAL
— RADIO: CIVIL ALERT SYSTEM BROADCAST

This is part of the Commonwealth Relay Tower Network. Authorized personnel only. Use the relay tower terminal to amplify three nearby radio signals.

## [3.11] FORT HAGEN FILLING STATION  THREAT LEVELS 15-25

FIG 3.11: FORT HAGEN (EXTERIOR)

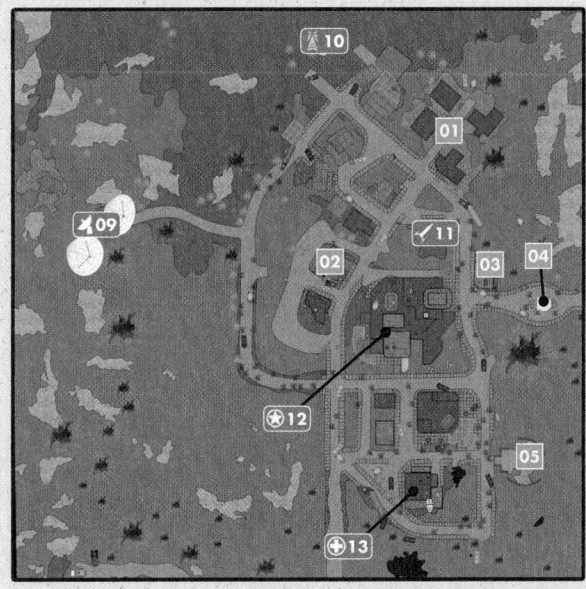

— CRAFTING: ARMOR WORKBENCH
— CRAFTING: COOKING STATION
— CRAFTING: POWER ARMOR STATION
— CRAFTING: WEAPONS WORKBENCH
— FACTION: BLOATFLIES

Red Rocket has all your automotive needs covered, though it has little of your post-apocalyptic necessities; the place has been thoroughly scavenged, aside from the workbenches. Use the Red Rocket awning as a landmark when situating yourself.
The following Secondary Locations are within the boundary of this township:

## [01] Barracks and Administration Buildings

These have been almost completely demolished. The barracks has some footlockers to scavenge, but the four buildings have little but the wind whistling through them.

## [02] Parked Tank

Alas, the tank isn't functional, but the cooking station is.

## [03] The Fort Hagen Bar

Half collapsed, with some scattered objet d'art and ammo on the upper floor.

### [04] Entrance Checkpoint

Scavenge some items from the pillbox on the road into the fort.

### [05] Playground

The only game you'll be playing is "dodge the Bloatfly spittle."

**HELPFUL HINT** *from Vault Boy!* Did You Know?

DON'T FORGET TO CHECK THE LARGE WAREHOUSES TO THE SOUTH FOR A LARGE DISPLAY OF PREWAR MIGHT AND NOW A ROW OF POWER ARMOR STATIONS. SECONDARY LOCATION [3.18]: POWER ARMOR WAREHOUSE IS WORTH THE TRIP.

## ⭐ [3.12] FORT HAGEN

THREAT LEVELS 15-25

- ARMAMENTS AND AMMO+++
- ARMAMENTS AND AMMO: MINI NUKE
- ARMAMENTS AND AMMO: MINI NUKE (FAT MAN)
- ARMAMENTS AND AMMO: TRUNK (2)
- ARMOR PART: FUSION CORE
- BOTTLECAPS
- COLLECTIBLE: BOBBLEHEAD: ENERGY WEAPONS
- COLLECTIBLE: REQUIRED READING: U.S. COVERT OPERATIONS MANUAL 6
- COLLECTIBLE: REQUIRED READING: GUNS AND BULLETS 2
- COLLECTIBLE: REQUIRED READING: ROBCO FUN!
- COLLECTIBLE: HOLOTAPE: PIPFALL
- COLLECTIBLE: NUKA COLA QUANTUM
- CRAFTING: ARMOR WORKBENCH
- CRAFTING: CHEMISTRY WORKBENCH (2)
- CRAFTING: COOKING STATION
- CRAFTING: WEAPONS WORKBENCH
- DANGER: OIL!
- DANGER: MINES!
- DANGER: TESLA ARC!
- DANGER: TENSION TRIGGER!
- DANGER: TURRETS!
- FACTION: SYNTHS (INSTITUTE)
- FACTION: CHARACTER: KELLOGG

- HEALTH OR CHEMS+++
- QUEST START: REVEILLE (BROTHERHOOD OF STEEL)
- QUEST VISIT: REUNIONS (MAIN)
- QUEST VISIT: DANGEROUS MINDS (MAIN)
- QUEST VISIT: SHADOW OF STEEL (BROTHERHOOD OF STEEL)
- QUEST VISIT: LAST VOYAGE OF THE U.S.S. CONSTITUTION (SIDE)
- UNIQUE ITEM: KELLOGG'S PISTOL

### FIG 3.12A: FORT HAGEN (INTERIOR)

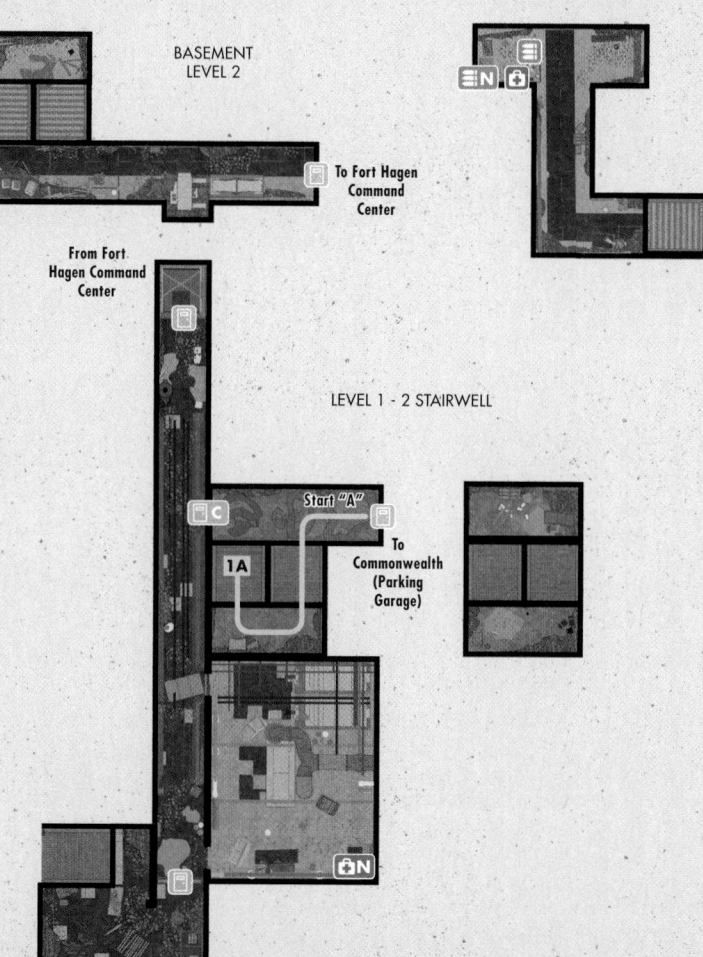

LEVEL 2

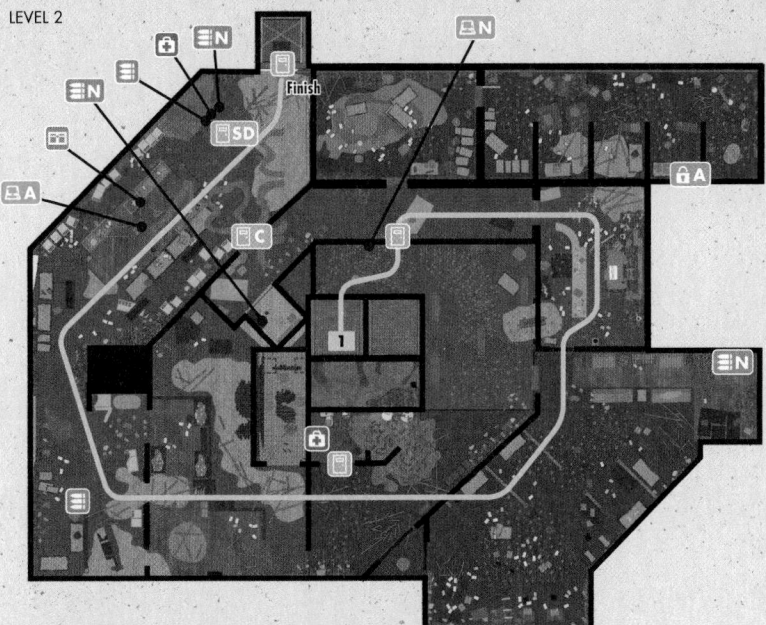

LEVEL 3

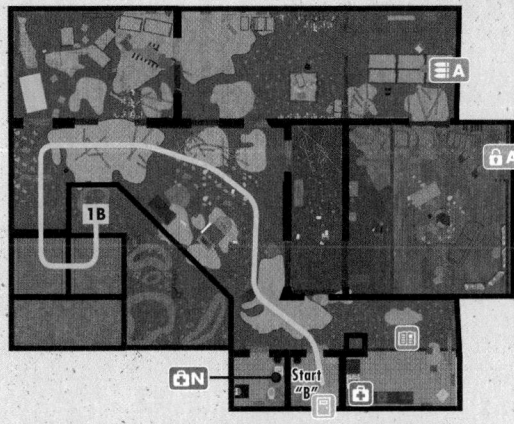

To Commonwealth (Fort Hagen Roof)

**FIG 3.12B: FORT HAGEN COMMAND CENTER
(INTERIOR)**

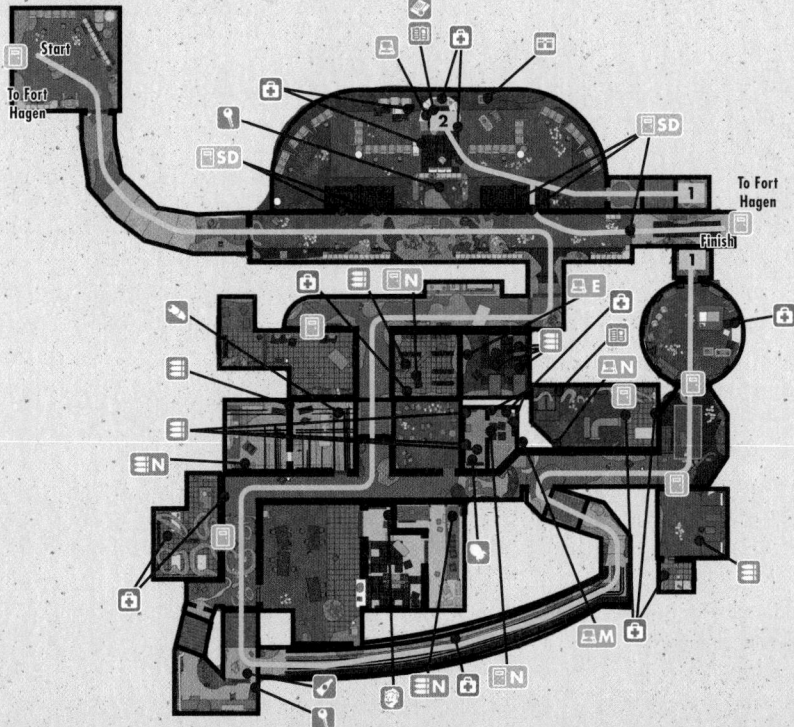

## VAULT-TEC RECOMMENDED LOOT

**ARMAMENTS AND AMMO:**
**MINI NUKE AND FAT MAN**
**BOBBLEHEAD: ENERGY WEAPONS**
**REQUIRED READING: GUNS AND BULLETS**

**REQUIRED READING: U.S. COVERT**
**OPERATIONS MANUAL**
**REQUIRED READING: ROBCO FUN!**
**HOLOTAPE: PIP FALL**

This location is not fully accessible unless
Main Quest: Reunions is active.

An old army base with a small
surrounding town and medical hospital,
Fort Hagen is now firmly sealed away
from scavengers. Inspect the exterior and
locate the parking structure under the
building, with the entrance to the south.
The first level down has a chemistry
station and some health.

It is the hideout of a man named Kellogg.
The main entrance is blocked, so seek
entry from a roof hatch or a door from the
lower parking garage. Either entrance
allows access to the ruined interior and
elevator down to the command center.
Before you head there, check the upper
floor kitchen for a magazine.

Command center: If you want an easier
time unlocking the terminal and security
gate to the armory (Master) that contains
the Mini Nuke and Fatman, locate the
toolbox in the pipe duct (southwest); it has
the Fort Hagen Armory password in it.
Look for the Fusion Core in the machine
room here, along with RobCo Fun! (and
the latest Holotape game) in the command
room. The Bobblehead is in the kitchens,
and there's yet another magazine in one of
the bedrooms. What a haul!

The Main Quests require you to find Kellogg and obtain the Cybernetic Brain Augmenter from him. The Brotherhood of Steel quests occur automatically as you leave Fort Hagen (look to the skies!). The Side Quest requires you to obtain an item for Captain Ironsides, which is inside the military chest close to the elevator on floor L2.

 ## [3.13] GREATER MASS BLOOD CLINIC

THREAT LEVELS 20+

- ARMAMENTS AND AMMO
- ARMAMENTS AND AMMO: TRUNK
- BOTTLECAPS
- COLLECTIBLE: REQUIRED READING: MASSACHUSETTS SURGICAL JOURNAL
- CRAFTING: CHEMISTRY STATION
- DANGER: OIL!
- DANGER: RADIATION (MILD)!
- FACTION: BLOATFLIES
- FACTION: BLOODBUGS
- HEALTH OR CHEMS++

### VAULT-TEC RECOMMENDED LOOT

**REQUIRED READING: MASSACHUSETTS SURGICAL JOURNAL**

**HEALTH OR CHEMS**

This is a small, heavily damaged outpatient clinic that once performed blood tests for the military base. The mutated wildlife has taken a liking to the blood packs here.

There are four levels to this ruin, including the remains of the roof, where you can gather a Caps stash and ammo from a duffel bag and container. Take the blood clinic key from a desk in the southwest upper area of this ruin.

Access the lab terminal (Advanced) to enter a tiny analysis room with a terminal (Novice) and a magazine to grab. There's also health and blood packs, a chemistry station, and a safe (Expert).

In the west part of the ground floor (which you can reach by dropping down through a hole in the second floor, or by unlocking the door (Expert) in the parking lot) are the remains of an office with a terminal (Novice) and some health. Next to it is a locked door (Expert) with a skeleton slumped by it. There's another blood clinic key here.

Down in the basement is a control room with yet another blood clinic key and a button opening a security gate. Beyond the gate is a steamer trunk and a large stash of chems and blood packs. The blood clinic key opens the safe in the tiny analysis room and the exit door (Expert) on the west perimeter wall.

 ## [3.14] BOSTON MAYORAL SHELTER

THREAT LEVELS 20+

### VAULT-TEC RECOMMENDED LOOT

**ARMAMENTS AND AMMO: MINI NUKE (AND FAT MAN)**

**COLLECTIBLE: MR. GUTSY MODEL KIT**

**REQUIRED READING: ASTOUNDINGLY AWESOME TALES**

When the bombs fell, the mayor of Boston and his wife were bundled into this hidden subterranean shelter. Though the bunker is sealed up tight, the wall terminal in the guard pod next door opens it without any problems. There's an explosives box here, too. Head inside and either enter the large pipe or take the corridors and find out what happened to Boston's mayor.

The Boston mayoral shelter bathroom key is inside the dresser in the bunk bed storeroom with the terminal (Master). The Boston mayoral shelter key is in the suitcase in the storeroom's southwest corner. It opens the safe.

Don't forget to check the blue wallpapered bedroom opposite the cigarette machine, east of the stairs (and the laundry room) and down from the bar; there's a rare robot model kit to snag!

- ARMAMENTS AND AMMO++
- ARMAMENTS AND AMMO: MINI NUKE
- ARMAMENTS AND AMMO: MINI NUKE (FAT MAN)
- ARMOR PART: FUSION CORE
- BOTTLECAPS
- COLLECTIBLE: ROBOT MODEL KIT (MR. GUTSY)
- COLLECTIBLE: HOLOTAPE: BOSTON SHELTER—GUARD UPDATE
- COLLECTIBLE: HOLOTAPE: BOSTON SHELTER—MAYOR'S GOODBYE
- COLLECTIBLE: HOLOTAPE: BOSTON SHELTER—WHERE ARE YOU?
- COLLECTIBLE: NUKA CHERRY (2)
- COLLECTIBLE: REQUIRED READING: ASTOUNDINGLY AWESOME TALES
- CRAFTING: ARMOR WORKBENCH
- CRAFTING: WEAPONS WORKBENCH
- DANGER: ESCAPING GAS!
- DANGER: OIL!
- FACTION: DEATHCLAW
- FACTION: SYNTHS (INSTITUTE)
- HEALTH OR CHEMS+++

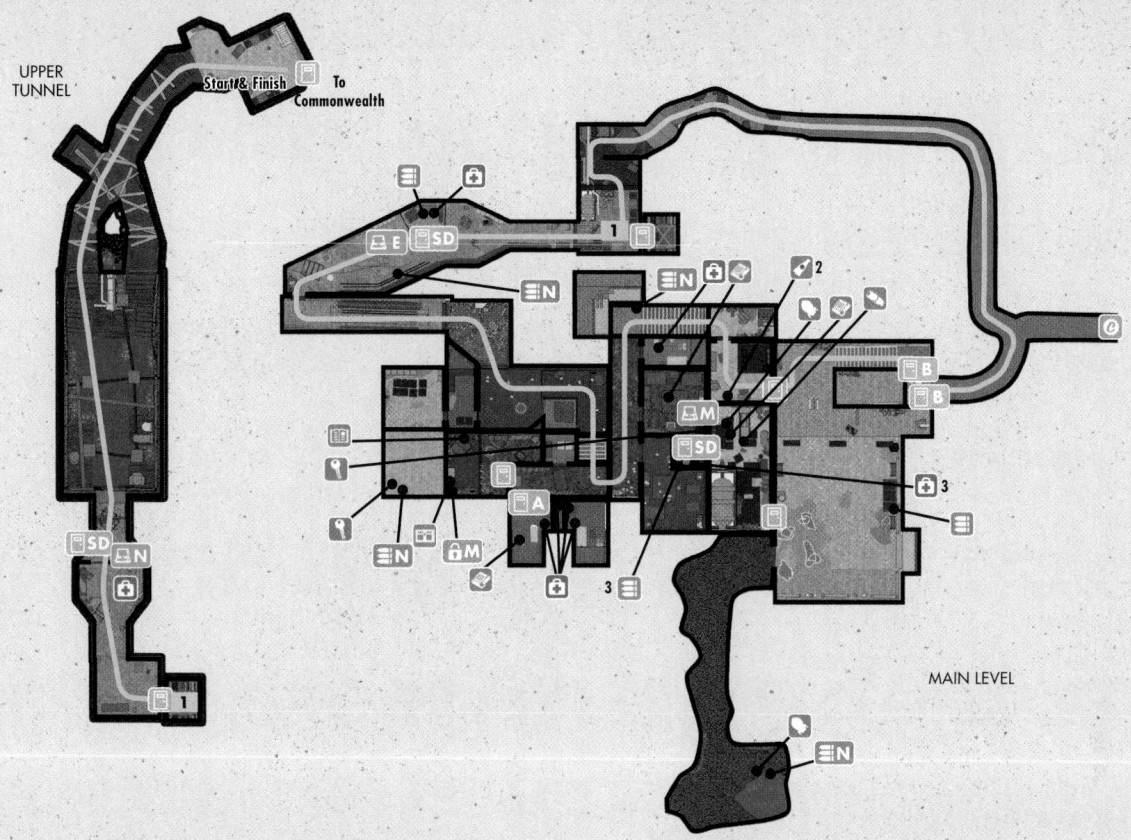

UPPER
TUNNEL

Start & Finish  To
Commonwealth

1

E  SD

N

N

N

M

SD

2

B

B

3

3

A

M

N

3

SD  N

M

1

MAIN LEVEL

N

## [3.15] FIDDLER'S GREEN TRAILER ESTATES

THREAT LEVELS 15-25

### FIG 3.15: FIDDLER'S GREEN TRAILER ESTATES (EXTERIOR)

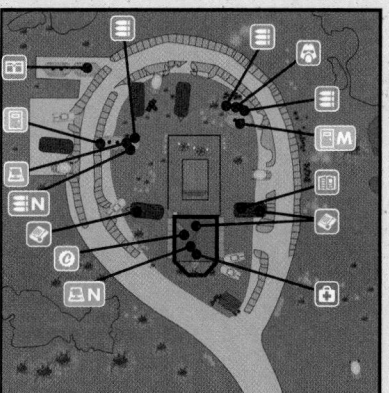

N

M

N

- ARMAMENTS AND AMMO
- ARMAMENTS AND AMMO: TRUNK
- ARMOR PART: POWER ARMOR (LEVELED)
- COLLECTIBLE: HOLOTAPE: THE NEW SQUIRREL TAPE 1
- COLLECTIBLE: HOLOTAPE: THE NEW SQUIRREL TAPE 2
- COLLECTIBLE: HOLOTAPE: THE NEW SQUIRREL TAPE 3
- COLLECTIBLE: REQUIRED READING: LIVE & LOVE
- CRAFTING: CHEMISTRY STATION
- CRAFTING: COOKING STATION
- DANGER: MINES!
- DANGER: RADIATION (MILD)!
- FACTION: FERAL GHOULS

This is a "retirement community" in every sense. Most of the residents had no family to speak of and ended up here due to improper financial planning. Now the residents are more of an infestation.

**VAULT-TEC RECOMMENDED LOOT**

ARMOR PART:
POWER ARMOR
(LEVELED)
REQUIRED
READING:
LIVE & LOVE

Harvest tarberries from the swimming pool. Hack the leasing office terminal (Novice) to access the wall safe (Novice). One of the caravans (Master) holds some Power Armor and ammo.

**FIG 3.16A: WESTON WATER TREATMENT PLANT (EXTERIOR)**

Elevator from
Treatment Plant
(Interior)

- ARMAMENTS AND AMMO
- ARMAMENTS AND AMMO: TRUNK
- COLLECTIBLE: REQUIRED READING: PICKET FENCES 5
- CRAFTING: CHEMISTRY STATION
- DANGER: CAN CHIMES!
- DANGER: EXPLOSIVE BARRELS!
- DANGER: GRENADES!
- DANGER: OIL!
- DANGER: RADIATION (MILD)!
- DANGER: TRIPWIRE!
- FACTION: MIRELURKS
- FACTION: SUPER MUTANTS
- HEALTH OR CHEMS
- QUEST VISIT: TROUBLED WATERS (MISCELLANEOUS)

**VAULT-TEC RECOMMENDED LOOT**

 **REQUIRED READING: PICKET FENCES**

This plant was built in 2051 as part of a decade-long plan to modernize the city's aging sanitation systems. In the decades after the bombs fell, the rising sea levels eventually overwhelmed the plant's retaining wall and began to flood the facility. As the pumps lost power, shorted out, and began to fail, the water output fell and grew more contaminated.

The exterior features a number of Super Mutant shacks dotted throughout the containment pools and some devious traps to wound the unwary. The roof of the structure, which has a terminal (Novice) and a safe (Expert) to hack, can only be accessed from a hatch inside.

RED ROCKET

GASOLINE DIESEL FUSION

*Car Wash While You Refuel? Our Robots Bring the Bubbles to You!*

GROUND FLOOR

To Commonwealth

Start "A"

1

A

Start "B"
To Commonwealth
(Roof)

SUBLEVEL 1

N

2

1

B

SUBLEVEL 2 (UPPER STRUCTURE)

CB

3

2

B

4

B

B

SUBLEVEL 3
(MIDDLE STRUCTURE)

A

B 5
CB

B

7

6

4

CB

E

SUBLEVEL 4
(LOWER STRUCTURE)

8

CB 8

7

Finish

To
Commonwealth

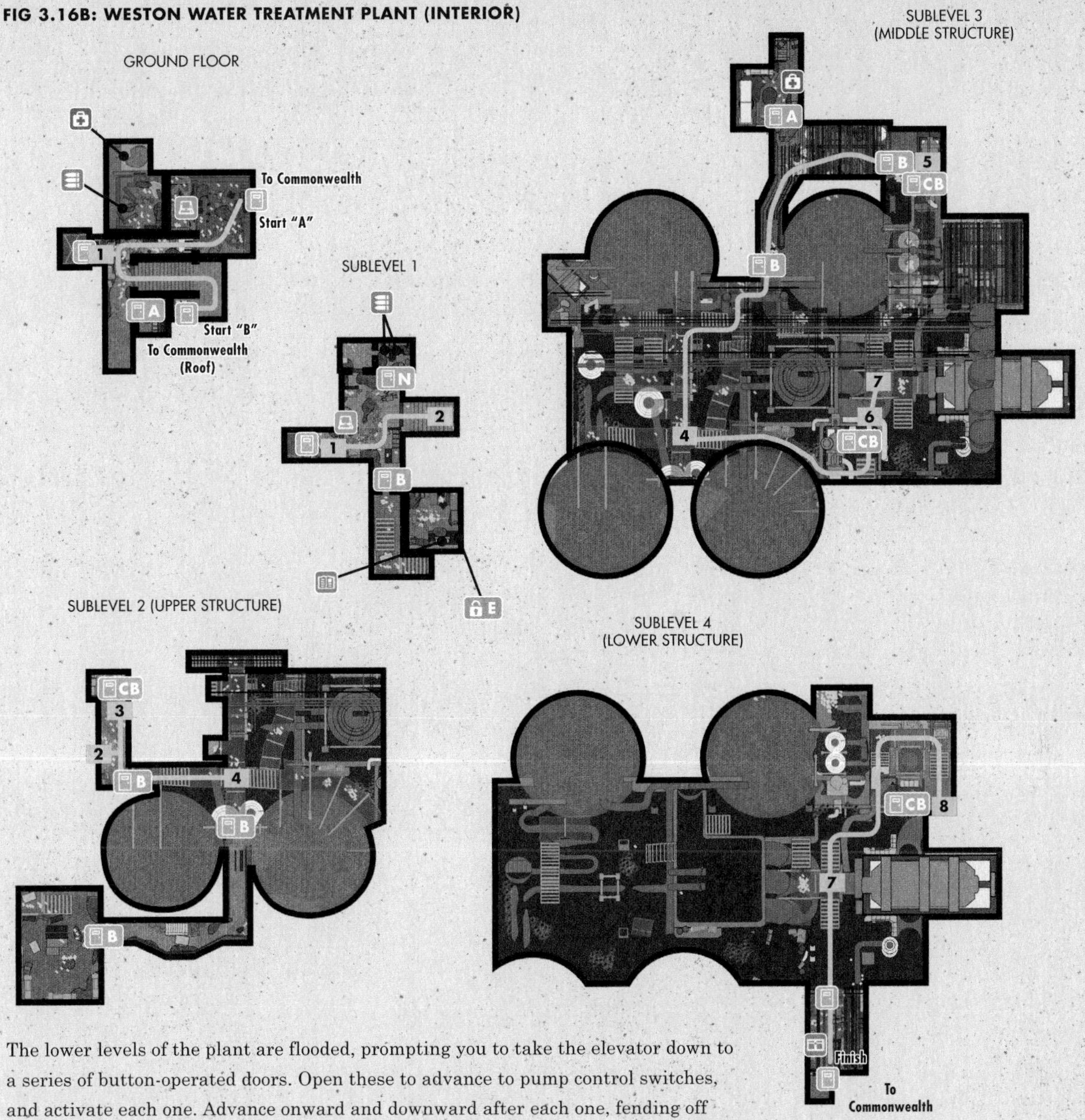

The lower levels of the plant are flooded, prompting you to take the elevator down to
a series of button-operated doors. Open these to advance to pump control switches,
and activate each one. Advance onward and downward after each one, fending off
Mirelurks. Then locate the lowest-level elevator that takes you back up to the surface.

SPOTTED A COMMIE DEVIL?

- ARMAMENTS AND AMMO+
- ARMAMENTS AND AMMO: TRUNK
- BOTTLECAPS
- COLLECTIBLE: HOLOTAPE: SHEILA'S HOLOTAPE
- CRAFTING: ARMOR WORKBENCH
- CRAFTING: WEAPONS WORKBENCH
- DANGER: RADIATION (MILD)!
- DANGER: TENSION TRIGGER!
- FACTION: FERAL GHOULS
- HEALTH OR CHEMS
- QUEST VISIT: BOTANY CLASS
  (DIAMOND CITY FREEFORM)

Forest Grove Marsh is a series of residential and other small buildings that have sunken and been flooded by the river. Some radioactive leak below the area has irradiated the water, and though scavengers have tried to put up walkways across the rooftops of the buildings to explore the houses, the numerous Ghouls in the area have stopped all but the most inquisitive or reckless scavengers. Proceed at your own risk.

**FIG 3.17: FOREST GROVE MARSH (EXTERIOR)**

## [01] South Bridge

Aside from the rusting remains of an accident, expect a few lurking ferals but little else. Enter town by heading north at the pub.

## [02] Pub and Buffet

South of town, this mostly dilapidated structure has a storeroom door with a tension trigger to investigate. Inside are health and chems. Upstairs is a chem cooler and an occupied couch.

## [03] Bakery Roof Tent

This structure has been flooded with irradiated water; enterprising scavengers have made a series of rickety bridges connecting many of the town's structures. Use them to navigate the area so you're not caught by advancing ferals. This blue tent has some chems and ammo to grab.

## [04] Red Tanker Trailer

You can break into the remains of a big-rig trailer (Advanced) and can gather some health and the contents of a toolbox.

## [05] Crab Shack and Pharmacy Roof

There's some strange mutated ferns growing here. Gather as many as you can; the specified quest depends on it. There are other buildings with this fern growing too.

## [06] The Gun Shop

This is one of the few buildings whose interior you can access. The badly damaged structure still has a functioning floor safe (Advanced) and cash register (Novice). Open some cabinets and grab any remaining hardware; there's a few rounds of each type and a weapons workbench upstairs with more ammo nearby. Don't forget the roof—there's a steamer trunk, Caps stash, more ammo and chems, a partly hidden explosives box, and a Holotape from Sheila.

### [07] Rusty Yellow Digging Machine

Search for this brightly colored machine holding up a plank bridge; this is a good place to return to the rooftops if you fall. The adjacent structure has more mutated ferns to harvest.

### [08] Charles River Lock and Dam

With the river waters rising to the south, the nonfunctioning river lock is at the root of the problems Forest Grove Marsh is experiencing. There's little you can do about it, save scavenging some health from the moored boat within the lock. The metal shack has an armor workbench to tinker on.

### [09] River Dam Camp

A small scavenger camp with a cooking station, this is occasionally used by scavengers and others passing through. The only permanent resident is a large stuffed space monkey.

MAP

ZONE 3

WESTERN COMMONWEALTH

##  [3.18] RELAY TOWER 1DL-109

THREAT LEVELS 15-25

– DANGER: OIL!          – RADIO: BOSTON CITY WORKS BEACON
– RADIO: DISTRESS SIGNAL

This is part of the Commonwealth Relay Tower Network. Authorized personnel only. Use the relay tower terminal to amplify both nearby radio signals.

## [3.19] OBERLAND STATION

THREAT LEVELS 6-14

– CRAFTING: COOKING STATION      – QUEST: MINUTEMEN RADIANT
– FACTION: SETTLER               – SERVICES: WORKSHOP

This small settlement is eking out an existence adjacent to the railroad. Tatos are the crop of choice here. Both the settlers and fruit are ripe for either exploiting or tending with care.

- ARMAMENTS AND AMMO
- ARMAMENTS AND AMMO: TRUNK
- COLLECTIBLE: REQUIRED READING: PICKET FENCES
- COLLECTIBLE: HOLOTAPE: GWINNETT BREW RECIPE
- BOTTLECAPS
- CRAFTING: CHEMISTRY STATION
- CRAFTING: COOKING STATION
- CRAFTING: WEAPONS WORKBENCH
- DANGER: CAN CHIMES!
- DANGER: TRIPWIRE!
- FACTION: RAIDERS
- FACTION: CHARACTER: TOWER TOM
- QUEST VISIT: CONFIDENCE MAN (SIDE)

## VAULT-TEC RECOMMENDED LOOT

**REQUIRED READING: PICKET FENCES**

**HOLOTAPE: GWINNETT BREW RECIPE**

There are additional entities here if the quest is active.

Renowned throughout the Commonwealth for its higher than normal alcohol content and lower than normal cost, Beantown Brown Beer was the favored drink among blue-collar workers after a long day on the job. Looked down upon by most discerning beer drinkers, the Beantown Brewery catered more to the "common man," which led to one of its more popular slogans, "Beantown Brown, because no one likes a snob." The beer was produced here. Currently, Raiders have taken over the location. They are here for the beer.

The main doors of this structure are locked up and require a little jimmying to open the main door (Advanced). Or, you can enter via the tasting room and store. Inside is more Gwinnett beer and lager than you'll ever need, as well as some Raiders to quiet down.

**FIG 3.20: BEANTOWN BREWERY (INTERIOR)**

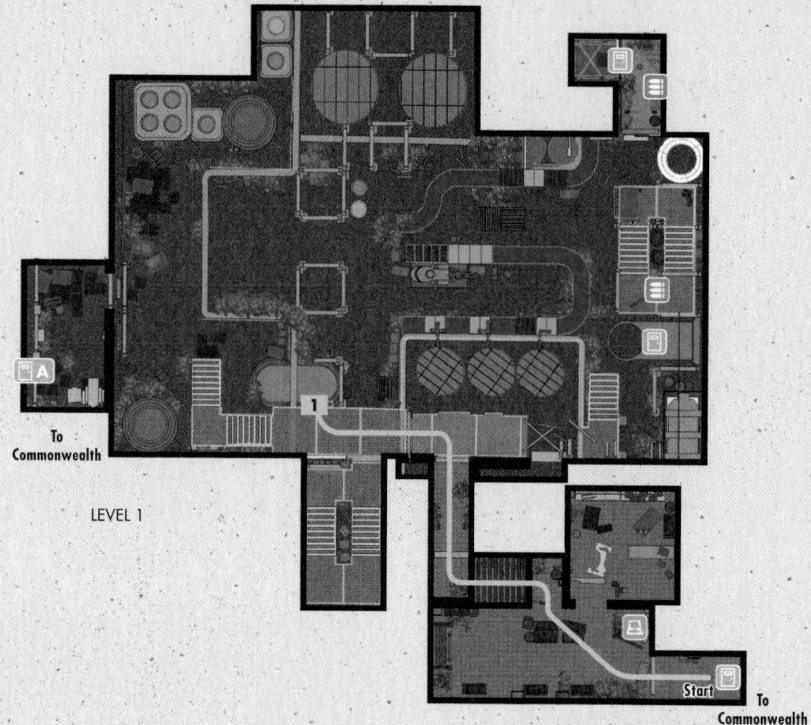

LEVEL 1

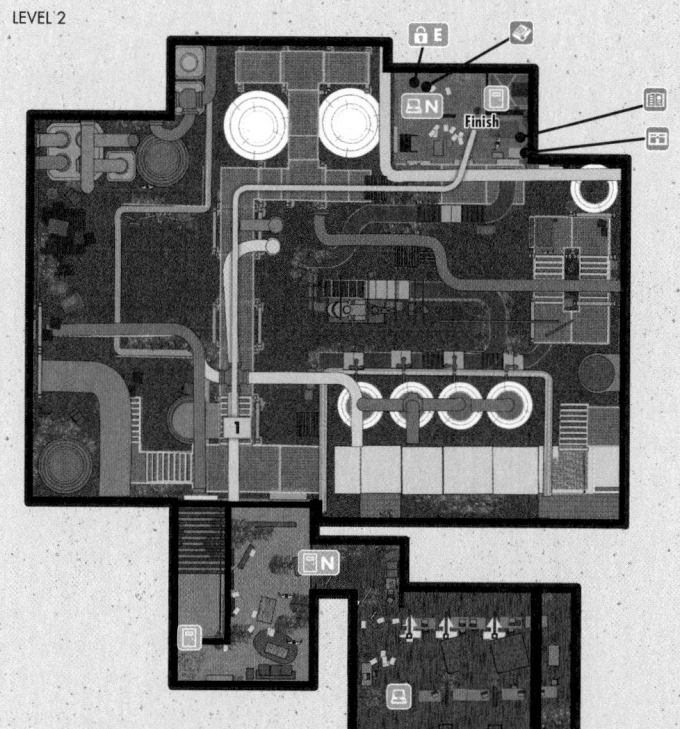

LEVEL 2

THREAT LEVELS 20+

- ARMAMENTS AND AMMO
- ARMAMENTS AND AMMO: TRUNK
- ARMOR PART: FUSION CORE
- ARMOR PART: POWER ARMOR (LEVELED)
- ARMOR PART: POWER ARMOR (LEVELED)
- COLLECTIBLE: REQUIRED READING: GROGNAK THE BARBARIAN
- BOTTLECAPS
- CRAFTING: POWER ARMOR STATION
- CRAFTING: WEAPONS WORKBENCH
- DANGER: LONG DROP!
- DANGER: TURRETS!
- FACTION: GUNNERS
- QUEST VISIT: LONG ROAD AHEAD (SIDE COMPANION)

**VAULT-TEC RECOMMENDED LOOT**

ARMOR PART: POWER ARMOR (LEVELED)

REQUIRED READING: GROGNAK THE BARBARIAN

This elevated highway interchange is now a well-defended and extremely defensible Gunner camp. There are two elevators to use; the one to the north has no nearby adversaries, whereas the one under the main central structure has a hut with Gunners waiting. The camp is behind the billboard signs, under the upper north-south freeway. However, by heading south and doubling back, you can climb and sneak above the camp. With careful maneuvering (and use of the curved elevated ramps), you can trek along the east-west freeway all the way to Mass Pike Tunnel West. A must for snipers.

**FIG 3.21: MASS PIKE INTERCHANGE (EXTERIOR)**

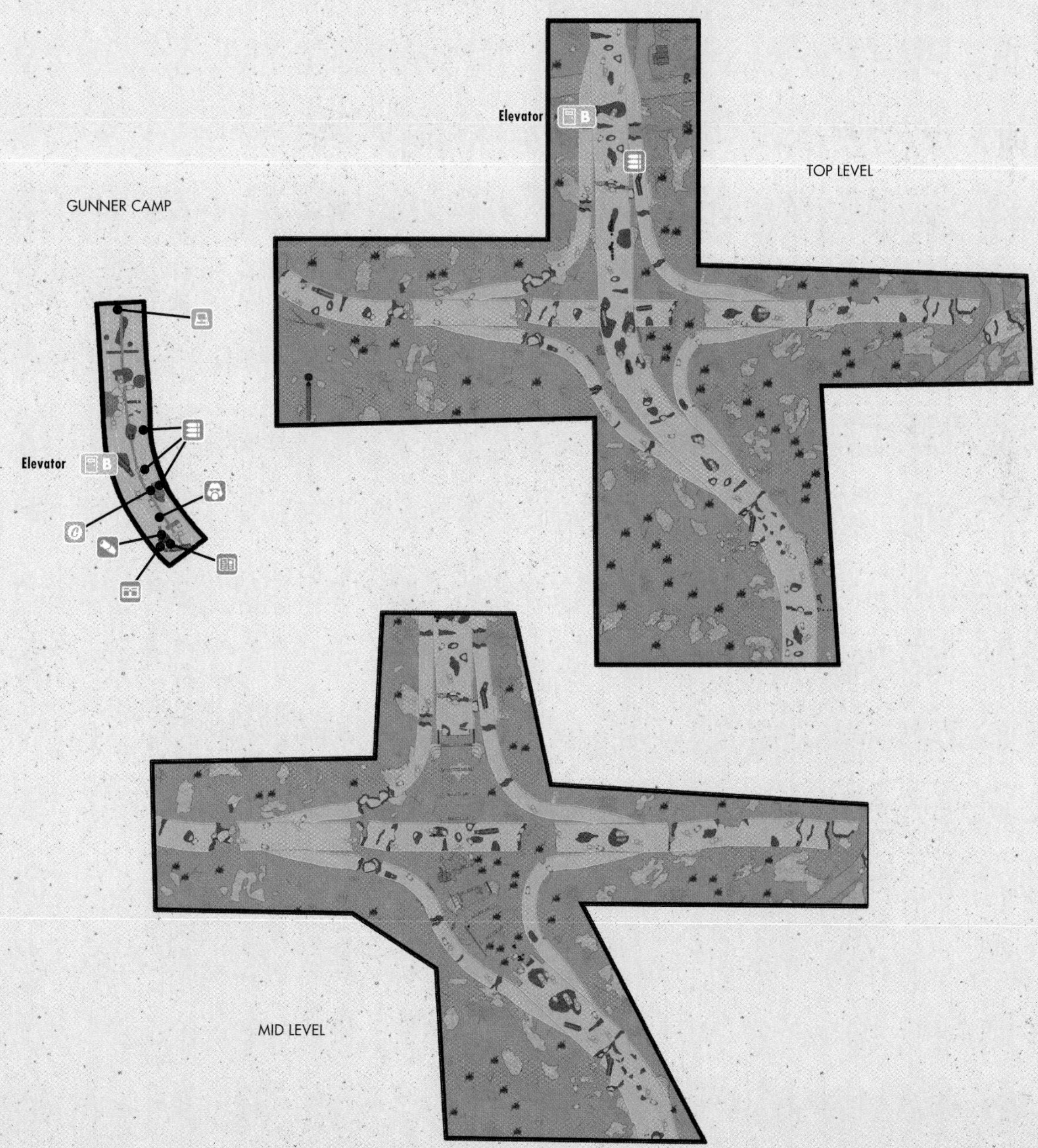

Elevator

TOP LEVEL

GUNNER CAMP

Elevator

MAP

**ZONE 3**

WESTERN COMMONWEALTH

MID LEVEL

- ARMAMENTS AND AMMO++
- ARMAMENTS AND AMMO: MINI NUKE
- ARMAMENTS AND AMMO: TRUNK
- BOTTLECAPS+++
- COLLECTIBLE: BOBBLEHEAD: MEDICINE
- COLLECTIBLE: REQUIRED READING: GROGNAK THE BARBARIAN
- COLLECTIBLE: REQUIRED READING: TABOO TATTOOS
- COLLECTIBLE: HOLOTAPE: VAULT 81 TECH PASSWORD
- COLLECTIBLE: NUKA CHERRY (4)
- COMPANION: CURIE
- DANGER: TURRETS!
- FACTION: SETTLER (VAULT DWELLER)
- FACTION: VAULT 81 LAB MOLE RATS
- FACTION: CHARACTER: MIRANDA
- FACTION: CHARACTER: NEIL
- FACTION: CHARACTER: CALVIN
- FACTION: CHARACTER: OVERSEER MCNAMARA
- FACTION: CHARACTER: OFFICER EDWARDS
- FACTION: CHARACTER: HOLT COMBES
- FACTION: CHARACTER: ALEXIS COMBES
- FACTION: CHARACTER: ERIN COMBES
- FACTION: CHARACTER: AUSTIN ENGILL
- FACTION: CHARACTER: MARK SUMMERSET

- FACTION: CHARACTER: MARIA SUMMERSET
- FACTION: CHARACTER: HORATIO
- FACTION: CHARACTER: DR. PENSKE
- FACTION: CHARACTER: KATY
- FACTION: CHARACTER: OLD RUSTY
- FACTION: CHARACTER: TINA DE LUCA
- FACTION: CHARACTER: BOBBY DE LUCA
- FACTION: CHARACTER: DOCTOR FORSYTHE
- FACTION: CHARACTER: RACHEL
- FACTION: CHARACTER: CURIE
- FACTION: CHARACTER: ASHES
- HEALTH OR CHEMS+++
- QUEST START: VAULT 81 (SIDE)
- QUEST START: HOLE IN THE WALL (SIDE)
- QUEST START: VAULT 81 TOUR (VAULT 81 FREEFORM)
- QUEST START: HERE KITTY, KITTY (VAULT 81 FREEFORM)
- QUEST START: MAINTENANCE MAN (VAULT 81 FREEFORM)
- QUEST START: FERTILIZER WOMAN (VAULT 81 FREEFORM)
- QUEST START: DEPENDENCY (VAULT 81 FREEFORM)
- QUEST START: SHORT STORIES (VAULT 81 FREEFORM)
- QUEST VISIT: EMERGENT BEHAVIOR (SIDE COMPANION)
- SERVICES: TRADER (ALEXIS COMBES)
- SERVICES: TRADER (MARIA SUMMERSET)
- SERVICES: TRADER (HORATIO)
- SERVICES: TRADER (DR. PENSKE)
- UNIQUE ITEM: SHORT SYRINGER RIFLE
- UNIQUE ITEM: VAULT ROOM

## VAULT-TEC RECOMMENDED LOOT

**ARMAMENTS AND AMMO: MINI NUKE**
**BOBBLEHEAD: MEDICINE**
**REQUIRED READING: GROGNAK THE BARBARIAN**
**REQUIRED READING: TABOO TATTOOS**

**COLLECTIBLE: NUKA CHERRY (4)**
**UNIQUE ITEM: SYRINGER RIFLE**
**UNIQUE ITEM: VAULT ROOM**

Somewhere in the Commonwealth is a vault that never fulfilled its secret purpose. The people just lived normal lives for generation after generation. They are aware of the outside world but choose to remain within the safety of the vault rather than brave the dangers of the Commonwealth. They do trade with the outside world since they aren't entirely self sufficient, so the people are used to seeing outsiders every couple of weeks or so. What secrets does Vault 81 contain?

Find the entrance to Vault 81 cut into the rocks inside a small shanty trading camp due west of the Fens Neighborhood.

### FIG 3.22A: VAULT 81 ENTRY (INTERIOR)

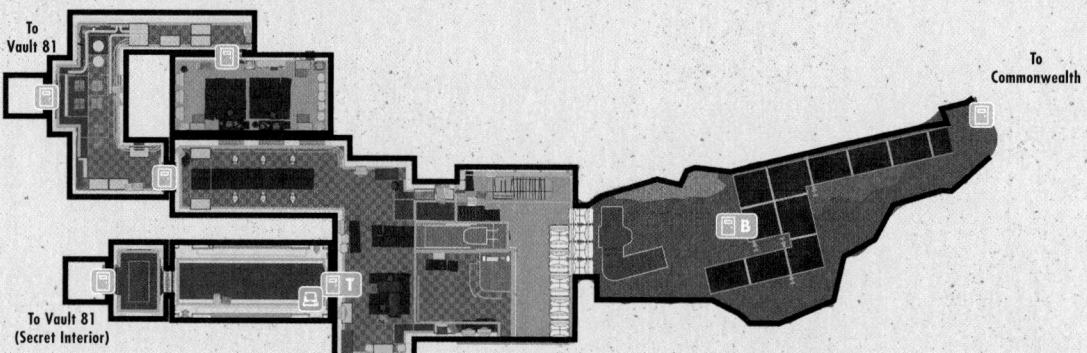

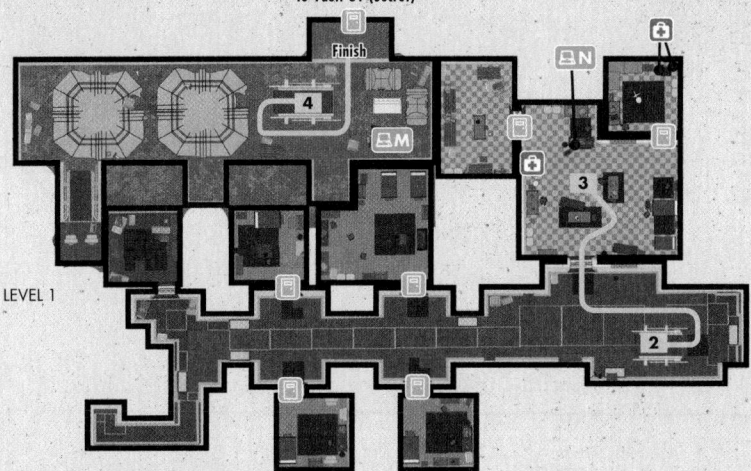

To Vault 81 (Secret)

Finish

LEVEL 1

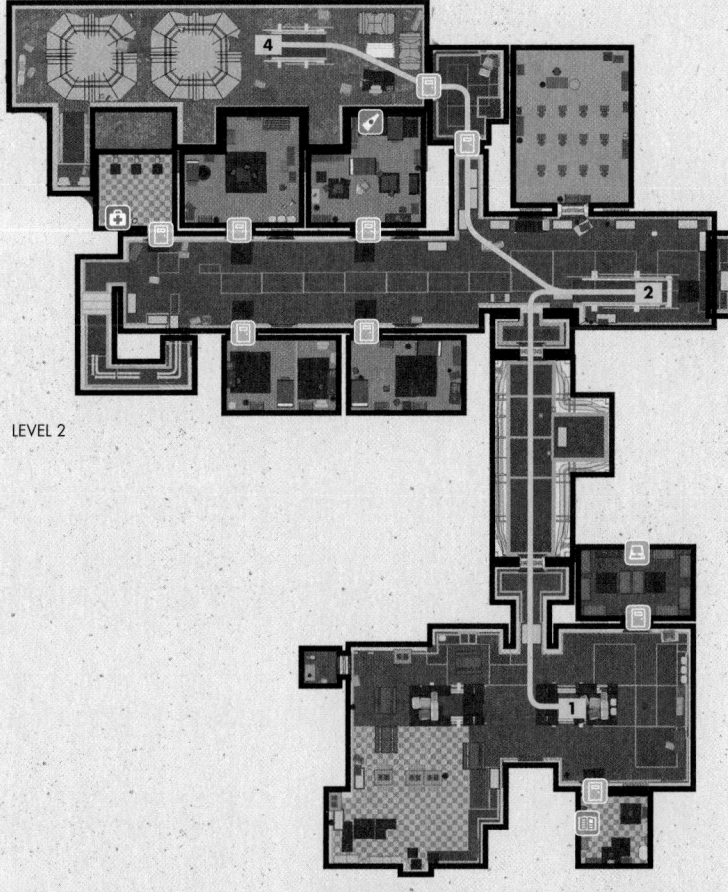

LEVEL 2

LEVEL 3

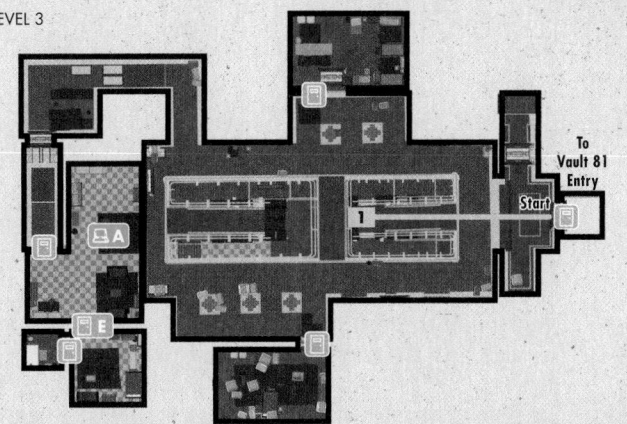

To Vault 81 Entry

Start

Not all areas are accessible unless the Side Quests are active. Once you've performed a small task for the overseer (bringing her a Fusion Core), you're free to move about the vault. Visit the different locations starting at the atrium:

- ALEXIS COMBES RUNS THE VAULT 81 DEPOT AND TRADES WITH YOU.
- HORATIO RUNS A BARBERSHOP WHERE YOU CAN GO FOR A QUICK HAIRCUT OR SOMETHING MORE INVOLVED.
- MARIA SUMMERSET RUNS THE SUNSHINE DINER AND TRADES WITH YOU.
- THE HYDROPONICS LABORATORY IS RUN BY DOCTOR PENSKE AND IS FOCUSED ON SOLVING LONG-TERM FOOD AND WATER SUPPLY PROBLEMS.
- KATY RUNS THE LEARNING CENTER, TEACHING THE VAULT'S CHILDREN.
- GWEN MCNAMARA IS THE OVERSEER OF THIS VAULT AND HAS BEEN FOR OVER A DECADE.
- FRATERNAL TWINS BOBBY AND TINA DE LUCA MAINTAIN THE REACTOR.
- DOCTOR FORSYTHE RUNS THE MEDICAL FACILITY WITH HIS ASSISTANT RACHEL.

In addition to the more involved quest in Vault 81, the following smaller tasks are available:

 **Freeform Quest: Vault 81 Tour**

When you first enter the vault, Austin hopes you'll pay him for a tour. You can accept, ask for a free tour, or ignore him. Break off the tour at any point and the quest fails. Continue, and you receive a reasonably adept understanding of this facility.

 **Freeform Quest: Maintenance Man**

Calvin the maintenance man needs any tools you scavenge and will pay you for any you bring back to him.

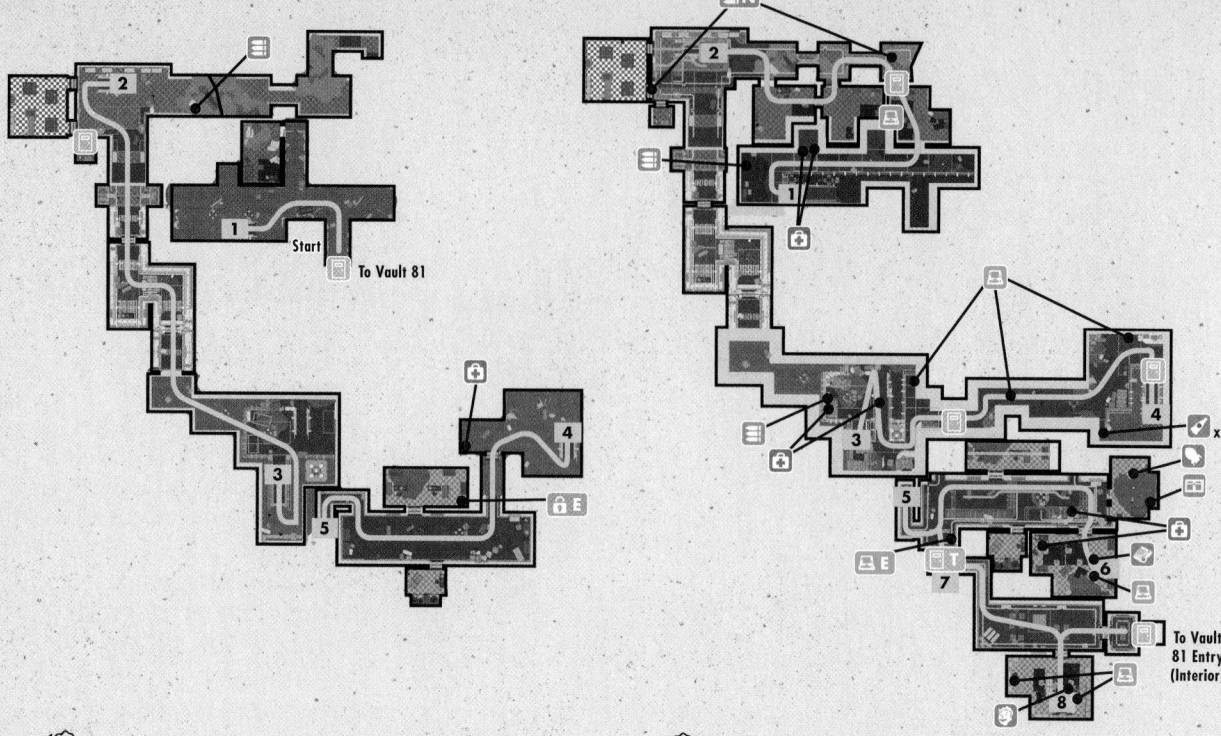

## Freeform Quest: Fertilizer Woman

Doctor Penske runs the hydroponics lab. She asks you to taste a Mutfruit for her. Answer how you wish. She needs fertilizer you scavenge and will pay you for any you bring back.

## Freeform Quest: Here Kitty, Kitty

Speak to Erin Combes and agree to help her find her lost cat. Find the wayward kitty at the Chestnut Hillock Reservoir, and let Erin Combes know afterward for a small reward.

## Freeform Quest: Dependency

Bobby and Tina DeLuca are in the reactor area. Bobby will buy chems off you. Tina wants Bobby off the Jet and Buffout. You can use your Charisma and challenge him to quit, or speak to Rachel in Doctor Forsythe's medical bay to help. Or encourage Bobby to continue using Jet, with quest (and heart) failure in mind.

## Freeform Quest: Short Stories

Katy is the teacher in the classroom. Complete Miscellaneous Quest: Short Stories here for a copy of Grognak the Barbarian.

## [3.23] CHESTNUT HILLOCK RESERVOIR     THREAT LEVELS 15-25

- ARMAMENTS AND AMMO
- ARMAMENTS AND AMMO: TRUNK
- BOTTLECAPS
- COLLECTIBLE: NUKA-COLA QUANTUM
- FACTION: BLOATFLIES
- FACTION: BLOODBUGS
- FACTION: RADROACHES
- FACTION: STINGWINGS
- HEALTH OR CHEMS
- QUEST START: MISCELLANEOUS (EDWIN'S TERMINAL)

### VAULT-TEC RECOMMENDED LOOT

**COLLECTIBLE: NUKA COLA QUANTUM**

This is a once-picturesque lake on the edge of the Fens, west of Diamond City. Find a Moon Monkey on the porch of the southeast house. Locate a Quantum clutched by a skeleton in a bathtub, on the east shore. Dive into the water to the southeast for a steamer trunk in a sunken trailer.

## Miscellaneous Quest (Edwin's Terminal)

Access Edwin's terminal inside the house on the east shore: Dive into the water under the capsized boat. Claim the key from the cooler on the lake bed. Use it to open the otherwise tricky-to-unlock safe (Master). Beware of Stingwings.

# SECONDARY LOCATIONS

## [3.01] CAR WRECKAGE

- ARMAMENTS AND AMMO
- FACTION: SUPER MUTANT

A rusting collection of cars, placed in a strangely primitive circle.

## [3.02] TRACTOR WAREHOUSE

- ARMOR PART: FUSION CORE
- DANGER: MINES!
- FACTION: STINGWINGS

Farm equipment is stored here, with a small generator out back. Watch your step.

## [3.03] GUNNER CAMP ON-RAMP

- ARMAMENTS AND AMMO
- DANGER: TURRETS!
- FACTION: GUNNERS

This metal shack has an entrance to the elevated Gunner camp with the windmills, on the freeway, over in Zone 1.

## [3.04] RAIDER GRAVES

- FACTION: RAIDERS

A Raider is laying their brethren to rest. Time to finish the job.

## [3.05] CARRIAGE DEN

- DANGER: MINES!
- ARMAMENTS AND AMMO

A rusting railcar with mines and a safe (Expert).

## [3.06] RUINED BRICK WAREHOUSE

- ARMAMENTS AND AMMO
- COLLECTIBLE: NUKA COLA QUANTUM

The blown-out remains of a small brick warehouse have a collection of bottles on the rusting air-conditioning duct, including a Quantum.

## [3.07] SCAVENGER'S TRAILER

- FACTION: SCAVENGER

A scavenger doesn't take kindly to your arrival. Are you here for his wild carrot flowers?

## [3.08] RUSTING APC

- ARMAMENTS AND AMMO
- DANGER: MINES!

A rusting tank north of Fort Hagen township. Scavenge for mines and other ammo here.

## [3.09] MIRELURK POND

- CRAFTING: COOKING STATION
- DANGER: RADIATION (MILD)!
- FACTION: MIRELURKS

A small pond on an upper rocky promontory, with a small camp and cooking stove.

## [3.10] CANISTER LAUNCH SHACK

- CRAFTING: COOKING STATION
- DANGER: EXPLOSIVE BARRELS!

A shack perched atop a rocky cliff with massive explosive potential.

## [3.11] SCHOELT PROPANE STORE

- ARMAMENTS AND AMMO

The remains of a propane refueling store. There's a floor safe that still hasn't been pillaged yet (Expert).

## [3.12] BRIDGE (SOUTH OF ARCJET SYSTEMS)

- ARMAMENTS AND AMMO
- DANGER: GRENADES!

This bridge has a secret stash below the concrete span but above the wooden raft planks.

## [3.13] ELEVATED FREEWAY ACCESS

- DANGER: LONG DROP!
- DANGER: RADIATION (MILD)!

The remains of a train carriage lie under the freeway rubble. Scavenge here, then climb onto and follow the freeway south, all the way to Mass Pike Interchange. A great route for snipers!

## [3.14] PULOWSKI PRESERVATION SHELTER CLUSTER

- ARMAMENTS AND AMMO
- FACTION: RAIDERS

Beware of this cluster of cut-rate fallout shelters; they aren't a patch on the quality and protection of the post-apocalyptic homesteads offered by Vault-Tec. Check the nearby bus for items.

## [3.15] CRASHED VERTIBIRD (ELEVATED FREEWAY)

- ARMAMENTS AND AMMO
- ARMAMENTS AND AMMO: TRUNK
- ARMOR PART: POWER ARMOR (LEVELED)
- DANGER: LONG DROP!

Check the ground directly below the remains of the Vertibird for ammo and a trunk. Appears at random. Access the construction lift to the east to reach the Vertibird and the Power Armor nearby.

## [3.16] CONSTRUCTION LIFT

- DANGER: LONG DROP!

This allows access to the elevated freeway to the southwest.

## [3.17] MILITARY CHECKPOINT (CAMBRIDGE OUTSKIRTS)

- ARMOR PART: POWER ARMOR (LEVELED)
- ARMAMENTS AND AMMO
- ARMAMENTS AND AMMO: TRUNK

This old military checkpoint has a trunk to scavenge within the locked green trailer (Advanced), as well as a security cage to extricate a suit of Power Armor from; use the terminal (Advanced).

## [3.18] POWER ARMOR WAREHOUSE

- ARMOR PART: POWER ARMOR (LEVELED)
- ARMAMENTS AND AMMO
- CRAFTING: POWER ARMOR STATION (4)

You'd think that the stockpile of ammunition and Power Armor stored at this location just south of Fort Hagen would have been mostly picked clean by now. And you'd be correct.

## [3.19] ARCJET ENGINE TRANSPORT

A big-rig with a flat trailer is carrying one of ArcJet's impressive engines. What would happen if you could access a terminal here and switch the engine on?

## [3.20] SCRAP MERCHANT

- **CRAFTING: COOKING STATION**
- **HEALTH OR CHEMS**
- **SERVICES: TRADER**

Perched on a cylindrical shack attached to the remains of the freeway on-ramp overlooking Forest Grove Marsh is a trader specializing in scrap. Pick the lock on his outside safe (Advanced) if you wish.

## [3.21] CAVE AND [3.22] CRASH SITE

- **FACTION: UNKNOWN**
- **FACTION: MOLE RAT**
- **UNIQUE ITEM: ALIEN BLASTER PISTOL**

Sometime during your adventure, you see something circular and metal whizzing past your head. It crashes here. Investigate the cave to see whether the pilot of this odd craft made it out alive.

## [3.23] MILITARY CHECKPOINT (SOUTH ZONE 3)

- **ARMOR PART: POWER ARMOR (LEVELED)**
- **ARMAMENTS AND AMMO**
- **ARMAMENTS AND AMMO: TRUNK**
- **FACTION: BLOODBUGS**

This rusting military checkpoint under the billboard warning of Communists is infested with bloodbugs. Scavenge for a (randomly appearing) trunk and suit of Power Armor.

## [3.24] WAYSTATION

- **ARMAMENTS AND AMMO**
- **FACTION: FERAL GHOULS**
- **HEALTH OR CHEMS**
- **QUEST VISIT: REUNIONS (MAIN)**

Head here with Dogmeat to uncover a trail. Visit here without the quest active, and this railway bridge, water tower, and waystation are empty. Access the hatch in the waystation for a small hideout. The rusting train cars are empty, too.

## [3.25] ROADSIDE STORE

- **COLLECTIBLE: NUKA CHERRY**
- **CRAFTING: CHEMISTRY STATION**
- **CRAFTING: COOKING STATION**
- **FACTION: SUPER MUTANTS**
- **HEALTH OR CHEMS**

This friendly store has a large number of grown produce and a chemistry station in the back storage area (Novice).

## [3.26] JOE'S SPUCKIES (FENS OUTSKIRTS)

Just north of Chestnut Hillock Reservoir are the western outskirts of the Fens, with the shell of a Joe's Spuckies to use as a landmark. There are a few minor scavengable items here.

## [3.27] RAIDER LOOKOUT CAMP (ELEVATED FREEWAY)

- **FACTION: RAIDERS**

A motley band of raiders and mongrels guard the remains of the freeway bridge.

# ZONE 4: COASTAL COMMONWEALTH

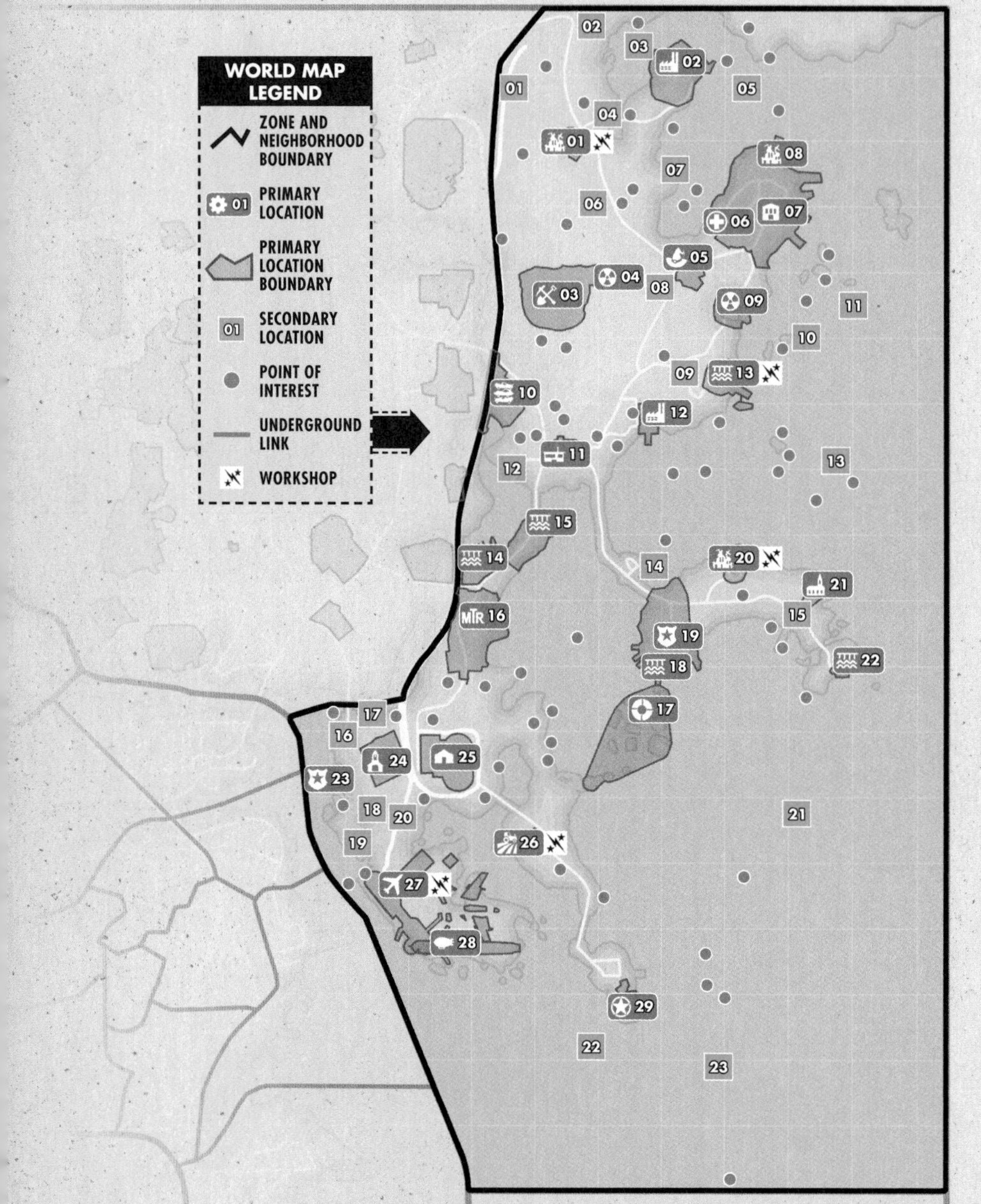

**WORLD MAP LEGEND**

- ⚙ 01 — ZONE AND NEIGHBORHOOD BOUNDARY
- ⚙ 01 — PRIMARY LOCATION
- ◈ — PRIMARY LOCATION BOUNDARY
- 01 — SECONDARY LOCATION
- ● — POINT OF INTEREST
- — UNDERGROUND LINK
- ✕ — WORKSHOP

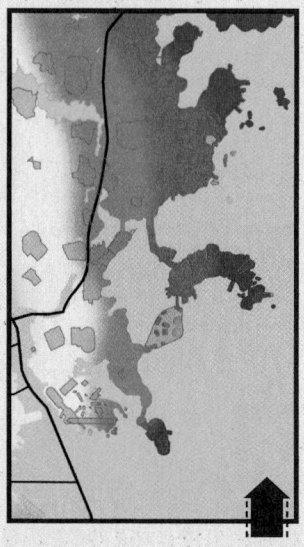

THREAT LEVEL MAP

1-5　6-14　15-25　20+　25+　30+　35+　40+　45+
EXPECTED LEVEL OF ENEMIES ENCOUNTERED

## Primary Locations

- [4.01] COASTAL COTTAGE
- [4.02] MAHKRA FISHPACKING
- [4.03] DUNWICH BORERS
- [4.04] HUGO'S HOLE
- [4.05] MUSEUM OF WITCHCRAFT
- [4.06] SANDY COVES CONVALESCENT HOME
- [4.07] SALEM
- [4.08] ROOK FAMILY HOUSE
- [4.09] CRATER HOUSE
- [4.10] HUB CITY AUTO WRECKERS
- [4.11] LYNN PIER PARKING
- [4.12] LONGNECK LUKOWSKI'S CANNERY
- [4.13] KINGSPORT LIGHTHOUSE
- [4.14] REEB MARINA
- [4.15] GIBSON POINT PIER
- [4.16] REVERE BEACH STATION
- [4.17] LIBERTALIA
- [4.18] NAHANT WHARF
- [4.19] NAHANT SHERIFF'S DEPARTMENT
- [4.20] CROUP MANOR
- [4.21] NAHANT CHAPEL
- [4.22] NAHANT OCEANOLOGICAL SOCIETY
- [4.23] EAST BOSTON POLICE STATION
- [4.24] EAST BOSTON PREPARATORY SCHOOL
- [4.25] EASY CITY DOWNS
- [4.26] NORDHAGEN BEACH
- [4.27] BOSTON AIRPORT
- [4.28] PRYDWEN
- [4.29] FORT STRONG

Those hoping to vacation on the eastern shores of the Commonwealth would do well to pack a copious supply of ammunition and have trained long and hard for this outing, as the threat level of the roaming miscreants in this zone is deemed "most dangerous." The township of Revere has been razed by Raiders. Nahant offers quiet walks interspersed with carnage, courtesy of ferals. Up north, Salem long continues its reputation for horror. Farther inland, toward East Boston and the airport, the ferociousness of your foes lessens just a little. The Brotherhood of Steel's imminent arrival at the airport should provide a brief respite should you agree to ally with them. Finally, those brave to dip their toes in the ocean may find one or two surprises under the waves.

## Secondary Locations

- [4.01] GUNNER CAMP (PARSONS ELEVATED FREEWAY)
- [4.02] MILTON GENERAL BILLBOARD
- [4.03] COASTAL VACATIONERS
- [4.04] COASTAL HIDEOUT
- [4.05] THE SUNKEN BATHTUB
- [4.06] SHANTY STORE
- [4.07] SALEM COASTAL DINER AND DOCK
- [4.08] RAIDER SHACK (SALEM OUTSKIRTS)
- [4.09] KINGSPORT RESTROOMS
- [4.10] OCEAN FISHING SHACK
- [4.11] SUNKEN FISHING BOAT
- [4.12] VITALE PUMPHOUSE
- [4.13] OCEAN RAFT
- [4.14] UNLOADING BARGE
- [4.15] NAHANT PIER RESTAURANT
- [4.16] DRUMLIN DINER (EAST BOSTON)
- [4.17] WATERFRONT WAREHOUSE
- [4.18] EAST BOSTON GARAGE
- [4.19] CONTAINER CRATES STASH
- [4.20] FREEWAY ROOFTOPS
- [4.21] UPSIDE DOWN ROWBOAT
- [4.22] DOOMED AIRLINES FLIGHT
- [4.23] FLOATING BARGE

### MAP LEGEND

| | | |
|---|---|---|
| 13 ——— 20 **OPTIMAL ROUTE** | C **BOTTLECAPS** | **HEALTH OR CHEMS** |
| | **SAFE** | **TERMINAL** |
| ● **AREA OF INTEREST** | **ARMAMENTS AND AMMO** | **STEAMER TRUNK** |
| | **DOOR** | |

- **FUSION CORE**
- **POWER ARMOR**
- **REQUIRED READING**

**Collectibles:**
- **BOBBLEHEAD**
- **NUKA CHERRY**
- **MINI NUKE**
- **NUKA COLA QUANTUM**
- **HOLOTAPE**
- **A KEY**

**N** – Novice (Locked)  
**A** – Advanced (Locked)  
**E** – Expert (Locked)  
**M** – Master (Locked)  
**T** – Terminal required to unlock  
**KEY** – Key or ID Card required to unlock  
**IN** – Inaccessible  
**C** – Chained  
**CB** – Circuit Breaker  
**B** – Button

# PRIMARY LOCATIONS

##  [4.01] COASTAL COTTAGE

THREAT LEVELS 40+

- COLLECTIBLE: NUKA CHERRY
- FACTION: MIRELURKS
- FACTION: SETTLER
- SERVICES: WORKSHOP

### VAULT-TEC RECOMMENDED LOOT

COLLECTIBLE: NUKA CHERRY

Offering windswept views of the ocean and Salem to the southeast, this ruined home and outbuildings are ripe for redevelopment as a settlement, once the Mirelurks are removed.

##  [4.02] MAHKRA FISHPACKING

THREAT LEVELS 45+

- ARMAMENTS AND AMMO
- ARMAMENTS AND AMMO: TRUNK
- BOTTLECAPS
- COLLECTIBLE: ROBOT MODEL KIT (PARTS)
- COLLECTIBLE: NUKA CHERRY (2)
- COLLECTIBLE: NUKA COLA QUANTUM
- COLLECTIBLE: REQUIRED READING: TESLA SCIENCE
- CRAFTING: CHEMISTRY STATION
- DANGER: GRENADES!
- DANGER: OIL!
- DANGER: MINES!
- DANGER: TRIPWIRE!
- FACTION: RAIDERS
- FACTION: SYNTHS (THE INSTITUTE)
- HEALTH OR CHEMS+

A seafood processing facility with a processing level deep underground. You can open both the locked doors (Advanced) using the key found on the Raider draped over the window of the eastern exterior hut. Beware of synths active on the lower level and reinforcements once you ascend on your way out.

Don't forget to also check the interior of the eastern hut for a rare robot model kit, sitting on a metal shelf inside, near the dead Raider.

### VAULT-TEC RECOMMENDED LOOT

COLLECTIBLE: NUKA CHERRY (2)
COLLECTIBLE: NUKA COLA QUANTUM
REQUIRED READING: TESLA SCIENCE
COLLECTIBLE: ROBOT MODEL KIT PARTS

MAP

**ZONE 4**

COASTAL COMMONWEALTH

## FIG 4.02A: MAHKRA FISHPACKING (EXTERIOR)

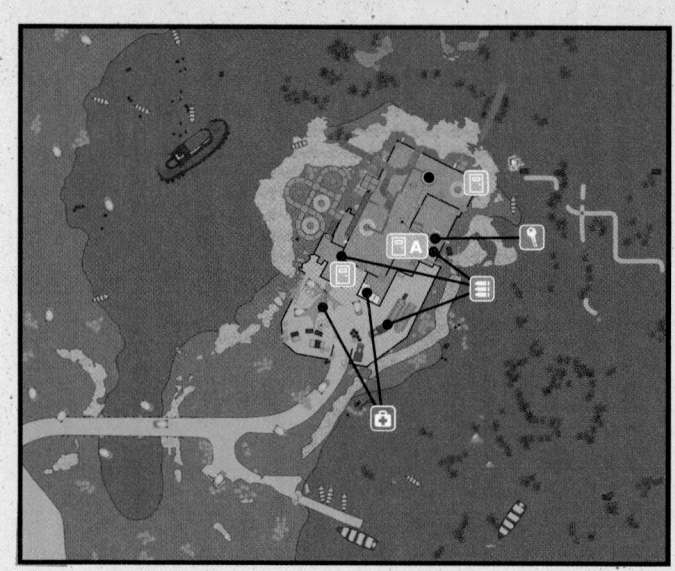

## FIG 4.02B: MAHKRA FISHPACKING (INTERIOR)

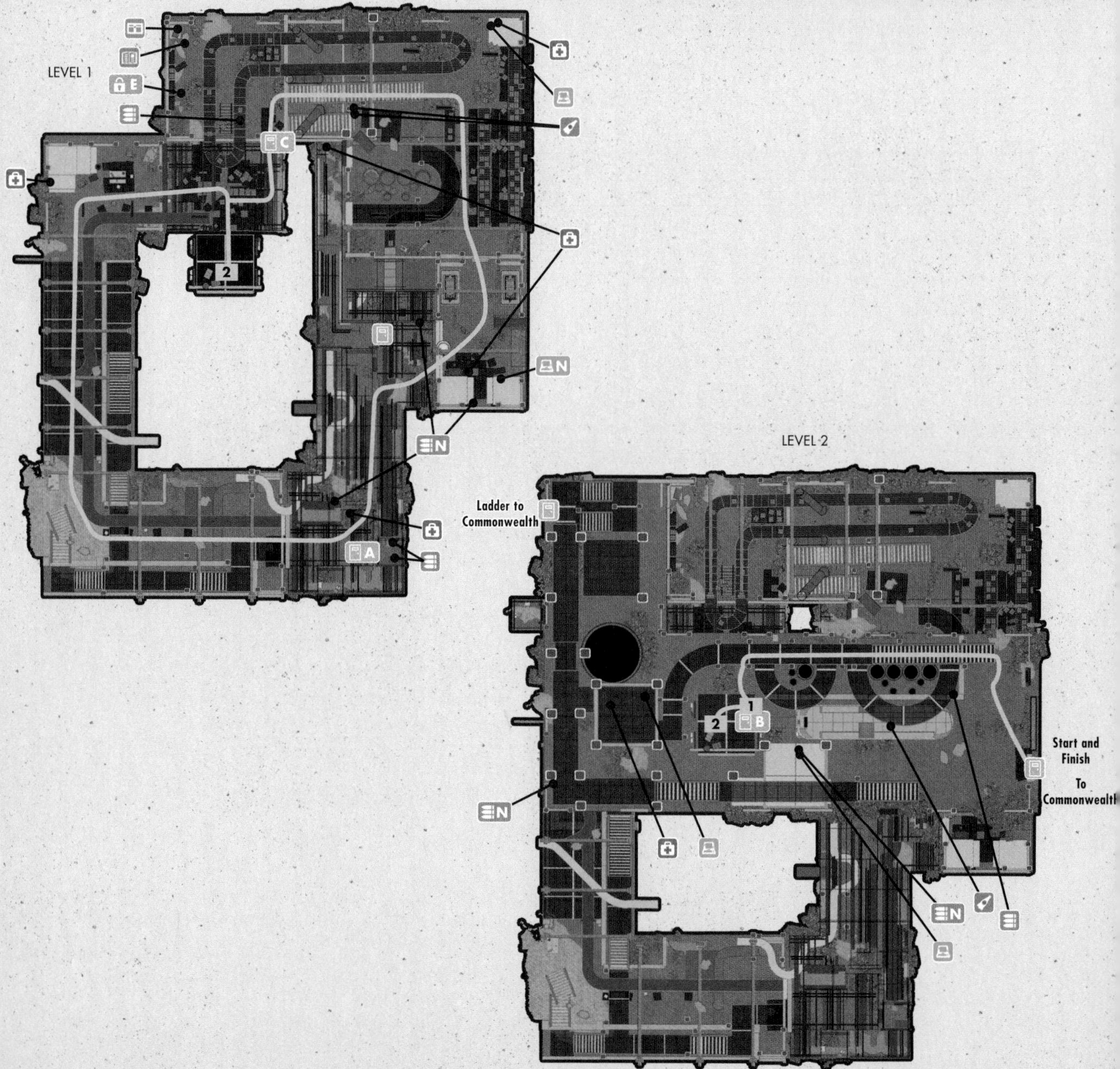

LEVEL 1

C

2

A

N

N

N

LEVEL 2

Ladder to
Commonwealth

2

B

1

Start and
Finish

To
Commonwealth

N

N

- ARMAMENTS AND AMMO+
- ARMAMENTS AND AMMO: MINI NUKE (3)
- ARMAMENTS AND AMMO: TRUNK
- COLLECTIBLE: BOBBLEHEAD: SNEAK
- COLLECTIBLE: REQUIRED READING: ASTOUNDINGLY AWESOME TALES
- CRAFTING: ARMOR WORKBENCH
- CRAFTING: COOKING STATION

- CRAFTING: WEAPONS WORKBENCH
- DANGER: ESCAPING GAS!
- DANGER: GRENADES!
- DANGER: LONG DROP!
- DANGER: MADNESS!
- DANGER: OIL!
- DANGER: RADIATION (MILD)!
- DANGER: TRIPWIRES!
- DANGER: TURRETS!
- FACTION: FERAL GHOULS
- FACTION: RAIDERS
- FACTION: CHARACTER: BEDLAM
- FACTION: CHARACTER: BRADLEY RAMONE
- FACTION: CHARACTER: BOB STANTON
- FACTION: CHARACTER: JOHN HATFIELD
- FACTION: CHARACTER: TIM SHOOTS
- HEALTH OR CHEMS
- QUEST START: MISCELLANEOUS (DUNWICH BORERS)
- UNIQUE ITEM: KREMVH'S TOOTH

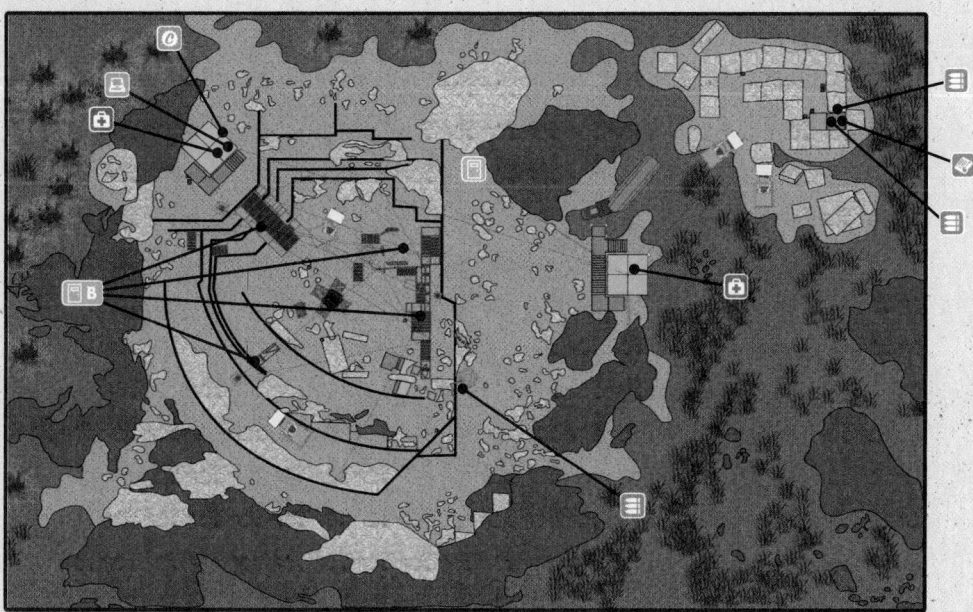

**FIG 4.03A: DUNWICH BORERS (EXTERIOR)**

This is an old marble quarry with deep subterranean fissures and tunnels. Many have attempted to fully explore this place, but none have ventured back up to the surface. The same can be said for a group of Raiders, some of whom have wisely kept to the surface. For it is said something unspeakable occurred within these depths...

## VAULT-TEC RECOMMENDED LOOT ⊚

**ARMAMENTS AND AMMO: MINI NUKE (3)**
**BOBBLEHEAD: SNEAK**
**REQUIRED READING: ASTOUNDINGLY AWESOME TALES**
**UNIQUE ITEM: KREMVH'S TOOTH**

👍 **Miscellaneous (Dunwich Borers)**

Wise wanderers should line up the numbered stations with the map provided in this guide to minimize confusion and insanity. Don't forget the magazine and trunk under station #3. Should you wish to try some diving, don hazmat attire (but not Power Armor, as you'll sink to the bottom and won't be able to get back out), and locate a ceremonial dagger and three collectible Mini Nukes before you surface.

**FIG 4.03B: DUNWICH BORERS (INTERIOR)**

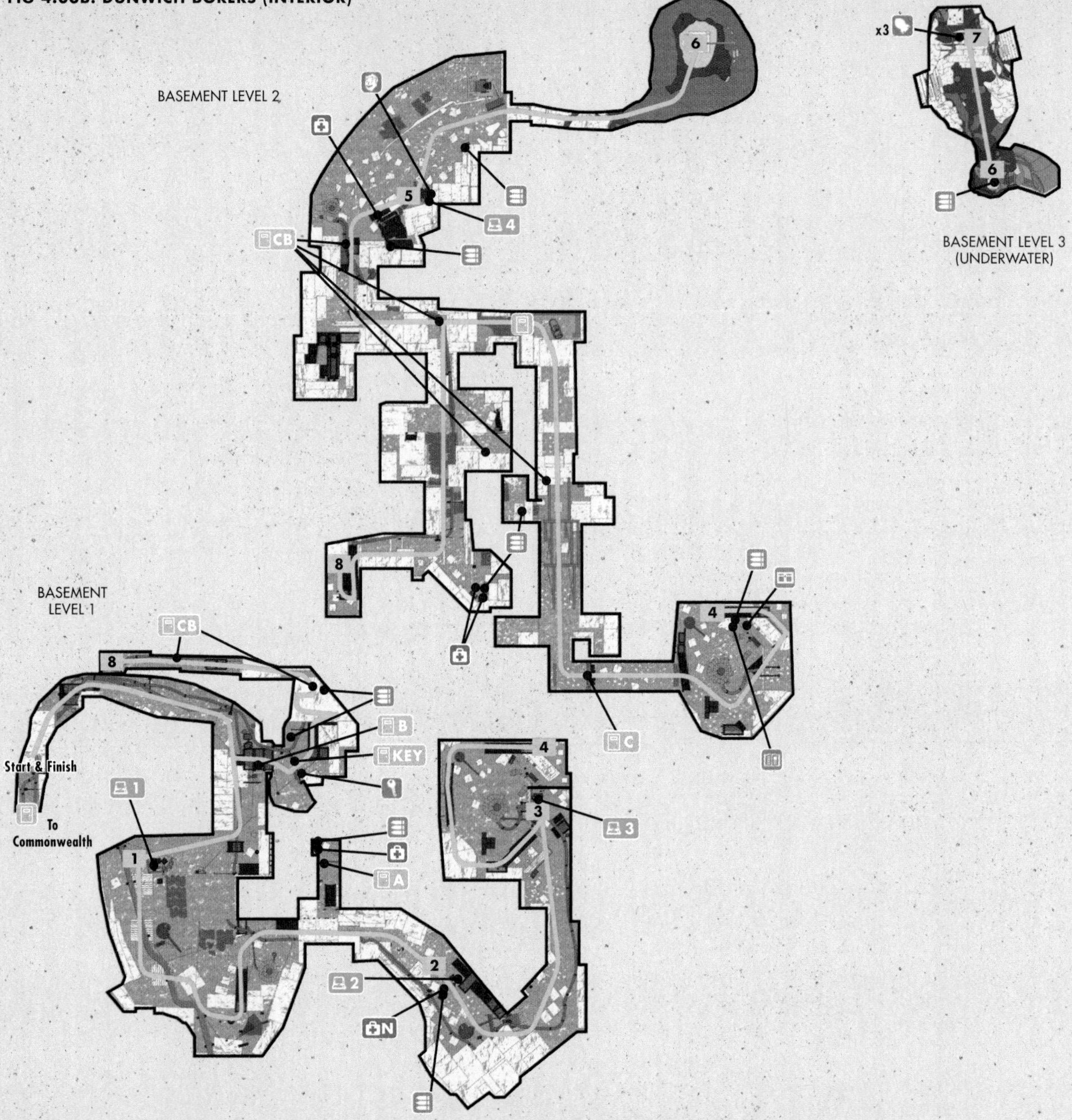

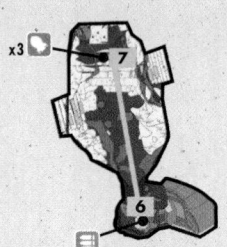

BASEMENT LEVEL 3
(UNDERWATER)

BASEMENT LEVEL 2

BASEMENT
LEVEL 1

Start & Finish

To
Commonwealth

☢ **[4.04] HUGO'S HOLE**      THREAT LEVELS 40+

– ARMAMENTS AND AMMO
– ARMAMENTS AND AMMO: TRUNK
– BOTTLECAPS
– COLLECTIBLE: ROBOT MODEL KIT
  (MR. HANDY)
– COLLECTIBLE: HOLOTAPE:
  HUGO'S HOLOTAPE
– CRAFTING: CHEMISTRY STATION
– DANGER: MAKESHIFT BOMBS!

– DANGER: RADIATION (SEVERE)!
– DANGER: TRIPWIRES!
– DANGER: TURRET!
– FACTION: RAIDER
– FACTION: CHARACTER: HUGO
– QUEST VISIT: MISCELLANEOUS
  (DUNWICH BORERS)

Between the thick cubes of marble on the northeast side of Dunwich Borers is the well-defended hidey-hole of Hugo, a local explorer. Listen to his Holotape for clues regarding the horrors at the adjacent quarry. Unlock his trunk (Expert) if you're the pilfering sort. There's a hazmat suit here, too, if you need to swim down an ancient irradiated well for some reason. Did you also check Hugo's sleeping area for a metal shelf with a robot model kit on it? Have you found them all yet?

**VAULT-TEC RECOMMENDED LOOT**  ⬡

 **COLLECTIBLE: ROBOT MODEL KIT (MR. HANDY)**

# [4.05—4.09] SALEM TOWNSHIP

## [4.05] MUSEUM OF WITCHCRAFT

THREAT LEVELS 45+

- ARMAMENTS AND AMMO
- ARMAMENTS AND AMMO: TRUNK
- COLLECTIBLE: REQUIRED READING: GROGNAK THE BARBARIAN
- FACTION: DEATHCLAW
- FACTION: GUNNER
- FACTION: CHARACTER: PRIVATE HART
- FACTION: CHARACTER: SERGEANT LEE
- HEALTH OR CHEMS
- QUEST START: THE DEVIL'S DUE (SIDE)

### FIG 4.05: MUSEUM OF WITCHCRAFT (INTERIOR)

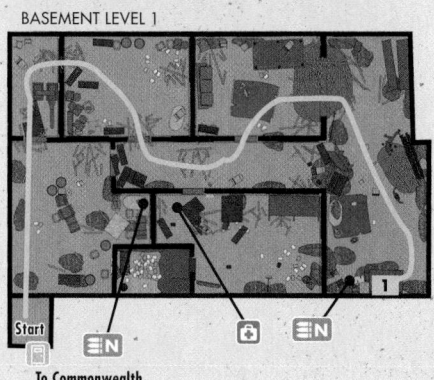

BASEMENT LEVEL 1

Start

To Commonwealth

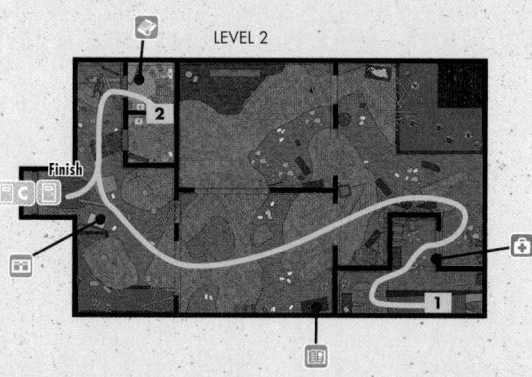

LEVEL 2

2

Finish

1

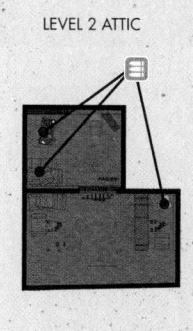

LEVEL 2 ATTIC

### VAULT-TEC RECOMMENDED LOOT

REQUIRED READING: GROGNAK THE BARBARIAN

A historic church greets visitors wishing to learn more about Salem's past, though the greeting is initially more subdued. The front door is chained, and the only entrance is via a basement hatch. Inside, it appears something terrifying is haunting this place. Need to reach the attic? A jetpack is in order

MAP

ZONE 4

COASTAL COMMONWEALTH

## [4.06] SANDY COVES CONVALESCENT HOME

THREAT LEVELS 45+

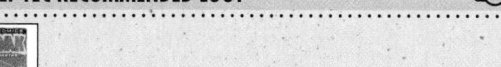

A nursing home for the elderly, the residents of Sandy Coves have been experiencing the very best in automated care now for over 200 years. The front desk terminal (Novice) near the book return terminal has locations of residents' keys to open the adjacent safes. Hunt for all six, and claim the contents (mainly chems) from the safes. Watch for a synth ambush on your way out.

### FIG 4.06: SANDY COVES CONVALESCENT HOME (INTERIOR)

- ARMAMENTS AND AMMO
- ARMAMENTS AND AMMO: TRUNK
- BOTTLECAPS
- COLLECTIBLE: REQUIRED READING: MASSACHUSETTS SURGICAL JOURNAL 9
- CRAFTING: CHEMISTRY STATION
- FACTION: RADROACHES
- FACTION: ROBOTS
- FACTION: SYNTHS (THE INSTITUTE)
- HEALTH OR CHEMS+++

### VAULT-TEC RECOMMENDED LOOT

REQUIRED READING: MASSACHUSETTS SURGICAL JOURNAL

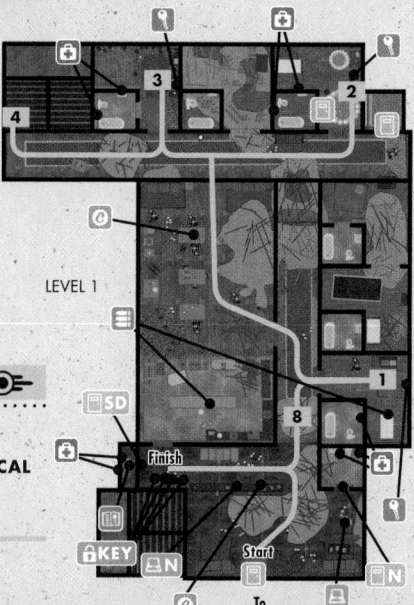

LEVEL 1

3

4

2

1

8

SD

KEY

Finish

Start

To Commonwealth

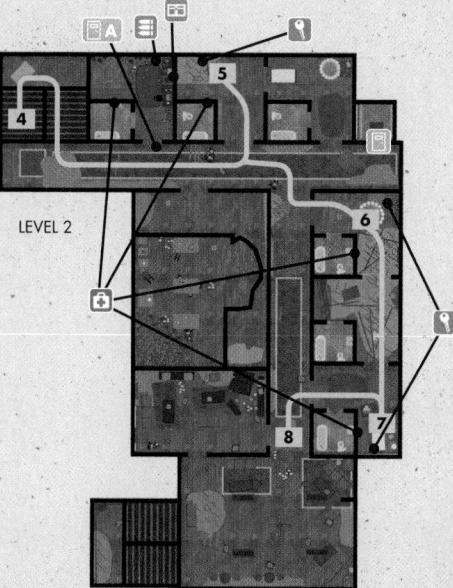

LEVEL 2

5

4

6

7

8

- ARMAMENTS AND AMMO+
- ARMAMENTS AND AMMO: MINI NUKE
- ARMAMENTS AND AMMO: MINI NUKE (FAT MAN)
- BOTTLECAPS+
- DANGER: RADIATION (MILD)!
- FACTION: MIRELURKS
- HEALTH OR CHEMS
- QUEST START: MISCELLANEOUS (BARNEY ROOK)

## VAULT-TEC RECOMMENDED LOOT

 **ARMAMENTS AND AMMO: MINI NUKE AND FAT MAN**

Once a quaint coastal town and seaport, this tourist destination was infamous for its witch trials of 1692. Nowadays the population has dwindled considerably due to Gunner activity in the area, the crazies worshipping a radiation crater down the road, and the large number of mating Mirelurks in the waters all around the bay. Proceed at your own risk.

**SALEM (EXTERIOR)**

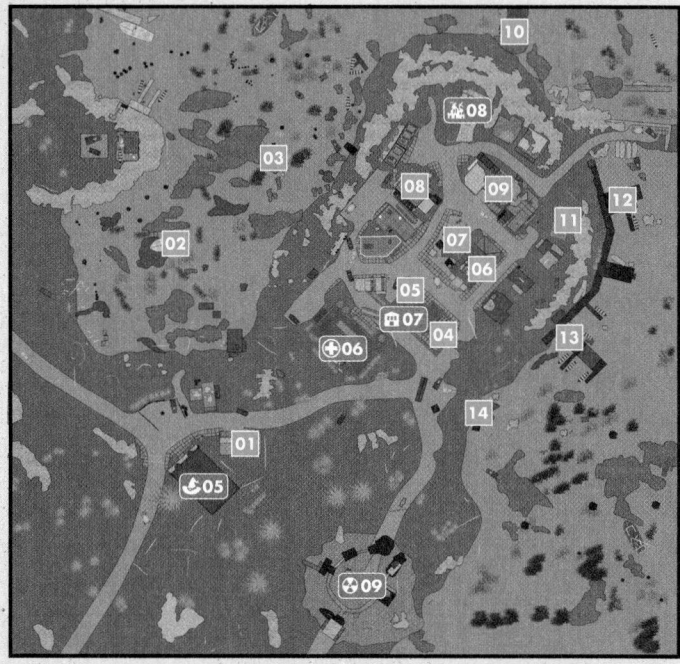

## [01] Museum Cottages

The ruins of the cottages have a safe (Expert) still intact on the upper level.

## [02] Fishing Boat

An impressive catch is on the deck. But you're here to scavenge the toolbox.

### [03] Flotsam and Jetsam

A few minor items and some playground equipment fashioned into stepping stones across the bay.

### [04] Drumlin Diner

Here for a quick meal? There's a few cans to gather, along with some health.

### [05] Clothing Store

Come for the fashionable items. They're a steal! Then check the small connecting bridge for the ammo. The chain-link area between the clothing store and diner has a terminal and a turret. Consult the Rook Family House Miscellaneous quest for more information.

### [06] Salem Church

There's very little to scavenge in this church, until you ascend to the upper floor (there's ammo). Climb the steeple for a terminal related to the Rook Family House Miscellaneous quest, as well as a Mini Nuke and caps stash.

### [07] Market Stalls

Mirelurks have terminated the once-thriving bartering market, though there's still some minor items to scavenge.

### [08] Rook Military Surplus

The upper floor of this gun shop belonging to Barney Rook houses a terminal and turret. Activate it during the specified quest. There's a Fat Man, caps stash, and safe (Master) for your troubles.

### [09] Ruined Restaurant and Offices

The buildings in this block are in a terrible state of repair. Ascend through the office building or via the scaffold steps near Barney Rook's place, and you can access two of the machine-gun turret terminals. Do this during the specified quest.

### [10] Submerged Barge

A small barge has run aground on the northern shore. Dive into the boat to secure some health.

### [11] Ruined Beach House

This beach house is one of the many dilapidated structures of Salem. It has a few scattered chems upstairs.

### [12] Wharf Warehouse

Both wharf warehouses have been picked clean of most supplies. Beware of Mirelurks.

### [13] Eastern Wharf

A small hut by the rocks has a stash of Caps, while the boathouse gently creaks in the breeze. The rocks to the southeast look interesting...

### [14] Salem Beach

This desolate stretch of sand has some strewn loungers and a small ocean-front shack with a safe to crack (Expert).

## VAULT-TEC RECOMMENDED LOOT

**REQUIRED READING: GUNS AND BULLETS**
**UNIQUE ITEM: REBA II**

Barney Rook was a keen survivalist and has defended his property with impressive fortitude. He is currently under Mirelurk attack.

- ARMAMENTS AND AMMO
- COLLECTIBLE: REQUIRED READING: GUNS AND BULLETS
- BOTTLECAPS
- CRAFTING: WEAPONS WORKBENCH
- FACTION: MIRELURKS
- FACTION: SCAVENGER
- FACTION: CHARACTER: BARNEY ROOK
- HEALTH OR CHEMS
- QUEST START: MISCELLANEOUS (BARNEY ROOK)
- UNIQUE WEAPON: REBA
- UNIQUE WEAPON: REBA II

 **Miscellaneous (Barney Rook)**

1. KILL THE MIRELURKS (3)
2. TALK TO BARNEY
3. MEET BARNEY IN HIS BUNKER
4. ACTIVATE BARNEY'S TURRETS (5)
5. REPORT BACK TO BARNEY

 (Easy, Medium) Ask for a reward for your troubles.

Crack open a few Mirelurk shells before speaking to the homeowner. He opens the previously inaccessible gate. Enter the ruined home and descend into the basement via the trapdoor. Here you meet Barney and his favorite gun, Reba. Agree to help him.

Activate his defense turrets around Salem (shown on the Salem Township map). Once complete, return to receive a key to his workshop and the unique weapon Reba II. Kill Barney for the previous iteration, Reba.

 **[4.09] CRATER HOUSE**

THREAT LEVELS 45+

- ARMAMENTS AND AMMO
- ARMAMENTS AND AMMO: TRUNK
- COLLECTIBLE: REQUIRED READING: WASTELAND SURVIVAL GUIDE
- CRAFTING: CHEMISTRY STATION
- CRAFTING: COOKING STATION
- DANGER: RADIATION (SEVERE)!
- DANGER: TURRETS!
- FACTION: CHILDREN OF THE ATOM
- HEALTH OR CHEMS

## VAULT-TEC RECOMMENDED LOOT

 **REQUIRED READING: WASTELAND SURVIVAL GUIDE**

The more lunatic of local cults has constructed a rickety shanty hamlet on top of an old, irradiated aircraft crash site. This seems to be some kind of gathering spot. Do not bathe in the water. Pick the safe (Expert) and access the terminal (Novice) to switch off the turrets and spotlights.

 **[4.10] HUB CITY AUTO WRECKERS**

THREAT LEVELS 35+

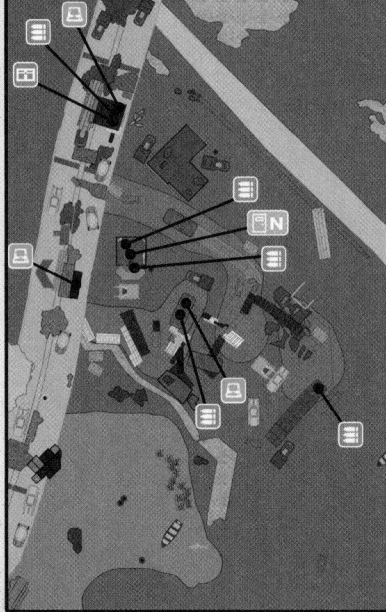

**FIG 4.10: HUB CITY AUTO WRECKERS (EXTERIOR)**

- ARMAMENTS AND AMMO
- ARMAMENTS AND AMMO: TRUNK
- BOTTLECAPS
- CRAFTING: POWER ARMOR STATION
- CRAFTING: WEAPONS WORKBENCH
- DANGER: CAN CHIMES!
- DANGER: FLAMETHROWER!
- DANGER: LONG DROP!
- DANGER: OIL!
- DANGER: TRIPWIRE!
- FACTION: GUNNERS
- FACTION: CHARACTER: CAPTAIN BRIDGET

Previously, Hub City Auto Wreckers had received several citations for the improper storage and disposal of radioactive materials. Currently, this location has been overrun by the altogether unreasonable Gunners faction. Utilize the Hub City terminal to raise or lower the crane, allowing access to the freeway defenses and steamer trunk in Captain Bridget's shack.

– **DANGER: RADIATION (MILD)!**
– **FACTION: IRRADIATED WILDLIFE (RADROACH)**

This low-rise parking structure once offered reasonable rates and a view of Gibson Point Pier. Now it is deserted and partly flooded.

 **[4.12] LONGNECK LUKOWSKI'S CANNERY**  THREAT LEVELS 40+

**FIG 4.12A: LONGNECK LUKOWSKI'S CANNERY (EXTERIOR)**

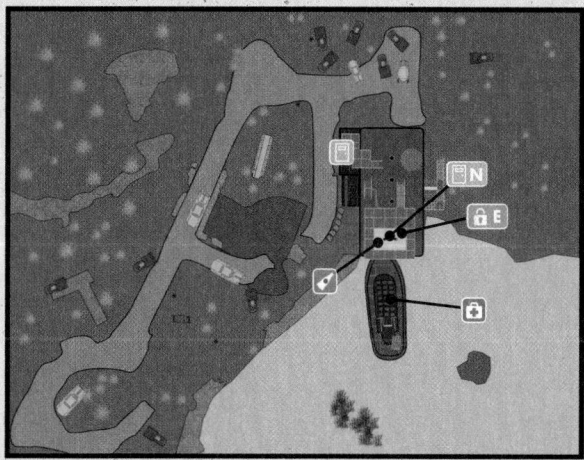

– ARMAMENTS AND AMMO
– ARMAMENTS AND AMMO: TRUNK
– ARMOR PART: FUSION CORE
– BOTTLECAPS
– COLLECTIBLE: BOBBLEHEAD: BARTER
– COLLECTIBLE: NUKA CHERRY
– COLLECTIBLE: REQUIRED READING: TALES OF A JUNKTOWN JERKY VENDOR
– CRAFTING: CHEMISTRY STATION
– CRAFTING: WEAPONS WORKBENCH
– DANGER: MAKESHIFT BOMB!
– DANGER: OIL!
– DANGER: MINES!
– DANGER: RADIATION (MILD)!
– DANGER: TESLA ARC!

– DANGER: TRIPWIRE!
– DANGER: TURRETS!
– FACTION: FERAL GHOULS
– FACTION: RADROACHES
– FACTION: SCAVENGER
– FACTION: CHARACTER: THEODORE COLLINS
– FACTION: CHARACTER: TRADER RYLEE
– HEALTH OR CHEMS
– QUEST START: MISCELLANEOUS (TRADER RYLEE)
– QUEST START: MYSTERY MEAT
– SERVICES: TRADER (THEODORE COLLINS)
– SERVICES: TRADER (TRADER RYLEE)

**VAULT-TEC RECOMMENDED LOOT**

**ARMOR PART: FUSION CORE**
**BOBBLEHEAD: BARTER**
**COLLECTIBLE: NUKA CHERRY**
**REQUIRED READING: TALES OF A JUNKTOWN JERKY VENDOR**

Famed for its quality potted meats, this cannery has recently been revitalized by the enterprising Theodore Collins, though the meats he produces have a strange, almost familiar taste.

When larking about outside, look for the rooftop metal hut (Novice); there's a thirst-quenching Nuka Cherry and safe (Expert) inside.

Inside, Trader Rylee and Theodore Collins are arguing about the quality of the potted meat product he's selling. Venture farther into the gantry hut for a collection of quality loot, including a Bobblehead and trunk.

 **Miscellaneous (Theodore Collins and Trader Rylee)**

Speak with Trader Rylee about the revolting potted meat Theodore has been selling; then trade with her if you wish.

 **Mystery Meat**

**1. CONFRONT THEODORE COLLINS**

Begin a thorough investigation of the facilities. When you ride the cargo elevator down to the lower level, this quest commences. Learn more about the meat production; then confront Theodore Collins when you unchain the door and head back into the factory. Collins has Longneck Lukowski's Key. If you almost kill him, he sometimes surrenders and asks if you're up for some caps in return for keeping quiet about the meat.

## FIG 4.12B: LONGNECK LUKOWSKI'S CANNERY (INTERIOR)

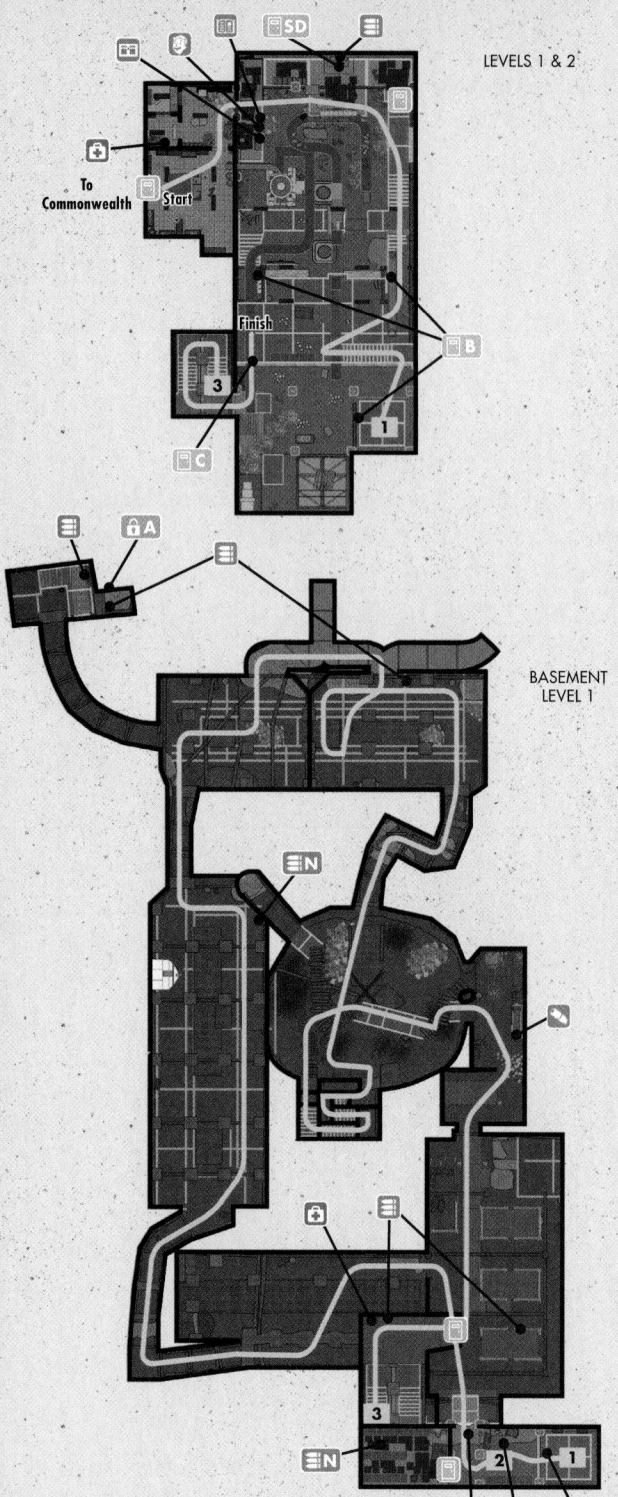

LEVELS 1 & 2

To Commonwealth

Start

Finish

3

BASEMENT LEVEL 1

THREAT LEVELS 45+

- ARMAMENTS AND AMMO: MINI NUKE
- ARMAMENTS AND AMMO: TRUNK
- BOTTLECAPS
- CRAFTING: WEAPONS WORKBENCH
- DANGER: MINE!
- DANGER: RADIATION (MILD)!
- DANGER: TRIPWIRE!
- FACTION: CHILDREN OF THE ATOM
- FACTION: FERAL GHOULS
- SERVICES: WORKSHOP

## VAULT-TEC RECOMMENDED LOOT

**ARMAMENTS AND AMMO: MINI NUKE**

Cultists from Crater House have sought to shine their light from the heavens and have an interesting glow for their beacon. Rid the area of these deviants and Kingsport Lighthouse could be an easily defendable settlement. Check the lighthouse keeper's home and the moored trawler; they each have a safe (Advanced) to crack.

## [4.14] REEB MARINA

THREAT LEVELS 35+

- ARMAMENTS AND AMMO
- ARMAMENTS AND AMMO: TRUNK
- COLLECTIBLE: REQUIRED READING: TESLA SCIENCE
- CRAFTING: ARMOR WORKBENCH
- CRAFTING: POWER ARMOR STATION
- CRAFTING: WEAPONS WORKBENCH
- FACTION: BLOODBUG
- FACTION: ROBOTS
- HEALTH OR CHEMS

### VAULT-TEC RECOMMENDED LOOT

 REQUIRED READING: TESLA SCIENCE

This small boating marina was home to brothers Eugene and Malcolm, who parted ways while not on the best of terms. Read more at Eugene's terminal or Malcolm's terminal (Novice), and be wary of surprises from robots. Check the trunk in the kitchen.

## [4.15] GIBSON POINT PIER

THREAT LEVELS 35+

- ARMAMENTS AND AMMO
- ARMAMENTS AND AMMO: TRUNK
- COLLECTIBLE: NUKA CHERRY
- COLLECTIBLE: NUKA-COLA QUANTUM
- DANGER: GRENADES!
- DANGER: TRIPWIRE!
- FACTION: MIRELURKS
- HEALTH OR CHEMS

### VAULT-TEC RECOMMENDED LOOT

COLLECTIBLE: NUKA CHERRY
COLLECTIBLE: NUKA COLA QUANTUM
COLLECTIBLE: PROTECTRON MODEL KIT

This is a small spit of land extending from Revere to Lynn. The original bridge was replaced with the current structure after a blizzard in the early 21st century. Cross the bridge with caution. Check the diner for a floor safe (Advanced) and some delicious Nuka! Beware of an ambush from the water. Wander into the small boathouse to find a trunk.

## [4.16] REVERE BEACH STATION

THREAT LEVELS 35+

- COLLECTIBLE: REQUIRED READING: LIVE & LOVE
- CRAFTING: CHEMISTRY STATION
- CRAFTING: COOKING STATION (2)
- CRAFTING: POWER ARMOR STATION
- DANGER: GRENADES!
- DANGER: MINES!
- DANGER: TENSION TRIGGER!
- DANGER: TURRETS!
- DANGER:
- FACTION: FERAL GHOULS
- FACTION: RADROACHES
- FACTION: RAIDERS
- FACTION: CHARACTER: CINDER
- HEALTH OR CHEMS

- ARMAMENTS AND AMMO
- ARMAMENTS AND AMMO: TRUNK (2)
- ARMOR PART: FUSION CORE
- BOTTLECAPS+
- COLLECTIBLE: ROBOT MODEL KIT (PROTECTION)
- COLLECTIBLE: NUKA CHERRY (2)

### FIG 4.16A: REVERE BEACH STATION (EXTERIOR)

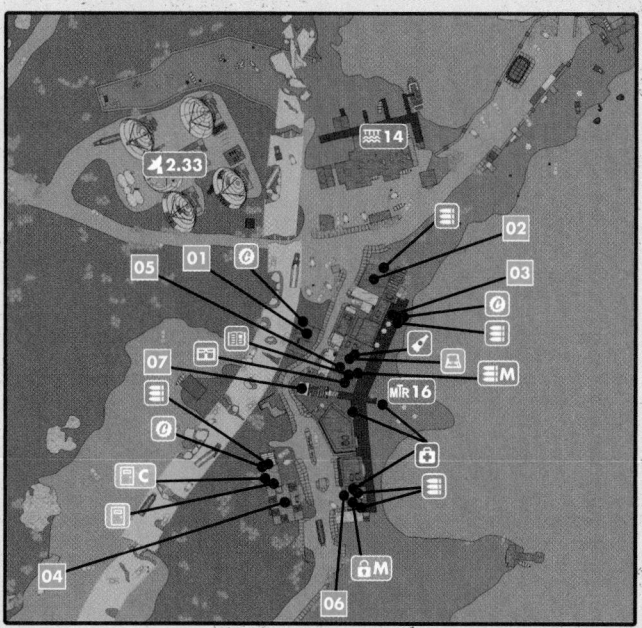

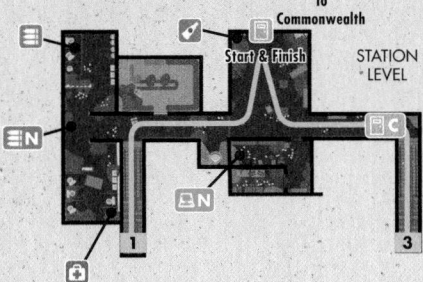

To Commonwealth

Start & Finish

STATION LEVEL

1

3

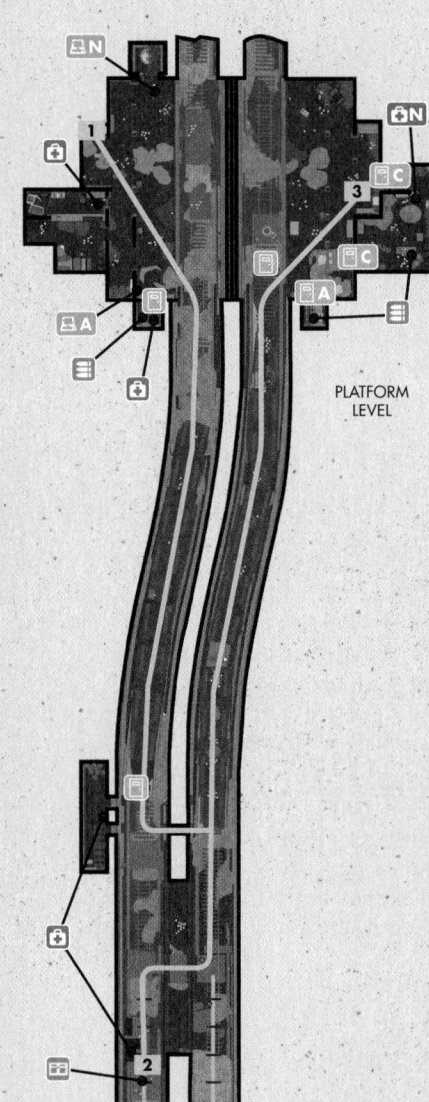

PLATFORM LEVEL

1

3

2

## VAULT-TEC RECOMMENDED LOOT

**ARMOR PART: FUSION CORE**
**COLLECTIBLE: NUKA CHERRY (2)**
**REQUIRED READING: LIVE & LOVE**

Prior to the war, Revere Beach Boardwalk was supposed to be a place where families and vacationers could come and have fun during the summer months. However, gangs of teens in black leather, racing their muscle cars, drove out most of the polite folks. The boardwalk turned into a hangout for this unsavory element.

Nowadays, if you fancy a stroll along the boardwalk with the sea breeze in your hair, you may need to remove the band of Raiders occupying this area.

### [01], [02] Outlying Houses (North)

The outlying houses to the north have a smattering of chems.

### [03] Railroad Stash

There's a Railroad stash below the promenade to the north.

### [04] Revere Garage

There are more goods on the roof of the southwest garage (where there's a Power Armor station). Use the fallen tree trunk to enter the garage.

Also check next to the power armor station for a robot model kit. It's the only one of its kind!

### [05] Revere Arcade

The central arcade has a book return terminal to use (spend 50 tokens on a Fusion Core in here), a Nuka Cherry on the counter, and a magazine to read upstairs, along with a tightly locked steamer trunk (Master).

### [06] Outlying House (South)

Don't leave without checking the accessible house to the south; that safe isn't going to unlock itself.

### [07] Revere Beach Station (Interior)

Between these two doomed subway trains is a Raider camp led by Cinder. Beware the Feral Ghouls behind the chained-off doors. Don't leave without a Nuka Cherry and the contents of the second trunk at this location.

## [4.17] LIBERTALIA

THREAT LEVELS 35+

- ARMAMENTS AND AMMO++
- ARMAMENTS AND AMMO: MINI NUKE
- ARMAMENTS AND AMMO: TRUNK
- BOTTLECAPS
- COLLECTIBLE: REQUIRED READING: U.S. COVERT OPERATIONS MANUAL
- CRAFTING: COOKING STATION
- CRAFTING: CHEMISTRY STATION
- DANGER: LONG DROP!
- DANGER: MINES!
- DANGER: RADIATION (MILD)!
- DANGER: TURRETS!
- FACTION: RAIDERS
- FACTION: CHARACTER: GABRIEL
- FACTION: CHARACTER: WIRE
- HEALTH OR CHEMS++
- QUEST VISIT: SYNTH RETENTION (THE INSTITUTE)
- UNIQUE WEAPON: LE FUSIL TERRIBLES

## VAULT-TEC RECOMMENDED LOOT

 **UNIQUE ITEM: LE FUSIL TERRIBLES**

 **ARMAMENTS AND AMMO: MINI NUKE**

 **REQUIRED READING: U.S. COVERT OPERATIONS MANUAL**

Some enterprising nutcases have gathered a variety of rusting ships, docks, and debris and fashioned a ship's graveyard into a stronghold. And a settler graveyard. The depravity on show here is frightful.

Approach from the north or south peninsula, and watch your footing. Assuming a north to south advance, check the first two shanty boats for a safe (Advanced) and a cage door (Expert) that leads to a storage area with ammo, chems, and another safe. There's another safe on the white boat in the middle of the cluster of hulks. One red and white boat has a locked door (Advanced) leading to a small stash of items. There's yet another safe (Advanced) on the top part of the tugboat and another safe (Advanced) in the green tower with the terminal (which unlocks this safe and controls the turrets and spotlight).

The captain's cabin (atop the stern of a sunken tanker) can be accessed via swimming or calling the shack platform from the trash boat. Locate a safe (Advanced) on the level just before accessing the captain's cabin. Inside the cabin is a Mini Nuke, a unique weapon, and Wire's terminal (Novice). Atop the cabin is a Raider leader (Wire, or Gabriel if the quest is active), guarding a terminal (Master) with a safe. There's a trunk in these parts, too.

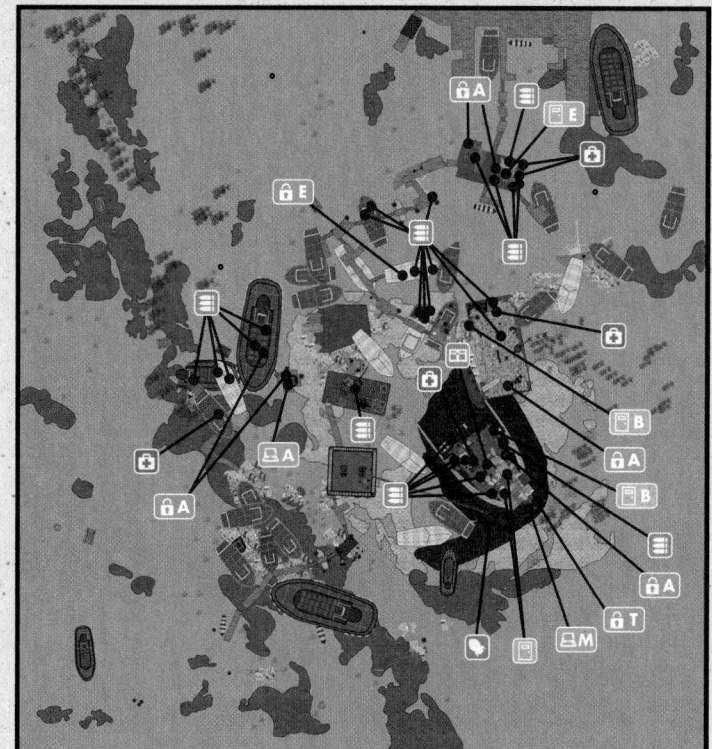

FIG 4.17: LIBERTALIA (EXTERIOR)

![threat level icon] **[4.18] NAHANT WHARF**    THREAT LEVELS 40+ ▮▮▮▮▮▮▮

FIG 4.18: NAHANT (TOWNSHIP)

– ARMAMENTS AND AMMO
– COLLECTIBLE: NUKA CHERRY
– DANGER: RADIATION (MILD)!

**VAULT-TEC RECOMMENDED LOOT** ⬢

**COLLECTIBLE: NUKA CHERRY**

This is a selection of outbuildings, a boathouse, and a warehouse overlooking Libertalia to the south, adjacent to the police station, slowly rusting away. Farther inland is the main cluster of rotting wood homes and a rusting Red Rocket Filling Station—all picked clean by scavengers, save for the roof.

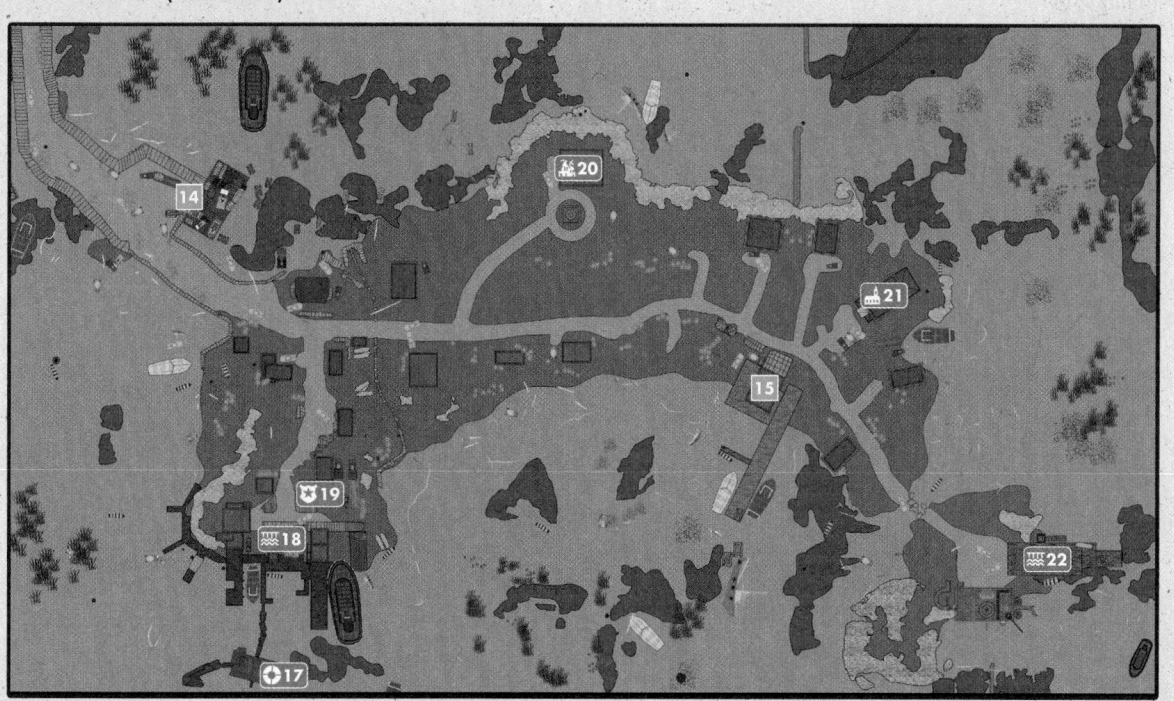

- ARMAMENTS AND AMMO
- BOTTLECAPS
- COLLECTIBLE: HOLOTAPE: EDDIE WINTER'S HOLOTAPE
- QUEST VISIT: LONG TIME COMING (SIDE)

The police department building is little more than a shell of concrete and rusting furniture. Another of Eddie Winter's Holotapes is upstairs on a filing cabinet.

 **[4.20] CROUP MANOR**   THREAT LEVELS 45+

- ARMAMENTS AND AMMO
- ARMAMENTS AND AMMO: MINI NUKE
- ARMAMENTS AND AMMO: TRUNK
- BOTTLECAPS
- CRAFTING: WEAPONS WORKBENCH

- FACTION: FERAL GHOULS
- FACTION: CHARACTER: THEODORE CROUP
- SERVICES: WORKSHOP

## VAULT-TEC RECOMMENDED LOOT

 **ARMAMENTS AND AMMO: MINI NUKE**

Through the gates from Nahant is a wooded area of once-lavish mansions. The most ostentatious of these is Croup Manor, belonging to a distinguished Nahant family.

The place is overrun with ferals; clean them up before attracting settlers to this place. Upstairs is a locked desk (Novice) containing a key and a door without a floor (Novice). There's also a top-floor door to pick (Advanced) or open using the bedroom key from the desk. The bedroom dresser has a basement key. The basement is locked (Master) and leads to a steamer trunk and a Croup family reunion. Of sorts. Unlock the safe (Advanced) if you wish.

**FIG 4.20A: CROUP MANOR (EXTERIOR)**

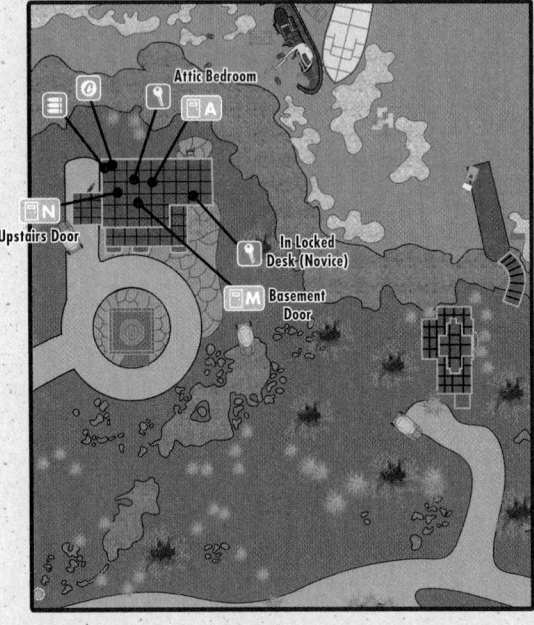

**FIG 4.20B: CROUP MANOR BASEMENT (INTERIOR)**

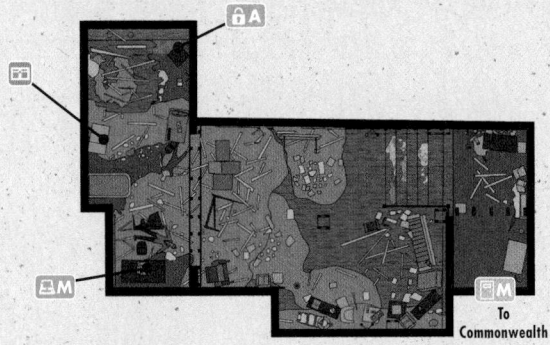

 **[4.21] NAHANT CHAPEL**   THREAT LEVELS 45+

- ARMAMENTS AND AMMO
- ARMAMENTS AND AMMO: TRUNK
- FACTION: MIRELURKS

Nahant's most intact structure is the chapel by the sea. Head upstairs for a steamer trunk and roof access allowing safe sniping should anything ambush you from the water. To the south is a ruined bar and restaurant house, also with a steamer trunk upstairs.

# [4.22] NAHANT OCEANOLOGICAL SOCIETY

THREAT LEVELS 45+

- ARMAMENTS AND AMMO
- ARMAMENTS AND AMMO: TRUNK (2)
- COLLECTIBLE: REQUIRED READING:
  WASTELAND SURVIVAL GUIDE
- CRAFTING: CHEMISTRY STATION
- CRAFTING: POWER ARMOR STATION
- CRAFTING: WEAPONS WORKBENCH

- DANGER: OIL!
- DANGER: RADIATION (MILD)!
- FACTION: MIRELURKS
- FACTION: ROBOTS
  (OCEANOLOGICAL INSTRUCTORS)
- HEALTH OR CHEMS

## FIG 4.22A: NAHANT OCEANOLOGICAL SOCIETY (INTERIOR)

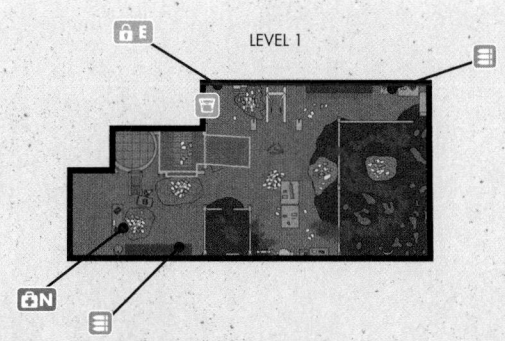

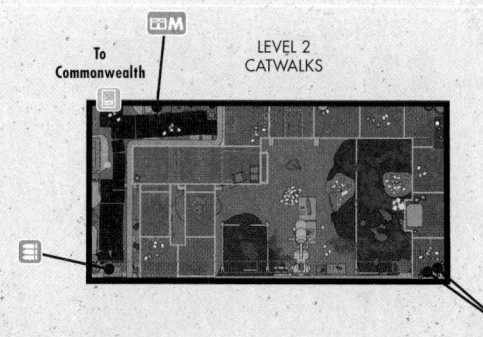

## FIG 4.22B: NAHANT OCEANOLOGICAL RESEARCH LAB (INTERIOR)

LEVEL 1

LEVEL 2
CATWALKS

To Commonwealth

### VAULT-TEC RECOMMENDED LOOT

REQUIRED READING:
WASTELAND SURVIVAL
GUIDE

The small Oceanological Society, perched at the end of the spit of land, is a former marine research laboratory but is now infamous for Mirelurk nests and spitting barnacles. Robots are still active and battling aquatic mutations coming up from the bay. There are two interior structures to investigate (each one has a trunk to open), as well as a tiny shack (Novice) at the edge of the tumbledown pier with some ammunition inside.

Look east out to sea to spot a beached fishing boat at the far end of the Mirelurk hatching area. Wade over and pry Casey's key from the toolbox in the cabin.

## [4.23] EAST BOSTON POLICE STATION

THREAT LEVELS 30+

- COLLECTIBLE: HOLOTAPE: EDDIE WINTER'S HOLOTAPE
- QUEST VISIT: LONG TIME COMING (SIDE)

Flooded in ankle-deep water, this police station has been ravaged by time and marauders. The sixth of Eddie Winter's Holotapes is upstairs inside a desk. Unless you're a fan of soggy sweet rolls, this place is devoid of major items to scavenge.

FIG 4.24A: EAST BOSTON PREPARATORY SCHOOL (EXTERIOR)

- ARMAMENTS AND AMMO+
- ARMAMENTS AND AMMO: MINI NUKE
- ARMAMENTS AND AMMO: TRUNK
- BOTTLECAPS++
- COLLECTIBLE: REQUIRED READING: ASTOUNDINGLY AWESOME TALES
- CHARACTER: JUDGE ZELLER
- CRAFTING: CHEMISTRY STATION
- CRAFTING: COOKING STATION
- DANGER: CAN CHIMES!
- DANGER: TRIPWIRE!
- FACTION: IRRADIATED WILDLIFE (RADROACHES)
- FACTION: RAIDERS
- HEALTH OR CHEMS

## VAULT-TEC RECOMMENDED LOOT

**ARMAMENTS AND AMMO: MINI NUKE**

**REQUIRED READING: ASTOUNDINGLY AWESOME TALES**

The Catholic Church founded East Boston Prep as religious preparatory school. As the priesthood and church funding declined, local activists took over the school as a secular institution serving the immigrant population in East Boston. The school was eventually abandoned during an economic downturn before the war.

FIG 4.24B: EAST BOSTON PREPARATORY SCHOOL (INTERIOR)

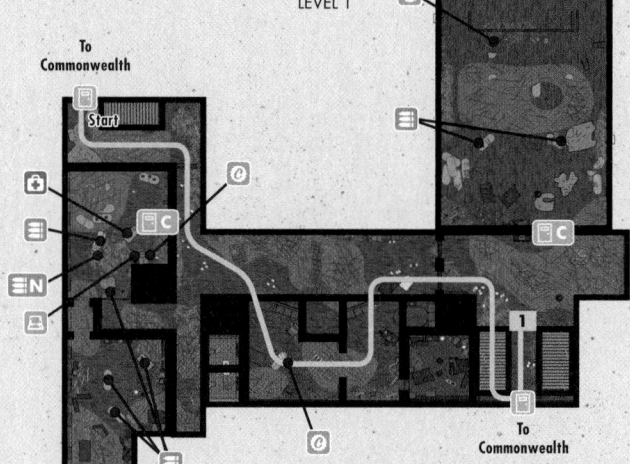

LEVEL 2

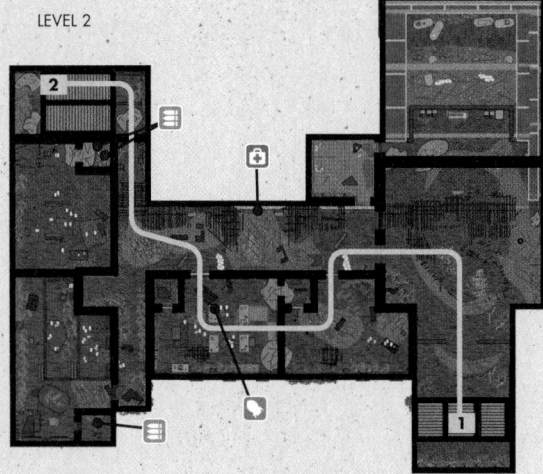

LEVEL 3

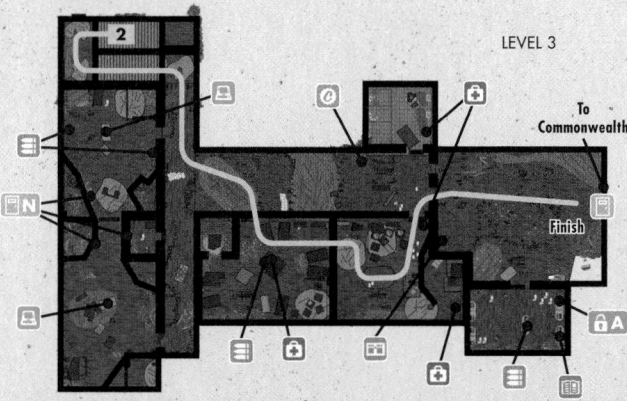

The "Traders Welcome" and other encouraging signs may be placed to coax the unwary: This location has been set up as a reeducation camp to recruit new Raiders.

Look for holes in floors and stairwells when navigating this mazelike location. The Blood Contract carried by Judge Zeller shows he was once tortured and forced into becoming a Raider.

THREAT LEVELS 25+

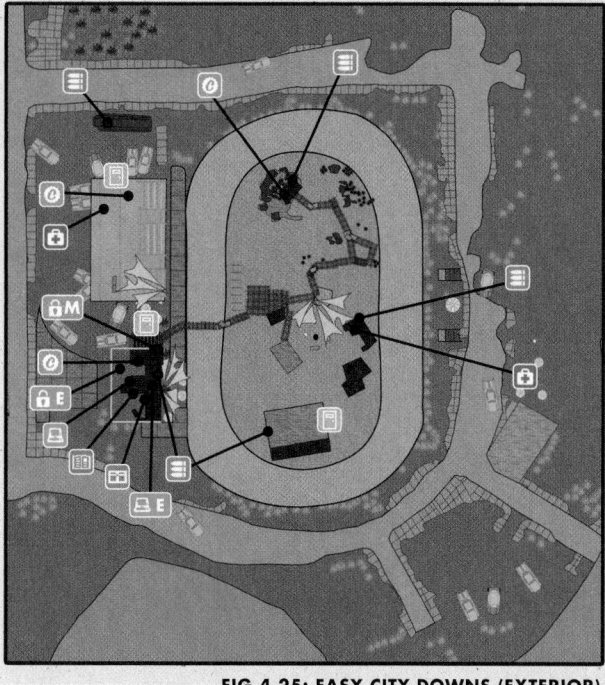

- ARMAMENTS AND AMMO+
- ARMAMENTS AND AMMO: TRUNK
- COLLECTIBLE: REQUIRED READING: TUMBLERS TODAY
- BOTTLECAPS+
- CRAFTING: ARMOR WORKBENCH
- CRAFTING: CHEMISTRY STATION
- CRAFTING: COOKING STATION
- CRAFTING: WEAPONS WORKBENCH
- DANGER: CAN CHIMES!
- DANGER: GAS LEAK!
- DANGER: GRENADES!
- DANGER: OIL!
- DANGER: MINES!
- FACTION: RAIDERS
- FACTION: ROBOTS
- FACTION: TRIGGERMEN
- FACTION: CHARACTER: ATOMIC DREAMZ
- FACTION: CHARACTER: BOB'S YOUR UNCLE
- FACTION: CHARACTER: EAGER ERNIE
- FACTION: CHARACTER: FUSION'S FOLLY
- FACTION: CHARACTER: IRON MAIDEN
- FACTION: CHARACTER: LADY LOVELACE
- FACTION: CHARACTER: OL' RUSTY
- FACTION: CHARACTER: PIECE O' JUNK
- FACTION: CHARACTER: THE BOSTON BLASTER
- FACTION: CHARACTER: TIN MAN
- HEALTH OR CHEMS

## VAULT-TEC RECOMMENDED LOOT

**REQUIRED READING:
TUMBLERS TODAY**

This was once a small, struggling racetrack with aging facilities. It is currently occupied by a gang of Raiders and Triggermen who use the track to host their robot races.

Eager Ernie is in charge here and has a key and password to unlock any doors, allowing easy access to the downstairs clubhouse terminal (Expert) and upstairs master control terminal (Expert), as well as the Repair Shop (Advanced) and Robot Control Terminal (Novice) out in the track. Both terminals allow you to control the racing robots; come evening, they turn against their masters. There are some reserve robots to activate in the south warehouse, too. Watch for items to scavenge everywhere; don't forget to check the bus (two are locked [Novice]).

 [4.26] NORDHAGEN BEACH    THREAT LEVELS 35+

- CRAFTING: CHEMISTRY STATION
- CRAFTING: COOKING STATION
- FACTION: SETTLER
- SERVICES: WORKSHOP

A meager existence outside the safety of a vault is on show here: Two settlers till the sand and grow gourds, waiting for protection.

- ARMAMENTS AND AMMO+++
- ARMAMENTS AND AMMO: MINI NUKE
- ARMAMENTS AND AMMO: MINI NUKE (FAT MAN)
- ARMAMENTS AND AMMO: TRUNK (3)
- ARMOR PART: FUSION CORE (2)
- BOTTLECAPS+
- DANGER: CAN CHIMES!
- DANGER: ESCAPING GAS!
- DANGER: EXPLOSIVE BARRELS!
- DANGER: OIL!
- DANGER: RADIATION (MILD)!
- FACTION: BROTHERHOOD OF STEEL
- FACTION: FERAL GHOULS
- FACTION: CHARACTER: INITIATE CLARKE
- FACTION: CHARACTER: KNIGHT-SERGEANT GAVIL

- FACTION: CHARACTER: KNIGHT LUCIA
- FACTION: CHARACTER: KNIGHT RYLAN
- HEALTH OR CHEMS
- QUEST VISIT: LIBERTY REPRIMED (BROTHERHOOD OF STEEL)
- QUEST VISIT SPOILS OF WAR (BROTHERHOOD OF STEEL)
- QUEST VISIT AD VICTORIAM (BROTHERHOOD OF STEEL)
- QUEST VISIT DUTY OR DISHONOR (BROTHERHOOD OF STEEL)
- QUEST VISIT LEARNING CURVE (BROTHERHOOD OF STEEL)
- SERVICES: WORKSHOP

## VAULT-TEC RECOMMENDED LOOT

**ARMAMENTS AND AMMO: MINI NUKE (AND FAT MAN)**

**ARMOR PART: FUSION CORE (2)**

**FIG 4.27A: BOSTON AIRPORT (EXTERIOR)**

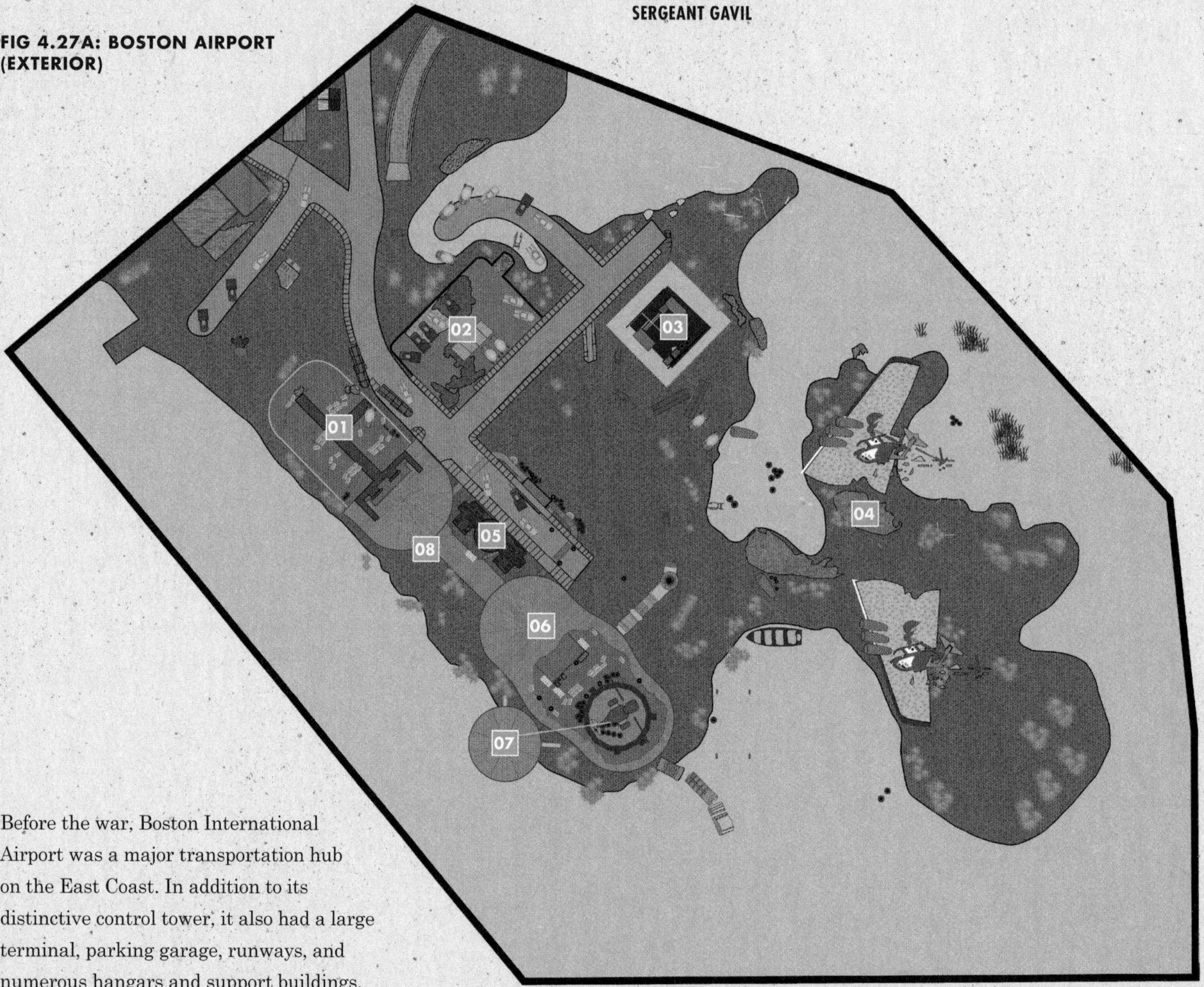

Before the war, Boston International Airport was a major transportation hub on the East Coast. In addition to its distinctive control tower, it also had a large terminal, parking garage, runways, and numerous hangars and support buildings.

The airport suffered heavily from the war. Most of its major buildings, including large sections of the terminal, have long since collapsed, and the rising sea levels have swamped the low-lying runways and outbuildings. Only the control tower and a few hangars remain relatively intact. After mooring the Prydwen at the airport in Act II, the Brotherhood occupy the area and turn it into the base of operations for their war machine in Act III.

The following assumes the Brotherhood of Steel has arrived at this location. If you explore prior to this point, expect fewer terminals and items and many more frothing ferals.

## [01] Arrivals Terminal

The workshop here allows you to build a settlement in relative safety, unless you decide not to ally yourself with the Brotherhood of Steel. Behind the two inaccessible security doors is an airport warehouse—a secret construction shop where a war machine is being built. This eventually is moved to Location 05. Attempt to access this airport warehouse from Location 06, and the wall terminal is inaccessible (only Proctor Ingram can access it). Don't forget to check the ruined "open air" upper floor above the workshop for a Mini Nuke.

## [02] Departure Terminal Parking Lot

Only the ground and roof levels of this structure are accessible (from the outer concrete stairs). There's health here and impressive views (or sniping opportunities) of the airport. Before the Brotherhood arrives, or if you've sided against them, you may also be able to access the Boston Airport Ruins from the elevator.

## [03] Maintenance Warehouse

A rusting exterior warehouse by the bay, with some health and an ammo box tucked away. Useful as a rest spot between battles.

## [04] Aircraft Wreckage

Picked clean by scavengers of the past, the aircraft fuselage and other pieces of twisted metal provide good cover if fighting foes from this location.

## [05] Main Concourse

Dominated by a giant scaffold gantry for one of the Brotherhood of Steel's war machines, this is where Proctor Ingram constructs the equipment needed to get this project online.

## [06] Departures Terminal

The Brotherhood of Steel will turn the ground floor into a supply depot. There are two side corridors that wrap around to a large set of steps up to a Vertibird landing area. There's a good amount of ammo and chems here. To the southwest is a corridor to the control tower. Look for two steamer trunks here, one on the ground floor and the other atop the tower. To the northwest is a corridor that leads to metal battlements and the main concourse (war machine scaffold access). To the northeast is a departure tube out to the remains of the airfield.

## [07] Control Tower (Prydwen Mooring)

Take the elevator from the arrivals terminal to reach the top of the control tower. This offers impressive views and whatever defenses (usually turrets) the Brotherhood of Steel have erected. There is a generator here, along with a mooring rope attached to Prydwen, when it docks here.

## [08] Boston Airport Ruins (Entrance)

You can access this door leading to an abandoned airport tunnel system at any time. However, the Brotherhood of Steel: Duty or Dishonor quest must be active to complete navigation of this location.

## FIG 4.27B: BOSTON AIRPORT RUINS (INTERIOR)

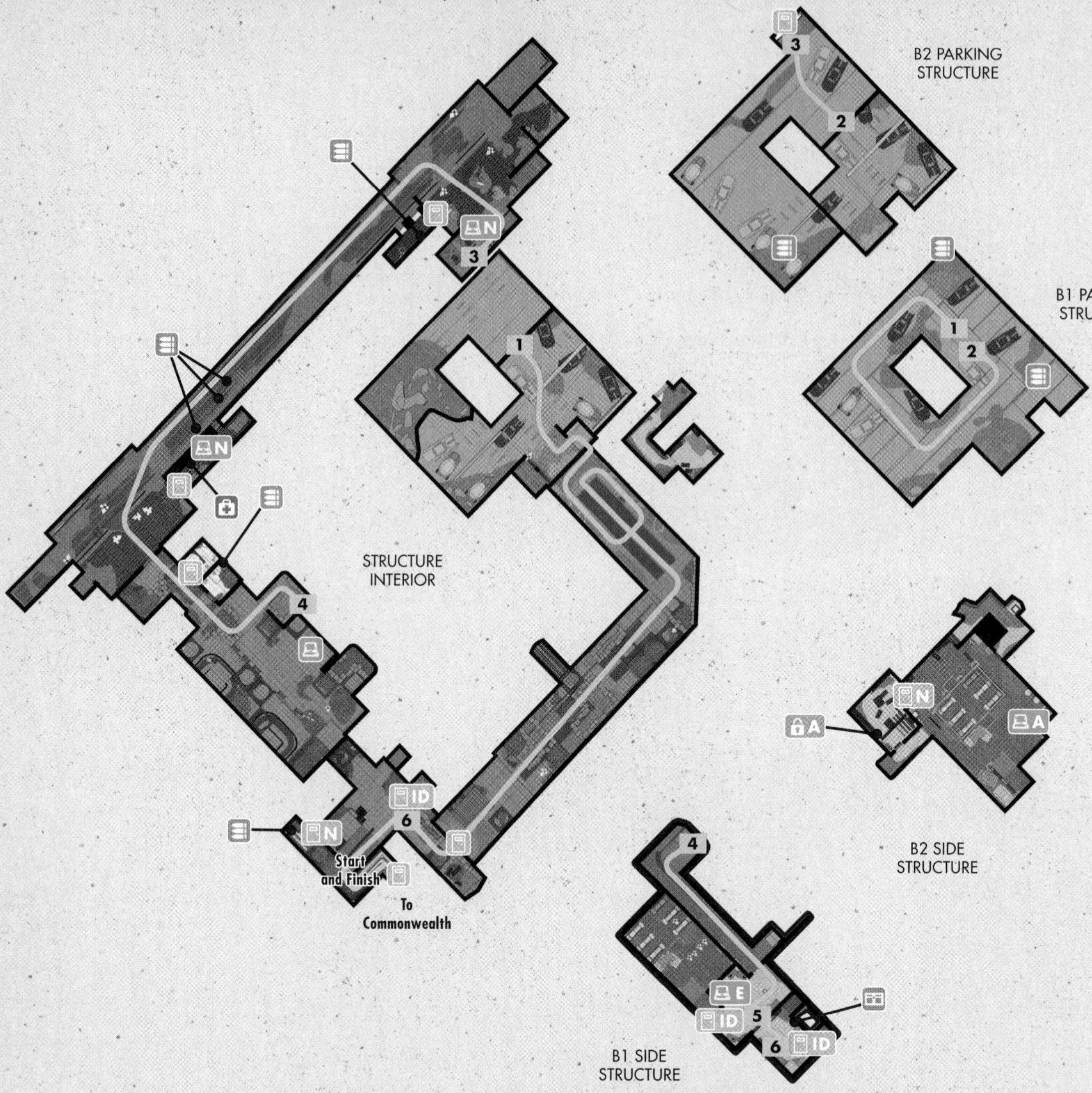
B2 PARKING STRUCTURE
B1 PARKING STRUCTURE
STRUCTURE INTERIOR
B2 SIDE STRUCTURE
B1 SIDE STRUCTURE
Start and Finish
To Commonwealth

Most of the Airport Ruins can only be explored during Brotherhood of Steel: Duty or Dishonor. You'll need the Airport Ruins ID Card, found on or near Initiate Clarke during the quest, to unlock the Airport Facilities elevator and several doors. The ruins consist of a partly flooded parking lot, a subway station, a baggage claim, and maintenance chambers. Be sure to loot a third trunk from here and a second Fusion Core.

Fly
Horizon Skyways

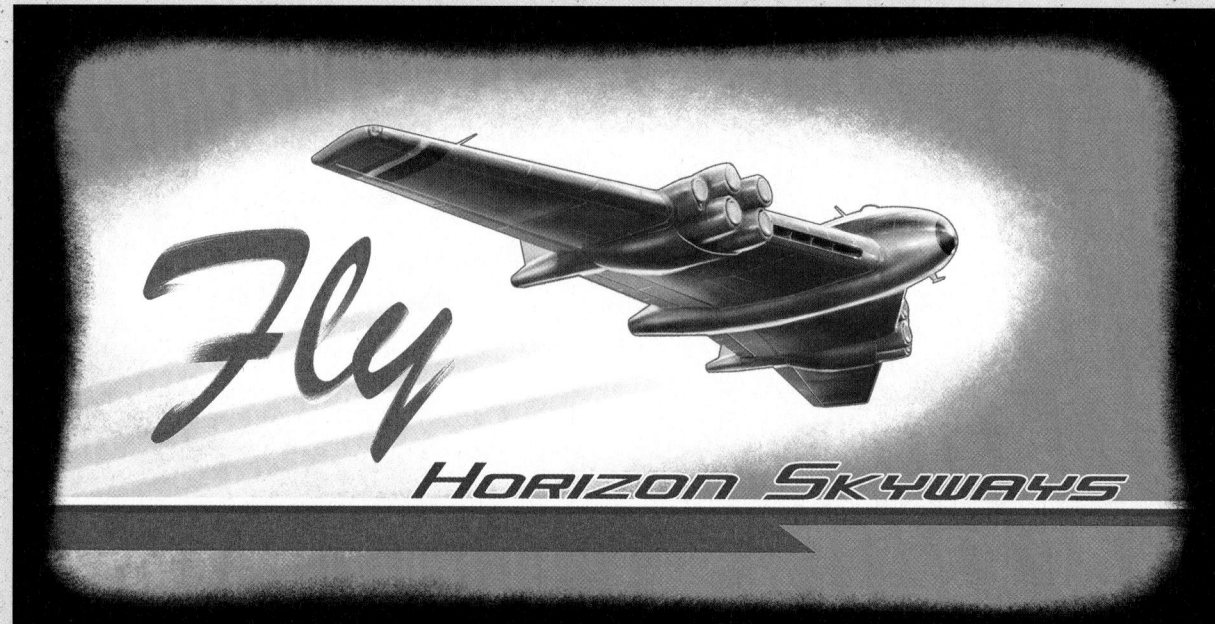

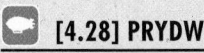

## VAULT-TEC RECOMMENDED LOOT

**ARMAMENTS AND AMMO: MINI NUKE (5+) AND FAT MAN**
**ARMOR PART: FUSION CORE**
**ARMOR PART: POWER ARMOR (T-60B)**
**COLLECTIBLE: NUKA COLA QUANTUM**

**UNIQUE ITEM: DEATH FROM ABOVE (WEAPON)**
**UNIQUE ITEM: EXEMPLAR'S T-60C TORSO**
**UNIQUE ITEM: FINAL JUDGEMENT (WEAPON)**
**UNIQUE ITEM: HONOR (APPAREL)**

**UNIQUE ITEM: SENTINEL'S PLASMACASTER (WEAPON)**
**UNIQUE ITEM: STEADFAST BOS COMBAT ARMOR CHEST PIECE (APPAREL)**
**UNIQUE ITEM: T-60 MEDIC PUMP (APPAREL)**
**UNIQUE ITEM: X-01 HELMET (APPAREL)**

**UNIQUE ITEM: VENGEANCE (APPAREL)**
**UNIQUE ITEM: VISIONARY'S T-60C HELM (APPAREL)**
**UNIQUE ITEM: VERTIBIRD SIGNAL GRENADES**
**COMPANION: PALADIN DANSE**

The Brotherhood of Steel know how to make an entrance! A giant dirigible appears once you complete Act I of your Main Quest. It is moored at Boston Airport. This becomes the base of operations for the Brotherhood of Steel for the remainder of your exploration. The ship is a marvel of engineering.

Your first access to this immense craft is during the Brotherhood of Steel quests. The craft can only be accessed by Vertibird (and Fast-Travel thereafter). Landing on the exterior flight deck, you see there are a number of Vertibird docks. The foredeck (accessed from the command deck) offers exceptional views of the Boston skyline.

- ARMAMENTS AND AMMO+++
- ARMAMENTS AND AMMO: MINI NUKE (5+)
- ARMAMENTS AND AMMO: MINI NUKE (FAT MAN)
- ARMAMENTS AND AMMO: TRUNK
- ARMOR PART: FUSION CORE
- ARMOR PART: POWER ARMOR (BOS II T-60B) (2)
- ARMOR PART: POWER ARMOR (T-60 MEDIC PUMP)
- ARMOR PART: POWER ARMOR (JETPACK)
- ARMOR PART: POWER ARMOR (VISIONARY'S T-60C HELM)
- BOTTLECAPS+++
- COLLECTIBLE: HOLOTAPE: KNIGHT-CAPTAIN CADE'S REPORT
- COLLECTIBLE: HOLOTAPE: MAXSON WAS RIGHT
- COLLECTIBLE: HOLOTAPE: PERSONAL LOG—142
- COLLECTIBLE: NUKA COLA QUANTUM
- COMPANION: PALADIN DANSE
- CRAFTING: ARMOR WORKBENCH (3)
- CRAFTING: CHEMISTRY STATION (2)
- CRAFTING: COOKING STATION
- CRAFTING: POWER ARMOR STATION (4)
- CRAFTING: WEAPONS WORKBENCH (3)
- DANGER: LONG DROP!
- FACTION: BROTHERHOOD OF STEEL
- FACTION: IRRADIATED WILDLIFE (MOLE RATS)
- FACTION: CHARACTER: ELDER MAXSON
- FACTION: CHARACTER: KNIGHT-CAPTAIN CADE
- FACTION: CHARACTER: LANCER-CAPTAIN KELLS
- FACTION: CHARACTER: PROCTOR INGRAM
- FACTION: CHARACTER: PROCTOR QUINLAN
- FACTION: CHARACTER: PROCTOR TEAGAN
- FACTION: CHARACTER: SENIOR SCRIBE NERIAH
- HEALTH OR CHEMS+++
- QUEST START: SHADOW OF STEEL (BROTHERHOOD OF STEEL)
- QUEST START: TOUR OF DUTY (BROTHERHOOD OF STEEL)
- QUEST START: SHOW NO MERCY (BROTHERHOOD OF STEEL)
- QUEST START: FROM WITHIN (BROTHERHOOD OF STEEL)
- QUEST START: OUTSIDE THE WIRE (BROTHERHOOD OF STEEL)
- QUEST START: LIBERTY REPRIMED (BROTHERHOOD OF STEEL)
- QUEST START: BLIND BETRAYAL (BROTHERHOOD OF STEEL)
- QUEST START: TACTICAL THINKING (BROTHERHOOD OF STEEL)
- QUEST START: SPOILS OF WAR (BROTHERHOOD OF STEEL)
- QUEST START: A NEW DAWN (BROTHERHOOD OF STEEL)
- QUEST START: THE LOST PATROL (BROTHERHOOD OF STEEL)
- QUEST START: DUTY OR DISHONOR (BROTHERHOOD OF STEEL)
- QUEST START: A LOOSE END (BROTHERHOOD OF STEEL)
- QUEST START: LEARNING CURVE (BROTHERHOOD OF STEEL)
- QUEST START: FEEDING THE TROOPS (BROTHERHOOD OF STEEL)
- QUEST START: GETTING TECHNICAL (BROTHERHOOD OF STEEL)
- QUEST START: BLOOD SAMPLES (BROTHERHOOD OF STEEL)
- QUEST VISIT: REVEILLE (BROTHERHOOD OF STEEL)
- QUEST VISIT: AIRSHIP DOWN (THE INSTITUTE)
- QUEST VISIT: ROCKETS RED GLARE (THE RAILROAD)
- QUEST VISIT: WITH OUR POWERS COMBINED (THE MINUTEMEN)
- SERVICES: TRADER (KNIGHT-CAPTAIN CADE)
- SERVICES: TRADER (PROCTOR TEAGAN)
- UNIQUE ITEM: BROTHERHOOD COMBAT ARMOR
- UNIQUE ITEM: T-60 MEDIC PUMP
- UNIQUE ITEM: X-01 HELMET
- UNIQUE ITEM: VERTIBIRD SIGNAL GRENADES
- UNIQUE ITEM: VISIONARY'S T-60C HELM

MAP

**ZONE 4**

COASTAL COMMONWEALTH

## FIG 4.28A: PRYDWEN MAIN DECK (INTERIOR)

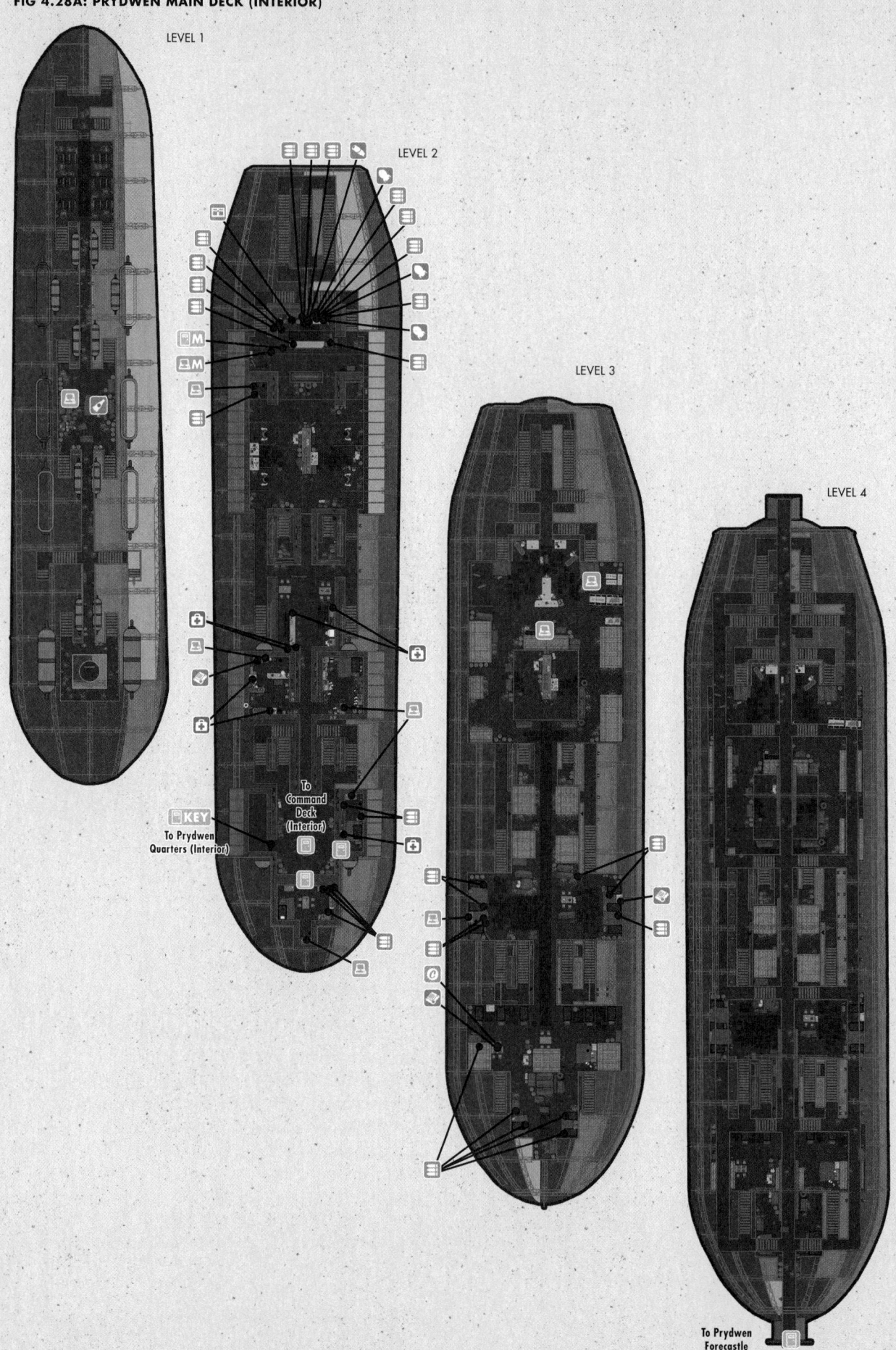

LEVEL 1

LEVEL 2

LEVEL 3

LEVEL 4

KEY

To Prydwen
Quarters (Interior)

To
Command
Deck
(Interior)

To Prydwen
Forecastle
(Exterior)

**FIG 4.28B: PRYDWEN COMMAND DECK (INTERIOR)**

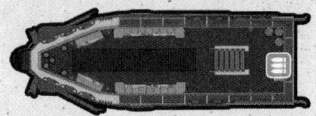

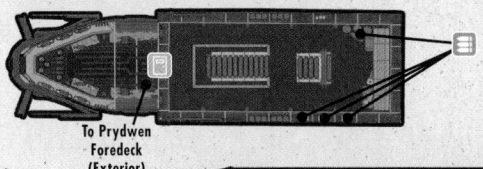

To Prydwen
Foredeck
(Exterior)

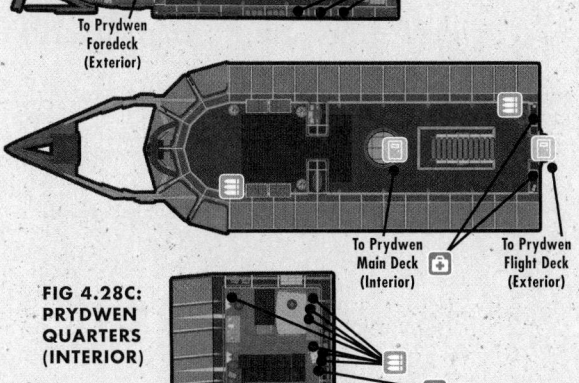

To Prydwen
Main Deck
(Interior)

To Prydwen
Flight Deck
(Exterior)

**FIG 4.28C:
PRYDWEN
QUARTERS
(INTERIOR)**

To Prydwen
Main Deck

The interior of this craft houses the various crew quarters, maintenance areas, medical facilities, and laboratories. Once allied with this faction, you are free to utilize the various workbenches, stations, and your own private quarters where items can be stored. Also visit the named personnel for a variety of tasks. Of particular note is Proctor Teagan, who has some excellent armor, ammunition, and weaponry for sale. However, as the quests for this faction progress, Mini Nukes can be appropriated from the weapons storage on the main deck.

**HELPFUL HINT** *from Vault Boy!*

*Did You Know?*

THOSE BROTHERHOOD OF STEEL TYPES HAVE QUITE THE COLLECTION OF GEAR, DON'T THEY? MOST OF THE GOODIES LISTED HERE MUST BE GIVEN AS QUEST REWARDS FOR A JOB WELL DONE OR ARE FOUND AT PROCTOR TEAGAN'S STORE. NATURALLY, IT'S BETTER TO GATHER ALL OF THESE ITEMS BEFORE PLANNING A POSSIBLE CHANGE OF ALLEGIANCE!

## [4.29] FORT STRONG

THREAT LEVELS 35+

**VAULT-TEC RECOMMENDED LOOT**

**ARMAMENTS AND AMMO: MINI NUKE (3) AND FAT MAN**
**ARMOR PART: FUSION CORE**
**ARMOR PART: POWER ARMOR (LEVELED)**
**REQUIRED READING: U.S. COVERT OPERATIONS MANUAL**

- ARMAMENTS AND AMMO++
- ARMAMENTS AND AMMO: MINI NUKE (3)
- ARMAMENTS AND AMMO: MINI NUKE (FAT MAN)
- ARMAMENTS AND AMMO: TRUNK
- ARMOR PART: FUSION CORE
- ARMOR PART: POWER ARMOR (LEVELED)
- ARMOR PART: POWER ARMOR (LEVELED)
- BOTTLECAPS
- COLLECTIBLE: HOLOTAPE: PRIVATE MURNAHAN'S HOLOTAPE
- COLLECTIBLE: REQUIRED READING: U.S. COVERT OPERATIONS MANUAL
- CRAFTING: ARMOR WORKBENCH
- DANGER: RADIATION (MILD)!
- FACTION: SUPER MUTANTS
- HEALTH OR CHEMS
- QUEST VISIT: SHOW NO MERCY (BROTHERHOOD OF STEEL)

**FIG 4.29A: FORT STRONG (EXTERIOR)**

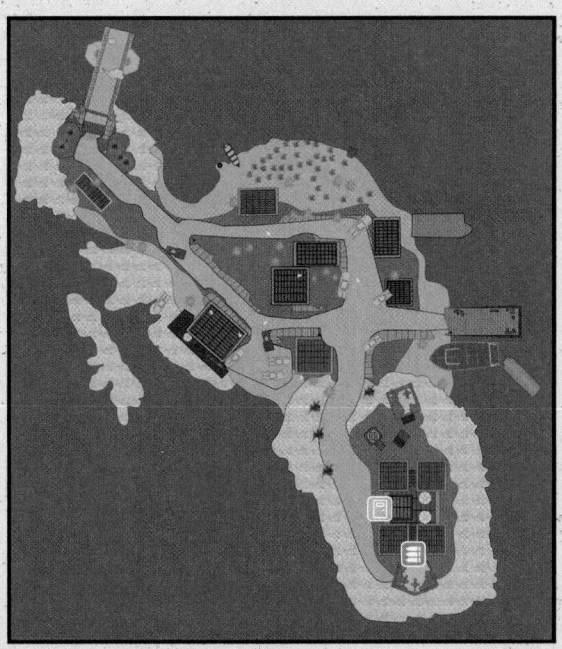

Fort Strong is an old military base. The island it sits on was used as a gun battery as far back as the Revolutionary War, and the fort itself dates to the Civil War. It had been abandoned for almost a century when the military quietly reoccupied it in the 2050s for use as a top-secret weapons research facility. The fort's exterior and outbuildings were left intact, but its interior was retrofitted and a basement level was dug to house the new laboratories and a sizable armory.

Live weapons testing began on the island in the early 2070s, with the fort's long-abandoned outbuildings used as targets. Among other weapons, the Fat Man and its Mini Nukes were invented here and first tested on the artillery range. But in October 2077, the island was hastily sealed up and its scientists evacuated.

To the north (not shown on the map) is a security kiosk with parts of a Power Armor suit and some ammo. Check under the bridge for a wooden crate. Otherwise, the road into the main armory building is devoid of scavengable items. Super Mutants are an ever-present danger; more so if the quest is active. Expect exceptionally heavy resistance if the quest is occurring.

**FIG 4.29B: FORT STRONG ARMORY (INTERIOR)**

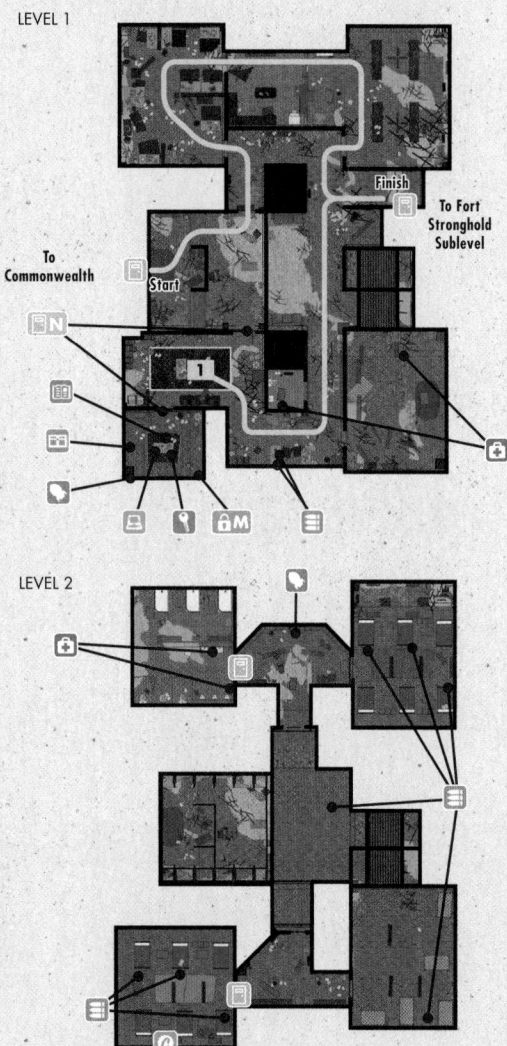

**FIG 4.29C: FORT STRONG SUBLEVEL (INTERIOR)**

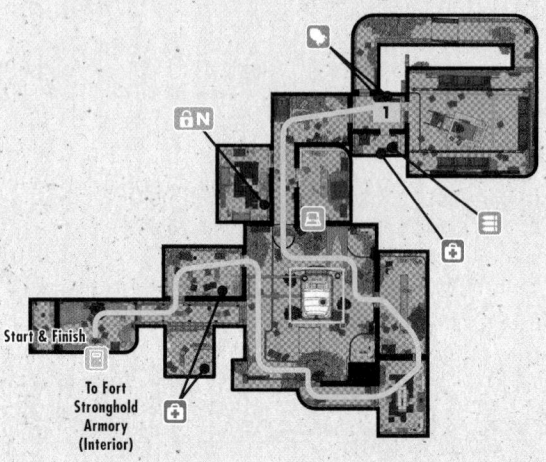

Additional Super Mutants are active in this lower level. Remove the threats as you wish. This is the place to stock up on Mini Nukes.

Once the specified quest has been completed, expect the Brotherhood of Steel to occupy this location. Return here if you're allied with them and wish to take advantage of their hospitality (though this does not extend to any additional quests).

Parts of this location, including the elevator to the sublevel, are inaccessible unless the specified quest is active.

The Fort Strong Key is found in the general's desk, in the locked (Novice) room to the southwest (along with a trunk and Mini Nuke). Reach the main part of the upper floor via the fallen section under the meat bags in the reception room. Reach the southern part of the upper floor by leaping up the fallen ceiling in the conference room to the southeast.

# SECONDARY LOCATIONS

## [4.01] GUNNER CAMP (PARSONS ELEVATED FREEWAY)

- ARMAMENTS AND AMMO
- DANGER: LONG DROP!
- FACTION: GUNNERS

A windmill-generated Gunner encampment is easy to spot; the windmill gives away its position. Use the construction lift at the location indicated, and assault the camp, gathering minor loot and ammo.

## [4.02] MILTON GENERAL BILLBOARD

- BOTTLECAPS

Go for a quick Bottlecaps run here, by the skeleton and gas canisters on the billboard gantry.

## [4.03] COASTAL VACATIONERS

- DANGER: OIL!
- DANGER: RADIATION (MILD)!
- FACTION: FERAL GHOULS

The irradiated inlet bay north of Mahkra Fishpacking has a number of frothing ferals to remove. Fortunately, they can't swim.

## [4.04] COASTAL HIDEOUT

- ARMOR PART: FUSION CORE
- FACTION: FERAL GHOULS

A door under the bridge to Mahkra Fishpacking reveals a small subterranean hideout, with some guests already inside. Open the cell door (Novice) for a quick toilet inspection.

## [4.05] THE SUNKEN BATHTUB

- ARMAMENTS AND AMMO: TRUNK

Dive below the red buoy to reach a sunken bathtub and nearby steamer trunk. The trunk appears randomly.

## [4.06] SHANTY STORE

- ARMAMENTS AND AMMO
- CHARACTER: LEONARD MOORE
- SERVICES: TRADER (LEONARD MOORE)

An enterprising soul trades scrap and ammo from here. His only companion is Jangles, a moon monkey.

## [4.07] SALEM COASTAL DINER AND DOCK

- ARMAMENTS AND AMMO
- DANGER: EXPLOSIVE BARRELS!

West of Salem is a small shack diner on a bluff overlooking a rickety dock. There's a floor safe (Expert) to inspect and some frightening-looking dead sea life on the shore.

## [4.08] RAIDER SHACK (SALEM OUTSKIRTS)

- ARMAMENTS AND AMMO
- CRAFTING: COOKING STATION

This makeshift tarp shack is in the scrubland outside Salem's Witchcraft Museum.

## [4.09] KINGSPORT RESTROOMS

- HEALTH OR CHEMS

The concrete brick structure provides some relief during your travels.

### [4.10] OCEAN FISHING SHACK

- ARMAMENTS AND AMMO

A collection of wood and metal roughly fashioned into a fishing platform attached to the rocks off the coast.

### [4.11] SUNKEN FISHING BOAT

- ARMAMENTS AND AMMO: TRUNK
- HEALTH OR CHEMS

At the bottom of the ocean is an overturned fishing boat. Look for the boat on your local map before diving. The trunk randomly appears.

### [4.12] VITALE PUMPHOUSE

- ARMAMENTS AND AMMO: TRUNK
- ARMOR PART: FUSION CORE
- DANGER: ESCAPING GAS!

A well-locked pumphouse with a trunk to rummage around in requires you to figure out the four-digit unlock code for the door. Fortunately, the wall under the stairs has the clue you need.

### [4.13] OCEAN RAFT

- HEALTH OR CHEMS

It's difficult to tell whether this is a collection of flotsam and jetsam or if someone actually nailed this together. Take in the views—ideally not of the gutted and mutated sea creature.

### [4.14] UNLOADING BARGE

- ARMAMENTS AND AMMO
- ARMOR PART: POWER ARMOR (LEVELED)
- FACTION: ROBOTS

A collection of cargo crates, two APCs, and some mechanical guards.

### [4.15] NAHANT PIER RESTAURANT

- ARMAMENTS AND AMMO: TRUNK
- COLLECTIBLE: NUKA CHERRY
- FACTION: FERAL GHOULS

This ruined café and Railroad dead drop has a (randomly appearing) trunk on the top floor (southeast corner). On a ground-floor table is a Nuka Cherry.

350

## [4.16] DRUMLIN DINER (EAST BOSTON)

– ARMAMENTS AND AMMO

Aside from some comestibles, the unlocked floor safe of this shoreline diner is where you should focus your scavenging.

## [4.17] WATERFRONT WAREHOUSE

– CRAFTING: ARMOR WORKBENCH
– CRAFTING: WEAPONS WORKBENCH

The remains of a warehouse with an equally decrepit truck rusting inside.

## [4.18] EAST BOSTON GARAGE

– ARMAMENTS AND AMMO
– ARMAMENTS AND AMMO: TRUNK

Look above water height in this warehouse-sized garage outside the police station; there's a steamer trunk on a larger crate and more ammo loot upstairs.

## [4.19] CONTAINER CRATES STASH

– ARMAMENTS AND AMMO
– CRAFTING: COOKING STATION

Climb the ramp of the rusting truck and hop across the containers to reach this loot.

## [4.20] FREEWAY ROOFTOPS

– ARMAMENTS AND AMMO
– HEALTH OR CHEMS

The rusting fire escape on this structure allows you (with some deft jumping) to reach the upper freeway. Stroll north and gather some loot from a blue tent.

## [4.21] UPSIDE DOWN ROWBOAT

– ARMAMENTS AND AMMO: TRUNK

After getting into choppy waters off the coast, a small rowboat sank. It is said there's a (randomly appearing) trunk of items to loot from under the hull. Look for the boat outline on your Pip-Boy's local map before diving.

## [4.22] DOOMED AIRLINES FLIGHT

– ARMAMENTS AND AMMO: TRUNK
– HEALTH OR CHEMS

The rusting fuselage of a doomed flight, which fell into the ocean southeast of Fort Strong. Swim through the cockpit window to find a trunk (appearing randomly).

## [4.23] FLOATING BARGE

– HEALTH OR CHEMS

Moored by a cable to the ocean floor, this is the perfect spot to relax in relative safety.

# ZONE 5: NATICK AND THE GLOWING SEA

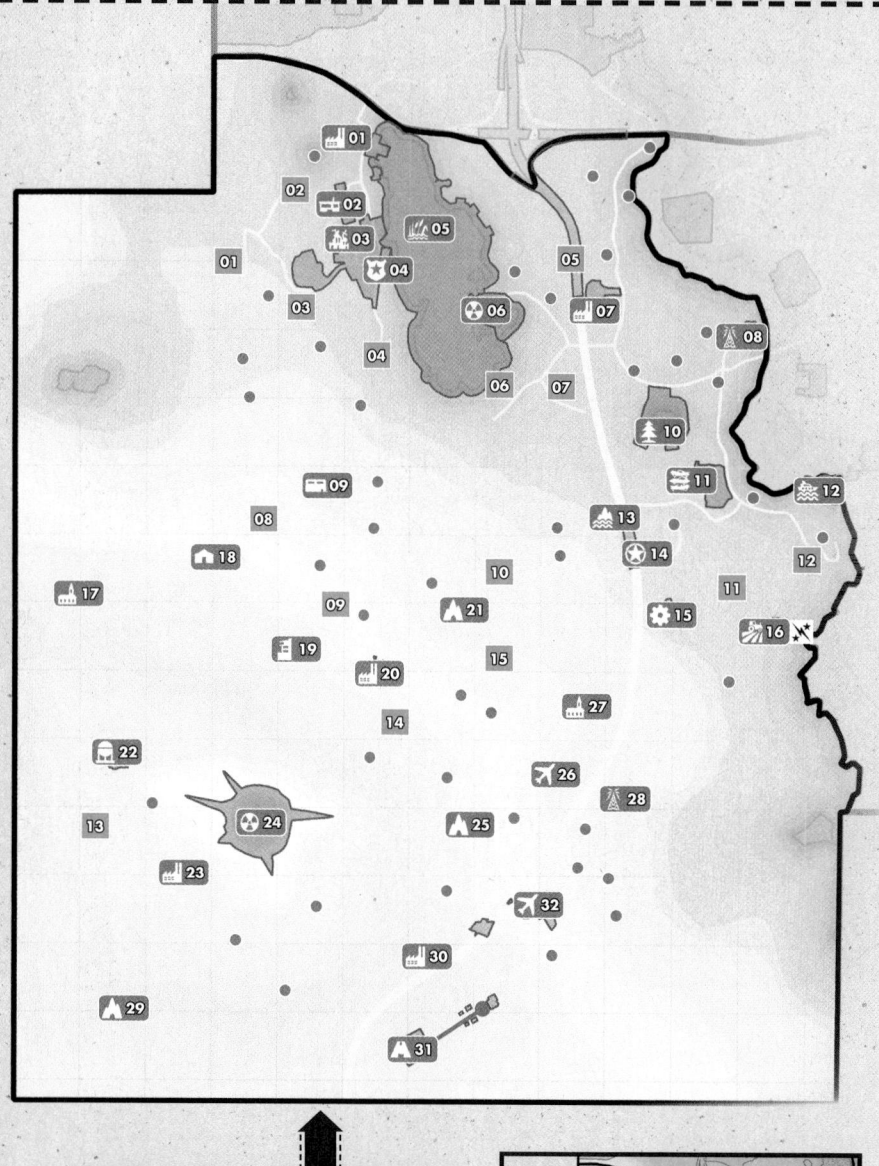

Complete and utter desolation as far as your blistered, irradiated eyes can see. A perpetual cloud of radiation haze. Fierce and toxic storms. If the Deathclaws and Radscorpions don't get you, the radiation sickness might. This is the epicenter of a massive (and highly successful) nuclear strike centered on what is known colloquially as the Crater of Atom. While the northern and riverside fringes of this zone are relatively free of radiation, be sure to stock up on chems and wear proper protective attire once you're south of Natick. Welcome to the Glowing Sea.

## Primary Locations

- [5.01] POSEIDON RESERVOIR
- [5.02] ROADSIDE PINES MOTEL
- [5.03] NATICK BANKS
- [5.04] NATICK POLICE DEPARTMENT
- [5.05] LAKE COCHITUATE
- [5.06] MASS FUSION DISPOSAL SITE
- [5.07] ELECTRICAL HOBBYIST'S CLUB
- [5.08] WRVR BROADCAST STATION
- [5.09] FEDERAL SUPPLY CACHE 84NE
- [5.10] ROBOTICS PIONEER PARK
- [5.11] SCRAP PALACE
- [5.12] CUTLER BEND
- [5.13] EDGE OF THE GLOWING SEA
- [5.14] WAYPOINT ECHO
- [5.15] VAULT 95
- [5.16] SOMERVILLE PLACE
- [5.17] FORGOTTEN CHURCH
- [5.18] ABANDONED SHACK
- [5.19] ATLANTIC OFFICES
- [5.20] CAPSIZED FACTORY
- [5.21] CAVE (RED ROCKET FILLING STATION)
- [5.22] DECAYED REACTOR SITE
- [5.23] DECREPIT FACTORY
- [5.24] CRATER OF ATOM
- [5.25] CAVE (SUPER DUPER MART)
- [5.26] VERTIBIRD WRECKAGE
- [5.27] HOPESMARCH PENTECOSTAL CHURCH
- [5.28] RELAY TOWER 0DB-521
- [5.29] ROCKY CAVE (VIRGIL'S LABORATORY)
- [5.30] O'NEILL FAMILY MANUFACTURING
- [5.31] SENTINEL SITE
- [5.32] SKYLANES FLIGHT 1665

## WORLD MAP LEGEND

- ∿ ZONE AND NEIGHBORHOOD BOUNDARY
- [01] SECONDARY LOCATION
- ● POINT OF INTEREST
- 🏠[01] PRIMARY LOCATION
- ⬡ PRIMARY LOCATION BOUNDARY
- ─ UNDERGROUND LINK
- ⚒ WORKSHOP

## THREAT LEVEL MAP

1-5  6-14  15-25  20+  25+  30+  35+  40+  45+

EXPECTED LEVEL OF ENEMIES ENCOUNTERED

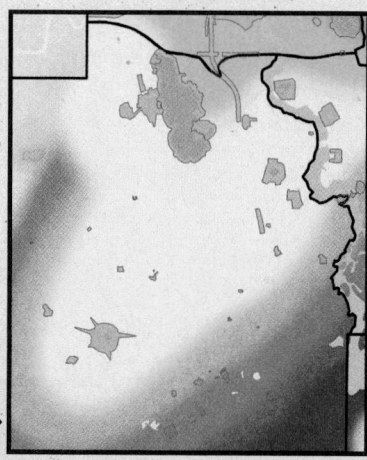

## Secondary Locations

- [5.01] NATICK POWER STATION
- [5.02] NATICK HILLSIDE HOME
- [5.03] SETTLER CAMPSITE (NATICK OUTSKIRTS)
- [5.04] MILITARY CHECKPOINT (LAKE COCHITUATE)
- [5.05] THE MAUSOLEUM

- [5.06] FISHING CABIN
- [5.07] TWO CABINS AND AN OUTHOUSE
- [5.08] COLLAPSED BILLBOARD (GLOWING SEA)
- [5.09] BURIED MANSION
- [5.10] RADIATION LAKE

- [5.11] MILITARY PILLBOX (SOMERVILLE)
- [5.12] THE SPLINTERED STATUE
- [5.13] DERELICT BUS
- [5.14] BURIED HOUSE
- [5.15] BUCKLED FREEWAY

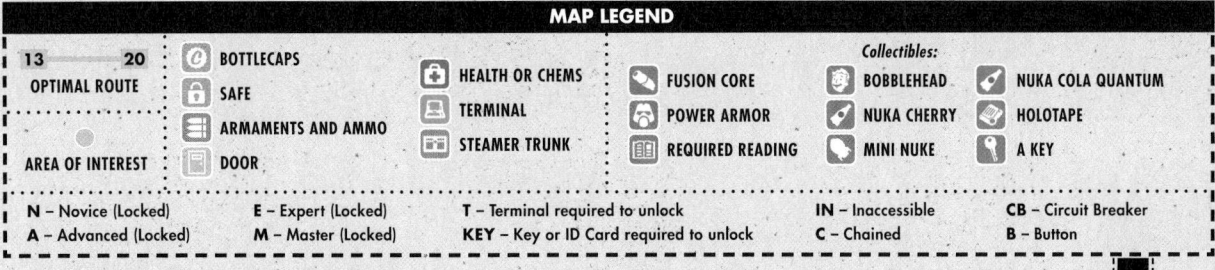

**MAP LEGEND**

| 13 ——— 20 OPTIMAL ROUTE | | |
| AREA OF INTEREST | | |

- C BOTTLECAPS
- SAFE
- ARMAMENTS AND AMMO
- DOOR

- HEALTH OR CHEMS
- TERMINAL
- STEAMER TRUNK

- FUSION CORE
- POWER ARMOR
- REQUIRED READING

Collectibles:
- BOBBLEHEAD
- NUKA CHERRY
- MINI NUKE

- NUKA COLA QUANTUM
- HOLOTAPE
- A KEY

| N – Novice (Locked) | E – Expert (Locked) | T – Terminal required to unlock | IN – Inaccessible | CB – Circuit Breaker |
| A – Advanced (Locked) | M – Master (Locked) | KEY – Key or ID Card required to unlock | C – Chained | B – Button |

# PRIMARY LOCATIONS

## [5.01] POSEIDON RESERVOIR

THREAT LEVELS 25+

- ARMAMENTS AND AMMO
- ARMAMENTS AND AMMO: TRUNK
- COLLECTIBLE: ROBOT MODEL KIT (PARTS)
- CRAFTING: ARMOR WORKBENCH
- CRAFTING: CHEMISTRY STATION
- CRAFTING: WEAPONS WORKBENCH
- DANGER: ESCAPING GAS!
- DANGER: EXPLOSIVE BARRELS!
- DANGER: OIL!
- DANGER: RADIATION (MILD)!
- FACTION: FERAL GHOULS
- HEALTH OR CHEMS

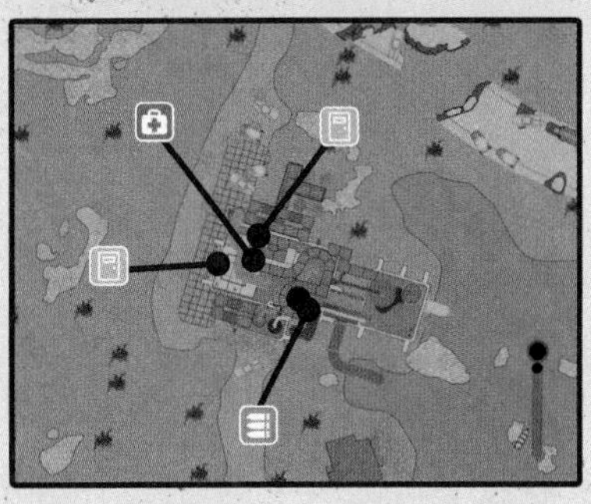

FIG 5.01A: POSEIDON RESERVOIR (EXTERIOR)

To Commonwealth

LEVEL 3

LEVEL 2

LEVEL 1

FIG 5.01B: POSEIDON RESERVOIR (INTERIOR)

MAP

ZONE 5

NATICK AND THE GLOWING SEA

## VAULT-TEC RECOMMENDED LOOT

COLLECTIBLE: ROBOT MODEL KIT PARTS

Poseidon Energy Reservoir not only distributed water to the surrounding farmlands and towns, but it was also a source of hydroelectric power. The power generated was used by Poseidon for its research facilities scattered about the Commonwealth. Currently, the reservoir is in a state of disrepair. The hydroelectric generators no longer operate and the water has become stagnant.

## [5.02–5.04] NATICK TOWNSHIP

**FIG 5.02: NATICK (TOWNSHIP)**

The roof gantries are easy to access, and the ferals up here can be wiped out while you gaze south at Natick and Lake Cochituate. Inside, the terminal in the first metal office pod opens the security doors leading deeper into the facility. The Poseidon Reservoir Safe Key is on top of the metal pod, near a locked toolbox (Expert). Also check the broken pipe on the south wall of the main building; it leads to a Railroad dead drop with some loot and a robot model kit. Nice!

### [5.02] ROADSIDE PINES MOTEL

THREAT LEVELS 25+

- ARMAMENTS AND AMMO
- ARMAMENTS AND AMMO: TRUNK
- ARMOR PARTS: FUSION CORE
- ARMOR PARTS: POWER ARMOR (RAIDER)
- CRAFTING: CHEMISTRY STATION
- DANGER: CAN CHIMES!
- DANGER: MAKESHIFT BOMB!
- DANGER: RADIATION (MILD)!
- DANGER: TRIPWIRE!
- FACTION: RAIDER

**VAULT-TEC RECOMMENDED LOOT**

ARMOR PART: FUSION CORE
ARMOR PART: POWER ARMOR (RAIDER)

On the north outskirts of Natick is a motel of ill repute, thanks to recent Raider activities. Check the reception floor for a safe (Novice). Grab items from the trunk in the room with the chemistry station outside. Head around the back to the generator with the Fusion Core.

### [5.03] NATICK BANKS

THREAT LEVELS 25+

- ARMAMENTS AND AMMO
- ARMAMENTS AND AMMO: TRUNK
- COLLECTIBLE: NUKA CHERRY
- CRAFTING: COOKING STATION
- CRAFTING: WEAPONS WORKBENCH
- DANGER: MINES!
- FACTION: DEATHCLAW
- FACTION: SCAVENGER
- FACTION: SUPER MUTANT
- FACTION: CHARACTER: GENE
- HEALTH OR CHEMS

**VAULT-TEC RECOMMENDED LOOT**

COLLECTIBLE: NUKA CHERRY

A small town on the banks of Lake Cochituate has suffered from major flooding and subsidence in recent times. Currently the Super Mutants that have mangled up and driven a group of Raiders north are experiencing their own demise, as a pack of Deathclaws has been active in this area.

For the scavenger about town, be certain to check the wall safe (Expert) in the ruined home west of the Red Rocket Filling Station. There's also a safe (Advanced) on the balcony upstairs in the warehouse overlooking the town. Enter the remains of the diner to secure a Nuka Cherry from the upstairs pool room. Look for the steamer trunk on the unsafe building by the water, opposite the diner.

## [5.04] NATICK POLICE DEPARTMENT

THREAT LEVELS 25+

- HEALTH OR CHEMS
- COLLECTIBLE: HOLOTAPE: EDDIE WINTER'S HOLOTAPE
- QUEST VISIT: LONG TIME COMING (SIDE)

Caution! This structure is slowly toppling into Lake Cochituate; beware of uneven flooring. The fourth of Eddie Winter's Holotapes is in an evidence locker near some first aid kits. Should you have any overdue books, return them to the book return terminal here for tokens, which you can exchange for a variety of (mainly plastic) toys.

**HELPFUL HINT** *from Vault Boy!* **Did You Know?**

ARE YOU AWARE THAT THE BOOK RETURN TERMINAL OVER AT REVERE BEACH STATION HAS A BETTER SELECTION OF ITEMS TO SWAP FOR TOKENS, INCLUDING A FUSION CORE AND STIMPAK? ARE YOU AWARE THAT THE BOOK RETURN TERMINAL OVER IN BOSTON PUBLIC LIBRARY HAS A SKILL MAGAZINE YOU CAN PURCHASE? SAVE THOSE TOKENS!

## [5.05] LAKE COCHITUATE

THREAT LEVELS 20+

THREAT LEVELS 25+

- ARMAMENTS AND AMMO
- ARMAMENTS AND AMMO: TRUNK (2)
- COLLECTIBLE: ROBOT MODEL KIT (PARTS)
- DANGER: RADIATION (MILD)!
- FACTION: MIRELURKS
- FACTION: RAIDERS
- HEALTH OR CHEMS

### VAULT-TEC RECOMMENDED LOOT

 **COLLECTIBLE: ROBOT MODEL KIT PARTS**

This was once a great fishing and recreation spot, until the contamination from the nearby disposal site shut down these activities. Now the lake stretches from the elevated freeway and Poseidon Reservoir area south by Natick to the devastated Mass Fusion Disposal Site to the south.

Check the abandoned homes on the northeastern shore for Raider and Mirelurk activity. Pay special attention to the northeast treehouse camp (there's a trunk here, and a robot model kit on an adjacent shelf). You can also find a second trunk at the bottom of the lake: Stand on the rickety jetty with the bathtub on it, facing west-southwest. Dive and swim straight ahead. The trunk is near a tree branch.

## [5.06] MASS FUSION DISPOSAL SITE

THREAT LEVELS 20+

- ARMAMENTS AND AMMO
- ARMAMENTS AND AMMO: MINI NUKE
- ARMAMENTS AND AMMO: TRUNK (2)
- DANGER: RADIATION (SEVERE)!
- FACTION: SUPER MUTANT
- HEALTH OR CHEMS

### VAULT-TEC RECOMMENDED LOOT

 **ARMAMENTS AND AMMO: MINI NUKE**

This was the property of Mass Fusion and used as a disposal site for coolants and other liquids. As much of the poisons were buried at this site, pressure has built up and the irradiated pools around the shores of the lake have bubbling gasses. Be wise: Wear radioactive protective gear at all times. Be perceptive: Locate the steamer trunk in the treehouse to the northeast. Be extra perceptive: There's a Mini Nuke inside the large tire by the yellow digging machine.

## [5.07] ELECTRICAL HOBBYIST'S CLUB

THREAT LEVELS 20+

- CRAFTING: ARMOR WORKBENCH (2)
- CRAFTING: CHEMISTRY STATION
- DANGER: MAKESHIFT BOMB!
- DANGER: MINES!
- DANGER: OIL!
- DANGER: RADIATION (MILD)!
- DANGER: TENSION TRIGGER!
- DANGER: TESLA ARC!
- DANGER: TRIPWIRES!
- DANGER: TURRETS!

A wealth of electrical junk rests inside this location, where tinkerers once met. The front door to this establishment is locked (Master), but the side entrance is heavily trapped. Both lead to a cellar, which is also heavily trapped. Listen to Hobbyist Holotapes and play with an Assaultron down here, if you're so inclined.

## [5.08] WRVR BROADCAST STATION

THREAT LEVELS 20+

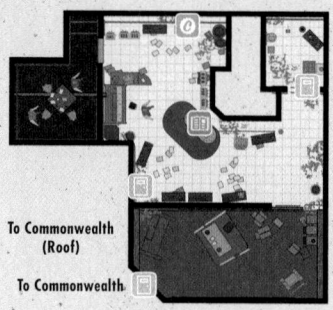

To Commonwealth
(Roof)

To Commonwealth

**FIG 5.08: WRVR BROADCAST CENTER
(INTERIOR)**

- ARMAMENTS AND AMMO
- BOTTLECAPS
- COLLECTIBLE: REQUIRED READING: LIVE & LOVE
- FACTION: SETTLER
- FACTION: CHARACTER: ANNE HARGRAVES
- FACTION: CHARACTER: GEORGE COOPER
- QUEST START: CURTAIN CALL (SIDE)
- RADIO: TRINITY TOWER RADIO

This local radio is home to the Charles River Trio and famous for their radio plays, though the third member of the group has gotten himself into a bit of a pickle. Listen to his panicked message and save him to help these folks out. Need a baseball bat? There's one on the roof.

## [5.09] FEDERAL SUPPLY CACHE 84NE

THREAT LEVELS 25+

- ARMAMENTS AND AMMO
- COLLECTIBLE: NUKA CHERRY
- CRAFTING: WEAPONS WORKBENCH
- DANGER: RADIATION (SEVERE)!
- FACTION: ROBOT (PROTECTRON)
- HEALTH OR CHEMS

Warning! Extreme radiation danger! This small federal bunker offers a brief respite from the terrors of the Glowing Sea. Check the footlockers for items, flip the circuit breaker to activate the two (hostile) Protectrons, and check the terminal (Expert). Did you find the Nuka Cherry behind the bed?

## [5.10] ROBOTICS PIONEER PARK

THREAT LEVELS 20+

- ARMAMENTS AND AMMO
- ARMAMENTS AND AMMO: TRUNK
- DANGER: RADIATION (MILD)!
- FACTION: DEATHCLAW
- FACTION: FERAL GHOUL
- FACTION: ROBOT (PROTECTRON)

A prewar memorial park built in honor of a roboticist of General Atomics International. Beware of Feral Ghouls. Of the two remaining cabins, one has a rear wall missing and a Deathclaw to face. The other has a Park Protectron Control Terminal (Novice) to hack, after which the four Protectron types can be activated. Don't leave without inspecting the cabin west of the podium for a trunk.

## [5.11] SCRAP PALACE

THREAT LEVELS 25+

- ARMAMENTS AND AMMO
- ARMAMENTS AND AMMO: TRUNK
- BOTTLECAPS
- CRAFTING: ARMOR WORKBENCH
- CRAFTING: WEAPONS WORKBENCH
- DANGER: TRIPWIRE!
- FACTION: SUPER MUTANT

This junkyard has been turned into sinew storage by a group of grotesque Super Mutants. Check upstairs in the warehouse for a safe (Expert) and steamer trunk. One of the sheds has a floor safe (Advanced) near the workbench.

**FIG 5.12: CUTLER BEND (EXTERIOR)**

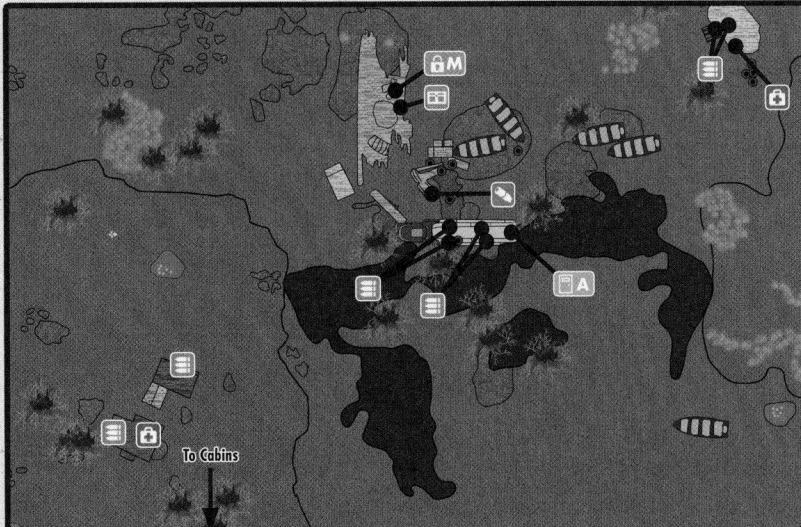

- ARMAMENTS AND AMMO
- ARMAMENTS AND AMMO: TRUNK (2)
- ARMOR PART: FUSION CORE
- BOTTLECAPS
- CRAFTING: COOKING STATION
- DANGER: MINES!
- FACTION: IRRADIATED WILDLIFE
  (MIRELURKS)
- FACTION: IRRADIATED WILDLIFE
  (STINGWINGS)
- HEALTH OR CHEMS

**VAULT-TEC RECOMMENDED LOOT**

**ARMOR PART: FUSION CORE**

A boggy mess of rusting boats, tires, and other debris forming a makeshift bridge across the Charles River. This has long been infested by Mirelurks, and the pickings are good for those with quick wits. The caravan on the east shore of the river is locked (Advanced). There's a shack on the west shore of the river.

Check the overturned white boat in the middle of this muck for a loose Fusion Core. Then make sure you inspect the small fishing boat on the river, attached to the plank, as well as the cabin southwest of the river crossing. Both locations have steamer trunks.

 **[5.13] EDGE OF THE GLOWING SEA**

THREAT LEVELS 20+

- ARMAMENTS AND AMMO          - FACTION: RAIDER
- DANGER: RADIATION (SEVERE!)

Warning! Extreme radiation danger! This small Raider encampment along the ruined freeway overpass marks the entrance to the Glowing Sea. You are strongly encouraged to wear protective clothing from this point. Climb the section of freeway to reach a rusting truck trailer to scavenge items from.

 **[5.14] WAYPOINT ECHO**

THREAT LEVELS 25+

- DANGER: TURRET!
- FACTION: BROTHERHOOD OF STEEL (QUEST ONLY)
- FACTION: CHARACTER: SCRIBE HAYLEN
- QUEST VISIT: LIBERTY REPRIMED (BROTHERHOOD OF STEEL)

Close to the entrance of the Glowing Sea is a single machine-gun turret. However, during the specified quest, this becomes a rendezvous point for you to reach.

MAP

**ZONE 5**

NATICK AND THE
GLOWING SEA

**FIG 5.15: VAULT 95 (INTERIOR)**

- ARMAMENTS AND AMMO+
- ARMAMENTS AND AMMO: TRUNK
- BOTTLECAPS
- COLLECTIBLE: BOBBLEHEAD: BIG GUNS
- COLLECTIBLE: NUKA CHERRY
- CRAFTING: ARMOR WORKBENCH
- CRAFTING: COOKING STATION (2)
- DANGER: GRENADES!
- DANGER: OIL!
- DANGER: TESLA ARC (REACTOR)!
- DANGER: TRIPWIRES!
- DANGER: TURRETS!
- FACTION: GUNNERS
- HEALTH OR CHEMS
- QUEST VISIT: BENIGN INTERVENTION

## VAULT-TEC RECOMMENDED LOOT ☢

**BOBBLEHEAD: BIG GUNS**

**COLLECTIBLE: NUKA CHERRY**

Gunners have overwhelmed the vault dwellers here and are utilizing this location for purposes other than those originally intended. You are encouraged to remove these threats. Beware of Assaultrons. Battle your way through the open vault door and reach the elevator to enter the vault's interior.

To access the facilities wing without impressive hacking skills (Master), head to the overseer's terminal on the upper floor. It is advisable to explore this location with Cait (companion). It is also advisable to check the classroom for a steamer trunk and the habitation quarters for a limited-edition Vault-Tec Bobblehead—one of a kind!

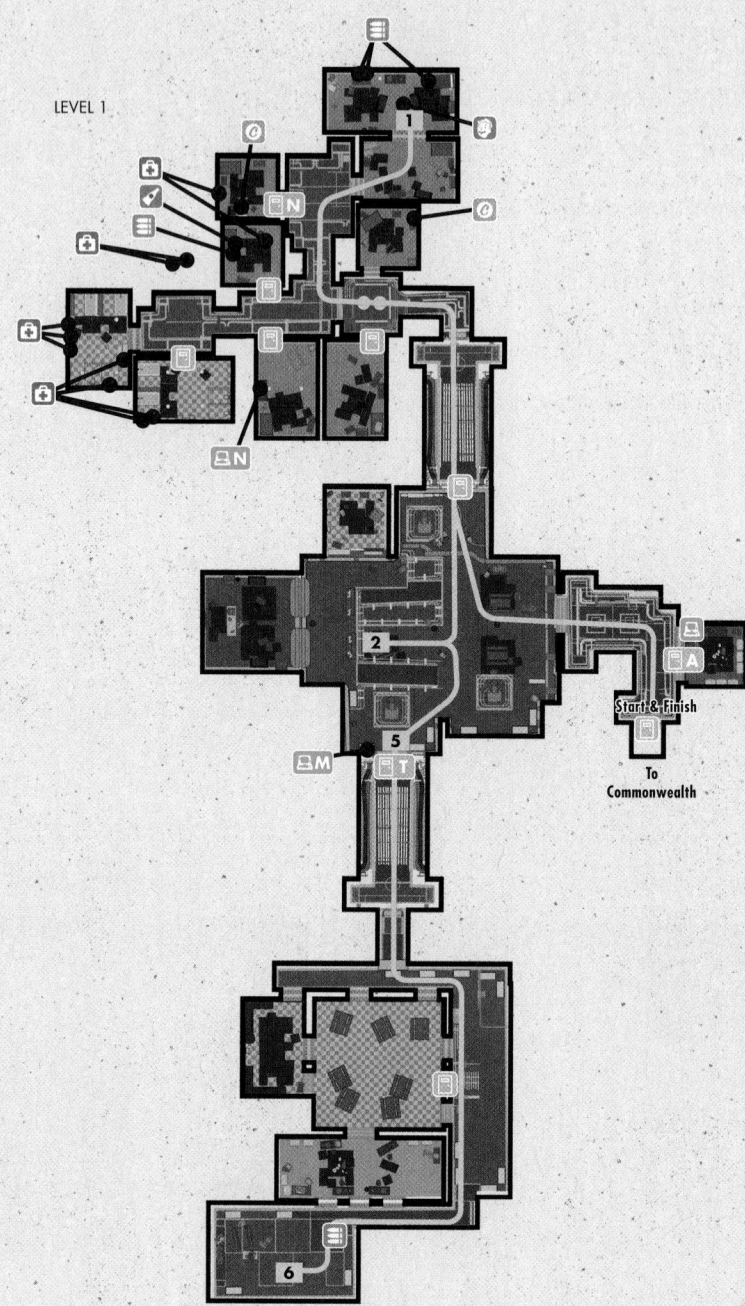

LEVEL 1

Start & Finish

To Commonwealth

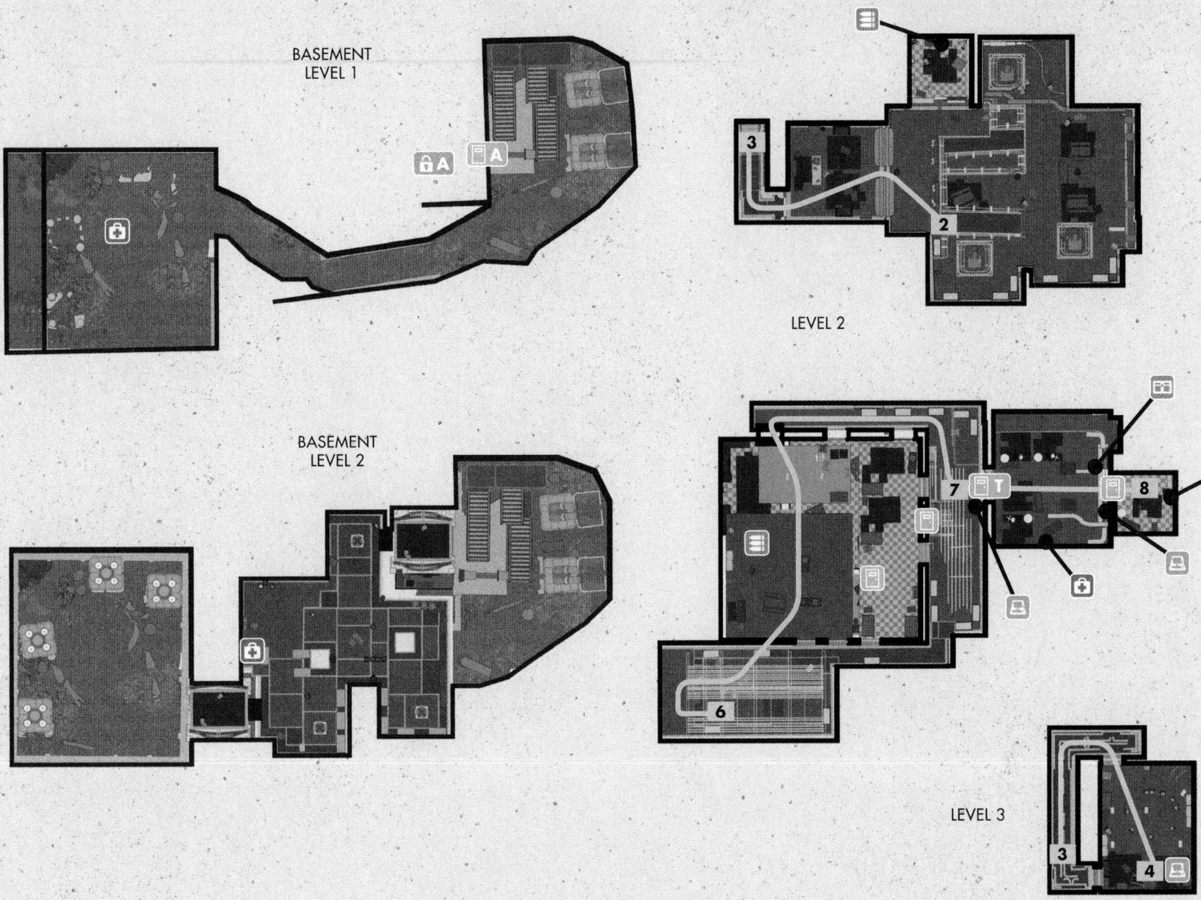
BASEMENT
LEVEL 1
A
A
3
2
LEVEL 2
BASEMENT
LEVEL 2
7
T
8
6
LEVEL 3
3
4

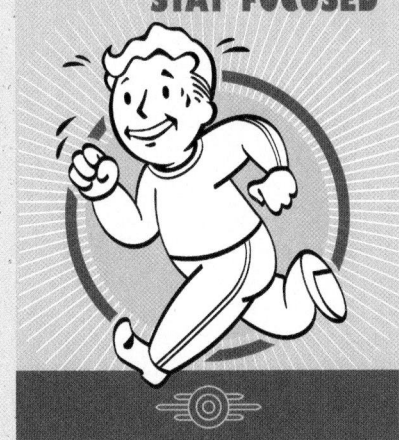

STAY FIT,
STAY FOCUSED

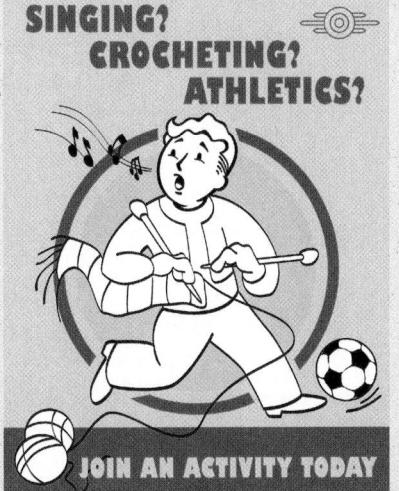

SINGING?
CROCHETING?
ATHLETICS?
JOIN AN ACTIVITY TODAY

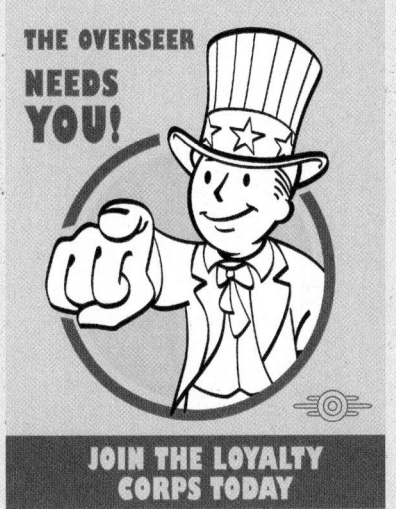

THE OVERSEER
NEEDS
YOU!
JOIN THE LOYALTY
CORPS TODAY

## [5.16] SOMERVILLE PLACE

THREAT LEVELS 35+

– FACTION: SETTLER      – SERVICES: WORKSHOP
– HEALTH OR CHEMS

A simple farmstead with settlers growing corn and being terrorized by nearby marauders. Helping them out guarantees loyalty and a settlement to tend to.

## [5.17] FORGOTTEN CHURCH

THREAT LEVELS 30+

– ARMAMENTS AND AMMO
– ARMAMENTS AND AMMO: TRUNK
– DANGER: LONG DROP!
– DANGER: RADIATION (SEVERE)!

Warning! Extreme radiation danger! Somewhere to the west of the Glowing Sea are the buried remains of a church. Make sure you descend to the trunk inside.

## [5.18] ABANDONED SHACK

THREAT LEVELS 25+

– ARMAMENTS AND AMMO
– ARMAMENTS AND AMMO: MINI NUKE
– ARMAMENTS AND AMMO: TRUNK
– ARMOR PART: POWER ARMOR (LEVELED)
– COLLECTIBLE: HOLOTAPE: EMPLOYEE 011985TP PERSONAL LOG
– COLLECTIBLE: REQUIRED READING: U.S. COVERT OPERATIONS MANUAL
– CRAFTING: ARMOR WORKBENCH
– CRAFTING: POWER ARMOR STATION
– DANGER: RADIATION (SEVERE)!
– DANGER: LONG DROP!
– DANGER: TESLA ARC!
– DANGER: TRIPWIRE!
– FACTION: SYNTHS (INSTITUTE)
– HEALTH OR CHEMS

FIG 5.18: BUNKER (INTERIOR)

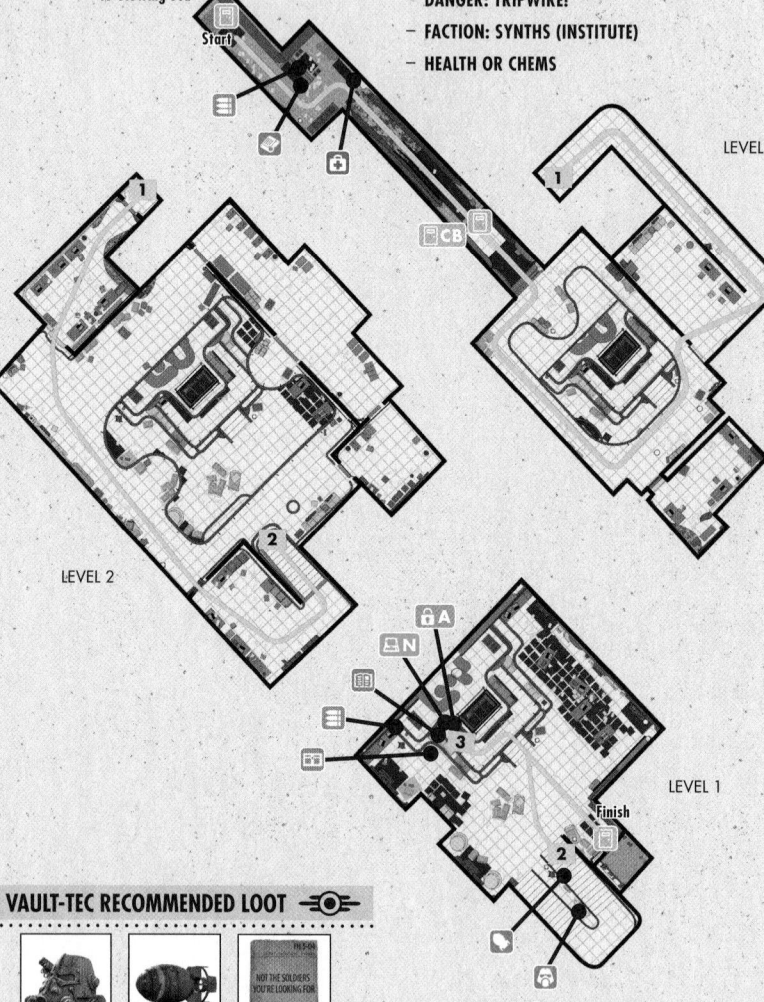

## VAULT-TEC RECOMMENDED LOOT

ARMOR PART: POWER ARMOR (LEVELED)
ARMAMENTS AND AMMO: MINI NUKE
REQUIRED READING: U.S. COVERT OPERATIONS MANUAL

Warning! Extreme radiation danger! An unassuming shack has a federal survival installation (codenamed K-21B) hidden beneath it. Enter the shack and open the trapdoor (Novice) or use the key in Bill the skeleton's suitcase.

Access the mainframe terminal if you wish to ride the elevator up to the surface bunker behind the shack and activate the Protectrons. The base of the main subterranean chamber is where you'll find a Mini Nuke, some essential reading, and a steamer trunk.

## [5.19] ATLANTIC OFFICES

THREAT LEVELS 20+

- ARMOR PART: FUSION CORE
- DANGER: GAS LEAK!
- DANGER: LONG DROP!
- DANGER: RADIATION (SEVERE)!
- DANGER: TRIPWIRES!
- FACTION: FERAL GHOUL
- HEALTH OR CHEMS

### VAULT-TEC RECOMMENDED LOOT

 ARMOR PART: FUSION CORE

Warning! Extreme radiation danger!
Atlantic Offices offers little more than
a reminder of the follies of man within
this hellscape. It is a tomb for ferals.
The lower levels are infested with them.
The "slightly above ground" floor has a
terminal allowing you to open a security
door. Reach the upper levels and ruined
roof via the elevator. Up here, the
women's bathroom is locked (Novice).
Check the safe too (Advanced).

## [5.20] CAPSIZED FACTORY

THREAT LEVELS 20+

- DANGER: RADIATION (SEVERE)!
- FACTION: FERAL GHOUL
- HEALTH OR CHEMS+

Warning! Extreme radiation danger!
Amid the mangled metal is a half-buried
factory filled with lolling ferals. Enter via
the hole or the remains of the doorway.
The base of the structure has a safe
(Advanced) and a variety of chems and
health to claim.

## [5.21] CAVE (RED ROCKET FILLING STATION)

THREAT LEVELS 20+

- DANGER: RADIATION (SEVERE)!
- FACTION: RADSCORPION
- HEALTH OR CHEMS

Warning! Extreme radiation danger! A
winding cave of twisted metal leads you to
a small pool of filthy water and the sagging
remains of a Red Rocket Filling Station.
Inside is a button to open the garage
(accessing a crate) and a safe (Master).

## [5.22] DECAYED REACTOR SITE

THREAT LEVELS 25+

- DANGER: RADIATION (SEVERE)!
- FACTION: DEATHCLAW

Warning! Extreme radiation danger! The
shell of a nuclear reactor, now home to
roaming Deathclaws. The small concrete
bunker has a circuit breaker to switch
the countdown on.

## [5.23] DECREPIT FACTORY

THREAT LEVELS 20+

- DANGER: RADIATION (SEVERE)!
- HEALTH OR CHEMS

Warning! Extreme
radiation danger!
Slowly sinking into
the irradiated ooze
are the remains of
a factory.

## [5.24] CRATER OF ATOM

THREAT LEVELS 20+

- ARMAMENTS AND AMMO
- COLLECTIBLE: REQUIRED READING: ASTOUNDINGLY AWESOME TALES
- DANGER: RADIATION (SEVERE)!
- FACTION: CHILDREN OF THE ATOM
- FACTION: CHARACTER: BROTHER GRIFFITH
- FACTION: CHARACTER: BROTHER OGDEN
- FACTION: CHARACTER: MOTHER ISOLDE
- FACTION: CHARACTER: SISTER LAYLA
- FACTION: CHARACTER: SISTER VERENA
- HEALTH OR CHEMS
- QUEST VISIT: THE GLOWING SEA (MAIN)

### VAULT-TEC RECOMMENDED LOOT

 REQUIRED READING: ASTOUNDINGLY AWESOME TALES

Warning! Extreme radiation danger!
The impact crater that created the
Glowing Sea is now a shrine and place
of pilgrimage for a strange cult called
the Children of the Atom. Ruled by
Mother Isolde, they are hostile unless the
specified quest is active.

## [5.25] CAVE (SUPER DUPER MART)  THREAT LEVELS 25+

**FIG 5.25: PARKING GARAGE (INTERIOR)**

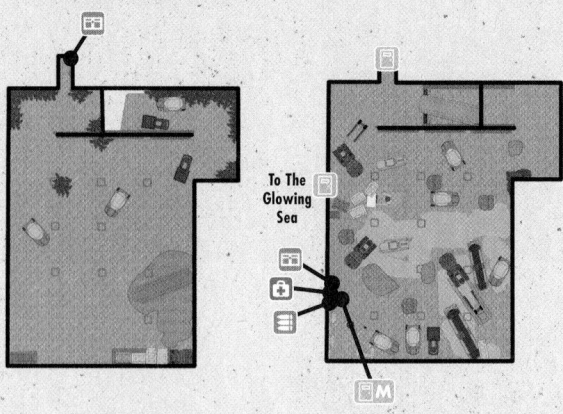

BASEMENT
LEVEL 1

LEVEL 1

- ARMAMENTS AND AMMO
- ARMAMENTS AND AMMO: TRUNK (2)
- ARMOR PART: FUSION CORE
- ARMOR PART: POWER ARMOR (RAIDER)
- CRAFTING: COOKING STATION
- DANGER: OIL!
- DANGER: RADIATION (SEVERE)!
- FACTION: IRRADIATED WILDLIFE (RADSCORPION)
- FACTION: DEATHCLAW
- HEALTH OR CHEMS

**VAULT-TEC RECOMMENDED LOOT**

  ARMOR PART; FUSION CORE

ARMOR PART: POWER ARMOR (RAIDER)

Warning! Extreme radiation danger! A cave mouth of bent metal leads to a weaving cave of debris, with Power Armor to claim. North is a half-buried Super Duper Mart. Take the exterior stairs entrance to the interior of the parking garage; the first of two steamer trunks is on this level. There is a security gate (Master) to unlock. Access the bus to drop down to the lower level where a Deathclaw is. Take the elevator atop the remains of the parking garage down to the lower flooded levels, where you can face the Deathclaw and open the steamer trunk.

 ## [5.26] VERTIBIRD WRECKAGE

THREAT LEVELS 30+

- DANGER: RADIATION (SEVERE)!

Warning! Extreme radiation danger! The tangled remains of a Vertibird lie in the eradicated zone, close to the remains of the freeway.

## [5.27] HOPESMARCH PENTECOSTAL CHURCH

THREAT LEVELS 25+

- ARMAMENTS AND AMMO
- ARMAMENTS AND AMMO: TRUNK
- DANGER: LONG DROP!
- DANGER: OIL!
- DANGER: RADIATION (SEVERE)!
- FACTION: FERAL GHOUL
- HEALTH OR CHEMS

Warning! Extreme radiation danger! The steeple of this church still points skyward and offers a modicum of familiarity in this vastness of despair. Avoid a long fall by descending through the steeple. Unlock a safe (Master) atop the stairs. Remaining on the balcony allows you to manage the congregation of ferals in this area. The exploration ends at the buried bus (check it for a trunk).

 ## [5.28] RELAY TOWER 0DB-521  THREAT LEVELS 30+

- DANGER: RADIATION (SEVERE)!
- RADIO: SKYLANES 1665 MAYDAY
- RADIO: DISTRESS SIGNAL

Warning! Extreme radiation danger! This is part of the Commonwealth Relay Tower Network. Authorized personnel only. Use the relay tower terminal to amplify both nearby radio signals.

**[5.29] ROCKY CAVE (VIRGIL'S LABORATORY)** THREAT LEVELS 20+

**FIG 5.29: VIRGIL'S LABORATORY (INTERIOR)**

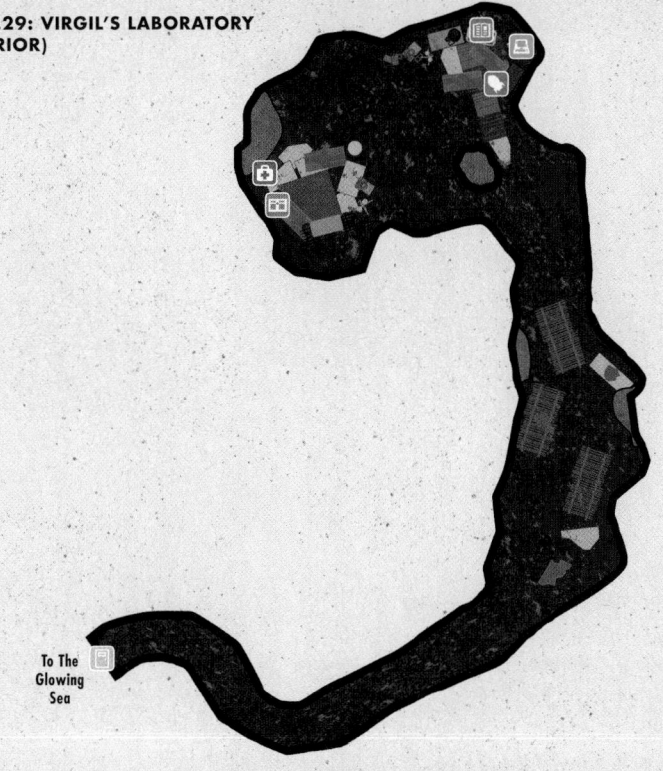

- ARMAMENTS AND AMMO
- ARMAMENTS AND AMMO: MINI NUKE
- ARMAMENTS AND AMMO: TRUNK
- BOTTLECAPS
- COLLECTIBLE: REQUIRED READING: TESLA SCIENCE
- CRAFTING: CHEMISTRY STATION
- DANGER: CAN CHIMES!
- DANGER: RADIATION (SEVERE)!
- DANGER: TURRETS!
- FACTION: DEATHCLAW
- FACTION: SUPER MUTANT (FRIENDLY)
- FACTION: CHARACTER: VIRGIL
- HEALTH OR CHEMS
- QUEST START: HUNTER HUNTED (MAIN)
- QUEST START: MISCELLANEOUS (VIRGIL'S CURE)
- QUEST VISIT: THE GLOWING SEA (MAIN)
- QUEST VISIT: THE MOLECULAR LEVEL (MAIN)
- QUEST VISIT: FROM WITHIN
  (BROTHERHOOD OF STEEL)
- QUEST VISIT: A LOOSE END
  (BROTHERHOOD OF STEEL)
- UNIQUE ITEM: VIRGIL'S RIFLE

To The Glowing Sea

A former scientist named Virgil still experiments out here in the loneliest corner of the Glowing Sea, with only a Protectron for company. He appears only if Quest: The Glowing Sea is active. Search his laboratory for a magazine and steamer trunk and a Mini Nuke under some metal shelving.

**VAULT-TEC RECOMMENDED LOOT**

**ARMAMENTS AND AMMO: MINI NUKE**
**COLLECTIBLE: NUKA COLA QUANTUM**
**REQUIRED READING: TESLA SCIENCE**
**UNIQUE ITEM: VIRGIL'S RIFLE**

 **Miscellaneous (Virgil's Cure)**

1. FIND VIRGIL'S SERUM   2. BRING THE SERUM TO VIRGIL   3. CHECK ON VIRGIL

Speak to Virgil and he mentions an experimental serum in his old laboratory that could reverse the effects of his Forced Evolutionary Virus. Continue your Main Quest until you're able to access the Institute. Once inside, explore the FEV Laboratory. Work your way through to the lab, and take the experimental serum. Give it to Virgil and leave his laboratory for 72 hours while he waits for the change. Upon your return, speak to Virgil again, and he rewards you by allowing you to loot his laboratory (though not his rifle, which must be pried from his cold, dead, green hands).

 **[5.30] O'NEILL FAMILY MANUFACTURING**

THREAT LEVELS 30+

- ARMAMENTS AND AMMO
- BOTTLECAPS
- COLLECTIBLE: ROBOT MODEL
  KIT (SENTRY BOT)
- CRAFTING: POWER ARMOR STATION
- FACTION: RADSCORPION
- FACTION: FERAL GHOULS
- HEALTH OR CHEMS

Warning! Extreme radiation danger! Only the roof section of this manufacturing plant is visible. Enter via the hole in the concrete. In the repair area, use the terminal to open the exterior door, then retrace your steps. Enter and open the steamer trunk at your own risk. Don't leave without the sentry bot model kit sitting near the wall terminal.

**VAULT-TEC RECOMMENDED LOOT**

 **COLLECTIBLE: SENTRY BOT MODEL KIT**

# [5.31] SENTINEL SITE

THREAT LEVELS 30+

- ARMAMENTS AND AMMO++
- ARMAMENTS AND AMMO: MINI NUKE
- COLLECTIBLE: HOLOTAPE: CAPTAIN
  DUNLEAVY'S HOLOTAPE
- COLLECTIBLE: HOLOTAPE: SENTINEL SITE BLAST
  DOOR OVERRIDE
- COLLECTIBLE: REQUIRED READING:
  ASTOUNDINGLY AWESOME TALES
- CRAFTING: CHEMISTRY STATION
- DANGER: LONG DROP!
- DANGER: RADIATION (SEVERE)!
- FACTION: CHILDREN OF THE ATOM
- FACTION: FERAL GHOULS
- FACTION: MOLE RATS
- FACTION: CHARACTER: BROTHER HENRI
- FACTION: CHARACTER: ATOM'S WRATH
- HEALTH OR CHEMS
- QUEST VISIT: LIBERTY REPRIMED
  (BROTHERHOOD OF STEEL)

## VAULT-TEC RECOMMENDED LOOT

ARMAMENTS AND AMMO: MINI NUKE

REQUIRED READING: ASTOUNDINGLY
AWESOME TALES

Warning! Extreme radiation danger! Not
all of this location is accessible until the
specified quest is active!

This secret military installation has
a stockpile of potent Mark 28 nuclear
warheads, many of them still intact. An
ominous pyramid surrounded by irradiated
sludge, this location was in the middle of
launching a missile strike when the bombs
dropped. It is now a tomb for ferals.

Inside, you must shut down the launch
at the terminal located at the base of the
pyramid. Work your way to the stockpile.
If you wish to use the cargo elevator
to exit this facility, exit atop one of the
towers to the southwest of the pyramid.

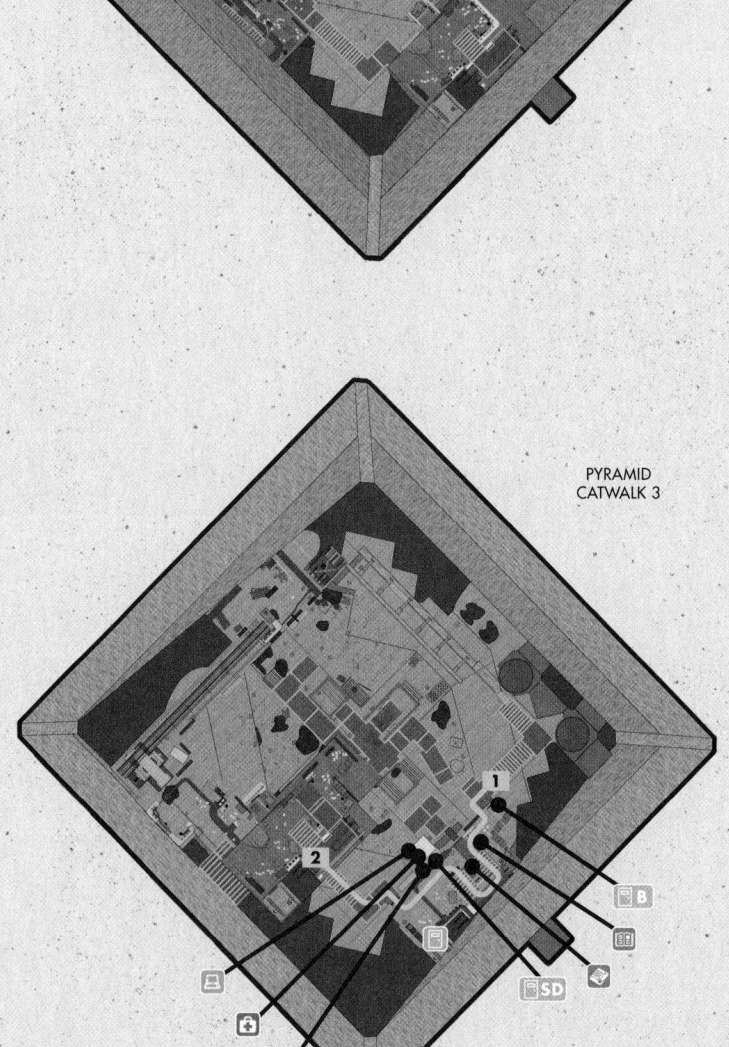

PYRAMID
CATWALK 3

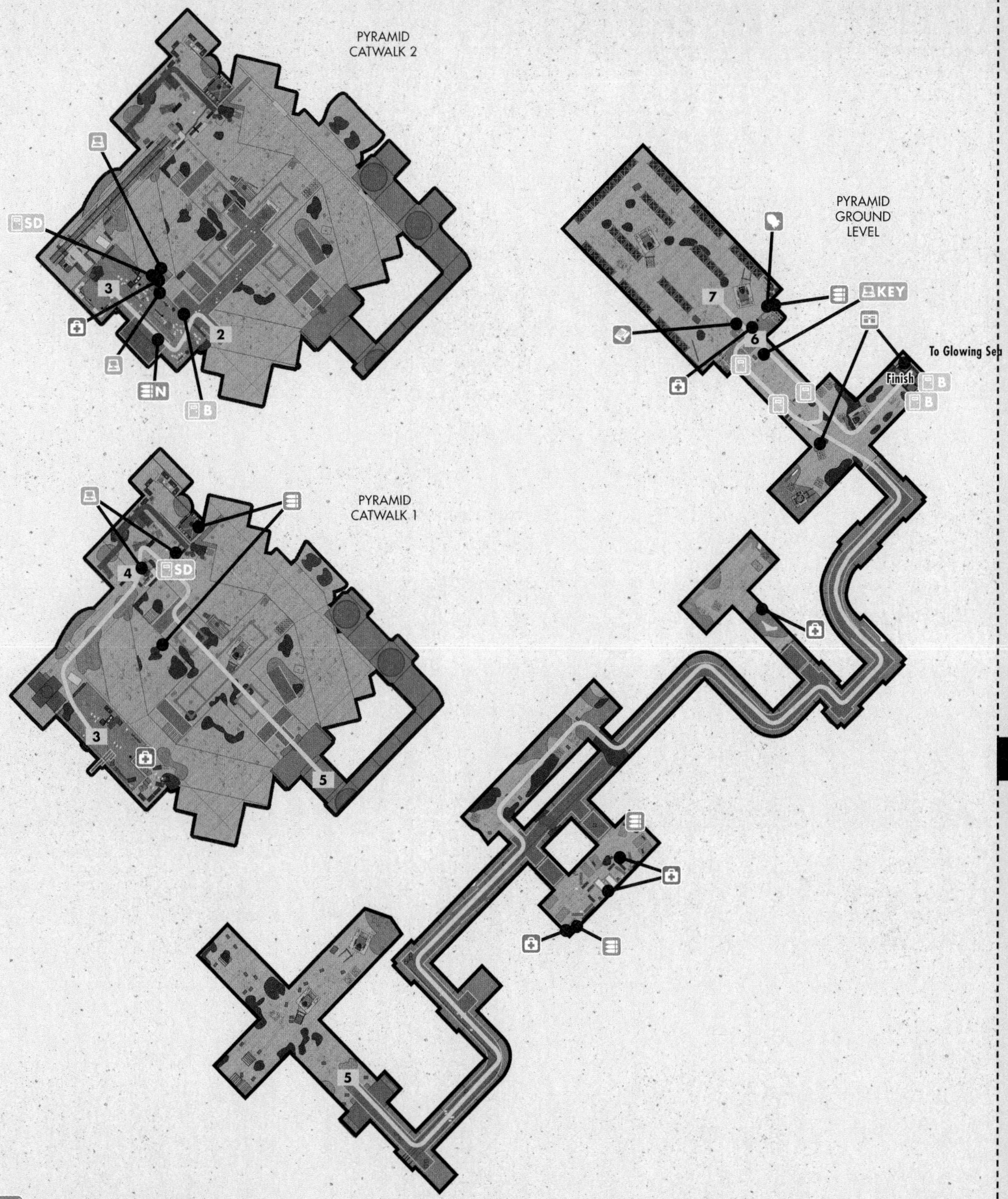

PYRAMID
CATWALK 2

SD

3
2

N
B

PYRAMID
GROUND
LEVEL

7
6

KEY

To Glowing Sea

Finish
B
B

PYRAMID
CATWALK 1

SD
4

3
5

MAP

ZONE 5

NATICK AND THE
GLOWING SEA

5

✈ [5.32] SKYLANES FLIGHT 1665

THREAT LEVELS 30+

- ARMAMENTS
  AND AMMO
- ARMAMENTS AND
  AMMO: TRUNK
- DANGER: RADIATION
  (SEVERE)!
- HEALTH OR CHEMS

Warning! Extreme radiation danger! Scattered pieces of the commercial flight 1665 lie here. The wing has a steamer trunk to ransack. The data recorder in the cockpit charts the final seconds of the doomed flight. There's also a secret compartment in the plane's cargo hold (Master). If you killed Ness (in a Random Encounter, or at Primary Location [2.10] Skylanes Flight 1983, her Skylanes Cargo Key will unlock it.

# SECONDARY LOCATIONS

## [5.01] NATICK POWER STATION

- ARMAMENTS AND AMMO
- FACTION: DEATHCLAWS
- FACTION: SUPER MUTANTS

The animosity between the two gigantic mutations vying for territory in Natick reaches its zenith in this abandoned power station. The Super Mutants, it seems, have brought out one of their heavy hitters.

## [5.02] NATICK HILLSIDE HOME

- ARMAMENTS AND AMMO
- FACTION: ATTACK DOGS
- FACTION: DEATHCLAWS
- HEALTH OR CHEMS

While the home owner has retired to the garage, this house overlooking Natick has a few scavengable items and some intruders to watch for.

## [5.03] SETTLER CAMPSITE (NATICK OUTSKIRTS)

- CRAFTING: COOKING STATION
- FACTION: DEATHCLAW

A settler has found out, to his cost, that even the outskirts of Natick are no place for anything without giant claws or green skin.

## [5.04] MILITARY CHECKPOINT (LAKE COCHITUATE)

- ARMAMENTS AND AMMO: TRUNK
- ARMOR PART: POWER ARMOR (LEVELED)

The remains of a military checkpoint still has a ghostly suit of Power Armor standing to attention. Check under one of the platforms for a (randomly appearing) trunk.

## [5.05] THE MAUSOLEUM

- ARMAMENTS AND AMMO
- FACTION: MIRELURKS

Under the freeway sits an old crypt, with a Mirelurk egg on the central dais. Perhaps no one (or nothing) will notice if you take it? Also check the open cargo container just south, by the freeway footing.

## [5.06] FISHING CABIN

- HEALTH OR CHEMS

This rotting hut overlooks the fetid lake, with scraps of loot to gather.

## [5.07] TWO CABINS AND AN OUTHOUSE

- ARMAMENTS AND AMMO: TRUNK
- CRAFTING: COOKING STATION
- FACTION: FERAL GHOULS

This is a small campsite just west of the remains of the freeway. The holidaymakers aren't the friendliest. Come for the trunk, as the views are slightly depressing.

## [5.08] COLLAPSED BILLBOARD (GLOWING SEA)

- DANGER: RADIATION (SEVERE)!
- FACTION: MOLE RATS

A half-buried billboard and the skeletal remains of buildings serve as a landmark in this inhospitable area.

## [5.09] BURIED MANSION

- DANGER: RADIATION (SEVERE)!
- FACTION: RADSCORPIONS
- HEALTH OR CHEMS

This is close to a half-sunk playground. Look for the roof sticking out of the rubble; it has a good number of chems to gather.

## [5.10] RADIATION LAKE

- DANGER: RADIATION (SEVERE)!
- FACTION: BLOODBUGS
- FACTION: FERAL GHOULS

Even by the inhospitable standards of this region, this Bloodbug-infested pool of irradiated slime isn't a place to venture to willingly.

## [5.11] MILITARY PILLBOX (SOMERVILLE)

- ARMAMENTS AND AMMO
- ARMAMENTS AND AMMO: TRUNK
- FACTION: ROBOTS

A docile sentry bot turns hostile if you attempt to raid the pillbox of its wooden box and trunk. The door inside is locked (Advanced).

## [5.12] THE SPLINTERED STATUE

- ARMAMENTS AND AMMO
- ARMAMENTS AND AMMO: TRUNK
- CRAFTING: COOKING STATION
- FACTION: RAIDERS
- FACTION: STINGWINGS
- HEALTH OR CHEMS

Everything is in place for the repainting of a long-forgotten statue—that is, until you arrive. Check the cabin to the northeast for a trunk.

## [5.13] DERELICT BUS

- ARMAMENTS AND AMMO: TRUNK
- DANGER: RADIATION (SEVERE)!
- FACTION: FERAL GHOULS

A bus of commuters is stuck in the mire here, with its passengers milling about nearby. Check inside for a steamer trunk.

## [5.14] BURIED HOUSE

- DANGER: RADIATION (SEVERE)!
- HEALTH OR CHEMS

If you're in danger of succumbing to the elements, head here and search out this ruined house for chems.

## [5.15] BUCKLED FREEWAY

- ARMAMENTS AND AMMO
- BOTTLECAPS
- DANGER: RADIATION (SEVERE)!
- FACTION: DEATHCLAWS

Close to the prowling Deathclaws is a section of buckled freeway where a container truck has spilled out its contents—a number of safes, both empty and full.

# ZONE 6: QUINCY AND SOUTHERN COMMONWEALTH

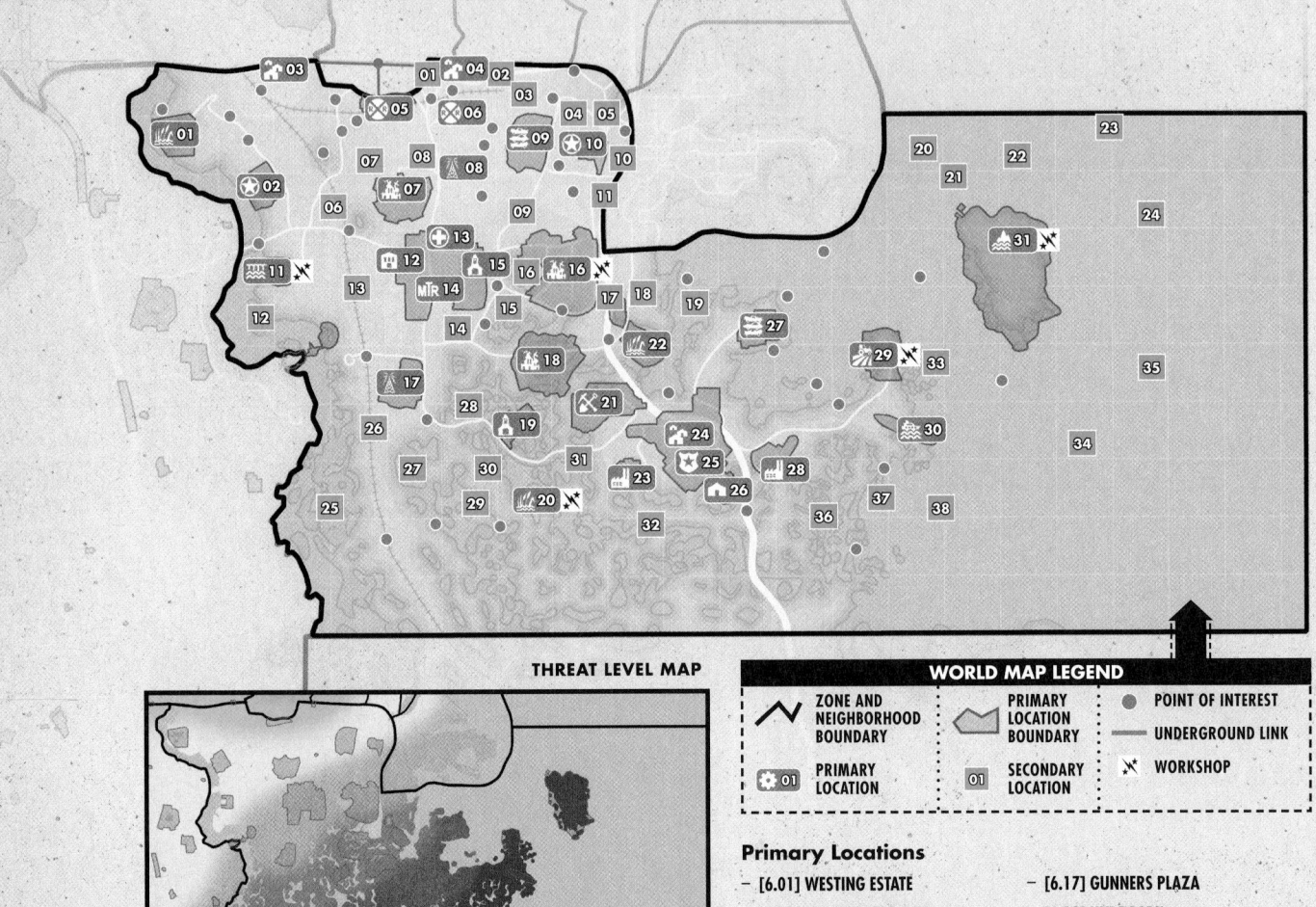

**THREAT LEVEL MAP**

**WORLD MAP LEGEND**

| | | |
|---|---|---|
| 〰 ZONE AND NEIGHBORHOOD BOUNDARY | ◢ PRIMARY LOCATION BOUNDARY | ● POINT OF INTEREST |
| | | ─ UNDERGROUND LINK |
| ⚙ 01 PRIMARY LOCATION | 01 SECONDARY LOCATION | ✕ WORKSHOP |

1-5  6-14  15-25  20+  25+  30+  35+  40+  45+
**EXPECTED LEVEL OF ENEMIES ENCOUNTERED**

Anywhere south of the Greater Boston Neighborhoods that isn't glowing with radiation can be considered the Southern Commonwealth. Head southwest to follow the river to the treacherous marshlands and across to the Glowing Sea. It's a straight shot south to both West Roxbury and Jamaica Plain—two townships with their fair share of secrets. Journey southeast into Quincy, which, like much of this zone, is under Gunner control. Only those impressively grizzled enough to have eked out an existence for months should venture to the most dangerous places of all—the coastal area past Quincy and the strange ruins of Spectacle Island, perhaps the most idyllic place for a settlement . . . if the locals can be convinced.

## Primary Locations

- [6.01] WESTING ESTATE
- [6.02] COAST GUARD PIER
- [6.03] MASS PIKE TUNNEL WEST
- [6.04] MASS PIKE TUNNEL EAST
- [6.05] BOSTON POLICE RATIONING SITE
- [6.06] NH&M FREIGHT DEPOT
- [6.07] FAIRLINE HILL ESTATES
- [6.08] RELAY TOWER 0SC-527
- [6.09] BIG JOHN'S SALVAGE
- [6.10] SOUTH BOSTON MILITARY CHECKPOINT
- [6.11] EGRET TOURS MARINA
- [6.12] FALLON'S DEPARTMENT STORE
- [6.13] MILTON GENERAL HOSPITAL
- [6.14] WEST ROXBURY STATION
- [6.15] SHAW HIGH SCHOOL
- [6.16] JAMAICA PLAIN
- [6.17] GUNNERS PLAZA
- [6.18] HYDE PARK
- [6.19] SUFFOLK COUNTY CHARTER SCHOOL
- [6.20] MURKWATER CONSTRUCTION SITE
- [6.21] QUINCY QUARRIES
- [6.22] NEPONSET PARK
- [6.23] WILSON ATOMATOYS FACTORY
- [6.24] QUINCY RUINS
- [6.25] QUINCY POLICE STATION
- [6.26] PEABODY HOUSE
- [6.27] ATOM CATS GARAGE
- [6.28] POSEIDON ENERGY
- [6.29] WARWICK HOMESTEAD
- [6.30] WRECK OF THE FMS NORTHERN STAR
- [6.31] SPECTACLE ISLAND

## Secondary Locations

- [6.01] RED ROCKET FILLING STATION (MASS PIKE EAST)
- [6.02] LAYTON TOWERS UNDERPASS ENTRANCE
- [6.03] CRATER AND SHACK
- [6.04] RED ROCKET FILLING STATION (BIG JOHN'S SALVAGE)
- [6.05] WICKED SHIPPING CONTAINER TRUCK #4
- [6.06] RAILROAD MAINTENANCE SHED
- [6.07] THE TRADING POST
- [6.08] DOG'S DINNER
- [6.09] MILITARY CHECKPOINT (WEST ROXBURY)
- [6.10] DESERTED CAMP (ELEVATED FREEWAY)
- [6.11] RAIDER CAMP (UNIVERSITY POINT OUTSKIRTS)
- [6.12] ISLAND CABIN
- [6.13] WAYSTATION (WEST ROXBURY)
- [6.14] MOONSHINER'S CABIN
- [6.15] THE HANGING TREE
- [6.16] JAMAICA PLAIN POND
- [6.17] MILITARY CONVOY (ELEVATED FREEWAY)
- [6.18] THE FRIDGE
- [6.19] MILITARY BARGE (UNIVERSITY POINT)
- [6.20] BOATING PLATFORMS
- [6.21] SUNKEN FISHING BOAT (SPECTACLE ISLAND)
- [6.22] BARGE PLATFORM
- [6.23] DEEP TRENCH WRECKAGE
- [6.24] SUNKEN SUPERTANKER
- [6.25] SNIPER'S HIDEOUT
- [6.26] WAYSTATION (GUNNERS' PLAZA)
- [6.27] RUINED GROVE ESTATES
- [6.28] THE SMALL DIG
- [6.29] CRASHED VERTIBIRD (MARSHLAND)
- [6.30] MILITARY PILLBOXES
- [6.31] OLD MILITARY MONUMENT
- [6.32] OVERFLOW OUTLET CAMP (ATOMATOYS FACTORY)
- [6.33] SCUPPERED BOAT
- [6.34] FLOATING BARGE
- [6.35] SKYLINES FLIGHT SALVAGE
- [6.36] BOAT GRAVEYARD
- [6.37] QUINCY LIGHTHOUSE
- [6.38] UNDERSEA HATCH PIPE

### MAP LEGEND

13    20    ●
OPTIMAL ROUTE   AREA OF INTEREST

- BOTTLECAPS
- SAFE
- ARMAMENTS AND AMMO
- DOOR
- HEALTH OR CHEMS
- TERMINAL
- STEAMER TRUNK

*Collectibles:*
- FUSION CORE
- POWER ARMOR
- ESSENTIAL READING
- BOBBLEHEAD
- NUKA CHERRY
- MINI NUKE
- NUKA COLA QUANTUM
- HOLOTAPE
- A KEY

N – Novice (Locked)
A – Advanced (Locked)
E – Expert (Locked)
M – Master (Locked)
T – Terminal required to unlock
KEY – Key or ID Card required to unlock
IN – Inaccessible
C – Chained
CB – Circuit Breaker
B – Button

MAP

**ZONE 6**

QUINCY AND
SOUTHERN
COMMONWEALTH

# PRIMARY LOCATIONS

## [6.01] WESTING ESTATE
THREAT LEVELS 15-25

- ARMAMENTS AND AMMO
- COLLECTIBLE: REQUIRED READING: UNSTOPPABLES
- FACTION: MIRELURKS
- HEALTH OR CHEMS
- QUEST VISIT: OUT IN LEFT FIELD (DIAMOND CITY FREEFORM ACTIVITY)
- UNIQUE ITEM: SIGNED BASEBALL
- UNIQUE ITEM: SIGNED BASEBALL CARD
- UNIQUE ITEM: SIGNED CATCHER'S MITT

### VAULT-TEC RECOMMENDED LOOT

REQUIRED READING: UNSTOPPABLES
UNIQUE ITEM: BASEBALL MEMORABILIA

The well-to-do Westing family once owned this idyllic slice of riverfront property. Now this is a Mirelurk swamp. Moe Cronin, of Swatters in Diamond City Market, is extremely keen on finding baseball relics from a bygone age. Unlock the safe (Novice), find the toolbox, and locate the cooler to find them.

## [6.02] COAST GUARD PIER
THREAT LEVELS 20+

- ARMAMENTS AND AMMO+
- ARMAMENTS AND AMMO: MINI NUKE
- ARMAMENTS AND AMMO: TRUNK
- BOTTLECAPS
- COLLECTIBLE: HOLOTAPE: EDDIE WINTER'S HOLOTAPE
- COLLECTIBLE: NUKA CHERRY
- COLLECTIBLE: REQUIRED READING: ASTOUNDINGLY AWESOME TALES
- CRAFTING: ARMOR WORKBENCH
- CRAFTING: WEAPONS WORKBENCH
- DANGER: DOOR TRAP!
- DANGER: OIL!
- DANGER: MINES!
- FACTION: SUPER MUTANT
- HEALTH OR CHEMS+
- QUEST VISIT: LONG TIME COMING (SIDE)

### VAULT-TEC RECOMMENDED LOOT

ARMAMENTS AND AMM1O: MINI NUKE
COLLECTIBLE: NUKA CHERRY

REQUIRED READING: ASTOUNDINGLY AWESOME TALES

The Coast Guard station along the Charles River had intercepted a shipment of smuggled chems. Now it is overrun by Super Mutants. The outside trailer (Advanced) allows access to an armor workbench and first aid. Another of Eddie Winter's Holotapes is on top of the main floor safe (Advanced). The upstairs restroom (Novice) contains first aid. The downstairs cell (Expert) holds a magazine and can be more easily opened at the adjacent lockup terminal. The evidence room terminal (Expert) is a trickier hack, but the room itself houses a good amount of ammo and chems, as well as two more safes (Novice, Expert).

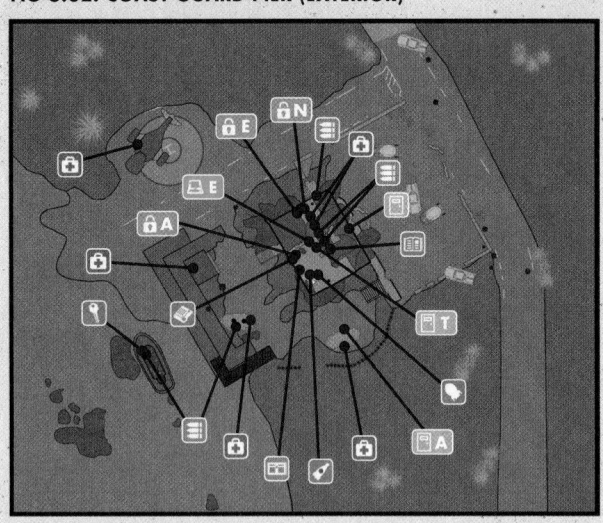

**FIG 6.02: COAST GUARD PIER (EXTERIOR)**

## 🏠 [6.03] MASS PIKE TUNNEL WEST    🏠 [6.04] MASS PIKE TUNNEL EAST

THREAT LEVELS 15-25          THREAT LEVELS 15-25

- ARMAMENTS AND AMMO
- ARMAMENTS AND AMMO: MINI NUKE
- ARMAMENTS AND AMMO: TRUNK
- ARMOR PART: FUSION CORE
- COLLECTIBLE: HOLOTAPE: DET. PERRY'S HOLOTAPE
- COLLECTIBLE: HOLOTAPE: MASS PIKE TUNNEL PASSWORD
- COLLECTIBLE: NUKA COLA QUANTUM (2)
- COLLECTIBLE: REQUIRED READING: TABOO TATTOOS
- CRAFTING: CHEMISTRY STATION
- CRAFTING: COOKING STATION
- CRAFTING: POWER ARMOR STATION
- DANGER: OIL!
- DANGER: MINES!
- DANGER: RADIATION (MILD)!
- DANGER: TURRETS!
- FACTION: FERAL GHOUL
- FACTION: MOLE RATS
- FACTION: RAIDERS
- HEALTH OR CHEMS

To Commonwealth (Mass Pike Tunnel West)

**FIG 6.04: MASS PIKE TUNNEL (INTERIOR)**

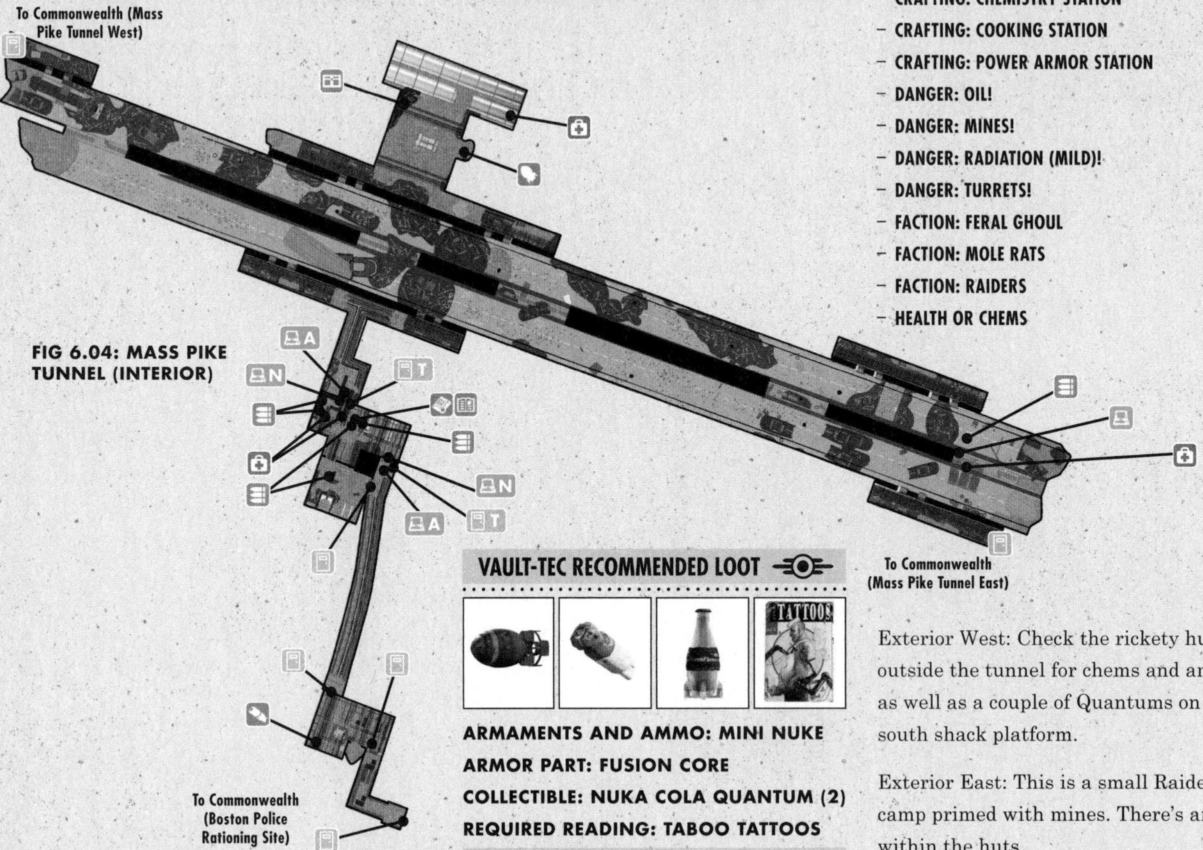

To Commonwealth (Mass Pike Tunnel East)

To Commonwealth (Boston Police Rationing Site)

### VAULT-TEC RECOMMENDED LOOT

**ARMAMENTS AND AMMO: MINI NUKE**
**ARMOR PART: FUSION CORE**
**COLLECTIBLE: NUKA COLA QUANTUM (2)**
**REQUIRED READING: TABOO TATTOOS**

Exterior West: Check the rickety huts outside the tunnel for chems and ammo, as well as a couple of Quantums on the south shack platform.

Exterior East: This is a small Raider camp primed with mines. There's ammo within the huts.

Interior: At the machinery chambers (south) by the skeleton are two Holotapes, one offering information and the other a password. Otherwise, prepare to be lightly irradiated and slathered upon by ferals. The interior links the west and east exits, as well as the Boston Police Rationing Site to the south.

THREAT LEVELS 20+

Just south of the Fens neighborhood is a pair of community basketball courts and a railway unloading depot. Boston PD set up a rationing site here, and the trailer, numerous crates, and an old warehouse are still standing. The police terminal has a Holotape regarding lost goods inside the warehouse with the barred door.

Access the warehouse via the blue train carriage, and leap to the roof. Then jump across the crates to the north side roof awning and enter. Inside is a steamer trunk (Expert) and an army terminal you can use to activate a nearby Protectron. Unbar the door and press the button to open the main sliding door before entering the utility tunnel (aka Mass Pike Tunnel). This tunnel links to Primary Locations: Mass Pike Tunnel West and Mass Pike Tunnel East. Consult those locations for the interior map.

- ARMAMENTS AND AMMO
- ARMAMENTS AND AMMO: TRUNK
- COLLECTIBLE: HOLOTAPE: DET. MCDONNELL'S HOLOTAPE
- FACTION: MOLE RATS
- HEALTH AND CHEMS

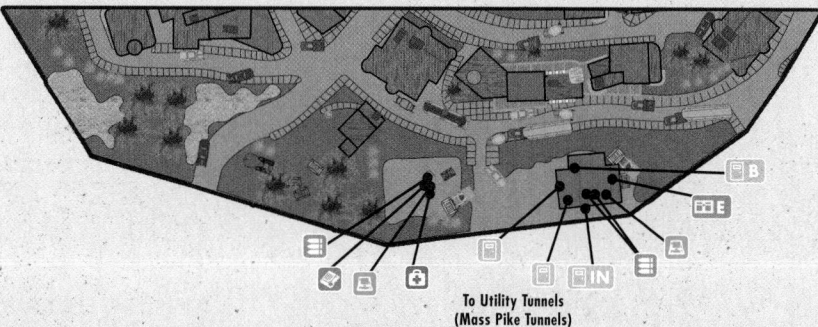

To Utility Tunnels
(Mass Pike Tunnels)

THREAT LEVELS 25+

- ARMAMENTS AND AMMO
- ARMOR PART: FUSION CORE (2)
- BOTTLECAPS
- COLLECTIBLE: NUKA CHERRY
- DANGER: EXPLOSIVE BARRELS!
- DANGER: OIL!
- FACTION: TRIGGERMEN
- HEALTH OR CHEMS
- QUEST VISIT: THE BIG DIG (SIDE)
- UNIQUE ITEM: ASHMAKER

### VAULT-TEC RECOMMENDED LOOT

  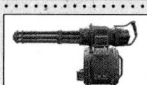

**ARMOR PART: FUSION CORE (2)**
**COLLECTIBLE: NUKA CHERRY**
**UNIQUE ITEM: ASHMAKER**

When the quest isn't active, the exterior door leads to a strongroom and is only accessible using Hancock's strongroom key (which isn't available). This is the alternate name of this location. As there's a security door directly inside, the only way you're getting in here is via an underground tunnel from Goodneighbor, during the quest. It's worth spending time ransacking the train cars full of loot, though! The unique weapon is awarded at the end of the quest, depending on who you side with.

### [6.07] FAIRLINE HILL ESTATES

THREAT LEVELS 25+

- ARMAMENTS AND AMMO+
- ARMAMENTS AND AMMO: TRUNK
- CRAFTING: CHEMISTRY STATION
- CRAFTING: POWER ARMOR STATION
- DANGER: CAN CHIMES!
- DANGER: DOOR TRAP!
- FACTION: FERAL GHOULS
- FACTION: YAO GUAI
- HEALTH OR CHEMS+

Since the bombs dropped, several Scavenger and Raider gangs have used the faded remains of this fairly upscale gated community. It is now home to a family of Yao Guai. The northeast house has an unlocked floor safe upstairs. The southwest house has an unlocked floor safe in the laundry porch. The west house is of most concern, especially once you see what's glowing in the garden. Enter this abode by ascending the rusty truck and debris and heading into the upstairs hole.

## [6.08] RELAY TOWER 0SC-527

THREAT LEVELS 25+

- ARMAMENTS AND AMMO
- BOTTLECAPS
- FACTION: MOLE RATS
- RADIO: SUPERMUTANT RADIO BROADCAST
- RADIO: DISTRESS SIGNAL
- RADIO: MILLER FAMILY RADIO SIGNAL

Warning! Extreme radiation danger! This is part of the Commonwealth Relay Tower Network. Authorized personnel only. Use the relay tower terminal to amplify three nearby radio signals.

## [6.09] BIG JOHN'S SALVAGE

THREAT LEVELS 25+

- ARMAMENTS AND AMMO+
- ARMAMENTS AND AMMO: MINI NUKE
- ARMAMENTS AND AMMO: TRUNK
- ARMOR PART: FUSION CORE
- COLLECTIBLE: REQUIRED READING: TALES OF A JUNKTOWN JERKY VENDOR
- BOTTLECAPS
- COLLECTIBLE: MINI NUKE
- CRAFTING: COOKING STATION
- FACTION: SUPER MUTANT
- HEALTH OR CHEMS+

**FIG 6.09: BIG JOHN'S SALVAGE (EXTERIOR)**

### VAULT-TEC RECOMMENDED LOOT

**ARMAMENTS AND AMMO: MINI NUKE**

**ARMOR PART: FUSION CORE**

**REQUIRED READING: TALES OF A JUNKTOWN JERKY VENDOR**

The Miller family home by the road is in ruins, with corpses of Raiders strewn about. Upstairs is John Miller's terminal and his safe (Master). The hardware store offers a back room (Novice) and counter safe (Advanced). Stairs leading up to a makeshift lookout shack with a button moving two rusty vehicles allow access from the road.

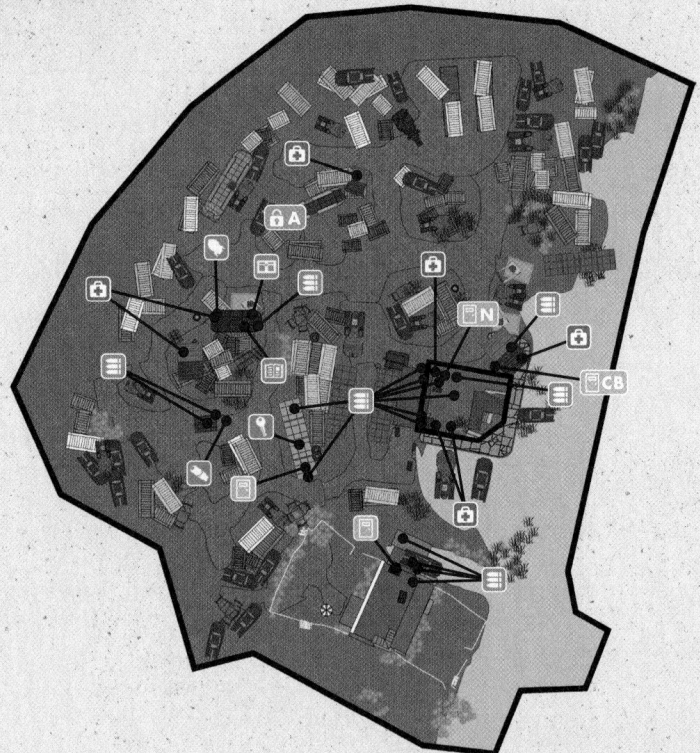

The salvage yard has numerous rickety walkways and rusting vehicles to inspect, including a bus with a safe (Advanced). There's also some makeshift ramps up to a trailer with a trunk and magazine to pilfer. Climb up a fridge and drop into a long blue container to reach a shelter trapdoor. It is sealed; follow the black electrical wire to a circuit breaker on a generator by the lookout hut and activate it. The shelter has a key to open the safes, revealing evidence of what happened to the Millers.

## [6.10] SOUTH BOSTON MILITARY CHECKPOINT

THREAT LEVELS 30+

Just west of South Boston Neighborhood, this was once a gathering place for military but is now an ambush spot for Gunners. There's a Fat Man inside the truck trailer, loot (including a magazine) inside the small bunker, and a wall safe (Master). Unlock the outside terminal (Expert) around the back to access a small secured area with Power Armor and a Mini Nuke.

### VAULT-TEC RECOMMENDED LOOT

**ARMAMENTS AND AMMO: MINI NUKE AND FAT MAN**
**ARMOR PART: FUSION CORE**
**ARMOR PART: POWER ARMOR (LEVELED)**
**REQUIRED READING: GUNS AND BULLETS**

- ARMAMENTS AND AMMO
- ARMAMENTS AND AMMO: MINI NUKE
- ARMAMENTS AND AMMO: MINI NUKE (FAT MAN)
- ARMAMENTS AND AMMO: TRUNK
- ARMOR PART: FUSION CORE
- ARMOR PART: POWER ARMOR (LEVELED)
- COLLECTIBLE: REQUIRED READING: GUNS AND BULLETS
- CRAFTING: POWER ARMOR STATION
- CRAFTING: WEAPONS WORKBENCH
- FACTION: GUNNERS
- HEALTH OR CHEMS

## [6.11] EGRET TOURS MARINA

 THREAT LEVELS 25+

- ARMAMENTS AND AMMO
- ARMAMENTS AND AMMO: TRUNK
- BOTTLECAPS
- COLLECTIBLE: NUKA COLA QUANTUM
- COLLECTIBLE: REQUIRED READING: WASTELAND SURVIVAL GUIDE
- CRAFTING: COOKING STATION
- CRAFTING: WEAPONS WORKBENCH
- DANGER: GRENADES!
- DANGER: MAKESHIFT BOMBS!
- DANGER: MINES!
- DANGER: OIL!
- DANGER: RADIATION (MILD)!
- DANGER: TRIPWIRE!
- FACTION: SETTLER
- FACTION: CHARACTER: PHYLLIS DAILY
- HEALTH OR CHEMS
- QUEST START: MISCELLANEOUS (PHYLLIS DAILY)
- SERVICES: WORKSHOP

### VAULT-TEC RECOMMENDED LOOT

**COLLECTIBLE: NUKA COLA QUANTUM**
**REQUIRED READING: WASTELAND SURVIVAL GUIDE**

### FIG 6.11: EGRET TOURS MARINA (EXTERIOR)

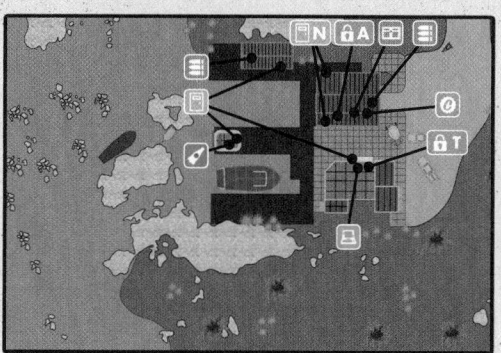

An inlet off the Charles River houses a boat landing and a brick building making up a marina. The place is home to (and has been booby-trapped by) an old woman named Phyllis. It could prove to be a valuable settlement. Phyllis's terminal upstairs unlocks her safe. The warehouse is locked (Novice) at both doors but is accessible via the water.

 **Miscellaneous (Phyllis Daily)**

#### 1. CONFRONT PHYLLIS ABOUT SAMUEL'S DEATH

A strange and angry old woman pulls a gun on you. Either slay her or speak to her.

 (Easy, Medium, Hard) Ask about her situation.

Learn more about her sorrows from the terminal upstairs. Speak to her again: You can kill her, tell her to leave, go to Covenant, or stay (you can console or entice her, turn her into the Covenant (if you're friendly with them), the Institute, or the Railroad). You're then able to use her workshop.

**FIG 6.12A: WEST ROXBURY (TOWNSHIP)**

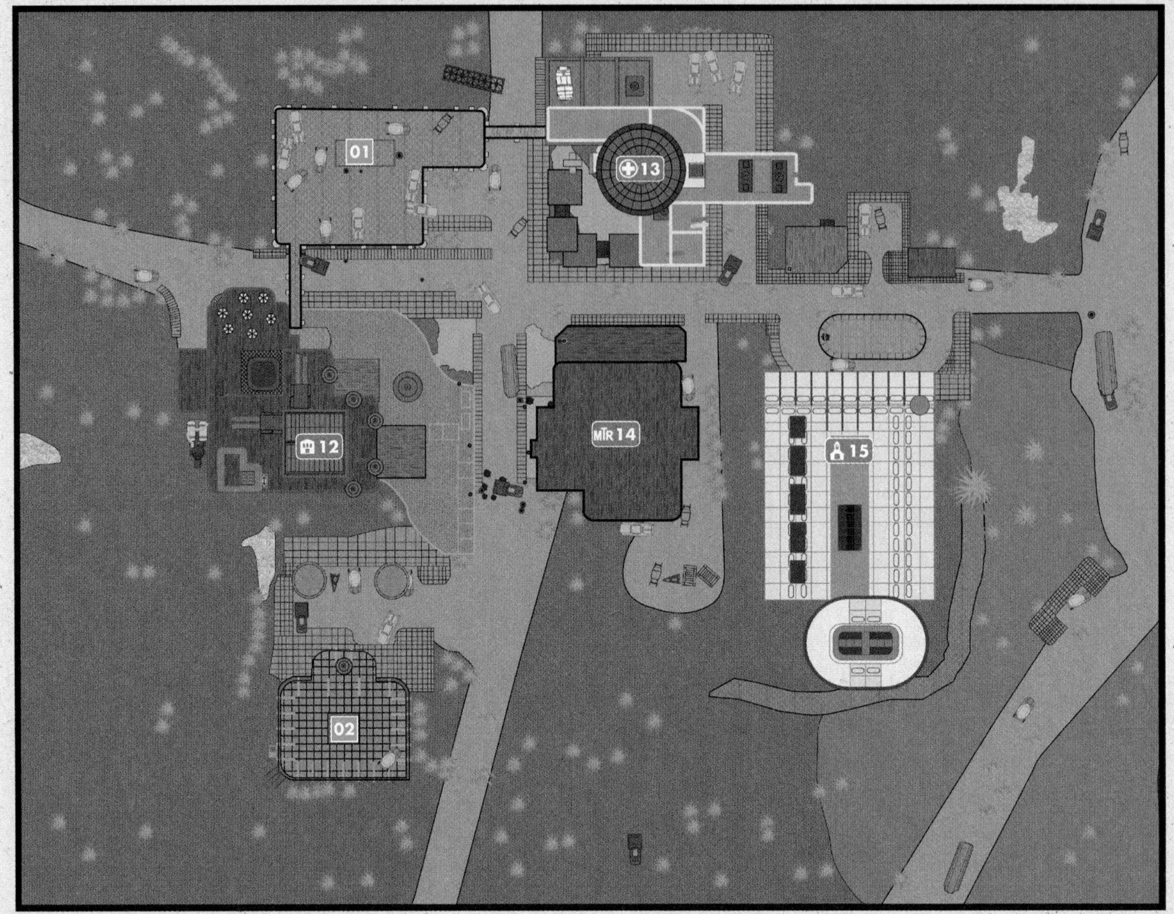

## [6.12] FALLON'S DEPARTMENT STORE

THREAT LEVELS 30+

- ARMAMENTS AND AMMO
- ARMAMENTS AND AMMO: TRUNK
- ARMOR PIECE: FUSION CORE
- BOTTLECAPS+++
- COLLECTIBLE:
  ROBOT MODEL KIT (EYEBOT)
- COLLECTIBLE: REQUIRED READING:
  LA COIFFE

- CRAFTING: CHEMISTRY STATION
- CRAFTING: COOKING STATION
- DANGER: LONG DROP!
- DANGER: MAKESHIFT BOMB!
- DANGER: RADIATION (MILD)!
- FACTION: SUPER MUTANT
- HEALTH OR CHEMS

### VAULT-TEC RECOMMENDED LOOT

ARMOR PART: FUSION CORE
REQUIRED READING: LA COIFFE
COLLECTIBLE: EYEBOT MODEL KIT

## FIG 6.12B: FALLON'S DEPARTMENT STORE (INTERIOR)

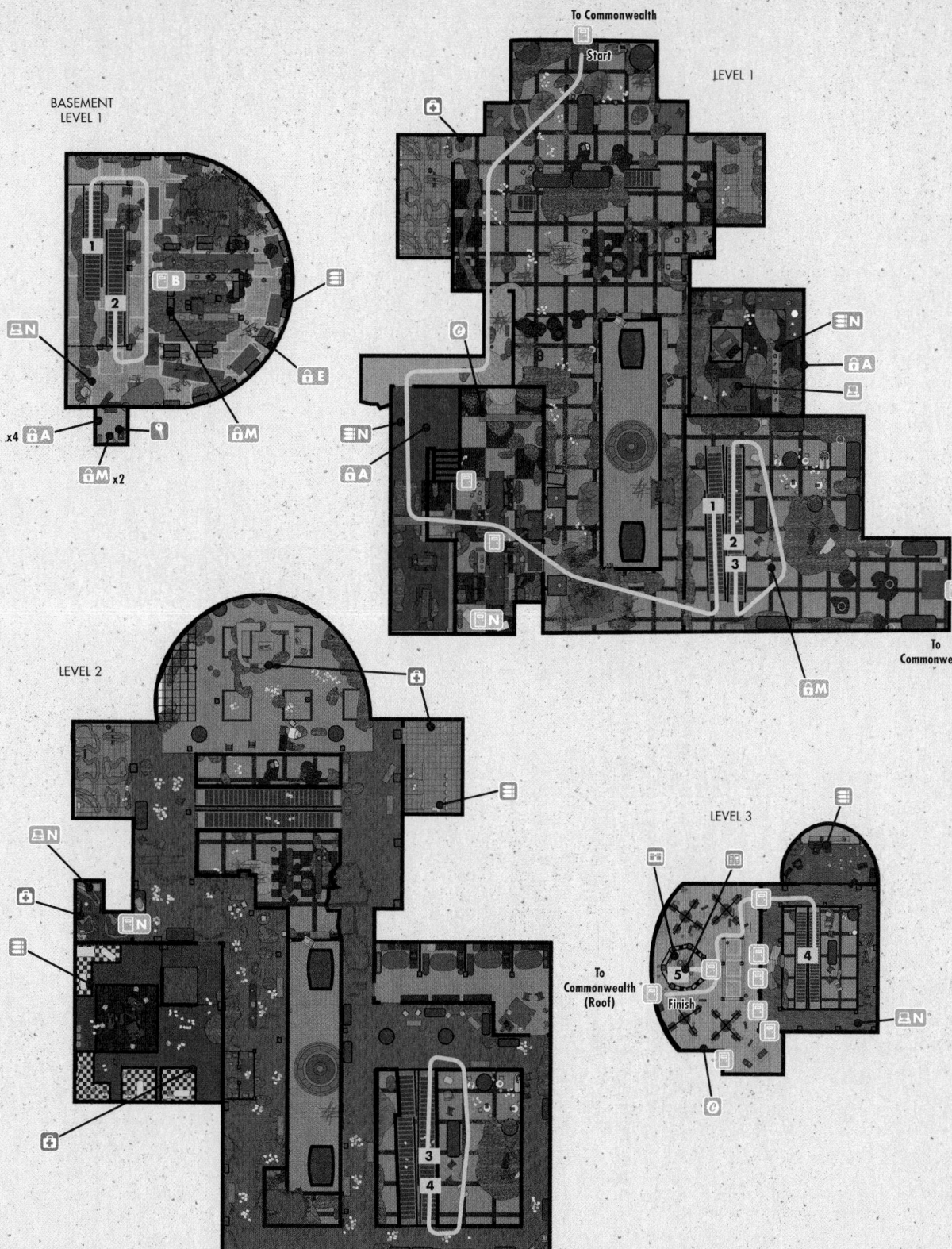

You can access this impressively vast department store from the heinous trap-festival funhouse (the parking lot to the north) or the concrete steps that lead from the ground to the roof entrance (the roof has a generator with a Fusion Core to grab). There are two entrances at street level, too.

Inside, prepare for combat with large green foes. Grab the magazine and search the trunk on the top floor, and don't forget to check the basement level—the remains of a jewelry store—to access a button near a Railroad sign. It opens a hidden bookcase in the southwest corner. Pry open six safes. Or just use the key in the toolbox if you're out of bobby pins or patience. Don't leave without heading to the Level 2 "Employees Only" storage room (Novice) on the west wall; there's an Eyebot model kit to take on the shelves near the Protectron and terminal (Novice).

## [6.13] MILTON GENERAL HOSPITAL

THREAT LEVELS 30+

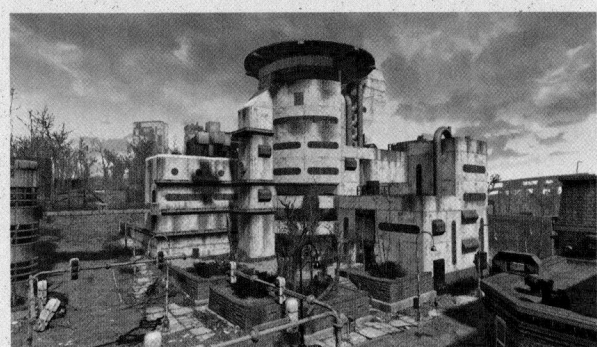

- ARMAMENTS AND AMMO
- ARMAMENTS AND AMMO: TRUNK
- COLLECTIBLE: NUKA COLA QUANTUM
- CRAFTING: CHEMISTRY STATION
- FACTION: ROBOTS
- FACTION: RAIDERS (QUEST ONLY)
- FACTION: CHARACTER: AVERY
- FACTION: CHARACTER: SHINJIN
- HEALTH OR CHEMS
- QUEST VISIT: THE SILVER SHROUD (SIDE)

### VAULT-TEC RECOMMENDED LOOT

COLLECTIBLE: NUKA COLA QUANTUM

**FIG 6.13: MILTON GENERAL HOSPITAL (INTERIOR)**

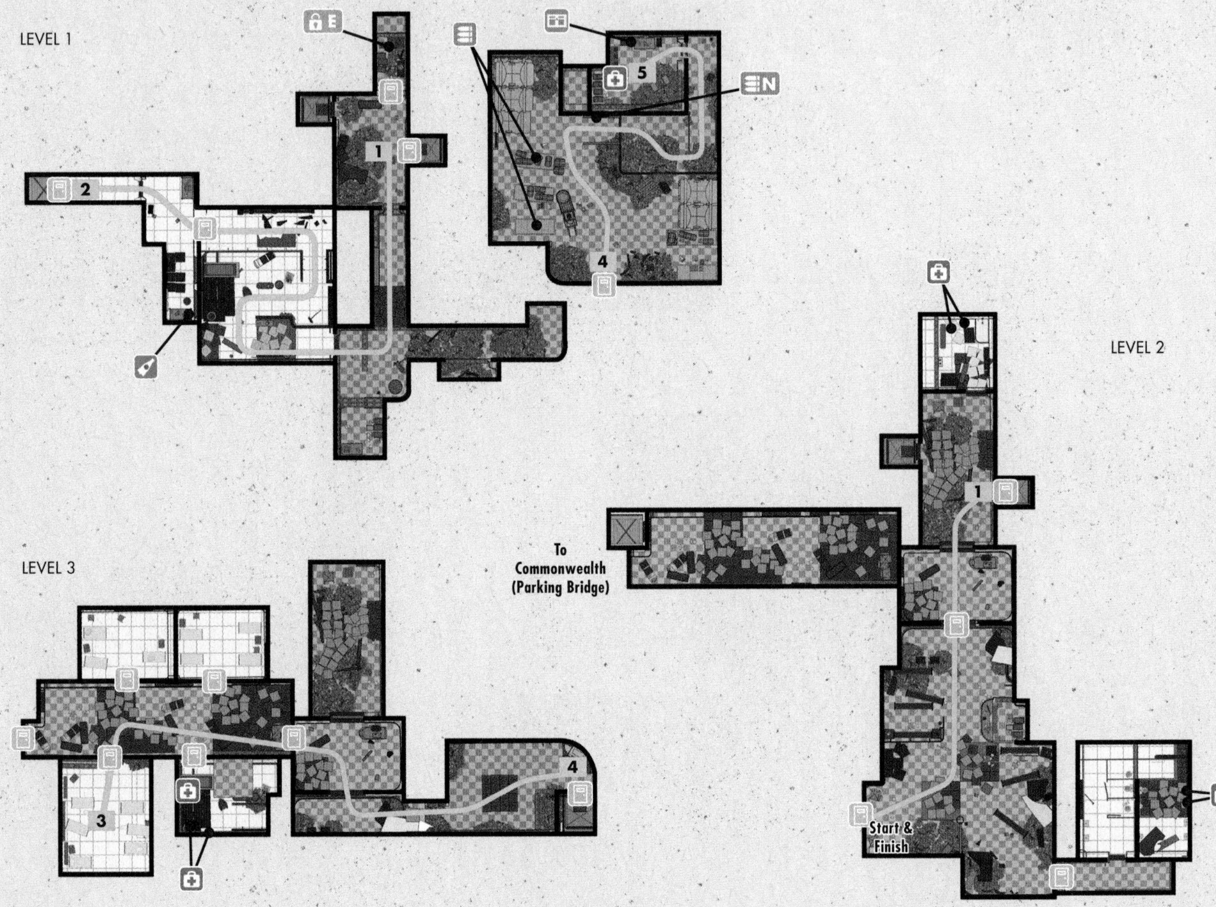

LEVEL 1
E
1
2
N
5
4
LEVEL 2
To Commonwealth (Parking Bridge)
1
Start & Finish
LEVEL 3
3
4

LEVEL 4
2
3

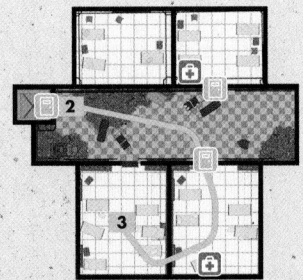

Historically, this hospital survived on donations from local churches and city funds until the invention of automated surgery. This hospital saw record earnings by employing a staff of Nurse Handys and Doctor Handy, MD, models and had a strong legal team to cover up any lawsuits. Then the bombs dropped.

There are two entrances to this confusing set of interior ruins (pause at the morgue for a refreshing Quantum). As long as you use each elevator once and don't fall through holes in the floor, you'll eventually reach the basement where the steamer trunk, or Shinjin if the quest is active, is located.

THREAT LEVELS 30+

- ARMAMENTS AND AMMO
- ARMAMENTS AND AMMO: TRUNK
- BOTTLECAPS
- COLLECTIBLE: NUKA CHERRY
- COLLECTIBLE: REQUIRED READING: TUMBLERS TODAY
- CRAFTING: ARMOR WORKBENCH
- CRAFTING: WEAPONS WORKBENCH
- DANGER: EXPLOSIVE BARRELS!
- DANGER: OIL!
- DANGER: MAKESHIFT BOMB!
- DANGER: TENSION TRIGGER!
- FACTION: RADROACHES
- FACTION: SUPER MUTANTS
- HEALTH OR CHEMS

## VAULT-TEC RECOMMENDED LOOT

COLLECTIBLE: NUKA CHERRY
REQUIRED READING: TUMBLERS TODAY

The exterior of this station is almost a shell of metal, with numerous meat bags and Super Mutants to encounter. Check behind the counter for a wall safe (Advanced) and some ammo in a nearby filing room before entering the station.

The interior involves pressing a series of buttons to move the subway carriages back and forth so you can access a hidden passage to the southwest; this winds back to the chained door area and a steamer trunk. The order of button pressing is shown on the map.

FIG 6.14: WEST ROXBURY STATION (INTERIOR)

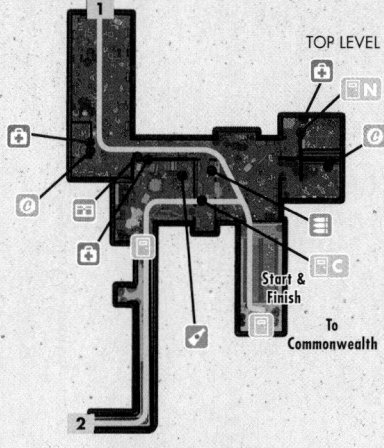

TOP LEVEL

Start & Finish

To Commonwealth

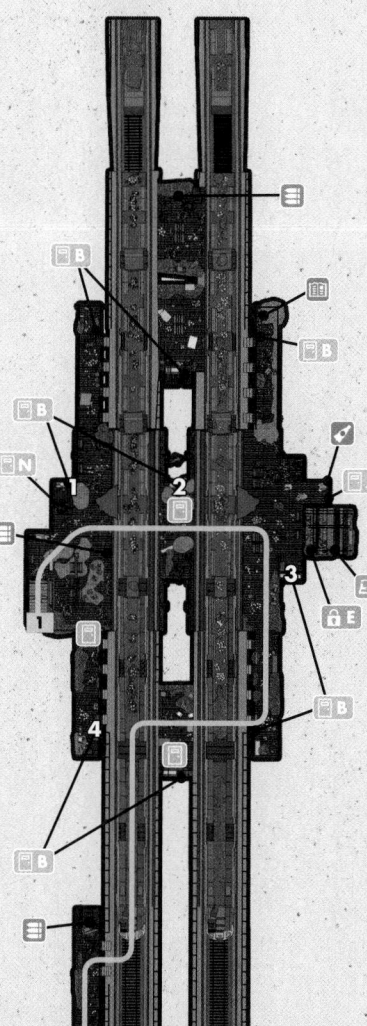

THREAT LEVELS 30+

- ARMAMENTS AND AMMO
- ARMAMENTS AND AMMO: TRUNK
- BOTTLECAPS
- COLLECTIBLE: HOLOTAPE: PROPERTY OF R. BURTON
- COLLECTIBLE: NUKA COLA QUANTUM (2)
- COLLECTIBLE: REQUIRED READING: UNSTOPPABLES
- CRAFTING: ARMOR WORKBENCH
- CRAFTING: CHEMISTRY STATION
- DANGER: CAN CHIMES!
- DANGER: MINES!
- DANGER: TESLA ARC!
- DANGER: TRIPWIRES!
- DANGER: TURRET!
- FACTION: SUPER MUTANT
- HEALTH OR CHEMS+

## VAULT-TEC RECOMMENDED LOOT

COLLECTIBLE: NUKA COLA QUANTUM (2)
REQUIRED READING: UNSTOPPABLES

A modern public school structure, now in rusting ruins with a strong Super Mutant presence in the halls. Do they seem more intelligent than normal?

Enter Principal Tanner's office, east of the entrance (Expert). Find the Library Key inside his locked desk (Novice). His terminal unlocks the nearby door (Master) and Mentats hoard. There's an abundance of this chem here. The library holds the steamer trunk, and the base of the northwest stairwell has some well-hidden Nuka Cola Quantums.

**FIG 6.15: SHAW HIGH SCHOOL (INTERIOR)**

LEVEL 1

LEVEL 2

BASEMENT
LEVEL 1

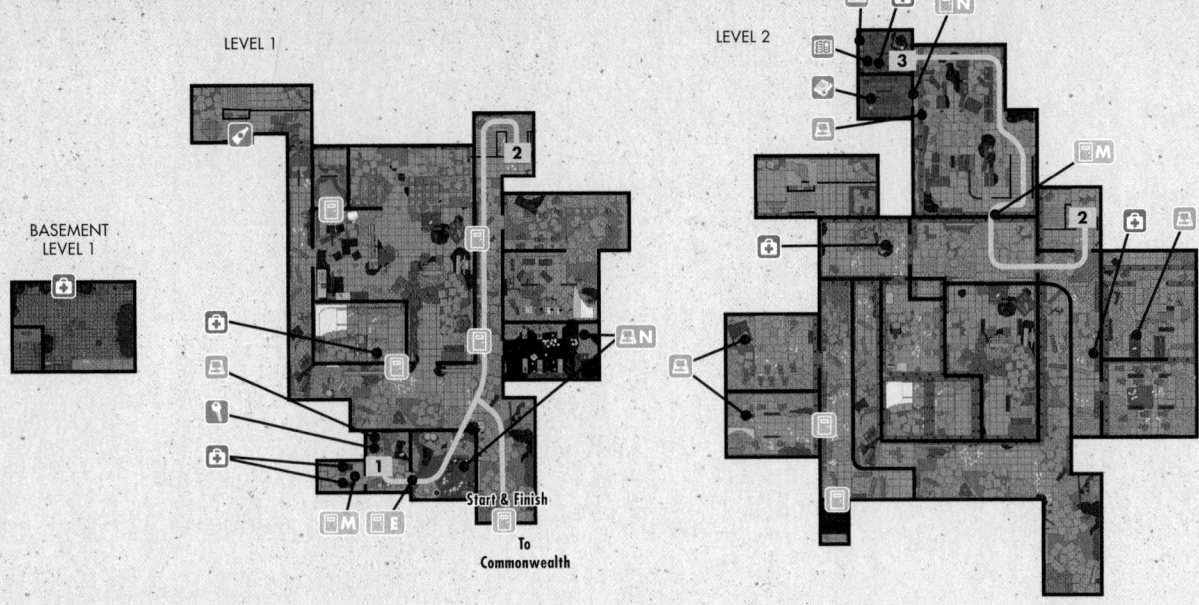

2

1

**N**

**N**

**M**

3

2

Start & Finish

To
Commonwealth

**M**  **E**

---

## WEST ROXBURY: SECONDARY LOCATIONS

### [01] Parking Lot Funhouse

– ARMAMENTS AND AMMO+++
– ARMAMENTS AND AMMO: MINI NUKE
– ARMAMENTS AND AMMO: TRUNK (2)
– ARMOR PART: FUSION CORE (4)
– BOTTLECAPS
– COLLECTIBLE: REQUIRED READING: HOT RODDERS
– CRAFTING: WEAPONS WORKBENCH
– DANGER: ESCAPING GAS!
– DANGER: GRENADES!
– DANGER: MAKESHIFT BOMBS!
– DANGER: TESLA ARCS!
– DANGER: TRIPWIRES!
– DANGER: TURRET!
– FACTION: RADROACHES
– FACTION: FERAL GHOULS
– HEALTH OR CHEMS+++

### VAULT-TEC RECOMMENDED LOOT ⟦⟧

**ARMAMENTS AND AMMO: MINI NUKE**
**ARMOR PART: FUSION CORE (4)**
**REQUIRED READING: HOT RODDER**

Some maniac with a penchant for carnage has set up a frightening series of death chambers in the abandoned parking structure between the hospital and department store. Try to enter via the hospital bridge (you need to access the hospital first or from the bridge to Fallon's), and you'll find your exit is barred. The only entrance is on the ground.

– LEVEL 1: HERE YOU'LL FIND RADROACHES AND SOME MAKESHIFT ROOMS WITH CAPS AND CRATES TO RANSACK. BURNING GAS BECKONS YOU TO SOLVE THE SIMPLE CELL DOOR PUZZLE (HIT BUTTON 1, THEN 3). CHECK THE RED DOOR FOR A TURRET AND FESTIVE DECORATIONS. CHECK THE ROOM OF MONKEYS FOR SOME HEALTH. EXIT VIA THE 18 BATHROOM SCALES; DEACTIVATE THEM ALL TO PREVENT A GRENADE EXPLOSION.

– LEVEL 2: WATCH FOR THE MISSILE LAUNCHER TRAP. KEEP TURNING LEFT TO REACH THE RAMP TO LEVEL 3. INVESTIGATE THE REST OF THIS LEVEL TO REACH SOME HEALTH ABOVE THE LOWER RAMP YOU JUST CAME FROM. THERE'S ALSO A SMALL ALCOVE WHERE SOME SETTLERS CAN BE FOUND (THEY AREN'T IN THE BEST HEALTH).

– LEVEL 3: A LARGE-SCALE FERAL GHOUL AMBUSH CAN BE THWARTED SLIGHTLY BY PLACING TRAPS OR REMAINING AT THE RAMP INSTEAD OF RUNNING BLINDLY AROUND THIS LEVEL. ONCE THE FERALS ARE FINISHED, PROCEED TO THE NEXT RAMP.

– LEVEL 4: BEWARE OF BATHROOM SCALES AND TRIPWIRES CONNECTED TO TESLA ARCS THROUGHOUT THIS AREA. THE BARRED DOOR LEADS TO FALLON'S DEPARTMENT STORE. BUT YOU'RE HERE TO PICK FROM DOORS #1, #2, AND #3:

• DOORS #1 AND #3: YOU MIGHT WANT TO SIDESTEP THESE AS SOON AS YOU OPEN THEM.

• DOOR #2: LEADS TO MORE ROOMS AND TRIPWIRES WITH MAKESHIFT BOMBS. CHECK THE SLEEPING QUARTERS FOR A MAGAZINE AND A WEAPONS WORKBENCH. THERE ARE TWO CELLS WITH A VARIETY OF EXCELLENT PRIZES! BUT YOU CAN ONLY PICK ONE, AS A FLAMETHROWER TRAP INCINERATES THE OTHER BEFORE THE CELL DOOR OPENS!

– THE LEFT CELL: A STEAMER TRUNK, MINI NUKE, A COMBAT ARMOR HELMET, AND FOUR FUSION CORES.
– THE RIGHT CELL: A STEAMER TRUNK AND A LARGE AMOUNT OF CHEMS.

Simply head to the ramp up to the roof from here to access Fallon's, the hospital, or a jump down to the ground and freedom.

## [02] Automobile Dealership

The buckled and twisted metal ruins of a once-shiny car dealership sits along the southern border of this township. There's little to pick through here.

  **[6.16] JAMAICA PLAIN** THREAT LEVELS 30+ THREAT LEVELS 35+

- ARMAMENTS AND AMMO+
- BOTTLECAPS
- COLLECTIBLE: HOLOTAPE: CARL'S LOG
- COLLECTIBLE: HOLOTAPE: SAL'S HOLOTAPE
- COLLECTIBLE: HOLOTAPE: THE TREASURES OF JAMAICA PLAIN
- COLLECTIBLE: HOLOTAPE: TREASURES INVENTORY
- CRAFTING: COOKING STATION
- CRAFTING: POWER ARMOR STATION
- DANGER: ESCAPING GAS!
- DANGER: OIL!
- DANGER: TRIPWIRES!
- DANGER: TURRETS!
- FACTION: FERAL GHOULS
- FACTION: ROBOTS
- FACTION: CHARACTER: CARL EVERETT
- FACTION: CHARACTER: LUKE SILVERHAND
- FACTION: CHARACTER: KEN STANDISH
- FACTION: CHARACTER: SAL
- FACTION: CHARACTER: TANYA STANDISH
- HEALTH OR CHEMS
- QUEST START: MISCELLANEOUS (TREASURE OF JAMAICA PLAIN)
- QUEST VISIT: MISCELLANEOUS (TREASURE OF JAMAICA PLAIN)
- QUEST VISIT: WORLD SERIES WIN (FREEFORM DIAMOND CITY)
- SERVICES: WORKSHOP
- UNIQUE ITEM: ANCHORAGE VETERAN'S FLAG
- UNIQUE ITEM: 2076 WORLD SERIES BASEBALL BAT

### VAULT-TEC RECOMMENDED LOOT

**UNIQUE ITEM: 2076 WORLD SERIES BASEBALL BAT**

**FIG 6.16A: JAMAICA PLAIN (EXTERIOR)**

Ask any Scavenger and they'll tell you, Jamaica Plain is known for both its inhospitable locals and the fabled treasures that lie somewhere inside this Feral Ghoul–infested town. Rumor has it that just before the bombs fell, the neighborhood's inhabitants sealed a vast wealth in a secure chamber somewhere near here. The aforementioned Ghouls have kept any treasure hunters at bay. Until now!

### [01] Jamaica Plain Diner

This diner is open, but not for business. Ferals lurk here.

### [02] Northeast Ruined House

A small amount of ammunition and a feral to set on fire in the locked (Novice) garage.

### [03] Jamaica Plain Duplex

A cluster of Feral Ghouls can be tricky to overcome in the confines of this ruined duplex. Upstairs you'll see Ken and Tanya Standish. They are carrying a Jamaica Plain Flyer. Tanya has a torn journal page. Ken has the Jamaica Plain Archives Key along with an invitation. There's also ammo loot to pocket here, too.

### [04] Eastern Barricade

Carl Everett is taking a rest at the traffic lights here. He's happy to part with the Jamaica Plain Town Hall Key and has a Holotape (Carl's Log) to read through.

### [05] Hardware Store

Two police Protectrons are housed in the remains of this hardware store. There's a terminal here to hack (Novice).

### [06] Jamaica Plain Church

Access this location via the rectory roof. Climb to the steeple, which holds some ammo. This is a good spot to snipe. Then descend into the church. The upper floor has some ammo and chems. Resting on a pew is a man named Luke Silverhand. There's a flyer and note pertinent to the location quest on his person. There's also the mayor's ID, which is critical to the task. Unchain the door to leave, but not before you pocket the Caps stash by Luke's pew.

### [07] Church Rectory

Open either door and watch for the gas leak in the kitchen. There's a light smattering of items and access to the open roof. This is the only way to reach the adjacent church.

### [08] Ruined House (South)

Check the mirror in the upstairs, open-air bathroom of this ruined home.

**FIG 6.16B: JAMAICA PLAIN TOWN HALL BASEMENT (INTERIOR)**

### [09] Jamaica Plain Workshop

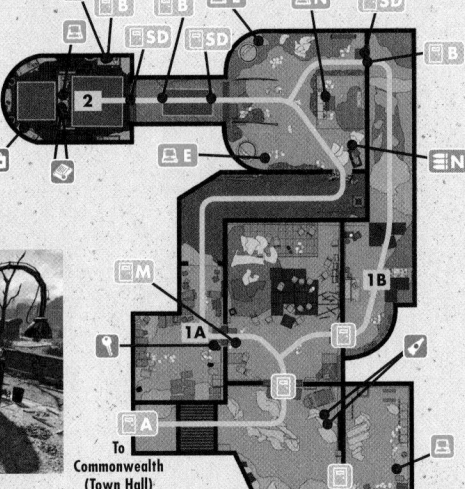

A modest and intact home next to a ruined garage hides a Power Armor station and workshop, allowing you to use this as a Minutemen settlement once all threats are removed.

### [10] Jamaica Plain Town Hall

Although there's no roof, the town hall still holds many secrets. Open the doors and secure the area. Inspect a wall safe (Expert) and terminal (Expert). Then access the blue metal door (or simply move around the hole in the wall), and descend to the basement door, unlocking it using the Town Hall Key you found when you met Carl or by lockpicking (Advanced).

Head through the holes in the bathroom walls and climb to the upper floor (without a roof). Here you'll find Sal, who has the Jamaica Plain Mayor's Password and a Holotape. Take that and any contents from the steamer trunk.

The method for clearing this area is detailed in the Miscellaneous quest:

---

 **Miscellaneous (Treasures of Jamaica Plain)**

**1. FIND THE TREASURES OF JAMAICA PLAIN**

During your exploration, you may stumble upon a flyer, spot a billboard poster, or interact with some ne'er-do-wells that reveal the location of Jamaica Plain and the supposed treasures hidden there.

Explore Jamaica Plain and find Carl Everett, Luke Silverhand, and both Ken and Tanya Standish. Gather the various keys and passwords they possess. Then visit the town hall and find Sal upstairs. Sal won't mind if you borrow the mayor's password.

Enter the town hall basement. In the meeting hall, you can:

- PLAN A: UNLOCK THE ARCHIVES ROOM USING A KEY OR BOBBY PINS (MASTER). WANDER THROUGH THE HOLE IN THE WALL AND ENTER THE INNER SECURITY ROOM.
- PLAN B: MOVE INTO THE SECURITY ROOM, AND IGNORE THE JANITOR'S ID PASSWORD ON THE CONSOLE. INSTEAD, SWIPE THE MAYOR'S ID TO DEACTIVATE THE TRIPWIRE FIELD AND TURRETS. THE SECURITY DOOR UNLOCKS, ALLOWING YOU TO ENTER THE INNER SECURITY ROOM.

Then activate the Treasures Access Terminal (Novice) using the Mayor's Password to open the fabled treasure room. Of course, you can force your way past most of these security systems, but be prepared for a fight.

- ARMAMENTS AND AMMO+++
- ARMAMENTS AND AMMO:
  MINI NUKE (2)
- ARMAMENTS AND AMMO:
  MINI NUKE (FAT MAN)
- ARMAMENTS AND AMMO:
  TRUNK (2)
- ARMOR PART: FUSION CORE
- BOTTLECAPS
- COLLECTIBLE: BOBBLEHEAD:
  SMALL GUNS
- COLLECTIBLE: HOLOTAPE:
  CRUZ'S HOLOTAPE
- COLLECTIBLE: HOLOTAPE:
  RYDER'S HOLOTAPE
- COLLECTIBLE: HOLOTAPE:
  WES'S HOLOTAPE
- COLLECTIBLE: NUKA CHERRY
- COLLECTIBLE: NUKA COLA
  QUANTUM
- COLLECTIBLE: REQUIRED
  READING: GUNS AND
  BULLETS
- CRAFTING: ARMOR
  WORKBENCH (2)
- CRAFTING: CHEMISTRY
  STATION
- CRAFTING: COOKING
  STATION (2)
- CRAFTING: WEAPONS
  WORKBENCH
- DANGER: CAN CHIMES!

- DANGER: GRENADES!
- DANGER: LONG DROP!
- DANGER: OIL!
- DANGER: MAKESHIFT BOMB!
- DANGER: MINES!
- DANGER: TENSION TRIGGER!
- DANGER: TRIPWIRE!
- DANGER: TURRETS!
- FACTION: GUNNERS
- FACTION: CHARACTER: CAPTAIN WES
- FACTION: CHARACTER: CRUZ
- FACTION: CHARACTER: RYDER
- HEALTH AND CHEMS+

## FIG 6.17A: GUNNERS PLAZA (EXTERIOR)

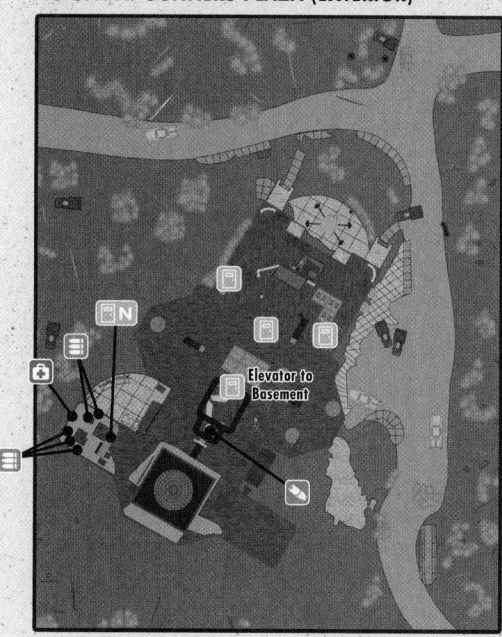

Elevator to Basement

## FIG 6.17B: GUNNERS PLAZA (INTERIOR)

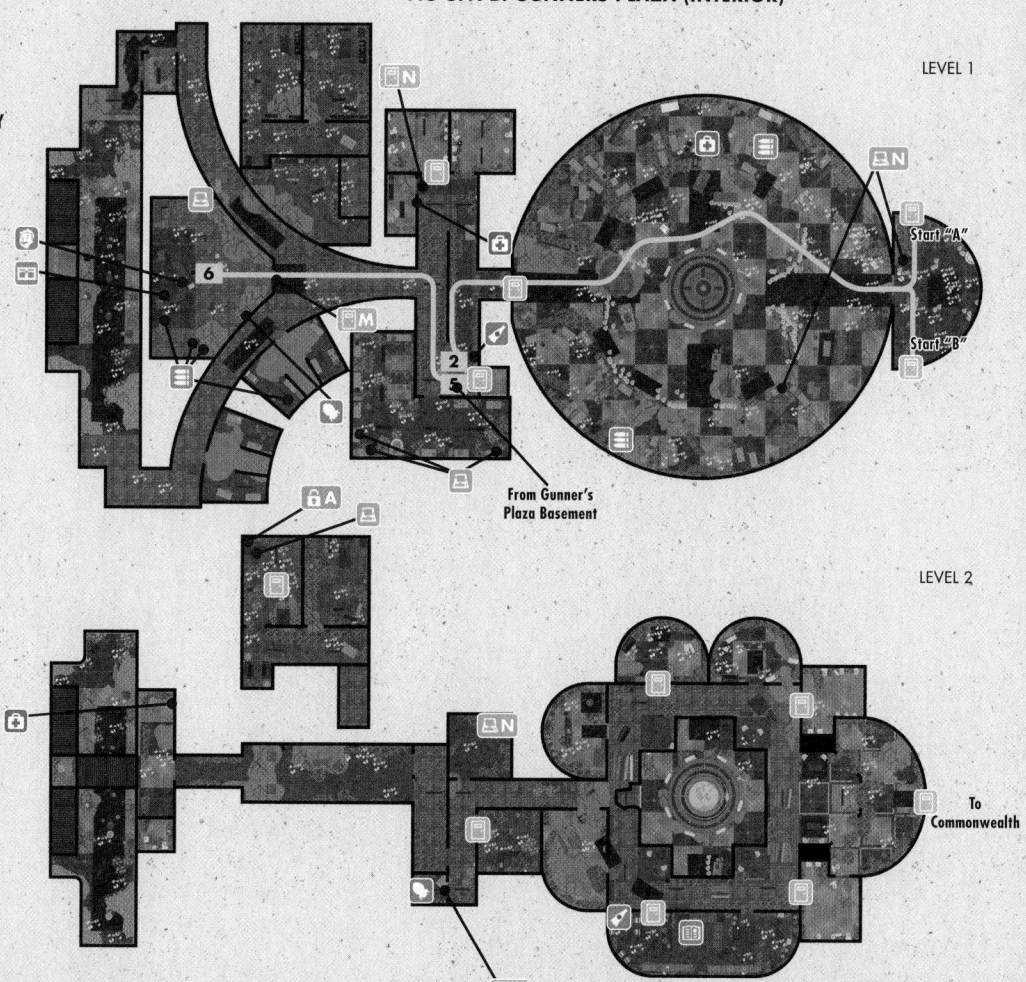

LEVEL 1

Start "A"

Start "B"

6

2
5

From Gunner's
Plaza Basement

LEVEL 2

To
Commonwealth

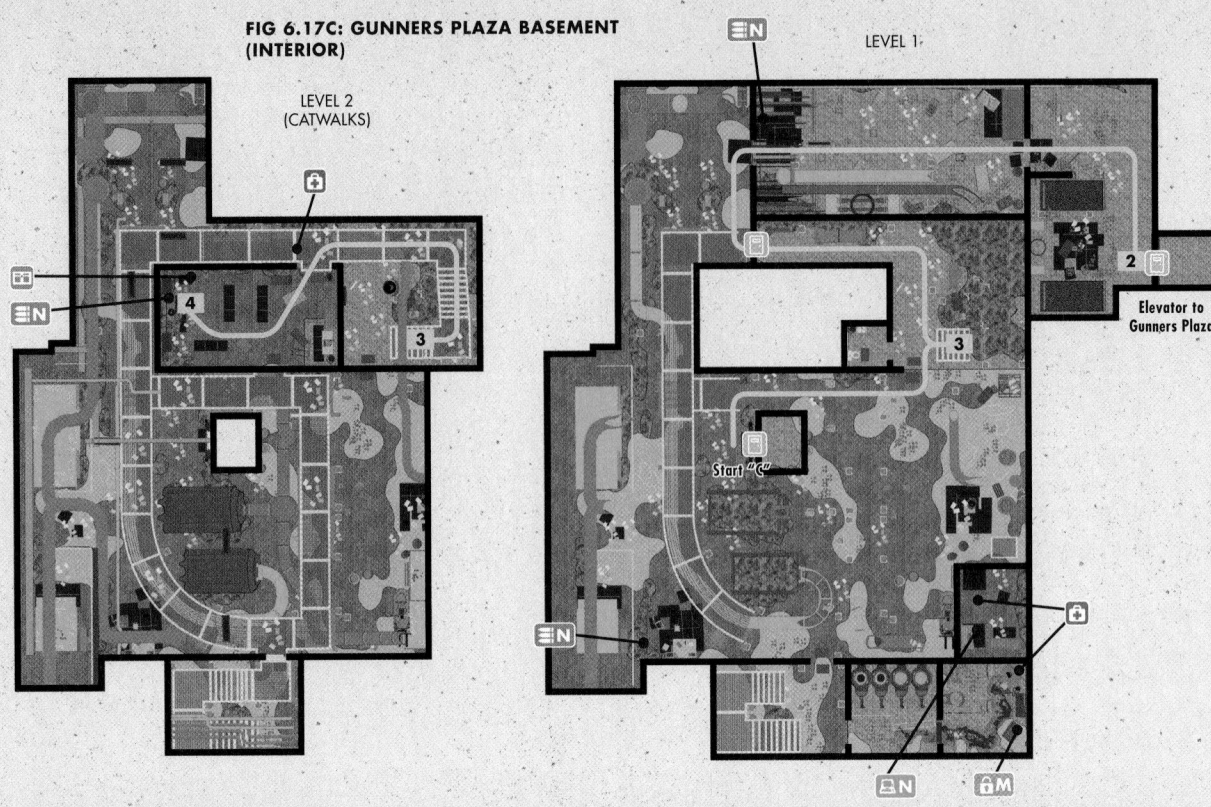

**FIG 6.17C: GUNNERS PLAZA BASEMENT (INTERIOR)**

LEVEL 2
(CATWALKS)

LEVEL 1

4

3

2

Elevator to
Gunners Plaza

3

Start "C"

---

## VAULT-TEC RECOMMENDED LOOT ☢

**ARMAMENTS AND AMMO: MINI NUKE (2) AND FAT MAN**
**ARMOR PART: FUSION CORE**
**BOBBLEHEAD: SMALL GUNS**
**COLLECTIBLE: NUKA CHERRY**
**COLLECTIBLE: NUKA COLA QUANTUM**
**REQUIRED READING: GUNS AND BULLETS**

This was once the headquarters of the Galaxy News Network, delivering pro-government televised newsreels. Since the bombs dropped, the station has changed hands and is now the main base of a gang of ruthless mercenaries known as the Gunners. Their insignia (the "targeted skull") is daubed on their defenses. You can use a side fire escape or mount a charge from the north to reach the roof (and Fusion Core). The two main doors to the ground floor rotunda are on the sides of the structure.

Inside, the Gunner Cruz (roaming the top floor) has the GNN Recording Room Key and a Holotape. Or, you can obtain the same key from Ryder in the basement, along with a key for the safe (Master) in the basement.

In the basement (accessed via the elevator), expect further Gunner confrontations. After making a sweep, use the elevator to return to the main floor (Optimal Path waypoint #5), head into the recording room (waypoint #6) where Captain Wes is stationed. He has a safe key on his person, which opens a safe (Master) with his holotape in it. Don't forget the Bobblehead on the recording room's main desk.

 **[6.18] HYDE PARK**  THREAT LEVELS 35+ ▮▮▮▮▮▯▯▯▯▯

- ARMAMENTS AND AMMO
- ARMAMENTS AND AMMO: TRUNK BOTTLECAPS
- COLLECTIBLE: REQUIRED READING: GROGNAK THE BARBARIAN
- CRAFTING: ARMOR WORKBENCH
- CRAFTING: POWER ARMOR STATION
- CRAFTING: WEAPONS WORKBENCH
- DANGER: GRENADES!

- DANGER: MINES!
- DANGER: RADIATION (MILD)!
- DANGER: TRIPWIRES!
- FACTION: RAIDERS
- FACTION: ROBOTS
- FACTION: SCAVENGERS
- FACTION: CHARACTER: SCUTTER
- HEALTH OR CHEMS

## VAULT-TEC RECOMMENDED LOOT ☢

 **REQUIRED READING: GROGNAK THE BARBARIAN**

Local reports state that this seemingly deserted town has been taken over by Raiders with a penchant for skinning and wearing their victims. Most neighborly. You are advised to remain away from the flooded main thoroughfare to maximize your chances of survival.

**FIG 6.18: HYDE PARK (EXTERIOR)**

### [01] Northwest Warehouse

A small warehouse with an armor workbench.

### [02] Northeast Ruined House

An overdosed settler provides some reasonable loot.

### [03] Northeast Access Bridges

Don't get your feet wet and enter the rooftops from this series of ramped planks. Mines and Raiders await inside. There's health on the level above the water and ammo on the blown-out roof area.

### [04] Northern Rooftops

Accessed this via the main bridge running north-south, or location #03.

### [05] South Access Bridges and Main Camp

Use the overturned car and ramps to reach the main Raider camp. The first dry floor has a room with a weapons workbench, ammo, chems, and health. The blown-out bedroom upstairs has some ammo and access to the main north-south bridge. But stay on the stairs to reach the upper camp where Scutter and his brethren reside. Come for the carnage. Stay for the copy of Grognak the Barbarian, steamer trunk, ammo, and neighborly note.

### [06] Southwest Rooftop

A lookout hut with ammo inside.

### [07] Workshop Warehouse (Southeast)

Though the meat on the barbecue isn't for eating, there's a Power Armor station to tinker on.

### [08] Waterlogged Warehouse (South)

Is wading and swimming through irradiated water worth the first aid box loot? That's a decision you'll have to make.

### [09] Hyde Park Church

You encounter two Scavengers and a couple of robots. Upstairs are some chems and ammo, but the real prize is on the roof; there's excellent sniping opportunities across Hyde Park to the northeast.

- ARMAMENTS AND AMMO
- ARMAMENTS AND AMMO: TRUNK
- ARMOR PART: FUSION CORE
- COLLECTIBLE: HOLOTAPE: SCHOOL ANNOUNCEMENTS OCT. 18TH
- COLLECTIBLE: HOLOTAPE: SCHOOL ANNOUNCEMENTS OCT. 20TH
- COLLECTIBLE: HOLOTAPE: SCHOOL ANNOUNCEMENTS OCT. 22ND
- COLLECTIBLE: REQUIRED READING: UNSTOPPABLES
- BOTTLECAPS
- CRAFTING: CHEMISTRY STATION
- CRAFTING: COOKING STATION
- DANGER: OIL!
- DANGER: RADIATION (MILD)!
- FACTION: FERAL GHOULS
- FACTION: IRRADIATED WILDLIFE (RADROACHES)
- UNIQUE ITEM: FOOD PASTE

The student base of this school consisted mostly of lower-income and disadvantaged students. These children were lucky enough to be chosen for trials of a new food substitute paste developed by Vault-Tec in conjunction with the U.S. government. The paste was intended to provide all necessary nutrition and have a shelf life of over 100 years. Despite some minor side effects, the paste is both nutritious and delicious. Why not try some yourself? You'll be in the pink!

The exterior of this school has a small playground teeming with Feral Ghouls. Wade through the slightly irradiated water to reach the main entrance by the bus. Or use the rear entrance by the marsh and playground.

Inside, you must fight off a group of Feral Ghouls with an odd hue to their complexions.

## VAULT-TEC RECOMMENDED LOOT

**ARMOR PART: FUSION CORE**
**REQUIRED READING: UNSTOPPABLES**
**UNIQUE ITEM: FOOD PASTE**

LEVEL 1

FIG 6.19: SUFFOLK COUNTY CHARTER SCHOOL (INTERIOR)

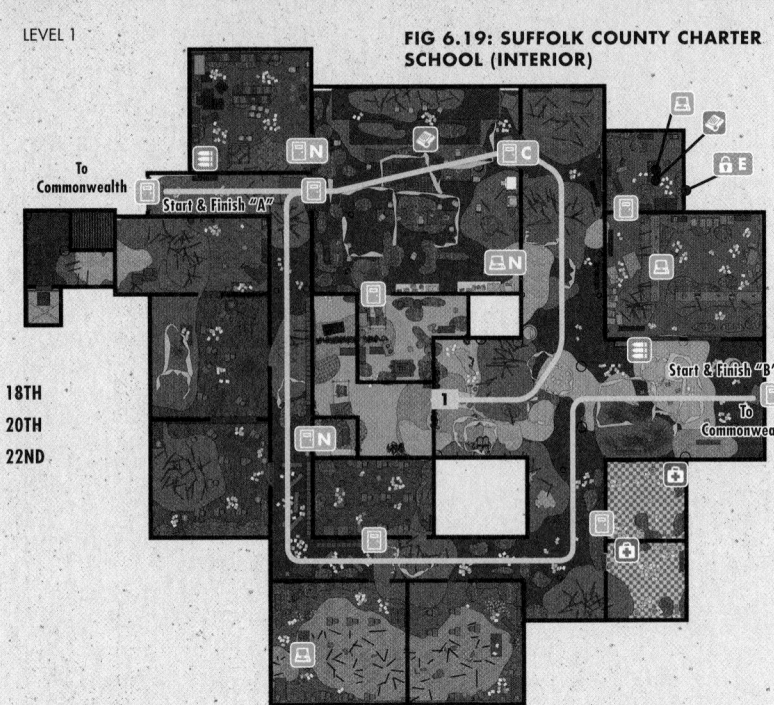

To Commonwealth

Start & Finish "A"

Start & Finish "B"

To Commonwealth

BASEMENT LEVEL 1

BASEMENT LEVEL 2

LEVEL 2

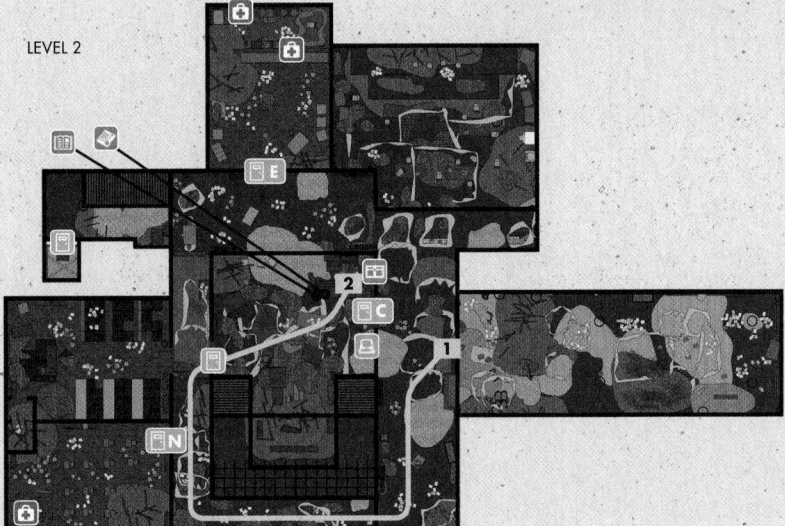

**[6.20] MURKWATER CONSTRUCTION SITE**  THREAT LEVELS 40+

- FACTION: MIRELURKS    - SERVICES: WORKSHOP

Despite the abundance of marshland south of Hyde Park, construction had begun on the outskirts of this area before the bombs dropped. Venture farther into the swamp to uncover some secondary locations. Currently, this area is teeming with wildlife of the irradiated and pincer-snapping kind. If made safe, this could be an excellent settlement location.

**[6.21] QUINCY QUARRIES**  THREAT LEVELS 40+

**FIG 6.21: QUINCY QUARRIES (EXTERIOR)**

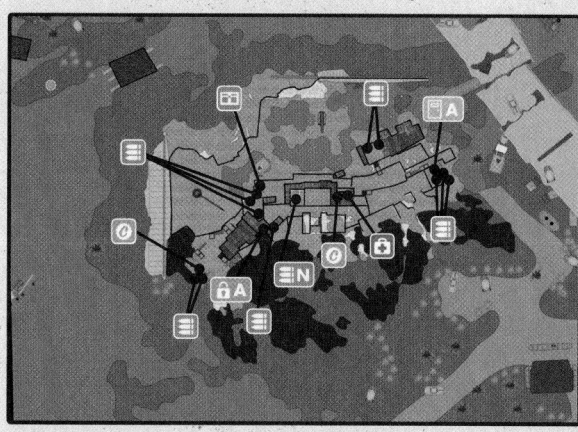

- ARMAMENTS AND AMMO++
- ARMAMENTS AND AMMO: TRUNK
- BOTTLECAPS++
- CRAFTING: COOKING STATION
- DANGER: RADIATION (MILD)!

- DANGER: TURRETS!
- FACTION: RAIDERS
- FACTION: CHARACTER: SLOUGH
- HEALTH OR CHEMS

 **VAULT-TEC RECOMMENDED LOOT**

 **BOTTLECAPS**

A large marble quarry northwest of Quincy is now flooded with water. Please refrain from drinking; the water is radioactive from the toxic dump of rusting barrels dumped here. A small contingent of Raiders spend their time huffing narcotics and growing paranoid. Use lockpicking prowess to open the trailer on the upper quarry (Expert). Farther along the marble-side pathway is a safe (Advanced). Check the cut marble lower level for a bedroom with a wooden crate (Novice) to pry open.

 **[6.22] NEPONSET PARK**  THREAT LEVELS 35+

- ARMAMENTS AND AMMO
- CRAFTING: COOKING STATION

- DANGER: RADIATION (MILD)!
- FACTION: MIRELURKS

Once a weekend getaway for the Dieter family, this small coast park is now infested with Mirelurks. Inspect the barnacle-clad trailer and two cabins; one is locked (Advanced) but has a steamer trunk and notes from the family on a terminal.

- ARMAMENTS AND AMMO
- ARMAMENTS AND AMMO: TRUNK (2)
- ARMOR PART: FUSION CORE
- CRAFTING: WEAPONS WORKBENCH
- DANGER: LONG DROP!

- DANGER: RADIATION (MILD)!
- FACTION: SUPER MUTANTS
- HEALTH OR CHEMS
- QUEST VISIT: MISCELLANEOUS
  (ARLEN GLASS)

This was a relatively new facility built in 2075 to produce the company's line of Giddyup Buttercup robotic toys. Records show that in late 2077, it was secretly being converted to produce mines for the war effort. Recently, a clan of Super Mutants have taken over.

**FIG 6.23: WILSON ATOMATOYS FACTORY (EXTERIOR AND INTERIOR)**

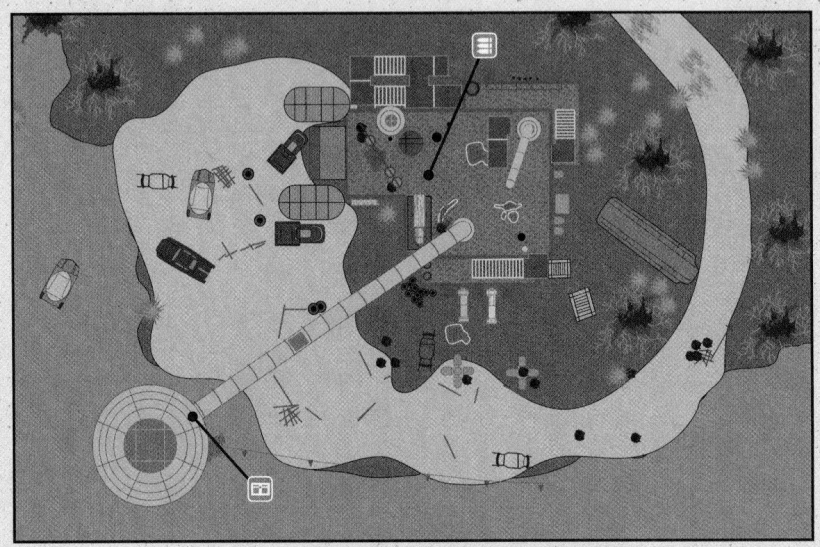

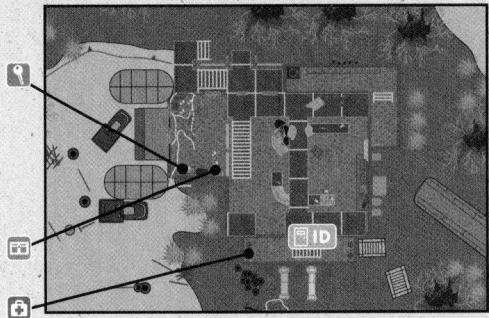

Access the roof and climb on the yellow machinery to reach the large pipe that connects the factory to the water tower (southwest). Drop into this horizontal pipe bridge to reach a cunningly hidden steamer trunk.

Inside the factory, one of the Super Mutants has a Wilson Atomatoys ID Card that you can use to enter a small storeroom, where you can find the Giddyup Buttercup parts needed by Arlen Glass. There's a steamer trunk on the balcony area, too.

# [6.24–26] QUINCY TOWNSHIP

QUINCY TOWNSHIP (EXTERIOR)

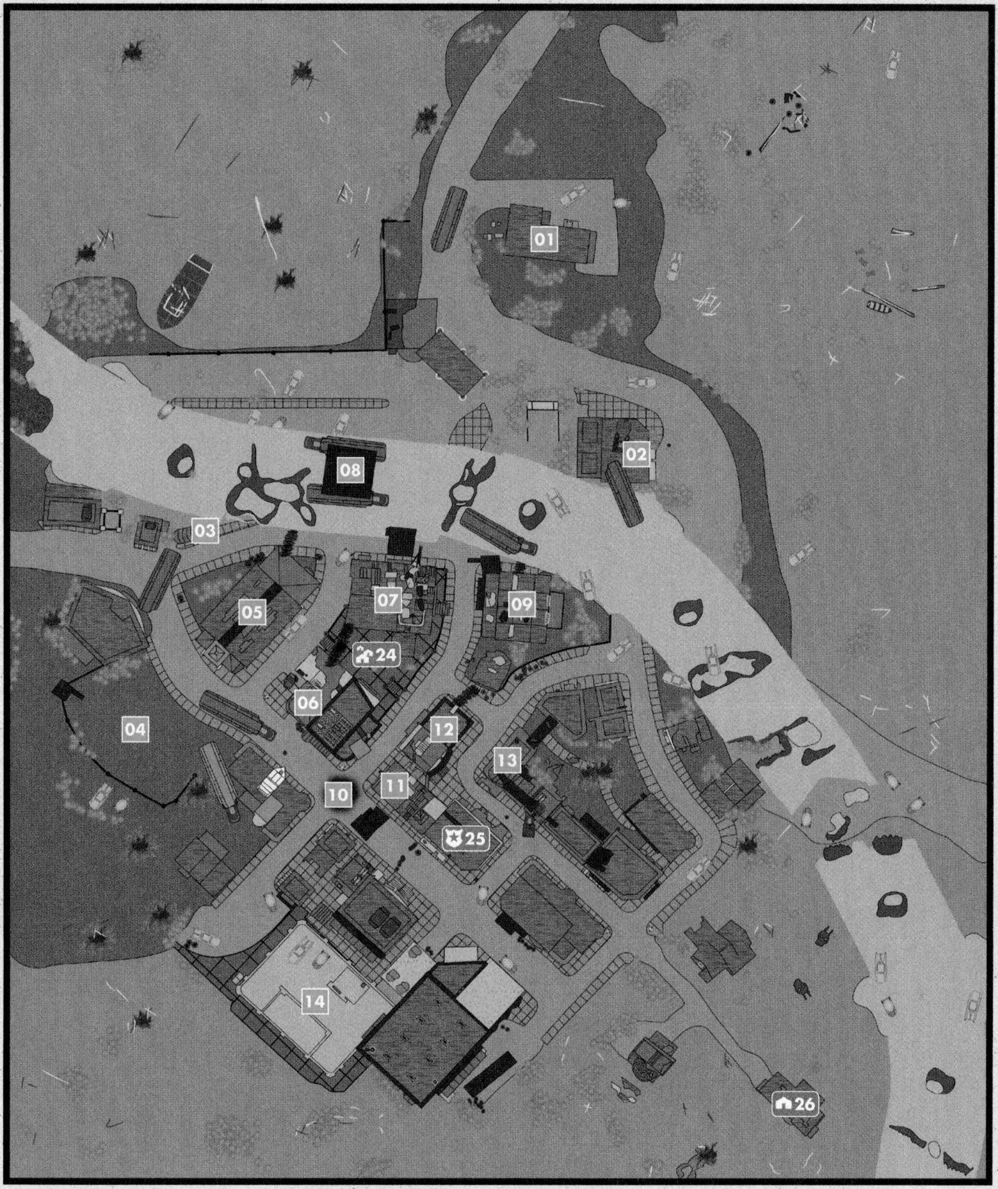


## [6.24] QUINCY RUINS

THREAT LEVELS 40+

THREAT LEVELS 45+

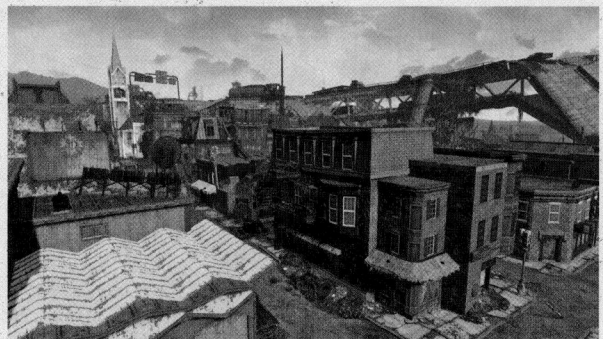

- ARMAMENTS AND AMMO++
- ARMAMENTS AND AMMO: MINI NUKE
- ARMAMENTS AND AMMO: MINI NUKE (FAT MAN)
- ARMAMENTS AND AMMO: TRUNK
- ARMOR PART: FUSION CORE
- ARMOR PART: POWER ARMOR (LEVELED)
- ARMOR PART: POWER ARMOR (LEVELED)
- BOTTLECAPS
- COLLECTIBLE: HOLOTAPE: TESSA'S HOLOTAPE
- COLLECTIBLE: NUKA COLA QUANTUM
- COLLECTIBLE: REQUIRED READING: GUNS AND BULLETS
- CRAFTING: CHEMISTRY STATION (2)
- CRAFTING: COOKING STATION (3)
- CRAFTING: POWER ARMOR STATION
- CRAFTING: WEAPONS WORKBENCH (2)
- DANGER: GRENADES!
- DANGER: LONG DROP!
- DANGER: MINES!
- DANGER: TRIPWIRES!
- DANGER: TURRETS!
- FACTION: GUNNERS
- FACTION: RADSCORPIONS
- FACTION: SETTLERS (GHOULS)
- FACTION: CHARACTER: BAKER
- FACTION: CHARACTER: BULLET (QUEST ONLY)
- FACTION: CHARACTER: CLINT
- HEALTH OR CHEMS++
- UNIQUE ITEM: GOOD INTENTIONS

**ARMAMENTS AND AMMO:**
**MINI NUKE AND FAT MAN**
**ARMOR PART: FUSION CORE**
**ARMOR PART: POWER ARMOR (LEVELED)**

**ARMOR PART: POWER ARMOR (LEVELED)**
**COLLECTIBLE: NUKA COLA QUANTUM**
**REQUIRED READING: GUNS AND BULLETS**
**UNIQUE ITEM: GOOD INTENTIONS**

Due to some controversial zoning, the freeway was run right over the main street, near the buildings of this once-picturesque and historical settlement. John Adams, John Quincy Adams, and John Hancock were all born here. Currently, Gunners have taken over the Quincy ruins and a section of freeway that runs through the town. This was once a Minutemen stronghold until the arrival of the Gunners and a defection of one of the Minutemen's own.

## [01] Beachside Warehouse

A small band of unpleasant Scavengers have made their home here.

## [02] Big Rig Rooftop

Head upstairs to gather some chems.

## [03] Quincy Station

The northwest entrance has a turret and barricades to worry about. Enter the train car, and disarm the tripwires to prevent a missile to the face.

## [04] Quincy Cemetery

Settlers have planted gourds here, which the Gunners are ignoring in favor of using the walled area as defenses. There's ammo at the rickety watchtower to the west.

## [05] Sturges' Church

The church where Sturges did some tinkering is here. Read about him at his terminal once the Gunner threats are met. There's a cooking station, weapons workbench, and Power Armor station inside here. Check a small wooden crate for the Fusion Core. There's health at the stairs and a safe (Expert) on the upper level. Climb the steeple to reach a good sniping spot for the Gunner camp at the freeway, or cross the rooftops for a closer inspection.

Active in this area is the Gunner named Baker. He usually carries a Fat Man, as well as Tessa's Holotape. There's direct access to the freeway from here, or a jump to location #07.

## [06] Diner and Gun Shop

Mama Murphy's Diner is seemingly picked clean, but climb the stairs and access the door onto the narrow balcony to claim her stash of chems (below the "Apartments" sign).

The gun shop has a few bits of ammo and weaponry, a weapons workbench, and a Caps stash under the counter. The wall terminal (Advanced) unlocks the floor safe. Open the barred door by dropping down the roof hole into the bathroom with the health and dead settler in it. Access location #07 from the ground or roof.

### [07] Fenton's Food Stuffs and Abandoned Apartment

A small shack store selling questionable meat is in the main market area in front of a ruined apartment structure. The apartments have four floors, including the roof. Watch the turret.

### [08] Gunners Freeway Stronghold

The main Gunner base overlooks Quincy and is therefore difficult to storm. Access is via one of the rickety bridges from the apartment building or church. Scavenge the area for a Nuka Cola Quantum and health, and use the collapsed freeway section to reach the top tier of the freeway.

When threats are abated, scrounge the camp for a Mini Nuke, ammo, a steam trunk, information from a Gunner terminal, and an issue of Guns and Bullets magazine. This is also where Clint is. He's wearing some impressive Power Armor and carries a unique laser rifle.

### [09] Old Headquarters (Abandoned)

There's a terminal revealing the goings-on that led to the Minutemen fleeing Quincy. There's also ammo here. Access this once-stately building from the roof bridges or ground.

### [10] Corpse Pile and Defenses

The main thoroughfare through Quincy has numerous obstacles, the most grotesque of which is a still-smoldering pile of bodies. At least the Gunners don't discriminate; there are dead Raiders and settlers here. To the southeast is a wall with a chained door to unlock.

### [11] Marcie & Jun Long's Store

In the middle of the Gunner encampment at ground level, the pharmacy can be entered from the corpse pile. Inside, the establishment has been mostly picked clean. But the terminal has interesting information on Jun Long, one of Preston Garvey's Minutemen. There's an unlocked safe under the stairs, a chemistry station, a cooking stove and ammo upstairs, and roof access to more gangplanks.

### [12] Quincy Liquor

The liquor store has a chemistry station and terminal, but little else. There's no roof access, and the alley door as part of the Gunner stronghold is locked (Advanced). Access this roof via locations #09 or #11.

### [13] Rooftops and Courtyard

Accessed from the police station, the rooftops to the northeast, or the fire escape in the courtyard, the rickety bridges allow you to crisscross above the streets. There's some health and chems up here.

### [14] Parking Lot

Watch for tripwires between here and the police station. Aside from a Radscorpion and a rusty Vault-Tec truck with a trunk in the back, the place has been picked clean. You can leap to the lot roof and across to the corner roof of the Super Duper Mart if you're fighting foes below.

THREAT LEVELS 45+

- ARMAMENTS AND AMMO
- ARMOR PART: FUSION CORE
- ARMOR PART: POWER ARMOR (LEVELED)
- COLLECTIBLE: HOLOTAPE: EDDIE WINTER'S HOLOTAPE
- COLLECTIBLE: HOLOTAPE: BAKER'S HOLOTAPE
- FACTION: GUNNERS
- FACTION: CHARACTER: TESSA
- HEALTH OR CHEMS
- QUEST VISIT: LONG TIME COMING (SIDE)
- UNIQUE ITEM: TESSA'S FIST (WEAPON)

**VAULT-TEC RECOMMENDED LOOT**

ARMOR PART: FUSION CORE
ARMOR PART: POWER ARMOR (LEVELED)
UNIQUE ITEM: TESSA'S FIST (WEAPON)

Expect heavy fire and punching power from a group of Gunners led by the Power Armor–clad Tessa. Inside the building is a book return terminal and another terminal where you can take Baker's Holotape for Tessa. Expect ammo and a series of precarious ramps across Quincy Ruins if you venture upstairs. Look for the door down into the lockup. Inside is a Protectron and a terminal you can use to unlock all the cell doors, including the locked one (Expert), and read up on Eddie Winter. Another of Eddie Winter's Holotapes is on one of the lockers.

 **[6.26] PEABODY HOUSE**   THREAT LEVELS 45+

- ARMAMENTS AND AMMO
- COLLECTIBLE: NUKA COLA QUANTUM
- FACTION: CHARACTER: CAROL PEABODY
- FACTION: CHARACTER: CLINT
- FACTION: CHARACTER: MATT PEABODY
- HEALTH OR CHEMS
- QUEST VISIT: KID IN A FRIDGE (SIDE)

**VAULT-TEC RECOMMENDED LOOT**

 COLLECTIBLE: NUKA COLA QUANTUM

Matt and Carol Peabody live here along with their son, who seems to have gone missing. These two friendly Ghouls are related to the specified quest. Look for a Caps stash in the oven, and head upstairs to find an unlocked wall safe with ammo and a first aid box.

**ARMOR PART: FUSION CORE**
**ARMOR PART: POWER ARMOR (VARIOUS)**
**BOBBLEHEAD: UNARMED**
**REQUIRED READING: HOT RODDER**
**UNIQUE ITEM: ZEKE'S JACKET AND JEANS**

- ARMAMENTS AND AMMO
- ARMOR PART: FUSION CORE
- ARMOR PART: POWER ARMOR (VARIOUS)
- COLLECTIBLE: BOBBLEHEAD: UNARMED
- COLLECTIBLE: REQUIRED READING: HOT RODDER
- CRAFTING: ARMOR WORKBENCH
- CRAFTING: POWER ARMOR STATION (2)
- CRAFTING: WEAPONS WORKBENCH
- DANGER: TRIPWIRES!
- FACTION: SETTLERS (ATOM CATS)
- FACTION: CHARACTER: BLUEJAY
- FACTION: CHARACTER: DUKE
- FACTION: CHARACTER: JOHNNY D.
- FACTION: CHARACTER: ROWDY
- FACTION: CHARACTER: ROXY
- FACTION: CHARACTER: ZEKE
- FACTION: GUNNERS
- HEALTH AND CHEMS
- QUEST START: MISCELLANEOUS (ATOM CATS)
- SERVICES: TRADER (BLUEJAY)
- SERVICES: TRADER (ROWDY)
- UNIQUE ITEM: ZEKE'S JACKET AND JEANS

**FIG 6.27: ATOM CATS GARAGE (EXTERIOR)**

A group of friendly Greasers make their base of operations from this abandoned garage and scrap yard. Be sure to get on the Cats' good side, daddio, as Rowdy offers some choice Power Armor mods. Zeke's terminal (Novice) is worth a hack. Their Holotape poetry? An acquired taste.

 **Miscellaneous (Atom Cats)**

| | | |
|---|---|---|
| 1. TALK TO ROWDY | 3. TELL JUNE WARWICK ABOUT THE FIX | 5. DEFEAT THE GUNNERS |
| 2. REPAIR THE WATER PUMP AT WARWICK | 4. RETURN TO ROWDY | 6. TALK TO ZEKE |

Speak with Zeke and refrain from violence. To join these cool Cats, speak with Rowdy, who wants you to install a water pump. Visit the nearby settlement, tinker with the pump, speak with June, and return to the Atom Cats. You're interrupted by a Gunner attack. Repel this before you're welcomed into the faction and given a groovy outfit.

FIG 6.28A: POSEIDON ENERGY (EXTERIOR)

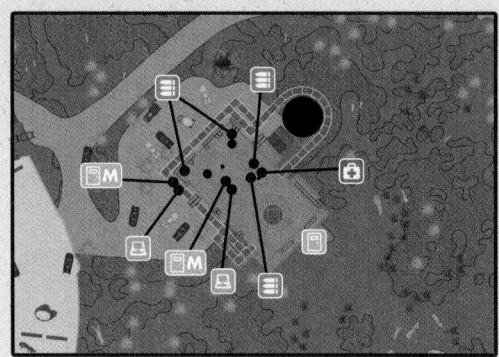

- ARMAMENTS AND AMMO++
- ARMAMENTS AND AMMO: TRUNK
- ARMOR PART: POWER ARMOR (RAIDER)
- COLLECTIBLE: BOBBLEHEAD: ENDURANCE
- COLLECTIBLE: NUKA CHERRY (2)
- COLLECTIBLE: REQUIRED READING: TESLA SCIENCE
- BOTTLECAPS+
- CRAFTING: CHEMISTRY STATION
- DANGER: CAN CHIMES!
- DANGER: LONG DROP!
- DANGER: MINES!
- DANGER: RADIATION (SEVERE)!
- DANGER: TRIPWIRE!
- FACTION: MIRELURKS
- FACTION: RAIDERS
- FACTION: ROBOTS
- FACTION: CHARACTER: CUTTY
- HEALTH OR CHEMS

FIG 6.28B: POSEIDON ENERGY SUBLEVELS (INTERIOR)

## VAULT-TEC RECOMMENDED LOOT

**ARMOR PART: POWER ARMOR (RAIDER)**
**BOBBLEHEAD: ENDURANCE**
**COLLECTIBLE: NUKA CHERRY (2)**
**REQUIRED READING: TESLA SCIENCE**

This Poseidon Energy corporation power plant uses natural gas and solar energy. Currently, a gang of raiders have set up defenses against the robot security active at this location, as well as encroaching mirelurks.

Currently, Raiders have set up here and fortified a safe zone in the upper floors of the power plant. Turrets and traps defend against the robots on the ground floor.

Both the ground-level entrance and the rooftop door access via the gantry are difficult to open (Master), and the adjacent terminal doesn't access it. Instead, try swimming up through an outflow pipe to the southeast.

Fancy being drenched by radioactive water as you swim and climb through a Mirelurk lair? Then you've come to the right place. Remember you must submerge and wade through underwater rooms to gain progress.

Cutty is carrying a most impressive minigun and is wearing Power Armor. His Poseidon Energy Key opens the ground and roof exits. Don't leave his metal hut chamber in the middle of the catwalks without claiming a limited-edition Vault-Tec Bobblehead and some light reading.

## FIG 6.28C: POSEIDON ENERGY (INTERIOR)

To Poseidon Energy
Sublevels

Start or
Finish "A"

N

SD

Start or
Finish "B"

M

To
Commonwealth

N

LEVEL 1

**1**

N

To
Commonwealth
(Roof)

**2**

**3**

**4**

**1**

LEVEL 2
(CATWALKS)

**2**

**3**

LEVEL 3
(CATWALKS)

## [6.29] WARWICK HOMESTEAD

THREAT LEVELS 45+

- ARMAMENTS AND AMMO
- ARMAMENTS AND AMMO:
  MINI NUKE
- ARMAMENTS AND AMMO:
  TRUNK BOTTLECAPS
- CRAFTING: COOKING STATION
- FACTION: SETTLER
- FACTION: CHARACTER: BILL SUTTON
- FACTION: CHARACTER:
  CEDRIC HOPTON
- FACTION: CHARACTER:
  JANEY WARWICK

- FACTION: CHARACTER:
  JUNE WARWICK
- FACTION: CHARACTER:
  ROGER WARWICK
- FACTION: CHARACTER:
  WALLY WARWICK
- HEALTH OR CHEMS
- QUEST START: MISCELLANEOUS
  (BILL SUTTON)
- QUEST VISIT: BUILDING A BETTER
  CROP (THE INSTITUTE)
- SERVICES: TRADER (JUNE WARWICK)
- SERVICES: WORKSHOP

The fertilizer from this old sewage facility offers great Mutfruit and tato plant growing conditions, if you can get over the stench. Need a Giddyup Buttercup? There's one here.

 **Miscellaneous (Bill Sutton)**

Chat to Bill Sutton, who's happy to hand over a few Caps for each tato you can bring him, from anywhere in the Commonwealth.

## 📟 [6.30] WRECK OF THE FMS NORTHERN STAR

- ARMAMENTS AND AMMO
- ARMAMENTS AND AMMO: MINI NUKE
- ARMAMENTS AND AMMO: TRUNK
- ARMOR PART: FUSION CORE
- BOTTLECAPS
- COLLECTIBLE: BOBBLEHEAD: AGILITY
- COLLECTIBLE: REQUIRED READING: TALES OF A JUNKTOWN JERKY VENDOR
- CRAFTING: CHEMISTRY STATION
- CRAFTING: COOKING STOVE
- DANGER: LONG DROP!
- DANGER: OIL!
- DANGER: RADIATION (MILD)!
- DANGER: TURRETS!
- FACTION: IRRADIATED WILDLIFE (MIRELURKS)
- FACTION: RAIDER
- FACTION: CHARACTER: RAGS
- HEALTH OR CHEMS

**FIG 6.30: WRECK OF THE FMS NORTHERN STAR (EXTERIOR)**

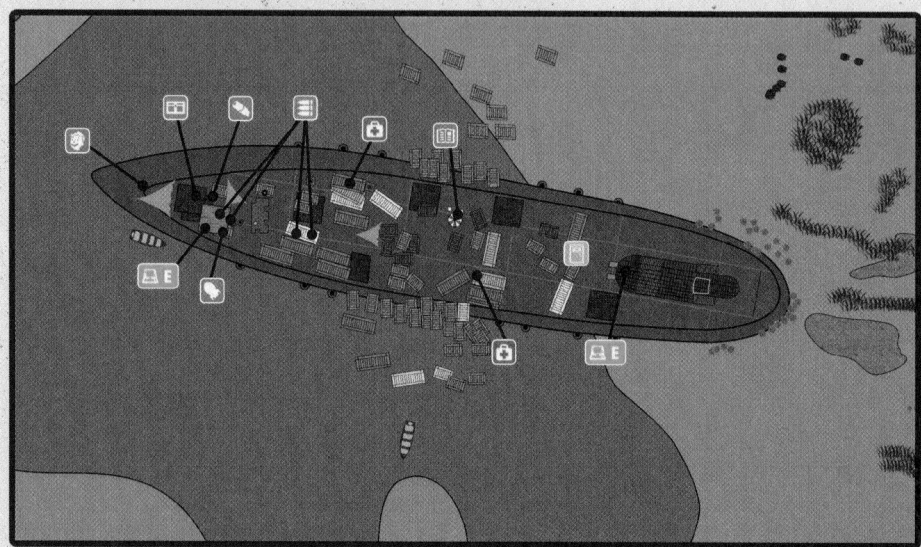

    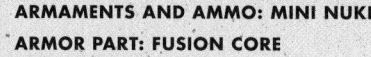

A rusting hulk with an interior hull of holes (with a generator containing a Fusion Core), containers, and Mirelurks. The top deck is a camp for a small Raider gang led by Rags. There are numerous entrances and a rowboat to lower via a button on its prow. Access the terminals (Expert) at either end of the top deck to switch off the spotlights and turrets. Check the area for a limited-edition Bobblehead in a precarious position, as well as a magazine, Mini Nuke, and trunk.

### VAULT-TEC RECOMMENDED LOOT

ARMAMENTS AND AMMO: MINI NUKE
ARMOR PART: FUSION CORE
BOBBLEHEAD: AGILITY
REQUIRED READING: TALES OF A JUNKTOWN JERKY VENDOR

## 🌊⭐ [6.31] SPECTACLE ISLAND

- ARMAMENTS AND AMMO
- ARMAMENTS AND AMMO: MINI NUKE
- ARMAMENTS AND AMMO: MINI NUKE (FAT MAN)
- ARMAMENTS AND AMMO: TRUNK
- BOTTLECAPS+
- COLLECTIBLE: BOBBLEHEAD: LUCK
- CRAFTING: CHEMISTRY STATION
- CRAFTING: COOKING STATION
- CRAFTING: POWER ARMOR STATION
- DANGER: RADIATION (MILD)!
- FACTION: MIRELURKS
- HEALTH OR CHEMS
- SERVICES: WORKSHOP

Once home to an eccentric millionaire who dreamed of creating his own private island paradise. His old mansion on the northwest shore has been abandoned for decades. Check the ground floor for an unexploded Mini Nuke. The rusting green boat to the south has a Fat Man inside, a Bobblehead, and a circuit breaker to power the signal cabin (though powering up the generator causes some interest from the local wildlife). The signal cabin circuit breaker sends out a frequency that scares off Mirelurks and allows the workshop to be accessed. The ruined shack to the northeast has a safe (Advanced). This place may be remote, but it's perfect for a settlement outpost.

### VAULT-TEC RECOMMENDED LOOT

ARMAMENTS AND AMMO: MINI NUKE AND FAT MAN
BOBBLEHEAD: LUCK

# SECONDARY LOCATIONS

## [6.01] RED ROCKET FILLING STATION (MASS PIKE EAST)

- CRAFTING: POWER ARMOR STATION
- CRAFTING: WEAPONS WORKBENCH
- HEALTH OR CHEMS

This rusting Red Rocket filling station has a couple of crafting areas and access into the Fens and Theater District neighborhoods.

## [6.02] LAYTON TOWERS UNDERPASS ENTRANCE

- DANGER: CAN CHIMES!
- DANGER: GRENADES!
- FACTION: RAIDERS

If you require quick access north into Back Bay or from the Layton Towers area of Back Bay into Zone 6, this is the concrete stairwell to take. Beware of numerous Raider traps as you encroach into their territory in Back Bay.

## [6.03] CRATER AND SHACK

- DANGER: RADIATION (MILD)!
- FACTION: BLOATFLIES
- FACTION: BLOODBUGS
- FACTION: STINGWINGS
- HEALTH OR CHEMS

Sewage pipes from the city poured out into this crater, mixing with the radioactive waste to create a particularly pungent sludge. Expect giant and revolting insects, as well as a fallen bridge up into Back Bay.

## [6.04] RED ROCKET FILLING STATION (BIG JOHN'S SALVAGE)

- CRAFTING: ARMOR WORKBENCH
- CRAFTING: POWER ARMOR STATION
- CRAFTING: WEAPONS WORKBENCH
- FACTION: SUPER MUTANTS

Near the road into the Theater District is a filling station with crafting opportunities. If you've been checking all the bathrooms in the Commonwealth, be prepared for a shock; someone left the toilet seat down in the restrooms here.

## [6.05] WICKED SHIPPING CONTAINER TRUCK #4

- ARMAMENTS AND AMMO
- ARMAMENTS AND AMMO: TRUNK
- BOTTLECAPS
- FACTION: RAIDERS
- QUEST VISIT: WICKED SHIPMENTS (LOCATION MISCELLANEOUS)

This is one of Wicked Shipping's trailers. The hatch is locked (Master), or use the key you found from the lockup in Zone 1. Access the trunk and Bottlecap mine inside.

## [6.06] RAILROAD MAINTENANCE SHED

- ARMAMENTS AND AMMO
- FACTION: ROBOTS

This location is not affiliated with The Railroad Faction. Two Protectron units can be controlled from a terminal (Expert) but first you must neutralize the guardian of the shed (a Sentry Bot). Check the brick shed for a safe (Novice).

## [6.07] THE TRADING POST

- ARMAMENTS AND AMMO
- DANGER: RADIATION (MILD)!
- FACTION: SETTLER
- FACTION: CHARACTER: ELEANOR
- SERVICES: TRADER (ELEANOR)

Just off the road by the sagging mansion (northwest of Fairline Hill Estates) is a metal trailer, campsite/graveyard, and tato orchard, near the small fetid pond. Visit Eleanor here for some trading opportunities (scrap and ammo).

## [6.08] DOG'S DINNER

- FACTION: SCAVENGER

A trapped hound inside a cage is whimpering for your attention. But is this a trap? Fend off the scavengers, and the dog runs home to Eleanor at her Trading Post (Secondary Location [6.07]). If the mutt makes it back, Eleanor will offer you a discount.

## [6.09] MILITARY CHECKPOINT (WEST ROXBURY)

- ARMAMENTS AND AMMO
- ARMAMENTS AND AMMO: TRUNK
- ARMOR PART: POWER ARMOR (LEVELED)
- FACTION: ROBOTS

A cluster of vehicles and an old checkpoint litter this road northeast of West Roxbury. Claim your rewards from the trunk under the platform.

## [6.10] DESERTED CAMP (ELEVATED FREEWAY)

- ARMOR PART: FUSION CORE
- BOTTLECAPS
- CRAFTING: CHEMISTRY STATION
- CRAFTING: COOKING STATION

Use the construction lift by the generators with the Fusion Core to reach this eagle's nest of a camp. Check the metal trailer for a safe (Master); the key can be found next to the skeleton on the lower level of the freeway. Then optionally make your way back and forth via the elevated freeway, all the way into the Financial District.

## [6.11] RAIDER CAMP (UNIVERSITY POINT OUTSKIRTS)

- ARMAMENTS AND AMMO
- CRAFTING: WEAPONS WORKBENCH
- DANGER: EXPLOSIVE BARRELS!
- DANGER: OIL!
- FACTION: RAIDERS
- HEALTH OR CHEMS

This small but well-defended Raider camp has a reasonable amount of loot to gather. Find it under the freeway, just west of University Point.

## [6.12] ISLAND CABIN

- ARMAMENTS AND AMMO
- FACTION: RADSTAG DOES

This cabin and treehouse just south of Egret Tours Marina was once a blissful retreat.

## [6.13] WAYSTATION (WEST ROXBURY)

- FACTION: SUPER MUTANT
- HEALTH OR CHEMS

The telltale signs of Super Mutant activity are all around this water tower and waystation. Unlock the station terminal (Novice), one of the few objects not covered in congealed blood.

## [6.14] MOONSHINER'S CABIN

- BOTTLECAPS
- CRAFTING: CHEMISTRY STATION

Approach this area with caution; the moonshiner inside this shack may not be competent with his still.

## [6.15] THE HANGING TREE

- ARMAMENTS AND AMMO
- DANGER: RADIATION (MILD)!
- DANGER: TURRETS!
- FACTION: RAIDERS

A small band of Raiders is encroaching into Gunner territory and decorating an old oak tree.

## [6.16] JAMAICA PLAIN POND

- ARMAMENTS AND AMMO
- BOTTLECAPS
- DANGER: RADIATION (MILD)!

An old rowboat still has some scavengable contents.

## [6.17] MILITARY CONVOY (ELEVATED FREEWAY)

- ARMAMENTS AND AMMO: TRUNK
- ARMOR PART: POWER ARMOR (LEVELED)

Three APCs have fallen off the collapsed freeway. The pond has Power Armor rusting in the mire, and you can climb on and enter the green trailer balanced precariously on the freeway; there's a trunk inside.

## [6.18] THE FRIDGE

- FACTION: SETTLER (GHOUL)
- FACTION: CHARACTER: BILLY PEABODY
- QUEST START: KID IN THE FRIDGE (SIDE)

A refrigerator has some muffled shouts coming from inside. Perhaps a kind soul should investigate.

## [6.19] MILITARY BARGE (UNIVERSITY POINT)

- ARMAMENTS AND AMMO
- ARMAMENTS AND AMMO: TRUNK
- ARMOR PART: POWER ARMOR
- DANGER: OIL!
- FACTION: ROBOTS

An unsteady barge still has robotic protection and a trunk in the back of the open APC.

## [6.20] BOATING PLATFORMS

- HEALTH OR CHEMS

A green buoy east of the Castle has a collection of old wood platforms and rowboats tangled together into a rustic boat platform. Come for the crops being grown in tires.

## [6.21] SUNKEN FISHING BOAT (SPECTACLE ISLAND)

- ARMAMENTS AND AMMO: TRUNK
- HEALTH OR CHEMS

A mast peeks out of the water just northwest of Spectacle Island. Dive down and investigate the cabin for a surprise. The trunk randomly appears.

## [6.22] BARGE PLATFORM

- HEALTH OR CHEMS

Two barge platforms, one sunk and anchoring the other, are moored north off Spectacle Island.

## [6.23] DEEP TRENCH WRECKAGE

Two boats amid a small cluster of flotsam marks the position of a deep trench. Check the rowboat for a safe (Advanced). A mass of tangled metal and boats includes a tugboat with a cabin of a cat fanatic.

## [6.24] SUNKEN SUPERTANKER

- ARMAMENTS AND AMMO

A green tugboat and two smaller police vessels congregate over a huge supertanker on the ocean floor.

## [6.25] SNIPER'S HIDEOUT

- ARMAMENTS AND AMMO
- CRAFTING: COOKING STATION
- DANGER: RADIATION (MILD)!
- FACTION: MIRELURKS

A stilt shack deep in the swamps. Come for the moonshine. Stay for the sniping.

## [6.26] WAYSTATION (GUNNERS' PLAZA)

- ARMAMENTS AND AMMO

A railroad waystation and signal tower southwest of the Gunners' plaza.

## [6.27] RUINED GROVE ESTATES

- ARMAMENTS AND AMMO
- FACTION: YAO GUAI
- DANGER: RADIATION (MILD)!
- HEALTH OR CHEMS

A collection of homes in moderate to severe states of disrepair. Scavenge them all and watch for irradiated wildlife.

## [6.28] THE SMALL DIG

- ARMAMENTS AND AMMO: TRUNK
- BOTTLECAPS
- FACTION: SUPER MUTANTS

Find the steamer trunk close to the skeleton with the shovel leaning on the rock. Watch for greenskin trouble.

## [6.29] CRASHED VERTIBIRD (MARSHLAND)

- ARMAMENTS AND AMMO: TRUNK (2)
- ARMOR PART: POWER ARMOR (LEVELED)
- DANGER: RADIATION (MILD)!
- FACTION: GUNNERS
- FACTION: ROBOTS

A downed Vertibird is being advanced on by Gunners exploring from their plaza and Hyde Park. There's a trunk by the Vertibird and Power Armor in the swamp. Check the rusting tank just north of here for the second trunk.

## [6.30] MILITARY PILLBOXES

- DANGER: RADIATION (MILD)!
- FACTION: ROBOTS

Five pillboxes gradually sink into this swamp. Open the door, and you may discover a fully operational sentry.

## [6.31] OLD MILITARY MONUMENT

- ARMAMENTS AND AMMO

A tattered flag still flies at this monument and memorial. Check the low wall for a weapon.

## [6.32] OVERFLOW OUTLET CAMP (ATOMATOYS FACTORY)

- ARMAMENTS AND AMMO
- BOTTLECAPS
- DANGER: RADIATION (MILD)!
- FACTION: FERAL GHOULS
- HEALTH OR CHEMS

Partly covered in low scrub is a long concrete outlet, turned into a makeshift settler camp, though the new inhabitants are a little more feral. Check the area for a safe (Expert).

## [6.33] SCUPPERED BOAT

- ARMAMENTS AND AMMO
- FACTION: MIRELURKS

This vessel has been dashed on the rocks to the east of Warwick Homestead. Scavenge it for ammo, a suitcase (Novice), and a great hat.

## [6.34] FLOATING BARGE

- HEALTH OR CHEMS

Two barges provided relative safety for a group of scientists. But that was decades ago. Now their bones have been picked clean. Inspect the barge for a safe to crack (Advanced).

## [6.35] SKYLINES FLIGHT SALVAGE

- HEALTH OR CHEMS

A sunken aircraft was being removed from the depths. Now the surface tugboat and barge are in much the same state.

## [6.36] BOAT GRAVEYARD

- ARMAMENTS AND AMMO
- BOTTLECAPS
- FACTION: MIRELURKS
- HEALTH OR CHEMS

A heavy Mirelurk presence roams this collection of two rusting ship hulls and rotting rowboats (check the green ship). There's a small stilt shack to the east with some Caps and chems to take.

## [6.37] QUINCY LIGHTHOUSE

- DANGER: LONG DROP!
- DANGER: RADIATION (MILD)!
- HEALTH OR CHEMS

Scale this severely waterlogged and leaning structure to reach the lamp room. There's a safe (Expert) here.

## [6.38] UNDERSEA HATCH PIPE

- ARMAMENTS AND AMMO: TRUNK
- HEALTH OR CHEMS

Dive down (using your local map to pinpoint the pipe) and open the hatch to discover a steamer trunk and a well-hidden first aid box. The trunk appears randomly.

# ZONE 7: NEIGHBORHOOD: CAMBRIDGE

**Primary Locations**

- [7.01] COLLEGE SQUARE
- [7.02] CAMBRIDGE POLICE STATION
- [7.03] COLLEGIATE ADMINISTRATION BUILDING
- [7.04] FRATERNAL POST 115
- [7.05] CAMBRIDGE CAMPUS DINER
- [7.06] CAMPUS LAW OFFICES
- [7.07] KENDALL HOSPITAL
- [7.08] CAMBRIDGE POLYMER LABS
- [7.09] C.I.T. RUINS
- [7.10] THE INSTITUTE
- [7.11] GREENETECH GENETICS
- [7.12] CAMBRIDGE CRATER
- [7.13] MONSIGNOR PLAZA

## Secondary Locations

- [7.01] BRIDGE DEN (CAMBRIDGE)
- [7.02] CHARLES RIVER BOATHOUSE
- [7.03] RED ROCKET FILLING STATION (COLLEGE SQUARE)
- [7.04] UNION'S HOPE CATHEDRAL
- [7.05] HARDWARE STORE (CAMBRIDGE)
- [7.06] PLUMBER'S SECRET
- [7.07] RAIDER BONFIRE CAMP
- [7.08] RED ROCKET FILLING STATION (NORTH CENTRAL CAMBRIDGE)

- [7.09] RAIDER CAMP (NARROW YARD)
- [7.10] CAMBRIDGE PARK AND OLD COVERED ALLEY
- [7.11] MASS CHEMICAL
- [7.12] SUPER MUTANT HIGH RISE
- [7.13] RAIDER PLATFORMS (CAMBRIDGE)
- [7.14] RAIDER ROOFTOP APARTMENTS (CAMBRIDGE)
- [7.15] CAMPUS OFFICE AND COVERED BRIDGE
- [7.16] KENDALL PARKING
- [7.17] KENDALL RAIDER APARTMENTS

- [7.18] TICONDEROGA SAFEHOUSE
- [7.19] PUBLIC WORKS MAINTENANCE AREA
- [7.20] SCIENCE CENTER GIFT SHOP

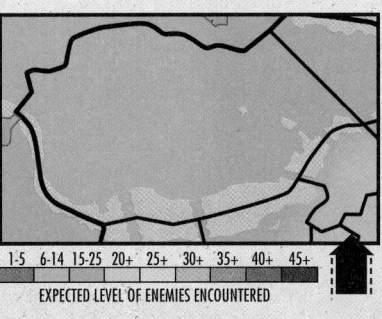

**THREAT LEVEL MAP**

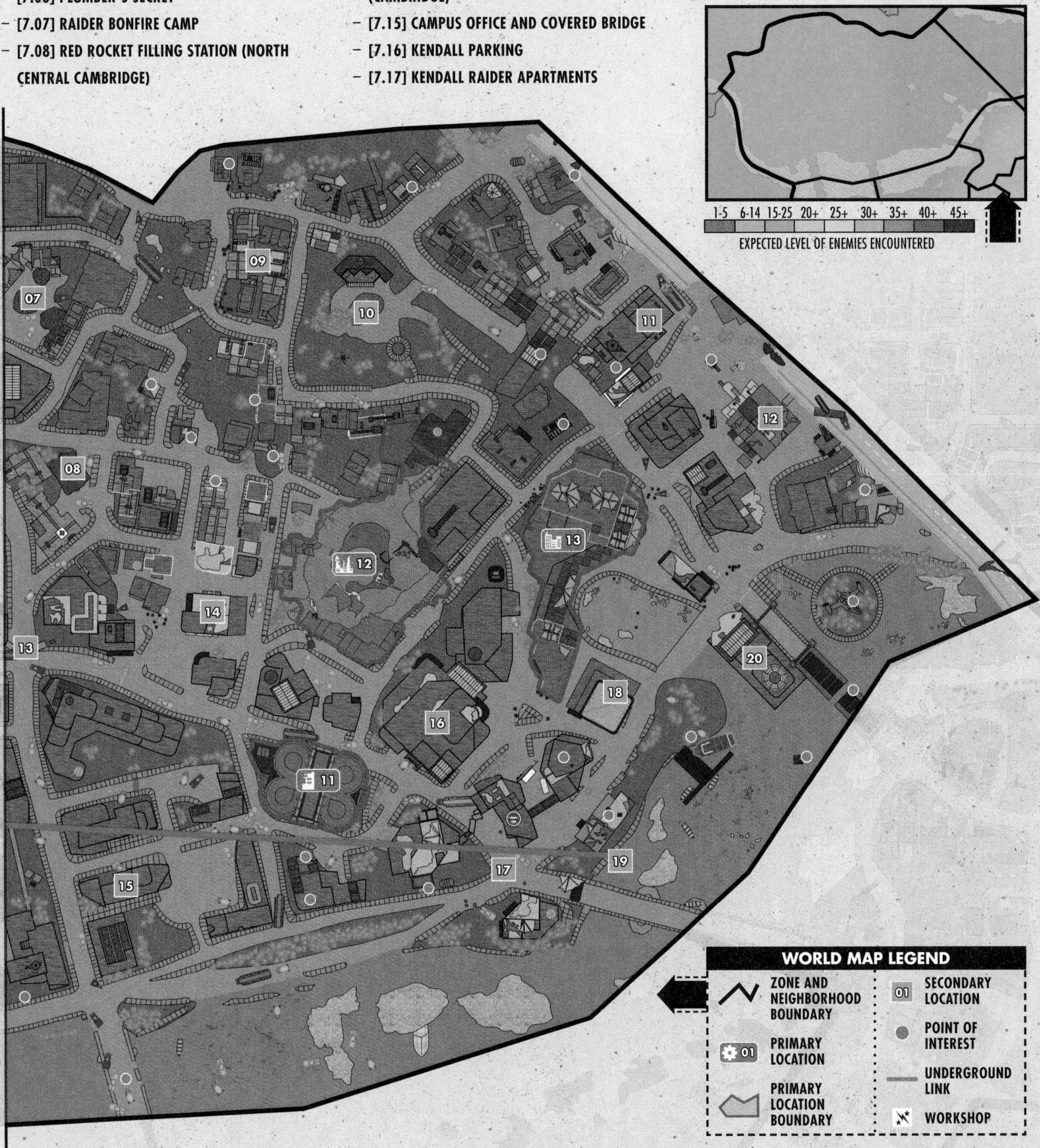

1-5  6-14  15-25  20+  25+  30+  35+  40+  45+

EXPECTED LEVEL OF ENEMIES ENCOUNTERED

**MAP**

**ZONE 7**

NEIGHBORHOOD: CAMBRIDGE

### WORLD MAP LEGEND

| | |
|---|---|
| ZONE AND NEIGHBORHOOD BOUNDARY | 01 SECONDARY LOCATION |
| 01 PRIMARY LOCATION | POINT OF INTEREST |
| PRIMARY LOCATION BOUNDARY | UNDERGROUND LINK |
| | WORKSHOP |

By far the largest of the Neighborhoods, and usually the first one travellers to Boston visit when heading in from Concord and Lexington, Cambridge is a sprawl of college structures and old homes (and even older feral inhabitants) from before the dawn of the 21st century. The closer to the Charles River you venture, the larger the structures, and the more dominated by raider gangs this zone becomes. The strangely silent C.I.T. Ruins still stand as a monument to past scientific discoveries, but the Institute scientists themselves are deep underground. For the sightseer, there's the impressively radioactive Cambridge Crater and its local feral population (don't forget to pack protective gear!), and taller structures like the landmark Greenetech Genetics tower. Venture eastwards to the freeway segmenting Cambridge and Charlestown, and you'll discover a sizable Super Mutant camp in a half-finished high-rise, as well as a secret Railroad safehouse.

## MAP LEGEND

| 13 ———— 20 | | BOTTLECAPS | | HEALTH OR CHEMS | | FUSION CORE | *Collectibles:* | BOBBLEHEAD | | NUKA COLA QUANTUM |
|---|---|---|---|---|---|---|---|---|---|---|
| OPTIMAL ROUTE | | SAFE | | TERMINAL | | POWER ARMOR | | NUKA CHERRY | | HOLOTAPE |
| | | ARMAMENTS AND AMMO | | STEAMER TRUNK | | REQUIRED READING | | MINI NUKE | | A KEY |
| AREA OF INTEREST | | DOOR | | | | | | | | |

| N – Novice (Locked) | E – Expert (Locked) | T – Terminal required to unlock | IN – Inaccessible | CB – Circuit Breaker |
|---|---|---|---|---|
| A – Advanced (Locked) | M – Master (Locked) | KEY – Key or ID Card required to unlock | C – Chained | B – Button |

# PRIMARY LOCATIONS

 **[7.01] COLLECTE SQUARE**     THREAT LEVELS 6-14

- ARMAMENTS AND AMMO++
- ARMAMENTS AND AMMO: TRUNK (2)
- BOTTLECAPS++
- COLLECTIBLE: NUKA CHERRY (2)
- COLLECTIBLE: REQUIRED READING:
  LIVE & LOVE
- DANGER: CAN CHIMES!

- DANGER: EXPLOSIVE BARRELS!
- DANGER: OIL!
- DANGER: MINES!
- DANGER: TRIPWIRE!
- FACTION: FERAL GHOULS
- HEALTH OR CHEMS+

### VAULT-TEC RECOMMENDED LOOT

  **COLLECTIBLE: NUKA CHERRY (2)**
**REQUIRED READING: LIVE & LOVE**

**FIG 7.01A: COLLEGE SQUARE
(EXTERIOR)**

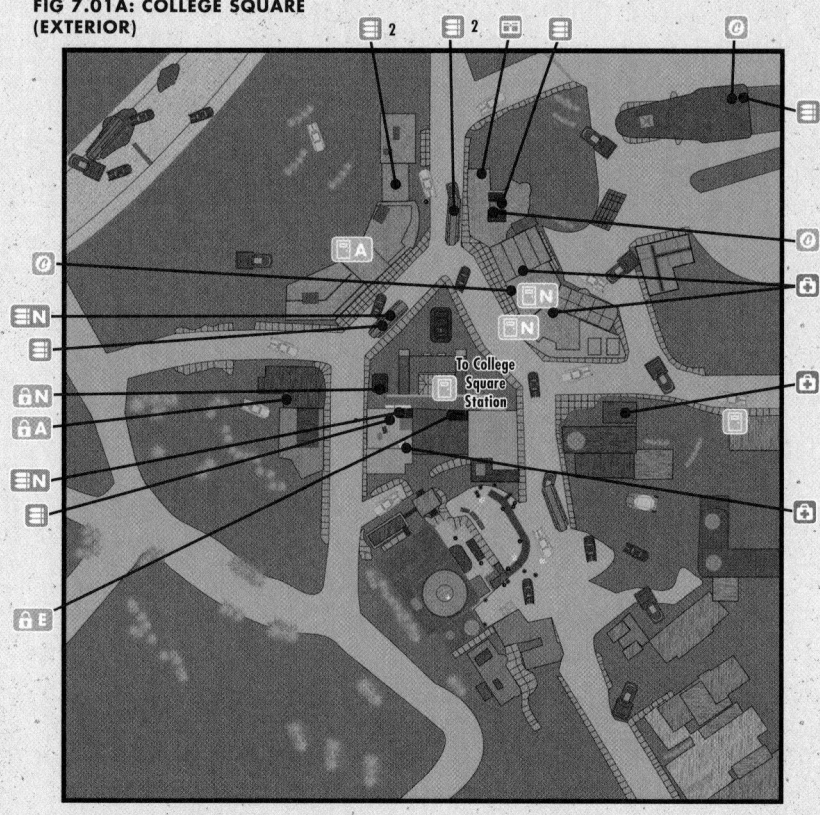

The northwest entrance to Cambridge was once a Raider stronghold, recently overrun by Feral Ghouls. It's worth removing a few rotting heads to gather the copious ammo and Caps here. Check the buildings you can access and don't forget to jimmy open the three safes and collect contents from a trunk on the northeast roof area.

## FIG 7.01B: COLLEGE SQUARE STATION (INTERIOR)

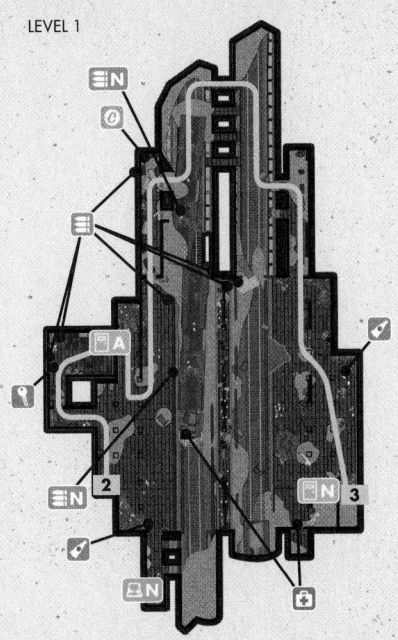

LEVEL 1

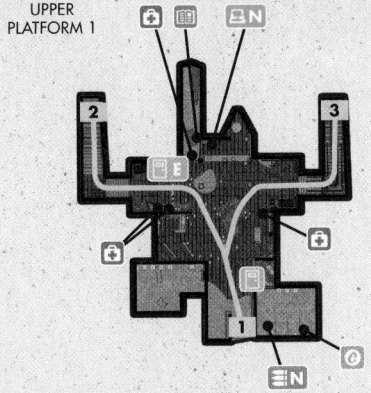

UPPER PLATFORM 1

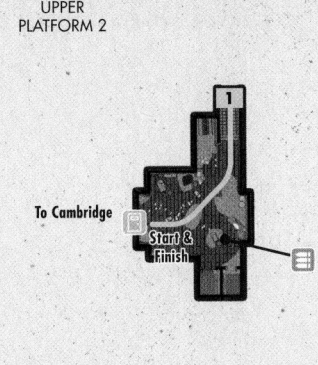

UPPER PLATFORM 2

To Cambridge

The interior station is a loop through an abandoned subway with numerous explosive barrels and copious ferals to make the journey harrowing. Pick up the key on the lower level to open the ticket office so you can claim the magazine. Don't forget to locate the trunk on the lower level.

## [7.02] CAMBRIDGE POLICE STATION

THREAT LEVELS 6-14

FIG 7.02A: CAMBRIDGE POLICE STATION (EXTERIOR)

To Cambridge Police Station

From Cambridge Police Station

- ARMAMENTS AND AMMO
- ARMAMENTS AND AMMO: MINI NUKE
- BOTTLECAPS
- COLLECTIBLE: HOLOTAPE: EDDIE WINTER'S HOLOTAPE
- COLLECTIBLE: HOLOTAPE: SCRIBE HAYLEN'S PERSONAL LOG
- COLLECTIBLE: REQUIRED READING: GUNS AND BULLETS
- COMPANION: PALADIN DANSE
- CRAFTING: POWER ARMOR STATION
- FACTION: BROTHERHOOD OF STEEL
- FACTION: FERAL GHOULS
- FACTION: CHARACTER: PALADIN DANSE
- FACTION: CHARACTER: SCRIBE HAYLEN
- FACTION: CHARACTER: KNIGHT RHYS
- HEALTH OR CHEMS
- QUEST VISIT: THE MOLECULAR LEVEL (MAIN)
- QUEST VISIT: REVEILLE (BROTHERHOOD OF STEEL)
- QUEST START: FIRE SUPPORT (BROTHERHOOD OF STEEL)
- QUEST START: CALL TO ARMS (BROTHERHOOD OF STEEL)
- QUEST START: SEMPER INVICTA (BROTHERHOOD OF STEEL)
- QUEST START: SHADOW OF STEEL (BROTHERHOOD OF STEEL)
- QUEST START: THE LOST PATROL (BROTHERHOOD OF STEEL)
- QUEST START: DUTY OR DISHONOR (BROTHERHOOD OF STEEL)
- QUEST START: QUARTERMASTERY (BROTHERHOOD OF STEEL)
- QUEST VISIT: PRECIPICE OF WAR (THE RAILROAD)
- QUEST VISIT: LONG TIME COMING (SIDE)
- RADIO: MILITARY FREQUENCY AF95

### VAULT-TEC RECOMMENDED LOOT

**ARMAMENTS AND AMMO: MINI NUKE**

**REQUIRED READING: GUNS AND BULLETS**

### AVAILABLE COMPANION

**COMPANION: PALADIN DANSE**

Paladin Danse and his recon team are valiantly holding the dilapidated remains of Cambridge Police Station from a horde of ferals. Help them to begin your working relationship with this faction. This is the Brotherhood's initial base of operations before the arrival of the Prydwen.

Access the Power Armor station in the garage from inside the structure, as well as the Vertibird landing spot on the roof (there's a Mini Nuke up there). Head here for numerous Brotherhood of Steel quests, prior to the Brotherhood's full force arriving. After Main Quest: Reunions and Brotherhood of Steel Quest: Call to Arms, a large contingent of Brotherhood soldiers occupy the police station, where they install a Cooking Station and Weapons Workbench outside, and a Chemistry Station inside. If you poke around inside the station, you can also find a copy of Guns and Bullets in the locked safe (Expert) in the old chief's office. Can't pick the lock? A key to the safe is on the front desk.

-- After Main Quest: The Molecular Level, the Brotherhood reinforces their position at the police station. Notably, this adds an Armor Workbench to the motor pool.

- If you're here for Side Quest: Long Time Coming, Eddie Winter's Holotape can be found on the terminal in the evidence room, in the back of the station.

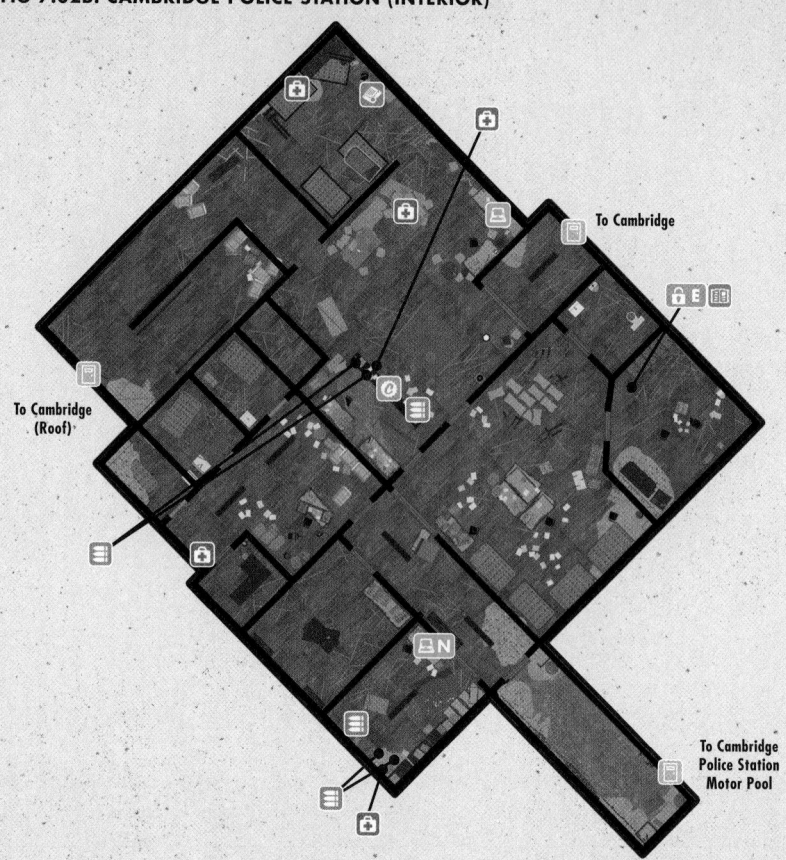

**FIG 7.02B: CAMBRIDGE POLICE STATION (INTERIOR)**

To Cambridge

To Cambridge (Roof)

To Cambridge Police Station Motor Pool

## [7.03] COLLEGIATE ADMINISTRATION BUILDING

THREAT LEVELS 6-14

This ancient structure was used for admitting students to a nearby place of learning. Now it is deserted and crumbling. Inside is a compact, three-floor structure. Locate the locked tool case atop the mezzanine (Novice), with a hole nearby allowing you to drop into the reception area. You can also visit the men's restroom, which now features an open-air feel. The third floor allows access to the ruins of the roof. Use this as a base of operations when scavenging the surrounding buildings.

Human Empathy— Robotic Precision

Milton General Hospital

# [7.04] FRATERNAL POST 115

THREAT LEVELS 6-14

- ARMAMENTS AND AMMO
- ARMAMENTS AND AMMO: TRUNK
- BOTTLECAPS
- COLLECTIBLE: NUKA COLA QUANTUM
- COLLECTIBLE: REQUIRED READING: GUNS AND BULLETS
- CRAFTING: ARMOR WORKBENCH
- DANGER: CAN CHIMES!
- DANGER: MINES!
- FACTION: SUPER MUTANT
- FACTION: CHARACTER: DEAD EYE
- HEALTH OR CHEMS

**FIG 7.04: FRATERNAL POST 115 (INTERIOR)**

LEVEL 2

LEVEL 1

Start

To Commonwealth (Cambridge)

Finish

To Commonwealth (Cambridge)

This location once served wounded veterans, helping with their recovery. Now it is a place of bloody despair: Choose either the front or rear entrance, depending on your predisposition to stealth combat. This two-floor mansion has a central pit where a new congregation gathers, led by the blind Dead Eye and his Super Mutant brethren. You can cut him off from flipping on an alarm, use the microphone and deliver part of a pre-war speech, and collect a magazine and copious ammunition in the process.

MAP

ZONE 7

NEIGHBORHOOD: CAMBRIDGE

**VAULT-TEC RECOMMENDED LOOT**

**COLLECTIBLE: NUKA COLA QUANTUM**

**REQUIRED READING: GUNS AND BULLETS**

# [7.05] CAMBRIDGE CAMPUS DINER

THREAT LEVELS 6-14

- HEALTH OR CHEMS

This thriving brick diner once served waffles and coffee, but its current patrons are decidedly less lively and more bony in appearance.

# [7.06] CAMPUS LAW OFFICES

THREAT LEVELS 6-14

- FACTION: RAIDERS

A few Raiders are picking through the debris in this blown-out building. Aside from a couple of rooms, there's nothing here but the screaming of any Raiders you dispatch. Note the secondary locations—including Union's Hope Cathedral—to the north.

- ARMAMENTS AND AMMO+
- ARMAMENTS AND AMMO: TRUNK
- ARMOR PIECE: FUSION CORE
- BOTTLECAPS
- CRAFTING: ARMOR WORKBENCH (2)
- CRAFTING: WEAPONS WORKBENCH

- DANGER: LONG DROP!
- DANGER: EXPLOSIVE BARREL!
- DANGER: TURRETS!
- FACTION: DEATHCLAW
- FACTION: RAIDERS
- HEALTH OR CHEMS

**FIG 7.07B: KENDALL HOSPITAL (INTERIOR)**

**VAULT-TEC RECOMMENDED LOOT** ⊰◉⊱

**ARMOR PART: FUSION CORE**

To Cambridge
Finish

LEVEL 1

Start

SD
B
11

LEVEL 2

9

10
CB

LEVEL 3

8
9

LEVEL 4

4
5
7
6

LEVEL 6

2
3

LEVEL 5

4
5
6

Those expecting a plentiful supply of stimpaks from this hospital location are in for disappointment. Despite this being used as a hiding point for the Railroad faction, Raiders discovered them, butchered everybody, and are either burning the corpses or throwing them down into a central pit to be consumed by a ravenous beast below. After discovering the bonfire camp, you'll move up and down this mainly vertical location.

- ARMAMENTS AND AMMO
- ARMOR PART: FUSION CORE
- ARMOR PART: PEIZONEUCLEIC POWER ARMOR CHEST
- COLLECTIBLE: REQUIRED READING: MASSACHUSETTS SURGICAL JOURNAL
- COLLECTIBLE: NUKA COLA QUANTUM
- CRAFTING: CHEMISTRY STATION
- DANGER: MINES!
- DANGER: RADIATION (SEVERE)!
- DANGER: TRIPWIRE!
- FACTION: ROBOTS
- FACTION: FERAL GHOULS
- FACTION: CHARACTER: DIRECTOR
- FACTION: CHARACTER: MOLLY
- HEALTH OR CHEMS
- QUEST START: CAMBRIDGE POLYMER LABS (MISCELLANEOUS)
- QUEST VISIT: UNDERGROUND UNDERCOVER (THE RAILROAD)
- UNIQUE ITEM: PEIZONEUCLEIC POWER ARMOR CHEST

## FIG 7.08: CAMBRIDGE POLYMER LABS (INTERIOR)

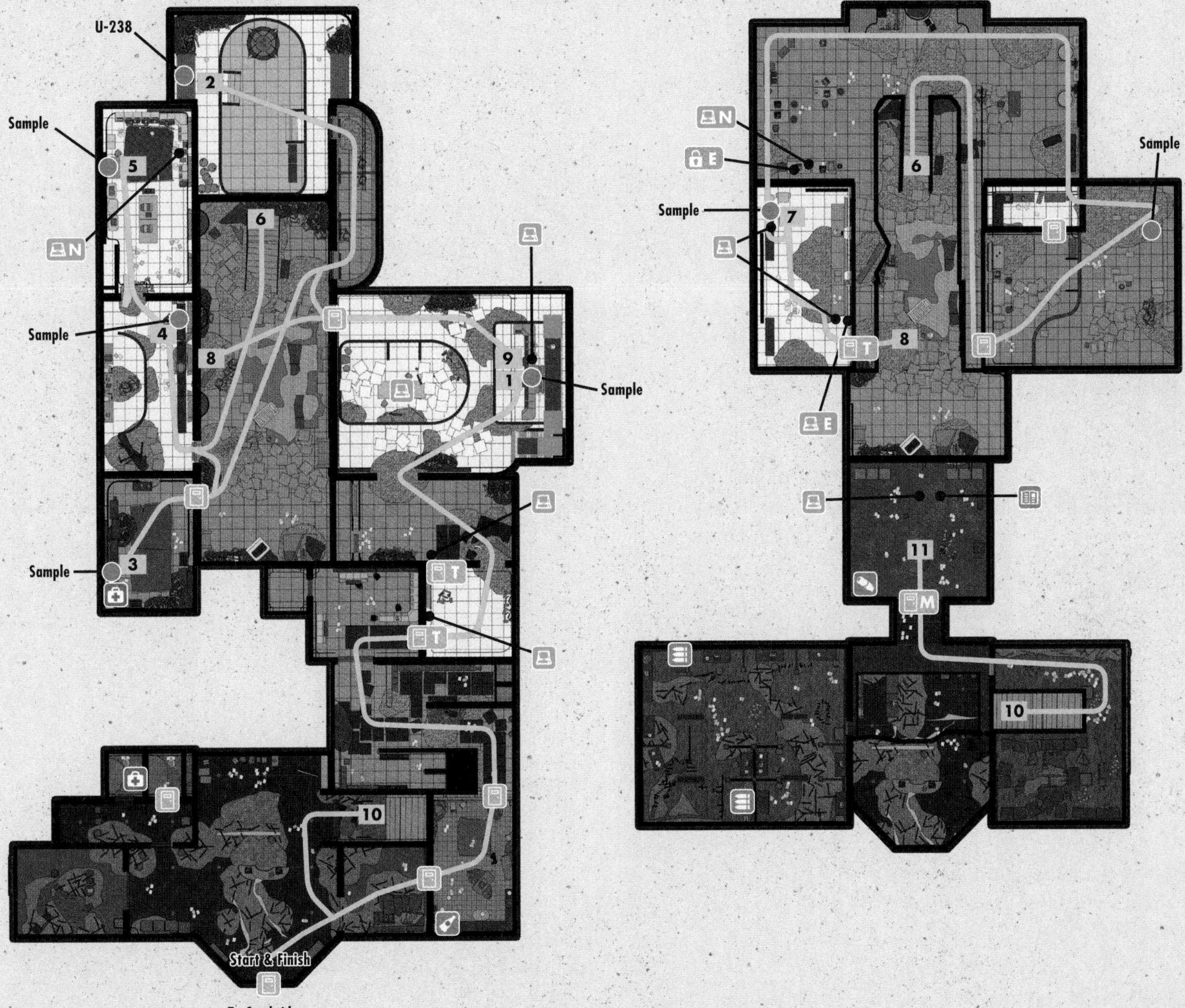

MAP

**ZONE 7**

NEIGHBORHOOD:
CAMBRIDGE

This laboratory was a research facility looking into the development of Smart Materials to convert radiation. It appears to have suffered a catastrophic failure after the bombs fell.

### VAULT-TEC RECOMMENDED LOOT

ARMOR PART: FUSION CORE
UNIQUE ITEM: PEIZONEUCLEIC POWER ARMOR CHEST
REQUIRED READING: MASSACHUSETTS SURGICAL JOURNAL

Perhaps you heard the radio advertising new and exciting opportunities in this field of research?

As you enter, a robot asks whether you're interested in becoming a researcher. Accept the position after a talk, if you wish. Take the orientation or ignore it. Enter the clean room, after which you're sealed inside. You're forced to complete either of the following objectives. Beware of Feral Ghouls.

**1. COMPLETE THE RESEARCH PROJECT**

**2. (OPTIONAL) FIND ANOTHER WAY TO ESCAPE THE LABORATORY**

Read messages on every terminal you come across. Progress through the labs, and locate the six unidentified samples. Return and place them (two at a time) on the Polymer Coating Applicator (terminal) to identify them:

- **UNIDENTIFIED SAMPLE 11317: HYDROCHLORIC ACID**
- **UNIDENTIFIED SAMPLE 3111: LITHIUM HYDRIDE**
- **UNIDENTIFIED SAMPLE 413: GALLIUM**
- **UNIDENTIFIED SAMPLE 65: TUNGSTEN**
- **UNIDENTIFIED SAMPLE 49: COBALT**
- **UNIDENTIFIED SAMPLE 611: GOLD**

To reach lab C5, access the hole in the wall at the end of lab C4. To reach lab C3, hack the wall terminal (Expert), or climb up the ramp, go across the ceiling crawlspace, and drop down the third hole you find in the floor. There's also a Holotape with the password for the radioactive containment area in lab C3.

Return to lab C5, and access the Isotope Containment Terminal (Novice). Open the door to the Isotope Containment Chamber. Enter the chamber and gather Isotope U-238.

Return to the Polymer Coating Applicator in lab C2. Place the isotope into the sample container. Then place Lithium Hydride and Gold into the chemical reagent slots. You receive a unique piece of Power Armor from the fabrication window.

The optional objective is completed at Bergman's terminal (upper floor, lab C3).

Inform Molly of your success, or free yourself at Bergman's terminal, and you can leave. To access the director's room door (Master), find the key on Molly, or use extreme lockpicking competence.

If the Railroad quest is active, seek the information you require on Bergman's terminal, inside lab C3.

## [7.09] C.I.T. RUINS          THREAT LEVELS 6-14

- **ARMAMENTS AND AMMO**
- **ARMAMENTS AND AMMO: MINI NUKE**
- **ARMAMENTS AND AMMO: TRUNK**
- **DANGER: EXPLOSIVE BARRELS!**
- **DANGER: LONG DROP!**
- **FACTION: SUPER MUTANT**
- **FACTION: SYNTHS (INSTITUTE)**
- **HEALTH OR CHEMS**
- **QUEST VISIT: THE BATTLE OF BUNKER HILL (THE INSTITUTE)**
- **QUEST VISIT: LIBERTY REPRIMED (BROTHERHOOD OF STEEL)**

### VAULT-TEC RECOMMENDED LOOT

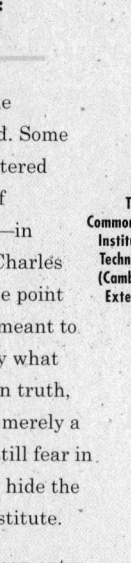

**ARMAMENTS AND AMMO: MINI NUKE**

**FIG 7.09: C.I.T. ROTUNDA (INTERIOR)**

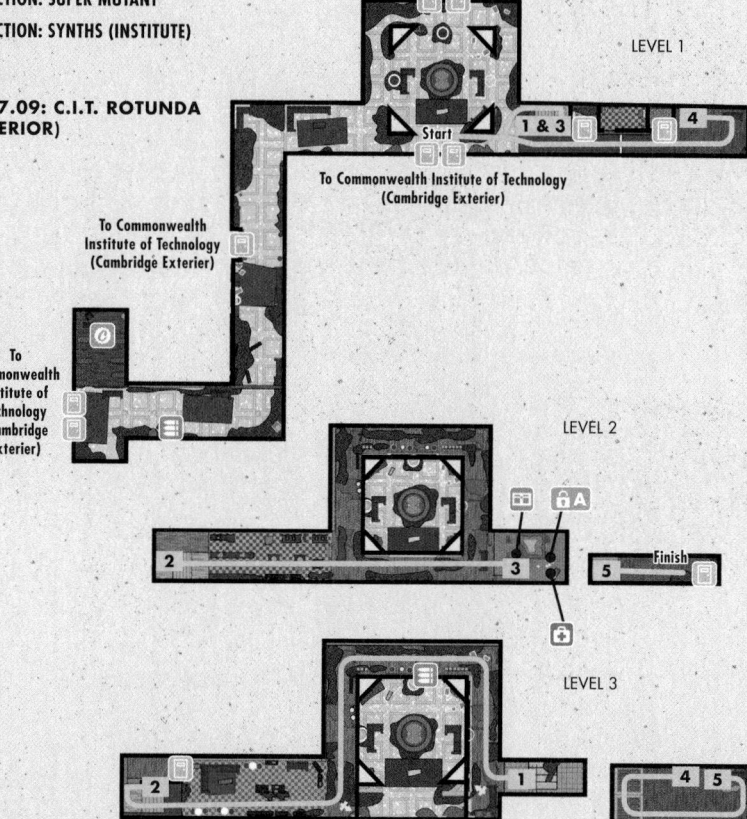

Perhaps the greatest fallacy about the Institute is where it's actually located. Some assume the organization is headquartered in the old Commonwealth Institute of Technology's central domed building—in Cambridge, on the north side of the Charles River. And why not? After all, at some point it had been fortified and was clearly meant to keep out intruders. And that's exactly what the Institute wants people to think. In truth, the above-ground Institute facility is merely a façade. A structure meant to both instill fear in the people of the Commonwealth and hide the true scope and depth of the actual Institute.

The perimeter has several doors you can enter and a small trailer in the southern courtyard. The southern courtyard has a central area where a large enough explosion could unearth passages into the Institute (if you're with the Brotherhood of Steel during the specified quests).

Inside, the structure has a central rotunda and two wings, along with Super Mutants battling synths. There are an abundances of exits on the ground floor, but the only stairwell that reaches the roof is on the eastern wing (close to the steamer trunk in the classroom). The roof views of Boston are impressive.

## AVAILABLE COMPANION

**COMPANION: X6-88**

Hidden from surface dwellers and only accessible via teleportation, this is the utopian dream of Father and his scientist colleagues who populate the Institute.

- ARMAMENTS AND AMMO++
- BOTTLECAPS+++
- COLLECTIBLE: NUKA CHERRY (2)
- COLLECTIBLE: NUKA COLA QUANTUM
- COLLECTIBLE: REQUIRED READING: ASTOUNDINGLY AWESOME TALES
- COMPANION: X6-88
- FACTION: THE INSTITUTE
- FACTION: CHARACTER (LEADER): FATHER
- FACTION: CHARACTER: SHAUN
- FACTION: CHARACTER: S9-23
- FACTION: CHARACTER: X6-88
- FACTION: CHARACTER: MADISON LI
- FACTION: CHARACTER: ALLIE FILMORE
- FACTION: CHARACTER: NATHAN FILMORE
- FACTION: CHARACTER: QUENTIN FILMORE
- FACTION: CHARACTER: LAWRENCE HIGGS
- FACTION: CHARACTER: ENRICO THOMPSON
- FACTION: CHARACTER: JANET THOMPSON
- FACTION: CHARACTER: ALICE THOMPSON
- FACTION: CHARACTER: JULIA THOMPSON
- FACTION: CHARACTER: NEWTON OBERLY
- FACTION: CHARACTER: CLAYTON HOLDREN
- FACTION: CHARACTER: ISAAC KARLIN
- FACTION: CHARACTER: DEAN VOLKERT
- FACTION: CHARACTER: BRENDAN VOLKERT
- FACTION: CHARACTER: MAX LOKEN
- FACTION: CHARACTER: ALAN BINET
- FACTION: CHARACTER: LIAM BINET
- FACTION: CHARACTER: EVAN WATSON
- FACTION: CHARACTER: ROSALIND ORMAN
- FACTION: CHARACTER: JANET THOMPSON
- FACTION: CHARACTER: JUSTIN AYO
- FACTION: CHARACTER: ALANA SECORD
- HEALTH OR CHEMS+++
- QUEST VISIT: INSTITUTIONALIZED (MAIN)

- QUEST START: THE NUCLEAR OPTION (MAIN)
- QUEST START: SYNTH RETENTION (THE INSTITUTE)
- QUEST START: THE BATTLE OF BUNKER HILL (THE INSTITUTE)
- QUEST START: MANKIND REDEFINED (THE INSTITUTE)
- QUEST START: POWERING UP (THE INSTITUTE)
- QUEST START: END OF THE LINE (THE INSTITUTE)
- QUEST START: AIRSHIP DOWN (THE INSTITUTE)
- QUEST START: NUCLEAR FAMILY (THE INSTITUTE)
- QUEST START: BUILDING A BETTER CROP (THE INSTITUTE)
- QUEST START: PLUGGING A LEAK (THE INSTITUTE)
- QUEST START: A HOUSE DIVIDED (THE INSTITUTE)
- QUEST START: MASS FUSION (THE INSTITUTE)
- QUEST START: PINNED (THE INSTITUTE)
- QUEST START: PEST CONTROL (THE INSTITUTE RADIANT)
- QUEST START: HYPOTHESIS (THE INSTITUTE RADIANT)
- QUEST START: APPROPRIATION (THE INSTITUTE RADIANT)
- QUEST START: RECLAMATION (THE INSTITUTE RADIANT)
- QUEST START: POLITICAL LEANINGS (THE INSTITUTE RADIANT)
- QUEST VISIT: FROM WITHIN (BROTHERHOOD OF STEEL)
- QUEST VISIT: OUTSIDE THE WIRE (BROTHERHOOD OF STEEL)
- QUEST VISIT: UNDERGROUND UNDERCOVER (THE RAILROAD)
- QUEST VISIT: INSIDE JOB (THE MINUTEMEN)
- QUEST VISIT: MISCELLANEOUS (FREEFORM: VIRGIL'S SERUM)
- SERVICES: TRADER (SYNTH FOOD VENDOR)
- SERVICES: TRADER (INSTITUTE REQUISITION VENDOR)
- UNIQUE ITEM: EXPERIMENT 18-A (WEAPON)
- UNIQUE ITEM: EXPERIMENTAL SERUM (ITEM)
- UNIQUE ITEM: INSTITUTE BEACON (ITEM)
- UNIQUE ITEM: LIAM'S GLASSES (APPAREL)
- UNIQUE ITEM: MARK 2 SYNTH HELMET (APPAREL)
- UNIQUE ITEM: MARK 2 SYNTH CHEST PIECE (APPAREL)
- UNIQUE ITEM: MARK 3 SYNTH CHEST PIECE (APPAREL)
- UNIQUE ITEM: MARK 3 RIGHT ARM (APPAREL)
- UNIQUE ITEM: WAZER WIFLE (FROM SHAUN, POST MAIN QUEST)

**MAP**

**ZONE 7**

NEIGHBORHOOD:
CAMBRIDGE

## VAULT-TEC RECOMMENDED LOOT

       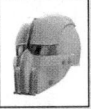

**ARMOR PART: FUSION CORE (2)**
**COLLECTIBLE: EXPERIMENTAL SERUM**
**COLLECTIBLE: NUKA CHERRY (2)**
**COLLECTIBLE: NUKA COLA QUANTUM (2)**

**REQUIRED READING: ASTOUNDINGLY AWESOME TALES**
**UNIQUE ITEM: EXPERIMENT 18-A**
**UNIQUE ITEM: MARK 2 SYNTH ARMOR (PIECES)**
**UNIQUE ITEM: MARK 3 SYNTH ARMOR (PIECES)**

## Main Atrium and Concourse

### FIG 7.10A: INSTITUTE CONCOURSE (INTERIOR)

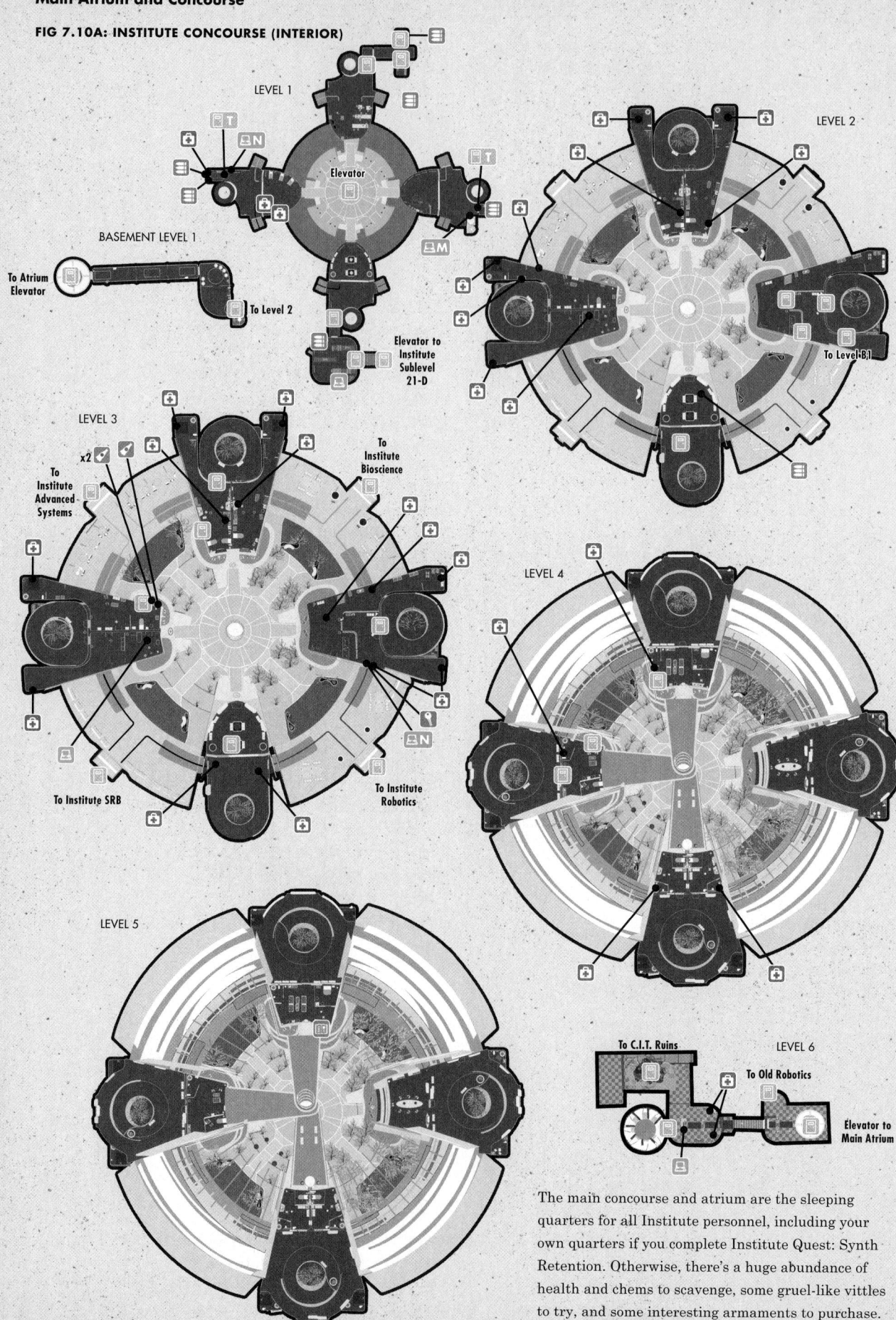

LEVEL 1

Elevator

BASEMENT LEVEL 1

To Atrium Elevator

To Level 2

Elevator to Institute Sublevel 21-D

LEVEL 2

To Level B1

LEVEL 3

x2

To Institute Advanced Systems

To Institute Bioscience

To Institute Robotics

To Institute SRB

LEVEL 4

LEVEL 5

To C.I.T. Ruins

LEVEL 6

To Old Robotics

Elevator to Main Atrium

The main concourse and atrium are the sleeping quarters for all Institute personnel, including your own quarters if you complete Institute Quest: Synth Retention. Otherwise, there's a huge abundance of health and chems to scavenge, some gruel-like vittles to try, and some interesting armaments to purchase.

## Institute Robotics

- **ARMAMENTS AND AMMO**
- **CHARACTER (DIVISION HEAD): ALAN BINET**

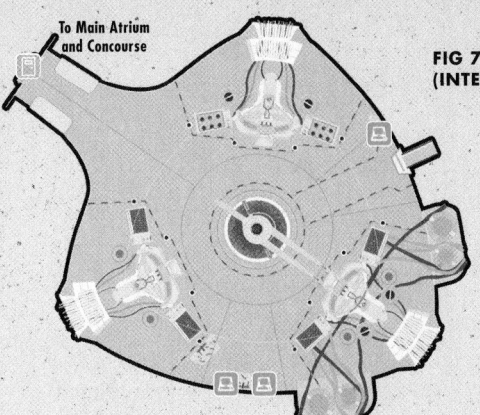

### FIG 7.10B: INSTITUTE ROBOTICS (INTERIOR)

Robotics works on synth production (with a factory floor of synth creation that's impressive to watch), quality control, and software/hardware improvements.

## Institute BioScience

- **ARMAMENTS AND AMMO**
- **CHARACTER (DIVISION HEAD): CLAYTON HOLDREN**
- **DANGER: TURRETS!**
- **HEALTH OR CHEMS**

### FIG 7.10C: INSTITUTE BIOSCIENCE (INTERIOR)

BioScience cultivates and maintains existing gardens and the food supply through hydroponics. Research into genetically modified crops and nutrition also occurs. A small synth gorilla enclosure that emulates a jungle habitat exists here, as well as entrances to an abandoned FEV laboratory.

## Institute Advanced Systems

- **ARMAMENTS AND AMMO**
- **CHARACTER (DIVISION HEAD): MADISON LI**
- **COLLECTIBLE: HOLOTAPE: ADVANCED SYSTEMS NOTES**

Advanced Systems works on applied physics (plasma weaponry and teleportation), as well as special projects currently classified. Access to the reactor is at this location but is currently off-limits until you undertake certain quests.

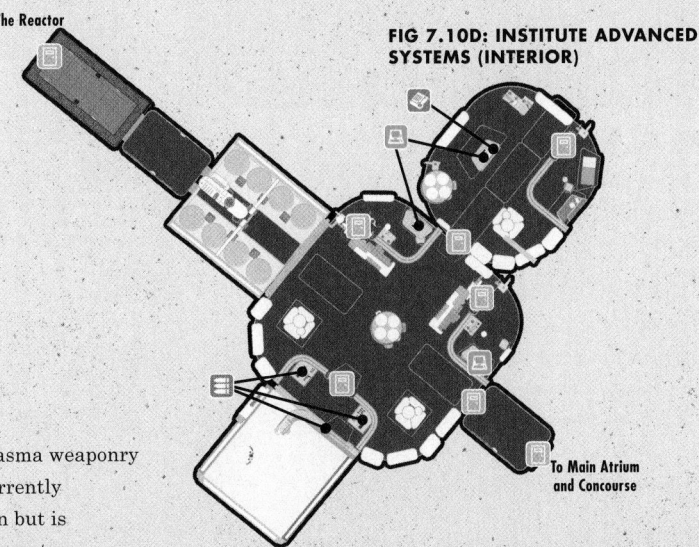

### FIG 7.10D: INSTITUTE ADVANCED SYSTEMS (INTERIOR)

## Institute Synth Retention Bureau

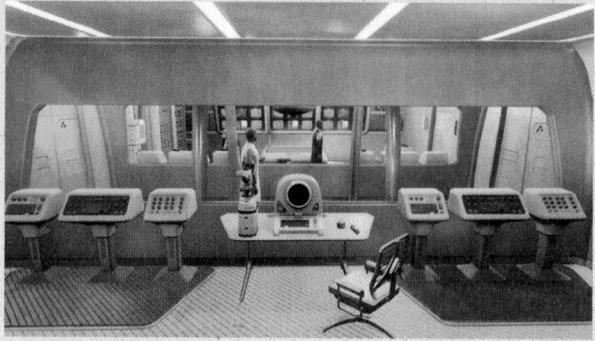

- ARMAMENTS AND AMMO+    – CHARACTER (DIVISION HEAD): JUSTIN AYO

Synth Retention (or SRB) supervises the coursers and their missions across the Commonwealth and repurposes any older Gen 1 and 2 synth models after interception on the surface.

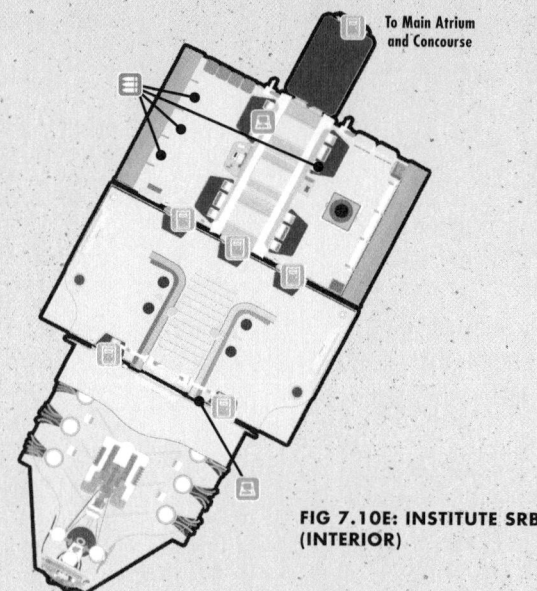

**FIG 7.10E: INSTITUTE SRB (INTERIOR)**

## Institute Sublevel 21-D

- DANGER: EXPLOSIVE BARRELS!

A partly excavated tunnel and old storage area accessed via a maintenance elevator.

**FIG 7.10F: INSTITUTE SUBLEVEL 21-D (INTERIOR)**

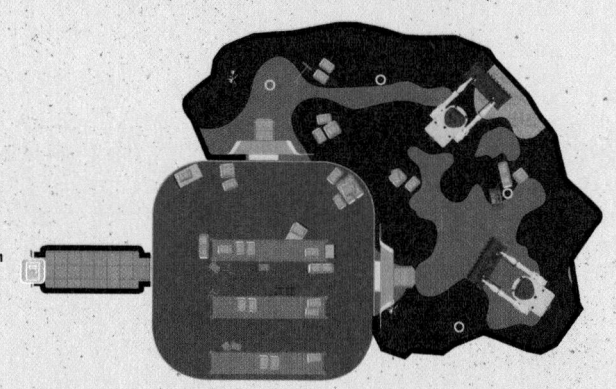

To Main Atrium and Concourse

## FEV Laboratory

**FIG 7.10G: FEV LAB (INTERIOR)**

- ARMAMENTS AND AMMO        – DANGER: TESLA ARCS!
- COLLECTIBLE: EXPERIMENTAL SERUM        – DANGER: TRIPWIRES!
- COLLECTIBLE: HOLOTAPE: BRIAN VIRGIL        – DANGER: TURRETS!
  PERSONAL LOG 0176        – HEALTH OR CHEMS

This is where Forced Evolutionary Viruses (FEV) were created and used on test subjects, forming the Super Mutants that roam the surface hellscape. This location doesn't have quite the sheen of the main locations. Beware of Assaultrons. Look for the Experimental Serum in the incubation lab, as well as one of Virgil's old Holotapes.

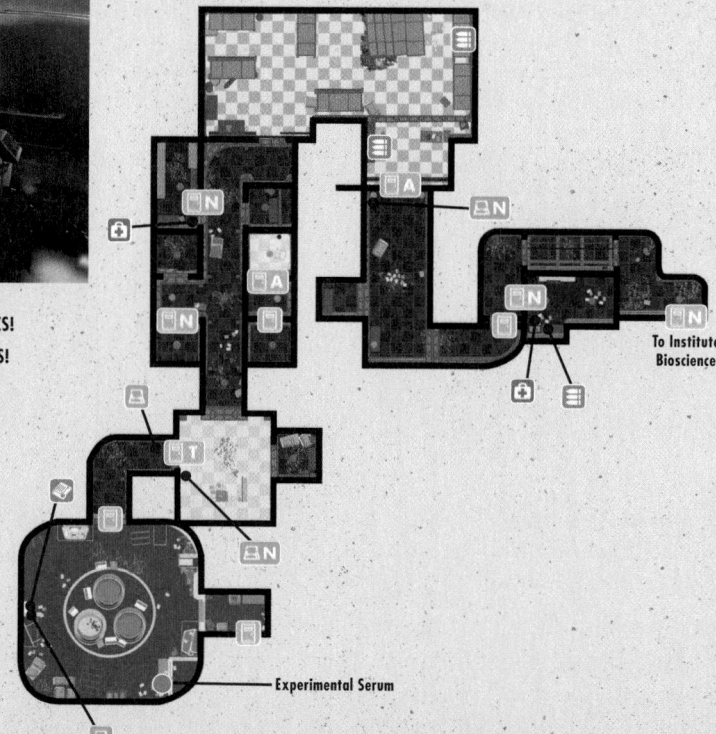

To Institute Bioscience

Experimental Serum

## Old Robotics

### FIG 7.10H: OLD ROBOTICS (INTERIOR)

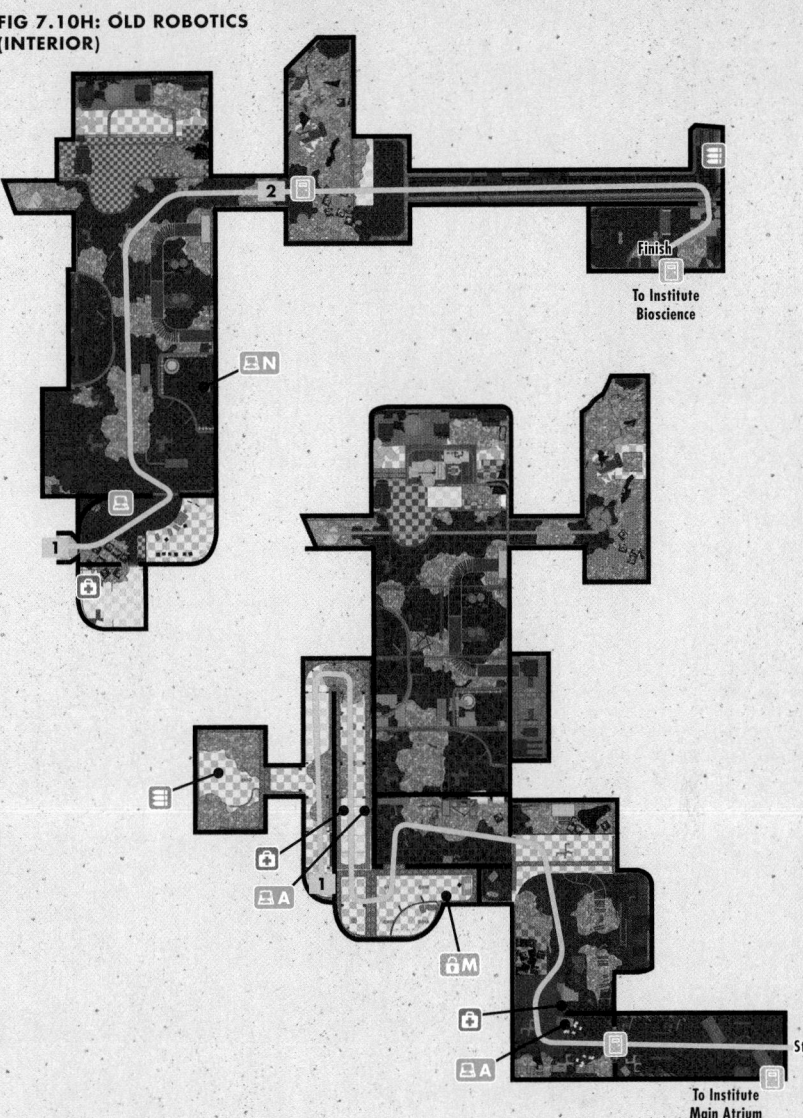

- ARMOR PART: FUSION CORE
- ARMAMENTS AND AMMO
- BOTTLECAPS
- DANGER: TURRETS!
- FACTION: ROBOT, SYNTH
- HEALTH OR CHEMS

This is where the earliest experimentations on synthetic life were carried out, and earlier generation synths still roam this area. The location is completely sealed off until Main Quest: The Nuclear Option is active. You may wish to access the terminal (unlocked) just before the lower level warehouse floor to activate an old Sentry Bot.

To Institute Bioscience

To Institute Main Atrium and Concourse

## Institute Reactor

- ARMAMENTS AND AMMO
- DANGER: TURRETS!
- DANGER: TESLA ARC!
- HEALTH OR CHEMS

Originally a research project from the old Commonwealth Institute, the reactor was salvaged and improved upon, allowing the Institute to stop relying on siphoning power from above-ground sources almost entirely. This location is completely sealed off until Main Quest: The Nuclear Option or Institute Quest: Powering Up is active.

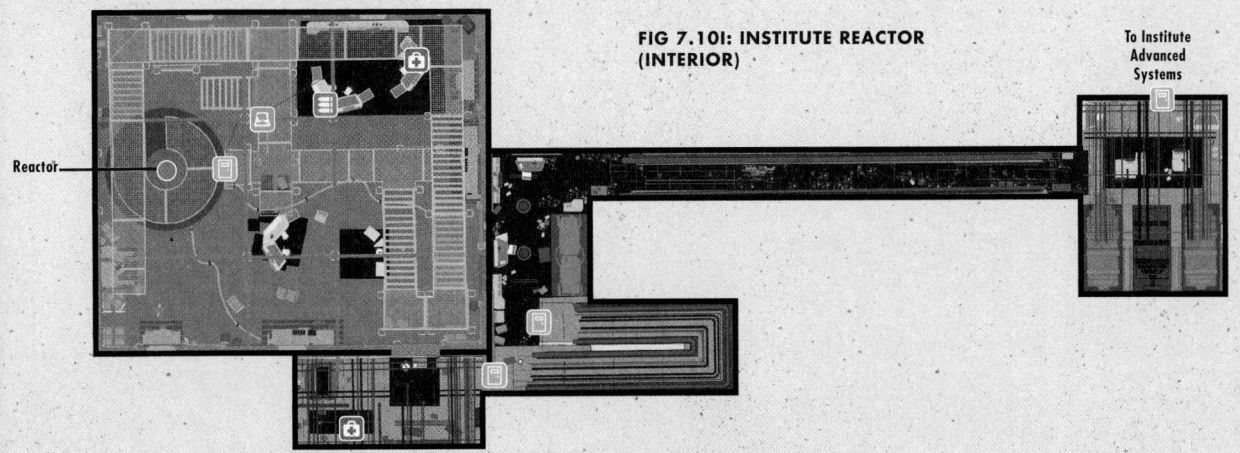

### FIG 7.10I: INSTITUTE REACTOR (INTERIOR)

To Institute Advanced Systems

Reactor

## Public Works Maintenance Area

- ARMAMENTS AND AMMO: TRUNK
- ARMOR PART: FUSION CORE
- CRAFTING: ARMOR WORKBENCH
- CRAFTING: CHEMISTRY STATION
- CRAFTING: POWER ARMOR STATION
- CRAFTING: WEAPONS WORKBENCH
- COLLECTIBLE: NUKA COLA QUANTUM
- DANGER: OIL!
- DANGER: RADIATION (MILD)!
- FACTION: FERAL GHOULS
- FACTION: MOLE RATS
- FACTION: THE INSTITUTE
- HEALTH AND CHEMS
- QUEST VISIT: THE NUCLEAR OPTION (MINUTEMEN)

**FIG 7.10J: PUBLIC WORKS MAINTENANCE AREA (INTERIOR)**

This location isn't accessed from the Institute itself; it is a medium-sized sewer complex under Cambridge that allows a cunning infiltration of the premises. Look for an underwater sewer pipe (Secondary Location 7.19) that's south of Greenetech Genetics on the northwest side of the Charles River and access the entrance. There is a wall terminal (Advanced) accessing a steamer trunk and a keypad on the east wall.

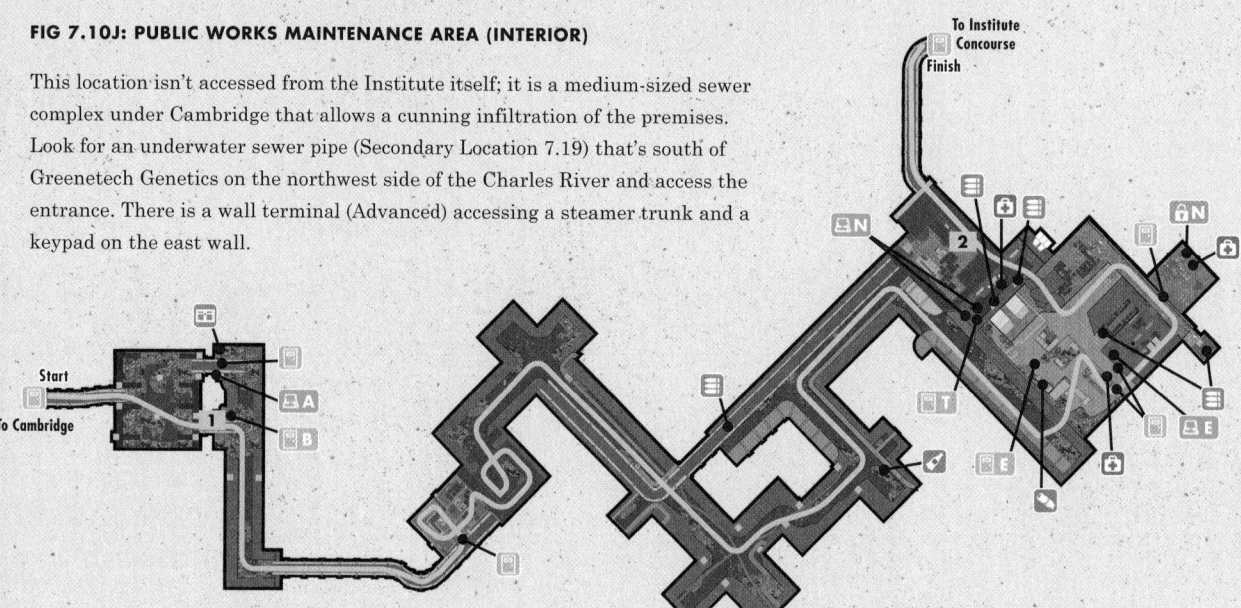

You cannot explore further until the quest is active and you've input the key code.

The interior is a series of tunnels where a large Institute pipe runs. Follow this pipe to access the maintenance area, and a secondary pipe brings you out into the Institute Concourse, near the relay chamber. As there's limited occasions to gather the available items, make your sweep during the quest.

THREAT LEVELS 6-14

- DANGER: GRENADES!
- DANGER: MAKESHIFT BOMB!
- DANGER: LONG DROP!
- DANGER: MINES!
- DANGER: TENSION TRIGGER!
- DANGER: TRIPWIRES!
- DANGER: TURRETS!

- FACTION: GUNNERS
- FACTION: SYNTHS (INSTITUTE)
- FACTION: CHARACTER: K1-98
- FACTION: CHARACTER: Z2-47 (COURSER)
- HEALTH OR CHEMS+
- QUEST VISIT: HUNTER/HUNTED (MAIN)
- QUEST START: MISCELLANEOUS (K1-98)

- ARMAMENTS AND AMMO++
- ARMAMENTS AND AMMO: MINI NUKE
- ARMAMENTS AND AMMO: MINI NUKE (FAT MAN)
- ARMOR PARTS: FUSION CORE (3)
- BOTTLECAPS+
- COLLECTIBLE: NUKA CHERRY
- COLLECTIBLE: REQUIRED READING:
  MASSACHUSETTS SURGICAL JOURNAL
- CRAFTING: CHEMISTRY STATION

**FIG 7.11A: GREENETECH GENETICS (BOTTOM FLOORS INTERIOR)**

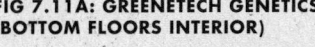

LEVEL 7

LEVEL 6

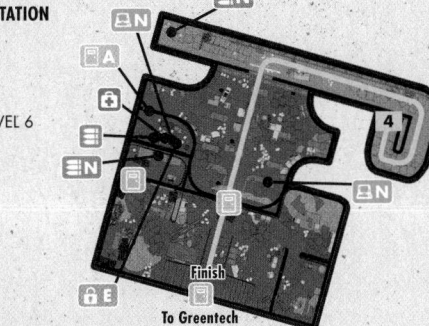

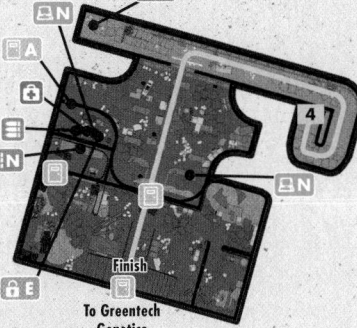

LEVEL 5

Finish

To Greentech Genetics

LEVELS 3 & 4

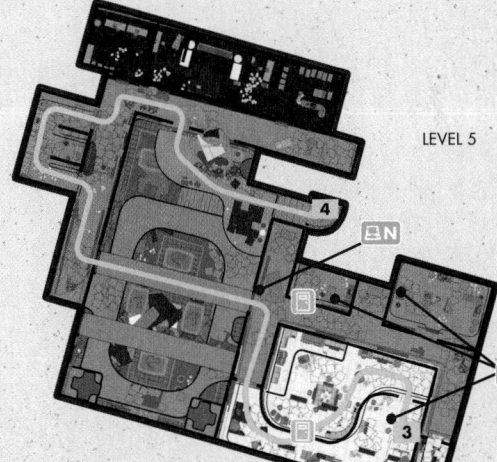

LEVEL 2

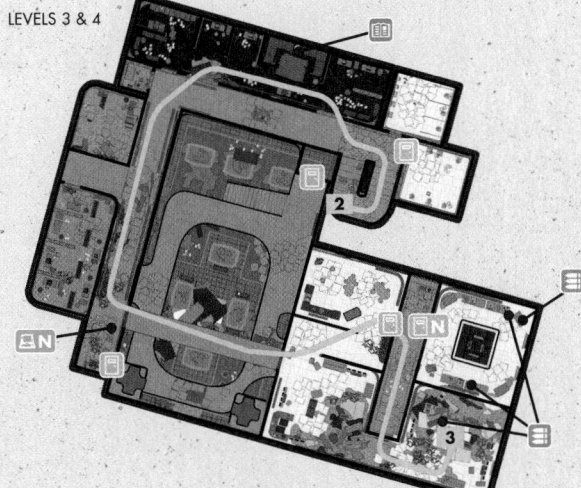

LEVEL 1

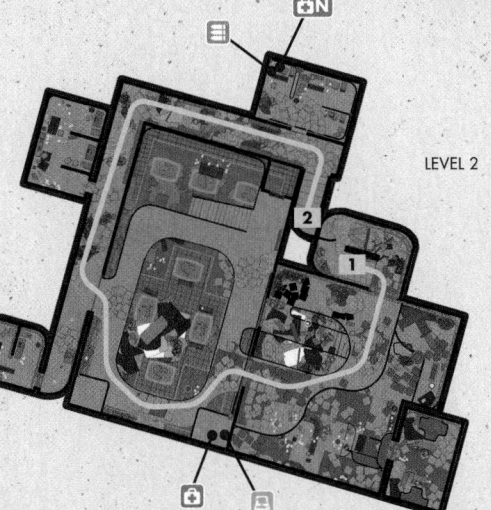

Start

MAP

ZONE 7

NEIGHBORHOOD:
CAMBRIDGE

## FIG 7.11B: GREENETECH GENETICS (TOP FLOORS INTERIOR)

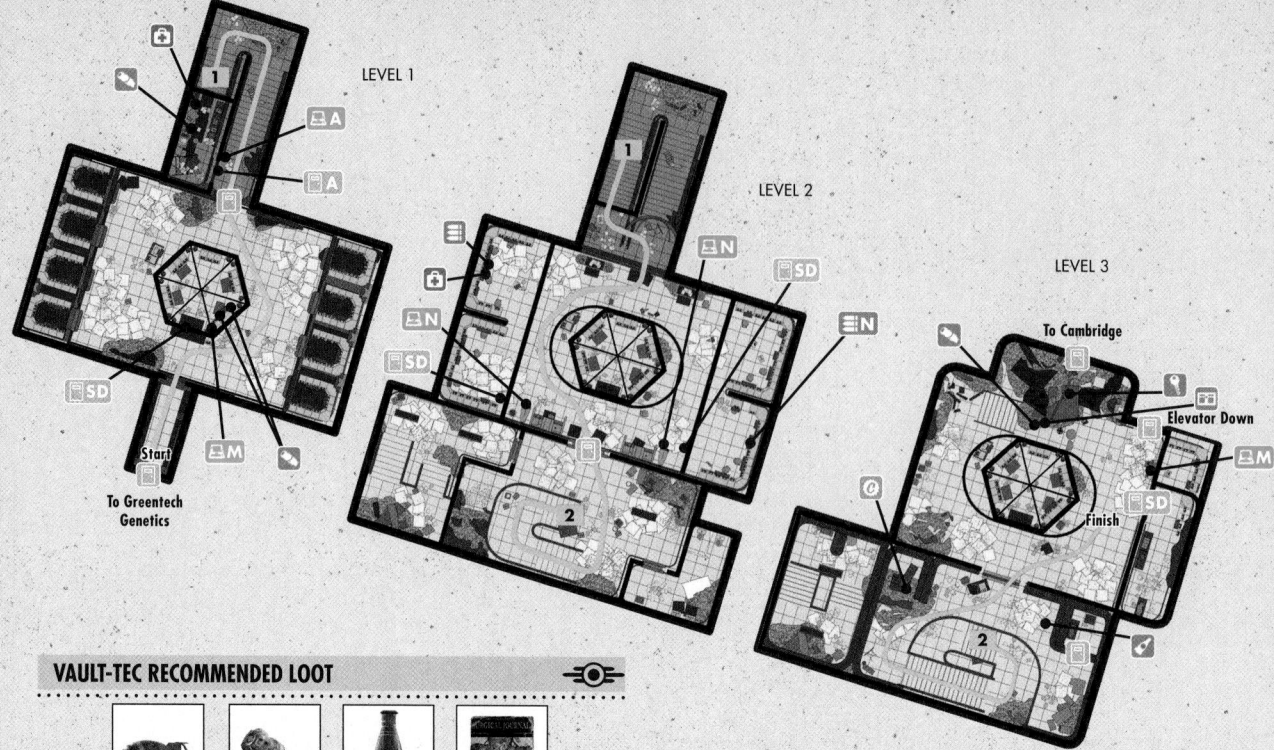

## VAULT-TEC RECOMMENDED LOOT

**ARMAMENTS AND AMMO: MINI NUKE AND FAT MAN**
**ARMOR PART: FUSION CORE (3)**
**COLLECTIBLE: NUKA CHERRY**
**REQUIRED READING: MASSACHUSETTS SURGICAL JOURNAL**

This location is not fully accessible unless the specified quest is active.

This vertical maze features the remains of the C.I.T.'s Greenetech building, where genetic manipulation and other secret experiments were undertaken. Once inside, prepare for a battle between Gunners as synths. Your target is located at the top of this structure's interior. The Courser Chip is your quest item to locate.

If you access the door to Cambridge at the top of the structure (up the stairs with the trunk and Fat Man on it), you reach a precarious roof deck with no railings and some of the best views of Boston around. Just watch your footing!

### Miscellaneous Quest (K1-98)

Once the quest at this location is over, speak with a trapped synth named K1-98. You can free her by hacking the terminal (Master) or by locating the passcode from the adjacent toolbox under the ruined staircase. She thanks you profusely. Perhaps you'll see her again at Ticonderoga Station? You can also execute or leave the three Gunner hostages.

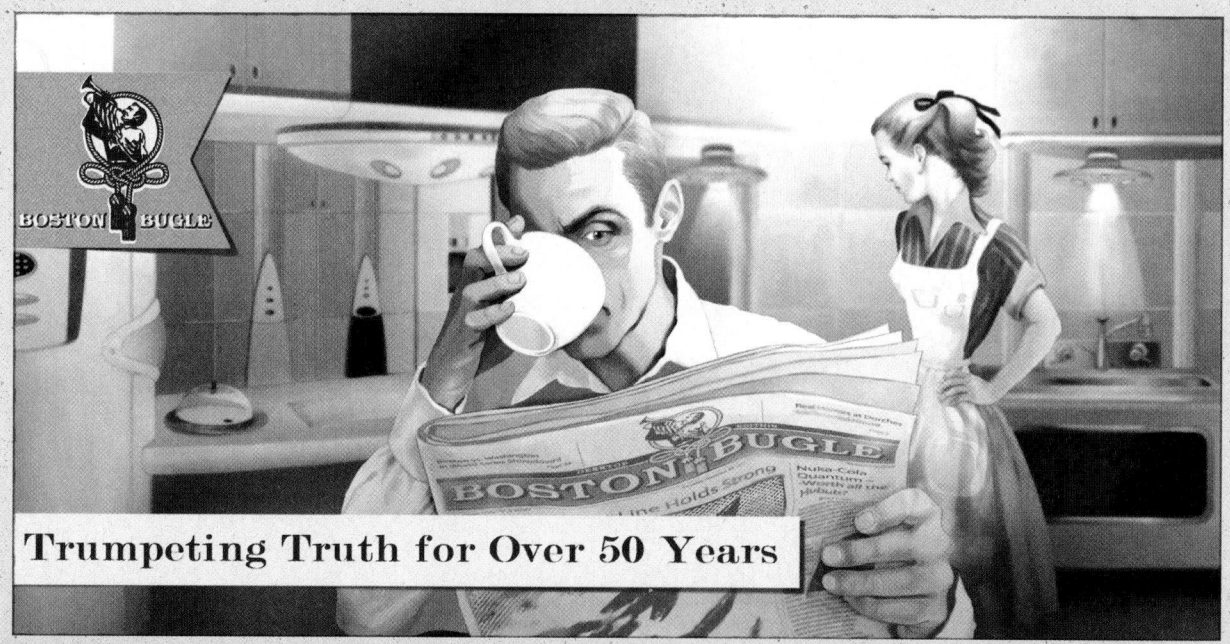

Trumpeting Truth for Over 50 Years

- – ARMAMENTS AND AMMO
- – ARMAMENTS AND AMMO: TRUNK
- – DANGER: LONG DROP!
- – DANGER: RADIATION (SEVERE)!
- – FACTION: FERAL GHOULS

This area was previously a city block in Cambridge. Non–Feral Ghouls moved here hoping it would be a safe haven for them. Unfortunately they turned feral over time. Exercise caution, as the ground is steep and the crater is difficult to climb out of and is full of ferals. A single ammo trunk is located close to the center of the crater.

**[7.13] MONSIGNOR PLAZA**   THREAT LEVELS 6-14

- – ARMAMENTS AND AMMO
- – ARMAMENTS AND AMMO: TRUNK
- – COLLECTIBLE: HOLOTAPE: GRISWOLD'S POETRY COLLECTION
- – CRAFTING: CHEMISTRY STATION
- – CRAFTING: COOKING STATION (2)
- – CRAFTING: WEAPONS WORKBENCH
- – DANGER: CAN CHIMES!
- – DANGER: GRENADES!
- – DANGER: TURRETS!
- – FACTION: RAIDERS
- – HEALTH OR CHEMS

The perimeter of this shopping plaza is now a fortified Raider camp, with most of the enemies lodged in makeshift barricades to the northeast. The location has a long perimeter around the water's edge, a Fallon's and Nuka Cherry sign to pinpoint, and a grotesque hanging tree of hook chains and corpses. Note both entrances, as well as a turret-control terminal and ammo in the camp.

Inside, Raiders have scorched and ruined an old shopping mall, although there's still some clothing to scavenge. Watch the turrets and other traps as you reach the third-floor steamer trunk. Up on Level 3, be sure to extract Griswold's poetry collection from his terminal.

**FIG 7:13: MONSIGNOR PLAZA (INTERIOR)**

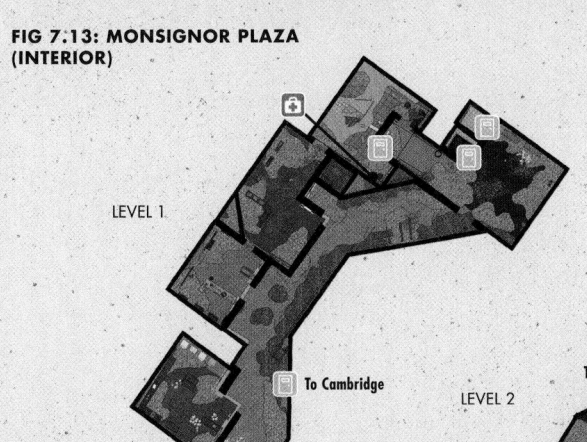

LEVEL 1

To Cambridge

To Cambridge

To Cambridge

Start

LEVEL 2

To Cambridge

LEVEL 3

Finish

# SECONDARY LOCATIONS

## [7.01] BRIDGE DEN (CAMBRIDGE)

- ARMAMENTS AND AMMO
- DANGER: TRIPWIRES!

Check under the bridge for a safe (Advanced) and an old tripwire trap, which might have already been triggered.

## [7.02] CHARLES RIVER BOATHOUSE

- ARMAMENTS AND AMMO: TRUNK
- DANGER: RADIATION (MILD)!
- FACTION: MIRELURKS

A locked boathouse (Advanced) with some radioactive spillage is worth braving, as there's a steamer trunk inside.

## [7.03] RED ROCKET FILLING STATION (COLLEGE SQUARE)

- ARMAMENTS AND AMMO
- CRAFTING: POWER ARMOR STATION
- CRAFTING: WEAPONS WORKBENCH

This is a handy dandy place to sit and mend your armor, work on your weapons, and use as a place to retreat to while attacking College Square to the southwest.

## [7.04] UNION'S HOPE CATHEDRAL

- ARMAMENTS AND AMMO
- FACTION: FERAL GHOUL
- FACTION: CHARACTER: FATHER GABE
- HEALTH OR CHEMS

The graveyard to the east of this imposing brick structure holds a band of frothing ferals. The front doors are closed, and the one on the east side is locked (Advanced), so use the front doors. Inside, Father Gabe is preaching. Grab the chems on the wall before leaving.

## [7.05] HARDWARE STORE (CAMBRIDGE)

- ARMAMENTS AND AMMO
- HEALTH OR CHEMS

This small and wrecked store with a locked back storage area (Master) is significantly easier to open if you find the locked storage key on a desk on the upper floor of the main building.

## [7.06] PLUMBER'S SECRET

- DANGER: MINES!
- HEALTH OR CHEMS
- FACTION: RADROACHES

The secret, in this case, is a small collection of mines to avoid setting off. Scour the supply shop for a safe (Advanced), and look upstairs for some chems.

## [7.07] RAIDER BONFIRE CAMP

- ARMAMENTS AND AMMO: TRUNK
- CRAFTING: COOKING STATION
- CRAFTING: WEAPONS WORKBENCH
- DANGER: MINES!
- DANGER: TURRETS!
- FACTION: RAIDERS
- HEALTH OR CHEMS

A large and well-guarded Raider camp with a central bonfire. Don't leave without massacring these deviants, and steal the contents of their steamer trunk afterward. Enter between the barrier to the southwest.

## [7.08] RED ROCKET FILLING STATION (NORTH CENTRAL CAMBRIDGE)

- ARMAMENTS AND AMMO
- CRAFTING: ARMOR WORKBENCH
- CRAFTING: POWER ARMOR STATION
- CRAFTING: WEAPONS WORKBENCH
- FACTION: RAIDERS

Just down the road from the Raider camp is a filling station where you can tinker on two workbenches and rummage around in an old desk safe (Novice).

## [7.09] RAIDER CAMP (NARROW YARD)

- ARMAMENTS AND AMMO
- FACTION: RAIDERS
- HEALTH OR CHEMS

A motley band of Raiders is roaming this local area. Check the southern ruined house upstairs for a duffel bag and safe (Novice).

## [7.10] CAMBRIDGE PARK AND OLD COVERED ALLEY

- ARMAMENTS AND AMMO
- COLLECTIBLE: NUKA CHERRY
- CRAFTING: CHEMISTRY STATION
- HEALTH OR CHEMS

A small and historically pleasant park is now scrub and stone with a tiny shop. Someone's left a Nuka Cherry in the old covered alley southwest of the park. Pry it out of their cold, bony hands. Then check the overhang to the northeast for a small chem lab and chemistry station.

## [7.11] MASS CHEMICAL

- ARMAMENTS AND AMMO
- CRAFTING: CHEMISTRY STATION
- CRAFTING: WEAPONS WORKBENCH
- DANGER: OIL!
- FACTION: SUPER MUTANTS

Part of the large Super Mutant camp in this vicinity, this old chemical factory now shows signs of greenskin offal collections. There's a Protectron terminal (Novice) and gantries to the exterior roof, where you can make use of an old sniper's nest.

## [7.12] SUPER MUTANT HIGH RISE

- ARMAMENTS AND AMMO: TRUNK (3)
- CRAFTING: WEAPONS WORKBENCH
- DANGER: LONG DROP!
- DANGER: TURRETS!
- DANGER: RADIATION (MILD)!
- FACTION: SUPER MUTANTS

A large construction site and partly completed high-rise is now home to a Super Mutant gang that terrorizes the border between Cambridge and Charlestown. The construction site warehouse to the north actually straddles both neighborhoods and has a place to sleep after the mayhem.

The main high-rise features an elevator door to open. Drop down into a flooded basement to claim a steamer trunk and unchain a door. Then climb up the stairwell. Including the basement, there are nine floors. As you ascend, look for a platform to the rooftops of the southwest warehouse.

When you run out of stairwell, use the collapsed floors to continue upward, all the way to another trunk atop the structure (expect a fight). Then head northeast, onto the elevated freeway, and unlock the overturned green trailer (Master) and ransack yet another trunk in here!

To the south is a small trailer, mostly filled with junk.

## [7.13] RAIDER PLATFORMS (CAMBRIDGE)

- ARMAMENTS AND AMMO
- FACTION: RAIDERS
- HEALTH OR CHEMS

A rusty bus and some debris masquerading as platforms allows you to scavenge the building northwest and northeast of this road junction. Use the fire escape to reach the upper floor of the northwest building for some extra loot crates.

## [7.14] RAIDER ROOFTOP APARTMENTS (CAMBRIDGE)

- ARMAMENTS AND AMMO
- ARMAMENTS AND AMMO: TRUNK
- FACTION: RAIDERS
- HEALTH OR CHEMS

This location features a collapsed radio mast linking the north and south structures together. Mop up the Raider scum en route to the penthouse apartment, where the tip of the mast lies; there's a trunk here to open.

## [7.15] CAMPUS OFFICE AND COVERED BRIDGE

- ARMAMENTS AND AMMO: TRUNK
- CRAFTING: CHEMISTRY STATION
- CRAFTING: COOKING STATION
- FACTION: RAIDERS
- HEALTH OR CHEMS

Some reasonably adept Raiders have made a fortified camp just east of the C.I.T. Ruins, but they've left the gates unlocked. Explore the two buildings linked by a small bridge. Enter the north building via an upper roof patio.

Inside the office building is an elevator leading down and more debris. Stay on the upper floor and take the exit door, cross the covered bridge with the unpleasant hanging decorations, and step into the upper floor of the south building. There's a small chem lab with a steamer trunk.

## [7.16] KENDALL PARKING

- ARMAMENTS AND AMMO
- COLLECTIBLE: NUKA CHERRY
- CRAFTING: COOKING STATION
- DANGER: MINES!
- FACTION: MOLE RATS
- FACTION: SCAVENGER

Watch for a scavenger and his pets in this rubble-filled parking structure just east of Greenetech Genetics. Grab a Nuka Cherry from his shopping cart. There's an upstairs floor if you're keen to see more rubble.

## [7.17] KENDALL RAIDER APARTMENTS

- ARMAMENTS AND AMMO
- ARMAMENTS AND AMMO: TRUNK
- CRAFTING: ARMOR WORKBENCH
- CRAFTING: COOKING STATION
- FACTION: RAIDERS
- FACTION: CHARACTER: BLACKBIRD
- HEALTH OR CHEMS
- QUEST VISIT: BUTCHER'S BILL 2 (THE RAILROAD)

A trio of high-rise buildings close to the river offer impressive defenses for this camp of Raiders. Follow the ramps up to the structure with the button and call the platform over; that way you'll be able to access the apartment tower to the south with the steamer trunk.

## [7.18] TICONDEROGA SAFEHOUSE

- ARMAMENTS AND AMMO
- ARMAMENTS AND AMMO: TRUNK
- ARMAMENTS AND AMMO: MINI NUKE
- ARMAMENTS AND AMMO: MINI NUKE (FAT MAN)
- COLLECTIBLE: NUKA COLA QUANTUM (2)
- COLLECTIBLE: REQUIRED READING: GUNS AND BULLETS
- CRAFTING: ARMOR WORKBENCH
- CRAFTING: CHEMISTRY STATION
- CRAFTING: COOKING STATION
- CRAFTING: WEAPONS WORKBENCH
- FACTION: THE RAILROAD
- FACTION: SYNTHS (THE INSTITUTE)
- FACTION: CHARACTER: HIGH RISE
- HEALTH OR CHEMS
- QUEST VISIT: BOSTON AFTER DARK (THE RAILROAD)
- QUEST VISIT: OPERATION TICONDEROGA

**FIG 7.18: TICONDEROGA (INTERIOR)**

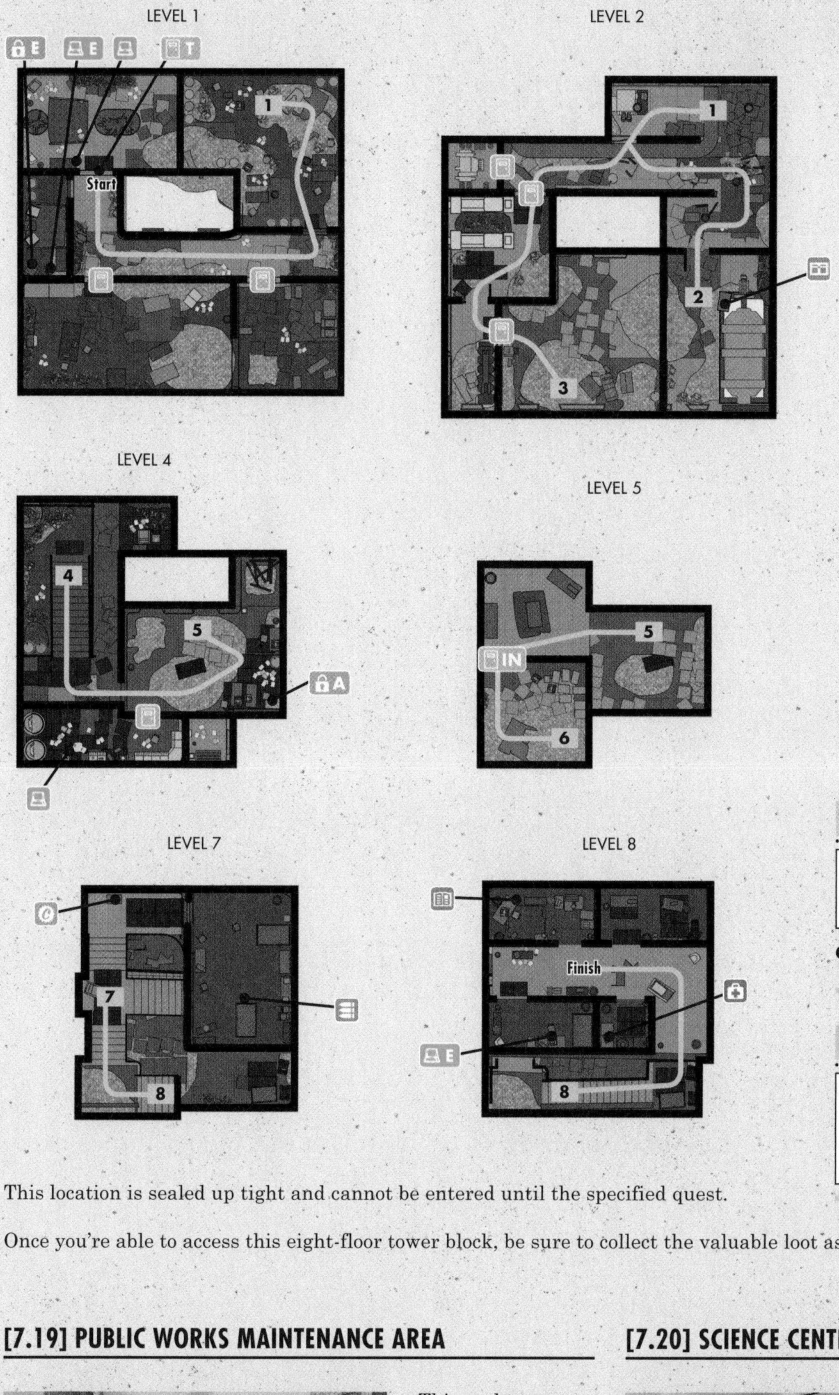

LEVEL 1

LEVEL 2

LEVEL 3

LEVEL 4

LEVEL 5

LEVEL 6

LEVEL 7

LEVEL 8

**VAULT-TEC RECOMMENDED LOOT**

ARMAMENTS AND
AMMO: MINI NUKE
AND FAT MAN

COLLECTIBLE: NUKA COLA QUANTUM (2)

**VAULT-TEC RECOMMENDED LOOT**

REQUIRED READING:
GUNS AND BULLETS

**MAP**

**ZONE 7**

NEIGHBORHOOD:
CAMBRIDGE

This location is sealed up tight and cannot be entered until the specified quest.

Once you're able to access this eight-floor tower block, be sure to collect the valuable loot as you ascend.

## [7.19] PUBLIC WORKS MAINTENANCE AREA

This underwater pipe marks a well-hidden entrance that allows access into the Institute's main facility. The map and information about the sewer tunnels are detailed in Primary Location 7.10: The Institute.

## [7.20] SCIENCE CENTER GIFT SHOP

– CRAFTING:
  CHEMISTRY STATION
– FACTION: ROBOTS
– HEALTH OR CHEMS

A small science store, mostly picked clean, with a friendly storekeeper.

# ZONE 8: NEIGHBORHOOD: CHARLESTOWN

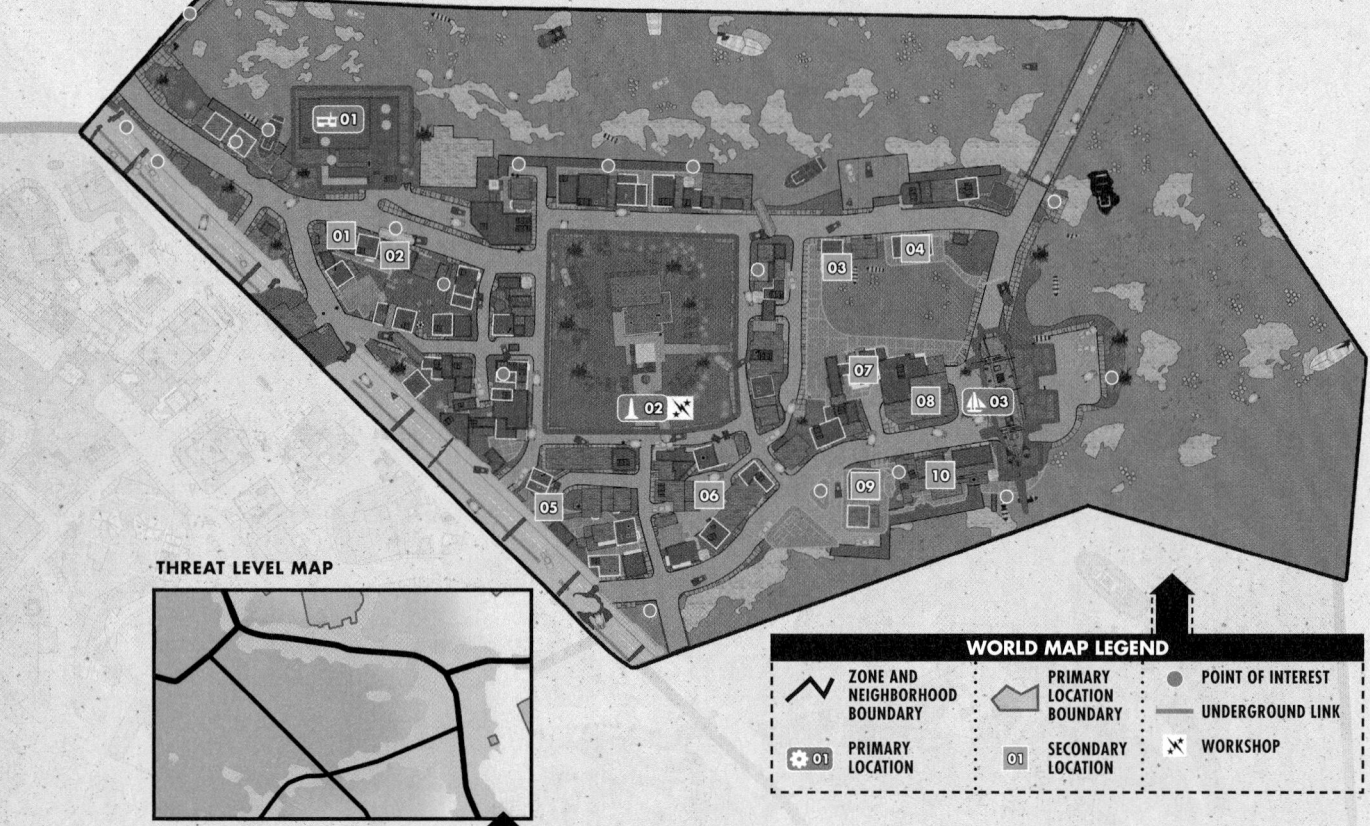

## THREAT LEVEL MAP

1-5  6-14  15-25  20+  25+  30+  35+  40+  45+
EXPECTED LEVEL OF ENEMIES ENCOUNTERED

### Primary Locations
- [8.01] BADTFL REGIONAL OFFICE
- [8.02] BUNKER HILL
- [8.03] U.S.S. CONSTITUTION

### Secondary Locations
- [8.01] RUINED TAVERN (CHARLESTOWN)
- [8.02] BACK ALLEY SCAFFOLD STEPS
- [8.03] GREEN AWNING MANSION
- [8.04] DRUG DEN
- [8.05] SOUTH ALLEY AND GARAGE
- [8.06] ABANDONED HOUSE
- [8.07] SCAVENGER CAMP (CHARLESTOWN)
- [8.08] SHELLED-OUT BUILDING
- [8.09] CHARLESTOWN LAUNDRY
- [8.10] SOUTH APARTMENTS (CHARLESTOWN)

## WORLD MAP LEGEND

| | | |
|---|---|---|
| ZONE AND NEIGHBORHOOD BOUNDARY | PRIMARY LOCATION BOUNDARY | ● POINT OF INTEREST |
| | | — UNDERGROUND LINK |
| ⚙ 01 PRIMARY LOCATION | 01 SECONDARY LOCATION | ✖ WORKSHOP |

West of Cambridge and north of the Charles River, Charlestown is the oldest of the Boston Neighborhoods, and the old wooden row houses reflect this past. Separated from Cambridge by the elevated freeway, this offers excellent exploration possibilities without feeling overwhelmed. It is primarily a Raider territory, with (sometimes hostile) Scavengers to the south and along the river. The neighborhood is dominated by two ancient monuments—Bunker Hill, which could be an exceptional settlement if your alliance with the locals is strong, and the U.S.S. Constitution, a prewar battleship that has been illegally moored for quite some time.

## MAP LEGEND

| 13 ——— 20 OPTIMAL ROUTE | ● AREA OF INTEREST |
|---|---|

| | | |
|---|---|---|
| ⓒ BOTTLECAPS | ▤ ARMAMENTS AND AMMO | ✚ HEALTH OR CHEMS |
| 🔒 SAFE | ▯ DOOR | ▯ TERMINAL |
| | | ▤ STEAMER TRUNK |

*Collectibles:*

| | | |
|---|---|---|
| 🔥 FUSION CORE | BOBBLEHEAD | NUKA COLA QUANTUM |
| POWER ARMOR | NUKA CHERRY | HOLOTAPE |
| 📖 ESSENTIAL READING | MINI NUKE | 🔑 A KEY |

N – Novice (Locked)
A – Advanced (Locked)
E – Expert (Locked)
M – Master (Locked)
T – Terminal required to unlock

KEY – Key or ID Card required to unlock
IN – Inaccessible
C – Chained
CB – Circuit Breaker
B – Button

# PRIMARY LOCATIONS

 **[8.01] BADTFL REGIONAL OFFICE** THREAT LEVELS 15-25

This is the local office for the Bureau of Alcohol, Drugs, Tobacco, Firearms, and Lasers (BADTFL). This location was responsible for investigations and was used as a holding cell and evidence locker housed in the facility. The locker has attracted Raiders, keen to loot it.

- ARMAMENTS AND AMMO++
- ARMAMENTS AND AMMO: MINI NUKE
- ARMAMENTS AND AMMO: MINI NUKE (FAT MAN)
- ARMAMENTS AND AMMO: TRUNK
- BOTTLECAPS
- COLLECTIBLE: HOLOTAPE: EDDIE WINTER HOLOTAPE
- COLLECTIBLE: HOLOTAPE: WE ARE DONE
- COLLECTIBLE: REQUIRED READING: GUNS AND BULLETS
- CRAFTING: ARMOR WORKBENCH
- CRAFTING: WEAPONS WORKBENCH
- FACTION: RAIDERS
- FACTION: ROBOT (PROTECTRON)
- FACTION: CHARACTER: SPARTA
- HEALTH AND CHEMS+
- QUEST VISIT: LONG TIME COMING (SIDE COMPANION)

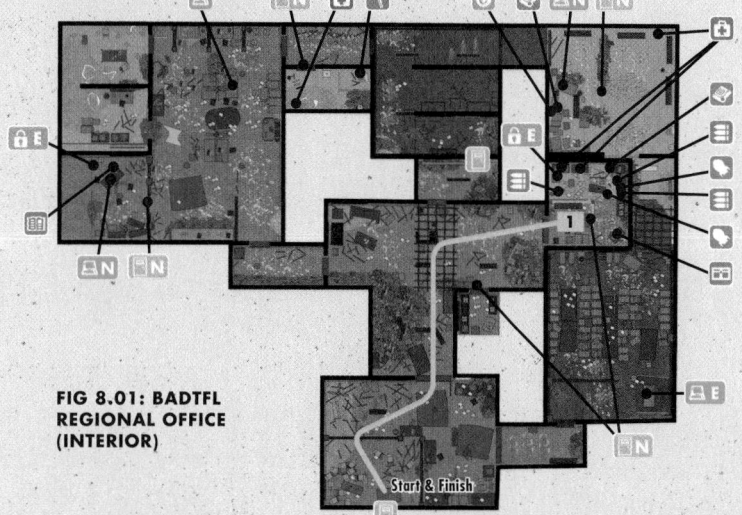

FIG 8.01: BADTFL
REGIONAL OFFICE
(INTERIOR)

MAP

**ZONE 8**

NEIGHBORHOOD:
CHARLESTOWN

The evidence terminal (northwest) has information pertaining to Eddie Winter, and his Holotape is in the lower cells area near a Caps stash and desk with a terminal on it. The chief's key is in the locked bathroom (Novice) to the north (unlock his office to obtain the magazine). Also be certain to visit the upper-level locker (Novice) for that massive haul of items!

 **[8.02] BUNKER HILL** THREAT LEVELS 15-25

- ARMAMENTS AND AMMO+++
- ARMAMENTS AND AMMO: MINI NUKE
- BOTTLECAPS
- COLLECTIBLE: REQUIRED READING: LIVE & LOVE
- DANGER: LONG DROP!
- DANGER: TURRETS!
- FACTION: SETTLER
- FACTION: CHARACTER: KAY

- FACTION: CHARACTER: KESSLER
- FACTION: CHARACTER: JOE SAVOLDI
- FACTION: CHARACTER: MEG
- FACTION: CHARACTER: OLD MAN STOCKTON
- FACTION: CHARACTER: TONY SAVOLDI
- HEALTH OR CHEMS+++
- QUEST START: FALLEN HERO
  (MISCELLANEOUS: FREEFORM)
- QUEST START: TRAFFIC JAM
  (MISCELLANEOUS: FREEFORM)
- QUEST START: PREP SCHOOL
  (MISCELLANEOUS: FREEFORM)
- QUEST START: MEG'S TOUR
  (MISCELLANEOUS: FREEFORM)
- QUEST VISIT: THE BATTLE OF BUNKER HILL
  (THE INSTITUTE)

- QUEST VISIT: LAST VOYAGE OF THE U.S.S.
  CONSTITUTION (SIDE)
- QUEST VISIT: BOSTON AFTER DARK (RAILROAD)
- QUEST VISIT: HUMAN ERROR (SIDE)
- SERVICES: TRADER (DEB)
- SERVICES: TRADER (JOE SAVOLDI)
- SERVICES: TRADER (KAY)
- SERVICES: TRADER (TONY SAVOLDI)
- SERVICES: WORKSHOP
- UNIQUE ITEM: BLACK OPS CHESTPIECE
- UNIQUE ITEM: BLACK OPS RIGHT SHINGUARD
- UNIQUE ITEM: DESTROYER'S LEFT ARM
- UNIQUE ITEM: WASTELANDER'S FRIEND

## FIG 8.02A: BUNKER HILL (EXTERIOR)

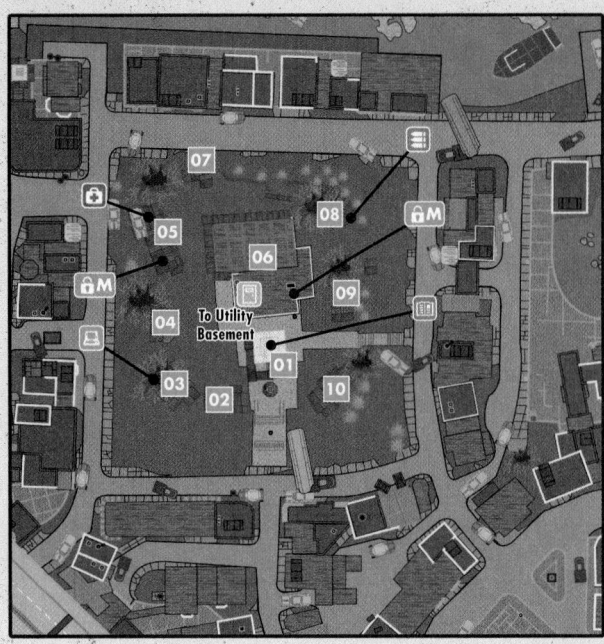

This large granite monument was erected to commemorate the Battle of Bunker Hill, which was the first main confrontation with the British back in 1775 during the American Revolutionary War. Today it serves as a reasonably well-defended settlement. The Railroad currently uses it as a pickup point for escaped synths, who are met and hidden by a local sympathizer until a Railroad agent can take them to safety.

This location has a workshop and can be converted into a settlement, but only after the Faction Quest: The Battle of Bunker Hill has been completed.

### [01] Entrance and Obelisk

This imposing landmark was erected between 1827 and 1843 using granite from quarries in Quincy.

### [02] Kay the Doctor

The workshop for this settlement is here, along with Deb's sleeping area and Kay the veterinarian.

### [03] Kessler's Shack

The leader of Bunker Hill sleeps here. Her terminal makes interesting reading.

### [04] Brahmin Pen and Crops

A couple of Brahmin and a crop of corn.

### [05] Savoldi's Rest Stop

Order drinks, catch up on gossip, and rent a room for the night. Old Man Stockton is here.

### [06] Bunker Hill Market

Deb runs the market from her stall in the remains of an old lodge (she has several unique items to sell), and caravans are sometimes found here. A trapdoor leads to the utility basement, which is inaccessible unless the Institute Quest is active.

### [07] The Latrines

The stench can sometimes be overpowering.

### [08-10] Caravan Shacks

Mattresses for caravan guards and tinkerers traveling here from parts both far and wide.

## FIG 8.02B: UTILITY BASEMENT (INTERIOR)

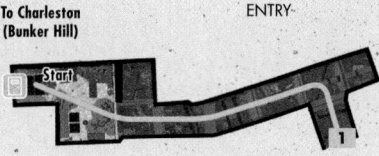

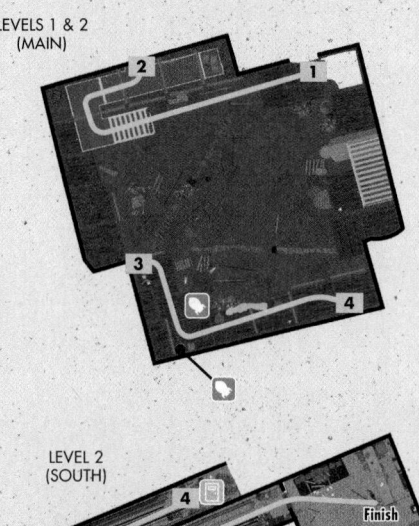

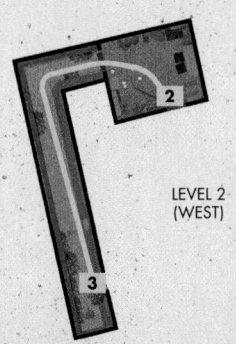

This interior location is only accessible during the specified Institute Quest. Don't forget to grab the Mini Nuke as you work your way through the fracas!

**Freeform Activities: Bunker Hill**

## Fallen Hero*

**1. MISCELLANEOUS: FIND ANY TRACE OF BRENT SAVOLDI**   **2. MISCELLANEOUS: RETURN HAT TO JOE SAVOLDI**

Get chatting with Joe Savoldi at his bar and ask for a job. Agree to help.

 (Easy) Talk him into paying you more for your help.

Locate and drop into the Old Gullet Sinkhole. Locate the hat. Return it to Joe Savoldi for your reward.

 **GRANDPA SAVOLDI'S HAT**

 **BOTTLECAPS (150–200)**

## Traffic Jam*

**1. MISCELLANEOUS: CLEAR THE TRAINING YARD**   **2. MISCELLANEOUS: REPORT BACK TO DEB**

Find Deb and ask her for a job. Agree to help remove the Feral Ghouls from the National Guard training yard to increase the flow of trade.

 (Easy, Medium, Hard) Ask for more Caps. Those Ghouls are filthy.

Head to the National Guard training yard. Beware of machine-gun turrets and Feral Ghouls. Kill all marked Ghouls until the quest updates. Return to Deb for your reward.

 **BOTTLECAPS (175–225)**

## Prep School*

**1. MISCELLANEOUS: RESCUE ANY CARAVAN SURVIVORS**
**2. MISCELLANEOUS: KILL ZELLER**
**3. MISCELLANEOUS: REPORT BACK TO KESSLER**

This is only available once Freeform Activity: Traffic Jam* has been completed. Speak with Kessler and agree to wipe out the Raider Gang nearby.

 (Easy, Medium, Hard) This might be tricky. Ask for more Caps.

Visit the East Boston Preparatory School. Beware of Raiders. Kill all foes and the named Raider "Zeller."

(Novice) Unlock the three cells and free the prisoners. Speak to them so they follow you.

Return to Kessler for your reward.

 **BOTTLECAPS (200–400)**

## Meg's Tour*

Meg is an urchin hanging around the obelisk and offers to take you on a tour of Bunker Hill for a price. Is that price worth paying?

**MAP**

**ZONE 8**

NEIGHBORHOOD: CHARLESTOWN

425

THREAT LEVELS 20+

– ARMAMENTS AND AMMO+
– ARMAMENTS AND AMMO: TRUNK (2)
– BOTTLECAPS+++
– COLLECTIBLE: REQUIRED READING:
  U.S. COVERT OPERATIONS MANUAL 2
– CRAFTING: CHEMISTRY STATION
– CRAFTING: WEAPONS WORKBENCH
– DANGER: RADIATION (MILD)!
– DANGER: TURRETS!
– FACTION: ROBOTS
– FACTION: CHARACTER: BOSUN
– FACTION: CHARACTER: CAPTAIN IRONSIDES
– FACTION: CHARACTER: FIRST MATE
– FACTION: CHARACTER: LOOKOUT
– FACTION: CHARACTER: MR. NAVIGATOR
– HEALTH OR CHEMS+
– QUEST START: LAST VOYAGE OF THE
  U.S.S. CONSTITUTION (SIDE)
– UNIQUE ITEM: BROADSIDER
– UNIQUE ITEM: CAPTAIN IRONSIDE'S HAT
– UNIQUE ITEM: LIEUTENANT'S HAT
– UNIQUE ITEM: ACCESS TO CAPTAIN'S CABIN

**FIG 8.03A: U.S.S. CONSTITUTION (BELOW DECK)**

LEVEL 1          LEVEL 2          LEVEL 3

## VAULT-TEC RECOMMENDED LOOT

**REQUIRED READING: UNSTOPPABLES**
**UNIQUE ITEM: BROADSIDER**
**UNIQUE ITEM: CAPTAIN IRONSIDE'S HAT**

This ancient maritime vessel was docked in the Boston Navy Yard and was primarily a tourist attraction. Before the war, it was populated by robots to give visitors a feel of what life was like back in the olden days. Due to an error in navigation, the ship is currently embedded in the remains of a harbor building, under constant threat of Scavenger and Raider attack. Access the interior of this vessel via a trapdoor in the hull that leads to the bow, through the building wreckage.

Once you navigate the interior, you can speak to Captain Ironsides and access the rowboat elevator on the vessel's stern, which is also stocked with health and ammo.

# SECONDARY LOCATIONS

## [8.01] RUINED TAVERN (CHARLESTOWN)

– CRAFTING: CHEMISTRY STATION

An old bar opposite the BADTFL regional office has seen better days.

## [8.02] BACK ALLEY SCAFFOLD STEPS

This area is inaccessible from the main streets, so weave through the fences to reach these metal scaffold steps up to a rooftop generator. There's a steamer trunk on the porch.

– ARMAMENTS AND AMMO          – ARMOR PART: FUSION CORE          – FACTION: WILD MONGRELS
– ARMAMENTS AND AMMO: TRUNK    – FACTION: FERAL GHOULS

## [8.03] GREEN AWNING MANSION

- ARMAMENTS AND AMMO: TRUNK

Turn west from the exterior roof of the drug den, and make a running leap onto the cottage rooftop and again into the open wall of this mansion. It's the only way to reach a locked closet (Novice) with a steamer trunk inside.

## [8.04] DRUG DEN

- ARMAMENTS AND AMMO: TRUNK
- FACTION: RAIDERS
- HEALTH OR CHEMS

Through the red door of this magazine store is a den of chem-addled Raiders. Climb to the top floor for a steamer trunk, and exit out to the open roof.

## [8.05] SOUTH ALLEY AND GARAGE

- COLLECTIBLE: NUKA COLA QUANTUM
- CRAFTING: ARMOR WORKBENCH

Check the Nuka Cola machine on the porch near this garage for a refreshing Quantum that sometimes appears.

## [8.06] ABANDONED HOUSE

- ARMAMENTS AND AMMO
- ARMAMENTS AND AMMO: TRUNK
- FACTION: FERAL GHOULS

Head into this Ghoul-infested three-floor home with severe rising damp. Unlock the top bedroom door (Advanced) for a storage attic with an unpleasant owner.

## [8.07] SCAVENGER CAMP (CHARLESTOWN)

- ARMAMENTS AND AMMO
- CRAFTING: COOKING STATION
- CRAFTING: WEAPONS WORKBENCH
- DANGER: MINES!
- FACTION: SCAVENGERS
- FACTION: CHARACTER: MANDY STILES
- FACTION: CHARACTER: DAVIES
- QUEST VISIT: LAST VOYAGE OF THE U.S.S. CONSTITUTION
- UNIQUE ITEM: NX-42 GUIDANCE CHIP

A group of scavengers have made their home here, along with a mercenary or two to dissuade invaders. You'll find Mandy Stiles most standoffish, unless the quest is active.

## [8.08] SHELLED-OUT BUILDING

- COLLECTIBLE: NUKA COLA QUANTUM
- QUEST VISIT: LAST VOYAGE OF THE U.S.S. CONSTITUTION

Amid the rubble is a mostly intact fridge and its thirst-quenching contents. Otherwise, Scavengers periodically launch attacks from here.

## [8.09] CHARLESTOWN LAUNDRY

- COLLECTIBLE: NUKA COLA QUANTUM
- COLLECTIBLE: REQUIRED READING: LA COIFFE

Turn west from the exterior roof of the drug den, and make a running leap onto the cottage rooftop and again into the open wall of this mansion. It's the only way to reach a locked closet (Novice) with a steamer trunk inside.

### VAULT-TEC RECOMMENDED LOOT

**REQUIRED READING: LA COIFFE**

Close to the large rusty anchor, this laundry and dry cleaners has an interior area to explore with a magazine and a locked employee office (Novice) where you'll find something refreshing to drink.

## [8.10] SOUTH APARTMENTS (CHARLESTOWN)

- ARMAMENTS AND AMMO
- QUEST VISIT: LAST VOYAGE OF THE U.S.S. CONSTITUTION

Including the waterlogged basement, there are five floors to this shop and upper apartment structure, with a ruined attic offering views across to the ship. You will utilize the circuit breaker on the attic roof balcony (southeast corner) during the quest. Otherwise, Scavengers periodically launch attacks from here.

# ZONE 09: NEIGHBORHOOD: THE FENS

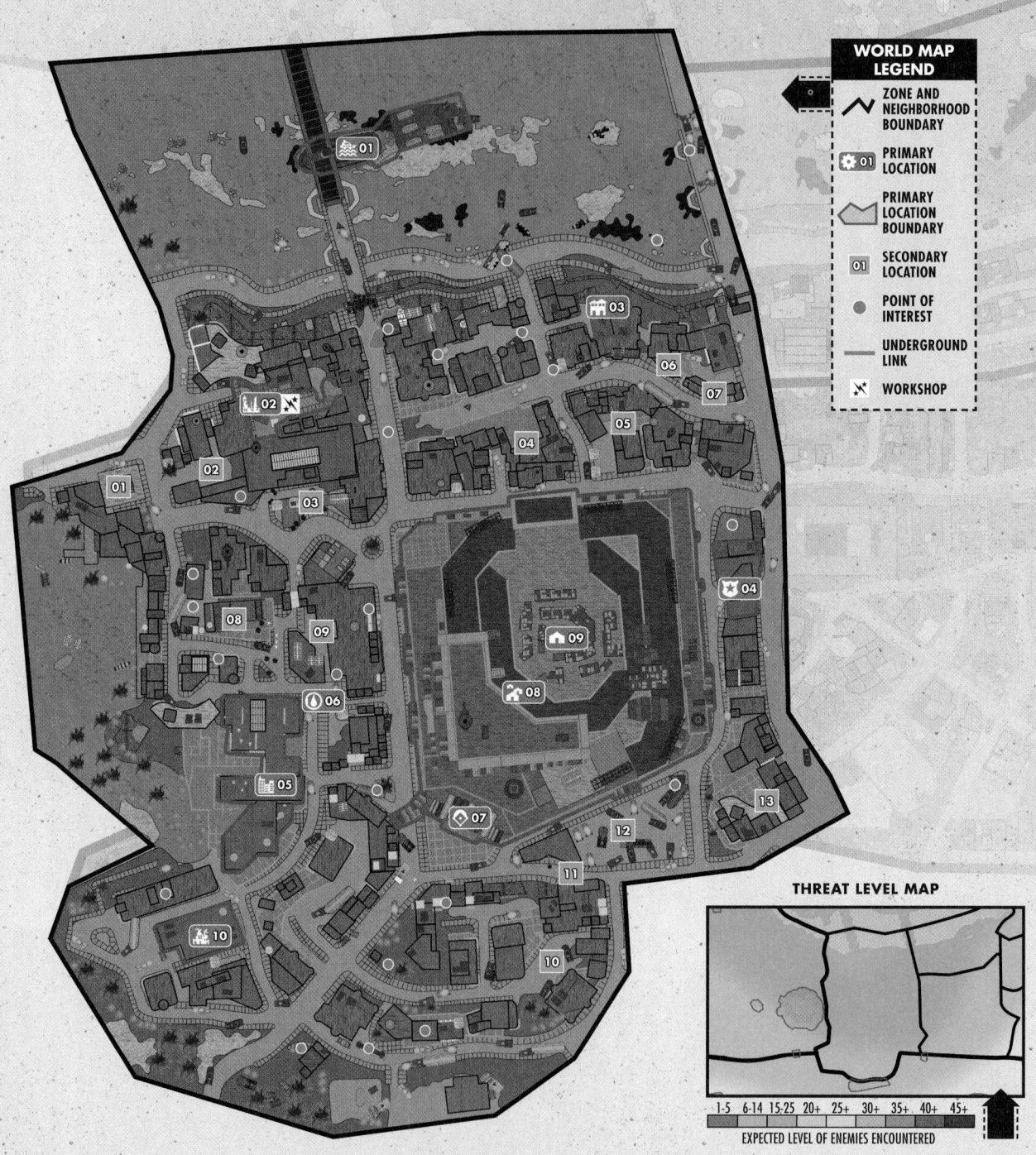

**WORLD MAP LEGEND**

〜 ZONE AND NEIGHBORHOOD BOUNDARY

⚙ 01 PRIMARY LOCATION

◥ PRIMARY LOCATION BOUNDARY

01 SECONDARY LOCATION

● POINT OF INTEREST

— UNDERGROUND LINK

✵ WORKSHOP

**THREAT LEVEL MAP**

1-5 6-14 15-25 20+ 25+ 30+ 35+ 40+ 45+
EXPECTED LEVEL OF ENEMIES ENCOUNTERED

This is perhaps the friendliest neighborhood in all of Boston. The giant green walled-off enclosure welcomes all travelers without ghoulish tendencies, and the threats to your life are manageable if you keep near the huge green walls. Venture farther afield and you may stray into danger: You'll run into Zone 3 if you keep heading west. Go up to Cambridge if you cross the Charles River, and journey east to Esplanade and Back Bay. South is Zone 6. Most of the outskirts of this neighborhood feature closed-off Raider camps, which have been decimated recently by the even-more carnage-hungry Super Mutants. But you're here for the trading, the questing, and the camaraderie offered here, in the great green jewel of the Commonwealth.

## Primary Locations

- [9.01] WRECK OF THE USS RIPTIDE
- [9.02] HANGMAN'S ALLEY
- [9.03] BACK STREET APPAREL
- [9.04] POLICE PRECINCT 8
- [9.05] PARKVIEW APARTMENTS
- [9.06] FENS STREET SEWER
- [9.07] DIAMOND CITY
- [9.08] DIAMOND CITY MARKET
- [9.09] HOME PLATE
- [9.10] HARDWARE TOWN

## Secondary Locations

- [9.01] FENS SUBWAY STATION (OUTSKIRTS)
- [9.02] FENS TUNNEL ENTRANCE
- [9.03] SUPER MUTANT ALLEY APARTMENTS
- [9.04] ANNA'S CAFÉ
- [9.05] RAIDER BACK-ALLEY CAMP (THE FENS)
- [9.06] BRIDGEWAY TRUST
- [9.07] BRIDGEWAY GARAGE
- [9.08] DINER AND APARTMENTS (THE FENS)
- [9.09] SETTLER'S STOP (THE FENS)
- [9.10] RAIDER CUL-DE-SAC (THE FENS)
- [9.11] SCAFFOLD BRIDGE (THE FENS)
- [9.12] DIAMOND CITY SCRAP
- [9.13] SCAVENGER'S REST (THE FENS)

---

### MAP LEGEND

| | | |
|---|---|---|
| 13 ——— 20 OPTIMAL ROUTE |  BOTTLECAPS | 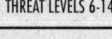 HEALTH OR CHEMS |
| | SAFE | TERMINAL |
| AREA OF INTEREST | ARMAMENTS AND AMMO | STEAMER TRUNK |
| | DOOR | |

FUSION CORE
POWER ARMOR
REQUIRED READING

**Collectibles:**
BOBBLEHEAD
NUKA CHERRY
MINI NUKE

NUKA COLA QUANTUM
HOLOTAPE
A KEY

N – Novice (Locked)
A – Advanced (Locked)

E – Expert (Locked)
M – Master (Locked)

T – Terminal required to unlock
KEY – Key or ID Card required to unlock

IN – Inaccessible
C – Chained

CB – Circuit Breaker
B – Button

---

# PRIMARY LOCATIONS

### [9.01] WRECK OF THE USS RIPTIDE    THREAT LEVELS 6-14

- ARMAMENTS AND AMMO
- ARMAMENTS AND AMMO: MINI NUKE
- ARMAMENTS AND AMMO: TRUNK
- ARMOR PART: POWER ARMOR (RAIDER)
- COLLECTIBLE: REQUIRED READING: WASTELAND SURVIVAL GUIDE
- CRAFTING: COOKING STATION

- DANGER: MINES!
- DANGER: OIL!
- DANGER: RADIATION (MILD)!
- DANGER: TURRETS!
- FACTION: RAIDERS
- HEALTH OR CHEMS

#### VAULT-TEC RECOMMENDED LOOT

  ARMAMENTS AND AMMO: MINI NUKE
ARMOR PART: POWER ARMOR (RAIDER)

Stuck under the half-open drawbridge on the Charles River between Cambridge and the Fens, this tugboat and barge is now a small Raider camp. Come for the survival guide and ammunition on the boat. Stay for the battle with a Power Armor–clad ruffian on the oil-soaked barge behind the boat.

###  [9.02] HANGMAN'S ALLEY    THREAT LEVELS 6-14

- ARMAMENTS AND AMMO
- ARMAMENTS AND AMMO: TRUNK
- CRAFTING: COOKING STATION
- CRAFTING: WEAPONS WORKBENCH

- FACTION: RAIDER
- HEALTH OR CHEMS
- SERVICES: WORKSHOP

This small Raider camp is in the northwest corner of the Fens. Approach from the west (heading east) to reach the locked main entrance (Novice). Approach from the northeast to access the chained door (which has an exit through the blown-out apartment building) and the other entrance (Novice). Beware of Super Mutants in the apartments to the east of here.

Inside this compact killing zone are multiple Raider threats. Clear the area and search for a steamer trunk (Advanced), chems near a weapons workbench, and most importantly a workshop. This allows you to rebuild this possible settlement, which is unique because there are very few in urban areas.

**[9.03] BACK STREET APPAREL** THREAT LEVELS 6-14

- ARMAMENTS AND AMMO
- ARMAMENTS AND AMMO: TRUNK
- BOTTLECAPS+
- COLLECTIBLE: REQUIRED READING: GROGNAK THE BARBARIAN
- CRAFTING: ARMOR WORKBENCH
- DANGER: GRENADES!
- DANGER: OIL!
- DANGER: TRIPWIRE!
- DANGER: TURRETS!
- FACTION: RAIDER
- FACTION: CHARACTER: CLUTCH
- HEALTH OR CHEMS

**FIG 9.03: BACK STREET APPAREL (INTERIOR)**

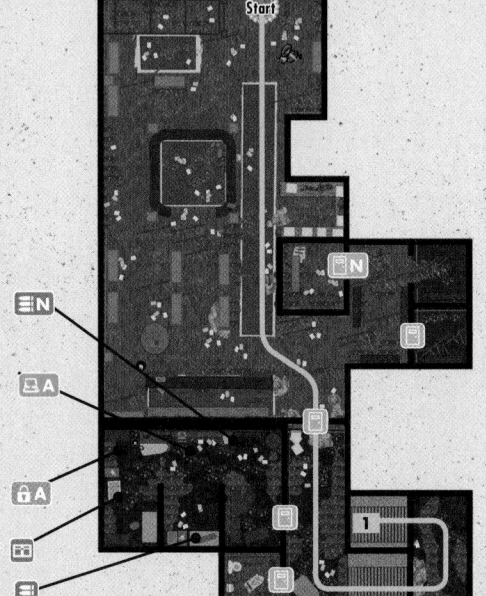

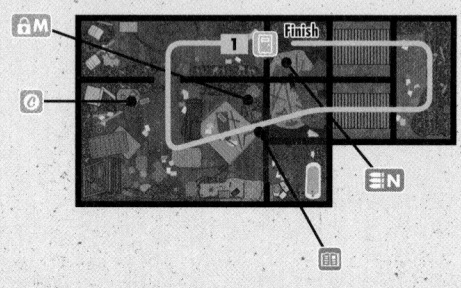

## VAULT-TEC RECOMMENDED LOOT

**REQUIRED READING: GROGNAK THE BARBARIAN**

Prewar customers of this clothing shop preferred the bargains found here. It is now overrun by Raiders, and a couple of turrets greet you at the only entrance, close to a pipe-laden truck used as a barricade. Climb to the upper floor for a comic and roof access.

 **[9.04] POLICE PRECINCT 8** THREAT LEVELS 15-25

- FACTION: RADROACHES
- COLLECTIBLE: HOLOTAPE: EDDIE WINTER'S HOLOTAPE
- HEALTH OR CHEMS
- QUEST VISIT: LONG TIME COMING (SIDE)

Just west of Boston Public Library and adjacent to Diamond City is a run-down police station. Clear any Radroaches you wish before optionally accessing the Precinct 8 evidence terminal. Anther of Eddie Winter's Holotapes is in one of the cells.

THREAT LEVELS 15-25

- ARMAMENTS AND AMMO+
- ARMAMENTS AND AMMO: TRUNK
- BOTTLECAPS
- CRAFTING: ARMOR WORKBENCH
- CRAFTING: WEAPONS WORKBENCH
- DANGER: CAN CHIMES!
- DANGER: LONG DROP!

- DANGER: TRIPWIRE!
- DANGER: TURRETS!
- FACTION: SUPER MUTANTS
- FACTION: RAIDERS
- HEALTH OR CHEMS
- QUEST VISIT: WEATHERVANE (THE RAILROAD)

**FIG 9.05A: PARKVIEW APARTMENTS (EXTERIOR)**

**FIG 9.05B: APARTMENT BUILDING (INTERIOR)**

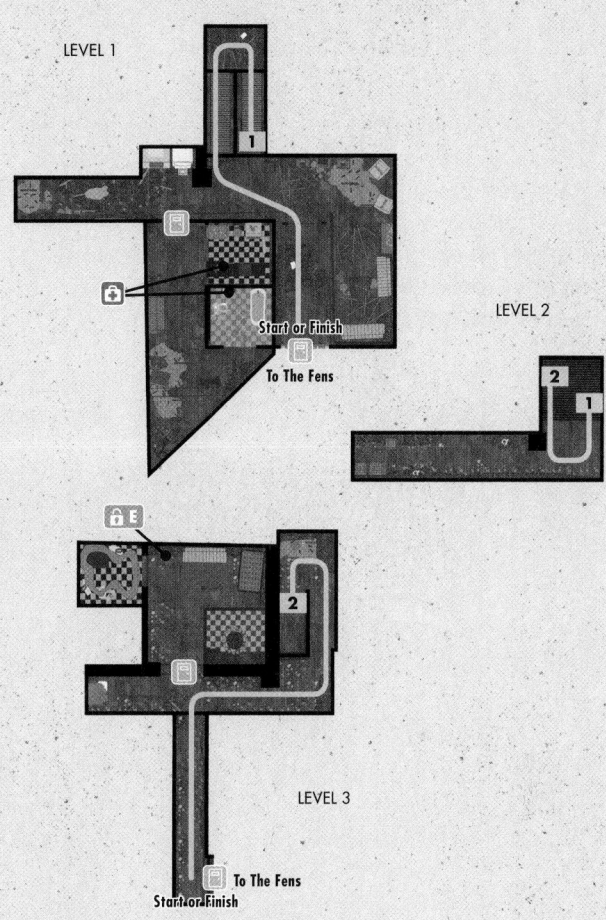

The exterior of Parkview Lounge has an entrance with turrets and Super Mutants, and metal stairs allow access into the lounge from an upper floor. Use the terminal to open the adjacent exterior garage, which allows a swift retreat toward Diamond City.

The entrance to the apartment building can be found close to Hardware City, under the "Apartments" sign.

The interior of Parkview Lounge is grotesque, with a gang of dead Raiders now strung up and gutted as Super Mutant decoration. The bar area has two exits outside. The one in the east wall allows you to climb scaffolding stairs to the roof.

The interior stairs allow access to a skylight area with a small office and wall safe (Expert) and another exit out to the Fens.

The upper exit from the Parkview Lounge allows access to a rooftop battle between Super Mutants and Raiders. Join in if you're game. Check the ruined office (northwest) for a steamer trunk. Take the bridge (south) to a separate rooftop with ammo and a vantage point overlooking Diamond City where you can place MILA if you're working on the specified quest.

Continue your rooftop excursion south, down a rusting fire escape to a blown-out building corner with chems and an armor workbench. Follow the rickety ledge around to a pair of Raiders guarding some ammo. But you're here to access the door leading into the apartment building (interior).

**FIG 9.05C: PARKVIEW LOUNGE (INTERIOR)**

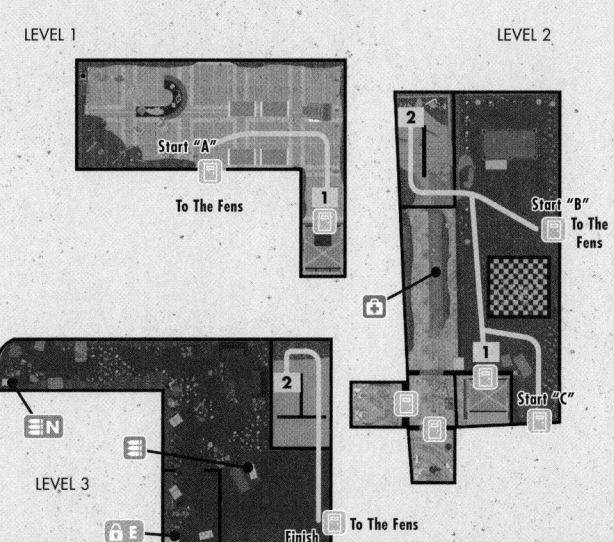

In prewar times, the deeper areas of the sewer were secluded and difficult to reach. Time has exposed parts of the upper tunnels to the sky and Feral Ghouls have since moved in, attracted to the nuclear power sources of the water pumps below.

An unassuming manhole cover and sprawled skeleton of an old sewer worker leads into this large labyrinthian tunnel system. When you find a series of skeletal remains, it becomes clear this was a place of suffering.

## VAULT-TEC RECOMMENDED LOOT

**REQUIRED READING: TUMBLERS TODAY**

- ARMAMENTS AND AMMO
- ARMAMENTS AND AMMO: TRUNK
- BOOK OR MAGAZINE: TUMBLERS TODAY
- BOTTLECAPS
- COLLECTIBLE: HOLOTAPE: DEAR DETECTIVE 1
- COLLECTIBLE: HOLOTAPE: DEAR DETECTIVE 2
- COLLECTIBLE: HOLOTAPE: DEAR DETECTIVE 3
- COLLECTIBLE: HOLOTAPE: DEAR DETECTIVE 4

- DANGER: ESCAPING GAS!
- DANGER: RADIATION (SEVERE)!
- FACTION: FERAL GHOULS
- FACTION: BLOATFLIES
- HEALTH OR CHEMS
- QUEST START: DEAR DETECTIVE (MISCELLANEOUS)

**FIG 9.06: FENS STREET SEWER (INTERIOR)**

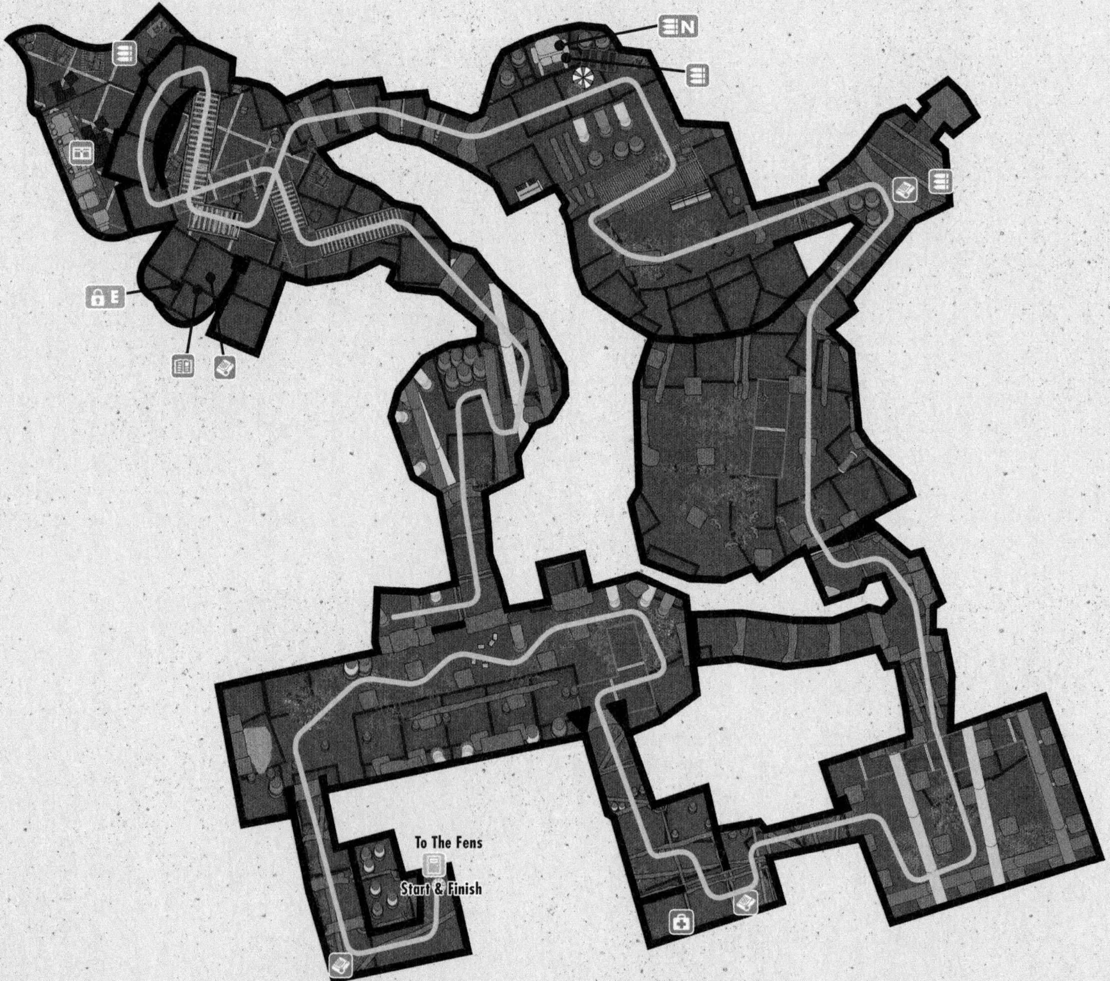

To The Fens

Start & Finish

 **Miscellaneous: Dear Detective**

The map shows the locations of four Holotapes with messages recorded on them. Listen, and figure out where the detective and her quarry finally came to rest.

## [9.07] DIAMOND CITY

THREAT LEVELS 15-25

- ARMAMENTS AND AMMO: MINI NUKE
- CRAFTING: ARMOR WORKBENCH
- FACTION: DIAMOND CITY (SETTLER)
- FACTION CHARACTER: DANNY SULLIVAN
- QUEST VISIT: JEWEL OF THE COMMONWEALTH (MAIN)
- QUEST START: ROAD TO FREEDOM (THE RAILROAD)

### VAULT-TEC RECOMMENDED LOOT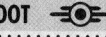

 **ARMAMENTS AND AMMO: MINI NUKE**

 **COLLECTIBLE: NUKA CHERRY (8)**

 **COLLECTIBLE: NUKA COLA QUANTUM (7)**

 **HOLOTAPE: GWINNETT ALE BREWING SUBROUTINES**

 **HOLOTAPE: ZETA INVADERS**

 **REQUIRED READING: LIVE & LOVE**

 **REQUIRED READING: ROBCO FUN!**

 **UNIQUE ITEM: BIG BOY**

 **UNIQUE ITEM: CHAMPION ARMOR (PIECES)**

 **UNIQUE ITEM: OLD FAITHFUL**

 **UNIQUE ITEM: PROTECTOR'S ARMOR (PIECES)**

 **UNIQUE ITEM: ROCKVILLE SLUGGER**

 **UNIQUE ITEM: WASTELANDER'S ARMOR (PIECES)**

## [9.08] DIAMOND CITY MARKET

THREAT LEVELS 15-25

This is the most well-known, well-defended settlement in the entire Commonwealth. Located in the remains of Boston's revered baseball stadium, the city houses several businesses and scores of people in divergent social classes. Every resident shares a common bond; they survived under the shadow of the great green wall—that monument to the ingenuity of humankind and their consummate protector.

### DIAMOND CITY MARKET

To The Fens

### AVAILABLE COMPANIONS

 **COMPANION: PIPER**

 **COMPANION: NICK VALENTINE**

- QUEST START: MISCELLANEOUS (FREEFORM: DIAMOND CITY'S MOST WANTED)
- QUEST START: MISCELLANEOUS (FREEFORM: HOME RUN!)
- QUEST START: MISCELLANEOUS (FREEFORM: BROTHER AGAINST BROTHER)
- QUEST START: MISCELLANEOUS (FREEFORM: NUKA COLA NEEDS)
- QUEST START: MISCELLANEOUS (FREEFORM: HOLIDAYS)
- QUEST START: MISCELLANEOUS (FREEFORM: END GAME)

Locate this large structure at night by looking for the light emitted from the area. Or during the day, when you're in the Fens, look for signs with a diamond icon. The giant, square-shaped structure has various barricades patrolled by Diamond City Security. The one to the west has a turret to hack (Advanced). There's a ruined forecourt to the northwest, which you can't enter from. To the east is a sleeping area with an armor workbench.

MAP

**ZONE 9**

NEIGHBORHOOD: THE FENS

The entrance is to the southwest, guarded by turrets. It has a terminal to hack (Advanced) and a massive metal door. Access Diamond City Market during Main Quest: Jewel of the Commonwealth by talking to Danny the guard.

## [01] All Faiths Chapel

- FACTION: CHARACTER: PASTOR CLEMENTS
- QUEST START: MISCELLANEOUS (FREEFORM: WEDDING DAY)

A multidenominational church open 24 hours a day, run by the friendly Pastor Clements. Sit on a pew in the church to gain benefits of the Quiet Reflection perk.

## [02] Publick Occurrences

- ARMAMENTS AND AMMO
- COMPANION: PIPER
- FACTION: CHARACTER: PIPER
- FACTION: CHARACTER: NAT
- HEALTH OR CHEMS
- QUEST START: STORY OF THE CENTURY (FREEFORM)
- QUEST START: IN SHEEP'S CLOTHING (FREEFORM)

This location is named after the newspaper, which is written, edited, and published by Piper. Her little sister Nat sells copies at the front of their office. She also publishes stories, such as "The Synthetic Truth," and is currently on the outs with the mayor. Inside the office, you can read her terminal notes and steal some chems and ammo.

## [03] Cathy & John's Super Salon

- ARMAMENTS AND AMMO
- FACTION: CHARACTER: CATHY
- FACTION: CHARACTER: JOHN
- QUEST START: MISCELLANEOUS (FREEFORM: NEW HAIR, NEW FACE)
- SERVICES: TRADER (JOHN)

Need a haircut (for 25 Caps)? Want to listen to constant bickering between mother and son? Aside from changing your hairstyle, there's a floor safe to steal from and a trapdoor (Novice) leading into their basement, which has ammo to steal from a suitcase.

## [04] Fallon's Basement

- COLLECTIBLE: HOLOTAPE: JOIN THE RAILROAD
- FACTION: CHARACTER: BECKY FALLON
- HEALTH OR CHEMS
- SERVICES: TRADER (BECKY FALLON)
- UNIQUE ITEM: WASTELANDER'S CHEST PIECE
- UNIQUE ITEM: CHAMPION RIGHT ARM

This premiere (and only) clothing store sells a variety of prewar attire at the best prices, as well as helpful outfits, like hazmat suits. The proprietor Becky Fallon tells everyone she's a direct descendant of the original Fallon family. Aside from a large supply of cram, the only item of note is a Holotape you can listen to regarding the Railroad.

## [05] Power Noodles

- COLLECTIBLE: NUKA COLA QUANTUM (2)
- CRAFTING: COOKING STATION
- FACTION: CHARACTER: TAKAHASHI
- SERVICES: TRADER (TAKAHASHI)

This noodle bar was built up against the fusion generator tower in the center of the settlement, where the pitcher's mound was. The Protectron chef, Takahashi, has a single phrase—"Nan-ni shimasho-ka?" or "What would you like to have?"—and a single item to trade. Noodles, naturally.

## [06] Security Office

- QUEST: MISCELLANEOUS (FREEFORM: DIAMOND CITY'S MOST WANTED)

Located in one of the old dugouts and connecting locker room, Diamond City Security runs a tight ship from here. They are usually throwing a drunk called Sheffield into the single cell (locked: Expert).

Inside is a notice board (for the quest) and a few chems and guns to steal. The automated security terminal (Expert) allows you to program a police Protectron.

## [07] Kellogg's House

- ARMAMENTS AND AMMO+
- COLLECTIBLE: NUKA CHERRY (3)
- COLLECTIBLE: NUKA COLA QUANTUM (2)
- FACTION: CHARACTER: KELLOGG
- QUEST START: GETTING A CLUE (MAIN)

This shack is home to a mercenary (and collector of Nuka Cola) named Kellogg. The front door (Master) can be opened prior to the quest (Master), but the items listed are only accessible during the quest, when a desk button is available for you to press.

## [08] Schoolhouse

- COLLECTIBLE: REQUIRED READING: LIVE & LOVE
- FACTION: CHARACTER: MISTER ZWICKY
- FACTION: CHARACTER: MISS EDNA
- FACTION: CHARACTER: GAVIN EVERITTS
- FACTION: CHARACTER: ERIN REISCHE
- FACTION: CHARACTER: PHIL WALLACE
- HEALTH OR CHEMS
- QUEST START: MISCELLANEOUS (FREEFORM: WEDDING DAY)

The two teachers here seem to have affection for each other, and the students appear to be well learned. Don't forget the magazine to steal (by the ground-floor bed).

## [09] Pembroke Residence

- FACTION: CHARACTER: PAUL PEMBROKE
- FACTION: CHARACTER: DARCY PEMBROKE
- QUEST START: DIAMOND CITY BLUES (SIDE)

This tiny house has a meager set of belongings inside, if you're the trespassing sort, as the front door is locked (Novice). Paul and Darcy are part of the specified quest, though their home isn't. You'll usually find these two in the Colonial Taphouse.

## [10] Swatters

- ARMAMENTS AND AMMO
- BOTTLECAPS++
- FACTION: CHARACTER: MOE CRONIN
- QUEST START: OUT IN LEFT FIELD (FREEFORM)
- QUEST START: MISCELLANEOUS (FREEFORM: WORLD SERIES WIN)
- SERVICES: TRADER (MOE CRONIN)
- UNIQUE ITEM: ROCKVILLE SLUGGER

"A swatter never runs out of bullets!" as Moe Cronin is fond of saying. He runs this store specializing in baseball equipment and almost nothing else. Barter with Moe to obtain a unique bat, and speak to him for a couple of quests that can net you some Caps.

Around back is Moe Cronin's house (Novice). Trespass here for a huge selection of soccer gear. Only joking; it's more baseball paraphernalia.

## [11] Commonwealth Weaponry (and Arturo's House)

- ARMAMENTS AND AMMO+++
- ARMAMENTS AND AMMO: MINI NUKE
- FACTION: CHARACTER: ARTURO RODRIGUEZ
- FACTION: CHARACTER: NINA RODRIGUEZ
- CRAFTING: WEAPONS WORKBENCH
- HEALTH OR CHEMS
- SERVICES: TRADER (ARTURO)
- UNIQUE ITEM: PROTECTOR'S LEFT ARMGUARD
- UNIQUE ITEM: PROTECTOR'S RIGHT ARMGUARD
- UNIQUE ITEM: BIG BOY
- UNIQUE ITEM: OLD FAITHFUL

This caters to anyone wanting the typical implements of death, including two unique (and expensive) weapons. Tinker on the workbench if you wish. Break into Arturo's locked house (Advanced) for a large amount of ammo and a Mini Nuke to steal.

## [12] Diamond City Surplus (and Myrna's House)

- ARMAMENTS AND AMMO
- COLLECTIBLE: NUKA CHERRY
- CRAFTING: ARMOR WORKBENCH
- FACTION: CHARACTER: MYRNA
- FACTION: CHARACTER: PERCY
- HEALTH OR CHEMS
- SERVICES: TRADER (MYRNA)
- SERVICES: TRADER (PERCY)
- UNIQUE ITEM: CHAMPION CHESTPIECE

Open 24 hours, this general store is run by Myrna and her robot shopkeeper. The prices might be steep, but the selection is good. Inside her house is her terminal (Novice) to snoop at and precarious steps up to the roof.

### [13] Chem-I-Care

- FACTION: CHARACTER: SOLOMON
- HEALTH OR CHEMS+++
- QUEST START: MISCELLANEOUS
  (FREEFORM: BOTANY CLASS)
- QUEST VISIT: THE DISAPPEARING ACT (SIDE)
- SERVICES: TRADER (SOLOMON)

This is a popular establishment, thanks to the genial owner, Solomon. Selling a complete variety of chems and healing supplies, Solomon may have convinced the populace that the benefits of his wares outweigh the risks. Pick the lock of his house (Novice) for a few more chems to steal inside.

### [14] Mega Surgery

- CRAFTING: CHEMISTRY STATION
- FACTION: CHARACTER: DOCTOR SUN
- FACTION: CHARACTER: DOC CROCKER
- HEALTH OR CHEMS++
- QUEST VISIT: THE DISAPPEARING ACT (SIDE)
- QUEST START: MISCELLANEOUS
  (FREEFORM: NEW HAIR, NEW FACE)
- QUEST START: IN SHEEP'S CLOTHING (FREEFORM)
- SERVICES: TRADER (DOCTOR SUN)

Despite the corrugated roof, this is a state-of-the-art medical facility offering healing, cybernetic grafts, and even facial reconstruction. Fancy a change in appearance? Sit down under Doctor Sun's scalpel! There are some other goings on here too; check the listed side quest before descending into the surgery cellar (Advanced).

### [15] Choice Chops

- FACTION: CHARACTER: POLLY
- HEALTH OR CHEMS
- SERVICES: TRADER (POLLY)

Fresh Brahmin meat is available from the sullen butcher, Polly (who's a frustrated poet), or Mole Rat meat if you're feeling adventurous. You can break into Polly's house (Novice) if you want to hack her terminal (Novice).

### [16] Greenhouse

- HEALTH OR CHEMS

A selection of Mutfruit grows under vaguely hydroponic conditions.

### [17] Valentine Detective Agency

- ARMAMENTS AND AMMO
- COLLECTIBLE: REQUIRED READING: ROBCO FUN!
- COLLECTIBLE: HOLOTAPE: ZETA INVADERS
- FACTION: CHARACTER: NICK VALENTINE
- FACTION: CHARACTER: ELLIE PERKINS
- HEALTH OR CHEMS
- QUEST VISIT: JEWEL OF THE
  COMMONWEALTH (MAIN)
- QUEST START: UNLIKELY VALENTINE (MAIN)
- QUEST VISIT: GETTING A CLUE (MAIN)
- QUEST START: THE DISAPPEARING ACT (SIDE)
- QUEST START: THE GILDED GRASSHOPPER (SIDE)
- QUEST START: LONG TIME COMING (SIDE)

Along the seedy back passage is a narrow alley leading to the neon signs of this small detective agency. Nick is initially indisposed, so chat to his secretary Ellie. Head here if you're unsure of how to proceed in your exploring.

### [18] The Wall

- FACTION: CHARACTER: ABBOT
- QUEST START: PAINTING THE TOWN (FREEFORM)

The great green wall has protected Diamond City for as long as anyone can remember. Only Abbot spends time here keeping the stage from falling into disrepair, the Brahmins fed, and the wall painted.

### [19] Abbot's House

- COLLECTIBLE: HOLOTAPE: JOIN THE RAILROAD

Across the Mutfruit field by the small lake is Abbot's shack (Novice). There's little to find inside, save for a Holotape.

### [20] Diamond City Radio

- ARMAMENTS AND AMMO
- FACTION: CHARACTER: TRAVIS MILES
- QUEST VISIT: POWERING UP (THE INSTITUTE)
- QUEST VISIT: CONFIDENCE MAN (SIDE)
- RADIO: RADIO FREEDOM

Have you tuned your radio to the socially inept talk station run by Travis Miles? This fellow's banter needs a dose of confidence applied; he isn't cut out to be a DJ.

## [21] Klean Watur (Sheng Kawolski's House)

- FACTION: CHARACTER: SHENG KAWOLSKI
- COLLECTIBLE: NUKA COLA QUANTUM
- DANGER: CAN CHIMES!
- DANGER: RADIATION (MILD)!
- QUEST START: MISCELLANEOUS (FREEFORM: POOL CLEANING)
- SERVICES: TRADER (KAWOLSKI)

Run by a young entrepreneur, the water filtration works over a small lake. Inside his hut (Novice) is a small storage area filled with sugar bombs.

## [22] Science! Center

- CRAFTING: ARMOR WORKBENCH
- CRAFTING: CHEMISTRY STATION
- CRAFTING: COOKING STATION
- CRAFTING: WEAPONS WORKBENCH
- FACTION: CHARACTER: DOCTOR DUFF
- FACTION: CHARACTER: PROFESSOR SCARA
- HEALTH OR CHEMS
- QUEST START: MISCELLANEOUS (FREEFORM: FLY FISHING)
- QUEST VISIT: LIBERTY REPRIMED (BROTHERHOOD OF STEEL)

The foremost center of scientific experimentation and discovery in Diamond City, run by the enthusiastic Doctor Duff. Her colleague is a little tired of Duff's prattling. Take a quiz with Duff if you want. Snoop on Scara's terminal (Master) if you can.

## [23] Doc Crocker's House

- ARMAMENTS AND AMMO
- COLLECTIBLE: NUKA CHERRY
- HEALTH OR CHEMS

Unlock this abode (Advanced) if you want to see where Crocker lives. The place seems spotless. Note the roof exit.

## [24] Doctor Sun's House

- HEALTH OR CHEMS

A small, locked house (Novice) where Doctor Sun retires to during the night.

## [25] Warehouse

- ARMAMENTS AND AMMO+
- ARMAMENTS AND AMMO: TRUNK
- HEALTH OR CHEMS

Snoop around the warehouse (Novice) if you're after a good amount of health, chems, and ammo to steal.

## [26] Earl Sterling's House

- ARMAMENTS AND AMMO+
- HEALTH OR CHEMS
- QUEST VISIT: THE DISAPPEARING ACT (SIDE)

The owner of this locked (Novice) and empty house has mysteriously disappeared. Most people assume he's been kidnapped by the Institute. Be sure the quest is active before investigating this place.

### [27] Dugout Inn

- ARMAMENTS AND AMMO
- COLLECTIBLE: HOLOTAPE: JOIN THE RAILROAD
- COLLECTIBLE: NUKA CHERRY (3)
- FACTION: CHARACTER: VADIM BOBROV
- FACTION: CHARACTER: YEFIM BOBROV
- FACTION: CHARACTER: SCARLETT
- FACTION: CHARACTER: COLETTE
- FACTION: CHARACTER: EDWARD DEEGAN
- HEALTH OR CHEMS
- QUEST START: CONFIDENCE MAN (SIDE)
- QUEST VISIT: DIAMOND CITY BLUES (SIDE)
- QUEST VISIT: THE DISAPPEARING ACT (SIDE)
- QUEST START: THE SECRET OF CABOT HOUSE (SIDE)
- QUEST START: MISCELLANEOUS (FREEFORM: DIAMOND CITY'S MOST WANTED)
- SERVICES: TRADER (VADIM BOBROV)
- SERVICES: TRADER (YEFIM BOBROV)

This is the primary watering hole of Diamond City. Many of the residents go here in the evenings to grab a drink. Occasionally, the place has guests who are traveling through the Commonwealth, as there are rooms available (and mattresses to sleep on) for 100 Caps. Though the Russian twins who run this place are identical in their features, their personalities are completely different.

This is one of the locations the Ghoul Edward Deegan hangs out in; speak to him to find out more about the Cabots. There's also a back room with a terminal (Novice) and Holotape regarding the Railroad. The locked storage room (Advanced) holds some chems and ammo.

### [28] Hawthorne Residence

- ARMAMENTS AND AMMO
- FACTION: CHARACTER: HAWTHORNE
- FACTION: CHARACTER: EUSTACE

Trespass into this upper-level home (Advanced) and uncover the reason why Hawthorne tends to spend most of his time at the Dugout Inn.

### [29] Cooke Residence

- ARMAMENTS AND AMMO
- COLLECTIBLE: NUKA COLA QUANTUM (2)
- HEALTH OR CHEMS+

This is the home of the Colonial Taphouse's owner. Trespass (Advanced) and discover the vittles of a man with a sweet tooth and a chem dependency.

### [30] Colonial Taphouse

- ARMAMENTS AND AMMO
- COLLECTIBLE: HOLOTAPE: GWINNETT ALE BREWING SUBROUTINES
- FACTION: CHARACTER: HENRY COOKE
- FACTION: CHARACTER: WELLINGHAM
- HEALTH OR CHEMS
- QUEST START: DIAMOND CITY BLUES (SIDE)
- QUEST VISIT: THE DEVIL'S DUE (SIDE)
- SERVICES: TRADER (HENRY COOKE)

The snobbish denizens of the upper area sip their alcohol from this establishment. Receive a dressing down from Wellington in the exterior seating area, then head inside for a pint and a punch if you're not careful. Look for the Holotape and a floor safe (Advanced) behind the bar.

### [31] Latimer Residence

- FACTION: CHARACTER: MALCOLM LATIMER
- FACTION: CHARACTER: NELSON LATIMER
- HEALTH OR CHEMS+
- QUEST VISIT: DIAMOND CITY BLUES (SIDE)

Pry open the front door (Advanced) and uncover the large (and partially wet) home of the Latimers, one of the major players in the quest.

### [32] Codman Residence

- FACTION: CHARACTER: CLARENCE CODMAN
- FACTION: CHARACTER: ANN CODMAN
- HEALTH OR CHEMS

Break in through the door (Advanced) to the home of the oldest family in Diamond City. The Codmans own the orchard.

### [33] The Mayor's Box

- FACTION: CHARACTER: MAYOR MCDONOUGH
- FACTION: CHARACTER: GENEVA
- QUEST VISIT: GETTING A CLUE (MAIN)
- QUEST START: MISCELLANEOUS (FREEFORM: HOME PLATE)
- QUEST START: IN SHEEP'S CLOTHING (FREEFORM)

Ride to the highest point in Diamond City via the yellow elevator. Speak to the mayor's secretary Geneva if you're interested in purchasing property for 2,000 Caps or if you have a quest to complete. Is that a button under Geneva's desk? Interesting . . .

Behind Geneva's reception room is the mayor's office with his terminal (Expert) and safe (Expert). The safe has Kellogg's house key. Through the double doors is a corridor with a few rooms to explore. One bedroom has a Giddyup Buttercup.

**[9.09] HOME PLATE** THREAT LEVELS 15-25

- ARMAMENTS AND AMMO
- CRAFTING: POWER ARMOR STATION
- FACTION: VAULT DWELLER
- HEALTH OR CHEMS

- QUEST VISIT: MISCELLANEOUS (FREEFORM: HOME PLATE)
- SERVICES: WORKSHOP

Head through any of the three entrances (including a roof trapdoor) to reach your own house, right on home plate! This must be purchased from Geneva as part of the quest. There's a place outside to park your Power Armor and a workshop to fill your home with furniture, decorations, and power (but not the full complement for a normal settlement and you can't summon workers here). This is a great Fast-Travel point and a place to store items you want to keep but can't carry. It comes fully stocked with ammo and health, too!

 **Side Quests: Freeform Activities: Diamond City**

## Diamond City's Most Wanted*

### 1. MISCELLANEOUS: CLEAR THE [ENEMIES] FROM THE [RANDOM LOCATION]

If you want a challenge, look for the "Wanted" poster on the wall in Diamond City, inside the security office and inside the entrance hall of the Dugout Inn (shown). If there's a note, read it.

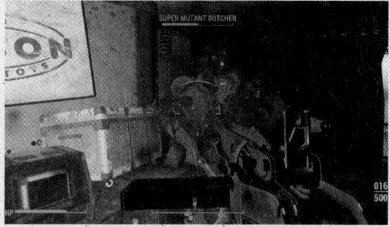 It requires you to remove a tagged foe or foes from a random location. In this example, it is a Super Mutant from inside the Wilson Atomatoys Corporate HQ. The quest completes when you neutralize the foe.

### Home Run!

 Try running the bases, beginning at home plate near the entrance of Diamond City.

## Painting the Town

### 1. SEARCH THE HARDWARE STORE FOR PAINT
### 2. RETURN TO ABBOT
### 3. APPLY PAINT TO THE WALL

Abbot in Diamond City wants you to find paint for the city's wall. There's a place called Hardware Town where you can start looking.

 (Easy, Medium, Hard) Fast-talk him to up his Caps amount for your troubles.

Enter Hardware Town. Beware of Raiders, especially the one named "Demo." Find the blue and yellow paint. You can:

Use the paint mixer to make green paint. Or not.

 **BLUE PAINT**   **YELLOW PAINT**   **GREEN PAINT**

Back with Abbot, paint the wall in any of the three colors you wish. Green is what Abbot requests, however. You can also complete this quest by finding the paint before speaking to Abbot.

 **BOTTLECAPS (100–200)**

MAP

ZONE 9

NEIGHBORHOOD: THE FENS

439

### Brother Against Brother*

This is only available prior to locating Nick Valentine during Main Quest: Unlikely Valentine. You may see two Diamond City inhabitants with one brother (Kyle) pointing a gun at the other (Riley), claiming he's a synth! You can:

– SHOOT RILEY.
– OR WAIT UNTIL DIAMOND CITY SECURITY SHOOTS RILEY.

Afterward, speak to the remaining brother or the security guard if you wish.

### Home Plate*

1. MISCELLANEOUS: VISIT YOUR HOME IN DIAMOND CITY

Visit Geneva in the mayor's office, and offer to purchase a residence in this location. Hand over 2,000 Caps, and you receive the following:

 .......................................
HOME PLATE KEY

Find your residence—called Home Plate—next to the Chem-I-Care store. There is a workshop here, and you can place furniture, decorations, and power items.

### New Hair, New Face*

Head to Cathy and John's Super Salon for a haircut to change your style.

Visit Doctor Sun and the Mega Surgery Center to change your face.

### Botany Class*

1. MISCELLANEOUS: BRING A MUTATED FERN FLOWER TO SOLOMON

Talk to Solomon, the proprietor of the Chem-I-Care store. Ask for work. He requests you find a rare mutated fern.

 (Easy, Medium, Hard) Fast-talk him to up his Caps amount for your troubles.

 Travel to Forest Grove Marsh. Locate the mutated fern flower. Beware of Feral Ghouls. Return to Solomon for the chem and Caps reward.

 MUTATED FERN FLOWER |  BUFFOUT, PSYCHO, JET |  BOTTLECAPS (100–200)

### Pool Cleaning*

1. MISCELLANEOUS: CLEAN THE WATER SUPPLY (5)

Head to the reservoir and speak to Sheng Kowalski. Agree to help.

2. MISCELLANEOUS: RETURN TO SHENG

 (Easy, Medium, Hard) Fast-talk him to up his Caps amount for your troubles.

Gather the detritus from the murky waters. Return to Sheng for your reward.

 ..............................
BOTTLECAPS (100–200)

## Fly Fishing*

**1. MISCELLANEOUS: BRING A BLOATFLY GLAND TO DOCTOR DUFF**

Head to the Science! Center, and listen to Doctor Duff's remarks. Offer to go on the field trip.

 (Easy, Medium, Hard) Fast-talk him to up his Caps to conduct this trip.

Defeat a Bloatfly anywhere. In this example, one was defeated at the Boston Police rationing site. Return to Duff and claim your reward.

 **BLOATFLY GLAND**

 **BOTTLECAPS (100–200)**

## Out in Left Field

**1. FIND A SIGNED BASEBALL**
**2. FIND A SIGNED CATCHER'S MITT**
**3. FIND A SIGNED BASEBALL CARD**
**4. RETURN TO MOE CRONIN**

Moe Cronin in Diamond City wants you to find three baseball relics said to have been left behind in the old Westing Estate. Offer to find them.

 (Easy, Medium, Hard) Fast-talk him to up his Caps to make it worth your while.

 **SIGNED BASEBALL**

 **SIGNED CATCHER'S MITT**

 **SIGNED BASEBALL CARD**

Enter the remains of the Westing Estate. Beware of Mirelurks. Find the three relics in a safe (Novice), toolbox, and chem cooler.

Return to Moe and accept your reward.

 **BOTTLECAPS (100–200)**

## World Series Win*

Visit Jamaica Plain. Beware of Feral Ghouls. Enter the Jamaica Plain Town Hall Basement. Complete Location Quest: Treasures of Jamaica Plain (see page 380). Obtain the following from the treasure room:

 **2076 WORLD SERIES BASEBALL BAT**

Return to Diamond City. Speak to Moe Cronin at Swatters, and tell him you have a 2076 World Series Bat. Sell it to him.

 (Easy, Medium, Hard) Sell for an increasingly ludicrous price.

 **BOTTLECAPS (200–400)**

## Story of the Century

**1. GO TO PIPER'S OFFICE**
**2. TALK TO PIPER**
**3. GET THE LATEST ISSUE OF PUBLICK OCCURRENCES**

Locate Piper after you enter Diamond City for the first time. Go to Publick Occurrences and talk to Piper when she's there (check inside). Agree to the interview. Answer the three questions as you wish. When you next return to Diamond City, talk to Nat for the latest edition with your interview in it. The article differs depending on your answers.

 **COMPANION: PIPER**

 **VIEW FROM THE VAULT, PARTS 1, 2, 3**

## Nuka-Cola Needs*

### 1. MISCELLANEOUS: GIVE SHEFFIELD A NUKA-COLA

Locate Sheffield the downtrodden. Hand him a Nuka-Cola. Then optionally tell him to join any of your settlements.

 **SETTLER: SHEFFIELD**

## Wedding Day*

Visit the Diamond City schoolhouse. Talk to Miss Edna. When she asks you about love, tell her "love conquers all."

 Leave Diamond City and return. The next time you visit, Miss Edna and Mister Zwicky are being married in front of the chapel.

## In Sheep's Clothing

### 1. CONFRONT MAYOR MCDONOUGH   2. (OPTIONAL) SAVE DANNY SULLIVAN

This quest is only accessible once the Institute reactor is online (during the Main Quest), and you must have sided with a faction other than the Institute (you should have been kicked out). Keep visiting Diamond City until you see Danny Sullivan, badly wounded by the sign for the mayor's office. You can:

- SPEAK TO DANNY AND OFFER HIM A STIMPAK.
- (CURIE) ASK CURIE TO ADMINISTER HELP.
- LOCATE DOC CROCKER OR DOCTOR SUN TO HELP.
- TELL DANNY HE'S BETTER OFF DEAD.
- OR IGNORE HIM. HE DIES IF YOU RESOLVE THE CRISIS WITH THE MAYOR

 Take the elevator up to the reception office. Piper is there, but the door is locked. You can:

- (NOVICE) PICK THE LOCK
- OR USE THE BUTTON UNDER THE DESK TO OPEN THE DOOR.

Once inside, confront the mayor. You can:

 (Medium) Demand he releases Geneva.

- ATTACK AND KILL HIM.
- ACCEPT HIS TERMS AND HE WALKS FREE.

The quest concludes. The next time you're in Diamond City, pick up a copy of Publick Occurrences for news of how this all went down.

## Holidays*

 For some festive spirit, be sure to visit Diamond City on Halloween (10/31) and Christmas (12/25). The dates are available on your Pip-Boy (easily seen when you are waiting).

## Diamond City: End Game

 Once you complete the Main Quest, you start to see a couple members from the faction you aligned with; they appear in Diamond City.

In this example, it is a Brotherhood of Steel Knight. Expect different greetings from residents, and a Publick Occurrence based on the victorious faction (Brotherhood of Steel, the Institute, the Minutemen, or the Railroad).

- ARMAMENTS AND AMMO
- ARMAMENTS AND AMMO: TRUNK
- BOTTLECAPS
- COLLECTIBLE: REQUIRED READING: PICKET FENCES
- CRAFTING: ARMOR WORKBENCH
- CRAFTING: POWER ARMOR STATION
- CRAFTING: WEAPONS WORKBENCH
- DANGER: OIL!
- FACTION: RAIDER
- FACTION: CHARACTER: DEMO
- HEALTH OR CHEMS
- QUEST VISIT: PAINTING THE TOWN (DIAMOND CITY)

## VAULT-TEC RECOMMENDED LOOT

    **REQUIRED READING: PICKET FENCES**

**FIG 10.01B: HARDWARE TOWN (INTERIOR)**

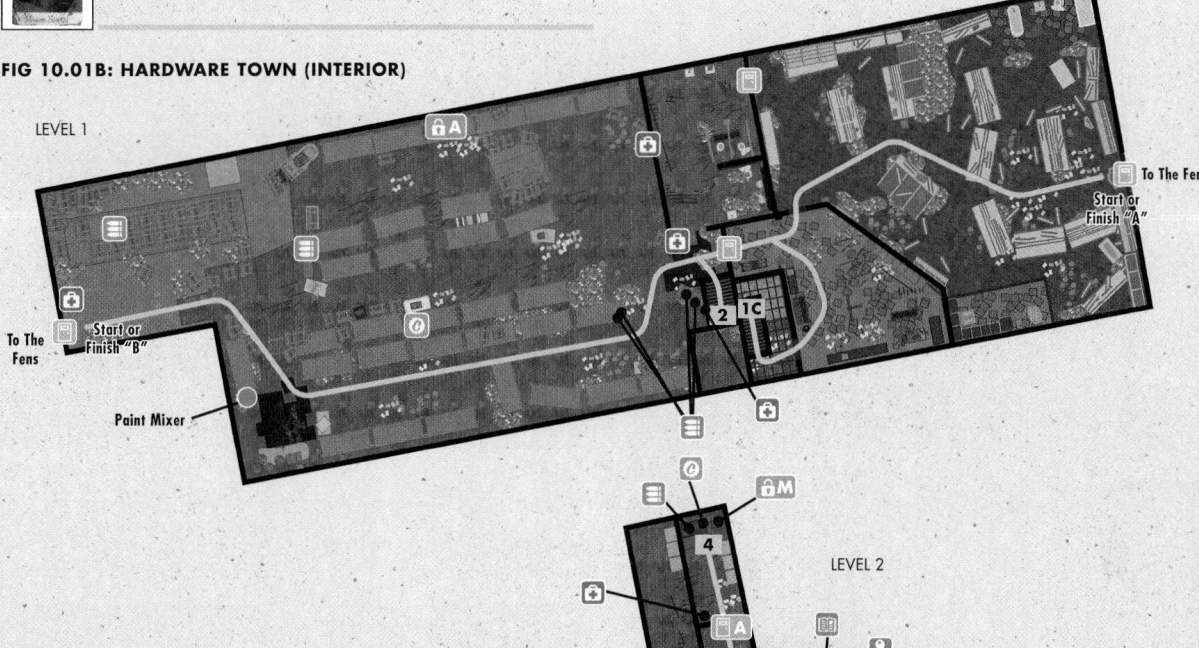

LEVEL 1

To The Fens   Start or Finish "A"

To The Fens   Start or Finish "B"

Paint Mixer

LEVEL 2

**MAP**

**ZONE 9**

NEIGHBORHOOD:
THE FENS

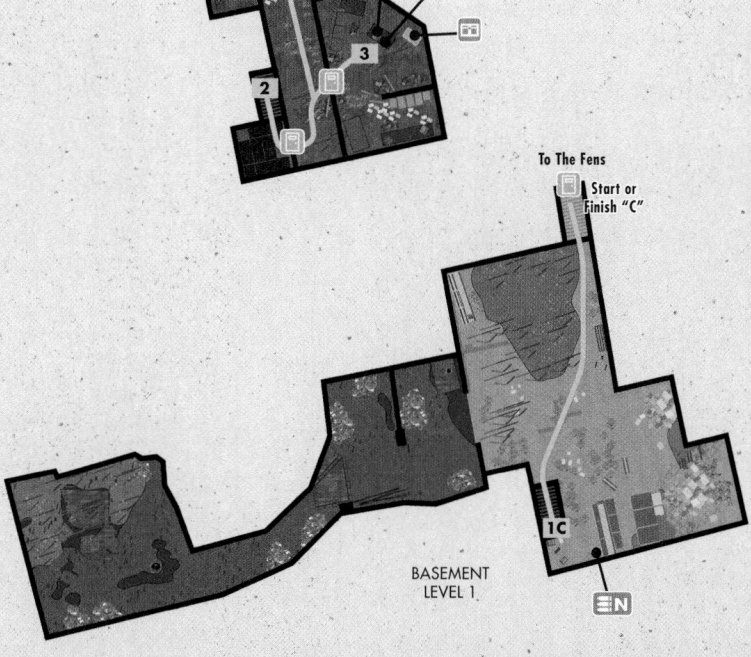

To The Fens   Start or Finish "C"

BASEMENT
LEVEL 1

This was once the most popular hardware store in town, but Raiders are active to the rear of the premises. They lure those of a more inquisitive (or idiotic) disposition into investigating the location, before slaying them and dumping their corpses.

There are three entrances. The main front entrance has a settler pleading for help; she disappears inside before you can speak with her. A basement entrance to the side allows stealthier explorers to enter. The rear entrance is close to a Power Armor station. You can also leap onto the roof from the small chem hideout to the north (accessed via scaffold steps).

# SECONDARY LOCATIONS

## [9.01] FENS SUBWAY STATION (OUTSKIRTS)

- CRAFTING: COOKING STATION
- FACTION: RADROACHES
- FACTION: BLOATFLIES

A subway platform infested with irradiated wildlife, this small interior location is mostly blocked with rubble.

## [9.02] FENS TUNNEL ENTRANCE

- ARMAMENTS AND AMMO
- FACTION: SUPER MUTANTS

Running east to west under Hangman's Alley is a small traffic tunnel. Approach from the west and you can cross a small bridge guarded by a Super Mutant hound. Check the south balcony before the tunnel for some loot.

## [9.03] SUPER MUTANT ALLEY APARTMENTS

- ARMAMENTS AND AMMO
- ARMAMENTS AND AMMO: TRUNK
- HEALTH OR CHEMS

This open-air low-rise apartment complex just northwest of Diamond City has been taken over by greenskins. Clear the scaffold and roof of foes before opening the steamer trunk on the rooftop.

## [9.04] ANNA'S CAFE

- HEALTH OR CHEMS

This once-thriving diner has been reduced to a ruin of clutter and rusting equipment. Check behind the counter for some health.

## [9.05] RAIDER BACK-ALLEY CAMP (THE FENS)

- ARMAMENTS AND AMMO
- FACTION: RAIDERS

A small group of Raiders has turned a section of old housing into a makeshift base, north of Diamond City.

## [9.06] BRIDGEWAY TRUST

- ARMAMENTS AND AMMO
- BOTTLECAPS+++
- HEALTH OR CHEMS

Enter this bank and have a go at hacking the safe room door (Master). It isn't easy, but once you've used the terminal to open the security door, you can ransack a new kind of vault. Aside from the gold bars, the following wall safes are accessible (along with the number of safes of each type):

- WALL SAFE (OPEN): 1
- WALL SAFE (EXPERT): 3
- WALL SAFE (NOVICE): 5
- WALL SAFE (MASTER): 2
- WALL SAFE (ADVANCED): 5

## [9.07] BRIDGEWAY GARAGE

– CRAFTING: POWER
ARMOR STATION

This small garage
is close to the
bank. Park your
Power Armor here
and tinker for a bit.

## [9.08] DINER AND APARTMENTS (THE FENS)

– ARMAMENTS
AND AMMO
– FACTION: SUPER
MUTANTS
– HEALTH OR CHEMS

Just north of
the main Super
Mutant forces is a small courtyard with a diner attached to
an apartment building. The place is awash with blood, and
the diner has access to the grim interior. This is a two-floor
apartment complex with an upper west door leading to a
balcony and an east (red) door leading to the area above the
diner, where you can grab some explosives from a box (Novice),
once you abate the greenskin threats.

## [9.09] SETTLER'S STOP (THE FENS)

– BOTTLECAPS        – CRAFTING: COOKING STATION

An open cargo container offers protection from the elements, but
not the greenskins roaming the bloody courtyard to the west.

## [9.10] RAIDER CUL-DE-SAC (THE FENS)

– ARMAMENTS
AND AMMO
– ARMAMENTS AND
AMMO: TRUNK
– DANGER: TURRETS!
– FACTION: RAIDERS

A band of Raiders
believe they're sealed in tight in the southern cul-de-sac close
to Zone 6. Though you can unlock any of the doors (Expert), you
are able (with some patience and clockwise jumping) to drop
onto the rooftops from the high office (scaffold bridge, below),
and work your way around the roofs before landing on the
western Raider roof. The height advantage is helpful.

## [9.11] SCAFFOLD BRIDGE (THE FENS)

– DANGER: MINES!    – DANGER: TRIPWIRES!    – HEALTH OR CHEMS

Climb the metal scaffold steps and check the ruined building
to the north and south, watching for traps. From the office
atop the flights of stairs, you can leap through the hole in the
window and access the rooftops to the south of Diamond City.

## [9.12] DIAMOND CITY SCRAP

– ARMAMENTS AND AMMO        – FACTION: RADROACHES
– HEALTH OR CHEMS           – FACTION: VICIOUS DOGS

A collection of rusting vehicles gives the southern side of
Diamond City a certain unkempt appearance.

## [9.13] SCAVENGER'S REST (THE FENS)

– CRAFTING: COOKING STATION

This small open-air alcove is nestled behind a low stone wall,
southeast of Diamond City.

# ZONE 10: ESPLANADE

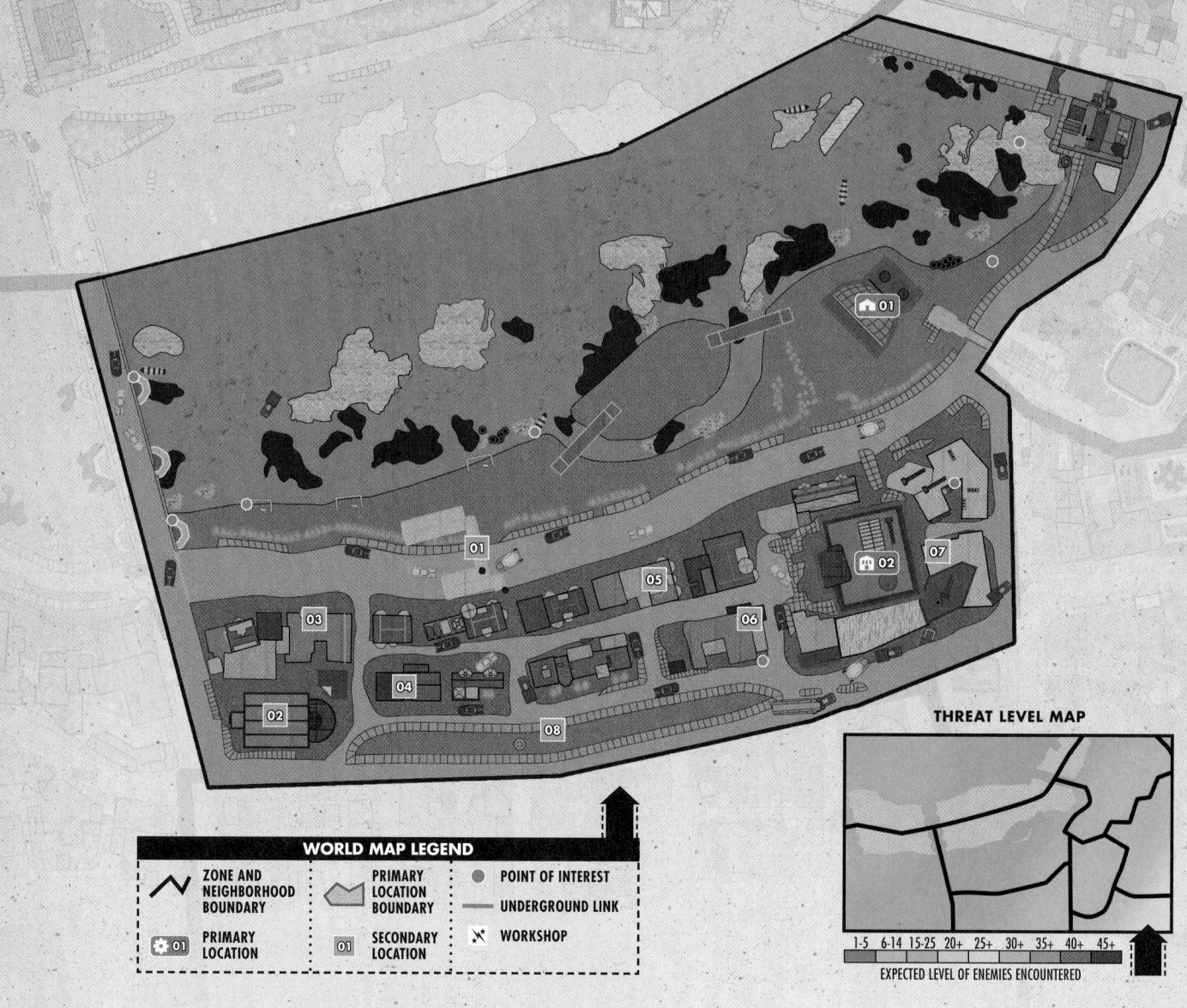

**WORLD MAP LEGEND**

| | | | |
|---|---|---|---|
| ⌇ | ZONE AND NEIGHBORHOOD BOUNDARY | ⬤ | POINT OF INTEREST |
| | | — | UNDERGROUND LINK |
| ⚙ 01 | PRIMARY LOCATION | ◁ | PRIMARY LOCATION BOUNDARY |
| | | ⚔ | WORKSHOP |
| 01 | SECONDARY LOCATION | | |

**THREAT LEVEL MAP**

1-5  6-14  15-25  20+  25+  30+  35+  40+  45+

EXPECTED LEVEL OF ENEMIES ENCOUNTERED

Technically part of the Back Bay Neighborhood, the Charles River Esplanade is comprised of the remains of a park, some waterfront mansions still exhibiting the faded grandeur of times gone by, and one of the main thoroughfares of Boston—Commonwealth Avenue. Currently, Raiders and Gunners are vying for control of this zone, though there are reports of strange smells (stranger than normal) emanating from the HalluciGen, Inc., building on the east side, close to Boston Common. If you fancy a stroll along the Charles River, you might want to pop in and say hello to the folks who've made the amphitheater their home; they're always looking for new recruits to join their secret society.

## Primary Locations
- [10.01] CHARLES VIEW AMPHITHEATER
- [10.02] HALLUCIGEN, INC.

## Secondary Locations
- [10.01] FOOTBRIDGE (ESPLANADE)
- [10.02] HOLY MISSION CONGREGATION CHURCH
- [10.03] BARRICADE AND ROOFTOPS
- [10.04] ROOFTOP DEN (ESPLANADE)
- [10.05] MALBOROUGH HOUSE
- [10.06] RAIDER LOOKOUT (ESPLANADE)
- [10.07] GUN SHOP GARAGE
- [10.08] COMMONWEALTH AVENUE

| 13 ——————— 20 | BOTTLECAPS | | HEALTH OR CHEMS | | ![] FUSION CORE | | Collectibles: | ![] BOBBLEHEAD | | ![] NUKA COLA QUANTUM |
| OPTIMAL ROUTE | SAFE | | ![] TERMINAL | | ![] POWER ARMOR | | | ![] NUKA CHERRY | | ![] HOLOTAPE |
| | ![] ARMAMENTS AND AMMO | | ![] STEAMER TRUNK | | ![] REQUIRED READING | | | ![] MINI NUKE | | ![] A KEY |
| AREA OF INTEREST | ![] DOOR | | | | | | | | | |

N – Novice (Locked)        E – Expert (Locked)        T – Terminal required to unlock        IN – Inaccessible        CB – Circuit Breaker
A – Advanced (Locked)      M – Master (Locked)        KEY – Key or ID Card required to unlock    C – Chained           B – Button

# PRIMARY LOCATIONS

## [10.01] CHARLES VIEW AMPHITHEATER    THREAT LEVELS 6-14 ▮▮▮▯▯▯▯▯▯▯

- ARMAMENTS AND AMMO
- ARMAMENTS AND AMMO: MINI NUKE
- FACTION: THE PILLARS (PILLARS OF THE COMMUNITY)
- FACTION: CHARACTER: BROTHER JAMES
- QUEST START: MISCELLANEOUS (A PILLAR OF THE COMMUNITY)
- QUEST VISIT: THE SECRET OF CABOT HOUSE (SIDE)

### VAULT-TEC RECOMMENDED LOOT

 ARMAMENTS AND AMMO: MINI NUKE

Pillars of the Community is ostensibly a missionary organization that hopes to restore the Commonwealth to prewar American values. Brother James is also a key player in the disappearance of Emogene Cabot from the well-to-do family of the same name. Visit here during the specified quest to uncover more about her. Need a Mini Nuke? Find one under one of the beds on the amphitheater stage.

 **Miscellaneous: A Pillar of the Community**

Speak with Brother Thomas. He is evasive to all of your questions. You can:

- JOIN HIS CULT, EVENTUALLY SHEDDING ALL OF YOUR CLOTHING AND EQUIPMENT AND GIVING IT TO HIM. THIS ISN'T RECOMMENDED.
- REFUSE TO JOIN HIS CULT. THEN SNEAK INTO HIS OFFICE AND OPEN THE LOCKED DOOR (ADVANCED).
- REFUSE TO JOIN HIS CULT. THEN SNEAK BEHIND AND PICKPOCKET THE AMPHITHEATER KEY AND UNLOCK THE DOOR IN THE SIDE OFFICE.
- GUN DOWN BROTHER THOMAS AND HIS CULTISTS. SEARCH HIS CORPSE FOR AN AMPHITHEATER KEY. USE IT ON THE DOOR IN HIS SIDE OFFICE.

## [10.02] HALLUCIGEN, INC.    THREAT LEVELS 15-25 ▮▮▮▮▯▯▯▯▯▯

- ARMAMENTS AND AMMO
- ARMAMENTS AND AMMO: TRUNK
- BOTTLECAPS++
- COLLECTIBLE: NUKA COLA QUANTUM
- COLLECTIBLE: REQUIRED READING: TESLA SCIENCE
- CRAFTING: CHEMISTRY STATION (3)
- DANGER: CAN CHIMES!
- DANGER: GAS LEAK!

- DANGER: OIL!
- DANGER: RADIATION (MILD)!
- FACTION: GUNNERS
- HEALTH OR CHEMS
- QUEST START: MISCELLANEOUS (HALLUCIGEN EXPLORATION)
- QUEST VISIT: MISCELLANEOUS (GOODNEIGHBOR: FRED ALLEN)
- UNIQUE ITEM: DRUGGED WATER
- UNIQUE ITEM: HALLUCIGEN GAS CANISTERS
- UNIQUE ITEM: HALLUCIGEN GAS GRENADES

### VAULT-TEC RECOMMENDED LOOT

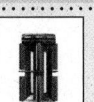  

COLLECTIBLE: NUKA COLA QUANTUM
UNIQUE ITEM:
HALLUCIGEN GAS GRENADES
REQUIRED READING: TESLA SCIENCE

The exterior of the building has the bodies of Gunners scattered everywhere. They appear to have been shot while running away. . . . You can enter through the main doors, or locate the side entrance (Master) on the northern side of the structure, facing the amphitheater.

**FIG 10.02B: HALLUCIGEN, INC. (INTERIOR)**

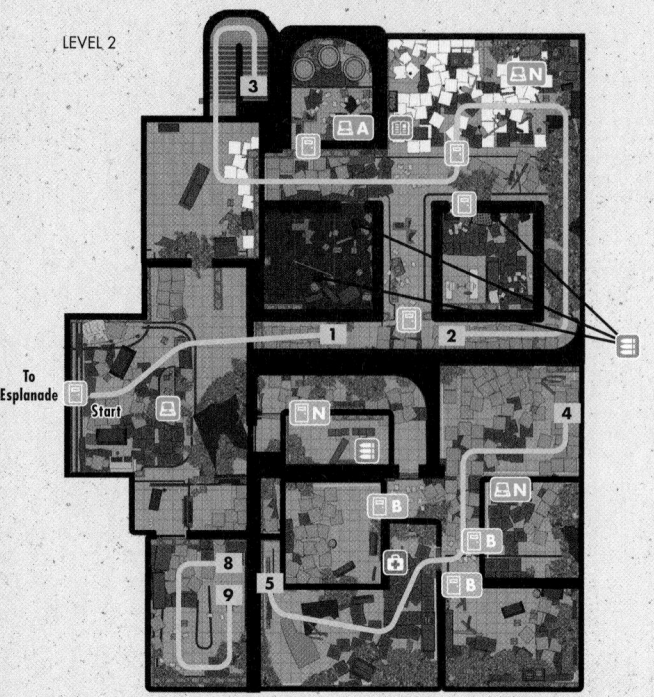

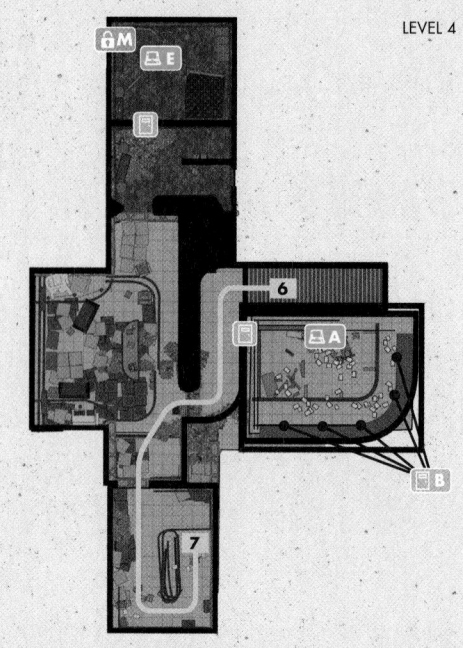

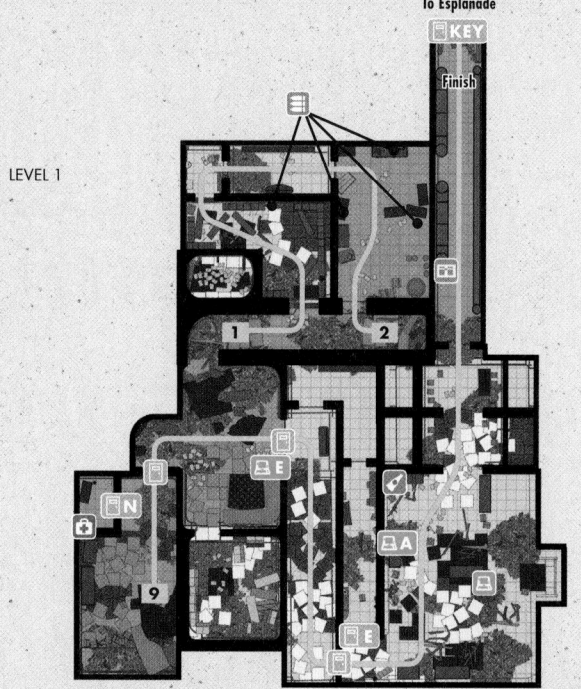

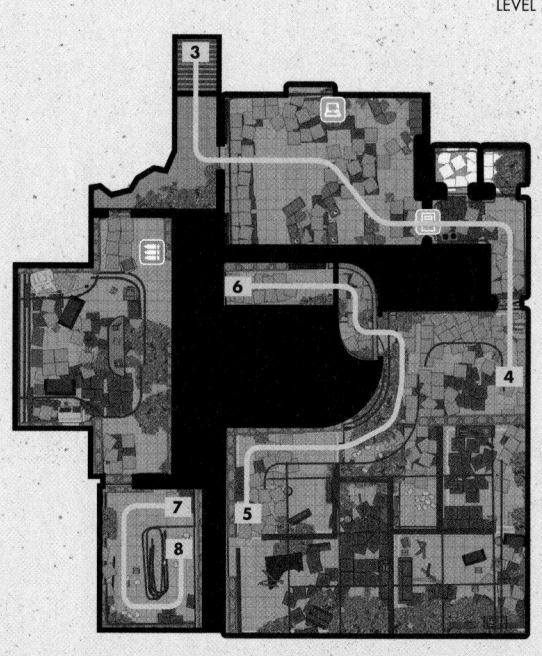

The reception room is ankle-deep in strange green gas. Read the "Help Wanted" note by the terminal for some interesting information. Gunners encountered here are fighting themselves as well as you.

Inside the research lab (north, L2) near the Tesla Science magazine, you can activate a suppressor prototype that paralyzes enemies it hits.

Drugged water is also available and is unique to this location. Inside the locked office (Advanced) is a Gunner.

 (Easy) Tell her to get out of here, that you're a friend or (hard) threaten her.

After breaching the lower-level pens, head up to the observation room and optionally press the buttons to start some "product demonstrations."

Continue through this maze until you reach the staircase down to the basement. Take the damage while running through, use Power Armor or a hazmat suit to breach the decontamination area, or use the terminal (Advanced) to dispel the gas, or pick the locked door (Expert) to reach the lab. The laboratory has a Gunner Commander with a key, mission brief, and note (the key unlocks the side entrance door). Gather HalluciGen Gas Canisters, which you can craft into unique HalluciGen Gas Grenades at any Chemistry Station-- but be warned, there's a limited supply of canisters. If Fred Allen of Goodneighbor (Hotel Rexford) sent you here for one, you can also find it in the lab.

# SECONDARY LOCATIONS

### [10.01] FOOTBRIDGE (ESPLANADE)

- ARMAMENTS AND AMMO
- FACTION: SUPER MUTANTS

Enabling access across the main road to the river, this is now a small Super Mutant camp. Feel free to butcher the inhabitant.

### [10.02] HOLY MISSION CONGREGATION CHURCH

- ARMAMENTS AND AMMO
- FACTION: FERAL GHOUL

The local church is still standing, though the sermons take on a more frenzied affair, as there are ferals present.

### [10.03] BARRICADE AND ROOFTOPS

- ARMAMENTS AND AMMO
- DANGER: LONG DROP!
- FACTION: RAIDERS
- HEALTH OR CHEMS

Access this small Raider camp via the barricade door to the east. Use the fire escape to climb to the roof, and back down a subsequent tenement building with loot and more foes to bring down.

### [10.04] ROOFTOP DEN (ESPLANADE)

- DANGER: LONG DROP!    - HEALTH OR CHEMS

Access the fire escape to reach a small rooftop hideaway with some minor chems and a good view of the neighborhood.

### [10.05] MALBOROUGH HOUSE

- ARMAMENTS AND AMMO    - FACTION: GUNNERS

This stately home has some of its ancient fineries still on display inside. This was recently used as a Gunner hideout, and there's the moderately impressive ammunition stashes here to prove it.

### [10.06] RAIDER LOOKOUT (ESPLANADE)

- ARMAMENTS AND AMMO
- FACTION: RAIDERS
- HEALTH OR CHEMS

A lone foe inside the attic of this once-grand mansion looks out at Gunner activity to the east.

### [10.07] GUN SHOP GARAGE

- CRAFTING: CHEMISTRY STATION
- CRAFTING: POWER ARMOR STATION
- CRAFTING: WEAPONS WORKBENCH

Park your Power Armor and tinker away at this garage, just behind HalluciGen, Inc.

### [10.08] COMMONWEALTH AVENUE

- FACTION: WILD MONGRELS

The main east-west thoroughfare along the southern edge of this neighborhood (to the south is Back Bay) offers access from the Fens (west) into Boston Common (east).

# ZONE 11: BACK BAY

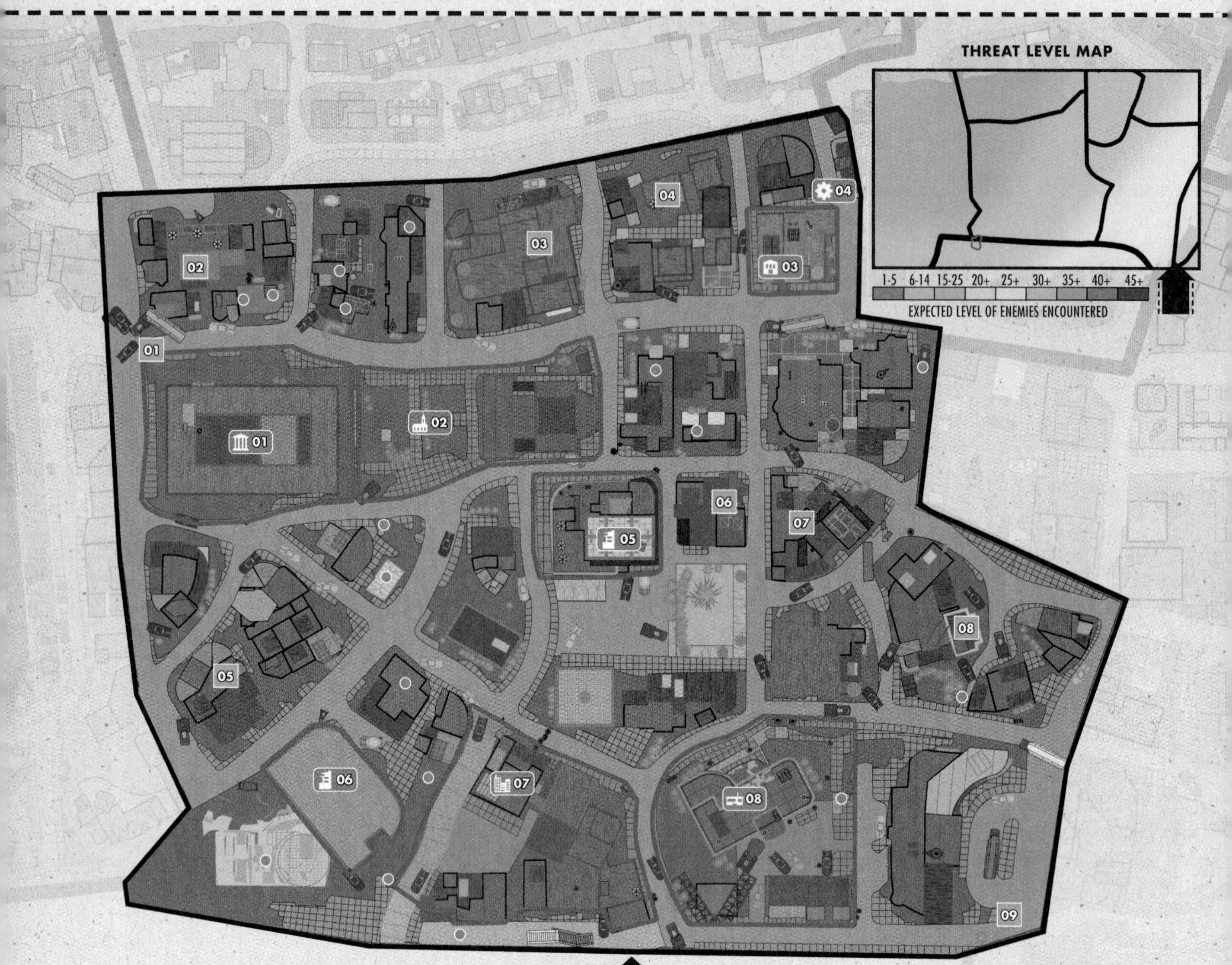

THREAT LEVEL MAP

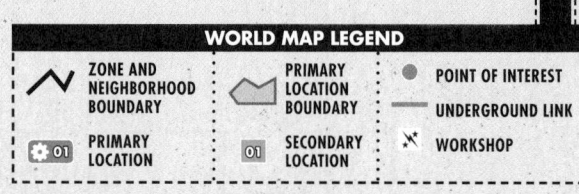

| 1-5 | 6-14 | 15-25 | 20+ | 25+ | 30+ | 35+ | 40+ | 45+ |
|------|------|------|------|------|------|------|------|------|

EXPECTED LEVEL OF ENEMIES ENCOUNTERED

## WORLD MAP LEGEND

- ∿ ZONE AND NEIGHBORHOOD BOUNDARY
- ⚙01 PRIMARY LOCATION
- ◿ PRIMARY LOCATION BOUNDARY
- 01 SECONDARY LOCATION
- ● POINT OF INTEREST
- ─ UNDERGROUND LINK
- ⚒ WORKSHOP

## Primary Locations

- [11.01] BOSTON PUBLIC LIBRARY
- [11.02] TRINITY PLAZA
- [11.03] HUBRIS COMICS
- [11.04] VAULT 114 (EXIT)
- [11.05] TRINITY TOWER
- [11.06] DARTMOUTH PROFESSIONAL BUILDING
- [11.07] LAYTON TOWERS
- [11.08] WILSON ATOMATOYS CORPORATE HQ

## Secondary Locations

- [11.01] THE CORNER OF MASS AND NEWBURY
- [11.02] HALF-DEMOLISHED APARTMENT (BACK BAY)
- [11.03] TRINITY PLAZA PARKING
- [11.04] SHENLEY'S OYSTER BAR
- [11.05] THE PATRIOT'S SLEEP SHACK
- [11.06] TRADER ROOFTOP (BACK BAY)
- [11.07] RAIDER ROOFTOPS (BACK BAY)
- [11.08] WARREN THEATER
- [11.09] RAIDER BLOCKADE (SOUTHEAST BACK BAY)

Back Bay was once known for its numerous brownstones of architectural significance. It is now dominated by the Trinity Tower skyscraper, an immense building constructed close to the old church and public library. Now the streets and alleyways are home to roving bands of Raiders, ferals, and packs of wild dogs. The tower still stands, which is more than can be said for another skyscraper, which has half toppled into the Dartmouth Professional Building. Keep going south to reach a Raider tenement block stronghold of Layton Towers. Super Mutants have a powerful grip on this part of the city, too, decorating the Wilson Atomatoys Corporate HQ and Trinity Tower with meat bags and bloody spikes.

## MAP LEGEND

| | | | | | |
|---|---|---|---|---|---|
| 13 ——— 20 | 🄲 BOTTLECAPS | | ➕ HEALTH OR CHEMS | ⚡ FUSION CORE | **Collectibles:** 🧠 BOBBLEHEAD | 🥤 NUKA COLA QUANTUM |
| OPTIMAL ROUTE | 🔒 SAFE | | 🖥 TERMINAL | ⚔ POWER ARMOR | 🥤 NUKA CHERRY | 📼 HOLOTAPE |
| ••••••••••• | 📦 ARMAMENTS AND AMMO | | 📟 STEAMER TRUNK | 📖 REQUIRED READING | ☢ MINI NUKE | 🔑 A KEY |
| ⚫ AREA OF INTEREST | 🚪 DOOR | | | | | |

| | | | | |
|---|---|---|---|---|
| N – Novice (Locked) | E – Expert (Locked) | T – Terminal required to unlock | IN – Inaccessible | CB – Circuit Breaker |
| A – Advanced (Locked) | M – Master (Locked) | KEY – Key or ID Card required to unlock | C – Chained | B – Button |

# PRIMARY LOCATIONS

## 🏛 [11.01] BOSTON PUBLIC LIBRARY

THREAT LEVELS 15-25

- ARMAMENTS AND AMMO
- ARMAMENTS AND AMMO: TRUNK
- BOTTLECAPS
- COLLECTIBLE: BOBBLEHEAD: INTELLIGENCE
- COLLECTIBLE: REQUIRED READING: MASSACHUSETTS SURGICAL JOURNAL
- CRAFTING: CHEMISTRY STATION (2)
- CRAFTING: COOKING STATION
- DANGER: GRENADES!
- DANGER: TRIPWIRES!
- DANGER: TURRETS!
- FACTION: SUPER MUTANTS
- FACTION: ROBOTS
- FACTION: CHARACTER: DALEN
- HEALTH OR CHEMS

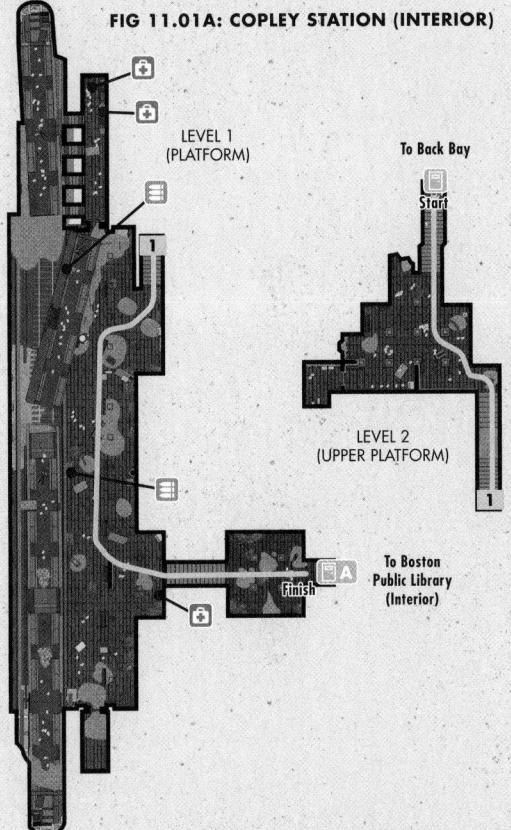

FIG 11.01A: COPLEY STATION (INTERIOR)

MAP

ZONE 11

NEIGHBORHOOD:
BACK BAY

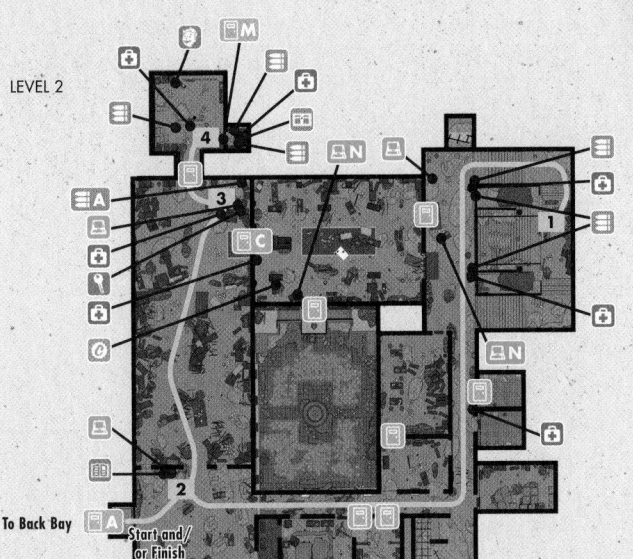

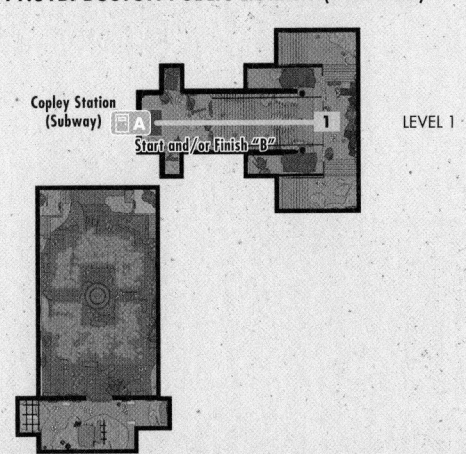

FIG 11.01B: BOSTON PUBLIC LIBRARY (INTERIOR)

451

This was the largest repository of historical documentation in the Commonwealth and a well-visited location before the bombs dropped. Decades of neglect, water damage, looting, and vandalism ruined all the books stored here. The building still has a grandeur and is accessed either by a side entrance (Advanced) or by a subterranean entrance at Copley Station, under the main building. Super Mutants roam these halls now.

The interior of Copley Station is a Super Mutant lair, with two traders already mauled in the north end of the subway car. There's another entrance into Boston Public Library here (Advanced).

The main library interior has only one magazine of required reading, but a lot of required bleeding on behalf of the Super Mutants you should be culling. Watch for Protectrons too; they are hostile if you break in, but if you use the intercom near every door into the library, and pass a speech challenge, you can get permission and have them allied to you. Be sure to investigate the west hall; the library storage room key is on the desk in the west hall (north end). It opens the door (Master) off the server room to the northwest. Don't leave without the Bobblehead!

Certain municipal buildings (like this library and police station) have book return terminals where overdue books you can scavenge can be dropped off in return for tickets. The book return terminals offer tokens as well as some plastic prizes (and toothpaste or gum) you can decorate your abodes (or mouth) with.

 **[11.02] TRINITY PLAZA**    THREAT LEVELS 15-25

– ARMAMENTS AND AMMO
– COLLECTIBLE: REQUIRED READING: ASTOUNDINGLY AWESOME TALES
– FACTION: SUPER MUTANT
– HEALTH OR CHEMS

**FIG 11.02: TRINITY CHURCH (INTERIOR)**

LEVEL 1                                 LEVEL 2

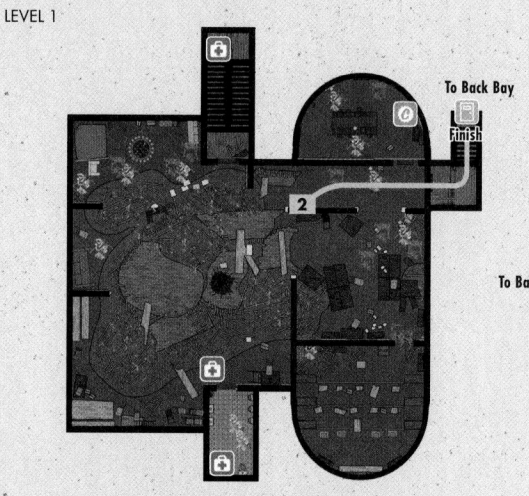 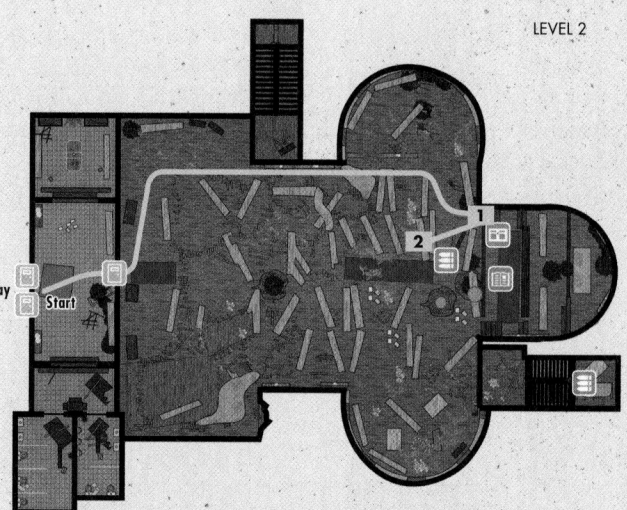

LEVEL 3

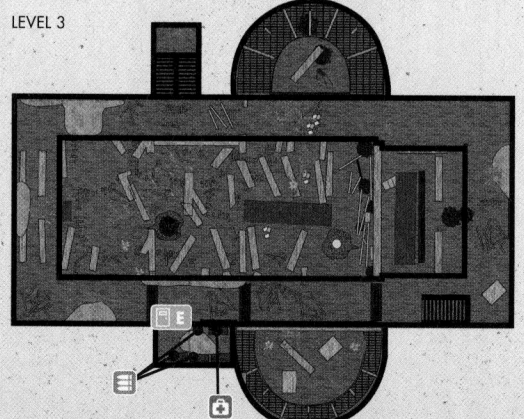

Still standing in the overgrown plaza that bears its name is Trinity Church. Founded in 1733, the present structure was completed in 1877 and now houses a small congregation of Super Mutants. The church has two entrances—the main doors and a hatch to the rear (east). Don't forget the magazine from the pulpit. The area is easy to spot from a distance; it is adjacent to the massive Trinity Tower.

# [11.03] HUBRIS COMICS

THREAT LEVELS 15-25

- ARMAMENTS AND AMMO
- ARMAMENTS AND AMMO: TRUNK
- BOTTLECAPS
- COLLECTIBLE: NUKA COLA QUANTUM
- COLLECTIBLE: REQUIRED READING: ASTOUNDINGLY AWESOME TALES
- COLLECTIBLE: REQUIRED READING: UNSTOPPABLES
- DANGER: EXPLOSIVE BARREL!
- FACTION: FERAL GHOULS
- FACTION: RADROACHES
- HEALTH OR CHEMS
- QUEST VISIT: THE SILVER SHROUD (SIDE)

- UNIQUE ITEM: GROGNAK COSTUME
- UNIQUE ITEM: GROGNAK'S AXE
- UNIQUE ITEM: SILVER SHROUD COSTUME
- UNIQUE ITEM: SILVER SHROUD HAT
- UNIQUE ITEM: SILVER SHROUD PHOTO
- UNIQUE ITEM: SILVER SUBMACHINE GUN PROP
- UNIQUE ITEM: SILVER SHROUD SCRIPT

## FIG 11.03: HUBRIS COMICS (INTERIOR)

LEVEL 1

LEVEL 2

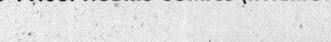

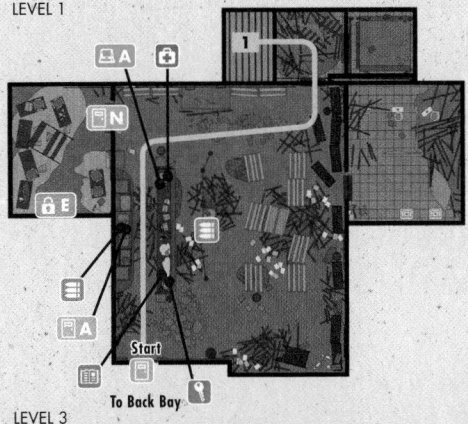

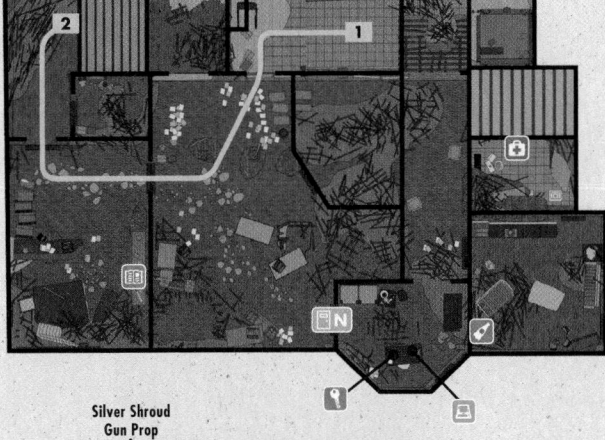

LEVEL 3

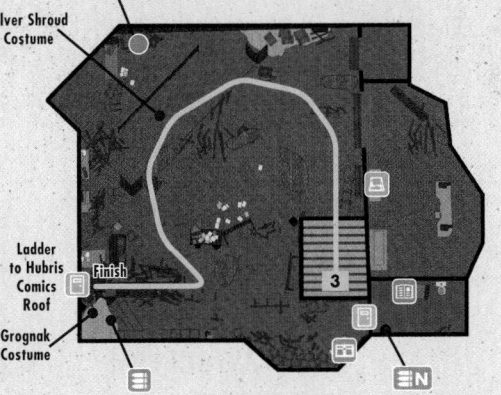

LEVEL 4

Silver Shroud Gun Prop

Silver Shroud Costume

Ladder to Hubris Comics Roof

Finish

Grognak Costume

## VAULT-TEC RECOMMENDED LOOT

**REQUIRED READING: ASTOUNDINGLY AWESOME TALES**
**REQUIRED READING: UNSTOPPABLES**
**UNIQUE ITEMS: GROGNAK'S COSTUME AND AXE**
**UNIQUE ITEMS: SILVER SHROUD PARAPHERNALIA**

This is the local store and office of Hubris Comics, publishers of classic graphic novels. In addition to the downstairs shop, the building also includes offices for the production staff a small television studio on the fourth floor.

Be sure to thoroughly inspect the store for collectibles! Look for the storeroom key in one of the cash registers and the office key in the desk upstairs. Don't forget Grognak's Axe in the display case, his costume by the exit ladder to the roof, and the Silver Shroud photo and costume (the latter of which is necessary for the specified quest). There's a prop gun hidden behind the stage backdrop, and one locked room even has an unreleased script!

## [11.04] VAULT 114 (EXIT)  THREAT LEVELS 20+

- ARMAMENTS AND AMMO
- ARMAMENTS AND AMMO: TRUNK
- BOTTLECAPS
- COLLECTIBLE: NUKA COLA QUANTUM
- COLLECTIBLE: REQUIRED READING: ASTOUNDINGLY AWESOME TALES
- COLLECTIBLE: REQUIRED READING: UNSTOPPABLES
- DANGER: EXPLOSIVE BARREL!
- FACTION: FERAL GHOULS

QUEST VISIT: UNLIKELY VALENTINE (MAIN)

This manhole cover leads down a ladder to the interior of Park Street Station (Boston Common Neighborhood), close to the entrance of Vault 114. It is only accessible once you complete the specified quest. It provides a quick access point if you wish to return to explore either location. Consult the Park Street Station location for maps and items you can find throughout the subway and vault.

## [11.05] TRINITY TOWER  THREAT LEVELS 15-25

- ARMAMENTS AND AMMO
- BOTTLECAPS++
- COLLECTIBLE: BOBBLEHEAD: MELEE
- CRAFTING: COOKING STATION
- CRAFTING: WEAPONS WORKBENCH
- COMPANION: STRONG
- DANGER: LONG DROP!
- FACTION: SUPER MUTANTS
- FACTION: CHARACTER: REX GOODMAN
- FACTION: CHARACTER: STRONG
- HEALTH OR CHEMS
- QUEST START: CURTAIN CALL (SIDE)
- UNIQUE ITEM: REGINALD'S SUIT (APPAREL)
- UNIQUE ITEM: AGATHA'S DRESS (APPAREL)

FIG 11.05A: TRINITY TOWER (EXTERIOR)

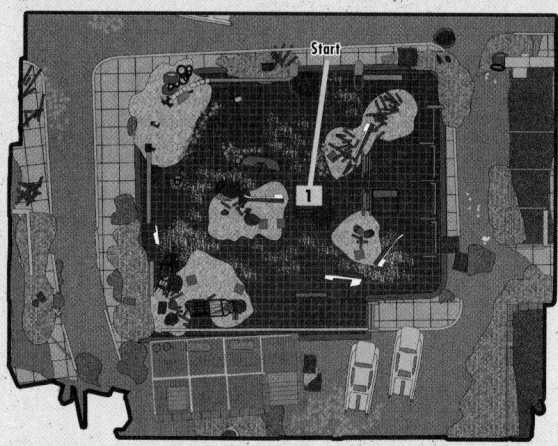

GROUND LEVEL 1

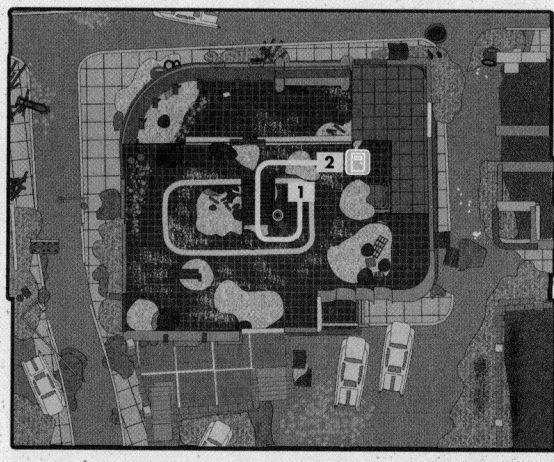

GROUND LEVEL 2

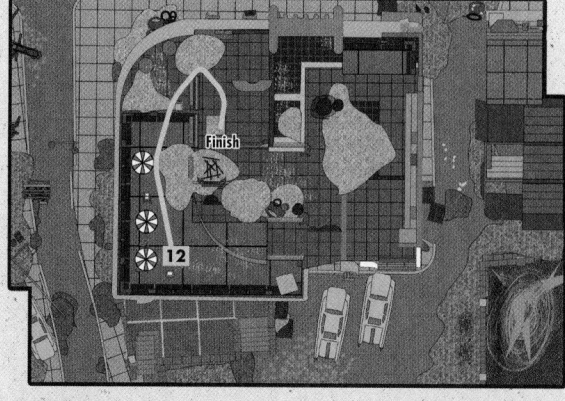

GROUND LEVEL 3

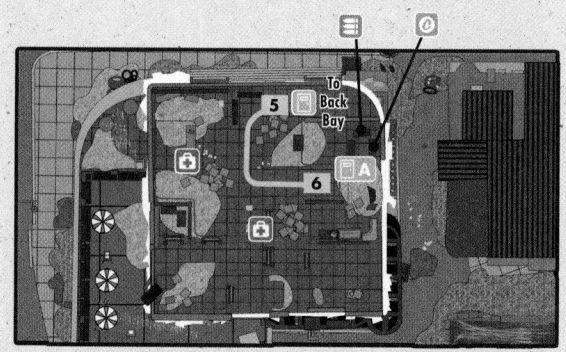

UPPER LEVEL 1

UPPER LEVEL 2

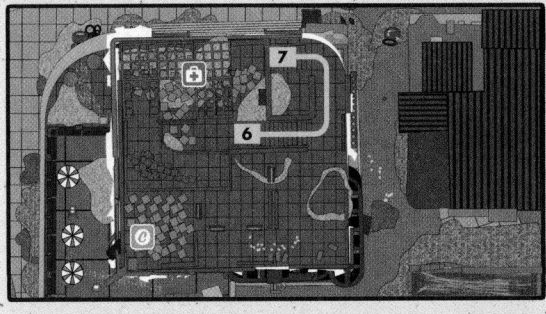

UPPER LEVEL 3

UPPER LEVEL 4

UPPER LEVEL 5
(ROOF)

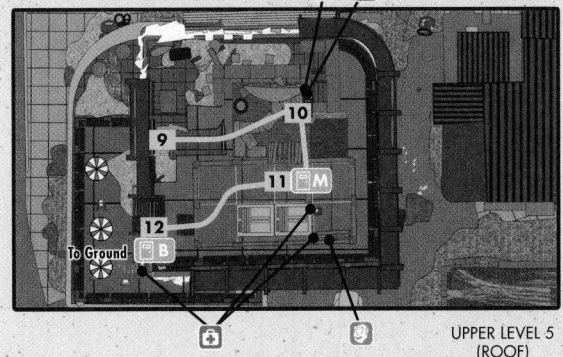

**FIG 11.05B: TRINITY TOWER MID-LEVEL (INTERIOR)**

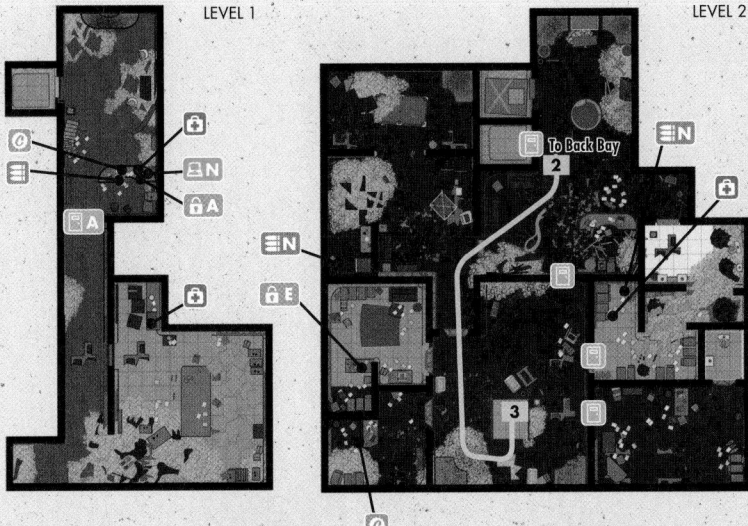

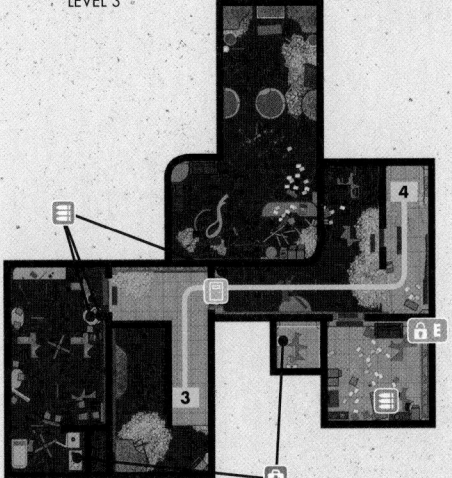

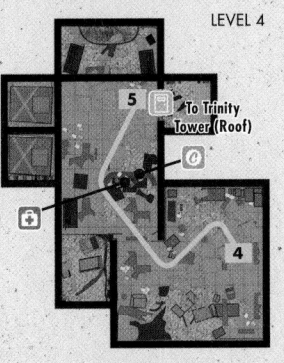

## VAULT-TEC RECOMMENDED LOOT

**BOBBLEHEAD: MELEE**

## AVAILABLE COMPANION

**COMPANION: STRONG**

The tallest building in Boston, this towering office skyscraper with a fancy plaza at ground level now features the "offal and splattering" aesthetic the Super Mutants are so keen on showcasing. You may have been summoned here by Trinity Tower Radio as part of the specified quest. The only way up into the structure is taking the mezzanine elevator to the mid-level. After scaling the interior, you appear on the final five floors leading to the roof. It's a very long way down, so watch your step. It is recommended to take in the sights via a window-washer elevator that takes you from the roof down to the plaza.

The Trinity Tower Cell Key is in the steamer trunk on the roof. Don't forget the Bobblehead and the Macbeth script inside the cell.

## [11.06] DARTMOUTH PROFESSIONAL BUILDING

THREAT LEVELS 15-25

- BOTTLECAPS
- FACTION: FERAL GHOULS
- FACTION: RADROACHES
- FACTION: SUPER MUTANT

An easily distinguished landmark, this huge tower has a second skyscraper half collapsed into its side. There's no access other than the initial interior room of this structure, which has a single Radroach and a Port-a-Diner to fiddle with.

## [11.07] LAYTON TOWERS

THREAT LEVELS 20+

- ARMAMENTS AND AMMO
- ARMAMENTS AND AMMO: TRUNK
- ARMOR PART: FUSION CORE
- BOTTLECAPS
- CRAFTING: CHEMISTRY STATION
- CRAFTING: COOKING STATION
- DANGER: LONG DROP!
- DANGER: MINES!
- DANGER: TURRETS!
- FACTION: RAIDERS
- HEALTH OR CHEMS

Two tenement blocks are separated by a courtyard, where Raiders roam and shout obscenities. Watch for spotlights and turrets. You can climb the fire escape to access the north tenement via the roof or barge in at ground level. The Mass Pike road is to the south, along with the other tenement and a window-washer lift prepped with mines. Ride that up to a second rooftop entry point (inside the ruined rooftop apartment). There's a steamer trunk and cooking station up here. Inside are five floors of boarded-up apartments overrun by Raiders.

**FIG 11.07: LAYTON TOWERS (INTERIOR)**

### VAULT-TEC RECOMMENDED LOOT

**ARMOR PART: FUSION CORE**

LEVEL 1

LEVEL 2

LEVEL 3

LEVEL 4

1

Start

To Back Bay

2

1

N

N

@

3

To Back Bay

Finish

2

To Back Bay

3

To Back Bay

THREAT LEVELS 20+

**FIG 11.08: WILSON ATOMATOYS CORPORATE HQ (INTERIOR)**

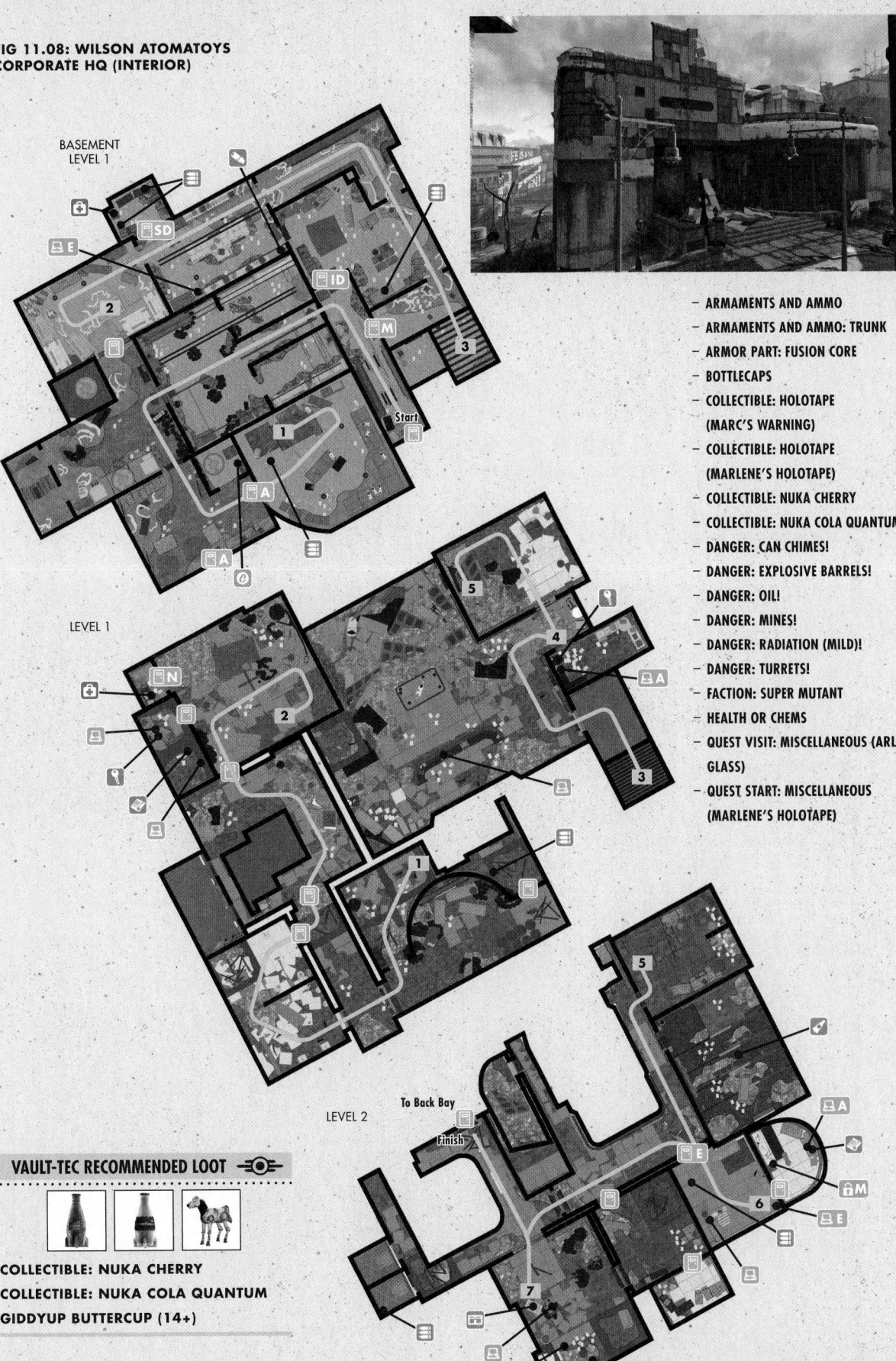

BASEMENT LEVEL 1

Start

LEVEL 1

LEVEL 2

To Back Bay

Finish

– ARMAMENTS AND AMMO
– ARMAMENTS AND AMMO: TRUNK
– ARMOR PART: FUSION CORE
– BOTTLECAPS
– COLLECTIBLE: HOLOTAPE (MARC'S WARNING)
– COLLECTIBLE: HOLOTAPE (MARLENE'S HOLOTAPE)
– COLLECTIBLE: NUKA CHERRY
– COLLECTIBLE: NUKA COLA QUANTUM
– DANGER: CAN CHIMES!
– DANGER: EXPLOSIVE BARRELS!
– DANGER: OIL!
– DANGER: MINES!
– DANGER: RADIATION (MILD)!
– DANGER: TURRETS!
– FACTION: SUPER MUTANT
– HEALTH OR CHEMS
– QUEST VISIT: MISCELLANEOUS (ARLEN GLASS)
– QUEST START: MISCELLANEOUS (MARLENE'S HOLOTAPE)

MAP

**ZONE 11**

NEIGHBORHOOD: BACK BAY

**VAULT-TEC RECOMMENDED LOOT**

COLLECTIBLE: NUKA CHERRY
COLLECTIBLE: NUKA COLA QUANTUM
GIDDYUP BUTTERCUP (14+)

Before the war, this was the headquarters of the Wilson Atomatoys Corporation, maker of the well-known Giddyup Buttercup horse. Only the senior officials at the company, including the lead designer Arlen Glass, were based here. The building lay abandoned for years until a gang of Super Mutants stormed it, using it as a base for raiding the surrounding area.

Up on the first floor, swipe the Wilson Atomatoys ID card from the secretary's desk in the northwest office, near the locked storage door (Novice). Don't miss the key by the security terminal in the small office northeast of the ruined entrance foyer.

On the upper floor, use lockpicking or the key to access the small, pristine development lab. Read the office terminal to receive a passcode that will allow access to the lab door without hacking the wall terminal (Master). The second lab terminal (Advanced, or use the password) has Marlene's Holotape and opens the safe (Master).

There's also a warning note by the president's terminal (which opens the wall safe [Advanced]), next to the steamer trunk. The desk has a key, too.

The roof offers more combat, some ammo, and a quick escape.

## Miscellaneous Quest (Arlen Glass)

Arlen Glass, a Ghoul at Primary Location: The Slog, sends you to find some toy parts at the old Atomatoys Factory. If you persuade him to give you his old ID Card, or you complete this misc objective and get the ID Card from the Factory, you can use it to open a door in the basement here, allowing you to bypass many of the Super Mutants waiting to ambush you.

## Miscellaneous Quest (Marlene's Holotape)

If you manage to find Marlene's Holotape here (inside the development lab terminal [Advanced]), return it to Arlen at the Slog. After an emotional moment, you're awarded with around 350 Caps, and a unique item—a Toy Buttercup horse.

TUNE INTO CHANNEL 314
THE SILVER SHROUD NEEDS YOU!

# SECONDARY LOCATIONS

### [11.01] THE CORNER OF MASS AND NEWBURY

– FACTION: FERAL GHOULS

When investigating this neighborhood, use this rusting big-rig container truck outside Boston Public Library to situate yourself. The rest of Back Bay is east and south of this general area, the Fens is west, and Esplanade is one block north.

### [11.02] HALF-DEMOLISHED APARTMENT (BACK BAY)

– HEALTH OR CHEMS

Use the fire escape or rubble pile to clamber down through the rooms of this small apartment structure. There are rooftop planks to the attic room to the southeast, too.

### [11.03] TRINITY PLAZA PARKING

– FACTION: RAIDERS

This small parking structure has openings east and west and Raiders in the middle.

## [11.04] SHENLEY'S OYSTER BAR

- ARMAMENTS AND AMMO
- ARMAMENTS AND AMMO: TRUNK
- CRAFTING: CHEMISTRY STATION
- DANGER: LONG DROP!
- DANGER: MINES!
- DANGER: TURRETS!
- FACTION: RAIDERS
- HEALTH OR CHEMS

This Raider camp has two chained doors and mines laid at the east and south entrances. Battle into the bar, and there's a door into the kitchens, a larder that's been picked clean, and stairs up to the roof. There are more foes up here, along with a steamer trunk. Keep climbing for more loot!

## [11.05] THE PATRIOT'S SLEEP SHACK

This may not be particularly safe, but the lean-to against the brick apartment is particularly patriotic.

## [11.06] TRADER ROOFTOP (BACK BAY)

- DANGER: LONG DROP!
- HEALTH OR CHEMS

If you make a running jump from the Raider rooftops (to the east), you can land safely on this roof—the last known whereabouts of a fleeing trader.

## [11.07] RAIDER ROOFTOPS (BACK BAY)

- ARMAMENTS AND AMMO
- ARMAMENTS AND AMMO: TRUNK
- CRAFTING: COOKING STATION
- CRAFTING: WEAPONS WORKBENCH
- DANGER: LONG DROP!
- DANGER: TURRETS!
- FACTION: RAIDERS
- HEALTH OR CHEMS

Enter the Raider camp at the road junction where barricades have been erected. Fight up the fire escape. A sweep of the rooftops allows you to ransack a steamer trunk in the southwest apartment ruin.

## [11.08] WARREN THEATER

- FACTION: SYNTHS (THE INSTITUTE)
- HEALTH OR CHEMS

The entrance foyer to this old theater still has a mystic grandeur to it, as well as some chems. Access the elevator to the theater. Jangles, Teddy, and their bony friends are watching a play, though the actors seem a bit stiff. Afterward, check the safe (Advanced) and some natty clothing.

## [11.09] RAIDER BLOCKADE (SOUTHEAST BACK BAY)

- ARMAMENTS AND AMMO
- FACTION: RAIDERS

Offering access out of Boston and into Zone 6, or infiltration east into the Theater District and D.B. Technical High School, this Raider camp is long on barricades but short on competent foes; they're all holed up at the Layton Apartments to the west.

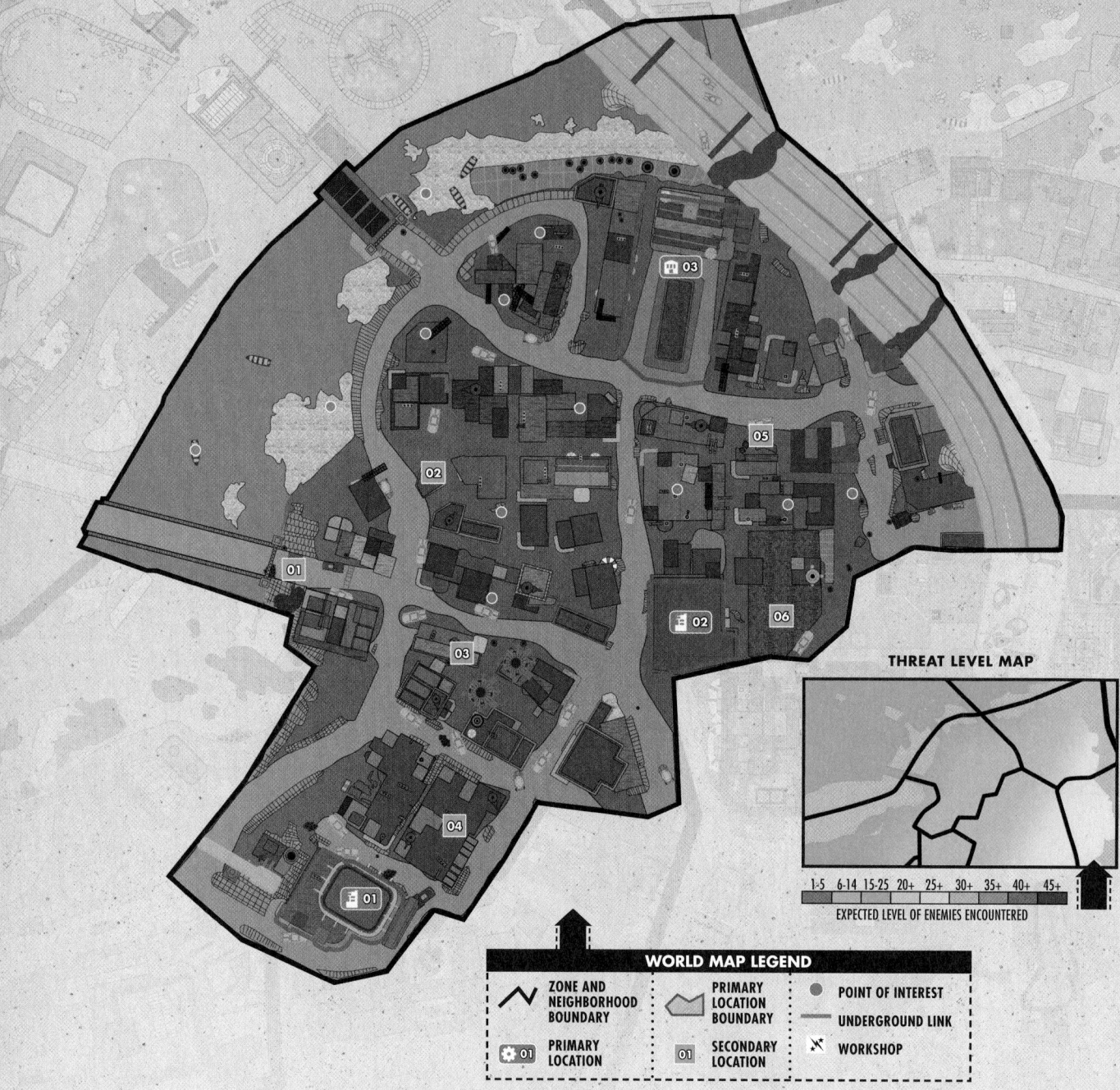

**THREAT LEVEL MAP**

| 1-5 | 6-14 | 15-25 | 20+ | 25+ | 30+ | 35+ | 40+ | 45+ |

EXPECTED LEVEL OF ENEMIES ENCOUNTERED

**WORLD MAP LEGEND**

| | | |
|---|---|---|
| ⋀ ZONE AND NEIGHBORHOOD BOUNDARY | ⬠ PRIMARY LOCATION BOUNDARY | ● POINT OF INTEREST |
| | | ── UNDERGROUND LINK |
| ⚙ 01 PRIMARY LOCATION | 01 SECONDARY LOCATION | ⤲ WORKSHOP |

South of the river from Charleston, this historic neighborhood of row houses, gas lights, and cobblestone alleys was once a pleasant place to live. Beacon Hill was the gateway to the Financial District but is now a far less desirable place, where bands of Raiders jostle for control and many structures have been decimated. You can scale the rooftops, pick through the rubble, and stop at Vault-Tec's Regional Headquarters (which may be closed, given the current circumstances). One area that still seems untouched by the ravages of war and time is the mysterious Cabot House, at the north end of this neighborhood.

## Primary Locations

– [12.01] VAULT-TEC REGIONAL HQ
– [12.02] BOSTON BUGLE BUILDING
– [12.03] CABOT HOUSE

## Secondary Locations

– [12.01] BEACON HILL APARTMENTS
– [12.02] DEMOLISHED APARTMENT TOWER (BEACON HILL)
– [12.03] PLAYGROUND GARAGE
– [12.04] ROOFTOP GENERATOR (BEACON HILL)
– [12.05] DESTROYED TENEMENT (BEACON HILL)
– [12.06] RUBBLE OVERLOOK

## MAP LEGEND

| | | | | | | | | | Collectibles: | | | |
|---|---|---|---|---|---|---|---|---|---|---|---|---|
| 13 — 20 OPTIMAL ROUTE | | 🄲 BOTTLECAPS | | ➕ HEALTH OR CHEMS | | 🔲 FUSION CORE | | | 🔲 BOBBLEHEAD | | 🔲 NUKA COLA QUANTUM | |
| | | 🔒 SAFE | | 🖥 TERMINAL | | 🔲 POWER ARMOR | | | 🔲 NUKA CHERRY | | 🔲 HOLOTAPE | |
| ● AREA OF INTEREST | | 🔲 ARMAMENTS AND AMMO | | 🔲 STEAMER TRUNK | | 📖 REQUIRED READING | | | 🔲 MINI NUKE | | 🔑 A KEY | |
| | | 🚪 DOOR | | | | | | | | | | |

**N** – Novice (Locked)      **E** – Expert (Locked)      **T** – Terminal required to unlock      **IN** – Inaccessible      **CB** – Circuit Breaker
**A** – Advanced (Locked)      **M** – Master (Locked)      **KEY** – Key or ID Card required to unlock      **C** – Chained      **B** – Button

# PRIMARY LOCATIONS

## 📑 [12.01] VAULT-TEC REGIONAL HQ      THREAT LEVELS 20+

- ARMAMENTS AND AMMO
- ARMAMENTS AND AMMO: MINI NUKE
- ARMAMENTS AND AMMO: TRUNK
- FACTION: FERAL GHOULS

### VAULT-TEC RECOMMENDED LOOT ⚙

ARMAMENTS AND AMMO: MINI NUKE

Welcome to Vault-Tec! Our regional representatives are pleased to assist you in all manner of vault-related requests and questions. Please use the main entrance or the basement door (Expert). Please note the views of Martin Reid do not reflect the values of Vault-Tec Corporation.

Additional Note: Due to the unwanted deposit of a Mini Nuke, the restrooms are currently out of order.

FIG 12.01: VAULT-TEC REGIONAL HQ

LEVEL 1

LEVEL 2

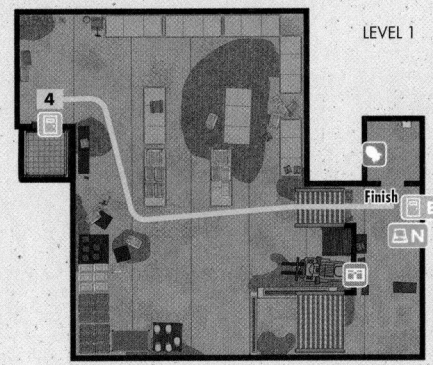

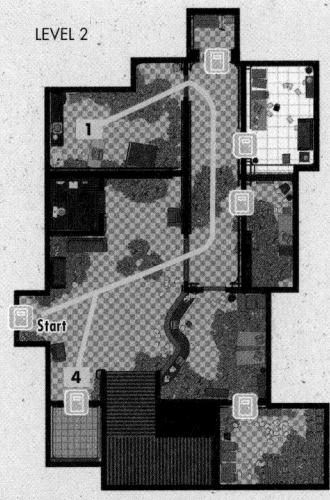

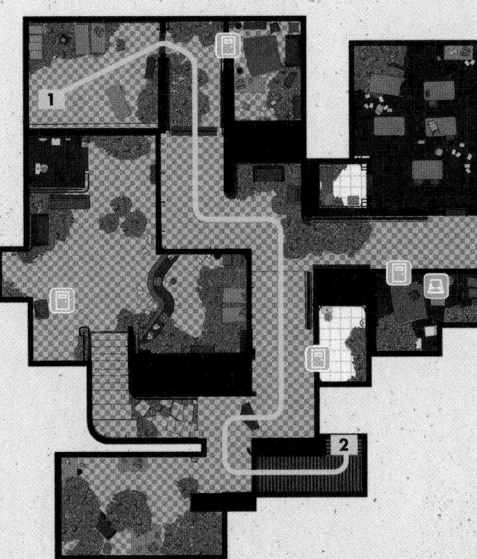

LEVEL 3

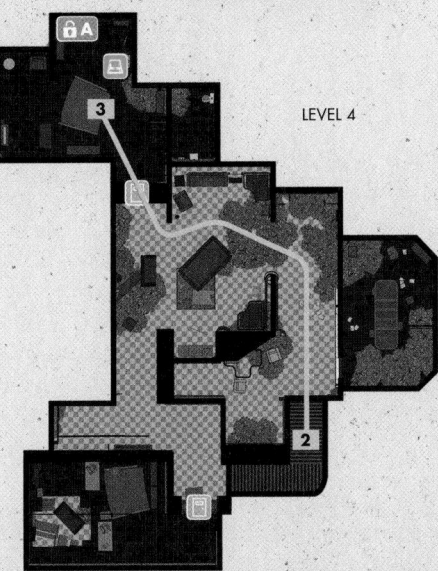

LEVEL 4

## [12.02] BOSTON BUGLE BUILDING

THREAT LEVELS 20+

- ARMAMENTS AND AMMO
- COLLECTIBLE: NUKA CHERRY
- DANGER: LONG DROP!
- FACTION: ROBOTS

LEVEL 1

To Beacon Hill

FIG 12.02: THE BOSTON BUGLE (INTERIOR)

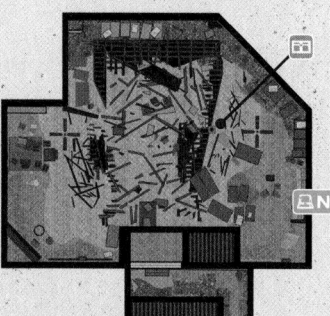

LEVEL 2B

LEVEL 2

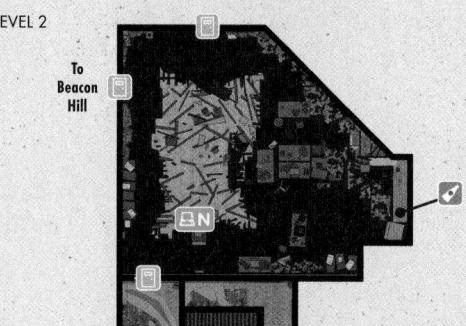

To Beacon Hill

### VAULT-TEC RECOMMENDED LOOT

COLLECTIBLE: NUKA CHERRY

Boston's largest circulation newspaper has been "Trumpeting the Truth for over 50 years." Its offices are in this upscale neighborhood. Now they are in a shocking state, though still patrolled by robot security.

The access door on the upper interior floor leads to a precarious open-air office with a death plummet should you trip. Simply access the floor safe (Novice) instead, before retracing your steps.

## [12.03] CABOT HOUSE

THREAT LEVELS 15-25

- ARMAMENTS AND AMMO+
- ARMAMENTS AND AMMO: MINI NUKE
- ARMAMENTS AND AMMO: MINI NUKE (FAT MAN)
- ARMAMENTS AND AMMO: TRUNK (2)
- COLLECTIBLE: NUKA CHERRY
- COLLECTIBLE: REQUIRED READING: MASSACHUSETTS SURGICAL JOURNAL
- CRAFTING: CHEMISTRY STATION
- FACTION: CABOT FAMILY
- FACTION: CHARACTER: EDWARD DEEGAN
- FACTION: CHARACTER: JACK CABOT
- FACTION: CHARACTER: EMOGENE CABOT
- FACTION: CHARACTER: WILHELMINA CABOT
- HEALTH OR CHEMS
- QUEST START: THE SECRET OF CABOT HOUSE (SIDE)

### VAULT-TEC RECOMMENDED LOOT

**ARMAMENTS AND AMMO: MINI NUKE AND FAT MAN**
**REQUIRED READING: MASSACHUSETTS SURGICAL JOURNAL**
**COLLECTIBLE: NUKA CHERRY**

This 1711 mansion is sealed up tighter than a T-60 Power Armor vacuum attachment: It is strangely preserved amid the general decay. Located on Louisburg Square, the park is still well maintained. The intercom at the front door allows you to ask to gain entry.

 (Easy, Medium) Though this isn't easy.

The door usually requires a key, given to you by a Ghoul named Edward Deegan at the start of the specified quest.

Explore the house, being mindful that this isn't your property. However, the magazine, gamma gun, Fat Man, and a plentiful supply of purified water in the pantry might galvanize you into pilfering some. Emogene's terminal (Master) on the upper floor offers surprising insights into the family.

**FIG 12.03: CABOT HOUSE (INTERIOR)**

LEVEL 3

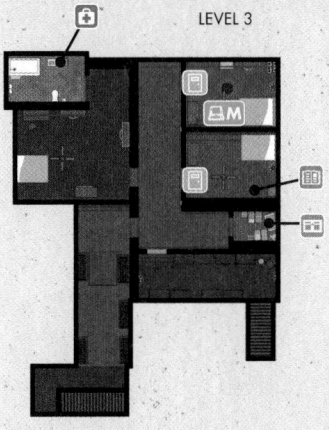

LEVEL 2

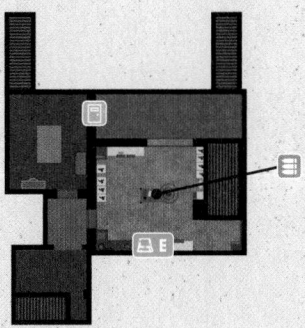

To Beacon Hill

LEVEL 1

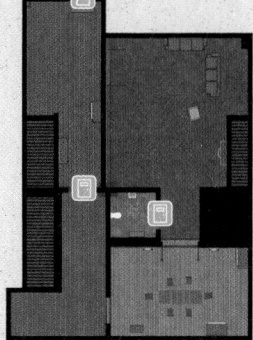

BASEMENT LEVEL 1

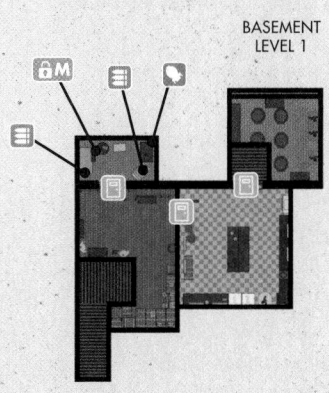

## [12.01] BEACON HILL APARTMENTS

- ARMAMENTS AND AMMO
- ARMAMENTS AND AMMO: TRUNK
- DANGER: LONG DROP!
- FACTION: RAIDERS
- HEALTH OR CHEMS

A fortified Raider camp with barricades facing the bridge (west) and a rickety bridge connecting two tower blocks. Enter the southern tower at ground level.

The southern apartments has a stairwell filled with alcohol and a few Raiders to execute. Exit via the tiny apartment at the top, crossing to the roof of the north apartments, which you can't enter. Gather ammo, open a steamer trunk, and unlock a safe (Advanced).

## [12.02] DEMOLISHED APARTMENT TOWER (BEACON HILL)

This pile of rubble is worth your time, as there's a safe to crack (Master).

## [12.03] PLAYGROUND GARAGE

- CRAFTING: POWER ARMOR STATION
- CRAFTING: WEAPONS WORKBENCH
- FACTION: YAO GUAI

Deal with any local wildlife roaming about, then use this as a tinkering station when you're in the Beacon Hill area.

## [12.04] ROOFTOP GENERATOR (BEACON HILL)

- ARMOR PART: FUSION CORE

Access this set of rooftops from the western rubble, and follow the fire escape stairs across to the eastern building. Pry a Fusion Core out of a generator here.

## [12.05] DESTROYED TENEMENT (BEACON HILL)

- HEALTH OR CHEMS

A mixture of rubble and brickwork, this structure holds some handy chems if you leap the gaps up from the rusty car.

## [12.06] RUBBLE OVERLOOK

This is a good spot to climb up, using the ladders from the alley to the north, as it allows you to peer into the Financial District and snipe at foes near Haymarket Mall and the Old Corner Bookstore.

MAP

ZONE 12

NEIGHBORHOOD: BEACON HILL

# ZONE 13: NEIGHBORHOOD: NORTH END

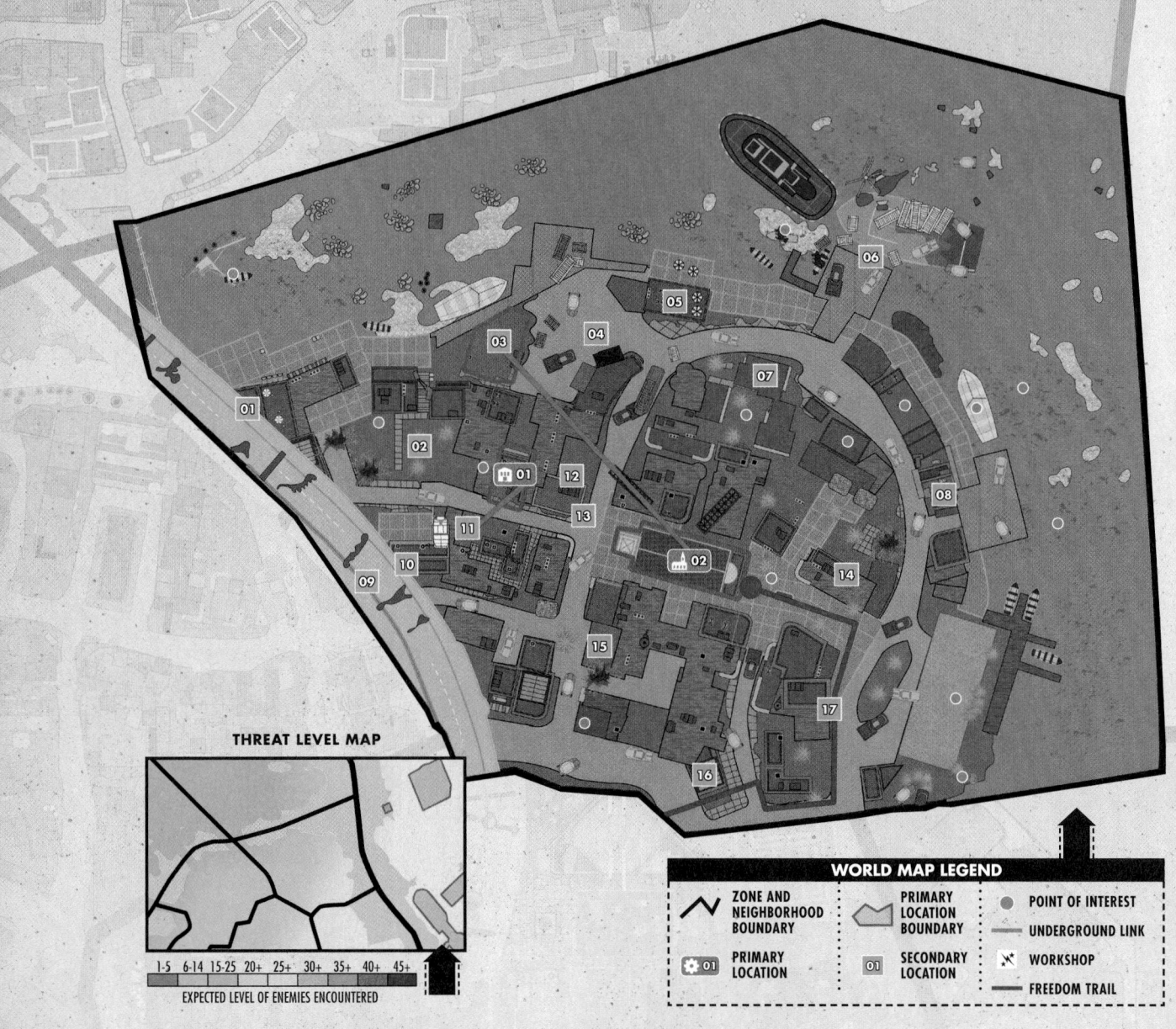

**THREAT LEVEL MAP**

1-5  6-14  15-25  20+  25+  30+  35+  40+  45+
EXPECTED LEVEL OF ENEMIES ENCOUNTERED

## WORLD MAP LEGEND

ZONE AND NEIGHBORHOOD BOUNDARY

PRIMARY LOCATION BOUNDARY

POINT OF INTEREST

UNDERGROUND LINK

PRIMARY LOCATION

SECONDARY LOCATION

WORKSHOP

FREEDOM TRAIL

This residential neighborhood once boasted continuous residential inhabitants since 1630. Currently, it boasts a variety of crumbling brick and wooden structures, some of historical significance, and is anchored by the Old North Church and the culmination of the Freedom Trail. It is deep in the catacombs under this church that the Railroad faction has holed up. Otherwise, this relatively small but dense zone should be approached with relative care; roving bands of Super Mutants and Raiders have been seen, and there's chatter regarding a fiendish serial killer who stalks the old alleyways after dark.

## Primary Locations

- [13.01] PICKMAN GALLERY
- [13.02] OLD NORTH CHURCH

## Secondary Locations

- [13.01] ROOFTOP APARTMENT (NORTH END)
- [13.02] NORTH END GRAVEYARD
- [13.03] RAILROAD HQ ESCAPE TUNNEL EXIT
- [13.04] RAIDER COURTYARD (NORTH END)
- [13.05] HOT PIZZA PIE SHOP
- [13.06] CRASHED VERTIBIRD (MILITARY BARGE)
- [13.07] WHARFSIDE COTTAGE
- [13.08] ROOFTOP LOUNGER
- [13.09] SKYTRAM (NORTH END ELEVATED FREEWAY)
- [13.10] MEAN PASTRIES
- [13.11] PICKMAN'S EXIT
- [13.12] BOXING GYM
- [13.13] SCAFFOLD STAIRS (NORTH END)
- [13.14] BILLBOARD ALLEY
- [13.15] RUINED BRICK APARTMENT (NORTH END)
- [13.16] SUBWAY STATION (NORTH END)
- [13.17] PAUL REVERE'S HOUSE

## MAP LEGEND

| 13 ——— 20 OPTIMAL ROUTE | | |
|---|---|---|
| AREA OF INTEREST | | |

- **BOTTLECAPS**
- **SAFE**
- **ARMAMENTS AND AMMO**
- **DOOR**
- **HEALTH OR CHEMS**
- **TERMINAL**
- **STEAMER TRUNK**
- **FUSION CORE**
- **POWER ARMOR**
- **REQUIRED READING**

Collectibles:
- **BOBBLEHEAD**
- **NUKA CHERRY**
- **MINI NUKE**
- **NUKA COLA QUANTUM**
- **HOLOTAPE**
- **A KEY**

N – Novice (Locked)
A – Advanced (Locked)
E – Expert (Locked)
M – Master (Locked)
T – Terminal required to unlock
KEY – Key or ID Card required to unlock
IN – Inaccessible
C – Chained
CB – Circuit Breaker
B – Button

# PRIMARY LOCATIONS

## [13.01] PICKMAN GALLERY     THREAT LEVELS 20+

- ARMAMENTS AND AMMO
- ARMAMENTS AND AMMO: TRUNK
- BOTTLECAPS
- COLLECTIBLE: BOBBLEHEAD: LOCKPICKING
- COLLECTIBLE: REQUIRED READING: ASTOUNDINGLY AWESOME TALES
- COLLECTIBLE: NUKA COLA QUANTUM (2)
- CRAFTING: CHEMISTRY STATION
- CRAFTING: COOKING STATION
- CRAFTING: WEAPONS WORKBENCH
- DANGER: MINES!
- DANGER: RADIATION (MILD)!
- DANGER: TRIPWIRES!
- DANGER: TURRETS!
- FACTION: RAIDERS
- FACTION: CHARACTER: PICKMAN
- FACTION: CHARACTER: SLAB
- HEALTH OR CHEMS
- QUEST START: PICKMAN'S GIFT (MISCELLANEOUS)
- QUEST VISIT: ART APPRECIATION* (GOODNEIGHBOR FREEFORM)
- UNIQUE ITEM: PICKMAN'S BLADE

FIG 13.01: PICKMAN GALLERY (INTERIOR)

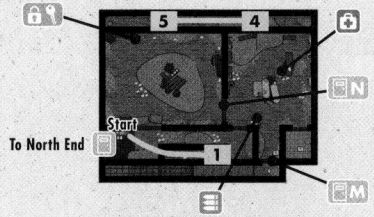

LEVEL 2

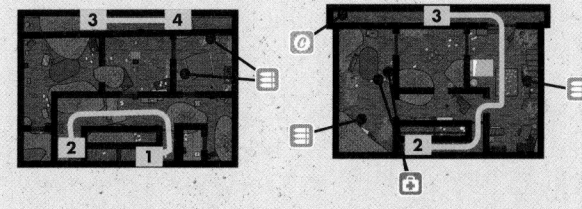

LEVEL 3     LEVEL 4

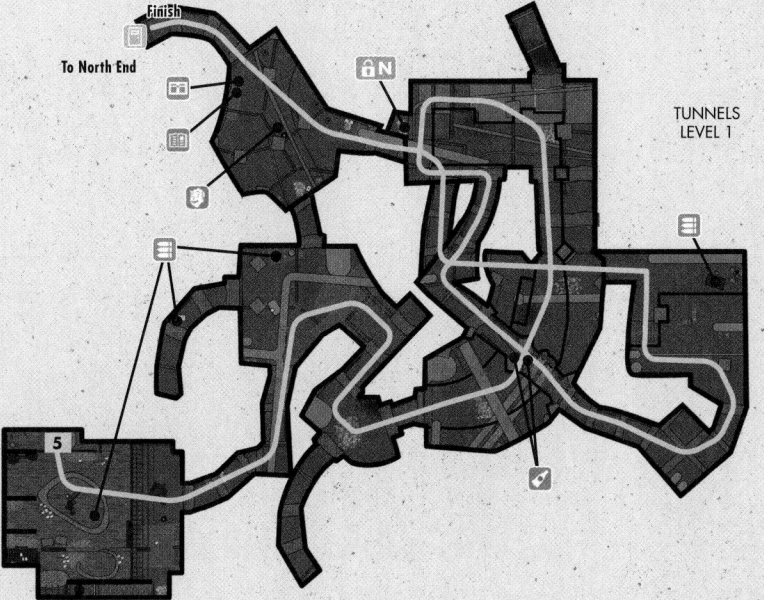

TUNNELS
LEVEL 1

## VAULT-TEC RECOMMENDED LOOT

**BOBBLEHEAD: LOCKPICKING**

**COLLECTIBLE: NUKA COLA QUANTUM (2)**

**REQUIRED READING: ASTOUNDINGLY AWESOME TALES**

**UNIQUE ITEM: PICKMAN'S BLADE**

A prolific serial killer stalks the alleys of North End and has recently been cornered in his lair by his prey of choice: Raiders. The rotting hulk of a row house Pickman calls home was chosen for its access to ancient subterranean smuggler tunnels beneath North End. He displays pictures of his victims on the walls.

Inside the dwelling, his blood-splattered daubing and corpse sculptures show the type of lunatic Pickman is. He has left a message to Jack in the front room and Pickman's Calling Card on many corpses. Fight your way to the end of the smuggler's sewer.

 **Quest: Pickman's Gift**

---

### 1. RECEIVE PICKMAN'S GIFT

You can choose to save or kill Pickman in the chamber where Slab the Raider has caught up with him. Either way, there's a key to find, which opens a hidden safe back in the first room of his row house, behind the picture named "Picnic for Stanley."

 **[13.02] OLD NORTH CHURCH**   THREAT LEVELS 25+

- ARMAMENTS AND AMMO+++
- ARMOR PART: FUSION CORE
- BOTTLECAPS+++
- COLLECTIBLE: NUKA CHERRY (2)
- COLLECTIBLE: REQUIRED READING: AWESOMELY ASTOUNDING TALES
- COMPANION: DEACON
- CRAFTING: ARMOR WORKBENCH
- CRAFTING: CHEMISTRY STATION
- CRAFTING: COOKING STATION
- CRAFTING: WEAPONS WORKBENCH (2)
- DANGER: EXPLOSIVE BARREL!
- DANGER: RADIATION (MILD)!
- FACTION: FERAL GHOULS
- FACTION: THE RAILROAD
- FACTION: CHARACTER: DESDEMONA
- FACTION: CHARACTER: DEACON
- FACTION: CHARACTER: DRUMMER BOY

- FACTION: CHARACTER: GLORY
- FACTION: CHARACTER: TINKER TOM
- FACTION: CHARACTER: DOCTOR CARRINGTON
- FACTION: CHARACTER: PAM
- HEALTH OR CHEMS+++
- QUEST START: TRADECRAFT (THE RAILROAD)
- QUEST START: UNDERGROUND UNDERCOVER (THE RAILROAD)
- QUEST START: OPERATION TICONDEROGA (THE RAILROAD)
- QUEST START: PRECIPICE OF WAR (THE RAILROAD)
- QUEST START: ROCKETS RED GLARE (THE RAILROAD)
- QUEST START: BURNING COVER (THE RAILROAD)
- QUEST START: ROAD TO FREEDOM (THE RAILROAD)
- QUEST START: BOSTON AFTER DARK (THE RAILROAD)
- QUEST START: MEMORY INTERRUPTED (THE RAILROAD)
- QUEST START: BUTCHER'S BILL 1 (THE RAILROAD RADIANT)
- QUEST START: BUTCHER'S BILL 2 (THE RAILROAD RADIANT)
- QUEST START: JACKPOT (THE RAILROAD RADIANT)
- QUEST START: MERCER STATION (THE RAILROAD RADIANT)
- QUEST START: CONCIERGE (THE RAILROAD RADIANT)

- QUEST START: WEATHERVANE (THE RAILROAD RADIANT)
- QUEST START: RANDOLPH SAFEHOUSE 1–6 (THE RAILROAD RADIANT)
- QUEST START: VARIABLE REMOVAL (THE RAILROAD RADIANT)
- QUEST START: TO THE MATTRESSES (THE RAILROAD RADIANT)
- QUEST START: LOST SOUL (THE RAILROAD RADIANT)
- QUEST START: A CLEAN EQUATION (THE RAILROAD RADIANT)
- QUEST START: HIGH GROUND (THE RAILROAD RADIANT)
- QUEST VISIT: ROAD TO FREEDOM (THE RAILROAD)
- QUEST VISIT: END OF THE LINE (THE INSTITUTE)
- QUEST VISIT: TACTICAL THINKING (BROTHERHOOD OF STEEL)
- SERVICES: TRADER (TINKER TOM)
- SERVICES: TRADER (DOCTOR CARRINGTON)
- UNIQUE ITEM: BALLISTIC WEAVE MK1-5 (APPAREL)
- UNIQUE ITEM: MAXIMUM CAPACITY ARMORED PIERCING SUBMACHINE GUN
- UNIQUE ITEM: RAILROAD STEALTH BOY
- UNIQUE ITEM: RAILWAY RIFLE

**FIG 13.02A: OLD NORTH CHURCH (INTERIOR)**

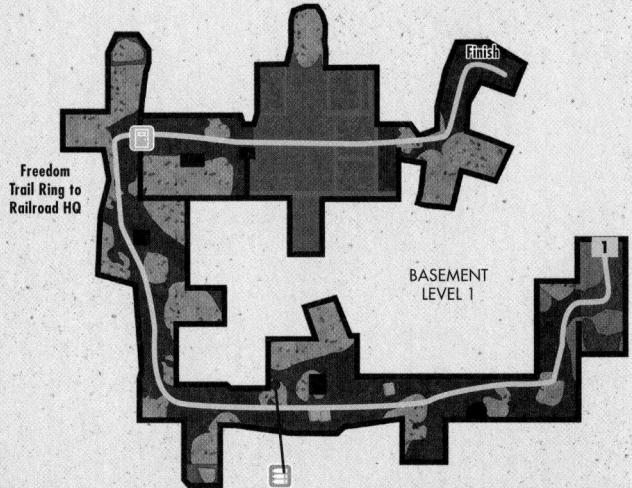

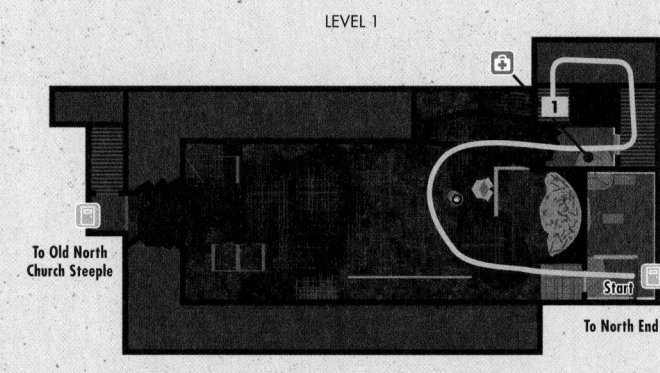

## FIG 13.02B RAILROAD HEADQUARTERS (INTERIOR)

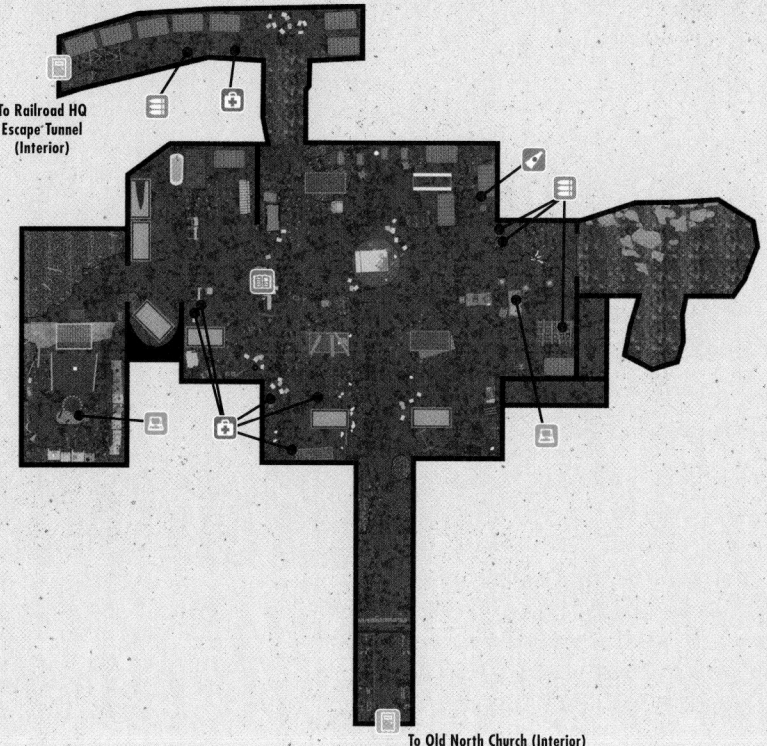

To Railroad HQ
Escape Tunnel
(Interior)

To Old North Church (Interior)

## FIG 13.02C: RAILROAD HQ ESCAPE TUNNEL (INTERIOR)

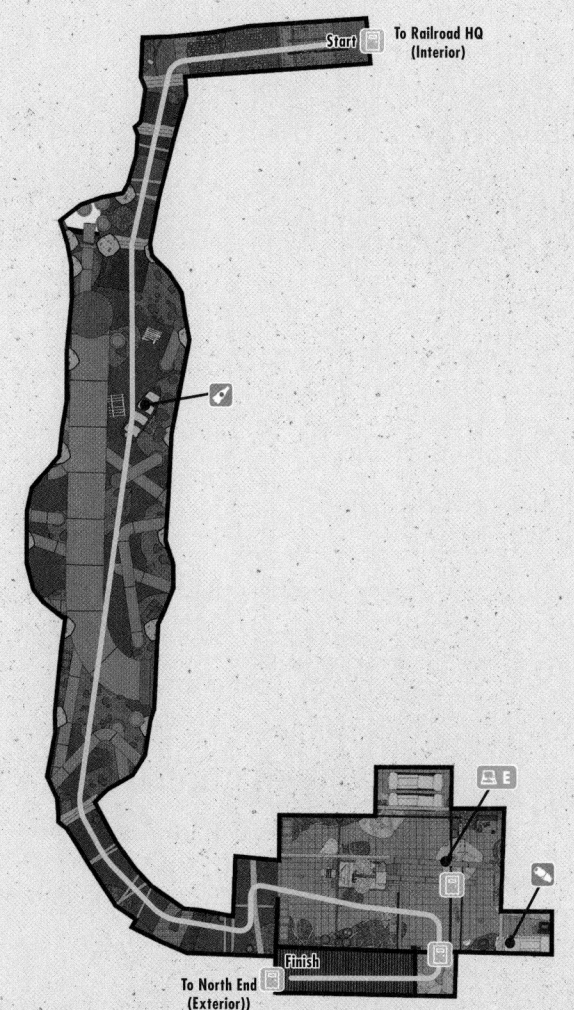

Start — To Railroad HQ
(Interior)

To North End
(Exterior))

Finish

Built in 1723, the Old North Church is the oldest standing church in Boston. Its 191-foot-tall steeple also makes it the tallest church in Boston. On the night of April 18, 1775, Lieutenant Colonel Smith marched with 700 British soldiers to Concord on a mission to disarm the rebels. Using a plan devised by Paul Revere, Robert Newman climbed to the top of this church and lit two lanterns to alert patriots that the Redcoats were coming up the Charles River. This inspired Longfellow's famous verse "One if by land, two if by sea." The battles of Lexington and Concord that followed would start the American Revolution.

This is part of the Freedom Trail. The number "1" is daubed on the circular ground plaque pointing at the letter "R." The insignia of the Railroad can be seen above the information plaque at the entrance.

Inside, fight off the Feral Ghouls. Access the Old North Church steeple from inside the structure. This allows you to collect some Caps and a sniper rifle and to look out across North End. Descend into the crypt. To solve the Railroad Trail Ring lock, spin it either clockwise or counterclockwise to spell out the word "RAILROAD." Head through the secret opening.

The Railroad Headquarters is the base of operations for this faction. It contains their senior members (two of whom offer excellent trading opportunities). There's a wall showing the "code" the Railroad uses for marking stashes and areas they've investigated. Be sure to utilize the escape tunnel, which allows quicker access to and from this location in the future. It brings you out by the river, northwest of the Old North Church.

# SECONDARY LOCATIONS

## [13.01] ROOFTOP APARTMENT (NORTH END)

– ARMAMENTS AND AMMO

Access this rooftop via the scaffold stairs (Secondary Location 13) just northwest of Old North Church, and cross the rooftops. This small apartment has some hoarded bric-a-brac.

## [13.02] NORTH END GRAVEYARD

– FACTION: FERAL GHOULS
– QUEST VISIT: THE GILDED GRASSHOPPER (SIDE)
– UNIQUE ITEM: SHEM DROWNE'S SWORD

Be sure to inspect the ancient gravestone in the northwest corner of this old, prewar graveyard, inhabited by North End's former residents.

## [13.03] RAILROAD HQ ESCAPE TUNNEL EXIT

– FACTION: RAILROAD
– FACTION: RAIDERS

Once you visit the Old North Church and wish to visit the Railroad faction, exit via this location (to unlock the chained door), and then return to this dilapidated warehouse and head back via the escape tunnel.

## [13.04] RAIDER COURTYARD (NORTH END)

– BOTTLECAPS
– FACTION: RAIDERS

With views of the U.S.S. Constitution to the north, this dockside courtyard is now part of the Raider territory extending into Pickman's Gallery to the south. Mooch around here to find a Caps stash between the large shipping containers. There's a ruined white brick building to the northeast with minimal loot and a rusting fire escape on the west side that allows roof access to this block.

## [13.05] HOT PIZZA PIE SHOP

– FACTION: RAIDERS

This wharfside pizza diner has more Raiders milling about. The roof terrace is inaccessible (unless you're using a jetpack). There's little here to entice a looter.

## [13.06] CRASHED VERTIBIRD (MILITARY BARGE)

– ARMAMENTS AND AMMO: TRUNK
– ARMOR PART: FUSION CORE
– ARMOR PART: POWER ARMOR (T-45)
– DANGER: RADIATION (MILD)!
– HEALTH OR CHEMS

A barge of military equipment has been stranded here for decades after the tugboat sank. Scavenge the area for a trunk (inside the blue container) and some Power Armor and a Fusion Core inside the locked cage. Use the terminal (Novice) to open the cage.

## [13.07] WHARFSIDE COTTAGE

– ARMAMENTS AND AMMO
– FACTION: RAIDER

You can enter the small cottage north of a once-quaint courtyard to see the contents of a cat lover's abode.

## [13.08] ROOFTOP LOUNGER

– CRAFTING: COOKING STATION
– HEALTH OR CHEMS

This rooftop rest spot offers great views and reasonable sniping opportunities. Access it via the rubble pile to the north.

## [13.09] SKYTRAM (NORTH END ELEVATED FREEWAY)

– ARMAMENTS AND AMMO: TRUNK
– FACTION: ROBOTS
– QUEST VISIT: WEATHERVANE (RAILROAD)

Look up at the freeway towering above this district to see the remains of the skytram. The cockpit has a trunk to ransack. However, you must access the skytram from the Garden Terrace, over in the Financial District.

## [13.10] MEAN PASTRIES

Once offering the best baked goods in town, this shop now offers a floor safe to pick (Expert) and an emaciated cat. Enter using either the north or south entrances.

## [13.11] PICKMAN'S EXIT

– QUEST VISIT: PICKMAN'S GIFT (MISCELLANEOUS)

An exit hatch links this narrow and ruined apartment to Pickman's Gallery to the north. The hatch requires a key to open, which is only available during the quest.

## [13.12] BOXING GYM

– ARMAMENTS AND AMMO
– HEALTH OR CHEMS

You're probably getting enough exercise, so use this place to scavenge for ammo and chems. There's a footlocker (Novice) and safe (Advanced) to unlock, and the smell of sweat still lingers.

## [13.13] SCAFFOLD STAIRS (NORTH END)

Just northwest of Old North Church, this allows access to the rooftops west and north of here. Head there if you need to escape foes on the ground, too.

## [13.14] BILLBOARD ALLEY

– ARMAMENTS AND AMMO: TRUNK
– FACTION: FERAL GHOULS

A small courtyard with a couple of ferals shambling about. Check the brick extension structure to the right of the GNN poster: Use the fallen tree to climb to the roof, and drop inside to access a steamer trunk. Then unlock the chained door.

## [13.15] RUINED BRICK APARTMENT (NORTH END)

Climb the rubble to reach the rooftops south of Old North Church, and pick the lock of the safe (Expert).

## [13.16] SUBWAY STATION (NORTH END)

– BOTTLECAPS
– HEALTH OR CHEMS

The subway station in this neighborhood has a small interior to search. Aside from the two cool customers facing a small (bloody) cage, there's chems and Caps behind the counter.

## [13.17] PAUL REVERE'S HOUSE

– FACTION: SUPER MUTANTS
– QUEST VISIT: ROAD TO FREEDOM (RAILROAD)

Built in 1680, this wooden building is the oldest structure in all of Boston. In 1770 this home was bought by famed patriot Paul Revere. He dwelled here with his family (including his 16 children) until 1800. Paul Revere was living here when he made his famous midnight ride to Lexington and Concord to warn Samuel Adams and John Hancock that Redcoats were en route to arrest them and seize the militia weaponry.

This is part of the Freedom Trail. The number "8" is daubed on the circular ground plaque pointing at the letter "D." This structure is mostly a shell, with a small Super Mutant encampment outside.

# ZONE 14: BOSTON COMMON

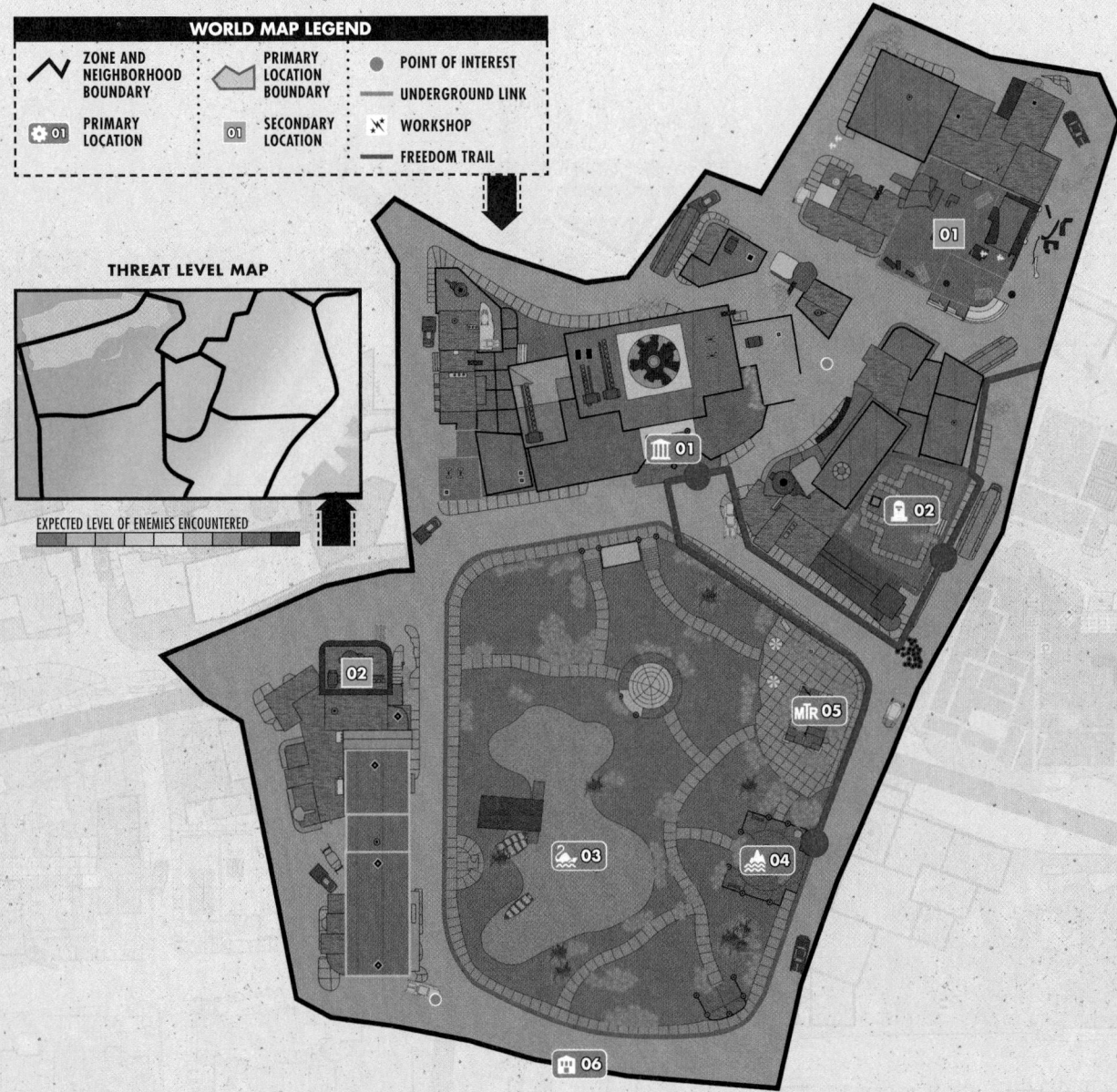

### WORLD MAP LEGEND

- ZONE AND NEIGHBORHOOD BOUNDARY
- PRIMARY LOCATION BOUNDARY
- POINT OF INTEREST
- PRIMARY LOCATION
- SECONDARY LOCATION
- UNDERGROUND LINK
- WORKSHOP
- FREEDOM TRAIL

**THREAT LEVEL MAP**

EXPECTED LEVEL OF ENEMIES ENCOUNTERED

The Freedom Trail starts here! Visit this once-idyllic park surrounded by ancient architectural prewar mansions and the remains of the State House, but be warned; there are numerous signs recommending you stay away from the pond at the park's west end. Perhaps it's better to start investigating the thin red line still visible along much of the sidewalks, a trail leading you through some of the most famous historical structures still (partly) standing. Surrounded by five other neighborhoods, Boston Common is at the nexus of the city south of the river.

## Primary Locations

- [14.01] MASSACHUSETTS STATE HOUSE
- [14.02] OLD GRANARY BURYING GROUND
- [14.03] SWAN'S POND
- [14.04] BOSTON COMMON
- [14.05] PARK STREET STATION (VAULT 114)
- [14.06] BOYLSTON CLUB

## Secondary Locations

- [14.01] SUPER MUTANT HOTEL SHELL
- [14.02] PROST BAR

## MAP LEGEND

| 13 — 20 OPTIMAL ROUTE | ⓒ BOTTLECAPS | 🏥 HEALTH OR CHEMS | 🗡 FUSION CORE | *Collectibles:* 🧠 BOBBLEHEAD | 🚀 NUKA COLA QUANTUM |
|---|---|---|---|---|---|
| | 🔒 SAFE | 💻 TERMINAL | 🛡 POWER ARMOR | 🍒 NUKA CHERRY | 📖 HOLOTAPE |
| ● AREA OF INTEREST | 🔫 ARMAMENTS AND AMMO | 📦 STEAMER TRUNK | 📕 REQUIRED READING | ☢ MINI NUKE | 🔑 A KEY |
| | 🚪 DOOR | | | | |

N – Novice (Locked)    E – Expert (Locked)    T – Terminal required to unlock    IN – Inaccessible    CB – Circuit Breaker
A – Advanced (Locked)    M – Master (Locked)    KEY – Key or ID Card required to unlock    C – Chained    B – Button

# PRIMARY LOCATIONS

## 🏛 [14.01] MASSACHUSETTS STATE HOUSE    THREAT LEVELS 20+

FIG 14.01: MASSACHUSETTS STATE HOUSE (INTERIOR)

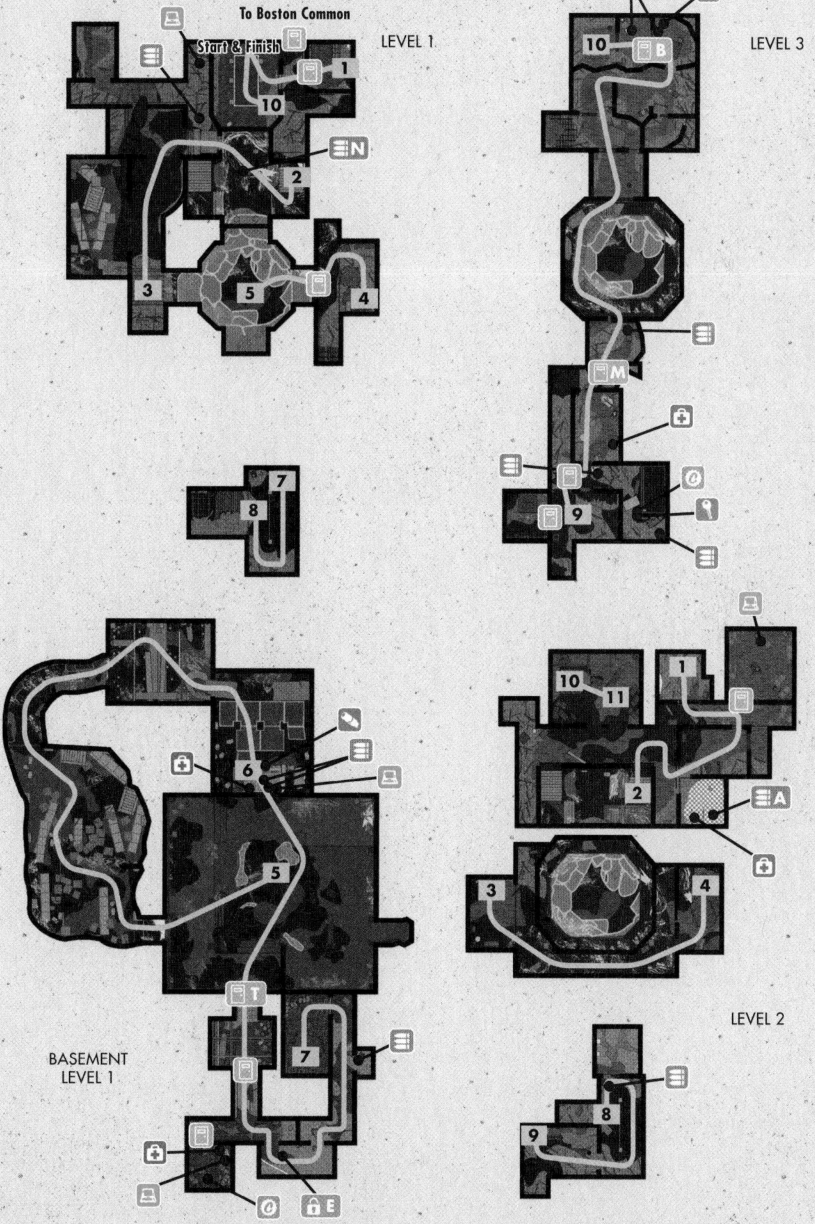

- ARMAMENTS AND AMMO
- ARMAMENTS AND AMMO: MINI NUKE
- ARMAMENTS AND AMMO: TRUNK
- ARMOR PART: FUSION CORE
- ARMOR PART: POWER ARMOR (RAIDER)
- BOTTLECAPS
- COLLECTIBLES: NUKA CHERRY
- CRAFTING: ARMOR WORKBENCH
- CRAFTING: COOKING STATION
- CRAFTING: WEAPONS WORKBENCH
- DANGER: EXPLOSIVE BARRELS!
- DANGER: GRENADES!
- DANGER: LONG DROP!
- DANGER: RADIATION (SEVERE)!
- DANGER: MINES!
- DANGER: TRIPWIRE!
- DANGER: TURRETS!
- FACTION: MIRELURKS
- FACTION: RAIDERS
- HEALTH AND CHEMS
- QUEST VISIT: ROAD TO FREEDOM (THE RAILROAD)

### VAULT-TEC RECOMMENDED LOOT ☢

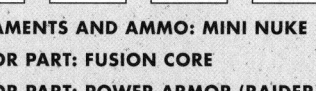

ARMAMENTS AND AMMO: MINI NUKE
ARMOR PART: FUSION CORE
ARMOR PART: POWER ARMOR (RAIDER)
COLLECTIBLE: NUKA CHERRY

**MAP**

**ZONE 14**

NEIGHBORHOOD:
BOSTON
COMMON

The "new" state house was completed in 1798 to house the government of Massachusetts State. The land selected was originally John Hancock's cow pastures. The first dome was constructed of wooden shingles and covered in copper smelted by Paul Revere. The state government used this building continuously until the formation of the Thirteen Commonwealths in 1969.

This is part of the Freedom Trail. The number "4" is daubed on the circular ground plaque pointing at the letter "L." Outside, one corner of the structure has collapsed, allowing lock-fiddlers the chance to open a wall safe (Novice).

Inside, the place is a messy maze of ruined history and blocked off corridors. Follow the optimal route on the nearby map to avoid palpitations, and beware of sizable threats from Mirelurks and Raiders vying for power in this location. Remember to look for the Atrium Key inside the metal box as you climb to the top floor and engage Raiders for the first time (the box is atop the stairs near the turret). Don't forget to take the rustic lift down to exit.

##  [14.02] OLD GRANARY BURYING GROUND    THREAT LEVELS 20+

– ARMAMENTS AND AMMO          – QUEST VISIT: ROAD TO FREEDOM (THE RAILROAD)
– FACTION: FERAL GHOUL

This burial ground was established in 1660, making it the oldest surviving burial ground in Boston. Many famous Revolutionary War heroes were buried here, including John Hancock, Paul Revere, Samuel Adams, and the victims of the Boston Massacre. In 2031, after the tragic death of Emilia Butler, the city council voted unanimously to have her remains interred here.

This is part of the Freedom Trail. The number "2" is daubed on the circular ground plaque pointing at the letter "A." It is overrun by ferals. The adjacent church is sealed and cannot be entered.

##  [14.03] SWAN'S POND    THREAT LEVELS 20+

– ARMAMENTS AND AMMO          – FACTION: SUPER MUTANT
– ARMAMENTS AND AMMO: TRUNK   – FACTION: CHARACTER: SWAN
– BOTTLECAPS                   – UNIQUE ITEM: FURIOUS POWER FIST
– DANGER: RADIATION (SEVERE)!

### VAULT-TEC RECOMMENDED LOOT

  UNIQUE ITEM: FURIOUS POWER FIST

The focal point of the Boston Common neighborhood since the early 1600s, the pond once featured ornate swan boats for visitors and citizens to take for a trip. This location is highly dangerous; even Raiders avoid the Common. Be sure to search the boathouse for five notes to understand more. Look for warnings about Swan's Pond around Boston Common.

##  [14.04] BOSTON COMMON    THREAT LEVELS 20+

– COLLECTIBLE: REQUIRED READING: GROGNAK THE BARBARIAN
– DANGER: RADIATION (MILD)!
– FACTION: SUPER MUTANT
– QUEST VISIT: ROAD TO FREEDOM (THE RAILROAD)

### VAULT-TEC RECOMMENDED LOOT

  REQUIRED READING: GROGNAK THE BARBARIAN

Established in 1634, Boston Common started as a communal grazing ground for cattle before it was made a public park (the oldest in the country). In the year before the Revolutionary War, a thousand Redcoats camped on the Common. The Redcoat brigades that marched on Lexington and Concord departed from this very ground.

Park Street Station is accessed to the northeast of this common. This is also the start of the Freedom Trail. On the east side, at the Protectron tour bot and fountain, the number "7" is daubed on the circular ground plaque pointing at the letter "A." Follow the red stripe along the ground from here to continue the specified quest.

There are numerous signs warning of the dangers of Swan's Pond. Aside from a Railroad warning and numerous verbal graffiti warnings, look for:

– A TORN NOTE ON KATH'S BODY, ON THE NORTHEAST SIDE OF THE POND.
– A TORN LETTER ON MIKAIL'S BODY, BY THE SOUTHEAST ENTRANCE TO THE COMMONS.
– A FUGITIVES' HOLOTAPE CLUTCHED IN THE SKELETAL HAND BY THE STATUE PLINTH, ON THE WEST SIDE OF THE POND.

FIG 14.05A: PARK STREET STATION (INTERIOR)

- ARMAMENTS AND AMMO
- COLLECTIBLE: BOBBLEHEAD: SPEECH
- COLLECTIBLE: REQUIRED READING: ASTOUNDINGLY AWESOME TALES
- BOTTLECAPS++
- COLLECTIBLE: NUKA COLA QUANTUM
- DANGER: GRENADES!
- DANGER: TRIPWIRE!
- FACTION: TRIGGERMEN
- FACTION: CHARACTER: DARLA
- FACTION: CHARACTER: DINO

- FACTION: CHARACTER: NICK VALENTINE
- FACTION: CHARACTER: SKINNY MALONE
- HEALTH OR CHEMS
- QUEST VISIT: UNLIKELY VALENTINE (MAIN)

LEVEL 1

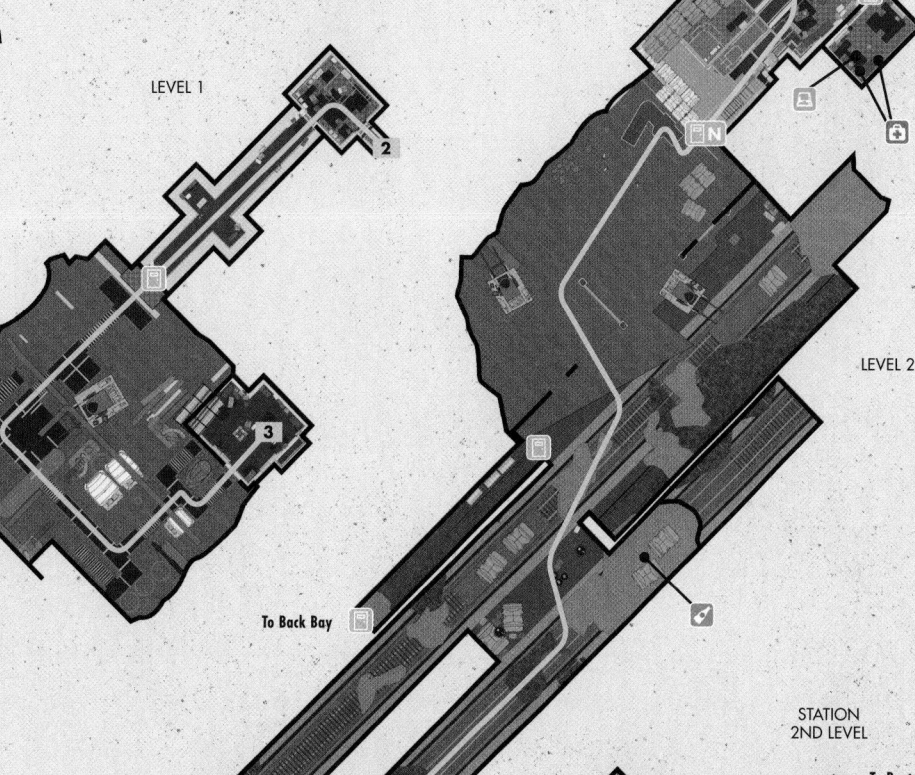

LEVEL 2

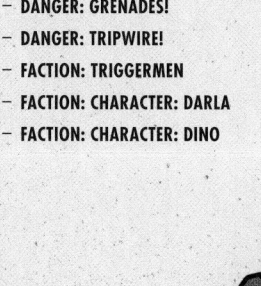

BASEMENT
LEVEL 1

To Vault 114

To Back Bay

STATION
2ND LEVEL

To Boston
Common

Start

**MAP**

**ZONE 14**

NEIGHBORHOOD:
BOSTON
COMMON

**FIG 14.05B: VAULT 114 (INTERIOR)**

To Park Street Station
LEVEL 2
Start
1
3
4
LEVEL 1
5
N
4
LEVEL 4
M
A
7
6
5
N
6
N
LEVEL 3
N
T
2
N
1
3
7
LEVEL 5
Finish
KEY
To Park Street Station (Interior)

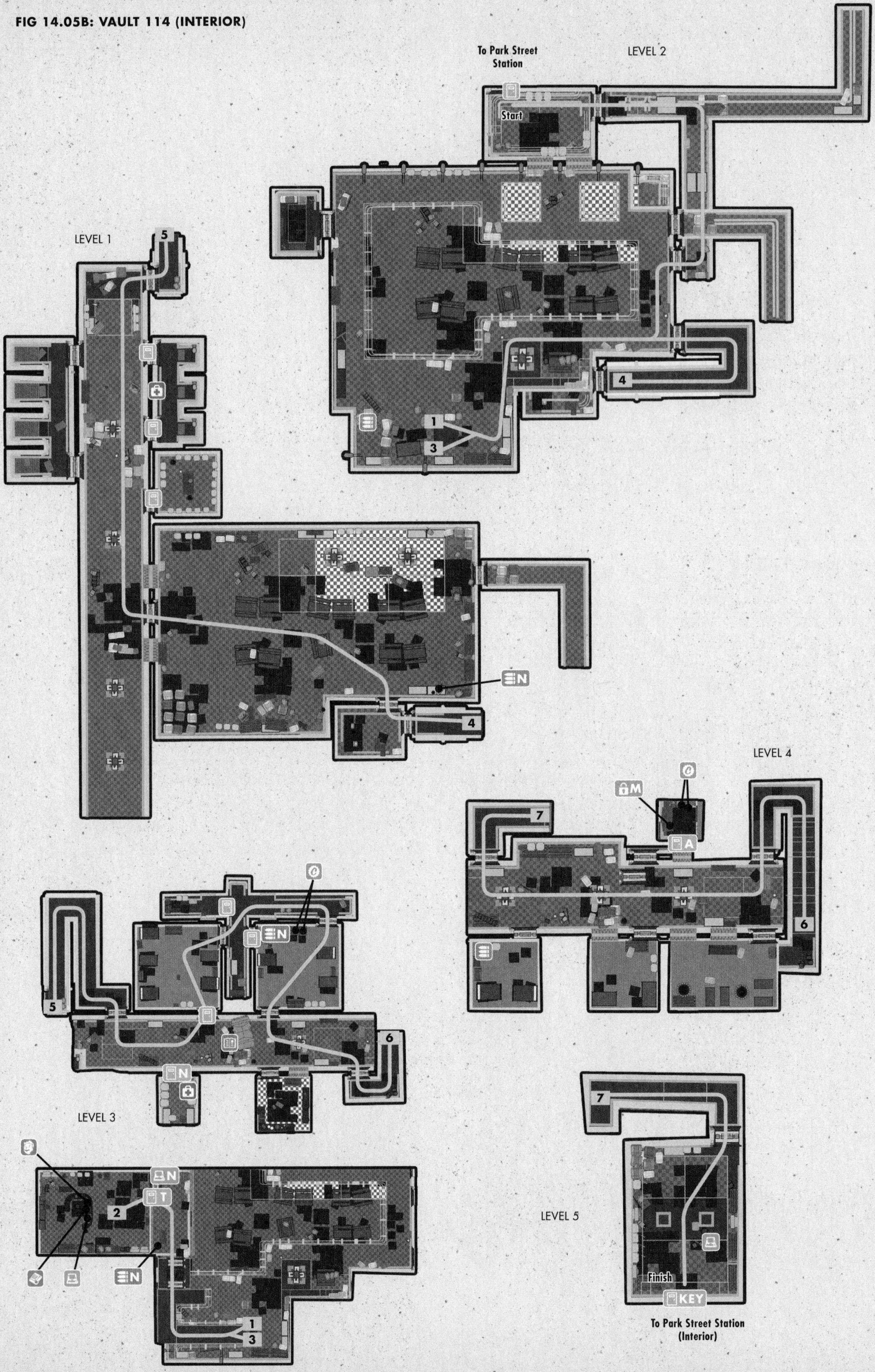

**BOBBLEHEAD: SPEECH**

**COLLECTIBLE: NUKA COLA QUANTUM**

**REQUIRED READING: ASTOUNDINGLY AWESOME TALES**

This location is not fully accessible unless the specified quest is active.

This has been identified as a low-traffic subway stop, and Vault-Tec industries is pleased to announce the purchase of this location for a new Vault, designated #114. Lower excavation costs, usage of existing tunneling equipment, and the repurposing of train cars into vault rooms should expedite the completion of this location.

After years of this location sitting half finished when the bombs fell, a local gang of Triggermen under the leadership of Skinny Malone chanced upon here; the numerous digging machines could be put to use in their nefarious operations.

Dino has the overseer door password. Nick Valentine is the only one who can open the door at the north end of the corridor on Level 1.

Along with the Bobblehead, there are three Holotapes (Vault 114 interviews) to pick up by the Vault-Tec terminal in Valentine's prison room. For best results, follow Valentine from the overseer's room (where you found him) to the exit, which can only be opened by him.

 **[14.06] BOYLSTON CLUB** THREAT LEVELS 20+

**- ARMAMENTS AND AMMO**

A ritzy social club for the most discerning of gentlemen, the small, deserted upper interior can be explored and the fate of the club members determined.

**FIG 14.06: THE BOYLSTON CLUB (INTERIOR)**

LEVEL 2

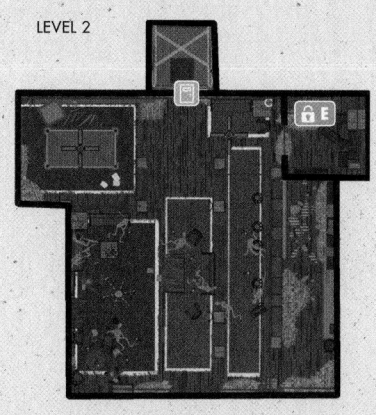

LEVEL 1

To Boston Common
(Exterior

# SECONDARY LOCATIONS

## [14.01] SUPER MUTANT HOTEL SHELL

- ARMAMENTS AND AMMO
- ARMAMENTS AND AMMO: TRUNK
- DANGER: LONG DROP!
- FACTION: SUPER MUTANTS

The shell of an old hotel is used to dump and carve up enemies of the Super Mutant. As one might imagine, there's blood everywhere. But there's also stairs up to the skeletal upper floors and precarious metal beams to cross to reach a steamer trunk. Approach from the ground or the fire escape to the north.

## [14.02] PROST BAR

- ARMAMENTS AND AMMO: TRUNK

Though this is still the place to come for a Gwinnett Lager, the patrons at the Prost Bar aren't as rowdy as they once were. Check the "Employees Only" office for a real baseball fan's trunk.

# ZONE 15: NEIGHBORHOOD: FINANCIAL DISTRICT

★

THREAT LEVEL MAP

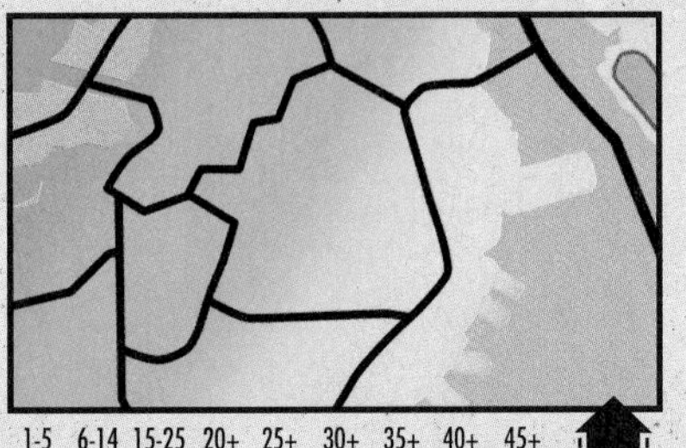

1-5 6-14 15-25 20+ 25+ 30+ 35+ 40+ 45+
**EXPECTED LEVEL OF ENEMIES ENCOUNTERED**

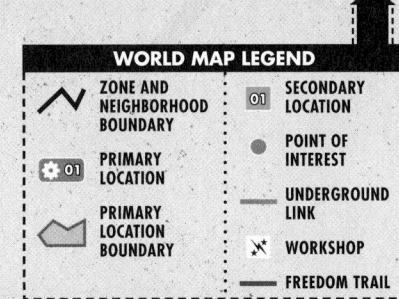

**WORLD MAP LEGEND**

ZONE AND NEIGHBORHOOD BOUNDARY

☼ 01 PRIMARY LOCATION

◢ PRIMARY LOCATION BOUNDARY

01 SECONDARY LOCATION

● POINT OF INTEREST

UNDERGROUND LINK

⚒ WORKSHOP

FREEDOM TRAIL

The Freedom Trail continues here! However, most of it is either covered in blood or the tons of rubble and mangled skyscraper metal from the numerous fallen structures. Simply put, this neighborhood is a disaster; structures have many holes, and the height of the skyscrapers dotted around the main thoroughfare of Congress Street means you're just as likely to fall to your death as succumb to Super Mutant or Gunner gunfire. As you're surrounded on all sides by other neighborhoods, it's sometimes difficult to know where you are, so study the maps presented here and understand that some of the locations of importance may be above or below you. Take in the sights steadily and methodically, including Boston's tallest structure, the immense Mass Fusion building.

**Primary Locations**
- [15.01] MASS FUSION BUILDING
- [15.02] OLD CORNER BOOKSTORE
- [15.03] HAYMARKET MALL
- [15.04] GARDEN TERRACE
- [15.05] FANEUIL HALL
- [15.06] GOODNEIGHBOR
- [15.07] FALLEN SKYBRIDGE
- [15.08] POSTAL SQUARE

**Secondary Locations**
- [15.01] WEATHERBY INVESTMENT TRUST
- [15.02] CONGRESS STREET GARAGE
- [15.03] BUS OF BONES
- [15.04] COMMONWEALTH BANK
- [15.05] THE SNOOZING SKELETON
- [15.06] ELEVATED ROAD (WEST ACCESS)
- [15.07] ELEVATED RAIDER CAMP (FINANCIAL DISTRICT)
- [15.08] ELEVATED ROAD (CENTRAL ACCESS)
- [15.09] RAILROAD HIDEOUT (FINANCIAL DISTRICT)
- [15.10] 35 COURT
- [15.11] ROOFTOP HIDEAWAY (FINANCIAL DISTRICT)
- [15.12] PEDESTRIAN UNDERPASS
- [15.13] PARKING GARAGE AND RAIDER ROOFTOPS
- [15.14] WATER STREET APARTMENTS

## MAP LEGEND

| 13 ——— 20 OPTIMAL ROUTE | | |
| --- | --- | --- |
| ● AREA OF INTEREST | | |

- BOTTLECAPS
- SAFE
- ARMAMENTS AND AMMO
- DOOR
- HEALTH OR CHEMS
- TERMINAL
- STEAMER TRUNK
- FUSION CORE
- POWER ARMOR
- REQUIRED READING

**Collectibles:**
- BOBBLEHEAD
- NUKA CHERRY
- MINI NUKE
- NUKA COLA QUANTUM
- HOLOTAPE
- A KEY

N – Novice (Locked)        E – Expert (Locked)        T – Terminal required to unlock        IN – Inaccessible        CB – Circuit Breaker
A – Advanced (Locked)    M – Master (Locked)      KEY – Key or ID Card required to unlock    C – Chained                  B – Button

# PRIMARY LOCATIONS

## [15.01] MASS FUSION BUILDING

THREAT LEVELS 20+

Before the war, Mass Fusion was the primary power supplier to Boston and most of the Commonwealth. It is the tallest building in Boston. With the proceeds from an enormously lucrative line of fusion wells, engines, and cores, this structure—their corporate headquarters—was built. Since the war, the structure has fallen into disrepair, though the reactor level hasn't yet been breached.

At ground level, Gunners fight through the rubble-strewn streets. Should you arrive on the roof (when the quest is active), prepare to fight your chosen rival faction, and hunt down a few choice items (including a Nuka Cherry). Beware the oil, gas leaks, and explosive barrels, or use them to your advantage.

- ARMAMENTS AND AMMO+
- ARMAMENTS AND AMMO: MINI NUKE
- ARMAMENTS AND AMMO: TRUNK (4)
- ARMOR PART: FUSION CORE
- BOTTLECAPS
- COLLECTIBLE: BOBBLEHEAD: STRENGTH
- COLLECTIBLE: HOLOTAPE: OSLOW'S OFFICE RECORDING
- COLLECTIBLE: NUKA CHERRY
- COLLECTIBLE: REQUIRED READING: TESLA SCIENCE
- CRAFTING: ARMOR WORKBENCH
- CRAFTING: CHEMISTRY STATION
- CRAFTING: WEAPONS WORKBENCH
- DANGER: CAN CHIMES!
- DANGER: ESCAPING GAS!
- DANGER: EXPLOSIVE BARRELS!
- DANGER: LONG DROP!
- DANGER: MINES!
- DANGER: OIL!
- DANGER: RADIATION (SEVERE)!
- DANGER: TENSION TRIGGER!
- DANGER: TESLA ARC!
- FACTION: BROTHERHOOD OF STEEL (QUEST ACTIVE)
- FACTION: GUNNERS (NO QUEST ACTIVE)
- FACTION: ROBOTS (QUEST ACTIVE)
- FACTION: SYNTHS (INSTITUTE) (QUEST ACTIVE)
- HEALTH OR CHEMS+
- QUEST VISIT: MASS FUSION (THE INSTITUTE)
- QUEST VISIT: SPOILS OF WAR (BROTHERHOOD OF STEEL)
- UNIQUE ITEM: FREEFALL ARMOR RIGHT LEG (APPAREL)
- UNIQUE ITEM: FREEFALL ARMOR LEFT LEG (APPAREL)

### VAULT-TEC RECOMMENDED LOOT

**ARMAMENTS AND AMMO: MINI NUKE**
**ARMOR PART: FUSION CORE**
**BOBBLEHEAD: STRENGTH**
**COLLECTIBLE: NUKA CHERRY**
**REQUIRED READING: TESLA SCIENCE**

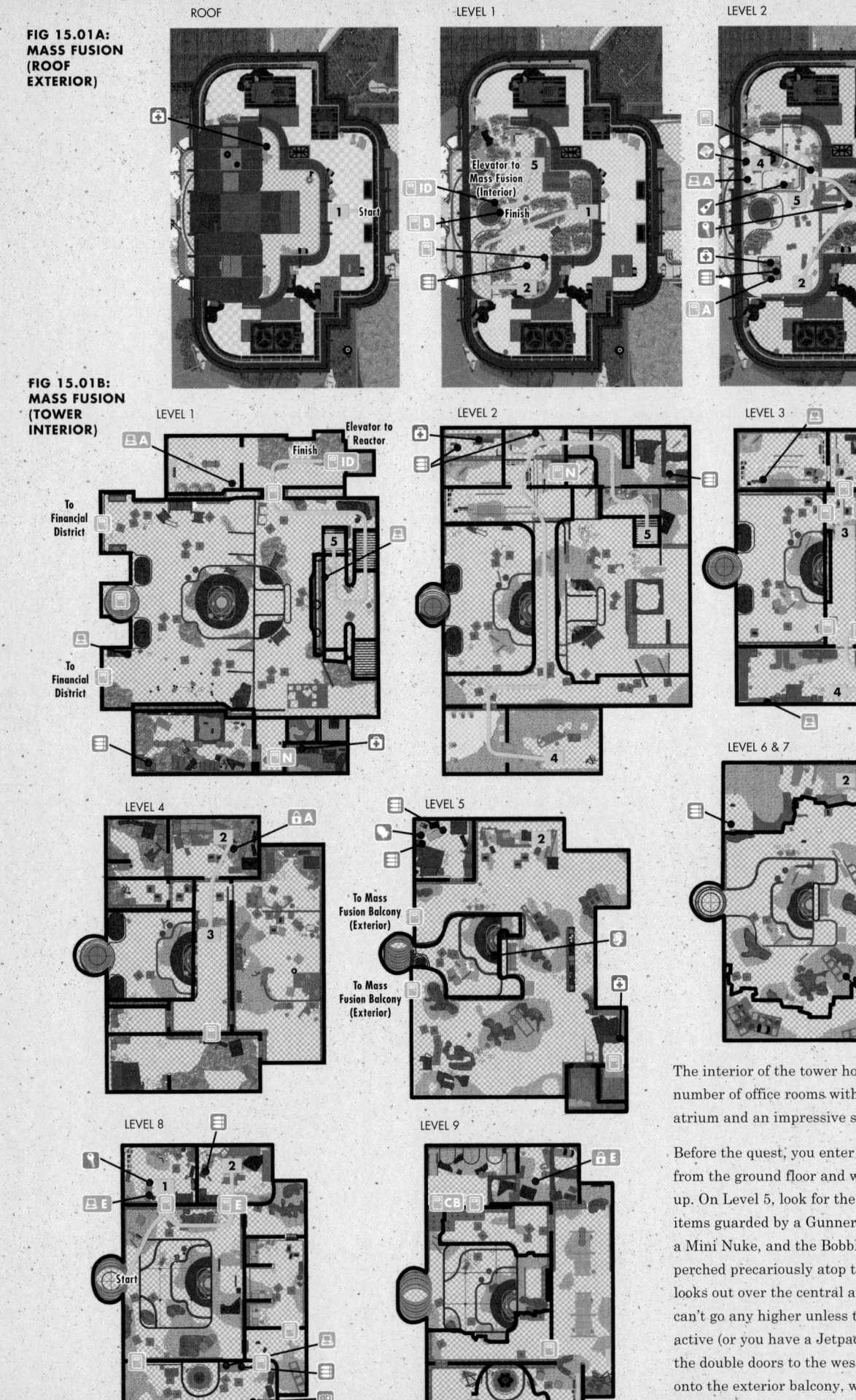

## FIG 15.01A: MASS FUSION (ROOF EXTERIOR)

**ROOF**

1  Start

**LEVEL 1**

Elevator to Mass Fusion (Interior)

Finish

5

1

2

**LEVEL 2**

4

A

5

3

2

A

## FIG 15.01B: MASS FUSION (TOWER INTERIOR)

**LEVEL 1**

A

Finish

Elevator to Reactor

ID

To Financial District

5

To Financial District

N

**LEVEL 2**

N

5

4

**LEVEL 3**

N

3

4

**LEVEL 4**

A

2

3

**LEVEL 5**

To Mass Fusion Balcony (Exterior)

To Mass Fusion Balcony (Exterior)

2

**LEVEL 6 & 7**

2

**LEVEL 8**

Start

1

E

2

E

**LEVEL 9**

E

CB

The interior of the tower houses a huge number of office rooms within a central atrium and an impressive sky elevator.

Before the quest, you enter Mass Fusion from the ground floor and work your way up. On Level 5, look for the main trunk of items guarded by a Gunner commander, a Mini Nuke, and the Bobblehead, perched precariously atop the statue that looks out over the central atrium. You can't go any higher unless the quest is active (or you have a Jetpack), so take the double doors to the west to exit out onto the exterior balcony, where you can fast-travel away. Or take the elevator on this level back down to the ground floor.

If you are here on the quest and have access to the upper levels, be sure to clear them of the scavengeable items as shown on the maps. Descend through the building, using the Executive ID Card you found on the roof to access the elevator to the Reactor Level. Come back with a jetpack, and you can reach some additional rewards on the highest levels of the building, which are otherwise inaccessible. These include a set of Freefall Armor for your legs inside the office of Jack Rockford on the 28th floor. Can you find it?

**FIG 15.01C: MASS FUSION REACTOR LEVEL**

REACTOR LEVEL
(UPPER FLOOR)

REACTOR LEVEL
(UPPER FLOOR)

From Mass
Fusion (Tower
Interior)

Start & Finish

This location cannot be reached unless one of the quests is active. Make sure to grab a Hazmat Suit from the locker room or one of the control rooms before entering the decontamination arches—the radiation level in the Reactor Chamber is extreme. If you can manage the (Master) lock, use the terminals in the Control Room and the side office to disable the security system, or prepare for a difficult fight with robots on your way out.

One steamer trunk can be found on the walkway above the decontamination hall. Another is submerged in the reactor room itself-- even with a hazmat suit, the radiation here is bad.

Power. People. Perfect. Mass Fusion

We Keep Boston Running

- ARMAMENTS AND AMMO
- ARMAMENTS AND AMMO: TRUNK
- BOTTLECAPS
- COLLECTIBLE: NUKA COLA QUANTUM

- DANGER: LONG DROP!
- FACTION: FERAL GHOULS
- HEALTH OR CHEMS
- QUEST VISIT: ROAD TO FREEDOM
  (THE RAILROAD)

**VAULT-TEC RECOMMENDED LOOT**

 **COLLECTIBLE: NUKA COLA QUANTUM**

**FIG 15.02: OLD CORNER BOOKSTORE (INTERIOR)**

LEVEL 1

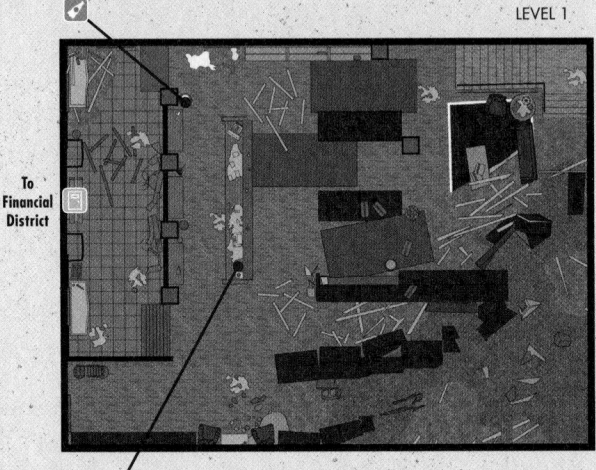

To Financial District

LEVEL 2

The Old Corner Bookstore was originally built as an apothecary after the devastating Great Fire of 1711. Originally the land belonged to Anne Hutchinson, the controversial puritan who was excommunicated and banished from Massachusetts for her "heretical" beliefs and sermons. During the mid-nineteenth century, the Old Corner Bookstore was the home of the leading American publisher Ticknor and Fields. They published the works of such luminaries as Charles Dickens, Ralph Waldo Emerson, Nathaniel Hawthorne, Henry Wadsworth Longfellow, Harriet Beecher Stowe, and Henry David Thoreau. Many of those were frequent visitors to this site.

The Old Corner Bookstore is a historic site on the Freedom Trail. The number "3" is daubed on the circular ground plaque pointing at the letter "I." The interior is mostly deserted. The exterior of the bookstore is cluttered with rubble and marauding ferals, along with encroaching Raiders and Super Mutants fighting for territory and food. However, don't miss the most difficult-to-find steamer trunk around; it's in the ruins of the skyscraper that was built atop of the bookstore.

Head east, following the Freedom Trail, then down into the Congress Street Garage [S15.02], where you can take an elevator up to the middle of the ruined building. Climb out onto the overpass, then leap from the overpass Leap from the overpass to a curved brown metal wall plate. Look southwest, then leap across and up to the remains of a tiled floor. Congratulations: jump northwest, and you should land on the roof you've attempted to reach, and find the contents of the trunk, close to some upturned desks.

## [15.03] HAYMARKET MALL

THREAT LEVELS 20+

- ARMAMENTS AND AMMO
- BOTTLECAPS
- CRAFTING: ARMOR WORKBENCH
- CRAFTING: COOKING STATION
- CRAFTING: WEAPONS WORKBENCH
- DANGER: EXPLOSIVE BARRELS!
- DANGER: LONG DROP!
- DANGER: TURRETS!
- FACTION: RAIDER
- FACTION: ROBOT (PROTECTRON)
- HEALTH OR CHEMS

The main entrance to this old skyscraper has been commandeered by Raiders. Inspect the rickety walkways here for some ammo. The eastern part of this stronghold—under the ruined freeway overpass and Primary Location: Garden Terrace—has a high wall and scaffolding. Climb it halfway until the ramps stop. To reach the roof, you need to enter the mall.

**FIG 15.03: HAYMARKET MALL (INTERIOR)**

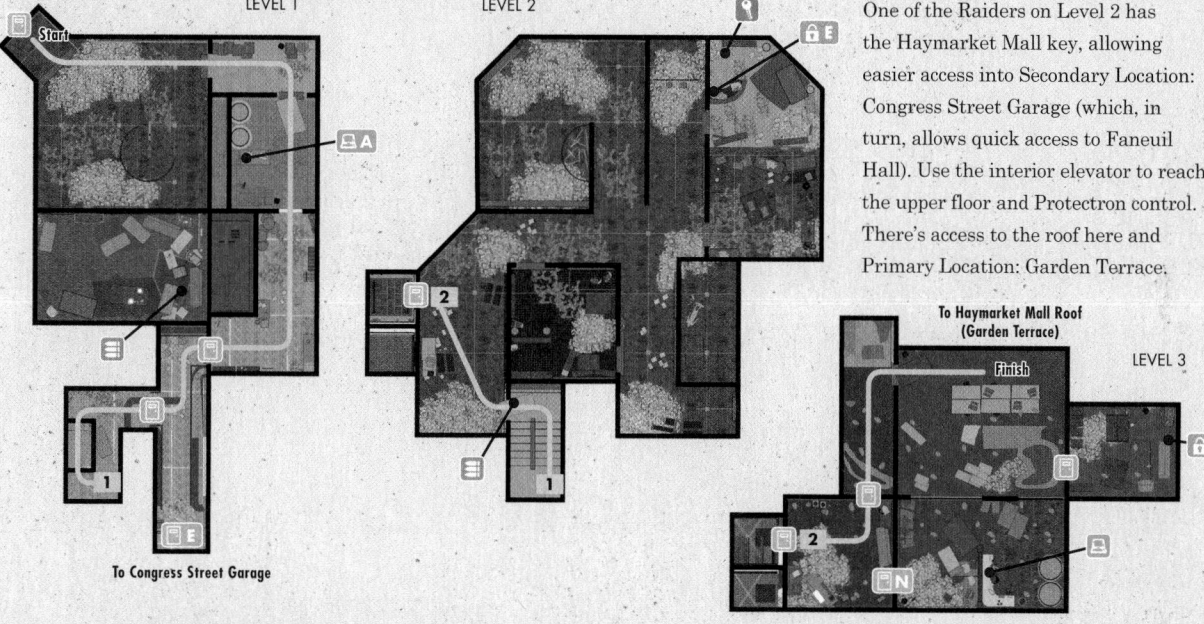

One of the Raiders on Level 2 has the Haymarket Mall key, allowing easier access into Secondary Location: Congress Street Garage (which, in turn, allows quick access to Faneuil Hall). Use the interior elevator to reach the upper floor and Protectron control. There's access to the roof here and Primary Location: Garden Terrace.

MAP
ZONE 15

NEIGHBORHOOD: FINANCIAL DISTRICT

## [15.04] GARDEN TERRACE

THREAT LEVELS 20+

- ARMAMENTS AND AMMO+
- COLLECTIBLE: NUKA COLA QUANTUM
- DANGER: LONG DROP!
- FACTION: DEATHCLAW
- FACTION: ROBOT (PROTECTRON)
- HEALTH OR CHEMS
- QUEST: WEATHERVANE (THE RAILROAD)

To reach the Garden Terrace, climb through the interior of Primary Location: Haymarket Mall, or leap down from the freeway that passes over it.

There's a reason Raiders don't venture up to this roof terrace. After you deal with any rabid wildlife, inspect the ruined corner to the northeast; open the steamer trunk, then use the elevator or drop through the holes where a sky train has hit the structure. Keep descending the structure to discover a safe (Advanced). Use the elevator to ascend back up.

For an even more precarious adventure, descend the scaffolding and enter the crashed sky train hanging below. Open the suitcases and the steamer trunk at the northwest end, guarded by the Protectron. The "plank" and open window is an optional location to place MILA during the specified quest.

**VAULT-TEC RECOMMENDED LOOT**

COLLECTIBLE: NUKA COLA QUANTUM

**HELPFUL HINT** from Vault Boy! *Did You Know?*

DID YOU KNOW THERE ARE SEVERAL OUT-OF-THE-WAY ITEMS TO GATHER, LIKE THE NUKA COLA QUANTUM CLUTCHED BY A SKELETON ON THE EXTERIOR ROOF (SOUTHWEST OF TERRACE)? FIND HIM ON THE BUILDING WITH THE "LIFE IS A RACE . . . WIN!" POSTER. ACCESS USING THE JETPACK, BOOSTING UP AND LANDING ON THE RED GIRDERS OF THE DEMOLISHED SKYSCRAPER TO THE SOUTH.

- ARMAMENTS AND AMMO
- ARMOR PART: FUSION CORE
- COLLECTIBLE: REQUIRED READING: LIVE & LOVE
- CRAFTING: CHEMISTRY STATION
- DANGER: CAN CHIMES!
- DANGER: GRENADES!
- DANGER: LONG DROP!

- FACTION: SUPER MUTANT
- HEALTH OR CHEMS
- QUEST START: MISCELLANEOUS
  (THE TREASURES OF JAMAICA PLAIN)
- QUEST VISIT: THE GILDED GRASSHOPPER (SIDE)
- UNIQUE ITEM: GILDED GRASSHOPPER

**FIG 15.05: FANEUIL HALL (INTERIOR)**

LEVEL 1

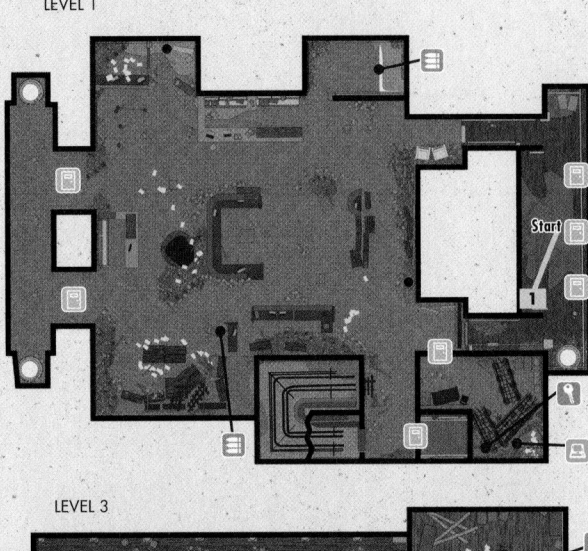

LEVEL 2

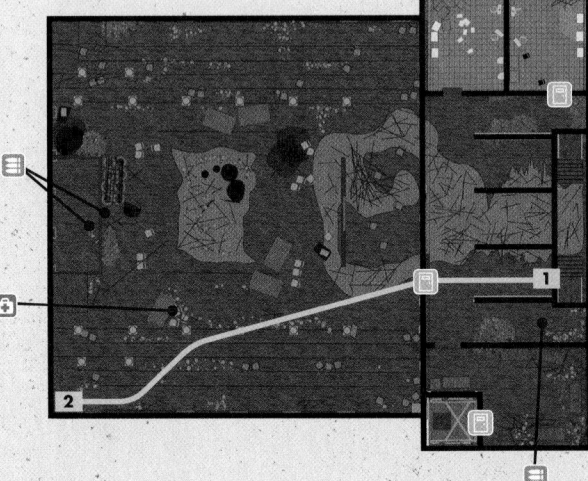

LEVEL 3

LEVEL 4

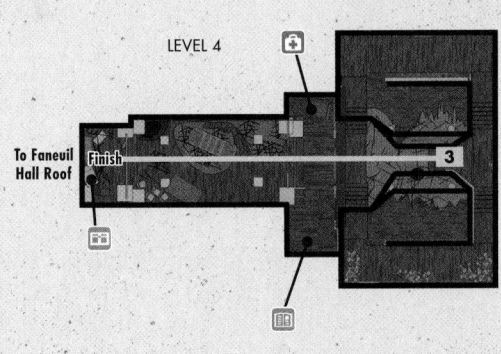

## VAULT-TEC RECOMMENDED LOOT ☢

**REQUIRED READING: LIVE & LOVE**
**UNIQUE ITEM: GILDED GRASSHOPPER**

Donated to the city of Boston in 1742 by French merchant Peter Faneuil, Faneuil Hall was a commercial hub in colonial Massachusetts. It played a notable role in the American Revolution. Protests against the British Sugar and Stamp Acts that began here led to the doctrine of "no taxation without representation." Later meetings were held here that culminated in the Boston Tea Party. Many of the Founding Fathers met here or gave speeches here (notably Samuel Adams), leading to the building's nickname, "the Cradle of Liberty."

This is part of the Freedom Trail. The number "5" is daubed on the circular ground plaque pointing at the letter "R." The exterior offers two entrances—the two main front doors and the three rear doors to the east. There is side scaffolding that doesn't reach all the way to the roof (look for a Fusion Core and ammo on the way up). Super Mutants are an ever-present threat.

The basement gift shop is overrun with bloody mutant types. If you have the time, peruse a magazine shelf for information on Easy City Downs, as well as the Treasures of Jamaica Plain (then visit that location for more information). Beware of traps and Super Mutants as you scale the interior. Take a ladder to the roof, where you'll find a strange Gilded Grasshopper, which is part of the specified quest.

- ARMAMENTS AND AMMO+++
- ARMAMENTS AND AMMO: MINI NUKE
- ARMAMENTS AND AMMO: MINI NUKE (FAT MAN)
- ARMAMENTS AND AMMO: TRUNK (3)
- BOTTLECAPS+++
- COLLECTIBLE: HOLOTAPE: FRED ALLEN'S PASSWORD
- COLLECTIBLE: HOLOTAPE: GWINNETT PILS RECIPE
- COLLECTIBLE: HOLOTAPE:
  HOTEL REGISTRY PASSWORD
- COLLECTIBLE: HOLOTAPE: JOIN THE RAILROAD (3)
- COLLECTIBLE: HOLOTAPE GAME:
  GROGNAK & THE RUBY RUINS
- COLLECTIBLE: NUKA CHERRY
- COLLECTIBLE: NUKA COLA QUANTUM
- COLLECTIBLE: REQUIRED READING: LIVE & LOVE (2)
- COLLECTIBLE: REQUIRED READING: ROBCOFUN!
- COMPANION: HANCOCK
- COMPANION: MACCREADY
- CRAFTING: ARMOR WORKBENCH
- CRAFTING: CHEMISTRY STATION
- CRAFTING: COOKING STATION
- CRAFTING: POWER ARMOR STATION
- CRAFTING: WEAPONS WORKBENCH
- FACTION: NEIGHBORHOOD WATCH
- FACTION: SETTLER (GOODNEIGHBOR)
- FACTION: TRIGGERMEN
- FACTION: CHARACTER: BARNES
- FACTION: CHARACTER: BOBBI NO-NOSE
- FACTION: CHARACTER: CLAIR HUTCHINS
- FACTION: CHARACTER: DAISY
- FACTION: CHARACTER: DOCTOR AMARI
- FACTION: CHARACTER: FAHRENHEIT
- FACTION: CHARACTER: FINN
- FACTION: CHARACTER: FRED ALLEN
- FACTION: CHARACTER: HAM
- FACTION: CHARACTER: IRMA
- FACTION: CHARACTER: KENT CONNOLLY

- FACTION: CHARACTER: KL-E-0
- FACTION: CHARACTER: MACCREADY
- FACTION: CHARACTER: MAGNOLIA
- FACTION: CHARACTER: MAROWSKI
- FACTION: CHARACTER: MAYOR HANCOCK
- FACTION: CHARACTER: RUFUS RUBINS
- FACTION: CHARACTER: SAMMY
- FACTION: CHARACTER: STAN SLAVIN
- FACTION: CHARACTER: VAULT-TEC REP
- FACTION: CHARACTER: WHITECHAPEL CHARLIE
- FACTION: CHARACTER: WINLOCK
- HEALTH OR CHEMS+++
- QUEST START: ART APPRECIATION* (FREEFORM)
- QUEST START: THE BIG DIG (SIDE)
- QUEST START: THE CLEANER* (FREEFORM)
- QUEST START: DANGEROUS MINDS (MAIN)
- QUEST START: FAMILIAR FACES* (FREEFORM)
- QUEST START: HAZARDOUS MATERIAL* (FREEFORM)
- QUEST START: LONG ROAD AHEAD (SIDE COMPANION)
- QUEST START: MACCREADY FOR ACTION* (FREEFORM)
- QUEST START: THE MEMORY DEN (FREEFORM)

- QUEST START: PUBLIC KNOWLEDGE (FREEFORM)
- QUEST START: RECRUITING HANCOCK* (FREEFORM)
- QUEST START: SHATTERED (MAIN)
- QUEST START: THE SILVER SHROUD (SIDE)
- QUEST START: TOUGH TIMES* (FREEFORM)
- QUEST START: TROUBLE BREWIN' (FREEFORM)
- QUEST VISIT: EMERGENT BEHAVIOR (SIDE
  COMPANION)
- QUEST VISIT: MEMORY INTERRUPTED
  (THE RAILROAD)
- QUEST VISIT: THE SECRET OF CABOT HOUSE (SIDE)
- SERVICES: TRADER (CLAIR HUTCHINS)
- SERVICES: TRADER (DAISY)
- SERVICES: TRADER (FRED ALLEN)
- SERVICES: TRADER (KL-E-0)
- SERVICES: TRADER (RUFUS RUBINS)
- SERVICES: TRADER (WHITECHAPEL CHARLIE)
- UNIQUE ITEM: DEVASTATOR'S CHESTPIECE
- UNIQUE ITEM: DEVASTATOR'S LEFT LEG
- UNIQUE ITEM: DEVASTATOR'S RIGHT GREAVE
- UNIQUE ITEM: PARTYSTARTER (MISSILE LAUNCHER)

**FIG 15.06A: GOODNEIGHBOR (EXTERIOR)**

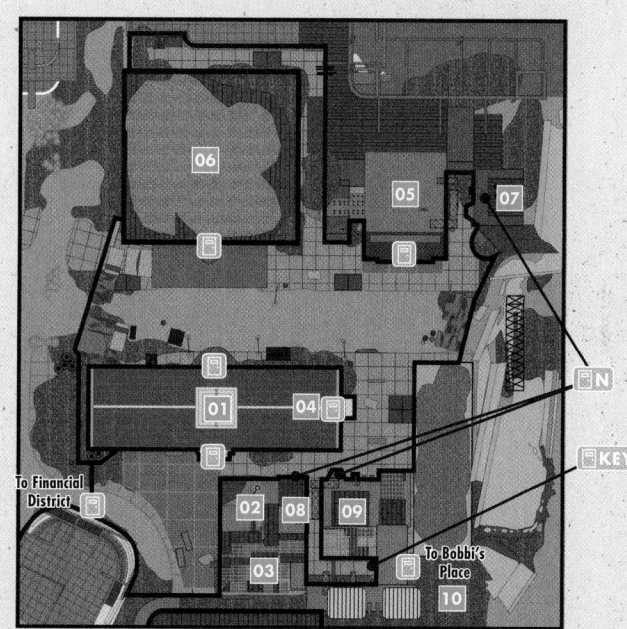

MAP

**ZONE 15**

NEIGHBORHOOD:
FINANCIAL
DISTRICT

## VAULT-TEC RECOMMENDED LOOT

ARMAMENTS AND AMMO: MINI NUKE AND FAT MAN
HOLOTAPE: GAME: GROGNAK & THE RUBY RUINS
HOLOTAPE: GWINNETT PILS RECIPE
COLLECTIBLE: NUKA CHERRY
COLLECTIBLE: NUKA COLA QUANTUM

REQUIRED READING: LIVE & LOVE
REQUIRED READING: LIVE & LOVE
REQUIRED READING: ROBCOFUN!
UNIQUE ITEM: DEVASTATOR ARMOR

**COMPANION: HANCOCK**

**COMPANION: MACCREADY**

Built on an ancient area of Boston once known as Scollay Square, Goodneighbor was founded in the year 2240 by a group of criminals banished from Diamond City. But appearances can be deceiving; although plagued with problems, Goodneighbor has its finer qualities: There are no social classes, so everyone is truly equal. There is no bigotry, and even Ghouls are accepted. Goodneighbor has proven instrumental in the success of the Railroad's operations.

## [01] Old State House

Mayor Hancock and his squeeze Fahrenheit are holed up here. The mayor is well liked, if a little cutthroat. He is guarded by the Neighborhood Watch; don't confuse them with the less friendly Triggermen! This four-floor mansion has a lot of chems to steal if you're so inclined and Holotapes extolling the virtues of the Railroad.

**FIG 15.06B: OLD STATE HOUSE (INTERIOR)**

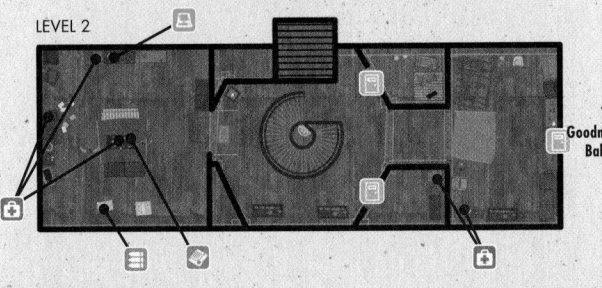

## [02] Kill or Be Killed

Everything here is guaranteed to kill or maim at your discretion except for the trader KL-E-0. This Assaultron has an excellent number of weapons and ammo to barter, including the unique weapon Partystarter and pieces of the infamous Devastator armor. There's a weapons workbench and Power Armor station here, as well as a Mini Nuke and Fat Man to steal. Upstairs there's little but a Railroad Holotape.

## [03] Daisy's Discounts

Daisy is a friendly, fresh-faced trader who deals in armor (including part of the Devastator armor) and comestibles. Barter with her, cook on her stove, or hammer out an armor improvement on her workbench.

## [04] The Third Rail

After Ham the doorman lets you in, take a restroom break for some light reading before visiting Whitechapel Charlie's bar, constructed from the remains of Scollay Square subway station. Downstairs you can chinwag with the governor (Charlie has a task he'd like assistance with), flirt with Magnolia the lounge singer, or steal a Holotape with a Gwinnett Pils recipe on it. The VIP area has MacCready and some rough types hanging around.

### FIG 15.06C: THE THIRD RAIL (INTERIOR)

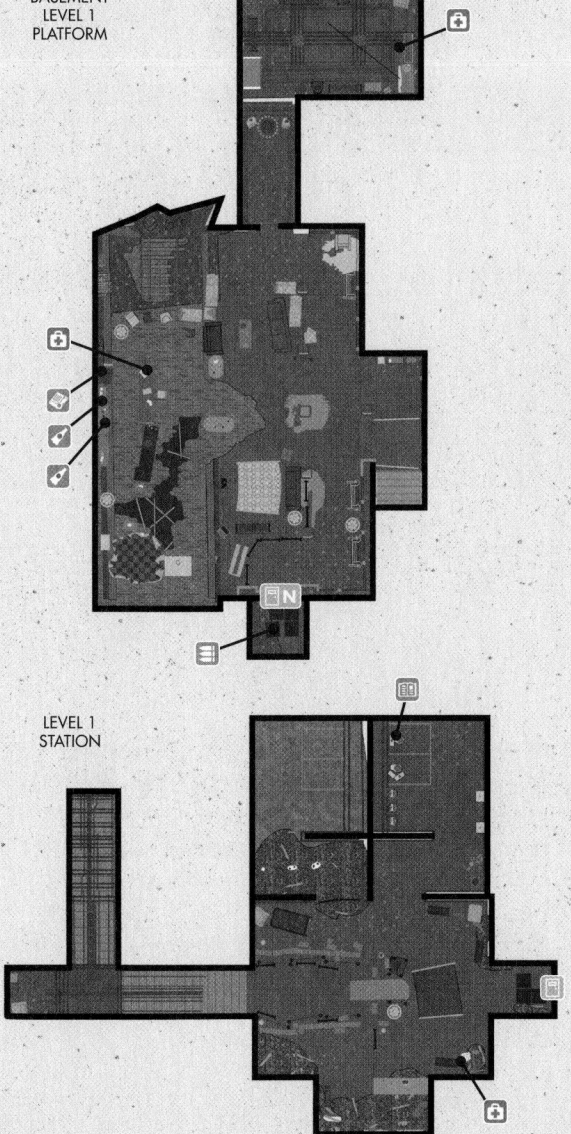

BASEMENT
LEVEL 1
PLATFORM

LEVEL 1
STATION

To
Goodneighbor

## [05] The Memory Den

If you're here to mooch around, Irma isn't happy to see you (unless you bribe or persuade her to take a trip down memory lane). Otherwise, this old theater holds few secrets. The mirrors behind the stage have chems, and Irma's upstairs room has a terminal to unlock (Novice), some ammo, and chems; otherwise, it's best to come here during the Main Quest with a detective friend in tow.

Kent Connolly, the Commonwealth's number one Silver Shroud fanatic, is in a side room. Speak to him to start the side quest.

Downstairs is the laboratory and two memory loungers, along with a good deal of chems, a copy of RobCoFUN! to read, and the Holotape Grognak game to play. The door is locked until the Main Quest is active.

### FIG 15.06D: THE MEMORY DEN (INTERIOR)

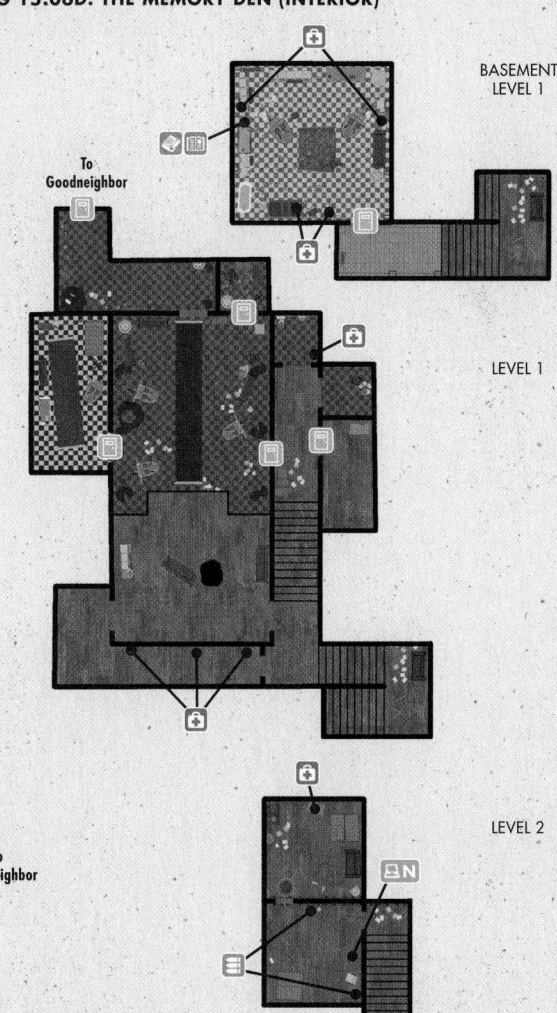

BASEMENT
LEVEL 1

To
Goodneighbor

LEVEL 1

LEVEL 2

## [06] Hotel Rexford

The place to sleep off your adventuring, this hotel lobby has a number of interesting folks to speak to. Rufus, the town's mechanic, has a job for you as well as items to trade. More abrupt is Clair Hutchins, who can offer you a room for the night, for a price. Don't forget the magazine behind the lobby bar and the password for the registry under the counter. A couple of known gangsters sometimes hang out here, too. And there's a special friend to say hello to (again) up on the top floor. He hasn't aged well.

If you need chems or a quick task to complete, seek out Fred Allen in the lobby or downstairs in his makeshift laboratory. He sells chems too. There's a Holotape under the stairs with his password.

**FIG 15.06E: HOTEL REXFORD (INTERIOR)**

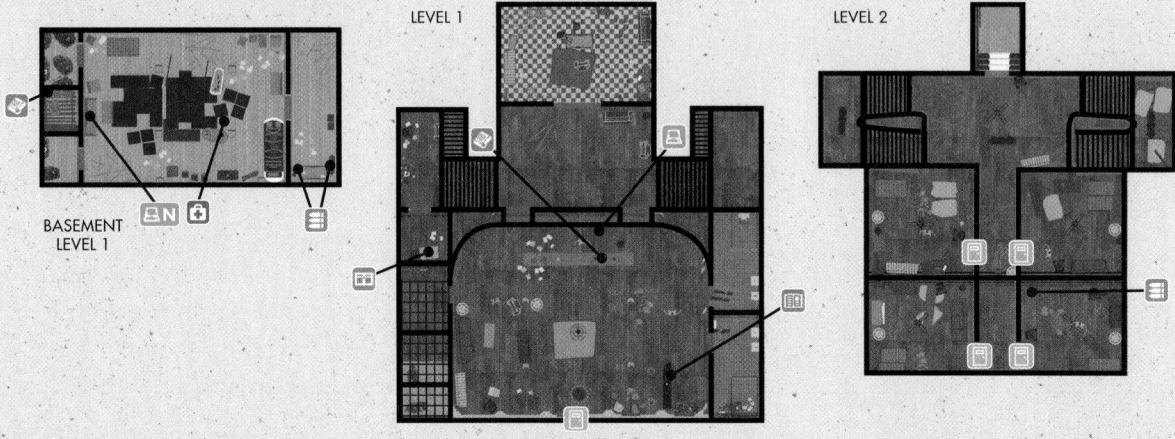

BASEMENT LEVEL 1

LEVEL 1

LEVEL 2

To Goodneighbor

## [07] Triggerman Warehouse #1

There's a chem cooler under the fallen ceiling ramp on the second floor, and chems plus a duffel bag are on the third (and final) floor, which consists of two separate rooms.

## [08] Triggerman Warehouse #2

This four-floor warehouse has Triggermen. There's also minimal chems, but a packed steamer trunk is on the top floor (southwest corner).

## [09] Triggerman Warehouse #3

There's ammo on the second floor, a small amount of scattered chems throughout, and a steamer trunk and duffel bag on the third (and final) floor.

## [10] Bobbi's Place

- ARMAMENTS AND AMMO
- ARMAMENTS AND AMMO: TRUNK
- ARMOR PART: FUSION CORE (3)
- ARMOR PART: POWER ARMOR (LEVELED)
- COLLECTIBLE: NUKA COLA QUANTUM (2)
- CRAFTING: CHEMISTRY STATION
- CRAFTING: COOKING STATION
- DANGER: RADIATION (MILD)!
- FACTION: FERAL GHOULS
- FACTION: IRRADIATED WILDLIFE (MIRELURKS)
- FACTION: TRIGGERMEN
- FACTION: CHARACTER: MEL
- FACTION: CHARACTER: SONJA
- HEALTH OR CHEMS
- QUEST START: THE BIG DIG (SIDE)
- UNIQUE ITEM: ASHMAKER (WEAPON)

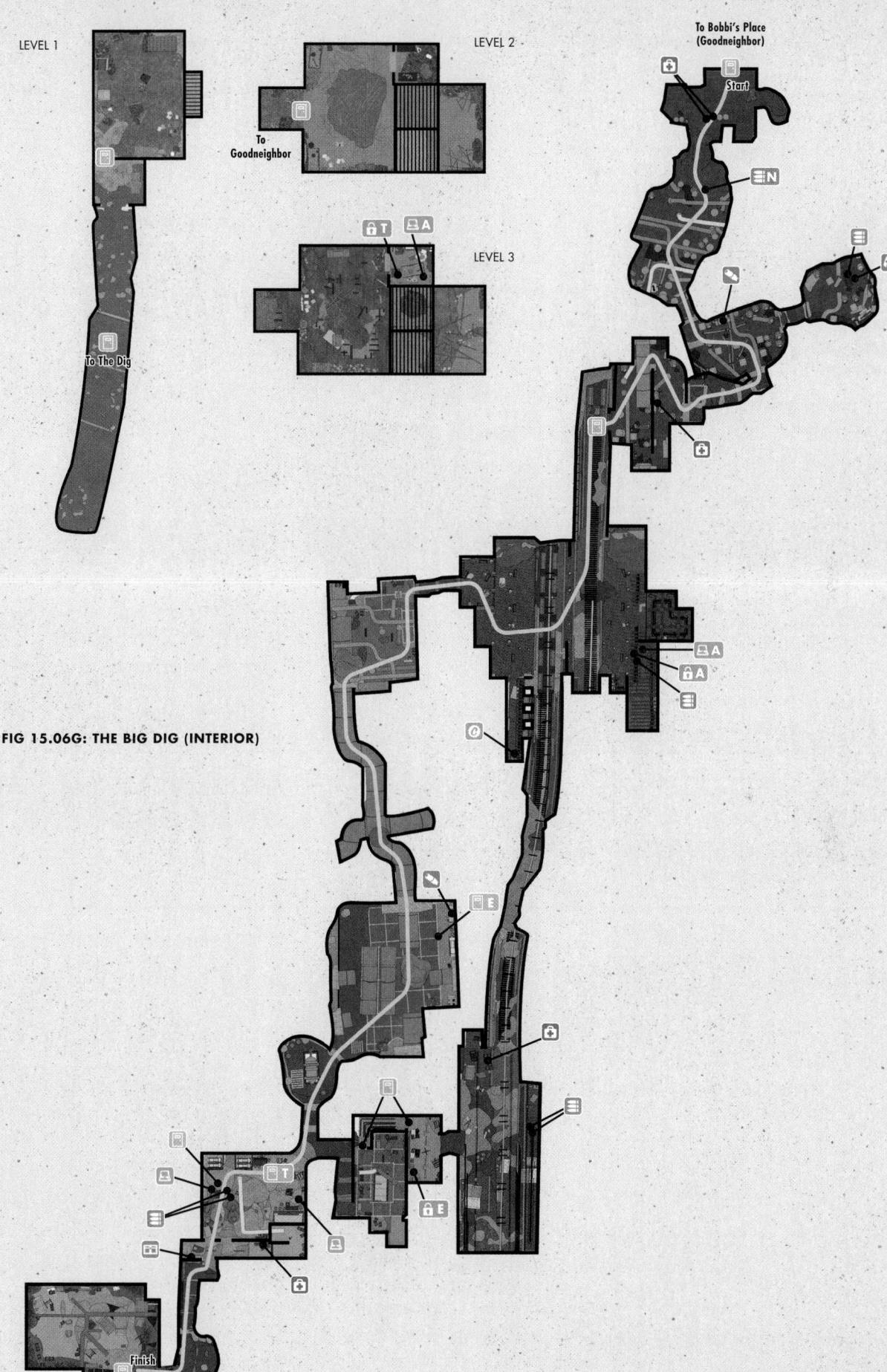

**FIG 15.06F: BOBBI'S PLACE (INTERIOR)**

LEVEL 1

LEVEL 2

To Goodneighbor

LEVEL 3

To Bobbi's Place (Goodneighbor)

Start

To The Dig

**FIG 15.06G: THE BIG DIG (INTERIOR)**

Finish

To Strongroom

## VAULT-TEC RECOMMENDED LOOT

   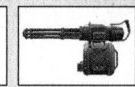

**ARMOR PART: FUSION CORE (3)**
**ARMOR PART: POWER ARMOR (LEVELED)**
**COLLECTIBLE: NUKA COLA QUANTUM (2)**
**UNIQUE ITEM: ASHMAKER**

Enter this location when you agree to help Bobbi as part of Side Quest: The Big Dig. This massive tunnel exploration involves digging through numerous fragile walls; finding three Fusion Cores, a steamer trunk, and two Nuka Cola Quantums; and eventually emerging at the NH&M Freight Depot, just south of the Mass Pike Tunnel East. If ever there was a need for a map, it's during this excursion!

 **Freeform Activities: Goodneighbor**

### The Memory Den

1. SIT IN THE MEMORY LOUNGER
2. RELIVE YOUR MEMORIES
3. TALK TO IRMA

You must attempt this quest before the end of Main Quest: Reunions. Enter the Memory Den, and relive a past memory from Vault 81. Afterward, speak to Irma.

 (Medium) Ask for a refund.

### Tough Times*

After visiting Goodneighbor for the first time and talking to Hancock, watch Hancock's speech from the balcony above the Third Rail. Leave Goodneighbor, then return. In the street close to Hotel Rexford, the Neighborhood Watch have slain a synth pretending to be a citizen.

### Public Knowledge

1. GO TO BOSTON PUBLIC LIBRARY
2. RETURN THE OVERDUE BOOK
3. CLEAR THE LIBRARY OF SUPER MUTANTS
4. RETURN TO DAISY

Speak with Daisy in Goodneighbor and agree to help her. She has asked you to clear out the Super Mutants that are threatening the old Boston Public Library. She also wants you to return her overdue book.

 (Easy, Medium, Hard) Request more Caps for your help.

 **OVERDUE BOOK**

Access Boston Public Library from the side door (Advanced) or Copley Station (Advanced).

Beware of Super Mutants, Mutant Hounds, Protectrons, and machine-gun turrets. Access the book return terminal and deposit the book to receive tokens. Collect more to receive prizes from this machine.

 **BOOK RETURN TOKEN (5)**

Make a sweep of the library and remove all Super Mutant threats. Then return to Daisy for your reward.

 **BOTTLECAPS (200–400)**

### Hazardous Material*

1. MISCELLANEOUS: BRING A HALLUCIGEN CANISTER TO FRED ALLEN
2. MISCELLANEOUS: RETURN TO FRED ALLEN

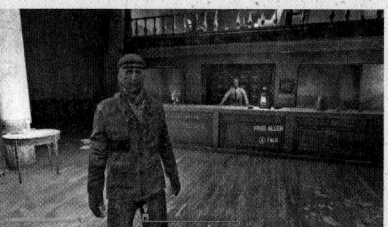

Visit Hotel Rexford and locate Fred Allen. Ask about work. He wants you to find a special canister for him.

 (Easy, Medium, Hard) Fast-talk him to up his Caps amount for your time.

Head to the HalluciGen. Beware of Gunners. Battle your way to locate the HalluciGen Canister. Return to Fred for the reward.

**HALLUCIGEN GAS CANISTER**

**BOTTLECAPS (200–400)**

## The Cleaner*

1. MISCELLANEOUS: CLEAR OUT THE GOODNEIGHBOR WAREHOUSES
2. MISCELLANEOUS: RETURN TO WHITECHAPEL CHARLIE

Visit Hotel Rexford and speak to Whitechapel Charlie. Agree to barter, then agree to help him.

 (Easy, Medium, Hard) Demand additional compensation.

Ask him who this warehouse clear-out is for.

(Novice) Pick the lock of each door. Enter and clear the warehouses of Triggermen. There are three warehouses to unlock and clear. Return to Whitechapel Charlie for your reward.

**BOTTLECAPS (200–400)**

## Art Appreciation*

1. MISCELLANEOUS: INVESTIGATE PICKMAN GALLERY
2. MISCELLANEOUS: RETURN TO HANCOCK

Enter the Old State House in Goodneighbor. Speak to Hancock and ask for work. Agree to help him.

 (Easy, Medium, Hard) Bargain a higher Cap amount for your services.

Find the entrance to Pickman Gallery. Beware of Raiders. Take the message from the tagged (and dead) foe. Head back to Hancock for a reward.

**MESSAGE TO JACK**

**BOTTLECAPS (200–400)**

## MacCready for Action*

1. MISCELLANEOUS: TALK TO MACCREADY

Visit the Third Rail and head into the VIP area. Wait for two Gunners (Barnes and Winlock) to stop talking to a third Gunner named MacCready. Afterward, hire him as a Mercenary Companion if you wish, for 250 Caps.

 (Medium) Or bargain him down to 200 Caps.

### VAULT-TEC AVAILABLE COMPANION

 **COMPANION (MERCENARY): MACCREADY**

## Familiar Faces*

Enter the Hotel Rexford and ascend to the top floor guest rooms. You meet an old friend. Speak with him.

 (Easy) Tell him to head to Sanctuary and help out as a settler.

 **SETTLER: VAULT-TEC REP**

## Recruiting Hancock*

1. MISCELLANEOUS: TALK TO HANCOCK

This becomes available once you end Side Quest: The Big Dig.

During the final decision you make at the NHM Freight Depot, you also have a choice to make when speaking to Bobbi. You can:

– **PLAN A: BETRAY BOBBI.**

 (Medium) Plan A: Convince Bobbi to leave.

– **PLAN B: STAY WITH BOBBI.**

Choose Plan A, then speak to Fahrenheit. Answer her as you wish. Complete Side Quest: The Big Dig. Now return to Hancock in Goodneighbor.

Choose Plan B, then kill Fahrenheit and all others except Bobbi. Complete Side Quest: The Big Dig. Now return to Hancock in Goodneighbor.

Plan A (continued): Speak to Hancock in the Old State House. Accept (or refuse) his offer to join you as a companion. The quest concludes.

Plan B (continued): Speak to Hancock at the entrance to Goodneighbor. You can:

- **IGNORE HIM.**
- **AGREE TO PAY HIM THE 1,000 CAPS HE'S OUT AND TAKE CARE OF BOBBI.**

 (Medium) Agree to pay him 750 Caps instead.

Locate Bobbi at her hideout in the Hawthorne Estate house (just north of University Point). You can:

- **KILL HER.**
- **TELL HER YOU'LL NEGOTIATE WITH HANCOCK.**

 (Medium) Urge her to flee.

Return to Hancock. Smooth things over with him, depending on your actions. Accept (or refuse) his offer to join you as a companion. The quest concludes.

### VAULT-TEC AVAILABLE COMPANION

 **COMPANION: HANCOCK**

 **Trouble Brewin'**

1. FIND THE BREWING MACHINE
2. SEND THE DRINKIN' BUDDY TO THE HOTEL REXFORD
3. (OPTIONAL) KEEP DRINKIN' BUDDY FOR YOURSELF
4. FOLLOW DRINKIN' BUDDY TO THE HOTEL REXFORD
5. TALK TO THE STAFF OF THE HOTEL REXFORD
6. TALK TO RUFUS
7. (OPTIONAL) SELL DRINKIN' BUDDY TO RUFUS
8. BRING DRINKIN' BUDDY INSIDE THE HOTEL REXFORD
9. COLLECT YOUR REWARD FROM RUFUS

Speak to Rufus Rubins over at Hotel Rexford in Goodneighbor. He wants you to find a brewing machine that was never delivered here. Head to the Shamrock Taphouse in Boston Harbor (Waterfront). In the cellar is the special "Drinkin' Buddy" Mister Brewer Protectron. Check him out near the terminal (Expert), or use the password from the Holotape on the shelves of the cellar.

At this point, you can chat to your new Buddy, feed him any brewing Holotapes you may have found, and point him in the direction of your nearest owned settlement so he becomes part of the ragtag collection of inhabitants there. Or you can return to Rufus after setting Drinkin' Buddy on his way back to Goodneighbor, and collect a reward from Rufus instead.

 **BOTTLECAPS**

Drinking Buddy is your real reward; he brews ice cold beer every few days, you can chill Nuka Cola (or Nuka Cherries or Quantums) and make it ice cold by putting it in his inventory. Also, why not give him new recipes to try?

**Recipes:**

| GWINNETT HOLOTAPE RECIPE | LOCATION |
|---|---|
| Gwinnett Ale Brewing Subroutines | Colonial Taphouse, Diamond City (Behind the bar) |
| Gwinnett Brew Recipe | Beantown Brewery, in the boss room next to the terminal |
| Gwinnett Lager Recipe | Shamrock Taphouse, behind the bar under the broken railing |
| Gwinnett Pils Recipe | The Third Rail, Goodneighbor (On the counter next to the fridge) |
| Gwinnett Stout Recipe | In a terminal in Gwinnett Brewery |

- ARMAMENTS AND AMMO
- ARMAMENTS AND AMMO: TRUNK
- DANGER: LONG DROP!
- FACTION: GUNNER
- FACTION: SUPER MUTANT

Gunners and Super Mutants are battling through a towering office building for the remains of a skybridge. Reaching this vantage point requires skill, good judgment, and topographical smarts. You're free to approach from Secondary Location 16: Hub 360 (Theater District), but an easier route is to find one of the following locations:

**FIG 15.07A: FALLEN SKY BRIDGE (EXTERIOR)**

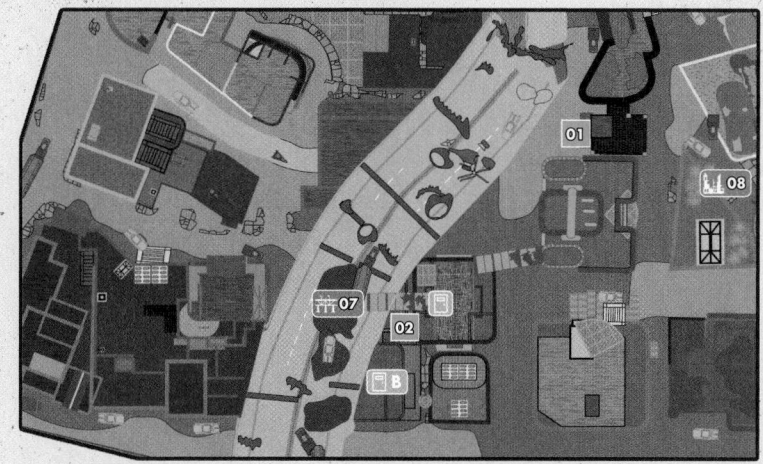

**FIG 15.07B: PINNACLE HIGH-RISE (RUINED SKYSCRAPER) (INTERIOR)**

LEVEL 1

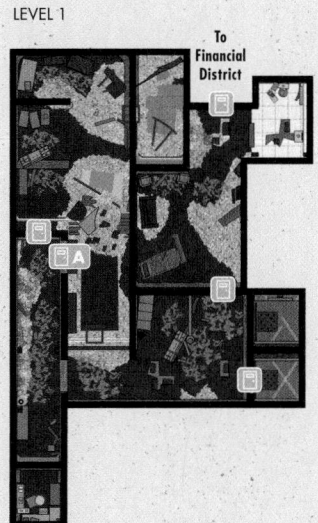

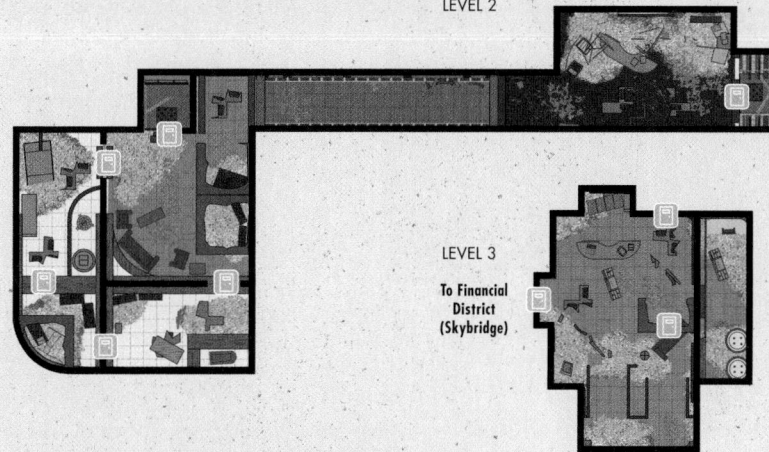

LEVEL 2

LEVEL 3

To Financial District (Skybridge)

### [01] Fire Escape Stairs (Financial District)

Find Primary Location: Postal Square. Head north, then make a sharp left at the rubble and traffic lights so you're facing south. Look for the red and blue ruined skyscrapers ahead. Climb the fire escape stairs between them to reach the entrance to Pinnacle High-Rise.

### [02] Hidden Fire Escape Stairs (Financial District)

Or, head east from Park Street Station (in Boston Common) down the main street until a Super Mutant barricade wall slows you down. Turn left (north) and enter the alley, and turn left again to find some fire escape stairs. Climb them to a second set of fire escape stairs. Climb those to a lift, activated by a button, which takes you to the Skybridge (without having to ascend through the Pinnacle High-Rise interior).

The exterior Skybridge area was a Gunner camp, recently taken over by Super Mutants. It is the exit from "Ruined Skyscraper," the upper area of the Pinnacle High-Rise.

It offers exceptional views of your surroundings and the ability to partake in dangerous parkour over the edge of the freeway overpass to the west. You can also access locations along the freeway into the Theater District to the south. Head northeast to access the rooftops above Primary Location: Postal Square.

FIG 15.08A: POSTAL SQUARE (EXTERIOR)

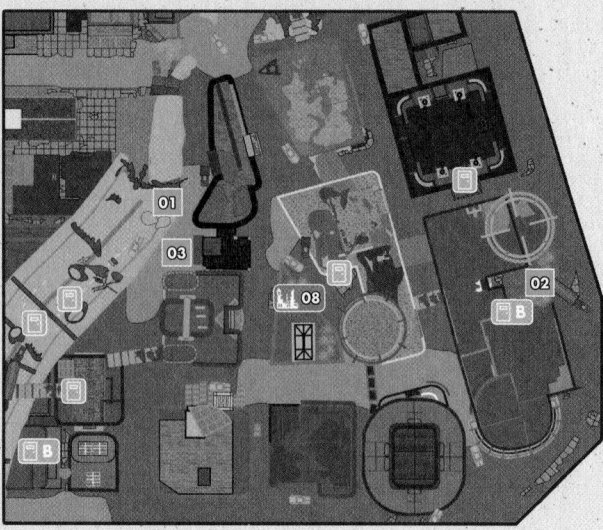

- ARMAMENTS AND AMMO++
- ARMAMENTS AND AMMO: TRUNK
- ARMOR PART: POWER ARMOR (LEVELED)
- BOTTLECAPS+
- CRAFTING: ARMOR WORKBENCH
- CRAFTING: WEAPONS WORKBENCH
- DANGER: CAN CHIMES!
- DANGER: GRENADES!

- DANGER: LONG DROP!
- DANGER: MINES!
- DANGER: TURRETS!
- FACTION: GUNNERS
- FACTION: RAIDERS
- FACTION: SUPER MUTANTS
- HEALTH OR CHEMS

FIG 15.08B: JOE'S SPUCKIES (INTERIOR)

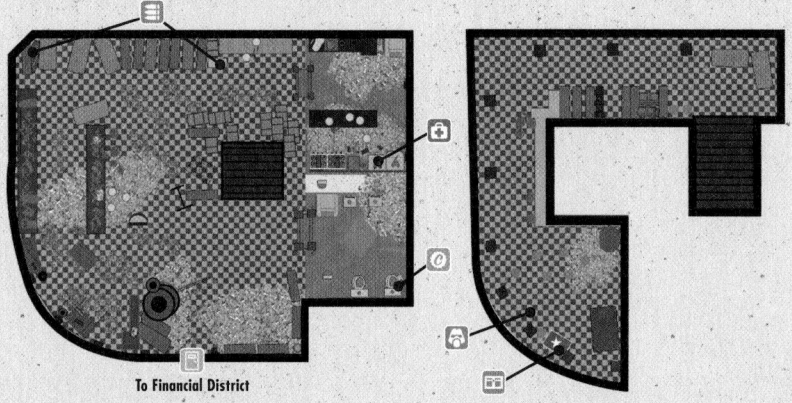

To Financial District

**VAULT-TEC RECOMMENDED LOOT**

**ARMOR PART: POWER ARMOR (LEVELED)**

Surrounded by ruined and impassable skyscrapers, this Gunner stronghold is well defended with turrets as the Gunners attempt to knock back Super Mutant incursions to the south, where most of the mines are.

While the Post Office Station is closed permanently, Joe's Spuckies is open and used as the Gunner's base of operations. It has a good supply of ammo and Caps.

Scaling the roof areas above this location is where it's at! There's a Safe (Advanced) directly above Joe's Spuckies on the ruined roof. There's a dead Raider with chems and ammo above the gantry bridge to the south, inside the white ruined skyscraper. To get up here, approach from one of the following directions:

### [01] Mangled Freeway Overpass

The Fallen Skybridge, dropping down from the mangled freeway overpass.

### [02] Rooftop Raider Camp (Postal Square Overlook)

Or, locate the lift near the bus and ruined green skyscraper, north of the Shamrock Taphouse. Ride the lift up to a small Raider camp. Clear them out, claim their chems and ammo, then head west (down the rusting roof).

### [03] Fire Escape Stairs (Financial District)

Or, locate the fire escape stairs to the northwest, just east of Secondary Location: Water Street Apartments (between the red and blue ruined skyscrapers).

# SECONDARY LOCATIONS

## [15.01] WEATHERBY INVESTMENT TRUST

- ARMAMENTS AND AMMO
- DANGER: LONG DROP!
- HEALTH OR CHEMS
- QUEST VISIT: LAST VOYAGE OF THE USS CONSTITUTION

This abandoned skyscraper just north of Faneuil Hall borders North End. Enter via the bus, and check the terminal (Advanced) to open the wall safe (Expert) before using the elevator. Enter an interior mezzanine to a second upper elevator that deposits you on the roof. Gaze at the incredible views all the way to Lexington, across the district, and even to Quincy! If you've completed the specified quest, the building has a new "extension" to it.

## [15.02] CONGRESS STREET GARAGE

- ARMAMENTS AND AMMO
- DANGER: LONG DROP!

Below the market stall and Freedom Trail to the west of Faneuil Hall is an exit from Haymarket Mall that leads into a two-level parking garage. Head down the ramp to find a safe (Advanced) and two working elevators.

Take the left elevator to ascend around five floors up to the blown-out shell of a building, close to the end of the collapsed freeway. Use the skybridge (head east) to reach the Commonwealth Bank upper access. Climb the stairs and maneuver around the girders until the platforms disappear. Access the freeway to the Garden Terrace if you wish. But watch your step!

Take the right elevator to ascend around 10 floors up to a tiny section of flooring at the top of this devastated structure. Carefully hop down from here, heading northwest so you can claim the steamer trunk atop the roof of the Old Corner Bookstore.

## [15.03] BUS WRECKAGE

- HEALTH OR CHEMS

The main thoroughfare running north to south has an astonishing amount of rubble. This overturned bus stops progress. Climb over it, or check inside for a chem cooler.

## [15.04] COMMONWEALTH BANK

- ARMAMENTS AND AMMO
- DANGER: LONG DROP!
- FACTION: ROBOTS
- HEALTH OR CHEMS
- QUEST VISIT: WEATHERVANE (THE RAILROAD)

### FIG S15.01: COMMONWEALTH BANK (INTERIOR)

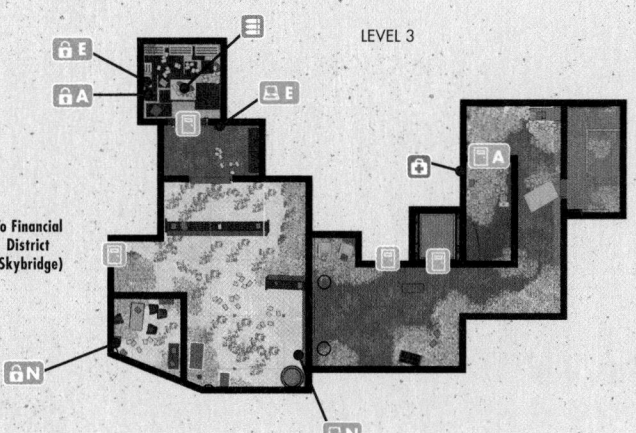

Enter this bank via a side alley door, the hole in the southeast corner of the structure, or the skybridge from the parking structure elevator. Inside is a second elevator that takes you to the dizzying heights of the roof. There a plank you use in the specified quest, along with some ammo.

### [15.05] SKYSCRAPER STASH

**– HEALTH OR CHEMS**

Tucked in a corner by a girder in the remains of the orange skyscraper southeast of Faneuil Hall is a well-hidden skeleton with chems to scavenge. A jetpack jump from the hall roof might be enough to leap across to this location.

### [15.06] ELEVATED ROAD (WEST ACCESS)

### [15.07] ELEVATED RAIDER CAMP (FINANCIAL DISTRICT)

### [15.08] ELEVATED ROAD (CENTRAL ACCESS)

**– ARMAMENTS AND AMMO**
**– CRAFTING: COOKING STATION**
**– FACTION: RAIDERS**
**– HEALTH OR CHEMS**

A small elevated road connects the western edge of the Financial District to the middle of the zone. Be sure to check under the road for points of interest, and approach a small Raider camp that is accessible from the road.

There's also elevator access to Secondary Location: Water Street Apartments from a plank on a rusting Vault-Tec van in the small southwest tunnel.

### [15.09] RAILROAD HIDEOUT (FINANCIAL DISTRICT)

**– ARMAMENTS AND AMMO**
**– CRAFTING: ARMOR WORKBENCH**
**– CRAFTING: COOKING STATION**
**– CRAFTING: WEAPONS WORKBENCH**
**– DANGER: GRENADES!**
**– DANGER: TRIPWIRES!**
**– HEALTH OR CHEMS**
**– SERVICES: TRADER (OPAL)**

Just south of the waterlogged junction, where the rubble is piled high, is a narrow brick alley. Use the fire escape to reach a pair of crafting workbenches and a terminal (Novice) for turning off the spotlight. There's a footlocker up here, too (Advanced), a safe to pick (Expert), and some rather natty formal gear.

### [15.10] 35 COURT

**– ARMAMENTS AND AMMO**
**– ARMOR PART: POWER ARMOR (LEVELED)**
**– DANGER: TRIPWIRES!**
**– FACTION: ROBOTS**
**– HEALTH OR CHEMS**

**VAULT-TEC RECOMMENDED LOOT**

 **ARMOR PART: POWER ARMOR (LEVELED)**

Evidence of a Protectron massacre is visible as you reach the entrance on the south side of this building. Enter the structure, watching for the tripwire by the desk that activates a Protectron. Ride the elevator to the open-air middle of the structure.

Open the door (Novice) to enter a small office with a safe (Expert). Head up the metal ramp, but beware an ambush when you reach the top. Enter the two side rooms and press the buttons to open a storage pod with Power Armor in it. Nice! Then feel free to leap west, landing on the rooftops north of Postal Square.

### [15.11] ROOFTOP HIDEAWAY (FINANCIAL DISTRICT)

**– HEALTH OR CHEMS**

A small hole in the stone building leads to a cubbyhole of chems. Approach using a jetpack from the raised road to the north to get to this tricky-to-reach locale.

### [15.12] PEDESTRIAN UNDERPASS

**– CRAFTING: COOKING STATION**
**– HEALTH OR CHEMS**

This allows access from the raised road to the north, south to the cluster of buildings. Check under the raised road for a cooking station, which sometimes hosts wandering traders.

## [15.13] PARKING GARAGE AND RAIDER ROOFTOPS

- ARMAMENTS AND AMMO
- ARMAMENTS AND AMMO: TRUNK
- DANGER: LONG DROP!
- FACTION: RAIDERS
- HEALTH OR CHEMS

Enter the parking structure from the north or south entrances, and work your way up the ramp or concrete stairwell. Continue to the low-rise rooftop with a steamer trunk and Raiders who don't take well to your trespassing. Scour the roof for additional ammo. To the east (and up) are the remains of a blue metal office tower and the Fallen Skybridge. Approach from the skybridge and drop down if you're wearing appropriate armor to cushion your falls.

## [15.14] WATER STREET APARTMENTS

- ARMAMENTS AND AMMO
- BOTTLECAPS
- CRAFTING: CHEMISTRY STATION
- FACTION: RAIDERS
- FACTION: CHARACTER: KENDRA
- HEALTH OR CHEMS
- QUEST VISIT: THE SILVER SHROUD (SIDE)

**FIG S15.14: WATER STREET APARTMENTS (INTERIOR)**

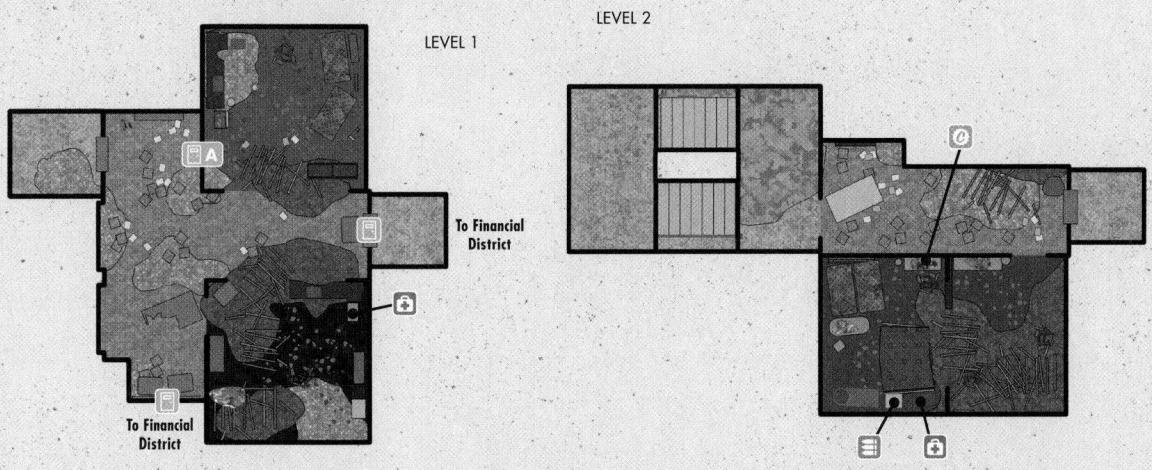

LEVEL 1

LEVEL 2

To Financial District

To Financial District

This set of run-down apartments has two accessible floors (the upper one is only available during the specified quest). The hangout of a known Raider, this has access from the raised road (via the elevator), but most of the structure's interior is inaccessible, until the quest is active.

# ZONE 16: NEIGHBORHOOD: THEATER DISTRICT

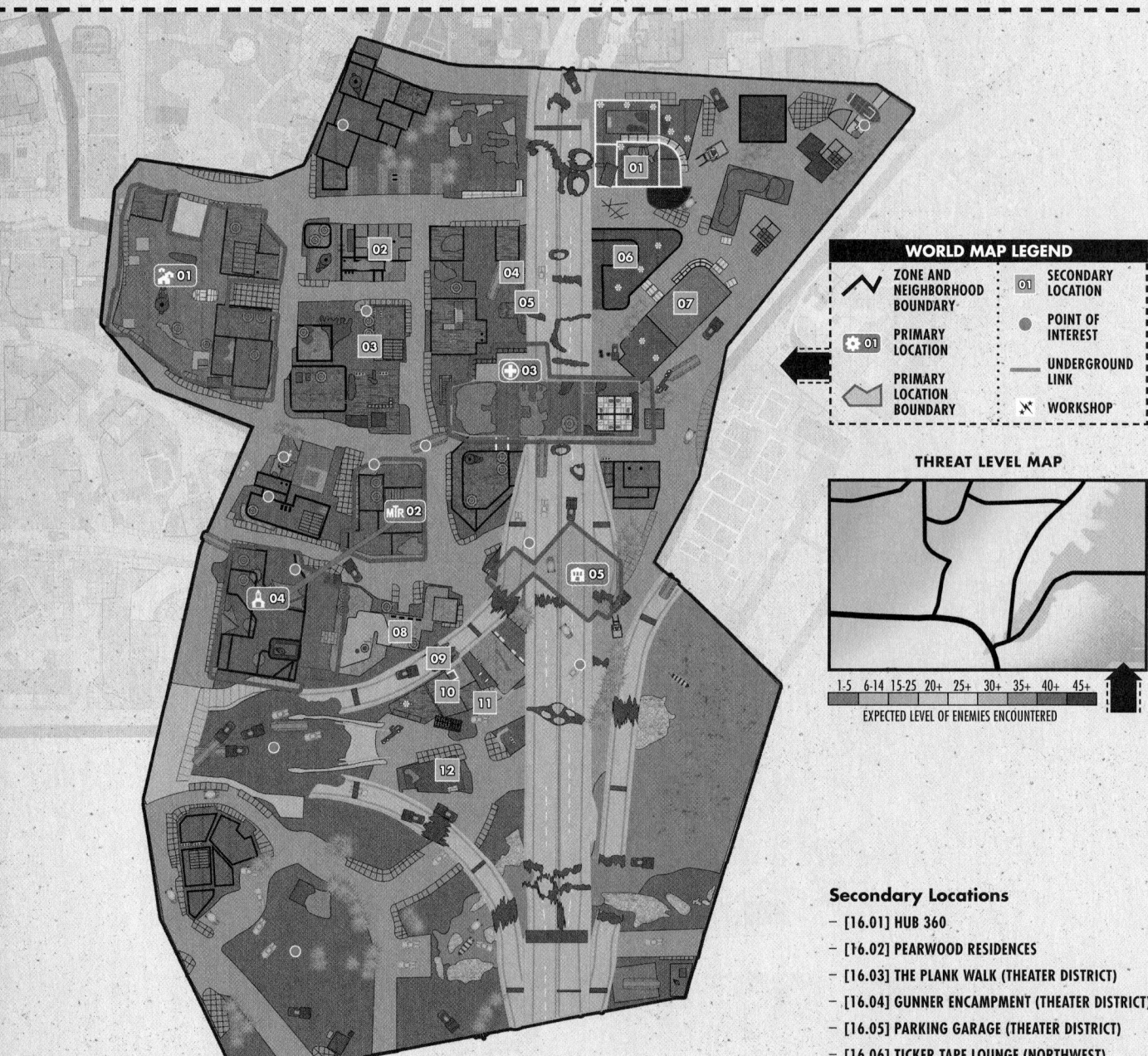

**WORLD MAP LEGEND**

- ╱╲ ZONE AND NEIGHBORHOOD BOUNDARY
- ⚙ 01 PRIMARY LOCATION
- ◢ PRIMARY LOCATION BOUNDARY
- 01 SECONDARY LOCATION
- ● POINT OF INTEREST
- ─── UNDERGROUND LINK
- ⚒ WORKSHOP

**THREAT LEVEL MAP**

1-5  6-14  15-25  20+  25+  30+  35+  40+  45+

EXPECTED LEVEL OF ENEMIES ENCOUNTERED

### Primary Locations

- [16.01] COMBAT ZONE
- [16.02] MEDICAL CENTER METRO
- [16.03] MASS BAY MEDICAL CENTER
- [16.04] D.B. TECHNICAL HIGH SCHOOL
- [16.05] HESTER'S CONSUMER ROBOTICS

### Secondary Locations

- [16.01] HUB 360
- [16.02] PEARWOOD RESIDENCES
- [16.03] THE PLANK WALK (THEATER DISTRICT)
- [16.04] GUNNER ENCAMPMENT (THEATER DISTRICT)
- [16.05] PARKING GARAGE (THEATER DISTRICT)
- [16.06] TICKER TAPE LOUNGE (NORTHWEST)
- [16.07] TICKER TAPE LOUNGE (SOUTHEAST)
- [16.08] UNDER THE ON-RAMP: CAMP AND GARAGE
- [16.09] THE ON-RAMP (THEATER DISTRICT)
- [16.10] RAILROAD DEAD DROP (THEATER DISTRICT)
- [16.11] STREET CORNER (THEATER DISTRICT)
- [16.12] OLD SNIPER CAMP

Bordering Zone 6 to the south, with access into both Back Bay and Boston Common to the west, the Financial District to the north, and Boston Harbor to the east, the Theater District offers height as well as width in many of its explorable locations. Though theatrical plays haven't been put on for 200 years, the largest of the theaters has its own form of violently bloody entertainment. Farther south is the sprawling Mass Bay Medical Center, offering (as many building do) access to the ground level and the elevated freeway above. Expect combat as Gunners attempt to hold on to territory while fending off Super Mutants encroaching on their facilities. Other locations are quieter, but no less dangerous, like the old robotics store close to the freeway. Remember that some map icons presented here may be above or below you.

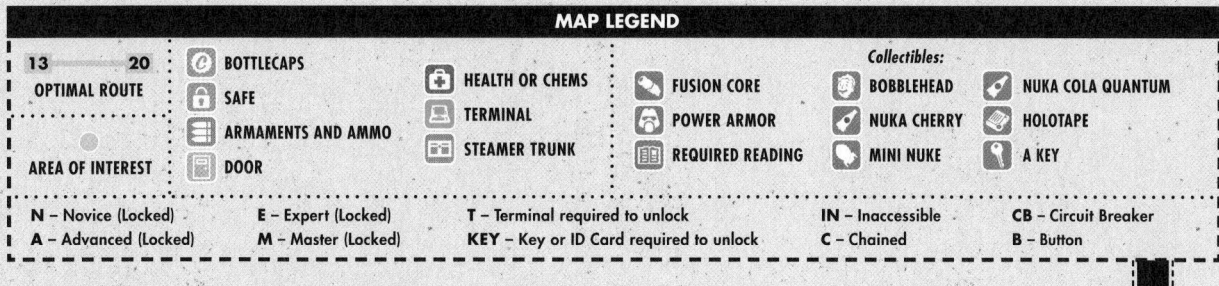

## MAP LEGEND

| 13 ——— 20 | |
|---|---|
| OPTIMAL ROUTE | |

- AREA OF INTEREST

- BOTTLECAPS
- SAFE
- ARMAMENTS AND AMMO
- DOOR

- HEALTH OR CHEMS
- TERMINAL
- STEAMER TRUNK

- FUSION CORE
- POWER ARMOR
- REQUIRED READING

**Collectibles:**
- BOBBLEHEAD
- NUKA CHERRY
- MINI NUKE

- NUKA COLA QUANTUM
- HOLOTAPE
- A KEY

N – Novice (Locked)      E – Expert (Locked)      T – Terminal required to unlock      IN – Inaccessible      CB – Circuit Breaker
A – Advanced (Locked)   M – Master (Locked)      KEY – Key or ID Card required to unlock      C – Chained      B – Button

# PRIMARY LOCATIONS

## [16.01] COMBAT ZONE    THREAT LEVELS 20+

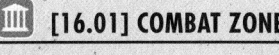

- ARMAMENTS AND AMMO
- ARMAMENTS AND AMMO: MINI NUKE
- COLLECTIBLE: NUKA CHERRY
- COLLECTIBLE: REQUIRED READING: PICKET FENCES
- COMPANION: CAIT
- CRAFTING: ARMOR WORKBENCH
- CRAFTING: CHEMISTRY STATION
- CRAFTING: COOKING STATION

- CRAFTING: WEAPONS STATION
- FACTION: RAIDERS
- FACTION: SETTLERS
- FACTION: CHARACTER: CAIT
- FACTION: CHARACTER: TOMMY LONEGAN
- HEALTH OR CHEMS
- QUEST START: BENIGN INTERVENTION (SIDE COMPANION)
- QUEST START: MISCELLANEOUS (COMBAT ZONE)

MAP

ZONE 16

NEIGHBORHOOD:
THEATER
DISTRICT

FIG 16.01: COMBAT ZONE (INTERIOR)

### VAULT-TEC RECOMMENDED LOOT

ARMAMENTS AND AMMO: MINI NUKE
COLLECTIBLE: NUKA CHERRY
REQUIRED READING: PICKET FENCES

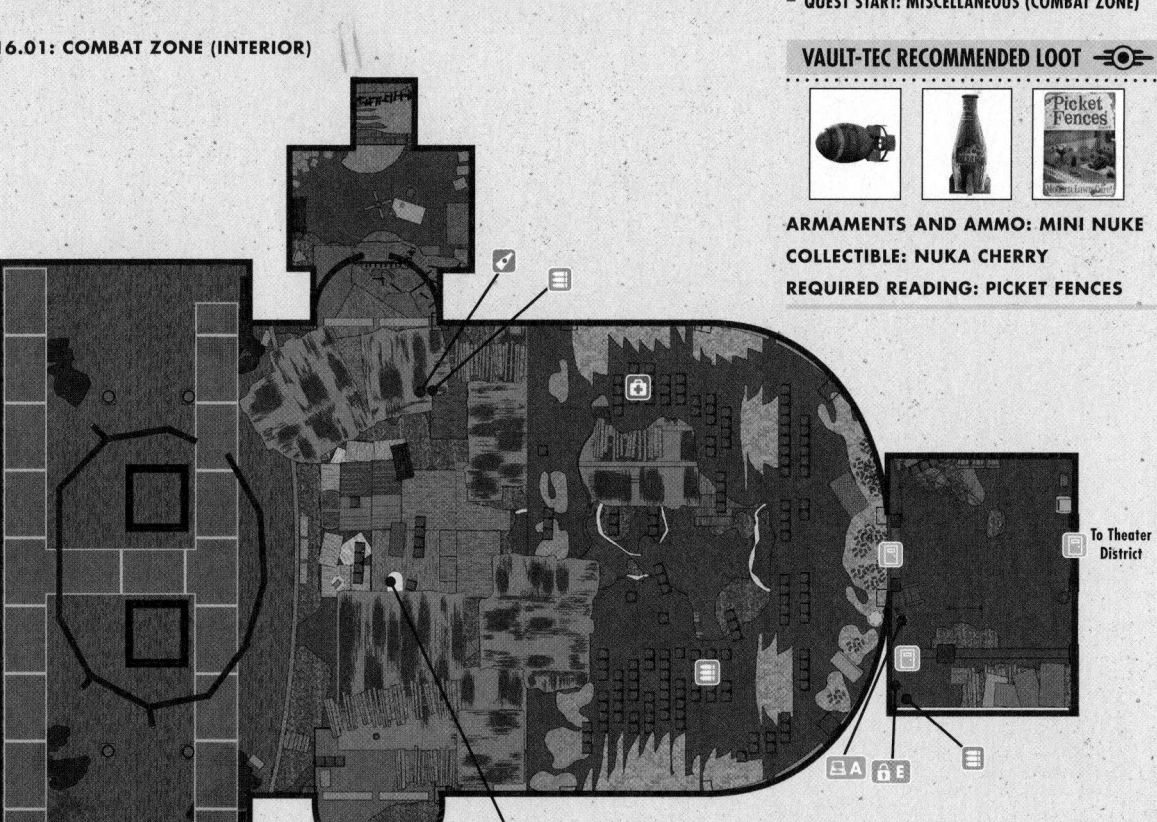

To Theater District

**COMPANION: CAIT**

Once an old-time theater and public arena, this location has been taken over by Raiders, who don't allow anyone in other than their own. Tommy Lonegan, a Southie Ghoul, announces the fights, while Cait, the headliner, cuts throats in the ring.

 **Miscellaneous Quest: Combat Zone**

1. **MISCELLANEOUS: ELIMINATE THE REMAINING RAIDERS**
2. **TALK TO TOMMY**

When all the Raiders are incapacitated, enter the arena and speak with Tommy Lonegan. He's hoping you'll partner up with Cait while he gets his arena back in order and gifts you some Caps to sweeten the deal.

 (Medium) Ask why you should partner with Cait.

Agree, and Cait becomes a possible companion.

##  [16.02] MEDICAL CENTER METRO

THREAT LEVELS 20+

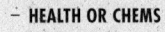

- ARMAMENTS AND AMMO
- ARMOR PART: FUSION CORE
- BOTTLECAPS
- COLLECTIBLE: NUKA COLA QUANTUM (2)
- DANGER: CAN CHIMES!
- DANGER: GRENADES!
- DANGER: MAKESHIFT BOMB!
- DANGER: OIL!
- DANGER: RADIATION (MILD)!
- DANGER: TRIPWIRES!
- DANGER: TURRET!
- FACTION: BLOODBUGS
- FACTION: RAIDERS
- HEALTH OR CHEMS

**FIG 16.02: MEDICAL CENTER STATION (INTERIOR)**

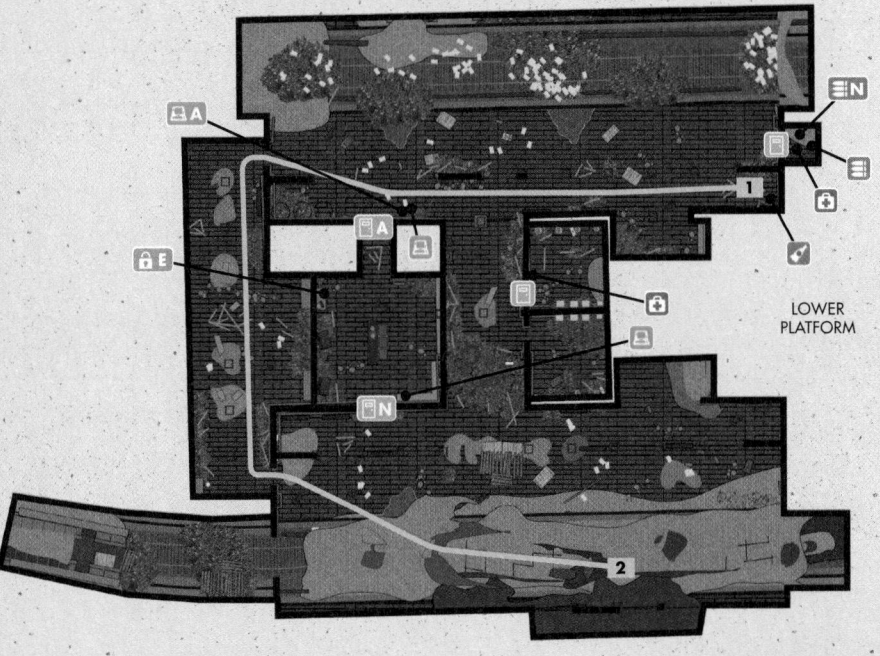

LOWER PLATFORM

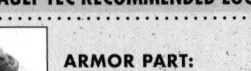

### VAULT-TEC RECOMMENDED LOOT

 **ARMOR PART: FUSION CORE**

**COLLECTIBLE: NUKA COLA QUANTUM (2)**

This subway station links to the D.B. Technical High School. Currently the tracks are flooded with slightly irradiated water, attracting Bloodbugs and drawing the Raider gang back aboveground.

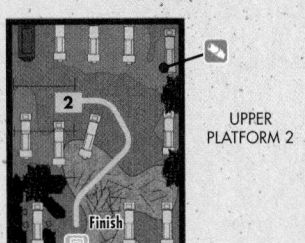

UPPER PLATFORM 2

UPPER PLATFORM 1

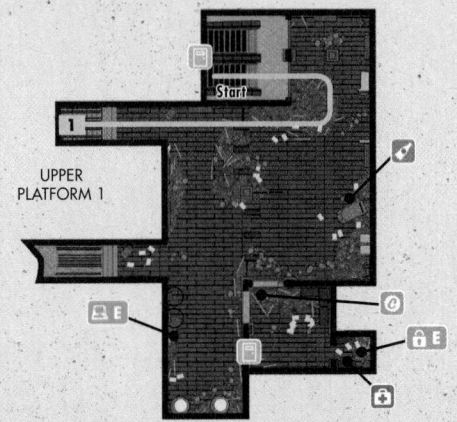

- ARMAMENTS AND AMMO
- ARMOR PART: POWER ARMOR (T-45)
- COLLECTIBLE: HOLOTAPE: BONNIE'S HOLOTAPE
- CRAFTING: CHEMISTRY STATION (2)
- CRAFTING: COOKING STATION (3)
- CRAFTING: POWER ARMOR STATION (2)
- DANGER: LONG DROP!

- DANGER: MINES!
- DANGER: TURRETS!
- FACTION: GUNNERS
- HEALTH OR CHEMS

**VAULT-TEC RECOMMENDED LOOT**

 **ARMOR PART: POWER ARMOR (LEVELED)**

This is one of the largest hospitals in the city of Boston. Gunners have a stronghold here, with makeshift and rusting pathways up to the roof and all the way to the elevated freeway south of the fallen skybridge. Be wary of the turrets before entering this facility. The rusting green structure towers over the elevated freeway.

Access inside is from one of five entrances. There are three on the ground level: the main one to the north, the side doors to the west (under the elevated freeway), and the emergency room with reception area (check it for an ammo box) to the northwest of this building. There's a small concrete bridge near the rubble tower and fallen bus below the freeway. There's also a monorail track with a train still attached, which you can take to the Medical Center Station from the roof of Hester's Consumer Robotics.

**FIG 16.03A: MASS BAY MEDICAL CENTER (INTERIOR)**

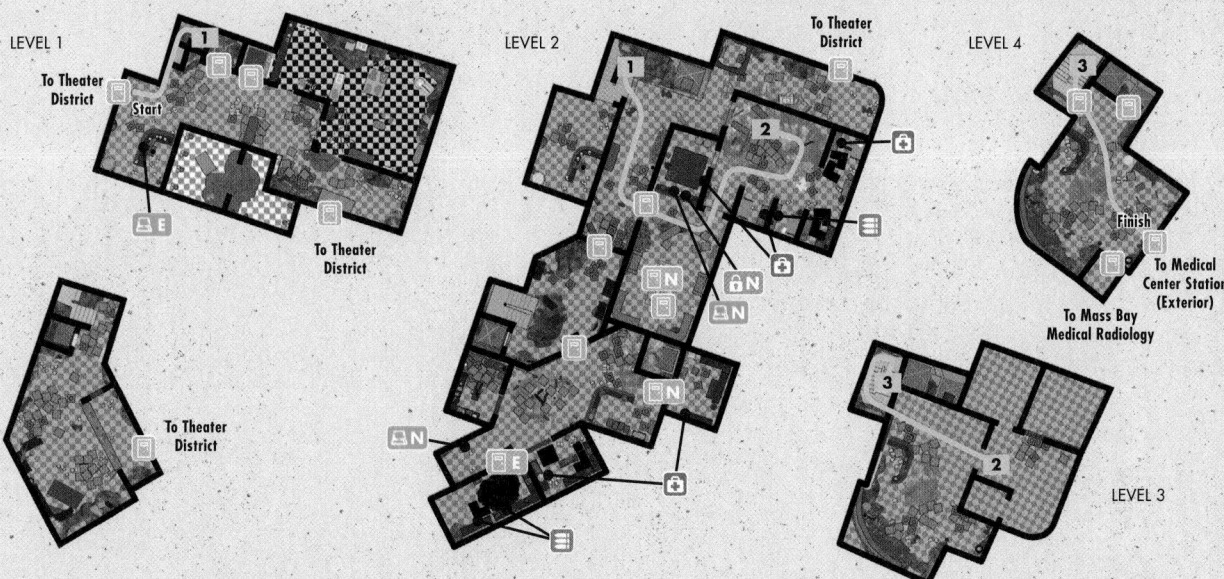

**MAP**

**ZONE 16**

NEIGHBORHOOD: THEATER DISTRICT

The top floor of the medical center has an elevator to the radiology department and double doors out to the Medical Center Station—a mezzanine with the remains of a coffee shop and a safe (Advanced). From the station, you can "take the train" south to the roof of Hester's Consumer Robotics or north to the rubble-filled remains of a parking structure under the elevated freeway.

**FIG 16.03B: MASS BAY MEDICAL RADIOLOGY (INTERIOR)**

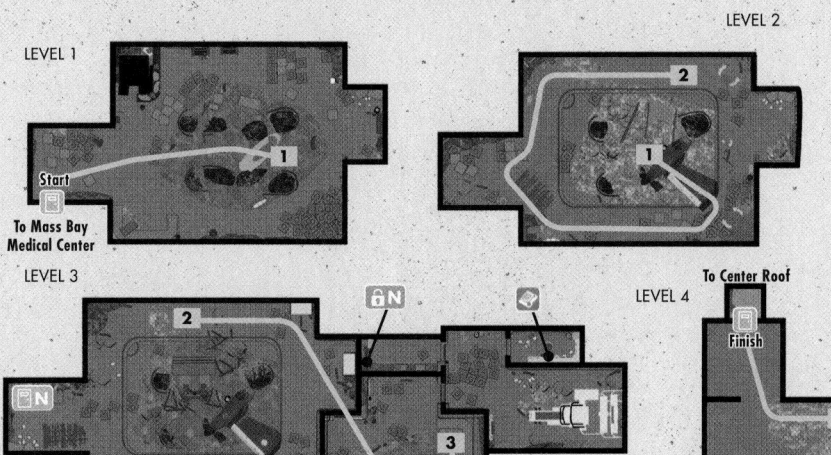

A Vertibird has crashed through the roof of the radiology department. Clear the area of Gunner scum if you wish before riding the elevator on the north to the roof where you can inspect the wreckage, grab a few chems, take in the vertigo-inducing views, and call a construction lift. Ride this to a lower roof, battle Gunners, and enter the Theater District Secondary Location: Ticker Tape Lounge from here. Or fall to your death. The latter isn't recommended.

**FIG 16.04: D.B. TECHNICAL HIGH SCHOOL (INTERIOR)**

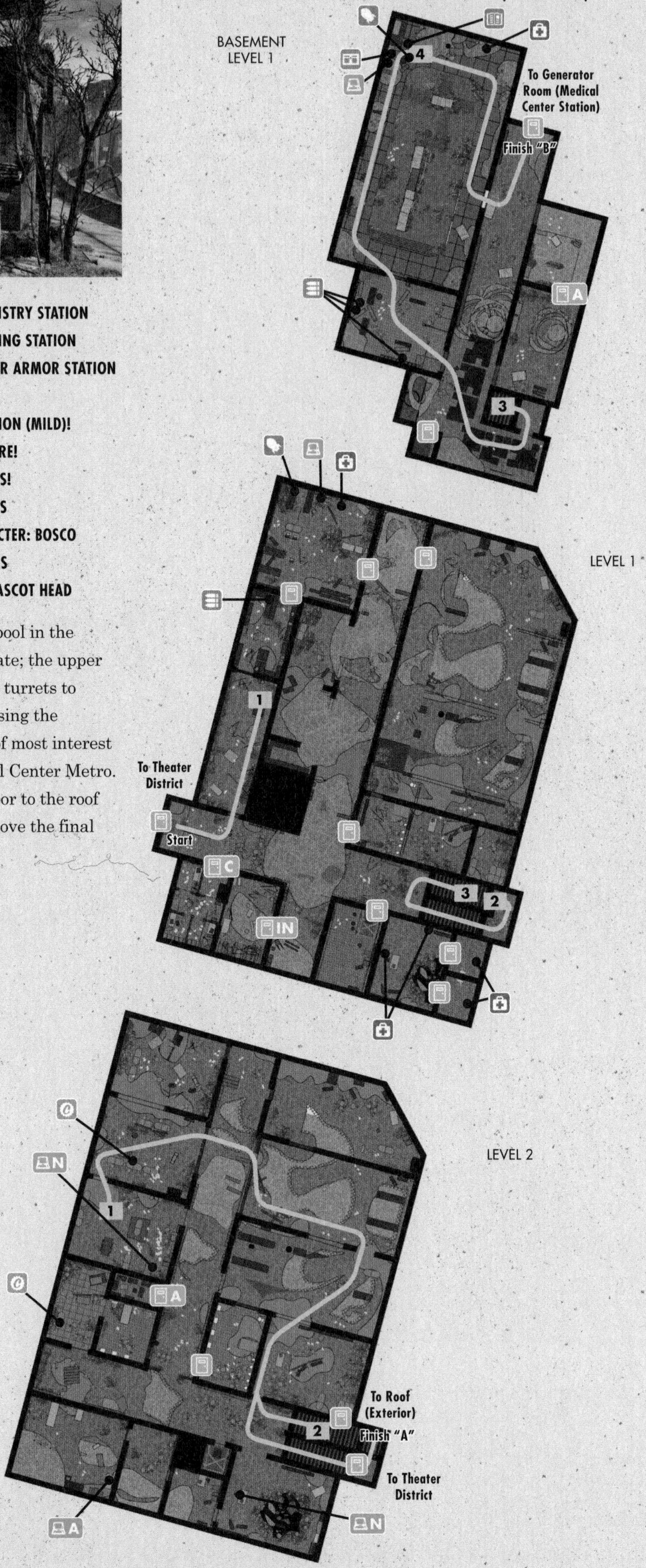

BASEMENT
LEVEL 1

To Generator
Room (Medical
Center Station)

Finish "B"

A

4

3

LEVEL 1

To Theater
District

Start

C

1

IN

3  2

LEVEL 2

To Roof
(Exterior)

Finish "A"

To Theater
District

N

A

1

A

2

N

C

C

- ARMAMENTS AND AMMO
- ARMAMENTS AND AMMO:
  MINI NUKE
- ARMAMENTS AND AMMO:
  MINI NUKE (FAT MAN)
- ARMAMENTS AND AMMO: TRUNK
- ARMOR PART: FUSION CORE
- BOTTLECAPS
- COLLECTIBLE: NUKA CHERRY
- COLLECTIBLE: REQUIRED READING:
  UNSTOPPABLES

- CRAFTING: CHEMISTRY STATION
- CRAFTING: COOKING STATION
- CRAFTING: POWER ARMOR STATION
- DANGER: OIL!
- DANGER: RADIATION (MILD)!
- DANGER: TRIPWIRE!
- DANGER: TURRETS!
- FACTION: RAIDERS
- FACTION: CHARACTER: BOSCO
- HEALTH OR CHEMS
- UNIQUE ITEM: MASCOT HEAD

This downtown high school has a large swimming pool in the basement. The interior of the school is in a right state; the upper floor has mostly collapsed, and Raiders have set up turrets to dissuade visitors. Work your way between floors, using the stairwell to the southeast if you get lost. The area of most interest is the basement. There's also a door here to Medical Center Metro. Otherwise, clear the area, scavenge, and use the door to the roof to catch a great view of the Boston skyline and remove the final Raider threats.

## VAULT-TEC RECOMMENDED LOOT

**ARMAMENTS AND AMMO:**
**MINI NUKE AND FAT MAN**
**ARMOR PART: FUSION CORE**
**COLLECTIBLE: NUKA CHERRY**

**REQUIRED READING: UNSTOPPABLES**
**UNIQUE ITEM:**
**D.B. TECH VARSITY UNIFORM**
**UNIQUE ITEM: MASCOT HEAD**

# [16.05] HESTER'S CONSUMER ROBOTICS

THREAT LEVELS 25+

- ARMAMENTS AND AMMO
- ARMAMENTS AND AMMO: TRUNK
- BOTTLECAPS
- CRAFTING: ARMOR WORKBENCH
- CRAFTING: POWER ARMOR STATION
- CRAFTING: WEAPONS WORKBENCH
- DANGER: EXPLODING BARRELS!
- FACTION: ROBOTS
- HEALTH OR CHEMS

This was a sales center and maintenance garage catering to the buyer of refurbished and upgraded consumer robots. Hester Geppetto was the long-dead proprietor. Nowadays the place is said to be a deceptive trap and is shunned by scavengers.

To the south and close to the water's edge, this structure has a few robots patrolling the perimeter and two entrances—the main doors to the southwest and a side door to the north.

## FIG 16.05: HESTER'S CONSUMER ROBOTICS (INTERIOR)

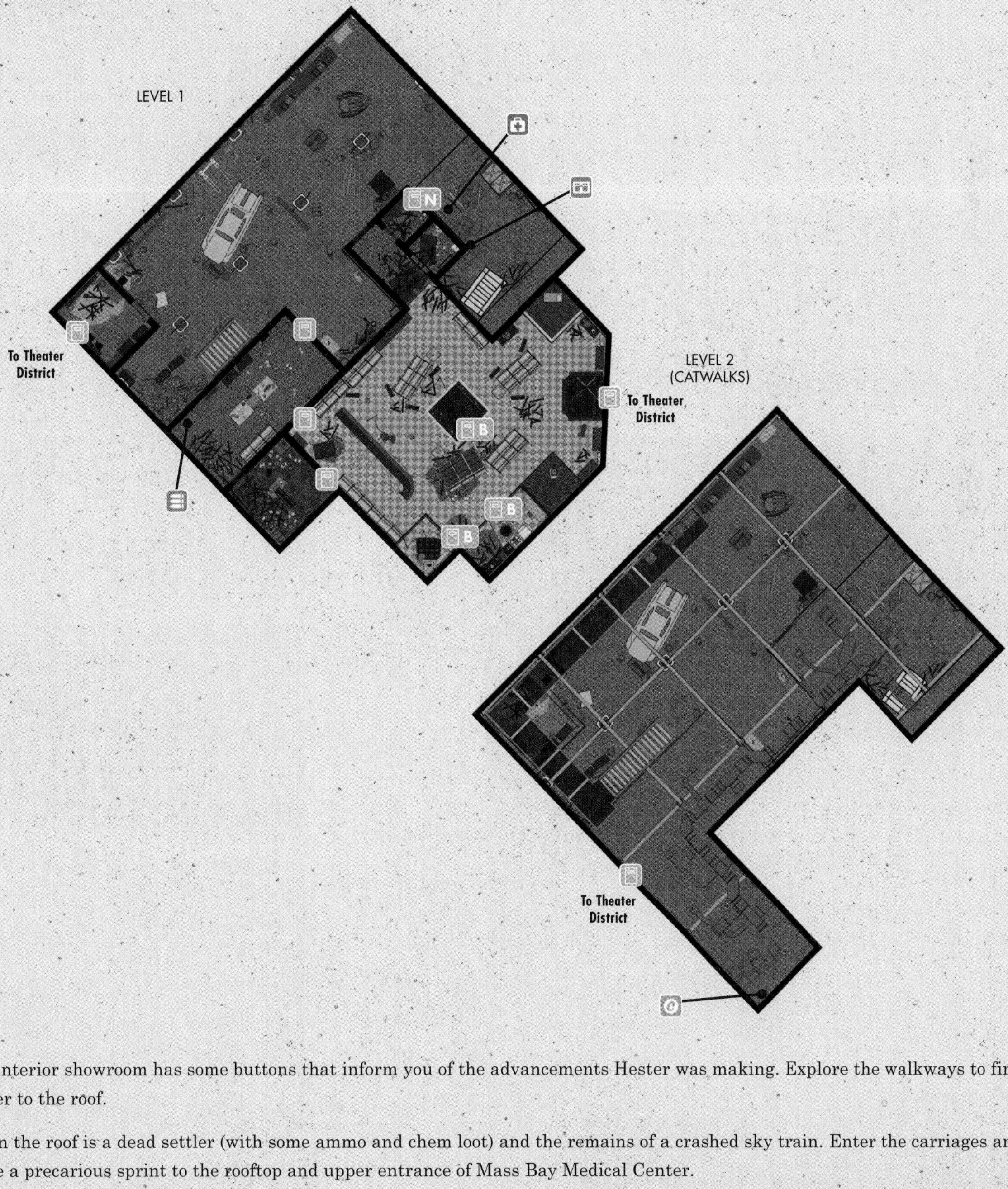

LEVEL 1

To Theater District

N

LEVEL 2 (CATWALKS)

To Theater District

B

B

B

To Theater District

The interior showroom has some buttons that inform you of the advancements Hester was making. Explore the walkways to find a ladder to the roof.

Up on the roof is a dead settler (with some ammo and chem loot) and the remains of a crashed sky train. Enter the carriages and make a precarious sprint to the rooftop and upper entrance of Mass Bay Medical Center.

# SECONDARY LOCATIONS

## [16.01] HUB 360

- ARMAMENTS AND AMMO
- ARMAMENTS AND AMMO: TRUNK
- DANGER: LONG DROP!
- DANGER: RADIATION (MILD)!
- FACTION: SUPER MUTANTS
- HEALTH OR CHEMS
- QUEST VISIT: WEATHERVANE (THE RAILROAD)

Access this sprawling Super Mutant camp from the ground or from the remains of the elevated freeway. Beginning at ground level, look for the structure and the rickety platforms stretching across the roads to the two other buildings to the east.

The ground-floor interior consists of a reception and dining area and a mezzanine staircase to a working elevator. Ascend to the next interior area, where you'll find kitchens and a door to Café Patio. Outside is a balcony offering views and more killing opportunities but no way out (except a long drop).

Back inside, climb the rubble pile and access either the rooftop pool (another greenskin hangout spot and access north to the fallen skybridge, or south to the Mass Bay Medical Center) or the elevator that takes you to the top of this structure. Here you can claim the contents of a steamer trunk and finish off the last mutated giant. There's a plank here for positioning the device in the specified quest.

Now, can you dive into the pool below?

## [16.02] PEARWOOD RESIDENCES

- ARMAMENTS AND AMMO
- DANGER: LONG DROP!
- DANGER: RADIATION (MILD)!
- FACTION: SUPER MUTANTS
- HEALTH OR CHEMS

This six-floor high-rise has been thoroughly ransacked, and the floor inside the structure has given way. Take the interior elevator up, and make some nimble drops to each ruined ledge to gather any items you wish. Exit via the top or bottom floor.

The top exit leads to perhaps the least private bathroom in Boston. Use the fire escape to descend or ascend here, just west of the building.

## [16.03] THE PLANK WALK (THEATER DISTRICT)

## [16.04] GUNNER ENCAMPMENT (THEATER DISTRICT)

- ARMAMENTS AND AMMO
- DANGER: LONG DROP!
- FACTION: GUNNERS
- HEALTH OR CHEMS

Starting at the fire escape or the Gunner encampment atop a ruined office block near the upper level of the elevated freeway, you can maneuver back and forth from the freeway to ground level using the fallen antenna and various planks to maneuver between rooftops. Gather any Railroad loot along the way (atop the fire escape).

## [16.05] PARKING GARAGE (THEATER DISTRICT)

- ARMAMENTS AND AMMO
- CRAFTING: COOKING STATION
- DANGER: LONG DROP!
- FACTION: GUNNERS

A section of the monorail has fallen into the roof of this garage. Check the green trailer at ground level (Advanced) near the concrete steps, or use the vehicle ramps to ascend the structure. The penultimate floor offers access south, into the medical center. Or head onto the roof and head south to reach the Mass Bay train station if you wish.

## [16.06] TICKER TAPE LOUNGE (NORTHWEST)

## [16.07] TICKER TAPE LOUNGE (SOUTHEAST)

- ARMAMENTS AND AMMO
- CRAFTING: CHEMISTRY STATION
- CRAFTING: COOKING STATION
- DANGER: LONG DROP!
- FACTION: GUNNERS

Once offering great food and better views, the lounge is comprised of two buildings linked via a small skybridge. Access the northwest structure from the elevated freeway. Access the southeast structure from the roof of the medical center by taking the construction lift down from the crashed Vertibird area. Inside are a couple of two-level lounges to traverse and some ammo and other supplies to covet.

## [16.08] UNDER THE ON-RAMP: CAMP AND GARAGE

- ARMAMENTS AND AMMO
- CRAFTING: CHEMISTRY STATION
- CRAFTING: COOKING STATION
- CRAFTING: POWER ARMOR STATION
- CRAFTING: WEAPONS WORKBENCH
- FACTION: SCAVENGERS
- FACTION: CHARACTER: SLIM

You may encounter wandering folk and a chap named Slim around here, but this is usually a good and safe place to tinker or sleep.

## [16.09] THE ON-RAMP (THEATER DISTRICT)

Use this entrance to access the elevated freeway, which you can traverse north into the Financial District and south into Zone 6, close to University Point.

## [16.10] RAILROAD DEAD DROP (THEATER DISTRICT)

- ARMAMENTS AND AMMO

A small run-down apartment has a roof generator where a thoughtful Railroad agent has placed a duffel bag and ammo crate. Access via the plank connected to the on-ramp.

## [16.11] STREET CORNER (THEATER DISTRICT)

- ARMOR PART: FUSION CORE

A pair of mannequins around the corner from the fallen Nuka Cola sign stand close to the small Raider camp under the on-ramp. Check the barrel by the dummies for a Fusion Core.

## [16.12] OLD SNIPER CAMP

- CRAFTING: COOKING STATION
- FACTION: SCAVENGER
- FACTION: CHARACTER: DANDO

A low-rise structure between the on-ramps provides a stairwell to keep you fit and a view of the Mass Pike to the west. Dando and his dog sometimes live here.

# ZONE 17: BOSTON HARBOR (WATERFRONT)

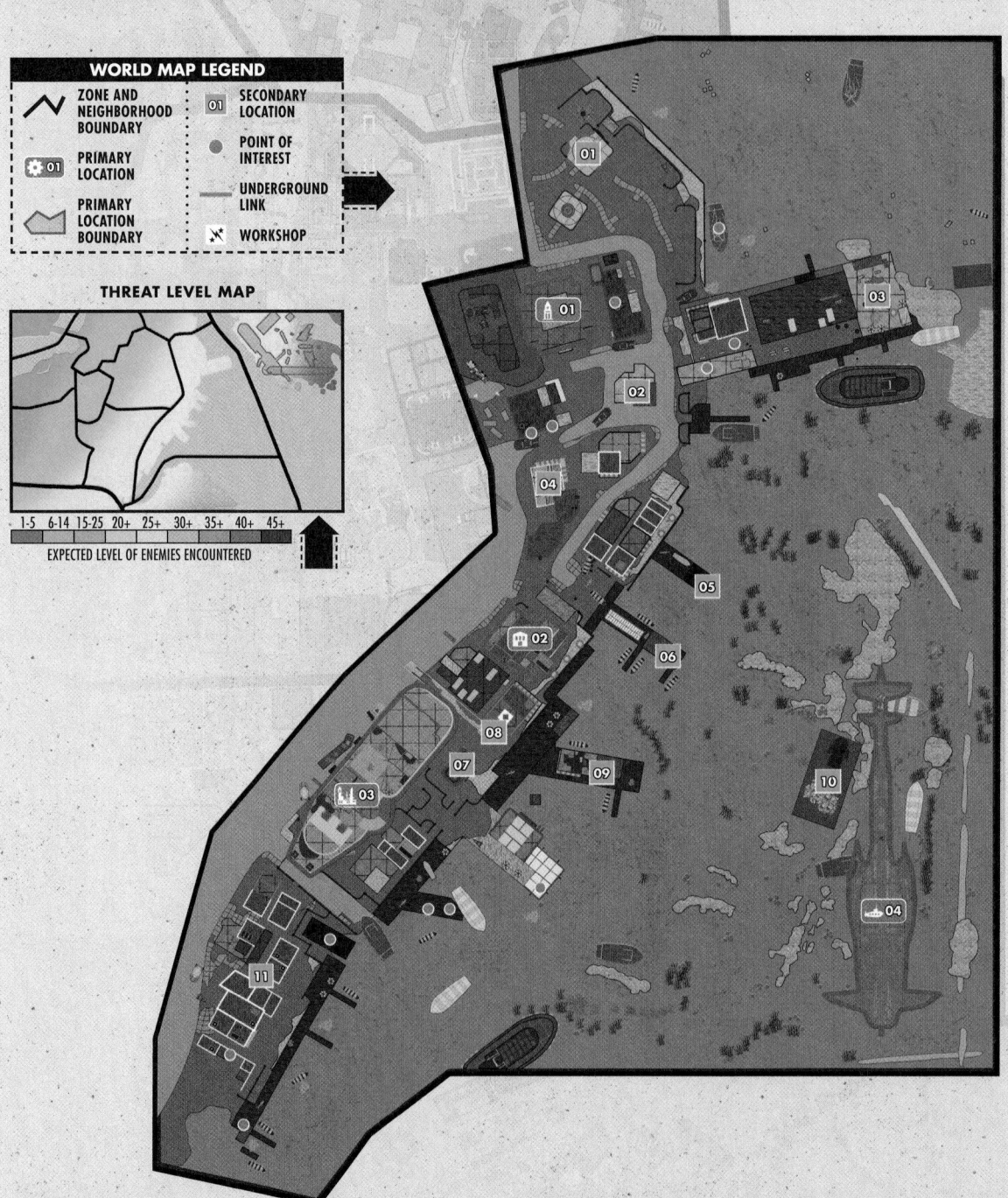

**WORLD MAP LEGEND**

| | | | |
|---|---|---|---|
| ∿ | ZONE AND NEIGHBORHOOD BOUNDARY | 01 | SECONDARY LOCATION |
| ⚙ 01 | PRIMARY LOCATION | ● | POINT OF INTEREST |
| ◿ | PRIMARY LOCATION BOUNDARY | — | UNDERGROUND LINK |
| | | ⚒ | WORKSHOP |

**THREAT LEVEL MAP**

1-5  6-14  15-25  20+  25+  30+  35+  40+  45+

EXPECTED LEVEL OF ENEMIES ENCOUNTERED

## Primary Locations

- [17.01] CUSTOM HOUSE TOWER
- [17.02] THE SHAMROCK TAPHOUSE
- [17.03] HARBORMASTER HOTEL
- [17.04] YANGTZE

## Secondary Locations

- [17.01] WATERFRONT PARK
- [17.02] CUSTOM HOUSE TOWER COURTYARD
- [17.03] WAREHOUSE AND WHARF
- [17.04] SCAVENGERS' ROOFTOPS (WATERFRONT)
- [17.05] TINKERER'S BOATHOUSE (WATERFRONT)
- [17.06] MAIN BOATHOUSE (WATERFRONT)
- [17.07] LOCKED DINER
- [17.08] PEDESTRIAN WALKWAY (WATERFRONT)
- [17.09] WATERFRONT CABIN
- [17.10] SCRAP METAL BARGE
- [17.11] DESOLATE PROMENADE

Just as the Charles River empties out into the Massachusetts Bay, so, too, did container vessels from across the Old World, about 400 years ago. Now the harbor is in serious need of dredging, with a variety of rusty hulks and rotting boats scattered about this waterway. Home to Mirelurks, pockets of Super Mutants and Raiders, and the odd roving Scavenger, Boston Harbor offers views out to the east, toward the airport. Head north to Charleston, west into the Theater District, and south toward Quincy and South Boston. Though there are few primary locations, this has the distinction of being among the most dangerous of neighborhoods, as the ground is sometimes soggy and the inhabitants never friendly. Also, did you hear tales of the sea monster lurking in the bay?

## MAP LEGEND

| | | | | | | |
|---|---|---|---|---|---|---|
| 13 ——— 20 OPTIMAL ROUTE | 🄲 BOTTLECAPS | | 🄰 HEALTH OR CHEMS | 🄵 FUSION CORE | 🄱 BOBBLEHEAD | 🄽 NUKA COLA QUANTUM |
| | 🔒 SAFE | | 🖥 TERMINAL | 🄿 POWER ARMOR | 🄽 NUKA CHERRY | 🄷 HOLOTAPE |
| | 🗄 ARMAMENTS AND AMMO | | 🧰 STEAMER TRUNK | 🄱🄱 REQUIRED READING | 🄼 MINI NUKE | 🄺 A KEY |
| AREA OF INTEREST | 🚪 DOOR | | | | *Collectibles:* | |

| | | | |
|---|---|---|---|
| **N** – Novice (Locked) | **E** – Expert (Locked) | **T** – Terminal required to unlock | **IN** – Inaccessible | **CB** – Circuit Breaker |
| **A** – Advanced (Locked) | **M** – Master (Locked) | **KEY** – Key or ID Card required to unlock | **C** – Chained | **B** – Button |

# PRIMARY LOCATIONS

### 🏛 [17.01] CUSTOM HOUSE TOWER

THREAT LEVELS 25+
THREAT LEVELS 30+

– ARMAMENTS AND AMMO
– FACTION: RAIDER
– FACTION: SUPER MUTANT
– HEALTH OR CHEMS

A landmark from the early 20th century, the Custom House served as a federal structure. Built on reclaimed shoreline and surviving the bombs, it now features a new and more bloody interior decoration due to recent Super Mutant activity.

### 🍺 [17.02] THE SHAMROCK TAPHOUSE

THREAT LEVELS 30+

## VAULT-TEC RECOMMENDED LOOT ⬢

**ARMAMENTS AND AMMO: MINI NUKE**
**HOLOTAPE: GWINNETT LAGER RECIPE**
**COLLECTIBLE: NUKA CHERRY**
**COLLECTIBLE: NUKA COLA QUANTUM (2)**
**REQUIRED READING: TOTAL HACK**

– ARMAMENTS AND AMMO
– ARMAMENTS AND AMMO: MINI NUKE
– ARMAMENTS AND AMMO: TRUNK
– BOTTLECAPS
– COLLECTIBLE: HOLOTAPE: DRINKIN'
  BUDDY PASSWORD
– COLLECTIBLE: HOLOTAPE:
  GWINNETT LAGER RECIPE
– COLLECTIBLE: HOLOTAPE: SPOTLIGHT
  HACKING SOURCE CODE
– COLLECTIBLE: NUKA CHERRY
– COLLECTIBLE: NUKA COLA QUANTUM (2)
– COLLECTIBLE: REQUIRED READING:
  TOTAL HACK
– CRAFTING: CHEMISTRY STATION

– CRAFTING: COOKING STATION
– DANGER: CAN CHIMES!
– DANGER: MAKESHIFT BOMB!
– DANGER: TENSION TRIGGER!
– FACTION: MOLE RATS
– FACTION: RADROACHES
– FACTION: RAIDERS
– FACTION: CHARACTER: GAFF
– FACTION: CHARACTER:
  DRINKIN' BUDDY
– HEALTH OR CHEMS
– QUEST START: MISCELLANEOUS
  (TROUBLE BREWIN')
– QUEST VISIT: MISCELLANEOUS
  (TROUBLE BREWIN')

This historic bar and pool club on the edge of the Theater District is run by one of the smaller Raider gangs active in this area. The bar has had a long and illustrious history since its establishment in 1787 . . . 500 years ago. Paul Revere was said to drink here.

On the sliver of land between the Waterfront and Financial District neighborhoods, this fortified Raider camp has a single entrance (the hatch from the cellar is cordoned off behind wire fencing). Expect turrets and harsh language. Mop up the Raider scum and loot their ammo. Then enter the establishment.

The place is run by Gaff, a Raider with a few cohorts scattered throughout the premises. The key to open the problematic doors of this establishment is in the cellar.

MAP

ZONE 17

NEIGHBORHOOD:
BOSTON HARBOR
(WATERFRONT)

**FIG 17.02: THE SHAMROCK TAPHOUSE (INTERIOR)**

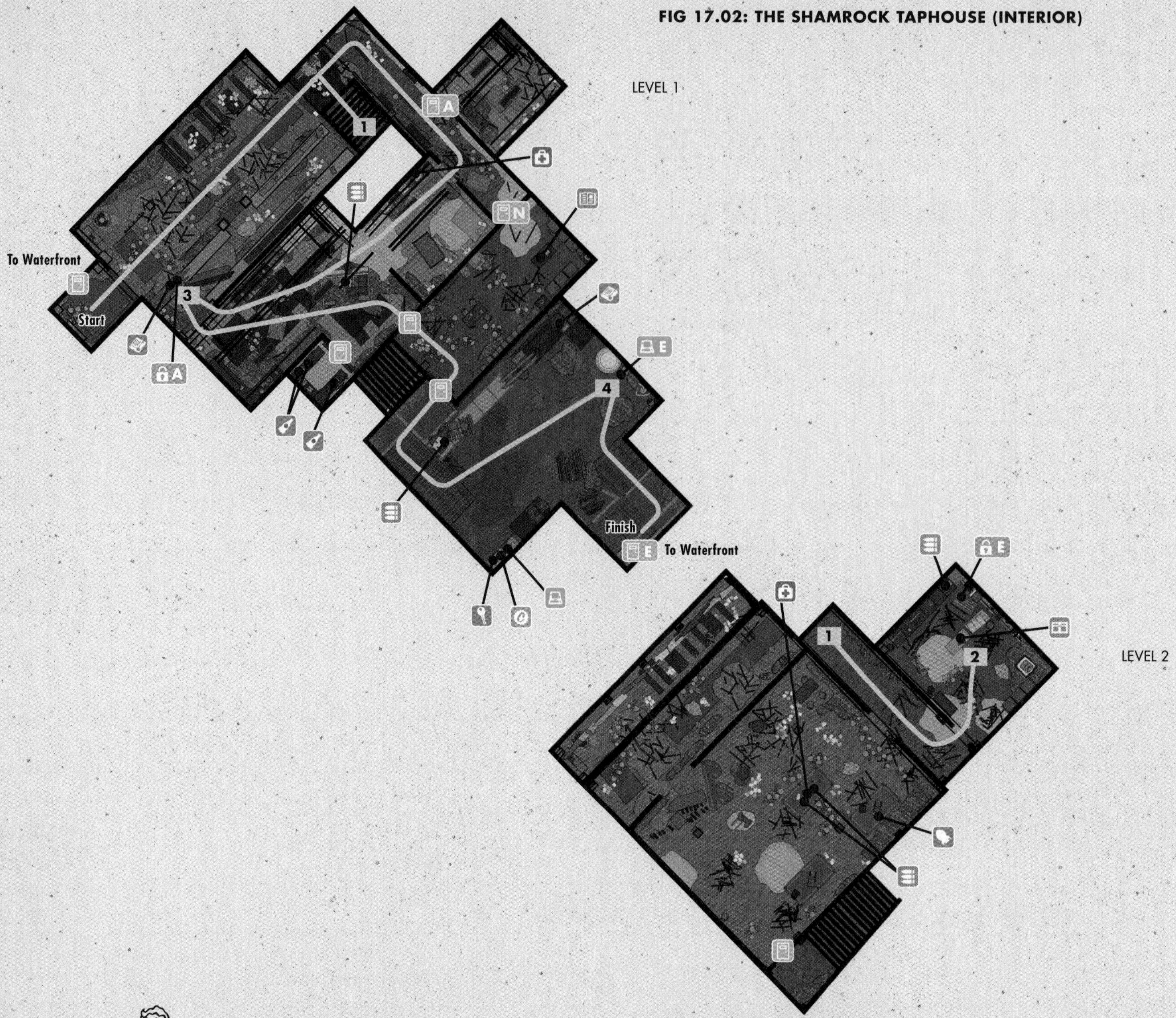

LEVEL 1

To Waterfront

Start

3

1

A

N

E

4

Finish

E   To Waterfront

2

LEVEL 2

E

![Vault Boy giving thumbs up] **Miscellaneous Quest: Trouble Brewin'**

Also in the cellar is a special "Drinkin' Buddy" Mister Brewer Protectron. Check him out near the terminal (Expert), or use the password from the Holotape on the cellar shelves. Consult the Goodneighbor Freeform quests for the full story.

 **[17.03] HARBORMASTER HOTEL**     THREAT LEVELS 30+

– ARMAMENTS AND AMMO
– BOTTLECAPS
– COLLECTIBLE: NUKA CHERRY
– DANGER: LONG DROP!

– FACTION: RAIDERS
– HEALTH AND CHEMS+
– UNIQUE ITEM: GIDDYUP
  BUTTERCUP (ITEM)

Close to the water's edge, this fortified Raider's camp has too many heads on poles and too few blockades, which allows you easy access into the hotel. Gather ammo before you enter.

Once inside, pick the foyer clean of minor items, then ride the elevator up to a ruined hallway with a locked door (Advanced). Inside, one of the older residents is hanging out with a couple of his toy pals. There's access out to the roof too.

On the rooftop pool deck, there's light resistance and a load of chems to scavenge, as well as a Nuka Cherry by the bar. Watch the sides; that drop looks lethal!

506

- ARMAMENTS AND AMMO+
- ARMAMENTS AND AMMO: MINI NUKE
- ARMOR PART: FUSION CORE
- BOTTLECAPS
- COLLECTIBLE: NUKA CHERRY
- COLLECTIBLE: NUKA COLA QUANTUM
- CRAFTING: CHEMISTRY STATION
- CRAFTING: WEAPONS WORKBENCH
- DANGER: OIL!
- DANGER: RADIATION (SEVERE)!

- FACTION: FERAL GHOULS
- FACTION: CHARACTER: CAPTAIN ZAO
- FACTION: CHARACTER: FIRST MATE
- HEALTH AND CHEMS+
- QUEST VISIT: HERE THERE BE MONSTERS (SIDE)
- UNIQUE ITEM: HOMING BEACONS

**FIG 17.04: YANGTZE (INTERIOR)**

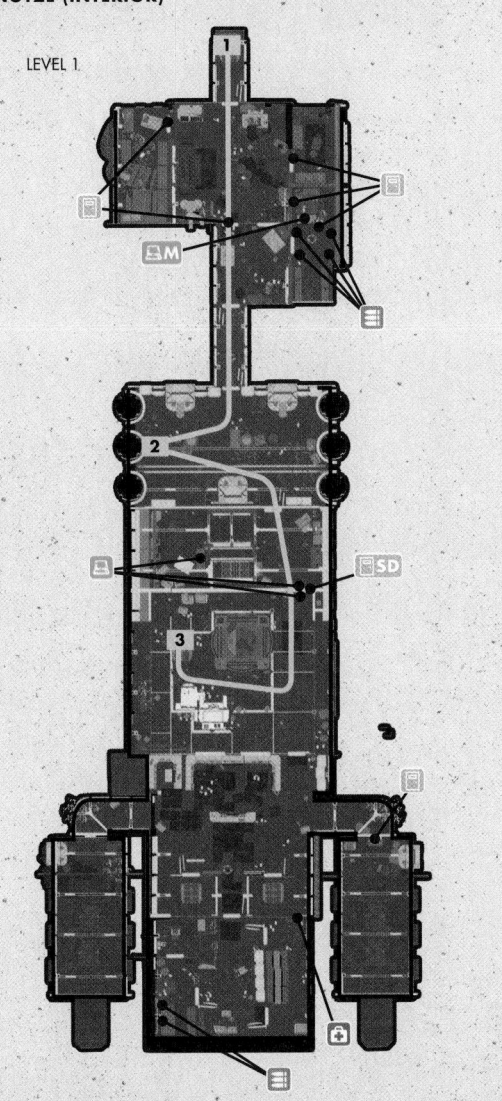

LEVEL 1

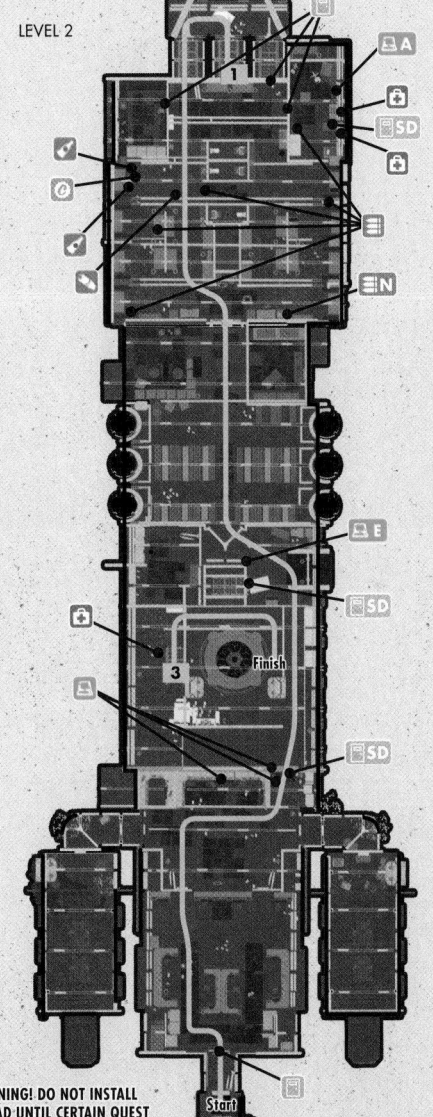

LEVEL 2

*WARNING! DO NOT INSTALL
WARHEAD UNTIL CERTAIN QUEST
OBJECTIVES ARE MET!

Start

To
Commonwealth

**MAP**

**ZONE 17**

NEIGHBORHOOD:
BOSTON HARBOR
(WATERFRONT)

## VAULT-TEC RECOMMENDED LOOT

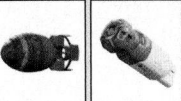    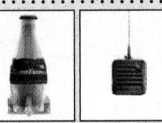

**ARMAMENTS AND AMMO: MINI NUKE**
**ARMOR PART: FUSION CORE**
**COLLECTIBLE: NUKA CHERRY**
**COLLECTIBLE: NUKA COLA QUANTUM**
**UNIQUE ITEM: HOMING BEACONS**

Easily mistaken for a strange aquatic monster, this Chinese nuclear submarine (Liao-Class Type 113) is hidden among the wrecks of other ships in the Boston Harbor. It is commanded by Captain Zao. Should you wish to access the terminal (Master) on the lower level, find the first mate's password from the fellow lurking down in these parts.

# SECONDARY LOCATIONS

## [17.01] WATERFRONT PARK

– FACTION: RADSTAG DOES       – HEALTH OR CHEMS

A small formal gardens on the waterfront, now home to roaming wildlife and a collection of withered skeletons gazing out into the harbor.

## [17.02] CUSTOM HOUSE TOWER COURTYARD

– ARMAMENTS AND AMMO

A podium and signs of a disagreement in the past. Scrabble around in the rubble for a few helpful items.

## [17.03] WAREHOUSE AND WHARF

– ARMAMENTS AND AMMO       – FACTION: SUPER MUTANTS
– CRAFTING: COOKING STATION

Greenskins have taken over the eastern wharf here. They have fashioned a couple of rowboats on a bloody pole and are wallowing in offal. The green tugboat to the south is a good place to snipe from. Enter the warehouse using the door on the south side, and gather some ammo inside.

## [17.04] SCAVENGERS' ROOFTOPS (WATERFRONT)

– ARMAMENTS AND AMMO    – FACTION: RAIDERS    – FACTION: SCAVENGER

Raiders have a habit of ambushing those below from this small rooftop. Scale the stairs to gather items and collect equipment from the corpses of those you recently slay.

## [17.05] TINKERER'S BOATHOUSE (WATERFRONT)

– CRAFTING: ARMOR WORKBENCH    – CRAFTING: POWER ARMOR STATION
– CRAFTING: CHEMISTRY STATION    – FACTION: MIRELURKS

A small boathouse still has a number of functioning crafting stations, if you can wade through the irradiated wildlife to get there.

## [17.06] MAIN BOATHOUSE (WATERFRONT)

– FACTION: MIRELURKS       A few scavengable items are still available from this rotting boathouse.

## [17.07] LOCKED DINER

– CRAFTING: COOKING STATION     – HEALTH OR CHEMS

Wrestle with the locked door (Advanced) before cooking up a recipe or two.

## [17.08] PEDESTRIAN WALKWAY (WATERFRONT)

– ARMAMENTS AND AMMO     – FACTION: RAIDERS

This L-shaped raised walkway allows you to enter the Theater District and the northwest side of the Harbormaster Hotel and gain a tactical height advantage on any foes below.

## [17.09] WATERFRONT CABIN

– FACTION: SETTLER     – QUEST START: HERE THERE BE
– FACTION: CHARACTER: DONNY KOWALSKI    MONSTERS (SIDE)

At the end of the wharf, a small boy named Donny is gazing out into the harbor, sure he's seen a monster poking its eye stalk out of the water. Perhaps you can humor him?

## [17.10] SCRAP METAL BARGE

– DANGER: RADIATION (MILD)!     – HEALTH OR CHEMS

Moored close to the "sea monster" is a rusting barge carrying scrap metal. Check inside for the remains of the crew and a safe to pry open (Expert).

## [17.11] DESOLATE PROMENADE

– FACTION: RADSCORPIONS

A series of once-quaint wooden stores line the waterfront. Irradiated wildlife prowls the alleyways adjacent to the Theater District. This location is now famous; it has the most difficult-to-reach cooler in all of Boston!

MAP

**ZONE 17**

NEIGHBORHOOD:
BOSTON HARBOR
(WATERFRONT)

# ZONE 18:
# NEIGHBORHOOD:
# SOUTH BOSTON

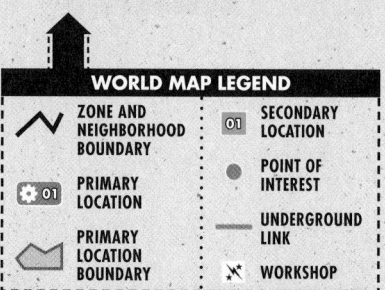

## WORLD MAP LEGEND

| | | | |
|---|---|---|---|
| 〰 | ZONE AND NEIGHBORHOOD BOUNDARY | 01 | SECONDARY LOCATION |
| ⚙01 | PRIMARY LOCATION | ● | POINT OF INTEREST |
| ◤ | PRIMARY LOCATION BOUNDARY | — | UNDERGROUND LINK |
| | | ✕ | WORKSHOP |

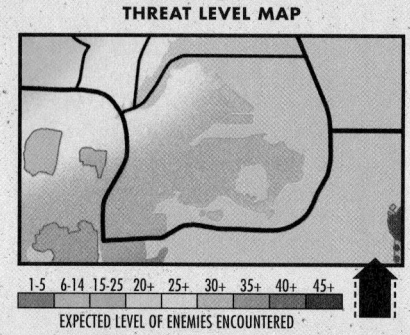

**THREAT LEVEL MAP**

| 1-5 | 6-14 | 15-25 | 20+ | 25+ | 30+ | 35+ | 40+ | 45+ |
|---|---|---|---|---|---|---|---|---|

EXPECTED LEVEL OF ENEMIES ENCOUNTERED

## Primary Locations

- [18.01] FOUR LEAF FISHPACKING PLANT
- [18.02] GENERAL ATOMICS FACTORY
- [18.03] ANDREW STATION
- [18.04] SOUTH BOSTON POLICE DEPARTMENT
- [18.05] GWINNETT BREWERY
- [18.06] THE GWINNETT RESTAURANT
- [18.07] SOUTH BOSTON HIGH SCHOOL
- [18.08] THE CASTLE
- [18.09] UNIVERSITY POINT

## Secondary Locations

- [18.01] BUS AND APARTMENT WRECKAGE
- [18.02] JOE'S SPUCKIES (SOUTHIE SPEAKEASY)
- [18.03] DOCKSIDE WAREHOUSE (SOUTH BOSTON)
- [18.04] FACTORY (SOUTH BOSTON)
- [18.05] FOUR LEAF FISHPACKING CONTAINER YARD
- [18.06] CONSTRUCTION YARD
- [18.07] ROOF GENERATOR (SOUTH BOSTON)
- [18.08] ROUNDABOUT RAIDER CAMP

- [18.09] HAWTHORNE ESTATE
- [18.10] DORCHESTER HEIGHT MONUMENT
- [18.11] ROOF CAMP (SOUTH BOSTON)
- [18.12] THE CANDY SHOP
- [18.13] SOUTH BOSTON CHURCH
- [18.14] SOUTH BOSTON WHARF AND RESTROOMS
- [18.15] RUSTING SHIP AND STILT CABIN

Featuring the most fearsome threats outside of Boston Common, South Boston is separated from the rest of the neighborhoods by the elevated freeway remains (to the west) and the bay (to the north and east). The lack of giant towering skyscrapers also means you're less likely to wander around in a bewildered fashion, but don't let your guard down. Powerful pincer-clapping Mirelurks roam the coast, and numerous pockets of Raiders, ferals, and a few Super Mutants are also active in this zone. The neighborhood has many impressive and ancient structures—none more so than the Castle, a fortification once belonging to the Minutemen. This could perhaps be the crowning achievement to the explorer who seeks to build and unite settlements both far and wide.

| MAP LEGEND | | | | | |
|---|---|---|---|---|---|
| 13 — 20 OPTIMAL ROUTE | C BOTTLECAPS | HEALTH OR CHEMS | FUSION CORE | Collectibles: BOBBLEHEAD | NUKA COLA QUANTUM |
| | SAFE | TERMINAL | POWER ARMOR | NUKA CHERRY | HOLOTAPE |
| AREA OF INTEREST | ARMAMENTS AND AMMO | STEAMER TRUNK | REQUIRED READING | MINI NUKE | A KEY |
| | DOOR | | | | |

N – Novice (Locked)   E – Expert (Locked)   T – Terminal required to unlock   IN – Inaccessible   CB – Circuit Breaker
A – Advanced (Locked)   M – Master (Locked)   KEY – Key or ID Card required to unlock   C – Chained   B – Button

# PRIMARY LOCATIONS

## [18.01] FOUR LEAF FISHPACKING PLANT

THREAT LEVELS 30+

FIG 18.01A: FOUR LEAF FISHPACKING PLANT (EXTERIOR)

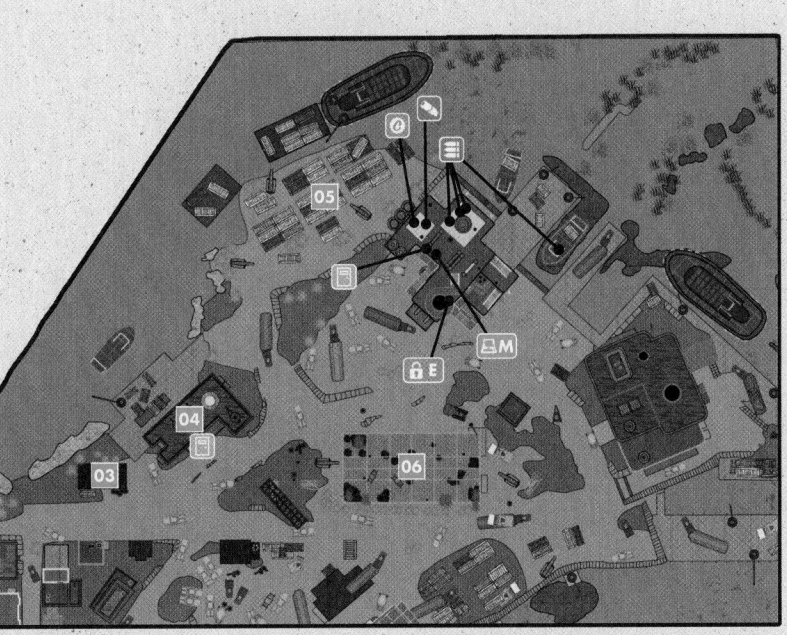

- ARMAMENTS AND AMMO
- ARMAMENTS AND AMMO: TRUNK
- ARMOR PART: FUSION CORE (3)
- BOTTLECAPS
- COLLECTIBLE: NUKA COLA QUANTUM
- COLLECTIBLE: REQUIRED READING: TALES OF A JUNKTOWN JERKY VENDOR
- CRAFTING: CHEMISTRY STATION (4)
- DANGER: OIL!
- DANGER: TRIPWIRES!
- FACTION: FERAL GHOULS
- FACTION: VICIOUS MONGRELS
- FACTION: CHARACTER: MAROWSKI
- HEALTH OR CHEMS++
- QUEST VISIT: DIAMOND CITY BLUES (SIDE)

**ARMOR PART: FUSION CORE (3)**
**COLLECTIBLE: NUKA COLA QUANTUM**
**REQUIRED READING: TALES OF A JUNKTOWN JERKY VENDOR**

This plant operated at a loss and was almost ready to shut down in October 2077. This was partly due to mismanagement, but the waste runoff from the nearby General Atomics Factory may have been a factor.

The exterior yard features stacks of rusting containers, a pack of mongrels, and some unpleasant feral types. There is an impressive tripwire system that can only be disarmed during the specified quest; it seems to forewarn whoever is behind the strange gantry terminal (Master) directly above the main entrance.

Clear the roof of rotting undesirables, then ammo. Check the chimney stack gantry for a safe (Expert). Access the gantry terminal (Master) to reveal Marowski's chem lab.

**FIG 18.01B: FOUR LEAF FISHPACKING PLANT (INTERIOR)**

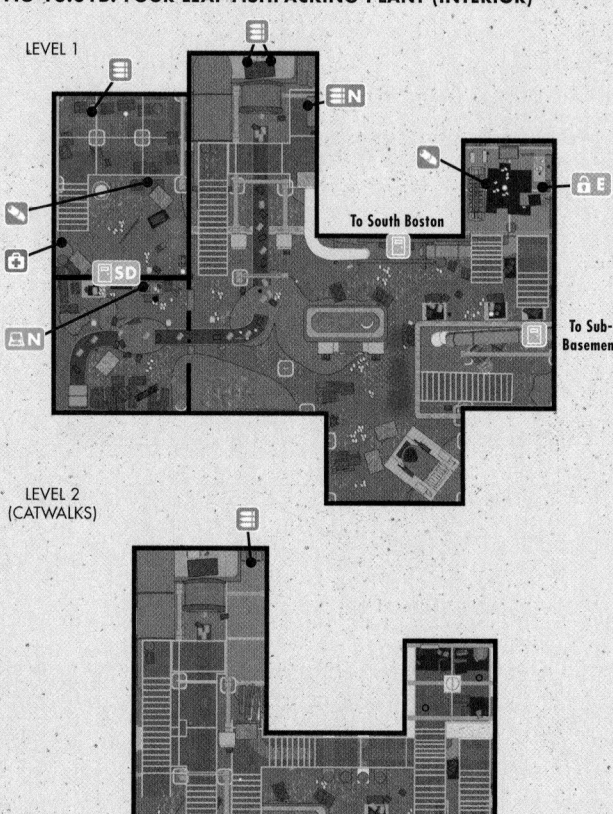

The interior offers a main area of pipes and conveyor belts to explore. There is also an infestation of ferals, especially in the sub-basement. Here you'll also find a steamer trunk.

**FIG 18.01C: MAROWSKI'S CHEM LAB (INTERIOR)**

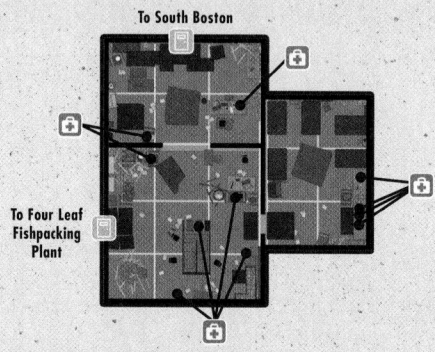

A local gangster's secret laboratory helps chems flow through Goodneighbor like water. This secret lab is completely separate from the main plant interior. You can investigate the area during the specified quest (where you can obtain notes to shut off the laser tripwires and open the secret door), or you can try hacking the exterior terminal on the catwalk (Master) to get in.

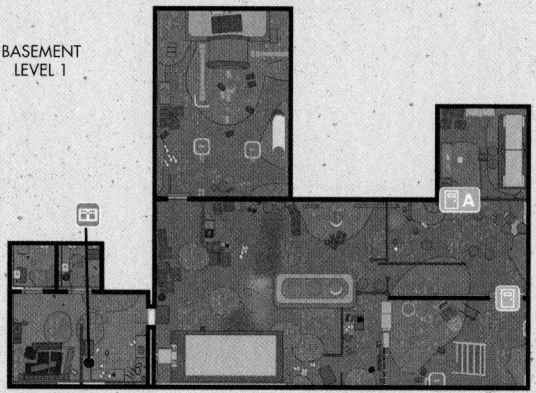

THREAT LEVELS 30+

- ARMAMENTS AND AMMO
- ARMAMENTS AND AMMO: TRUNK BOTTLECAPS
- COLLECTIBLE: NUKA CHERRY
- COLLECTIBLE: NUKA COLA QUANTUM
- COLLECTIBLE: REQUIRED READING: TESLA SCIENCE
- CRAFTING: ARMOR WORKBENCH
- DANGER: TURRETS!
- FACTION: ROBOTS
- HEALTH OR CHEMS
- QUEST START: MISCELLANEOUS (CURIE)
- QUEST START: MISCELLANEOUS (QUALITY ASSURANCE)

## VAULT-TEC RECOMMENDED LOOT

COLLECTIBLE: NUKA CHERRY
COLLECTIBLE: NUKA COLA QUANTUM
REQUIRED READING: TESLA SCIENCE

As civil unrest heightened across the country, General Atomics moved their focus away from this factory, which specialized in creating Ms. Nanny units for child care. A General Atomics nuclear reactor powers the facility to the current day. While the production equipment has since degraded with no one around to repair it, the Quality Assurance Department remains functional.

FIG 18.02A: GENERAL ATOMICS FACTORY (EXTERIOR)

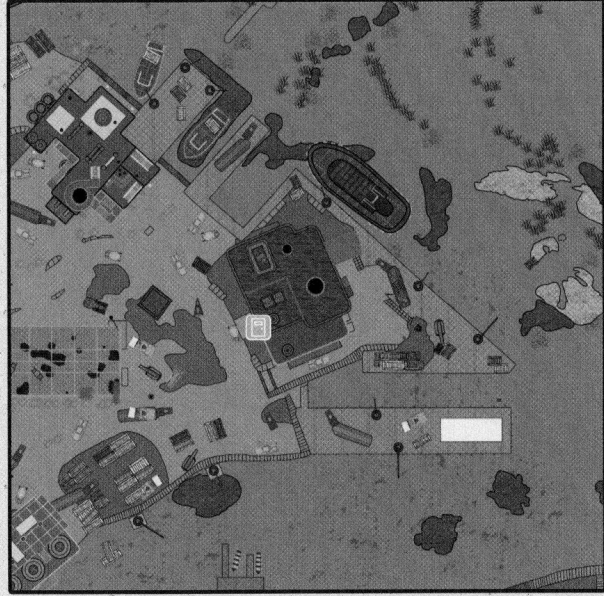

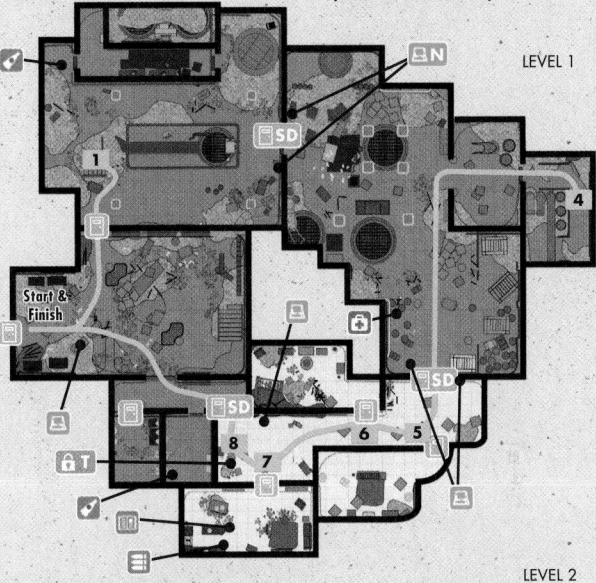

LEVEL 1

Start & Finish

LEVEL 2

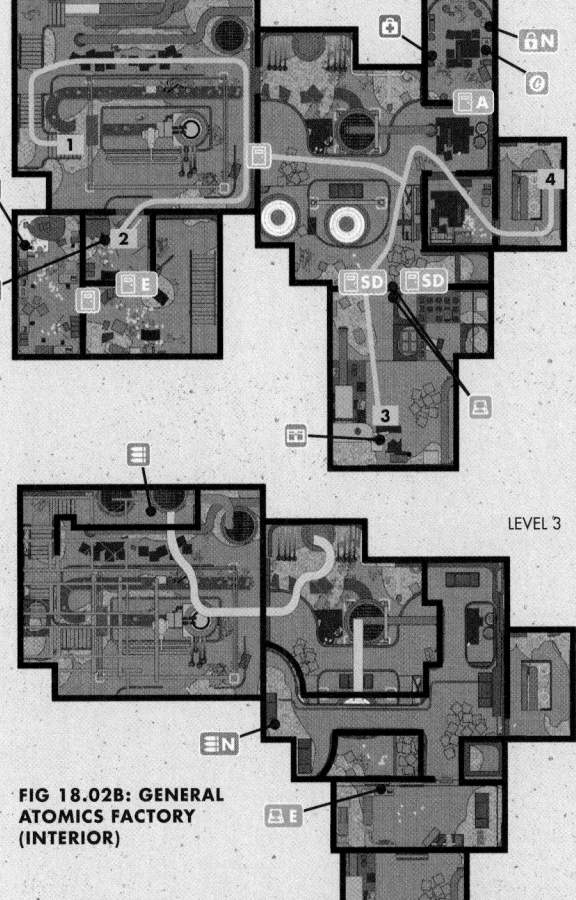

LEVEL 3

FIG 18.02B: GENERAL ATOMICS FACTORY (INTERIOR)

MAP

**ZONE 18**

NEIGHBORHOOD: SOUTH BOSTON

The interior is spread over three floors, with various Mr. Handy robots engaged in hostile protocols, led by Major Gutsy. Aside from other items to gather (including a Giddyup Buttercup), the Quality Assurance wing has some chambers to investigate.

## Miscellaneous: Curie

Should you visit here with Curie, she has some remarks about this location.

## Miscellaneous: Quality Assurance

The Quality Assurance wing of the factory has three tests to complete. Listen to the instructions.

- **TEST 1: SHUT OFF THE RADIO TO PUNISH THE CHILD.**
- **TEST 2: DROP THE BABY BOTTLE INTO THE CRIB NEXT TO THE "BABY" (THE TEDDY BEAR), OR PLACE IT INTO THE INVENTORY OF THE "BABY."**
- **TEST 3: REMOVE DANGEROUS OBJECTS FROM THE CHAMBER (THE WRENCH BENEATH THE OTTOMAN, THE ABRAXO CLEANER FROM THE END TABLE, AND THE MACHETE FROM THE FRIDGE).**

Once complete, the safe (Terminal) unlocks. Also of note is the General Atomics ID card, shown on the map as a "Key", which you can present at location [2.11] General Atomics Galleria to the Director and avoid confrontation.

 **[18.03] ANDREW STATION**     THREAT LEVELS 30+

- ARMAMENTS AND AMMO+
- ARMAMENTS AND AMMO: TRUNK
- BOTTLECAPS+
- COLLECTIBLE: HOLOTAPE: TO CLAIRE
- COLLECTIBLE: NUKA CHERRY (2)
- CRAFTING: ARMOR WORKBENCH
- CRAFTING: CHEMISTRY STATION (2)
- CRAFTING: COOKING STATION (2)
- CRAFTING: WEAPONS WORKBENCH (2)
- DANGER: CAN CHIMES!
- DANGER: MINES!
- DANGER: TURRETS!
- FACTION: ATTACK DOG
- FACTION: RAIDER
- FACTION: CHARACTER: CHANCER
- FACTION: CHARACTER: EDDIE WINTER
- HEALTH OR CHEMS
- QUEST VISIT: LONG TIME COMING (SIDE COMPANION)
- UNIQUE WEAPON: EDDIE'S PEACE

### VAULT-TEC RECOMMENDED LOOT

 COLLECTIBLE: NUKA CHERRY (2)
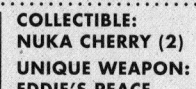 UNIQUE WEAPON: EDDIE'S PEACE

FIG 18.03B: ANDREW STATION (INTERIOR)

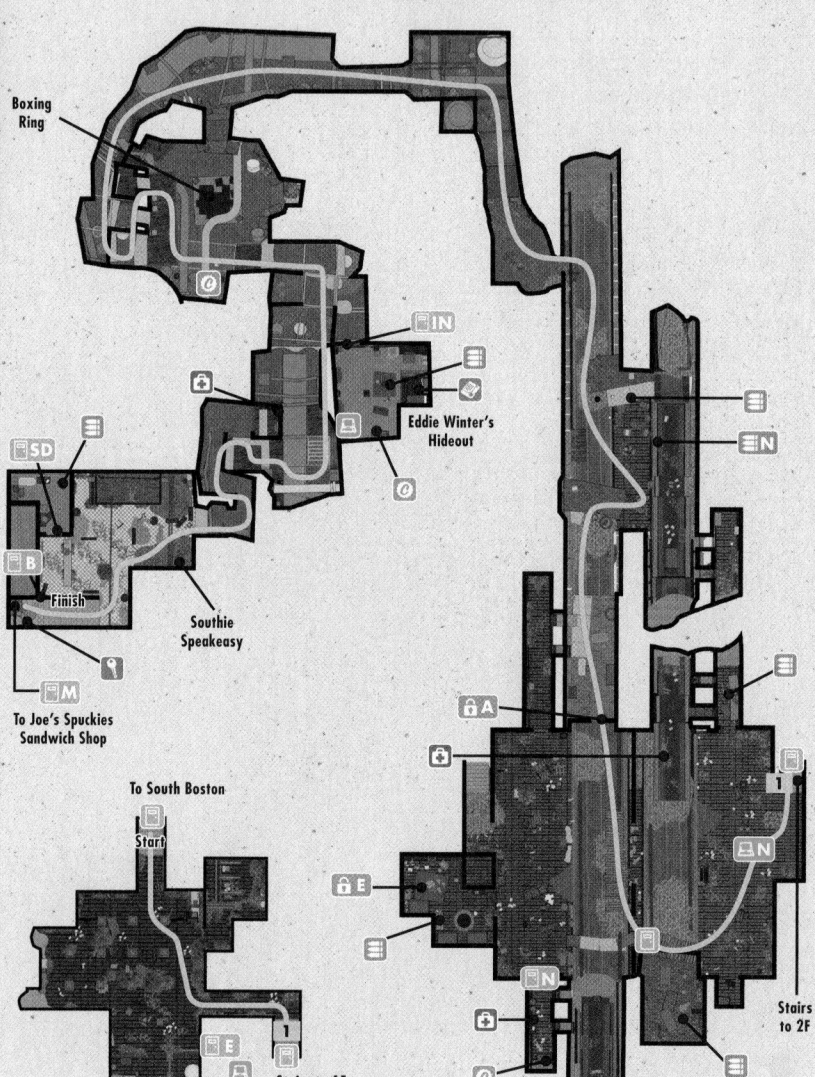

This bus station and subway system is said to contain a number of secret smuggling passageways used by the infamous prewar gangster Eddie Winter. Currently, Raiders are combing the tunnels for evidence of Winter's stash. The exterior station is well defended by Raiders. Note the wall safe (Advanced) at one of the counters.

As you enter the station, optionally unlock the food court door (Expert) to program a Protectron. Descend into the subway and beware of traps, turrets, and a number of Raiders. Eddie Winter's hideout is only accessible during the quest. The speakeasy is where you find Chancer. Use your lockpicking chutzpah to open the trapdoor, which leads into the sandwich shop, or unlock the trapdoor with Joe's Spuckies basement key, found nearby.

## [18.04] SOUTH BOSTON POLICE DEPARTMENT

THREAT LEVELS 30+

– ARMAMENTS AND AMMO
– COLLECTIBLE: HOLOTAPE: EDDIE WINTER HOLOTAPE
– FACTION: RAIDER
– FACTION: ROBOT (PROTECTRON)
– HEALTH OR CHEMS
– QUEST VISIT: LONG TIME COMING (SIDE COMPANION)

Partly blocked from Andrew Station by barricades, the police station has held up well since the bombs dropped. Check the rooftop to the southwest (use the fire escape) to locate some ammo. Inside the police station, there's a terminal to hack (Expert), a cell door to open (Expert), and a police evidence terminal to check for information on Eddie Winter. Aside from a Protectron and two mongrel guard dogs, the upstairs houses the usual scavengable items and a terminal (Novice) to control the Protectron. Eddie Winter's Holotape is on the captain's desk in the north corner, near a wall safe (Expert).

## [18.05] GWINNETT BREWERY

THREAT LEVELS 30+

This venerable brewing operation was started by a local beer maker named Button Gwinnett, namesake of one of the founding fathers. Their Southie Stout was voted "Boston's Best Beer of 2051 and 2062." Currently, the brewing factory is dilapidated. There is roof access, but only from the interior. Outside, beware of flammable oil, shoot through the broken windows to remove the bar from the door to the metal hut, allowing access to a brewing systems terminal, and a recipe for Gwinnett Stout.

– ARMAMENTS AND AMMO
– ARMAMENTS AND AMMO: TRUNK
– COLLECTIBLE: REQUIRED READING:
  TALES OF A JUNKTOWN JERKY VENDOR
– COLLECTIBLE: HOLOTAPE: GWINNETT STOUT RECIPE
– DANGER: OIL!
– DANGER: RADIATION (MILD)!
– FACTION: MIRELURKS

### VAULT-TEC RECOMMENDED LOOT

**REQUIRED READING:
TALES OF A JUNKTOWN
JERKY VENDOR**

Inside, use your hacking or lockpicking abilities to enter the facility, and maneuver along the pipe to reach the roof access door. Otherwise, access the large interior pipe, which leads directly into the Gwinnett Restaurant (Primary Location).

**MAP**

**ZONE 18**

NEIGHBORHOOD:
SOUTH BOSTON

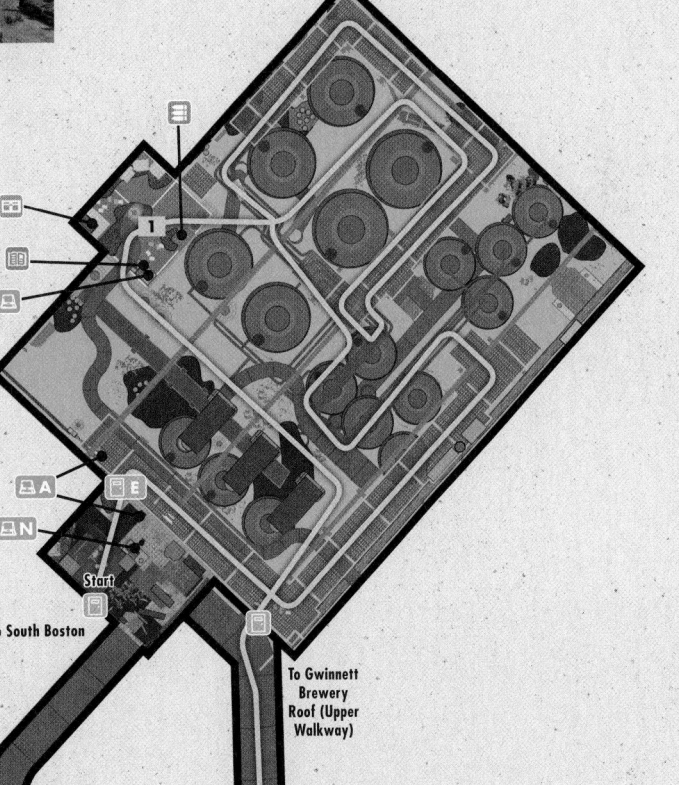

FIG 18.05B: MAIN GWINNETT BREWERY
(INTERIOR)

## [18.06] THE GWINNETT RESTAURANT

THREAT LEVELS 30+

**FIG 18.06 GWINNETT RESTAURANT (INTERIOR)**

- ARMAMENTS AND AMMO
- BOTTLECAPS
- COLLECTIBLE: HOLOTAPE: GWINNETT BREWERY PASSWORD
- COLLECTIBLE: NUKA CHERRY
- COLLECTIBLE: NUKA COLA QUANTUM
- CRAFTING: CHEMISTRY STATION
- DANGER: CAN CHIMES!
- DANGER: ESCAPING GAS!
- DANGER: MINES!
- DANGER: RADIATION (MILD)!
- FACTION: MIRELURKS
- FACTION: SUPER MUTANTS
- HEALTH OR CHEMS

This front-of-house restaurant allowed beer aficionados to sample such fine products as Gwinnett's Pale Ale, Peabody Pilsner, Dead Redcoat Ale, and the infamous Bunker Hill Brew. "Give a Man . . . a Taste of Freedom!" the slogan said. Now the place is piled high with offal and half demolished by Super Mutants. There is a main entrance, as well as a rear entrance (Advanced) for those of a stealthy disposition. The Gwinnett Brewery (Primary Location) can be accessed via the security door and large Mirelurk-infested pipes. If you aren't competent at hacking, find the Gwinnett Brewery password, but approach from the brewery side, not via the restaurant.

If you can't hack into the brewery, feel free to head through the restaurant, into the kitchen, and use the hole in the wall to jump into the craft brewing area (attached to the bar), and enter the water-filled pipe that leads into the Brewery.

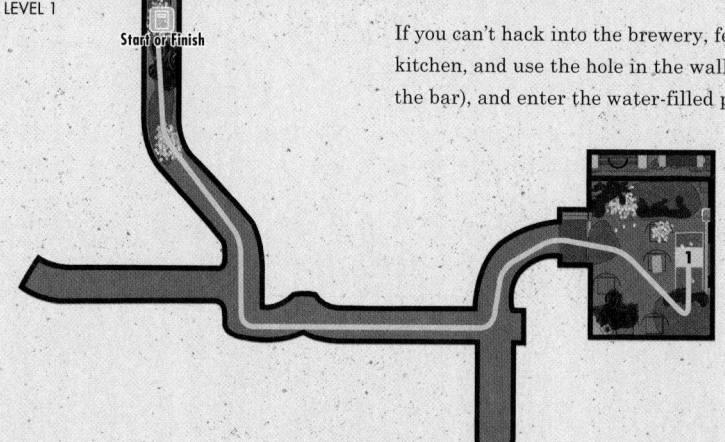

LEVEL 1

**VAULT-TEC RECOMMENDED LOOT**

COLLECTIBLE: NUKA CHERRY
COLLECTIBLE: NUKA COLA QUANTUM

LEVEL 2

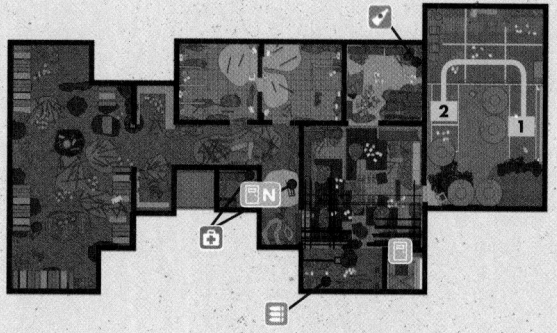

LEVEL 3

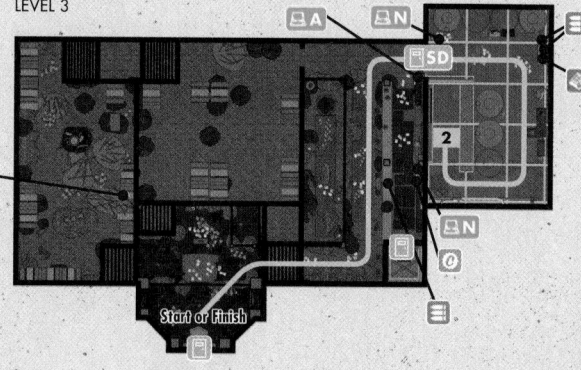

## [18.07] SOUTH BOSTON HIGH SCHOOL

THREAT LEVELS 35+

- ARMAMENTS AND AMMO
- CRAFTING: CHEMISTRY STATION
- FACTION: RAIDER
- HEALTH OR CHEMS

A high school close to the Dorchester Height monument is in a terrible state, with a northern wing (overlooking the Gwinnett Restaurant) exposed to the elements. The main entrance is blocked, meaning access is via the southern wing, now surrounded by wreckage of a small Raider camp. Inside, the few accessible rooms have mostly been picked clean, aside from the contents of a safe (Advanced).

516

- ARMAMENTS AND AMMO+++
- ARMAMENTS AND AMMO: MINI NUKE
- ARMAMENTS AND AMMO: MINI NUKE (FAT MAN)
- ARMOR PART: FUSION CORE
- COLLECTIBLE: REQUIRED READING:
  GUNS AND BULLETS
- CRAFTING: ARMOR WORKBENCH
- CRAFTING: CHEMISTRY STATION (2)
- CRAFTING: WEAPONS WORKBENCH
- DANGER: ESCAPING GAS!
- DANGER: MINES!
- DANGER: TURRETS!
- FACTION: MINUTEMEN
- FACTION: MIRELURKS
- FACTION: RADROACHES
- FACTION: CHARACTER: GENERAL MCGANN
- FACTION: CHARACTER: RONNIE SHAW
- FACTION: CHARACTER: SARGE
- HEALTH OR CHEMS
- QUEST START: DEFEND THE CASTLE
  (THE MINUTEMEN)
- QUEST START: FORM RANKS (THE MINUTEMEN)
- QUEST START: OLD GUNS (THE MINUTEMEN)
- QUEST START: WITH OUR POWERS COMBINED
  (THE MINUTEMEN)
- QUEST VISIT: TAKING INDEPENDENCE
  (THE MINUTEMEN)
- RADIO: RADIO FREEDOM
- SERVICES: TRADER (RONNIE SHAW)
- SERVICES: WORKSHOP
- UNIQUE ITEM: AUTOMATIC LASER MUSKET (WEAPON)
- UNIQUE ITEM: ARTILLERY SCHEMATIC
- UNIQUE ITEM: ARTILLERY SMOKE GRENADES
- UNIQUE ITEM: COLONIAL WOOL COAT
- UNIQUE ITEM: GENERAL'S HAT

**FIG 18.08A THE CASTLE (EXTERIOR)**

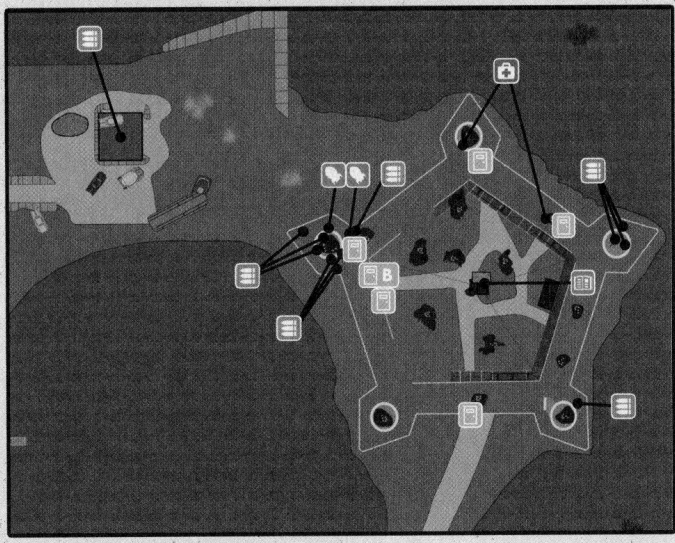

## VAULT-TEC RECOMMENDED LOOT

**ARMAMENTS AND AMMO: MINI NUKE AND FAT MAN**
**ARMOR PART: FUSION CORE**
**REQUIRED READING: GUNS AND BULLETS**
**UNIQUE ITEM: ARTILLERY SCHEMATIC**
**UNIQUE ITEM: ARTILLERY SMOKE GRENADES**
**UNIQUE ITEM: GENERAL'S HAT AND COLONIAL WOOL COAT**

Historians have noted the original name for this settlement was Fort Independence, but the people of the Commonwealth now refer to it simply as the Castle. This place has a long and storied history; it is one of the first forts in America and predates the Revolutionary War. In recent times, it served as the base of operations for the Minutemen as they attempted (and failed) to establish a Provisional government. In 2240, the Castle was partly destroyed by gigantic Mirelurk, and most of the Minutemen leadership died.

Still, it is generally agreed that the location could yet become an excellent base of operations for the Minutemen (and an exceptional settlement) if it can be reclaimed from the sea creatures. Note that the map information refers to interior corridors within the fortification walls.

This location cannot be accessed unless Minutemen Quest: Old Guns is active. It allows you to reach the armory and unlock the otherwise-sealed outer door in the southwest courtyard wall.

**FIG 18.08B THE CASTLE TUNNELS (INTERIOR)**

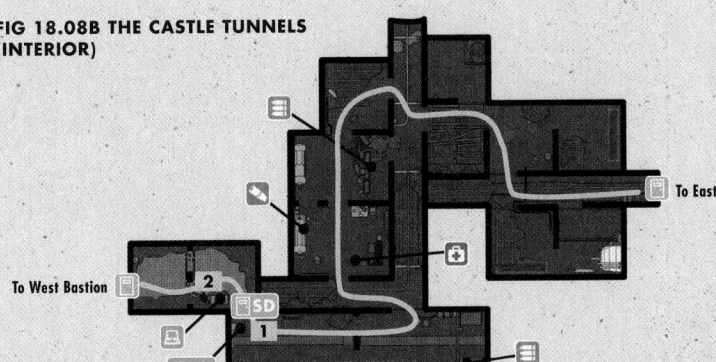

MAP

**ZONE 18**

NEIGHBORHOOD:
SOUTH BOSTON

- ARMAMENTS AND AMMO
- ARMAMENTS AND AMMO: MINI NUKE
- ARMAMENTS AND AMMO: TRUNK
- BOTTLECAPS
- COLLECTIBLE: HOLOTAPE: JACQ'S HOLOTAPE
- COLLECTIBLE: HOLOTAPE: SYLVIA'S HOLOTAPE
- COLLECTIBLE: HOLOTAPE: UNIVERSITY POINT
  COUNCIL MEETING
- COLLECTIBLE: NUKA CHERRY
- COLLECTIBLE: REQUIRED READING: TESLA SCIENCE
- CRAFTING: ARMOR WORKBENCH
- CRAFTING: CHEMISTRY STATION (2)
- CRAFTING: COOKING STATION (3)
- CRAFTING: WEAPONS WORKBENCH (2)
- DANGER: MINES!
- DANGER: RADIATION (MILD)!
- DANGER: TENSION TRIGGER!
- FACTION: MIRELURKS
- FACTION: SYNTHS (THE INSTITUTE)
- HEALTH OR CHEMS
- UNIQUE ITEM: PROTOTYPE PA77 (WEAPON)

**FIG 18.09A UNIVERSITY POINT (EXTERIOR)**

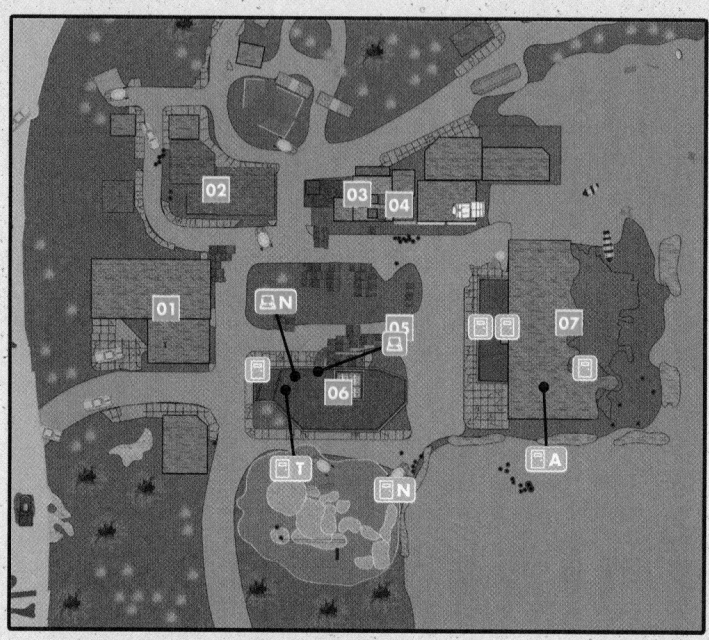

This once-thriving settlement was built into the ruins of the old university. Approximately one year before current events, synths from the Institute wiped this trading post off the map after a disagreement regarding classified research. An explosion in the service tunnels under Sedgwick Hall killed many, released a large amount of radioactive material, and caused the building to partly collapse.

### [01] Traders' Welcome (Basketball Court)

The main entrance to this settlement was through a repurposed basketball court and hall. The place is deserted now. You can also enter via the Credit Union (south) or water (east).

### [02] The Armor Store

Synths have removed any settlers from this location, though the trappings of an armor trader still remain. There are some clothing options and an upstairs access to an elevated shack.

## [03] The Weapons Store

This location has almost been picked clean, but there's a weapons workbench and a couple of ammo boxes to pilfer from. Upstairs has access to the roof of the liquor store.

## [04] The Liquor Store

The place is in a real state, but the abundance of alcohol makes up for it. Open the toolbox on the counter to find Sylvia's Holotape. Upstairs, you can access the interior of this location or escape to the north.

## [05] Settlement Shacks

Warning! Hostile synths may have taken over the four ruined shacks at this location.

## [06] University Credit Union

The customer entrance (northwest) only allows you to the counter. Instead, enter the Credit Union via the hackable terminal (Novice). Before entering, climb two floors to reach the mayor's office. His terminal and Holotape within illuminate your knowledge, and there's a shack built onto the side of this building you can shoot from.

The interior of the credit union features a vault to ransack and a strange laboratory accessible if you look hard enough. Did you find a strange prototype weapon in here?

## [07] Sedgwick Hall

**FIG 18.09B UNIVERSITY CREDIT UNION (INTERIOR)**

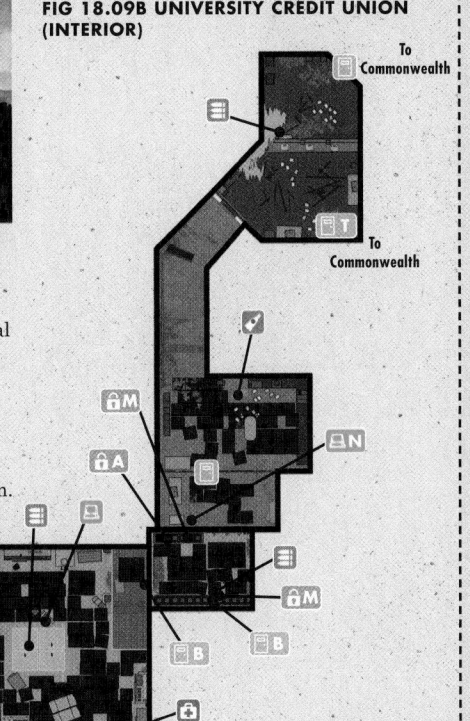

Slowly sagging and slipping into the waters, this once-grand hall is a mess of barricades and broken floors. The entire eastern side has already fallen away, allowing access up to the roof and an upper door. There's an undisturbed safe (Expert) on the hall's southeast exterior corner; reach it by carefully leaping the ruins of the upper floors overlooking the bay.

**FIG 18.09C UNIVERSITY POINT: SEDGWICK HALL (INTERIOR)**

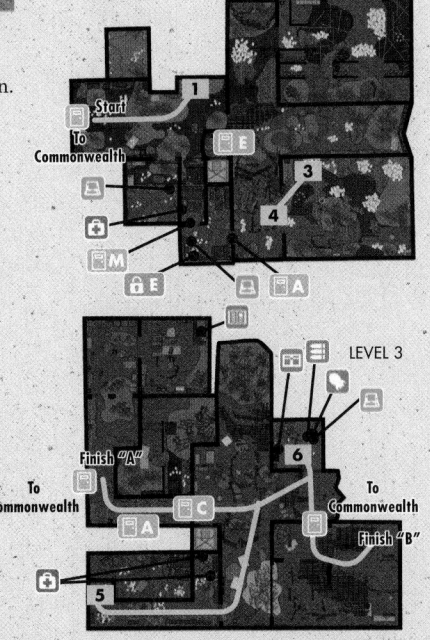

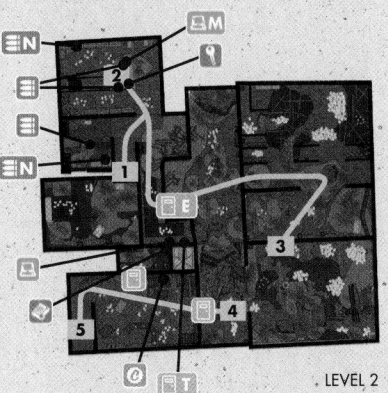

Make methodical work of this Mirelurk nest. Gerald's barricade key is in the tool shop upstairs (northwest).

# SECONDARY LOCATIONS

### [18.01] BUS AND APARTMENT WRECKAGE

- ARMAMENTS AND AMMO
- COLLECTIBLE: REQUIRED READING: GROGNAK THE BARBARIAN

**VAULT-TEC RECOMMENDED LOOT** ⬤

**REQUIRED READING: GROGNAK THE BARBARIAN**

Next to the Southie Speakeasy is a precariously perched bus atop the roof of a ruined house. Scour the upstairs for a comic-book fan's bedroom and a copy of Grognak for your records.

### [18.02] JOE'S SPUCKIES (SOUTHIE SPEAKEASY)

- QUEST VISIT: LONG TIME COMING (SIDE COMPANION)

A Joe's Spuckies coffee and sandwich emporium is simply a front for an old speakeasy; there's a hatch behind the counter (Master). However, you'll usually appear here after navigating Andrew Station.

### [18.03] DOCKSIDE WAREHOUSE (SOUTH BOSTON)

- ARMAMENTS AND AMMO
- CRAFTING: ARMOR WORKBENCH
- CRAFTING: POWER ARMOR STATION
- FACTION: BLOODBUGS

Park your Power Armor here and tinker away. Bloodbugs are active in this area, so keep your wits about you and your blood away from their probing proboscises.

### [18.04] FACTORY (SOUTH BOSTON)

- ARMOR PART: FUSION CORE
- DANGER: RADIATION (MILD)!
- FACTION: BLOODBUGS
- FACTION: RADROACHES
- HEALTH OR CHEMS

This is a medium-sized abandoned factory on the waterfront. Enter the structure and work your way through the machine room to the stairs. Unlock the upstairs door (Novice) to reach the foreman's terminal. Use the terminal to open the security door downstairs, accessing the first aid kits on the wall.

### [18.05] FOUR LEAF FISHPACKING CONTAINER YARD

- ARMAMENTS AND AMMO

A container yard with a rusting barge ready to unlock more metal containers. Search the open ones for a modicum of equipment.

### [18.06] CONSTRUCTION YARD

- ARMAMENTS AND AMMO
- FACTION: SUPER MUTANTS
- HEALTH OR CHEMS

A warehouse under construction has been left in a state of disrepair and now comes decorated with bloody meat, courtesy of a small group of Super Mutants. Check the middle level for a safe (Advanced).

## [18.07] ROOF GENERATOR (SOUTH BOSTON)

- ARMOR PART: FUSION CORE

Climb the fire escape to the west in the alley to locate a generator with a Fusion Core to pry out.

## [18.08] ROUNDABOUT RAIDER CAMP

- ARMAMENTS AND AMMO
- FACTION: RAIDERS
- HEALTH OR CHEMS

A group of thugs has strung up a good view of corpses in this circular road junction. Scavenge for ammo after you've returned the favor.

## [18.09] HAWTHORNE ESTATE

- QUEST VISIT: RECRUITING HANCOCK (GOODNEIGHBOR FREEFORM)

Enter this structure of faded grandeur to scrape together a few meager items. Bobbi No Nose makes her home here during the specified quest and installs a security system. Check the corner for a safe (Advanced).

## [18.10] DORCHESTER HEIGHT MONUMENT

- HEALTH OR CHEMS

Constructed on the raised oval park just west of South Boston High School, this monument is helpful to look for when attempting to navigate this neighborhood. Use it as a landmark.

## [18.11] ROOF CAMP (SOUTH BOSTON)

- ARMAMENTS AND AMMO
- CRAFTING: COOKING STATION
- HEALTH OR CHEMS

This settler camp offers access across three rooftops and reasonable protection from ground dwellers. Unfortunately, it's not bulletproof protection.

## [18.12] THE CANDY SHOP

- DANGER: OIL!
- DANGER: MINES!
- ARMAMENTS AND AMMO

Close to an old playground and on the western outskirts of the Castle is a small candy shop. Watch for the primed mine.

## [18.13] SOUTH BOSTON CHURCH

- DANGER: RADIATION (MILD)!
- FACTION: FERAL GHOULS

An overgrown graveyard is home to ferals. A hatch allows access into the remains of the church cellar, where an altar to Mr. Tiddles and sacrificial dog meat can be found.

## [18.14] SOUTH BOSTON WHARF AND RESTROOMS

- DANGER: RADIATION (MILD)!
- HEALTH AND CHEMS

Once known to locals as the L Street Bath House, the shell of this ornate wharfside facility is now cloaked in dead plant life and lightly irradiated water pools. Check the restrooms for a spot of health.

## [18.15] RUSTING SHIP AND STILT CABIN

- ARMAMENTS AND AMMO
- DANGER: RADIATION (MILD)!
- FACTION: MIRELURKS
- HEALTH OR CHEMS

This boat once ferried visitors to the mysterious Spectacle Island off the coast to the east. Now you need to swim there after collecting any loot you fancy.

# A COLLECTION OF APPENDICES

The final chapter of this guide focuses on the most pertinent data of all—the gathering of the largest collection of highly desirable items, methods to claim the most impressive deeds, and knowledge of where a likely companion or two may reside.

## APPENDIX I: ACHIEVEMENTS AND TROPHIES

Learn the tasks to undertake in order to set your claim to being a professional wasteland wanderer.

| INDEX | ACHIEVEMENT | GAMER SCORE | TROPHIES | DESCRIPTION | NOTES |
|---|---|---|---|---|---|
| **MAIN QUESTS** | | | | | |
| 1 | War Never Changes | 10 | Bronze | Enter The Wasteland | Leave Vault 111. |
| 2 | When Freedom Calls | 10 | Bronze | Complete "When Freedom Calls" | |
| 3 | Unlikely Valentine | 20 | Bronze | Complete "Unlikely Valentine" | |
| 4 | Reunions | 20 | Bronze | Complete "Reunions" | |
| 5 | Dangerous Minds | 20 | Bronze | Complete "Dangerous Minds" | |
| 6 | Hunter/Hunted | 20 | Bronze | Complete "Hunter/Hunted" | |
| 7 | The Molecular Level | 20 | Bronze | Complete "The Molecular Level" | |
| 8 | The Nuclear Option | 30 | Silver | Complete "The Nuclear Option" | You can receive this OR The Institute's "Nuclear Family" achievement - not both (in a single playthrough). |
| **INSTITUTE** | | | | | |
| 9 | Institutionalized | 10 | Bronze | Complete "Institutionalized" | |
| 10 | Mankind-Redefined | 10 | Bronze | Complete "Mankind-Redefined" | |
| 11 | Powering Up | 10 | Bronze | Complete "Powering Up" | |
| 12 | Complete "Nuclear Family" | 30 | Silver | Complete "Nuclear Family" | You can receive this OR the other factions' "The Nuclear Option" achievement - not both. |
| **MINUTEMEN** | | | | | |
| 13 | The First Step | 10 | Bronze | Join the Minutemen | Complete "When Freedom Calls." |
| 14 | Taking Independence | 10 | Bronze | Complete "Taking Independence" | |
| 15 | Old Guns | 30 | Silver | Complete "Old Guns" | |
| **BROTHERHOOD OF STEEL** | | | | | |
| 16 | Semper Invicta | 10 | Bronze | Join the Brotherhood of Steel | Complete "Shadow of Steel." |
| 17 | Blind Betrayal | 10 | Bronze | Complete "Blind Betrayal" | |
| 18 | Ad Victoriam | 30 | Silver | Complete "Ad Victoriam" | |
| **RAILROAD** | | | | | |
| 19 | Tradecraft | 10 | Bronze | Join the Railroad | Complete "Tradecraft." |
| 20 | Underground Undercover | 10 | Bronze | Complete "Underground Undercover" | |
| 21 | Rockets' Red Glare | 30 | Silver | Complete "Rockets' Red Glare" | |
| **WORKSHOP/SETTLEMENT** | | | | | |
| 22 | Complete Sanctuary | 20 | Bronze | Complete "Sanctuary" | |
| 23 | Community Organizer | 20 | Bronze | Ally with 3 Settlements | |
| 24 | Benevolent Leader | 20 | Bronze | Reach Maximum Happiness in a Large Settlement | Consult the Workshops Chapter for strategies to complete this. |
| **GENERAL** | | | | | |
| 25 | Gun-For-Hire | 20 | Silver | Complete 10 Side Quests | Complete any quest flagged as "Side" in this guide. |
| 26 | Mercenary | 30 | Silver | Complete 50 Misc. Objectives | Complete any objective or quest flagged as "Miscellaneous" in this guide, with an Objective that appears on your Pip-Boy. |
| 27 | Scavver | 20 | Bronze | Gather 1000 Resources Used For Crafting | Consult the Crafting chapter for some interesting combinations to make, but this achievement simply requires searching the Commonwealth for resources. |

| INDEX | ACHIEVEMENT | GAMER SCORE | TROPHIES | DESCRIPTION | NOTES |
|---|---|---|---|---|---|
| **GENERAL (CONTINUED)** | | | | | |
| 28 | What's Yours Is Mine | 30 | Silver | Pick 50 Locks | |
| 29 | RobCo's Worst Nightmare | 30 | Silver | Hack 50 Terminals | |
| 30 | Armed and Dangerous | 30 | Silver | Mod 50 Weapons | |
| 31 | Wasteland D.I.Y. | 30 | Silver | Craft 100 Items | |
| 32 | Never Go It Alone | 20 | Bronze | Recruit 5 Separate Companions | Consult the Companions section of the STAT chapter for locations of each. |
| 33 | Lovable | 20 | Bronze | Reach Maximum Relationship Level with a Companion | Consult the Companions section of the STAT chapter for methods of increasing your affinity with a Companion. |
| 34 | Fix-Er-Upper | 20 | Bronze | Build 100 Workshop Items | Consult the Workshop chapter for planning to complete this. |
| 35 | Future Retro | 10 | Bronze | Play a Holotape Game | Simply find the Holotape game in the Vault 111 Terminal before leaving for the first time, to complete this easily. |
| 36 | ...The Harder They Fall | 20 | Bronze | Kill 5 Giant Creatures | Seek out Super Mutant Behemoths and Mirelurks Queens. |
| 37 | Ranger Corps | 40 | Silver | Discover 100 Locations | The MAP chapter is particularly helpful here. |
| 38 | Print's Not Dead | 20 | Bronze | Read 20 Magazines | Consult the Required Reading Appendix for locations of all magazines. |
| 39 | Prankster's Return | 10 | Bronze | Placed A Grenade Or Mine While Pickpocketing | You need Pickpocket Perk Rank 2 to attempt this. |
| 40 | Masshole | 20 | Bronze | Kill 300 People | This includes Raiders, Gunners, The Forged, and and any other humans, including those not hostile to you. |
| 41 | Animal Control | 20 | Bronze | Kill 300 Creatures | This includes Deathclaws, Feral Ghouls, Super Mutants, Mirelurks, any of the other irradiated wildlife, and anything not human. |
| 42 | Homerun! | 10 | Bronze | Get a Homerun | Run around the bases surrounding Diamond City Market. |
| 43 | Touchdown! | 10 | Bronze | Get a Touchdown | Have you fired your Fat Man at your feet again? |
| 44 | They're Not Dolls... | 10 | Bronze | Collect 10 Vault-Tec Bobbleheads | Consult the Bobblehead Appendix for locations of all of these. |
| 45 | ...They're Action Figures | 20 | Silver | Collect 20 Vault-Tec Bobbleheads | Consult the Bobblehead Appendix for locations of all of these. |
| 46 | Born Survivor | 5 | Bronze | Reach Level 5 | |
| 47 | Commonwealth Citizen | 10 | Bronze | Reach Level 10 | |
| 48 | Unstoppable Wanderer | 25 | Silver | Reach Level 25 | |
| 49 | Legend Of The Wastes | 50 | Silver | Reach Level 50 | |
| 50 | Prepared for the Future | 50 | Platinum | Decide the Fate of the Commonwealth | This is awarded once you completely finish one of the four main Faction Quest paths, working with the Brotherhood of Steel, Institute, Minutemen, or Railroad. |

# APPENDIX II: BOBBLEHEADS

Strictly limited edition, there are only 20 unique Bobbleheads in known existence. Sadly these have already been taken out of the packaging. But they do bestow a fancy improvement and look great on the display case in your hovel.

| BOBBLEHEAD | ZONE LOCATION | LOCATION NAME | NOTES |
|---|---|---|---|
| Agility | [P6.30] | Wreck of the FMS Northern Star | On the very edge of the bow of the ship, on a rickety wooden platform past the deck huts. |
| Barter | [P4.12] | Longneck Lukowski's Cannery | Inside the metal catwalk hut, northwest upper area of the main cannery room. |
| Big Guns | [P5.15] | Vault 95 | In the living quarters area, north most room, on a radio. |
| Charisma | [P2.07] | Parsons State Insane Asylum | Inside Jack Cabot's office, on his desk, close to the elevator, in the Administration area. |
| Endurance | [P6.28] | Poseidon Energy | On the metal desk with the magazine, near the steamer trunk, in the central metal catwalk hut. |
| Energy Weapons | [P3.12] | Fort Hagen | In the Command Center, southwest kitchens, on a small table between two fridges. |
| Explosives | [P2.19] | Saugus Ironworks | In the Blast Furnace area, with the magazine and steamer trunk, on the catwalk. |
| Intelligence | [P11.01] | Boston Public Library | On the computer bank, in the mechanical room, northwest corner of the Library. |
| Lock Picking | [P13.01] | Pickman Gallery | On the ground between the brick pillars in the last tunnel chamber, where you meet Pickman. |
| Luck | [P6.31] | Spectacle Island | In a locker by the steamer trunk, on the green boat moored south of the island. |
| Medicine | [P3.22] | Vault 81 | In Secret Vault 81, in Curie's office, southeast corner of the Vault. |
| Melee | [P11.05] | Trinity Tower | In the cage where Rex and Strong are being held, at the very top of Trinity Tower. |
| Perception | [P1.12] | Museum of Freedom | In the chamber above the front doors, where Preston is holed up, on a metal desk. |
| Repair | [P3.06] | Corvega Assembly Plant | On the very end of the top exterior ganty, southwest roof section of the plant building. |
| Science | [P2.23] | Malden Middle School (Vault 75) | On the desk overlooking the subterranean "Diner" area, inside the vault building, Basement level 3. |
| Small Guns | [P6.17] | Gunners Plaza | On the broadcast desk in the on-air room, ground floor, west side of the building. |
| Sneak | [P4.03] | Dunwich Borers | On a small metal table by a lantern, right next to the metal post terminal for area #4. |
| Speech | [P14.05] | Park Street Station (Vault 114) | In the Overseer's office, where Nick Valentine is being held. |
| Strength | [P15.01] | Mass Fusion Building | On the metal wall sculpture high above the lobby desk. |
| Unarmed | [P6.27] | Atom Cats Garage | On the hood of the rusty car in the main warehouse. |

# APPENDIX III: REQUIRED READING: MAGAZINES

There are 17 different magazine publications for you to collect, including five with a free Holotape game you simply must try! The following is a complete catalog. Alas, none of these could be categorized as being in mint condition.

| | | ZONE LOC # | ZONE NAME | NOTES |
|---|---|---|---|---|
| **YOU'RE S.P.E.C.I.A.L.! & ASTOUNDINGLY AWESOME TALES** | [01] | [P1.02] | Sanctuary | You're S.P.E.C.I.A.L. magazine is inside your own home, where Codsworth is located. |
| | [01] | [P2.01] | Outpost Zimonja | On the workshop. |
| | [02] | [P2.10] | Skylanes Flight 1981 | On the restroom toilet below the cockpit. |
| | [03] | [P3.14] | Boston Mayoral Shelter | Lower level bedroom, southwest corner, on a small table. |
| | [04] | [P4.03] | Dunwich Borers | At the bottom of the pit below terminal #3, on a table near the steamer trunk. |
| | [05] | [P4.24] | East Boston Preparatory School | On a desk in the computer room, top floor, southeast corner. |
| | [06] | [P5.24] | Crater of Atom | Top floor of the central metal shack built into the northern rocks. |
| | [07] | [P5.31] | Sentinel Site | In the metal hut, at the very end of the tunnels, overlooking the stockpile chamber. |
| | [08] | [P6.02] | Coast Guard Pier | On the toilet inside the locked cell by the secured storage room. |
| | [09] | [P7.10] | The Institute | On the triangular table of the outside balcony, accessed via Holdren's quarters. North of atrium. |
| | [10] | [P11.02] | Trinity Plaza | On the lecturn, by the steamer trunk at the east side of the church interior. |
| | [11] | [P11.03] | Hubris Comics | Top floor, in the "star" restroom on a table, near the steamer trunk. |
| | [12] | [P13.01] | Pickman Gallery | To the right of the steamer trunk in the last tunnel chamber, where you meet Pickman. |
| | [13] | [P13.02] | Old North Church | Inside Railroad HQ, on a metal desk in the brick crypt area, west area of the room. |
| | [14] | [P14.05] | Park Street Station (Vault 114) | In the living quarters area, on a container in the blocked corridor, under the "Laundry" sign. |
| **GROGNAK THE BARBARIAN** | | [P1.02] | Sanctuary | On the kitchen table of your old house, where Codsworth resides. |
| | [01] | [P1.09] | Wicked Shipping Fleet Lockup | East end of the main warehouse in the small office, on the desk with the key. |
| | [02] | [P2.23] | Malden Middle School (Vault 75) | On the bed, inside the Overseer's office, top floor. |
| | [03] | [P3.06] | Corvega Assembly Plant | Assembly level (top floor), in the Raider metal hut accessed via catwalk bridge, near Steamer Trunk. |
| | [04] | [P3.21] | Mass Pike Interchange | On the toilet inside the Gunner camp, by the Power Armor Station. |
| | [05] | [P3.22] | Vault 81 | Given as a reward by Katy the teacher for completing Miscellaneous Quest: Short Stories in the Classroom. |
| | [06] | [P4.05] | Museum of Witchcraft | On the table in the "dungeon" room, upper floor, south wall. |
| | [07] | [P6.18] | Hyde Park | In the raider camp on the roof of the buildings south of the main drag. |
| | [08] | [P9.03] | Back Street Apparel | On a living room table in the ruined upstairs apartment, near the TV and safe. |
| | [09] | [P14.04] | Boston Common | In the bandstand, near the skeleton, close to Park Street Station entrance. |
| | [10] | [S18.01] | Bus and Apartment Wreckage | On the bed of the comic book fan's apartment, with the bus crashed into it, close to Andrew Street Station. |
| **GUNS AND BULLETS** | [01] | [P3.12] | Fort Hagen | On the oval table in the kitchen area, top floor, southeast area. |
| | [02] | [P4.08] | Rook Family House | Inside Barney's bunker, on a metal desk near the lantern and filing cabinet. |
| | [03] | [P6.10] | South Boston Military Checkpoint | Inside the checkpoint, on a metal desk, east wall. |
| | [04] | [P6.17] | Gunners Plaza | Top floor lounge, in the table surrounded by sofas, south mezzanine offices. |
| | [05] | [P6.24] | Quincy Ruins | On the desk with the terminal, elevated freeway Gunners camp, between the two big-rig trailers. |
| | [06] | [P7.02] | Cambridge Police Station | In a locked safe in the station chief's office. Available only after Brotherhood reinforcements arrive at the station. |
| | [07] | [P7.04] | Fraternal Post 115 | On the lecturn in the stage area, by the American flag and sandbags. |
| | [08] | [S7.18] | Ticonderoga Safehouse | On the desk of the corner office, northwest corner, top floor. |
| | [09] | [P8.01] | BADTFL Regional Office | On a desk in the chief's office, bullpen room in the western part of the building. |
| | [10] | [P18.08] | The Castle | On the radio operator's desk, in the middle of the Castle grounds, outside. |
| **HOT RODDER** | [01] | [P1.04] | Robotics Disposal Ground | Inside the small concrete hut, on the desk with the terminal on it. |
| | [02] | [P6.27] | Atom Cats Garage | On the bedside table in Zeke's trailer. |
| | [03] | [P6.13] | West Roxbury: Parking Lot Funhouse | Inside the parking lot, to the west of the Hospital. Top floor sleeping quarters, near the prize cells. |
| **LA COIFFE** | [01] | [P6.12] | Fallon's Department Store | In the upper floor octagonal room, by the Steamer Trunk, west side of the building near the roof exit. |
| | [02] | [S8.09] | Charlestown Laundry | In a shopping basket on top of one of the washing machines. |
| **LIVE & LOVE** | [01] | [P3.15] | Fiddler's Green Trailer Estates | Inside the caravan trailer, east side of the estates (and swimming pool). |
| | [02] | [P4.16] | Revere Beach Station | On the concrete blocks by the cooking pot and steamer trunk, inside the promenade building, upper floor. |
| | [03] | [P5.08] | WRVR Broadcast Station | On the table near the recording desk and wall computer. |
| | [04] | [P7.01] | College Square | On the safe behind the counter, at the station entrance interior, before descending the stairs. |
| | [05] | [P8.02] | Bunker Hill | At the top of the monument. |
| | [06] | [P9.08] | Diamond City Schoolhouse | Inside the Schoolhouse bedroom, ground floor, on the bedside table. |
| | [07] | [P15.05] | Faneuil Hall | On the small table, attic level, just after climbing the main staircase. |
| | [08] | [P15.06] | Goodneighbor | On top of the toilet, The Third Rail restroom, entrance area (north). |
| | [09] | [P15.06] | Goodneighbor | On the bar counter, just right of the entrance, in the lobby of Hotel Rexford. |
| **MASSACHUSETTS SURGICAL JOURNAL** | [01] | [P2.07] | Parsons State Insane Asylum | Inside Lorenzo's living quarters, at the very bottom floor of the facility. |
| | [02] | [P2.20] | Medford Memorial Hospital | In the filing and storage room, west side balcony above the main lobby, one floor up from the ground. |
| | [03] | [P2.24] | Med-Tek Research | On the large central laboratory table, lowest floor of the sub-level, where the Prevent is located. |
| | [04] | [P3.13] | Greater Mass Blood Clinic | In the analyst's room (accessed via the wall terminal), on the desk. |
| | [05] | [P4.06] | Sandy Coves Convalescent Home | Behind the security door, next to the wall of safes, near the reception. |
| | [06] | [P7.08] | Cambridge Polymer Labs | On the desk inside the Director's office, above the reception area. |
| | [07] | [P7.11] | Greenetech Genetics | On the table between the two red sofas and dark carpet, in the long room mid-way up the north side of the building. |
| | [08] | [P11.01] | Boston Public Library | In the overdue book vending machine (southeast area). Purchase with 50 Tokens via the terminal. |
| | [09] | [P12.03] | Cabot House | Top floor bedroom, west side, on the wooden desk. |

| | | ZONE LOC # | ZONE NAME | NOTES |
|---|---|---|---|---|
| **PICKET FENCES** | [01] | [P2.19] | Saugus Ironworks | Blast Furnace area, on the catwalk just below the steamer trunk and Bobblehead. |
| | [02] | [P3.16] | Weston Water Treatment Plant | In the metal office overlooking the generator room, before descending to the main treatment chamber. |
| | [03] | [P3.20] | Beantown Brewery | In the foreman's concrete wall office, upper walkways of the main vat room, near the steamer trunk. |
| | [04] | [P9.10] | Hardware Town | In the upstairs office on the desk with the key, center of the building, near the steamer trunk. |
| | [05] | [P16.01] | Combat Zone | On the formica table, ground level near the bar, in front of the main stage. |
| **ROBCO FUN!** | [01] | [P1.01] | Vault 111 | Inside the cafeteria terminal, northeast area. Only the game is available. |
| | [02] | [P1.12] | Museum of Freedom | In the chamber above the front doors, where Preston is holed up, on Sturges' desk. |
| | [03] | [P3.12] | Fort Hagen | Command Center, adjacent to Kellogg's Terminal, in the chamber where you speak with Kellogg. |
| | [04] | [P9.08] | Diamond City Market: Valentine's Detective Agency | On a desk, inside the Valentine's Detective Agency. |
| | [05] | [P15.06] | Goodneighbor | In the Memory Den, basement Memory Lounger area, on a metal desk against one of the brick walls. |
| **TABOO TATTOOS** | [01] | [P1.05] | Thicket Excavations | In the metal trailer caravan on the marble edge (south) of the excavation area, close to two other trailers. |
| | [02] | [P1.11] | Concord | Concord Civic Access, in the scavenger's sleeping area, close to the steamer trunk, western area near exit stairs. |
| | [03] | [P2.30] | Irish Pride Industries Shipyard | On the metal bench, inside the docked ship, in the shipyard interior. |
| | [04] | [P3.22] | Vault 81 | Inside Horatio's barber's shop, main atrium area. |
| | [05] | [P6.03] and [P6.04] | Mass Pike Tunnel West and East | In the south central interior tunnels, by the skeletal corpse, close to the power armor station. |
| **TALES OF A JUNKTOWN JERKY VENDOR** | [01] | [P1.19] | Walden Pond | On the barrel with the lantern on it, inside the pipe tunnel interior cave. |
| | [02] | [P1.20] | Mystic Pines | On the sideboard table by the TV, west wall, inside the building, just north of the main entrance. |
| | [03] | [P1.21] | Super Duper Mart | On the magazine stand, northwest wall, just right of the Milton General Hospital poster. |
| | [04] | [P4.12] | Longneck Lukowski's Cannery | Inside the metal catwalk hut, northwest upper area of the main cannery room, with the Bobblehead. |
| | [05] | [P6.09] | Big John's Salvage | On the small table with the lantern, inside the caravan perched atop the containers, adjacent to the steamer trunk. |
| | [06] | [P6.30] | Wreck of the FMS Northern Star | Upper level, mid-deck, on the parasol table, north side of the ship. |
| | [07] | [P18.01] | Four Leaf Fishpacking Plant | Basement locker room, on the bench, western side of the plant. |
| | [08] | [P18.05] | Gwinnett Brewery | Catwalk metal hut, upper level, along the northwest wall. Climb the pipes and catwalks to reach it. |
| **TESLA SCIENCE** | [01] | [P3.02] | Arcjet Systems | In the CEO's office on the second floor, next to his terminal. |
| | [02] | [P4.02] | Mahkra Fishpacking | Lowest floor filleting room, on a small table, north east corner. Room below the one with the Steamer Trunk. |
| | [03] | [P4.14] | Reeb Marina | On the wooden bench in the kitchen of the warehouse, near the birthday sweetroll. |
| | [04] | [P5.29] | Rocky Cave (Virgil's Laboratory) | On a broken fridge, just left of Virgil's terminal. |
| | [05] | [P6.28] | Poseidon Energy | On the metal desk with the Bobblehead near the steamer trunk, in the central metal catwalk hut. |
| | [06] | [P10.02] | HalluciGen, Inc. | First floor, in the Weaponization Research lab, in the northeast corner. |
| | [07] | [P15.01] | Mass Fusion Building | On the computer bank, southeast mezzanine room, upper offices above the glass floor. |
| | [08] | [P18.02] | General Atomics Factory | In the upper floor office, on a metal desk against the east wall, directly above the entrance lobby. |
| | [09] | [P18.09] | University Point | Top floor, northern computer room, northeast corner on a small table. Access via the open curtains. |
| **TOTAL HACK** | [01] | [P2.09] | Wildwood Cemetery | Under the tree in the center of the cemetery. |
| | [02] | [P3.08] | Wattz Consumer Electronics | Basement server room, on the terminal desk, north wall. |
| | [03] | [P17.02] | The Shamrock Taphouse | Held by the female mannequin standing on the table in the "game" room with the checkers board. |
| **TUMBLERS TODAY** | [01] | [P2.21] | Malden Center | Inside one of the cargo carriages at the station, in the Raider camp at the deepest part of this location. |
| | [02] | [P2.28] | Poseiden Energy Turbine #18-F | In the metal control room, northwest corner of the facility, by the steamer trunk, on a metal shelf. |
| | [03] | [P4.25] | Easy City Downs | On the side chest by the black sofa, in the commentator's area, southwest side of the racetrack |
| | [04] | [P6.14] | West Roxbury Station | In the open locker, eastern platform maintenance room, next wall button. |
| | [05] | [P9.06] | Fens Street Sewer | Next to the holotape on the metal drawers, inside the "cell" area of the sewers, northwest catwalks and tunnels. |
| **U.S. COVERT OPERATIONS MANUAL** | [01] | [P1.06] | USAF Satellite Station Olivia | Inside the computer room unlocked by terminal (southeast interior), on the desk with the mini nuke. |
| | [02] | [P1.22] | Lexington: Switchboard | On the desk by the terminal in the executive office above the open office and double stairwell area. |
| | [03] | [P2.32] | National Guard Training Yard | On a table in the cafeteria of the Barracks, near a cooler. |
| | [04] | [P2.34] | Revere Satellite Array | In the shanty hut atop the central satellite support (without the dish). |
| | [05] | [P3.01] | Federal Ration Stockpile | On the main table in front of the sofa, in Red Tourette's base, southeast tunnels near exit. |
| | [06] | [P3.12] | Fort Hagen | Command Center, on the side table of the bedroom and kitchenette room, just east of the armory. |
| | [07] | [P4.17] | Libertalia | By the red chair on the main shanty ship, halfway up, same level as the white metal window wall. |
| | [08] | [P4.29] | Fort Strong | On the desk of General Brock, southwest corner of the ground floor. |
| | [09] | [P5.18] | Abandoned Shack | In the Federal Survival Center, deepest area, on the light blue metal computer bank, near the steamer trunk and terminal. |
| | [10] | [P8.03] | USS Constitution | Ship interior, on a corner table inside the Captain's cabin. |
| **UNSTOPPABLES** | [01] | [P6.01] | Westing Estate | On the shack closest to the river, with the lantern on the wooden floor near the mattress. |
| | [02] | [P6.15] | Shaw High School | Library office on the lower level, with the Steamer Trunk. North area. |
| | [03] | [P6.19] | Suffolk County Charter School | In the library room, upper floor, by the holotape and steamer trunk. |
| | [04] | [P11.03] | Hubris Comics | On the shop counter, in front of the cheeky monkey and Grognak's Axe in the display case. |
| | [05] | [P16.04] | D.B. Technical High School | Basement level swimming pool, northwest corner wall, on a table above a Fat Man and near the steamer trunk. |
| **WASTELAND SURVIVAL GUIDE** | [01] | [P1.08] | Ranger Cabin | On the sideboard table in the cabin. |
| | [02] | [P1.14] | Gorski Cabin | In the underground bunker, by the journal terminal, on a metal desk. |
| | [03] | [P1.18] | Sunshine Tidings Co-op | In the locked cabin near the silos, on the floor near a mattress and steamer trunk. |
| | [04] | [P2.05] | Lynn Woods | On the sleeping bag, inside the main shack with the steamer trunk. |
| | [05] | [P2.14] | Old Gullet Sinkhole | On a concrete block inside the sinkhole, by the cooking pot station. |
| | [06] | [P4.09] | Crater House | Western side of the crater, on the table, lower level of a stilt shack with a lantern and caps stash on a table. |
| | [07] | [P4.22] | Nahant Oceanological Society | On the metal desk with the typewriter, entrance room area, ground floor. |
| | [08] | [P6.11] | Egret Tours Marina | On the counter of the diner and coolant recharge station. |
| | [09] | [P9.01] | Wreck of the USS Riptide | Inside the ship, on a table, under the bridge on the water's level. |

You may be hoping to figure out the best places to find overdue library books so you can trade them in for tokens. Don't swap those tokens for any old junk, though; use the library book terminal in the southeast corner of Boston Public Library to spend 50 tokens and receive a copy of the *Massachusetts Surgical Journal* to complete your magazine collection. So where should you rummage around to find overdue books? There are almost 100 to find across the Commonwealth. But go here to get a few in one place:

– EAST BOSTON PREPARATORY SCHOOL (9 BOOKS)
– SHAW HIGH SCHOOL (8 BOOKS)
– BOSTON PUBLIC LIBRARY (6 BOOKS)
– SUFFOLK COUNTY CHARTER SCHOOL (5 BOOKS)
– COLLEGIATE ADMINISTRATION BUILDING (4 BOOKS)
– SANDY COVES CONVALESCENCE HOME (4 BOOKS)

## APPENDIX IV: UNIQUE OR EXCEPTIONAL ITEMS

There are many thousands of items to classify across the Commonwealth. We know, as our Mr. Handy author malfunctioned during the cataloging of every item and had to be forcibly dismantled. Fortunately, some of the earlier read-outs weren't mangled, and the following table details every item, whether it's an extremely rare or unique weapon, apparel piece, or even a house you can call home.

| UNIQUE OR EXCEPTIONAL ITEM | LOC # | LOCATION NAME | NOTES |
|---|---|---|---|
| 2076 World Series Baseball Bat (Weapon) | [P6.16] | Jamaica Plain | Reward under Jamaica Plain City Hall. Sell it to Moe Cronin if you wish; he'll buy it at a premium. |
| Agatha's Dress (Apparel) | [P11.05] | Trinity Tower | Found at this location. |
| Alien Blaster Pistol (Weapon) | [S3.21] | Cave | Found once the nearby Crash Site has been investigated for Zetan activity. |
| Artillery Schematic (Item) | [P18.08] | The Castle | Found during your exploration of The Castle's tunnels during The Minutemen Quest: Old Guns. |
| Artillery Smoke Grenades (Weapon) | [P18.08] | The Castle | Found during your exploration of The Castle's tunnels during The Minutemen Quest: Old Guns. |
| Ashmaker (Weapon) | [P6.06] | NH&M Freight Depot | Reward for siding with (or killing) Farenheit at the end of Side Quest: The Big Dig. |
| Automatic Laser Musket (Weapon) | [P18.08] | The Castle | Given to you while talking to Sturges at the conclusion of The Minutemen Quest: The Nuclear Option. |
| Ballistic Weave Mk1-5 (Apparel) | [P13.02] | Old North Church | Sold by Tinker Tom once you complete The Railroad Radiant Quest: Jackpot. |
| Big Boy (Weapon) | [P9.08] | Diamond City Market: Commonwealth Weaponry (and Arturo's House) | Sold by this vendor. |
| Big Jim (Weapon) | [P1.19] | Walden Pond | Find this unique Pipe Wrench lying in Walden Pond. |
| Black Ops Chestpiece (Apparel) | [P8.02] | Bunker Hill | Sold by Deb. |
| Black Ops Right Shinguard (Apparel) | [P8.02] | Bunker Hill | Sold by Deb. |
| Broadsider (Weapon) | [P8.03] | USS Constitution | Reward as part of Side Quest: Last Voyage of the U.S.S. Constitution. |
| Captain Ironside's Hat (Apparel) | [P8.03] | USS Constitution | Reward as part of Side Quest: Last Voyage of the U.S.S. Constitution. |
| Champion Chestpiece (Apparel) | [P9.08] | Diamond City Market: Diamond City Surplus (and Myrna's House) | Sold by this vendor. |
| Champion Right Arm (Apparel) | [P9.08] | Diamond City Market: Fallon's Basement | Sold by this vendor. |
| Cryolator (Weapon) | [P1.01] | Vault 111 | Found in Vault 111 under lock and key (Master) in the Overseer's office. |
| DB Tech Varsity Uniform (Apparel) | [P16.04] | D.B. Technical High School | Found at this location. |
| Death from Above (Weapon) | [P4.28] | Prydwen | Missile Launcher sold by Proctor Teagan once you reach the rank of Paladin. |
| Deathclaw Gauntlet (Weapon) | [P2.05] | Deathclaw Nest (Lynn Woods) | Reward for completing Side Quest: The Devil's Due. |
| Deliverer (Weapon) | [P13.02] | Old North Church | Reward after completing The Railroad Quest: Tradecraft. |
| Destroyer's Left Arm (Apparel) | [P8.02] | Bunker Hill | Sold by Deb. |
| Devastator's Chestpiece (Apparel) | [P15.06] | Goodneighbor | Sold by KL-E-0 at Kill or Be Killed. |
| Devastator's Right Greave (Apparel) | [P15.06] | Goodneighbor | Sold by KL-E-0 at Kill or Be Killed. |
| Drugged Water (Item) | [P10.02] | HalluciGen, Inc. | Found throughout this location. |
| Eddie's Peace (Weapon) | [P18.03] | Andrew Station | Reward for removing Eddie as a threat during Side Quest: Long Time Coming. |
| Exemplar's T-60c Torso | [P4.28] | Prydwen | Reward for Clarke turning himself in, during Brotherhood of Steel Quest: Duty or Dishonor. |
| Experiment 18-A (Weapon) | [P6.10] | The Institute | Sold by the Institute Requisition Vendor. |
| Experimental Serum (Item) | [P6.10] | The Institute | Found in the FEV Laboratory, as part of Miscellaneous Quest: Virgil's Cure. |
| Final Judgment (Weapon) | [P4.28] | Prydwen | Carried by Elder Maxson; remove it from him during Institute Quest: Airship Down, or The Railroad Quest: Precipice of War. |
| Food Paste (Item) | [P6.19] | Suffolk County Charter School | A disgusting foodstuff splattered all over this location. |
| Freefall Armor Left Leg (Apparel) | [P15.01] | Mass Fusion Building | In Mass Fusion, in the safe in Jack Rockford's office on the 28th floor. Keep ascending the interior of this structure to reach it (a Brotherhood of Steel Jet Pack is helpful here). |
| Freefall Armor Right Leg (Apparel) | [P15.01] | Mass Fusion Building | In Mass Fusion, in the safe in Jack Rockford's office on the 28th floor. Keep ascending the interior of this structure to reach it (a Brotherhood of Steel Jet Pack is helpful here). |
| Furious Power Fist (Weapon) | [P14.03] | Swan's Pond | Remove the threat of Swan in Boston Common. |
| Gamma Gun (Weapon) | [P2.07] | Parsons State Insane Asylum | Reward for completing Side Quest: The Secret of Cabot House. |
| General's Hat (Apparel) | [P18.08] | The Castle | Found during your exploration of The Castle's tunnels during The Minutemen Quest: Old Guns. |
| General's Wool Coat (Apparel) | [P18.08] | The Castle | Found during your exploration of The Castle's tunnels during The Minutemen Quest: Old Guns. |
| Giddyup Buttercup Parts | [P6.23] | Wilson Atomatoys Factory | In the sealed storage room; you'll need the Atomatoys ID Card to gain access. Your objective for Miscellaneous Quest: Arlen Glass (The Slog). |
| Good Intentions (Weapon) | [P6.24] | Quincy Ruins | Carried by the Gunner leader Clint on the elevated freeway camp. |
| Grandpa Savoldi's Hat (Apparel) | [P2.14] | Old Gullet Sinkhole | Found here if Miscellaneous Quest (Freeform Bunker Hill): Fallen Hero is active. |
| Grognak Costume (Apparel) | [P11.03] | Hubris Comics | In one of the open lockers on the fourth floor. |
| Grognak's Axe (Weapon) | [P11.03] | Hubris Comics | In the locked display case (Advanced) on the first floor. |

| UNIQUE OR EXCEPTIONAL ITEM | LOC # | LOCATION NAME | NOTES |
|---|---|---|---|
| HalluciGen Gas Canister (Item) | [P10.02] | HalluciGen, Inc. | Found in the basement laboratory at this location. |
| HalluciGen Gas Grenades (Weapon) | [P10.02] | HalluciGen, Inc. | Craft these grenades at a Chemistry Workbench. Requires a HalluciGen Gas Canister. |
| Home Plate (House) | [P9.09] | Home Plate | Purchased for 2,000 Caps at the Mayor's Office. |
| Homing Beacons (Item) | [P17.04] | Yangtze | Reward for completing Side Quest: Here There Be Monsters. |
| Honor (Apparel) | [P4.28] | Prydwen | Armor sold by Proctor Teagan once you reach the rank of Paladin. |
| Institute Beacon (Item) | [P6.10] | The Institute | Supplied by the Institute for your mission in The Institute Quest: Airship Down. |
| Junk Jet (Weapon) | [P3.02] | Arcjet Systems | In the utility room on the lower level of the Arcjet Engine Core, accessible during Brotherhood of Steel Quest: Call to Arms. |
| Kellogg's .44 Pistol (Weapon) | [P3.12] | Fort Hagen | Carried by Kellogg at this location. |
| Kremvh's Tooth (Weapon) | [P4.03] | Dunwich Borers | Found in the darkest depths of this location. |
| Le Fusil Terribles (Weapon) | [P4.17] | Libertalia | Found in the Captain's cabin area of this location. |
| Liam's Glasses (Apparel) | [P6.10] | The Institute | Reward for completing The Institute Quest: Plugging a Leak. |
| Lieutenant's Hat (Apparel) | [P8.03] | USS Constitution | Reward as part of Side Quest: Last Voyage of the U.S.S. Constitution. |
| Lorenzo's Artifact (Weapon) | [P2.07] | Parsons State Insane Asylum | Reward for completing Side Quest: The Secret of Cabot House. |
| Lorenzo's Suit (Apparel) | [P2.07] | Parsons State Insane Asylum | Reward for completing Side Quest: The Secret of Cabot House. |
| Mark 2 Synth Chest Piece (Apparel) | [P6.10] | The Institute | Sold by the Institute Requisition Vendor. |
| Mark 2 Synth Helmet (Apparel) | [P6.10] | The Institute | Sold by the Institute Requisition Vendor. |
| Mark 3 Right Arm (Apparel) | [P6.10] | The Institute | Sold by the Institute Requisition Vendor. |
| Mark 3 Synth Chest Piece (Apparel) | [P6.10] | The Institute | Sold by the Institute Requisition Vendor. |
| Mascot Head (Apparel) | [P16.04] | D.B. Technical High School | Found at this location. |
| Mysterious Serum (Item) | [P2.07] | Parsons State Insane Asylum | Reward for completing Side Quest: The Secret of Cabot House. |
| Old Faithful (Weapon) | [P9.08] | Diamond City Market: Commonwealth Weaponry (and Arturo's House) | Sold by this vendor. |
| Partystarter (Weapon) | [P15.06] | Goodneighbor | Sold by KL-E-0 at Kill or Be Killed. |
| Peizoneucleic Power Armor Chest (Apparel) | [P7.08] | Cambridge Polymer Labs | Complete the Miscellaneous Quest: Cambridge Polymer Labs quest. |
| Pickman's Blade | [P13.01] | Pickman Gallery | Reward if you side with Pickman. |
| Prevent (Item) | [P2.24] | Med-Tek Research | Found at the sub-level laboratory, as part of Side Companion Quest: Long Road Ahead. |
| Protector's Left Armguard (Apparel) | [P9.08] | Diamond City Market: Commonwealth Weaponry (and Arturo's House) | Sold by this vendor. |
| Protector's Right Armguard (Apparel) | [P9.08] | Diamond City Market: Commonwealth Weaponry (and Arturo's House) | Sold by this vendor. |
| Prototype PA77 (Weapon) | [P18.09] | University Point | In the locked safe (Master) inside the University Credit Union. |
| Railroad Stealth Boy (Item) | [P13.02] | Old North Church | Reward after completing The Railroad Quest: Memory Interrupted. |
| Railway Rifle (Weapon) | [P13.02] | Old North Church | Reward after completing The Railroad Quest: Underground Undercover. |
| Reba (Weapon) | [P4.08] | Rook Family House | Carried by Barney Rook. |
| Reba II (Weapon) | [P4.08] | Rook Family House | Reward for helping Barney during Miscellaneous Quest: Barney Rook. |
| Reginald's Suit (Apparel) | [P11.05] | Trinity Tower | Found at this location. |
| Righteous Authority (Weapon) | [P3.02] | Arcjet Systems | A reward for completing Brotherhood of Steel Quest: Call to Arms. |
| Rockville Slugger (Weapon) | [P9.08] | Diamond City Market: Swatters | Sold by this vendor. |
| Sentinel's Plasmacaster (Weapon) | [P4.28] | Prydwen | Plasma Rifle sold by Proctor Teagan once you reach the rank of Sentinel. |
| Shem Drowne's Sword (Weapon) | [S13.02] | North End Graveyard | Reward after completing Side Quest: The Gilded Grasshopper. |
| Shishkebab (Weapon) | [P2.19] | Saugus Ironworks | Found in the Blast Furnace, carried by Slag. |
| Short Syringer Rifle (Weapon) | [P3.22] | Vault 81 | Reward for completing Side Quest: Hole in the Wall. |
| Signed Baseball | [P6.01] | Westing Estate | Found here, and sold to Moe Cronin at Swatters in Diamond City (Freeform Quest: Out in Left Field). |
| Signed Baseball Card | [P6.01] | Westing Estate | Found here, and sold to Moe Cronin at Swatters in Diamond City (Freeform Quest: Out in Left Field). |
| Signed Catcher's Mitt | [P6.01] | Westing Estate | Found here, and sold to Moe Cronin at Swatters in Diamond City (Freeform Quest: Out in Left Field). |
| Silver Shroud Costume (Apparel) | [P11.03] | Hubris Comics | Found at this location. |
| Silver Shroud Hat (Apparel) | [P11.03] | Hubris Comics | Found at this location. |
| Silver Shroud Photo (Item) | [P11.03] | Hubris Comics | Found at this location. |
| Silver Submachine Gun Prop (Item) | [P11.03] | Hubris Comics | On the fourth floor, on a crate behind the TV set backdrop. |
| Silver Shroud Script | [P11.03] | Hubris Comics | On the third floor, in the locked office. |
| Slocum's BuzzBites Recipe (Item) | [P2.22] | Slocum's Joe Corporate HQ | Found inside the safe (Advanced). |
| Steadfast BOS Combat Armor Chest Piece (Apparel) | [P4.28] | Prydwen | Reward for completing Brotherhood of Steel Quest: The Lost Patrol, if you turn the quest in to Captain Kells. |
| Survivor's Special (Weapon) | [P2.04] | Recon Bunker Theta | Kill Paladin Brandis, steal it from him, or receive it from him as a reward if you convince him to rejoin the Brotherhood, as part of Brotherhood of Steel Quest: The Lost Patrol. |
| T-60 Medic Pump (Apparel) | [P4.28] | Prydwen | Reward for completing Brotherhood of Steel Quest: Liberty Reprimed. |
| Tessa's Fist (Weapon) | [P6.25] | Quincy Police Station | Carried by Tessa. |
| The Gainer (Weapon) | [S4.12] | Vitale Pumphouse | Solve the number puzzle and this .44 Pistol is in the room with the steamer trunk. |
| The Gilded Grasshopper (Item) | [P15.05] | Faneuil Hall | Found atop this structure, on the roof. |
| Toy Buttercup (Item) | [P2.18] | The Slog | Reward for completing Miscellaneous Quest: Arlen Glass. |
| Vault Room (House) | [P3.22] | Vault 81 | Reward for completing Side Quest: Hole in the Wall. |
| Vengeance (Apparel) | [P4.28] | Prydwen | Armor sold by Proctor Teagan once you reach the rank of Sentinel. |
| Vertibird Signal Grenades (Weapon) | [P4.28] | Prydwen | Reward for completing Brotherhood of Steel Quest: Show No Mercy. Also available from either the Railroad or Preston Garvey (Minutemen) after the removal of the Prydwen, if allied to either of those factions. |

| UNIQUE OR EXCEPTIONAL ITEM | LOC # | LOCATION NAME | NOTES |
|---|---|---|---|
| Virgil's Rifle (Weapon) | [P5.29] | Rocky Cave (Virgil's Laboratory) | Kill Virgil or steal it from him. |
| Visionary's T-60c Helm (Apparel) | [P4.28] | Prydwen | Reward after completing Brotherhood of Steel Quest: A Loose End. |
| Wastelander's Chest Piece (Apparel) | [P9.08] | Diamond City Market: Fallon's Basement | Sold by this vendor. |
| Wastelander's Friend (Weapon) | [P8.02] | Bunker Hill | Sold by Deb. |
| Wazer Wifle | [P6.10] | The Institute | Reward for completing Shaun's three quests once the Main and Faction quests are over. |
| X-01 Helmet (Apparel) | [P4.28] | Prydwen | Sometimes seen behind the counter at Proctor Teagan's store. |
| Your Quarters (Brotherhood of Steel House) | [P4.28] | Prydwen: Your Quarters | Reward for completing Brotherhood of Steel: Tour of Duty. |
| Your Quarters (Institute House) | [P4.28] | The Institute: Your Quarters | Reward for completing The Institute Quest: Synth Retention. |
| Zeke's Jacket and Jeans (Apparel) | [P6.27] | Atom Cats Garage | Reward for helping the Atom Cats repel some Gunner scum. |

## APPENDIX V: THE COMMONWEALTH COLLECTION (LOCATION INDEX)

Although the Map chapter allows quick access to every location in the Commonwealth, sometimes you need to look up information on a location in alphabetical order. This is the chart to use. It comes with the following parcels of information:

– LOCATION NAME, PAGE #, AND LOCATION #: THE NAME OF THE LOCATION, PAGE IN THE MAP CHAPTER WHERE IT APPEARS, AND THE ZONE CODE FOR THE LOCATION, SO YOU CAN LOOK IT UP IN THE MAP CHAPTER. FOR EXAMPLE, [P1.15] ABANDONED SHACK IS THE FIFTEENTH PRIMARY LOCATION IN ZONE 05. PRIMARY LOCATIONS ARE LISTED IN RED. SECONDARY LOCATIONS ARE LISTED IN GREEN.
– ARMAMENTS AND AMMO: IF THE LOCATION HAS A GOOD SUPPLY OF AMMO AND WEAPONS, MINI NUKES AND/OR FAT MEN, AND STEAMER TRUNKS, IT IS NOTED.
– FUSION CORES AND POWER ARMOR: COMPLETE YOUR POWER ARMOR SCAVENGING BY QUICKLY ASCERTAINING IF A LOCATION HAS ANY PARTS YOU MIGHT NEED.
– BOTTLECAPS: DOES THE LOCATION HAVE A PLENTIFUL SUPPLY? CHECK HERE.
– COLLECTIBLES: NOTES FOR BOBBLEHEADS, NUKA CHERRY, AND NUKA COLA QUANTUMS AND ANY REQUIRED READING MAGAZINES ARE HERE.
– COMPANIONS: IF A PARTICULARLY FRIENDLY OR HELPFUL INDIVIDUAL RESIDES HERE, IT IS NOTED.
– FACTION: WHO LIVES HERE? IT'S IMPORTANT TO KNOW WHAT KIND OF FACTION HAS SET UP HOME AT EACH LOCATION SO YOU CAN PLAN YOUR VISIT ACCORDINGLY.
– HEALTH OR CHEMS: IF THIS LOCATION HAS A PLENTIFUL SUPPLY OF LIFE-SUSTAINING GOODIES, THESE ARE FLAGGED.
– TRADERS, WORKSHOPS, AND RADIOS: IF A LOCATION HAS SOMEONE TO BARTER WITH, IT IS NOTED. IF THE LOCATION CAN BE TURNED INTO A SETTLEMENT WITH A WORKSHOP, CHECK HERE. FINALLY, IF A RADIO SIGNAL EMANATES FROM A LOCATION, YOU'LL FIND OUT HERE.
– UNIQUE ITEM: DOES THIS LOCATION HAVE ONE OR MORE UNIQUE ITEMS, WEAPONS, OR EXCEPTIONAL EQUIPMENT? IF IT DOES, CROSS-REFERENCE IT TO THE EARLIER APPENDIX TO FIND OUT THE EXACT NATURE OF THE EQUIPMENT AVAILABLE.

| LOCATION NAME | PAGE NUMBER | ZONE LOCATION NUMBER | AMMO | MINI NUKE OR FAT MAN | TRUNK | FUSION CORE | POWER ARMOR | BOTTLECAPS | BOBBLEHEAD | NUKA CHERRY | NUKA COLA QUANTUM | REQUIRED READING | COMPANION | FACTION | HEALTH OR CHEMS | TRADER | WORKSHOP | RADIO | UNIQUE ITEM |
|---|---|---|---|---|---|---|---|---|---|---|---|---|---|---|---|---|---|---|---|
| 35 Court | 494 | [S15.10] | x | – | – | – | x | – | – | – | – | – | – | Robots | x | – | – | – | – |
| A Cooking Spot | 266 | [S1.21] | x | – | – | – | – | – | – | – | – | – | – | – | – | – | – | – | – |
| Abandoned Caravan | 271 | [S1.14] | x | – | – | – | – | – | – | – | – | – | – | – | – | x | – | – | – |
| Abandoned House | 427 | [S8.06] | x | – | x | – | – | – | – | – | – | – | – | Feral Ghouls | – | – | – | – | – |
| Abandoned Raider Camp (Elevated Freeway) | 287 | [S2.23] | x | – | – | – | – | – | – | – | – | – | – | Raiders | – | – | – | – | – |
| Abandoned Shack | 360 | [P5.18] | x | x | x | – | x | – | – | – | – | U.S. Covert Operations Manual | – | Synths (The Institute) | x | – | – | – | – |
| Abbot's House (Diamond City) | 433 | [P9.08] | – | – | – | – | – | – | – | – | – | – | – | – | – | – | – | – | – |
| Abernathy Farm | 261 | [P1.10] | x | – | – | – | – | – | – | – | – | – | – | Settler | – | Blake Abernathy, Connie Abernathy | x | – | – |
| All Faiths Chapel (Diamond City) | 434 | [P9.08] | – | – | – | – | – | – | – | – | – | – | – | – | – | – | – | – | – |
| Andrew Station | 514 | [P18.03] | x+ | – | x | – | x+ | – | x (2) | – | – | – | – | Attack Dogs, Raiders | x | – | – | – | x |
| Anna's Café | 444 | [S9.04] | – | – | – | – | – | – | – | – | – | – | – | – | – | x | – | – | – |
| ArcJet Engine Transport | 323 | [S3.19] | – | – | – | – | – | – | – | – | – | – | – | – | – | – | – | – | – |
| Arcjet Systems | 322 | [P3.02] | x++ | – | x (2) | x | – | x | – | – | – | – | – | Robots, Synths (Institute - quest only) | x | – | – | – | x |
| Atlantic Offices | 361 | [P5.19] | – | – | – | x | – | – | – | – | – | – | – | Feral Ghouls | x | – | – | – | – |
| Atom Cats Garage | 391 | [P6.27] | x | – | – | x | x | – | Unarmed | – | – | Hot Rodder | – | Settlers (Atom Cats), Gunners | x | Bluejay, Rowdy | – | – | x |
| Back Alley Scaffold Steps | 426 | [S8.02] | x | – | x | x | – | – | – | – | – | – | – | Feral Ghouls, Wild Mongrels | – | – | – | – | – |
| Back Street Apparel | 430 | [P9.03] | x | – | x | – | x+ | – | – | – | – | Grognak the Barbarian | – | Raiders | x | – | – | – | – |

| LOCATIONS | | | ARMAMENTS AND AMMO | | | ARMOR PARTS | | | COLLECTIBLES | | | | | | | SERVICES | | | |
|---|---|---|---|---|---|---|---|---|---|---|---|---|---|---|---|---|---|---|---|
| LOCATION NAME | PAGE NUMBER | ZONE LOCATION NUMBER | AMMO | MINI NUKE OR FAT MAN | TRUNK | FUSION CORE | POWER ARMOR | BOTTLECAPS | BOBBLEHEAD | NUKA CHERRY | NUKA COLA QUANTUM | REQUIRED READING | COMPANION | FACTION | HEALTH OR CHEMS | TRADER | WORKSHOP | RADIO | UNIQUE ITEM |
| BADTFL Regional Office | 423 | [P8.01] | x++ | x (2) | x | — | — | x | — | — | — | Guns and Bullets | — | Raiders, Robots | x+ | — | — | — | — |
| Barge Platform | 397 | [S6.22] | — | — | — | — | — | — | — | — | — | — | — | — | x | — | — | — | — |
| Barricade and Rooftops | 449 | [S10.03] | x | — | — | — | — | — | — | — | — | — | — | Raiders | x | — | — | — | — |
| Beacon Hill Apartments | 463 | [S12.01] | x | — | x | — | — | — | — | — | — | — | — | Raiders | x | — | — | — | — |
| Beantown Brewery | 316 | [P3.20] | x | — | x | — | — | x | — | — | — | Picket Fences | — | Raiders | — | — | — | — | — |
| Bedford Station | 264 | [P1.13] | x | — | x | — | — | — | — | — | — | — | — | Feral Ghouls | x | — | — | — | — |
| Big John's Salvage | 372 | [P6.09] | x+ | x | x | x | — | x | — | — | — | Tales of a Junktown Jerky Vendor | — | Super Mutants | x+ | — | — | — | — |
| Billboard Alley | 469 | [S13.14] | — | — | x | — | — | — | — | — | — | — | — | Feral Ghouls | — | — | — | — | — |
| Billboard Scavenger Shack | 297 | [S2.08] | — | — | — | — | — | — | — | — | — | — | — | — | — | — | — | — | — |
| Bloatfly Camp | 297 | [S2.07] | x | — | — | — | — | — | — | — | — | — | — | Bloatflies | — | — | — | — | — |
| Boat Graveyard | 399 | [S6.36] | x | — | — | — | — | x | — | — | — | — | — | Mirelurks | x | — | — | — | — |
| Boating Platforms | 397 | [S6.20] | — | — | — | — | — | — | — | — | — | — | — | — | x | — | — | — | — |
| Bobbi's Place (The Big Dig) | 486 | [P15.06] | x | — | x | x (3) | x | — | — | — | x (2) | — | — | Feral Ghouls, Mirelurks | x | — | — | — | — |
| Boston Airport | 342 | [P4.27] | x+++ | x (2) | x (3) | x (2) | — | — | x+ | — | — | — | — | Brotherhood of Steel, Feral Ghouls | — | — | x | — | — |
| Boston Bugle Building | 462 | [P12.02] | x | — | — | — | — | — | — | x | — | — | — | Robots | — | — | — | — | — |
| Boston Common | 472 | [P14.04] | — | — | — | — | — | — | — | — | — | Grognak the Barbarian | — | Super Mutants | — | — | — | — | — |
| Boston Mayoral Shelter | 310 | [P3.14] | x++ | x (2) | — | x | — | x | — | x (2) | — | Astoundingly Awesome Tales | — | Deathclaw, Synths (The Institute) | x+++ | — | — | — | — |
| Boston Police Rationing Site | 371 | [P6.05] | x | — | x | — | — | — | — | — | — | — | — | Mole Rats | x | — | — | — | — |
| Boston Public Library | 451 | [P11.01] | x | — | x | — | — | x | Intelligence | — | — | Massachusetts Surgical Journal | — | Super Mutants, Robots | x | — | — | — | — |
| Boxing Gym | 469 | [S13.12] | x | — | — | — | — | — | — | — | — | — | — | — | x | — | — | — | — |
| Boylston Club | 475 | [P14.06] | x | — | — | — | — | — | — | — | — | — | — | — | — | — | — | — | — |
| Breakheart Banks | 282 | [P2.16] | x | — | x | — | — | x | — | — | x | — | — | Super Mutants | x | — | — | — | — |
| Bridge (South of ArcJet Systems) | 322 | [S3.12] | x | — | — | — | — | — | — | — | — | — | — | — | — | — | — | — | — |
| Bridge Den (Cambridge) | 418 | [S7.01] | x | — | — | — | — | — | — | — | — | — | — | — | — | — | — | — | — |
| Bridgeway Garage | 445 | [S9.07] | — | — | — | — | — | — | — | — | — | — | — | — | — | — | — | — | — |
| Bridgeway Trust | 444 | [S9.06] | x | — | — | — | — | x+++ | — | — | — | — | — | — | x | — | — | — | — |
| Brotherhood of Steel Battle Site | 299 | [S2.21] | x | — | — | — | — | — | — | — | — | — | — | Brotherhood of Steel | — | — | — | — | — |
| Buckled Freeway | 367 | [S5.15] | x | — | — | — | — | x | — | — | — | — | — | Deathclaws | — | — | — | — | — |
| Bunker Hill | 423 | [P8.02] | x+++ | x | — | — | — | x | — | — | — | Live & Love | — | Settlers | x+++ | Deb, Joe Savoldi, Kay, Tony Savoldi | x | — | x |
| Buried House | 367 | [S5.14] | — | — | — | — | — | — | — | — | — | — | — | — | x | — | — | — | — |
| Buried Mansion | 366 | [S5.09] | — | — | — | — | — | — | — | — | — | — | — | Radscorpions | x | — | — | — | — |
| Bus and Apartment Wreckage | 520 | [S18.01] | x | — | — | — | — | — | — | — | — | Grognak the Barbarian | — | — | — | — | — | — | — |
| Bus Ramp | 272 | [S1.29] | — | — | — | — | — | — | — | — | — | — | — | Feral Ghouls, The Railroad | — | — | — | — | — |
| Bus Wreckage | 493 | [S15.03] | — | — | — | — | — | — | — | — | — | — | — | — | x | — | — | — | — |
| C.I.T. Ruins | 408 | [P7.09] | x | x | x | — | — | — | — | — | — | — | — | Super Mutants, Synths (The Institute) | x | — | — | — | — |
| Cabot House | 462 | [P12.03] | x+ | x (2) | x (2) | — | — | — | — | x | — | Massachusetts Surgical Journal | — | Cabot Family | x | — | — | — | — |
| Cambridge Campus Diner | 405 | [P7.05] | — | — | — | — | — | — | — | — | — | — | — | — | x | — | — | — | — |
| Cambridge Crater | 417 | [P7.12] | x | — | x | — | — | — | — | — | — | — | — | Feral Ghouls | — | — | — | — | — |
| Cambridge Park and Old Covered Alley | 419 | [S7.10] | x | — | — | — | — | — | — | x | — | — | — | — | x | — | — | — | — |
| Cambridge Police Station | 403 | [P7.02] | x | — | — | — | — | x | — | — | — | Guns and Bullets | Paladin Danse | Brotherhood of Steel, Feral Ghouls | x | — | — | Military Frequency AF95 | — |
| Cambridge Polymer Labs | 407 | [P7.08] | x | — | — | x | x | — | — | — | x | Massachusetts Surgical Journal | — | Feral Ghouls, Robots | x | — | — | — | x |

| LOCATIONS | | | ARMAMENTS AND AMMO | | | ARMOR PARTS | | | COLLECTIBLES | | | | | | | | SERVICES | | |
|---|---|---|---|---|---|---|---|---|---|---|---|---|---|---|---|---|---|---|---|
| LOCATION NAME | PAGE NUMBER | ZONE LOCATION NUMBER | AMMO | MINI NUKE OR FAT MAN | TRUNK | FUSION CORE | POWER ARMOR | BOTTLECAPS | BOBBLEHEAD | NUKA CHERRY | NUKA COLA QUANTUM | REQUIRED READING | COMPANION | FACTION | HEALTH OR CHEMS | TRADER | WORKSHOP | RADIO | UNIQUE ITEM |
| Campus Law Offices | 405 | [P7.06] | — | — | — | — | — | — | — | — | — | — | — | Raiders | — | — | — | — | — |
| Campus Office and Covered Bridge | 420 | [S7.15] | — | — | x | — | — | — | — | — | — | — | — | Raiders | x | — | — | — | — |
| Canister Launch Shack | 307 | [S3.10] | — | — | — | — | — | — | — | — | — | — | — | — | — | — | — | — | — |
| Capsized Factory | 361 | [P5.20] | — | — | — | — | — | — | — | — | — | — | — | Feral Ghouls | x+ | — | — | — | — |
| Car Tree Camp | 297 | [S2.03] | x | — | — | — | — | x+ | — | — | — | — | — | Radscorpions | — | — | — | — | — |
| Car Wreckage | 321 | [S3.01] | x | — | — | — | — | — | — | — | — | — | — | Super Mutants | — | — | — | — | — |
| Caravan Crossroads | 298 | [S2.19] | — | — | — | — | — | x | — | — | — | — | — | — | — | — | — | — | — |
| Carriage Den | 321 | [S3.05] | x | — | — | — | — | — | — | — | — | — | — | — | — | — | — | — | — |
| Cathy & John's Super Salon (Diamond City) | 445 | [P9.08] | x | — | — | — | — | — | — | — | — | — | — | — | — | John | — | — | — |
| Cave | 323 | [S3.21] | — | — | — | — | — | — | — | — | — | — | — | Unknown (Zetan), Mole Rat | — | — | — | — | x |
| Cave (Red Rocket Filling Station) | 361 | [P5.21] | — | — | — | — | — | — | — | — | — | — | — | Radscorpions | x | — | — | — | — |
| Cave (Super Duper Mart) | 362 | [P5.25] | x | — | x (2) | x | x | — | — | — | — | — | — | Deathclaws, Radscorpions | x | — | — | — | — |
| Charles River Boathouse | 418 | [S7.02] | — | — | x | — | — | — | — | — | — | — | — | Mirelurks | — | — | — | — | — |
| Charles View Amphitheater | 447 | [P10.01] | x | x | — | — | — | — | — | — | — | — | — | The Pillars (Pillars of the Community) | — | — | — | — | — |
| Charlestown Laundry | 427 | [S8.09] | — | — | — | — | — | — | — | — | x | La Coiffe | — | — | — | — | — | — | — |
| Chem-I-Care (Diamond City) | 445 | [P9.08] | — | — | — | — | — | — | — | — | — | — | — | — | x+++ | Solomon | — | — | — |
| Chestnut Hillock Reservoir | 320 | [P3.23] | x | — | x | — | — | x | — | — | x | — | — | Bloatflies, Radroaches, Stingwings | x | — | — | — | — |
| Choice Chops (Diamond City) | 445 | [P9.08] | — | — | — | — | — | — | — | — | — | — | — | — | x | Polly | — | — | — |
| Coast Guard Pier | 369 | [P6.02] | x+ | x | x | — | — | x | — | x | — | Astoundingly Awesome Tales | — | Super Mutants | x+ | — | — | — | — |
| Coastal Cottage | 325 | [P4.01] | — | — | — | — | — | — | — | x | — | — | — | Mirelurks, Settlers | — | — | x | — | — |
| Coastal Hideout | 349 | [S4.04] | — | — | — | x | — | — | — | — | — | — | — | Feral Ghouls | — | — | — | — | — |
| Coastal Vacationers | 349 | [S4.03] | — | — | — | — | — | — | — | — | — | — | — | Feral Ghouls | — | — | — | — | — |
| Cadman Residence (Diamond City) | 445 | [P9.08] | — | — | — | — | — | — | — | — | — | — | — | — | x | — | — | — | — |
| Collapsed Billboard (Glowing Sea) | 366 | [S5.08] | — | — | — | — | — | — | — | — | — | — | — | Mole Rats | — | — | — | — | — |
| College Square | 402 | [P7.01] | x++ | — | x (2) | — | — | x++ | — | x (2) | — | Live & Love | — | Feral Ghouls | x+ | — | — | — | — |
| Collegiate Administration Building | 404 | [P7.03] | — | — | — | — | — | — | — | — | — | — | — | Robots | — | — | — | — | — |
| Colonial Taphouse (Diamond City) | 438 | [P9.08] | x | — | — | — | — | — | — | — | — | — | — | — | x | Henry Cooke | — | — | — |
| Combat Zone | 497 | [P16.01] | x | x | — | — | — | — | — | x | — | Picket Fences | Cait | Raiders, Settlers | x | — | — | — | — |
| Commonwealth Avenue | 449 | [S10.08] | — | — | — | — | — | — | — | — | — | — | — | Wild Mongrels | — | — | — | — | — |
| Commonwealth Bank | 493 | [S15.04] | x | — | — | — | — | — | — | — | — | — | — | Robots | x | — | — | — | — |
| Commonwealth Weaponry (and Arturo's House) (Diamond City) | 435 | [P9.08] | x+++ | x | — | — | — | — | — | — | — | — | — | — | x | Arturo Rodriguez | — | — | x |
| Concord | 262 | [P1.11] | x+ | — | x (2) | — | — | x++ | — | — | — | Taboo Tattoos | — | Deathclaws, Mirelurks, Mole Rats, Radroaches, Raiders | x | — | — | — | — |
| Concord Campfire | 271 | [S1.18] | — | — | — | — | — | — | — | — | — | — | — | Raiders | — | — | — | — | — |
| Concord Outskirts Ruined House | 271 | [S1.17] | — | — | — | — | — | — | — | — | x | — | — | — | — | — | — | — | — |
| Congress Street Garage | 493 | [S15.02] | x | — | — | — | — | — | — | — | — | — | — | — | — | — | — | — | — |
| Construction Lift | 322 | [S3.16] | — | — | — | — | — | — | — | — | — | — | — | — | — | — | — | — | — |
| Construction Lift to Gunners' Den | 272 | [S1.23] | x | — | x | — | — | — | — | — | — | — | — | Gunners | — | — | — | — | — |
| Construction Yard | 520 | [S18.06] | x | — | — | — | — | — | — | — | — | — | — | Super Mutants | x | — | — | — | — |
| Container Crates Stash | 351 | [S4.19] | x | — | — | — | — | — | — | — | — | — | — | — | — | — | — | — | — |
| Container Truck Camp | 297 | [S2.01] | x | — | — | — | — | — | — | — | — | — | — | Raiders | x | — | — | — | — |

| LOCATION NAME | PAGE NUMBER | ZONE LOCATION NUMBER | ARMAMENTS AND AMMO | | | ARMOR PARTS | | BOTTLECAPS | COLLECTIBLES | | | | COMPANION | FACTION | HEALTH OR CHEMS | SERVICES | | | UNIQUE ITEM |
|---|---|---|---|---|---|---|---|---|---|---|---|---|---|---|---|---|---|---|---|
| | | | AMMO | MINI NUKE OR FAT MAN | TRUNK | FUSION CORE | POWER ARMOR | | BOBBLEHEAD | NUKA CHERRY | NUKA COLA QUANTUM | REQUIRED READING | | | | TRADER | WORKSHOP | RADIO | |
| Cooke Residence (Diamond City) | 438 | [P9.08] | x | — | — | — | — | — | — | — | x (2) | — | — | — | x+ | — | — | — | — |
| Cooling Vats | 299 | [S2.26] | x | — | — | — | — | — | — | — | — | — | — | Bloodbugs | — | — | — | — | — |
| Corvega Assembly Plant | 304 | [P3.06] | x+ | — | x | — | — | — | Repair | x | — | Grognak the Barbarian | — | Feral Ghouls, Raiders | x | — | — | — | — |
| County Crossing | 295 | [P2.33] | — | — | — | — | — | — | — | — | — | — | — | Settlers | — | — | x | — | — |
| Covenant | 290 | [P2.25] | x | — | x | x | — | x++ | — | — | — | — | — | Settlers (Covenant) | x | Doctor Patricia, Deezer, Penny Fitzgerald, Talia McGovern | x | — | — |
| Crash Site | 323 | [S3.22] | — | — | — | — | — | — | — | — | — | — | — | Unknown (Zetan) | — | — | — | — | — |
| Crashed Vertibird (Covenant Lake) | 298 | [S2.14] | — | — | — | — | x | — | — | — | — | — | — | — | — | — | — | — | — |
| Crashed Vertibird (Elevated Freeway) | 322 | [S3.15] | x | — | x | — | x | — | — | — | — | — | — | — | — | — | — | — | — |
| Crashed Vertibird (Marshland) | 398 | [S6.29] | — | — | x (2) | — | x | — | — | — | — | — | — | Gunners, Robots | — | — | — | — | — |
| Crashed Vertibird (Military Barge) | 468 | [S13.06] | — | — | x | x | x | — | — | — | — | — | — | — | x | — | — | — | — |
| Crashed Vertibird (Near Robotics Disposal Ground) | 270 | [S1.07] | — | — | x | — | — | — | — | — | — | — | — | Radstag Does | — | — | — | — | — |
| Crater and Shack | 395 | [S6.03] | — | — | — | — | — | — | — | — | — | — | — | Bloatflie, Bloodbugs, Stingwings | x | — | — | — | — |
| Crater House | 332 | [P4.09] | x | — | x | — | — | — | — | — | — | Wasteland Survival Guide | — | Children of the Atom | x | — | — | — | — |
| Crater of Atom | 361 | [P5.24] | x | — | — | — | — | — | — | — | — | Astoundingly Awesome Tales | — | Children of the Atom | x | — | — | — | — |
| Croup Manor | 338 | [P4.20] | x | x | x | — | — | x | — | — | — | — | — | Feral Ghouls | — | — | x | — | — |
| Custom House Tower | 505 | [P17.01] | x | — | — | — | — | — | — | — | — | — | — | Super Mutants, Raiders | x | — | — | — | — |
| Custom House Tower Courtyard | 508 | [S17.02] | x | — | — | — | — | — | — | — | — | — | — | — | — | — | — | — | — |
| Cutler Bend | 357 | [P5.12] | x | — | x (2) | x | — | x | — | — | — | — | — | Mirelurks, Stingwings | x | — | — | — | — |
| D.B. Technical High School | 500 | [P16.04] | x | x (2) | x | x | — | x | — | x | — | Unstoppables | — | Raiders | x | — | — | — | x |
| Dark Hollow Pond | 281 | [P2.12] | — | — | — | — | — | — | — | — | — | — | — | Mirelurks, Raiders | — | — | — | — | — |
| Dartmouth Professional Building | 456 | [P11.06] | — | — | — | — | x | — | — | — | — | — | — | Feral Ghouls, Radroaches, Super Mutants | — | — | — | — | — |
| Deathclaw Nest (Lynn Woods) | 297 | [S2.05] | — | — | — | — | — | — | — | — | — | — | — | Deathclaws | — | — | — | — | x |
| Decayed Reactor Site | 361 | [P5.22] | — | — | — | — | — | — | — | — | — | — | — | Deathclaws | — | — | — | — | — |
| Decrepit Factory | 361 | [P5.23] | — | — | — | — | — | — | — | — | — | — | — | — | x | — | — | — | — |
| Deep Trench Wreckage | 398 | [S6.23] | — | — | — | — | — | — | — | — | — | — | — | — | — | — | — | — | — |
| Demolished Apartment Tower (Beacon Hill) | 463 | [S12.02] | — | — | — | — | — | — | — | — | — | — | — | — | — | — | — | — | — |
| Derelict Bus | 367 | [S5.13] | — | — | x | — | — | — | — | — | — | — | — | Feral Ghouls | — | — | — | — | — |
| Derelict Mansion | 299 | [S2.24] | x | — | — | — | — | — | — | — | — | — | — | — | x | — | — | — | — |
| Deserted Camp (Elevated Freeway) | 396 | [S6.10] | — | — | — | x | — | x | — | — | — | — | — | — | — | — | — | — | — |
| Deserted Picnic Area | 297 | [S2.04] | — | — | — | — | — | — | — | — | — | — | — | — | — | — | — | — | — |
| Desolate Promenade | 509 | [S17.11] | — | — | — | — | — | — | — | — | — | — | — | Radscorpions | x | — | — | — | — |
| Destroyed Tenement (Beacon Hill) | 463 | [S12.05] | — | — | — | — | — | — | — | — | — | — | — | — | x | — | — | — | — |
| Diamond City | 433 | [P9.07] | — | x | — | — | — | — | — | — | — | — | — | Diamond City Settlers | — | — | — | — | — |
| Diamond City Market | 433 | [P9.08] | — | — | — | — | — | — | — | — | — | — | — | — | — | — | — | — | — |
| Diamond City Radio (Diamond City) | 436 | [P9.08] | x | — | — | — | — | — | — | — | — | — | — | — | — | — | — | Radio Freedom | — |
| Diamond City Scrap | 445 | [S9.12] | x | — | — | — | — | — | — | — | — | — | — | Radroaches, Vicious Dogs | x | — | — | — | — |
| Diamond City Surplus (and Myrna's House) (Diamond City) | 435 | [P9.08] | x | — | — | — | — | — | — | x | — | — | — | — | x | — | — | — | x |

531

| LOCATION NAME | PAGE NUMBER | ZONE LOCATION NUMBER | ARMAMENTS AND AMMO | | | ARMOR PARTS | | BOTTLECAPS | COLLECTIBLES | | | | COMPANION | FACTION | HEALTH OR CHEMS | SERVICES | | | UNIQUE ITEM |
|---|---|---|---|---|---|---|---|---|---|---|---|---|---|---|---|---|---|---|---|
| | | | AMMO | MINI NUKE OR FAT MAN | TRUNK | FUSION CORE | POWER ARMOR | | BOBBLEHEAD | NUKA CHERRY | NUKA COLA QUANTUM | REQUIRED READING | | | | TRADER | WORKSHOP | RADIO | |
| Dilapidated Trailer Shack | 272 | [S1.22] | x | – | – | – | – | – | – | – | – | – | – | Bloatflies, Radroaches | – | – | – | – | – |
| Diner and Apartments (The Fens) | 445 | [S9.08] | x | – | – | – | – | – | – | – | – | – | – | Super Mutants | x | – | – | – | – |
| Doc Crocker's House (Diamond City) | 437 | [P9.08] | x | – | – | – | – | – | – | x | – | – | – | – | x | – | – | – | – |
| Dockside Warehouse (South Boston) | 520 | [S18.03] | x | – | – | – | – | – | – | – | – | – | – | Bloodbugs | – | – | – | – | – |
| Doctor Sun's House (Diamond City) | 437 | [P9.08] | – | – | – | – | – | – | – | – | – | – | – | – | x | – | – | – | – |
| Dog's Dinner | 396 | [S6.08] | – | – | – | – | – | – | – | – | – | – | – | Scavenger | – | – | – | – | – |
| Doomed Airlines Flight | 351 | [S4.22] | – | – | x | – | – | – | – | – | – | – | – | – | x | – | – | – | – |
| Dorchester Height Monument | 521 | [S18.10] | – | – | – | – | – | – | – | – | – | – | – | – | x | – | – | – | – |
| Drug Den | 427 | [S8.04] | – | – | x | – | – | – | – | – | – | – | – | Raiders | x | – | – | – | – |
| Drumlin Diner | 264 | [P1.15] | – | – | – | – | – | x | – | – | – | – | – | Raider, Scavenger | x | Trudy | – | – | – |
| Drumlin Diner (East Boston) | 351 | [S4.16] | x | – | – | – | – | – | – | – | – | – | – | – | – | – | – | – | – |
| Dry Creek Bed | 270 | [S1.01] | – | – | – | – | – | – | – | – | x | – | – | – | – | – | – | – | – |
| Dry Creek Shack | 271 | [S1.15] | – | – | – | – | – | – | – | – | – | – | – | – | x | – | – | – | – |
| Dugout Inn (Diamond City) | 438 | [P9.08] | x | – | – | – | – | – | – | x (3) | – | – | – | – | x | Vadim Bobrov, Yefim Bobrov | – | – | – |
| Dunwich Borers | 327 | [P4.03] | x+ | x (3) | x | – | – | – | Sneak | – | – | Astoundingly Awesome Tales | – | Feral Ghouls, Raiders | x | – | – | – | x |
| Earl Sterling's House (Diamond City) | 437 | [P9.08] | x+ | – | – | – | – | – | – | – | – | – | – | – | x | – | – | – | – |
| East Boston Garage | 351 | [S4.18] | x | – | x | – | – | – | – | – | – | – | – | – | – | – | – | – | – |
| East Boston Police Station | 339 | [P4.23] | – | – | – | – | – | – | – | – | – | – | – | – | – | – | – | – | – |
| East Boston Preparatory School | 340 | [P4.24] | x+ | x | x | – | – | x++ | – | – | – | Astoundingly Awesome Tales | – | Raiders, Radroaches | x | – | – | – | – |
| Easy City Downs | 341 | [P4.25] | x+ | – | x | – | – | x+ | – | – | – | Tumblers Today | – | Raiders, Robots, Triggermen | x | – | – | – | – |
| Edge of the Glowing Sea | 357 | [P5.13] | x | – | – | – | – | – | – | – | – | – | – | Raiders | – | – | – | – | – |
| Egret Tours Marina | 373 | [P6.11] | x | – | x | – | – | x | – | – | x | Wasteland Survival Guide | – | Settlers | x | – | x | – | – |
| Electrical Hobbyist's Club | 355 | [P5.07] | – | – | – | – | – | – | – | – | – | – | – | – | – | – | – | – | – |
| Elevated Freeway Access | 322 | [S3.13] | – | – | – | – | – | – | – | – | – | – | – | – | – | – | – | – | – |
| Elevated Freeway Access (Lexington) | 273 | [S1.36] | – | – | – | – | – | – | – | – | – | – | – | – | – | – | – | – | – |
| Elevated Freeway Access (Lexington) | 273 | [S1.39] | – | – | – | – | – | – | – | – | – | – | – | – | – | – | – | – | – |
| Elevated Freeway Access (North Wilderness) | 270 | [S1.10] | x | – | – | – | – | – | – | – | – | – | – | – | – | – | – | – | – |
| Elevated Freeway: Derelict Bus | 273 | [S1.35] | – | – | – | – | – | – | – | – | x | – | – | Feral Ghouls, The Railroad | – | – | – | – | – |
| Elevated Freeway: Elevated Trailer | 298 | [S2.13] | – | – | x | – | – | – | – | – | – | – | – | – | – | – | – | – | – |
| Elevated Gunner Camp | 297 | [S2.09] | x | – | – | – | – | – | – | – | – | – | – | Gunners | x | – | – | – | – |
| Elevated Gunners' Den | 272 | [S1.27] | x | – | – | – | – | – | – | – | – | – | – | Gunners | – | – | – | – | – |
| Elevated Jumping-Off Point | 273 | [S1.40] | – | – | – | – | – | – | – | – | – | – | – | – | – | – | – | – | – |
| Elevated Road (West Access), Elevated Raider Camp (Financial District), and Elevated Road (Central Access) | 494 | [S15.06], [S15.07], and [S15.08] | x | – | – | – | – | – | – | – | – | – | – | Raiders | – | – | – | – | – |
| Factory (South Boston) | 520 | [S18.04] | – | – | – | x | – | – | – | – | – | – | – | Bloodbugs, Radroaches | x | – | – | – | – |
| Fairline Hill Estates | 371 | [P6.07] | x+ | – | x | – | – | – | – | – | – | – | – | Feral Ghouls, Yao Guai | x+ | – | – | – | – |
| Fallen Skybridge | 491 | [P15.07] | x | – | x | – | – | – | – | – | – | – | – | Gunners, Super Mutants | – | – | – | – | – |

| LOCATIONS | | | ARMAMENTS AND AMMO | | | ARMOR PARTS | | | COLLECTIBLES | | | | | | | | SERVICES | | | |
|---|---|---|---|---|---|---|---|---|---|---|---|---|---|---|---|---|---|---|---|
| LOCATION NAME | PAGE NUMBER | ZONE LOCATION NUMBER | AMMO | MINI NUKE OR FAT MAN | TRUNK | FUSION CORE | POWER ARMOR | BOTTLECAPS | BOBBLEHEAD | NUKA CHERRY | NUKA COLA QUANTUM | REQUIRED READING | COMPANION | FACTION | HEALTH OR CHEMS | TRADER | WORKSHOP | RADIO | UNIQUE ITEM |
| Fallon's Basement (Diamond City) | 434 | [P9.08] | – | – | – | – | – | – | – | – | – | – | – | – | x | Becky Fallon | – | – | x |
| Fallon's Department Store | 374 | [P6.12] | x | – | x | x | – | x+++ | – | – | – | La Coiffe | – | Super Mutants | x | – | – | – | – |
| Faneuil Hall | 482 | [P15.05] | x | – | – | x | – | – | – | – | – | Live & Love | – | Super Mutants | x | – | – | – | x |
| Federal Ration Stockpile | 301 | [P3.01] | x | x (2) | x | x | x | x | – | x | x (2) | U.S. Covert Operations Manual | – | Raiders | x | – | – | – | – |
| Federal Supply Cache 84NE | 356 | [P5.09] | x | – | – | – | – | – | – | x | – | – | – | Robots | x | – | – | – | – |
| Fens Street Sewer | 432 | [P9.06] | x | – | x | – | – | x | – | – | – | Tumblers Today | – | Bloatflies, Feral Ghouls | x | – | – | – | – |
| Fens Subway Station (Outskirts) | 444 | [S9.01] | – | – | – | – | – | – | – | – | – | – | – | Bloatflies, Radroaches | – | – | – | – | – |
| Fens Tunnel Entrance | 444 | [S9.02] | x | – | – | – | – | – | – | – | – | – | – | Super Mutants | – | – | – | – | – |
| Fiddler's Green Trailer Estates | 311 | [P3.15] | x | – | x | – | x | – | – | – | – | Live & Love | – | Feral Ghouls | x | – | – | – | – |
| Finch Farm | 296 | [P2.35] | – | – | – | – | – | x+ | – | – | – | – | – | Settlers | – | Finch | x | – | – |
| Fishing Cabin | 366 | [S5.06] | – | – | – | – | – | – | – | – | – | – | – | – | x | – | – | – | – |
| Floating Barge | 351 | [S4.23] | – | – | – | – | – | – | – | – | – | – | – | – | – | – | – | – | – |
| Floating Barge | 399 | [S6.34] | – | – | – | – | – | – | – | – | – | – | – | – | – | – | – | – | – |
| Footbridge (Esplanade) | 449 | [S10.01] | x | – | – | – | – | – | – | – | – | – | – | Super Mutants | – | – | – | – | – |
| Forest Grove Marsh | 314 | [P3.17] | x+ | – | x | – | – | x | – | – | – | – | – | Feral Ghouls | x | – | – | – | – |
| Forgotten Church | 360 | [P5.17] | x | – | x | – | – | – | – | – | – | – | – | – | – | – | – | – | – |
| Fort Hagen | 308 | [P3.12] | x+++ | x (2) | x (2) | x | – | x | Energy Weapons | – | x | Guns and Bullets, Robco FUN! (and Pipfall Game), U.S. Covert Operations Manual | – | Synths (The Institute) | x+++ | – | – | – | x |
| Fort Hagen Filling Station | 307 | [P3.11] | – | – | – | – | – | – | – | – | – | – | – | Bloatflies | – | – | – | – | – |
| Fort Hagen Satellite Array | 307 | [P3.09] | x | – | – | – | – | – | – | – | – | – | – | – | – | – | – | – | – |
| Fort Strong | 347 | [P4.29] | x++ | x (4) | x | x | x | x | – | – | – | U.S. Covert Operations Manual | – | Super Mutants | x | – | – | – | – |
| Four Leaf Fishpacking Container Yard | 520 | [S18.05] | x | – | – | – | – | – | – | – | – | – | – | – | – | – | – | – | – |
| Four Leaf Fishpacking Plant | 511 | [P18.01] | x | – | x | x (3) | – | x | – | – | x | Tales of a Junktown Jerky Vendor | – | Feral Ghouls, Vicious Mongrels | x++ | – | – | – | – |
| Fraternal Post 115 | 405 | [P7.04] | x | – | x | – | – | x | – | – | – | Guns and Bullets | – | Super Mutants | x | – | – | – | – |
| Freeway Rooftops | 351 | [S4.20] | x | – | – | – | – | – | – | – | – | – | – | – | x | – | – | – | – |
| Freeway Shack and Cage | 273 | [S1.37] | – | – | – | – | – | x | – | – | – | – | – | Radscorpions | x | – | – | – | – |
| Garden Terrace | 481 | [P15.04] | x+ | – | – | – | – | – | – | – | x | – | – | Deathclaws, Robots | x | – | – | – | – |
| General Atomics Factory | 513 | [P18.02] | x | – | x | – | – | x | – | x | x | Tesla Science | – | Robots | x | – | – | – | – |
| General Atomics Galleria | 280 | [P2.11] | x | – | – | – | – | x | – | – | – | – | – | Robots | x | Bean, Crisp, Danny, Reg, Sprocket, Waitron | – | – | – |
| Gibson Point Pier | 335 | [P4.15] | x | – | x | – | – | – | – | x | x | – | – | Mirelurks | x | – | – | – | – |
| Goodneighbor | 483 | [P15.06] | x+++ | x (2) | x (3) | – | – | x+++ | – | – | x | Live & Love (2), RobCo FUN! (and Grognak & The Ruby Ruins Game) | Hancock, MacCready | Settler (Goodneighbor), Neighborhood Watch, Triggermen | x+++ | KL-E-O, Daisy, Whitechapel Charlie, Rufus Rubins, Clair Hutchins, Fred Allen | – | – | x |
| Gorski Cabin | 264 | [P1.14] | x | – | – | – | – | – | – | – | – | Wasteland Survival Guide | – | Feral Ghouls | – | – | – | – | – |
| Graygarden | 304 | [P3.04] | – | – | – | – | – | x | – | – | – | – | – | Settler (Robots) | x | Robots | x | – | – |
| Greater Mass Blood Clinic | 310 | [P3.13] | x | – | x | – | – | x | – | – | – | Massachusetts Surgical Journal | – | Bloatflies, Bloodbugs | x++ | – | – | – | – |
| Green Awning Mansion | 427 | [S8.03] | – | – | x | – | – | – | – | – | – | – | – | – | – | – | – | – | – |
| Greenetech Genetics | 415 | [P7.11] | x++ | x (2) | – | x (3) | – | x+ | – | – | x | Massachusetts Surgical Journal | – | Gunners, Synths (The Institute) | x+ | – | – | – | – |
| Greenhouse (Diamond City) | 436 | [P9.08] | – | – | – | – | – | – | – | – | – | – | – | – | x | – | – | – | – |

| LOCATION NAME | PAGE NUMBER | ZONE LOCATION NUMBER | AMMO | MINI NUKE OR FAT MAN | TRUNK | FUSION CORE | POWER ARMOR | BOTTLECAPS | BOBBLEHEAD | NUKA CHERRY | NUKA COLA QUANTUM | REQUIRED READING | COMPANION | FACTION | HEALTH OR CHEMS | TRADER | WORKSHOP | RADIO | UNIQUE ITEM |
|---|---|---|---|---|---|---|---|---|---|---|---|---|---|---|---|---|---|---|---|
| Greentop Nursery | 281 | [P2.15] | – | – | – | – | – | – | – | – | – | – | – | Settlers, Stingwings | – | – | x | – | – |
| Gun Shop Garage | 449 | [S10.07] | – | – | – | – | – | – | – | – | – | – | – | – | – | – | – | – | – |
| Gunner Camp (Parsons Elevated Freeway) | 349 | [S4.01] | x | – | – | – | – | – | – | – | – | – | – | Gunners | – | – | – | – | – |
| Gunner Camp On-ramp | 321 | [S3.03] | x | – | – | – | – | – | – | – | – | – | – | Gunners | – | – | – | – | – |
| Gunners Plaza | 381 | [P6.17] | x+++ | x (3) | x (2) | x | – | x | Small Guns | x | x | Guns and Bullets | – | Gunners | x+ | – | – | – | – |
| Gwinnett Brewery | 515 | [P18.05] | x | – | x | – | – | – | – | – | – | Tales of a Junktown Jerky Vendor | – | Mirelurks | – | – | – | – | – |
| Half-Buried Stash | 271 | [S1.16] | – | – | x | – | – | – | – | – | – | – | – | – | – | – | – | – | – |
| Half-Demolished Apartment (Back Bay) | 458 | [S11.02] | – | – | – | – | – | – | – | – | – | – | – | – | x | – | – | – | – |
| HalluciGen, Inc. | 447 | [P10.02] | x | – | x | – | – | – | – | – | x | Tesla Science | – | Gunners | x | – | – | – | x |
| Hangman's Alley | 429 | [P9.02] | x | – | x | – | – | – | – | – | – | – | – | Raiders, Settlers | – | – | x | – | – |
| Harbormaster Hotel | 506 | [P17.03] | x | – | – | – | – | x | – | x | – | – | – | Raiders | x+ | – | – | – | – |
| Hardware Store (Cambridge) | 418 | [S7.05] | x | – | – | – | – | – | – | – | – | – | – | – | x | – | – | – | – |
| Hardware Town | 443 | [P9.10] | x | – | x | – | – | x | – | – | – | Picket Fences | – | Raiders | x | – | – | – | – |
| Hawthorne Estate | 521 | [S18.09] | – | – | – | – | – | – | – | – | – | – | – | – | – | – | – | – | – |
| Hawthorne Residence (Diamond City) | 438 | [P9.08] | x | – | – | – | – | – | – | – | – | – | – | – | – | – | – | – | – |
| Haymarket Mall | 481 | [P15.03] | x | – | – | – | – | x | – | – | – | – | – | Raiders, Robots | x | – | – | – | – |
| Hester's Consumer Robotics | 501 | [P16.05] | x | – | – | – | – | x | – | – | – | – | – | Robots | x | – | – | – | – |
| Hilltop Hut | 297 | [S2.02] | – | – | – | – | – | – | – | – | – | – | – | Robots | – | – | – | – | – |
| Holy Mission Congregation Church | 449 | [S10.02] | x | – | – | – | – | – | – | – | – | – | – | Feral Ghouls | – | – | – | – | – |
| Home Plate | 439 | [P9.09] | x | – | – | – | – | – | – | – | – | – | – | Vault Dweller | x | – | x | – | x |
| Hopesmarch Pentecostal Church | 362 | [P5.27] | x | – | x | – | – | – | – | – | – | – | – | Feral Ghouls | x | – | – | – | – |
| Hot Pizza Pie Shop | 468 | [S13.05] | – | – | – | – | – | – | – | – | – | – | – | Raiders | – | – | – | – | – |
| Hub 360 | 502 | [S16.01] | x | – | x | – | – | – | – | – | – | – | – | Super Mutants | x | – | – | – | – |
| Hub City Auto Wreckers | 352 | [P4.10] | x | – | x | – | – | x | – | – | – | – | – | Gunners | – | – | – | – | – |
| Hubris Comics | 453 | [P11.03] | x | – | x | – | – | x | – | – | x | Astoundingly Awesome Tales, Unstoppables | – | Feral Ghouls, Radroaches | x | – | – | – | x |
| Hugo's Hole | 328 | [P4.04] | x | – | x | – | – | x | – | – | – | – | – | Raider | – | – | – | – | – |
| Hyde Park | 382 | [P6.18] | x | – | x | – | – | – | – | – | – | Grognak the Barbarian | – | Raiders, Robots, Scavengers | x | – | – | – | – |
| Irish Pride Industries Shipyard | 292 | [P2.30] | x | – | x | – | – | x | – | – | – | Taboo Tattoos | – | Bloodbugs, Mirelurks | x | – | – | – | – |
| Island Cabin | 396 | [S6.12] | x | – | – | – | – | – | – | – | – | – | – | Radstag Does | – | – | – | – | – |
| Jalbert Brothers Disposal | 304 | [P3.05] | x | x | x | – | – | – | – | – | – | – | – | Mole Rats, Children of the Atom | x | – | – | – | – |
| Jamaica Plain | 379 | [P6.16] | x+ | – | – | – | – | – | – | – | – | – | – | Feral Ghouls, Robots | x | – | x | – | x |
| Jamaica Plain Pond | 397 | [S6.16] | x | – | – | – | – | x | – | – | – | – | – | – | – | – | – | – | – |
| Joe's Spuckies (Southie Speakeasy) | 520 | [S18.02] | – | – | – | – | – | – | – | – | – | – | – | – | – | – | – | – | – |
| Joe's Spuckies Coffee Shop (Fens Outskirts) | 323 | [S3.26] | – | – | – | – | – | – | – | – | – | – | – | – | – | – | – | – | – |
| Kellogg's House (Diamond City) | 435 | [P9.08] | x+ | – | – | – | – | – | – | x (3) | x (2) | – | – | – | – | – | – | – | – |
| Kendall Hospital | 406 | [P7.07] | x+ | – | x | x | – | x | – | – | – | – | – | Deathclaws, Raiders | x | – | – | – | – |
| Kendall Parking | 420 | [S7.16] | x | – | – | – | – | – | – | x | – | – | – | Mole Rats, Scavengers | – | – | – | – | – |
| Kendall Raider Apartments | 420 | [S7.17] | x | – | x | – | – | – | – | – | – | – | – | Raiders | x | – | – | – | – |
| Kingsport Lighthouse | 334 | [P4.13] | – | x | x | – | – | x | – | – | – | – | – | Children of the Atom, Feral Ghouls | – | – | x | – | – |
| Kingsport Restrooms | | [S4.09] | – | – | – | – | – | – | – | – | – | – | – | – | x | – | – | – | – |
| Klean Watur (Sheng Kawolski's House) (Diamond City) | 437 | [P9.08] | – | – | – | – | – | – | – | – | x | – | – | – | – | Kawolski | – | – | – |

534

| LOCATION NAME | PAGE NUMBER | ZONE LOCATION NUMBER | AMMO | MINI NUKE OR FAT MAN | TRUNK | FUSION CORE | POWER ARMOR | BOTTLECAPS | BOBBLEHEAD | NUKA CHERRY | NUKA COLA QUANTUM | REQUIRED READING | COMPANION | FACTION | HEALTH OR CHEMS | TRADER | WORKSHOP | RADIO | UNIQUE ITEM |
|---|---|---|---|---|---|---|---|---|---|---|---|---|---|---|---|---|---|---|---|
| Lake Cochituate | 355 | [P5.05] | x | — | x (2) | — | — | — | — | — | — | — | — | Mirelurks, Raiders | x | — | — | — | — |
| Lake Quannapowitt | 275 | [P2.02] | x | — | x | — | — | — | — | — | — | — | — | Bloatflies, Bloodbugs, Mirelurks | — | — | — | — | — |
| Latimer Residence (Diamond City) | 438 | [P9.08] | — | — | — | — | — | — | — | — | — | — | — | — | x+ | — | — | — | — |
| Layton Towers | 456 | [P11.07] | x | — | x | x | — | x | — | — | — | — | — | Raiders | x | — | — | — | — |
| Layton Towers Underpass Entrance | 395 | [S6.02] | — | — | — | — | — | — | — | — | — | — | — | Raiders | — | — | — | — | — |
| Lexington | 267 | [P1.22] | x | x | x | — | — | — | — | — | — | — | — | Feral Ghouls, Raiders | x | — | — | — | — |
| Lexington Apartments | 269 | [P1.23] | x | — | — | — | — | x | — | — | — | — | — | Raiders | — | — | — | — | — |
| Lexington: Switchboard | 268 | [P1.22] | x | x | x | x (2) | — | x | — | — | — | — | U.S. Covert Operations Manual | — | Radroaches, Radscorpions, Synths (The Institute) | x | — | — | — | — |
| Libertalia | 336 | [P4.17] | x++ | x | x | — | — | x | — | — | — | — | U.S. Covert Operations Manual | — | Raiders | x++ | — | — | — | x |
| Listening Post Bravo | 282 | [P2.17] | x | — | x | — | — | — | — | — | — | — | — | — | Brotherhood of Steel, Robots, Yao Guai | x | — | — | — | — |
| Locked Diner | 509 | [S17.07] | — | — | — | — | — | — | — | — | — | — | — | — | x | — | — | — | — |
| Lonely Chapel | 265 | [P1.17] | — | — | — | — | — | — | — | — | — | — | — | Raiders | — | — | — | — | — |
| Longneck Lukowski's Cannery | 333 | [P4.12] | x | — | x | x | — | x | Barter | x | — | Tales of a Junktown Jerky Vendor | — | Feral Ghouls, Radroaches, Scavengers | x | Theodore Collins, Trader Rylee | — | — | — |
| Lynn Pier Parking | 333 | [P4.11] | — | — | — | — | — | — | — | — | — | — | — | Radroaches | — | — | — | — | — |
| Lynn Woods | 276 | [P2.05] | x | — | x | — | — | x | — | — | — | Wasteland Survival Guide | — | Deathclaws, Raiders | x | — | — | — | — |
| Mahkra Fishpacking | 325 | [P4.02] | x | — | x | — | — | x | — | x (2) | x | Tesla Science | — | Raiders, Synths (The Institute) | x+ | — | — | — | — |
| Main Boathouse (Waterfront) | 508 | [S17.06] | — | — | — | — | — | — | — | — | — | — | — | Mirelurks | — | — | — | — | — |
| Malborough House | 449 | [S10.05] | x | — | — | — | — | — | — | — | — | — | — | Gunners | — | — | — | — | — |
| Malden Center | 286 | [P2.21] | x+ | x (2) | x | x | — | x+ | — | x | — | Tumblers Today | — | Raiders, Synths (the Institute) | x | — | — | — | — |
| Malden Drainage | 299 | [S2.20] | — | — | — | — | — | — | — | — | — | — | — | Bloodbugs | — | — | — | — | — |
| Malden Middle School (Vault 75) | 287 | [P2.23] | x+++ | — | x | — | — | x | Science | — | — | Grognak the Barbarian | — | Brotherhood of Steel, Gunners, The Institute | x+ | — | — | — | — |
| Mass Bay Medical Center | 499 | [P16.03] | x | — | — | — | x | — | — | — | — | — | — | Gunners | x | — | — | — | — |
| Mass Chemical | 419 | [S7.11] | x | — | — | — | — | — | — | — | — | — | — | Super Mutants | — | — | — | — | — |
| Mass Fusion Building | 477 | [P15.01] | x+ | x | x (4) | x | — | x | Strength | x | — | Tesla Science | — | Gunners, Brotherhood of Steel (Quest active), Synths (The Institute, Quest active), Robots (Quest active) | x+ | — | — | — | x |
| Mass Fusion Containment Shed | 281 | [P2.13] | x | — | — | x | — | — | — | — | — | — | — | Feral Ghouls, Radroaches | — | — | — | — | — |
| Mass Fusion Disposal Site | 355 | [P5.06] | x | x (2) | — | — | — | — | — | — | — | — | — | Super Mutants | x | — | — | — | — |
| Mass Gravel & Sand | 306 | [P3.07] | — | — | — | — | — | — | — | — | — | — | — | Mole Rats, Raider | — | — | — | — | — |
| Mass Pike Interchange | 317 | [P3.21] | x | — | x | x | x | x | — | — | — | Grognak the Barbarian | — | Gunners | — | — | — | — | — |
| Mass Pike Tunnel West and East | 370 | [P6.03] and [04] | x | x | x | x | — | — | — | — | x (2) | Taboo Tattoos | — | Feral Ghouls, Mole Rats, Raiders | x | — | — | — | — |
| Massachusetts State House | 471 | [P14.01] | x | x | x | x | x | x | — | x | — | — | — | Mirelurks, Raiders | x | — | — | — | — |
| Mean Pastries | 469 | [S13.10] | — | — | — | — | — | — | — | — | — | — | — | — | — | — | — | — | — |
| Med-Tek Research | 288 | [P2.24] | x++ | — | x | x | — | — | — | x | — | Massachusetts Surgical Journal | — | Feral Ghouls | x | — | — | — | x |
| Medford Memorial Hospital | 285 | [P2.20] | x | — | x (2) | x | — | x | — | x | x | Massachusetts Surgical Journal | — | Super Mutants | x | — | — | — | — |
| Medical Center Metro | 498 | [P16.02] | x | — | — | x | — | x | — | — | x (2) | — | — | Bloodbugs, Raiders | x | — | — | — | — |
| Mega Surgery (Diamond City) | 436 | [P9.08] | — | — | — | — | — | — | — | — | — | — | — | — | x++ | Doctor Sun | — | — | — |
| Military APC (Sanctuary Lake) | 271 | [S1.13] | — | — | — | — | — | — | — | — | — | — | — | Bloatflies | x | — | — | — | — |

| LOCATION NAME | PAGE NUMBER | ZONE LOCATION NUMBER | ARMAMENTS AND AMMO | | | ARMOR PARTS | | BOTTLECAPS | COLLECTIBLES | | | | COMPANION | FACTION | HEALTH OR CHEMS | SERVICES | | | |
|---|---|---|---|---|---|---|---|---|---|---|---|---|---|---|---|---|---|---|---|
| | | | AMMO | MINI NUKE OR FAT MAN | TRUNK | FUSION CORE | POWER ARMOR | | BOBBLEHEAD | NUKA CHERRY | NUKA COLA QUANTUM | REQUIRED READING | | | | TRADER | WORKSHOP | RADIO | UNIQUE ITEM |
| Military APCs | 299 | [S2.25] | – | – | – | – | x | – | – | – | – | – | – | Robots | x | – | – | – | – |
| Military Armor Transport (Lexington) | 273 | [S1.33] | x | – | x | x | x | – | – | – | – | – | – | – | – | – | – | – | – |
| Military Armor Transport (North Wilderness) | 271 | [S1.11] | – | – | – | x | x | – | – | – | – | – | – | – | – | – | – | – | – |
| Military Barge (University Point) | 397 | [S6.19] | x | – | x | – | – | – | – | – | – | – | – | Robots | – | – | – | – | – |
| Military Checkpoint (Cambridge Outskirts) | 322 | [S3.17] | x | – | x | – | x | – | – | – | – | – | – | – | – | – | – | – | – |
| Military Checkpoint (Commie Devil Billboard) | 323 | [S3.23] | x | – | x | – | x | – | – | – | – | – | – | Bloodbugs | – | – | – | – | – |
| Military Checkpoint (Lake Cochituate) | 366 | [S5.04] | x | – | x | – | x | – | – | – | – | – | – | – | – | – | – | – | – |
| Military Checkpoint (Lexington) | 273 | [S1.38] | x | – | x | – | – | – | – | – | – | – | – | – | – | – | – | – | – |
| Military Checkpoint (West Roxbury) | 396 | [S6.09] | x | – | x | – | x | – | – | – | – | – | – | Robots | – | – | – | – | – |
| Military Convoy (APCs and Trailer) | 298 | [S2.12] | x | – | x | – | – | – | – | – | – | – | – | – | – | – | – | – | – |
| Military Convoy (Elevated Freeway) | 397 | [S6.17] | – | – | x | – | x | – | – | – | – | – | – | – | – | – | – | – | – |
| Military Convoy (Training Yard) | 299 | [S2.22] | x | – | x | – | x | – | – | – | – | – | – | Robots, Stingwings | – | – | – | – | – |
| Military Pillbox (Somerville) | 367 | [S5.11] | – | – | – | – | – | – | – | – | – | – | – | Robots | – | – | – | – | – |
| Military Pillbox (Walden) | 272 | [S1.30] | x | – | – | – | – | – | – | – | – | – | – | – | – | – | – | – | – |
| Military Pillboxes | 399 | [S6.30] | – | – | – | – | – | – | – | – | – | – | – | Robots | – | – | – | – | – |
| Milton General Billboard | 349 | [S4.02] | – | – | – | – | – | x | – | – | – | – | – | – | – | – | – | – | – |
| Milton General Hospital | 376 | [P6.13] | x | – | x | – | – | – | – | – | x | – | – | Robots, Raiders (Quest only) | x | – | – | – | – |
| Mirelurk Pond | 321 | [S3.09] | – | – | – | – | – | – | – | – | – | – | – | Mirelurks | – | – | – | – | – |
| Monsignor Plaza | 417 | [P7.13] | x | – | x | – | – | – | – | – | – | – | – | Raiders | x | – | – | – | – |
| Moonshiner's Cabin | 397 | [S6.14] | – | – | – | – | – | x | – | – | – | – | – | – | – | – | – | – | – |
| Murkwater Construction Site | 385 | [P6.20] | – | – | – | – | – | – | – | – | – | – | – | Mirelurks | – | – | – | x | – |
| Museum of Freedom | 263 | [P1.12] | x | – | – | x | x | x | Perception | – | – | – | RobCo FUN! (and Atomic Command Game) | Preston Garvey | Minutemen, Raiders, Settlers | x | – | – | – | – |
| Museum of Witchcraft | 329 | [P4.05] | x | – | x | – | – | – | – | – | – | – | Grognak the Barbarian | – | Deathclaw, Gunner | x | – | – | – | – |
| Mystic Pines | 266 | [P1.20] | – | – | – | x | – | – | – | – | x | x | Tales of a Junktown Jerky Vendor | – | – | x | – | – | – | – |
| Nahant Chapel | 338 | [P4.21] | x | – | x | – | – | – | – | – | – | – | – | – | Mirelurks | – | – | – | – | – |
| Nahant Oceanological Society | 339 | [P4.22] | x | – | x (2) | – | – | – | – | – | – | – | Wasteland Survival Guide | – | Mirelurks, Robots | x | – | – | – | – |
| Nahant Pier Restaurant | 350 | [S4.15] | – | – | x | – | – | – | – | – | x | – | – | – | Feral Ghouls | – | – | – | – | – |
| Nahant Sheriff's Department | 338 | [P4.19] | x | – | – | – | – | x | – | – | – | – | – | – | – | – | – | – | – | – |
| Nahant Wharf | 337 | [P4.18] | x | – | – | – | – | – | – | – | x | – | – | – | – | – | – | – | – | – |
| Natick Banks | 354 | [P5.03] | x | – | x | – | – | – | – | – | x | – | – | – | Deathclaws, Scavengers, Super Mutants | x | – | – | – | – |
| Natick Hillside Home | 366 | [S5.02] | x | – | – | – | – | – | – | – | – | – | – | – | Attack Dogs, Deathclaws | x | – | – | – | – |
| Natick Police Department | 355 | [P5.04] | – | – | – | – | – | – | – | – | – | – | – | – | – | x | – | – | – | – |
| Natick Power Station | 366 | [S5.01] | x | – | – | – | – | – | – | – | – | – | – | – | Deathclaws, Super Mutants | x | – | – | – | – |
| National Guard Training Yard | 293 | [P2.32] | x+ | – | x | x (2) | x | – | – | – | – | – | U.S. Covert Operations Manual | – | Brotherhood of Steel, Feral Ghouls, Robots | x | – | – | – | – |
| Neponset Park | 385 | [P6.22] | x | – | – | – | – | – | – | – | – | – | – | – | Mirelurks | – | – | – | – | – |
| NH&M Freight Depot | 371 | [P6.06] | x | – | – | x (2) | – | x | – | – | x | – | – | – | Triggermen | – | – | – | – | x |

| LOCATIONS | | | ARMAMENTS AND AMMO | | | ARMOR PARTS | | | COLLECTIBLES | | | | | | | | SERVICES | | | |
|---|---|---|---|---|---|---|---|---|---|---|---|---|---|---|---|---|---|---|---|---|
| LOCATION NAME | PAGE NUMBER | ZONE LOCATION NUMBER | AMMO | MINI NUKE OR FAT MAN | TRUNK | FUSION CORE | POWER ARMOR | BOTTLECAPS | BOBBLEHEAD | NUKA CHERRY | NUKA COLA QUANTUM | REQUIRED READING | COMPANION | FACTION | HEALTH OR CHEMS | TRADER | WORKSHOP | RADIO | UNIQUE ITEM |
| Nordhagen Beach | 341 | [P4.26] | — | — | — | — | — | — | — | — | — | — | — | Settler | — | — | x | — | — |
| North End Graveyard | 468 | [S13.02] | — | — | — | — | — | — | — | — | — | — | — | Feral Ghouls | — | — | — | — | x |
| O'Neill Family Manufacturing | 363 | [P5.30] | x | — | — | — | — | x | — | — | — | — | — | Feral Ghouls, Radscorpions | x | — | — | — | — |
| Oberland Station | 315 | [P3.19] | — | — | — | — | — | — | — | — | — | — | — | Settler | — | — | x | — | — |
| Ocean Fishing Shack | 350 | [S4.10] | x | — | — | — | — | — | — | — | — | — | — | — | — | — | — | — | — |
| Ocean Raft | 350 | [S4.13] | — | — | — | — | — | — | — | — | — | — | — | — | x | — | — | — | — |
| Old Caravan Trailer | 298 | [S2.17] | — | — | — | — | — | x | — | — | — | — | — | Robots | — | — | — | — | — |
| Old Corner Bookstore | 480 | [P15.02] | x | — | x | — | — | x | — | — | x | — | — | Feral Ghouls | x | — | — | — | — |
| Old Firing Range | 270 | [S1.03] | x | — | — | — | — | — | — | — | — | — | — | Scavengers | — | — | — | — | — |
| Old Granary Burying Ground | 472 | [P14.02] | x | — | — | — | — | — | — | — | — | — | — | Feral Ghouls | — | — | — | — | — |
| Old Gullet Sinkhole | 281 | [P2.14] | x | — | x | — | — | x | — | — | — | Wasteland Survival Guide | — | Deathclaws, Feral Ghouls, Radroaches | — | — | — | — | x |
| Old Military Monument | 399 | [S6.31] | x | — | — | — | — | — | — | — | — | — | — | — | — | — | — | — | — |
| Old North Church | 466 | [P13.02] | x+++ | — | — | x | — | — | — | x (2) | — | Astoundingly Awesome Tales | Deacon | Feral Ghouls, The Railroad | x+++ | Tinker Tom, Doctor Carrington | — | — | x |
| Old Sniper Camp | 503 | [S16.12] | — | — | — | — | — | — | — | — | — | — | — | Scavengers | — | — | — | — | — |
| On-Ramp Gunners' Den | 272 | [S1.28] | — | — | — | — | — | — | — | — | — | — | — | Gunners | — | — | — | — | — |
| Outpost Zimonja | 275 | [P2.01] | x | x | — | — | — | — | — | — | — | Astoundingly Awesome Tales | — | Raiders | — | — | x | — | — |
| Overflow Outlet Camp (Atomatoys Factory) | 399 | [S6.32] | x | — | — | — | — | x | — | — | — | — | — | Feral Ghouls | x | — | — | — | — |
| Park Street Station (Vault 114) | 473 | [P14.05] | x | — | — | — | — | x++ | Speech | — | x | Astoundingly Awesome Tales | Nick Valentine | Triggermen | x | — | — | — | — |
| Parking Garage (Theater District) | 502 | [S16.05] | x | — | — | — | — | — | — | — | — | — | — | Gunners | — | — | — | — | — |
| Parking Garage and Raider Rooftops | 495 | [S15.13] | x | — | x | — | — | — | — | — | — | — | — | Raiders | x | — | — | — | — |
| Parkview Apartments | 431 | [P9.05] | x+ | — | x | — | — | x | — | — | — | — | — | Super Mutants, Raiders | x | — | — | — | — |
| Parsons Creamery | 276 | [P2.06] | x | — | — | — | — | — | — | — | — | — | — | Raiders | — | — | — | — | — |
| Parsons State Insane Asylum | 276 | [P2.07] | x | — | — | — | — | x | Charisma | — | — | Massachusetts Surgical Journal | — | Radroaches, Mercenaries, Raiders | x | — | — | — | x |
| Paul Revere's House | 469 | [S13.17] | — | — | — | — | — | — | — | — | — | — | — | Super Mutants | — | — | — | — | — |
| Peabody House | 390 | [P6.26] | x | — | — | — | — | — | — | — | x | — | — | Settlers (Ghouls) | x | — | — | — | — |
| Pearwood Residences | 502 | [S16.02] | x | — | — | — | — | — | — | — | — | — | — | Super Mutants | x | — | — | — | — |
| Pedestrian Underpass | 494 | [S15.12] | — | — | — | — | — | — | — | — | — | — | — | — | x | — | — | — | — |
| Pedestrian Walkway (Waterfront) | 509 | [S17.08] | x | — | — | — | — | — | — | — | — | — | — | Raiders | — | — | — | — | — |
| Pembroke Residence (Diamond City) | 435 | [P9.08] | — | — | — | — | — | — | — | — | — | — | — | — | — | — | — | — | — |
| Pickman Gallery | 465 | [P13.01] | x | — | x | — | — | x | Lock Picking | — | x (2) | Astoundingly Awesome Tales | — | Raiders | x | — | — | — | x |
| Pickman's Exit | 469 | [S13.11] | — | — | — | — | — | — | — | — | — | — | — | — | — | — | — | — | — |
| Playground Garage | 463 | [S12.03] | — | — | — | — | — | — | — | — | — | — | — | Yao Guai | — | — | — | — | — |
| Plumber's Secret | 418 | [S7.06] | — | — | — | — | — | — | — | — | — | — | — | Radroaches | x | — | — | — | — |
| Police Precinct 8 | 430 | [P9.04] | — | — | — | — | — | — | — | — | — | — | — | Radroaches | x | — | — | — | — |
| Pond and Freeway Shack | 270 | [S1.09] | x | — | — | — | — | — | — | — | — | — | — | — | x | — | — | — | — |
| Poseiden Energy Turbine #18-F | 291 | [P2.28] | — | — | x | — | — | — | — | — | — | Tumblers Today | — | Bloatflies, Mirelurks, Radroaches | x | — | — | — | — |
| Poseiden Energy | 392 | [P6.28] | x++ | — | — | — | x | x+ | Endurance | x (2) | — | Tesla Science | — | Mirelurks, Raiders, Robots | x | — | — | — | — |
| Poseiden Reservoir | 353 | [P5.01] | x | — | — | — | — | — | — | — | — | — | — | Feral Ghouls | — | — | — | — | — |
| Postal Square | 492 | [P15.08] | x++ | — | x | — | x | x+ | — | — | — | — | — | Gunners, Super Mutants | x | — | — | — | — |
| Power Armor Warehouse | 322 | [S3.18] | x | — | — | — | x | — | — | — | — | — | — | — | x | — | — | — | — |
| Power Noodles (Diamond City) | 434 | [P9.08] | — | — | — | — | — | — | — | — | x (2) | — | — | — | — | Takahashi | — | — | — |

| LOCATIONS | | | ARMAMENTS AND AMMO | | | ARMOR PARTS | | | COLLECTIBLES | | | | | | | SERVICES | | | |
|---|---|---|---|---|---|---|---|---|---|---|---|---|---|---|---|---|---|---|---|
| LOCATION NAME | PAGE NUMBER | ZONE LOCATION NUMBER | AMMO | MINI NUKE OR FAT MAN | TRUNK | FUSION CORE | POWER ARMOR | BOTTLECAPS | BOBBLEHEAD | NUKA CHERRY | NUKA COLA QUANTUM | REQUIRED READING | COMPANION | FACTION | HEALTH OR CHEMS | TRADER | WORKSHOP | RADIO | UNIQUE ITEM |
| Prost Bar | 475 | [S14.02] | – | – | x | – | – | – | – | – | – | – | – | – | – | – | – | – | – |
| Protectron Trailer | 299 | [S2.28] | – | – | – | – | – | – | – | – | – | – | – | Robots | – | – | – | – | – |
| Prydwen | 345 | [P4.28] | x+++ | x (5+) | x | x | x | x+++ | – | – | x | – | Paladin Danse | Brotherhood of Steel, Mole Rats | x+++ | Knight-Captain Cade, Proctor Teagan | – | – | x |
| Public Works Maintenance Area | 421 | [S7.19] | – | – | x | x | – | – | – | – | x | – | – | Feral Ghouls, Mole Rats, Synths (The Institute) | x | – | – | – | – |
| Publick Occurrences (Diamond City) | 434 | [P9.08] | x | – | – | – | – | – | – | – | – | – | Piper | – | x | – | – | – | – |
| Pulowski Preservation Shelter Cluster | 322 | [S3.14] | x | – | – | – | – | – | – | – | – | – | – | Raiders | – | – | – | – | – |
| Quincy Lighthouse | 399 | [S6.37] | – | – | – | – | – | – | – | – | – | – | – | – | – | x | – | – | – |
| Quincy Police Station | 390 | [P6.25] | x | – | – | x | x | – | – | – | – | – | – | Gunners | x | – | – | – | x |
| Quincy Quarries | 385 | [P6.21] | x++ | – | x | – | – | x++ | – | – | – | – | – | Raiders | x | – | – | – | – |
| Quincy Ruins | 387 | [P6.24] | x++ | x (2) | x | x | x | x | – | – | x | Guns and Bullets | – | Gunners, Radscorpions, Settlers (Ghouls) | x++ | – | – | – | x |
| Radiation Lake | 367 | [S5.10] | – | – | – | – | – | – | – | – | – | – | – | Bloodbugs, Feral Ghouls | – | – | – | – | – |
| Radio Tower 3SM-U81 | 275 | [P2.03] | – | – | – | – | – | – | – | – | – | – | – | Bloodbugs | – | – | – | Automated Radio Alarm, Greenbriar Radio Signal, Nautical Radio Signal | – |
| Radroach Outhouse | 271 | [S1.20] | – | – | – | – | – | – | – | – | – | – | – | Radroaches | x | – | – | – | – |
| Raider Back-Alley Camp (The Fens) | 444 | [S9.05] | x | – | – | – | – | – | – | – | – | – | – | Raiders | – | – | – | – | – |
| Raider Blockade (Southeast Back Bay) | 459 | [S11.09] | x | – | – | – | – | – | – | – | – | – | – | Raiders | – | – | – | – | – |
| Raider Bonfire Camp | 418 | [S7.07] | – | – | x | – | – | – | – | – | – | – | – | Raiders | x | – | – | – | – |
| Raider Camp (Narrow Yard) | 419 | [S7.09] | x | – | – | – | – | – | – | – | – | – | – | Raiders | x | – | – | – | – |
| Raider Camp (University Point Outskirts) | 396 | [S6.11] | x | – | – | – | – | – | – | – | – | – | – | Raiders | x | – | – | – | – |
| Raider Chem Lab Shack | 272 | [S1.25] | – | – | – | – | – | – | – | – | – | – | – | Raiders | x | – | – | – | – |
| Raider Courtyard (North End) | 468 | [S13.04] | – | – | – | – | – | x | – | – | – | – | – | Raiders | – | – | – | – | – |
| Raider Cul-de-Sac (The Fens) | 445 | [S9.10] | x | – | x | – | – | – | – | – | – | – | – | Raiders | – | – | – | – | – |
| Raider Graves | 321 | [S3.04] | – | – | – | – | – | – | – | – | – | – | – | Raiders | – | – | – | – | – |
| Raider Hilltop Den | 270 | [S1.06] | – | – | – | – | – | – | – | – | – | – | – | Raiders | x | – | – | – | – |
| Raider Lookout (Esplanade) | 449 | [S10.06] | x | – | – | – | – | – | – | – | – | – | – | Raiders | x | – | – | – | – |
| Raider Lookout Camp (Elevated Freeway) | 323 | [S3.27] | – | – | – | – | – | – | – | – | – | – | – | Raiders | – | – | – | – | – |
| Raider Platforms (Cambridge) | 420 | [S7.13] | x | – | – | – | – | – | – | – | – | – | – | Raiders | x | – | – | – | – |
| Raider Rooftop Apartments (Cambridge) | 420 | [S7.14] | x | – | x | – | – | – | – | – | – | – | – | Raiders | x | – | – | – | – |
| Raider Rooftops (Back Bay) | 459 | [S11.07] | x | – | x | – | – | – | – | – | – | – | – | Raiders | x | – | – | – | – |
| Raider Shack | 270 | [S1.02] | x | – | – | – | – | – | – | – | – | – | – | Raiders | x | – | – | – | – |
| Raider Shack (Salem Outskirts) | 349 | [S4.08] | x | – | – | – | – | – | – | – | – | – | – | – | – | – | – | – | – |
| Railroad Dead Drop (Theater District) | 503 | [S16.10] | x | – | – | – | – | – | – | – | – | – | – | – | – | – | – | – | – |
| Railroad Hideout (Financial District) | 494 | [S15.09] | x | – | – | – | – | – | – | – | – | – | – | – | x | Opal | – | – | – |
| Railroad HQ Escape Tunnel Exit | 468 | [S13.03] | x | – | – | – | – | – | – | – | – | – | – | The Railroad, Raiders | – | – | – | – | – |
| Railroad Maintenance Shed | 395 | [S6.06] | x | – | – | – | – | – | – | – | – | – | – | Robots | – | – | – | – | – |
| Ranger Cabin | 261 | [P1.08] | – | – | – | – | – | – | – | – | – | Wasteland Survival Guide | – | Bloatflies | – | – | – | – | – |
| Recon Bunker Theta | 276 | [P2.04] | x | – | x | x | – | x | – | – | – | – | – | – | – | – | – | – | x |
| Red Rocket Filling Station (Big John's Salvage) | 395 | [S6.04] | – | – | – | – | – | – | – | – | – | – | – | Super Mutants | – | – | – | – | – |

| LOCATION NAME | PAGE NUMBER | ZONE LOCATION NUMBER | AMMO | MINI NUKE OR FAT MAN | TRUNK | FUSION CORE | POWER ARMOR | BOTTLECAPS | BOBBLEHEAD | NUKA CHERRY | NUKA COLA QUANTUM | REQUIRED READING | COMPANION | FACTION | HEALTH OR CHEMS | TRADER | WORKSHOP | RADIO | UNIQUE ITEM |
|---|---|---|---|---|---|---|---|---|---|---|---|---|---|---|---|---|---|---|---|
| Red Rocket Filling Station (College Square) | 418 | [S7.03] | x | – | – | – | – | – | – | – | – | – | – | – | – | – | – | – | – |
| Red Rocket Filling Station (Mass Pike East) | 395 | [S6.01] | – | – | – | – | – | – | – | – | – | – | – | – | x | – | – | – | – |
| Red Rocket Filling Station (North Central Cambridge) | 418 | [S7.08] | x | – | – | – | – | – | – | – | – | – | – | Raiders | – | – | – | – | – |
| Red Rocket Truck Stop | 258 | [P1.03] | x | – | – | x | – | x | – | – | – | – | Dogmeat | Mole Rats | – | – | – | x | – |
| Reeb Marina | 335 | [P4.14] | x | – | x | – | – | – | – | – | – | Tesla Science | – | Bloodbugs, Robots | x | – | – | – | – |
| Relay Tower 0BB-915 | 307 | [P3.10] | – | – | – | – | – | – | – | – | – | – | – | – | – | – | – | Distress Signal, Raider Radio Signal, Civil Alert System Broadcast | – |
| Relay Tower 0DB-521 | 362 | [P5.28] | – | – | – | – | – | – | – | – | – | – | – | – | – | – | – | Skylanes 1665 Mayday, Distress Signal | – |
| Relay Tower 0SC-527 | 372 | [P6.08] | x | – | – | – | – | x | – | – | – | – | – | Mole Rats | – | – | – | Supermutant Radio Broadcast, Distress Signal, Miller Family Radio Signal | – |
| Relay Tower 1DL-109 | 315 | [P3.18] | – | – | – | – | – | – | – | – | – | – | – | – | – | – | – | Distress Signal, Boston City Works Beacon | – |
| Relay Tower 0MC-810 | 293 | [P2.31] | – | – | – | – | – | – | – | – | – | – | – | – | – | – | – | Default Radio Signal, Separated Family Radio Signal | – |
| Revere Beach Station | 335 | [P4.16] | x | – | x (2) | x | – | x+ | – | x (2) | – | Live & Love | – | Feral Ghouls, Radroaches, Raiders | x | – | – | – | – |
| Revere Satellite Array | 296 | [P2.34] | x+ | x (2) | x | – | x | – | – | – | – | U.S. Covert Operations Manual | – | Brotherhood of Steel, Super Mutants | x | – | – | – | – |
| River's End Shack | 299 | [S2.27] | – | – | – | – | – | – | – | – | – | – | – | Feral Ghouls | – | – | – | – | – |
| River's End Warehouse | 299 | [S2.29] | – | – | – | – | – | – | – | – | – | – | – | – | – | – | – | – | – |
| Roadside Pines Motel | 354 | [P5.02] | x | – | x | x | – | x | – | – | – | – | – | Raiders | – | – | – | – | – |
| Roadside Store | 323 | [S3.25] | – | – | – | – | – | – | – | x | – | – | – | Super Mutants | x | – | – | – | – |
| Robotics Disposal Ground | 259 | [P1.04] | x+ | x (2) | x | – | – | – | – | – | – | Hot Rodder | – | Mole Rats | x | – | – | – | – |
| Robotics Pioneer Park | 356 | [P5.10] | x | – | x | – | – | – | – | – | – | – | – | Deathclaws, Feral Ghouls, Robots | – | – | – | – | – |
| Rocky Cave (Virgil's Laboratory) | 363 | [P5.29] | x | x | x | – | – | x | – | – | – | Tesla Science | – | Deathclaws, Robots, Super Mutant (Friendly) | x | – | – | – | x |
| Rocky Narrows Park | 303 | [P3.03] | x | – | x | – | – | – | – | – | – | – | – | Yao Guai, Radstag Doe | – | – | – | – | – |
| Roof Camp (South Boston) | 521 | [S18.11] | x | – | – | – | – | – | – | – | – | – | – | – | x | – | – | – | – |
| Roof Generator (South Boston) | 521 | [S18.07] | – | – | – | x | – | – | – | – | – | – | – | – | – | – | – | – | – |
| Rooftop Apartment (North End) | 468 | [S13.01] | x | – | – | – | – | – | – | – | – | – | – | – | – | – | – | – | – |
| Rooftop Den (Esplanade) | 449 | [S10.04] | – | – | – | – | – | – | – | – | – | – | – | – | x | – | – | – | – |
| Rooftop Generator (Beacon Hill) | 463 | [S12.04] | – | – | – | x | – | – | – | – | – | – | – | – | – | – | – | – | – |
| Rooftop Hideaway (Financial District) | 494 | [S15.11] | – | – | – | – | – | – | – | – | – | – | – | – | x | – | – | – | – |
| Rooftop Lounger | 468 | [S13.08] | – | – | – | – | – | – | – | – | – | – | – | – | x | – | – | – | – |
| Rook Family House | 332 | [P4.08] | x | – | – | – | – | x | – | – | – | Guns and Bullets | – | Mirelurks, Scavengers | x | – | – | – | x |

| LOCATIONS | | | ARMAMENTS AND AMMO | | | ARMOR PARTS | | | COLLECTIBLES | | | | | | | | SERVICES | | | |
|---|---|---|---|---|---|---|---|---|---|---|---|---|---|---|---|---|---|---|---|
| LOCATION NAME | PAGE NUMBER | ZONE LOCATION NUMBER | AMMO | MINI NUKE OR FAT MAN | TRUNK | FUSION CORE | POWER ARMOR | BOTTLECAPS | BOBBLEHEAD | NUKA CHERRY | NUKA COLA QUANTUM | REQUIRED READING | COMPANION | FACTION | HEALTH OR CHEMS | TRADER | WORKSHOP | RADIO | UNIQUE ITEM |
| Rotten Landfill | 279 | [P2.08] | x | – | x | – | – | – | – | – | – | – | – | Mole Rats, Settlers | x | Trader | – | – | – |
| Roundabout Raider Camp | 521 | [S18.08] | x | – | – | – | – | – | – | – | – | – | – | Raiders | x | – | – | – | – |
| Rubble Overlook | 463 | [S12.06] | – | – | – | – | – | – | – | – | – | – | – | – | – | – | – | – | – |
| Ruined Brick Apartment (North End) | 469 | [S13.15] | – | – | – | – | – | – | – | – | – | – | – | – | – | – | – | – | – |
| Ruined Brick Warehouse | 321 | [S3.06] | x | – | – | – | – | – | – | – | x | – | – | – | – | – | – | – | – |
| Ruined Grove Estates | 398 | [S6.27] | x | – | – | – | – | – | – | – | – | – | – | Yao Guai | x | – | – | – | – |
| Ruined Tavern (Charlestown) | 426 | [S8.01] | – | – | – | – | – | – | – | – | – | – | – | – | – | – | – | – | – |
| Rusting APC | 321 | [S3.08] | x | – | – | – | – | – | – | – | – | – | – | – | – | – | – | – | – |
| Rusting Ship and Stilt Cabin | 521 | [S18.15] | x | – | – | – | – | – | – | – | – | – | – | Mirelurks | x | – | – | – | – |
| Rusty Tractor | 298 | [S2.16] | – | – | – | – | – | x | – | – | – | – | – | Feral Ghouls | – | – | – | – | – |
| Rusty Trailer | 297 | [S2.06] | – | – | x | – | – | – | – | – | – | – | – | – | – | – | – | – | – |
| Salem | 330 | [P4.07] | x+ | x (2) | – | – | – | x+ | – | – | – | – | – | Mirelurks | x | – | – | – | – |
| Salem Coastal Diner and Dock | 349 | [S4.07] | x | – | – | – | – | – | – | – | – | – | – | – | – | – | – | – | – |
| Sanctuary | 258 | [P1.02] | x | – | – | – | – | x | – | x (2) | – | Grognak the Barbarian, You're S.P.E.C.I.A.L. | Codsworth | Bloatflies, Radroaches | x+ | – | x | – | – |
| Sandy Caves Convalescent Home | 329 | [P4.06] | x | – | x | – | – | x | – | – | – | Massachusetts Surgical Journal | – | Radroaches, Robots, Synths (The Institute) | x+++ | – | – | – | – |
| Saugus Ironworks | 283 | [P2.19] | x+ | – | x | – | – | – | Explosives | x | – | Picket Fences | – | Forged (Raiders) | x | – | – | – | x |
| Scaffold Bridge (The Fens) | 445 | [S9.11] | – | – | – | – | – | – | – | – | – | – | – | – | x | – | – | – | – |
| Scaffold Stairs (North End) | 469 | [S13.13] | – | – | – | – | – | – | – | – | – | – | – | – | – | – | – | – | – |
| Scavenger Camp | 298 | [S2.11] | x | – | – | – | – | – | – | – | – | – | – | Yao Guai | – | – | – | – | – |
| Scavenger Camp (Charlestown) | 427 | [S8.07] | x | – | – | – | – | – | – | – | – | – | – | Scavengers | – | – | – | – | – |
| Scavenger's Rest (The Fens) | 445 | [S9.13] | – | – | – | – | – | – | – | – | – | – | – | – | – | – | – | – | – |
| Scavenger's Shack | 270 | [S1.08] | – | – | – | – | – | – | – | – | – | – | – | Scavengers | x | – | – | – | – |
| Scavenger's Trailer | 321 | [S3.07] | – | – | – | – | – | – | – | – | – | – | – | Scavenger | – | – | – | – | – |
| Scavengers' Rooftops (Waterfront) | 508 | [S17.04] | x | – | – | – | – | – | – | – | – | – | – | Scavengers, Raiders | – | – | – | – | – |
| Schoelt Propane Store | 322 | [S3.11] | x | – | – | – | – | – | – | – | – | – | – | – | – | – | – | – | – |
| Schoolhouse (Diamond City) | 435 | [P9.08] | – | – | – | – | – | – | – | – | – | Live & Love | – | – | x | – | – | – | – |
| Science Center Gift Shop | 421 | [S7.20] | – | – | – | – | – | – | – | – | – | – | – | Robots | x | – | – | – | – |
| Science! Center (Diamond City) | 437 | [P9.08] | – | – | – | – | – | – | – | – | – | – | – | – | x | – | – | – | – |
| Scrap Merchant | 323 | [S3.20] | – | – | – | – | – | – | – | – | – | – | – | Settler | x | Scrap Merchant | – | – | – |
| Scrap Metal Barge | 509 | [S17.10] | – | – | – | – | – | – | – | – | – | – | – | – | x | – | – | – | – |
| Scrap Palace | 356 | [P5.11] | x | – | x | – | – | x | – | – | – | – | – | Super Mutants | – | – | – | – | – |
| Scuppered Boat | 399 | [S6.33] | x | – | – | – | – | – | – | – | – | – | – | Mirelurks | – | – | – | – | – |
| Security Office (Diamond City) | 434 | [P9.08] | – | – | – | – | – | – | – | – | – | – | – | – | – | – | – | – | – |
| Sentinel Site | 364 | [P5.31] | x++ | x | – | – | – | – | – | – | – | Astoundingly Awesome Tales | – | Children of the Atom, Feral Ghouls, Mole Rats | x | – | – | – | – |
| Settler Campsite (Natick Outskirts) | 366 | [S5.03] | – | – | – | – | – | – | – | – | – | – | – | Deathclaws | – | – | – | – | – |
| Settler's Stop (The Fens) | 445 | [S9.09] | – | – | – | – | – | x | – | – | – | – | – | – | – | – | – | – | – |
| Settlers' Tent | 272 | [S1.24] | – | – | – | – | – | – | – | – | – | – | – | Settlers | – | – | – | – | – |
| Shanty Store | 349 | [S4.06] | x | – | – | – | – | – | – | – | – | – | – | Settler | – | Leonard Moore | – | – | – |
| Shaw High School | 377 | [P6.15] | x | – | x | – | – | x | – | – | x (2) | Unstoppables | – | Super Mutants | x+ | – | – | – | – |
| Shelled-Out Building | 427 | [S8.08] | – | – | – | – | – | – | – | – | x | – | – | – | – | – | – | – | – |
| Shenley's Oyster Bar | 459 | [S11.04] | x | – | x | – | – | – | – | – | – | – | – | Raiders | x | – | – | – | – |
| Shopping Cart of Goodies | 271 | [S1.19] | – | – | – | – | – | – | – | x | – | – | – | – | – | – | – | – | – |

| LOCATION NAME | PAGE NUMBER | ZONE LOCATION NUMBER | AMMO | MINI NUKE OR FAT MAN | TRUNK | FUSION CORE | POWER ARMOR | BOTTLECAPS | BOBBLEHEAD | NUKA CHERRY | NUKA COLA QUANTUM | REQUIRED READING | COMPANION | FACTION | HEALTH OR CHEMS | TRADER | WORKSHOP | RADIO | UNIQUE ITEM |
|---|---|---|---|---|---|---|---|---|---|---|---|---|---|---|---|---|---|---|---|
| Skylanes Flight 1665 | 365 | [P5.32] | x | — | x | — | — | — | — | — | — | — | — | — | x | — | — | — | — |
| Skylanes Flight 1981 | 279 | [P2.10] | x | — | x | — | — | x++ | — | — | — | Astoundingly Awesome Tales | — | Feral Ghouls, Raiders, Robots | x | — | — | — | — |
| Skylines Flight Salvage | 399 | [S6.35] | — | — | — | — | — | — | — | — | — | — | — | — | x | — | — | — | — |
| Skyscraper Stash | 494 | [S15.05] | — | — | — | — | — | — | — | — | — | — | — | — | x | — | — | — | — |
| Skytram (North End Elevated Freeway) | 468 | [S13.09] | — | — | — | — | — | — | — | — | — | — | — | Robots | — | — | — | — | — |
| Slocum's Joe Corporate HQ | 287 | [P2.22] | x | — | x | — | — | x | — | — | — | — | — | Raiders | — | — | — | — | x |
| Small Trading Shack | 272 | [S1.26] | — | — | — | — | — | — | — | — | — | — | — | — | — | Trader | — | — | — |
| Sniper's Hideout | 398 | [S6.25] | x | — | — | — | — | — | — | — | — | — | — | Mirelurks | — | — | — | — | — |
| Somerville Place | 362 | [P5.16] | — | — | — | — | — | — | — | — | — | — | — | Settlers | x | — | x | — | — |
| South Alley and Garage | 427 | [S8.05] | — | — | — | — | — | — | — | — | x | — | — | — | — | — | — | — | — |
| South Apartments (Charlestown) | 427 | [S8.10] | x | — | — | — | — | — | — | — | — | — | — | — | — | — | — | — | — |
| South Boston Church | 521 | [S18.13] | — | — | — | — | — | — | — | — | — | — | — | Feral Ghouls | — | — | — | — | — |
| South Boston High School | 516 | [P18.07] | — | — | — | — | — | — | — | — | — | — | — | Raiders | x | — | — | — | — |
| South Boston Military Checkpoint | 373 | [P6.10] | x | x (2) | x | x | x | — | — | — | — | Guns and Bullets | — | Gunners | x | — | — | — | — |
| South Boston Police Department | 515 | [P18.04] | x | — | — | — | — | — | — | — | — | — | — | Raider, Robots | x | — | — | — | — |
| South Boston Wharf and Restrooms | 521 | [S18.14] | — | — | — | — | — | — | — | — | — | — | — | — | x | — | — | — | — |
| Spectacle Island | 394 | [P6.31] | x | x (2) | x | — | — | x+ | Luck | — | — | — | — | Mirelurks | x | — | x | — | — |
| Starlight Drive In | 265 | [P1.16] | x | — | — | x | — | — | — | x | x | — | — | Mole Rats, Radroaches | — | — | x | — | — |
| Street Corner (Theater District) | 503 | [S16.11] | — | — | — | x | — | — | — | — | — | — | — | — | — | — | — | — | — |
| Subway Station (North End) | 469 | [S13.16] | — | — | — | — | — | x | — | — | — | — | — | — | x | — | — | — | — |
| Suffolk County Charter School | 384 | [P6.19] | x | — | x | x | — | x | — | — | — | Unstoppables | — | Feral Ghouls, Radroaches | — | — | — | — | x |
| Sunken Fishing Boat | 350 | [S4.11] | — | — | x | — | — | — | — | — | — | — | — | — | x | — | — | — | — |
| Sunken Fishing Boat (Spectacle Island) | 397 | [S6.21] | — | — | x | — | — | — | — | — | — | — | — | — | x | — | — | — | — |
| Sunken Rowboat Stash | 270 | [S1.04] | — | — | x | — | — | — | — | — | — | — | — | — | — | — | — | — | — |
| Sunken Supertanker | 398 | [S6.24] | x | — | — | — | — | — | — | — | — | — | — | — | — | — | — | — | — |
| Sunshine Tidings Co-op | 265 | [P1.18] | — | — | x | — | — | x | — | — | — | Wasteland Survival Guide | — | Feral Ghouls, Radroaches | x | — | x | — | — |
| Super Duper Mart | 266 | [P1.21] | x+ | — | x | x | — | x | — | x (3) | x (2) | Tales of a Junktown Jerky Vendor | — | Feral Ghouls | x+ | — | — | — | — |
| Super Mutant Alley Apartments | 444 | [S9.03] | x | — | x | — | — | — | — | — | — | — | — | Super Mutants | x | — | — | — | — |
| Super Mutant High Rise | 419 | [S7.12] | — | — | x (3) | — | — | — | — | — | — | — | — | Super Mutants | — | — | — | — | — |
| Super Mutant Hotel Shell | 475 | [S14.01] | x | — | x | — | — | — | — | — | — | — | — | Super Mutants | — | — | — | — | — |
| Swan's Pond | 472 | [P14.03] | x | — | x | — | — | x | — | — | — | — | — | Super Mutants | — | — | — | — | x |
| Swatters (Diamond City) | 435 | [P9.08] | x | — | — | — | — | x++ | — | — | — | — | — | — | — | Moe Cronin | — | — | x |
| Switchboard Entrance (Sewer) | 273 | [S1.34] | — | — | — | — | — | — | — | — | — | — | — | — | — | — | — | — | — |
| Taffington Boat House | 291 | [P2.26] | x | — | x (2) | x | — | x+ | — | — | — | — | — | Bloodbugs | x | — | x | — | — |
| Tenpines Bluff | 260 | [P1.07] | — | — | — | — | — | — | — | — | — | — | — | Radroaches, Settlers | — | — | x | — | — |
| The Candy Shop | 521 | [S18.12] | x | — | — | — | — | — | — | — | — | — | — | — | — | — | — | — | — |
| The Castle | 517 | [P18.08] | x+++ | x (2) | — | x | — | — | — | — | — | Guns and Bullets | — | The Minutemen, Mirelurks, Radroaches | x | Ronnie Shaw | x | Radio Freedom | x |
| The Corner of Mass and Newbury | 458 | [S11.01] | — | — | — | — | — | — | — | — | — | — | — | Feral Ghouls | — | — | — | — | — |
| The Fishing Spot (Covenant Compound) | 298 | [S2.15] | — | — | — | — | — | — | — | — | — | — | — | Settlers (Covenant) | — | — | — | — | — |
| The Fridge | 397 | [S6.18] | — | — | — | — | — | — | — | — | — | — | — | Settler (Ghoul) | — | — | — | — | — |

| LOCATION NAME | PAGE NUMBER | ZONE LOCATION NUMBER | ARMAMENTS AND AMMO | | | ARMOR PARTS | | BOTTLECAPS | COLLECTIBLES | | | | COMPANION | FACTION | HEALTH OR CHEMS | SERVICES | | | |
|---|---|---|---|---|---|---|---|---|---|---|---|---|---|---|---|---|---|---|---|
| | | | AMMO | MINI NUKE OR FAT MAN | TRUNK | FUSION CORE | POWER ARMOR | | BOBBLEHEAD | NUKA CHERRY | NUKA COLA QUANTUM | REQUIRED READING | | | | TRADER | WORKSHOP | RADIO | UNIQUE ITEM |
| The Gwinnett Restaurant | 516 | [P18.06] | x | — | — | — | — | x | — | x | x | — | — | Mirelurks, Super Mutants | x | — | — | — | — |
| The Hanging Tree | 397 | [S6.15] | x | — | — | — | — | — | — | — | — | — | — | Raiders | — | — | — | — | — |
| The Institute | 409 | [P7.10] | x++ | — | — | x | — | x+++ | — | x (2) | x | Astoundingly Awesome Tales | X6-88 | The Institute | x+++ | Synth Food Vendor, Institute Requisition Vendor | — | — | x |
| The Locked Trailer | 298 | [S2.18] | x | — | — | — | — | — | — | — | — | — | — | — | — | — | — | — | — |
| The Mausoleum | 366 | [S5.05] | x | — | — | — | — | — | — | — | — | — | — | Mirelurks | — | — | — | — | — |
| The Mayor's Box (Diamond City) | 438 | [P9.08] | — | — | — | — | — | — | — | — | — | — | — | — | — | — | — | — | — |
| The On-Ramp (Theater District) | 503 | [S16.09] | — | — | — | — | — | — | — | — | — | — | — | — | — | — | — | — | — |
| The Patriot's Sleep Shack | 459 | [S11.05] | — | — | — | — | — | — | — | — | — | — | — | — | — | — | — | — | — |
| The Plank Walk (Theater District) and Gunner Encampment (Theater District) | 502 | [S16.03] and [S16.04] | x | — | — | — | — | — | — | — | — | — | — | Gunners | x | — | — | — | — |
| The Shamrock Taphouse | 505 | [P17.02] | x | x | x | — | — | x | — | x | x (2) | Total Hack | — | Mole Rats, Radroaches, Raiders | x | — | — | — | — |
| The Slog | 282 | [P2.18] | — | — | — | — | — | x+++ | — | — | — | — | — | Settlers (Ghouls) | — | Deirdre | x | — | x |
| The Small Dig | 398 | [S6.28] | — | — | x | — | — | x | — | — | — | — | — | Super Mutants | — | — | — | — | — |
| The Splintered Statue | 367 | [S5.12] | x | — | — | — | — | — | — | — | — | — | — | Raiders, Stingwings | x | — | — | — | — |
| The Sunken Bathtub | 349 | [S4.05] | — | — | x | — | — | — | — | — | — | — | — | — | — | — | — | — | — |
| The Trading Post | 396 | [S6.07] | x | — | — | — | — | — | — | — | — | — | — | Settler | — | Eleanor | — | — | — |
| The Wall (Diamond City) | 436 | [P9.08] | — | — | — | — | — | — | — | — | — | — | — | — | — | — | — | — | — |
| Thicket Excavations | 259 | [P1.05] | x+ | — | x | — | — | x+ | — | — | — | Taboo Tattoos | — | Mirelurks, Raiders | x | — | — | — | — |
| Ticker Tape Lounge (Northwest and Southeast) | 503 | [S16.06] and [S16.07] | x | — | — | — | — | — | — | — | — | — | — | Gunners | — | — | — | — | — |
| Ticonderoga Safehouse | 420 | [S7.18] | x | x (2) | x | — | — | — | — | — | x (2) | Guns and Bullets | — | The Railroad, Synths (The Institute) | x | — | — | — | — |
| Tinkerer's Boathouse (Waterfront) | 508 | [S17.05] | — | — | — | — | — | — | — | — | — | — | — | Mirelurks | — | — | — | — | — |
| Tractor Warehouse | 321 | [S3.02] | — | — | — | x | — | — | — | — | — | — | — | Stingwings | — | — | — | — | — |
| Trader Rooftop (Back Bay) | 459 | [S11.06] | — | — | — | — | — | — | — | — | — | — | — | — | x | — | — | — | — |
| Trader's Shack (West of Ranger Cabin) | 271 | [S1.12] | — | — | — | — | — | — | — | — | — | — | — | — | — | Trader | — | — | — |
| Trinity Plaza | 452 | [P11.02] | x | — | x | — | — | — | — | — | — | Astoundingly Awesome Tales | — | Super Mutants | x | — | — | — | — |
| Trinity Plaza Parking | 458 | [S11.03] | — | — | — | — | — | — | — | — | — | — | — | Raiders | — | — | — | — | — |
| Trinity Tower | 454 | [P11.05] | x | — | — | — | — | x++ | Melee | — | — | — | Strong | Super Mutants | x | — | — | — | x |
| Tucker Memorial Bridge | 291 | [P2.27] | — | — | — | — | — | — | — | — | — | — | — | — | — | — | — | — | — |
| Two Cabins and an Outhouse | 366 | [S5.07] | — | — | x | — | — | — | — | — | — | — | — | Feral Ghouls | — | — | — | — | — |
| Under the On-Ramp: Camp and Garage | 503 | [S16.08] | x | — | — | — | — | — | — | — | — | — | — | Scavengers | — | — | — | — | — |
| Undersea Hatch Pipe | 399 | [S6.38] | — | — | x | — | — | — | — | — | — | — | — | — | x | — | — | — | — |
| Union's Hope Cathedral | 418 | [S7.04] | x | — | — | — | — | — | — | — | — | — | — | Feral Ghouls | x | — | — | — | — |
| University Point | 518 | [P18.09] | x | x | x | — | — | x | — | x | — | Tesla Science | — | Mirelurks, Synths (The Institute) | — | — | — | — | x |
| Unloading Barge | 350 | [S4.14] | x | — | — | — | x | — | — | — | — | — | — | Robots | — | — | — | — | — |
| Upside Down Rowboat | 351 | [S4.21] | — | — | x | — | — | — | — | — | — | — | — | — | — | — | — | — | — |
| USAF Satellite Station Olivia | 260 | [P1.06] | x+ | x | x | x | — | — | — | — | — | U.S. Covert Operations Manual | — | Radroaches, Raiders | x | — | — | — | — |
| USS Constitution | 426 | [P8.03] | x+ | — | x (2) | — | — | x+++ | — | — | — | U.S. Covert Operations Manual | — | Robots | x+ | — | — | — | x |
| Valentine's Detective Agency (Diamond City) | 436 | [P9.08] | — | — | — | — | — | — | — | — | — | RobCo FUN! (and Zeta Invaders Game) | — | — | x | — | — | — | — |
| Vault 111 | 257 | [P1.01] | x | — | — | — | — | — | — | — | — | Red Menace Game (no Magazine) | — | Radroaches | x | — | — | — | x |

| LOCATION NAME | PAGE NUMBER | ZONE LOCATION NUMBER | AMMO | MINI NUKE OR FAT MAN | TRUNK | FUSION CORE | POWER ARMOR | BOTTLECAPS | BOBBLEHEAD | NUKA CHERRY | NUKA COLA QUANTUM | REQUIRED READING | COMPANION | FACTION | HEALTH OR CHEMS | TRADER | WORKSHOP | RADIO | UNIQUE ITEM |
|---|---|---|---|---|---|---|---|---|---|---|---|---|---|---|---|---|---|---|---|
| Vault 114 (Exit) | 454 | [P11.04] | — | — | — | — | — | — | — | — | — | — | — | — | — | — | — | — | — |
| Vault 81 | 318 | [P3.22] | x++ | x | x | — | — | x+++ | Medicine | x (4) | — | Grognak the Barbarian, Taboo Tattoos | Curie | Settlers (Vault Dwellers), Vault 81 Lab Mole Rats | x+++ | Alexis Combes, Maria Summerset, Horatio, Dr. Penske | — | — | x |
| Vault 95 | 358 | [P5.15] | x+ | — | x | — | — | x | Big Guns | x | — | — | — | Gunners | x | — | — | — | — |
| Vault-Tec Regional HQ | 461 | [P12.01] | x | x | x | — | — | — | — | — | — | — | — | Feral Ghouls | — | — | — | — | — |
| Vending Machine Truck Transport | 272 | [S1.31] | — | — | — | — | — | — | — | — | x | — | — | — | — | — | — | — | — |
| Vertibird Wreckage | 362 | [P5.26] | — | — | — | — | — | — | — | — | — | — | — | — | — | — | — | — | — |
| Vitale Pumphouse | 350 | [S4.12] | — | — | x | x | — | — | — | — | — | — | — | — | — | — | — | — | x |
| Walden Pond | 265 | [P1.19] | x | — | — | — | — | x | — | — | — | Tales of a Junktown Jerky Vendor | — | Raiders | x | — | — | — | x |
| Warehouse (Diamond City) | 437 | [P9.08] | x+ | — | x | — | — | — | — | — | — | — | — | — | x | — | — | — | — |
| Warehouse and Wharf | 508 | [S17.03] | x | — | — | — | — | — | — | — | — | — | — | Super Mutants | — | — | — | — | — |
| Warren Theater | 459 | [S11.08] | — | — | — | — | — | — | — | — | — | — | — | Synths (The Institute) | x | — | — | — | — |
| Warwick Homestead | 393 | [P6.29] | x | x | x | — | — | x | — | — | — | — | — | Settler | x | June Warwick | x | — | — |
| Water Filtration Caps Stash | 270 | [S1.05] | — | — | — | — | — | x+ | — | — | — | — | — | — | x | — | — | — | — |
| Water Street Apartments | 495 | [S15.14] | x | — | — | — | — | x | — | — | — | — | — | Raiders | x | — | — | — | — |
| Waterfront Cabin | 509 | [S17.09] | — | — | — | — | — | — | — | — | — | — | — | Settler | — | — | — | — | — |
| Waterfront Park | 508 | [S17.01] | — | — | — | — | — | — | — | — | — | — | — | Radstag Does | x | — | — | — | — |
| Waterfront Warehouse | 351 | [S4.17] | — | — | — | — | — | — | — | — | — | — | — | — | — | — | — | — | — |
| Wattz Consumer Electronics | 306 | [P3.08] | x | x | — | — | — | — | — | — | — | Total Hack | — | Radroaches, Robots | x | — | — | — | — |
| Waypoint Echo | 357 | [P5.14] | — | — | — | — | — | — | — | — | — | — | — | Brotherhood of Steel (Quest only) | — | — | — | — | — |
| Waystation | 323 | [S3.24] | x | — | — | — | — | — | — | — | — | — | — | Feral Ghouls | x | — | — | — | — |
| Waystation (Gunners' Plaza) | 395 | [S6.26] | x | — | — | — | — | — | — | — | — | — | — | — | — | — | — | — | — |
| Waystation (West Roxbury) | 396 | [S6.13] | — | — | — | — | — | — | — | — | — | — | — | Super Mutants | x | — | — | — | — |
| Weatherby Investment Trust | 493 | [S15.01] | x | — | — | — | — | — | — | — | — | — | — | — | x | — | — | — | — |
| West Everett Estates | 292 | [P2.29] | x | — | x (2) | — | — | x | — | — | x (2) | — | — | Super Mutants | x | — | — | — | — |
| West Roxbury Station | 377 | [P6.14] | x | — | x | — | — | x | — | x | — | Tumblers Today | — | Radroaches, Super Mutants | x | — | — | — | — |
| West Roxbury: Parking Lot Funhouse | 378 | [P6.15] | x+++ | x | x (2) | x (4) | — | — | — | — | — | Hot Rodders | — | Radroaches, Feral Ghouls | x+++ | — | — | — | — |
| Westing Estate | 369 | [P6.01] | x | — | — | — | — | — | — | — | — | Unstoppables | — | Mirelurks | x | — | — | — | x |
| Weston Water Treatment Plant | 312 | [P3.16] | x | — | x | — | — | — | — | — | — | Picket Fences | — | Mirelurks, Super Mutants | x | — | — | — | — |
| Wharfside Cottage | 468 | [S13.07] | x | — | — | — | — | — | — | — | — | — | — | Raiders | — | — | — | — | — |
| Wicked Shipping Container Truck #2 | 273 | [S1.32] | — | — | x | — | — | — | — | — | — | — | — | — | — | — | — | — | — |
| Wicked Shipping Container Truck #3 | 297 | [S2.10] | x | — | x | — | — | — | — | — | — | — | — | — | — | — | — | — | — |
| Wicked Shipping Container Truck #4 | 395 | [S6.05] | x | — | x | — | — | x | — | — | — | — | — | Raiders | — | — | — | — | — |
| Wicked Shipping Fleet Lockup | 261 | [P1.09] | x+ | — | x | — | — | — | — | — | — | Grognak the Barbarian | — | Feral Ghouls | x | — | — | — | — |
| Wildwood Cemetery | 279 | [P2.09] | x | — | — | — | — | — | — | — | — | Total Hack | — | Mole Rats, Raiders | x | — | — | — | — |
| Wilson Atomatoys Corporate HQ | 457 | [P11.08] | x | — | x | x | — | x | — | x | x | — | — | Super Mutants | x | — | — | — | — |
| Wilson Atomatoys Factory | 386 | [P6.23] | x | — | x (2) | x | — | — | — | — | — | — | — | Super Mutants | — | — | — | — | x |
| Wreck of the FMS Northern Star | 394 | [P6.30] | x | x | x | x | — | x | Agility | — | — | Tales of a Junktown Jerky Vendor | — | Mirelurks, Raiders | x | — | — | — | — |
| Wreck of the USS Riptide | 429 | [P9.01] | x | x | x | — | x | — | — | — | — | Wasteland Survival Guide | — | Raiders | x | — | — | — | — |
| WRVR Broadcast Station | 356 | [P5.08] | x | — | — | — | — | x | — | — | — | Live & Love | — | Settlers | — | — | — | Trinity Tower Radio | — |
| Yangtze | 407 | [P17.04] | x+ | x | — | x | — | x | — | x | x | — | — | Feral Ghouls | x+ | — | — | — | x |

543

Written by David S. J. Hodgson and Nick von Esmarch

SE ISBN: 978-0-7440-1630-7
CE ISBN: 978-07440-1631-4
Printed at RRDK

Printing Code: The rightmost double-digit number is the year of the book's printing; the rightmost single-digit number is the number of the book's printing. For example, 15-1 shows that the first printing of the book occurred in 2015.

18  17  16  15        4  3  2  1

Printed in the USA.

## CREDITS

**Senior Development Editor**
Chris Hausermann

**Book Designers**
*In Color Design:*
*Targa Funk & Mark Bernard*
Brent Gann
Dan Caparo

**Production Designers**
*In Color Design:*
*Targa Funk & Mark Bernard*
Justin Lucas

**Production**
Angela Graef

**Copy Editor**
Carrie Andrews

**Cartography Coordinator**
Adam Brackenbury

**Map Illustration**
DK Delhi Team

**Map Illustration work:**
Rajesh Chhibber
Rahul Kumar
Manish Bhatt
Rohit Rojal
Arun Pottirayil
Alok Kumar Singh
Nain Singh Rawat

**Head of Department, Digital Operations Delhi:**
Manjari Rathi Hooda

**Map Editing**
Miguel Lopez
Evan Walters
Darren Strecker

## PRIMA GAMES STAFF

**VP & Publisher**
Mike Degler

**Editorial Manager**
Tim Fitzpatrick

**Design and Layout Manager**
Tracy Wehmeyer

**Licensing**
Christian Sumner
Paul Giacomotto
Aaron Lockhart

**Marketing**
Katie Hemlock

**Digital Publishing**
Julie Asbury
Tim Cox
Shaida Boroumand

**Operations Manager**
Stacey Beheler

## ACKNOWLEDGMENTS

**David S. J. Hodgson**

Trilby hats off, and a Gwinnett Stout raised to the *Fallout 4* team at Bethesda for their steadfast support and aid during the creation of this guide. Thanks also to the Documentation Department at Vault-Tec, for use of the SimTek 5000. A firm handshake and spot of backslapping to the best co-author in the business; thank you Nick. Thanks to Chris, Shaida, Tracy, Dan, Tim, Mike, and all at Prima for their patience and help during my extended trip to Boston. Thank you to my loving wife Melanie; Mum, Dad, and Ian; Loki; The Moon Wiring Club, Laibach, Kraftwerk, The Benningtons; and O for the Old Ones, known also as Elder Things, just a terrible, terrible spawn, who contacts humans only through possession, and simply just cannot be drawn.

**Nick von Esmarch**

Thanks to everyone at Bethesda for their support and patience. Thanks to all at Prima, with special thanks to Chris, Shaida, Dan, Mike, Tim, and Tracy. Big thanks to David for being a patient and reliable source of advice. Seriously, David—you've been awesome.

Of course, I thank every member of my family (whether bound by blood or by choice). Too many names to list, but the folks, siblings, in-laws, little ones, and super-best friends mean everything. Extra-special thanks to Kurt and Damien for putting up with my nonsense and providing a bit of their own. Nonsense is important.